The Cambridge Edition of the Poets

ENGLISH AND SCOTTISH
POPULAR BALLADS

EDITED BY

HELEN CHILD SARGENT

AND

GEORGE LYMAN KITTREDGE

𝕿𝖍𝖊 𝕮𝖆𝖒𝖇𝖗𝖎𝖉𝖌𝖊 𝕻𝖔𝖊𝖙𝖘

Edited by

BROWNING	HORACE E. SCUDDER
MRS. BROWNING	HARRIET WATERS PRESTON
BURNS	W. E. HENLEY
BYRON	PAUL E. MORE
CHAUCER	F. N. ROBINSON
DRYDEN	GEORGE R. NOYES
ENGLISH AND SCOTTISH }	HELEN CHILD SARGENT
POPULAR BALLADS }	GEORGE L. KITTREDGE
HOLMES	HORACE E. SCUDDER
KEATS	HORACE E. SCUDDER
LONGFELLOW	HORACE E. SCUDDER
LOWELL	HORACE E. SCUDDER
MILTON	WILLIAM VAUGHN MOODY
POPE	HENRY W. BOYNTON
SCOTT	HORACE E. SCUDDER
SHAKESPEARE	W. A. NEILSON
SHELLEY	GEORGE E. WOODBERRY
SPENSER	R. E. NEIL DODGE
TENNYSON	WILLIAM J. ROLFE
WHITTIER	HORACE E. SCUDDER
WORDSWORTH	A. J. GEORGE

HOUGHTON MIFFLIN COMPANY

BOSTON   NEW YORK   CHICAGO

English
and
Scottish Popular
BALLADS

Carnarvan Castle

HOUGHTON MIFFLIN COMPANY BOSTON

Cambridge Edition

The Riverside Press Cambridge

PREFACE

THE English and Scottish Popular Ballads, edited by the late Francis James Child, was published in ten parts, forming five large volumes, from 1882 to 1898. It contains three hundred and five distinct ballads, but the number of texts printed in full is much larger than this, for Professor Child's plan was to give every extant version of every ballad. Thus of No. 4, 'Lady Isabel and the Elf-Knight,' he published nine different versions; of No. 58, 'Sir Patrick Spens,' eighteen; of No. 173, 'Mary Hamilton,' twenty-eight, — and so on. Each ballad has an introduction dealing with the history and bibliography of the piece, and containing a full account of parallels in foreign languages, and, in general, of the diffusion of the story, with other pertinent matter. There are also exhaustive collations, elaborate bibliographies, an index of published ballad airs, a collection of tunes, — and, in a word, all the apparatus necessary for the study of this kind of literature.

The present volume offers a selection from the materials collected and edited by Mr Child, and is prepared in accordance with a plan which he had approved. Each of the three hundred and five ballads in his large collection (except Nos. 33, 279, 281, 290, and 299) is represented by one or more versions, without the *apparatus criticus*, and with very short introductions. The notes, which are necessarily brief, give specimens (and specimens only) of significant stanzas from versions not included in the volume. The numbers (1–305) and letters (A, B, etc.) correspond to the designations used in the large collection, and there is, in every case, an implied reference to that work for further information. For instance, 'The Twa Sisters' (No. 10) is here represented by two versions, A and B, selected from those published by Mr Child, which (as the note on p. 642 indicates) are twenty-seven in number. To A is prefixed (both in this volume and in the large collection) a memorandum of the four sources (a, b, c, d) from which Mr Child derived this version. The text, as printed on pp. 18, 19, is identical with the text of a as edited by Mr Child, but the variant readings, fully registered in the large collection, are omitted. The short introduction to No. 10 is extracted from Mr Child's eight-page introduction, to which the student who wishes to pursue the subject will naturally have recourse. Mr Child's own words are retained whenever that was possible. The present volume, it will be observed, is neither a new edition of the collection of Mr Child nor a substitute for it. It differs from that work in scope and purpose. Yet it is, in a manner, complete in itself. It affords a conspectus of English and Scottish ballad literature which, it is hoped, may be useful to the general reader and may lead those who feel a more particular interest in the subject to acquaint themselves at first hand with the full collection of texts and other apparatus in Mr Child's admirable volumes.

The Glossary is based on that in the larger work. It is not intended to furnish material for linguistic investigations, but merely to assist the reader.

For obvious reasons, it has seemed best to reproduce the List of Sources entire. For other bibliographical lists the large collection may be consulted.

The general Introduction has been written especially for this book. It attempts to sum up, as simply and judicially as may be, the present state of a very complicated discussion.

The portrait of Mr Child is from a photograph belonging to Miss Catharine Innes Ireland.

Professor Neilson has had the great kindness to relieve the editors of the difficult task of preparing the glossary, and Miss Ireland has rendered invaluable assistance in proof-reading. Without the help of these generous and self-sacrificing friends the appearance of the book would have been long delayed.

CAMBRIDGE, MASS., March 16, 1904.

CONTENTS

CONTENTS

INTRODUCTION

A BALLAD is a song that tells a story, or — to take the other point of view — a story told in song. More formally, it may be defined as a short narrative poem, adapted for singing, simple in plot and metrical structure, divided into stanzas, and characterized by complete impersonality so far as the author or singer is concerned. This last trait is of the very first consequence in determining the quality or qualities which give the ballad its peculiar place in literature. A ballad has no author. At all events, it appears to have one. The teller of the story for the time being is as much the author as the unknown and for our purposes unimportant) person who first put it into shape. In most forms of artistic literature the personality of the writer is a matter of deep concern to the reader. The style, we say, is the man. The individuality of one poet distinguishes his works, however they may vary among themselves, from the works of all other poets. Chaucer, for instance, has his way, or his ways, of telling a tale that are not the way, or the ways, of William Morris. If a would-be creative literary artist has no individuality that we can detect, we set him down as conventional, and that is an end of him and of his works. In the ballad it is not so. There the author is of no account. He is not even present. We do not feel sure that he ever existed. At most, we merely infer his existence, at some indefinite time in the past, from the fact of his product : a poem, we think, implies a poet ; therefore somebody must have composed this ballad. Until we begin to reason, we have no thought of the author of any ballad, because, so far as we can see, he had no thought of himself.

We may go a step farther in this matter of impersonality. Not only is the author of a ballad invisible, and, so far as the effect which the poem produces on the hearer is concerned, practically non-existent, but the teller of the tale has no rôle in it. Unlike other songs, it does not purport to give utterance to the feelings or the mood of the singer.[1] The first person does not occur at all, except in the speeches of the several characters. Finally, there are no comments or reflections by the narrator. He does not dissect or psychologize. He does not take sides for or against any of the *dramatis personae*. He merely tells what happened and what people said, and he confines the dialogue to its simplest and most inevitable elements. The story exists for its own sake. If it were possible to conceive a tale as *telling itself*, without the instrumentality of a conscious speaker, the ballad would be such a tale.[2]

So far we have dealt in generalities and impressions. What has been said is obvious enough, and it is admitted by everybody. There is, as we shall see presently, no agreement among scholars as to the origin and history of what are called popular ballads, but as to the fact of their impersonal quality there is no dispute. Nor will it be denied that this quality puts them in a class by themselves. Whatever the cause or causes,

---

[1] This distinguishes the ballad, strictly so called, from the purely lyrical poem. Such a song as Waly, waly, gin love be bony ' (p. 667) is, then, not a ballad, though it tells a story. It should be noted that, in common parlance, the term ballad is very loosely applied.

[2] There are, of course, slight departures from the type in particular cases, but these are readily accounted for, and do not affect the integrity of the type.

the bare fact is clear and undeniable. No one can read 'The Hunting of the Cheviot' or 'Mary Hamilton,' or 'Johnie Armstrong,' or 'Robyn and Gandeleyn,' or 'The Wife of Usher's Well,' and fail to recognize that, different as they are from each other in theme and in effect, they belong together. Yet no two of them are the works of the same author. Their common element is not the personality of the writer but his impersonality, and this distinguishes the ballad, as a class, from the productions of the conscious literary artist. In studying ballads, then, we are studying the "poetry of the folk," and the "poetry of the folk" is different from the "poetry of art."

Poetry of the folk is, perhaps, a dangerous phrase; but it is too convenient to be lightly rejected, and, if we proceed with caution, we may employ it without disaster. Let us hasten to acknowledge that in introducing the term at this stage of our discussion we have gone somewhat farther than the logic of the situation warrants. We have seen, to be sure, that all poetry is divisible into two great classes, — that which is manifestly the work of the conscious artist, and that which is not. We have recognized a characteristic difference between 'The Prioress's Tale' and 'Julian and Maddalo' on the one hand and 'Johnie Armstrong' and 'The Wife of Usher's Well' on the other. But we have not yet discovered anything that justifies us in calling the ballads *folk*-poetry, and we have not defined the folk, though that is a term which assuredly requires explanation.

The alphabet was no doubt a great invention, and everybody should be happy to know that he can write. But now and then it would be convenient if one's thoughts could dissociate literature for a moment from the written or printed page. In theory this is easy enough to do. Practically, however, it is difficult for even a professed student of linguistics to remember that a word is properly a sign made with the vocal organs, and that the written word is merely a conventional symbol standing for the word that is spoken. We are in the habit of thinking that a word should be pronounced as it is spelled, rather than that it should be spelled as it is pronounced. *Author* means to us a man with a pen in his hand, — a *writer*, as we call him. It requires a combined effort of the reason and the imagination to conceive a poet as a person who cannot write, singing or reciting his verses to an audience that cannot read. History, as we understand it, is the written record or even the printed volume; it is no longer the accumulated fund of tribal memories, handed down from father to son by oral tradition. Yet everybody knows that, quite apart from what we usually call literature, there is a great mass of song and story and miscellaneous lore which circulates among those who have neither books nor newspapers. To this oral literature, as the French call it, education is no friend. Culture destroys it, sometimes with amazing rapidity. When a nation learns to read, it begins to disregard its traditional tales; it feels a little ashamed of them; and finally it loses both the will and the power to remember and transmit them. What was once the possession of the folk as a whole, becomes the heritage of the illiterate only, and soon, unless it is gathered up by the antiquary, vanishes altogether.

To this oral literature belong the popular ballads, and we are justified, therefore, in calling them "folk-poetry." They are not, like written literature, the exclusive possession of the cultivated classes in any community. They belonged, in the first instance, to the whole people, at a time when there were no formal divisions of literate and illiterate; when the intellectual interests of all were substantially identical, from the king to the peasant. As civilization advanced, they were banished from polite society, but they lived on among the humble, among shepherds and ploughboys and "the spinsters and the knitters in the sun," until even these became too sophisticated to care for them and they were heard no more.

The process just sketched is not imaginary or merely inferential. It is, to be sure, impossible, from the nature of the case, to cite documentary evidence for every step in the history of the ballads of a given people. But we are not confined to the limits of a single nationality. Every country of Europe may be laid under contribution for evidence, and not a little testimony has come in from other continents. All stages of civilization are represented in the material that scholars have brought together, so that we are enabled to speak with entire confidence. Positive chronology may be out of the question, but relative chronology is all that one can require in such matters. The hostility between education and balladry is not conjectural; its history is known in Great Britain for at least two hundred years. The homogeneous folk — that is, the community whose intellectual interests are the same from the top of the social structure to the bottom — is no fiction; examples in abundance have been observed and recorded. The ability of oral tradition to transmit great masses of verse for hundreds of years is proved and admitted. Ballads themselves exist in plenty, fortunately preserved in old manuscripts or broadsides or taken down from singing or recitation in recent years. It is possible to be ignorant of the evidence, no doubt, but it is not possible to doubt when once the evidence is known. *The popular ballads are really popular, that is, they belong to the folk.* So much is clear. There are problems enough remaining, — the relation of the ballads to written literature, their sources, their origin, the manner of composition, and so on. But these are secondary questions. The main point is established, and, indeed, there has never been any reason to dispute it.

The authorship of popular ballads is a question of great difficulty, which must be considered in due season, but which may be deferred for the present. Before discussing the different theories that have been proposed it is well to refer to other matters that admit of a more satisfactory settlement.

Professor Child's great collection, The English and Scottish Popular Ballads, in five volumes (Boston, 1882–98), comprises the whole extant mass of this material. It includes three hundred and five pieces, most of them in a number of different versions, with full collations and other pertinent apparatus. A few variants of this or that ballad have come to light since the publication of this admirable work, but no additional ballads have been discovered. Ballad-making, so far as the English-speaking nations are concerned, is a lost art; and the same may be said of ballad-singing. A few of the ballads in Mr Child's collection are still in oral circulation; but most of them are completely forgotten or are known only in versions derived from print. Among those which survive may be mentioned 'Lord Randal,' 'The Wife of Usher's Well,' 'The Maid Freed from the Gallows,' 'Sir Hugh,' and 'The Twa Sisters.' Much has been lost, and some of the most precious relics of tradition that we possess have been saved by mere accident and in a sadly mutilated condition. Yet what has been preserved is considerable in amount and, on the whole, of excellent quality. No country has better ballads than those of England and Scotland.

On pages 677–684 of the present volume will be found a chronological list of the manuscripts, broadsides, and printed books from which Professor Child derived the texts which make up his collection. Only eleven ballads, it will be observed, are extant in manuscripts older than the seventeenth century. The unique copy of 'Judas' (No. 29) dates from the thirteenth century; next, by a long interval, comes 'Riddles Wisely Expounded' (No. 1), which occurs in a manuscript of about 1445; slightly later, perhaps, are the manuscripts which contain 'Robin Hood and the Monk' (No. 119), 'St Stephen and Herod' (No. 22), and 'Robyn and Gandeleyn' (No. 115); from about 1500 come our

copies of ‘Robin Hood and the Potter’ (No. 121) and ‘Crow and Pie’ (No. 111) ; fr‹
about 1550 those of ‘The Battle of Otterburn’ (No. 161) and the older version of ‘T‹
Hunting of the Cheviot’ (No. 162); ‘Sir Andrew Barton’ (No. 167) and ‘Captain Ca‹
(No. 178) occur in manuscripts of the seventeenth century. The Percy Folio, which‹
the most important of all our ballad manuscripts, is in a hand of about 1650. A f‹
ballads are found in printed copies of the fifteenth and sixteenth centuries. Miscellan‹
of the seventeenth century preserve a number of texts, and broadsides of the same ce‹
tury are plentiful. Then we come to the collectors of the eighteenth and nineteen‹
centuries, to whose enthusiasm for popular poetry are due the majority of the texts whi‹
we possess.

Evidently, then, the written and printed documents which we are studying are, in t‹
main, modern documents. But we are not to infer that the ballads themselves are nece‹
sarily of recent origin. A sharp distinction must be made between the date of the bo‹
or manuscript in which a ballad occurs and the date of the ballad itself.

There is ample evidence for the antiquity of popular ballads in England. Nobo‹
doubts that the Angles and Saxons had them in abundance when they invaded Britai‹
and the mediæval chroniclers testify to the continuance of the ballad-singing hab‹
Indeed, there is no difficulty in proving beyond a reasonable doubt that there we‹
ballads in plenty from the dawn of English history (not to speak of what lies before th‹
epoch) down to the seventeenth century, when written and printed documents begin‹
abound. From the nature of the case, however, such songs very seldom got writt‹
down. The substance of many Anglo-Saxon ballads may be preserved in Béowulf, b‹
this is an epic poem of considerable pretensions to artistic structure and finish, and w‹
cannot hope to extract from it the separate songs which its author or authors utilize‹
Much ballad material is doubtless preserved in chronicles, but the ballads themselves a‹
not there. Only a limited class of ballads (those of an heroic or historical character‹
were likely to afford material to chroniclers and epic poets. What the people sang woul‹
only be recorded by accident. Thus it is not surprising that we have but a single balla‹
written down in the thirteenth century. The existence of this one text, the ‘Judas,’ com‹
pletely popular in metre, in phraseology, and in what we call atmosphere, is a valuabl‹
piece of evidence. The lack of similar texts for the next two hundred years is no ev‹
dence at all, except, perhaps, of the fact that such pieces were in the possession of th‹
folk and circulated from mouth to mouth, but that nobody cared to commit them t‹
writing. ‘St Stephen and Herod’ is just such another piece as ‘Judas’ and may b‹
quite as old, yet it did not achieve the perpetuity of pen and ink until about 1450. ‘Th‹
Maid and the Palmer’ (No. 21), which is a popular version of the story of the Samarita‹
woman in the gospel, belongs to the same class. So far as we know, however, it was no‹
written down until about 1650, when it was included in that extraordinary miscellan‹
known as Bishop Percy’s Folio Manuscript. When Percy discovered this manuscript i‹
was lying under a bureau in the parlor of a country gentleman’s house, and the maid‹
were using it to light fires. Suppose it had escaped Percy’s notice. Another month‹
another week, would have sent it up Humphrey Pitts’s chimney in smoke. We shoul‹
then have no knowledge of the existence of ‘The Maid and the Palmer’ in Englis‹
except for three stanzas and half of the burden, which Sir Walter Scott remembered an‹
which were first printed in 1880 in the second edition of Sharpe’s Ballad Book ; but w‹
should make a great mistake if we inferred that ‘The Maid and the Palmer’ was t‹
be dated in accordance with the time when it was first printed or even the time when i‹
was communicated to Sharpe by Scott. To avoid a possible misapprehension it may b‹

added that Scott was not aware that this ballad occurs in the Percy Manuscript. His knowledge of it, in other words, came from pure oral tradition which was in no manner affected by the accident that some scribe in the seventeenth century wrote down a version that was then in circulation. The case of 'The Maid and the Palmer' is so instructive that we must dwell on it a little longer. The ballad is not confined to England. There are versions in Danish, in Färöe, in Norwegian, in Swedish, and in Finnish. The Danish ballad was printed as a broadside about 1700, and was also taken down from recitation in 1848 and again in 1869. The Färöe version is known from about the end of the eighteenth century, and the same is true of one of the Swedish texts. A memorandum in the handwriting of Arne Magnusson proves that the ballad existed in Icelandic in the seventeenth or early eighteenth century. All these facts are quite independent of the scribe of the Percy Manuscript and of the recollection of Sir Walter Scott. Geographical distribution, then, may give valuable testimony to the antiquity of a ballad. A striking example is 'Lady Isabel and the Elf-Knight' (No. 4). This was first printed, so far as we know, in a broadside of about 1765,[1] and next in 1776 by Herd, who took it down from singing or recitation. But these dates are of no value in determining the age of the ballad. What convinces us that 'Lady Isabel and the Elf-Knight' came to the printer of the broadside and to Herd from an oral tradition of indeterminable antiquity is its existence among all the nations of Europe. "It is nearly as well known to the southern as to the northern nations. It has an extraordinary currency in Poland. The Germans, Low and High, and the Scandinavians, preserve it, in a full and evidently ancient form, even in the tradition of this generation."[2] No one can turn over the pages of Mr Child's introduction to 'Lady Isabel' without perceiving that nothing has less significance for the date of any ballad than the precise moment at which it first excited the interest of some collector who reduced it to writing, or of some catchpenny publisher who had it struck off on poor paper in battered type for the gratification of those who, like Mopsa, love a ballad in print a-life.

So long as a ballad continues to be handed down by oral tradition, it is, of course, continuously subjected to the processes of change which every language undergoes. Hence, a version derived from recitation or singing in the nineteenth century will conform, in the main, to the habitual dialect of the singer or reciter, and thus will be, in a real sense, modern. But this has nothing to do with the age of the ballad itself. In printed versions, the linguistic forms may be considerably older than the date of publication, and the same is true of copies preserved in manuscript. Thus, the language of the 'Gest of Robin Hood' (No. 117) is much earlier than 1500, the approximate date of the first edition that we know of. There is nothing surprising in this, for Robin Hood ballads were in circulation a good while before 1377, as the casual mention of them in Piers Plowman proves.

The considerations set forth in the preceding paragraphs have an important bearing on another question which has been much debated,— the relation between ballads and metrical romances. Such romances are, on the whole, preserved in manuscripts much older than the sources from which we derive our ballad texts, and it has therefore seemed natural to many scholars to assume without argument that when a romance and a ballad tell the same story, the ballad is merely a *rifacimento* of the romance. Such an inference is, however, by no means a matter of course. Most romances were literary productions, composed as modern novels are composed, pen in hand. Clearly, then, if a written

---

[1] Roxburghe Ballads, Ballad Society, VII, 383-4.
[2] Child, English and Scottish Popular Ballads, I, 22 (1882).

romance was in a given case based upon a ballad which had never been committed to writing, and which continued to circulate from mouth to mouth for a century or two before anybody took it down, the romance, though in fact later than the ballad, would appear, so far as documentary evidence is concerned, to be the older of the two. No doubt certain ballads are based upon metrical romances. Such appears to be the case with 'The Lord of Lorn and the False Steward' (No. 271), which may probably be a retelling of 'Roswall and Lillian,' but in general, there is no presumption in favor of the priority of the romance; and even when the extant ballad does demonstrably go back to a romance, it is sometimes probable that the romance itself goes back to a still older ballad which has perished. A priori considerations are of little or no value in solving these problems. Each case requires to be investigated by itself. The reader may find abundant materials for such investigation in Professor Child's introductions to 'Hind Horn' (No. 17), 'Sir Lionel' (No. 18), 'King Orfeo' (No. 19), 'Sir Aldingar' (No. 59), and 'Fair Annie' (No. 62). What has been said of ballads and romances is equally true of ballads and literary material in general. 'Lady Diamond' (No. 269) is unquestionably derived in some way from Boccaccio's Decameron, but nothing is more certain than that Boccaccio's own tale goes back in the long run to distinctly popular sources. Certain historical ballads may come from chronicles, but, on the other hand, it is well known that chroniclers have often drawn without scruple from legendary songs and other forms of oral tradition. Only by comparative study of extensive material and patient scrutiny of details can one hope to arrive at a satisfactory result in these matters, and it often happens that the truth lies too far back for us to discover.

Some ballads are historical, or at least are founded on actual occurrences. In such cases, we have a manifest point of departure for our chronological investigation. The ballad is likely to have sprung up shortly after the event and to represent the common rumor of the time. Accuracy is not to be expected, and indeed too great historical fidelity in detail is rather a ground of suspicion than a certificate of the genuinely popular character of the piece. There can be no object in enumerating the obviously historical ballads in the present collection ; the reader will easily find most of them for himself by running through the Table of Contents. But two cautionary observations are necessary. Since history repeats itself, the possibility and even the probability must be entertained that every now and then a ballad which had been in circulation for some time was adapted to the circumstances of a recent occurrence and has come down to us only in such an adaptation. It is also far from improbable that many ballads which appear to have no definite localization or historical antecedents may be founded on fact, since one of the marked tendencies of popular narrative poetry is to alter or eliminate specific names of persons and places in the course of oral tradition. A good example, though not in a case of historical derivation, may be seen in 'Hind Horn' (No. 17), and another in 'King Orfeo' (No. 19). In 'Hind Horn,' but one name is kept, that of the hero himself, which happened to afford the opportunity for a kind of pun ("Drink to Horn from the horn "), and so was preserved. Were it not for this name, we could only say that the ballad belongs to a great class of stories of which the romance of 'King Horn' is also a member ; we should have no right to postulate any special connection between the romance and the ballad. The pretty little Shetland ballad of 'King Orfeo' comes in some way from the classical tale of Orpheus and Eurydice, apparently by way of a Middle English lay or romance, but it has lost the name of the hero and has transformed that of the heroine into Isabel.

A popular ballad, as we have seen, seldom or never has an ascertainable date. In fact he precise date of its composition is not significant in the sense in which the date of an ode or a sonnet is significant. An artistic poem receives its final form at the hands of the author at the time of composition. That form is fixed and authoritative. Nobody either has or supposes that he has the right to modify it. Any such alteration is an offence, a corruption, and the critic's duty is to restore the text to its integrity so that we may have before us what the poet wrote and nothing else.[1] The composition of an ode or a sonnet, then, may be regarded as a single creative act. And with the accomplishment of this creative act, the account is closed ; once finished, the poem is a definite entity, no longer subject to any process of development. Not so with the popular ballad. Here the mere act of composition (which is quite as likely to be oral as written) is not the conclusion of the matter ; it is rather the beginning. The product as it comes from the author is handed over to the folk for oral transmission, and thus passes out of his control. If it is accepted by those for whom it is intended, it ceases to be the property of the author ; it becomes the possession of the folk, and a new process begins, that of oral tradition, which is hardly second in importance to the original creative act. As it passes from singer to singer it is changing unceasingly. Old stanzas are dropped and new ones are added ; rhymes are altered ; the names of the characters are varied ; portions of other ballads work their way in ; the catastrophe may be transformed completely. Finally, if the tradition continues for two or three centuries, as it frequently does continue, the whole linguistic complexion of the piece may be so modified with the development of the language in which it is composed, that the original author would not recognize his work if he heard it recited. Taken collectively, these processes of oral tradition amount to a second act of composition, of an inextricably complicated character, in which many persons share (some consciously, others without knowing it), which extends over many generations and much geographical space, and which may be as efficient a cause of the ballad in question as the original creative act of the individual author. It would be a great mistake to regard the results of what we may call, for want of a better term, collective composition, as identical with the corruptions of scribes and editors in the case of a classical text.[2] Individually they are sometimes indistinguishable from such corruptions, but in the aggregate they amount to a distinct kind of authorship which every student of popular literature is obliged to recognize, not only as actually operative in the production of ballads, but as legitimate. They may even result in the production of new ballads to which no individual author can lay claim, so completely is the initial act of creative authorship overshadowed by the secondary act of collective composition. We may compare the processes of language. A word is created by somebody. It then becomes the property of the whole body of those who speak the language, and is subjected to continuous modification from generation to generation. The primary act of the original creator of the word is not more important, and may be far less so, than the secondary acts of his countrymen who transmit his creation and make it their own as they pass it on.

It follows that a genuinely popular ballad can have no fixed and final form, no sole authentic version. There are *texts*, but there is no *text*. Version **A** may be nearer the

---

[1] The author, of course, may revise his own work from time to time ; but that does not affect the principle involved. If such revisions are made, the author's latest revised text becomes the authoritative version, and, for our present purpose, simply supersedes the first draught, which, except for minute questions of literary history, is cancelled and practically ceases to exist.

[2] Of course there are also headlong, blundering corruptions which are comparable to those that take place in the transmission of a written or printed text ; but these may, if necessary, be distinguished from the proper and lawful modifications which are of the very nature of oral tradition.

original than versions **B** and **C**, but that does not affect the pretensions of **B** and **C** to exist and hold up their heads among their fellows. It would be interesting if we could have every one of Mr Child's three hundred and five ballads exactly as it came from the lips or hands of its first composer ; but such versions, if we could arrive at them, would not cancel the variants that have come down to us. Oral transmission and its concomitants are not the accidents of the ballad, they are essential to it ; they are constituent elements of its very nature. Without them the ballad would not be the ballad.

Hitherto we have assumed that ballads are initially the work of individual authors like any other poem, and this may probably be the truth with respect to most and perhaps all of the English and Scottish ballads which have survived, although, as we have seen, the function of the individual author is far less significant in the production of a genuinely popular ballad than in the case of poems which are made by the well-defined process of artistic composition. A different theory of ballad origins was held by James Grimm ; and the mystery in which his indistinct utterances involved the subject has long been a matter of controversy. Grimm's general views on myth, popular poetry, and fairy tales are well known, and need not here be particularized. He held that they were, in the fullest sense, the expression of the spirit of the folk, and that they perpetuated themselves, ever changing and continually fitting themselves to new environments, but with little or no intentional alteration on the part of any given reciter. That these theories were somewhat too far-reaching was pointed out by his own contemporaries. In the main, however, if understood with some reserves in particular cases and with ample allowance for exceptions, little fault can be found with them. The " mystery" is reached when Grimm declares that the people, as a whole, composes poetry ; *das Volk dichtet.*[1] It is easy enough to understand that the material for ballads is in the possession of the folk. It is not more difficult to see that a ballad, when once it exists, becomes the possession of the folk, and is subjected to those vicissitudes of oral tradition which, as we have seen, are hardly less important than the initial act of composition. But the difficulty comes when we try to figure to ourselves the actual production of a ballad in the first instance without the agency of an individual author. For this difficulty Grimm has nowhere provided, nor is it certain that he was entirely clear in his own mind as to the scope or the bearings of his theory in this crucial point.

Modern criticism has made merry with Grimm's theory of ballad authorship. Composition, it is held, must be the act of an individual ; it is inconceivable otherwise ; ballads were composed like other poems ; the folk has no voice as a community; it cannot pour forth unpremeditated and original song in unison. Thus baldly stated, the objections to Grimm's theory are unanswerable, for they speak the words of truth and soberness. But Grimm, though he has not expressed himself with precision, — though perhaps he may even be charged with avoiding the direct issue, — cannot have meant anything so grossly unreasonable as the tenets which his opponents ascribe to him. He was not deficient in common sense, and he certainly had a profound and rarely sympathetic knowledge of popular literature and of the popular spirit in all its manifestations. No doubt he uttered dark oracles, but, though we cannot accept his doctrine in any literal sense, still that is no valid reason for flying off to the opposite pole, — for denying the existence of any problem and asserting that the only difference between ballads and other poems turns on the question of anonymity. Such an explanation is far too simple ; it ignores too many

---

[1] This famous phrase is to be regarded as a summing up of Grimm's theory rather than as a direct quotation. Professor Gummere notes that A. W. Schlegel anticipated Grimm, though he subsequently protested against Grimm's doctrine (Beginnings of Poetry, p. 134).

served facts and leaves uncorrelated too many phenomena which seem to be connected
l which bear at least the appearance of being significant. Before we allow ourselves to
quite so radical as this, we should at all events examine Professor Gummere's theories
to the beginnings of poetry and as to the connection between communal composition
d the ballad.[1]

"Folk" is a large word. It suggests a whole nation, or at all events a huge concourse
people. Let us abandon it, then, for the moment, and think rather of a small tribal
thering, assembled, in very early times, or — what for the anthropologist amounts to
e same thing — under very simple conditions of life, for the purpose of celebrating some
casion of common interest, — a successful hunt, or the return from a prosperous foray,
the repulse of a band of marauding strangers. The object of the meeting is known to
; the deeds which are to be sung, the dance which is to accompany and illustrate the
ging, are likewise familiar to every one. There is no such diversity of intellectual
terests as characterizes even the smallest company of civilized men. There is unity of
eling and a common stock, however slender, of ideas and traditions. The dancing and
nging, in which all share, are so closely related as to be practically complementary parts
a single festal act. Here, now, we have the "folk" of our discussion, reduced, as it
ere, to its lowest terms, — a singing, dancing throng subjected as a unit to a mental and
notional stimulus which is not only favorable to the production of poetry, but is almost
rtain to result in such production. And this is no fancy picture. It is the soberest
nd of science, — a mere brief chapter of descriptive anthropology, for which authorities
ight be cited without number.

Let us next consider the manner in which poetry (the word is of course used under
rdon) is produced in such an assembly. Here again we can proceed upon just grounds
anthropological evidence. Different members of the throng, one after another, may
ant each his verse, composed on the spur of the moment, and the sum of these various
ntributions makes a song. This is communal composition, though each verse, taken by
self, is the work of an individual. A song made in this way is no man's property and
is no individual author. *The folk is its author.*

Communal composition, as just described, is a very simple matter and its products are
finitely crude. That, however, was to be expected. Nobody will hold that 'Robin Hood
nd the Monk' or 'King Estmere' is the direct result of communal composition. It is
nlikely that even the simplest of our extant ballads were made in this fashion. We are
ot now concerned with the connection, if any there be, between the ballad and the compos-
ng folk. That question will come up presently. What is of importance at this stage
f the discussion is to get clearly in mind not merely the theoretical possibility of com-
unal composition on a small scale, but the actual fact of its occurrence. The danger of
isapprehension comes from attaching too dignified a sense to the phrase or from con-
eiving the process which it designates as something systematic or elaborate. All that is
equired is a starting-place. It is necessary to know whether men in a low stage of
dvancement are familiar with this method of composing, and that point is satisfactorily
stablished. Further, the persistence of the habit among civilized peoples in modern

[1] These are based on a profound and extensive acquaintance with the material, and are devel-
ped with great originality and acuteness. See Old English Ballads (Athenæum Press Series), Bos-
on, 1894 (Introduction); The Ballad and Communal Poetry, in the Child Memorial Volume of
tudies and Notes in Philology and Literature, Boston, 1896; a series of three papers on Primitive
oetry and the Ballad, in Modern Philology, vol. I, Chicago, 1903-4; and especially, The Begin-
ings of Poetry, New York and London, 1901.

times is a matter of common knowledge. In the Färöe Islands, a few generations ago,
was common for a group to surround some fisherman who had been unlucky, or ha
otherwise laid himself open to ridicule, and to improvise a song about him, each con
tributing his verse or stanza. In the Russian cigarette factories, the girls who roll th
cigarettes amuse themselves, while at work, by composing songs about each other in
similar way. One girl begins the song, another follows, and so on, till the result of th
act of strictly communal composition is a piece of verse which, in some instances,
retained in the memory and achieves a more or less permanent local reputation. Every
body has heard children engaged in the communal composition of satirical rhymes.

Communal composition, then, is nothing unusual or paradoxical. Not only do we fin
it among simple peoples in a low state of civilization, but everybody can remember in
stances of it which have come under his own observation among his contemporaries o
in which he has taken part himself. With us it has sunk to the position of a mer
amusement, a children's game perhaps, just as the elaborate dances of our forefather
have survived only in such childish dancing games as " Here we go round the gooseberr
bush." [1] The products of communal composition among us are trivial and ephemera
and we fail to observe them, or, at all events, we seldom think of associating them wit
literature. We have come to associate " authorship " with something quite differen
from the singing and dancing throng. To us, as has already been said, an author is
solitary individual sitting in his study, pen in hand. When, therefore, we read of " com
munal authorship," the very idea seems strange and even preposterous. Yet as soon a
we begin to consider, we perceive that we have always been familiar with the phenomeno
in some form or other ; only we have not associated it in our minds with " authorship
at all.

The origin of poetry, like the origin of language, lies too far back for us to find. Th
singing, dancing throng, with its few rude staves, primitive as it seems in compariso
with the multifariousness of artistic literature, must still be very far from primitive i
the literal sense. For our purpose, however, we need follow the trail no farther bacl
than this throng. What came before it is, like the probably arboreal, no concern o
ours in the present discussion. Our business is with the later history of poetry. Ou
task is to discern the connection between the authorship of the extant English and Scot
tish ballads and the conditions of communal composition as described by the anthropo
logists.

As we examine the most characteristic of these extant ballads with a view to any
peculiarities of technique that may distinguish them from other poetry, we immediatel
note certain features which point straight back to the singing, dancing throng and to
communal composition. These elements have been carefully studied by Mr Gummere
so that their significance is unmistakable. First comes the refrain, which, though it
history is one of the obscurest chapters in literature and art, is manifestly a point of con
nection between the ballad and the throng. The refrain can never have been the inven
tion of the solitary, brooding author of our modern conditions. It presupposes a crowd
of singers and dancers. Accordingly, as ballads get farther and farther away from the
people or from singing, they tend to lose their refrains ; the recited ballad has no need
of them. It is not meant that all the ballads in this collection were composed for sing
ing; still less that all of them once possessed the refrain. Mr Child's three hundred and
five numbers include, as we shall see in a moment, ballads of many kinds and illustrat

[1] For proof that games of this kind are descended from dances that were once popular in society
see W. W. Newell, The Games and Songs of American Children.

very grade of popularity. What is meant is rather that there is abundant evidence for regarding the refrain in general as a characteristic feature of ballad poetry which gradually ceased to be essential. Some ballads, therefore, retain this feature; others occur both with and without the refrain; still others took shape at a time when its use was no longer obligatory. Exact dates in a matter of this sort are quite out of the question, and indeed would be destitute of significance if we could arrive at them, for periods in the history of literary forms are not like dynasties; one does not come to an end when the next begins. The refrain, wherever it occurs, whether in 'Robyn and Gandeleyn,' which was written down about 1450, or in 'The Bonny Birdy,' as sung by Mrs Brown about 1783, is a very ancient survival which brings the whole category of ballads into close relations with the singing, dancing throng.

Other elements which point in the same direction are commonplaces, or recurrent passages, varying from a line to several stanzas in length. These are to the ballad very much what idiomatic phrases are to language. Each of them must, at some time, have been the creation of an individual, but all of them have become common property. The balladist who utilizes, for example, the stock stanzas —

> ' Whare will I get a bonny boy,
>   Wad fain wun hos and shoon,
> That wud rin on to my Wayets,
>   And quickly cume again ? '

> ' Here am I, a bonny boy,
>   Wad fain wun hoes and shoon,
> Wha wull run on to your Wayets,
>   And quickly cume again,' [1]

is not inventing. We may go farther. He is not even quoting from an individual predecessor, any more than you and I are when, in the course of conversation, we say " That depends upon circumstances," or " without let or hindrance." [2] The testimony of commonplaces is, indeed, to some extent ambiguous. Their occurrence is consistent with several different theories of ballad authorship and ballad growth. Yet they warn us away from our modern prepossession for the solitary writer, and direct our thoughts toward less sophisticated and more communal conditions of authorship.

Simple repetition is so familiar a feature of the ballad style that it may be dismissed with a word. A message, for instance, is regularly delivered at full length and in precisely the terms in which it was entrusted to the messenger. A similar trait, to which Mr Gummere has given the apposite name of " incremental repetition," is even more noteworthy. It may be seen, for instance, in 'The Twa Sisters' (No. 10), 'The Cruel Brother' (No. 11), and many other ballads. Thus in stanzas 21–26 of 'The Cruel Brother' we have : —

> ' O what will you leave to your father dear ? '
> ' The silver-shod steed that brought me here.'

> ' What will you leave to your mother dear ? '
> ' My velvet pall and my silken gear.'

[1] No. 66 C (Child, II, 131).

[2] Examples of commonplaces are No. 82, st. 4, lines 1, 2 ; No. 39, A 8 ; No. 42, A 6, lines 1, 2 ; No. 47, A 2, lines 1, 2 ; No. 49, B 3 ; No. 63, A 2. lines 1, 2 ; No. 64, B 21, lines 1, 2. For a long list, see Child, V, 474, 475 (Index, s. v.).

'What will you leave to your sister Anne?'
'My silken scarf and my gowden fan.'

'What will you leave to your sister Grace?'
'My bloody cloaths to wash and dress.'

'What will you leave to your brother John?'
'The gallows-tree to hang him on.'

'What will you leave to your brother John's wife?'
'The wilderness to end her life.'

With these stanzas before us, incremental repetition defines itself :— each stanza repeat the substance of the preceding, but with some variation which advances the story. Her again, a composing throng is not necessary to explain the phenomenon, but, given th composing throng as an historical fact, we cannot fail to recognize this kind of repetitio as a stylistic feature that suits the conditions admirably, and may probably have arise in the communal period. Once established, such a feature would become what we fin it — a bit of ballad technique.

It appears, then, that there is no lack of characteristic traits — besides the general ai of impersonality — which justify the conjecture that the history of balladry, if we coul follow it back in a straight line without interruptions, would lead us to very simple con ditions of society, to the singing and dancing throng, to a period of communal compos tion. Demonstration, however, is not to be expected, since, from the very nature of th material, the evidence can never be even approximately complete in the case of any par ticular people. Fortunately, we are not confined to the boundaries of a single nation o language. What has perished in one country has often survived in another, and for th earlier stages of the process we can adduce the plentiful materials which travellers an anthropologists have collected, — materials which have the greater value for our purpose because they were gathered by men who had no thought of any theory of ballad authorshi and were not concerned with the origin of poetry.

So far we have said nothing of the professional minstrel, to whom it was formerly th practice of scholars to ascribe the authorship of ballads. Undoubtedly the minstrel is very ancient figure ; we can trace him, in various guises, to remote antiquity. In Eng land, for example, we can follow him back to a time earlier by many centuries than th oldest ballad text that has come down to us.[1] But, during the periods which we are abl to study, we do not find that the minstrel stands in any such relation to the genuine anc characteristic popular ballad as justifies us in imagining that he is to have the credit o originating or perpetuating that class of popular literature. Such ballads as have beer recovered from oral tradition in recent times (and these, as we have seen, comprise the vast majority of our texts) have not, except now and then, been taken down from the recitation or the singing of minstrels, or of any order of men who can be regarded as the descendants or the representatives of minstrels. They have almost always beer found in the possession of simple folk whose relation to them was in no sense professional. They were the property of the people, not of a limited class or guild of entertainers. A great number of them (among all nations) have been derived from women, — the most stationary part of the community and the farthest removed, by every instinct and habit, from the roving and irresponsible professionalism which characterizes the minstrel.

[1] This, it will be remembered, is 'Judas' (No. 23), which is preserved in a thirteenth-century manuscript.

Take an example. 'The Cruel Brother' (No. 11) was furnished to Professor Child by Miss Margaret Reburn in a version [1] current in Ireland about 1860. With this as a starting-point, let us see how far back we can trace the ballad as actually in oral circulation. In 1858 Aytoun remarks that "this is, perhaps, the most popular of all the Scottish ballads, being commonly sung and recited even at the present day." In 1846 Dixon notes that it is still popular among the peasantry in the west of England. In 1827 Kinloch recorded it in his manuscripts from the recitation of Mary Barr of Clydesdale. In 1800 Alexander Fraser Tytler obtained a copy from Mrs Brown of Falkland, to whose well-stored memory we owe some of the best versions of the Scottish ballads. In the last years of the eighteenth century Mrs Harris learned the piece, as a child, and she recited it to her daughter long afterward. In 1869 it was printed in Notes and Queries as "sung in Cheshire amongst the people" in the preceding century. In 1776 David Herd recorded it in his manuscript as he had heard it sung. Thus we have a succession of *testimonia* for 'The Cruel Brother' from 1860 back to 1776. Nowhere is there any contact with professional minstrelsy. So much for very modern times.

With 'Johnie Armstrong' (No. 169) the test may be applied for a century earlier. Goldsmith, who was born in 1728, recalls, in a famous passage in his Essays (1765), the effect which this ballad had upon him when a child : "The music of the finest singer is dissonance to what I felt when our old dairymaid sung me into tears with Johnny Armstrong's Last Good Night, or the Cruelty of Barbara Allen." In 1658 the ballad was in existence and was printed in Wit Restor'd under the title of 'A Northern Ballet,' and there is no more reason for supposing that it had been in the possession of the minstrel class between that date and Goldsmith's boyhood than for supposing that it was their property between Goldsmith's boyhood and the middle of the nineteenth century. It is superfluous to multiply examples. The reader can collect as many as he likes from Mr Child's volumes. The following proposition will hardly be controverted by any scholar who is familiar with the subject : It is capable of practically formal proof, that for the last two or three centuries the English and Scottish ballads have not, as a general thing, been sung and transmitted by professional minstrels or their representatives. There is no reason whatever for believing that the state of things between 1300 and 1600 was different, in this regard, from that between 1600 and 1900, — and there are many reasons for believing that it was not different.

One other piece of evidence, complementary to that which we have been discussing, makes the case against minstrel authorship almost superfluously convincing. We not only fail to find any special connection between the professional minstrel and the great mass of popular ballads, but we do find an intimate connection between the minstrels and works of an altogether different order. Ballads are one thing: the mediæval *Spielmannsdichtung* or minstrel poetry is another. The two categories are recognized as distinct by all literary historians. In fact, they are much more than distinct, — they are incommensurable. It is not conceivable that the same order of mind and the same habits of thought should have produced them both. The ballads, then, belong to the folk; they are not the work of a limited professional class, whether of high or of low degree.

Let us not misunderstand the situation. It is not maintained that the minstrels never meddled with ballads at all. It was their business to know all kinds of poetry so as to make themselves acceptable to all sorts and conditions of men. No doubt they had a share in carrying ballads from place to place and in transmitting them to posterity. There is direct proof of this. We owe our early copy of the 'Hunting of the Cheviot'

[1] Child's J, not printed in this volume.

(No. 162) to Richard Sheale, a humble member of the guild; but we know that he did not compose the ballad, for we have not only strong external evidence to the contrary but also four pieces of Sheale's own (not ballads) which settle the question forever. Of course the minstrels did sometimes compose in the popular strain. We have a few minstrel ballads, like 'The Boy and the Mantle' (No. 29) and 'Crow and Pie' (No. 111), which put this beyond a peradventure. Not all ballads are of the same origin, as we shall see presently. But the existence of such ballads is only additional proof that the bulk of our traditional material is not of minstrel authorship. The difference between 'The Boy and the Mantle' and the ballads that come straight from the folk is very striking. It is the difference between sophistication and artlessness.

It is time to gather up the threads of our discussion. We have examined the popular ballad from various points of view, and have weighed and measured a good many opinions about it. Let us apply our conclusions to the material that survives, and, so far as possible, let us see what is to be thought of the origin of the three hundred and five ballads that lie before us in Professor Child's collection.

The extant ballads of England and Scotland represent, in the main, the end of a process of which the beginning may not improbably be discovered in the period of communal composition. They were not themselves composed in this way, but were, in the first instance, the work of individual authors, at least in the great majority of cases. These authors, however, were not professional poets or minstrels, but members of the folk, and their function was in many respects different from that which we ascribe to an author to-day. Let us try to figure to ourselves a typical instance. In the first place, the ballad poet stands in a relation both to his material and to his audience that distinguishes his activity from that of the conscious literary artist. His subject is not his own, — it belongs to the folk. It is a popular tradition of immemorial antiquity, or a situation so simple and obvious as to be matter of general experience, or a recent occurrence which has been taken up by the mouth of common fame. He has no wish to treat the theme in a novel way, — no desire to utter his peculiar feelings about it or to impress it with his individuality. He is not, like the artistic poet among us, an exceptional figure with a message, either of substance or form. He takes no credit to himself, for he deserves none. What he does, many of his neighbors could do as well. Accordingly, he is impersonal and without self-consciousness. He utters what everybody feels, — he is a voice rather than a person. Further, his composition is not a solitary act. He improvises orally,[1] with his audience before him, — or rather, with his audience about him. There is the closest emotional contact between him and his hearers, — a contact which must have a distinct effect on the composer, so that the audience, even if they kept silence (as they can hardly be supposed to do), would still have a kind of share in his poetic act. Here is the strongest contrast to the situation of the modern literary artist, who, in the solitude of his sound-proof study, writes down his own thoughts and feelings, uncertain who will read them, or even if anybody will read them, — addressing himself to an audience *in posse*, who know neither his face nor his voice, nor even his handwriting. And the difference, it will be observed, consists in the function which the throng (the "folk") performs — by its mere presence, if nothing more — in the production (the "authorship") of ballad poetry.

---

[1] Improvisation in verse is a lost art among us, and we instinctively regard it as a very special mark of exceptional genius. But this is a serious misapprehension. It survives in full vigor among the folk in most countries, and is well known to be far less difficult, in itself, than the art of speaking extempore in well-turned prose sentences. The point needs no argument, for it is generally admitted.

Commonly, however, the audience will have a far larger function than that of sympathetic and stimulative emotional contact with the author, as we must still call him for want of a better name. As he composes, the author draws freely on a large stock of commonplaces which are public property. These are, of course, entirely familiar to every person in the company, as well as the points in any narrative (for these are also fixed by long-standing tradition) at which the conventional stanzas must come in. When the author arrives at such a point, the audience join their voices with his. So also in passages which merely repeat, in identical terms, what has already been said or sung, as in the delivery of a message. Again, in a succession of stanzas constructed on the principle of incremental repetition, the author and the audience may become merged in the same way, even if the first stanza of the series is in some degree original. Thus we have arrived at a state of things which is in effect scarcely to be distinguished from the supposedly inconceivable phenomenon of a unanimous throng composing poetry with one voice. That dark oracle *das Volk dichtet* has interpreted itself in action, though not without the license which every Delphic utterance may claim.

For the sake of concreteness, let us apply what has just been said to a specific example, — ' The Hangman's Tree,' [1] — taken down from singing in America a few years ago. Miss Backus, who obtained the ballad, remarks, on the basis of local information : " This is an old English song, . . . which was brought over to Virginia before the Revolution. It has not been written for generations, for none of the family have been able to read or write."

THE HANGMAN'S TREE

1 ' Hangman, hangman, howd yo hand,
   O howd it wide and far !
For theer I see my feyther coomin,
   Riding through the air.

2 ' Feyther, feyther, ha yo brot me goold ?
   Ha yo paid my fee ?
Or ha yo coom to see me hung,
   Beneath tha hangman's tree ? '

3 ' I ha naw brot yo goold,
   I ha naw paid yo fee,
But I ha coom to see yo hung
   Beneath tha hangman's tree.'

4 ' Hangman, hangman, howd yo hand,
   O howd it wide and far !
For theer I see my meyther coomin,
   Riding through the air.

5 ' Meyther, meyther, ha yo brot me goold ?
   Ha yo paid my fee ?
Or ha yo coom to see me hung,
   Beneath tha hangman's tree ? '

6 ' I ha naw brot yo goold,
   I ha naw paid yo fee,
But I ha coom to see yo hung
   Beneath tha hangman's tree.'

---

[1] ' The Hangman's Tree ' is a version of ' The Maid Freed from the Gallows ' (No. 95), and was first printed in the Additions and Corrections in Mr Child's fifth volume (p. 296).

7 ' Hangman, hangman, howd yo hand,
   O howd it wide and far !
For theer I see my sister coomin,
   Riding through the air.

8 ' Sister, sister, ha yo brot me goold ?
   Ha yo paid my fee ?
Or ha yo coom to see me hung,
   Beneath tha hangman's tree ? '

9 ' I ha naw brot yo goold,
   I ha naw paid yo fee,
But I ha coom to see yo hung
   Beneath tha hangman's tree.'

10 ' Hangman, hangman, howd yo hand,
   O howd it wide and far !
For theer I see my sweetheart coomin,
   Riding through the air.

11 ' Sweetheart, sweetheart, ha yo brot me goold ˊ
   Ha yo paid my fee ?
Or ha yo coom to see me hung,
   Beneath tha hangman's tree ? '

12 ' O I ha brot yo goold,
   And I ha paid yo fee,
And I ha coom to take yo froom
   Beneath tha hangman's tree.'

Suppose now that ' The Hangman's Tree ' is a new ballad, sung for the first time by the improvising author. The audience are silent for the first two stanzas and until the first line of the third has been finished. After that, they join in the song. So inevitable is the course of the narrative, so conventionally fixed the turn of the phraseology, that they could almost finish the piece by themselves if the author remained silent. At most they would need his prompting for " meyther," " sister," and " sweetheart " in stanzas 4, 7, and 10, and for a few words in stanza 12. If, in accordance with an hypothesis which is justifiable in many cases, they were familiar with the outline of the plot, though they had never heard a ballad on the subject, they would not require even so much assistance as this. The song is ended, the creative act of composition is finished, — and what has become of the author ? He is lost in the throng.

' The Hangman's Tree ' is, to be sure, an extreme instance of simplicity in plot and of inevitableness in both structure and diction; but that does not make it an unfair example. It is a survival [1] of an archaic type-specimen, in full vigor of traditional life, at a very late date, when most of our ballads belong to much more highly developed genera. As we study it, we are carried farther back in the direction of communal composition than we could reasonably hope to get at this age of the world, — so far, in truth, that a sanguine theorist might regard the broken line as repaired again. And ' The Hangman's Tree ' is by no means a solitary specimen of its kind. The ballad literature of Europe affords examples enough of almost or quite as high a degree of structural and stylistic simplicity,

[1] Or, if one prefers, a reversion to the type. The distinction is of no consequence, since we are here concerned not with ' The Hangman's Tree ' itself, but with what it stands for.

and similar traits are visible in many English and Scottish pieces, though seldom to quite the same extent.

We have described the characteristic method of ballad authorship as improvisation in the presence of a sympathetic company which may even, at times, participate in the process. Such a description is in general warranted by the evidence; and though it cannot be proved for any of the English and Scottish ballads, is not improbable for some of them. The actual facts with regard to any particular piece in this collection are beyond our knowledge, and the matter need not be insisted on. Even if none of our ballads were composed in this way, still many of them conform to a type which was established under the conditions of authorship referred to. It makes no difference whether a given ballad was in fact composed in the manner described, or whether it was composed (or even written) in solitude, provided the author belonged to the folk, derived his material from popular sources, made his ballad under the inherited influence of the method described, and gave it to the folk as soon as he had made it, — and provided, moreover, the folk accepted the gift and subjected it to that course of oral tradition which, as we have seen, is essential to the production of a genuine ballad. That most of the three hundred and five numbers in Mr Child's collection satisfy these conditions is beyond question. In other words, most of these poems are genuine popular ballads within the limits of any reasonable definition of that term. It remains to speak of certain other pieces and to account for their inclusion in the book.[1]

The "minstrel ballad" has already been referred to. Three undoubted examples, all of first-rate quality, are 'The Boy and the Mantle' (No. 29), 'King Arthur and King Cornwall' (No. 30), and 'The Marriage of Sir Gawain' (No. 31). Their characteristics are felicitously summed up by Professor Child in his introduction to 'The Boy and the Mantle.' They are, he says, "clearly not of the same rise, and not meant for the same ears, as those which go before. They would come down by professional rather than by domestic tradition, through minstrels rather than knitters and weavers. They suit the hall better than the bower, the tavern or public square better than the cottage, and would not go to the spinning-wheel at all." All three, it should be noticed, stand in close relation to the materials of mediæval romantic fiction, even if they are not directly derived from metrical romances. Yet they are indubitably ballads, composed in the popular style and perpetuated for a time by oral tradition. With them should be compared 'Sir Cawline' (No. 61). This looks as if it were simplified from a romance in stanzas, which, however, would very probably itself have been constructed on the basis of ballads now lost. Minstrel ballads of a later and less popular type are such historical pieces as 'Durham Field' (No. 159), 'The Rising in the North' (No. 175), 'Northumberland Betrayed by Douglas' (No. 176), and 'The Rose of England' (No. 166). The last-mentioned is remarkable for its use of allegory, which makes it seem far more artificial than the others. 'The Earl of Westmoreland' (No. 177) is a curious combination of historical material with romantic fiction of a conventional order. The cynical 'Crow and Pie' (No. 111) is clearly the work of a minstrel, and stands in a class by itself; as a whole, it might be refused the designation of popular ballad, but it contains one passage (stanzas 9–14) which justifies its inclusion in a collection of this kind, especially in view of the age of the manuscript.

"Broadside ballads" are of two main classes, which are really quite distinct: those that are traditional and those that are not. In the seventeenth century there was a great demand for printed ballads, and there grew up a class of professional "purveyors to the press," as Mr Child calls them, who were kept busy in supplying materials for the single-

---

[1] In what follows no complete enumeration is made under the several categories.

page issues which were hawked about by pedlars and with which every alehouse seems to have been papered. Many traditional ballads were printed in this form, usually in debased versions. Now and then a good old ballad was made over by some hack-writer, and when this was the case, the broadside text, though a pitiful specimen of Grub Street versification, may preserve the substance of a lost traditional ballad. A probable instance is 'The Famous Flower of Serving-Men' (No. 106). Still more remarkable is 'The Suffolk Miracle' (No. 272), which is the only representative in English of the so-called Lenore cycle. The great majority of the broadside ballads, however, belong to the second, or non-traditional class, and have no claim to be admitted into a collection like that of Professor Child. It is to rubbish of this character that the scornful allusions to ballad-mongers in Shakspere and the other Elizabethan dramatists have reference. Hundreds of such pieces have been reprinted by the Ballad Society. They are generally composed in some form of the ballad stanza, and they use some of the commonplaces of the ballad style, but they are destitute of merit, and, though they are of value to the student of language and manners, they have nothing to do with the subject of this essay.

Several broadside ballads of the poorer sort will be found among the thirty-eight numbers (117–154) relating to Robin Hood. Some of these are inserted because they presumably or conceivably are based on earlier and more traditional pieces; others because they embody a situation which occurs in genuine ballads; still others because, though of no value in themselves and destitute of any claim to traditional antecedents, they are a part of the evidence about the famous outlaw and illustrate the literary history of balladry. Taken as a whole, the Robin Hood pieces afford materials of the highest interest for the study of ballad and epic. The older ballads are in the best traditional vein. The 'Gest' (No. 117) is, as Mr Child says, "a popular epic, composed from several ballads by a poet of a thoroughly congenial spirit. No one of the ballads from which it is made up is extant in a separate shape, and some portions of the story may have been of the compiler's own invention." It may be contrasted with Nos. 149 and 154. The former, 'Robin Hood's Birth, Breeding, Valor, and Marriage,' is a jocular piece, the work of some seventeenth-century rhymester who cared nothing for tradition and to whom the simplicity of the ballad style suggested only a temptation to good-humored caricature. The latter, Martin Parker's 'True Tale of Robin Hood,' is a prosaic *omnium gatherum*, professing to be authentic biography. It is the only text in Mr Child's whole collection which is the work of a known author. 'Robin Hood and the Prince of Aragon' (No. 129) is a kind of metrical romance in the ballad stanza. Garlands, or little pamphlets of verse, differing from broadsides only in their form, are the authorities for several of our Robin Hood texts.[1]

The mere fact that a ballad is derived from recitation is of course no positive proof that it is traditional. Imitations and counterfeits may be fabricated orally or may be written down and furnished to guileless collectors as from the mouths of the people. Some of the later pieces in this collection are very suspicious and others are almost certainly spurious. What to include and what to reject is a difficult question, which no two scholars would answer in precisely the same way. It is fitting, however, that the student of literary history should have before him specimens of the decadent period. Occasionally, too, such imitations contain stanzas of value, or are otherwise significant. Thus 'Willie's Fatal Visit' (No. 255) is a hotch-potch of three ballads with one stanza from a fourth; yet it contains a very spirited passage (stanzas 15–17) which is unknown elsewhere and worthy of preservation for its own sake. Who put the piece together we

[1] See the bibliographical notes prefixed to the several ballads.

cannot tell, — perhaps the blind beggar whom Buchan employed to collect for him. In any case, the conglomerate is instructive; for it shows how new ballads may come into existence by a process of amalgamation, and this is a process which is quite as active among the folk as in the laboratory of the counterfeiter. David Herd is above suspicion, and he lived at a time when good ballads were abundant and tradition was still pure and vigorous; whatever occurs in his manuscripts may be unhesitatingly accepted as a faithful transcript from the lips of the people. Yet he records a copy of 'Clerk Saunders' (No. 69) consisting of forty-one stanzas, the last fifteen of which are merely 'Sweet William's Ghost' (No. 77) slightly modified so as to fit what precedes. This is the simplest kind of traditional compounding. A similar example may be seen in the copy of 'The Clerk's Twa Sons o Owsenford' (No. 72) preserved in the memory of the grandmother of Robert Chambers, which concludes with a beautiful fragment of 'The Wife of Usher's Well' (No. 79). Complications less easy to disentangle may be seen by studying the relations of 'Willie o Douglas Dale' (No. 101), 'Willie and Earl Richard's Daughter' (No. 102), and 'Rose the Red and White Lily' (No. 103) to each other and to 'Leesome Brand' (No. 15). Here both tradition and manufacture have been operative. A good example of contamination which has not resulted in the genesis of a new ballad occurs in the "old lady's" version of 'The Mother's Malison' (No. 216 A), which has appropriated an incident that belongs to 'The Lass of Roch Royal' (No. 76). To appreciate the full effects of oral tradition in this and other directions, the investigator must have recourse to the full body of variants printed by Professor Child in his large collection. The present volume, however, contains examples enough to illustrate and enforce what has been said of the significance of oral tradition in the problem of ballad "authorship." [1] It was no doubt the feeling that the popular ballad is a fluid and unstable thing that has prompted so many editors — among them Sir Walter Scott, whom it is impossible to assail, however much the scholarly conscience may disapprove — to deal freely with the versions that came into their hands. "Doch Homeride zu seyn, auch nur als letzter, ist schön"!

Of literary "imitations of the ancient ballad" little need be said. Even when the polite authors of such pieces have palmed them off as genuine, one must rather wonder that the imposture succeeded than give way to anger at the attempt. Nobody who is at all well-read in genuine "oral literature" can be deceived. Lady Wardlaw's 'Hardycnute,' which puzzled many brains in its time, has not a single ballad touch; its two good lines, —

> Stately stept he east the wa'
> And stately stept he west,

have nothing popular about them. The Rev. Mr Lamb's 'Laidley Worm of Spindleston Heughs,' which he gave out as "made by the old Mountain Bard, Duncan Frasier, living on Cheviot, A. D. 1270," [2] was hardly meant to deceive, and would not be dangerous if it had been so meant. In short, the traditional ballad appears to be inimitable by any person of literary cultivation, and we may well feel grateful to those poets and poetasters who have tried their hands at it, for their invariable failure is one of the strongest proofs — amounting almost to demonstration — that there *is* a difference between the "poetry of the folk" and "the poetry of art." A solitary, though doubtful, exception is 'Kinmont Willie" (No. 186), which is under vehement suspicion of being the work of Sir

---

[1] See p. xvii, above.
[2] See Child, English and Scottish Popular Ballads, I, 308.

Walter Scott. Sir Walter's success, however, in a special kind of balladry for which he was better adapted by nature and habit of mind than for any other, would only emphasize the universal failure. And it must not be forgotten that 'Kinmont Willie,' if it be Scott's work, is not made out of whole cloth; it is a working-over of one of the best traditional ballads known ('Jock o the Side'), with the intention of fitting it to an historical exploit of Buccleuch's. Further, the exploit itself was of such a nature that it might well have been celebrated in a ballad, — indeed, one is tempted to say that it must have been so celebrated. And finally, Sir Walter Scott felt towards "the Kinmont" and "the bold Buccleuch" precisely as the moss-trooping author of such a ballad would have felt. For once, then, the miraculous happened, — and, when we study the situation, we perceive that, for this once, it was not so great a miracle after all.

Peter Buchan's blind beggar has been casually mentioned, but he is too notorious a personage to dismiss without more formality. There is a good deal of his work in Mr Child's collection (most of it omitted in the present volume), and an attempt must be made to determine his position, and in particular his significance, in the history of oral tradition. It is hard to be patient with James Rankin (for that was his name), but perhaps we may see occasion for something better than patience before we have done with him. Liar though he was, his falsehoods may give evidence that a truthteller could not afford us.

Buchan's Ancient Ballads and Songs of the North of Scotland, for which Rankin's industry as collector, composer, and rhapsodist furnished much of the material, appeared in 1828. Some of the ballads which it contains are found nowhere else, and most of these are suspicious enough, though several of them are reproduced by Mr Child, and repeated in this volume, on the same principle which has led to the inclusion of certain dubious broadsides — because they may preserve more or less genuine material in a disguised shape. Most of Buchan's texts, however, are versions of ballads otherwise vouched for. In this case, they are almost always the longest versions known, padded with superfluous details (often silly beyond expression), tricked out with pinchbeck finery, and thoroughly vulgarized in style and spirit. Here we have the work of Rankin, who seems to have been paid by the yard, and who found his honest patron an easy man to cajole. Now the significance of James Rankin lies in the fact that he was in effect a professional minstrel of the humbler order, or at least the lineal descendant or representative of the minstrel class of former times. When we compare his own productions, or the versions which he has recomposed, with those which other collectors were deriving at about the same time from non-professional sources, — shepherds, ploughmen, nurses, and other simple bodies who had no touch of literature and no ambition except to sing the old songs as they had heard them sung, — we see in a moment the absurdity of the notion that our popular ballads were composed or even largely transmitted by minstrels. And thus one chapter, and a troublesome one, of our investigation is brought to a satisfactory close.

We have touched upon most of the problems that confront the investigator of the popular ballad. Certain others, like that of the transmission of ballads from country to country, which includes the special question of kinship between the English and Scottish ballads and those of Scandinavia, do not come within the scope of this introduction. The same is true of the history of ballad collections, which would take much space, and in lieu of which the reader is referred once more to the List of Sources on pp. 677–684.

Of the merit of the English and Scottish ballads nothing need be said. It is unhesitatingly admitted by all persons who care for ballads at all. There is no occasion to make comparisons as to excellence between these pieces and the poetry of art. Such

parisons are misleading; they tend only to confound the distinctions between two
y different categories of literature. The ballads must stand or fall by themselves,
by reason of their likeness or unlikeness to Dante or Shakspere or Milton or Brown-
. Above all things, they should not be judged indiscriminately or in the lump. There
good ballads and poor ballads, as there are good dramas and poor dramas, and this
ume contains an abundance of both sorts. On the whole, however, the average of
ellence is probably as high as in most volumes of verse of equal dimensions. Finally,
popular ballad, though it may be despised, cannot be ignored by the student of
rature. Whatever may be thought of the importance of such verse in its bearing on
origin of poetry in general, or of epic poetry in particular, the ballad, like other forms
popular material, has in the last two centuries exercised a powerful influence on artis-
literature, and it will always have to be reckoned with by the literary historian.

G. L. K.

1

IDDLES WISELY EXPOUNDED

In the oldest version (A*) the devil threatens
carry off a maiden if she cannot answer cer-
n riddles. She solves them all, and (at the
l) calls the devil by his right name, thus no
bt putting him to flight. The "good end-
" of **A** (sts. 19–23) is a modern perversion.
Riddles play an important part in popular
ry, and that from very remote times. No
e needs to be reminded of Samson, Œdipus,
ollonius of Tyre. Riddle tales, which, if
; so old as the oldest of these, may be carried
all likelihood some centuries beyond our era,
l live in Asiatic and European tradition, and
ve their representatives in popular ballads.
e largest class of these tales is that in which
e party has to guess another's riddles, or two
als compete in giving or guessing, under
nalty in either instance of forfeiting life or
me other heavy wager (see No. 45). In a
ond class, a suitor can win a lady's hand
ly by guessing riddles (see No. 46); there is
netimes a penalty of loss of life for the un-
ccessful. Thirdly, there is the tale of the
ever Lass, who wins a husband, and some-
mes a crown, by guessing riddles, solving
ficult but practicable problems, or matching
d evading impossibilities (see No. 2).

A*

Rawlinson MS. D. 328, fol. 174 b, Bodleian
brary, in a hand of about 1450.

Inter diabolus et virgo.

Wol ȝe here a wonder thynge
Betwyxt a mayd *and* þe fovle fende ?

Thys spake þe fend to þe mayd:
'Beleue on me, mayd, to day.

'Mayd, mote y thi leman be,
Wyssedom y wolle teche the:

4 'All þe wyssedom off the world,
Hyf þou wolt be true *and* forward holde

5 'What ys hyer þan ys [þe] tre ?
What ys dypper þan ys the see ?

6 'What ys scharpper þan ys þe þorne ?
What ys loder þan ys þe horne ?

7 'What [ys] longger þan ys þe way ?
What is rader þan ys þe day ?

8 'What [ys] bether than is þe bred ?
What ys scharpper than ys þe dede ?

9 'What ys grenn*er* þan ys þe wode ?
What ys sweett*er* þan ys þe note ?

10 'What ys swifter þan ys the wynd ?
What ys recher þan ys þe kyng*e* ?

11 'What ys ȝelu*er* þan ys þe wex ?
What [ys] soft*er* þan ys þe flex ?

12 'But þou now answery me,
Thu schalt for soþe my leman be.'

13 'Ihesu, for þy myld myȝth,
As thu art kynge and knyȝt,

14 'Lene me wisdome to answere here ryȝth,
And schylde me fram the fovle wyȝth !

15 'Hewene ys heyer than ys the tre,
Helle ys dypper þan ys the see.

16 'Hongyr ys scharpp*er* than [ys] þe
thorne,
Þonder ys lodder than ys þe horne.

17 'Loukyng*e* ys long*er* than ys þe way,
Syn ys rader þan ys þe day.

18 'Godys flesse ys bet*ur* þan ys the brede,
Payne ys streng*er* þan ys þe dede.

19 'Gras ys grenner þan ys þe wode.
  Loue ys swetter þan ys the notte.

20 'Þowt ys swifter þan ys the wynde,
  Ihesus ys recher þan ys the kynge.

21 'Safer is ʒeluer than ys the wexs,
  Selke ys softer þan ys the flex.

22 'Now, thu fende, styl thu be;
  Nelle ich speke no more with the !'

A

a. 'A Noble Riddle Wisely Expounded,'
broadside in the Rawlinson collection, 4to, 566,
fol. 193, Wood, E. 25, fol. 15.   b. Pepys, III,
19, No. 17.   c. Douce, II, fol. 168 b.   d. Pills
to Purge Melancholy, IV, 130, ed. 1719.

1 THERE was a lady of the North Country,
  Lay the bent to the bonny broom
  And she had lovely daughters three.
  Fa la la la, fa la la la ra re

2 There was a knight of noble worth
  Which also lived in the North.

3 The knight, of courage stout and brave,
  A wife he did desire to have.

4 He knocked at the ladie's gate
  One evening when it was late.

5 The eldest sister let him in,
  And pin'd the door with a silver pin.

6 The second sister she made his bed,
  And laid soft pillows under his head.

7 The youngest daughter that same night,
  She went to bed to this young knight.

8 And in the morning, when it was day,
  These words unto him she did say :

9 'Now you have had your will,' quoth she,
  'I pray, sir knight, will you marry
  me ?'

10 The young brave knight to her replyed,
  'Thy suit, fair maid, shall not be deny'd.

11 'If thou canst answer me questions
  three,
  This very day will I marry thee.'

12 'Kind sir, in love, O then,' quoth sh
  'Tell me what your [three] quest
  be.'

13 'O what is longer than the way,
  Or what is deeper than the sea ?

14 'Or what is louder than the horn,
  Or what is sharper than a thorn ?

15 'Or what is greener than the grass,
  Or what is worse then a woman was

16 'O love is longer than the way,
  And hell is deeper than the sea.

17 'And thunder is louder than the hor
  And hunger is sharper than a thorn.

18 'And poyson is greener than the gra
  And the Devil is worse than won
  was.'

19 When she these questions answered b
  The knight became exceeding glad.

20 And having [truly] try'd her wit,
  He much commended her for it.

21 And after, as it is verifi'd,
  He made of her his lovely bride.

22 So now, fair maidens all, adieu,
  This song I dedicate to you.

23 I wish that you may constant prove
  Vnto the man that you do love.

C

'The Unco Knicht's Wowing,' Motherwe
MS., p. 647. From the recitation of Mrs Sto

1 THERE was a knicht riding frae the ea
  Sing the Cather banks, the bon
  brume
  Wha had been wooing at monie a pla
  And ye may beguile a young th
  sune

2 He came unto a widow's door,
  And speird whare her three docht
  were.

3 The auldest ane 's to a washing gane,
  The second 's to a baking gane.

4 The youngest ane 's to a wedding gane,
And it will be nicht or she be hame.

5 He sat him doun upon a stane,
Till thir three lasses came tripping hame.

6 The auldest ane 's to the bed making,
And the second ane's to the sheet spreading.

7 The youngest ane was bauld and bricht,
And she was to lye with this unco knicht.

8 ' Gin ye will answer me questions ten,
The morn ye sall be made my ain.

9 ' O what is heigher nor the tree ?
And what is deeper nor the sea ?

10 ' Or what is heavier nor the lead ?
And what is better nor the breid ?

11 ' O what is whiter nor the milk ?
Or what is safter nor the silk ?

12 ' Or what is sharper nor a thorn ?
Or what is louder nor a horn ?

13 ' Or what is greener nor the grass ?
Or what is waur nor a woman was ? '

14 ' O heaven is higher nor the tree,
And hell is deeper nor the sea.

15 ' O sin is heavier nor the lead,
The blessing 's better nor the bread.

16 ' The snaw is whiter nor the milk,
And the down is safter nor the silk.

17 ' Hunger is sharper nor a thorn.
And shame is louder nor a horn,

18 ' The pies are greener nor the grass,
And Clootie's waur nor a woman was.'

19 As sune as she the fiend did name,
He flew awa in a blazing flame.

2

THE ELFIN KNIGHT

This ballad is related to a remarkable group of stories, covering, by representatives which are still extant or may be shown to have existed, a large part of Asia and Europe. In the particular type to which our ballad belongs, a clever girl wins a husband by her quickness of wit ; the man imposes tasks, of which the girl stands acquitted if she can match each of them with another of no less difficulty. The elf is an interloper from some other ballad (cf. No. 4); the suitor should be a mortal.

A

' A proper new ballad entituled The Wind hath blown my Plaid away, or, A Discourse betwixt a young [Wo]man and the Elphin Knight;' a black letter broadside, of about 1670, in the Pepysian library, bound up at the end of a copy of Blind Harry's ' Wallace,' Edinburgh, 1673.

My plaid awa, my plaid awa,
And ore the hill and far awa,
And far awa to Norrowa,
My plaid shall not be blown awa.

1 The elphin knight sits on yon hill,
Ba, ba, ba, lilli ba
He blaws his horn both lowd and shril.
The wind hath blown my plaid awa

2 He blowes it east, he blowes it west,
He blowes it where he lyketh best.

3 'I wish that horn were in my kist,
Yea, and the knight in my armes two.'

4 She had no sooner these words said,
When that the knight came to her bed.

5 'Thou art over young a maid,' quoth he,
' Married with me thou il wouldst be.'

6 'I have a sister younger than I,
And she was married yesterday.'

7 'Married with me if thou wouldst be,
A courtesie thou must do to me.

8 'For thou must shape a sark to me,
Without any cut or heme,' quoth he.

9 'Thou must shape it knife-and-sheer-lesse,
And also sue it needle-threedlesse.'

10 'If that piece of courtesie I do to thee,
Another thou must do to me.

11 ' I have an aiker of good ley-land,
    Which lyeth low by yon sea-strand.

12 ' For thou must eare it with thy horn,
    So thou must sow it with thy corn.

13 ' And bigg a cart of stone and lyme,
    Robin Redbreast he must trail it hame.

14 ' Thou must barn it in a mouse-holl,
    And thrash it into thy shoes soll.

15 ' And thou must winnow it in thy looff,
    And also seek it in thy glove.

16 ' For thou must bring it over the sea,
    And thou must bring it dry home to me.

17 ' When thou hast gotten thy turns well
        done,
    Then come to me and get thy sark then.'

18 ' I 'l not quite my plaid for my life ;
    It haps my seven bairns and my wife.'
        The wind shall not blow my plaid awa

19 ' My maidenhead I 'l then keep still,
    Let the elphin knight do what he will.'
        The wind's not blown my plaid awa

3

THE FALSE KNIGHT UPON
THE ROAD

This singular ballad is known only through
Motherwell. The idea at the bottom of the
piece is that the devil will carry off the wee boy
if he can nonplus him. There is a curious
Swedish ballad of the same description, in
which an old crone, possibly a witch, is substituted for the false knight.

A

Motherwell's Minstrelsy, Introduction, p.
lxxiv. From Galloway.

1 ' O WHARE are ye gaun ? '
    Quo the fause knicht upon the road :
  ' I 'm gaun to the scule,'
    Quo the wee boy, and still he stude.

2 ' What is that upon your back ? ' quo etc.
  ' Atweel it is my bukes,' quo etc.

3 ' What 's that ye 've got in your arm ?
  ' Atweel it is my peit.'

4 ' Wha 's aucht they sheep ? '
  ' They are mine and my mither's.'

5 ' How monie o them are mine ? '
  ' A' they that hae blue tails.'

6 ' I wiss ye were on yon tree : '
  ' And a gude ladder under me.'

7 ' And the ladder for to break : '
  ' And you for to fa down.'

8 ' I wiss ye were in yon sie : '
  ' And a gude bottom under me.'

9 ' And the bottom for to break : '
  ' And ye to be drowned.'

4

LADY ISABEL AND THE ELF-
KNIGHT

Of all ballads this has perhaps obtained the
widest circulation. It is nearly as well known
to the southern as to the northern nations o
Europe. It has an extraordinary currency in
Poland. The Germans, Low and High, and the
Scandinavians, preserve it, in a full and evidently ancient form, even in the tradition of
this generation. Among the Latin nations it
has, indeed, shrunk to very meagre propor-
tions, and though the English forms are not
without ancient and distinctive marks, most of
these have been eliminated, and the better ballads are very brief. In A and B the supernatural character of the Elf-Knight is retained
(less clearly in B) ; in others it is lost completely, and he has become merely " false Sir
John " or the like.

The Dutch ballad, ' Halewijn,' is far better
preserved than the English. Heer Halewijn
sang such a song that those who heard it longed
to be with him. A king's daughter asked her
father if she might go to Halewijn. "No,'
he said ; " those who go that way never come
back." So said mother and sister, but her
brother's answer was, " I care not where you
go, so long as you keep your honor." She
dressed herself splendidly, took the best horse
from her father's stable, and rode to the wood,
where she found Halewijn waiting for her.
They then rode on further, till they came to a
gallows, on which many women were hanging

Halewijn offers her the choice between hanging and the sword. She chooses the sword. Only take off your coat first; for a maid's blood spirts a great way, and it would be a pity to spatter you.'' His head was off before his coat, but the tongue still spake. This dialogue ensues : —

'Go yonder into the corn,
  And blow upon my horn,
  That all my friends you may warn.'

'Into the corn I will not go,
  And on your horn I will not blow :
  A murderer's bidding I will not do !

'Go yonder under the gallows-tree,
  And fetch a pot of salve for me,
  And rub my red neck lustily.'

'Under the gallows I will not go,
  Nor will I rub your red neck, no,
  A murderer's bidding I will not do.'

She takes the head by the hair and washes it in a spring, and rides back through the wood. Half-way through she meets Halewijn's mother, who asks after her son ; and she tells her that he is gone hunting, that he will never be seen again, that he is dead, and she has his head in her lap. When she came to her father's gate, she blew the horn like any man.

And when the father heard the strain,
He was glad she had come back again.

Thereupon they held a feast,
The head was on the table placed.

A

a. 'The Gowans sae gay,' Buchan's Ballads of the North of Scotland, I, 22. b. Motherwell's MS., p. 563.

1 FAIR lady Isabel sits in her bower sewing,
        Aye as the gowans grow gay
    There she heard an elf-knight blawing his horn.
        The first morning in May

2 'If I had yon horn that I hear blawing,
    And yon elf-knight to sleep in my bosom.'

3 This maiden had scarcely these words spoken,
    Till in at her window the elf-knight has luppen.

4 'It 's a very strange matter, fair maiden,'' said he,
    'I canna blaw my horn but ye call on me.

5 'But will ye go to yon greenwood side ?
    If ye canna gang, I will cause you to ride.'

6 He leapt on a horse, and she on another,
    And they rode on to the greenwood together.

7 'Light down, light down, lady Isabel,' said he,
    'We are come to the place where ye are to die.'

8 'Hae mercy, hae mercy, kind sir, on me,
    Till ance my dear father and mother I see.'

9 'Seven king's-daughters here hae I slain,
    And ye shall be the eight o them.'

10 'O sit down a while, lay your head on my knee,
    That we may hae some rest before that I die.'

11 She stroak'd him sae fast, the nearer he did creep,
    Wi a sma charm she lulld him fast asleep.

12 Wi his ain sword-belt sae fast as she ban him,
    Wi his ain dag-durk sae sair as she dang him.

13 'If seven king's-daughters here ye hae slain,
    Lye ye here, a husband to them a'.'

B

a. 'The Water o Wearie's Well,' Buchan's MSS., II, fol. 80. b. Buchan's Ballads of the North of Scotland, II, 201. c. Motherwell's MS., p. 561. d. Harris MS., No. 19.

1 THERE came a bird out o a bush,
    On water for to dine,
  An sighing sair, says the king's daughter,
    'O wae's this heart o mine!'

2 He's taen a harp into his hand,
    He's harped them all asleep,
  Except it was the king's daughter,
    Who one wink couldna get.

3 He's luppen on his berry-brown steed,
    Taen 'er on behind himsell,
  Then baith rede down to that water
    That they ca Wearie's Well.

4 'Wide in, wide in, my lady fair,
    No harm shall thee befall ;
  Oft times I've watered my steed
    Wi the waters o Wearie's Well.'

5 The first step that she stepped in,
    She stepped to the knee ;
  And sighend says this lady fair,
    'This water's nae for me.'

6 'Wide in, wide in, my lady fair,
    No harm shall thee befall ;
  Oft times I've watered my steed
    Wi the water o Wearie's Well.'

7 The next step that she stepped in,
    She stepped to the middle ;
  'O,' sighend says this lady fair,
    'I've wat my gowden girdle.'

8 'Wide in, wide in, my lady fair,
    No harm shall thee befall ;
  Oft times have I watered my steed
    Wi the water o Wearie's Well.'

9 The next step that she stepped in,
    She stepped to the chin ;
  'O,' sighend says this lady fair,
    'They sud gar twa loves twin.'

10 'Seven king's-daughters I've drownd
    there,
    In the water o Wearie's Well,
  And I'll make you the eight o them,
    And ring the common bell.'

11 'Since I am standing here,' she says,
    'This dowie death to die,
  One kiss o your comely mouth
    I'm sure wad comfort me.'

12 He louted him oer his saddle bow,
    To kiss her cheek and chin ;
  She's taen him in her arms twa,
    And thrown him headlong in.

13 'Since seven king's daughters ye'v
    drowned there,
    In the water o Wearie's Well,
  I'll make you bridegroom to them a',
    An ring the bell mysell.'

14 And aye she warsled, and aye sh
    swam,
    And she swam to dry lan ;
  She thanked God most cheerfully
    The dangers she oercame.

H

'May Collin,' MS. at Abbotsford. Scot
Ballads, Materials for Border Minstrels
No. 146.

1 MAY COLLIN . . .
    . . . was her father's heir
  And she fell in love with a falsh priest
  And she rued it ever mair.

2 He followd her butt, he followd he
    benn,
    He followd her through the hall,
  Till she had neither tongue nor teeth
    Nor lips to say him naw.

3 'We'll take the steed out where he is,
    The gold where eer it be,
  And we'll away to some unco land,
    And married we shall be.'

4 They had not riden a mile, a mile,
    A mile but barely three,
  Till they came to a rank river,
    Was raging like the sea.

5 'Light off, light off now, May Collin,
    It's here that you must die ;
  Here I have drownd seven king'
    daughters,
    The eight now you must be.

6 'Cast off, cast off now, May Collin,
    Your gown that's of the green ;
  For it's oer good and oer costly
    To rot in the sea-stream.

7 'Cast off, cast off now, May Collin,
    Your coat that 's of the black ;
For it 's oer good and oer costly
    To rot in the sea-wreck.

8 'Cast off, cast off now, May Collin,
    Your stays that are well laced ;
For thei 'r oer good and costly
    In the sea's ground to waste.

9 'Cast [off, cast off now, May Collin,]
    Your sark that 's of the holland ;
For [it 's oer good and oer costly]
    To rot in the sea-bottom.'

10 'Turn you about now, falsh Mess John,
    To the green leaf of the tree ;
It does not fit a mansworn man
    A naked woman to see.'

11 He turnd him quickly round about,
    To the green leaf of the tree ;
She took him hastly in her arms
    And flung him in the sea.

12 'Now lye you there, you falsh Mess
        John,
    My mallasin go with thee !
Youthought todrownmenaked andbare,
    But take your cloaths with thee,
And if there be seven king's daughters
        there
    Bear you them company.'

13 She lap on her milk steed
    And fast she bent the way,
And she was at her father's yate
    Three long hours or day.

14 Up and speaks the wylie parrot,
    So wylily and slee :
'Where is the man now, May Collin,
    That gaed away wie thee ?'

15 'Hold your tongue, my wylie parrot,
    And tell no tales of me,
And where I gave a pickle befor
    It 's now I 'll give you three.'

5

GIL BRENTON

'Gil Brenton' was taken down from recitation in Scotland about 1783. It has many
Scandinavian relatives. In some of these the
father of the heroine had built her bower by
the sea-strand, and it was broken open by a
company of men, one of whom had robbed
her of her honor. This knight proves to be
the hero of the ballad. (So, for example, in
Grundtvig, No. 274.)

A

a. Jamieson-Brown MS., No. 16, p. 34. b.
William Tytler's Brown MS., No. 3. Both
from the recitation of Mrs. Brown of Falkland,
1783, Aberdeenshire.

1 GIL BRENTON has sent oer the fame,
    He 's woo'd a wife an brought her
        hame.

2 Full sevenscore o ships came her wi,
    The lady by the greenwood tree.

3 There was twal an twal wi beer an wine,
    An twal an twal wi muskadine:

4 An twall an twall wi bouted flowr,
    An twall an twall wi paramour :

5 An twall an twall wi baken bread,
    An twall an twall wi the goud sae red.

6 Sweet Willy was a widow's son,
    An at her stirrup-foot he did run

7 An she was dressd i the finest pa,
    But ay she loot the tears down fa.

8 An she was deckd wi the fairest flowrs,
    But ay she loot the tears down pour.

9 'O is there water i your shee ?
    Or does the win blaw i your glee ?

10 'Or are you mourning i your meed
    That eer you left your mither gueede ?

11 'Or are ye mourning i your tide
    That ever ye was Gil Brenton's bride ?

12 'The[re] is nae water i my shee,
    Nor does the win blaw in my glee:

13 'Nor am I mourning i my tide
    That eer I was Gil Brenton's bride :

14 'But I am mourning i my meed
    That ever I left my mither gueede.

15 ' But, bonny boy, tell to me
 What is the customs o your country.'

16 ' The customs o 't, my dame,' he says,
 ' Will ill a gentle lady please.

17 ' Seven king's daughters has our king
  wedded,
 An seven king's daughters has our
  king bedded.

18 ' But he 's cutted the paps frae their
  breast-bane,
 An sent them mourning hame again.

19 ' But whan you come to the palace yate,
 His mither a golden chair will set.

20 ' An be you maid or be you nane,
 O sit you there till the day be dane.

21 ' An gin you 're sure that you are a
  maid,
 Ye may gang safely to his bed.

22 ' But gin o that you be na sure,
 Then hire some woman o youre bowr.'

23 O whan she came to the palace yate,
 His mither a golden chair did set.

24 An was she maid or was she nane,
 She sat in it till the day was dane.

25 An she 's calld on her bowr woman,
 That waiting was her bowr within.

26 ' Five hundred pound, maid, I 'll gi to
  the,
 An sleep this night wi the king for
  me.'

27 Whan bells was rung, an mass was sung,
 An a' man unto bed was gone,

28 Gil Brenton an the bonny maid
 Intill ae chamber they were laid.

29 ' O speak to me, blankets, an speak to
  me, sheets,
 An speak to me, cods, that under me
  sleeps ;

30 ' Is this a maid that I ha wedded ?
 Is this a maid that I ha bedded ? '

31 ' It 's nae a maid that you ha wedded
 But it 's a maid that you ha bedded.

32 ' Your lady 's in her bigly bowr,
 An for you she drees mony sharp showr

33 O he has taen him thro the ha,
 And on his mither he did ca.

34 ' I am the most unhappy man
 That ever was in christend lan.

35 ' I woo 'd a maiden meek an mild,
 An I 've marryed a woman great w
  child.'

36 ' O stay, my son, intill this ha,
 An sport you wi your merry men a'.

37 ' An I 'll gang to yon painted bowr,
 An see how 't fares wi yon base whore

38 The auld queen she was stark an
  strang;
 She gard the door flee aff the ban.

39 The auld queen she was stark an steer
 She gard the door lye i the fleer.

40 ' O is your bairn to laird or loon ?
 Or is it to your father's groom ? '

41 ' My bairn 's na to laird or loon,
 Nor is it to my father's groom.

42 ' But hear me, mither, on my knee,
 An my hard wierd I 'll tell to thee.

43 ' O we were sisters, sisters seven,
 We was the fairest under heaven.

44 ' We had nae mair for our seven year
  wark
 But to shape and sue the king's son
  sark.

45 ' O it fell on a Saturday's afternoon,
 Whan a' our langsome wark was dane,

46 ' We keist the cavils us amang,
 To see which shoud to the greenwoo
  gang.

47 ' Ohone, alas! for I was youngest,
 An ay my wierd it was the hardest.

58 'The cavil it did on me fa,
Which was the cause of a' my wae.

59 'For to the greenwood I must gae,
To pu the nut but an the slae ;

60 'To pu the red rose an the thyme,
To strew my mother's bowr and mine.

61 'I had na pu'd a flowr but ane,
Till by there came a jelly hind greeme,

62 'Wi high-colld hose an laigh-colld
shoone,
An he 'peard to be some kingis son.

63 'An be I maid or be I naue,
He kept me there till the day was dane.

64 'An be I maid or be I nae,
He kept me there till the close of day.

65 'He gae me a lock of yallow hair,
An bade me keep it for ever mair.

66 'He gae me a carket o gude black beads,
An bade me keep them against my
needs.

67 'He gae to me a gay gold ring,
An bade me ke[e]p it aboon a' thing.

68 'He gae to me a little pen-kniffe,
An bade me keep it as my life.'

59 'What did you wi these tokens rare
That ye got frae that young man there ?'

60 'O bring that coffer hear to me,
And a' the tokens ye sal see.'

61 An ay she rauked, an ay she flang,
Till a' the tokens came till her han.

62 'O stay here, daughter, your bowr within,
Till I gae parley wi my son.'

63 O she has taen her thro the ha,
An on her son began to ca.

64 'What did you wi that gay gold ring
I bade you keep aboon a' thing ?

65 'What did you wi that little pen-kniffe
I bade you keep while you had life ?

66 'What did you wi that yallow hair
I bade you keep for ever mair ?

67 'What did you wi that good black beeds
I bade you keep against your needs ?'

68 'I gae them to a lady gay
I met i the greenwood on a day.

69 'An I would gi a' my father's lan,
I had that lady my yates within.

70 'I would gi a' my ha's an towrs,
I had that bright burd i my bowrs.'

71 'O son, keep still your father's lan;
You hae that lady your yates within.

72 'An keep you still your ha's an towrs;
You hae that bright burd i your bowrs.'

73 Now or a month was come and gone,
This lady bare a bonny young son.

74 An it was well written on his breast-
bane
'Gil Brenton is my father's name.'

6
WILLIE'S LADY

This ballad, like No. 5, was written down,
from recitation, about 1783. It is extant in
two copies, differing very slightly and both derived from Mrs. Brown of Falkland. Danish
versions are numerous (see Grundtvig, Nos. 84,
85).

A

a. A copy, by Miss Mary Fraser Tytler, of
a transcript made by her grandfather from
William Tytler's manuscript. b. Jamieson-
Brown MS., No. 15, p. 33.

1 WILLIE has taen him oer the fame,
He 's woo'd a wife and brought her
hame.

2 He 's woo'd her for her yellow hair,
But his mother wrought her mickle
care.

3 And mickle dolour gard her dree,
For lighter she can never be.

4 But in her bower she sits wi pain,
   And Willie mourns oer her in vain.

5 And to his mother he has gone,
   That vile rank witch of vilest kind.

6 He says : 'My ladie has a cup,
   Wi gowd and silver set about.

7 'This goodlie gift shall be your ain,
   And let her be lighter o her young
      bairn.'

8 'Of her young bairn she 'll neer be
      lighter,
   Nor in her bower to shine the brighter.

9 'But she shall die and turn to clay,
   And you shall wed another may.'

10 'Another may I 'll never wed,
    Another may I 'll neer bring home.'

11 But sighing says that weary wight,
    'I wish my life were at an end.'

12 'Ye doe [ye] unto your mother again,
    That vile rank witch of vilest kind.

13 'And say your ladie has a steed,
    The like o 'm 's no in the lands of Leed.

14 'For he [i]s golden shod before,
    And he [i]s golden shod behind.

15 'And at ilka tet of that horse's main,
    There 's a golden chess and a bell ring-
      ing.

16 'This goodlie gift shall be your ain,
    And let me be lighter of my young
      bairn.'

17 'O her young bairn she 'll neer be
      lighter,
    Nor in her bower to shine the brighter.

18 'But she shall die and turn to clay,
    And ye shall wed another may.'

19 'Another may I ['ll] never wed,
    Another may I ['ll] neer bring hame.'

20 But sighing said that weary wight,
    'I wish my life were at an end.'

21 'Ye doe [ye] unto your mother again,
    That vile rank witch of vilest kind.

22 'And say your ladie has a girdle,
    It 's red gowd unto the middle.

23 'And ay at every silver hem,
    Hangs fifty silver bells and ten.

24 'That goodlie gift has be her ain,
    And let me be lighter of my young
      bairn.'

25 'O her young bairn she 's neer be
      lighter,
    Nor in her bower to shine the brighter

26 'But she shall die and turn to clay,
    And you shall wed another may.'

27 'Another may I 'll never wed,
    Another may I 'll neer bring hame.'

28 But sighing says that weary wight,
    'I wish my life were at an end.'

29 Then out and spake the Belly Blind ;
    He spake aye in good time.

30 'Ye doe ye to the market place,
    And there ye buy a loaf o wax.

31 'Ye shape it bairn and bairnly like,
    And in twa glassen een ye pit ;

32 'And bid her come to your boy's christ-
      ening ;
    Then notice weel what she shall do.

33 'And do you stand a little fore bye,
    And listen weel what she shall say.'

34 'Oh wha has loosed the nine witch
      knots
    That was amo that ladie's locks ?

35 'And wha has taen out the kaims of care
    That hangs amo that ladie's hair ?

36 'And wha 's taen down the bush o wood-
      bine
    That hang atween her bower and mine?

37 'And wha has killd the master kid
    That ran beneath that ladie's bed ?

'And wha has loosed her left-foot shee,
And lotten that ladie lighter be?'

O Willie has loosed the nine witch
    knots
That was amo that ladie's locks.

And Willie 's taen out the kaims o care
That hang amo that ladie's hair.

And Willie 's taen down the bush o
    woodbine
That hang atween her bower and thine.

And Willie has killed the master kid
That ran beneath that ladie's bed.

And Willie has loosed her left-foot
    shee,
And letten his ladie lighter be.

And now he 's gotten a bonny young
    son,
And mickle grace be him upon.

7

EARL BRAND

'Earl Brand' has preserved most of the in-
dents of a very ancient story with a faithful-
ss unequalled by any ballad that has been
covered from English oral tradition. It has,
wever, all but lost a circumstance that forms
e turning-point in related Scandinavian bal-
ds with which it must once have agreed in
important particulars. This is the so-called
"lead-naming," which has an important place
popular superstition. The incident appears
follows in the Danish 'Ribold and Guldborg,'
'rundtvig, No. 82): Ribold is fleeing with his
ve Guldborg. They are pursued by Guld-
rg's father and her brothers. Ribold bids
uldborg hold his horse, and, whatever may
 appen, not to call him by name. Ribold cuts
wn six or seven of her brothers and her
ther, besides others of her kin; the youngest
other only is left, and Guldborg in an agony
lls upon Ribold to spare him, to carry tidings
her mother. No sooner was his name pro-
ounced than Ribold received a mortal wound.
he English and Scottish ballads preserve only
e faintest trace of the knight's injunction
ot to name him. Cf. A*, st. 27, with 'Erlin-
n,' A*, st. 15, B, st. 14.
  'Earl Brand,' with the many Scandinavian
allads of the same group, would seem to belong among the numerous ramifications of the
Hildesaga. Of these, the second lay of Helgi
Hundingslayer, in the Poetic Edda. and 'Wal-
tharius,' the beautiful poem of Ekkehard, are
most like the ballads. See also 'Erlinton'
(No. 8). Percy, in his Reliques, expanded the
fragmentary version C to five times its actual
length.

A*

' The Earl o Bran,' "Scotch Ballads, Materials for Border Minstrelsy," No. 22 b, Abbotsford; in the handwriting of Richard Heber.

1 DID ye ever hear o guid Earl o Bran
    An the queen's daughter o the south-
        lan?

2 She was na fifteen years o age
    Till she came to the Earl's bed-side.

3 'O guid Earl o Bran, I fain wad see
    My grey hounds run over the lea.'

4 'O kind lady, I have no steeds but one,
    But ye shall ride, an I shall run.'

5 'O guid Earl o Bran, but I have tua,
    An ye shall hae yere wael o those.'

6 The 're ovr moss an the 're over muir,
    An they saw neither rich nor poor.

7 Till they came to ald Carl Hood,
    He 's ay for ill, but he 's never for good.

8 'O guid Earl o Bran, if ye loe me,
    Kill Carl Hood an gar him die.'

9 'O kind lady, we had better spare;
    I never killd ane that wore grey hair.

10 'We 'll gie him a penny-fie an let him
        gae,
    An then he 'll carry nae tiddings away.'

11 'Where hae been riding this lang sim-
        mer-day?
    Or where hae stolen this lady away?'

12 'O I hae not riden this lang simmer-
        day,
    Nor hae I stolen this lady away.

13 'For she is my sick sister
    I got at the Wamshester.'

14 'If she were sick an like to die,
    She wad na be wearing the gold sae
        high.'

15 Ald Carl Hood is over the know,
    Where they rode one mile, he ran
        four.

16 Till he came to her mother's yetts,
    An I wat he rapped rudely at.

17 'Where is the lady o this ha ?'
    'She 's out wie her maidens, playing at
        the ba.'

18 'O na ! fy na !
    For I met her fifteen miles awa.

19 'She 's over moss, an she 's over muir,
    An a' to be the Earl o Bran's whore.'

20 Some rode wie sticks, an some wie
        rungs,
    An a' to get the Earl o Bran slain.

21 That lady lookd over her left shoudder-
        bane :
    'O guid Earl o Bran, we 'll a' be taen !
    For yond 'r a' my father's men.

22 'But if ye 'll take my claiths, I 'll take
        thine,
    An I 'll fight a' my father's men.'

23 'It 's no the custom in our land
    For ladies to fight an knights to stand.

24 'If they come on me ane by ane,
    I 'll smash them a' doun bane by bane.

25 'If they come on me ane and a',
    Ye soon will see my body fa.'

26 He has luppen from his steed,
    An he has gein her that to had.

27 An bad her never change her cheer
    Untill she saw his body bleed.

28 They came on him ane by ane,
    An he smashed them doun a' bane by
        bane.

29 He sat him doun on the green grass,
    For I wat a wearit man he was.

30 But ald Carl Hood came him behind
    An I wat he gae him a deadly woun

31 He 's awa to his lady then,
    He kissed her, and set her on
        steed again.

32 He rode whistlin out the way.
    An a' to hearten his lady gay.

33 'Till he came to the water-flood :
    'O guid Earl o Bran, I see blood !'

34 'O it is but my scarlet hood,
    That shines upon the water-flood.'

35 They came on 'till his mother's yett,
    An I wat he rappit poorly at.

36 His mother she 's come to the door :
    'O son, ye 've gotten yere dead wie
        English whore !'

37 'She was never a whore to me ;
    Sae let my brother her husband be.'

38 Sae ald Carl Hood was not the dead
        ane,
    But he was the dead o hale seeventee

B

'The Douglas Tragedy,' Scott's Minstrels
III, 246, ed. 1803 ; III, 6, ed. 1833 : the co
principally used supplied by C. K. Sharpe, t
last three stanzas from a penny pamphlet a
from tradition.

1 'RISE up, rise up, now, Lord Dougla
        she says,
    'And put on your armour so bright
    Let it never be said that a daughter
        thine
    Was married to a lord under night.

2 'Rise up, rise up, my seven bold sons,
    And put on your armour so bright,
    And take better care of your younge
        sister,
    For your eldest 's awa the last night

3 He 's mounted her on a milk-white stee
    And himself on a dapple grey,
    With a bugelet horn hung down by h
        side,
    And lightly they rode away.

Lord William lookit oer his left shoulder,
 To see what he could see,
And there he spy'd her seven brethren bold,
 Come riding over the lee.

'Light down, light down, Lady Margret,' he said,
 'And hold my steed in your hand,
Until that against your seven brethren bold,
 And your father, I mak a stand.'

She held his steed in her milk-white hand,
 And never shed one tear,
Until that she saw her seven brethren fa,
 And her father hard fighting, who lovd her so dear.

'O hold your hand, Lord William!' she said,
 'For your strokes they are wondrous sair;
True lovers I can get many a ane,
 But a father I can never get mair.'

8 O she's taen out her handkerchief,
 It was o the holland sae fine,
And aye she dighted her father's bloody wounds,
 That were redder than the wine.

9 'O chuse, O chuse, Lady Margret,' he said,
 'O whether will ye gang or bide?'
'I'll gang, I'll gang, Lord William,' she said,
 'For ye have left me no other guide.'

10 He's lifted her on a milk-white steed,
 And himself on a dapple grey,
With a bugelet horn hung down by his side,
 And slowly they baith rade away.

11 O they rade on, and on they rade,
 And a' by the light of the moon,
Until they came to yon wan water,
 And there they lighted down.

12 They lighted down to tak a drink
 Of the spring that ran sae clear,

And down the stream ran his gude heart's blood,
 And sair she gan to fear.

13 'Hold up, hold up, Lord William,' she says,
 'For I fear that you are slain;'
''T is naething but the shadow of my scarlet cloak,
 That shines in the water sae plain.'

14 O they rade on, and on they rade,
 And a' by the light of the moon,
Until they cam to his mother's ha door,
 And there they lighted down.

15 'Get up, get up, lady mother,' he says,
 'Get up, and let me in!
Get up, get up, lady mother,' he says,
 'For this night my fair lady I've win.

16 'O mak my bed, lady mother,' he says,
 'O mak it braid and deep,
And lay Lady Margret close at my back,
 And the sounder I will sleep.'

17 Lord William was dead lang ere midnight,
 Lady Margret lang ere day,
And all true lovers that go thegither,
 May they have mair luck than they!

18 Lord William was buried in St. Mary's kirk,
 Lady Margret in Mary's quire;
Out o the lady's grave grew a bonny red rose,
 And out o the knight's a briar.

19 And they twa met, and they twa plat,
 And fain they wad be near;
And a' the warld might ken right weel
 They were twa lovers dear.

20 But bye and rade the Black Douglas,
 And wow but he was rough!
For he pulld up the bonny brier,
 And flang 't in St. Mary's Loch.

F

'The Child of Ell,' Percy MS., p. 57; ed. Hales and Furnivall, I, 133.

1 .   .   .   .   .   .

Sayes 'Christ thee saue, good Child of
    Ell !
    Christ saue thee and thy steede!

2 'My father sayes he will [eat] noe
        meate,
    Nor his drinke shall doe him noe
        good,
    Till he haue slaine the Child of Ell,
    And haue seene his harts blood.'

3 'I wold I were in my sadle sett,
    And a mile out of the towne;
    I did not care for your father
    And all his merry men !

4 'I wold I were in my sadle sett,
    And a little space him froe;
    I did not care for your father
    And all that long him to!'

5 He leaned ore his saddle bow
    To kisse this lady good;
    The teares *that* went them *two* betweene
    Were blend water and blood.

6 He sett himselfe on one good steed,
    This lady on a palfray,
    And sett his litle horne to his mouth,
    And roundlie he rode away.

7 He had not ridden past a mile,
    A mile out of the towne,

    .   .   .   .   .   .

8 Her father was readye with her *seuen*
        brether,
    He said, 'Sett thou my daughter
        downe !
    For it ill beseemes thee, thou false
        churles sonne,
    To carry her forth of this towne!'

9 'But lowd thou lyest, Sir Iohn the
        knight,
    Thou now doest lye of me ;
    A knight me gott, and a lady me bore ;
    Soe neuer did none by thee.

10 'But light now downe, my lady gay,
    Light downe and hold my horsse,
    Whilest I and your father and your
        brether
    Doe play vs at this crosse.

11 'But light now downe, my owne tr
        loue,
    And meeklye hold my steede,
    Whilest your father [and your se
        brether] bold
    *   *   *   *   *

8

ERLINTON

This ballad has only with much hesitati
been separated from the foregoing. Versi
A and B have one correspondence with t
Scandinavian Ribold ballad not found in ' E
Brand,' — the strict watch kept over the la
But notwithstanding the resemblances to t
Ribold story, there is a difference in the larg
part of the details, and all the ' Erlinton ' ba
lads have a fortunate ending. The copy
Scott's Minstrelsy, III, 235, ed. 1803, w
compounded from A* and a closely relat
version.

A*

Abbotsford MS., Scotch Ballads, Materi
for Border Minstrelsy, No. 20, obtained fr
Nelly Laidlaw, and in the handwriting of W
liam Laidlaw.

1 LORD ERLINTON had ae daughter,
    I trow he 's weird her a grit sin ;
    For he has bugn a bigly bower,
    An a' to pit his ae daughter in.
        An he has buggin, etc.

2 An he has warn her sisters six,
    Her sisters six an her brethren se'e
    Thei 'r either to watch her a' the nigh
    Or than to gang i the mornin soon.

3 She had na been i that bigly bower
    Not ae night but only ane
    Untill that Willie, her true-love,
    Chappit at the bower-door, no at th
        gin.

4 'Whae 's this, whae 's this chaps at m
        bower-door,
    At my bower-door, no at the gin ?'
    'O it is Willie, thy ain true-love ;
    O will ye rise an let me in ?'

5 'In my bower, Willie, there is a wane,
    An in the wane there is a wake ;
    But I will come to the green woods
    The morn, for my ain true-love's sake.

6 This lady she 's lain down again,
    An she has lain till the cock crew
      thrice ;
  She said unto her sisters baith,
    Lasses, it 's time at we soud rise.

7 She 's putten on her breast a silver tee,
    An on her back a silken gown ;
  She 's taen a sister in ilka hand,
    An away to the bonnie green wood
    she 's gane.

8 They hadna gane a mile in that bonnie
    green wood,
    They had na gane a mile but only
    ane,
  Till they met wi Willie, her ain true-
    love,
    An thrae her sisters he has her taen.

9 He 's taen her sisters ilk by the hand,
    He 's kissd them baith, an he 's sent
    them hame ;
  He 's muntit his ladie him high behind,
    An thro the bonnie green wood thei 'r
    gane.

10 They 'd ridden a mile i that bonnie
    green wood,
    They hadna ridden but only ane,
  When there cam fifteen o the baldest
    knights
    That ever boor flesh, bluid an bane.

11 Than up bespak the foremost knight,
    He woor the gray hair on his chin ;
  'Yield me yer life or your lady fair,
    An ye sal walk the green woods
    within.'

12 'For to gie my wife to thee,
    I wad be very laith,' said he ;
  'For than the folk wad think I was gane
    mad,
    Or that the senses war taen frae me.'

13 Up than bespak the niest foremost
    knight,
    I trow he spak right boustrouslie ;
  'Yield me yer life or your ladie fair,
    An ye sall walk the green woods wi
    me.'

14 'My wife, she is my warld's meed,
    My life, it lyes me very near ;

But if ye be man o your manhood
    I serve will while my days are near.'

15 He 's luppen off his milk-white steed,
    He 's gien his lady him by the head :
  'See that ye never change yer cheer
    Till ance ye see my body bleed.'

16 An he 's killd a' the fifteen knights,
    He 's killed them a' but only ane ;
  A' but the auld grey-headed knight,
    He bade him carry the tiddins hame.

17 He 's gane to his lady again,
    I trow he 's kissd her, baith cheek an
    chin ;
  'Now ye 'r my ain, I have ye win,
    An we will walk the green woods
    within.'

B

'True Tammas,' MS. of Robert White, Esq.,
of Newcastle, from James Telfer's collection.

1 THERE was a knight, an he had a daugh-
    ter,
    An he wad wed her, wi muckle sin ;
  Sae he has biggit a bonnie bower, love,
    An a' to keep his fair daughter in.

2 But she hadna been in the bonnie bower,
    love,
    And no twa hours but barely ane,
  Till up started Tammas, her ain true
    lover,
    And O sae fain as he wald been in.

3 'For a' sae weel as I like ye, Tammas,
    An for a' sae weel as I like the gin,
  I wadna for ten thousand pounds, love,
    Na no this night wad I let thee in.

4 'But yonder is a bonnie greenwud,
    An in the greenwud there is a wauk,
  An I 'll be there an sune the morn, love,
    It 's a' for my true love's sake.

5 'On my right hand I 'll have a glove,
    love,
    An on my left ane I 'll have nane;
  I 'll have wi' me my sisters six, love,
    An we will wauk the wuds our lane.'

6 They hadna waukd in the bonnie green-
    wud,
    Na no an hour but barely ane,

Till up start Tammas, her ain true lover,
  He 's taen her sisters her frae mang.

7 An he has kissed her sisters six, love,
    An he has sent them hame again,
  But he has keepit his ain true lover,
    Saying, ' We will wauk the wuds our
      lane.'

8 They hadna waukd in the bonnie green-
    wud
    Na no an hour but barely ane,
  Till up start fifteen o the bravest out-
    laws
    That ever bure either breath or bane.

9 An up bespake the foremost man, love,
    An O but he spake angrily:
  ' Either your life — or your lady fair,
      sir,
    This night shall wauk the wuds wi
      me.'

10 ' My lady fair, O I like her weel, sir,
    An O my life, but it lies me near!
  But before I lose my lady fair, sir,
    I 'll rather lose my life sae dear.'

11 Then up bespak the second man, love,
    An aye he spake mair angrily,
  Saying, ' Baith your life, and your lady
      fair, sir,
    This night shall wauk the wuds wi
      me.'

12 ' My lady fair, O I like her weel, sir,
    An O my life, but it lies me near!
  But before I lose my lady fair, sir,
    I 'll rather lose my life sae dear.

13 ' But if ye 'll be men to your manhood,
    As that I will be unto mine,
  I 'll fight ye every ane man by man,
    Till the last drop's blude I hae be
      slain.

14 ' O sit ye down, my dearest dearie,
    Sit down and hold my noble steed,
  And see that ye never change your cheer
    Until ye see my body bleed.'

15 He 's feughten a' the fifteen outlaws,
    The fifteen outlaws every ane,
  He 's left naething but the auldest man
    To go and carry the tidings hame.

16 An he has gane to his dearest dear,
    An he has kissed her, cheek and chin
  Saying, ' Thou art mine ain, I hav
    bought thee dear,
    An we will wauk the wuds our lane.

9

THE FAIR FLOWER OF NORTHUMBERLAND

The earliest copy of this ballad is introduce
as ' The Maiden's Song ' in Deloney's Pleasan
History of John Winchcomb, in his younge
yeares called Jacke of Newberie, a book writter
as early as 1597. Halliwell reprinted the " 9th
edition, of the date 1633, in 1859. We do no
find the story of this ballad repeated as a whol
among other European nations, but there are
interesting agreements in parts with Scandi
navian, Polish, and German ballads. Ther
is also some resemblance in the first half to a
pretty ballad of the northern nations whicl
treats in a brief way the theme of our exquisite
romance of ' The Nutbrown Maid ' (see Grundt
vig, No. 249). The ballad of ' Young Andrew
(No. 48) has points in common with ' The Fair
Flower of Northumberland.'

A

a. Deloney's Pleasant History of John
Winchcomb, 9th ed., London, 1633, reprinted
by Halliwell, p. 61. b. ' The Ungrateful
Knight and the Fair Flower of Northumberland,' Ritson's Ancient Songs, 1790, p. 169.

1 IT was a knight in Scotland borne
    Follow, my love, come over the strand
  Was taken prisoner, and left forlorne,
    Even by the good Earle of Northum
      berland.

2 Then was he cast in prison strong,
    Where he could not walke nor lie along.
  Even by the goode Earle of Northum-
      berland.

3 And as in sorrow thus he lay,
    The Earle's sweete daughter walkt that
      way,
    And she the faire flower of Northum-
      berland.

4 And passing by, like an angell bright,
    The prisoner had of her a sight,

And she the faire flower of Northumberland.

5 And loud to her this knight did crie,
  The salt teares standing in his eye,
    And she the faire flower of Northumberland.

6 'Faire lady,' he said, 'take pity on me,
  And let me not in prison dye,
    And you the faire flower of Northumberland.'

7 'Faire Sir, how should I take pity on thee,
  Thou being a foe to our countrey,
    And I the faire flower of Northumberland.'

8 'Faire lady, I am no foe,' he said,
  'Through thy sweet love heere was I stayd,
    For thee, the faire flower of Northumberland.'

9 'Why shouldst thou come heere for love of me,
  Having wife and children in thy countrie?
    And I the faire flower of Northumberland.'

10 'I sweare by the blessed Trinitie,
   I have no wife nor children, I,
     Nor dwelling at home in merrie Scotland.

11 'If curteously you will set me free,
   I vow that I will marrie thee,
     So soone as I come in faire Scotland.

12 'Thou shalt be a lady of castles and towers,
   And sit like a queene in princely bowers,
     When I am at home in faire Scotland.'

13 Then parted hence this lady gay,
   And got her father's ring away,
     To helpe this sad knight into faire Scotland.

14 Likewise much gold she got by sleight,
   And all to helpe this forlorne knight
     To wend from her father to faire Scotland.

15 Two gallant steedes, both good and able,
   She likewise tooke out of the stable,
     To ride with this knight into faire Scotland.

16 And to the jaylor she sent this ring,
   The knight from prison forth to bring,
     To wend with her into faire Scotland.

17 This token set the prisoner free,
   Who straight went to this faire lady,
     To wend with her into faire Scotland.

18 A gallant steede he did bestride,
   And with the lady away did ride,
     And she the faire flower of Northumberland.

19 They rode till they came to a water cleare:
   'Good Sir, how should I follow you heere,
     And I the faire flower of Northumberland?

20 The water is rough and wonderfull deepe,
   An[d] on my saddle I shall not keepe,
     And I the faire flower of Northumberland.'

21 'Feare not the foord, faire lady,' quoth he,
   'For long I cannot stay for thee,
     And thou the faire flower of Northumberland.'

22 The lady prickt her wanton steed,
   And over the river swom with speede,
     And she the faire flower of Northumberland.

23 From top to toe all wet was shee:
   'This have I done for love of thee,
     And I the faire flower of Northumberland.'

24 Thus rode she all one winter's night,
   Till Edenborow they saw in sight,
     The chiefest towne in all Scotland.

25 'Now chuse,' quoth he, 'thou wanton flower,

Whe'r thou wilt be my paramour,
    Or get thee home to Northumber-
        land.

26 'For I have wife, and children five,
    In Edenborow they be alive;
        Then get thee home to faire England.

27 'This favour shalt thou have to boote,
    Ile have thy horse, go thou on foote,
        Go, get thee home to Northumber-
            land.'

28 'O false and faithlesse knight,' quoth
        shee,
    'And canst thou deale so bad with me,
        And I the faire flower of Northum-
            berland ?

29 'Dishonour not a ladie's name,
    But draw thy sword and end my shame,
        And I the faire flower of Northum-
            berland.'

30 He tooke her from her stately steed,
    And left her there in extreme need,
        And she the faire flower of Northum-
            berland.

31 Then sate she downe full heavily;
    At length two knights came riding by,
        Two gallant knights of faire England.

32 She fell downe humbly on her knee,
    Saying, 'Courteous knights, take pittie
        on me,
    And I the faire flower of Northum-
        berland.

33 'I have offended my father deere,
    And by a false knight that brought me
        heere,
    From the good Earle of Northumber-
        land.'

34 They tooke her up behind them then,
    And brought her to her father's againe,
        And he the good Earle of Northum-
            berland.

35 All you faire maidens be warned by
        me,
    Scots were never true, nor never will
        be,
    To lord, nor lady, nor faire England.

10

THE TWA SISTERS

This is one of the very few old ballads which
are not extinct as tradition in the British Isles.
Even drawing-room versions are spoken of as
current, " generally traced to some old nurse,
who sang them to the young ladies." It has
been found in England, Scotland, Wales, and
Ireland, and was very early in print. The ballad is as popular with the Scandinavians as with
their Saxon cousins: we have Danish, Icelandic, Norwegian, Färöe, and Swedish versions.
There is a remarkable agreement between the
Norse and English ballads till we approach
the conclusion of the story, with a natural diversity as to some of the minuter details. According to all complete and uncorrupted forms
of the ballad, either some part of the body of
the drowned girl is taken to furnish a musical
instrument, a harp or a viol, or the instrument
is wholly made from the body. Perhaps the
original conception was the simple and beautiful one which we find in English B and also in
the Icelandic ballads, that the king's harper,
or the girl's lover, takes three locks of her yellow hair to string his harp with. Infelicitous
additions were, perhaps, successively made ;
as a harp-frame from the breast-bone, and fid-
dle-pins formed of the finger joints, and so one
thing and another added or substituted, till we
end with the buffoonery of English A. All
the Norse ballads (see Grundtvig, No. 95) make
the harp or fiddle to be taken to a wedding,
which chances to be that of the elder sister
with the drowned girl's betrothed. Unfortunately, many of the English versions are so
injured towards the close that the full story
cannot be made out. There is no wedding
feast preserved in any of them.

Though the range of the ballad proper is
somewhat limited, popular tales equivalent as
to the characteristic circumstances are very
widely diffused.

A

a. 'The Miller and the King's Daughter,'
broadside of 1656, Notes and Queries, 1st Series, v, 591. b. Wit Restor'd, 1658, in the reprint of 1817, p. 153. c. 'The Miller and the
King's Daughters,' Wit and Drollery, ed. 1682,
p. 87. d. 'The Miller and the King's Daughter,' Jamieson's Popular Ballads, I, 315.

1 THERE were two sisters, they went
        playing,
    With a hie downe downe a downe-a

To see their father's ships come sayling in.
With a hy downe downe a downe-a

And when they came unto the sea-brym,
The elder did push the younger in.

'O sister, O sister, take me by the gowne,
And drawe me up upon the dry ground.'

'O sister, O sister, that may not bee,
Till salt and oatmeale grow both of a tree.'

Somtymes she sanke, somtymes she swam,
Until she came unto the mill-dam.

The miller runne hastily downe the cliffe,
And up he betook her withouten her life.

What did he doe with her brest-bone ?
He made him a violl to play thereupon.

What did he doe with her fingers so small ?
He made him peggs to his violl withall.

What did he doe with her nose-ridge ?
Unto his violl be made him a bridge.

What did he doe with her veynes so blew ?
He made him strings to his violl thereto.

What did he doe with her eyes so bright ?
Upon his violl he played at first sight.

What did he doe with her tongue so rough ?
Unto the violl it spake enough.

What did he doe with her two shinnes ?
Unto the violl they danc'd Moll Syms.

Then bespake the treble string,
'O yonder is my father the king.'

Then bespake the second string,
'O yonder sitts my mother the queen.'

16 And then bespake the strings all three,
'O yonder is my sister that drowned mee.'

17 'Now pay the miller for his payne,
And let him bee gone in the divel's name.'

B

a. 'The Twa Sisters,' Jamieson-Brown MS., p. 39. b. Wm. Tytler's Brown MS., No. 15. c. Abbotsford MS., Scottish Songs, fol. 21. d. Jamieson's Popular Ballads, i, 48.

1 THERE was twa sisters in a bowr,
   Edinburgh, Edinburgh
   There was twa sisters in a bowr,
   Stirling for ay
   There was twa sisters in a bowr,
   There came a knight to be their wooer.
   Bonny Saint Johnston stands upon Tay

2 He courted the eldest wi glove an ring,
   But he lovd the youngest above a' thing.

3 He courted the eldest wi brotch an knife,
   But lovd the youngest as his life.

4 The eldest she was vexed sair,
   An much envi'd her sister fair.

5 Into her bowr she could not rest,
   Wi grief an spite she almos brast.

6 Upon a morning fair an clear,
   She cried upon her sister dear :

7 'O sister, come to yon sea stran,
   An see our father's ships come to lan.'

8 She 's taen her by the milk-white han,
   An led her down to yon sea stran.

9 The younges[t] stood upon a stane,
   The eldest came an threw her in.

10 She tooke her by the middle sma,
   An dashd her bonny back to the jaw.

11 'O sister, sister, tak my han,
   An Ise mack you heir to a' my lan.'

12 'O sister, sister, tak my middle,
  An yes get my goud and my gouden
    girdle.

13 'O sister, sister, save my life,
  An I swear Ise never be nae man's
    wife.'

14 'Foul fa the han that I should tacke,
  It twin'd me an my wardles make.

15 'Your cherry cheeks an yallow hair
  Gars me gae maiden for evermair.'

16 Sometimes she sank, an sometimes she
    swam,
  Till she came down yon bonny mill-
    dam.

17 O out it came the miller's son,
  An saw the fair maid swimmin in.

18 'O father, father, draw your dam,
  Here 's either a mermaid or a swan.'

19 The miller quickly drew the dam,
  An there he found a drownd woman.

20 You coudna see her yellow hair
  For gold and pearle that were so rare.

21 You coudna see her middle sma
  For gouden girdle that was sae braw.

22 You coudna see her fingers white,
  For gouden rings that was sae gryte.

23 An by there came a harper fine,
  That harped to the king at dine.

24 When he did look that lady upon,
  He sighd and made a heavy moan.

25 He 's taen three locks o her yellow hair,
  An wi them strung his harp sae fair.

26 The first tune he did play and sing,
  Was, 'Farewell to my father the king.'

27 The nextin tune that he playd syne,
  Was, 'Farewell to my mother the
    queen.'

28 The lasten tune that he playd then,
  Was, 'Wae to my sister, fair Ellen.'

11
THE CRUEL BROTHER

This was formerly one of the most popula
of Scottish ballads. There are many version
most of which agree in all essentials. Th
point of the story is the mortal offense give
by the neglect to ask the brother's consent t
the marriage. The same idea occurs in a num
ber of Scandinavian ballads. In a very commo
German ballad, 'Graf Friedrich' (Uhland, N
122), the bride receives a fatal wound durin
the bringing home, but accidentally, and fro
the bridegroom's hand. The peculiar testa
ment made by the bride in 'The Cru
Brother,' by which she bequeaths good thing
to her friends, but ill things to the author o
her death, is highly characteristic of balla
poetry. See 'Lord Randal' (No. 12) and 'E
ward' (No. 13).

A

'[The] Cruel Brother, or the Bride's Testa
ment.' a. Alex. Fraser Tytler's Brown MS
b. Jamieson's Popular Ballads, i, 66, purpor
ing to be from the recitation of Mrs Arrot o
Aberbrothick (probably by mistake for M
Brown).

1 THERE was three ladies playd at the b
    With a hey ho and a lillie gay
  There came a knight and played oe
    them a'.
    As the primrose spreads so sweetly

2 The eldest was baith tall and fair,
  But the youngest was beyond compar

3 The midmost had a graceful mien,
  But the youngest lookd like beautie
    queen.

4 The knight bowd low to a' the three,
  But to the youngest he bent his knee.

5 The ladie turned her head aside,
  The knight he woo'd her to be his brid

6 The ladie blushd a rosy red,
  And sayd, 'Sir knight, I 'm too youn
    to wed.'

7 'O ladie fair, give me your hand,
  And I 'll make you ladie of a' my land

8 'Sir knight, ere ye my favor win,
  You maun get consent frae a' my kin.'

He 's got consent frae her parents dear,
And likewise frae her sisters fair.

He 's got consent frae her kin each
    one,
But forgot to spiek to her brother
    John.

Now, when the wedding day was come,
The knight would take his bonny bride
    home.

And many a lord and many a knight
Came to behold that ladie bright.

And there was nae man that did her
    see,
But wishd himself bridegroom to be.

Her father dear led her down the stair,
And her sisters twain they kissd her
    there.

Her mother dear led her thro the closs,
And her brother John set her on her
    horse.

She leand her oer the saddle-bow,
To give him a kiss ere she did go.

He has taen a knife, baith lang and
    sharp,
And stabbd that bonny bride to the
    heart.

She hadno ridden half thro the town,
Until her heart's blude staind her gown.

'Ride softly on,' says the best young
    man,
'For I think our bonny bride looks pale
    and wan.'

'O lead me gently up yon hill,
And I 'll there sit down, and make my
    will.'

'O what will you leave to your father
    dear ?'
'The silver-shode steed that brought me
    here.'

2 'What will you leave to your mother
    dear ?'
'My velvet pall and my silken gear.'

23 'What will you leave to your sister
        Anne ?'
    'My silken scarf and my gowden fan.'

24 'What will you leave to your sister
        Grace ?'
    'My bloody cloaths to wash and dress.'

25 'What will you leave to your brother
        John ?'
    'The gallows-tree to hang him on.'

26 'What will you leave to your brother
        John's wife ?'
    'The wilderness to end her life.'

27 This ladie fair in her grave was laid,
    And many a mass was oer her said.

28 But it would have made your heart
        right sair,
    To see the bridegroom rive his haire.

B

Kinloch's MSS., i, 21, from Mary Barr, May,
1827, Clydesdale.

1 A GENTLEMAN cam oure the sea,
        Fine flowers in the valley
    And he has courted ladies three.
        With the light green and the yellow

2 One o them was clad in red :
    He asked if she wad be his bride.

3 One o them was clad in green :
    He asked if she wad be his queen.

4 The last o them was clad in white :
    He asked if she wad be his heart's
        delight.

5 'Ye may ga ask my father, the king :
    Sae maun ye ask my mither, the queen.

6 'Sae maun ye ask my sister Anne :
    And dinna forget my brither John.'

7 He has asked her father, the king :
    And sae did he her mither, the queen.

8 And he has asked her sister Anne :
    But he has forgot her brother John.

9 Her father led her through the ha,
  Her mither danced afore them a'.

10 Her sister Anne led her through the closs,
   Her brither John set her on her horse.

11 It 's then he drew a little penknife,
   And he reft the fair maid o her life.

12 'Ride up, ride up,' said the foremost
   man ;
   'I think our bride comes hooly on.'

13 'Ride up, ride up,' said the second man;
   'I think our bride looks pale and wan.'

14 Up than cam the gay bridegroom,
   And straucht unto the bride he cam.

15 'Does your side-saddle sit awry ?
   Or does your steed . . .

16 'Or does the rain run in your glove ?
   Or wad ye chuse anither love ?'

17 'The rain runs not in my glove,
   Nor will I e'er chuse anither love.

18 'But O an I war at Saint Evron's well,
   There I wad licht, and drink my fill !

19 'Oh an I war at Saint Evron's closs,
   There I wad licht, and bait my horse !'

20 Whan she cam to Saint Evron's well,
   She dought na licht to drink her fill.

21 Whan she cam to Saint Evron's closs,
   The bonny bride fell aff her horse.

22 'What will ye leave to your father, the
   king ?'
   'The milk-white steed that I ride on.'

23 'What will ye leave to your mother, the
   queen ?'
   'The bluidy robes that I have on.'

24 'What will ye leave to your sister
   Anne ?'
   'My gude lord, to be wedded on.'

25 'What will ye leave to your brither
   John ?'
   'The gallows pin to hang him on.'

26 'What will ye leave to your brither
   wife ?'
   'Grief and sorrow a' the days o her lif

27 'What will ye leave to your brithe
   bairns ?'
   'The meal-pock to hang oure the arm

28 Now does she neither sigh nor groan
   She lies aneath yon marble stone.

12

LORD RANDAL

This ballad may be traced back about
century in English. In Italy it has been pop
lar for more than 250 years. According to th
Italian tradition, a young man and his tru
love are the object and the agent of the crim
This is also the case in several of the Englis
versions and in some of the German. It is n
unlikely, as Scott suggests, that the young m
was changed to a child poisoned by a stepm
ther when the ballad was sung to children.

A

From a small manuscript volume, lent
Professor Child by Mr. William Macmath,
Edinburgh, containing four pieces written
or about 1710, and this ballad in a later han
(probably of the beginning of the 19th century
Charles Mackie, August, 1808, is scratched up
the binding.

1 'O WHERE ha you been, Lord Randa
   my son ?
   And where ha you been, my handsom
   young man ?'
   'I ha been at the greenwood ; mothe
   mak my bed soon,
   For I 'm wearied wi hunting, and fai
   wad lie down.'

2 'An wha met ye there, Lord Randa
   my son ?
   An wha met you there, my handsom
   young man ?'
   'O I met wi my true-love ; mothe
   mak my bed soon,
   For I 'm wearied wi huntin, an fain wa
   lie down.'

3 'And what did she give you, Lord Ran
   dal, my son ?

And what did she give you, my handsome young man ? '
' Eels fried in a pan ; mother, mak my
bed soon,
For I 'm wearied wi huntin, and fain
wad lie down.'

4 ' And wha gat your leavins, Lord Randal, my son ?
And wha gat your leavins, my handsom young man ? '
' My hawks and my hounds ; mother,
mak my bed soon,
For I 'm wearied wi hunting, and fain
wad lie down.'

5 ' And what becam of them, Lord Randal, my son ?
And what becam of them, my handsome
young man ? '
' They stretched their legs out an died ;
mother, mak my bed soon,
For I 'm wearied wi huntin, and fain wad
lie down.'

6 ' O I fear you are poisoned, Lord Randal, my son !
I fear you are poisoned, my handsome
young man ! '
' O yes, I am poisoned ; mother, mak
my bed soon,
For I 'm sick at the heart, and I fain
wad lie down.'

7 ' What d' ye leave to your mother, Lord
Randal, my son ?
What d' ye leave to your mother, my
handsome young man ? '
' Four and twenty milk kye ; mother,
mak my bed soon,
For I 'm sick at the heart, and I fain
wad lie down.'

8 ' What d' ye leave to your sister, Lord
Randal, my son ?
What d' ye leave to your sister, my
handsome young man ? '
' My gold and my silver ; mother, mak
my bed soon,
For I 'm sick at the heart, an I fain wad
lie down.'

9 ' What d' ye leave to your brother, Lord
Randal, my son ?

What d' ye leave to your brother, my
handsome young man ? '
' My houses and my lands ; mother, mak
my bed soon,
For I 'm sick at the heart, and I fain
wad lie down.'

10 ' What d' ye leave to your true-love,
Lord Randal, my son ?
What d' ye leave to your true-love, my
handsome young man ? '
' I leave her hell and fire ; mother, mak
my bed soon,
For I 'm sick at the heart, and I fain
wad lie down.'

B

' Lord Donald,' Kinloch MSS., VII, 89.   Kinloch's Ancient Scottish Ballads, p. 110.   From
Mrs. Comie, Aberdeen.

1 ' O WHARE hae ye been a' day, Lord
Donald, my son ?
O whare hae ye been a' day, my jollie
young man ? '
' I 've been awa courtin ; mither, mak my
bed sune,
For I 'm sick at the heart, and I fain
wad lie doun.'

2 ' What wad ye hae for your supper,
Lord Donald, my son ?
What wad ye hae for your supper, my
jollie young man ? '
' I 've gotten my supper ; mither, mak
my bed sune,
For I 'm sick at the heart, and I fain
wad lie doun.'

3 ' What did ye get to your supper, Lord
Donald, my son ?
What did ye get to your supper, my
jollie young man ? '
' A dish of sma fishes ; mither, mak my
bed sune,
For I 'm sick at the heart, and I fain
wad lie doun.'

4 ' Whare gat ye the fishes, Lord Donald,
my son ?
Whare gat ye the fishes, my jollie
young man ? '
' In my father's black ditches ; mither,
mak my bed sune,

For I 'm sick at the heart, and I fain
wad lie doun.'

5 ' What like were your fishes, Lord
Donald, my son ?
What like were your fishes, my jollie
young man ? '
' Black backs and spreckld bellies ;
mither, mak my bed sune,
For I 'm sick at the heart, and I fain
wad lie doun.'

6 ' O I fear ye are poisond, Lord Donald,
my son !
O I fear ye are poisond, my jollie young
man ! '
' O yes ! I am poisond ; mither mak
my bed sune,
For I 'm sick at the heart, and I fain
wad lie doun.'

7 ' What will ye leave to your father,
Lord Donald my son ?
What will ye leave to your father, my
jollie young man ? '
' Baith my houses and land ; mither,
mak my bed sune,
For I 'm sick at the heart, and I fain
wad lie doun.'

8 ' What will ye leave to your brither,
Lord Donald, my son ?
What will ye leave to your brither, my
jollie young man ? '
' My horse and the saddle ; mither, mak
my bed sune,
For I 'm sick at the heart, and I fain
wad lie doun.'

9 ' What will ye leave to your sister,
Lord Donald, my son ?
What will ye leave to your sister, my
jollie young man ? '
' Baith my gold box and rings ; mither,
mak my bed sune,
For I 'm sick at the heart, and I fain
wad lie doun.'

10 ' What will ye leave to your true-love,
Lord Donald, my son ?
What will ye leave to your true-love,
my jollie young man ? '
' The tow and the halter, for to hang on
yon tree,
And lat her hang there for the poyson-
ing c me.'

J

' The Bonnie Wee Croodlin Dow,' Mother
well's MS., p. 238. From the recitation of Mis.
Maxwell, of Brediland.

1 ' O WHARE hae ye been a' day, my bonnie wee croodlin dow ?
O whare hae ye been a' day, my bonnie
wee croodlin dow ? '
' I 've been at my step-mother's ; oh mak
my bed, mammie, now !
I 've been at my step-mother's ; oh mak
my bed, mammie, now ! '

2 ' O what did ye get at your step-
mother's, my bonnie wee croodlin
dow ? ' [Twice.]
' I gat a wee wee fishie ; oh mak my
bed, mammie, now ! ' [Twice.]

3 ' O whare gat she the wee fishie, my
bonnie wee croodlin dow ? '
' In a dub before the door ; oh mak my
bed, mammie, now ! '

4 ' What did ye wi the wee fishie, my bonnie wee croodlin dow ? '
' I boild it in a wee pannie ; oh mak my
bed, mammy, now ! '

5 ' Wha gied ye the banes o the fishie till,
my bonnie wee croodlin dow ? '
' I gied them till a wee doggie ; oh mak
my bed, mammie, now ! '

6 ' O whare is the little wee doggie, my
bonnie wee croodlin dow ?
O whare is the little wee doggie, my
bonnie wee croodlin doo ? '
' It shot out its fit and died, and sae
maun I do too ;
Oh mak my bed, mammy, now, now,
oh mak my bed, mammy, now ! '

13

EDWARD

The affectedly antique spelling in Percy's
copy (B) has given rise to vague suspicions
concerning the authenticity of the ballad or of
the language : but as spelling will not make
an old ballad, so it will not unmake one. We
have, but do not need, the later traditional
copy (A) to prove the other genuine. ' Edward ' is not only unimpeachable, but has ever

n regarded as one of the noblest and most
rling specimens of the popular ballad. It has
exact counterpart in Swedish and Danish;
o in Finnish, probably from the Swedish,
c with traits of its own. The last stanza of
dward' is peculiar in implicating the mother
the guilt of the murder.

A

a. Motherwell's MS., p. 139. From Mrs
ng, Kilbarchan. b. Motherwell's Minstrelsy,
339.

'WHAT bluid 's that on thy coat lap,
　　Son Davie, son Davie?
What bluid 's that on thy coat lap?
　　And the truth come tell to me.'

' It is the bluid of my great hawk,
　　Mother lady, mother lady :
It is the bluid of my great hawk,
　　And the truth I have told to thee.'

3 'Hawk's bluid was neer sae red,
　　Son Davie, son Davie :
Hawk's bluid was neer sae red,
　　And the truth come tell to me.'

4 ' It is the bluid of my greyhound,
　　Mother lady, mother lady :
It is the bluid of my greyhound,
　　And it wadna rin for me.'

5 'Hound's bluid was neer sae red,
　　Son Davie, son Davie :
Hound's bluid was neer sae red,
　　And the truth come tell to me.'

6 ' It is the bluid o my brither John,
　　Mother lady, mother lady :
It is the bluid o my brither John,
　　And the truth I have told to thee.'

7 'What about did the plea begin,
　　Son Davie, son Davie?'
' It began about the cutting of a willow
　　　wand
That would never been a tree.'

8 'What death dost thou desire to die,
　　Son Davie, son Davie?
What death dost thou desire to die?
　　And the truth come tell to me.'

9 ' I 'll set my foot in a bottomless ship,
　　Mother lady, mother lady :

I 'll set my foot in a bottomless ship,
　　And ye 'll never see mair o me.'

10 ' What wilt thou leave to thy poor wife,
　　Son Davie, son Davie?'
' Grief and sorrow all her life,
　　And she 'll never see mair o me.'

11 ' What wilt thou leave to thy old son,
　　Son Davie, son Davie?'
' I 'll leave him the weary world to wan-
　　　der up and down,
And he 'll never get mair o me.'

12 ' What wilt thou leave to thy mother
　　　dear,
　　Son Davie, son Davie?'
' A fire o coals to burn her, wi hearty
　　　cheer,
And she 'll never get mair o me.'

B

Percy's Reliques, 1765, i, 53. Communicated by Sir David Dalrymple (Lord Hailes).

1 'WHY dois your brand sae drap wi bluid,
　　　　　Edward, Edward,
Why dois your brand sae drap wi bluid,
　　And why sae sad gang yee O?'
' O I hae killed my hauke sae guid,
　　　　　Mither, mither,
O I hae killed my hauke sae guid,
　　And I had nae mair bot hee O.'

2 'Your haukis bluid was nevir sae reid,
　　　　　Edward, Edward,
Your haukis bluid was nevir sae reid,
　　My deir son I tell thee O.'
' O I hae killed my reid-roan steid,
　　　　　Mither, mither,
O I hae killed my reid-roan steid,
　　That erst was sae fair and frie O.'

3 'Your steid was auld, and ye hae gat
　　　mair,
　　　　　Edward, Edward,
Your steid was auld, and ye hae gat
　　　mair,
　　Sum other dule ye drie O.'
' O I hae killed my fadir deir,
　　　　　Mither, mither,
O I hae killed my fadir deir,
　　Alas, and wae is mee O !'

4 'And whatten penance wul ye drie for
       that,
                        Edward, Edward ?
  And whatten penance will ye drie for
       that ?
  My deir son, now tell me O.'
  'Ile set my feit in yonder boat,
                        Mither, mither,
  Ile set my feit in yonder boat,
  And Ile fare ovir the sea O.'

5 'And what wul ye doe wi your towirs
       and your ha,
                        Edward, Edward ?
  And what wul ye doe wi your towirs
       and your ha,
  That were sae fair to see O ? '
  'Ile let thame stand tul they doun fa,
                        Mither, mither,
  Ile let thame stand tul they doun fa,
  For here nevir mair maun I bee O.'

6 'And what wul ye leive to your bairns
       and your wife,
                        Edward, Edward ?
  And what wul ye leive to your bairns
       and your wife,
  Whan ye gang ovir the sea O ? '
  'The warldis room, late them beg thrae
       life,
                        Mither, mither,
  The warldis room, late them beg thrae
       life,
  For thame nevir mair wul I see O.'

7 'And what wul ye leive to your ain
       mither deir,
                        Edward, Edward ?
  And what wul ye leive to your ain
       mither deir ?
  My deir son, now tell me O.'
  'The curse of hell frae me sall ye beir,
                        Mither, mither,
  The curse of hell frae me sall ye beir,
  Sic counseils ye gave to me O.'

14

BABYLON; OR, THE BONNIE
BANKS O FORDIE

This ballad, with additional circumstances,
is familiar to all branches of the Scandinavian
race. The Danish 'Herr Truels' Daughters'

(Grundtvig-Olrik, No. 338) may serve as
specimen : — Herr Truels' three daughte
oversleep their matins one morning, and a
roused by their mother. If we have oversley
our matins, they say, we will make up at hig
mass. They set out for church, and in a woo
fall in with three robbers, who say :

'Whether will ye be three robbers' wives,
  Or will ye rather lose your lives ? '

Much rather death, say they. The two elde
sisters submitted to their fate without a word
the third made a hard resistance. With he
last breath she adjured the robbers to seek
lodging at Herr Truels' that night. This the
did. They drank so long that they drank Hei
Truels to bed. Then they asked his wife t
promise herself to all three. First. she sai
she must look into their bags. In their bag
she saw her daughters' trinkets. She excuse
herself for a moment, barred the door strongl
roused her husband, and made it known to hir
that these guests had killed his three daugh
ters. Herr Truels called on all his men t
arm. He asked the robbers who was thei
father. They said that they had been stole
by robbers, on their way to school, one day
had had a hard life for fourteen years; an
the first crime they had committed was killin
three maids yesterday. Herr Truels reveale
to them that they had murdered their sisters
and offered them new clothes, in which the
might go away. "Nay," they said, "not so
life for life is meet." They were taken out o
the town, and their heads struck off.

A

'Babylon; or, The Bonnie Banks o Fordie
a. Motherwell's Minstrelsy, p. 88. b. Th
same. c. Appendix, p. xxii, No. xxvi, ap
parently from South Perthshire.

1 THERE were three ladies lived in
       bower,
         Eh vow bonnie
  And they went out to pull a flower.
     On the bonnie banks o Fordie

2 They hadna pu'ed a flower but ane,
  When up started to them a banisht man

3 He's taen the first sister by her hand,
  And he's turned her round and made
       her stand.

4 'It's whether will ye be a rank robber'
       wife,
  Or will ye die by my wee pen-knife ? '

5 ' It 's I 'll not be a rank robber's wife,
   But I 'll rather die by your wee pen-
       knife.'

6 He 's killed this may, and he 's laid her
   by,
   For to bear the red rose company.

7 He 's taken the second ane by the hand,
   And he 's turned her round and made
   her stand.

8 ' It 's whether will ye be a rank robber's
   wife,
   Or will ye die by my wee pen-knife ? '

9 ' I 'll not be a rank robber's wife,
   But I 'll rather die by your wee pen-
       knife.'

10 He 's killed this may, and he 's laid
   her by,
   For to bear the red rose company.

11 He 's taken the youngest ane by the
   hand,
   And he 's turned her round and made
   her stand.

12 Says, ' Will ye be a rank robber's wife,
   Or will ye die by my wee pen-knife ? '

13 ' I 'll not be a rank robber's wife,
   Nor will I die by your wee pen-knife.

14 ' For I hae a brother in this wood,
   And gin ye kill me, it 's he 'll kill thee.'

15 ' What 's thy brother's name ? come
   tell to me.'
   ' My brother's name is Baby Lon.'

16 ' O sister, sister, what have I done !
   O have I done this ill to thee !

17 ' O since I 've done this evil deed,
   Good sall never be seen o me.'

18 He 's taken out his wee pen-knife,
   And he 's twyned himsel o his ain sweet
   life.

15

LEESOME BRAND

This is one of the cases in which a remarkably fine ballad has been worse preserved in
Scotland than anywhere else. Without light
from abroad we cannot fully understand even
so much as we have saved. Though injured
by the commixture of foreign elements, A
has still much of the original story. B has,
on the contrary, so little that distinctively and
conclusively belongs to this story that it might
almost as well have been put with No. 16.

The ballad which ' Leesome Brand ' represents is preserved among the Scandinavian races
under four forms. One form of the story in
Danish, ' Redselille og Medelvold ' (Grundtvig,
No. 271), runs thus : A daughter is forced to
acknowledge to her mother that she has been
beguiled by a knight. The mother threatens
both with punishment, and the daughter,
alarmed, goes to her lover's house at night,
and informs him of the fate that awaits them.
They ride off on his horse and come to a wood.
Then her pangs seize her, but unwilling that a
man should help her, she sends the knight in
search of water. When he comes to the spring,
there sits a nightingale and sings, " Redselille
lies dead in the wood, with two sons in her
bosom." All that the nightingale has said is
found to be true. In some versions the knight
digs a grave, and lays mother and children
in it ; in two versions he lays himself in the
grave with them. It is not said whether the
children are dead or living, and the point
would hardly be raised, but for what follows.
In certain Danish and Swedish versions, however, it is expressly mentioned that the children are *alive*, and in some Danish and Norwegian versions the children are heard, or
seem to be heard, shrieking from under the
ground. Nearly all the versions make the
knight run himself through with his sword,
either immediately after the others are laid in
the grave, or after he has ridden far and wide,
because he cannot endure the cries of the children from under the earth. This would seem
to be the original conclusion of the story ; the
horrible circumstance of the children being
buried alive is much more likely to be slurred
over or omitted at a later day than to be
added.

A

' Leesome Brand.'   a. Buchan's Ballads of
the North of Scotland, i, 38.   b. Motherwell's
MS., p. 626.

1 My boy was scarcely ten years auld,
    Whan he went to an unco land,
  Where wind never blew, nor cocks ever
    crew,
    Ohon for my son, Leesome Brand !

2 Awa to that king's court he went,
    It was to serve for meat an fee ;
  Gude red gowd it was his hire,
    And lang in that king's court stayd
    he.

3 He hadna been in that unco land
    But only twallmonths twa or three,
  Till by the glancing o his ee,
    He gaind the love o a gay ladye.

4 This ladye was scarce eleven years auld,
    When on her love she was right
    bauld ;
  She was scarce up to my right knee,
    When oft in bed wi men I 'm tauld.

5 But when nine months were come and
    gane,
  This ladye's face turnd pale and wane.

6 To Leesome Brand she then did say,
   'In this place I can nae mair stay.

7 'Ye do you to my father's stable,
  Where steeds do stand baith wight and
    able.

8 'Strike ane o them upo the back,
  The swiftest will gie his head a wap.

9 'Ye take him out upo the green,
  And get him saddled and bridled seen.

10 'Get ane for you, anither for me,
  And lat us ride out ower the lee.

11 'Ye do you to my mother's coffer,
  And out of it ye 'll take my tocher.

12 'Therein are sixty thousand pounds,
  Which all to me by right belongs.'

13 He 's done him to her father's stable,
  Where steeds stood baith wicht and
    able.

14 Then he strake ane upon the back,
  The swiftest gae his head a wap.

15 He 's taen him out upo the green,
  And got him saddled and bridle
    seen.

16 Ane for him, and another for her,
  To carry them baith wi might an
    virr.

17 He 's done him to her mother's coffer,
  And there he 's taen his lover's tocher ;

18 Wherein were sixty thousand pound,
  Which all to her by right belongd.

19 When they had ridden about six mile,
  His true love than began to fail.

20 'O wae 's me,' said that gay ladye,
  'I fear my back will gang in three !

21 'O gin I had but a gude midwife,
  Here this day to save my life,

22 'And ease me o my misery,
  O dear, how happy I woud be !'

23 'My love, we 're far frae ony town,
  There is nae midwife to be foun.

24 'But if ye 'll be content wi me,
  I 'll do for you what man can dee.'

25 'For no, for no, this maunna be,'
  Wi a sigh, replied this gay ladye.

26 'When I endure my grief and pain,
  My companie ye maun refrain.

27 'Ye 'll take your arrow and your bow,
  And ye will hunt the deer and roe.

28 'Be sure ye touch not the white hynde,
  For she is o the woman kind.'

29 He took sic pleasure in deer and roe,
  Till he forgot his gay ladye.

30 Till by it came that milk-white hynde,
  And then he mind on his ladye syne.

31 He hasted him to yon greenwood tree,
  For to relieve his gay ladye ;

32 But found his ladye lying dead,
  Likeways her young son at her head.

33 His mother lay ower her castle wa,
    And she beheld baith dale and down ;
    And she beheld young Leesome Brand,
    As he came riding to the town.

34 ' Get minstrels for to play,' she said,
    ' And dancers to dance in my room ;
    For here comes my son, Leesome Brand,
    And he comes merrilie to the town.'

35 ' Seek nae minstrels to play, mother,
    Nor dancers to dance in your room ;
    But tho your son comes, Leesome Brand,
    Yet he comes sorry to the town.

36 ' O I hae lost my gowden knife ;
    I rather had lost my ain sweet life !

37 ' And I hae lost a better thing,
    The gilded sheath that it was in.'

38 ' Are there nae gowdsmiths here in Fife,
    Can make to you anither knife ?

39 ' Are there nae sheath-makers in the land,
    Can make a sheath to Leesome Brand ? '

40 ' There are nae gowdsmiths here in Fife,
    Can make me sic a gowden knife ;

41 ' Nor nae sheath-makers in the land,
    Can make to me a sheath again.

42 ' There ne'er was man in Scotland born,
    Ordaind to be so much forlorn.

43 ' I 've lost my ladye I lovd sae dear,
    Likeways the son she did me bear.'

44 ' Put in your hand at my bed head,
    There ye 'll find a gude grey horn ;
    In it three draps o' Saint Paul's ain blude,
    That hae been there sin he was born.

45 ' Drap twa o them o your ladye,
    And ane upo your little young son ;
    Then as lively they will be
    As the first night ye brought them hame.'

46 He put his hand at her bed head,
    And there he found a gude grey horn,

Wi three draps o' Saint Paul's ain blude,
    That had been there sin he was born.

47 Then he drappd twa on his ladye,
    And ane o them on his young son,
    And now they do as lively be,
    As the first day he brought them hame.

B

'The Broom blooms bonnie,' etc., Motherwell's MS., p. 365. From the recitation of Agnes Lyle, Kilbarchan.

1 ' THERE is a feast in your father's house,
    The broom blooms bonnie and so is it fair
    It becomes you and me to be very douce.
    And we 'll never gang up to the broom nae mair

2 ' You will go to yon hill so hie;
    Take your bow and your arrow wi thee.'

3 He 's tane his lady on his back,
    And his auld son in his coat lap.

4 ' When ye hear me give a cry,
    Ye 'll shoot your bow and let me lye.

5 ' When ye see me lying still,
    Throw away your bow and come running me till.'

6 When he heard her gie the cry,
    He shot his bow and he let her lye.

7 When he saw she was lying still,
    He threw away his bow and came running her till.

8 It was nae wonder his heart was sad
    When he shot his auld son at her head.

9 He houkit a grave, long, large and wide,
    He buried his auld son doun by her side.

10 It was nae wonder his heart was sair
    When he shooled the mools on her yellow hair.

11 'Oh,' said his father, 'son, but thou 'rt
    sad !
    At our braw meeting you micht be glad.'

12 'Oh,' said he, 'Father, I 've lost my
    knife
    I loved as dear almost as my own life.

13 'But I have lost a far better thing,
    I lost the sheath that the knife was in.'

14 'Hold thy tongue, and mak nae din;
    I 'll buy thee a sheath and a knife
    therein.'

15 'A' the ships eer sailed the sea
    Neer 'll bring such a sheath and a knife
    to me.

16 'A' the smiths that lives on land
    Will neer bring such a sheath and knife
    to my hand.'

16

SHEATH AND KNIFE

Other ballads with a like theme are Nos. 50,
51, 52. See also the introduction to 'Leesome
Brand,' No. 15.

A

a. Motherwell's MS., p. 286. From the recitation of Mrs. King, Kilbarchan Parish, February 9, 1825. b. 'The broom blooms bonnie
and says it is fair,' Motherwell's Minstrelsy,
p. 189.

1 IT is talked the warld all over,
    The brume blooms bonnie and says it
    is fair
    That the king's dochter gaes wi child to
    her brither.
    And we 'll never gang doun to the
    brume onie mair

2 He 's taen his sister doun to her fa-
    ther's deer park,
    Wi his yew-tree bow and arrows fast
    slung to his back.

3 'Now when that ye hear me gie a loud
    cry,
    Shoot frae thy bow an **arrow** and there
    let me lye.

4 'And when that ye see I am lying dead,
    Then ye 'll put me in a grave, wi a
    turf at my head.'

5 Now when he heard her gie a loud
    cry,
    His silver arrow frae his bow he sud-
    denly let fly.
    Now they 'll never, etc.

6 He has made a grave that was lang and
    was deep,
    And he has buried his sister, wi her babe
    at her feet.
    And they 'll never, etc.

7 And when he came to his father's court
    hall,
    There was music and minstrels and dan-
    cing and all.
    But they 'll never, etc.

8 'O Willie, O Willie, what makes thee
    in pain ? '
    'I have lost a sheath and knife that I 'll
    never see again.'
    For we 'll never, etc.

9 'There is ships o your father's sailing
    on the sea
    That will bring as good a sheath and a
    knife unto thee.'

10 'There is ships o my father's sailing on
    the sea,
    But sic a sheath and a knife they can
    never bring to me.'
    Now we 'll never, etc.

B

From a half-sheet of paper in Motherwell's
handwriting.

1 ONE king's daughter said to anither,
    Brume blumes bonnie and grows sae
    fair
    'We 'll gae ride like sister and brither.'
    And we 'll neer gae doun to the
    brume nae mair

2 'We 'll ride doun into yonder valley,
    Whare the greene green trees are bud-
    ding sae gaily.

3 ' Wi hawke and hounde we will hunt sae
      rarely,
   And we 'll come back in the morning
      early.'

4 They rade on like sister and brither,
   And they hunted and hawket in the
      valley thegether.

5 ' Now, lady, hauld my horse and my
      hawk,
   For I maun na ride, and I downa walk.

6 ' But set me doun be the rute o this tree,
   For there hae I dreamt that my bed sall
      be.'

7 The ae king's dochter did lift doun the
      ither,
   And she was licht in her armis like ony
      fether.

8 Bonnie Lady Ann sat doun be the tree,
   And a wide grave was houkit whare
      nane suld be.

9 The hawk had nae lure, and the horse
      had nae master,
   And the faithless hounds thro the woods
      ran faster.

10 The one king's dochter has ridden awa,
    But bonnie Lady Ann lay in the deed-
      thraw.

17

HIND HORN

   The story of ' Horn,' of which this ballad
gives little more than the catastrophe, is related at full in (i) ' King Horn,' a *gest* in about
1550 short verses, preserved in three manuscripts: the oldest regarded as of the second
half of the 13th century, or older; the others
put at 1300 and a little later. (ii) ' Horn et
Rymenhild,' a romance in about 5250 heroic
verses, preserved likewise in three manuscripts;
the best in the Public Library of the University of Cambridge, and of the 14th century.
(iii) ' Horn Childe and Maiden Rimnild,' from
a manuscript of the 14th century, in not quite
100 twelve-line stanzas. The relations of these
versions to each other and to the ballad are not
entirely clear. For the whole matter, see Schofield, Publications of the Modern Language
Association of America, **XVIII**, 1 ff., where full
references will be found.

   Certain points in the story of Horn — the
long absence, the sudden return, the appearance under disguise at the wedding feast, and
the dropping of the ring into a cup of wine
obtained from the bride — repeat themselves
in a great number of romantic tales. More commonly it is a husband who leaves his wife for
seven years, is miraculously informed on the
last day that she is to be remarried on the
morrow, and is restored to his home in the nick
of time, also by superhuman means. Examples
of such stories are the sixteenth-century chap-
book of Henry the Lion; the Middle High German Reinfrid von Braunschweig; Der edle
Moringer; Torello, in Boccaccio's Decameron,
x, 9.

A

' Hindhorn,' Motherwell's MS., p. 106. From
Mrs King, Kilbarchan.

1 IN Scotland there was a babie born,
      Lill lal, etc.
   And his name it was called young Hind
      Horn.
      With a fal lal, etc.

2 He sent a letter to our king
   That he was in love with his daughter
      Jean.

3 He 's gien to her a silver wand,
   With seven living lavrocks sitting
      thereon.

4 She 's gien to him a diamond ring,
   With seven bright diamonds set therein.

5 ' When this ring grows pale and wan,
   You may know by it my love is gane.'

6 One day as he looked his ring upon,
   He saw the diamonds pale and wan.

7 He left the sea and came to land,
   And the first that he met was an old
      beggar man.

8 ' What news, what news? ' said young
      Hind Horn;
   ' No news, no news,' said the old beggar
      man.

9 ' No news,' said the beggar, ' no news
      at a',
   But there is a wedding in the king's ha.

10 'But there is a wedding in the king's ha,
That has halden these forty days and
twa.'

11 'Will ye lend me your begging coat ?
And I 'll lend you my scarlet cloak.

12 'Will you lend me your beggar's rung ?
And I 'll gie you my steed to ride upon.

13 'Will you lend me your wig o hair,
To cover mine, because it is fair ? '

14 The auld beggar man was bound for the
mill,
But young Hind Horn for the king's hall.

15 The auld beggar man was bound for to
ride,
But young Hind Horn was bound for
the bride.

16 When he came to the king's gate,
He sought a drink for Hind Horn's sake.

17 The bride came down with a glass of
wine,
When he drank out the glass, and dropt
in the ring.

18 'O got ye this by sea or land ?
Or got ye it off a dead man's hand ? '

19 'I got not it by sea, I got it by land,
And I got it, madam, out of your own
hand.'

20 'O I 'll cast off my gowns of brown,
And beg wi you frae town to town.

21 'O I 'll cast off my gowns of red,
And I 'll beg wi you to win my bread.'

22 'Ye needna cast off your gowns of
brown,
For I 'll make you lady o many a town.

23 'Ye needna cast off your gowns of red,
It 's only a sham, the begging o my
bread.'

24 The bridegroom he had wedded the
bride,
But young Hind Horn he took her to
bed.

G

Kinloch's MSS., VII, 117 ; Kinloch's A▪
cient Scottish Ballads, p. 135.   From the nor▪
of Scotland.

1 'HYNDE Horn 's bound, love, and Hynd▪
Horn 's free ;
Whare was ye born ? or frae what cu▪
trie ? '

2 'In gude greenwud whare I was born,▪
And all my friends left me forlorn.

3 'I gave my love a gay gowd wand,
That was to rule oure all Scotland.

4 'My love gave me a silver ring,
That was to rule abune aw thing.

5 'Whan that ring keeps new in hue,
Ye may ken that your love loves you.

6 'Whan that ring turns pale and wan,
Ye may ken that your love loves anithe▪
man.'

7 He hoisted up his sails, and away saile▪
he
Till he cam to a foreign cuntree.

8 Whan he lookit to his ring, it was turn▪
pale and wan ;
Says, I wish I war at hame again.

9 He hoisted up his sails, and hame saile▪
he
Until he cam till his ain cuntree.

10 The first ane that he met with,
It was with a puir auld beggar-man.

11 'What news ? what news, my puir aul▪
man ?
What news hae ye got to tell to me ? '

12 'Na news, na news,' the puir man di▪
say,
'But this is our queen's wedding-day.'

13 'Ye 'll lend me your begging-weed,
And I 'll lend you my riding-steed.'

14 'My begging-weed is na for thee,
Your riding-steed is na for me.'

5 He has changed wi the puir auld beg-
    gar-man.

6 'What is the way that ye use to
    gae ?
  And what are the words that ye beg
    wi ? '

7 'Whan ye come to yon high hill,
  Ye 'll draw your bent bow nigh until.

8 'Whan ye come to yon town-end,
  Ye 'll lat your bent bow low fall doun.

9 'Ye 'll seek meat for St Peter, ask for
    St Paul,
  And seek for the sake of your Hynde
    Horn all.

10 ' But tak ye frae nane o them aw
   Till ye get frae the bonnie bride her-
     sel O.'

1 Whan he cam to yon high hill,
  He drew his bent bow nigh until.

2 And when he cam to yon toun-end,
  He loot his bent bow low fall doun.

3 He sought for St Peter, he askd for St
    Paul,
  And he sought for the sake of his Hynde
    Horn all.

4 But he took na frae ane o them aw
  Till he got frae the bonnie bride her-
    sel O.

5 The bride cam tripping doun the stair,
  Wi the scales o red gowd on her hair.

6 Wi a glass o red wine in her hand,
  To gie to the puir beggar-man.

7 Out he drank his glass o wine,
  Into it he dropt the ring.

8 'Got ye 't by sea, or got ye 't by land,
  Or got ye 't aff a drownd man's hand ? '

9 'I got na 't by sea, I got na 't by land,
  Nor gat I it aff a drownd man's hand ;

30 ' But I got it at my wooing,
   And I 'll gie it to your wedding.'

31 'I 'll tak the scales o gowd frae my
     head,
   I 'll follow you, and beg my bread.

32 'I 'll tak the scales o gowd frae my hair,
   I 'll follow you for evermair.'

33 She has tane the scales o gowd frae her
     head,
   She 's followed him, to beg her bread.

34 She has tane the scales o gowd frae her
     hair,
   And she has followd him evermair.

35 Atween the kitchen and the ha,
   There he loot his cloutie cloak fa.

36 The red gowd shined oure them aw,
   And the bride frae the bridegroom was
     stown awa.

18

SIR LIONEL

One half of **A** (the second and fourth quarters) is wanting in the Percy MS. **B** can be
traced in Banffshire for more than a hundred
years, through the old woman that sang it, and
her forbears. What we can gather of the story
is this. A knight finds a lady sitting in (or
under) a tree, who tells him that a wild boar
has slain (or worried) her lord and killed (or
wounded) thirty of his men. The knight kills
the boar, and seems to have received bad
wounds in the process. The boar belonged to
a giant, or to a wild woman. The knight is
required to forfeit his hawks and leash and the
little finger of his right hand (or his horse, his
hound, and his lady). He refuses to submit to
such disgrace, though in no condition to resist ;
the giant allows him time to heal his wounds,
and he is to leave his lady as security for his
return. At the end of the time the knight
comes back sound and well, and kills the giant
as he had killed the boar. **C** and **D** say
nothing of the knight having been wounded.
The wild woman, to revenge her " pretty
spotted pig," flies fiercely at him, and he cleaves
her in two. The last quarter of the Percy copy
would, no doubt, reveal what became of the
lady who was sitting in the tree, as to which
traditional copies give no light.

The ballad has much in common with the
romance of ' Sir Eglamour of Artois ' (Percy
MS., Hales and Furnivall, ii, 338 ; Thornton

Romances, ed. Halliwell, p. 121). It has also
taken up something from the romance of
' Eger and Grime ' (Percy MS., I, 341 ; Laing,
Early Metrical Tales, p. 1).

A

' Sir Lionell,' Percy MS., p. 32, Hales and
Furnivall, I, 75.

1 SIR Egrabell had sonnes three,
    Blow thy horne, good hunter
  Sir Lyonell was one of these.
    As I am a gentle hunter

2 Sir Lyonell wold on hunting ryde,
  Vntill the forrest him beside.

3 And as he rode thorrow the wood,
  Where trees and harts and all were good,

4 And as he rode over the plaine,
  There he saw a knight lay slaine.

5 And as he rode still on the plaine,
  He saw a lady sitt in a graine.

6 ' Say thou, lady, and tell thou me,
  What blood shedd heere has bee.'

7 ' Of this blood shedd we may all rew,
  Both wife and childe and man alsoe.

8 ' For it is not past 3 days right
  Since Sir Broninge was mad a knight.

9 ' Nor it is not more than 3 dayes agoe
  Since the wild bore did him sloe.'

10 ' Say thou, lady, and tell thou mee,
   How long thou wilt sitt in that tree.'

11 She said, ' I will sitt in this tree
   Till my friends doe feitch me.'

12 ' Tell me, lady, and doe not misse,
   Where that your friends dwellings is.'

13 ' Downe,' shee said, ' in yonder towne,
   There dwells my freinds of great re-
     nowne.'

14 Says, ' Lady, Ile ryde into yonder towne
   And see wether your friends beene
   bowne.

15 ' I my self wilbe the formost man
   That shall come, lady, to feitch you
     home.'

16 But as he rode then by the way,
   He thought it shame to goe away ;

17 And vmbethought him of a wile,
   How he might that wilde bore beguile.

18 ' Sir Egrabell,' he said, ' my father was ;
   He neuer left lady in such a case ;

19 ' Noe more will I ' . . .

    *   *   *   *   *

20 ' And a[fter] that thou shalt doe mee
   Thy hawkes and thy lease alsoe.

21 ' Soe shalt thou doe at my command
   The litle fingar on thy right hand.'

22 ' Ere I wold leaue all this with thee,
   Vpoon this ground I rather dyee.'

23 The gyant gaue Sir Lyonell such a blow,
   The fyer out of his eyen did throw.

24 He said then, ' If I were saffe and sound,
   As with-in this hower I was in this
     ground,

25 ' It shold be in the next towne told
   How deare thy buffett it was sold ;

26 ' And it shold haue beene in the next
     towne said
   How well thy buffett it were paid.'

27 ' Take 40 daies into spite,
   To heale thy wounds that beene soe wide.

28 ' When 40 dayes beene at an end,
   Heere meete thou me both safe and
     sound.

29 ' And till thou come to me againe,
   With me thoust leaue thy lady alone.'

30 When 40 dayes was at an end,
   Sir Lyonell of his wounds was healed
     sound.

31 He tooke with him a litle page,
   He gaue to him good yeomans wage.

2 And as he rode by one hawthorne,
   Even there did hang his hunting horne.

3 He sett his bugle to his mouth,
   And blew his bugle still full south.

4 He blew his bugle lowde and shrill ;
   The lady heard, and came him till.

5 Sayes, 'The gyant lyes vnder yond low,
   And well he heares your bugle blow.

6 'And bidds me of good cheere be,
   This night heele supp with you and me.'

7 Hee sett that lady vppon a steede,
   And a litle boy before her yeede.

8 And said, 'Lady, if you see that I must
   dye,
   As euer you loued me, from me flye.

9 'But, lady, if you see *that* I must liue,'
     *   *   *   *   *

B

'Isaac-a-Bell and Hugh the Græme,' Christie,
Traditional Ballad Airs, I, 110. From the singing of an old woman in Buckie, Enzie, Banffshire.

1 A KNICHT had two sons o sma fame,
       Hey nien nanny
   Isaac-a-Bell and Hugh the Græme.
       And the norlan flowers spring bonny

2 And to the youngest he did say,
   'What occupation will you hae ?
       When the, etc.

3 'Will you gae fee to pick a mill ?
   Or will you keep hogs on yon hill ?
       While the, etc.

4 'I winna fee to pick a mill,
   Nor will I keep hogs on yon hill.
       While the, etc.

5 'But it is said, as I do hear,
   That war will last for seven year,
       And the, etc.

6 'With a giant and a boar
   That range into the wood o Tore.
       And the, etc.

7 'You'll horse and armour to me provide,
   That through Tore wood I may safely
   ride.'
       When the, etc.

8 The knicht did horse and armour provide,
   That through Tore wood Græme micht
   safely ride.
       When the, etc.

9 Then he rode through the wood o Tore,
   And up it started the grisly boar.
       When the, etc.

10 The firsten bout that he did ride,
   The boar he wounded in the left side.
       When the, etc.

11 The nexten bout at the boar he gaed,
   He from the boar took aff his head.
       And the, etc.

12 As he rode back through the wood o
   Tore,
   Up started the giant him before.
       And the, etc.

13 'O cam you through the wood o Tore,
   Or did you see my good wild boar ?'
       And the, etc.

14 'I cam now through the wood o Tore,
   But woe be to your grisly boar.
       And the, etc.

15 'The firsten bout that I did ride,
   I wounded your wild boar in the side.
       And the, etc.

16 'The nexten bout at him I gaed,
   From your wild boar I took aff his
   head.'
       And the, etc.

17 'Gin you have cut aff the head o my
   boar,
   It's your head shall be taen therfore.
       And the, etc.

18 'I'll gie you thirty days and three,
   To heal your wounds, then come to
   me.'
       While the, etc.

19 'It's after thirty days and three,
   When my wounds heal, I'll come to
     thee.'
   When the, etc.

20 So Græme is back to the wood o
     Tore,
   And he's killd the giant, as he killd the
     boar.
   And the, etc.

C

a. 'The Jovial Hunter of Bromsgrove,'
Allies, The British, Roman, and Saxon Antiquities and Folk-Lore of Worcestershire,
2d ed., p. 116. From the recitation of Benja-
min Brown, of Upper Wick, about 1845. b.
Ancient Poems, Ballads and Songs of the
Peasantry of England, edited by Robert Bell,
p. 124.

1 SIR ROBERT BOLTON had three sons,
   Wind well thy horn, good hunter
   And one of them was called Sir Ryalas.
   For he was a jovial hunter

2 He rang'd all round down by the wood-
     side,
   Till up in the top of a tree a gay lady he
     spy'd.
   For he was, etc.

3 'O what dost thou mean, fair lady?'
     said he ;
   'O the wild boar has killed my lord and
     his men thirty.'
   As thou beest, etc.

4 'O what shall I do this wild boar to
     see?'
   'O thee blow a blast, and he'll come
     unto thee.'
   As thou beest, etc.

5 [Then he put his horn unto his mouth],
   Then he blowd a blast full north, east,
     west and south.
   As he was, etc.

6 And the wild boar heard him full into
     his den ;
   Then he made the best of his speed unto
     him.
   To Sir Ryalas, etc.

7 Then the wild boar, being so stout and
     so strong,
   He thrashd down the trees as he came
     along.
   To Sir Ryalas, etc.

8 'O what dost thou want of me?' the
     wild boar said he;
   'O I think in my heart I can do enough
     for thee.'
   For I am, etc.

9 Then they fought four hours in a long
     summer's day,
   Till the wild boar fain would have got-
     ten away.
   From Sir Ryalas, etc.

10 Then Sir Ryalas drawd his broad sword
     with might,
   And he fairly cut his head off quite.
   For he was, etc.

11 Then out of the wood the wild woman
     flew :
   'Oh thou hast killed my pretty spotted
     pig !
   As thou beest, etc.

12 'There are three things I do demand of
     thee,
   It's thy horn, and thy hound, and thy
     gay lady.'
   As thou beest, etc.

13 'If these three things thou dost demand
     of me,
   It's just as my sword and thy neck can
     agree.'
   For I am, etc.

14 Then into his locks the wild woman flew,
   Till she thought in her heart she had
     torn him through.
   As he was, etc.

15 Then Sir Ryalas drawd his broad sword
     again,
   And he fairly split her head in twain.
   For he was, etc.

16 In Bromsgrove church they both do
     lie ;
   There the wild boar's head is picturd by
     Sir Ryalas, etc.

19

KING ORFEO

Mr Edmonston, from whose memory this ballad was derived, notes that though stanzas are probably lost after the first, which would give some account of the king in the east wooing the lady in the west, no such verses were sung to him. He had forgotten some stanzas after the fourth, of which the substance was that the lady was carried off by fairies, that the king went in quest of her, and one day saw a company passing along a hillside, among whom he recognized his lost wife. The troop went to what seemed a great "ha-house," or castle, on the hillside. Stanzas after the eighth were also forgotten, the purport being that a messenger from behind the grey stane appeared and invited the king in.

We have here in traditional song the story of the mediæval romance of Orpheus, in which fairy-land supplants Tartarus, faithful love is rewarded, and Eurydice (Heurodis, Erodys, Eroudys) is retrieved. There are three versions of this tale (edited respectively by Laing, Select Remains of the Ancient Popular Poetry of Scotland, No. 3; Halliwell, Illustrations of Fairy Mythology, p. 37; and Ritson, Metrical Romanceës. II, 248). See the critical edition by O. Zielke, Breslau, 1880.

A

The Leisure Hour, February 14, 1880, No. 468, p. 109: Folk-Lore from Unst, Shetland, by Mrs Saxby. Obtained from the singing of Andrew Coutts, an old man in Unst, Shetland, by Mr Biot Edmondston.

1 DER lived a king inta da aste,
        Scowan ürla grün
   Der lived a lady in da wast.
        Whar giorten han grün oarlac

2 Dis king he has a huntin gaen,
   He 's left his Lady Isabel alane.

3 'Oh I wis ye 'd never gaen away,
   For at your hame is döl an wae.

4 'For da king o Ferrie we his daert,
   Has pierced your lady to da hert.'
        *   *   *   *   *

5 And aifter dem da king has gaen,
   But whan he cam it was a grey stane.

6 Dan he took oot his pipes ta play,
   Bit sair his hert wi döl an wae.

7 And first he played da notes o noy,
   An dan he played da notes o joy.

8 An dan he played da göd gabber reel,
   Dat meicht ha made a sick hert hale.
        *   *   *   *   *

9 'Noo come ye in inta wir ha,
   An come ye in among wis a'.'

10 Now he 's gaen in inta der ha,
    An he 's gaen in among dem a'.

11 Dan he took out his pipes to play,
    Bit sair his hert wi döl an wae.

12 An first he played da notes o noy,
    An dan he played da notes o joy.

13 An dan he played da göd gabber reel,
    Dat meicht ha made a sick hert hale.

14 'Noo tell to us what ye will hae :
    What sall we gie you for your play ?'

15 'What I will hae I will you tell,
    An dat 's me Lady Isabel.'

16 'Yees tak your lady, an yees gaeng hame,
    An yees be king ower a' your ain.'

17 He 's taen his lady, an he 's gaen hame,
    An noo he 's king ower a' his ain.

20

THE CRUEL MOTHER

The Cruel Mother ' is strikingly similar to a Danish ballad, recovered by Kristensen in 1870 (Jydske Folkeviser, I, 329). Versions A and B of the English ballad, which are fragmentary, were printed in the last quarter of the eighteenth century. P is from a broadside of about 1690.

A

Herd's MSS, I, 132, II, 191. Herd's Ancient and Modern Scottish Songs, 1776, II, 237.

        *   *   *   *   *

1 AND there she 's leand her back to a thorn,
        Oh and alelladay, oh and alelladay

And there she has her baby born.
   Ten thousand times good night and be
     wi thee

2 She has houked a grave ayont the sun,
   And there she has buried the sweet
     babe in.

3 And she 's gane back to her father's ha,
   She 's counted the leelest maid o them a'.

   *   *   *   *   *

4 ' O look not sae sweet, my bonie babe,
   Gin ye smyle saè, ye 'll smyle me dead.'

   *   *   *   *   *

B

a. ' Fine Flowers in the Valley,' Johnson's
Museum, p. 331. b. Scott's Minstrelsy, 1803,
III, 259, preface.

1 SHE sat down below a thorn,
     Fine flowers in the valley
   And there she has her sweet babe born.
     And the green leaves they grow rarely

2 ' Smile na sae sweet, my bonie babe,
   And ye smile sae sweet, ye 'll smile me
     dead.'

3 She 's taen out her little pen-knife,
   And twinnd the sweet babe o its life.

4 She 's howket a grave by the light o the
     moon,
   And there she 's buried her sweet babe
     in.

5 As she was going to the church,
   She saw a sweet babe in the porch.

6 ' O sweet babe, and thou were mine,
   I wad cleed thee in the silk so fine.'

7 ' O mother dear, when I was thine,
   You did na prove to me sae kind.'

   *   *   *   *   *

C

' The Cruel Mother,' Motherwell's Minstrelsy, p. 161.

1 SHE leaned her back unto a thorn,
     Three, three, and three by three

And there she has her two babes born
     Three, three, and thirty-three

2 She took frae 'bout her ribbon-belt,
   And there she bound them hand an
     foot.

3 She has taen out her wee pen-knife,
   And there she ended baith their life.

4 She has howked a hole baith deep an
     wide,
   She has put them in baith side b
     side.

5 She has covered them oer wi a marbl
     stane,
   Thinking she would gang maiden hame

6 As she was walking by her father'
     castle wa,
   She saw twa pretty babes playing at th
     ba.

7 ' O bonnie babes, gin ye were mine,
   I would dress you up in satin fine.

8 ' O I would dress you in the silk,
   And wash you ay in morning milk.'

9 ' O cruel mother, we were thine,
   And thou made us to wear the twine.

10 ' O cursed mother, heaven 's high,
   And that 's where thou will neer wi
     nigh.

11 ' O cursed mother, hell is deep,
   And there thou 'll enter step by step.'

P

' The Duke's Daughter's Cruelty,' broadsid
from the Osterley Park library, British Mu
seum, C. 39, k. 6 (60). About 1690.

1 THERE was a duke's daughter lived in
     York,
     Come bend and bear away the bow
       of yew
     So secretly she loved her father's clark
       Gentle hearts, be to me true.

2 She lovd him long and many a day,
   Till big with child she went away.

3 She went into the wide wilderness;
   Poor she was to be pitied for her heaviness.

4 She leant her back against a tree,
   And there she endurd much misery.

5 She leant her back against an oak,
   With bitter sighs these words she spoke.

6 She set her foot against a thorne,
   And there she had two pritty babes born.

7 She took her filliting off her head,
   And there she ty'd them hand and leg.

8 She had a penknife long and sharp,
   And there she stuck them to the heart.

9 She dug a grave, it was long and deep,
   And there she laid them in to sleep.

10 The coldest earth it was their bed,
   The green grass was their coverlid.

11 As she was a going by her father's hall,
   She see three children a playing at ball.

12 One was drest in scarlet fine,
   And the other as naked as ere they was born.

13 'O mother, O mother, if these children was mine,
   I would dress them [in] scarlet fine.'

14 'O mother, O mother, when we was thine,
   You did not dress us in scarlet fine.

15 'You set your back against a tree,
   And there you endured great misery.

16 'You set your foot against a thorne,
   And there you had us pritty babes born.

17 'You took your filliting off your head,
   And there you bound us, hand to leg.

18 'You had a penknife long and sharp,
   And there you stuck us to the heart.

19 'You dug a grave, it was long and deep,
   And there you laid us in to sleep.

20 'The coldest earth it was our bed,
   The green grass was our coverlid.

21 'O mother, O mother, for your sin
   Heaven-gate you shall not enter in.

22 'O mother, O mother, for your sin
   Hell-gates stands open to let you in.'

23 The lady's cheeks lookd pale and wan,
   'Alass!' said she, 'what have I done!

24 She tore her silken locks of hair,
   And dy'd away in sad despair.

25 Young ladies all, of beauty bright,
   Take warning by her last good-night.

21

THE MAID AND THE PALMER

The only English copy of this ballad that approaches completeness is furnished by the Percy manuscript, A. Sir Walter Scott remembered, and communicated to Kirkpatrick Sharpe, three stanzas, and half of the burden, of another version, B. The English ballad speaks only of a maid, who does not appear to be any particular person, and of a mysterious palmer, who seems authorized to impose on the sinner certain penances, but whose identity is not declared. In the Scandinavian versions, as well as in a Finnish version, their true characters are seen. In all of these the story of the woman of Samaria (John, iv) is blended with mediæval traditions concerning Mary Magdalen, who is assumed to be the same with the woman "which was a sinner," in Luke, vii, 37, and also with Mary, sister of Lazarus. This is the view of the larger part of the Latin ecclesiastical writers, while most of the Greeks distinguish the three. It was reserved for ballads, says Grundtvig, to confound the Magdalen with the Samaritan woman. The names Maria, or Magdalena, Jesus, or Christ, are found in most of the Scandinavian ballads. There are several Slavic ballads which blend the story of the Samaritan woman and that of 'The Cruel Mother,' without admixture of the Magdalen. The popular ballads of some of the southern nations give us the legend of the Magdalen uncombined.

A

Percy MS. p. 461; Hales and Furnivall, IV, 96.

1 THE maid shee went to the well to
    washe,
  Lillumwham, lillumwham !
  The mayd shee went to the well to
    washe,
  Whatt then ? what then ?
  The maid shee went to the well to
    washe,
  Dew ffell of her lilly white fleshe.
  Grandam boy, grandam boy, heye !
  Leg a derry, leg a merry, mett, mer,
    whoope, whir !
  Driuance, larumben, grandam boy,
    heye !

2 While shee washte and while shee ronge,
  While shee hangd o the hazle wand.

3 There came an old palmer by the way,
  Sais, 'God speed thee well, thou faire
    maid !

4 'Hast either cupp or can,
  To giue an old palmer drinke therin ?'

5 Sayes, ' I have neither cupp nor cann,
  To giue an old palmer drinke therin.'

6 'But an thy lemman came from Roome,
  Cupps and canns thou wold ffind soone.'

7 Shee sware by God & good St John,
  Lemman had shee neuer none.

8 Saies, ' Peace, ffaire mayd, you are ffor-
    sworne !
  Nine children you haue borne.

9 'Three were buryed vnder thy bed's
    head,
  Other three vnder thy brewing leade.

10 ' Other three on yon play greene ;
   Count, maid, and there be 9.'

11 'But I hope you are the good old man
   That all the world beleeues vpon.

12 ' Old palmer, I pray thee,
   Pennaunce that thou wilt giue to me.'

13 ' Penance I can giue thee none,
   But 7 yeere to be a stepping-stone.

14 'Other seauen a clapper in a bell,
   Other 7 to lead an ape in hell.

15 ' When thou hast thy penance done,
   Then thoust come a mayden home.'

B

A Ballad Book, by Charles Kirkpatrick
Sharpe, edited by David Laing, p. 157 f, VII
from Sir Walter Scott's recollection.

1 'SEVEN years ye shall be a stone,
  .   .   .   .   .   .
  For many a poor palmer to rest him
    upon.
  And you the fair maiden of Gowden-gane

2 ' Seven years ye 'll be porter of hell,
  And then I 'll take you to mysell.'
  *   *   *   *   *

3 'Weel may I be a' the other three,
  But porter of hell I never will be.'
  And I, etc.

22

ST STEPHEN AND HEROD

The manuscript which preserves this de
lightful little legend has been judged by the
handwriting to be of the age of Henry VI
The manuscript was printed entire by Thomas
Wright, in 1856, for the Warton Club, under
the title, Songs and Carols, from a manuscript
in the British Museum of the fifteenth century.
The story, with the Wise Men replacing Stephen, is also found in the carol, still current
of ' The Carnal and the Crane ' (No. 55). The
legend of Stephen and Herod, with the miracle of the roasted cock, occurs in a number
of Scandinavian ballads. The same miracle is
found in other ballads, which, for the most
part, relate to the wide-spread legend of the
Pilgrims of St James. The miracle occurs as
an interpolation in two late Greek manuscripts
of the so-called Gospel of Nicodemus (Tischen-
dorf, Evangelia Apocrypha, p. 269, note 3), and
seems to have originated in the East.

Sloane MS., 2593, fol. 22 b, British Museum.

1 SEYNT Steuene was a clerk in kyng
    Herowdes halle,
  And seruyd him of bred and cloþ as
    euery kyng befalle.

2 Steuyn out of kechone cam, wyth boris
    hed on honde;
  He saw a sterre was fayr and bryȝt ouer
    Bedlem stonde.

3 He kyst adoun þe boris hed and went in
    to þe halle:
  ' I forsak þe, kyng Herowdes, and þi
    werkes alle.

4 ' I forsak þe, kyng Herowdes, and þi
    werkes alle;
  þer is a chyld in Bedlem born is beter
    þan we alle.'

5 ' Quat eylyt þe, Steuene ? quat is þe be-
    falle ?
  Lakkyt þe eyþer mete or drynk in kyng
    Herowdes halle ? '

6 ' Lakit me neyþer mete ne drynk in kyng
    Herowdes halle;
  þer is a chyld in Bedlem born is beter
    þan we alle.'

7 ' Quat eylyt þe, Steuyn ? art þu wod, or
    þu gynnyst to brede ?
  Lakkyt þe eyþer gold or fe, or ony ryche
    wede ? '

8 ' Lakyt me neyþer gold ne fe, ne non
    ryche wede;
  þer is a chyld in Bedlem born xal hel-
    pyn vs at our nede.'

9 ' þat is al so soþ, Steuyn, al so soþ,
    iwys,
  As þis capoun crowe xal þat lyþ here in
    myn dysh.'

10 þat word was not so sone seyd, þat word
    in þat halle,
  þe capoun crew Cristus natus est ! among
    þe lordes alle.

11 ' Rysyt vp, myn turmentowres, be to and
    al be on,
  And ledyt Steuyn out of þis town, and
    stonyt hym wyth ston! '

12 Tokyn he Steuene, and stonyd hym in
    the way,
  And þerfore is his euyn on Crystes
    owyn day.

23

JUDAS

This legend, which was first printed (in 1845) in Wright and Halliwell's Reliquiæ Antiquæ, I, 144, is, so far as is known, unique in several particulars. The common tradition gives Judas an extraordinary domestic history, but does not endow him with a sister as perfidious as himself. Neither is his selling his Master for thirty pieces accounted for elsewhere as it is here, if it may be strictly said to be accounted for here. A popular explanation, founded upon John, xii, 3–6, and current for six centuries and more, is that Judas, bearing the bag, was accustomed to take tithes of all moneys that came into his hands, and that he considered he had lost thirty pieces on the precious ointment which had not been sold for three hundred pence, and took this way of indemnifying himself. There is a Wendish ballad (Haupt and Schmaler, I, 276) in which Judas receives from Jesus thirty pieces of silver to buy bread, and loses them while gambling with the Jews. At their suggestion he then sells his Master for thirty pieces.

MS. B 14, 39, of the 13th century, library of Trinity College, Cambridge.

1 Hit wes upon a Scereþorsday þat vre
    louerd aros;
  Ful milde were þe wordes he spec to
    Iudas.

2 ' Iudas, þou most to Iurselem, oure
    mete for to bugge;
  þritti platen of seluer þou bere up oþi
    rugge.

3 ' þou comest fer iþe brode stret, fer iþe
    brode strete;
  Summe of þine tunesmen þer þou meist
    i-mete.'

4 Imette wid is soster, þe swikele wimon:
  ' Iudas, þou were wrþe me stende þe
    wid ston;

5 [' Iudas, þou were wrþe me stende þe
    wid ston,]
  For þe false prophete þat tou bileuest
    upon.'

6 ' Be stille, leue soster, þin herte þe to-
    breke!
  Wiste min louerd Crist, ful wel he wolde
    be wreke.'

7 'Iudas, go þou on þe roc, heie up-on þe
          ston;
    Lei þin heued i my barm, slep þou þe
          anon.'

8 Sone so Iudas of slepe was awake,
    Þritti platen of seluer from hym weren
          itake.

9 He drou hym selue bi þe cop, þat al it
          lauede ablode;
    Þe Iewes out of Iurselem awenden he
          were wode.

10 Foret hym com þe riche Ieu þat heiste
          Pilatus:
    'Wolte sulle þi louerd, þat hette Ie-
          sus ?'

11 'I nul sulle my louerd for nones cunnes
          eiste,
    Bote hit be for þe þritti platen þat he
          me bi-taiste.'

12 'Wolte sulle þi lord Crist for enes cunnes
          golde ?'
    'Nay, bote hit be for þe platen þat he
          habben wolde.'

13 In him com ur lord gon, as is postles
          seten at mete:
    'Wou sitte ye, postles, ant wi nule ye
          ete ?

14 ['Wou sitte ye, postles, ant wi nule ye
          ete?]
    Ic am iboust ant isold to day for oure
          mete.'

15 Vp stod him Iudas: 'Lord, am I þat ... ?
    I nas neuer oþe stude þer me þe euel
          spec.'

16 Vp him stod Peter, ant spec wid al is
          miste,
    Þau Pilatus him come wid ten hundred
          cnistes,

17 ['Þau Pilatus him com wid ten hundred
          cnistes,]
    Yet ic wolde, louerd, for þi loue fiste.'

18 'Still þou be, Peter, wel I þe i-cnowe;
    Þou wolt fur-sake me þrien ar þe coc
          him crowe.'

24

BONNIE ANNIE

Had an old copy of this still pretty and
touching, but much disordered, ballad been
saved, we should perhaps have had a story
like this: Bonnie Annie, having stolen her
father's gold and her mother's fee, and fled
with her paramour, the ship in which she is
sailing encounters a storm and cannot get on.
Annie is seized with the pangs of travail, and
deplores the absence of women. The sailors
say there is somebody on board who is marked
for death, or flying from a just doom. They
cast lots, and the lot falls on Annie. Conscious
only of her own guilt, she asks to be thrown
overboard. Her paramour offers great sums
to the crew to save her, but their efforts prove
useless, and Annie again begs, or they now in-
sist, that she shall be cast into the sea with her
babe. This done, the ship is able to sail on;
Annie floats to shore and is buried there.

If the narrative in Jonah, i, is the ultimate
source of this and similar stories, it must be
owned that the tradition has maintained its
principal traits in this ballad remarkably well.
Cf. also 'Brown Robyn's Confession' (No.
57).

A

'Bonnie Annie,' Kinloch's Ancient Scottish
Ballads, p. 123.

1 THERE was a rich lord, and he lived in
          Forfar,
    He had a fair lady, and one only doch-
          ter.

2 O she was fair, O dear, she was bon-
          nie !
    A ship's captain courted her to be his
          honey.

3 There cam a ship's captain out owre the
          sea sailing,
    He courted this young thing till he got
          her wi bairn.

4 'Ye 'll steal your father's gowd, and
          your mother's money,
    And I 'll mak ye a lady in Ireland bon-
          nie.'

5 She 's stown her father's gowd, and her
          mother's money,

But she was never a lady in Ireland
    bonnie.

*   *   *   *   *

6 ' There 's fey fowk in our ship, she win-
    na sail for me,
    There 's fey fowk in our ship, she winna
    sail for me.'

7 They 've casten black bullets twice six
    and forty,
    And ae the black bullet fell on bonnie
    Annie.

8 ' Ye 'll tak me in your arms twa, lo, lift
    me cannie,
    Throw me out owre board, your ain dear
    Annie.'

9 He has tane her in his arms twa, lo,
    lifted her cannie,
    He has laid her on a bed of down, his
    ain dear Annie.

10 ' What can a woman do, love, I 'll do
    for ye ; '
    ' Muckle can a woman do, ye canna do
    for me.'

11 ' Lay about, steer about, lay our ship
    cannie,
    Do all ye can to save my dear Annie.'

12 ' I 've laid about, steerd about, laid
    about cannie,
    But all I can do, she winna sail for me.'

13 ' Ye 'll tak her in your arms twa, lo, lift
    her cannie,
    And throw her out owre board, your ain
    dear Annie.'

14 He has tane her in his arms twa, lo,
    lifted her cannie,
    He has thrown her out owre board, his
    ain dear Annie.

15 As the ship sailed, bonnie Annie she
    swam,
    And she was at Ireland as soon as them.

16 He made his love a coffin of the gowd
    sae yellow,
    And buried his bonnie love doun in a
    sea valley.

B

' The High Banks o Yarrow,' Motherwell's
MS., p. 652. From the singing of a boy, Henry
French, Ayr.

1 Down in Dumbarton there wonnd a
    rich merchant,
    Down in Dumbarton there wond a rich
    merchant,
    And he had nae family but ae only
    dochter.
    Sing fal lal de deedle, fal lal de deedle
    lair, O a day

2 There cam a rich squire, intending to
    woo her,
    He wooed her until he had got her wi
    babie.

3 ' Oh what shall I do ! oh what shall
    come o me !
    Baith father and mither will think nae-
    thing o me.'

4 ' Gae up to your father, bring down
    gowd and money,
    And I 'll take ye ower to a braw Irish
    ladie.'

5 She gade to her father, brought down
    gowd and money,
    And she 's awa ower to a braw Irish
    ladie.

6 She hadna sailed far till the young thing
    cried ' Women ! '
    ' What women can do, my dear, I 'll do
    for you.'

7 ' O haud your tongue, foolish man, dinna
    talk vainly,
    For ye never kent what a woman driet
    for you.

8 ' Gae wash your hands in the cauld
    spring water,
    And dry them on a towel a' giltit wi
    silver.

9 ' And tak me by the middle, and lift me
    up saftlie,
    And throw me ower shipboard, baith
    me and my babie.'

10 He took her by the middle, and lifted
    her saftly,
    And threw her ower shipboard, baith
    her and her babie.

11 Sometimes she did sink, sometimes she
    did float it,
    Until that she cam to the high banks o
    Yarrow.

12 'O captain tak gowd, O sailors tak
    money,
    And launch out your sma boat till I sail
    for my honey.'

13 'How can I tak gowd, how can I tak
    money ?
    My ship 's on a sand bank, she winna
    sail for me.'

14 The captain took gowd, the sailors took
    money,
    And they launchd out their sma boat
    till he sailed for his honey.

15 'Mak my love a coffin o the gowd sae
    yellow,
    Whar the wood it is dear, and the
    planks they are narrow,
    And bury my love on the high banks o
    Yarrow.'

16 They made her a coffin o the gowd sae
    yellow,
    And buried her deep on the high banks
    o Yarrow.

25

WILLIE'S LYKE–WAKE

Of this piece there is a broadside version of
1810 (not here printed).   All other copies that
have been recovered date from about 1825.
The device of a lover's feigning death as a
means of winning a shy mistress enjoys considerable popularity in European ballads.   Even
more favorite is a ballad in which the woman
adopts this expedient, in order to escape from
the control of her relations.   See the 'Gay
Goshawk' (No. 96).   A Danish ballad answer-
ing to our Feigned Lyke-Wake is preserved in
many manuscripts. some of them of the 16th
century, and is still living in tradition.   The
corresponding south-European ballad, which is
very gay and pretty, is well represented by the

Italian 'Il Genovese' (Ferraro, Canti popolar
monferrini, No. 40).

A

'Willie, Willie,' Kinloch's MSS., I, 53, from
the recitation of Mary Barr, Lesmahagow
aged upwards of seventy.   May, 1827.

1 'WILLIE, Willie, I 'll learn you a wile,'
    And the sun shines over the valleys
    and a'
    'How this pretty fair maid ye may be-
    guile.'
    Amang the blue flowrs and the yel-
    low and a'

2 'Ye maun lie doun just as ye were dead,
    And tak your winding-sheet around your
    head.

3 'Ye maun gie the bellman his bell-groat,
    To ring your dead-bell at your lover's
    yett.'

4 He lay doun just as he war dead,
    And took his winding-sheet round his
    head.

5 He gied the bellman his bell-groat,
    To ring his dead-bell at his lover's yett.

6 'O wha is this that is dead, I hear ? '
    'O wha but Willie that loed ye sae dear.'

7 She is to her father's chamber gone,
    And on her knees she 's fallen down.

8 'O father, O father, ye maun grant me
    this ;
    I hope that ye will na tak it amiss.

9 'That I to Willie's burial should go;
    For he is dead, full well I do know.'

10 'Ye 'll tak your seven bauld brethren
    wi thee,
    And to Willie's burial straucht go ye.'

11 It 's whan she cam to the outmost yett,
    She made the silver fly round for his
    sake.

12 It 's whan she cam to the inmost yett,
    She made the red gowd fly round for his
    sake.

3　As she walked frae the court to the
　　parlour there,
　The pretty corpse syne began for to
　　steer.

4　He took her by the waist sae neat and
　　sae sma,
　And threw her atween him and the wa.

5　'O Willie, O Willie, let me alane this
　　nicht,
　O let me alane till we 're wedded richt.'

6　'Ye cam unto me baith sae meek and
　　mild,
　But I 'll mak ye gae hame a wedded
　　wife wi child.'

26

THE THREE RAVENS

First printed in Melismata, 1611. Chappell
remarked, about 1855 (Popular Music of the
Olden Time, I, 59), that the ballad was still so
popular in some parts of the country that he
had " been favored with a variety of copies of
it, written down from memory, and all differing in some respects, both as to words and
tune, but with sufficient resemblance to prove
a similar origin."
'The Twa Corbies,' first printed in Scott's
Minstrelsy, and known in several versions in
Scotland, is, as Scott says, " rather a counterpart than a copy " of ' The Three Ravens.'

Melismata. Musicall Phansies. Fitting the
Court, Cittie, and Countrey Humours. London, 1611. [T. Ravenscroft.]

1　THERE were three rauens sat on a tree,
　　Downe a downe, hay down, hay
　　downe
　There were three rauens sat on a tree,
　　With a downe
　There were three rauens sat on a tree,
　They were as blacke as they might be.
　　With a downe derrie, derrie, derrie,
　　downe, downe

2　The one of them said to his mate,
　'Where shall we our breakfast take ?'

3　'Downe in yonder greene field,
　There lies a knight slain vnder his
　　shield.

4　'His hounds they lie downe at his feete,
　So well they can their master keepe.

5　'His haukes they flie so eagerly,
　There 's no fowle dare him come nie.'

6　Downe there comes a fallow doe,
　As great with yong as she might goe.

7　She lift vp his bloudy hed,
　And kist his wounds that were so red.

8　She got him vp vpon her backe,
　And carried him to earthen lake.

9　She buried him before the prime,
　She was dead herselfe ere euen-song
　　time.

10　God send euery gentleman,
　Such haukes, such hounds, and such a
　　leman.

THE TWA CORBIES

Minstrelsy of the Scottish Border, III, 239, ed.
1803, communicated by C. K. Sharpe, as written down from tradition by a lady (cf. Sharpe's
Letters, ed. Allardyce, I, 136).

1　As I was walking all alane,
　I heard twa corbies making a mane ;
　The tane unto the t'other say,
　'Where sall we gang and dine to-day ?'

2　'In behint yon auld fail dyke,
　I wot there lies a new slain knight ;
　And naebody kens that he lies there,
　But his hawk, his hound, and lady fair.

3　'His hound is to the hunting gane,
　His hawk to fetch the wild-fowl hame,
　His lady 's ta'en another mate,
　So we may mak our dinner sweet.

4　'Ye 'll sit on his white hause-bane,
　And I 'll pike out his bonny blue een ;
　Wi ae lock o his gowden hair
　We 'll theek our nest when it grows
　　bare.

5　'Mony a one for him makes mane,
　But nane sall ken where he is gane ;
　Oer his white banes, when they are bare,
　The wind sall blaw for evermair.'

27

THE WHUMMIL BORE

This ballad, if it ever were one, seems not to have been met with, or at least to have been thought worth notice, by anybody but Motherwell.

a. Motherwell's MS., p. 191. b. Motherwell's Minstrelsy, Appendix, p. xvi, No. III.

1 SEVEN lang years I hae served the king,
    Fa fa fa fa lilly
  And I never got a sight of his daughter
      but ane.
    With my glimpy, glimpy, glimpy
      eedle,
    Lillum too tee a ta too a tee a ta a tally

2 I saw her thro a whummil bore,
  And I neer got a sight of her no more.

3 Twa was putting on her gown,
  And ten was putting pins therein.

4 Twa was putting on her shoon,
  And twa was buckling them again.

5 Five was combing down her hair,
  And I never got a sight of her nae mair.

6 Her neck and breast was like the snow,
  Then from the bore I was forced to go.

28

BURD ELLEN AND YOUNG TAMLANE

This fragment seems to have no connection with what is elsewhere handed down concerning Tamlane (see No. 39), or with the story of any other ballad.

Maidment's North Countrie Garland, 1824, p. 21. Communicated by R. Pitcairn, "from the recitation of a female relative, who had heard it frequently sung in her childhood," about sixty years before the above date. Here from Pitcairn's MSS., III, 49.

1 BURD ELLEN sits in her bower windowe,
    With a double laddy double, and for
    the double dow

Twisting the red silk and the blue.
    With the double rose and the Machey

2 And whiles she twisted, and whiles sh
      twan,
  And whiles the tears fell down amang.

3 Till once there by cam Young Tamlane
  'Come light, O light, and rock you
      young son.'

4 'If you winna rock him, you may le'
      him rair,
  For I hae rocked my share and mair.'

    *   *   *   *   *

5 Young Tamlane to the seas he 's gane,
  And a' women's curse in his company 's
      gane.

29

THE BOY AND THE MANTLE

This ballad and the two which follow it are clearly not of the same rise, and not meant for the same ears, as those which go before. They would come down by professional rather than by domestic tradition, through minstrels rather than knitters and weavers. They suit the hall better than the bower, the tavern or public square better than the cottage, and would not go to the spinning-wheel at all. 'The Boy and the Mantle' is an exceedingly good piece of minstrelsy; much livelier than most of the numerous variations on the somewhat overhandled theme. Its nearest relative is the fabliau or "romance" of Le Mantel Mautaillié, 'Cort Mantel' (Montaiglon et Raynaud, Recueil Général des Fabliaux, III, 1), of which there are manuscripts of the thirteenth century. The outline of a similar tale is preserved in the Lanzelet of Ulrich von Zatzikhoven.

The probation by the Horn runs parallel with that of the Mantle, with which it is combined in the English ballad. Whether this or that is the anterior creation it is not possible to say, though the 'Lai du Corn' is of a more original stamp, fresher and more in the popular vein than the fabliau of the Mantle, as we have it. The 'Lai du Corn,' by Robert Bikez, is ascribed to the middle of the twelfth century. Like the ballad, it makes Caradoc (Garadue) the hero. This is also the case in the 'Livre de Caradoc,' inserted in the verse romance of Percival li Gallois (ed. Potvin, vv. 15,640 ff.). There are several other versions.

Besides the stories of probation by the Mantle and by the Horn or cup there are a number

others in which other objects have the same
sting power; — viz.: a crown; a bridge; a
rdle; an arch; a glove; a garland; a cup of
ngealed tears; bedclothes and bed (as in No.
; a stepping-stone by the bed-side; a chair;
wers; a shirt, a sword, a picture; a wax im-
e; a ring (as in the romance of Horn Child);
mirror; a harp; a crystal brook; a stone; a
agnet; a statue; a shield; a chess-board,
3.

Percy MS., p. 284; Hales and Furnivall, II,
4.

1 In the third day of May
    to Carleile did come
A kind curteous child,
    that cold much of wisdome.

2 A kirtle and a mantle
    this child had vppon,
With brauches and ringes
    full richelye bedone.

3 He had a sute of silke,
    about his middle drawne;
Without he cold of curtesye,
    he thought itt much shame.

4 'God speed thee, King Arthur,
    sitting att thy meate!
And the goodly Queene Gueneuer!
    I canott her fforgett.

5 'I tell you lords in this hall,
    I hett you all heede,
Except you be the more surer,
    is you for to dread.'

6 He plucked out of his potewer,
    and longer wold not dwell,
He pulled forth a pretty mantle,
    betweene two nut-shells.

7 'Haue thou here, King Arthure,
    haue thou heere of mee;
Giue itt to thy comely queene,
    shapen as itt is alreadye.

8 'Itt shall neuer become that wiffe
    that hath once done amisse:'
Then euery knight in the kings court
    began to care for his.

9 Forth came dame Gueneuer,
    to the mantle shee her bed;

The ladye shee was new-fangle,
    but yett shee was affrayd.

10 When shee had taken the mantle,
    shee stoode as she had beene madd;
It was from the top to the toe
    as sheeres had itt shread.

11 One while was itt gaule,
    another while was itt greene;
Another while was itt wadded;
    ill itt did her beseeme.

12 Another while was it blacke,
    and bore the worst hue;
'By my troth,' quoth King Arthur,
    'I thinke thou be not true.'

13 Shee threw downe the mantle,
    that bright was of blee,
Fast with a rudd redd
    to her chamber can shee flee.

14 Shee curst the weauer and the walker
    that clothe that had wrought,
And bade a vengeance on his crowne
    that hither hath itt brought.

15 'I had rather be in a wood,
    vnder a greene tree,
Then in King Arthurs court
    shamed for to bee.'

16 Kay called forth his ladye,
    and bade her come neere;
Saies, 'Madam, and thou be guiltye,
    I pray thee hold thee there.'

17 Forth came his ladye
    shortlye and anon,
Boldlye to the mantle
    then is shee gone.

18 When she had tane the mantle,
    and cast it her about,
Then was shee bare
    all aboue the buttocckes.

19 Then euery knight
    that was in the kings court
Talked, laughed, and showted,
    full oft att that sport.

20 Shee threw downe the mantle,
    that bright was of blee,

Ffast with a red rudd
　to her chamber can shee flee.

21 Forth came an old knight,
　　pattering ore a creede,
　And he proferred to this little boy
　　twenty markes to his meede,

22 And all the time of the Christmasse
　　willinglye to ffeede;
　For why, this mantle might
　　doe his wiffe some need.

23 When shee had tane the mantle,
　　of cloth that was made,
　Shee had no more left on her
　　but a tassell and a threed :
　Then euery knight in the kings court
　　bade euill might shee speed.

24 Shee threw downe the mantle,
　　that bright was of blee,
　And fast with a redd rudd
　　to her chamber can shee flee.

25 Craddocke called forth his ladye,
　　and bade her come in ;
　Saith, ' Winne this mantle, ladye,
　　with a litle dinne.

26 ' Winne this mantle, ladye,
　　and it shalbe thine
　If thou neuer did amisse
　　since thou wast mine.'

27 Forth came Craddockes ladye
　　shortlye and anon,
　But boldlye to the mantle
　　then is shee gone.

28 When shee had tane the mantle,
　　and cast itt her about,
　Vpp att her great toe
　　itt began to crinkle and crowt;
　Shee said, ' Bowe downe, mantle,
　　and shame me not for nought.

29 ' Once I did amisse,
　　I tell you certainlye,
　When I kist Craddockes mouth
　　vnder a greene tree,
　When I kist Craddockes mouth
　　before he marryed mee.'

30 When shee had her shreeuen,
　　and her sines shee had tolde,

The mantle stoode about her
　right as shee wold ;

31 Seemelye of coulour,
　　glittering like gold ;
　Then euery knight in Arthurs court
　　did her behold.

32 Then spake dame Gueneuer
　　to Arthur our king:
　' She hath tane yonder mantle,
　　not with wright but with wronge !

33 ' See you not yonder woman
　　that maketh her selfe soe clene ?
　I haue seene tane out of her bedd
　　of men fiueteene;

34 ' Preists, clarkes, and wedded men,
　　from her by-deene;
　Yett shee taketh the mantle,
　　and maketh her-selfe cleane ! '

35 Then spake the litle boy
　　that kept the mantle in hold;
　Sayes ' King, chasten thy wiffe;
　　of her words shee is to bold.

36 ' Shee is a bitch and a witch,
　　and a whore bold;
　King, in thine owne hall
　　thou art a cuchold.'

37 The litle boy stoode
　　looking ouer a dore;
　He was ware of a wyld bore,
　　wold haue werryed a man.

38 He pulld forth a wood kniffe,
　　fast thither that he ran;
　He brought in the bores head,
　　and quitted him like a man.

39 He brought in the bores head,
　　and was wonderous bold;
　He said there was neuer a cucholds
　　kniffe
　　carue itt that cold.

40 Some rubbed their kniues
　　vppon a whetstone;
　Some threw them vnder the table,
　　and said they had none.

41 King Arthur and the child
　　stood looking them vpon;

All their kniues edges
turned backe againe.

2 Craddoccke had a litle kniue
of iron and of steele;
He birtled the bores head
wonderous weele,
That euery *knight* in the *king*s court
had a morssell.

3 The litle boy had a horne,
of red gold *that* ronge;
He said, ' there was noe cuckolde
shall drinke of my horne,
But he shold itt sheede,
either behind o* beforne.'

4 Some shedd on their shoulder,
and some on their knee;
He *that* cold not hitt his mouth
put it in his eye;
And he *that* was a cuckold,
euery man might him see.

5 Craddoccke wan the horne
and the bores head;
His ladye wan the mantle
vnto her meede;
Euerye such a louely ladye,
God send her well to speede!

30

KING ARTHUR AND KING CORNWALL

The mutilation of the eariy pages of the Percy manuscript leaves us in possession of only one half of this ballad, and that half in eight fragments, so that even the outline of the story cannot be fully made out. Apparently it should run as follows: King Arthur, while boasting to Gawain of his Round Table, is told by Guenever that she knows of one immeasurably finer, and the palace it srands in is worth all Little Britain besides, but not a word will she say as to where this table and this goodly building may be. Arthur makes a vow never to sleep two nights in one place till he sees that round table; and, taking for companions Gawain, Tristram, Sir Bredbeddle, and Sir Marramiles, sets out on the quest. The five assume a palmer's weed simply for disguise, and travel east and west, only to arrive at Cornwall, so very little a way from home. The proud porter of Cornwall's gate, clad in a suit of gold, for his master is the richest king in Christen-

dom, or yet in heathenesse, is evidently impressed with Arthur's bearing. Cornwall, finding that the pilgrims come from Little Britain, asks if they ever knew King Arthur, and boasts that he had lived seven years in Arthur's kingdom, and had had a daughter by Arthur's wife, now a lady of radiant beauty. He then sends for his wonderful steed and probably his horn and sword (which also have remarkable properties), and a Burlow-Beanie, or Billy-Blin, a seven-headed, fire-breathing fiend, whom he has in his service. Arthur is then conducted to bed, and the Billy-Blin, shut up, as far as we can make out, in some sort of barrel or other vessel (called a thrub chadler, or trub chandler), is set by Arthur's bedside to hear and report the talk of the pilgrims. Now it would seem that the knights make each their vow or brag. Arthur's is that he will be the death of Cornwall King before he sees Little Britain. Gawain will have Cornwall's daughter home with him. Here there is a gap. Tristram should undertake to blow the horn, Marramiles to ride the steed, and Arthur to kill Cornwall with the sword. But first it would be necessary to subdue the loathly fiend. Bredbeddle bursts open the " rub-chadler," and fights the monster in a style that is a joy to see ; but sword, knife, and axe all break, and he is left without a weapon. Yet he had something better to fall back on, and that was a little book which he had found by the seaside. It was probably a book of Evangiles ; our Lord had written it with his hands and sealed it with his blood. With this little book Bredbeddle conjures the Burlow-Beanie, and shuts him up till wanted in a " wall of stone." He then reports to Arthur, who has a great desire to see the fiend in all his terrors, and makes the fiend start out again. The Billy-Blin is now entirely amenable to command. Bredbeddle has only to conjure him to do a thing, and it is done. First he fetches down the steed. Marramiles considers that he is the man to ride him, but finds he can do nothing with him, and has to call on Bredbeddle for help. The Billy-Blin is required to tell how the steed is to be ridden, and reveals that three strokes of a gold wand which stands in Cornwall's study-window will make him spring like spark from brand. And so it comes out that Cornwall is a magician. Next the horn has to be fetched, but, when brought, it cannot be sounded. For this a certain powder is required. This the fiend procures. Tristram blows a blast which rends the horn up to the midst. Finally, the Billy-Blin is conjured to fetch the sword, and with this sword Arthur goes and strikes off Cornwall's head. So Arthur keeps his vow, and so far as we can see all the rest are in a condition to keep theirs.

The ballad bears a close relation to the eleventh-century *chanson de geste* of Charlemagne's Journey to Jerusalem and Constantinople. Perhaps the two are derived from a common source.

Percy MS., p. 24. Hales and Furnivall, I, 61; Madden's Syr Gawayne, p. 275.

*   *   *   *

1 [SAIES, 'Come here, cuzen Gawaine so
    gay,]
    My sisters sonne be yee;
  Ffor you shall see one of the fairest
    round tables
    That euer you see with your eye.'

2 Then bespake Lady Queen Gueneuer,
    And these were the words said shee:
  'I know where a round table is, thou
    noble king,
    Is worth thy round table and other
    such three.

3 'The trestle that stands vnder this
    round table,' she said,
  'Lowe downe to the mould,
  It is worth thy round table, thou worthy
    king,
    Thy halls, and all thy gold.

4 'The place where this round table
    stands in,
    . . . . .
  It is worth thy castle, thy gold, thy
    fee,
    And all good Litle Britaine.'

5 'Where may that table be, lady?'
    quoth hee,
  'Or where may all that goodly build-
    ing be?'
  'You shall it seeke,' shee says, 'till you
    it find,
    For you shall neuer gett more of
    me.'

6 Then bespake him noble King Arthur
    These were the words said hee:
  'Ile make mine avow to God,
    And alsoe to the Trinity,

7 'Ile never sleepe one night there as I
    doe another,
    Till that round table I see:

Sir Marramiles and Sir Tristeram,
    Fellowes that ye shall bee.

8 .   .   .   .   .
    .   .   .   .
  'Weele be clad in palmers weede,
    Fiue palmers we will bee;

9 'There is noe outlandish man will
    abide,
    Nor will vs come nye.'
  Then they riued east and the riue
    west,
    In many a strange country.

10 Then they tranckled a litle further,
    They saw a battle new sett:
  'Now, by my faith,' saies noble Kin
    Arthur,
    .   .   .   .   well

*   *   *   *   *

11 But when he cam to this . . c
    And to the palace gate,
  Soe ready was ther a proud porter,
    And met him soone therat.

12 Shooes of gold the porter had on,
    And all his other rayment was vnt
    the same:
  'Now, by my faith,' saies noble Kin
    Arthur,
    'Yonder is a minion swaine.'

13 Then bespake noble King Arthur,
    These were the words says hee:
  'Come hither, thou proud porter,
    I pray thee come hither to me.

14 'I haue two poore rings of my finger,
    The better of them Ile giue to thee;
  Tell who may be lord of this castle,' h
    sayes,
    'Or who is lord in this cuntry?'

15 'Cornewall King,' the porter sayes,
    'There is none soe rich as hee;
  Neither in christendome, nor yet ii
    heathennest,
    None hath soe much gold as he.'

16 And then bespake him noble King Ar
    thur,
    These were the words sayes hee:

'I haue two poore rings of my finger,
 The better of them Ile giue thee,
If thou wilt greete him well, Cornewall
 King,
 And greete him well from me.

7 'Pray him for one nights lodging and
 two meales meate,
For his love that dyed vppon a tree;
Of one ghesting and two meales meate,
 For his loue that dyed vppon a tree.

8 'Of one ghesting, of two meales meate,
 For his love that was of virgin borne,
And in the morning *that* we may scape
 away,
 Either *w*ithout scath or scorne.'

9 Then forth is gone this proud porter,
 As fast as he cold hye,
And when he came befor Cornewall
 King,
 He kneeled downe on his knee.

0 Says, 'I haue beene porter-man, at thy
 gate,
 This thirty winter and three . .

. . . .

* * * * *

1 . . . . . .

Our Lady was borne; then thought
 Cornewall King
 These palmers had beene in Brit*taine*.

2 Then bespake him Cornewall King,
 These were the words he said there:
'Did you euer know a comely king,
 His name was King Arthur?'

3 And then bespake him noble King Ar-
 thur,
 These were the words said hee :
'I doe not know that comly king,
 But once my selfe I did him see.'
Then bespake Cornewall King againe,
 These were the words said he :

4 Says, 'Seuen yeere I was clad and fed,
 In Litle Brittaine, in a bower ;
I had a daughter by King Arthurs wife,
 That now is called my flower ;

For King Arthur, that kindly cockward,
 Hath none such in his bower.

25 'For I durst sweare, and saue my othe,
 That same lady soe bright,
That a man *that* were laid on his death
 bed
 Wold open his eyes on her to haue
 sight.'
'Now, by my faith,' sayes noble King
 Arthur,
 'And that's a full faire wight !'

26 And then bespake Cornewall [King]
 againe,
 And these were the words he said :
'Come hither, fiue or three of my
 knights,
 And feitch me downe my steed ;
King Arthur, that foule cockeward,
 Hath none such, if he had need.

27 'For I can ryde him as far on a day
 As King Arthur can doe any of his
 on three ;
And is it not a pleasure for a king
 When he shall ryde forth on his iour-
 ney ?

28 'For the eyes that beene in his head,
 The glister as doth the gleed.'
'Now, by my faith,' says noble King
 Arthur,
 '*That* is a well faire steed.'

* * * * *

29 . . . . . .

'Nobody say . . . .
 But one *that*'s learned to speake.'

30 Then King Arthur to his bed was
 brought,
 A greeiued man was hee ;
And soe were all his fellowes *w*ith him,
 From him the thought neuer to flee.

31 Then take they did that lodly groome,
 And under the rub-chadler closed was
 hee,
And he was set by King Arthurs bed-
 side,
 To heere theire talke and theire comunye ;

32 *That* he might come forth, and make
       proclamation,
    Long before it was day ;
    It was more for K*ing* Cornwalls plea-
       sure,
    Then it was for K*ing* Arthurs pay.

33 And when K*ing* Arthur in his bed was
       laid,
    These were the words said hee :
 ' Ile make mine avow to God,
    And alsoe to the Trinity,
    That Ile be the bane of Cornwall Kinge,
    Litle Brittaine or euer I see ! '

34 ' It is an vnaduised vow,' saies Gawaine
       the gay,
    ' As ever k*ing* hard make I ;
    But wee *that* beene fiue christian men,
    Of the christen faith are wee,
    And we shall fight against anoynted
       k*ing*
    And all his armorie.'

35 And then bespake him noble Arthur,
    And these were the words said he :
 ' Why, if thou be afraid, S*ir* Gawaine
       the gay,
    Goe home, and drinke wine in thine
       owne country.'

36 And then bespake S*ir* Gawaine the
       gay,
    And these were the words said hee :
 ' Nay, seeing you have made such a
       hearty vow,
    Heere another vow make will I.

37 ' Ile make mine avow to God,
    And alsoe to the Trinity,
    That I will haue yonder faire lady
    To Litle Brittaine w*ith* mee.

38 ' Ile hose her hourly to my heart,
    And w*ith* her Ile worke my will ; '

    .   .   .   .   .   .

    *   *   *   *   *

39 .   .   .   .   .
    These were the words sayd hee :
 ' Befor I wold wrestle with yonder
       feend,
    It is better be drowned in the sea.'

40 And then bespake S*ir* Bredbeddle,
    And these were the words said he :
 ' Why, I will wrestle with yon lod*l*
       feend,
    God, my gouernor thou wilt bee ! '

41 Then bespake him noble Arthur,
    And these were the words said he :
 ' What weapons wilt thou haue, tho*u*
       gentle knight ?
    I pray thee tell to me.'

42 He sayes, ' Collen brand Ile haue in m*y*
       hand,
    And a Millaine knife fast by me kne*e*
    And a Danish axe fast in my hands,
    That a sure weapon I thinke wilbe.'

43 Then w*ith* his Collen brand *that* he ha*d*
       in his hand
    The bunge of that rub-chaudler b*e*
       burst in three ;
    With that start out a lodly feend,
    With seuen heads, and one body.

44 The fyer towards the element flew,
    Out of his mouth, where was grea*t*
       plentie ;
    The knight stoode in the middle an*d*
       fought,
    That it was great ioy to see.

45 Till his Collaine brand brake in hi*s*
       hand,
    And his Millaine knife burst on hi*s*
       knee,
    And then the Danish axe burst in hi*s*
       hand first,
    That a sur weapon he thought shol*d*
       be.

46 But now is the knight left without an*y*
       weapons,
    And alacke ! it was the more pitty ;
    But a surer weapon then he had one,
    Had neuer l*ord* in Christentye ;
    And all was but one litle booke,
    He found it by the side of the sea.

47 He found it at the sea-side,
    . Wrucked upp in a floode ;
    Our L*ord* had written it w*ith* his hands
    And sealed it w*ith* his bloode.

    *   *   *   *   *

8 'That thou doe not s . . . .
   But ly still in that wall of stone,
Till I haue beene with noble King Ar-
   thur,
   And told him what I haue done.'

9 And when he came to the kings cham-
   ber,
   He cold of his curtesie :
Says, 'Sleepe you, wake you, noble
   King Arthur ?
   And euer Iesus waken yee !'

0 'Nay, I am not sleeping, I am waking,'
   These were the words said hee ;
'Ffor thee I haue card; how hast thou
   fared ?
   O gentle knight, let me see.'

1 The knight wrought the king his booke,
   Bad him behold, reede and see ;
And euer he found it on the backside of
   the leafe
   As noble Arthur wold wish it to be.

2 And then bespake him King Arthur,
   'Alas ! thow gentle knight, how may
   this be,
That I might see him in the same lick-
   nesse
   That he stood vnto thee ?'

3 And then bespake him the Greene
   Knight,
   These were the words said hee :
'If youle stand stifly in the battell
   stronge,
   For I haue won all the victory.'

4 Then bespake him the king againe,
   And these were the words said hee :
'If wee stand not stifly in this battell
   strong,
   Wee are worthy to be hanged all on
   a tree.'

5 Then bespake him the Greene Knight,
   These were the words said he :
Saies, 'I doe coniure thee, thou fowle
   feend,
   In the same licknesse thou stood vnto
   me.'

6 With that start out a lodly feend,
   With seuen heads, and one body ;

The fier towards the element flaugh,
   Out of his mouth, where was great
   plenty.

57 The knight stood in the middle p . .

   .   .   .   .   .

   .   .   .   .   .

  *   *   *   *   *

58 .   .   .   .   .

   . . they stood the space of an
   houre,
   I know not what they did.

59 And then bespake him the Greene
   Knight,
   And these were the words said he:
Saith, 'I coniure thee, thou fowle feend,
   That thou feitch downe the steed that
   we see.'

60 And then forth is gone Burlow-beanie,
   As fast as he cold hie,
And feitch he did that faire steed,
   And came againe by and by.

61 Then bespake him Sir Marramiles,
   And these were the words said hee:
'Riding of this steed, brother Bredbed-
   dle,
   The mastery belongs to me.'

62 Marramiles tooke the steed to his hand,
   To ryd him he was full bold;
He cold noe more make him goe
   Then a child of three yeere old.

63 He laid vppon him with heele and hand,
   With yard that was soe fell;
'Helpe ! brother Bredbeddle,' says Mar-
   ramile,
   'For I thinke he be the devill of hell.

64 'Helpe! brother Bredbeddle,' says Mar-
   ramile,
   'Helpe ! for Christs pittye;
Ffor without thy help, brother Bred-
   beddle,
   He will neuer be rydden for me.'

65 Then bespake him Sir Bredbeddle,
   These were the words said he:

'I coniure thee, thou Burlow-beane,
  Thou tell me how this steed was rid-
    din in his country.'

66 He saith, ' there is a gold wand
    Stands in King Cornwalls study win-
      dowe;

  .   .   .   .   .   .

  .   .   .   .   .   .

67 'Let him take that wand in *that* win-
      dow,
    And strike three strokes on that
      steed;
    And then he will spring forth of his
      hand
    As sparke doth out of gleede.'

68 And then bespake him the Greene
    Knight,

  .   .   .   .   .

  .   .   .   .   .

  *   *   *   *   *

69 .   .   .   .   .   .

  .   .   .   .   .

    A lowd blast he may blow then.

70 And then bespake Sir Bredebeddle,
    To the ffeend these words said hee :
    Says, 'I coniure thee, thou Burlow-
      beanie,
    The powder-box thou feitch me.'

71 Then forth is gone Burlow-beanie,
    As fast as he cold hie,
    And feich he did the powder-box,
    And came againe by and by.

72 Then Sir Tristeram tooke powder forth
      of *that* box,
    And blent it with warme sweet milke,
    And there put it vnto that horne,
    And swilled it about in that ilke.

73 Then he tooke the horne in his hand,
    And a lowd blast he blew;
    He rent the horne vp to the midst,
    All his ffellowes this the knew.

74 Then bespake him the Greene Knight,
    These were the words said he:

Saies, 'I coniure thee, thou Burlow
  beanie,
  That thou feitch me the sword *the*
  I see.'

75 Then forth is gone Burlow-beanie,
    As fast as he cold hie,
    And feitch he did that faire sword,
    And came againe by and by.

76 Then bespake him Sir Bredbeddle,
    To the king these words said he :
    'Take this sword in thy hand, tho
      noble King Arthur,
    For the vowes sake *that* thou mad
    Ile giue it th[ee,]
    And goe strike off King Cornewall
      head,
    In bed were he doth lye.'

77 Then forth is gone noble King Arthur,
    As fast as he cold hye,
    And strucken he hath off King Corn
      walls head,
    And came againe by and by.

78 He put the head vpon a swords point,

  .   .   .   .   .

  .   .   .   .   .

  *   *   *   *   *

31

THE MARRIAGE OF SIR GA-
  WAIN

We have here again half a ballad, in seven
fragments, but the essentials of the story
which is well known from other versions
happen to be preserved, or may be inferred
Arthur, apparently some day after Christmas
had been encountered at Tarn Wadling, in the
forest of Inglewood, by a bold baron armed
with a club, who offered him the choice of
fighting or ransoming himself by coming back
on New Year's day and bringing word what
women most desire. Arthur puts this question
in al. quarters, and having collected many answers, in which, possibly, he had little confidence, he rides to keep his day. On the way
he meets a frightfully ugly woman ; she inti-
mates that she can help him. Arthur promises
her Gawain in marriage, if she will, and she
imparts to him the right answer. Arthur finds

...e baron waiting for him at the tarn, and pre-
...nts first the answers which he had collected
...d written down. These are contemptuously
...jected. Arthur then says that he had met
...lady on a moor, who had told him that a
...oman would have her will. The baron says
...at the misshapen lady on the moor was his
...ster, and he will burn her if he can get hold
...f her. Upon Arthur's return he tells his
...nights that he has a wife for one of them.
...When they see the bride they decline the
...atch in vehement terms, all but Gawain, who
...s somehow led to waive "a little foul sight and
...isliking." He takes her in all her repulsive-
...ess, and she turns to a beautiful young woman.
...he asks Gawain whether he will have her in
...nis likeness by night only or only by day.
...Gawain leaves the choice to her, and this is all
...nat is needed to keep her perpetually beau-
...ful. For a stepmother had bewitched her
...o go on the wild moor in that fiendly shape
...ntil she should meet some knight who would
...et her have all her will. Her brother, under a
...ke spell, was to challenge men either to fight
...vith him at odds or to answer his hard ques-
...ions.

These incidents, with the variation that
...rthur waits for Gawain's consent before he
...romises him in marriage, are found in a
...omance, probably of the fifteenth century,
...rinted in Madden's Syr Gawayne, and some-
...vhat hastily pronounced by the editor to be
... unquestionably the original of the mutilated
...oem in the Percy folio." Gower (Confessio
...Amantis, Book I, vv. 1407 ff.) and Chaucer
Wife of Bath's Tale) both have this tale,
...hough with a different setting, and with the
...variation, beyond doubt original in the story,
...hat the man whose life is saved by rightly an-
...wering the question has himself to marry the
...nonstrous woman in return for her prompting
...im. The ballad of 'The Knight and Shep-
...erd's Daughter' (No. 110) has much in com-
...non with The Wife of Bath's Tale and should
...lso be compared. The incident of a hag turned
...nto a beautiful woman after a man has bedded
...with her occurs several times in ancient Irish
...story, one text being found in the Book of
...Leinster, a twelfth-century manuscript. For a
...full discussion of the whole cycle of tales see
...Maynadier, The Wife of Bath's Tale, its
...Sources and Analogues, 1901.

Percy MS., p. 46, Hales and Furnivall, I,
105; Madden's Syr Gawayne, p. 288; Percy's
Reliques, ed. 1794, III, 350.

1 KINGE ARTHUR liues in merry Carleile,
  And seemely is to see,

And there he hath with him Queene
  Genev*er*,
  That bride soe bright of blee.

2 And there he hath with [him] Queene
  Genever,
  That bridé soe bright in bower,
And all his barons about him stoode,
  That were both stiffe and stowre.

3 The k*i*ng kept a royall Christmasse,
  Of mirth and great honor,
  And when . . . .

    .   .   .   .   .

  *   *   *   *   *

4 'And bring me word what thing it is
  That a woman [will] most desire ;
This shalbe thy ransome, Arthur,' he
  sayes,
  'For Ile haue noe other hier.'

5 K*i*ng Arthur then held vp his hand,
  According thene as was the law ;
He tooke his leaue of the baron there,
  And homward can he draw.

6 And when he came to merry Carlile,
  To his chamber he is gone,
And ther came to him his cozen S*i*r
  Gawaine,
  As he did make his mone.

7 And there came to him his cozen S*i*r
  Gawaine,
  That was a curteous knight ;
' Why sigh you soe sore, vnckle Arthur,'
  he said,
  ' Or who hath done thee vnright ? '

8 ' O peace, O peace, thou gentle Gawaine,
  That faire may thee beffall !
For if thou knew my sighing soe deepe,
  Thou wold not meruaile att all.

9 'Ffor when I came to Tearne Wadling,
  A bold barron there I fand,
With a great club vpon his backe,
  Standing stiffe and strong.

10 'And he asked me wether I wold fight
  Or from him I shold begone,
O[r] else I must him a ransome pay,
  And soe dep*art* him from.

11 ' To fight with him I saw noe cause;
    Methought it was not meet;
    For he was stiffe and strong with-all,
      His strokes were nothing sweete.

12 ' Therefor this is my ransome, Gawaine,
    I ought to him to pay;
    I must come againe, as I am sworne,
      Vpon the New Yeers day;

13 ' And I must bring him word what thing
      it is

      .   .   .   .   .   .

      .   .   .   .   .   .

      *   *   *   *   *

14 Then king Arthur drest him for to
      ryde,
    In one soe rich array,
    Toward the fore-said Tearne Wadling,
      That he might keepe his day.

15 And as he rode over a more,
    Hee see a lady where shee sate
    Betwixt an oke and a greene hollen;
      She was cladd in red scarlett.

16 Then there as shold haue stood her
      mouth,
    Then there was sett her eye;
    The other was in her forhead fast,
      The way that she might see.

17 Her nose was crooked and turnd out-
      ward,
    Her mouth stood foule a-wry;
    A worse formed lady than shee was,
      Neuer man saw with his eye.

18 To halch vpon him, King Arthur,
    This lady was full faine,
    But King Arthur had forgott his lesson,
      What he shold say againe.

19 ' What knight art thou,' the lady sayd,
    ' That will not speak to me ?
    Of me be thou nothing dismayd,
      Tho I be vgly to see.

20 ' For I haue halched you curteouslye,
    And you will not me againe;
    Yett I may happen Sir Knight,' shee
      said,
    ' To ease thee of thy paine.'

21 ' Giue thou ease me, lady,' he said,
    ' Or helpe me any thing,
    Thou shalt have gentle Gawaine, n
      cozen,
    And marry him with a ring.'

22 ' Why, if I help thee not, thou nob
      King Arthur,
    Of thy owne hearts desiringe,
    Of gentle Gawaine .   .   .   .

      *   *   *   *   *

23 And when he came to the Tearne Wa
      ling,
    The baron there cold he finde,
    With a great weapon on his backe,
      Standing stiffe and stronge.

24 And then he tooke King Arthurs letter
      in his hands,
    And away he cold them fling,
    And then he puld out a good browm
      sword,
    And cryd himselfe a king.

25 And he sayd, ' I have thee and thy land
      Arthur,
    To doe as it pleaseth me,
    For this is not thy ransome sure,
      Therfore yeeld thee to me.'

26 And then bespoke him noble Arthur,
    And bad him hold his hand:
    ' And giue me leaue to speake m
      mind
    In defence of all my land.'

27 He said, ' As I came over a more,
    I see a lady where shee sate
    Betweene an oke and a green hollen;
      Shee was clad in red scarlett.

28 ' And she says a woman will haue he
      will,
    And this is all her cheef desire:
    Doe me right, as thou art a baron o
      sckill,
    This is thy ransome and all thy hyer.'

29 He sayes, ' An early vengeance light on
      her !
    She walkes on yonder more;
    It was my sister that told thee this,
    And she is a misshappen hore.

0 ' But heer Ile make mine avow to God
 To doe her an euill turne,
For an euer I may thate fowle theefe get,
 In a fyer I will her burne.'

*   *   *   *   *

81 Sir Lancelott and Sir Steven bold,
 They rode with them that day,
And the formost of the company
 There rode the steward Kay.

82 Soe did Sir Banier and Sir Bore,
 Sir Garrett with them soe gay,
Soe did Sir Tristeram that gentle
 knight,
 To the forrest fresh and gay.

33 And when he came to the greene for-
 rest,
Vnderneath a greene holly tree,
Their sate that lady in red scarlet
 That vnseemly was to see.

34 Sir Kay beheld this ladys face,
 And looked vppon her swire ;
' Whosoeuer kisses this lady,' he sayes,
 ' Of his kisse he stands in feare.'

35 Sir Kay beheld the lady againe,
 And looked vpon her snout;
' Whosoeuer kisses this lady,' he saies,
 ' Of his kisse he stands in doubt.'

36 ' Peace, cozen Kay,' then said Sir Ga-
 waine,
 ' Amend thee of thy life;
For there is a knight amongst vs all
 That must marry her to his wife.'

37 ' What ! wedd her to wiffe !' then said
 Sir Kay,
 ' In the diuells name anon !
Gett me a wiffe where-ere I may,
 For I had rather be slaine !'

88 Then some tooke vp their hawkes in
 hast,
 And some tooke vp their hounds,
And some sware they wold not marry
 her
 For citty nor for towne.

89 And then be-spake him noble King Arthur,

And sware there by this day,
 For a litle foule sight and misliking

 .   .   .   .   .

*   *   *   *   *

40 Then shee said, ' Choose thee, gentle Ga-
 waine,
 Truth as I doe say,
Wether thou wilt haue me in this lik-
 nesse
 In the night or else in the day.'

41 And then bespake him gentle Gawaine,
 Was one soe mild of moode,
Sayes, ' Well I know what I wold say,
 God grant it may be good !

42 ' To haue thee fowle in the night
 When I with thee shold play —
Yet I had rather, if I might,
 Haue thee fowle in the day.'

43 ' What ! when lords goe with ther
 feires,' shee said,
 ' Both to the ale and wine,
Alas ! then I must hyde my selfe,
 I must not goe withinne.'

44 And then bespake him gentle Gawaine,
 Said, ' Lady, that 's but skill;
And because thou art my owne lady,
 Thou shalt haue all thy will.'

45 Then she said, ' Blesed be thou, gentle
 Gawain,
 This day that I thee see,
For as thou seest me att this time,
 From henceforth I wilbe.

46 ' My father was an old knight,
 And yett it chanced soe
That he marryed a younge lady
 That brought me to this woe.

47 ' Shee witched me, being a faire young
 lady,
 To the greene forrest to dwell,
And there I must walke in womans lik-
 nesse,
 Most like a feend of hell.

48 ' She witched my brother to a carlish
 b . . .

*   *   *   *   *

49 .   .   .   .   .   .

    'That looked soe foule, and that was
        wont
       On the wild more to goe.'

50 'Come kisse her, brother Kay,' then
       said Sir Gawaine,
    'And amend thé of thy liffe ;
    I sweare this is the same lady
       That I marryed to my wiffe.'

51 Sir Kay kissed that lady bright,
       Standing vpon his ffeete;
    He swore, as he was trew knight,
       The spice was neuer soe sweete.

52 'Well, cozen Gawaine,' sayes Sir Kay,
    'Thy chance is fallen arright,
    For thou hast gotten one of the fairest
       maids
       I euer saw with my sight.'

53 'It is my fortune,' said Sir Gawaine ;
    'For my vnckle Arthurs sake
    I am glad as grasse wold be of raine,
       Great ioy that I may take.'

54 Sir Gawaine tooke the lady by the one
       arme,
    Sir Kay tooke her by the tother,
    They led her straight to King Arthur,
       As they were brother and brother.

55 King Arthur welcomed them there all,
       And soe did Lady Geneuer his queene,
    With all the knights of the Round
       Table,
       Most seemly to be seene.

56 King Arthur beheld that lady faire
       That was soe faire and bright,
    He thanked Christ in Trinity
       For Sir Gawaine that gentle knight.

57 Soe did the knights, both more and
       lesse,
    Reioyced all that day
    For the good chance that hapened was
       To Sir Gawaine and his lady gay.

32

KING HENRY

Scott describes his copy of 'King Henry' as
"edited from the MS. of Mrs. Brown, corrected
by a recited fragment." This manuscript was
William Tytler's, now lost. The story is a
variety of that which is found in 'The Marriage of Sir Gawain' (No. 31), and has its parallel, as Scott observes, in an episode in the
saga of Hrólfr Kraki. Every point of the
Norse saga, except the stepmother's weird, is
found in the Gaelic tale 'The Daughter of
King Under-waves' (Campbell's Popular Tales
of the West Highlands, No. 86, III, 403 f.).
Campbell had a fragment of a Gaelic ballad
upon this story (vol. XVII, p. 212, of his manuscript collection), 'Collun gun Cheann,' or
'The Headless Trunk,' twenty-two lines. In
this case, as the title imports, a body without
a head replaces the hideous, dirty, and un-
kempt draggle-tail who begs shelter of the
Finn successively and obtains her boon only
from Diarmaid (see Campbell's Gaelic Ballads,
p. ix). On the whole matter see Dr. Maynadier's monograph on The Wife of Bath's Tale
(p. 55, above).

'King Henry.' a. Jamieson-Brown MS., p.
31. b. Minstrelsy of the Scottish Border,
1802, II, 132.

1 LAT never a man a wooing wend
       That lacketh thingis three;
    A routh o gold, an open heart,
       Ay fu o charity.

2 As this I speak of King Henry,
       For he lay burd-alone ;
    An he's doen him to a jelly hunt's ha,
       Was seven miles frae a town.

3 He chas'd the deer now him before,
       An the roe down by the den,
    Till the fattest buck in a' the flock
       King Henry he has slain.

4 O he has doen him to his ha,
       To make him beerly cheer ;
    An in it came a griesly ghost,
       Steed stappin i the fleer.

5 Her head hat the reef-tree o the house,
       Her middle ye mot wel span ;
    He's thrown to her his gay mantle,
       Says, 'Lady, hap your lingcan.'

6 Her teeth was a' like teather stakes,
    Her nose like club or mell ;
    An I ken naething she 'peard to be,
    But the fiend that wons in hell.

7 'Some meat, some meat, ye King Henry,
    Some meat ye gie to me !'
  'An what meat 's in this house, lady,
    An what ha I to gie ?'
  'O ye do kill your berry-brown steed,
    An you bring him here to me.'

8 O whan he slew his berry-brown steed,
    Wow but his heart was sair !
  Shee eat him [a'] up, skin an bane,
    Left naething but hide an hair.

9 'Mair meat, mair meat, ye King Henry,
    Mair meat ye gi to me !'
  'An what meat 's in this house, lady,
    An what ha I to gi ?'
  'O ye do kill your good gray-hounds,
    An ye bring them a' to me.'

10 O whan he slew his good gray-hounds,
    Wow but his heart was sair !
  She eat them a' up, skin an bane,
    Left naething but hide an hair.

11 'Mair meat, mair meat, ye King Henry,
    Mair meat ye gi to me !'
  'An what meat 's i this house, lady,
    An what ha I to gi ?'
  'O ye do kill your gay gos-hawks,
    An ye bring them here to me.'

12 O whan he slew his gay gos-hawks,
    Wow but his heart was sair !
  She eat them a' up, skin an bane,
    Left naething but feathers bare.

13 'Some drink, some drink, now, King
    Henry,
    Some drink ye bring to me !'
  'O what drink 's i this house, lady,
    That you 're nae welcome ti ?'
  'O ye sew up your horse's hide,
    An bring in a drink to me.'

14 And he 's sewd up the bloody hide,
    A puncheon o wine put in ;
  She drank it a' up at a waught,
    Left na ae drap ahin.

15 'A bed, a bed, now, King Henry,
    A bed you mak to me !

    For ye maun pu the heather green,
    An mak a bed to me.'

16 O pu'd has he the heather green,
    An made to her a bed,
  An up has he taen his gay mantle,
    An oer it has he spread.

17 'Tak aff your claiths, now, King Henry,
    An lye down by my side !'
  'O God forbid,' says King Henry,
    'That ever the like betide ;
  That ever the fiend that wons in hell
    Shoud streak down by my side.'

*   *   *   *   *

18 Whan night was gane, and day was
    come,
    An the sun shone throw the ha,
  The fairest lady that ever was seen
    Lay atween him an the wa.

19 'O well is me !' says King Henry,
    'How lang 'll this last wi me ?'
  Then out it spake that fair lady,
    'Even till the day you dee.

20 'For I 've met wi mony a gentle knight
    That 's gien me sic a fill,
  But never before wi a courteous knight
    That ga me a' my will.'

34

KEMP OWYNE

The Icelandic saga of 'Hjálmter and Olver'
comes near enough to the story of the ballad
to show where its connections lie (Rafn, Forn-
aldar Sögur. III, 473 ff., 514 ff.). In many
tales of the sort a single kiss suffices to undo
the spell and reverse the transformation ; in
others, as in the ballad, three are required.
The incidents have been carefully studied by
Schofield in his investigation of the romance
of Li Beaus Desconeüs (Studies and Notes in
Philology and Literature, IV, 199 ff.).

A

'Kemp Owyne,' Buchan, Ballads of the
North of Scotland, II. 78, from Mr Nicol of
Strichen, as learned in his youth from old peo-
ple ; Motherwell's Minstrelsy, p. 374 ; 'Kemp
Owayne,' Motherwell's MS., p. 448.

1 HER mother died when she was young,
 Which gave her cause to make great
  moan;
 Her father married the warst woman
  That ever lived in Christendom.

2 She served her with foot and hand,
 In every thing that she could dee,
 Till once, in an unlucky time,
  She threw her in ower Craigy's sea.

3 Says, 'Lie you there, dove Isabel,
 And all my sorrows lie with thee;
 Till Kemp Owyne come ower the sea,
  And borrow you with kisses three,
 Let all the warld do what they will,
  Oh borrowed shall you never be!'

4 Her breath grew strang, her hair grew
  lang,
 And twisted thrice about the tree,
 And all the people, far and near,
  Thought that a savage beast was she.

5 These news did come to Kemp Owyne,
 Where he lived, far beyond the sea;
 He hasted him to Craigy's sea,
  And on the savage beast lookd he.

6 Her breath was strang, her hair was
  lang,
 And twisted was about the tree,
 And with a swing she came about:
  'Come to Craigy's sea, and kiss with
   me.

7 'Here is a royal belt,' she cried,
  'That I have found in the green
   sea;
 And while your body it is on,
  Drawn shall your blood never be;
 But if you touch me, tail or fin,
  I vow my belt your death shall be.'

8 He stepped in, gave her a kiss,
  The royal belt he brought him wi;
 Her breath was strang, her hair was
  lang,
 And twisted twice about the tree,
 And with a swing she came about:
  'Come to Craigy's sea, and kiss with
   me.

9 'Here is a royal ring,' she said,
  'That I have found in the green sea;

And while your finger it is on,
 Drawn shall your blood never be;
But if you touch me, tail or fin,
 I swear my ring your death shall be

10 He stepped in, gave her a kiss,
  The royal ring he brought him wi;
 Her breath was strang, her hair wa
  lang,
 And twisted ance about the tree,
 And with a swing she came about:
  'Come to Craigy's sea, and kiss wit
   me.

11 'Here is a royal brand,' she said,
  'That I have found in the green sea
 And while your body it is on,
  Drawn shall your blood never be;
 But if you touch me, tail or fin,
  I swear my brand your death shal
   be.'

12 He stepped in, gave her a kiss,
  The royal brand he brought him wi;
 Her breath was sweet, her hair grew
  short,
 And twisted nane about the tree,
 And smilingly she came about,
  As fair a woman as fair could be.

B

'Kempion.' a. Jamieson-Brown MS., p. 29
b. Scott's Minstrelsy, II, 93, 1802, from Wil
liam Tytler's Brown MS., No. 9, " with correc
tions from a recited fragment."

1 'COME here, come here, you freel
  feed,
 An lay your head low on my knee;
 The hardest weird I will you read
  That eer was read to a lady.

2 'O meikle dollour sall you dree,
  An ay the sat seas oer ye ['s] swim;
 An far mair dollour sall ye dree
  On Eastmuir craigs, or ye them clim

3 'I wot ye's be a weary wight,
  An relieved sall ye never be
 Till Kempion, the kingis son,
  Come to the craig and thrice kiss
   thee.'

4 O meickle dollour did she dree,
  An ay the sat seas oer she swam;

An far mair dollour did she dree
  On Eastmuir craigs, or them she
    clam;
An ay she cried for Kempion,
  Gin he would come till her han.

5 Now word has gane to Kempion
  That sich a beast was in his lan,
An ay be sure she would gae mad
  Gin she gat nae help frae his han.

6 'Now by my sooth,' says Kempion,
  'This fiery beast I ['ll] gang to see;'
'An by my sooth,' says Segramour,
  'My ae brother, I 'll gang you wi.'

7 O biggit ha they a bonny boat,
  An they hae set her to the sea,
An Kempion an Segramour
  The fiery beast ha gane to see:
A mile afore they reachd the shore,
  I wot she gard the red fire flee.

8 'O Segramour, keep my boat afloat,
  An lat her no the lan so near;
For the wicked beast she 'll sure gae
    mad,
  An set fire to the land an mair.'

9 'O out o my stye I winna rise —
  An it is na for the fear o thee —
Till Kempion, the kingis son,
  Come to the craig an thrice kiss me.'

10 He 's louted him oer the Eastmuir
    craig,
  An he has gien her kisses ane;
Awa she gid, an again she came,
  The fieryest beast that ever was
    seen.

11 'O out o my stye I winna rise —
  An it is na for fear o thee —
Till Kempion, the kingis son,
  Come to the craig an thrice kiss me.'

12 He louted him oer the Eastmuir craig,
  An he has gien her kisses twa;
Awa she gid, an again she came,
  The fieryest beast that ever you saw.

13 'O out o my stye I winna rise —
  An it is na for fear o ye —
Till Kempion, the kingis son,
  Come to the craig an thrice kiss me.'

14 He 's louted him oer the Eastmuir
    craig,
  An he has gien her kisses three;
Awa she gid, an again she came,
  The fairest lady that ever coud be.

15 'An by my sooth,' say[s] Kempion,
  'My ain true love — for this is she —
O was it wolf into the wood,
  Or was it fish intill the sea,
Or was it man, or wile woman,
  My true love, that misshapit thee ?'

16 'It was na wolf into the wood,
  Nor was it fish into the sea,
But it was my stepmother,
  An wae an weary mot she be.

17 'O a heavier weird light her upon
  Than ever fell on wile woman;
Her hair 's grow rough, an her teeth 's
    grow lang,
  An on her four feet sal she gang.

18 'Nane sall tack pitty her upon,
  But in Wormie's Wood she sall ay
    won,
An relieved sall she never be,
  Till St Mungo come oer the sea.'

35

ALLISON GROSS

    The queen of the fairies undoing the spell
of the witch is a remarkable feature, not paralleled in English or northern tradition. The
Greek nereids, however, who do pretty much
everything, good or bad, that is ascribed to
northern elves or fairies, and even bear an appellation resembling that by which fairies are
spoken of in Scotland and Iceland, "the good
damsels," "the good ladies," have a queen
who is described as taking no part in the un-
friendly acts of her subjects, but as being
kindly disposed towards mankind, and even as
repairing the mischief which subordinate spirits
have done against her will. If now the fairy
queen might interpose in behalf of men against
her own kith and kin, much more likely would
she be to exert herself to thwart the malignity
of a witch.

'Allison Gross,' Jamieson-Brown MS , p. 40 ;
Jamieson's Popular Ballads, II, 187.

1 O Allison Gross, that lives in yon
  towr,
  The ugliest witch i the north country,
Has trysted me ae day up till her
  bowr,
  An monny fair speech she made to
  me.

2 She stroaked my head, an she kembed
  my hair,
  An she set me down saftly on her
  knee;
Says, Gin ye will be my lemman so
  true,
  Sae monny braw things as I woud
  you gi.

3 She showd me a mantle o red scarlet,
  Wi gouden flowrs an fringes fine;
Says, Gin ye will be my lemman so
  true,
  This goodly gift it sal be thine.

4 ' Awa, awa, ye ugly witch,
  Haud far awa, an lat me be;
I never will be your lemman sae true,
  An I wish I were out o your com-
  pany.'

5 She neist brought a sark o the saftest
  silk,
  Well wrought wi pearles about the
  ban;
Says, Gin you will be my ain true love,
  This goodly gift you sal comman.

6 She showd me a cup of the good red
  gold,
  Well set wi jewls sae fair to see;
Says, Gin you will be my lemman sae
  true,
  This goodly gift I will you gi.

7 ' Awa, awa, ye ugly witch,
  Had far awa, and lat me be ;
For I woudna ance kiss your ugly mouth
  For a' the gifts that ye coud gi.'

8 She 's turnd her right and roun about,
  An thrice she blaw on a grass-green
  horn,
An she sware by the meen and the stars
  abeen,
  That she 'd gar me rue the day I was
  born.

9 Then out has she taen a silver wand,
  An she 's turnd her three times ro
  an roun ;
She 's mutterd sich words till n
  strength it faild,
  An I fell down senceless upon t
  groun.

10 She 's turnd me into an ugly worm,
  And gard me toddle about the tree
An ay, on ilka Saturdays night,
  My sister Maisry came to me,

11 Wi silver bason an silver kemb,
  To kemb my heady upon her knee ;
But or I had kissd her ugly mouth,
  I 'd rather a toddled about the tree.

12 But as it fell out on last Hallow-even,
  When the seely court was ridin by,
The queen lighted down on a gowan
  bank,
  Nae far frae the tree where I wont t
  lye.

13 She took me up in her milk-white han,
  An she 's stroakd me three times oe
  her knee ;
She chang'd me again to my ain prope
  shape,
  An I nae mair maun toddle about th
  tree.

36

THE LAILY WORM AND TH
MACHREL OF THE SEA

Though this ballad is somewhat mutilate
and defaced, it is pure tradition, and neve
been retouched by a pen. It has the firs
stanza in common with ' Kemp Owyne ' (N
34), and shares more than that with ' Alliso
Gross ' (No. 35). But it is independent c
' Allison Gross,' and has a far more origina
sound.

The Old Lady's MS., No. 2.

1 ' I was bat seven year alld
  Fan my mider she did dee,
My father marrëd the ae warst woma
  The wardle did ever see.

2 ' For she has made me the lailly worm
  That lays att the fitt of the tree,

An o my sister Meassry
   The machrel of the sea.

3 ' An every Saterday att noon
   The machrl comes to me,
An she takes my laylë head,
   An lays it on her knee,
   An keames it we a silver kemm,
   An washes it in the sea.

4 ' Seven knights ha I slain
   Sane I lay att the fitt of the tree ;
An ye war na my ain father,
   The eight an ye sud be.'

5 ' Sing on your song, ye l[a]ily worm,
   That ye sung to me ; '
' I never sung that song
   But fatt I wad sing to ye.

6 ' I was but seven year aull
   Fan my mider she [did] dee,
My father marrëd the a warst woman
   The wardle did ever see.

7 ' She changed me to the layel[y] worm
   That layes att the fitt of the tree,
An my sister Messry
   [To] the makrell of the sea.

8 ' And every Saterday att noon
   The machrell comes to me,
An she takes my layly head,
   An layes it on her knee,
   An kames it weth a siller kame,
   An washes it in the sea.

9 ' Seven knights ha I slain
   San I lay att the fitt of the tree ;
An ye war na my ain father,
   The eight ye sud be.'

10 He sent for his lady
   As fast as sen cod he :
' Far is my son,
   That ye sent fra me,
And my daughter,
   Lady Messry ? '

11 ' Yer son is att our king's court,
   Sarving for meatt an fee,
And yer daugh[t]er is att our quin's
   court,
   A mary suit an free.'

12 ' Ye lee, ye ill woman,
   Sa loud as I hear ye lea,
For my son is the layelly worm
   That lays at the fitt of the tree,
An my daughter Messry
   The machrell of the sea.'

13 She has tain a silver wan
   An gine him stroks three,
An he started up the bravest knight
   Your eyes did ever see.

14 She has tane a small horn
   An loud an shill blue she,
An a' the fish came her tell but the proud
   machrell,
   An she stood by the sea :
Ye shaped me ance an unshemly shape,
   An ye 's never mare shape me.'

15 He has sent to the wood
   For hathorn an fun,
An he has tane that gay lady,
   An ther he did her burne.

37

THOMAS RYMER

Thomas of Erceldoune, otherwise Thomas the Rhymer, has had a fame as a seer, which, though progressively narrowed, is, after the lapse of nearly or quite six centuries, far from being extinguished. The common people throughout the whole of Scotland, according to Mr Robert Chambers (1870), continue to regard him with veneration, and to preserve a great number of his prophetic sayings, which they habitually seek to connect with " dear years " and other notable public events. A prediction of Thomas of Erceldoune's is recorded in a manuscript which is put at a date before 1320, and he is referred to with other soothsayers in the Scalacronica, a French chronicle of English history begun in 1355. Erceldoune is spoken of as a poet in Robert Mannyng's translation of Langtoft's Chronicle, finished in 1338, and in the Auchinleck copy of ' Sir Tristrem,' thought to have been made about 1350, a Thomas is said to have been consulted at Erþeldoun touching the history of Tristrem. So that we seem safe in holding that Thomas of Erceldoune had a reputation both as prophet and poet in the earlier part of the fourteenth century. The vaticinations of

Thomas are cited by various late chroniclers,
and had as much credit in England as in Scotland. All this might have been if Thomas of
Erceldoune had not been more historical than
Merlin. But the name is known to have belonged to a real person. Just when he lived
is not certain, but it was somewhere between
1210 and 1296 or 1297.

Thomas of Erceldoune's prophetic power
was a gift of the queen of the elves; the modern elves, equally those of northern Europe
and of Greece, resembling in respect to this
attribute the nymphs of the ancient Hellenic
mythology. How Thomas attained this grace
is set forth in the first three fits of a poem
which bears his name. This poem has come
down in four somewhat defective copies: the
earliest written a little before the middle of
the fifteenth century, two others about 1450,
the fourth later. There is a still later manuscript copy of the second and third fits. All
the manuscripts are English, but it is manifest
from the nature of the topics that the original
poem was the work of a Scotsman. All four
of the complete versions speak of an older
story. This was undoubtedly a romance which
narrated the adventure of Thomas with the
elf-queen *simply*, without specification of his
prophecies. In all probability it concluded
with Thomas's return to fairy-land after a certain time passed in this world. The story of
Thomas and the Elf-queen is but another version of what is related of Ogier le Danois and
Morgan the Fay. The fairy adventures of
Thomas and of Ogier have the essential points
in common, and even the particular trait that
the fairy is taken to be the Virgin. The occurrence of this trait again in the ballad,
viewed in connection with the general similarity of the two, will leave no doubt that the
ballad had its source in the romance. Yet it
is an entirely popular ballad as to style, and
must be of considerable age, though the earliest
version (A) can be traced at furthest only into
the first half of the eighteenth century.

A

'Thomas Rymer and Queen of Elfland,'
Alexander Fraser Tytler's Brown MS., No. 1;
Jamieson's Popular Ballads, II, 7.

1 TRUE THOMAS lay oer yond grassy
    bank,
    And he beheld a ladie gay,
  A ladie that was brisk and bold,
    Come riding oer the fernie brae.

2 Her skirt was of the grass-green silk,
    Her mantel of the velvet fine,

At ilka tett of her horse's mane
  Hung fifty silver bells and nine.

3 True Thomas he took off his hat,
    And bowed him low down till h
      knee:
  ' All hail, thou mighty Queen of Hea
      en !
  For your peer on earth I never di
      see.'

4 ' O no, O no, True Thomas,' she says,
    ' That name does not belong to me;
  I am but the queen of fair Elfland,
    And I 'm come here for to visit thee

    *   *   *   *   *

5 ' But ye maun go wi me now, Thomas,
    True Thomas, ye maun go wi me,
  For ye maun serve me seven years,
    Thro weel or wae as may chance t
      be.'

6 She turned about her milk-white steed
    And took True Thomas up behind,
  And aye wheneer her bridle rang,
    The steed flew swifter than the wind

7 For forty days and forty nights
    He wade thro red blude to the knee,
  And he saw neither sun nor moon,
    But heard the roaring of the sea.

8 O they rade on, and further on,
    Until they came to a garden green:
  ' Light down, light down, ye ladie free
    Some of that fruit let me pull to thee.

9 ' O no, O no, True Thomas,' she says,
    ' That fruit maun not be touched by
      thee,
  For a' the plagues that are in hell
    Light on the fruit of this countrie.

10 ' But I have a loaf here in my lap,
    Likewise a bottle of claret wine,
  And now ere we go farther on,
    We 'll rest a while, and ye may
      dine.'

11 When he had eaten and drunk his fill,
    ' Lay down your head upon my knee,'
  The lady sayd, ' ere we climb yon hill,
    And I will show you fairlies three.

2 'O see not ye yon narrow road,
    So thick beset wi thorns and briers ?
  That is the path of righteousness,
    Tho after it but few enquires.

3 ' And see not ye that braid braid road,
    That lies across yon lillie leven ?
  That is the path of wickedness,
    Tho some call it the road to heaven.

4 ' And see not ye that bonny road,
    Which winds about the fernie brae ?
  That is the road to fair Elfland,
    Whe[re] you and I this night maun
      gae.

5 'But Thomas, ye maun hold your
      tongue,
    Whatever you may hear or see,
  For gin ae word you should chance to
      speak,
    You will neer get back to your ain
      countrie.'

6 He has gotten a coat of the even cloth,
    And a pair of shoes of velvet green,
  And till seven years were past and gone
    True Thomas on earth was never
      seen.

C*

'Thomas the Rhymer,' Scotch Ballads,
Materials for Border Minstrelsy, No. 97, Abbotsford ; communicated to Sir Walter Scott
by Mrs Christiana Greenwood, London, May
7, 1806 (Letters, I, 189), from the recitation
of her mother and of her aunt, both then above
sixty, who learned it in their childhood from
Kirstan Scot, a very old woman, at Longnew-
on, near Jedburgh.

1 THOMAS lay on the Huntlie bank,
    A spying ferlies wi his eee,
  And he did spy a lady gay,
    Come riding down by the lang lee.

2 Her steed was o the dapple grey,
    And at its mane there hung bells nine;
  He thought he heard that lady say,
    ' They gowden bells sall a' be thine.'

3 Her mantle was o velvet green,
    And a' set round wi jewels fine;
  Her hawk and hounds were at her side,
    And her bugle-horn wi gowd did
      shine.

4 Thomas took aff baith cloak and cap,
    For to salute this gay lady:
  'O save ye, save ye, fair Queen o
      Heavn,
    And ay weel met ye save and see ! '

5 ' I 'm no the Queen o Heavn, Thomas;
    I never carried my head sae hee;
  For I am but a lady gay,
    Come out to hunt in my follee.

6 ' Now gin ye kiss my mouth, Thomas,
    Ye mauna miss my fair bodee;
  Then ye may een gang hame and tell
    That ye 've lain wi a gay ladee.'

7 'O gin I loe a lady fair,
    Nae ill tales o her wad I tell,
  And it 's wi thee I fain wad gae,
    Tho it were een to heavn or hell.'

8 ' Then harp and carp, Thomas,' she
      said,
    ' Then harp and carp alang wi me;
  But it will be seven years and a day
    Till ye win back to yere ain coun-
      trie.'

9 The lady rade, True Thomas ran,
    Untill they cam to a water wan;
  O it was night, and·nae delight,
    And Thomas wade aboon the knee.

10 It was dark night, and nae starn-light,
    And on they waded lang days three,
  And they heard the roaring o a flood,
    And Thomas a waefou man was he.

11 Then they rade on, and farther on,
    Untill they came to a garden green;
  To pu an apple he put up his hand,
    For the lack o food he was like to
      tyne.

12 'O haud yere hand, Thomas,' she cried,
    ' And let that green flourishing be;
  For it 's the very fruit o hell,
    Beguiles baith man and woman o yere
      countrie.

13 ' But look afore ye, True Thomas,
    And I shall show ye ferlies three;
  Yon is the gate leads to our land,
    Where thou and I sae soon shall
      be.

14 ' And dinna ye see yon road, Thomas,
      That lies out-owr yon lilly lee ?
   Weel is the man yon gate may gang,
      For it leads him straight to the heav-
         ens hie.

15 ' But do you see yon road, Thomas,
      That lies out-owr yon frosty fell ?
   Ill is the man yon gate may gang,
      For it leads him straight to the pit o
         hell.

16 ' Now when ye come to our court,
         Thomas,
      See that a weel-learnd man ye be;
   For they will ask ye, one and all,
      But ye maun answer nane but me.

17 ' And when nae answer they obtain,
      Then will they come and question
         me,
   And I will answer them again
      That I gat yere aith at the Eildon
         tree.

        *   *   *   *   *

18 ' Ilka seven years, Thomas,
      We pay our teindings unto hell,
   And ye 're sae leesome and sae strang
      That I fear, Thomas, it will be yere-
         sell.'

38

THE WEE WEE MAN

There is a poem in eight-line stanzas, in a
fourteenth-century manuscript (Cotton, Julius,
A, v), edited by Wright (Pierre de Langtoft,
II, 452), which stands in somewhat the same
relation to this ballad as the poem of Thomas
of Erceldoune does to the ballad of ' Thomas
Rymer ' (No. 37), but with the important difference that there is no reason for deriving the
ballad from the poem in this instance.   There
seems to have been an intention to make it,
like Thomas of Erceldoune, an introduction
to a string of prophecies which follows, but no
junction has been effected.

A

' The Wee Wee Man,' Herd's MSS., I, 153;
Herd's Ancient and Modern Scottish Songs,
1776, I, 95.

1 As I was wa'king all alone,
      Between a water and a wa,
   And there I spy'd a wee wee man,
      And he was the least that ere I saw.

2 His legs were scarce a shathmont'
         length,
      And thick and thimber was his thigh
   Between his brows there was a span,
      And between his shoulders there wa
         three.

3 He took up a meikle stane,
      And he flang 't as far as I could see
   Though I had been a Wallace wight,
      I couldna liften 't to my knee.

4 ' O wee wee man, but thou be strang !
      O tell me where thy dwelling be ? '
   ' My dwelling 's down at yon bonny
         bower ;
      O will you go with me and see ? '

5 On we lap, and awa we rade,
      Till we came to yon bonny green ;
   We lighted down for to bait our horse,
      And out there came a lady fine.

6 Four and twenty at her back,
      And they were a' clad out in green ;
   Though the King of Scotland had been
         there,
      The warst o them might hae been hi
         queen.

7 On we lap, and awa we rade,
      Till we came to yon bonny ha,
   Whare the roof was o the beaten gould,
      And the floor was o the cristal a'.

8 When we came to the stair-foot,
      Ladies were dancing, jimp and sma,
   But in the twinkling of an eye,
      My wee wee man was clean awa.

39

TAM LIN

' The Tayl of the ȝong Tamlene ' is spoken
of as told among a company of shepherds, in
Vedderburn's Complaint of Scotland, 1549
' Thom of Lyn ' is mentioned as a dance of the
same party, a little further on, and ' Young
Thomlin ' is the name of an air in a medley

Wood's MS., inserted, as David Laing thought, between 1600 and 1620, and printed in Forbes's Cantus, 1666 (Stenhouse's ed. of the Scots Musical Museum, 1853, IV, 440). A ballett of Thomalyn' is licensed to Master John Wallye and Mistress Toye in 1558 (Arber, Registers of the Company of Stationers, I, 22).

This fine ballad stands by itself, and is not, as might have been expected, found in possession of any people but the Scottish. Yet it has connections, through the principal feature in the story, the retransformation of Tam Lin, with Greek popular tradition older than Homer. There is a Cretan fairy tale cited by Bernhard Schmidt (Volksleben der Neugriechen, pp. 115–117) which comes surprisingly near to the principal event of the Scottish ballad. A young peasant, who was a good player on the flute, used to be taken by the nereids into their grotto, for the sake of his music. He fell in love with one of them, and, not knowing how to help himself, had recourse to an old woman of his village. She gave him this advice : that just before cock-crow he should seize his beloved by the hair, and hold on, unterrified, till the cock crew, whatever forms she should assume. The peasant gave good heed, and the next time he was taken into the cave fell to playing, as usual, and the nereids to dancing. But as cock-crow drew nigh, he put down his instrument, sprang upon the object of his passion, and grasped her by her locks. She instantly changed shape ; became a dog, a snake, a camel, fire. But he kept his courage and held on, and presently the cock crew, and the nereids vanished, all but one. His love returned to her proper beauty, and went with him to his home. After the lapse of a year she bore a son, but in all this time never uttered a word. The good husband was fain to ask counsel of the old woman again, who told him to heat the oven hot, and say to his wife that if she would not speak he would throw the boy into the oven. He acted upon this prescription ; the nereid cried out, ' Let go my child, dog ! ' tore the infant from his arms, and vanished.

This Cretan tale, recovered from tradition even later than our ballad, repeats all the important circumstances of the forced marriage of Thetis with Peleus (Apollodorus, Bibliotheca, III, 13, 5, 6). The Cretan tale does not differ from the one repeated by Apollodorus from earlier writers a couple of thousand years ago more than two versions of a story gathered from oral tradition in these days are apt to do. Whether it has come down to our time from mouth to mouth through twenty-four centuries or more, or whether, having died out of the popular memory, it was reintroduced through literature, is a question that cannot be decided with certainty ; but there will be nothing unlikely in the former supposition to those who bear in mind the tenacity of tradition among people who have never known books.

A

' Tam Lin,' Johnson's Museum, 1792, p. 423, No. 411. Communicated by Robert Burns.

1 O I FORBID you, maidens a',
   That wear gowd on your hair,
To come or gae by Carterhaugh,
   For young Tam Lin is there.

2 There 's nane that gaes by Carterhaugh
   But they leave him a wad,
Either their rings, or green mantles,
   Or else their maidenhead.

3 Janet has kilted her green kirtle
   A little aboon her knee,
And she has broded her yellow hair
   A little aboon her bree,
And she 's awa to Carterhaugh,
   As fast as she can hie.

4 When she came to Carterhaugh
   Tam Lin was at the well,
And there she fand his steed standing,
   But away was himsel.

5 She had na pu'd a double rose,
   A rose but only twa,
Till up then started young Tam Lin,
   Says, Lady, thou 's pu nae mae.

6 Why pu's thou the rose, Janet,
   And why breaks thou the wand ?
Or why comes thou to Carterhaugh
   Withoutten my command ?

7 ' Carterhaugh, it is my ain,
   My daddie gave it me ;
I 'll come and gang by Carterhaugh,
   And ask nae leave at thee.'

*   *   *   *   *

8 Janet has kilted her green kirtle
   A little aboon her knee,
And she has snooded her yellow hair
   A little aboon her bree,
And she is to her father's ha,
   As fast as she can hie.

9 Four and twenty ladies fair
    Were playing at the ba,
And out then cam the fair Janet,
    Ance the flower amang them a'.

10 Four and twenty ladies fair
    Were playing at the chess,
And out then cam the fair Janet,
    As green as onie glass.

11 Out then spak an auld grey knight,
    Lay oer the castle wa,
And says, Alas, fair Janet, for thee
    But we 'll be blamed a'.

12 'Haud your tongue, ye auld fac'd
        knight,
    Some ill death may ye die!
Father my bairn on whom I will,
    I 'll father nane on thee.'

13 Out then spak her father dear,
    And he spak meek and mild;
'And ever alas, sweet Janet,' he says,
    'I think thou gaes wi child.'

14 'If that I gae wi child, father,
    Mysel maun bear the blame;
There 's neer a laird about your ha
    Shall get the bairn's name.

15 'If my love were an earthly knight,
    As he 's an elfin grey,
I wad na gie my ain true-love
    For nae lord that ye hae.

16 'The steed that my true-love rides on
    Is lighter than the wind;
Wi siller he is shod before,
    Wi burning gowd behind.'

17 Janet has kilted her green kirtle
    A little aboon her knee,
And she has snooded her yellow hair
    A little aboon her bree,
And she 's awa to Carterhaugh,
    As fast as she can hie.

18 When she cam to Carterhaugh,
    Tam Lin was at the well,
And there she fand his steed standing,
    But away was himsel.

19 She had na pu'd a double rose,
    A rose but only twa,

Till up then started young Tam Lin,
    Says, Lady, thou pu's nae mae.

20 Why pu's thou the rose, Janet,
    Amang the groves sae green,
And a' to kill the bonie babe
    That we gat us between?

21 'O tell me, tell me, Tam Lin,' sł
        says,
    'For 's sake that died on tree,
If eer ye was in holy chapel,
    Or christendom did see?'

22 'Roxbrugh he was my grandfather,
    Took me with him to bide,
And ance it fell upon a day
    That wae did me betide.

23 'And ance it fell upon a day,
    A cauld day and a snell,
When we were frae the hunting come,
    That frae my horse I fell;
The Queen o Fairies she caught me,
    In yon green hill to dwell.

24 'And pleasant is the fairy land,
    But, an eerie tale to tell,
Ay at the end of seven years
    We pay a tiend to hell;
I am sae fair and fu o flesh,
    I 'm feard it be mysel.

25 'But the night is Halloween, lady,
    The morn is Hallowday;
Then win me, win me, an ye will,
    For weel I wat ye may.

26 'Just at the mirk and midnight hour
    The fairy folk will ride,
And they that wad their true-love win,
    At Miles Cross they maun bide.'

27 'But how shall I thee ken, Tam Lin,
    Or how my true-love know,
Amang sae mony unco knights
    The like I never saw?'

28 'O first let pass the black, lady,
    And syne let pass the brown,
But quickly run to the milk-white steed
    Pu ye his rider down.

29 'For I 'll ride on the milk-white steed,
    And ay nearest the town:

Because I was an earthly knight
They gie me that renown.

9 'My right hand will be glovd, lady,
My left hand will be bare,
Cockt up shall my bonnet be,
And kaimd down shall my hair,
And thae 's the takens I gie thee,
Nae doubt I will be there.

10 'They 'll turn me in your arms, lady,
Into an esk and adder;
But hold me fast, and fear me not,
I am your bairn's father.

11 'They 'll turn me to a bear sae grim,
And then a lion bold;
But hold me fast, and fear me not,
As ye shall love your child.

12 'Again they 'll turn me in your arms
To a red het gaud of airn;
But hold me fast, and fear me not
I 'll do to you nae harm.

13 'And last they 'll turn me in your arms
Into the burning gleed;
Then throw me into well water,
O throw me in wi speed.

14 'And then I 'll be your ain true-love,
I 'll turn a naked knight;
Then cover me wi your green mantle,
And cover me out o sight.'

15 Gloomy, gloomy was the night,
And eerie was the way,
As fair Jenny in her green mantle
To Miles Cross she did gae.

16 About the middle o the night
She heard the bridles ring;
This lady was as glad at that
As any earthly thing.

17 First she let the black pass by,
And syne she let the brown;
But quickly she ran to the milk-white
steed,
And pu'd the rider down.

18 Sae weel she minded what he did say,
And young Tam Lin did win:
Syne coverd him wi her green mantle,
As blythe 's a bird in spring.

40 Out then spak the Queen o Fairies,
Out of a bush o broom:
'Them that has gotten young Tam Lin
Has gotten a stately groom.'

41 Out then spak the Queen o Fairies,
And an angry woman was she:
'Shame betide her ill-far'd face,
And an ill death may she die,
For she 's taen awa the boniest knight
In a' my companie.

42 'But had I kend, Tam Lin,' she says,
'What now this night I see,
I wad hae taen out thy twa grey een,
And put in twa een o tree.'

40

THE QUEEN OF ELFAN'S NOURICE

We learn from this pretty fragment, which, after the nature of the best popular ballad, forces you to chant it and will not be read, that a woman had been carried off, four days after bearing a son, to serve as nurse in the Elf-queen's family. Stanzas 10-12 are out of place here, and properly belong to No. 37. It is well known that elves and water spirits have frequently solicited the help of mortal women at lying-in time.

Skene MS., No. 8, p. 25; Sharpe's Ballad Book, ed. Laing, p. 169.

1 I HEARD a cow low, a bonnie cow low,
An a cow low down in yon glen;
Lang, lang will my young son greet
Or his mither bid him come ben.

2 I heard a cow low, a bonnie cow low,
An a cow low down in yon fauld;
Lang, lang will my young son greet
Or his mither take him frae cauld.

*   *   *   *   *

3 .   .   .   .   .

Waken, Queen of Elfan,
An hear your nourice moan.'

4 'O moan ye for your meat,
Or moan ye for your fee,

Or moan ye for the ither bounties
    That ladies are wont to gie ? '

5 'I moan na for my meat,
    Nor moan I for my fee,
Nor moan I for the ither bounties
    That ladies are wont to gie.

6 .   .   .   .   .   .

But I moan for my young son
    I left in four nights auld.

7 'I moan na for my meat,
    Nor yet for my fee,
But I mourn for Christen land,
    It 's there I fain would be.'

8 'O nurse my bairn, nourice,' she says,
    'Till he stan at your knee,
An ye 's win hame to Christen land,
    Whar fain it 's ye wad be.

9 'O keep my bairn, nourice,
    Till he gang by the hauld,
An ye 's win hame to your young son
    Ye left in four nights auld.'

    *   *   *   *   *

10 'O nourice lay your head
    Upo my knee :
See ye na that narrow road
    Up by yon tree ?

11 .   .   .   .   .   .

That 's the road the righteous goes,
    And that 's the road to heaven.

12 ' An see na ye that braid road,
    Down by yon sunny fell ?
Yon 's the road the wicked gae,
    An that 's the road to hell.'

    *   *   *   *   *

41

HIND ETIN

This ballad has suffered severely by the accidents of tradition. A has been not simply damaged by passing through low mouths, but has been worked over by low hands. Something considerable has been lost from the story, and fine romantic features, preserved in Norse and German ballads, have been quite effaced. The etin of the Scottish story is in Norse and German a dwarf-king, elf-king, hill-king, or even a merman. The ballad is still sung in Scandinavia and Germany, but only the Danes have versions taken down before the nineteenth century (see Grundtvig, No. 37). One of the three Danish sixteenth-century versions tells how a knight, expressing a strong desire to obtain a king's daughter, is overheard by a dwarf, who says this shall never be. The dwarf pretends to bargain with the knight for his services in forwarding the knight's object, but consults meanwhile with his mother how he may get the lady for himself. The mother tells him that the princess will go to even-song, and the dwarf writes runes on the way she must go by, which compel her to come to the hill. The dwarf holds out his hand and asks, "How came ye to this strange land ?" to which the lady answers mournfully, " I wot never how." The dwarf says, "You have pledged yourself to a knight, and he has betrayed you with runes : this eve you shall be the dwarf's guest." She stayed there the night, and was taken back to her mother in the morning. Eight years went by ; her hand was sought by five kings, nine counts, but no one of them could get a good answer. One day her mother asked, " Why are thy cheeks so faded ? Why can no one get thee ?" She then revealed that she had been beguiled by the dwarf, and had seven sons and a daughter in the hill, none of whom she ever saw. She thought she was alone, but the dwarf-king was listening. He strikes her with an elf-rod, and bids her hie to the hill after him. Late in the evening the poor thing dons her cloak, knocks at her father's door, and says good night to the friends that never will see her again, then sadly turns to the hill. Her seven sons advance to meet her, and ask why she told of their father. Her tears run sore ; she gives no answer ; she is dead ere midnight.

In another series of Scandinavian versions, which offers the type of the much-corrupted Scottish ballad, the woman has been living eight or nine years in the hill, and has there borne her children. She longs to go home or to church, and permission is granted on condition that she keep silence about the hill-man and observe certain other restrictions. These terms she violates, with the consequence that the hill-man appears and orders her back to his abode. The German versions, from which the Norse are derived, are somewhat nearer the Scottish.

A

'Young Akin,' Buchan's Ballads of the North of Scotland, I, 6; Motherwell's MS., p. 554.

1 LADY MARGARET sits in her bower
        door,
    Sewing at her silken seam;
    She heard a note in Elmond's wood,
    And wishd she there had been.

2 She loot the seam fa frae her side,
    And the needle to her tae,
    And she is on to Elmond's wood
    As fast as she coud gae.

3 She hadna pu'd a nut, a nut,
    Nor broken a branch but ane,
    Till by it came a young hind chiel,
    Says, Lady, lat alane.

4 O why pu ye the nut, the nut,
    Or why brake ye the tree?
    For I am forester o this wood:
    Ye shoud spier leave at me.

5 'I 'll ask leave at no living man,
    Nor yet will I at thee;
    My father is king oer a' this realm,
    This wood belongs to me.'

6 She hadna pu'd a nut, a nut,
    Nor broken a branch but three,
    Till by it came him Young Akin,
    And gard her lat them be.

7 The highest tree in Elmond's wood,
    He 's pu'd it by the reet,
    And he has built for her a bower,
    Near by a hallow seat.

8 He 's built a bower, made it secure
    Wi carbuncle and stane;
    Tho travellers were never sae nigh,
    Appearance it had nane.

9 He 's kept her there in Elmond's wood,
    For six lang years and one,
    Till six pretty sons to him she bear,
    And the seventh she 's brought home.

10 It fell ance upon a day,
    This guid lord went from home,
    And he is to the hunting gane,
    Took wi him his eldest son.

11 And when they were on a guid way,
    Wi slowly pace did walk,
    The boy's heart being something wae,
    He thus began to talk:

12 'A question I woud ask, father,
    Gin ye woudna angry be:'
    'Say on, say on, my bonny boy,
    Ye 'se nae be quarrelld by me.'

13 'I see my mither's cheeks aye weet,
    I never can see them dry;
    And I wonder what aileth my mither,
    To mourn continually.'

14 'Your mither was a king's daughter,
    Sprung frae a high degree,
    And she might hae wed some worthy
        prince,
    Had she nae been stown by me.

15 'I was her father's cup-bearer,
    Just at that fatal time;
    I catchd her on a misty night,
    Whan summer was in prime.

16 'My luve to her was most sincere,
    Her luve was great for me,
    But when she hardships doth endure,
    Her folly she does see.'

17 'I 'll shoot the buntin o the bush,
    The linnet o the tree,
    And bring them to my dear mither,
    See if she 'll merrier be.'

18 It fell upo another day,
    This guid lord he thought lang,
    And he is to the hunting gane,
    Took wi him his dog and gun.

19 Wi bow and arrow by his side,
    He 's aff, single, alane,
    And left his seven children to stay
    Wi their mither at hame.

20 'O I will tell to you, mither,
    Gin ye wadna angry be:'
    'Speak on, speak on, my little wee boy,
    Ye 'se nae be quarrelld by me.'

21 'As we came frae the hynd-hunting,
    We heard fine music ring:'
    'My blessings on you, my bonny boy,
    I wish I 'd been there my lane.'

22 He 's taen his mither by the hand,
    His six brithers also,
  And they are on thro Elmond's wood,
    As fast as they coud go.

23 They wistna weel where they were gaen,
    Wi the stratlins o their feet;
  They wistna weel where they were
    gaen,
    Till at her father's yate.

24 'I hae nae money in my pocket,
    But royal rings hae three;
  I 'll gie them you, my little young son,
    And ye 'll walk there for me.

25 'Ye 'll gie the first to the proud porter,
    And he will lat you in;
  Ye 'll gie the next to the butler-boy,
    And he will show you ben;

26 'Ye 'll gie the third to the minstrel
    That plays before the king;
  He 'll play success to the bonny boy
    Came thro the wood him lane.'

27 He gae the first to the proud porter,
    And he opend an let him in;
  He gae the next to the butler-boy,
    And he has shown him ben;

28 He gae the third to the minstrel
    That playd before the king;
  And he playd success to the bonny boy
    Came thro the wood him lane.

29 Now when he came before the king,
    Fell low down on his knee;
  The king he turned round about,
    And the saut tear blinded his ee.

30 'Win up, win up, my bonny boy,
    Gang frae my companie;
  Ye look sae like my dear daughter,
    My heart will birst in three.'

31 'If I look like your dear daughter,
    A wonder it is none;
  If I look like your dear daughter,
    I am her eldest son.'

32 'Will ye tell me, ye little wee boy,
    Where may my Margaret be?'
  'She 's just now standing at your yates,
    And my six brithers her wi.'

33 'O where are all my porter-boys
    That I pay meat and fee,
  To open my yates baith wide and braid?
    Let her come in to me.'

34 When she came in before the king,
    Fell low down on her knee;
  'Win up, win up, my daughter dear,
    This day ye 'll dine wi me.'

35 'Ae bit I canno eat, father,
    Nor ae drop can I drink,
  Till I see my mither and sister dear,
    For lang for them I think.'

36 When she came before the queen,
    Fell low down on her knee;
  'Win up, win up, my daughter dear,
    This day ye 'se dine wi me.'

37 'Ae bit I canno eat, mither,
    Nor ae drop can I drink,
  Until I see my dear sister,
    For lang for her I think.'

38 When that these two sisters met,
    She haild her courteouslie;
  'Come ben, come ben, my sister dear,
    This day ye 'se dine wi me.'

39 'Ae bit I canno eat, sister,
    Nor ae drop can I drink,
  Until I see my dear husband,
    For lang for him I think.'

40 'O where are all my rangers bold
    That I pay meat and fee,
  To search the forest far an wide,
    And bring Akin to me?'

41 Out it speaks the little wee boy:
    Na, na, this maunna be;
  Without ye grant a free pardon,
    I hope ye 'll nae him see.

42 'O here I grant a free pardon,
    Well seald by my own han;
  Ye may make search for Young Akin,
    As soon as ever you can.'

43 They searchd the country wide and
    braid,
    The forests far and near,
  And found him into Elmond's wood,
    Tearing his yellow hair.

4 'Win up, win up now, Young Akin,
　　Win up, and boun wi me;
　We 're messengers come from the
　　　court,
　　The king wants you to see.'

5 'O lat him take frae me my head,
　　Or hang me on a tree;
　For since I 've lost my dear lady,
　　Life 's no pleasure to me.'

6 'Your head will nae be touchd, Akin,
　　Nor hangd upon a tree;
　Your lady 's in her father's court,
　　And all he wants is thee.'

47 When he came in before the king,
　　Fell low down on his knee;
　'Win up, win up now, Young Akin,
　　This day ye 'se dine wi me.'

48 But as they were at dinner set,
　　The boy asked a boun:
　'I wish we were in the good church,
　　For to get christendoun.

49 'We hae lived in guid green wood
　　This seven years and ane;
　But a' this time, since eer I mind,
　　Was never a church within.'

50 'Your asking 's nae sae great, my boy,
　　But granted it shall be;
　This day to guid church ye shall gang,
　　And your mither shall gang you wi.'

51 When unto the guid church she came,
　　She at the door did stan;
　She was sae sair sunk down wi shame,
　　She coudna come farer ben.

52 Then out it speaks the parish priest,
　　And a sweet smile gae he:
　'Come ben, come ben, my lily flower,
　　Present your babes to me.'

53 Charles, Vincent, Sam and Dick,
　　And likewise James and John;
　They calld the eldest Young Akin,
　　Which was his father's name.

54 Then they staid in the royal court,
　　And livd wi mirth and glee,
　And when her father was deceasd,
　　Heir of the crown was she.

B

'Hynde Etin,' Kinloch's Ancient Scottish
Ballads, p. 228.

1 MAY MARGRET stood in her bouer door,
　　Kaiming doun her yellow hair;
　She spied some nuts growin in the wud,
　　And wishd that she was there.

2 She has plaited her yellow locks
　　A little abune her bree,
　And she has kilted her pettticoats
　　A little below her knee,
　And she 's aff to Mulberry wud,
　　As fast as she could gae.

3 She had na pu'd a nut, a nut,
　　A nut but barely ane,
　Till up started the Hynde Etin,
　　Says, Lady, let thae alane !

4 'Mulberry wuds are a' my ain;
　　My father gied them me,
　To sport and play when I thought lang;
　　And they sall na be tane by thee.'

5 And ae she pu'd the tither berrie
　　Na thinking o the skaith,
　And said, To wrang ye, Hynde Etin,
　　I wad be unco laith.

6 But he has tane her by the yellow locks,
　　And tied her till a tree,
　And said, For slichting my commands,
　　An ill death sall ye dree.

7 He pu'd a tree out o the wud,
　　The biggest that was there,
　And he howkit a cave monie fathoms
　　　deep,
　　And put May Margret there.

8 'Now rest ye there, ye saucie may;
　　My wuds are free for thee;
　And gif I tak ye to mysell,
　　The better ye 'll like me.'

9 Na rest, na rest May Margret took,
　　Sleep she got never nane;
　Her back lay on the cauld, cauld floor,
　　Her head upon a stane.

10 'O tak me out,' May Margret cried,
　　'O tak me hame to thee,

And I sall be your bounden page
    Until the day I dee.'

11 He took her out o the dungeon deep,
       And awa wi him she 's gane;
   But sad was the day an earl's dochter
       Gaed hame wi Hynde Etin.

     *   *   *   *

12 It fell out ance upon a day
       Hynde Etin 's to the hunting gane,
   And he has tane wi him his eldest son,
       For to carry his game.

13 'O I wad ask ye something, father,
       An ye wadna angry be;'
   'Ask on, ask on, my eldest son,
       Ask onie thing at me.'

14 'My mother's cheeks are aft times
       weet,
       Alas! they are seldom dry;'
   'Na wonder, na wonder, my eldest son,
       Tho she should brast and die.

15 'For your mother was an earl's dochter,
       Of noble birth and fame,
   And now she 's wife o Hynde Etin,
       Wha neer got christendame.

16 'But we 'll shoot the laverock in the
       lift,
       The buntlin on the tree,
   And ye 'll tak them hame to your
       mother,
   And see if she 'll comforted be.'

    *   *   *   *   *

17 'I wad ask ye something, mother,
       An ye wadna angry be;"
   'Ask on, ask on, my eldest son,
       Ask onie thing at me.'

18 'Your cheeks they are aft times weet,
       Alas! they 're seldom dry;'
   'Na wonder, na wonder, my eldest son,
       Tho I should brast and die.

19 'For I was ance an earl's dochter,
       Of noble birth and fame,
   And now I am the wife of Hynde Etin,
       Wha neer got christendame.'

    *   *   *   *   *

42

CLERK COLVILL

All the English versions are deplorably imperfect. Clerk Colvill is not, as his representative is or may be in other ballads, the guil-
less and guileless object of the love or envy of
water-sprite or elf. It is clear that before hi
marriage with his gay lady he had been in th
habit of resorting to this mermaid, and equall
clear, from the impatient answer which he ren-
ders his dame, that he means to visit her again
His death is the natural penalty of his de-
sertion of the water-nymph; for no point i
better established than the fatal consequence
of inconstancy in such connections. His history
were it fully told, would closely resemble tha
of the Knight of Staufenberg, as narrated in a
German poem of about the year 1310. Clerk
Colvill and the mermaid are represented by Si
Oluf and an elf in Scandinavian ballads to th
number of about seventy. The oldest of these
is derived from a Danish manuscript of 1550
two centuries and a half later than the Staufenberg poem, but two earlier than Clerk Colvill
the oldest ballad outside of the Scandinavian
series (see Grundtvig, No. 47). The Breton
'Seigneur Nann' is closely akin to the Scandinavian versions, and the ballad has spread
apparently from Brittany, over all France
('Jean Renaud').

A

'Clark Colven,' from a transcript of No. 1:
of William Tytler's Brown MS.

1 CLARK COLVEN and his gay ladie,
       As they walked to yon garden green
   A belt about her middle gimp,
       Which cost Clark Colven crowns fif-
       teen:

2 'O hearken weel now, my good lord,
       O hearken weel to what I say;
   When ye gang to the wall o Stream,
       O gang nae neer the well-fared may.'

3 'O haud your tongue, my gay ladie,
       Tak nae sic care o me;
   For I nae saw a fair woman
       I like so well as thee.'

4 He mounted on his berry-brown steed,
       And merry, merry rade he on,
   Till he came to the wall o Stream,
       And there he saw the mermaiden.

5 'Ye wash, ye wash, ye bonny may,
    And ay 's ye wash your sark o silk:'
  'It 's a' for you, ye gentle knight,
    My skin is whiter than the milk.'

6 He 's taen her by the milk-white hand,
    He 's taen her by the sleeve sae green,
  And he 's forgotten his gay ladie,
    And away with the fair maiden.

*   *   *   *   *

7 'Ohon, alas!' says Clark Colven,
    'And aye sae sair 's I mean my head!'
  And merrily leugh the mermaiden,
    'O win on till you be dead.

8 'But out ye tak your little pen-knife,
    And frae my sark ye shear a gare;
  Row that about your lovely head,
    And the pain ye 'll never feel nae
      mair.'

9 Out he has taen his little pen-knife,
    And frae her sark he 's shorn a
      gare,
  Rowed that about his lovely head,
    But the pain increased mair and
      mair.

10 'Ohon, alas!' says Clark Colven,
    'An aye sae sair 's I mean my head!'
  And merrily laughd the mermaiden,
    'It will ay be war till ye be dead.'

11 Then out he drew his trusty blade,
    And thought wi it to be her dead,
  But she 's become a fish again,
    And merrily sprang into the fleed.

12 He 's mounted on his berry-brown steed,
    And dowy, dowy rade he home,
  And heavily, heavily lighted down
    When to his ladie's bower-door he
      came.

13 'Oh, mither, mither, mak my bed,
    And, gentle ladie, lay me down;
  Oh, brither, brither, unbend my bow,
    'T will never be bent by me again.'

14 His mither she has made his bed,
    His gentle ladie laid him down,
  His brither he has unbent his bow,
    'T was never bent by him again.

B

'Clerk Colvill, or, The Mermaid,' Herd's
Ancient and Modern Scots Songs, 1769, p. 302;
ed. 1776, I, 161.

1 CLERK COLVILL and his lusty dame
    Were walking in the garden green ;
  The belt around her stately waist
    Cost Clerk Colvill of pounds fifteen.

2 'O promise me now, Clerk Colvill,
    Or it will cost ye muckle strife,
  Ride never by the wells of Slane,
    If ye wad live and brook your life.'

3 'Now speak nae mair, my lusty dame,
    Now speak nae mair of that to me;
  Did I neer see a fair woman,
    But I wad sin with her body ?'

4 He 's taen leave o his gay lady,
    Nought minding what his lady said,
  And he 's rode by the wells of Slane,
    Where washing was a bonny maid.

5 'Wash on, wash on, my bonny maid,
    That wash sae clean your sark of silk;'
  'And weel fa you, fair gentleman,
    Your body whiter than the milk.'

*   *   *   *   *

6 Then loud, loud cry'd the Clerk Colvill,
    'O my head it pains me sair;'
  'Then take, then take,' the maiden said,
    'And frae my sark you 'll cut a gare.'

7 Then she 's gied him a little bane-knife,
    And frae her sark he cut a share;
  She 's ty'd it round his whey-white face,
    But ay his head it aked mair.

8 Then louder cry'd the Clerk Colvill,
    'O sairer, sairer akes my head;'
  'And sairer, sairer ever will,'
    The maiden crys, 'till you be dead.'

9 Out then he drew his shining blade,
    Thinking to stick her where she stood,
  But she was vanishd to a fish,
    And swam far off, a fair mermaid.

10 'O mother, mother, braid my hair;
    My lusty lady, make my bed;
  O brother, take my sword and spear,
    For I have seen the false mermaid.'

43

THE BROOMFIELD HILL

A song of 'Brume, brume on hil' is named in The Complaint of Scotland, 1549 (ed. Murray, p. 64). The foot of the song is sung in Wager's comedy "The Longer thou Livest, the More Fool thou art" (about 1568), as follows: —

> Brome, brome on hill,
> The gentle brome on hill, hill,
> Brome, brome on Hive hill,
> The gentle brome on Hive hill,
> The brome stands on Hive hill a.

If "Hive Hill" in A, st. 8, is a genuine traditional reading, the song and the ballad are doubtless identical; but we cannot be quite sure of this stanza.

The main features of the story are widely known, in ballads, romances, and tales. The magic may be vulgarized into a sleeping draught (as in the Pecorone of Ser Giovanni Fiorentino, iv, 1), and the tables are sometimes turned on the maiden.

A

'The Broomfield Hill.' a. Scott's Minstrelsy, III, 271, ed. 1803. b. Sts. 8–14; the same, II, 229, ed. 1802.

1 THERE was a knight and a lady bright,
    Had a true tryste at the broom;
  The ane gaed early in the morning,
    The other in the afternoon.

2 And ay she sat in her mother's bower door,
    And ay she made her mane:
  'O whether should I gang to the Broomfield Hill,
    Or should I stay at hame?

3 'For if I gang to the Broomfield Hill,
    My maidenhead is gone;
  And if I chance to stay at hame,
    My love will ca me mansworn.'

4 Up then spake a witch-woman,
    Ay from the room aboon:
  'O ye may gang to the Broomfield Hill,
    And yet come maiden hame.

5 'For when ye gang to the Broomfield Hill,
    Ye 'll find your love asleep,

With a silver belt about his head,
    And a broom-cow at his feet.

6 'Take ye the blossom of the broom,
    The blossom it smells sweet,
  And strew it at your true-love's head,
    And likewise at his feet.

7 'Take ye the rings off your fingers,
    Put them on his right hand,
  To let him know, when he doth awake,
    His love was at his command.'

8 She pu'd the broom flower on Hive Hill,
    And strewd on 's white hals-bane,
  And that was to be wittering true
    That maiden she had gane.

9 'O where were ye, my milk-white steed,
    That I hae coft sae dear,
  That wadna watch and waken me
    When there was maiden here?'

10 'I stamped wi my foot, master,
    And gard my bridle ring,
  But na kin thing wald waken ye,
    Till she was past and gane.'

11 'And wae betide ye, my gay goss-hawk,
    That I did love sae dear,
  That wadna watch and waken me
    When there was maiden here.'

12 'I clapped wi my wings, master,
    And aye my bells I rang,
  And aye cry'd, Waken, waken, master,
    Before the ladye gang.'

13 'But haste and haste, my gude white steed,
    To come the maiden till,
  Or a' the birds of gude green wood
    Of your flesh shall have their fill.'

14 'Ye need na burst your gude white steed
    Wi racing oer the howm;
  Nae bird flies faster through the wood,
    Than she fled through the broom.'

B

'I 'll wager, I 'll wager,' etc., Herd, Ancient and Modern Scots Songs, 1769, p. 310.

1 'I 'LL wager, I 'll wager, I 'll wager with
        you
    Five hundred merks and ten,
    That a maid shanae go to yon bonny
        green wood,
    And a maiden return agen.'

2 'I 'll wager, I 'll wager, I 'll wager with
        you
    Five hundred merks and ten,
    That a maid shall go to yon bonny green
        wood,
    And a maiden return agen.'

*   *   *   *   *

3 She 's pu'd the blooms aff the broom-
        bush,
    And strewd them on 's white hass-bane:
    'This is a sign whereby you may know
        That a maiden was here, but she 's
        gane.'

4 'O where was you, my good gray steed,
        That I hae loed sae dear ?
    O why did you not awaken me
        When my true love was here ? '

5 'I stamped with my foot, master,
        And gard my bridle ring,
    But you wadnae waken from your sleep
        Till your love was past and gane.'

6 'Now I may sing as dreary a sang
        As the bird sung on the brier,
    For my true love is far removd,
        And I 'll neer see her mair.'

44

THE TWA MAGICIANS

This is a base-born cousin of a pretty ballad
known over all Southern Europe, and elsewhere (as among the Slavs), but in especially
graceful forms in France. The French ballad
generally begins with a young man's announ-
cing that he has won a mistress, and intends
to pay her a visit on Sunday, or to give her an
aubade. She declines his visit or his music.
To avoid him she will turn, for example, into a
rose ; then he will turn bee, and kiss her. She
will turn quail ; he sportsman, and bag her.
She will turn carp ; he angler, and catch her.
She will turn hare ; and he hound. She will
turn nun ; he priest, and confess her day and
night. She will fall sick ; he will watch with

her, or be her doctor. She will become a star;
he a cloud, and muffle her. She will die ; he
will turn earth, into which they will put her,
or St Peter, and receive her into Paradise. In
the end she says, " Since you are inevitable,
you may as well have me as another; " or
more complaisantly, " Je me donnerai à toi,
puisque tu m'aimes tant."

There can be little doubt that the ballads
are derived, or take their hint, from popular
tales, in which (1) a youth and maid, pursued
by a sorcerer, fiend, giant, ogre, are transformed by the magical powers of one or the
other into such shapes as enable them to elude,
and finally to escape, apprehension; or (2) a
young fellow, who has been apprenticed to a
sorcerer, fiend, etc., and has acquired the black
art by surreptitious reading in his master's
books, being pursued, as before, assumes a
variety of forms, and his master others, adapted
to the destruction of his intended victim, until
the tables are turned by the fugitive's taking
on the stronger figure and despatching his ad-
versary.

Buchan's Ballads of the North of Scotland,
i, 24 ; Motherwell's MS., p. 570.

1 THE lady stands in her bower door,
        As straight as willow wand;
    The blacksmith stood a little forebye,
        Wi hammer in his hand.

2 ' Weel may ye dress ye, lady fair,
        Into your robes o red;
    Before the morn at this same time,
        I 'll gain your maidenhead.'

3 ' Awa, awa, ye coal-black smith,
        Woud ye do me the wrang
    To think to gain my maidenhead,
        That I hae kept sae lang ! '

4 Then she has hadden up her hand,
        And she sware by the mold,
    ' I wudna be a blacksmith's wife
        For the full o a chest o gold.

5 ' I 'd rather I were dead and gone,
        And my body laid in grave,
    Ere a rusty stock o coal-black smith
        My maidenhead shoud have.'

6 But he has hadden up his hand,
        And he sware by the mass,
    ' I 'll cause ye be my light leman
        For the hauf o that and less.'

O bide, lady, bide,
　And aye he bade her bide;
　The rusty smith your leman shall
　　be,
　For a' your muckle pride.

7 Then she became a turtle dow,
　　To fly up in the air,
　And he became another dow,
　　And they flew pair and pair.
　　　O bide, lady, bide, &c.

8 She turnd hersell into an eel,
　　To swim into yon burn,
　And he became a speckled trout,
　　To gie the eel a turn.
　　　O bide, lady, bide, &c.

9 Then she became a duck, a duck,
　　To puddle in a peel,
　And he became a rose-kaimd drake,
　　To gie the duck a dreel.
　　　O bide, lady, bide, &c.

10 She turnd hersell into a hare,
　　To rin upon yon hill,
　And he became a gude grey-hound,
　　And boldly he did fill.
　　　O bide, lady, bide, &c.

11 Then she became a gay grey mare,
　　And stood in yonder slack,
　And he became a gilt saddle,
　　And sat upon her back.
　　　Was she wae, he held her sae,
　　　And still he bade her bide;
　　The rusty smith her leman was,
　　For a' her muckle pride.

12 Then she became a het girdle,
　　And he became a cake,
　And a' the ways she turnd hersell,
　　The blacksmith was her make.
　　　Was she wae, &c.

13 She turnd hersell into a ship,
　　To sail out ower the flood;
　He ca'ed a nail intill her tail,
　　And syne the ship she stood.
　　　Was she wae, &c.

14 Then she became a silken plaid,
　　And stretchd upon a bed,
　And he became a green covering,
　　And gaind her maidenhead.
　　　Was she wae, &c.

45

KING JOHN AND THE BISHOP

Version B was printed for P. Brooksby, who published from 1672 to 1695. It was "allowed" by Roger L'Estrange, who was licenser from 1663 to 1685. The title of B is 'A New Ballad of King John and the Abbot of Canterbury. To the Tune of The King and the Lord Abbot.' The older ballad seems not to have come down.

The story is apparently of Oriental origin. The oldest known version was discovered by Professor C. C. Torrey in the Conquest of Egypt, an Arabic historical work of about 850 A. D., and is thought by him to be " a genuine bit of Coptic folk-lore," current in Egypt long before the Arab invasion in the seventh century. In this tale a wicked king gives his vezirs certain questions : if they answer them, he promises to increase their pay ; if they fail, he will cut off their heads. They are assisted by a potter, who disguises himself as a vezir and tricks the king (Journal of the American Oriental Society, xx, 209). There are a multitude of other versions, Oriental and Occidental. Among those which resemble the ballad closely may be mentioned the Middle High German tale of Âmîs and the Bishop, in the Stricker's Pfaffe Âmîs (about 1236), and the fourth novella of Sacchetti. In the latter we have the prizing of the questioner at twenty-nine deniers, as in the English. Riddle stories in which a forfeit is to be paid by the vanquished party are a very extensive class. The oldest example is that of Samson's riddle in Judges xiv, 12 ff. Death is often the penalty, as in the Poetic Edda (Vafþrúðnismál).

A

' Kinge John and the Bishoppe,' Percy MS., p. 184 ; Hales and Furnivall, i, 508.

1 OFF an ancient story Ile tell you anon,
　Of a notable prince that was called King
　　Iohn,
　In England was borne, with maine and
　　with might;
　Hee did much wrong and mainteied
　　litle right.

2 This noble prince was vexed in veretye,
　For he was angry with the Bishopp of
　　Canterbury;
　Ffor his house-keeping and his good
　　cheere,
　Thé rode post for him, as you shall
　　heare.

3 They rode post for him verry hastilye;
  The king sayd the bishopp kept a better
    house then hee:
  A hundred men euen, as I [have heard]
    say,
  The bishopp kept in his house euerye
    day,
  And fifty gold chaines, without any
    doubt,
  In veluett coates waited the bishopp
    about.

4 The bishopp, he came to the court anon,
  Before his prince that was called King
    Iohn.
  As soone as the bishopp the king did
    see,
  ' O,' quoth the king, ' bishopp, thow art
    welcome to mee.
  There is noe man soe welcome to towne
  As thou that workes treason against my
    crowne.'

5 ' My leege,' quoth the bishopp, ' I wold
    it were knowne
  I spend, your grace, nothing but that
    that 's my owne;
  I trust your grace will doe me noe
    deare
  For spending my owne trew gotten
    geere.'

6 ' Yes,' quoth the king, ' bishopp, thou
    must needs dye,
  Eccept thou can answere mee questions
    three;
  Thy head shalbe smitten quite from
    thy bodye,
  And all thy liuing remayne vnto mee.

7 ' First,' quoth the king, ' tell me in this
    steade,
  With this crowne of gold heere vpon
    my head,
  Amongst my nobilitye, with ioy and
    much mirth,
  Lett me know within one pennye what
    I am worth.

8 ' Secondlye, tell me without any dowbt
  How soone I may goe the whole world
    about;
  And thirdly, tell mee or euer I stinte,
  What is the thing, bishopp, that I doe
    thinke.

  Twenty dayes pardon thoust haue
    trulye,
  And come againe and answere mee.'

9 The bishopp bade the king god night att
    a word;
  He rode betwixt Cambridge and Oxen-
    ford,
  But neuer a doctor there was soe wise
  Cold shew him these questions or enter-
    prise.

10 Wherewith the bishopp was nothing
    gladd,
  But in his hart was heauy and sadd,
  And hyed him home to a house in the
    countrye,
  To ease some part of his melanchollye.

11 His halfe-brother dwelt there, was feirce
    and fell,
  Noe better but a shepard to the bish-
    oppe himsell;
  The shepard came to the bishopp anon,
  Saying, My Lord, you are welcome
    home !

12 ' What ayles you,' quoth the shepard,
    ' that you are soe sadd,
  And had wonte to haue beene soe merry
    and gladd ? '
  ' Nothing,' quoth the bishopp, ' I ayle
    att this time;
  Will not thee availe to know, brother
    mine.'

13 ' Brother,' quoth the shepeard, ' you
    haue heard itt,
  That a ffoole may teach a wisemane
    witt;
  Say me therfore whatsoeuer you will,
  And if I doe you noe good, Ile doe you
    noe ill.'

14 Quoth the bishop: I haue beene att the
    court anon,
  Before my prince is called King Iohn,
  And there he hath charged mee
  Against his crowne with traitorye.

15 If I cannott answer his misterye,
  Three questions hee hath propounded to
    mee,
  He will haue my land soe faire and free,
  And alsoe the head from my bodye.

16 The first question was, to tell him in
     that stead,
     With the crowne of gold vpon his head,
     Amongst his nobilitye, with ioy and
       much mirth,
     To lett him know within one penye
       what hee is worth.

17 And secondlye, to tell him with-out any
       doubt
     How soone he may goe the whole world
       about;
     And thirdlye, to tell him, or ere I stint,
     What is the thinge *that* he does thinke.

18 'Brother,' quoth the shepard, 'you are
       a man of learninge;
     What neede you stand in doubt of soe
       small a thinge?
     Lend me,' quoth the shepard, 'your
       ministers apparrell,
     Ile ryde to the court and answere your
       quarrell.

19 'Lend me your serving men, say me
       not nay,
     With all your best horsses *that* ryd on
       the way;
     Ile to the court, this matter to stay;
     Ile speake with King Iohn and heare
       what heele say.'

20 The bishopp with speed prepared then
     To sett forth the shepard with horsse
       and man;
     The shepard was liuely without any
       doubt;
     I wott a royall companye came to the
       court.

21 The shepard hee came to the court anon
     Before [his] prince *that* was called
       King Iohn.
     As soone as the king the shepard did see,
     'O,' quoth the king, 'bishopp, thou art
       welcome to me.'
     The shepard was soe like the bishopp
       his brother,
     The king cold not know the one from
       the other.

22 Quoth the king, Bishopp, thou art wel-
       come to me
     If thou can answere me my questions
       three.

Said the shepeard, If it please you
       grace,
     Show mee what the first quest[i]o.
       was.

23 'First,' quoth the king, 'tell mee in thi
       stead,
     With the crowne of gold vpon my head
     Amongst my nobilitye, with ioy and
       much mirth,
     Within one pennye what I am worth.'

24 Quoth the shepard, To make your grace
       noe offence,
     I thinke you are worth nine and twenty
       pence;
     For our Lord Iesus, *that* bought vs all,
     For thirty pence was sold into thrall
     Amongst the cursed Iewes, as I to you
       doe showe;
     But I know Christ was one penye bet
       ter then you.

25 Then the king laught, and swore by S
       Andrew
     He was not thought to bee of such a
       small value.
     'Secondlye, tell mee with-out any doub
     How soone I may goe the world round
       about.'

26 Saies the shepard, It is noe time with
       your grace to scorne.
     But rise betime with the sun in the
       morne,
     And follow his course till his vprising,
     And then you may know without any
       leasing.

27 And this [to] your grace shall proue the
       same,
     You are come to the same place from
       whence you came;
     [In] twenty-four houres, with-out any
       doubt,
     Your grace may the world goe round
       about;
     The world round about, euen as I doe
       say,
     If with the sun you can goe the next
       way.

28 'And thirdlye tell me or euer I stint,
     What is the thing, bishoppe, *that* I doe
       thinke.'

' *That* shall I doe,' q*uoth* the shepeard;
 ' for veretye,
You thinke I am the bishopp of Canter-
   burye.'

' Why, art not thou ? the truth tell to
   me;
For I doe thinke soe,' q*uoth* the k*ing*,
 ' by St Marye.'
' Not soe,' q*uoth* the shepeard; ' the
   truth shalbe knowne,
I am his poore shepeard; my brother is
   att home.

' Why,' q*uoth* the k*ing*, ' if itt soe bee,
Ile make thee bishopp here to mee.'
' Noe, Sir,' q*uoth* the shepard, ' I pray
   you be still,
For Ile not bee bishop but against my
   will;
For I am not fitt for any such deede,
For I can neither write nor reede.'

' Why then,' q*uoth* the k*ing*, ' Ile giue
   thee cleere
A pattent of three hundred pound a
   yeere;
That I will giue thee franke and free;
Take thee *that*, shepard, for coming to
   me.

2 ' Free p*ardon* Ile giue,' the k*ing*s grace
   said,
 ' To saue the bishopp, his land and his
   head;
With him nor thee Ile be nothing
   wrath;
Here is the p*ardon* for him and thee
   both.'

3 Then the shepard he had noe more to
   say,
But tooke the p*ardon* and rode his
   way:
When he came to the bishopps place,
The bishopp asket anon how all things
   was.

34 ' Brother,' q*uoth* the shepard, ' I haue
   well sped,
For I haue saued both y*our* land and
   y*our* head;
The k*ing* with you is nothing wrath,
For heere is the p*ardon* for you and mee
   both.'

35 Then the bishopes hart was of a merry
   cheere:
 ' Brother, thy paines Ile quitt them
   cleare;
For I will giue thee a patent to thee
   and to thine
Of fifty pound a yeere, land good and
   fine.'

36 .   .   .   .   .   .

 ' I will to thee noe longer croche nor
   creepe,
Nor Ile serue thee noe more to keepe
   thy sheepe.'

37 Whereeu*er* wist you shepard before,
That had in his head witt such store
To pleasure a bishopp in such a like case,
To answer three questions to the k*ing*s
   grace ?
Whereeu*er* wist you shepard gett cleare
Three hundred and fifty pound a yeere ?

38 I neu*er* hard of his fellow before,
Nor I neu*er* shall : now I need to say
   noe more.
I neu*er* knew shepeard *that* gott such a
   liuinge
But David, the shepeard, *that* was a
   k*ing*.

B

' King John and the Abbot of Canterbury,'
broadside, printed for P. Brooksby, at the
Golden Ball in Pye-corner (1672–95).

1 I'll tell you a story, a story anon,
   Of a noble prince, and his name was
      King John;
   For he was a prince, and a prince of
      great might,
   He held up great wrongs, he put down
      great right.
   Derry down, down hey, derry down.

2 I'll tell you a story, a story so merry,
   Concerning the Abbot of Canterbury,
   And of his house-keeping and high re-
      nown,
   Which made him resort to fair London
      town.

3 ' How now, father abbot ? 'T is told
      unto me

That thou keepest a far better house
   than I;
And for [thy] house-keeping and high
   renown,
I fear thou has treason against my
   crown.'

4 'I hope, my liege, that you owe me no
   grudge
For spending of my true-gotten goods.'
'If thou dost not answer me questions
   three,
Thy head shall be taken from thy
   body.

5 'When I am set so high on my steed,
With my crown of gold upon my head,
Amongst all my nobility, with joy and
   much mirth,
Thou must tell me to one penny what I
   am worth.

6 'And the next question you must not
   flout,
How long I shall be riding the world
   about;
And the third question thou must not
   shrink,
But tell to me truly what I do think.'

7 'O these are hard questions for my shallow wit,
For I cannot answer your grace as
   yet;
But if you will give me but three days
   space,
I 'll do my endeavor to answer your
   grace.'

8 'O three days space I will thee give,
For that is the longest day thou hast to
   live.
And if thou dost not answer these questions right,
Thy head shall be taken from thy body
   quite.'

9 And as the shepherd was going to his
   fold,
He spy'd the old abbot come riding
   along:
'How now, master abbot? You 'r wel-
   come home;
What news have you brought from good
   King John?'

10 'Sad news, sad news I have thee to giv
For I have but three days space for
   live;
If I do not answer him questions three
My head will be taken from my body.

11 'When he is set so high on his steed,
With his crown of gold upon his head,
Amongst all his nobility, with joy an
   much mirth,
I must tell him to one penny what he
   worth.

12 'And the next question I must not flou
How long he shall be riding the worl
   about;
And the third question I must not shrink
But tell him truly what he does think.

13 'O master, did you never hear it yet,
That a fool may learn a wiseman wit?
Lend me but your horse and your ap
   parel,
I 'll ride to fair London and answer th
   quarrel.'

14 'Now I am set so high on my steed,
With my crown of gold upon my head,
Amongst all my nobility, with joy an
   much mirth,
Now tell me to one penny what I an
   worth.'

15 'For thirty pence our Saviour was sold
Amongst the false Jews, as you have
   been told,
And nine and twenty 's the worth of thee
For I think thou are one penny worse
   than he.'

16 'And the next question thou mayst no
   flout;
How long I shall be riding the world
   about.'
'You must rise with the sun, and ride
   with the same,
Until the next morning he rises again,
And then I am sure you will make no
   doubt
But in twenty-four hours you 'l ride it
   about.'

17 'And the third question you must not
   shrink,
But tell me truly what I do think.'

'All that I can do, and 't will make you
   merry;
For you think I 'm the Abbot of Canterbury,
But I 'm his poor shepherd, as you may
   see,
And am come to beg pardon for he and
   for me.'

18 The king he turned him about and did
   smile,
   Saying, Thou shalt be the abbot the
     other while:
'O no, my grace, there is no such need,
   For I can neither write nor read.'

19 'Then four pounds a week will I give
   unto thee
   For this merry jest thou hast told unto
     me;
And tell the old abbot, when thou comest
   home,
   Thou hast brought him a pardon from
     good King John.'

46

CAPTAIN WEDDERBURN'S COURTSHIP

'Captain Wedderburn's Courtship' is a counterpart of the ballad in which a maid wins a
husband by guessing riddles (cf. Nos. 1 and 2).
The ingenious suitor, though not so favorite a
subject as the clever maid, is of an old and
celebrated family. We find him in the Gesta
Romanorum (cap. 70, Oesterley, p. 383), in
Apollonius of Tyre (which has been carried
back to the third or fourth century), in a Persian poem by Nisami (died 1180), and in the
Persian story of Prince Calaf in Pétis de La
Croix's Thousand and One Days. On Prince
Calaf is founded Carlo Gozzi's play of La
Turandot, now best known through Schiller's
translation. There are also parallels in European popular tales. The Elder Edda presents
us with a similar story in the lay of Alvíss.

A

a. 'I 'll no ly neist the wa,' Herd's MS., I,
161. b. The same, II, 100.

1 THE laird of Bristoll's daughter was in
   the woods walking,
   And by came Captain Wetherbourn, a
     servant to the king;

And he said to his livery man, Wer 't
   not against the law,
I would tak her to mine ain bed, and
   lay her neist the wa.

2 'I 'm into my father's woods, amongst
   my father's trees,
   O kind sir, let mee walk alane, O kind
     sir, if you please;
The butler's bell it will be rung, and
   I 'll be mist awa;
I 'll lye into mine ain bed, neither at
   stock nor wa.

3 'O my bonny lady, the bed it 's not be
   mine,
   For I 'll command my servants for to
     call it thine;
The hangings are silk satin, the sheets
   are holland sma,
And we 's baith lye in ae bed, but you 's
   lye neist the wa.

4 'And so, my bonny lady, — I do not
   know your name, —
   But my name 's Captain Wetherburn,
     and I 'm a man of fame;
Tho your father and a' his men were
   here, I would na stand in awe
To tak you to mine ain bed, and lay you
   neist the wa.

5 'Oh my bonny, bonny lady, if you 'll gie
   me your hand,
   You shall hae drums and trumpets to
     sound at your command;
Wi fifty men to guard you, sae weel
   their swords can dra,
And wee 's baith lye in ae bed, but you 's
   lye neist the wa.'

6 He 's mounted her upon a steid, behind
   his gentleman,
   And he himself did walk afoot, to had
     his lady on,
With his hand about her midle sae jimp,
   for fear that she should fa;
She man lye in his bed, but she 'll not
   lye neist the wa.

7 He 's taen her into Edinburgh, his landlady cam ben:
'And monny bonny ladys in Edinburgh
   hae I seen,

But the like of this fine creature my
 eyes they never sa;'
'O dame bring ben a down-bed, for she's
 lye neist the wa.'

8 'Hold your tongue, young man,' she
 said, 'and dinna trouble me,
Unless you get to my supper, and that
 is dishes three;
Dishes three to my supper, tho I eat
 nane at a',
Before I lye in your bed, but I winna
 lye neist the wa.

9 'You maun get to my supper a cherry
 but a stane,
And you man get to my supper a capon
 but a bane,
And you man get a gentle bird that flies
 wanting the ga,
Before I lye in your bed, but I'll not
 lye neist the wa.'

10 'A cherry whan in blossom is a cherry
 but a stane;
A capon when he's in the egg canna
 hae a bane;
The dow it is a gentle bird that flies
 wanting the ga;
And ye man lye in my bed, between me
 and the wa.'

11 'Hold your tongue, young man,' she
 said, 'and dinna me perplex,
Unless you tell me questions, and that
 is questions six;
Tell me them as I shall ask them, and
 that is twa by twa,
Before I lye in your bed, but I'll not
 lye neist the wa.'

12 'What is greener than the grass, what's
 higher than the tree?
What's war than a woman's wiss, what's
 deeper than the sea?
What bird sings first, and whereupon
 the dew down first does fa?
Before I lye in your bed, but I'll not
 lye neist the wa.'

13 'Virgus is greener than the grass,
 heaven's higher than the tree;
The deil's war than a woman's wish,
 hell's deeper than the sea;

The cock sings first, on the Sugar Loa
 the dew down first does fa;
And ye man lye in my bed, betweest me
 and the wa.'

14 'Hold your tongue, young man,' she
 said, 'I pray you give it oer,
Unless you tell me questions, and tha
 is questions four;
Tell me them as I shall ask them, and
 that is twa by twa,
Before I lye in your bed, but I winna
 lye neist the wa.'

15 'You man get to me a plumb that does
 in winter grow;
And likewise a silk mantle that never
 waft gaed thro;
A sparrow's horn, a priest unborn, this
 night to join us twa,
Before I lye in your bed, but I winna
 lye neist the wa.'

16 'There is a plumb in my father's yeard
 that does in winter grow;
Likewise he has a silk mantle that never
 waft gaed thro;
A sparrow's horn, it may be found,
 there's ane in every tae,
There's ane upo the mouth of him, perhaps there may be twa.

17 'The priest is standing at the door, just
 ready to come in;
Nae man could sae that he was born, to
 lie it is a sin;
For a wild boar bored his mother's side,
 he out of it did fa;
And you man lye in my bed, between
 me and the wa.'

18 Little kent Grizey Sinclair, that morning when she raise,
'T was to be the hindermost of a' her
 single days;
For now she's Captain Wetherburn's
 wife, a man she never saw,
And she man lye in his bed, but she'll
 not lye neist the wa.

B

a. 'The Earl of Rosslyn's Daughter,' Kinloch MSS., i. 83, from Mary Barr's recitation.
b. 'Lord Roslin's Daughter's Garland.' c. Bu-

chan's MSS., ii, 34. **d.** ' Captain Wedderburn's
Courtship,' Jamieson's Popular Ballads, ii, 159.
e. Harris MS., fol. 19 b, No. 14, from Mrs Harris's recitation. **f.** Notes and Queries, 2d S.,
iv, 170, " as sung among the peasantry of the
Mearns," 1857.

1 THE Lord of Rosslyn's daughter gaed
    through the wud her lane,
  And there she met Captain Wedder-
    burn, a servant to the king.
  He said unto his livery-man, Were 't na
    agen the law,
  I wad tak her to my ain bed, and lay
    her at the wa.

2 ' I 'm walking here my lane,' she says,
    ' amang my father's trees;
  And ye may lat me walk my lane, kind
    sir, now gin ye please.
  The supper-bell it will be rung, and I 'll
    be missd awa;
  Sae I 'll na lie in your bed, at neither
    stock nor wa.'

3 He said, My pretty lady, I pray lend
    me your hand,
  And ye 'll hae drums and trumpets al-
    ways at your command;
  And fifty men to guard ye wi, that weel
    their swords can draw;
  Sae we 'll baith lie in ae bed, and ye 'll
    lie at the wa.

4 ' Haud awa frae me, kind sir, I pray let
    go my hand;
  The supper-bell it will be rung, nae
    langer maun I stand.
  My father he 'll na supper tak, gif I be
    missd awa;
  Sae I 'll na lie in your bed, at neither
    stock nor wa.'

5 ' O my name is Captain Wedderburn,
    my name I 'll neer deny,
  And I command ten thousand men, upo
    yon mountains high.
  Tho your father and his men were here,
    of them I 'd stand na awe,
  But should tak ye to my ain bed, and
    lay ye neist the wa.'

6 Then he lap aff his milk-white steed, and
    set the lady on,
  And a' the way he walkd on foot, he
    held her by the hand;

He held her by the middle jimp, for fear
    that she should fa;
  Saying, I 'll tak ye to my ain bed, and
    lay thee at the wa.

7 He took her to his quartering-house, his
    landlady looked ben,
  Saying, Monie a pretty ladie in Edin-
    bruch I 've seen;
  But sic 'na pretty ladie is not into
    it a':
  Gae, mak for her a fine down-bed, and
    lay her at the wa.

8 ' O haud awa frae me, kind sir, I pray
    ye lat me be,
  For I 'll na lie in your bed till I get
    dishes three;
  Dishes three maun be dressd for me,
    gif I should eat them a',
  Before I lie in your bed, at either stock
    or wa.

9 ' 'T is I maun hae to my supper a chicken
    without a bane;
  And I maun hae to my supper a cherry
    without a stane;
  And I maun hae to my supper a bird
    without a gaw,
  Before I lie in your bed, at either stock
    or wa.'

10 ' Whan the chicken 's in the shell, I am
    sure it has na bane;
  And whan the cherry 's in the bloom, I
    wat it has na stane;
  The dove she is a genty bird, she flees
    without a gaw;
  Sae we 'll baith lie in ae bed, and ye 'll
    be at the wa.'

11 ' O haud awa frae me, kind sir, I pray
    ye give me owre,
  For I 'll na lie in your bed, till I get
    presents four;
  Presents four ye maun gie me, and that
    is twa and twa,
  Before I lie in your bed, at either stock
    or wa.

12 ' 'T is I maun hae some winter fruit that
    in December grew;
  And I maun hae a silk mantil that waft
    gaed never through;

A sparrow's horn, a priest unborn, this
nicht to join us twa,
Before I lie in your bed, at either stock
or wa.'

13 'My father has some winter fruit that
in December grew;
My mither has a silk mantil the waft
gaed never through;
A sparrow's horn ye soon may find,
there 's ane on evry claw,
And twa upo the gab o it, and ye shall
get them a'.

14 'The priest he stands without the yett,
just ready to come in;
Nae man can say he eer was born, nae
man without he sin;
He was haill cut frae his mither's side,
and frae the same let fa;
Sae we 'll baith lie in ae bed, and ye 'se
lie at the wa.'

15 'O haud awa frae me, kind sir, I pray
don't me perplex,
For I 'll na lie in your bed till ye answer
questions six:
Questions six ye maun answer me, and
that is four and twa,
Before I lie in your bed, at either stock
or wa.

16 'O what is greener than the gress,
what 's higher than thae trees ?
O what is worse than women's wish,
what 's deeper than the seas ?
What bird craws first, what tree buds
first, what first does on them fa ?
Before I lie in your bed, at either stock
or wa.'

17 'Death is greener than the gress,
heaven higher than thae trees;
The devil 's waur than women's wish,
hell 's deeper than the seas;
The cock craws first, the cedar buds first,
dew first on them does fa;
Sae we 'll baith lie in ae bed, and ye 'se
lie at the wa.'

18 Little did this lady think, that morning
whan she raise,
That this was for to be the last o a' her
maiden days.

But there 's na into the king's realm to
be found a blither twa,
And now she 's Mrs. Wedderburn, and
she lies at the wa.

47

PROUD LADY MARGARET

A was communicated to Scott " by Mr. Hamilton, music-seller, Edinburgh, with whose
mother it had been a favorite." Two stanzas
(sts. 6 and 11 of the present text) and one line
were wanting, and were supplied by Scott
" from a different ballad, having a plot somewhat similar." Later Hamilton sent Scott certain verses " to come in at the first break."
There were still four lines, which should come
before these, which he could not recollect.
The present text is Scott's, with the insertion
of the verses sent by Hamilton (sts. 7–8). A is
plainly compounded of two ballads, the conclusion being derived from E. The lady's "looking oer her castle wa," her putting riddles, and
her having " gard so mony die," make the supposition far from incredible that the Proud
Lady Margaret of the first part of the ballad
may have originally been one of the Perilous
Princesses well-known in popular story (cf. No.
46).

A

'Proud Lady Margaret,' Scott's Minstrelsy,
III, 275, ed. 1803. Communicated " by Mr.
Hamilton, music-seller, Edinburgh." Sts. 7, 8.
Abbotsford MS., Scotch Ballads, Materials for
Border Minstrelsy, No. 117 (also from Hamil-
ton).

1 'T WAS on a night, an evening bright,
When the dew began to fa,
Lady Margaret was walking up and
down,
Looking oer her castle wa.

2 She looked east and she looked west,
To see what she could spy,
When a gallant knight came in her
sight,
And to the gate drew nigh.

3 'You seem to be no gentleman,
You wear your boots so wide;
But you seem to be some cunning
hunter,
You wear the horn so syde.'

4 'I am no cunning hunter,' he said,
   'Nor neer intend to be;
But I am come to this castle
   To seek the love of thee.
And if you do not grant me love,
   This night for thee I'll die.'

5 'If you should die for me, sir knight,
   There's few for you will meane;
For mony a better has died for me,
   Whose graves are growing green.

6 ['But ye maun read my riddle,' she
      said,
   'And answer my questions three;
And but ye read them right,' she
      said,
   'Gae stretch ye out and die.]

7 'O wherein leems the beer?' she said,
   'Or wherein leems the wine?
O wherein leems the gold?' she said,
   'Or wherein leems the twine?'

8 'The beer is put in a drinking-horn,
   The wine in glasses fine,
There's gold in store between two
      kings,
   When they are fighting keen,
And the twine is between a lady's two
      hands
   When they are washen clean.'

9 'Now what is the flower, the ae first
      flower,
   Springs either on moor or dale?
And what is the bird, the bonnie bon-
      nie bird,
   Sings on the evening gale?'

10 'The primrose is the ae first flower
   Springs either on moor or dale,
And the thristlecock is the bonniest
      bird
   Sings on the evening gale.'

11 ['But what's the little coin,' she said,
   'Wald buy my castle bound?
And what's the little boat,' she said,
   'Can sail the world all round?']

12 'O hey, how mony small pennies
      Make thrice three thousand pound?
Or hey, how mony salt fishes
   Swims a' the salt sea round?'

13 'I think you maun be my match,' she
      said,
   'My match and something mair;
You are the first eer got the grant
   Of love frae my father's heir.

14 'My father was lord of nine castles,
   My mother lady of three;
My father was lord of nine castles,
   And there's nane to heir but me.

15 'And round about a' thae castles
   You may baith plow and saw,
And on the fifteenth day of May
   The meadows they will maw.'

16 'O hald your tongue, Lady Margaret,'
      he said,
   'For loud I hear you lie;
Your father was lord of nine castles,
   Your mother was lady of three;
Your father was lord of nine castles,
   But ye fa heir to but three.

17 'And round about a' thae castles
   You may baith plow and saw,
But on the fifteenth day of May
   The meadows will not maw.

18 'I am your brother Willie,' he said,
   'I trow ye ken na me;
I came to humble your haughty heart,
   Has gard sae mony die.'

19 'If ye be my brother Willie,' she said,
   'As I trow weel ye be,
This night I'll neither eat nor drink,
   But gae alang wi thee.'

20 'O hold your tongue, Lady Margaret,'
      he said,
   'Again I hear you lie;
For ye've unwashen hands and ye've
      unwashen feet,
   To gae to clay wi me.

21 'For the wee worms are my bedfellows,
   And cauld clay is my sheets,
And when the stormy winds do blow,
   My body lies and sleeps.'

E

'Fair Margret,' Alex. Laing, Ancient Ballads and Songs, etc., etc., from the recitation of
old people. Never published. MS., 1829, p. 6.

1 FAIR MARGRET was a young ladye,
      An come of high degree;
   Fair Margret was a young ladye,
      An proud as proud coud be.

2 Fair Margret was a rich ladye,
      The king's cousin was she;
   Fair Margaret was a rich ladye,
      An vain as vain coud be.

3 She war'd her wealth on the gay cleedin
      That comes frae yont the sea,
   She spent her time frae morning till
         night
      Adorning her fair bodye.

4 Ae night she sate in her stately ha,
      Kaimin her yellow hair,
   When in there cum like a gentle knight,
      An a white scarf he did wear.

5 'O what's your will wi me, sir knight,
      O what's your will wi me?
   You 're the likest to my ae brother
      That ever I did see.

6 'You 're the likest to my ae brother
      That ever I hae seen,
   But he 's buried in Dunfermline kirk,
      A month an mair bygane.'

7 'I'm the likest to your ae brother
      That ever ye did see,
   But I canna get rest into my grave,
      A' for the pride of thee.

8 'Leave pride, Margret, leave pride,
         Margrct,
      Leave pride an vanity;
   Ere ye see the sights that I hae seen,
      Sair altered ye maun be.

9 'O ye come in at the kirk door
      Wi the gowd plaits in your hair;
   But wud ye see what I hae seen,
      Ye maun them a' forbear.

10 'O ye come in at the kirk-door
      Wi the gowd prins i your sleeve;
   But wad ye see what I hae seen,
      Ye maun gie them a' their leave.

11 'Leave pride, Margret, leave pride,
         Margret,
      Leave pride an vanity;

Ere ye see the sights that I hae seen,
   Sair altered ye maun be.'

12 He got her in her stately ha,
      Kaimin her yellow hair,
   He left her on her sick sick bed,
      Sheding the saut saut tear.

48

YOUNG ANDREW

'Young Andrew' is known only from the Percy manuscript. The story recalls both 'Lady Isabel and the Elf-Knight' (No. 4) an 'The Fair Flower of Northumberland' (No. 9. The conclusion is mutilated and hard to make out. Young Andrew seems to have been pursued and caught. Why he was not promptly disposed of, and how the wolf comes into th story, will probably never be known.

Percy MS., p. 292; Hales and Furnivall, π 328.

1 As I was cast in my ffirst sleepe,
      A dreadffull draught in my mind I
         drew,
   Ffor I was dreamed of a yong man,
      Some men called him yonge Andrew.

2 The moone shone bright, and itt cast a
         ffayre light,
      Sayes shee, Welcome, my honey, my
         hart, and my sweete !
   For I haue loued thee this seuen long
         yeere,
      And our chance itt was wee cold
         neuer meete.

3 Then he tooke her in his armes two,
      And kissed her both cheeke and chin,
   And twise or thrise he pleased this may
      Before they tow did part in twinn.

4 Saies, Now, good sir, you haue had your
         will,
      You can demand no more of mee;
   Good sir, remember what you said be-
         fore,
      And goe to the church and marry
         mee.

5 Ffaire maid, I cannott doe as I wold;
      .   .   .   .   .   .

Goe home and fett thy fathers redd gold,
  And I 'le goe to the church and marry
    thee.

6 This ladye is gone to her ffathers hall,
  And well she knew where his red gold
    lay,
  And counted fforth five hundred pound,
    Besides all other iuells and chaines :

7 And brought itt all to younge Andrew,
  Itt was well counted vpon his knee;
  Then he tooke her by the lillye white
    hand,
  And led her vp to an hill soe hye.

8 Shee had vpon a gowne of blacke vel-
    uett,
    (A pittyffull sight after yee shall
      see:)
  ' Put of thy clothes, bonny wenche,' he
    says,
    ' For noe ffoote further thoust gang
    with mee.'

9 But then shee put of her gowne of vel-
    uett,
  With many a salt teare from her eye,
  And in a kirtle of ffine breaden silke
  Shee stood beffore young Andrews
    eye.

10 Sais, O put off thy kirtle of silke,
  Ffor some and all shall goe with mee;
  And to my owne lady I must itt beare,
  Who I must needs loue better then
    thee.

11 Then shee put of her kirtle of silke,
  With many a salt teare still ffrom her
    eye;
  In a peticoate of scarlett redd
  Shee stood before young Andrewes
    eye.

12 Saies, O put of thy peticoate,
  For some and all of itt shall goe with
    mee;
  And to my owne lady I will itt beare,
  Which dwells soe ffarr in a strange
    countrye.

13 But then shee put of her peticoate,
  With many a salt teare still from her
    eye,

And in a smocke of braue white silke
  Shee stood before young Andrews
    eye.

14 Saies, O put of thy smocke of silke,
  For some and all shall goe with mee;
  Vnto my owne ladye I will itt beare,
    That dwells soe ffarr in a strange
    countrye.

15 Sayes, O remember, young Andrew,
  Once of a woman you were borne;
  And ffor *that* birth *that* Marye bore,
  I pray you let my smocke be vpon !

16 ' Yes, ffayre ladye, I know itt well,
  Once of a woman I was borne;
  Yett ffor noe birth *that* Mary bore,
  Thy smocke shall not be left here
    vpon.'

17 But then shee put of her head-geere
    ffine;
  Shee hadd billaments worth a hun-
    dred pound;
  The hayre *that* was vpon this bony
    wench head
  Couered her bodye downe to the
    ground.

18 Then he pulled forth a Scottish brand,
  And held itt there in his owne right
    hand;
  Saies, Whether wilt thou dye vpon my
    swords point, ladye,
  Or thow wilt goe naked home againe ?

19 ' Liffe is sweet,' then, ' sir,' said shee,
    'Therfore I pray you leaue mee with
    mine;
  Before I wold dye on your swords point,
  I had rather goe naked home againe.

20 ' My ffather,' shee sayes, ' is a right good
    erle
  As any remaines in his countrye;
  If euer he doe your body take,
  You 'r sure to fflower a gallow tree.

21 ' And I haue seuen brethren,' shee sayes,
    ' And they are all hardy men and
    bold;
  Giff euer the doe your body take,
    You must neuer gang quicke ouer the
    mold.'

22 'If your ffather be a right good erle
　　As any remaines in his owne coun-
　　　trye,
　Tush! he shall neuer my body take,
　　I 'le gang soe ffast ouer the sea.

23 'If you haue seuen brethren,' he sayes,
　　'If they be neuer soe hardy or bold,
　Tush! they shall neuer my body take,
　　I 'le gang soe ffast into the Scottish
　　　mold.'

24 Now this ladye is gone to her fathers
　　　hall,
　When euery body their rest did take;
　But the Erle which was her ffather
　　Lay waken for his deere daughters
　　　sake.

25 'But who is that,' her ffather can say,
　　'That soe priuilye knowes the pinn?'
　'It 's Hellen, your owne deere daugh-
　　　ter, ffather,
　　I pray you rise and lett me in.'

26 .　　.　　.　　.　　.
　　'Noe, by my hood!' quoth her ffa-
　　　ther then,
　'My [house] thoust neuer come within,
　　Without I had my red gold againe.'

27 'Nay, your gold is gone, ffather!' said
　　　shee,
　　.　　.　　.　　.　　.
　'Then naked thou came into this world,
　　And naked thou shalt returne againe.'

28 'Nay! God fforgaue his death, father,'
　　　shee sayes,
　　'And soe I hope you will doe mee;'
　'Away, away, thou cursed woman,
　　I pray God an ill death thou may
　　　dye!'

29 Shee stood soe long quacking on the
　　　ground
　Till her hart itt burst in three;
　And then shee ffell dead downe in a
　　　swoond,
　　And this was the end of this bonny
　　　ladye.

30 Ithe morning, when her ffather gott
　　　vpp,
　A pittyffull sight there he might see;

His owne deere daughter was dead,
　　without clothes,
　The teares they trickeled fast ffrom
　　his eye.

31 .　　.　　.　　.　　.
　　Sais, Fye of gold, and ffye of ffee!
　For I sett soe much by my red gold
　　That now itt hath lost both my
　　daughter and mee!'

32 .　　.　　.　　.　　.
　But after this time he neere dought
　　good day,
　But as flowers doth fade in the frost,
　　Soe he did wast and weare away.

33 But let vs leaue talking of this ladye,
　　And talke some more of young An-
　　　drew;
　Ffor ffalse he was to this bonny ladye,
　　More pitty that he had not beene
　　true.

34 He was not gone a mile into the wild
　　　forrest,
　Or halfe a mile into the hart of
　　Wales,
　But there they cought him by such a
　　braue wyle
　　That hee must come to tell noe more
　　tales.

　　　*　　*　　*　　*　　*

35 .　　.　　.　　.　　.
　　Ffull soone a wolfe did of him
　　smell,
　And shee came roaring like a beare,
　　And gaping like a ffeend of hell.

36 Soe they ffought together like two
　　　lyons,
　　And fire betweene them two glashet
　　out;
　The raught eche other such a great
　　rappe,
　　That there young Andrew was slaine,
　　well I wott.

37 But now young Andrew he is dead,
　　But he was neuer buryed vnder
　　mold,
　For ther as the wolfe devoured him,
　　There lyes all this great erles gold.

49

THE TWA BROTHERS

All the Scottish versions (six in number) ere obtained within the first third of the nineteenth century, and since then no others ave been heard of, but the ballad has been obtained within recent years from the singing of poor children in American cities. B is conderably corrupted. It need hardly be mentioned that the age of the boys in the first two anzas does not suit the story. The conclusion f B belongs to 'Sweet William's Ghost' (No. 7).

A

a. C. K. Sharpe's papers (watermark of 1817) rom Elizabeth Kerry; Sharpe's Ballad Book, , 56, No. 19. b. 'The Two Brothers,' Walks ear Edinburgh, by Margaret Warrender, 890, p. 60. Given to Lady John Scott many ears ago by Campbell Riddell, brother of Sir ohn Riddell, of Ardnamurchan.

1 THERE were twa brethren in the north,
    They went to school thegithar;
  The one unto the other said,
    Will you try a warsle afore?

2 They wrestled up, they wrestled down,
    Till Sir John fell to the ground,
  And there was a knife in Sir Willie's
        pouch,
    Gied him a deadlie wound.

3 'Oh brither dear, take me on your back,
    Carry me to yon burn clear,
  And wash the blood from off my wound,
    And it will bleed nae mair.'

4 He took him up upon his back,
    Carried him to yon burn clear,
  And washd the blood from off his
        wound,
    And aye it bled the mair.

5 'Oh brother dear, take me on your
        back,
    Carry me to yon kirk-yard,
  And dig a grave baith wide and deep,
    And lay my body there.'

6 He 's taen him up upon his back,
    Carried him to yon kirk-yard,
  And dug a grave both deep and wide,
    And laid his body there.

7 'But what will I say to my father dear,
    Should he chance to say, Willie,
        whar's John?'
  'Oh say that he 's to England gone,
    To buy him a cask of wine.'

8 'And what shall I say to my mother
        dear,
    Should she chance to say, Willie,
        whar's John?'
  'Oh say that he 's to England gone,
    To buy her a new silk gown.'

9 'And what will I say to my sister dear,
    Should she chance to say, Willie,
        whar's John?'
  'Oh say that he 's to England gone,
    To buy her a wedding ring.'

10 'What will I say to her you loe dear,
    Should she cry, Why tarries my
        John?'
  'Oh tell her I lie in fair Kirk-land,
    And home will never come.'

B

'The Cruel Brother,' Motherwell's MS., p. 259. From the recitation of Widow McCormick, January 19, 1825.

1 THERE was two little boys going to the
        school,
    And twa little boys they be,
  They met three brothers playing at the
        ba,
    And ladies dansing hey.

2 'It 's whether will ye play at the ba,
        brither,
    Or else throw at the stone?'
  'I am too little, I am too young,
    O brother let me alone.'

3 He pulled out a little penknife,
    That was baith sharp and sma,
  He gave his brother a deadly wound
    That was deep, long and sair.

4 He took the holland sark off his back,
    He tore it frae breast to gare,
  He laid it to the bloody wound,
    That still bled mair and mair.

5 'It 's take me on your back, brother,'
        he says,

'And carry me to yon kirk-yard,
And make me there a very fine grave,
   That will be long and large.

6 'Lay my bible at my head,' he says,
   'My chaunter at my feet,
My bow and arrows by my side,
   And soundly I will sleep.

7 'When you go home, brother,' he says,
   'My father will ask for me;
You may tell him I am in Saussif town,
   Learning my lesson free.

8 'When you go home, brother,' he says,
   'My mother will ask for me;
You may tell her I am in Sausaf town,
   And I'll come home merrily.

9 'When you go home, brother,' he says,
   'Lady Margaret will ask for me;
You may tell her I'm dead and in
      grave laid,
   And buried in Sausaff toun.'

10 She put the small pipes to her mouth,
   And she harped both far and near,
Till she harped the small birds off the
      briers,
   And her true love out of the grave.

11 'What's this? what's this, lady Mar-
      garet?' he says,
   'What's this you want of me?'
'One sweet kiss of your ruby lips,
   That's all I want of thee.'

12 'My lips they are so bitter,' he says,
   'My breath it is so strong,
If you get one kiss of my ruby lips,
   Your days will not be long.'

50

THE BONNY HIND

This piece is transcribed three times in
Herd's manuscripts, with a note prefixed in
each instance that it was copied from the
mouth of a milkmaid in 1771. In the first
half of the story 'The Bonny Hind' comes
very near to the fine Scandinavian ballad of
'Margaret' (Grundtvig and Sigurðsson, No.
14). The conclusions differ altogether. The
story of Kullervo, incorporated in what is
called the national epic of the Finns, the Ka-
levala, has striking resemblances with the ballads of the 'Bonny Hind' class (Schiefner, run
35, 36).

'The Bonny Hyn,' Herd's MSS., II, fol. 6.
"Copied from the mouth of a milkmaid, by
W. L., in 1771."

1 O MAY she comes, and may she goes,
   Down by yon gardens green,
And there she spied a gallant squire
   As squire had ever been.

2 And may she comes, and may she goes,
   Down by yon hollin tree,
And there she spied a brisk young
      squire,
   And a brisk young squire was he.

3 'Give me your green manteel, fair maid,
   Give me your maidenhead;
Gif ye winna gie me your green manteel,
   Gie me your maidenhead.'

4 He has taen her by the milk-white
      hand,
   And softly laid her down,
And when he's lifted her up again
   Given her a silver kaim.

5 'Perhaps there may be bairns, kind
      sir,
   Perhaps there may be nane;
But if you be a courtier,
   You'll tell to me your name.'

6 'I am nae courtier, fair maid,
   But new come frae the sea;
I am nae courtier, fair maid,
   But when I court 'ith thee.

7 'They call me Jack when I'm abroad,
   Sometimes they call me John;
But when I'm in my father's bower
   Jock Randal is my name.'

8 'Ye lee, ye lee, ye bonny lad,
   Sae loud's I hear ye lee!
Ffor I'm Lord Randal's yae daughter,
   He has nae mair nor me.'

9 'Ye lee, ye lee, ye bonny may,
   Sae loud's I hear ye lee!
For I'm Lord Randal's yae yae son,
   Just now come oer the sea.'

She 's putten her hand down by her
    spare,
And out she 's taen a knife,
And she has putn 't in her heart's
    bluid,
And taen away her life.

4 And he 's taen up his bonny sister,
    With the big tear in his een,
And he has buried his bonny sister
    Amang the hollins green.

2 And syne he 's hyed him oer the dale,
    His father dear to see:
'Sing O and O for my bonny hind,
    Beneath yon hollin tree !'

3 'What needs you care for your bonny
    hyn ?
For it you needna care;
There 's aught score hyns in yonder
    park,
And five score hyns to spare.

4 'Four score of them are siller-shod,
    Of thae ye may get three ;'
'But O and O for my bonny hyn,
    Beneath yon hollin tree !'

5 'What needs you care for your bonny
    hyn ?
For it you need na care;
Take you the best, gi me the warst,
    Since plenty is to spare.'

6 'I care na for your hyns, my lord,
    I care na for your fee;
But O and O for my bonny hyn,
    Beneath the hollin tree !'

7 'O were ye at your sister's bower,
    Your sister fair to see,
Ye 'll think na mair o your bonny
    hyn
    Beneath the hollin tree.'

*   *   *   *   *

51

LIZIE WAN

First printed in Herd's Scottish Songs, 1776,
and here given from his manuscript.

A

'Lizie Wan,' Herd's MSS., i, 151 ; stanzas 1–
6, ii, p. 78.   Herd's Scottish Songs, 1776, i, 91.

1 LIZIE WAN sits at her father's bower-
    door,
Weeping and making a mane,
And by there came her father dear:
    'What ails thee, Lizie Wan ?'

2 'I ail, and I ail, dear father,' she said,
    'And I 'll tell you a reason for why;
There is a child between my twa sides,
    Between my dear billy and I.'

3 Now Lizie Wan sits at her father's
    bower-door,
Sighing and making a mane,
And by there came her brother dear:
    'What ails thee, Lizie Wan ?'

4 'I ail, I ail, dear brither,' she said,
    'And I 'll tell you a reason for why;
There is a child between my twa sides,
    Between you, dear billy, and I.'

5 'And hast thou tald father and mother
    o that ?
And hast thou tald sae o me ?'
And he has drawn his gude braid sword,
    That hang down by his knee.

6 And he has cutted aff Lizie Wan's head,
    And her fair body in three,
And he 's awa to his mothers bower,
    And sair aghast was he.

7 'What ails thee, what ails thee, Geordy
    Wan ?
What ails thee sae fast to rin ?
For I see by thy ill colour
    Some fallow's deed thou hast done.'

8 'Some fallow's deed I have done, moth-
    er,
And I pray you pardon me;
For I 've cutted aff my greyhound's head;
    He wadna rin for me.'

9 'Thy greyhound's bluid was never sae
    red,
O my son Geordy Wan !
For I see by thy ill colour
    Some fallow's deed thou hast done.'

10 'Some fallow's deed I hae done, mother,
    And I pray you pardon me;
For I hae cutted aff Lizie Wan's head
    And her fair body in three.'

11 'O what wilt thou do when thy father comes hame,
    O my son Geordy Wan?'
'I'll set my foot in a bottomless boat,
    And swim to the sea-ground.'

12 'And when will thou come hame again,
    O my son Geordy Wan?'
'The sun and the moon shall dance on the green
    That night when I come hame.'

52

THE KING'S DOCHTER LADY JEAN

At the beginning of this ballad there is resemblance to 'Tam Lin' (No. 39) and to 'Hind Etin' (No. 41).

A

a. 'The King's Dochter Lady Jean,' Motherwell's MS., p. 657. From the recitation of Mrs Storie, Lochwinnich. b. 'Lady Jean,' Motherwell's Minstrelsy, Appendix, p. xxi, No. XXIII, one stanza (st. 1).

1 THE king's young dochter was sitting in her window,
    Sewing at her silken seam;
She lookt out o the bow-window,
    And she saw the leaves growing green, my luve,
    And she saw the leaves growing green.

2 She stuck her needle into her sleeve,
    Her seam down by her tae,
And she is awa to the merrie greenwood,
    To pu the nit and slae.

3 She hadna pu't a nit at a',
    A nit but scarcely three,
Till out and spak a braw young man,
    Saying, How daur ye bow the tree?

4 'It's I will pu the nit,' she said,
    'And I will bow the tree,
And I will come to the merrie green wu
    And na ax leive o thee.'

5 He took her by the middle sae sma,
    And laid her on the gerss sae gree
And he has taen his will o her,
    And he loot her up agen.

6 'Now syn ye hae got your will o me,
    Pray tell to me your name;
For I am the king's young dochter,' s said,
    'And this nicht I daurna gang ham

7 'Gif ye be the king's young dochte he said,
    'I am his auldest son;
I wish I had died on some frem isle,
    And never had come hame!

8 'The first time I came hame, Jeanie,
    Thou was na here nor born;
I wish my pretty ship had sunk,
    And I had been forlorn.

9 'The neist time I came hame, Jeanie,
    Thou was sittin on the nourice knee
And I wish my pretty ship had sunk,
    And I had never seen thee!

10 'And the neist time I came hame, Jean
    I met thee here alane;
I wish my pretty ship had sunk,
    And I had neer come hame!'

11 She put her hand down by her side,
    And doun into her spare,
And she pou't out a wee pen-knife,
    And she wounded hersell fu sair.

12 Hooly, hooly rase she up,
    And hooly she gade hame,
Until she came to her father's parlou
    And there she did sick and mane.

13 'O sister, sister, mak my bed,
    O the clean sheets and strae,
O sister, sister, mak my bed,
    Down in the parlour below.'

14 Her father he came tripping down t stair,
    His steps they were fu slow;

'I think, I think, Lady Jean,' he said,
    'Ye 're lying far ower low.'

15 'O late yestreen, as I came hame,
    Down by yon castil wa,
    O heavy, heavy was the stane
    That on my briest did fa !'

16 Her mother she came tripping doun the
        stair,
    Her steps they were fu slow;
    'I think, I think, Lady Jean,' she
        said,
    'Ye 're lying far ower low.'

17 'O late yestreen, as I cam hame,
    Down by yon castil wa,
    O heavy, heavy was the stane
    That on my breast did fa !'

18 Her sister came tripping doun the
        stair,
    Her steps they were fu slow;
    'I think, I think, Lady Jean,' she said,
    'Ye 're lying far ower low.'

19 'O late yestreen, as I cam hame,
    Doun by yon castil wa,
    O heavy, heavy was the stane
    That on my breast did fa !'

20 Her brither he cam trippin doun the
        stair,
    His steps they were fu slow;
    He sank into his sister's arms,
    And they died as white as snaw.

53

YOUNG BEICHAN

Professor Child prints fifteen versions of this
ballad, all but one from Scotland. The story
of Beichan agrees in the general outline and
also in some details, with a well-known legend
about Gilbert Beket, father of St Thomas.
The earlier and more authentic biographies lack
this particular bit of romance, but the legend
nevertheless goes back to a date not much later
than a century after the death of the saint, being found in a poetical narrative preserved in
a manuscript of about 1300. That our ballad
has been affected by the legend of Gilbert
Beket is altogether likely. But the ballad is
not derived from the legend. Stories and ballads of the general cast of 'Young Beichan'

are extremely frequent. The legend lacks
some of the main points of these stories, and
the ballad (in one version or another) has them.
A number of heroes, — among them Henry of
Brunswick, Alexander von Metz, and the Noble
Moringer, go to the East and have adventures
similar to Young Beichan's. Just as Susie
Pye is warned that Beichan is to be married
next day, and is conveyed to Beichan's hall with
miraculous dispatch, so are Henry and others
warned, and transported to their homes by
devil, angel, or necromancer. Norse, Spanish,
and Italian ballads likewise preserve a story
essentially the same as that of 'Young Beichan.'
It should also be compared with 'Hind Horn'
(No. 17).

A

'Young Bicham,' Jamieson-Brown MS., p.
13, c. 1783.

1 IN London city was Bicham born,
    He longd strange countries for to see,
    But he was taen by a savage Moor,
    Who handld him right cruely.

2 For thro his shoulder he put a bore,
    An thro the bore has pitten a tree,
    An he 's gard him draw the carts o wine,
    Where horse and oxen had wont to be.

3 He 's casten [him] in a dungeon deep,
    Where he coud neither hear nor see;
    He 's shut him up in a prison strong,
    An he 's handld him right cruely.

4 O this Moor he had but ae daughter,
    I wot her name was Shusy Pye;
    She 's doen her to the prison-house,
    And she 's calld Young Bicham one
        word by.

5 'O hae ye ony lands or rents,
    Or citys in your ain country,
    Coud free you out of prison strong,
    An coud mantain a lady free ?'

6 'O London city is my own,
    An other citys twa or three,
    Coud loose me out o prison strong,
    An coud mantain a lady free.

7 O she has bribed her father's men
    Wi meikle goud and white money,
    She 's gotten the key o the prison doors,
    An she has set Young Bicham free.

8 She 's gi'n him a loaf o good white bread,
    But an a flask o Spanish wine,
An she bad him mind on the ladie's love
    That sae kindly freed him out o pine.

9 'Go set your foot on good ship-board,
    An haste you back to your ain country,
An before that seven years has an end,
    Come back again, love, and marry me.'

10 It was long or seven years had an end
    She longd fu sair her love to see;
She 's set her foot on good ship-board,
    An turnd her back on her ain country.

11 She 's saild up, so has she doun,
    Till she came to the other side;
She 's landed at Young Bicham's gates,
    An I hop this day she sal be his
    bride.

12 'Is this Young Bicham's gates?' says
    she,
    'Or is that noble prince within?'
'He 's up the stairs wi his bonny bride,
    An monny a lord and lady wi him.'

13 'O has he taen a bonny bride,
    An has he clean forgotten me!'
An sighing said that gay lady,
    I wish I were in my ain country!

14 But she 's pitten her han in her pocket,
    An gin the porter guineas three;
Says, Take ye that, ye proud porter,
    An bid the bridegroom speak to me.

15 O whan the porter came up the stair,
    He 's fa'n low down upon his knee:
'Won up, won up, ye proud porter,
    An what makes a' this courtesy?'

16 'O I 've been porter at your gates
    This mair nor seven years an three,
But there is a lady at them now
    The like of whom I never did see.'

17 'For on every finger she has a ring,
    An on the mid-finger she has three,
An there 's as meikle goud aboon her
    brow
    As woud buy an earldome o lan to me.'

18 Then up it started Young Bicham,
    An sware so loud by Our Lady,

'It can be nane but Shusy Pye,
    That has come oer the sea to me.'

19 O quickly ran he down the stair,
    O fifteen steps he has made but three
He 's tane his bonny love in his arms,
    An a wot he kissd her tenderly.

20 'O hae you tane a bonny bride?
    An hae you quite forsaken her
An hae ye quite forgotten her
    That gae you life an liberty?'

21 She 's lookit oer her left shoulder
    To hide the tears stood in her ee;
'Now fare thee well, Young Bicham
    she says,
    'I 'll strive to think nae mair on thee

22 'Take back your daughter, madam,' h
    says,
    'An a double dowry I 'll gi her wi;
For I maun marry my first true love,
    That 's done and suffered so much fo
    me.'

23 He 's take his bonny love by the han,
    And led her to yon fountain stane;
He 's changd her name frae Shusy Pye
    An he 's cald her his bonny love, Lad
    Jane.

C

'Young Bekie.' **a.** Jamieson-Brown MS
p. 11, c. 1783. **b.** Jamieson's Popular Ballads
II, 127.

1 YOUNG BEKIE was as brave a knight
    As ever saild the sea;
An he 's doen him to the court of France
    To serve for meat and fee.

2 He had nae been i the court of France
    A twelvemonth nor sae long,
Til he fell in love with the king'
    daughter,
    An was thrown in prison strong.

3 The king he had but ae daughter,
    Burd Isbel was her name;
An she has to the prison-house gane,
    To hear the prisoner's mane.

4 'O gin a lady woud borrow me,
    At her stirrup-foot I woud rin;

Or gin a widow wad borrow me,
    I woud swear to be her son.

5 'Or gin a virgin woud borrow me,
    I woud wed her wi a ring;
I'd gi her ha's, I'd gie her bowers,
    The bonny towrs o Linne.'

6 O barefoot, barefoot gaed she but,
    An barefoot came she ben;
It was no for want o hose an shoone,
    Nor time to put them on.

7 But a' for fear that her father dear
    Had heard her making din:
She's stown the keys o the prison-house
    dor
An latten the prisoner gang.

8 O whan she saw him, Young Bekie,
    Her heart was wondrous sair!
For the mice but an the bold rottons
    Had eaten his yallow hair.

9 She's gien him a shaver for his beard,
    A comber till his hair,
Five hunder pound in his pocket,
    To spen, an nae to spair.

10 She's gien him a steed was good in
    need,
An a saddle o royal bone,
A leash o hounds o ae litter,
    An Hector called one.

11 Atween this twa a vow was made,
    'T was made full solemnly,
That or three years was come an gane,
    Well married they shoud be.

12 He had nae been in 's ain country
    A twelvemonth till an end,
Till he's forcd to marry a duke's daugh-
    ter,
Or than lose a' his land.

13 'Ohon, alas!' says Young Beckie,
    'I know not what to dee;
For I canno win to Burd Isbel,
    And she kensnae to come to me.'

14 O it fell once upon a day
    Burd Isbel fell asleep,
An up it starts the Belly Blin,
    An stood at her bed-feet.

15 'O waken, waken, Burd Isbel,
    How [can] you sleep so soun,
Whan this is Bekie's wedding day,
    An the marriage gain on?

16 'Ye do ye to your mither's bowr,
    Think neither sin nor shame;
An ye tak twa o your mither's marys,
    To keep ye frae thinking lang.

17 'Ye dress yoursel in the red scarlet,
    An your marys in dainty green,
An ye pit girdles about your middles
    Woud buy an earldome.

18 'O ye gang down by yon sea-side,
    An down by yon sea-stran;
Sae bonny will the Hollans boats
    Come rowin till your han.

19 'Ye set your milk-white foot abord,
    Cry, Hail ye, Domine!
An I shal be the steerer o't,
    To row you oer the sea.'

20 She's tane her till her mither's bowr,
    Thought neither sin nor shame,
An she took twa o her mither's marys,
    To keep her frae thinking lang.

21 She dressd hersel i the red scarlet,
    Her marys i dainty green,
And they pat girdles about their mid-
    dles
Woud buy an earldome.

22 An they gid down by yon sea-side,
    An down by yon sea-stran;
Sae bonny did the Hollan boats
    Come rowin to their han.

23 She set her milk-white foot on board,
    Cried, Hail ye, Domine!
An the Belly Blin was the steerer o't,
    To row her oer the sea.

24 Whan she came to Young Bekie's gate,
    She heard the music play;
Sae well she kent frae a' she heard,
    It was his wedding day.

25 She's pitten her han in her pocket,
    Gin the porter guineas three;
'Hae, tak ye that, ye proud porter,
    Bid the bride-groom speake to me.'

26 O whan that he cam up the stair,
   He fell low down on his knee:
   He haild the king, an he haild the
      queen,
   An he haild him, Young Bekie.

27 'O I 've been porter at your gates
   This thirty years an three;
   But there 's three ladies at them now,
   Their like I never did see.

28 'There 's ane o them dressd in red scar-
      let,
   And twa in dainty green,
   An they hae girdles about their mid-
      dles
   Woud buy an earldome.'

29 Then out it spake the bierly bride,
   Was a' goud to the chin;
   'Gin she be braw without,' she says,
   'We 's be as braw within.'

30 Then up it starts him, Young Bekie,
   An the tears was in his ee:
   'I 'll lay my life it 's Burd Isbel,
   Come oer the sea to me.'

31 O quickly ran he down the stair,
   An whan he saw 't was shee,
   He kindly took her in his arms,
   And kissd her tenderly.

32 'O hae ye forgotten, Young Bekie,
   The vow ye made to me,
   Whan I took you out o the prison
      strong,
   Whan ye was condemnd to die?

33 'I gae you a steed was good in need,
   An a saddle o royal bone,
   A leash o hounds o ae litter,
   An Hector called one.'

34 It was well kent what the lady said,
   That it wasnae a lee,
   For at ilka word the lady spake,
   The hound fell at her knee.

35 'Tak hame, tak hame your daughter
      dear,
   A blessing gae her wi,
   For I maun marry my Burd Isbel,
   That 's come oer the sea to me.'

36 'Is this the custom o your house
   Or the fashion o your lan,
   To marry a maid in a May mornin,
   An send her back at even?'

54

THE CHERRY-TREE CAROL

The proper story of this highly popul
carol is derived from the Pseudo-Matthew
gospel, chapter xx. What succeeds after A
B 8, is probably founded on the angel's wor
to the shepherds in Luke ii, and on Jesus's pr
dictions in the authentic gospels.

A

a. 'Joseph was an old man,' Sandys, Chris
mas Carols, p. 123, West of England. b
Sandys, Christmastide, p. 241.

1 JOSEPH was an old man,
      and an old man was he,
   When he wedded Mary,
      in the land of Galilee.

2 Joseph and Mary walked
      through an orchard good,
   Where was cherries and berries,
      so red as any blood.

3 Joseph and Mary walked
      through an orchard green,
   Where was berries and cherries,
      as thick as might be seen.

4 O then bespoke Mary,
      so meek and so mild:
   'Pluck me one cherry, Joseph,
      for I am with child.'

5 O then bespoke Joseph,
      with words most unkind:
   'Let him pluck thee a cherry
      that brought thee with child.'

6 O then bespoke the babe,
      within his mother's womb:
   'Bow down then the tallest tree,
      for my mother to have some.'

7 Then bowed down the highest tree
      unto his mother's hand;

Then she cried, See, Joseph,
  I have cherries at command.

8 O then bespake Joseph:
  'I have done Mary wrong;
  But cheer up, my dearest,
    and be not cast down.'

9 Then Mary plucked a cherry,
    as red as the blood,
  Then Mary went home
    with her heavy load.

10 Then Mary took her babe,
    and sat him on her knee,
  Saying, My dear son, tell me
    what this world will be.

11 'O I shall be as dead, mother,
    as the stones in the wall;
  O the stones in the streets, mother,
    shall mourn for me all.

12 'Upon Easter-day, mother,
    my uprising shall be;
  O the sun and the moon, mother,
    shall both rise with me.'

B

a. 'The Cherry-Tree Carol,' Husk, Songs
of the Nativity, p. 59, from a Worcester broadside of the eighteenth century. b. Hone's
Ancient Mysteries, p. 90, from various copies.
c. Sylvester, A Garland of Christmas Carols,
45. d. Birmingham chap-book, of about
1843, in B. Harris Cowper's Apocryphal Gospels, p. xxxviii.

1 JOSEPH was an old man,
    and an old man was he,
  And he married Mary,
    the Queen of Galilee.

2 When Joseph was married,
    and Mary home had brought,
  Mary proved with child,
    and Joseph knew it not.

3 Joseph and Mary walked
    through a garden gay,
  Where the cherries they grew
    upon every tree.

4 O then bespoke Mary,
    with words both meek and mild:

'O gather me cherries, Joseph,
    they run so in my mind.'

5 And then replied Joseph,
    with words so unkind:
  'Let him gather thee cherries
    that got thee with child.'

6 O then bespoke our Saviour,
    all in his mother's womb:
  'Bow down, good cherry-tree,
    to my mother's hand.'

7 The uppermost sprig
    bowed down to Mary's knees:
  'Thus you may see, Joseph,
    these cherries are for me.'

8 'O eat your cherries, Mary,
    O eat your cherries now;
  O eat your cherries, Mary,
    that grow upon the bough.'

9 As Joseph was a walking,
    he heard an angel sing:
  'This night shall be born
    our heavenly king.

10 'He neither shall be born
    in housen nor in hall,
  Nor in the place of Paradise,
    but in an ox's stall.

11 'He neither shall be clothed
    in purple nor in pall,
  But all in fair linen,
    as were babies all.

12 'He neither shall be rocked
    in silver nor in gold,
  But in a wooden cradle,
    that rocks on the mould.

13 'He neither shall be christened
    in white wine nor red,
  But with fair spring water,
    with which we were christened.

14 Then Mary took her young son,
    and set him on her knee:
  'I pray thee now, dear child,
    tell how this world shall be.'

15 'O I shall be as dead, mother,
    as the stones in the wall;

O the stones in the street, mother,
  shall mourn for me all.

16 ' And upon a Wednesday
    my vow I will make,
  And upon Good Friday
    my death I will take.

17 ' Upon Easter-day, mother,
    my rising shall be;
  O the sun and the moon
    shall uprise with me.

18 'The people shall rejoice,
    and the birds they shall sing,
  To see the uprising
    of the heavenly king.'

55

THE CARNAL AND THE CRANE

Mr Husk, who had access to a remarkably good collection of carols, had met with no copy of ' The Carnal and the Crane ' of earlier date than the middle of the eighteenth century. Internal evidence points us much further back. The carol had obviously been transmitted from mouth to mouth before it was fixed in its present incoherent and corrupted form by print. The well-informed Crane instructs his cate-chumen, the Crow, in several matters pertaining to the birth and earliest days of Jesus : the Nativity, the conference of Herod with the Wise Men, including the miracle of the roasted cock ; the Flight into Egypt, with the Adoration of the Beasts and the Instantaneous Harvest ; the Massacre of the Innocents. Of the apocryphal incidents, the miracle of the cock has been spoken of under ' Stephen and Herod ' (No. 22). The adoration of the beasts is derived from the Historia de Nativitate Mariae, etc. (Pseudo-Matthaei Evangelium), and is of course frequent in legendaries of the infancy of the Saviour, but is not remarkable enough to be popular in carols. The miraculous harvest by which the Holy Family evaded Herod's pursuit, is, on the contrary, a favorite subject with popular poetry, as also, like the bowing of the palm-tree, with pictorial art.

' The Carnal and the Crane.' a. Sandys, Christmas Carols, p. 152, Christmastide, p. 246, from a broadside. b. Husk, Songs of the Nativity, p. 97, apparently from a Worcester broadside. c. Birmingham chap-book, of about 1843, in B. Harris Cowper's Apocryphal Gospels, p. xli.

1 As I passd by a river side,
    And there as I did reign,
  In argument I chanced to hear
    A Carnal and a Crane.

2 The Carnal said unto the Crane,
    If all the world should turn,
  Before we had the Father,
    But now we have the Son !

3 ' From whence does the Son come,
    From where and from what place ?
  He said, In a manger,
    Between an ox and ass.

4 ' I pray thee,' said the Carnal,
    ' Tell me before thou go,
  Was not the mother of Jesus
    Conceivd by the Holy Ghost ? '

5 She was the purest virgin,
    And the cleanest from sin;
  She was the handmaid of our Lord
    And mother of our king.

6 ' Where is the golden cradle
    That Christ was rocked in ?
  Where are the silken sheets
    That Jesus was wrapt in ? '

7 A manger was the cradle
    That Christ was rocked in:
  The provender the asses left
    So sweetly he slept on.

8 There was a star in the east land,
    So bright it did appear,
  Into King Herod's chamber,
    And where King Herod were.

9 The Wise Men soon espied it,
    And told the king on high
  A princely babe was born that night
    No king could eer destroy.

10 ' If this be true,' King Herod said,
    ' As thou tellest unto me,
  This roasted cock that lies in the dish
    Shall crow full fences three.'

11 The cock soon freshly featherd was,
    By the work of God's own hand,
  And then three fences crowed he,
    In the dish where he did stand.

12 'Rise up, rise up, you merry men all,
   See that you ready be;
   All children under two years old
   Now slain they all shall be.'

13 Then Jesus, ah, and Joseph,
   And Mary, that was so pure,
   They travelld into Egypt,
   As you shall find it sure.

14 And when they came to Egypt's land,
   Amongst those fierce wild beasts,
   Mary, she being weary,
   Must needs sit down to rest.

15 'Come sit thee down,' says Jesus,
   'Come sit thee down by me,
   And thou shalt see how these wild
      beasts
   Do come and worship me.'

16 First came the lovely lion,
   Which Jesus's grace did bring,
   And of the wild beasts in the field
   The lion shall be king.

17 We'll choose our virtuous princes
   Of birth and high degree,
   In every sundry nation,
   Whereer we come and see.

18 Then Jesus, ah, and Joseph,
   And Mary, that was unknown,
   They travelled by a husbandman,
   Just while his seed was sown.

19 'God speed thee, man,' said Jesus,
   'Go fetch thy ox and wain,
   And carry home thy corn again
   Which thou this day hast sown.'

20 The husbandman fell on his knees,
   Even upon his face:
   'Long time hast thou been looked for,
   But now thou art come at last.

21 'And I myself do now believe
   Thy name is Jesus called;
   Redeemer of mankind thou art,
   Though undeserving all.'

22 'The truth, man, thou hast spoken,
   Of it thou mayst be sure,
   For I must lose my precious blood
   For thee and thousands more.

23 'If any one should come this way,
   And enquire for me alone,
   Tell them that Jesus passed by
   As thou thy seed did sow.'

24 After that there came King Herod,
   With his train so furiously,
   Enquiring of the husbandman
   Whether Jesus passed by.

25 'Why, the truth it must be spoke,
   And the truth it must be known;
   For Jesus passed by this way
   When my seed was sown.

26 'But now I have it reapen,
   And some laid on my wain,
   Ready to fetch and carry
   Into my barn again.'

27 'Turn back,' says the captain,
   'Your labor and mine's in vain;
   It's full three quarters of a year
   Since he his seed has sown.'

28 So Herod was deceived,
   By the work of God's own hand,
   And further he proceeded
   Into the Holy Land.

29 There's thousands of children young
   Which for his sake did die;
   Do not forbid those little ones,
   And do not them deny.

30 The truth now I have spoken,
   And the truth now I have shown;
   Even the Blessed Virgin
   She's now brought forth a son.

56

DIVES AND LAZARUS

A ballet " of the Ryche man and poor Lazarus " was licensed to Master John Wallye and Mistress Toye, 19 July, 1557 – 9 July, 1558. W. Pekerynge pays his license for printing " of a ballett, Dyves and Lazarus," 22 July, 1570 – 22 July, 1571 (Arber, Registers of the Company of Stationers, I, 76, 436). A fiddler in Fletcher's Monsieur Thomas, printed 1639, says he can sing The merry ballad of Diverus and Lazarus (act iii, scene 3).

'Dives and Lazarus.' **a.** Sylvester, A Garland of Christmas Carols, p. 50, from an old Birmingham broadside. **b.** Husk, Songs of the Nativity, p. 94, from a Worcestershire broadside of the eighteenth century.

1 As it fell out upon a day,
    Rich Dives he made a feast,
And he invited all his friends,
    And gentry of the best.

2 Then Lazarus laid him down and down,
    And down at Dives' door:
' Some meat, some drink, brother Dives,
    Bestow upon the poor.'

3 ' Thou art none of my brother, Lazarus,
    That lies begging at my door;
No meat nor drink will I give thee,
    Nor bestow upon the poor.'

4 Then Lazarus laid him down and down,
    And down at Dives's wall:
' Some meat, some drink, brother Dives,
    Or with hunger starve I shall.'

5 ' Thou art none of my brother, Lazarus,
    That lies begging at my wall;
No meat nor drink will I give thee,
    But with hunger starve you shall.'

6 Then Lazarus laid him down and down,
    And down at Dives's gate:
' Some meat, some drink, brother Dives,
    For Jesus Christ his sake.'

7 ' Thou art none of my brother, Lazarus,
    That lies begging at my gate;
No meat nor drink will I give thee,
    For Jesus Christ his sake.'

8 Then Dives sent out his merry men,
    To whip poor Lazarus away;
They had no power to strike a stroke,
    But flung their whips away.

9 Then Dives sent out his hungry dogs,
    To bite him as he lay;
They had no power to bite at all,
    But licked his sores away.

10 As it fell out upon a day,
    Poor Lazarus sickened and died;
Then came two angels out of heaven
    His soul therein to guide.

11 ' Rise up, rise up, brother Lazarus,
    And go along with me;
For you 've a place prepared in heaven,
    To sit on an angel's knee.'

12 As it fell out upon a day,
    Rich Dives sickened and died;
Then came two serpents out of hell,
    His soul therein to guide.

13 ' Rise up, rise up, brother Dives,
    And go with us to see
A dismal place, prepared in hell,
    From which thou canst not flee.'

14 Then Dives looked up with his eyes,
    And saw poor Lazarus blest:
' Give me one drop of water, brother
        Lazarus,
    To quench my flaming thirst.

15 ' Oh had I as many years to abide
    As there are blades of grass,
Then there would be an end, but now
    Hell's pains will ne'er be past.

16 ' Oh was I now but alive again,
    The space of one half hour !
Oh that I had my peace secure !
    Then the devil should have no power.

57

BROWN ROBYN'S CONFESSION

The only version of ' Brown Robyn's Confession ' is the one printed in Ballads of the North of Scotland, the copy in Motherwell' MS. having been derived from Buchan. The ballad celebrates a miracle of the Virgin, and is our only example of that extensive class of legends, unless we choose to include ' The Jew's Daughter' (No. 155) and to take Robin Hood's view of the restoration of his loan, in the fourth Fit of the Little Gest (No. 117). A fine ballad very common in Sweden ('Sir Peder's Voyage '), and preserved by tradition also in Denmark and Norway, has the same story with a tragical termination for the hero, saving a single instance, in which there is also supernatural interference in his behalf. Compare also the throwing over of Bonnie Annie in No. 24.

Buchan's Ballads of the North of Scotland, I, 110 ; Motherwell's MS., p. 580.

It fell upon a Wodensday
  Brown Robyn's men went to sea,
But they saw neither moon nor sun,
  Nor starlight wi their ee.

' We 'll cast kevels us amang,
  See wha the unhappy man may be; '
The kevel fell on Brown Robyn,
  The master-man was he.

' It is nae wonder,' said Brown Robyn,
  ' Altho I dinna thrive,
For wi my mither I had twa bairns,
  And wi my sister five.

' But tie me to a plank o wude,
  And throw me in the sea;
And if I sink, ye may bid me sink,
  But if I swim, just lat me bee.'

They 've tyed him to a plank o wude,
  And thrown him in the sea;
He didna sink, tho they bade him sink;
  He swimd, and they bade lat him bee.

He hadna been into the sea
  An hour but barely three,
Till by it came Our Blessed Lady,
  Her dear young son her wi.

' Will ye gang to your men again,
  Or will ye gang wi me ?
Will ye gang to the high heavens,
  Wi my dear son and me ? '

' I winna gang to my men again,
  For they would be feared at mee;
But I woud gang to the high heavens,
  Wi thy dear son and thee.'

' It's for nae honour ye did to me, Brown
  Robyn,
It 's for nae guid ye did to mee;
But a' is for your fair confession
  You 've made upon the sea.'

58

SIR PATRICK SPENS

This ballad is one of many which were first
de known to the world through Percy's
liques. Percy's version remains, poetically,
best. It may be a fragment, but the imagi-
tion easily supplies all that may be wanting.

The versions fall into two classes. Of the
copies here printed, A and B belong to the
first group ; G belongs to the second, which
is distinguished by additional circumstances.
Thus in the second group the destination of
the ship is Norway; the object of the voyage
(not told in G) is to bring home the king of
Norway's daughter (or the Scottish king's
daughter), or to take out the Scottish king's
daughter to Norway, where she is to be queen.

The ballad may or may not be historical.
Motherwell has suggested a sufficiently plausible foundation. Margaret, daughter of Alexander III, was married, in 1281, to Eric, King of
Norway. She was conducted to her husband,
" brought home," in August of that year, by
many knights and nobles. Many of these were
drowned on the return voyage. Margaret died
in 1283, leaving a newly-born daughter, to
whom the crown of Scotland fell in 1286. A
match was proposed between the infant Margaret, called the Maid of Norway, and the eldest son of Edward I of England. A deputation
was sent to Norway in 1290 to bring the princess over, but she died on the voyage. According to one (untrustworthy) account she
perished, apparently in a storm, on the coasts
of Boghan (Buchan ?). No such name as Patrick Spens is historically connected with any
of these occurrences; but the ballad might
be substantially historical though the command of the ship were invariably given (as
it is in one version) to Sir Andrew Wood, a
distinguished admiral, who was born a couple
of centuries after the supposed event, and it
might be substantially historical though we
could prove that Patrick Spens was only a ship-
master, of purely local fame, who was lost off
Aberdour a couple of hundred years ago. The
question cannot be decided, and is of slight
importance.

A

a. Sir Patrick Spence,' Percy's Reliques,
1765, I, 71: " given from two MS. copies, transmitted from Scotland." b. ' Sir Andrew
Wood,' Herd's Scots Songs, 1769, p. 243.

1 THE king sits in Dumferling toune,
  Drinking the blude-reid wine:
' O whar will I get guid sailor,
  To sail this schip of mine ? '

2 Up and spak an eldern knicht,
  Sat at the kings richt kne:
' Sir Patrick Spence is the best sailor
  That sails upon the se.'

3 The king has written a braid letter,
  And signd it wi his hand,

And sent it to Sir Patrick Spence,
 Was walking on the sand.

4 The first line that Sir Patrick red,
 A loud lauch lauched he;
The next line that Sir Patrick red,
 The teir blinded his ee.

5 'O wha is this has don this deid,
 This ill deid don to me,
To send me out this time o' the yeir,
 To sail upon the se !

6 ' Mak hast, mak haste, my mirry men all,
 Our guid schip sails the morne:'
' O say na sae, my master deir,
 For I feir a deadlie storme.

7 ' Late late yestreen I saw the new moone,
 Wi the auld moone in hir arme,
And I feir, I feir, my deir master,
 That we will cum to harme.'

8 O our Scots nobles wer richt laith
 To weet their cork-heild schoone;
Bot lang owre a' the play wer playd,
 Thair hats they swam aboone.

9 O lang, lang may their ladies sit,
 Wi thair fans into their hand,
Or eir they se Sir Patrick Spence
 Cum sailing to the land.

10 O lang, lang may the ladies stand,
 Wi thair gold kems in their hair,
Waiting for thair ain deir lords,
 For they 'll se thame na mair.

11 Haf owre, haf owre to Aberdour,
 It 's fiftie fadom deip,
And thair lies guid Sir Patrick Spence,
 Wi the Scots lords at his feit.

B

'Sir Patrick Spence,' Herd's MSS., II, 27,
I, 49.

1 THE king he sits in Dumferling,
 Drinking the blude reid wine: O
'O where will I get a gude sailor,
 That 'l sail the ships o mine ?' O

2 Up then started a yallow-haird man,
 Just be the kings right knee:

'Sir Patrick Spence is the best sailor
 That ever saild the see.'

3 Then the king he wrote a lang letter,
 And sealld it with his hand,
And sent it to Sir Patrick Spence,
 That was lyand at Leith Sands.

4 When Patrick lookd the letter on,
 He gae loud laughters three;
But afore he wan to the end of it
 The teir blindit his ee.

5 'O wha is this has tald the king,
 Has tald the king o me ?
Gif I but wist the man it war,
 Hanged should he be.

6 'Come eat and drink, my merry men all,
 For our ships maun sail the morn;
Bla'd wind, bla'd weet, bla'd sna or sleet,
 Our ships maun sail the morn.'

7 ' Alake and alas now, good master,
 For I fear a deidly storm;
For I saw the new moon late yestreen,
 And the auld moon in her arms.'

8 They had not saild upon the sea
 A league but merely three,
When ugly, ugly were the jaws
 That rowd unto their knee.

9 They had not saild upon the sea
 A league but merely nine,
When wind and weit and snaw and sleet
 Came blawing them behind.

10 ' Then where will I get a pretty boy
 Will take my steer in hand,
Till I go up to my tap-mast,
 And see gif I see dry land ?'

11 ' Here am I, a pretty boy
 That 'l take your steir in hand,
Till you go up to your tap-mast,
 And see an you see the land.'

12 Laith, laith were our Scottish lords
 To weit their coal-black shoon;
But yet ere a' the play was playd,
 They wat their hats aboon.

13 Laith, laith war our Scottish lords
 To weit their coal-black hair;

But yet ere a' the play was playd,
    They wat it every hair.

4 The water at St Johnston's wall
    Was fifty fathom deep,
And there ly a' our Scottish lords,
    Sir Patrick at their feet.

5 Lang, lang may our ladies wait
    Wi the tear blinding their ee,
Afore they see Sir Patrick's ships
    Come sailing oer the sea.

6 Lang, lang may our ladies wait,
    Wi their babies in their hands,
Afore they see Sir Patrick Spence
    Come sailing to Leith Sands.

G

'Sir Patrick Spence,' Jamieson's Popular
Ballads, i, 157, communicated by Scott.

1 THE king sits in Dunfermlin town,
    Sae merrily drinkin the wine:
'Whare will I get a mariner,
    Will sail this ship o mine?'

2 Then up bespak a bonny boy,
    Sat just at the king's knee:
'Sir Patrick Spence is the best seaman,
    That eer set foot on sea.'

3 The king has written a braid letter,
    Seald it wi his ain hand;
He has sent word to Sir Patrick,
    To come at his command.

4 'O wha is this, or wha is that,
    Has tald the king o me?
For I was never a good seaman,
    Nor ever intend to be.'

5 They mounted sail on Munenday morn,
    Wi a' the haste they may,
And they hae landed in Norraway,
    Upon the Wednesday.

6 They hadna been a month, a month
    In Norraway but three,
Till lads o Norraway began to say,
    Ye spend a' our white monie.

7 'Ye spend a' our good kingis goud,
    But and our queenis fee:'

'Ye lie, ye lie, ye liars loud,
    Sae weel 's I hear you lie.

8 'For I brought as much white money
    As will gain my men and me;
I brought half a fou o good red goud
    Out oer the sea with me.

9 'Be 't wind or weet, be 't snaw or
    sleet,
    Our ships maun sail the morn:'
'O ever alack! my master dear,
    I fear a deadly storm.

10 'I saw the new moon late yestreen,
    Wi the auld moon in her arm;
And if we gang to sea, master,
    I fear we 'll suffer harm.'

11 They hadna sailed a league on sea,
    A league but barely ane,
Till anchors brak, and tap-masts lap;
    There came a deadly storm.

12 'Whare will I get a bonny boy
    Will tak thir sails in hand,
That will gang up to the tap-mast,
    See an he ken dry land?'

13 Laith, laith were our good Scots lords
    To weet their leathern shoon;
But or the morn at fair day-light,
    Their hats were wat aboon.

14 Mony was the feather bed,
    That flotterd on the faem,
And mony was the good Scots lord
    Gaed awa that neer cam hame,
And mony was the fatherless bairn
    That lay at hame greetin.

15 It 's forty miles to Aberdeen,
    And fifty fathoms deep;
And there lyes a' our good Scots lords,
    Wi Sir Patrick at their feet.

16 The ladies crackt their fingers white,
    The maidens tore their hair,
A' for the sake o their true loves,
    For them they neer saw mair.

17 Lang, lang may our ladies stand,
    Wi their fans in their hand,
Ere they see Sir Patrick and his men
    Come sailing to the land.

59

SIR ALDINGAR

This ballad, one of the most important of all that the Percy manuscript has saved from oblivion, was first given to the world in the Reliques of Ancient English Poetry (II, 48, ed. 1765; II, 49, ed. 1767), with conjectural emendations by the editor, and the insertion of some stanzas to complete the story. A second version (B), very much humbled in diction, and otherwise corrupted, but of indubitable antiquity, as Scott remarks, was published in the Minstrelsy of the Scottish Border in 1803. Tales of the same general description as this ballad are extremely often to be met with in ballad, romance, chronicle, or saga; nor is the number small of those which have the special traits that the accusation is made by a trusted officer of the husband, who has attempted to seduce the lady, and has failed, and that the wife is cleared by a judgment of God. Our ballad belongs with a very distinct Scandinavian variety of these last, but has adopted one characteristic trait from another source. The Scandinavian ballad in question is 'Ravengaard og Memering,' (Grundtvig, No. 13), of which there are versions from Denmark, Iceland, and the Färöes, as well as a Norwegian prose redaction.

A story essentially the same as that of the English and Scandinavian ballads is told by William of Malmesbury (De Gestis Regum Anglorum, ii, 12), of Gunhild, daughter of Cnut the Great and Emma, who was married in 1036 to King Henry, afterwards the Emperor Henry III. William was apparently following ballad authority. Gunhild never had any trouble with her husband. The story was probably transferred to her from St Cunigund, the consort of the Emperor St Henry II, in whose legendary history there is a passage essentially similar. A still earlier instance is that of Gundeberg, wife of the Lombard king Arioald (about 630 A. D.).

The incident of the leper, which does not occur in 'Ravengaard og Memering,' links the English ballad with the story of Oliva, or Sibilla, in the Charlemagne cycle (see the Karlamagnus Saga, Unger, p. 51; the old French chanson de geste of Doon l'Alemanz, etc.). Compare also the Middle English romances Sir Triamour and The Erl of Tolous (the latter professedly a "lay of Britain"), and the old French romance of Joufrois.

A

'Sir Aldingar,' Percy MS., p. 68; Hales and Furnivall, I, 166.

1 OUR king he kept a ffalse steward,
    Men called him Sir Aldingar.
    . . . . . .
    . . . . . .

2 He wold haue layen by our comel
        queene,
    Her deere worshipp to haue betraide
    Our queene shee was a good woman,
        And euer more said him nay.

3 Aldingar was offended in his mind,
        With her hee was neuer content,
    But he sought what meanes he cold fin
        out,
    In a fyer to haue her brent.

4 There came a lame lazer to the king
        gates,
    A lazar was blind and lame;
    He tooke the lazar vpon his backe,
    Vpon the queenes bed he did him lay

5 He said, Lye still, lazar, wheras thou
        lyest;
    Looke thou goe not away;
    Ile make thee a whole man and a sound
    In two howres of a day.

6 And then went forth Sir Aldingar,
        Our queene for to betray,
    And then he mett with our comlye king,
    Saies, God you saue and see!

7 'If I had space, as I haue grace,
        A message I wold say to thee:'
    'Say on, say on, Sir Aldingar,
        Say thou on and vnto me.'

8 'I can let you now see one of [the]
        greiuos[est] sights
    That euer Christen king did see;
    Our queene hath chosen a new, new
        loue,
    She will haue none of thee.

9 'If shee had chosen a right good knight,
        The lesse had beene her shame;
    But she hath chosen a lazar man,
        Which is both blinde and lame.'

10 'If this be true, thou Aldingar,
        That thou dost tell to me,
    Then will I make thee a rich knight
        Both of gold and fee.

1 ' But if it be false, Sir Aldingar,
 That thou doest tell to me,
Then looke for noe other death
 But to be hangd on a tree.
Goe with me,' saide our comly king,
 ' This lazar for to see.'

2 When the king he came into the queenes
  chamber,
 Standing her bed befor,
' There is a lodly lome,' says Harry
  King,
 ' For our dame Queene Elinor !

3 ' If thou were a man, as thou art none,
 Here thou sholdest be slaine;
But a paire of new gallowes shall be built,
 Thoust hang on them soe hye.

4 ' And [a] fayre fyer there shalbe bett,
 And brent our queene shalbee : '
Fforth then walked our comlye king,
 And mett with our comly queene.

5 Saies, God you saue, our queene, Madam,
 And Christ you saue and see !
Heere you [haue] chosen a new, new
  loue,
 And you will haue none of mee.

6 ' If you had chosen a right good knight,
 The lesse had beene your shame;
But you haue chosen a lazar man,
 That is both blind and lame.'

7 ' Euer alacke !' said our comly queene,
 ' Sir Aldingar is false to mee;
But euer alacke !' said our comly queene,
 ' Euer alas, and woe is mee !

8 ' I had thought sweuens had neuer been
  true;
 I haue prooued them true at the last;
I dreamed in my sweauen on Thursday
  at eueninge,
 In my bed wheras I lay,

9 ' I dreamed a grype and a grimlie beast
 Had carryed my crowne away,
My gorgett and my kirtle of golde,
 And all my faire heade-geere.

20 ' How he wold haue worryed me with his
  tush,
 And borne me into his nest,

Saving there came a little hawk,
 Flying out of the east.

21 ' Saving there came a little hawke,
 Which men call a merlion;
Vntill the ground he stroke him downe,
 That dead he did fall downe.

22 ' Giffe I were a man, as I am none,
 A battell I would proue;
I wold fight with that false traitor;
 Att him I cast my gloue !

23 ' Seing I am able noe battell to make,
 You must grant me, my leege, a
  knight,
To fight with that traitor, Sir Aldingar,
 To maintaine me in my right.'

24 ' I 'le giue thee forty dayes,' said our
  king,
 ' To seeke thee a man therin;
If thou find not a man in forty dayes,
 In a hott fyer thou shall brenn.'

25 Our queene sent forth a messenger;
 He rode fast into the south;
He rode the countryes through and
  through,
 Soe ffar vnto Portsmouth.

26 . . . . . .

 He cold find never a man in the south
  country
 That wold fight with the knight soe
  keene.

27 The second messenger the queen forth
  sent
 Rode far into the east;
But, blessed be God made sunn and
  moone !
 He sped then all of the best.

28 As he rode then by one riuer side,
 There he mett with a little child;
He seemed noe more in a mans likenesse
 Then a child of four yeeres old.

29 He askt the queenes messenger how far
  he rode;
 Loth he was him to tell;
The little one was offended att him,
 Bid him adew, farwell.

30 Said, Turne thou againe, thou messenger,
  Greete our queene well from me;
  When bale is att hyest, boote is att next;
  Helpe enough there may bee.

31 'Bid our queene remember what she did
    dreame
  In her bedd wheras shee lay;
  Shee dreamed the grype and the grimly
    beast
  Had carryed her crowne away;

32 'Her gorgett and her kirtle of gold,
  Alsoe her faire head-geere;
  He wold haue werryed her with his
    tushe,
  And borne her into his nest.

33 'Saving there came a little hawke,
  Men call him a merlyon;
  Vntill the ground he did strike him
    downe,
  That dead he did ffall downe.

34 'Bidd the queene be merry att her hart,
  Euermore light and glad;
  When bale is att hyest, boote is at
    next,
  Helpe enoughe there shalbe.'

35 Then the queenes messenger rode backe,
  A gladed man then was hee;
  When he came before our queene,
  A gladd woman then was shee.

36 Shee gaue the messenger twenty pound,
  O lord, in gold and ffee;
  Saies, Spend and spare not while this
    doth last,
  Then feitch thou more of me.

37 Our queene was put in a tunne to burne,
  She thought no thing but death;
  The were ware of the little one
  Came ryding forth of the east.

38 With a mu . . . . .
  A louelie child was hee;
  When he came to that fier,
  He light the queene full nigh.

39 Said, Draw away these brands of fire
  Lie burning before our queene,
  And feitch me hither Sir Aldingar,
  That is a knight soe keene.

40 When Aldingar see that little one,
  Ffull litle of him hee thought;
  If there had beene halfe a hundred such,
  Of them he wold not haue wrought.

41 Hee sayd, Come hither, Sir Aldingar;
  Thou seemust as bigge as a ffooder;
  I trust to God, ere I haue done with
    thee,
  God will send to vs [an] auger.

42 Saies, The first stroke that 's giuen, Sir
    Aldingar,
  I will giue vnto thee,
  And if the second giue thou may,
  Looke then thou spare not mee.

43 The litle one pulld forth a well good
    sword,
  I-wis itt was all of guilt;
  It cast light there over that feild,
  It shone soe all of guilt.

44 He stroke the first stroke att Aldingar,
  He stroke away his leggs by his knee;
  .   .   .   .
  .   .   .   .   .   .

45 Sayes, Stand vp, stand vp, thou false
    traitor,
  And fight vpon thy feete;
  For and thou thriue as thou begins,
  Of a height wee shalbe meete.

46 'A preist, a preist,' sayes Aldingar,
  'Me for to houzle and shriue!
  A preist, a preist,' sayes Aldingar,
  'While I am a man liuing a-liue!

47 'I wold haue laine by our comlie queene;
  To it shee wold neuer consent;
  I thought to haue betrayd her to our king,
  In a fyer to haue had her brent.

48 'There came a lame lazar to the kings
    gates,
  A lazar both blind and lame;
  I tooke the lazar vpon my backe,
  In the Queenes bed I did him lay.

49 'I bad him, Lie still, lazar, where he lay,
  Looke he went not away;
  I wold make him a whole man and a
    sound
  In two houres of a day.

0 . . . . .

'Euer alacke!' sayes Sir Aldingar,
　'Falsing neuer doth well;

1 'Forgiue, forgiue me, queene, Madam!
　　For Christs loue forgiue me!'
　'God forgaue his death, Aldingar,
　　And freely I forgiue thee.'

2 'Now take thy wife, thou King Harry,
　　And loue her as thou shold;
　Thy wiffe shee is as true to thee
　　As stone *that* lies on the castle
　　　wall.'

3 The lazar vnder the gallow tree
　　Was a pretty man and small;
　The lazar vnder the gallow tree
　　Was made steward in King Henerys
　　　hall.

B

'Sir Hugh le Blond,' Minstrelsy of the Scottish Border, III, 51, 1803. Communicated to
Scott by K. Williamson Burnet, of Monboddo,
as written down from the recitation of an old
woman, long in the service of the Arbuthnot
family.

1 THE birds sang sweet as ony bell,
　　The world had not their make;
　The queen she's gone to her cham-
　　ber,
　　With Rodingham to talk.

2 'I love you well, my queen, my dame,
　　Bove land and rents so clear,
　And for the love of you, my queen,
　　Would thole pain most severe.'

3 'If well you love me, Rodingham,
　　I'm sure so do I thee;
　I love you well as any man,
　　Save the king's fair bodye.'

4 'I love you well, my queen, my dame,
　　'Tis truth that I do tell;
　And for to lye a night with you,
　　The salt seas I would sail.'

5 'Away, away, O Rodingham!
　　You are both stark and stoor;
　Would you defile the king's own bed,
　　And make his queen a whore?

6 'To-morrow you'd be taken sure,
　　And like a traitor slain,
　And I'd be burned at a stake,
　　Altho I be the queen.'

7 He then steppd out at her room-door,
　　All in an angry mood,
　Untill he met a leper-man,
　　Just by the hard way-side.

8 He intoxicate the leper-man,
　　With liquors very sweet,
　And gave him more and more to drink,
　　Until he fell asleep.

9 He took him in his arms two,
　　And carried him along,
　Till he came to the queen's own bed,
　　And there he laid him down.

10 He then steppd out of the queen's
　　　bower,
　　As swift as any roe,
　Till he came to the very place
　　Where the king himself did go.

11 The king said unto Rodingham,
　　What news have you to me?
　He said, Your queen's a false woman,
　　As I did plainly see.

12 He hastend to the queen's chamber,
　　So costly and so fine,
　Until he came to the queen's own bed,
　　Where the leper-man was lain.

13 He looked on the leper-man,
　　Who lay on his queen's bed;
　He lifted up the snaw-white sheets,
　　And thus he to him said.

14 'Plooky, plooky are your cheeks,
　　And plooky is your chin,
　And plooky are your armis twa,
　　My bonny queen's layne in.

15 'Since she has lain into your arms,
　　She shall not lye in mine;
　Since she has kissd your ugsome mouth,
　　She never shall kiss mine.'

16 In anger he went to the queen,
　　Who fell upon her knee;
　He said, You false, unchaste woman,
　　What's this you've done to me?

17 The queen then turnd herself about,
    The tear blinded her ee:
    ' There 's not a knight in a' your court
    Dare give that name to me.'

18 He said, 'T is true that I do say;
    For I a proof did make;
    You shall be taken from my bower,
    And burned at a stake.

19 ' Perhaps I 'll take my word again,
    And may repent the same,
    If that you 'll get a Christian man
    To fight that Rodingham.'

20 ' Alass ! alass ! ' then cried our queen,
    ' Alas, and woe to me !
    There 's not a man in all Scotland
    Will fight with him for me.'

21 She breathed unto her messengers,
    Sent them south, east, and west;
    They could find none to fight with
      him,
    Nor enter the contest.

22 She breathed on her messengers,
    She sent them to the north;
    And there they found Sir Hugh le
      Blond,
    To fight him he came forth.

23 When unto him they did unfold
    The circumstance all right,
    He bade them go and tell the queen
    That for her he would fight.

24 The day came on that was to do
    That dreadful tragedy;
    Sir Hugh le Blond was not come up,
    To fight for our lady.

25 ' Put on the fire,' the monster said,
    ' It is twelve on the bell; '
    ''T is scarcely ten, now,' said the
      king,
    ' I heard the clock mysell.'

26 Before the hour the queen is brought,
    The burning to proceed;
    In a black velvet chair she 's set,
    A token for the dead.

27 She saw the flames ascending high,
    The tears blinded her ee:

    ' Where is the worthy knight,' she said
    ' Who is to fight for me ? '

28 Then up and spak the king himsell:
    ' My dearest, have no doubt,
    For yonder comes the man himsel,
    As bold as eer set out.'

29 They then advanced to fight the duel,
    With swords of temperd steel;
    Till down the blood of Rodingham
    Came running to his heel.

30 Sir Hugh took out a lusty sword,
    'T was of the metal clear,
    And he has pierced Rodingham
    Till 's heart-blood did appear.

31 'Confess your treachery, now,' he said,
    ' This day before you die;'
    ' I do confess my treachery,
    I shall no longer lye.

32 ' I like to wicked Haman am,
    This day I shall be slain:'
    The queen was brought to her chamber,
    A good woman again.

33 The queen then said unto the king,
    Arbattle 's near the sea;
    Give it unto the northern knight,
    That this day fought for me.

34 Then said the king, Come here, Sir
      Knight,
    And drink a glass of wine,
    And, if Arbattle 's not enough,
    To it we 'll Fordoun join.

C

' Sir Hugh le Blond,' Dr. Joseph Robertson's
Note-Book, January 1, 1830, p. 6.

1 THEY 've putten her into prison strang,
    A twalmon lang and mair,
    Until the mice and wild rottens
    Did tear her yellow hair.

    *   *   *   *   *

2 'One shake o your han,' said Rodingham,
    ' One shak o your han gie me: '
    ' I cam na here for shaking hans,
    But to fight maist desperatelie.'

3 ' It 's nae ten strucken on the clock,
  Nor eleven on the bell: '
  ' We 'll doe ill deeds anew ere night,
  Tho it were strucken twall.'

60

KING ESTMERE

' King Estmere ' occurred at page 249 of
Percy's folio manuscript, but the three leaves
on which it was written were " unfortunately
torn out " by Percy to send to the press, and
the genuine form of the ballad was thereby put
beyond recovery.

We are told by Percy in a note to stanza 63,
that though liberties have been taken with that
portion of the ballad which follows, yet wherever the fourth edition differs from the preceding ones it has been brought nearer to the
folio. Some notes of readings of the folio
are also furnished in the fourth edition (and are
here restored) which were not given in the
others. While we cannot but be vexed that
so distinguished a ballad, not injured much, so
far as we can see, by time, should not come
down to us as it came to Percy, our loss must
not be exaggerated. The changes made by
the editor, numerous enough, no doubt, cannot
be very material until we approach the end.
Stanzas 63–66 are entirely suspicious.

' King Estmere ' resembles in a general way
a series of German poems in which a young
king (or his guardians) is nice about a wife,
and the princess proposed to him is won only
with great difficulty : Ornit, Hugdietrich, Os-
wald, Orendel, Dietwart (in Dietrichs Flucht).
The names of Adler and Estmere appear again
in a short romance in the Percy manuscript
(Hales and Furnivall, II, 296), in which the
story is that of Hugdietrich in the Helden-
buch.

  a. Percy's Reliques, ed. of 1794, I, 64. b.
Edition of 1765, I, 58.

1 HEARKEN to me, gentlemen,
  Come and you shall heare;
  Ile tell you of two of the boldest brether
  That ever borne were.

2 The tone of them was Adler Younge,
  The tother was Kyng Estmere;
  The were as bolde men in their deeds
  As any were, farr and neare.

3 As they were drinking ale and wine
  Within his brother's hall,

' When will ye marry a wyfe, brother,
  A wyfe to glad us all ? '

4 Then bespake him Kyng Estmere,
  And answered him hartilye:
  ' I know not that ladye in any land,
  That 's able to marrye with mee.'

5 ' Kyng Adland hath a daughter, bro-
     ther,
  Men call her bright and sheene;
  If I were kyng here in your stead,
  That ladye shold be my queene.'

6 Saies, Reade me, reade me, deare bro-
     ther,
  Throughout merry England,
  Where we might find a messenger
  Betwixt us towe to sende.

7 Saies, You shal ryde yourselfe, brother,
  Ile beare you companye;
  Many a man throughe fals messengers
     is deceived,
  And I feare lest soe shold wee.

8 Thus the renisht them to ryde,
  Of twoe good renisht steeds,
  And when the came to King Adlands
     halle,
  Of redd gold shone their weeds.

9 And when the came to Kyng Adlands
     hall,
  Before the goodlye gate,
  There they found good Kyng Adland
  Rearing himselfe theratt.

10 ' Now Christ thee save, good Kyng
      Adland;
  Now Christ you save and see: '
  Sayd, You be welcome, King Estmere,
  Right hartilye to mee.

11 ' You have a daughter,' said Adler
      Younge,
  ' Men call her bright and sheene;
  My brother wold marrye her to his
     wiffe,
  Of Englande to be queene.'

12 ' Yesterday was att my deere daughter
  The king his sonne of Spayn,
  And then she nicked him of naye,
  And I doubt sheele do you the same.

13 'The kyng of Spayne is a foule paynim,
    And 'leeveth on Mahound,
    And pitye it were that fayre ladye
    Shold marry a heathen hound.'

14 ' But grant to me,' sayes Kyng Estmere,
    ' For my love I you praye,
    That I may see your daughter deere
    Before I goe hence awaye.'

15 ' Although itt is seven yeers and more
    Since my daughter was in halle,
    She shall come once downe for your
        sake,
    To glad my guestës alle.'

16 Downe then came that mayden fayre,
    With ladyes laced in pall,
    And halfe a hundred of bold knightes,
    To bring her [from] bowre to hall,
    And as many gentle squiers,
    To tend upon them all.

17 The talents of golde were on her head
        sette
    Hanged low downe to her knee,
    And everye ring on her small finger
    Shone of the chrystall free.

18 Saies, God you save, my deere madam,
    Saies, God you save and see:
    Said, You be welcome, Kyng Estmere,
    Right welcome unto mee.

19 ' And, if you love me, as you saye,
    Soe well and hartilee,
    All that ever you are comen about
    Soone sped now itt shal bee.'

20 Then bespake her father deare:
    My daughter, I saye naye;
    Remember well the kyng of Spayne,
    What he sayd yesterdaye.

21 ' He wold pull downe my halles and
        castles,
    And reave me of my lyfe;
    I cannot blame him if he doe,
    If I reave him of his wyfe.

22 ' Your castles and your towres, father,
    Are stronglye built aboute,
    And therefore of the king his sonne of
        Spaine
    Wee neede not stande in doubt.

23 ' Plight me your troth, nowe, Kyn|
        Estmere,
    By heaven and your righte hand,
    That you will marrye me to your wyfe
    And make me queene of your land.'

24 Then Kyng Estmere he plight hi'
        troth,
    By heaven and his righte hand,
    That he wolde marrye her to his wyfe,
    And make her queene of his land.

25 And he tooke leave of that ladye fayre
    To goe to his owne countree,
    To fetche him dukes and lordes an|
        knightes,
    That marryed the might bee.

26 They had not ridden scant a myle,
    A myle forthe of the towne,
    But in did come the kyng of Spayne,
    With kempës many one.

27 But in did come the kyng of Spayne,
    With manye a bold barone,
    Tone day to marrye Kyng Adland
        daughter,
    Tother daye to carrye her home.

28 Shee sent one after Kyng Estmere,
    In all the spede might bee,
    That he must either turne againe an|
        fighte,
    Or goe home and loose his ladye.

29 One whyle then the page he went,
    Another while he ranne;
    Till he had oretaken King Estmere,
    I-wis he never blanne.

30 ' Tydings, tydings, Kyng Estmere ! '
    ' What tydings nowe, my boye ? '
    ' O tydinges I can tell to you,
    That will you sore annoye.

31 ' You had not ridden scant a mile,
    A mile out of the towne,
    But in did come the kyng of Spayne,
    With kempës many a one.

32 ' But in did come the kyng of Spayne,
    With manye a bold barone,
    Tone daye to marrye King Adland
        daughter,
    Tother daye to carry her home.

3 'My ladye fayre she greetes you well,
  And ever-more well by mee;
You must either turne againe and fighte,
  Or goe home and loose your ladye.'

4 Saies, Reade me, reade me, deere brother,
  My reade shall ryse at thee,
Whether it is better to turne and fighte,
  Or goe home and loose my ladye.

5 'Now hearken to me,' sayes Adler
    Yonge,
  'And your reade must rise at me;
I quicklye will devise a waye
  To sette thy ladye free.

6 'My mother was a westerne woman,
  And learned in gramarye,
And when I learned at the schole,
  Something shee taught itt mee.

7 'There growes an hearbe within this field,
  And iff it were but knowne,
His color, which is whyte and redd,
  It will make blacke and browne.

8 'His color, which is browne and blacke,
  Itt will make redd and whyte;
That sworde is not in all Englande
  Upon his coate will byte.

9 'And you shal be a harper, brother,
  Out of the north countrye,
And Ile be your boy, soe faine of fighte,
  And beare your harpe by your knee.

10 'And you shal be the best harper
  That ever tooke harpe in hand,
And I wil be the best singer
  That ever sung in this lande.

11 'Itt shal be written in our forheads,
  All and in grammarye,
That we towe are the boldest men
  That are in all Christentye.'

12 And thus they renisht them to ryde,
  Of tow good renisht steedes,
And when they came to King Adlands
    hall,
  Of redd gold shone their weedes.

13 And whan the came to Kyng Adlands
    hall
  Untill the fayre hall-yate,

There they found a proud porter,
  Rearing himselfe thereatt.

44 Sayes, Christ thee save, thou proud por-
    ter,
  Sayes, Christ thee save and see:
'Nowe you be welcome,' sayd the porter,
  'Of what land soever ye bee.'

45 'Wee beene harpers,' sayd Adler Younge,
  'Come out of the northe countrye;
Wee beene come hither untill this place
  This proud weddinge for to see.'

46 Sayd, And your color were white and
    redd,
  As it is blacke and browne,
I wold saye King Estmere and his brother
  Were comen untill this towne.

47 Then they pulled out a ryng of gold,
  Layd itt on the porters arme:
'And ever we will thee, proud porter,
  Thow wilt saye us no harme.'

48 Sore he looked on Kyng Estmere,
  And sore he handled the ryng,
Then opened to them the fayre hall-yates,
  He lett for no kind of thyng.

49 Kyng Estmere he stabled his steede
  Soe fayre att the hall-bord;
The froth that came from his brydle
    bitte
  Light in Kyng Bremors beard.

50 Saies, Stable thy steed, thou proud
    harper,
  Saies, Stable him in the stalle;
It doth not beseeme a proud harper
  To stable his steed in a kyngs halle.

51 'My ladde he is so lither,' he said,
  'He will doe nought that's meete;
And is there any man in this hall
  Were able him to beate?'

52 'Thou speakst proud words,' sayes the
    king of Spaine,
  'Thou harper, here to mee;
There is a man within this halle
  Will beate thy ladd and thee.

53 'O let that man come downe,' he said,
  A sight of him wold I see;

And when hee hath beaten well my ladd,
 Then he shall beate of mee.'

54 Downe then came the kemperye man,
 And looked him in the eare;
For all the gold that was under hea-
  ven,
 He durst not neigh him neare.

55 'And how nowe, kempe,' said the kyng
  of Spaine,
 'And how, what aileth thee ?'
He saies, It is writt in his forhead,
 All and in gramarye,
That for all the gold that is under
  heaven,
 I dare not neigh him nye.

56 Then Kyng Estmere pulld forth his
  harpe,
 And plaid a pretty thinge;
The ladye upstart from the borde,
 And wold have gone from the king.

57 'Stay thy harpe, thou proud harper,
 For Gods love I pray thee;
For and thou playes as thou beginns,
 Thou 'lt till my bryde from mee.'

58 He stroake upon his harpe againe,
 And playd a pretty thinge;
The ladye lough a loud laughter,
 As shee sate by the king.

59 Saies, Sell me thy harpe, thou proud
  harper,
 And thy stringës all;
For as many gold nobles thou shalt have,
 As heere bee ringes in the hall.

60 'What wold ye doe with my harpe,' he
  sayd,
 'If I did sell itt yee ?'
'To playe my wiffe and me a fitt,
 When abed together wee bee.'

61 'Now sell me,' quoth hee, 'thy bryde
  soe gay,
 As shee sitts by thy knee;
And as many gold nobles I will give
 As leaves been on a tree.'

62 'And what wold ye doe with my bryde
  soe gay,
 Iff I did sell her thee ?

More seemelye it is for her fayre body
 To lye by mee then thee.'

63 Hee played agayne both loud and shrille
 And Adler he did syng,
'O ladye, this is thy owne true love,
 Noe harper, but a kyng.

64 'O ladye, this is thy owne true love,
 As playnlye thou mayest see,
And Ile rid thee of that foule paynim
 Who partes thy love and thee.'

65 The ladye looked, the ladye blushte,
 And blushte and lookt agayne,
While Adler he hath drawne his brande
 And hath the sowdan slayne.

66 Up then rose the kemperye men,
 And loud they gan to crye:
'Ah ! traytors, yee have slayne our
  kyng,
 And therefore yee shall dye.'

67 Kyng Estmere threwe the harpe asyde
 And swith he drew his brand,
And Estmere he and Adler Yonge
 Right stiffe in stour can stand.

68 And aye their swordes soe sore can byte,
 Throughe help of gramarye,
That soone they have slayne the kem-
  pery men,
 Or forst them forth to flee.

69 Kyng Estmere tooke that fayre ladye,
 And marryed her to his wiffe,
And brought her home to merry Eng-
  land,
 With her to lead his life.

61

SIR CAWLINE

The copy of this ballad in the Percy manuscript, the only one known to exist, shows very
great carelessness on the part of the transcriber, or of some predecessor. It begins
with two stanzas, which manifestly belong to
an historical ballad, and have only a verbal
connection with what follows. There is a
large omission after the 125th verse (the 28th
stanza as here printed), though the writing is
continuous. There are also several difficult or

nintelligible passages, even more than are
sually met with in this manuscript. As
ublished in the Reliques of Ancient Eng-
sh Poetry, ' Sir Cawline ' is extended to nearly
wice the amount of what is found in the
anuscript, and a tragical turn is forced upon
he story.

' Sir Cawline ' may possibly be formed upon
romance in stanzas which itself was composed
rom earlier ballads. The first adventure re-
embles one in the romance of Eger, Grime and
ray-Steel. Gervase of Tilbury has a story of
n ancient entrenchment in the bishopric of Ely,
here anybody could have a passage at arms
ith an unearthly warrior, by moonlight only,
y simply calling out, " Come, knight, and meet
night." Scott has introduced a spectral com-
at of this sort into his Marmion, Canto iii,
s. 23–25. Cf. also the Old French Lai de
Espine, wrongly ascribed to Marie de France.
'here is a close resemblance between ' Sir
awline ' and the story of Sir Eglamour (Thorn-
n Romances, p. 121 ; Percy MS., Hales and
urnivall, II, 341).

Percy MS., p. 368 ; Hales and Furnivall,
I, 3.

*   *   *   *   *

1 AND in *tha*t land dwells a king
     W*h*ich does beare the bell ouer all,
     And wi*th* him there dwelled a curteous
         k*n*ight,
     Sir Cawline men him call.

2 And he hath a ladye to his daughter,
     Of ffashyon shee hath noe peere;
     K*n*igh*t*s and lordes they woed her both,
     Trusted to haue beene her feere.

3 Sir Cawline loues her best of onë,
     But nothing durst hee say
     To discreeue his councell to noe man,
     But deerlye loued this may.

4 Till itt beffell vpon a day,
     Great dill to him was dight;
     The maydens loue remoued his mind,
     To care-bed went the knight.

5 And one while he spread his armes him
         ffroe,
     And cryed soe pittyouslye:
     ' Ffor the maydens loue *tha*t I haue
         most minde
     This day may comfort mee,

Or else ere noone I shalbe dead '
     Thus can S*i*r Cawline say.

6 When our p*a*rish masse *tha*t itt was
         done,
     And our king was bowne to dine,
     He sayes, Where is S*i*r Cawline,
     *Tha*t was wont to serue me wi*th* ale
         and wine ?

7 But then answered a curteous k*n*igh*t*,
     Ffast his hands wringinge:
     ' S*i*r Cawline 's sicke, and like to be de*a*d
     W*i*thout and a good leedginge.'

8 ' Ffeitch yee downe my daughter deere,
     Shee is a leeche ffull ffine;
     I, and take you doe and the baken
         bread,
     And drinke he on the wine soe red,
     And looke no daynti is ffor him to deare,
     For ffull loth I wold him tine.'

9 This ladye is gone to his chamber,
     Her maydens ffollowing nye;
     ' O well,' shee sayth, ' how doth my
         lord ? '
     ' O sicke ! ' againe saith hee.

10 ' I, but rise vp wightlye, man, for
         shame !
     Neuer lye here soe cowardlye !
     Itt is told in my ffathers hall,
     Ffor my loue you will dye.'

11 ' Itt is ffor your loue, ffayre ladye,
     *Tha*t all this dill I drye;
     Ffor if you wold comfort me wi*th* a kisse,
     Then were I brought ffrom bale to blisse,
     Noe longer here wold I lye.'

12 ' Alas ! soe well you know, S*i*r k*n*ight,'
     .   .   .   .   .

     .   .   .   .   .

13 .   .   .   .   .   .
     I cannott bee yo*u*r peere:
     ' Ffor some deeds of armes ffaine wold
         I doe,
     To be yo*u*r bacheeleere.'

14 ' Vpon Eldrige Hill there growes a
         thorne,
     Vpon the mores brodinge;

And wold you, sir knight, wake there
  all night
To day of the other morninge ?

15 ' Ffor the eldrige king, that is mickle of
    might,
  Will examine you beforne;
  And there was neuer man that bare his
    liffe away
  Since the day that I was borne.'

16 ' But I will ffor your sake, ffaire ladye,
  Walke on the bents [soe] browne,
  And Ile either bring you a readye token,
  Or Ile neuer come to you againe.'

17 But this ladye is gone to her chamber,
  Her maydens ffollowing bright,
  And Sir Cawlin 's gone to the mores soe
    broad,
  Ffor to wake there all night.

18 Vnto midnight [that] the moone did
    rise,
  He walked vp and downe,
  And a lightsome bugle then heard he
    blow,
  Ouer the bents soe browne;
  Saies hee, And if cryance come vntill my
    hart,
  I am ffarr ffrom any good towne.

19 And he spyed, ene a litle him by,
  A ffuryous king and a ffell,
  And a ladye bright his brydle led,
  That seemlye itt was to see.

20 And soe fast hee called vpon Sir Caw-
    line,
  Oh man, I redd the fflye !
  Ffor if cryance come vntill thy hart,
  I am a-feard least thou mun dye.

21 He sayes, [No] cryance comes to my
    hart,
  Nor ifaith I ffeare not thee;
  Ffor because thou minged not Christ be-
    fore,
  Thee lesse me dreadeth thee.

22 But Sir Cawline he shooke a speare;
  The king was bold, and abode;
  And the timber these two children
    bore
  Soe soone in sunder slode;

Ffor they tooke and two good swords,
  And they layden on good loade.

23 But the elridge king was mickle
    might,
  And stiffly to the ground did stand;
  But Sir Cawline, with an aukewar
    stroke,
  He brought ffrom him his hand,
  I, and fflying ouer his head soe hye,
  [It] ffell downe of that lay land.

24 And his lady stood a litle thereby,
  Ffast ringing her hands:
  ' For the maydens loue that you hau
    most minde,
  Smyte you my lord no more.

25 ' And hees neuer come vpon Eldrig
    [Hill],
  Him to sport, gamon, or play,
  And to meete noe man of middle-eart
  And that liues on Christs his lay.'

26 But he then vp and that eldryge king,
  Sett him in his sadle againe,
  And that eldryge king and his ladye
  To their castle are they gone.

27 And hee tooke then vp and that eldryg
    sword,
  As hard as any fflynt,
  And soe he did those ringes fiue,
  Harder then ffyer, and brent.

28 Ffirst he presented to the kings daughte
  The hand, and then the sword,
  .   .   .   .

*   *   *   *   *

29 ' But a serre buffett you haue him giuen
  The king and the crowne,' shee sayd;
  ' I, but four and thirty stripes
  Comen beside the rood.'

30 And a gyant that was both stiffe [and
    strong,
  He lope now them amonge,
  And vpon his squier fiue heads he bare
  Vnmackley made was hee.

31 And he dranke then on the kings wine,
  And hee put the cup in his sleeue,

And all thé trembled and were wan,
Ffor feare he shold them greeffe.

32 ' Ile tell thee mine arrand, king,' he
    says,
  ' Mine errand what I doe heere;
Ffor I will bren thy temples hye,
  Or Ile haue thy daughter deere;
I, or else vpon yond more soe brood
  Thou shalt ffind mee a ppeare.'

33 The king he turned him round about,
  Lord, in his heart he was woe !
Says, Is there noe knight of the Round
    Table
  This matter will vndergoe ?

34 ' I, and hee shall haue my broad lands,
  And keepe them well his liue;
I, and soe hee shall my daughter deere,
  To be his weded wiffe.'

35 And then stood vp Sir Cawline,
  His owne errand ffor to say:
' Ifaith, I wold to God, Sir,' sayd Sir
    Cawline,
  ' That soldan I will assay.

36 ' Goe ffeitch me downe my eldrige
    sword,
  Ffor I woone itt att ffray:'
' But away, away ! ' sayd the hend sol-
    dan,
  ' Thou tarryest mee here all day ! '

37 But the hend soldan and Sir Cawline
  Thé ffought a summers day;
Now has hee slaine that hend soldan,
  And brought his fiue heads away.

38 And the king has betaken him his broade
    lands,
  And all his venison;

  .   .   .   .   .   .
    .   .   .   .   .

39 ' But take you doo and your lands [soe]
    broad,
  And brooke them well your liffe;
Ffor you promised mee your daughter
    deere,
  To be my weded wiffe.'

40 ' Now by my ffaith,' then sayes our king,
  ' Ffor that wee will not striffe,

Ffor thou shalt haue my daughter dere,
  To be thy weded wiffe.'

41 The other morninge Sir Cawline rose
  By the dawning of the day,
And vntill a garden did he goe
  His mattins ffor to say;
And that bespyed a ffalse steward,
  A shames death that he might dye !

42 And he lett a lyon out of a bande,
  Sir Cawline ffor to teare;
And he had noe wepon him vpon,
  Nor noe wepon did weare.

43 But hee tooke then his mantle of greene,
  Into the lyons mouth itt thrust;
He held the lyon soe sore to the wall
  Till the lyons hart did burst.

44 And the watchmen cryed vpon the walls
  And sayd, ' Sir Cawline 's slaine !
And with a beast is not ffull litle,
  A lyon of mickle mayne:'
Then the kings daughter shee ffell
    downe,
  ' For peerlesse is my payne ! '

45 ' O peace, my lady ! ' sayes Sir Caw-
    line,
  ' I haue bought thy loue ffull deere;
O peace, my lady ! ' sayes Sir Cawline,
  ' Peace, lady, ffor I am heere ! '

46 Then he did marry this kings daughter,
  With gold and siluer bright,
And fiftene sonnes this ladye beere
  To Sir Cawline the knight.

62

FAIR ANNIE

A and B were not printed till the beginning
of the nineteenth century. A was obtained
" chiefly from the recitation of an old woman,"
but we are not informed who supplied the rest.
A fragment (D) printed by Herd in 1769 (before any of the nine other versions), furnished
stanzas 2–6, 12, 17, 19. A doubt may be hazarded whether stanzas 8–10 came from the old
woman.

The Scandinavian ballad of ' Fair Annie '
(Grundtvig, No. 258) is preserved in Danish
and Swedish, and is in the main identical in

plot with the English. It was perhaps transmitted from Low German. Various Dutch and German versions are also preserved. The story is also told in the Lai del Fresne of Marie de France (about 1180). This tale, of Breton origin, is some four hundred years older than any manuscript of the ballad. Comparison, however, shows that it is not the source either of the English or of the Low German and Scandinavian ballad. The tale and the ballad have a common source, which lies too far back for us to find.

A

'Lord Thomas and Fair Annie,' Minstrelsy of the Scottish Border, II, 102, 1802, chiefly from the recitation of an old woman residing near Kirkhill, in West Lothian.

1 'It 's narrow, narrow, make your bed,
    And learn to lie your lane;
For I 'm ga'n oer the sea, Fair Annie,
    A braw bride to bring hame.
Wi her I will get gowd and gear;
    Wi you I neer got nane.

2 'But wha will bake my bridal bread,
    Or brew my bridal ale?
And wha will welcome my brisk bride,
    That I bring oer the dale?'

3 'It 's I will bake your bridal bread,
    And brew your bridal ale,
And I will welcome your brisk bride,
    That you bring oer the dale.'

4 'But she that welcomes my brisk bride
    Maun gang like maiden fair;
She maun lace on her robe sae jimp,
    And braid her yellow hair.'

5 'But how can I gang maiden-like,
    When maiden I am nane?
Have I not born seven sons to thee,
    And am with child again?'

6 She 's taen her young son in her arms,
    Another in her hand,
And she 's up to the highest tower,
    To see him come to land.

7 'Come up, come up, my eldest son,
    And look oer yon sea-strand,
And see your father's new-come bride,
    Before she come to land.'

8 'Come down, come down, my mother dear,
    Come frae the castle wa!
I fear, if langer ye stand there,
    Ye 'll let yoursell down fa.'

9 And she gaed down, and farther down,
    Her love's ship for to see,
And the topmast and the mainmast
    Shone like the silver free.

10 And she 's gane down, and farther down,
    The bride's ship to behold,
And the topmast and the mainmast
    They shone just like the gold.

11 She 's taen her seven sons in her hand,
    I wot she didna fail;
She met Lord Thomas and his bride,
    As they came oer the dale.

12 'You 're welcome to your house, Lord Thomas,
    You 're welcome to your land;
You 're welcome with your fair ladye,
    That you lead by the hand.

13 'You 're welcome to your ha's, ladye,
    You 're welcome to your bowers;
You 're welcome to your hame, ladye,
    For a' that 's here is yours.'

14 'I thank thee, Annie; I thank thee, Annie,
    Sae dearly as I thank thee;
You 're the likest to my sister Annie,
    That ever I did see.

15 'There came a knight out oer the sea,
    And steald my sister away;
The shame scoup in his company,
    And land whereer he gae!'

16 She hang ae napkin at the door,
    Another in the ha,
And a' to wipe the trickling tears,
    Sae fast as they did fa.

17 And aye she served the lang tables,
    With white bread and with wine,
And aye she drank the wan water,
    To had her colour fine.

18 And aye she served the lang tables,
    With white bread and with brown;

And ay she turned her round about,
Sae fast the tears fall down.

19 And he's taen down the silk napkin,
Hung on a silver pin,
And aye he wipes the tear trickling
A' down her cheik and chin.

20 And aye he turn'd him round about,
And smil'd amang his men;
Says, Like ye best the old ladye,
Or her that's new come hame?

21 When bells were rung, and mass was
sung,
And a' men bound to bed,
Lord Thomas and his new-come bride
To their chamber they were gaed.

22 Annie made her bed a little forbye,
To hear what they might say;
'And ever alas!' Fair Annie cried,
'That I should see this day!

23 'Gin my seven sons were seven young
rats,
Running on the castle wa,
And I were a grey cat mysell,
I soon would worry them a'.

24 'Gin my seven sons were seven young
hares,
Running oer yon lilly lee,
And I were a grew hound mysell,
Soon worried they a' should be.'

25 And wae and sad Fair Annie sat,
And drearie was her sang,
And ever, as she sobbd and grat,
'Wae to the man that did the wrang!'

26 'My gown is on,' said the new-come
bride,
'My shoes are on my feet,
And I will to Fair Annie's chamber,
And see what gars her greet.

27 'What ails ye, what ails ye, Fair
Annie,
That ye make sic a moan?
Has your wine barrels cast the girds,
Or is your white bread gone?

28 'O wha was't was your father, Annie,
Or wha was't was your mother?

And had ye ony sister, Annie,
Or had ye ony brother?'

29 'The Earl of Wemyss was my father,
The Countess of Wemyss my mother;
And a' the folk about the house
To me were sister and brother.'

30 'If the Earl of Wemyss was your father,
I wot sae was he mine;
And it shall not be for lack o gowd
That ye your love sall tine.

31 'For I have seven ships o mine ain,
A' loaded to the brim,
And I will gie them a' to thee,
Wi four to thine eldest son:
But thanks to a' the powers in heaven
That I gae maiden hame!'

B

'Burd Helen,' Jamieson's Popular Ballads,
II, 376, from the recitation of Mrs Arrot, of
Aberbrothick.

1 THERE livd a lord on yon sea-side,
And he thought on a wile,
How he would go over the saut sea
A lady to beguile.

2 'O learn to mak your bed, Helen,
And learn to ly your lane,
For I'm gaun over the saut seas
A bright bride to bring hame.'

3 'How can I mak my bed,' she says,
'Unless I mak it wide,
Whan I have seven o your sons
To lie down by my side?

4 'And the first o your seven sons,
He rides a milk-white steed;
The second o your seven sons
He wears a milk-white weed.

5 'The third ane o your seven sons,
He draws baith ale and wine;
The fourth ane o your seven sons,
He serves you when you dine.

6 'The fifth ane o your seven sons,
He can baith read and write;
And the sixth ane o your seven sons,
He is a' your heart's delight.

7 ' And the youngest o your seven sons,
    He sleeps on my breast-bane;
Whan him and I ly down at night,
    For him rest get I nane.'

8 ' O wha will bake my bridal bread,
    And brew my bridal ale ?
And wha will welcome my gae lady,
    That I bring oer the dale ?

9 ' And sin ye 've taen the turn in hand,
    See that ye do it right,
And ilka chimly o the house,
    That they be dearly dight.'

10 O a' the day she washd and wrang,
    And a' the night she buik,
And she 's awa to her chamber,
    To gie her young son suck.

11 ' Come here, come here, my eldest son,
    And see what ye may see;
For yonder comes your father dear,
    Your mother-in-law side be.'

12 She 's taen a cake o the best bread,
    A bottle o the best wine,
And a' the keys upon her arm,
    And to the yates she 's gaen.

13 ' Ye are welcome hame, gay lady,' she
    said,
    ' And ay ye are welcome hame;
And sae is a' the gentlewomen
    That 's wi you ridden and gane.

14 ' You are welcome hame, gay lord,' she
    said,
    ' And ay ye are welcome hame;
And sae is a' the gentlemen
    That 's wi you ridden and gane.'

15 She saird them up, she saird them down,
    She saird them till and frae;
But when she went behind their backs,
    The tear did blind her ee.

16 Whan day was gane, and night was
    come,
    And a' man boun to bed,
The bridegroom and the bonny bride
    In their chamber was laid.

17 Burd Helen and her seven sons
    Lay in a bower near by;

. . . . .
   . . . . . .

18 ' If my seven sons were seven grey ratts,
    To rin frae wa to wa,
And I mysel a good grey cat,
    I would bite their back a-twa.

19 ' If my seven sons were seven grey hares,
    And them to rin a race,
And I mysel a good greyhound,
    I would gie them a chace.'

20 Up and spak the bonny bride,
    In chamber where she lay:
' There is a lady in this bower,
    She will gae mad or day.'

21 ' Lye still, lye still, my bonny bride,
    Lie still and tak a sleep;
It 's but ane o my wine puncheons;
    Nae langer wad it keep.'

22 ' King Henry was my father dear,
    Queen Catherine was my mother,
Lady Anne she was my sister dear,
    And Frederick was my brother.

23 ' And whan I was six years of age,
    They ca'd me Mary Mild;
I was stown frae my father's yate,
    Whan I was but a child.'

24 Then up and spak the bonny bride,
    By her lord as she lay:
' Lye down, lye down, my dear sister,
    There 's nae ill done for me.

25 ' O seven ships conveyd me here,
    And seven came oer the main;
And four o them shall stay wi you,
    And three convey me hame.

26 ' But when I gae hame to my father's
    house,
    They will laugh me to scorn,
To come awa a wedded wife,
    Gae hame a maid the morn.'

E

' Lady Jane,' Jamieson-Brown MS., p. 20 ;
Jamieson's Popular Ballads, II, 371.

1 ' O WHA will bake my bridal bread,
    And brew my bridal ale ?

Wha will welcome my bright bride,
   That I bring oer the dale?'

2 'O I will bake your bridal bread,
   An brew your bridal ale;
An I will welcome your bright bride,
   That you bring oer the dale.'

3 'O she that welcomes my bright bride
   Maun gang like maiden fair;
She maun lace her in her green cloathin,
   And braid her yellow hair.'

4 'O how can I gang maiden like,
   Whan maiden I am nane?
Whan I ha born you seven sons,
   An am wi bairn again?'

5 The lady stood in her bowr door
   An lookit oer the lan,
An there she saw her ain good lord,
   Leadin his bride by the han.

6 She's dressd her sons i the scarlet
   red,
   Hersel i the dainty green,
An tho her cheek lookd pale and wan,
   She well might ha been a queen.

7 She calld upon her eldest son:
   'Look yonder what you see;
For yonder comes your father dear,
   Your step-mother him wi.

8 'O you'r welcome hame, my ain good
   lord,
   To your ha's but an your bowrs;
You'r welcome hame, my ain good
   lord,
   To your castles an your towrs:
Sae is your bright bride you beside,
   She's fairer nor the flowers.'

9 'O whatn a lady's that?' she says,
   'That welcoms you an me?
If I'm lang lady about this place,
   Some good I will her dee.
She looks sae like my sister Jane,
   Was stoln i the bowr frae me.'

10 O she has servd the lang tables,
   Wi the white bread an the wine;
But ay she drank the wan water,
   To keep her colour fine.

11 An she gid by the first table,
   An leugh amo them a';
But ere she reachd the second table,
   She let the tears down fa.

12 She's taen a napkin lang an white,
   An hung't upon a pin;
It was to dry her watry eyes,
   As she went out and in.

13 Whan bells were rung, an mass was
   sung,
   An a' man boun to bed,
The bride but an the bonny bridegroom
   In ae chamber was laid.

14 She's taen her harp intill her han,
   To harp this twa asleep;
An ay as she harped an she sang,
   Full sorely did she weep.

15 'O seven fu fair sons I have born
   To the good lord o this place,
An I wish that they were seven hares,
   To run the castle race,
An I mysel a good gray houn,
   An I woud gi them chase.

16 'O seven fu fair sons I have born
   To the good lord o this ha;
I wish that they were seven rottons,
   To rin the castle wa,
An I mysell a good gray cat,
   I wot I woud worry them a'.

17 'The earle o Richmond was my father,
   An the lady was my mother,
An a' the bairns bisides mysel
   Was a sister an a brother.'

18 'Sing on, sing on, ye gay lady,
   I wot ye hae sung in time;
Gin the earle o Richmond was your
   father,
   I wot sae was he mine.'

19 'Rise up, rise up, my bierly bride;
   I think my bed's but caul;
I woudna hear my lady lament
   For your tocher ten times taul.

20 'O seven ships did bring you here,
   An an sal tak you hame;
The leve I'll keep to your sister Jane,
   For tocher she gat nane.'

63

CHILD WATERS

The variations in the several versions of this charming ballad, which has perhaps no superior in English, and if not in English perhaps nowhere, are not material. An exceedingly popular Scandinavian ballad (Grundtvig, No. 267) is manifestly of the same source, though the story is told in a very different way, the cruel trials to which the woman's love is put being entirely lacking. Another Scandinavian ballad (Grundtvig, No. 249) has a limited resemblance to 'Child Waters,' and there is a Piedmontese ballad (Nigra, No. 35) which has a good many similar incidents.

A

'Childe Waters,' Percy MS., p. 274; Hales and Furnivall, II, 269.

1 CHILDE WATTERS in his stable stoode,
 And stroaket his milke-white steede;
To him came a ffaire young ladye
 As ere did weare womans wee[de].

2 Saies, Christ you saue, good Chyld Waters !
Sayes, Christ you saue and see !
My girdle of gold, which was too longe,
Is now to short ffor mee.

3 ' And all is with one chyld of yours,
 I ffeele sturre att my side;
My gowne of greene, it is to strayght;
 Before it was to wide.'

4 'If the child be mine, Faire Ellen,' he sayd,
' Be mine, as you tell mee,
Take you Cheshire and Lancashire both,
Take them your owne to bee.

5 'If the child be mine, Ffaire Ellen,' he said,
' Be mine, as you doe sweare,
Take you Cheshire and Lancashire both,
And make that child your heyre.'

6 Shee saies, I had rather haue one kisse,
Child Waters, of thy mouth,
Then I wold haue Cheshire and Lancashire both,
That lyes by north and south.

7 ' And I had rather haue a twinkling,
 Child Waters, of your eye,
Then I wold haue Cheshire and Lanca-
shire both,
 To take them mine oune to bee.'

8 'To-morrow, Ellen, I must forth ryde
 Soe ffarr into the north countrye;
The ffairest lady that I can ffind,
 Ellen, must goe with mee.'
' And euer I pray you, Child Watters,
 Your ffootpage let me bee !'

9 'If you will my ffootpage be, Ellen,
 As you doe tell itt mee,
Then you must cutt your gownne of
greene
 An inche aboue your knee.

10 ' Soe must you doe your yellow lockes,
 Another inch aboue your eye;
You must tell noe man what is my
name;
 My ffootpage then you shall bee.'

11 All this long day Child Waters rode,
 Shee ran bare ffoote by his side;
Yett was he neuer soe curteous a knight
 To say, Ellen, will you ryde ?

12 But all this day Child Waters rode,
 Shee ran barffoote thorow the broome;
Yett he was neuer soe curteous a knight
 As to say, Put on your shoone.

13 ' Ride softlye,' shee said, ' Child Waters;
 Why doe you ryde soe ffast ?
The child which is no mans but yours
 My bodye itt will burst.'

14 He says, Sees thou yonder water, Ellen,
 That fflowes from banke to brim ?
'I trust to God, Child Waters,' shee said,
 ' You will neuer see mee swime.'

15 But when shee came to the waters side,
 Shee sayled to the chinne:
' Except the lord of heauen be my speed,
 Now must I learne to swime.'

16 The salt waters bare vp Ellens clothes,
 Our Ladye bare vpp he[r] chinne,

And Child Waters was a woe man, good
    Lord,
    To ssee Faire Ellen swime.

7 And when shee ouer the water was,
    Shee then came to his knee:
    He said, 'Come hither, Ffaire Ellen,
    Loe yonder what I see !

8 'Seest thou not yonder hall, Ellen ?
    Of redd gold shine the yates;
    There 's four and twenty ffayre ladyes,
    The ffairest is my wordlye make.

9 'Seest thou not yonder hall, Ellen ?
    Of redd gold shineth the tower;
    There is four and twenty ffaire ladyes,
    The fairest is my paramoure.'

0 'I doe see the hall now, Child Waters,
    That of redd gold shineth the yates;
    God giue good then of *your* selfe,
    And of *your* wordlye make !

1 'I doe see the hall now, Child Waters,
    That of redd gold shineth the tower;
    God giue good then of *your* selfe,
    And of *your* paramoure ! '

2 There were four and twenty ladyes,
    Were playing att the ball,
    And Ellen, was the ffairest ladye,
    Must bring his steed to the stall.

3 There were four and twenty faire ladyes
    Was playing att the chesse;
    And Ellen, shee was the ffairest ladye,
    Must bring his horsse to grasse.

4 And then bespake Child Waters sister,
    And these were the words said shee:
    You haue the prettyest ffootpage, bro-
      ther,
    That euer I saw *with* mine eye;

5 'But *that* his belly it is soe bigg,
    His girdle goes wonderous hye;
    And eu*er* I pray you, Child Waters,
    Let him goe into the chamber *with*
      mee.'

6 'It is more meete for a little ffootpage,
    That has run through mosse and mire,
    To take his supper vpon his knee
    And sitt downe by the kitchin fyer,

Then to goe into the chamber *with* any
    ladye
    That weares soe [rich] attyre.'

27 But when thé had supped euery one,
    To bedd they took the way;
    He sayd, Come hither, my little footpage,
    Harken what I doe say.

28 And goe thee downe into yonder towne,
    And low into the street;
    The ffairest ladye *that* thou can find,
    Hyer her in mine armes to sleepe,
    And take her vp in thine armes two,
    For filinge of her ffeete.

29 Ellen is gone into the towne,
    And low into the streete;
    The fairest ladye *that* shee cold find
    Shee hyred in his armes to sleepe,
    And tooke her in her armes two,
    For filing of her ffeete.

30 'I pray you now, good Child Waters,
    That I may creepe in att *your* bedds
      feete;
    For there is noe place about this house
    Where I may say a sleepe.'

31 This [night] and itt droue on affterward
    Till itt was neere the day:
    He sayd, Rise vp, my litle ffoote-page,
    And giue my steed corne and hay;
    And soe doe thou the good blacke oates,
    That he may carry me the better away.

32 And vp then rose Ffaire Ellen,
    And gaue his steed corne and hay,
    And soe shee did and the good blacke
      oates,
    That he might carry him the better
      away.

33 Shee layned her backe to the manger
      side,
    And greiuouslye did groane;
    And *that* beheard his mother deere,
    And heard her make her moane.

34 Shee said, Rise vp, thou Child Waters,
    I thinke thou art a cursed man;
    For yonder is a ghost in thy stable,
    That greiuouslye doth groane,
    Or else some woman laboures of child,
    Shee is soe woe begone.

35 But vp then rose Child Waters,
    And did on his shirt of silke;
Then he put on his other clothes
    On his body as white as milke.

36 And when he came to the stable-dore,
    Full still *that* hee did stand,
That hee might heare now Faire Ellen,
    How shee made her monand.

37 Shee said, Lullabye, my owne deere
    child !
    Lullabye, deere child, deere !
I wold thy father were a king,
    Thy mother layd on a beere !

38 'Peace now,' he said, 'good Faire Ellen,
    And be of good cheere, I thee pray,
And the bridall and the churching both,
    They shall bee vpon one day.'

B

a. 'Burd Ellen,' Jamieson-Brown MS., p. 22, taken down from Mrs Brown's recitation before 1783. **b.** A. Fraser Tytler's Brown MS., No. 9, as recited by Mrs Brown in 1800.

1 'I WARN ye all, ye gay ladies,
    That wear scarlet an brown,
That ye dinna leave your father's house,
    To follow young men frae town.'

2 'O here am I, a lady gay,
    That wears scarlet an brown,
Yet I will leave my father's house,
    An follow Lord John frae the town.'

3 Lord John stood in his stable-door,
    Said he was bound to ride;
Burd Ellen stood in her bowr-door,
    Said she 'd rin by his side.

4 He 's pitten on his cork-heeld shoone,
    An fast awa rade he;
She 's clade hersel in page array,
    An after him ran she.

5 Till they came till a wan water,
    An folks do ca it Clyde;
Then he 's lookit oer his left shoulder,
    Says, Lady, can ye wide ?

6 'O I learnt it i my father house,
    An I learnt it for my weal,

Wenneer I came to a wan water,
    To swim like ony eel.'

7 But the firstin stap the lady stappit,
    The water came til her knee;
'Ohon, alas !' said the lady,
    'This water 's oer deep for me.'

8 The nextin stap the lady stappit,
    The water came till her middle;
An sighin says that gay lady,
    I 've wat my gouden girdle.

9 The nextin stap the lady stappit,
    The water came till her pap;
An the bairn that was in her twa sides
    For caul begane to quake.

10 'Lye still, lye still, my ain dear babe,
    Ye work your mither wae;
Your father rides on high horse-back,
    Cares little for us twae.'

11 O about the midst o Clyden water
    There was a yeard-fast stane;
He lightly turnd his horse about,
    An took her on him behin.

12 'O tell me this now, good Lord John,
    An a word ye dinna lee,
How far it is to your lodgin,
    Whare we this night maun be ?'

13 'O see you nae yon castle, Ellen,
    That shines sae fair to see ?
There is a lady in it, Ellen,
    Will sunder you an me.

14 'There is a lady in that castle
    Will sunder you and I:'
'Betide me well, betide me wae,
    I sal go there an try.'

15 'O my dogs sal eat the good white bread,
    An ye sal eat the bran;
Then will ye sigh, an say, alas !
    That ever I was a man !'

16 'O I sal eat the good white bread,
    An your dogs sal eat the bran;
An I hope to live an bless the day,
    That ever ye was a man.'

17 'O my horse sal eat the good white meal,
    An ye sal eat the corn;

Then will ye curse the heavy hour
   That ever your love was born.'

28 'O I sal eat the good white meal,
   An your horse sal eat the corn;
An I ay sall bless the happy hour
   That ever my love was born.'

29 O four an twenty gay ladies
   Welcomd Lord John to the ha,
But a fairer lady then them a'
   Led his horse to the stable sta.

30 An four an twenty gay ladies
   Welcomd Lord John to the green,
But a fairer lady than them a'
   At the manger stood alane.

31 Whan bells were rung, an mass was sung,
   An a' men boun to meat,
Burd Ellen at a bye-table
   Amo the foot-men was set.

32 'O eat an drink, my bonny boy,
   The white bread an the beer:'
'The never a bit can I eat or drink,
   My heart's sae full of fear.'

33 'O eat an drink, my bonny boy,
   The white bread an the wine:'
'O I canna eat nor drink, master,
   My heart's sae full of pine.'

34 But out it spake Lord John's mother,
   An a wise woman was she:
'Whare met ye wi that bonny boy,
   That looks sae sad on thee?

35 'Sometimes his cheek is rosy red,
   An sometimes deadly wan;
He's liker a woman big wi bairn,
   Than a young lord's serving man.'

36 'O it makes me laugh, my mother dear,
   Sic words to hear frae thee;
He is a squire's ae dearest son,
   That for love has followd me.

37 'Rise up, rise up, my bonny boy,
   Gi my horse corn an hay:'
'O that I will, my master dear,
   As quickly as I may.'

38 She's taen the hay under her arm,
   The corn intill her han,

An she's gane to the great stable,
   As fast as eer she can.

29 'O room ye roun, my bonny broun steeds,
   O room ye near the wa;
For the pain that strikes me thro my sides
   Full soon will gar me fa.'

30 She's leand her back against the wa;
   Strong travail seizd her on;
An even amo the great horse feet
   Burd Ellen brought forth her son.

31 Lord John'[s] mither intill her bowr
   Was sitting all alone,
Whan, i the silence o the night,
   She heard fair Ellen's moan.

32 'Won up, won up, my son,' she says,
   'Go se how a' does fare;
For I think I hear a woman's groans,
   An a bairn greeting sair.'

33 O hastily he gat him up,
   Stayd neither for hose nor shoone,
An he's doen him to the stable-door,
   Wi the clear light o the moon.

34 He strack the door hard wi his foot,
   An sae has he wi his knee,
An iron locks an iron bars
   Into the floor flung he:
'Be not afraid, Burd Ellen,' he says,
   'Ther's nane come in but me.'

35 Up he has taen his bonny young son,
   An gard wash him wi the milk;
An up has he taen his fair lady,
   Gard row her in the silk.

36 'Cheer up your heart, Burd Ellen,' he
   says,
'Look nae mair sad nor wae;
For your marriage an your kirkin too
   Sal baith be in ae day.'

64

FAIR JANET

There are points of resemblance between
'Fair Janet' and a ballad very popular in
Scandinavia, 'King Valdemar and his Sister'
(Grundtvig, No. 126), and also in Germany

(e. g., Müllenhoff, Sagen u. s. w. der Herzog-thümer Schleswig-Holstein und Lauenburg, p. 492; Wunderhorn, 1808, II, 272). In both the Scandinavian and the German, however, the dancing is expressly devised as a test, and there are unspeakably ferocious features which are wanting in the Scottish ballad. A Breton ballad (Luzel, II, 6–15) likewise has the probation by dancing.

A

'Fair Janet,' Sharpe's Ballad Book, p. 1, as sung by an old woman in Perthshire.

1 'Ye maun gang to your father, Janet,
　Ye maun gang to him soon;
　Ye maun gang to your father, Janet,
　In case that his days are dune.'

2 Janet's awa to her father,
　As fast as she could hie:
'O what's your will wi me, father?
　O what's your will wi me?'

3 'My will wi you, Fair Janet,' he said,
'It is both bed and board;
　Some say that ye loe Sweet Willie,
　But ye maun wed a French lord.'

4 'A French lord maun I wed, father?
　A French lord maun I wed?
　Then, by my sooth,' quo Fair Janet,
'He's neer enter my bed.'

5 Janet's awa to her chamber,
　As fast as she could go;
　Wha's the first ane that tapped there,
　But Sweet Willie her jo?

6 'O we maun part this love, Willie,
　That has been lang between;
　There's a French lord coming oer the sea,
　To wed me wi a ring;
　There's a French lord coming oer the sea,
　To wed and tak me hame.'

7 'If we maun part this love, Janet,
　It causeth mickle woe;
　If we maun part this love, Janet,
　It makes me into mourning go.'

8 'But ye maun gang to your three sisters,
　Meg, Marion, and Jean;

Tell them to come to Fair Janet,
　In case that her days are dune.'

9 Willie's awa to his three sisters,
　Meg, Marion, and Jean:
'O haste, and gang to Fair Janet,
　I fear that her days are dune.'

10 Some drew to them their silken hose,
　Some drew to them their shoon,
　Some drew to them their silk manteils
　Their coverings to put on,
　And they're awa to Fair Janet,
　By the hie light o the moon.

*　　*　　*　　*　　*

11 'O I have born this babe, Willie,
　Wi mickle toil and pain;
　Take hame, take hame, your babe, Willie,
　For nurse I dare be nane.'

12 He's tane his young son in his arms,
　And kisst him cheek and chin,
　And he's awa to his mother's bower,
　By the hie light o the moon.

13 'O open, open, mother,' he says,
'O open, and let me in;
　The rain rains on my yellow hair,
　And the dew drops oer my chin,
　And I hae my young son in my arms,
　I fear that his days are dune.'

14 With her fingers lang and sma
　She lifted up the pin,
　And with her arms lang and sma
　Received the baby in.

15 'Gae back, gae back now, Sweet Willie,
　And comfort your fair lady;
　For where ye had but ae nourice,
　Your young son shall hae three.'

16 Willie he was scarce awa,
　And the lady put to bed,
　Whan in and came her father dear:
'Make haste, and busk the bride.'

17 'There's a sair pain in my head, father,
　There's a sair pain in my side;
　And ill, O ill, am I, father,
　This day for to be a bride.'

18 'O ye maun busk this bonny bride,
      And put a gay mantle on;
   For she shall wed this auld French
          lord,
      Gin she should die the morn.'

19 Some pat on the gay green robes,
      And some pat on the brown;
   But Janet put on the scarlet robes,
      To shine foremost throw the town.

20 And some they mounted the black steed,
      And some mounted the brown;
   But Janet mounted the milk-white steed,
      To ride foremost throw the town.

21 'O wha will guide your horse, Janet?
      O wha will guide him best?'
   'O wha but Willie, my true-love?
      He kens I loe him best.'

22 And when they cam to Marie's kirk,
      To tye the haly ban,
   Fair Janet's cheek looked pale and wan,
      And her colour gaed an cam.

23 When dinner it was past and done,
      And dancing to begin,
   'O we 'll go take the bride's maidens,
      And we 'll go fill the ring.'

24 O ben than cam the auld French lord,
      Saying, Bride, will ye dance with me?
   'Awa, awa, ye auld French lord,
      Your face I downa see.'

25 O ben than cam now Sweet Willie,
      He cam with ane advance:
   'O I 'll go tak the bride's maidens,
      And we 'll go tak a dance.'

26 'I 've seen ither days wi you, Willie,
      And so has mony mae,
   Ye would hae danced wi me mysel,
      Let a' my maidens gae.'

27 O ben than cam now Sweet Willie,
      Saying, Bride, will ye dance wi me?
   'Aye, by my sooth, and that I will,
      Gin my back should break in three.'

28 She had nae turned her throw the dance,
      Throw the dance but thrice,
   Whan she fell doun at Willie's feet,
      And up did never rise.

29 Willie 's taen the key of his coffer,
      And gien it to his man:
   'Gae hame, and tell my mother dear
      My horse he has me slain;
   Bid her be kind to my young son,
      For father he has nane.'

30 The tane was buried in Marie's kirk,
      And the tither in Marie's quire;
   Out of the tane there grew a birk,
      And the tither a bonny brier.

B

'Fair Janet and Sweet William,' Motherwell's MS., p. 357, from the recitation of
Agnes Lyle, Kilbarchan.

1 'IF you do love me weel, Willie,
      Ye 'll shew to me truelie;
   Ye 'll build to me a bonnie ship,
      And set her on the sea.'

2 He did love her very weel,
      He shewed to her trulie;
   He builded her a bonnie ship,
      And set her on the sea.

3 They had not sailed one league, one
          league,
      One league but only three,
   Till sharp, sharp showers fair Janet took,
      She grew sick and like to die.

4 'If you do love me weel, Willie,
      Ye 'll shew to me trulye;
   Ye 'll tak me to my mother's bower,
      Whare I was wont to be.'

5 He did love her very weel,
      He shewed to her trulye;
   He took her to her mother's bower,
      Whare she was wont to be.

6 'It 's ye 'll stand up at my richt side,
      You will on tiptaes stand,
   Until you hear your auld son weep,
      But an your Janet mourn.

7 'Come take your auld son in your arms,
      He is both large and lang;
   Come take your auld son in your arms,
      And for a nourice gang.'

8 He is to his mother's bowers,
      An hour or it struck nine:

'I have a babe into my arms,
  He'll die for nouricing.'

9 'Goe home, go home, my son,' she
      says,
  'And mak thy Jenny blythe;
  If ae nurse winna sere her son,
  It's I'll provide him five.'

10 Fair Janet was nae weel lichter,
   Nor weel doun on her side,
   Till ben and cam her father dear,
   Saying, Wha will busk our bride?

11 Ben and cam her brethren dear,
   Saying, Wha will busk our bride?
   And wha will saddle our bride's horse?
   Whom ahint will she ride?

12 'Hold your tongue, my brethren dear,
   And let your folly be,
   For I'm sae fair and full of hair
   Sma busking will serve me.

13 'Hold your tongue, my brethren dear,
   And let your folly be,
   For I will ride behint William,
   He will best wait on me.

14 'Willie, lay the saddle saft,
   And lead the bridle soun,
   And when we come to Mary's Kirk,
   Ye'll set me hooly down.'

15 Supper scarslie was owre,
   Nor musick weel fa'n to,
   Till ben and cam the bride's brethren,
   Saying, Bride, ye'll dance wi me:
   'Awa, awa, my brethren dear,
   For dancing's no for me.'

16 Ben and came her ain bridegroom,
   Saying, Bride, ye'll dance wi me;
   She says, Awa, awa, ye southland dog,
   Your face I downa see.

17 Ben and cam then Sweet Willie,
   Saying, Bride, ye'll dance wi me:
   'Oh I will dance the floor once owre,
   Tho my heart should break in three.'

18 'Oh no, oh no,' said Sweet William,
   'Let no such things eer be;
   But I will cut my glove in two,
   And I'll dance for thee and me.'

19 She hadna danced the floor once owre,
   I'm sure she hadna thrice,
   Till she fell in a deadly swound,
   And from it neer did rise.

20 Out and spak her ain bridegroom,
   And an angry man was he:
   'This day she has gien me the gecks,
   Yet she must bear the scorn;
   There's not a bell in merry Linkum
   Shall ring for her the morn.'

21 Out and spoke then Sweet William,
   And a sorry man was he:
   'Altho she has gien you the gecks,
   She will not bear the scorn;
   There's not a bell in merry Linkum
   But shall ring for her the morn.'

22 There was not a bell in merry Linkum
   But they tinkled and they rang,
   And a' the birds that flew above,
   They changed their notes and sang.

65

LADY MAISRY

'Lady Maisry' has a limited, and perhaps quite accidental resemblance to the Scandinavian-German ballad spoken of in the preface to 'Fair Janet' (No. 64).

A

'Lady Maisry,' Jamieson-Brown MS., p. 24; Jamieson's Popular Ballads, I, 73.

1 THE young lords o the north country
  Have all a wooing gone,
  To win the love of Lady Maisry,
  But o them she woud hae none.

2 O they hae courted Lady Maisry
  Wi a' kin kind of things;
  An they hae sought her Lady Maisry
  Wi brotches an wi rings.

3 An they ha sought her Lady Maisry
  Frae father and frae mother;
  An they ha sought her Lady Maisry
  Frae sister an frae brother.

4 An they ha followd her Lady Maisry
  Thro chamber an thro ha;

But a' that they coud say to her,
 Her answer still was Na.

5 'O had your tongues, young men,' she
  says,
 'An think nae mair o me;
For I 've gien my love to an English
  lord,
 An think nae mair o me.'

6 Her father's kitchy-boy heard that,
 An ill death may he dee !
An he is on to her brother,
 As fast as gang coud he.

7 'O is my father an my mother well,
 But an my brothers three ?
Gin my sister Lady Maisry be well,
 There 's naething can ail me.'

8 'Your father and your mother is well,
 But an your brothers three;
Your sister Lady Maisry 's well,
 So big wi bairn gangs she.'

9 'Gin this be true you tell to me,
 My mailison light on thee !
But gin it be a lie you tell,
 You sal be hangit hie.'

10 He 's done him to his sister's bowr,
 Wi meikle doole an care;
An there he saw her Lady Maisry,
 Kembing her yellow hair.

11 'O wha is aught that bairn,' he says,
 'That ye sae big are wi ?
And gin ye winna own the truth,
 This moment ye sall dee.'

12 She turnd her right an roun about,
 An the kem fell frae her han;
A trembling seizd her fair body,
 An her rosy cheek grew wan.

13 'O pardon me, my brother dear,
 An the truth I 'll tell to thee;
My bairn it is to Lord William,
 An he is betrothd to me.'

14 'O coud na ye gotten dukes, or lords,
 Intill your ain country,
That ye draw up wi an English dog,
 To bring this shame on me ?

15 'But ye maun gi up the English lord,
 Whan youre young babe is born;
For, gin you keep by him an hour
  langer,
 Your life sall be forlorn.'

16 'I will gi up this English blood,
 Till my young babe be born;
But the never a day nor hour langer,
 Tho my life should be forlorn.'

17 'O whare is a' my merry young men,
 Whom I gi meat and fee,
To pu the thistle and the thorn,
 To burn this wile whore wi ?'

18 'O whare will I get a bonny boy,
 To help me in my need,
To rin wi hast to Lord William,
 And bid him come wi speed ?'

19 O out it spake a bonny boy,
 Stood by her brother's side:
'O I would rin your errand, lady,
 Oer a' the world wide.

20 'Aft have I run your errands, lady,
 Whan blawn baith win and weet;
But now I 'll rin your errand, lady,
 Wi sat tears on my cheek.'

21 O whan he came to broken briggs,
 He bent his bow and swam,
An whan he came to the green grass
  growin,
 He slackd his shoone and ran.

22 O whan he came to Lord William's
  gates,
 He baed na to chap or ca,
But set his bent bow till his breast,
 An lightly lap the wa;
An, or the porter was at the gate,
 The boy was i the ha.

23 'O is my biggins broken, boy ?
 Or is my towers won ?
Or is my lady lighter yet,
 Of a dear daughter or son ?'

24 'Your biggin is na broken, sir,
 Nor is your towers won;
But the fairest lady in a' the lan
 For you this day maun burn.'

25 ' O saddle me the black, the black,
    Or saddle me the brown;
    O saddle me the swiftest steed
    That ever rade frae a town.'

26 Or he was near a mile awa,
    She heard his wild horse sneeze:
    ' Mend up the fire, my false brother,
    It 's na come to my knees.'

27 O whan he lighted at the gate,
    She heard his bridle ring:
    ' Mend up the fire, my false brother,
    It 's far yet frae my chin.

28 ' Mend up the fire to me, brother,
    Mend up the fire to me;
    For I see him comin hard an fast
    Will soon men 't up to thee.

29 ' O gin my hands had been loose, Willy,
    Sae hard as they are boun,
    I would have turnd me frae the gleed,
    And castin out your young son.'

30 ' O I 'll gar burn for you, Maisry,
    Your father an your mother;
    An I 'll gar burn for you, Maisry,
    Your sister an your brother.

31 ' An I 'll gar burn for you, Maisry,
    The chief of a' your kin;
    An the last bonfire that I come to,
    Mysel I will cast in.'

B

Motherwell's MS., p. 422, communicated by
Charles Kirkpatrick Sharpe.

1 IN came her sister,
    Stepping on the floor;
    Says, It 's telling me, my sister Janet,
    That you 're become a whore.

2 ' A whore, sister, a whore, sister ?
    That 's what I 'll never be;
    I 'm no so great a whore, sister,
    As liars does on me lee.'

3 In came her brother,
    Stepping on the floor;
    Says, It 's telling me, my sister Janet,
    That you 're become a whore.

4 ' A whore, brother, a whore, brother ?
    A whore I 'll never be;
    I 'm no so bad a woman, brother,
    As liars does on me lee.'

5 In came her mother,
    Stepping on the floor:
    ' They are telling me, my daughter,
    That you 're so soon become a whore.'

6 ' A whore, mother, a whore, mother ?
    A whore I 'll never be;
    I 'm only with child to an English lord,
    Who promised to marry me.'

7 In came her father,
    Stepping on the floor;
    Says, They tell me, my daughter Janet,
    That you are become a whore.

8 ' A whore, father, a whore, father ?
    A whore I 'll never be;
    I 'm but with child to an English lord,
    Who promisd to marry me.'

9 Then in it came an old woman,
    The lady's nurse was she,
    And ere she could get out a word
    The tear blinded her ee.

10 ' Your father 's to the fire, Janet,
    Your brother 's to the whin;
    All for to kindle a bold bonfire,
    To burn your body in.'

11 ' Where will I get a boy,' she said,
    ' Will gain gold for his fee,
    That would run unto fair England
    For my good lord to me ? '

12 ' O I have here a boy,' she said,
    ' Will gain gold to his fee,
    For he will run to fair England
    For thy good lord to thee.'

13 Now when he found a bridge broken,
    He bent his bow and swam,
    And when he got where grass did grow,
    He slacked it and ran.

14 And when he came to that lord's gate,
    Stopt not to knock or call,
    But set his bent bow to his breast
    And lightly leapt the wall:

And ere the porter could open the
    gate,
    The boy was in the hall,

5 In presence of that noble lord,
    And fell down on his knee:
    ' What is it, my boy,' he cried,
    ' Have you brought unto me ?

6 ' Is my building broke into ?
    Or is my towers won ?
    Or is my true-love delivered
    Of daughter or of son ? '

7 ' Your building is not broke,' he cried,
    ' Nor is your towers won,
    Nor is your true-love delivered
    Of daughter nor of son;
    But if you do not come in haste,
    Be sure she will be gone.

8 ' Her father is gone to the fire,
    Her brother to the whin,
    To kindle up a bold bonfire,
    To burn her body in.'

9 ' Go saddle to me the black,' he cried,
    ' And do it very soon;
    Get unto me the swiftest horse
    That ever rade from the town.'

10 The first horse that he rade upon,
    For he was raven black,
    He bore him far, and very far,
    But failed in a slack.

11 The next horse that he rode upon,
    He was a bonny brown;
    He bore him far, and very far,
    But did at last fall down.

12 The next horse that he rode upon,
    He as the milk was white;
    Fair fall the mare that foaled that foal
    Took him to Janet's sight !

13 And boots and spurs, all as he was,
    Into the fire he lap,
    Got one kiss of her comely mouth,
    While her body gave a crack.

14 ' O who has been so bold,' he says,
    ' This bonfire to set on ?
    Or who has been so bold,' he says,
    ' Her body for to burn ? '

25 ' O here are we,' her brother said,
    ' This bonfire who set on;
    And we have been so bold,' he said,
    ' Her body for to burn.'

26 ' O I 'll cause burn for you, Janet,
    Your father and your mother;
    And I 'll cause die for you, Janet,
    Your sister and your brother.

27 ' And I 'll cause mony back be bare,
    And mony shed be thin,
    And mony wife be made a widow,
    And mony ane want their son.'

66

LORD INGRAM AND CHIEL WYET

There is a Danish ballad (Grundtvig-Olrik,
No. 354) which has certain resemblances to
our English ballad. Ebbe Skammelsøn, being
obliged to absent himself from his plighted
maid for a considerable time, loses her through
the artifices of his brother, who pretends first
that Ebbe is unfaithful, and then that he is
dead. Ebbe is warned by a dream that his
brother is about to wed his mistress, goes home
in great haste, and arrives on the wedding day.
He kills the bride, and then his brother, who,
at the last moment, offers to cede the bride to
him, as Lord Ingram, in B 17, says he meant
to do. Ebbe after this begs his bread, or goes
on a pilgrimage weighted with iron on his hands
and loins ; wherein his part resembles Maisry's.

A

a. ' Lord Ingram and Chiel Wyet,' C. K.
Sharpe's MS., " second collection "; Mother-
well's Minstrelsy. p. 173, communicated by
Charles Kirkpatrick Sharpe. b. Maidment's
North Countrie Garland, p. 24, from tradition
in Aberdeenshire.

1 LORD INGRAM and Chiel Wyet
    Was baith born in one bower;
    Laid baith their hearts on one lady,
    The less was their honour.

2 Chiel Wyet and Lord Ingram
    Was baith born in one hall;
    Laid baith their hearts on one lady,
    The worse did them befall.

3 Lord Ingram wood her Lady Maisery
   From father and from mother;
   Lord Ingram wood her Lady Maisery
   From sister and from brother.

4 Lord Ingram wood her Lady Maisery
   With leave of a' her kin;
   And every one gave full consent,
   But she said no to him.

5 Lord Ingram wood her Lady Maisery
   Into her father's ha;
   Chiel Wyet wood her Lady Maisery
   Amang the sheets so sma.

6 Now it fell out upon a day,
   She was dressing her head,
   That ben did come her father dear,
   Wearing the gold so red.

7 He said, Get up now, Lady Maisery,
   Put on your wedding gown;
   For Lord Ingram he will be here,
   Your wedding must be done.

8 'I 'd rather be Chiel Wyet's wife,
   The white fish for to sell,
   Before I were Lord Ingram's wife,
   To wear the silk so well.

9 'I 'd rather be Chiel Wyet's wife,
   With him to beg my bread,
   Before I were Lord Ingram's wife,
   To wear the gold so red.

10 'Where will I get a bonny boy,
    Will win gold to his fee,
    And will run unto Chiel Wyet's,
    With this letter from me ?'

11 'O here I am,' the boy says,
    'Will win gold to my fee,
    And carry away any letter
    To Chiel Wyet from thee.'

12 And when he found the bridges broke,
    He bent his bow and swam;
    And when he found the grass growing,
    He hastened and he ran.

13 And when he came to Chiel Wyet's
    castle,
    He did not knock nor call,
    But set his bent bow to his breast,
    And lightly leaped the wall;

And ere the porter opend the gate,
   The boy was in the hall.

14 The first line that he looked on,
    A grieved man was he;
    The next line that he looked on,
    A tear blinded his ee:
    Says, I wonder what ails my one brothe
    He 'll not let my love be !

15 'But I 'll send to my brother's bridal –
    The bacon shall be mine —
    Full four and twenty buck and roe,
    And ten tun of the wine:
    And bid my love be blythe and glad,
    And I will follow syne.'

16 There was not a groom about that castl
    But got a gown of green,
    And all was blythe, and all was glad,
    But Lady Maisery was neen.

17 There was no cook about that kitchen
    But got a gown of gray,
    And all was blythe, and all was glad,
    But Lady Maisery was wae.

18 Between Mary Kirk and that castle
    Was all spread ower with garl,
    To keep Lady Maisery and her maiden
    From tramping on the marl.

19 From Mary Kirk to that castle
    Was spread a cloth of gold,
    To keep Lady Maisery and her maiden
    From treading on the mold.

20 When mass was sung, and bells wa
    rung,
    And all men bound for bed,
    Then Lord Ingram and Lady Maisery
    In one bed they were laid.

21 When they were laid into their bed —
    It was baith saft and warm —
    He laid his hand over her side,
    Says, I think you are with bairn.

22 'I told you once, so did I twice,
    When ye came me to woo,
    That Chiel Wyet, your only brother,
    One night lay in my bower.

23 'I told you twice, so did I thrice,
    Ere ye came me to wed,

That Chiel Wyet, your one brother,
   One night lay in my bed.'

24 'O will you father your bairn on me,
      And on no other man ?
   And I 'll give him to his dowry
      Full fifty ploughs of land.'

25 'I will not father my bairn on you,
      Nor on no wrongeous man,
   Though ye would give him to his dowry
      Five thousand ploughs of land.'

26 Then up did start him Chiel Wyet,
      Shed by his yellow hair,
   And gave Lord Ingram to the heart
      A deep wound and a sair.

27 Then up did start him Lord Ingram,
      Shed by his yellow hair,
   And gave Chiel Wyet to the heart
      A deep wound and a sair.

28 There was no pity for that two lords,
      Where they were lying slain;
   But all was for her Lady Maisery,
      In that bower she gaed brain.

29 There was no pity for that two lords,
      When they were lying dead;
   But all was for her Lady Maisery,
      In that bower she went mad.

30 Said, Get to me a cloak of cloth.
      A staff of good hard tree;
   If I have been an evil woman,
      I shall beg till I dee.

31 'For a bit I 'll beg for Chiel Wyet,
      For Lord Ingram I 'll beg three;
   All for the good and honorable marriage
      At Mary Kirk [he] gave me.'

B

'Lord Ingram and Gil Viett,' Skene MS.,
p. 16; taken down in the North of Scotland,
1802–1803.

1 LORD INGRAM and Gil Viett
      Were baith born in ae ha;
   They laid their love on ae lady,
      An fate they coud na fa.

2 Lord Ingram and Gil Viett
      Were baith laid in ae wame;

They laid their love on ae lady,
   The greater was their shame.

3 Lord Ingram wood her Lady Masery
      Frae father and frae mither;
   Gil Viett wood her Lady Masery
      Frae sister and frae brither.

4 Lord Ingram courted her Lady Masery
      Among the company a';
   Jill Viett he wood her Lady Masery
      Among the sheets so sma.

5 'Get up, my daughter dear,
      Put on your bridal gown;
   This day 's your bridal day
      Wi Lord Ingram.'

6 'How can I get up,
      An put on my bridal gown,
   Or how marry the ae brither,
      An the tither's babe in my womb ?'

   *   *   *   *   *

7 'O laugh you at mysell, brither,
      Or at my companie ?
   Or laugh ye at my bonnie bride,
      She wad na laugh at thee ?'

8 'I laugh na at yoursel, brither,
      Nor at your companie;
   Nor laugh I at your buirlie bride,
      She wad na laugh at me.

9 'But there 's a brotch on a breast-bane,
      A garlan on ane's hair;
   Gin ye kend what war under that,
      Ye wad neer love woman mair.

10 'There is a brotch on a breast-bane,
      An roses on ane's sheen;
   Gin ye kend what war under that,
      Your love wad soon be deen.'

11 Whan bells were rung, and mass was
         sung,
      And a' man boun to bed,
   Lord Ingram and Lady Masery
      In ae chamer were laid.

12 He put his hand out oure his bonnie bride,
      The babe between her sides did quake·

   .   .   .   .   .   .
      .   .   .   .   .

13 'O father your babe on me, Lady
        Masery,
    O father your babe on me.'

.   .   .   .   .   .

.   .   .   .   .   .

14 'I may father my babe on a stock,
    Sae may I on a stane,
    But my babe shall never hae
    A father but its ain.'

15 He took out a brand,
    And laid it atween them twa;

.   .   .   .   .

.   .   .   .   .

16 Gill Viett took out a long brand,
    And stroakd it oer a stro,
    An thro and thro Lord Ingram's bodie
    He made it come and go.

17 'Wae mat worth ye, Gill Viett,
    An ill died mat ye die!
    For I han the cup in my hand
    To hae drunken her oer to thee.'

18 '[For] ae mile [I wad gae] for Gil Viett,
    For Lord Ingram I wad hae gaen
        three;
    An a' for that in good kirk-door
    Fair wedding he gave me.'

19 Gil Viett took a long brand,
    An stroakd it on a stro,
    An through and thro his ain bodie
    He made it come and go.

20 There was nae mean made for that godd
        lords,
    In bowr whar they lay slain,
    But a' was for that lady,
    In bowr whar she gaed brain.

21 There was nae mean made for that lady,
    In bowr whar she lay dead,
    But a' was for the bonnie babe
    That lay blabbering in her bleed.

C

'Auld Ingram,' Herd's MSS., i, 169, ii, 84;
'Lord Wa'yates and Auld Ingram,' Jamieson's
Popular Ballads, ii, 265.

1. LADY MAISDRY was a lady fair,
    She maid her mither's bed;

Auld Ingram was an aged knight,
    And hee sought her to wed.

2 ''T is I forbid ye, Auld Ingram,
    For to seek me to spouse;
    For Lord Wayets, your sister's son,
    Has been into my bowrs.

3 ''T is I forbid ye, Auld Ingram,
    For to seek me to wed;
    For Lord Wayets, your sister's son,
    Has been into my bed.'

4 'T is he has bought to this lady
    The robes of the brown;
    'And ever alas,' says this lady,
    'The robs will pit mee down!'

5 And he has bought to this lady
    The robs of the red;
    'And ever alas,' says this lady,
    'The robs will be my dead!'

6 And he has bought to this lady
    The chrystal and the lammer,
    Sae has hee bought to her mither
    The curches of the cammer.

7 Every ane o her se'n brethren
    They had a hawk in hand,
    And every lady i the place
    They got a goud garland.

8 Every cuk in that kitchen
    They gat a noble claith;
    A' was blyth at Auld Ingram's cuming
    But Lady Maisdrey was wraith.

9 'Whare will I get a bonny boy,
    Wad fain wun hos and shoon,
    That wud rin on to my Wayets,
    And quickly cume again?'

10 'Here am I, a bonny boy,
    Wad fain wun hoes and shoon,
    Wha wull rin on to your Wayets,
    And quickly cume again.'

11 'Ye 'l bid him, and ye 'l pray him baith,
    Gif ony prayer can dee,
    To Mary Kirk to cume the morn,
    My weary wadding to see.'

12 Lord Wayets lay our his castle wa,
    Beheld baith dale and down,

And he beheld a bonny boy
  Cume rinnen to the town.

3 'What news, what news, ye bonny boy?
  What news ye hae to mee?

. . . . . .

. . . . . .

4 'O is my ladie's fauldis brunt?
  Or is her towrs wun?
Or is my Maisdrey lighter yet
  A dear dochter or sun?'

5 'Your ladie's faulds they are not brunt,
  Nor yet are her towrs wun,
Neither is Maisdrey lighter yet
  A dear dochter or sun.

6 'But she bids ye and she prays ye
    baith,
  Gif ony prayer can dee,
To Mary Kirk to cume the morn,
  Her weary wadding to see.'

7 He dung the boord up wi his fit,
  Sae did he wi his tae;
The silver cup that sat upon 't
  I the fire he gard it flee:
'O what na a lord in a' Scotland
  Dare marry my Maisdrey?'

8 'O 't is but a feeble thought
  To tell the tane and not the tither;
O 't is but a feeble thought
  To tell 't is your mither's brither.'

9 ''T is I wull send to that wadding,
  And I wul follow syne,
The fitches o the fallow deer
  An the gammons o the swine,
An the nine hides o the noble cow;
  'T was slain in season time.

10 ''T is I wul send to that wadding
  Ten ton of the red wyne;
Much more I 'll send to that wadding,
  An I wul follow syne.'

11 When he came in unto the ha,
  Lady Maisdrey she did ween,
And twenty times he kist her mou
  Before Auld Ingram's een.

12 Nor to the kirk she wud ne gae,
  Nor til 't she wudn ride,

Till four and twunty men she gat her
    before,
  An twunty on ilka side,
An four and twunty milk-white dows
  To flee aboon her head.

23 A loud laughter gae Lord Wayets
  Mang the mids o his men:
'Marry the lady wham they weel,
  A maiden she is nane.'

24 'O laugh ye at my men, Wayets?
  Or di ye laugh at me?
Or laugh ye at the beerly bride,
  That 's gane to marry me?'

25 'I laugh na at your men, uncle,
  Nor yet dive I at thee,
Bit I laugh at my lands sae braid,
  Sae weel 's I do them see.'

26 Whan ene was cume, and ene-bells rung,
  An a' man gane to bed,
The bride bit and the silly bridegroom
  In chambers they were laid.

27 Was na it a fell thing for to see,
  Twa heads lye on a coad,
Lady Maisdrey like the moten goud,
  Auld Ingram like a toad?

28 He turnd his face unto the stock,
  And sound he fell asleep;
She turnd her fair face unto the wa,
  An sa't tears she did weep.

29 It fell about the mark midnight,
  Auld Ingram began to turn him;
He pat his hands on 's lady's sides,
  An waly, sair was she murnin.

30 'What aileth thee, my lady dear?
  Ever alas and wae 's me,
There is a baube betwixt thy sides!
  O sae sair 's it grieves me.'

31 'Didn I tell ye that, Auld Ingram,
  Or ye saught me to wed,
That Lord Wayets, your sister's son,
  Had been into my bed?'

32 'O father that bairn on me, Maisdrey,
  O father it on me,
An ye sall hae a rigland shire
  Your mornin's gift to bee.'

33 'O sarbit,' says the Lady Maisdrey,
   'That ever the like me befa,
  To father my bairn on Auld Ingram,
   Lord Wayets in my father's ha !

34 'O sarbit,' says the Lady Maisdrey,
   'That ever the like me betide,
  To father my bairn on Auld Ingram,
   An Lord Wayets beside !'

67

GLASGERION

'Glasgerion' was first printed in Percy's
Reliques, III, 43, 1765, and was not thought by
the editor to require much correction. Certainly the English ballad is one which it would
be hard to mend. Scottish B is mainly of
good derivation (a poor old woman in Aberdeenshire), and has some good stanzas, but
Jamieson unfortunately undertook to improve
a copy in which the story was complete, but
"the diction much humbled," by combining
with it a fragment of another version. 'The
Bret Glascurion' is joined in Chaucer's House
of Fame, iii, 111–118, with the harpers Orpheus, Orion (Arion), and Chiron. 'Bret' is
Briton, and Y Bardd Glas Keraint, in English
Keraint the Blue Bard (Blue Bard being an
appellation of a chief bard, who wore an offi-
cial robe of blue), is recorded to have been an
eminent poet of distinguished birth, son of
Owain, Prince of Glamorgan. There is at
least no absurdity in the suggestion that the
Glascurion of Chaucer and the Glasgerion of
the ballad may represent the Welsh Glas
Keraint.

A

'Glasgerion,' Percy MS., p. 94; Hales and
Furnivall, I, 248.

1 GLASGERION was a kings owne sonne,
   And a harper he was good;
  He harped in the kings chamber,
   Where cuppe and candle stoode,
  And soe did hee in the queens chamber,
   Till ladies waxed wood.

2 And then bespake the kings daughter,
   And these words thus sayd shee:

  .   .   .   .   .
    .   .   .   .

3 Saide, Strike on, strike on, Glasgerrion,
   Of thy striking doe not blinne;

There 's neuer a stroke comes ouer th
   harpe
  But it glads my hart within.

4 'Faire might you fall, lady !' quoth he
   'Who taught you now to speake ?
  I haue loued you, lady, seuen yeere;
   My hart I durst neere breake.'

5 'But come to my bower, my Glasgerryo
   When all men are att rest;
  As I am a ladie true of my promise,
   Thou shalt bee a welcome guest.'

6 But hom then came Glasgerryon,
   A glad man, Lord, was hee:
  'And come thou hither, Iacke, my bo
   Come hither vnto mee.

7 'For the kings daughter of Normandy
   Her loue is granted mee,
  And beffore the cocke haue crowen,
   Att her chamber must I bee.'

8 'But come you hither, master,' quoth he
   'Lay your head downe on this stone
  For I will waken you, master deere,
   Afore it be time to gone.'

9 But vpp then rose that lither ladd,
   And did on hose and shoone;
  A coller he cast vpon his necke,
   Hee seemed a gentleman.

10 And when he came to that ladies cham
   ber,
  He thrild vpon a pinn;
  The lady was true of her promise,
   Rose vp and lett him in.

11 He did not take the lady gay
   To boulster nor to bedd,
  But downe vpon her chamber-flore
   Full soone he hath her layd.

12 He did not kisse that lady gay
   When he came nor when he youd;
  And sore mistrusted that lady gay
   He was of some churlës blood.

13 But home then came that lither ladd,
   And did of his hose and shoone,
  And cast that coller from about h
   necke;
  He was but a churlës sonne:

'Awaken,' quoth hee, 'my master deere,
    I hold it time to be gone.

4 'For I haue sadled your horsse, master,
    Well bridled I haue your steed;
Haue not I serued a good breakfast,
    When time comes I haue need.'

5 But vp then rose good Glasgerryon,
    And did on both hose and shoone,
And cast a coller about his necke;
    He was a kingës sonne.

6 And when he came to that ladies cham-
        ber,
    He thrild vpon a pinn;
The lady was more then true of promise,
    Rose vp and let him in.

17 Saies, Whether haue you left with me
    Your braclett or your gloue?
Or are you returned backe againe
    To know more of my loue?

18 Glasgerryon swore a full great othe,
    By oake and ashe and thorne,
'Lady, I was neuer in your chamber
    Sith the time that I was borne.'

19 'O then it was your litle foote-page
    Falsly hath beguiled me:'
And then shee pulld forth a litle pen-
        kniffe,
    That hanged by her knee,
Says, There shall neuer noe churlës blood
    Spring within my body.

20 But home then went Glasgerryon,
    A woe man, good [Lord], was hee;
Sayes, Come hither, thou Iacke, my boy,
    Come thou hither to me.

21 Ffor if I had killed a man to-night,
    Iacke, I wold tell it thee;
But if I haue not killed a man to-night,
    Iacke, thou hast killed three!

22 And he puld out his bright browne
        sword,
    And dryed it on his sleeue,
And he smote off that lither ladds head,
    And asked noe man noe leaue.

23 He sett the swords poynt till his brest,
    The pumill till a stone;

Thorrow that falsenese of that lither ladd
    These three liues werne all gone.

B

'Glenkindie,' Jamieson's Popular Ballads, 1
93, taken from the recitation of an old woman
by Professor Scott, of Aberdeen, and "somewhat improved" by a fragment communicated
by the Rev. William Gray, of Lincoln.

1 GLENKINDIE was ance a harper gude,
    He harped to the king;
And Glenkindie was ance the best harper
    That ever harpd on a string.

2 He'd harpit a fish out o saut water,
    Or water out o a stane,
Or milk out o a maiden's breast,
    That bairn had never nane.

3 He's taen his harp intil his hand,
    He harpit and he sang,
And ay as he harpit to the king,
    To haud him unthought lang.

4 'I'll gie you a robe, Glenkindie,
    A robe o the royal pa,
Gin ye will harp i the winter's night
    Afore my nobles a'.'

*   *   *   *   *

5 He's taen his harp intill his hand,
    He's harpit them a' asleep,
Except it was the young countess,
    That love did waukin keep.

6 And first he has harpit a grave tune,
    And syne he has harpit a gay,
And mony a sich atween hands
    I wat the lady gae.

7 Says, Whan day is dawen, and cocks hae
        crawen,
    And wappit their wings sae wide,
It's ye may come to my bower-door,
    And streek you by my side.

8 But look that ye tell na Gib, your man,
    For naething that ye dee;
For, an ye tell him Gib, your man,
    He'll beguile baith you and me.

9 He's taen his harp intill his hand,
    He harpit and he sang,

And he is hame to Gib, his man,
　　As fast as he could gang.

10 'O mith I tell you, Gib, my man,
　　Gin I a man had slain?'
　'O that ye micht, my gude master,
　　Altho ye had slain ten.'

11 'Then tak ye tent now, Gib, my
　　man,
　　My bidden for to dee;
　And but an ye wauken me in time,
　　Ye sall be hangit hie.

12 'Whan day has dawen, and cocks hae
　　crawen,
　　And wappit their wings sae wide,
　I 'm bidden gang till yon lady's
　　bower,
　　And streek me by her side.'

13 'Gae hame to your bed, my good mas-
　　ter;
　　Ye 've waukit, I fear, oer lang;
　For I 'll wauken you in as good time
　　As ony cock i the land.'

14 He 's taen his harp intill his hand,
　　He harpit and he sang,
　Until he harpit his master asleep,
　　Syne fast awa did gang.

15 And he is till that lady's bower,
　　As fast as he could rin;
　When he cam till that lady's bower,
　　He chappit at the chin.

16 'O wha is this,' says that lady,
　　'That opens nae and comes in?'
　'It 's I, Glenkindie, your ain true-
　　love,
　　O open and lat me in!'

17 She kent he was nae gentle knicht
　　That she had latten in,
　For neither when he gaed nor cam,
　　Kist he her cheek or chin.

18 He neither kist her when he cam,
　　Nor clappit her when he gaed,
　And in and at her bower window,
　　The moon shone like the gleed.

19 'O ragged is your hose, Glenkindie,
　　And riven is your sheen,

And reaveld is your yellow hair,
　　That I saw late yestreen.'

20 'The stockings they are Gib, my man'
　　They came first to my hand,
　And this is Gib, my man's shoon,
　　At my bed-feet they stand;
　I 've reavelld a' my yellow hair
　　Coming against the wind.'

21 He 's taen the harp intill his hand,
　　He harpit and he sang,
　Until he cam to his master,
　　As fast as he could gang.

22 'Won up, won up, my good master,
　　I fear ye sleep oer lang;
　There 's nae a cock in a' the land
　　But has wappit his wings and crawn.

23 Glenkindie 's tane his harp in hand,
　　He harpit and he sang,
　And he has reachd the lady's bower
　　Afore that eer he blan.

24 When he cam to the lady's bower,
　　He chappit at the chin:
　'O wha is that at my bower-door,
　　That opens na and comes in?'
　'It 's I, Glenkindie, your ain true-love,
　　And in I canna win.'

*　　*　　*　　*　　*

25 'Forbid it, forbid it,' says that lady,
　　'That ever sic shame betide,
　That I should first be a wild loon's lass,
　　And than a young knight's bride.'

26 He 's taen his harp intill his hand,
　　He harpit and he sang,
　And he is hame to Gib, his man,
　　As fast as he could gang.

27 'Come forth, come forth, now, Gib, my
　　man,
　　Till I pay you your fee;
　Come forth, come forth, now, Gib, my
　　man,
　　Weel payit sall ye be.'

28 And he has taen him Gib, his man,
　　And he has hangd him hie,
　And he 's hangit him oer his ain yate,
　　As high as high could be.

29 There was nae pity for that lady,
    For she lay cald and dead,
  But a' was for him, Glenkindie,
    In bower he must go mad.

68

YOUNG HUNTING

Scott's 'Earl Richard' is mainly from Herd's copies A and G, here given, but partly from independent tradition (Minstrelsy, 1802, II, 42; ed. 1803, II, 44).

A Scandinavian ballad (Grundtvig, No. 208), begins somewhat like 'Young Hunting,' but ends like 'Elveskud,' or 'Clerk Colvill' (No. 42). A young man who has made up his mind to marry is warned by his mother against the wiles of a former mistress. He rides to his old love's house and is welcomed to beer and wine. He tells her that he is on the way to his bride. She wants a word with him, or a kiss, and as he leans over to her on the horse, stabs him to the heart. He rides home bleeding, pretends that he has hurt himself by running against a tree, asks that his bed may be made and a priest sent for, and dies.

A

'Young Hunting.' **a**. Herd's MSS., I, 182.
b. The same, II, 67.

1 O LADY, rock never your young son young
    One hour longer for me,
  For I have a sweetheart in Garlick's
      Wells
  I love thrice better than thee.

2 'The very sols of my love's feet
    Is whiter then thy face:'
  'But nevertheless na, Young Hunting,
    Ye 'l stay wi me all night.'

3 She has birld in him Young Hunting
    The good ale and the beer,
  Till he was as fou drunken
    As any wild-wood steer.

4 She has birld in him Young Hunting
    The good ale and the wine,
  Till he was as fou drunken
    As any wild-wood swine.

5 Up she has tain him Young Hunting,
    And she has had him to her bed,

  .   .   .   .
    .   .   .   .

6 And she has minded her on a little pen-
      knife,
    That hangs low down by her gare,
  And she has gin him Young Hunting
    A deep wound and a sare.

7 Out an spake the bonny bird,
    That flew abon her head:
  'Lady, keep well thy green clothing
    Fra that good lord's blood.'

8 'O better I 'll keep my green clothing
    Fra that good lord's blood
  Nor thou can keep thy flattering toung,
    That flatters in thy head.

9 'Light down, light down, my bonny
      bird,
    Light down upon my hand,

  .   .   .   .
    .   .   .   .

10 'O siller, O siller shall be thy hire,
    An goud shall be thy fee,
  An every month into the year
    Thy cage shall changed be.'

11 'I winna light down, I shanna light
      down,
    I winna light on thy hand;
  For soon, soon wad ye do to me
    As ye done to Young Hunting.'

12 She has booted an spird him Young
      Hunting
    As he had been gan to ride,
  A hunting-horn about his neck,
    An the sharp sourd by his side.

13 And she has had him to yon wan
      water,
    For a' man calls it Clyde,

  .   .   .   .
    .   .   .   .

14 The deepest pot intill it all
    She has puten Young Hunting in;
  A green truff upon his breast,
    To hold that good lord down.

15 It fell once upon a day
    The king was going to ride,

And he sent for him Young Hunting,
 To ride on his right side.

16 She has turnd her right and round about,
 She sware now by the corn,
'I saw na thy son, Young Hunting,
 Sen yesterday at morn.'

17 She has turnd her right and round about,
 She swear now by the moon,
'I saw na thy son, Young Hunting,
 Sen yesterday at noon.'

18 'It fears me sair in Clyde Water
 That he is drownd therein:'
O thay ha sent for the king's duckers,
 To duck for Young Hunting.

19 They ducked in at the tae water-bank,
 Thay ducked out at the tither:
'We 'll duck no more for Young Hunt-
  ing,
All tho he wear our brother.'

20 Out an spake the bonny bird,
 That flew abon their heads,

 . . . . .

21 'O he 's na drownd in Clyde Water,
 He is slain and put therein;
The lady that lives in yon castil
 Slew him and put him in.

22 'Leave aff your ducking on the day,
 And duck upon the night;
Whear ever that sakeless knight lys
  slain,
The candels will shine bright.'

23 Thay left off their ducking o the day,
 And ducked upon the night,
And where that sakeless knight lay
  slain,
The candles shone full bright.

24 The deepest pot intill it a'
 Thay got Young Hunting in;
A green turff upon his brest,
 To hold that good lord down.

25 O thay ha sent aff men to the wood
 To hew down baith thorn an fern,
That they might get a great bonefire
 To burn that lady in.

'Put na the wyte on me,' she says,
 'It was her May Catheren.'

26 Whan thay had tane her May Catheren,
 In the bonefire set her in;
It wad na take upon her cheeks,
 Nor take upon her chin,
Nor yet upon her yellow hair,
 To healle the deadly sin.

27 Out they hae tain her May Catheren,
 And they hay put that lady in;
O it took upon her cheek, her cheek,
 An it took upon her chin,
An it took on her fair body,
 She burnt like hoky-gren.

C

'Young Riedan,' Harris MS., fol. 8, from Mrs
Harris, Perthshire.

1 THE ladie stude in her bour-door,
 In her bour-door as she stude,
She thocht she heard a bridle ring,
 That did her bodie gude.

2 She thocht it had been her father dear,
 Come ridin owre the sand;
But it was her true-love Riedan,
 Come hiean to her hand.

3 'You 're welcome, you 're welcome,
  Young Riedan,' she said,
'To coal an cannel-licht;
You 're welcome, you 're welcome, Young
  Riedan,
To sleep in my bour this nicht.'

4 'I thank you for your coal, madame,
 An for your cannel tae;
There 's a fairer maid at Clyde's Water,
 I love better than you.'

5 'A fairer maid than me, Riedan?
 A fairer maid than me?
A fairer maid than ten o me
 You shurely neer did see.'

6 He leant him owre his saddle-bow,
 To gie her a kiss sae sweet;
She keppit him on a little penknife,
 An gae him a wound sae deep.

7 'Oh hide! oh hide! my bourswoman,
 Oh hide this deed on me!

An the silks that waur shappit for me
    at Yule
  At Pasch sall be sewed for thee.'

8 They saidled Young Riedan, they bri-
    dled Young Riedan,
  The way he was wont to ride;
  Wi a huntin-horn aboot his neck,
  An a sharp sword by his side.

9 An they are on to Clyde's Water,
  An they rade it up an doon,
  An the deepest linn in a' Clyde's Water
  They flang him Young Riedan [in].

10 'Lie you there, you Young Riedan,
   Your bed it is fu wan;
  The [maid] you hae at Clyde's Water,
  For you she will think lang.'

11 Up it spak the wily bird,
   As it sat on the tree:
  'Oh wae betide you, ill woman,
  An an ill death may you dee !
  For he had neer anither love,
  Anither love but thee.'

12 'Come doon, come doon, my pretty
    parrot,
  An pickle wheat aff my glue;
  An your cage sall be o the beaten goud,
  Whan it 's of the willow tree.'

13 'I winna come doon, I sanna come doon,
   To siccan a traitor as thee;
  For as you did to Young Riedan,
  Sae wald you do to mee.'

14 'Come doon, come doon, my pretty
    parrot,
  An pickle wheat aff my hand;
  An your cage sall be o the beaten goud,
  Whan it 's o the willow wand.'

15 'I winna come doon, I sanna come
    doon,
  To siccan a traitor as thee;
  You wald thraw my head aff my hase-
    bane,
  An fling it in the sea.'

16 It fell upon a Lammas-tide
   The king's court cam ridin bye:
  'Oh whare is it him Young Riedan ?
  It 's fain I wald him see.'

17 'Oh I hae no seen Young Riedan
   Sin three lang weeks the morn;
  It bodes me sair, and drieds me mair,
  Clyde's Water 's him forlorn.'

18 Up it spak the wily bird,
   As it sat on the tree;
.   .   .   .   .

.   .   .   .   .

19 'Leave aff, leave aff your day-seekin,
   An ye maun seek by nicht;
  Aboon the place Young Riedan lies,
  The cannels burn bricht.'

20 They gae up their day-seekin,
   An they did seek by nicht;
  An owre the place Young Riedan lay,
  The cannels burnt bricht.

21 The firsten grip his mother got
   Was o his yellow hair;
  An was na that a dowie grip,
  To get her ae son there !

22 The nexten grip his mother got
   Was o his milk-white hand;
  An wasna that a dowie grip,
  To bring sae far to land !

23 White, white waur his wounds washen,
   As white as ony lawn;
  But sune 's the traitor stude afore,
  Then oot the red blude sprang.

   *   *   *   *   *

24 Fire wadna tak on her bourswoman,
   Niether on cheek nor chin;
  But it took fast on thae twa hands
  That flang Young Riedan in.

25 'Come oot, come oot, my bourswoman,
   Come oot, lat me win in;
  For as I did the deed mysell,
  Sae man I drie the pine.'

G

Herd's MSS., i, 34; Herd's Scottish Songs,
1776, i, 148.

1 SHE has calld to her her bower-maidens,
   She has calld them one by one:
  'There is a dead man in my bower,
  I wish that he was gone.'

2 They have booted him, and spurred him,
   As he was wont to ride,
A hunting-horn around his waist,
   A sharp sword by his side.

3 Then up and spake a bonie bird,
   That sat upon the tree:
' What hae ye done wi Earl Richard ?
   Ye was his gay lady.'

4 ' Cum down, cum down, my bonie bird,
   Cum sit upon my hand;
And ye sall hae a cage o the gowd,
   Where ye hae but the wand.'

5 ' Awa, awa, ye ill woman,
   Nae ill woman for me;
What ye hae done to Earl Richard,
   Sae wad ye do to mee.'

*   *   *   *   *

6 ' O there 's a bird intill your bowir
   That sings sae sad and sweet;
O there 's a bird intill your bour
   Kept me frae my nicht's sleep.'

*   *   *   *   *

7 And she sware by the grass sae greene,
   Sae did she by the corn,
That she had not seen Earl Richard
   Sen yesterday at morn.

*   *   *   *   *

69

CLERK SAUNDERS

' Clerk Saunders ' was first given to the world
in the Minstrelsy of the Scottish Border, and
was there said to be " taken from Herd's MS.,
with several corrections from a shorter and
more imperfect copy in the same volume, and
one or two conjectural emendations in the arrangement of the stanzas." Sir Walter arranged
his ballad with much good taste, but this account of his dealing with Herd's copies is far
from precisely accurate. A, the longer of these,
does not end, in Herd's MS., with Margaret's
refusal to be comforted, a rather unsufficing
conclusion it must be owned. The story is continued by annexing the ballad of ' Sweet William's Ghost,' the lack of which in B makes

Scott call that version imperfect. This sequel,
found also in F, is omitted here, and will be
given under No. 77. F (Jamieson's Ballads) is
like Scott's, a made-up copy, " the stanzas
where the seven brothers are introduced " having been " enlarged from two fragments, which,
though very defective . . . . , furnished lines
which, when incorporated in the text, seemed
to improve it." But F is important, since it
connects ' Clerk Saunders ' with a Scandinavian ballad (Grundtvig-Olrik, No. 304) which
seems to be preserved, in abbreviated and some
times perverted forms, by other races as well.
Nos. 70 and 71 have connections with ' Clerk
Saunders.'

A

' Clerk Saunders,' Herd's MSS., **a**, I, 177; **b**
II, 419.

1 CLARK SANDERS and May Margret
   Walkt ower you graveld green,
And sad and heavy was the love,
   I wat, it fell this twa between.

2 ' A bed, a bed,' Clark Sanders said,
   ' A bed, a bed for you and I;'
' Fye no, fye no,' the lady said,
   ' Until the day we married be.

3 ' For in it will come my seven brothers,
   And a' their torches burning bright;
They 'll say, We hae but ae sister,
   And here her lying wi a knight.'

4 ' Ye 'l take the sourde fray my scabbord,
   And lowly, lowly lift the gin,
And you may say, your oth to save,
   You never let Clark Sanders in.

5 ' Yele take a napken in your hand,
   And ye 'l ty up baith your een,
An ye may say, your oth to save,
   That ye saw na Sandy sen late yes-
      treen.

6 ' Yele take me in your armes twa,
   Yele carrey me ben into your bed,
And ye may say, your oth to save,
   In your bower-floor I never tread.'

7 She has taen the sourde fray his scab-
      bord,
   And lowly, lowly lifted the gin;
She was to swear, her oth to save,
   She never let Clerk Sanders in.

She has tain a napkin in her hand,
    And she ty'd up baith her eeen;
She was to swear, her oth to save,
    She saw na him sene late yestreen.

She has taen him in her armes twa,
    And carried him ben into her bed;
She was to swear, her oth to save,
    He never in her bower-floor tread.

In and came her seven brothers,
    And all their torches burning bright;
Says thay, We hae but ae sister,
    And see there her lying wi a knight.

Out and speaks the first of them,
    ' A wat they hay been lovers dear;'
Out and speaks the next of them,
    ' They hay been in love this many a
      year.'

2 Out an speaks the third of them,
    ' It wear great sin this twa to twain;'
Out an speaks the fourth of them,
    ' It wear a sin to kill a sleeping man.'

3 Out an speaks the fifth of them,
    ' A wat they 'll near be twained by
      me;'
Out an speaks the sixt of them,
    ' We 'l tak our leave an gae our way.'

4 Out an speaks the seventh of them,
    ' Altho there wear no a man but me,
 .   .   .   .   .
    I bear the brand, I 'le gar him die.'

5 Out he has taen a bright long brand,
    And he has striped it throw the straw,
And throw and throw Clarke Sanders'
      body
A wat he has gard cold iron gae.

16 Sanders he started, an Margret she lapt,
    Intill his arms whare she lay,
And well and wellsom was the night,
    A wat it was between these twa.

17 And they lay still, and sleeped sound,
    Untill the day began to daw;
And kindly till him she did say
    ' It 's time, trew-love, ye wear awa.'

18 They lay still, and sleeped sound,
    Untill the sun began to shine;

She lookt between her and the wa,
    And dull and heavy was his eeen.

19 She thought it had been a loathsome
      sweat,
    A wat it had fallen this twa between;
But it was the blood of his fair body,
    A wat his life days wair na lang.

20 ' O Sanders, I 'le do for your sake
    What other ladys would na thoule;
When seven years is come and gone,
    There 's near a shoe go on my sole.

21 ' O Sanders, I 'le do for your sake
    What other ladies would think mare;
When seven years is come an gone,
    Ther 's nere a comb go in my hair.

22 ' O Sanders, I 'le do for your sake
    What other ladies would think lack;
When seven years is come an gone,
    I 'le wear nought but dowy black.'

23 The bells gaed clinking throw the towne,
    To carry the dead corps to the clay,
An sighing says her May Margret,
    ' A wat I bide a doulfou day.'

24 In an come her father dear,
    Stout steping on the floor;
 .   .   .   .   .

25 ' Hold your toung, my doughter dear,
    Let all your mourning a bee;
I 'le carry the dead corps to the clay,
    An I 'le come back an comfort thee.'

26 ' Comfort well your seven sons,
    For comforted will I never bee;
For it was neither lord nor loune
    That was in bower last night wi mee.'

B

' Clerk Saunders,' Herd's MSS., a, I, 163; b
II, 46.

1 CLERK SAUNDERS and a gay lady
    Was walking in yonder green,
And heavy, heavy was the love
    That fell this twa lovers between.

2 ' A bed, a bed,' Clerk Saunders said,
    ' And ay a bed for you and me;'

'Never a ane,' said the gay lady,
  'Till ance we twa married be.'

3 'There would come a' my seven breth-
    ern,
  And a' their torches burning bright,
  And say, We hae but ae sister,
    And behad, she 's lying wi you the
    night.'

4 'You 'll take a napkain in your hand,
  And then you will tie up your een;
  Then you may swear, and safe your aith,
    You sawna Sandy sin yestreen.

5 'You 'll take me up upo your back,
  And then you 'll carry me to your bed;
  Then you may swear, and save your aith,
    Your board [-floor] Sandy never tred.'

6 She 's taen him upo her back,
  And she 's carried him unto her bed,
  That she might swear, and safe her aith,
    Her board-floor Sandy never tread.

7 She 's taen a napkin in her hand,
  And lo she did tie up her een,
  That she might swear, and safe her aith,
    She sawna Sandy syne yestreen.

8 They were na weel into the room,
  Nor yet laid weel into the bed,

  .   .   .   .   .

9 When in came a' her seven brethern,
  And a' their torches burning bright;
  Says they, We hae but ae sister,
    And behold, she 's lying wi you this
    night.

10 'I,' bespake the first o them,
   A wat an ill death mat he die!
  'I bear a brand into my hand
    Shall quickly gar Clerk Saunders die.'

11 'I,' bespake the second of them,
   A wat a good death mat he die!
  'We will gae back, let him alane,
    His father has nae mair but he.'

12 'I,' bespake the third o them,
   A wat an ill death mat he die!
  'I bear the brand into my hand
    Shall quickly help to gar him die.'

13 'I,' bespake the fourth o them,
   A wat a good death mat he die!
  'I bear the brand into my hand
    Shall never help to gar him die.'

14 'I,' bespake the fifth o them,
   A wat an ill death mat he die!
  'Altho his father hae nae mair,
    I 'll quickly help to gar him die.'

15 'I,' bespake the sixth o them,
   A wat a good death mat he die!
  'He 's a worthy earl's son,
    I 'll never help to gar him die.'

16 'I,' bespake the seventh of them,
   A wat an ill death mat he die!
  'I bear the brand into my hand
    Shall quickly gar Clerk Saunders die'

17 They baith lay still, and sleeped soun
  Untill the sun began to sheen;
  She drew the curtains a wee bit,
    And dull and drowsie was his een.

18 'This night,' said she, 'the sleepie
    man
  That ever my twa eyes did see
  Hay lyen by me, and sweat the sheets
    A wite they 're a great shame to see

19 She rowd the claiths a' to the foot,
  And then she spied his deadly wound
  'O wae be to my seven brethern,
    A wat an ill death mat they die!

20 'I 'm sure it was neither rogue nor lou
  I had into my bed wi me;
  'T was Clerk Saunders, that good earl'
    son,
  That pledgd his faith to marry me.'

F

'Clerk Saunders,' Jamieson's Popular Ba
lads, I, 83, communicated by Mrs Arrot, o
Aberbrothick, but enlarged from two frag
ments.

1 CLERK SAUNDERS was an earl's son,
  He livd upon sea-sand;
  May Margaret was a king's daughter,
    She livd in upper land.

2 Clerk Saunders was an earl's son,
  Weel learned at the scheel;

May Margaret was a king's daughter,
    They baith loed ither weel.

3 He 's throw the dark, and throw the
      mark,
    And throw the leaves o green,
    Till he came to May Margaret's door,
    And tirled at the pin.

4 'O sleep ye, wake ye, May Margaret,
    Or are ye the bower within?'
    'O wha is that at my bower-door,
    Sae weel my name does ken?'
    'It 's I, Clerk Saunders, your true-love,
    You 'll open and lat me in.

5 'O will ye to the cards, Margaret,
    Or to the table to dine?
    Or to the bed, that 's weel down spread,
    And sleep when we get time?'

6 'I 'll no go to the cards,' she says,
    'Nor to the table to dine;
    But I 'll go to a bed, that 's weel down
      spread,
    And sleep when we get time.'

7 They were not weel lyen down,
    And no weel fa'en asleep,
    When up and stood May Margaret's
      brethren,
    Just up at their bed-feet.

8 'O tell us, tell us, May Margaret,
    And dinna to us len,
    O wha is aught yon noble steed,
    That stands your stable in?'

9 'The steed is mine, and it may be thine,
    To ride whan ye ride in hie;

   .   .   .   .   .

10 'But awa, awa, my bald brethren,
    Awa, and mak nae din;
    For I am as sick a lady the nicht
    As eer lay a bower within.'

11 'O tell us, tell us, May Margaret,
    And dinna to us len,
    O wha is aught yon noble hawk,
    That stands your kitchen in?'

12 'The hawk is mine, and it may be thine,
    To hawk whan ye hawk in hie;

   .   .   .   .   .

13 'But awa, awa, my bald brethren,
    Awa, and mak nae din;
    For I 'm ane o the sickest ladies this
      nicht
    That eer lay a bower within.'

14 'O tell us, tell us, May Margaret,
    And dinna to us len,
    O wha is that, May Margaret,
    You and the wa between?'

15 'O it is my bower-maiden,' she says,
    'As sick as sick can be;
    O it is my bower-maiden,' she says,
    'And she 's thrice as sick as me.'

16 'We hae been east, and we 've been
      west,
    And low beneath the moon;
    But a' the bower-women eer we saw
    Hadna goud buckles in their shoon.'

17 Then up and spak her eldest brither,
    Ay in ill time spak he:
    'It is Clerk Saunders, your true-love,
    And never mat I the
    But for this scorn that he has done
    This moment he sall die.'

18 But up and spak her youngest brother,
    Ay in good time spak he:
    'O but they are a gudelie pair!
    True lovers an ye be,
    The sword that hangs at my sword-belt
    Sall never sinder ye.'

19 Syne up and spak her nexten brother,
    And the tear stood in his ee:
    'You 've loed her lang, and loed her
      weel,
    And pity it wad be
    The sword that hangs at my sword-
      belt
    Shoud ever sinder ye.'

20 But up and spak her fifthen brother:
    'Sleep on your sleep for me;
    But we baith sall never sleep again,
    For the tane o us sall die.'

21 And up and spak her thirden brother,
    Ay in ill time spak he:

' Curse on his love and comeliness !
  Dishonourd as ye be,
The sword that hangs at my sword-belt
  Sall quickly sinder ye.'

22 The eldest brother has drawn his sword,
   The second has drawn anither,
Between Clerk Saunders' hause and col-
     lar-bane
   The cald iron met thegither.

23 ' O wae be to you, my fause brethren,
     And an ill death mat ye die !
   Ye mith slain Clerk Saunders in open
       field,
     And no in bed wi me.'

70

WILLIE AND LADY MAISRY

' Willie and Lady Maisry,' preserved in two
versions, has much in common with ' Clerk
Saunders.' The chief point of difference is
that of Willie's killing Maisry's brother and
the guard (in **A**, only the guard). Here the
ballad has probably been affected by another
now represented in English only by a very corrupt version, 'The Bent sae Brown' (No. 71).

A

' Willie, the Widow's Son,' Motherwell's
MS., p. 498 ; ' Sweet Willie and Lady Margerie,'
Motherwell's Minstrelsy, p. 370. From the
recitation of Mrs Notman, then far advanced
in years, with whose grandmother it was a
favorite : September 9, 1826.

1 WILLIE was a widow's son,
    And he wore a milk-white weed, O
  And weel could Willie read and write,
    Far better ride on steed. O

2 Lady Margerie was the first lady
    That drank to him the wine,
  And aye as the healths gade round and
      round,
    ' Laddy, your love is mine.'

3 Lady Margerie was the first ladye
    That drank to him the beer,
  And aye as the healths gade round and
      round,
    ' Laddy, you 're welcome here.'

4 ' You must come into my bower
    When the evening bells do ring,
  And you must come into my bower
    When the evening mass doth sing.'

5 He 's taen four and twenty braid arrow
    And laced them in a whang,
  And he 's awa to Lady Margerie's bow
    As fast as he can gang.

6 He set ae foot on the wall,
    And the other on a stane,
  And he 's killed a' the king's life-guard
    And he 's killed them every man.

7 ' Oh open, open, Lady Margerie,
    Open and let me in ;
  The weet weets a' my yellow hair,
    And the dew draps on my chin.'

8 With her feet as white as sleet
    She strode her bower within,
  And with her fingers long and small
    She 's looten Sweet Willie in.

9 She 's louten down unto her foot
    To loose Sweet Willie's shoon ;
  The buckles were sa stiff they wud
      lowse,
    The blood had frozen in.

10 ' O Willie, Willie, I fear that thou
     Has bred me dule and sorrow ;
   The deed that thou has dune this nich
     Will kythe upon the morrow.'

11 In then came her father dear,
     And a broad sword by his gare,
   And he 's gien Willie, the widow's son
     A deep wound and a sair.

12 ' Lye yont, lye yont, Willie,' she says,
     ' Your sweat weets a' my side ;
   Lye yont, lye yont, Willie,' she says,
     ' For your sweat I downa bide.'

13 She turned her back unto the wa,
     Her face unto the room,
   And there she saw her auld father,
     Walking up and down.

14 ' Woe be to you, father,' she said,
     ' And an ill deed may you die !
   For ye 've killd Willie, the widow's son
     And he would have married me.'

5 She turned her back unto the room,
  Her face unto the wa,
And with a deep and heavy sich
  Her heart it brak in twa.

B

'Willie and Lady Maisry,' Buchan's Ballads
f the North of Scotland, i, 155.

1 SWEET WILLIE was a widow's son,
  And milk-white was his weed;
It sets him weel to bridle a horse,
  And better to saddle a steed, my dear,
  And better to saddle a steed.

2 But he is on to Maisry's bower-door,
  And tirled at the pin:
' Ye sleep ye, wake ye, Lady Maisry,
  Ye 'll open, let me come in.'

3 ' O who is this at my bower-door,
  Sae well that knows my name ? '
' It is your ain true-love, Willie,
  If ye love me, lat me in.'

4 Then huly, huly raise she up,
  For fear o making din,
Then in her arms lang and bent,
  She caught sweet Willie in.

5 She leand her low down to her toe,
  To loose her true-love's sheen,
But cauld, cauld were the draps o bleed
  Fell fae his trusty brand.

6 ' What frightfu sight is that, my love ?
  A frightfu sight to see !
What bluid is this on your sharp brand ?
  O may ye not tell me ? '

7 ' As I came thro the woods this night,
  The wolf maist worried me;
O shoud I slain the wolf, Maisry ?
  Or shoud the wolf slain me ? '

8 They hadna kissd, nor love clapped,
  As lovers when they meet,
Till up it starts her auld father,
  Out o his drowsy sleep.

9 ' O what 's become o my house-cock,
  Sae crouse at ane did craw ?
I wonder as much at my bold watch,
  That 's nae shooting ower the wa.

10 ' My gude house-cock, my only son,
  Heir ower my land sae free,
If ony ruffian hae him slain,
  High hanged shall he be.'

11 Then he 's on to Maisry's bower-door,
  And tirled at the pin:
' Ye sleep ye, wake ye, daughter Maisry,
  Ye 'll open, lat me come in.'

12 Between the curtains and the wa
  She rowd her true-love then,
And huly went she to the door,
  And let her father in.

13 ' What 's become o your maries, Maisry,
  Your bower it looks sae teem ?
What 's become o your green claithing,
  Your beds they are sae thin ? '

14 ' Gude forgie you, father,' she said,
  ' I wish ye be 't for sin;
Sae aft as ye hae dreaded me,
  But never found me wrang.'

15 He turnd him right and round about,
  As he 'd been gaun awa;
But sae nimbly as he slippet in
  Behind a screen sae sma.

16 Maisry, thinking a' dangers past,
  She to her love did say,
' Come, love, and take your silent rest;
  My auld father 's away.'

17 Then baith lockd in each other's arms,
  They fell full fast asleep,
When up it starts her auld father,
  And stood at their bed-feet.

18 ' I think I hae the villain now
  That my dear son did slay;
But I shall be revengd on him
  Before I see the day.'

19 Then he 's drawn out a trusty brand,
  And stroakd it oer a stray,
And thro and thro Sweet Willie's
      middle
  He 's gart cauld iron gae.

20 Then up it wakend Lady Maisry,
  Out o her drowsy sleep,
And when she saw her true-love slain,
  She straight began to weep.

21 'O gude forgie you now, father,' she
    said,
    ' I wish ye be 't for sin;
    For I never lovd a love but ane,
    In my arms ye 've him slain.'

22 ' This night he 's slain my gude bold
    watch,
    Thirty stout men and twa;
    Likewise he 's slain your ae brother,
    To me was worth them a'.'

23 ' If he has slain my ae brither,
    Himsell had a' the blame,
    For mony a day he plots contriv'd,
    To hae Sweet Willie slain.

24 ' And tho he 's slain your gude bold watch,
    He might hae been forgien;
    They came on him in armour bright,
    When he was but alane.'

25 Nae meen was made for this young
    knight,
    In bower where he lay slain,
    But a' was for sweet Maisry bright,
    In fields where she ran brain.

71

THE BENT SAE BROWN

' The Bent sae Brown ' combines the story
of ' Clerk Saunders ' (No. 69) with that of
another ballad, not found in an independent
form in English, but sufficiently common in
Danish and Swedish (Kristensen, No. 80, etc.);
whence the non-tragical conclusion, for the
killing of a certain number of brothers is not
regarded as a very serious matter by the
heroine, whether in English or Norse. The
introduction and conclusion, and some inciden-
tal decorations, of the Scottish ballad will
not be found in the Norse, but are an outcome
of the invention and the piecing and shaping of
that humble but enterprising rhapsodist who
has left his trail over so large a part of Buchan's
volumes.

Stanzas 21–34 contain the substance of the
Norse ballad referred to. A youth has passed
the night with his love, either in her bower or
in a wood. When they are about to part in
the morning, she begs him to be on his guard
against her seven brothers, on his way through
the wood and over the heath. He makes
light of the danger, and in the wood meets the
seven brothers. They demand how he come
to be there, and he feigns to have been ou
with his hawk and hounds. No, they say, yo
were with our sister last night. He makes n
denial. They ask whether he will fly or figh
He has no thought of flight, kills all seven, an
goes back to his love. She will not forsak
him for killing her brothers; nor would she, i
some versions, had he killed her father too.

Buchan's Ballads of the North of Scotland
I, 30.

1 ' THERE are sixteen lang miles, I 'n
    sure,
    Between my love and me;
    There are eight o them in gude dry land
    And other eight by sea.

2 ' Betide me life, betide me death,
    My love I 'll gang and see;
    Altho her friends they do me hate,
    Her love is great for me.

3 ' Of my coat I 'll make a boat,
    And o my sark a sail,
    And o my cane a gude tapmast,
    Dry land till I come till.'

4 Then o his coat he 's made a boat,
    And o his sark a sail;
    And o his cane a gude tapmast,
    Dry land till he came till.

5 He is on to Annie's bower-door,
    And tirled at the pin:
    ' O sleep ye, wake ye, my love, Annie,
    Ye 'll rise, lat me come in.'

6 ' O who is this at my bower-door,
    Sae well that kens my name ? '
    ' It is your true-love, Sweet Willie,
    For you I 've crossd the faem.'

7 ' I am deeply sworn, Willie,
    By father and by mother;
    At kirk or market where we meet,
    We darna own each other.

8 ' And I am deeply sworn, Willie,
    By my bauld brothers three;
    At kirk or market where we meet,
    I darna speak to thee.'

9 ' Ye take your red fan in your hand,
    Your white fan ower your een,

And ye may swear, and save your oath,
    Ye sawna me come in.

10 'Ye take me in your arms twa,
    And carry me to your bed;
    And ye may swear, and save your oath,
    Your bower I never tread.'

11 She 's taen her red fan in her hand,
    The white fan ower her een;
    It was to swear, and save her oath,
    She sawna him come in.

12 She 's taen him in her arms twa,
    And carried him to her bed;
    It was to swear, and save her oath,
    Her bower he never tread.

13 They hadna kissd, nor love clappd,
    As lovers do when they meet,
    Till up it waukens her mother,
    Out o her drowsy sleep.

14 'Win up, win up, my three bauld sons,
    Win up and make ye boun;
    Your sister's lover 's in her bower,
    And he 's but new come in.'

15 Then up it raise her three bauld sons,
    And girt to them their brand,
    And they are to their sister's bower,
    As fast as they coud gang.

16 When they came to their sister's bower,
    They sought it up and down;
    But there was neither man nor boy
    In her bower to be foun.

17 Then out it speaks the first o them:
    'We 'll gang and lat her be;
    For there is neither man nor boy
    Intill her companie.'

18 Then out it speaks the second son:
    'Our travel 's a' in vain;
    But mother dear, nor father dear,
    Shall break our rest again.'

19 Then out it speaks the third o them,
    An ill death mat he die !
    'We 'll lurk amang the bent sae brown,
    That Willie we may see.'

20 He stood behind his love's curtains,
    His goud rings showd him light;

And by this ye may a' weell guess
    He was a renowned knight.

21 He 's done him to his love's stable,
    Took out his berry-brown steed;
    His love stood in her bower-door,
    Her heart was like to bleed.

22 'O mourn ye for my coming, love ?
    Or for my short staying ?
    Or mourn ye for our safe sindring,
    Case we never meet again ?'

23 'I mourn nae for your here coming,
    Nor for your staying lang;
    Nor mourn I for our safe sindring,
    I hope we 'll meet again.

24 'I wish ye may won safe away,
    And safely frae the town;
    For ken you not my brothers three
    Are mang the bent sae brown ?'

25 'If I were on my berry-brown steed,
    And three miles frae the town,
    I woudna fear your three bauld bro-
      thers,
    Amang the bent sae brown.'

26 He leint him ower his saddle-bow,
    And kissd her lips sae sweet;
    The tears that fell between these twa,
    They wat his great steed's feet.

27 But he wasna on his berry-brown steed,
    Nor twa miles frae the town,
    Till up it starts these three fierce men,
    Amang the bent sae brown.

28 Then up they came like three fierce
      men,
    Wi mony shout and cry:
    'Bide still, bide still, ye cowardly youth,
    What makes your haste away ?

29 'For I must know before you go,
    Tell me, and make nae lie;
    If ye 've been in my sister's bower,
    My hands shall gar ye die.'

30 'Tho I 've been in your sister's bower.
    I have nae fear o thee ;
    I 'll stand my ground, and fiercely
      fight,
    And shall gain victorie.'

31 'Now I entreat you for to stay,
    Unto us gie a wad;
  If ye our words do not obey,
    I 'se gar your body bleed.'

32 'I have nae wad,' says Sweet Willie,
    'Unless it be my brand,
  And that shall guard my fair body,
    Till I win frae your hand.'

33 Then two o them stept in behind,
    All in a furious meed;
  The third o them came him before,
    And seizd his berry-brown steed.

34 O then he drew his trusty brand,
    That hang down by his gare,
  And he has slain these three fierce men,
    And left them sprawling there.

35 Then word has gane to her mother,
    In bed where she slept soun,
  That Willie had killd her three bauld
    sons,
    Amang the bent sae brown.

36 Then she has cut the locks that hung
    Sae low down by her ee,
  Sae has she kiltit her green claithing
    A little aboon her knee.

37 And she has on to the king's court,
    As fast as gang coud she;
  When Fair Annie got word o that,
    Was there as soon as she.

38 Her mother, when before the king,
    Fell low down on her knee;
  'Win up, win up, my dame,' he said,
    'What is your will wi me?'

39 'My wills they are not sma, my liege,
    The truth I 'll tell to thee;
  There is ane o your courtly knights
    Last night hae robbed me.'

40 'And has he broke your bigly bowers?
    Or has he stole your fee?
  There is nae knight into my court
    Last night has been frae me;

41 'Unless 't was Willie o Lauderdale,
    Forbid that it be he!'
  'And by my sooth,' says the auld woman,
    'That very man is he.

42 'For he has broke my bigly bowers,
    And he has stole my fee,
  And made my daughter Ann a whore,
    And an ill woman is she.

43 'That was not all he did to me,
    Ere he went frae the town;
  My sons sae true he fiercely slew,
    Amang the bent sae brown.'

44 Then out it spake her daughter Ann,
    She stood by the king's knee:
  'Ye lie, ye lie, my mother dear,
    Sae loud 's I hear you lie.

45 'He has not broke your bigly bowers,
    Nor has he stole your fee,
  Nor made your daughter Ann a whore;
    A good woman I 'll be.

46 'Altho he slew your three bauld sons,
    He weel might be forgien;
  They were well clad in armour bright,
    Whan my love was him lane.'

47 'Well spoke, well spoke,' the king re-
    plied,
    'This tauking pleases me;
  For ae kiss o your lovely mouth,
    I 'll set your true-love free.'

48 She 's taen the king in her arms,
    And kissd him cheek and chin;
  He then set her behind her love,
    And they went singing hame.

72

THE CLERK'S TWA SONS O OWSENFORD

There are ballads both in Northern and Southern Europe which have a certain amount of likeness with 'The Clerk's Twa Sons,' but if the story of all derives from one original, time has introduced great and even unusual variations. A very well known German ballad ('Das Schloss in Oesterreich,' Böhme's Erk, No. 61), found also in the Low Countries and in Scandinavia, has the following story. A youth is lying in a dungeon, condemned to be hanged. His father comes to the town and they exchange words about the severity of his prison. The father then goes to the lord of the place and offers three hundred florins as a ransom.

Ransom is refused: the boy has a gold chain on his neck which will be his death. The father says that the chain was not stolen, but the gift of a young lady, who reared the boy as a page, or what not. There is no dear-bought love in the case. The father, standing by the gallows, threatens revenge, but his son deprecates that: he cares not so much for his life as for his mother's grief. Within a half year, more than three hundred men pay with their lives for the death of the boy. A Catalan and Italian ballad (Milá, Romancerillo, No. 208; Nigra, No. 4) has resemblances with the Scottish and the German, and may possibly be a common link. Three students meet three girls, and attempt some little jests with them: ask them for a kiss, or throw some pebbles at them; or meet one girl on a bridge and kiss her. For this the girls have them arrested by an accommodating catchpoll, and they are hanged by a peremptory judge. This Southern ballad is originally French (see Journal des Savants, Sept.–Nov., 1889, p. 614).

A

'The Clerk's Twa Sons o Owsenford,' Kinloch MSS., v, 403, in the handwriting of James Chambers, as sung to his maternal grandmother, Janet Grieve, seventy years before, by an old woman, a Miss Ann Gray, of Neidpath Castle, Peeblesshire; January 1, 1829.

1　O I WILL sing to you a sang,
　　But oh my heart is sair!
　The clerk's twa sons in Owsenford
　　Has to learn some unco lair.

2　They hadna been in fair Parish
　　A twelvemonth an a day,
　Till the clerk's twa sons o Owsenford
　　Wi the mayor's twa daughters lay.

3　O word 's gaen to the mighty mayor,
　　As he saild on the sea,
　That the clerk's twa sons o Owsenford
　　Wi his twa daughters lay.

4　'If they hae lain wi my twa daughters,
　　Meg an Marjorie,
　The morn, or I taste meat or drink,
　　They shall be hangit hie.'

5　O word 's gaen to the clerk himself,
　　As he sat drinkin wine,
　That his twa sons in fair Parish
　　Were bound in prison strong.

6　Then up and spak the clerk's ladye,
　　And she spak powrfully:
　'O tak with ye a purse of gold,
　　Or take with ye three,
　And if ye canna get William,
　　Bring Andrew hame to me.'

*　　*　　*　　*　　*

7　'O lye ye here for owsen, dear sons,
　　Or lie ye here for kye?
　Or what is it that ye lie for,
　　Sae sair bound as ye lie?'

8　'We lie not here for owsen, dear father,
　　Nor yet lie here for kye,
　But it 's for a little o dear bought love
　　Sae sair bound as we lie.'

9　O he 's gane to the mighty mayor,
　　And he spoke powerfully:
　'Will ye grant me my twa sons' lives,
　　Either for gold or fee?
　Or will ye be sae gude a man
　　As grant them baith to me?'

10　'I 'll no grant ye yere twa sons' lives,
　　Neither for gold or fee,
　Nor will I be sae gude a man
　　As gie them back to thee;
　Before the morn at twelve o'clock
　　Ye 'll see them hangit hie.'

11　Up an spak his twa daughters,
　　An they spak powrfully:
　'Will ye grant us our twa loves' lives,
　　Either for gold or fee?
　Or will ye be sae gude a man
　　As grant them baith to me?'

12　'I 'll no grant ye yere twa loves' lives,
　　Neither for gold or fee,
　Nor will I be sae gude a man
　　As grant their lives to thee;
　Before the morn at twelve o'clock
　　Ye 'll see them hangit hie.'

13　O he 's taen out these proper youths,
　　And hangd them on a tree,
　And he 's bidden the clerk o Owsenford
　　Gang hame to his ladie.

14　His lady sits on yon castle-wa,
　　Beholding dale an doun,

An there she saw her ain gude lord
Come walkin to the toun.

15 'Ye're welcome, welcome, my ain gude
  lord,
 Ye're welcome hame to me;
But where away are my twa sons?
 Ye should hae brought them wi ye.'

16 'It's I've putten them to a deeper lair,
 An to a higher schule;
Yere ain twa sons ill no be here
 Till the hallow days o Yule.'

17 'O sorrow, sorrow come mak my bed,
 An dool come lay me doon!
For I'll neither eat nor drink,
 Nor set a fit on ground.'

73

LORD THOMAS AND FAIR ANNET

The English version of this ballad, 'Lord
Thomas and Fair Ellinor' (D), given, with al-
terations, in Percy's Reliques, III, 82, 1765, is
a broadside of Charles the Second's time and
licensed by L'Estrange, who was censor from
1663 to 1685. This copy has become traditional in Scotland and Ireland. The Scottish
traditional copy, A, given by Percy in the
Reliques (unfortunately with some corrections,
but these cannot have been many), is far superior, and one of the most beautiful of all ballads.
'Fair Margaret and Sweet William' (No. 74)
begins in the same way, but the conclusion is
that the forsaken maid dies of grief, not by
the hand of her incensed rival. It is most natural that the two stories should be blended in
tradition, as they are here in I (and in versions
E–H). Sts. 31 ff. of I belong to 'Fair Margaret
and Sweet William' (No. 74). Norse ballads
(see Grundtvig, IV, 219) have the story of 'Lord
Thomas and Fair Annet,' coming very close in
details. Those forms which are nearest to the
English resemble more the mixed versions
than the simple version A. A southern ballad
has something of the outline of the English
and Norse, and sounds like a thin echo of them.

A

'Lord Thomas and Fair Annet,' Percy's Reliques, 1765, II, 593, " given, with some corrections, from a MS. copy transmitted from Scotland;" III, 240, ed. 1767.

1 LORD THOMAS and Fair Annet
 Sate a' day on a hill;
Whan night was cum, and sun wa
 sett,
 They had not talkt their fill.

2 Lord Thomas said a word in jest,
 Fair Annet took it ill:
'A, I will nevir wed a wife
 Against my ain friends' will.'

3 'Gif ye wull nevir wed a wife,
 A wife wull neir wed yee:'
Sae he is hame to tell his mither,
 And knelt upon his knee.

4 'O rede, O rede, mither,' he says,
 'A gude rede gie to mee;
O sall I tak the nut-browne bride,
 And let Faire Annet bee?'

5 'The nut-browne bride haes gowd an
  gear,
 Fair Annet she has gat nane;
And the little beauty Fair Annet haes
 O it wull soon be gane.'

6 And he has till his brother gane:
 'Now, brother, rede ye mee;
A, sall I marrie the nut-browne bride,
 And let Fair Annet bee?'

7 'The nut-browne bride has oxen, brother
 The nut-browne bride has kye;
I wad hae ye marrie the nut-browne
 bride,
 And cast Fair Annet bye.'

8 'Her oxen may dye i the house, billie,
 And her kye into the byre,
And I sall hae nothing to mysell
 Bot a fat fadge by the fyre.'

9 And he has till his sister gane:
 'Now, sister, rede ye mee;
O sall I marrie the nut-browne bride,
 And set Fair Annet free?'

10 'I'se rede ye tak Fair Annet, Thomas,
 And let the browne bride alane;
Lest ye sould sigh, and say, Alace,
 What is this we brought hame!'

11 'No, I will tak my mither's counsel,
 And marrie me cwt o hand;

And I will tak the nut-browne bride,
　Fair Annet may leive the land.'

2 Up then rose Fair Annet's father,
　Twa hours or it wer day,
　And he is gane into the bower
　Wherein Fair Annet lay.

3 ' Rise up, rise up, Fair Annet,' he says,
　' Put on your silken sheene;
　Let us gae to St Marie's kirke,
　And see that rich weddeen.'

4 ' My maides, gae to my dressing-roome,
　And dress to me my hair;
　Whaireir yee laid a plait before,
　See yee lay ten times mair.

5 ' My maids, gae to my dressing-room,
　And dress to me my smock;
　The one half is o the holland fine,
　The other o needle-work.'

16 The horse Fair Annet rade upon,
　He amblit like the wind;
　Wi siller he was shod before,
　Wi burning gowd behind.

17 Four and twenty siller bells
　Wer a' tyed till his mane,
　And yae tift o the norland wind,
　They tinkled ane by ane.

18 Four and twenty gay gude knichts
　Rade by Fair Annet's side,
　And four and twenty fair ladies,
　As gin she had bin a bride.

19 And whan she cam to Marie's kirk,
　She sat on Marie's stean:
　The cleading that Fair Annet had on
　It skinkled in their een.

20 And whan she cam into the kirk,
　She shimmerd like the sun;
　The belt that was about her waist
　Was a' wi pearles bedone.

21 She sat her by the nut-browne bride,
　And her een they wer sae clear,
　Lord Thomas he clean forgat the bride,
　Whan Fair Annet drew near.

22 He had a rose into his hand,
　He gae it kisses three,

And reaching by the nut-browne bride,
　Laid it on Fair Annet's knee.

23 Up than spak the nut-browne bride,
　She spak wi meikle spite:
　' And whair gat ye that rose-water,
　That does mak yee sae white ? '

24 ' O I did get the rose-water
　Whair ye wull neir get nane,
　For I did get that very rose-water
　Into my mither's wame.'

25 The bride she drew a long bodkin
　Frae out her gay head-gear,
　And strake Fair Annet unto the heart,
　That word spak nevir mair.

26 Lord Thomas he saw Fair Annet wex
　pale,
　And marvelit what mote bee;
　But whan he saw her dear heart's blude,
　A' wood-wroth wexed hee.

27 He drew his dagger, that was sae sharp,
　That was sae sharp and meet,
　And drave it into the nut-browne bride,
　That fell deid at his feit.

28 ' Now stay for me, dear Annet,' he sed,
　' Now stay, my dear,' he cry'd;
　Then strake the dagger untill his heart,
　And fell deid by her side.

29 Lord Thomas was buried without kirk-
　wa,
　Fair Annet within the quiere,
　And o the tane thair grew a birk,
　The other a bonny briere.

30 And ay they grew, and ay they threw,
　As they wad faine be neare;
　And by this ye may ken right weil
　They were twa luvers deare.

D

' Lord Thomas and Fair Ellinor.' **a.** Pepys
Ballads, III, 316, No. 312. **b.** A Collection of
Old Ballads, I, 249, 1723. **c.** Ritson, Select
Collection of English Songs, II, 187, 1783. **d.**
Buchan's Gleanings, p. 86. **e, f, g, h, i,** re-
cited copies.

1 LORD THOMAS he was a bold forrester,
　And a chaser of the king's deer;

Faire Ellinor was a fair woman,
  And Lord Thomas he loved her dear.

2 'Come riddle my riddle, dear mother,'
    he said,
  'And riddle us both as one,
Whether I shall marry Fair Ellinor,
  And let the brown girl alone.'

3 'The brown girl she has got houses and
    lands,
  And Fair Ellinor she has got none;
Therefore I charge you on my blessing
  To bring me the brown girl home.'

4 And as it befell on a high holidaye,
  As many did more beside,
Lord Thomas he went to Fair Ellinor,
  That should have been his bride.

5 But when he came to Fair Ellinor's
    bower,
  He knocked there at the ring;
But who was so ready as Fair Ellinor
  For to let Lord Thomas in.

6 'What news, what news, Lord Thomas,'
    she said,
  'What news hast thou brought unto
    me?'
  'I am come to bid thee to my wedding,
  And that is bad news to thee.'

7 'Oh God forbid, Lord Thomas,' she
    said,
  'That such a thing should be done;
I thought to have been thy bride my
    own self,
  And you to have been the brid's-
    groom.

8 'Come riddle my riddle, dear mother,'
    she sayd,
  'And riddle it all in one;
Whether I shall go to Lord Thomas's
    wedding,
  Or whether I shall tarry at home.'

9 'There's many that are your friends,
    daughter,
  And many that are your fo;
Therefore I charge you on my bless-
    ing,
  To Lord Thomas's wedding don't
    go.'

10 'There's many that are my friend
    mother,
  If a thousand more were my foe,
Betide my life, betide my death,
  To Lord Thomas's wedding I'le go.

11 She cloathed herself in gallant attyre,
  And her merry men all in green,
And as they rid thorough everye town
  They took her to have been a queen

12 But when she came to Lord Thomas
    gate,
  She knocked there at the ring;
But who was so ready as Lord Thoma
  To lett Fair Ellinor in.

13 'Is this your bride?' Fair Ellin sh
    sayd,
  'Methinks she looks wondrous browne
Thou mightest have had as fair a woma
  As ever trod on the ground.'

14 'Despise her not, Fair Ellin,' he sayd,
  'Despise her not now unto mee;
For better I love thy little finger
  Than all her whole body.'

15 This browne bride had a little penknife
  That was both long and sharp,
And betwixt the short ribs and the lon
  Prickd Fair Ellinor to the heart.

16 'Oh Christ now save thee,' Lord Thoma
    he said,
  'Methinks thou lookst wondrous wan
Thou wast usd for to look with as fres
    a colour
  As ever the sun shin'd on.'

17 'Oh art thou blind, Lord Thomas?' sh
    sayd,
  'Or canst thou not very well see?
Oh dost thou not see my own heart'
    blood
  Runs trickling down my knee?'

18 Lord Thomas he had a sword by his side
  As he walked about the hall;
He cut off his bride's head from her
    shoulders,
  And he threw it against the wall.

19 He set the hilte against the ground,
  And the point against his heart;

There was never three lovers that ever
    met
More sooner they did depart.

I

Abbotsford MS., Scotch Ballads, Materials
for Border Minstrelsy, No. 22 h ; in the handwriting of William Laidlaw. From Jean Scott.

1 FAIR ANNIE an Sweet Willie
    Sat a' day on yon hill;
    Whan day was gane an night was
        comd,
    They hadna said their fill.

2 Willie spak but ae wrang word,
    An Annie took it ill:
'I 'll never marry a fair woman
    Against my friends's will.'

3 Annie spak but ae wrang word,
    An Willy lookit down:
'If I binna gude eneugh for yer wife,
    I 'm our-gude for yer loun.'

4 Willie 's turnd his horse's head about,
    He 's turnd it to the broom,
    An he 's away to his father's bower,
    I the ae light o the moon.

5 Whan he cam to his father's bower,
    [He tirlt at the pin;
    Nane was sae ready as his father
    To rise an let him in.]

6 ' An askin, an askin, dear father,
    An askin I 'll ask thee; '
' Say on, say on, my son Willie,
    Whatever your askin be.'

7 'O sall I marry the nit-brown bride,
    Has corn, caitle an kye,
    Or sall I marry Fair Annie,
    Has nought but fair beauty ? '

8 ' Ye ma sit a gude sate, Willy,
    Wi corn, caitle an kye;
    But ye 'll but sit a silly sate
    Wi nought but fair beauty.'

9 Up than spak his sister's son,
    Sat on the nurse's knee,
    Sun-bruist in his mother's wame,
    Sun-brunt on his nurse's knee:

10 'O yer hogs will die out i the field,
    Yer kye ill die i the byre;
    An than, whan a' yer gear is gane,
    A fusom fag by yer fire !
    But a' will thrive at is wi you
    An ye get yer heart's desire.'

11 Willie 's turnd his horse's head about,
    He 's away to his mother's bour,
    etc.

12 'O my hogs ill die out i the field,
    My kye die i the byre,
    An than, whan a' my gear is gane,
    A fusom fag bi my fire !
    But a' will thrive at is wi me
    Gin I get my heart's desire.'

13 Willie 's, etc.,
    He 's awae to his brother's bower, etc.

14 "   "   "   " sister's bower, etc.

15 Than Willie has set his wadin-day
    Within thirty days an three,
    An he has sent to Fair Annie
    His waddin to come an see.

16 The man that gade to Fair Annie
    Sae weel his errant coud tell:
' The morn it 's Willie's wadin-day,
    Ye maun be there yer sell.'

17 'T was up an spak her aged father,
    He spak wi muckle care;
' An the morn be Willie's wadin-day,
    I wate she maun be there.

18 ' Gar take a steed to the smiddie,
    Caw on o it four shoon;
    Gar take her to a merchant's shop,
    Cut off for her a gown.'

19 She wadna ha 't o the red sae red
    Nor yet o the grey sae grey,
    But she wad ha 't o the sky couler
    That she woor ilka day.

*   *   *   *   *

20 There war four-a-twontie gray goss-
        hawks
    A' flaffin their wings sae wide,
    To flaff the stour thra off the road
    That Fair Annie did ride.

21 The[re] war four-an-twontie milk-white
      dows
   A' fleein aboon her head,
   An four-an-twontie milk-white swans
      Her out the gate to lead.

22 Whan she cam to St Marie's kirk,
      She lightit on a stane;
   The beauty o that fair creature
      Shone oer mony ane.

23 'T was than out cam the nit-brown
      bride,
      She spak wi muckle spite;
   'O where gat ye the water, Annie,
      That washes you sae white?'

24 'I gat my beauty
      Where ye was no to see;
   I gat it i my father's garden,
      Aneath an apple tree.

25 'Ye ma wash i dubs,' she said,
      'An ye ma wash i syke,
   But an ye wad wash till doomsday
      Ye neer will be as white.

26 'Ye ma wash i dubs,' she said,
      'An ye ma wash i the sea,
   But an ye soud wash till doomsday
      Ye'll neer be as white as me.

27 'For I gat a' this fair beauty
      Where ye gat never none,
   For I gat a' this fair beauty
      Or ever I was born.'

28 It was than out cam Willie,
      Wi hats o silks and flowers;
   He said, Keep ye thae, my Fair Annie,
      An brook them weel for yours.

29 'Na, keep ye thae, Willie,' she said,
      'Gie them to yer nit-brown bride;
   Bid her wear them wi mukle care,
      For woman has na born a son
      Sal mak my heart as sair.'

30 Annie's luppen on her steed
      An she has ridden hame,
   Than Annie's luppen of her steed
      An her bed she has taen.

31 When mass was sung, an bells war
      rung,
      An a' man bound to bed,

An Willie an his nit-brown bride
   I their chamber war laid,

32 They war na weel laid in their bed,
      Nor yet weel faen asleep,
   Till up an startit Fair Annie,
      Just up at Willie's feet.

33 'How like ye yer bed, Willie?
      An how like ye yer sheets?
   An how like ye yer nut-brown bride,
      Lies in yer arms an sleeps?'

34 'Weel eneugh I like my bed, Annie,
      Weel eneugh I like my sheets;
   But wae be to the nit-brown bride
      Lies in my arms an sleeps!'

35 Willie's ca'd on his merry men a'
      To rise an pit on their shoon;
   'An we'll awae to Annie's bower,
      Wi the ae light o the moon.'

36 An whan he cam to Annie's bower,
      He tirlt at the pin;
   Nane was sae ready as her father
      To rise an let him in.

37 There was her father a[n] her se'e[n]
      brethren
   A' makin to her a bier,
   Wi ae stamp o the melten goud,
      Another o siller clear.

38 When he cam to the chamber-door
      Where that the dead lay in,
   There was her mother an six sisters
      A' makin to her a sheet,
   Wi ae drap o   .   .   .   .
      Another o silk sae white.

39 'Stand by, stand by now, ladies a',
      Let me look on the dead;
   The last time that I kiss[t] her lips
      They war mair bonny red.'

40 'Stand by, stand by now, Willie,' the[y]
      said,
      'An let ye her alane;
   Gin ye had done as ye soud done,
      She wad na there ha lien.'

41 'Gar deal, gar deal at Annie's burrial
      The wheat bread an the wine,
   For or the morn at ten o clock
      Ye's deal'd as fast at mine.'

74

AIR MARGARET AND SWEET WILLIAM

A, a, b, c, are broadside or stall copies, a of
e end of the seventeenth century, b "mod-
n" in Percy's time. The ballad is twice
oted in Beaumont and Fletcher's Knight of
e Burning Pestle, 1611 (ii, 8; iii, 5). David
allet published as his own, in 1724, 'Mar-
ret's Ghost,' which turns out to be simply
Villiam and Margaret, an Old Ballad,' printed
1711, with a few changes. The 1711 text is
nply 'Fair Margaret and Sweet William'
written in what used to be called an elegant
yle.
' Fair Margaret and Sweet William ' begins
e No. 73, and from the fifth stanza on is
ended with a form of that ballad. The
tastrophe of ' Fair Margaret and Sweet Wil-
,m ' is repeated in ' Lord Lovel ' (No. 75).

A

a. ' Fair Margaret's Misfortune,' etc., Douce
allads, I, fol. 72. b. ' Fair Margaret and
veet William,' Ritson, A Select Collection
English Songs, 1783, II, 190. c. ' Fair Mar-
ret and Sweet William,' Percy's Reliques,
65, III, 121. d. Percy's Reliques, 1767, III,
9.

As it fell out on a long summer's day,
  Two lovers they sat on a hill;
They sat together that long summer's
    day,
  And could not talk their fill.

' I see no harm by you, Margaret,
  Nor you see none by me;
Before tomorrow eight a clock
  A rich wedding shall you see.'

Fair Margaret sat in her bower-window,
  A combing of her hair,
And there she spy'd Sweet William and
    his bride,
  As they were riding near.

Down she layd her ivory comb,
  And up she bound her hair;
She went her way forth of her bower,
  But never more did come there.

When day was gone, and night was
    come,
  And all men fast asleep,

Then came the spirit of Fair Margaret,
  And stood at William's feet.

6 'God give you joy, you two true lovers,
    In bride-bed fast asleep;
  Loe I am going to my green grass grave,
    And am in my winding-sheet.'

7 When day was come, and night was
      gone,
    And all men wak'd from sleep,
  Sweet William to his lady said,
    ' My dear, I have cause to weep.

8 'I dreamd a dream, my dear lady;
    Such dreams are never good;
  I dreamd my bower was full of red
      swine,
    And my bride-bed full of blood.'

9 'Such dreams, such dreams, my hon-
      oured lord,
    They never do prove good,
  To dream thy bower was full of swine,
    And [thy] bride-bed full of blood.'

10 He called up his merry men all,
    By one, by two, and by three,
  Saying, I 'll away to Fair Margaret's
      bower,
    By the leave of my lady.

11 And when he came to Fair Margaret's
      bower,
    He knocked at the ring;
  So ready was her seven brethren
    To let Sweet William in.

12 He turned up the covering-sheet:
    ' Pray let me see the dead;
  Methinks she does look pale and wan,
    She has lost her cherry red.

13 'I 'll do more for thee, Margaret,
    Than any of thy kin;
  For I will kiss thy pale wan lips,
    Tho a smile I cannot win.'

14 With that bespeak her seven brethren,
    Making most pitious moan:
  ' You may go kiss your jolly brown bride
    And let our sister alone.'

15 'If I do kiss my jolly brown bride,
    I do but what is right;

For I made no vow to your sister dear,
  By day or yet by night.

16 ' Pray tell me then how much you 'll deal
  Of your white bread and your wine;
  So much as is dealt at her funeral today
  Tomorrow shall be dealt at mine.'

17 Fair Margaret dy'd today, today,
  Sweet William he dy'd the morrow;
  Fair Margaret dy'd for pure true love,
  Sweet William he dy'd for sorrow.

18 Margaret was buried in the lower chan-
    cel,
  Sweet William in the higher;
  Out of her breast there sprung a rose,
  And out of his a brier.

19 They grew as high as the church-top,
  Till they could grow no higher,
  And then they grew in a true lover's
    knot,
  Which made all people admire.

20 There came the clerk of the parish,
  As you this truth shall hear,
  And by misfortune cut them down,
  Or they had now been there.

B

Percy Papers; communicated by the Dean
of Derry, as written down from memory by
his mother, Mrs Bernard; February, 1776.

1 SWEET WILLIAM would a wooing ride,
  His steed was lovely brown;
  A fairer creature than Lady Margaret
  Sweet William could find none.

2 Sweet William came to Lady Margaret's
    bower,
  And knocked at the ring,
  And who so ready as Lady Margaret
  To rise and to let him in.

3 Down then came her father dear,
  Clothed all in blue:
  ' I pray, Sweet William, tell to me
  What love 's between my daughter
    and you ? '

4 ' I know none by her,' he said,
  ' And she knows none by me;

Before tomorrow at this time
  Another bride you shall see.'

5 Lady Margaret at her bower-window,
  Combing of her hair,
  She saw Sweet William and his brow
    bride
  Unto the church repair.

6 Down she cast her iv'ry comb,
  And up she tossd her hair,
  She went out from her bowr alive,
  But never so more came there.

7 When day was gone, and night was com
  All people were asleep,
  In glided Margaret's grimly ghost,
  And stood at William's feet.

8 ' How d' ye like your bed, Sweet W
    liam ?
  How d' ye like your sheet ?
  And how d 'ye like that brown lady,
  That lies in your arms asleep ? '

9 ' Well I like my bed, Lady Margaret,
  And well I like my sheet;
  But better I like that fair lady
  That stands at my bed's feet.'

10 When night was gone, and day w
    come,
  All people were awake,
  The lady waket out of her sleep,
  And thus to her lord she spake.

11 ' I dreamd a dream, my wedded lord,
  That seldom comes to good;
  I dreamd that our bowr was lin'd wi
    white swine,
  And our brid-chamber full of blood

12 He called up his merry men all,
  By one, by two, by three,
  ' We will go to Lady Margaret's bow
  With the leave of my wedded lady

13 When he came to Lady Margare
    bower,
  He knocked at the ring,
  And who were so ready as her brethr
  To rise and let him in.

14 ' Oh is she in the parlor,' he said,
  ' Or is she in the hall ?

Or is she in the long chamber,
    Amongst her merry maids all ? '

5 ' She 's not in the parlor,' they said,
    ' Nor is she in the hall;
But she is in the long chamber,
    Laid out against the wall.'

6 ' Open the winding sheet,' he cry'd,
    ' That I may kiss the dead;
That I may kiss her pale and wan
    Whose lips used to look so red.'

7 Lady Margaret [died] on the over night,
    Sweet William died on the morrow;
Lady Margaret died for pure, pure
    love,
Sweet William died for sorrow.

8 On Margaret's grave there grew a rose,
    On Sweet William's grew a briar;
They grew till they joind in a true
    lover's knot,
And then they died both together.

75

LORD LOVEL

In ' Fair Margaret and Sweet William '
(No. 74), as also in ' Lord Thomas and Fair
Annet ' (No. 73), a lover sacrifices his inclination to make a marriage of interest. In ' Lord
Lovel ' the woman dies, not of affections betrayed, but of hopes too long deferred, and
her laggard but not unfaithful lover sinks
under his remorse and grief. There are several sets of ballads, very common in Germany
and in Scandinavia, which, whether they are
or are not variations of the same original,
at least have a great deal in common with
' Lord Lovel ' and ' Fair Margaret and Sweet
William.' Of these, one which more closely
resembles the English is ' Der Ritter und die
Maid,' of German origin (see Uhland, No. 97;
Erk, Liederhort, No. 26), but found also in
Scandinavia. A Romaic ballad (Passow, No.
415) has the characteristic features of the English, German, and Scandinavian stories, with a
beginning of its own, as these also have.

A

' Lady Ouncebell,' Percy Papers, communicated by the Rev. P. Parsons, of Wye, from
singing · May 22, 1770, and April 19, 1775.

1 ' AND I fare you well, Lady Ouncebell,
    For I must needs be gone,
And this time two year I 'll meet you
    again,
To finish the loves we begun.'

2 ' That is a long time, Lord Lovill,' said
    she,
    ' To live in fair Scotland; '
' And so it is, Lady Ouncebell,
    To leave a fair lady alone.'

3 He had not been in fair Scotland
    Not half above half a year,
But a longin mind came into his head,
    Lady Ouncebell he woud go see her.

4 He called up his stable-groom,
    To sadle his milk-white stead;
Dey down, dey down, dey down dery
    down,
I wish Lord Lovill good speed.

5 He had not been in fair London
    Not half above half a day,
But he heard the bells of the high chapel
    ring,
They rang with a ceserera.

6 He asked of a gentleman,
    That set there all alone,
What made the bells of the high chapel
    ring,
The ladys make all their moan.

7 ' One of the king's daughters are dead,'
    said he,
    ' Lady Ouncebell was her name;
She died for love of a courtous young
    night,
Lord Lovill he was the same.'

8 He caused her corps to be set down,
    And her winding sheet undone,
And he made a vow before them all
    He 'd never kiss wowman again.

9 Lady Ouncebell died on the yesterday,
    Lord Lovill on the morrow;
Lady Ouncebell died for pure true love,
    Lord Lovill died for sorrow.

10 Lady Ouncebell was buried in the high
    chancel,
Lord Lovill in the choir:

Lady Ouncebell's breast sprung out a
        sweet rose,
    Lord Lovill's a bunch of sweet
        brier.

11 They grew till they grew to the top of
        the church,
    And then they could grow no higher;
    They grew till they grew to a true-lover's
        not,
    And then they tyed both together.

12 An old wowman coming by that way,
    And a blessing she did crave,
    To cut off a bunch of that true-lover's
        not,
    And buried them both in one grave.

B

'Lord Lavel,' Kinloch MSS., I, 45, from the
recitation of Mary Barr, of Lesmahago, " aged
upwards of 70," May, 1827.

1 LORD LAVEL he stands at his stable-
        door,
    Kaiming his milk-white steed;
    And by and cam Fair Nancybelle,
    And wished Lord Lavel good speed.

2 'O whare are ye goiug, Lord Lavel ? '
        she said,
    'I pray ye tell to me:'
    'O I am going to merry England,
    To win your love aff me.'

3 'And whan will ye return again ? ' she
        said,
    'Lord Lavel, pray tell to me: '
    'Whan seven lang years are past and
        gane,
    Fair Nancybelle, I 'll return to thee.'

4 ''T is too lang, Lord Lavel,' she said,
    ''T is too lang for me;
    'T is too lang, Lord Lavel,' she said,
    ' A true lover for to see.'

*   *   *   *   *

5 He had na been in merry England
    A month but barely three,
    Till languishing thoughts cam into his
        mind,
    Ard Nancybelle fain wad he see.

6 He rade, and he rade, alang the hieway
    Till he cam to yonder toun;
    He heard the sound o a fine chapel-bell
    And the ladies were mourning roun.

7 He rade, and he rade, alang the hieway
    Till he cam to yonder hall;
    He heard the sound o a fine chapel-bell
    And the ladies were mourning all.

8 He asked wha it was that was dead,
    The ladies did him tell:
    They said, It is the king's daughter,
    Her name is Fair Nancybelle;
    She died for the love of a courteous
        young knicht,
    His name is Lord Lavel.

9 'O hast thou died, Fair Nancybelle,
    O hast thou died for me !
    O hast thou died, Fair Nancybelle !
    Then I will die for thee.'

10 Fair Nancybelle died, as it might be,
        this day,
    Lord Lavel he died tomorrow;
    Fair Nancybelle died with pure, pure
        love,
    Lord Lavel he died with sorrow.

11 Lord Lavel was buried in Mary's kirk,
    Nancybelle in Mary's quire;
    And out o the ane there grew a birk,
    Out the other a bonny brier.

12 And ae they grew, and ae they threw,
    Until they twa did meet,
    That ilka ane might plainly see
    They war twa lovers sweet.

D

' Lord Lovel,' Kinloch MSS.. VII, 83, from
the recitation of a lady of Roxburghshire;
Kinloch's Ancient Scottish Ballads, p. 31.

1 LORD LOVEL stands at his stable-door,
    Mounted upon a grey steed,
    And bye cam Ladie Nanciebel,
    And wishd Lord Lovel much speed.

2 'O whare are ye going, Lord Lovel ?
    My dearest, tell unto me:'
    'I am going a far journey,
    Some strange countrey to see.'

3 'But I 'll return in seven long years,
   Lady Nanciebel to see:'
  'Oh seven, seven, seven long years,
   They are much too long for me.'

*   *   *   *   *

4 He was gane about a year away,
   A year but barely ane,
  Whan a strange fancy cam intil his
   head
  That fair Nanciebel was gane.

5 It 's then he rade, and better rade,
   Untill he cam to the toun,
  And there he heard a dismal noise,
   For the church bells aw did soun.

6 He asked what the bells rang for;
   They said, It 's for Nanciebel;
  She died for a discourteous squire,
   And his name is Lord Lovel.

7 The lid of the coffin he opened up,
   The linens he faulded doun,
  And ae he kissd her pale, pale lips,
   And the tears cam trinkling doun.

8 'Weill may I kiss these pale, pale lips,
   For they will never kiss me;
  I 'll mak a vow, and I 'll keep it true,
   That I 'll neer kiss ane but thee.'

9 Lady Nancie died on Tuesday's nicht,
   Lord Lovel upon the niest day;
  Lady Nancie died for pure, pure love,
   Lord Lovel for deep sorraye.

76

THE LASS OF ROCH ROYAL

A, the oldest copy, published for the first
time in Child's English and Scottish Popular
Ballads, is from a manuscript of the first half
of the eighteenth century. A has a preliminary history wanting in all others, but the story
is somewhat obscure and two different relations
may have been confounded. The conclusion
of A is that of 'Lord Lovel' (No. 75) and
'Fair Margaret and Sweet William' (No. 74),
and must perhaps be set aside as not the original one.

A

'Fair Isabell of Rochroyall,' Elizabeth Cochrane's Song-Book, MS., p. 151, No. 114.

1 FAIR ISABELL of Rochroyall,
   She dreamed where she lay,
  She dreamd a dream of her love Gregory,
   A litle before the day.

2 O huly, huly rose she up,
   And huly she put on,
  And huly, huly she put on
   The silks of crimsion.

3 'Gar sadle me the black,' she sayes,
  'Gar sadle me the broun;
  Gar sadle me the swiftest steed
   That ever rode the toun.

4 'Gar shoe him with the beat silver,
   And grind him with the gold;
  Gar put two bells on every side,
   Till I come to some hold.'

5 She had not rode a mile, a mile,
   A mile but barely three,
  Till that she spyed a companie
   Come rakeing oere the lee.

6 'O whether is this the first young may,
   That lighted and gaed in;
  Or is this the second young may,
   That neer the sun shined on?
  Or is this Fair Isabell of Roch Royall,
   Banist from kyth and kin?'

7 'O I am not the first young may,
   That lighted and gaed in;
  Nor neither am I the second young
   may,
   That neer the sun shone on;

8 'But I 'm Fair Isabell of Roch Royall
   Banist from kyth and kin;
  I 'm seeking my true-love Gregory,
   And I woud I had him in.'

9 'O go your way to yon castle,
   And ride it round about,
  And there you 'll find Love Gregory;
   He 's within, without any doubt.'

10 O she 's away to yon castle,
   She 's tirled at the pin:
  'O open, open, Love Gregory,
   And let your true-love in.'

11 'If you be the lass of the Rochroyall,
   As I trow not you be,

You will tell me some of our love-
tokens,
That was betwixt you and me.'

12 'Have you not mind, Love Gregory,
Since we sat at the wine;
When we changed the rings off our
fingers,
And ay the worst fell mine?

13 'Mine was of the massy gold,
And thine was of the tin;
Mine was true and trusty both,
And thine was false within.'

14 'If you be [the] lass of the Roch Royall,
As I trow not you be,
You will tell me some other love-token
That was betwixt you and me.'

15 'Have you not mind, Love Gregory,
Since we sat at the wine,
We changed the smocks off our two
backs,
And ay the worst fell mine?

16 'Mine was of the holland fine,
And thine was course and thin;
So many blocks have we two made,
And ay the worst was mine.'

17 'Love Gregory, he is not at home,
But he is to the sea;
If you have any word to him,
I pray you leave 't with me.'

*   *   *   *   *

18 'O who will shoe my bony foot?
Or who will glove my hand?
Or who will bind my midle jimp
With the broad lilly band?

19 'Or who will comb my bony head
With the red river comb?
Or who will be my bairn's father
Ere Gregory he come home?'

20 'O I's gar shoe thy bony foot,
And I's gar glove thy hand,
And I's gar bind thy midle jimp
With the broad lilly band.

21 'And I's gar comb thy bony head
With the red river comb;

But there is none to be thy bairn's fa
ther
Till Love Gregory he come home.'

22 'I'll set my foot on the ship-board,
God send me wind and more!
For there's never a woman shall bear a
son
Shall make my heart so sore.'

23 'I dreamed a dream now since yestreen
That I never dreamed before;
I dreamd that the lass of the Roch
royall
Was knocking at the door.'

24 'Ly still, ly still, my 6 dear son,
Ly still, and take a sleep;
For it's neither ane hour, nor yet a half
Since she went from the gate.'

25 'O wo be to you, ill woman,
And ane ill death mott you die!
For you might have come to my bedside
And then have wakened me.

26 'Gar sadle me the black,' he sayes,
'Gar sadle me the broun;
Gar sadle me the swiftest steed
That ever rode the toun.

27 'Gar shoe him with the beat silver,
Gar grind him with the gold;
Cause put two bells on every side,
Till I come to some hold.'

28 They sadled him the black, the black,
So did they him the broun;
So did they him the swiftest steed
That ever rode to toun.

29 They shoed him with the beat silver,
They grind him with the gold;
They put two bells on every side,
Till he came to some hold.

30 He had not rode a mile, a mile,
A mile but barely three,
Till that he spyed her comely corps
Come raking oere the lee.

31 'Set doun, set doun these comely corps,
Let me look on the dead:'
And out he's ta'en his little pen-knife,
And slitted her winding sheet.

32 And first he kist her cheek, her cheek,
　　And then he kist her chin;
　　And then he kist her rosy lips,
　　But there was no breath within.

33 'Gar deall, gar deall for my love sake
　　The spiced bread and the wine;
　　For ere the morn at this time
　　So shall you deall for mine.

34 'Gar deall, gar deall for my love sake
　　The pennys that are so small;
　　For ere the morn at this time
　　So shall you deall for all.'

35 The one was buried in Mary kirk,
　　The other in Mary quire;
　　Out of the one there sprung a birk,
　　Out of the other a bryar;
　　So thus you may well know by that
　　They were two lovers dear.

D

'Fair Anny,' Jamieson-Brown MS., p. 27;
Fair Annie of Lochroyan,' Jamieson's Popular Ballads, I, 36.

1 'O WHA will shoe my fu fair foot?
　　An wha will glove my han?
　　An wha will lace my middle gimp
　　Wi the new made London ban?

2 'Or wha will kemb my yallow hair,
　　Wi the new made silver kemb?
　　Or wha 'll be father to my young bairn,
　　Till Love Gregor come hame?'

3 Her father shoed her fu fair foot,
　　Her mother glovd her han;
　　Her sister lac'd her middle gimp
　　Wi the new made London ban.

4 Her brother kembd her yallow hair,
　　Wi the new made silver kemb,
　　But the king o heaven maun father her
　　　bairn,
　　Till Love Gregor come hame.

5 'O gin I had a bony ship,
　　An men to sail wi me,
　　It 's I would gang to my true-love,
　　Since he winna come to me.'

6 Her father 's gien her a bonny ship,
　　An sent her to the stran;

She 's tane her young son in her arms,
　　An turnd her back to the lan.

7 She had na been o the sea saillin
　　About a month or more,
　　Till landed has she her bonny ship
　　Near her true-love's door.

8 The night was dark, an the win blew
　　　caul,
　　An her love was fast asleep,
　　An the bairn that was in her twa
　　　arms
　　Fu sair began to weep.

9 Long stood she at her true-love's door,
　　An lang tirld at the pin;
　　At length up gat his fa'se mither,
　　Says, Wha 's that woud be in?

10 'O it is Anny of Roch-royal,
　　Your love, come oer the sea,
　　But an your young son in her arms;
　　So open the door to me.'

11 'Awa, awa, you ill woman,
　　You 've na come here for gude;
　　You 're but a witch, or wile warlock,
　　Or mermaid o the flude.'

12 'I 'm na a witch, or wile warlock,
　　Nor mermaiden,' said she;
　　'I 'm but Fair Anny o Roch-royal;
　　O open the door to me.'

13 'O gin ye be Anny o Roch-royal,
　　As [I] trust not ye be,
　　What taiken can ye gie that ever
　　I kept your company?'

14 'O dinna ye mind, Love Gregor,' she
　　　says,
　　'Whan we sat at the wine,
　　How we changed the napkins frae our
　　　necks,
　　It 's na sae lang sin syne?

15 'An yours was good, an good enough,
　　But nae sae good as mine;
　　For yours was o the cumbruk clear,
　　But mine was silk sae fine.

16 'An dinna ye mind, Love Gregor,' she
　　　says,
　　'As we twa sat at dine,

How we changed the rings frae our
fingers,
But ay the best was mine ?

17 'For yours was good, an good enough,
Yet nae sae good as mine;
For yours was of the good red gold,
But mine o the diamonds fine.

18 'Sae open the door now, Love Gregor,
An open it wi speed,
Or your young son that is in my arms
For cauld will soon be dead.'

19 'Awa, awa, you ill woman,
Gae frae my door for shame;
For I hae gotten another fair love,
Sae ye may hye you hame.'

20 'O hae you gotten another fair love,
For a' the oaths you sware ?
Then fair you well now, fa'se Gregor,
For me you 's never see mair.'

21 O heely, heely gi'd she back,
As the day began to peep;
She set her foot on good ship-board,
An sair, sair did she weep.

22 Love Gregor started frae his sleep,
An to his mither did say,
I dreamd a dream this night, mither,
That maks my heart right wae.

23 'I dreamd that Anny of Roch-royal,
The flowr o a' her kin,
Was standin mournin at my door,
But nane would lat her in.'

24 'O there was a woman stood at the
door,
Wi a bairn intill her arms,
But I woud na lat her within the
bowr,
For fear she had done you harm.'

25 O quickly, quickly raise he up,
An fast ran to the stran,
An there he saw her Fair Anny,
Was sailin frae the lan.

26 An 'Heigh, Anny !' an 'Hou, Anny !
O Anny, speak to me !'
But ay the louder that he cried Anny,
The louder roard the sea.

27 An 'Heigh, Anny !' an 'Hou, Anny !
O Anny, winna you bide ?'
But ay the langer that he cried Anny,
The higher roard the tide.

28 The win grew loud, an the sea grew
rough,
An the ship was rent in twain,
An soon he saw her Fair Anny
Come floating oer the main.

29 He saw his young son in her arms,
Baith tossd aboon the tide;
He wrang his hands, than fast he ran,
An plung'd i the sea sae wide.

30 He catchd her by the yallow hair,
An drew her to the strand,
But cauld an stiff was every limb
Before he reachd the land.

31 O first he kissd her cherry cheek,
An then he kissd her chin;
An sair he kissd her ruby lips,
But there was nae breath within.

32 O he has mournd oer Fair Anny
Till the sun was gaing down,
Then wi a sigh his heart it brast,
An his soul to heaven has flown.

77

SWEET WILLIAM'S GHOST

The story of this ballad seems to have become
disordered in most of the versions. A alone, the
first published, has perhaps retained the original form. The principal idea is, however, preserved in all the full versions : the dead lover
returns to ask back his unfulfilled troth-plight.
His grave is wrongly said in A to be far beyond
the sea. B constitutes, in Herd's MSS, and F,
in Jamieson's Popular Ballads, the termination
of a copy of 'Clerk Saunders' (No. 69).
'Sweet William's Ghost' has much in common with one of the most beautiful and celebrated of the Scandinavian ballads, 'The Betrothed in the Grave' (Grundtvig, No. 90), and
may well be a different development of the same
story. A man dies as he is to be married. His
love grieves for him passionately. The dead
hears her under the ground. comes to her bower
with his coffin on his back, and knocks. She
lets him in after he has proved himself to be
"a spirit of health" by uttering the name of

esus. combs his hair, and asks him how it is
nder the black earth. It is like the bliss of
eaven. May she follow him into the grave?
; is like blackest hell. Every time she weeps
r him his coffin is filled with lappered blood.
ut when she sings and is happy, his grave is
ll hung with rose-leaves. The cock crows, the
hite, the red, the black ; he takes up his coffin
nd goes wearily back to the graveyard. His
ve follows through the mirk wood, to the
urchyard and into the church. Then his
ellow hair falls away, his rosy color wanes.
e bids her go home and never weep for him
ore. " Look up at the sky, the night is go-
g !" and as she looks he slips into his grave.
he goes sadly home, prays God that she may
ot live out a year and a day, falls sick, and
es within a month. The Scandinavian ballad
grees in many particulars with the conclusion
f the second lay of Helgi Hundingsbani in the
lder Edda.

A

'Sweet William's Ghost,' Ramsay's Tea
able Miscellany, "4th volume, 1740 ;" here
rom the London edition of 1750, p. 324.

1 THERE came a ghost to Margret's
      door,
    With many a grievous groan,
  And ay he tirled at the pin,
    But answer made she none.

2 'Is that my father Philip,
    Or is 't my brother John ?
  Or is 't my true-love, Willy,
    From Scotland new come home ? '

3 ''T is not thy father Philip,
    Nor yet thy brother John;
  But 't is thy true-love, Willy,
    From Scotland new come home.

4 'O sweet Margret, O dear Margret,
    I pray thee speak to me;
  Give me my faith and troth, Margret,
    As I gave it to thee.'

5 'Thy faith and troth thou's never
      get,
    Nor yet will I thee lend,
  Till that thou come within my bower,
    And kiss my cheek and chin.'

6 'If I shoud come within thy bower,
    I am no earthly man;

And shoud I kiss thy rosy lips,
    Thy days will not be lang.

7 'O sweet Margret, O dear Margret,
    I pray thee speak to me;
  Give me my faith and troth, Margret,
    As I gave it to thee.'

8 'Thy faith and troth thou 's never get,
    Nor yet will I thee lend,
  Till you take me to yon kirk,
    And wed me with a ring.'

9 'My bones are buried in yon kirk-yard,
    Afar beyond the sea,
  And it is but my spirit, Margret,
    That 's now speaking to thee.'

10 She stretchd out her lilly-white hand,
    And, for to do her best,
  'Hae, there 's your faith and troth,
        Willy,
    God send your soul good rest.'

11 Now she has kilted her robes of green
      A piece below her knee,
  And a' the live-lang winter night
    The dead corp followed she.

12 'Is there any room at your head, Willy ?
    Or any room at your feet ?
  Or any room at your side, Willy,
    Wherein that I may creep ? '

13 'There 's no room at my head, Margret,
    There 's no room at my feet;
  There 's no room at my side, Margret,
    My coffin 's made so meet.'

14 Then up and crew the red, red cock,
    And up then crew the gray:
  'Tis time, tis time, my dear Margret,
    That you were going away.'

15 No more the ghost to Margret said,
    But, with a grievous groan,
  Evanishd in a cloud of mist,
    And left her all alone.

16 'O stay, my only true-love, stay,'
    The constant Margret cry'd;
  Wan grew her cheeks, she closd her
        een,
    Stretchd her soft limbs, and dy'd.

B

Herd's MSS., I, 177, II, 49, stanzas 27 ff.

1 WHAN bells war rung, an mass was
　　sung,
　　A wat a' man to bed were gone,
　Clark Sanders came to Margret's win-
　　dow,
　　With mony a sad sigh and groan.

2 'Are ye sleeping, Margret,' he says,
　　'Or are ye waking, presentlie?
　Give me my faith and trouthe again,
　　A wat, trew-love, I gied to thee.'

3 'Your faith and trouth ye's never get,
　　Nor our trew love shall never twain,
　Till ye come with me in my bower,
　　And kiss me both cheek and chin.'

4 'My mouth it is full cold, Margret,
　　It has the smell now of the ground;
　And if I kiss thy comely mouth,
　　Thy life-days will not be long.

5 'Cocks are crowing a merry mid-larf,
　　I wat the wild fule boded day;
　Gie me my faith and trouthe again,
　　And let me fare me on my way.'

6 'Thy faith and trouth thou shall na get,
　　Nor our trew love shall never twin,
　Till ye tell me what comes of women
　　Awat that dy's in strong traveling.'

7 'Their beds are made in the heavens
　　high,
　　Down at the foot of our good Lord's
　　knee,
　Well set about wi gilly-flowers,
　　A wat sweet company for to see.

8 'O cocks are crowing a merry midd-
　　larf,
　　A wat the wilde foule boded day;
　The salms of Heaven will be sung,
　　And ere now I 'le be misst away.'

9 Up she has tain a bright long wand,
　　And she has straked her trouth there-
　　on;
　She has given [it] him out at the shot-
　　window,
　　Wi many a sad sigh and heavy groan.

10 'I thank you, Margret, I thank you
　　Margret,
　　And I thank you hartilie;
　Gine ever the dead come for the quick,
　　Be sure, Margret, I 'll come again fc
　　thee.'

11 It 's hose an shoon an gound alane
　　She clame the wall and followed hin
　Untill she came to a green forest,
　　On this she lost the sight of him.

12 'Is their any room at your head, Sar
　　ders?
　　Is their any room at your feet?
　Or any room at your twa sides?
　　Whare fain, fain woud I sleep.'

13 'Their is na room at my head, Margret
　　Their is na room at my feet;
　There is room at my twa sides,
　　For ladys for to sleep.

14 'Cold meal is my covering owre,
　　But an my winding sheet;
　My bed it is full low, I say,
　　Down among the hongerey worms
　　sleep.

15 'Cold meal is my covering owre,
　　But an my winding sheet;
　The dew it falls na sooner down
　　Then ay it is full weet.'

F

Jamieson's Popular Ballads, I, 83, stanzas 26 ff

1 WHEN seven years were come and gane
　　Lady Margaret she thought lang;
　And she is up to the hichest tower,
　　By the lee licht o the moon.

2 She was lookin oer her castle high,
　　To see what she might fa,
　And there she saw a grieved ghost,
　　Comin waukin oer the wa.

3 'O are ye a man of mean,' she says,
　　'Seekin ony o my meat?
　Or are you a rank robber,
　　Come in my bower to break?'

4 'O I 'm Clerk Saunders, your true-love
　　Behold, Margaret, and see,

And mind, for a' your meikle pride,
Sae will become of thee.'

5 'Gin ye be Clerk Saunders, my true-
love,
This meikle marvels me;
O wherein is your bonny arms,
That wont to embrace me?'

6 'By worms they're eaten, in mools
they're rotten,
Behold, Margaret, and see,
And mind, for a' your mickle pride,
Sae will become o thee.'

* * * * *

7 O, bonny, bonny sang the bird,
Sat on the coil o hay;
But dowie, dowie was the maid
That followd the corpse o clay.

8 'Is there ony room at your head, Saun-
ders?
Is there ony room at your feet?
Is there ony room at your twa sides,
For a lady to lie and sleep?'

9 'There is nae room at my head, Mar-
garet,
As little at my feet;
There is nae room at my twa sides,
For a lady to lie and sleep.

10 'But gae hame, gae hame now, May
Margaret,
Gae hame and sew your seam;
For if ye were laid in your weel made
bed,
Your days will nae be lang.'

G

Abbotsford MS., Scotch Ballads, Materials
for Border Minstrelsy, No. 141; in the handwriting of James Hogg. Minstrelsy of the
Scottish Border, III, 183, ed. 1833.

1 'But plett a wand o bonnie birk
An lay it on my breast,
An drap a tear upon my grave,
An wiss my saul gude rest.

2 'But fair Marget, an rare Marget,
An Marget, o verity,

If eer ye loe another man,
Neer loe him as ye did me.'

3 But up then crew the milk-white cock,
An up then crew the grey;
Her lover vanishd in the air,
An she gaed weepin away.

78

THE UNQUIET GRAVE

This fragmentary ballad exhibits the universal popular belief that excessive grieving
for the dead interferes with their repose. There
are many tales and ballads that express this
superstition. One of the most striking is contained in the second lay of Helgi Hundingsbani
in the Elder Edda (see introduction to No. 77).
Cf. 'The Twa Brothers,' No. 49, B, sts. 10–12.

A

'The Unquiet Grave,' communicated to the
Folk Lore Record, I, 60, 1868, by Miss Charlotte Latham, as written down from the lips of
a girl in Sussex.

1 'The wind doth blow today, my love,
And a few small drops of rain;
I never had but one true-love,
In cold grave she was lain.

2 'I'll do as much for my true-love
As any young man may;
I'll sit and mourn all at her grave
For a twelvemonth and a day.'

3 The twelvemonth and a day being up,
The dead began to speak:
'Oh who sits weeping on my grave,
And will not let me sleep?'

4 ''T is I, my love, sits on your grave,
And will not let you sleep;
For I crave one kiss of your clay-cold
lips,
And that is all I seek.'

5 'You crave one kiss of my clay-cold lips;
But my breath smells earthy strong;
If you have one kiss of my clay-cold lips,
Your time will not be long.

6 ''T is down in yonder garden green,
Love, where we used to walk,

The finest flower that ere was seen
Is withered to a stalk.

7 'The stalk is withered dry, my love,
So will our hearts decay;
So make yourself content, my love,
Till God calls you away.'

79

THE WIFE OF USHER'S WELL

A motive for the return of the Wife's three
sons is not found in A and B. The mother
had cursed the sea when she first heard they
were lost, and can only go mad when she finds
that after all she has not recovered them; nor
will a little wee while make any difference.
There is no indication that the sons come back
to forbid obstinate grief, as the dead often do.
C and D, however, say that they return in
answer to prayer. But supplying a motive
would add nothing to the impressiveness of the
verses. Nothing that we have is more pro-
foundly affecting.

A

'The Wife of Usher's Well,' Minstrelsy of
the Scottish Border, II, 111, 1802, from the recitation of an old woman residing near Kirkhill,
in West Lothian.

1 THERE lived a wife at Usher's Well,
And a wealthy wife was she;
She had three stout and stalwart sons,
And sent them oer the sea.

2 They hadna been a week from her,
A week but barely ane,
Whan word came to the carline wife
That her three sons were gane.

3 They hadna been a week from her,
A week but barely three,
Whan word came to the carlin wife
That her sons she 'd never see.

4 'I wish the wind may never cease,
Nor fashes in the flood,
Till my three sons come hame to me,
In earthly flesh and blood.'

5 It fell about the Martinmass,
When nights are lang and mirk,
The carlin wife's three sons came hame,
And their hats were o the birk.

6 It neither grew in syke nor ditch,
Nor yet in ony sheugh;
But at the gates o Paradise,
That birk grew fair eneugh.

*   *   *   *

7 'Blow up the fire, my maidens,
Bring water from the well;
For a' my house shall feast this night,
Since my three sons are well.'

8 And she has made to them a bed,
She 's made it large and wide,
And she 's taen her mantle her about,
Sat down at the bed-side.

*   *   *   *   *

9 Up then crew the red, red cock,
And up and crew the gray;
The eldest to the youngest said,
'T is time we were away.

10 The cock he hadna crawd but once,
And clappd his wings at a',
When the youngest to the eldest said,
Brother, we must awa.

11 'The cock doth craw, the day doth daw
The channerin worm doth chide;
Gin we be mist out o our place,
A sair pain we maun bide.

12 ' Fare ye weel, my mother dear !
Fareweel to barn and byre !
And fare ye weel, the bonny lass
That kindles my mother's fire !

B

Kinloch MSS., v, 403, stanzas 18–23 (as conclusion to No. 72, A). In the handwriting of
James Chambers, as sung to his maternal
grandmother, Janet Grieve, seventy years before, by an old woman, a Miss Ann Gray, of
the Neidpath Castle, Peeblesshire : January 1,
1829.

1 THE hallow days o Yule are come,
The nights are lang an dark,
An in an cam her ain twa sons,
Wi their hats made o the bark.

2 'O eat an drink, my merry men a.'
The better shall ye fare,

For my twa sons the are come hame
  To me for evermair.'

3 O she has gaen an made their bed,
  An she 's made it saft an fine,
An she 's happit them wi her gay mantel,
  Because they were her ain.

4 O the young cock crew i the merry
    Linkem,
  An the wild fowl chirpd for day;
The aulder to the younger did say,
  Dear brother, we maun away.

5 ' Lie still, lie still a little wee while,
  Lie still but if we may;
For gin my mother miss us away
  She 'll gae mad or it be day.'

6 O it 's they 've taen up their mother's
    mantel,
  An they 've hangd it on the pin:
' O lang may ye hing, my mother's
    mantel,
  Or ye hap us again ! '

C

' The Widow-Woman,' Shropshire Folk-
Lore, edited by Charlotte Sophia Burne, 1883–
86, p. 541; " taken down by Mr Hubert Smith,
24th March, 1883, from the recitation of an
elderly fisherman at Bridgworth, who could
neither read nor write, and had learnt it some
forty years before from his grandmother in
Corve Dale."

1 THERE was a widow-woman lived in far
    Scotland,
  And in far Scotland she did live,
And all her cry was upon sweet Jesus,
  Sweet Jesus so meek and mild.

2 Then Jesus arose one morning quite
    soon,
  And arose one morning betime,
And away he went to far Scotland,
  And to see what the good woman
    want.

3 And when he came to far Scotland,

  Crying, What, O what, does the good
    woman want,
  That is calling so much on me ?

4 ' It 's you go rise up my three sons,
  Their names, Joe, Peter, and John,
And put breath in their breast,
  And clothing on their backs,
And immediately send them to far Scot-
    land,
  That their mother may take some
    rest.'

5 Then he went and rose up her three
    sons,
  Their names, Joe, Peter, and John,
And did immediately send them to far
    Scotland,
  That their mother may take some
    rest.

6 Then she made up a supper so neat,
  As small, as small, as a yew-tree leaf,
But never one bit they could eat.

7 Then she made up a bed so soft,
  The softest that ever was seen,
And the widow-woman and her three
    sons
  They went to bed to sleep.

8 There they lay ; about the middle of
    the night,
  Bespeaks the youngest son:
' The white cock he has crowed once,
  The second has, so has the red.'

9 And then bespeaks the eldest son:
' I think, I think it is high time
  For the wicked to part from their
    dead.'

10 Then they laid [= led] her along a
    green road,
  The greenest that ever was seen,
Until they came to some far chaperine,
  Which was builded of lime and sand;
Until they came to some far chaperine,
  Which was builded with lime and
    stone.

11 And then he opened the door so big,
  And the door so very wide;
Said he to her three sons, Walk in !
  But told her to stay outside.

12 ' Go back, go back ! ' sweet Jesus re-
    plied,
  ' Go back, go back ! ' says he;

' For thou hast nine days to repent
    For the wickedness that thou hast
    done.'

13 Nine days then was past and gone,
    And nine days then was spent,
    Sweet Jesus called her once again,
    And took her to heaven with him.

D

Communicated, 1896, by Miss Emma M.
Backus, of North Carolina, who notes that it
has long been sung by the " poor whites " in
the mountains of Polk County in that State.

1 THERE was a lady fair and gay,
    And children she had three:
    She sent them away to some northern
        land,
    For to learn their grammeree.

2 They had n't been gone but a very short
        time,
    About three months to a day,
    When sickness came to that land
    And swept those babes away.

3 There is a king in the heavens above
    That wears a golden crown:
    She prayed that he would send her
        babies home
    To-night or in the morning soon.

4 It was about one Christmas time,
    When the nights was long and cool,
    She dreamed of her three little lonely
        babes
    Come running in their mother's room.

5 The table was fixed and the cloth was
        spread,
    And on it put bread and wine:
    ' Come sit you down, my three little
        babes,
    And eat and drink of mine.'

6 ' We will neither eat your bread, dear
        mother,
    Nor we 'll neither drink your wine;
    For to our Saviour we must return
    To-night or in the morning soon.'

7 The bed was fixed in the back room;
    On it was some clean white sheet,

And on the top was a golden cloth,
    To make those little babies sleep.

8 ' Wake up ! wake up !' says the oldest
        one,
    ' Wake up ! it 's almost day.
    And to our Saviour we must return
    To-night or in the morning soon.'

9 'Green grass grows at our head, dear
        mother,
    Green moss grows at our feet;
    The tears that you shed for us three
        babes
    Won't wet our winding sheet.'

80

OLD ROBIN OF PORTINGALE

The information given by a page, the reward promised and the alternative punishment
threatened him, the savage vengeance taken
on the lady, and the immediate remorse are
repeated in No. 81.

Percy MS., p. 90 ; Hales and Furnivall,
235.

1 GOD let neuer soe old a man
    Marry soe yonge a wiffe
    As did Old Robin of Portingale;
    He may rue all the dayes of his liffe.

2 Ffor the maiors daughter of Lin, God
        wott,
    He chose her to his wife,
    And thought to have liued in quiettnesse
    With her all the dayes of his liffe.

3 They had not in their wed-bed laid,
    Scarcely were both on sleepe,
    But vpp shee rose, and forth shee goes
    To Sir Gyles, and fast can weepe.

4 Saies, Sleepe you, wake you, faire Sir
        Gyles ?
    Or be not you within ?

    .   .   .   .   .   .

5 ' But I am waking, sweete,' he said,
    ' Lady, what is your will ?'
    ' I haue vnbethought me of a wile,
    How my wed lord we shall spill.

6 'Four and twenty knights,' she sayes,
    'That dwells about this towne,
Eene four and twenty of my next cozens,
    Will helpe to dinge him downe.'

7 With that beheard his litle foote-page,
    As he was watering his masters steed;
Soe s . . . .
    His verry heart did bleed.

8 He mourned, sikt, and wept full sore;
    I sweare by the holy roode,
The teares he for his master wept
    Were blend water and bloude.

9 With that beheard his deare master,
    As [he] in his garden sate;
Says, Euer alacke, my litle page,
    What causes thee to weepe?

10 'Hath any one done to thee wronge,
    Any of thy fellowes here?
Or is any of thy good friends dead,
    Which makes thee shed such teares?

11 'Or if it be my head-kookes-man,
    Greiued againe he shalbe,
Nor noe man within my howse
    Shall doe wrong vnto thee.'

12 'But it is not your head-kookes-man,
    Nor none of his degree;
But [f]or to morrow, ere it be noone,
    You are deemed to die.

13 'And of that thanke your head-stew-
        ard,
    And after, your gay ladie:'
'If it be true, my litle foote-page,
    Ile make thee heyre of all my land.'

14 'If it be not true, my deare master,
    God let me neuer thye:'
'If it be not true, thou litle foot-page,
    A dead corse shalt thou be.'

15 He called downe his head-kookes-man,
    Cooke in kitchen super to dresse:
'All and anon, my deare master,
    Anon att your request.'

16 . . . . .
    . . . . .
    'And call you downe my faire lady,
    This night to supp with mee.'

17 And downe then came that fayre lady,
    Was cladd all in purple and palle;
The rings that were vpon her fingers
    Cast light thorrow the hall.

18 'What is your will, my owne wed lord,
    What is your will with mee?'
'I am sicke, fayre lady,
    Sore sicke, and like to dye.'

19 'But and you be sicke, my owne wed lord,
    Soe sore it greiueth mee;
But my fiue maydens and my selfe
    Will goe and make your bedd.

20 'And at the wakening of your first sleepe
    You shall haue a hott drinke made,
And at the wakening of your next sleepe
    Your sorrowes will haue a slake.'

21 He put a silke cote on his backe,
    Was thirteen inches folde,
And put a steele cap vpon his head,
    Was gilded with good red gold.

22 And he layd a bright browne sword by
        his side,
    And another att his ffeete,
And full well knew Old Robin then
    Whether he shold wake or sleepe.

23 And about the middle time of the night
    Came twenty four good knights in;
Sir Gyles he was the formost man,
    Soe well he knew that ginne.

24 Old Robin, with a bright browne sword,
    Sir Gyles head he did winne;
Soe did he all those twenty four,
    Neuer a one went quicke out [agen].

25 None but one litle foot-page,
    Crept forth at a window of stone,
And he had two armes when he came in,
    And [when he went out he had none].

26 Vpp then came that ladie light,
    With torches burning bright;
Shee thought to haue brought Sir Gyles
        a drinke,
    But shee found her owne wedd knight.

27 And the first thinge that this ladye stum-
        bled vpon
    Was of Sir Gyles his ffoote;

Sayes, Euer alacke, and woe is me,
Here lyes my sweete hart-roote !

28 And the *second* thing *that* this ladie
    stumbled on
    Was of S*i*r Gyles his head;
    Sayes, Euer alacke, and woe is me,
    Heere lyes my true-loue deade !

29 Hee cutt the papps beside he[r] brest,
    And bad her wish her will;
    And he cutt the eares beside her heade,
    And bade her wish on still.

30 'Mickle is the mans blood I haue
    spent,
    To doe thee and me some good;'
    Sayes, Euer alacke, my fayre lady,
    I thinke *that* I was woode !

31 He calld then vp his litle foote-page,
    And made him heyre of all his land,

.   .   .   .   .

.   .   .   .   .

32 And he shope the crosse in his right
    sholder,
    Of the white flesh and the redd,
    And he went him into the holy land,
    Wheras Christ was quicke and dead.

81

LITTLE MUSGRAVE AND LADY BARNARD

A broadside printed for Henry Gosson (C) appears to be the earliest impression known, but it has not so good a text as **A**. The ballad is quoted in Beaumont and Fletcher's Knight of the Burning Pestle (about 1611), act v, scene 3, and in other old plays. 'Little Musgrave' is entered to Francis Coules in the Stationers' Registers, June 24, 1630.

A

'Little Musgrave and the Lady Barnard.' **a.** Wit Restord, 1658, in the reprint 'Facetiæ,' London, 1817, i, 293. **b.** Wit and Drollery, 1682, p. 81.

1 As it fell one holy-day,
    Hay downe
    As many be in the yeare,

    When young men and maids togeth
      did goe,
    Their mattins and masse to heare,

2 Little Musgrave came to the churc
    dore;
    The preist was at private masse;
    But he had more minde of the fai
      women
    Then he had of our lady['s] grace.

3 The one of them was clad in green,
    Another was clad in pall,
    And then came in my lord Bernard
      wife,
    The fairest amonst them all.

4 She cast an eye on Little Musgrave,
    As bright as the summer sun;
    And then bethought this Little Mus
      grave,
    This lady's heart have I woonn.

5 Quoth she, I have loved thee, Littl
    Musgrave,
    Full long and many a day;
    'So have I loved you, fair lady,
    Yet never word durst I say.'

6 'I have a bower at Buckelsfordbery,
    Full daintyly it is deight;
    If thou wilt wend thither, thou Littl
      Musgrave,
    Thou 's lig in mine armes all night.'

7 Quoth he, I thank yee, faire lady,
    This kindnes thou showest to me;
    But whether it be to my weal or woe,
    This night I will lig with thee.

8 With that he heard, a little tynë page,
    By his ladye's coach as he ran:
    'All though I am my ladye's foot-page
    Yet I am Lord Barnard's man.

9 'My lord Barnard shall knowe of this,
    Whether I sink or swim;'
    And ever where the bridges were broake
    He laid him downe to swimme.

10 'A sleepe or wake, thou Lord Barnard,
    As thou art a man of life,
    For Little Musgrave is at Bucklesford-
      bery,
    A bed with thy own wedded wife.'

11 'If this be true, thou little tinny page,
    This thing thou tellest to me,
Then all the land in Bucklesfordbery
    I freely will give to thee.

12 'But if it be a ly, thou little tinny
        page,
    This thing thou tellest to me,
On the hyest tree in Bucklesfordbery
    Then hanged shalt thou be.'

13 He called up his merry men all:
    'Come saddle me my steed;
This night must I to Buckellsford-
        bery,
    For I never had greater need.'

14 And some of them whistld, and some of
        them sung,
    And some these words did say,
And ever when my lord Barnard's horn
        blew,
    'Away, Musgrave, away!'

15 'Methinks I hear the thresel-cock,
    Methinks I hear the jaye;
Methinks I hear my lord Barnard,
    And I would I were away.'

16 'Lye still, lye still, thou Little Mus-
        grave,
    And huggell me from the cold;
'T is nothing but a shephard's boy,
    A driving his sheep to the fold.

17 'Is not thy hawke upon a perch?
    Thy steed eats oats and hay;
And thou a fair lady in thine armes,
    And wouldst thou bee away?'

18 With that my lord Barnard came to the
        dore,
    And lit a stone upon;
He plucked out three silver keys,
    And he opend the dores each one.

19 He lifted up the coverlett,
    He lifted up the sheet:
'How now, how now, thou Littell Mus-
        grave,
    Doest thou find my lady sweet?'

20 'I find her sweet,' quoth Little Mus-
        grave,
    'The more 't is to my paine;

I would gladly give three hundred
        pounds
    That I were on yonder plaine.'

21 'Arise, arise, thou Littell Musgrave,
    And put thy clothës on;
It shall nere be said in my country
    I have killed a naked man.

22 'I have two swords in one scabberd,
    Full deere they cost my purse;
And thou shalt have the best of them,
    And I will have the worse.'

23 The first stroke that Little Musgrave
        stroke,
    He hurt Lord Barnard sore;
The next stroke that Lord Barnard
        stroke,
    Little Musgrave nere struck more.

24 With that bespake this faire lady,
    In bed whereas she lay:
'Although thou 'rt dead, thou Little
        Musgrave,
    Yet I for thee will pray.

·25 'And wish well to thy soule will I,
    So long as I have life;
So will I not for thee, Barnard,
    Although I am thy wedded wife.'

26 He cut her paps from off her brest;
    Great pitty it was to see
That some drops of this ladie's heart's
        blood
    Ran trickling downe her knee.

27 'Woe worth you, woe worth, my mery
        men all,
    You were nere borne for my good;
Why did you not offer to stay my
        hand,
    When you see me wax so wood?

28 'For I have slaine the bravest sir knight
    That ever rode on steed;
So have I done the fairest lady
    That ever did woman's deed.

29 'A grave, a grave,' Lord Barnard
        cryd,
    'To put these lovers in;
But lay my lady on the upper hand,
    For she came of the better kin.'

B

Percy MS., p. 53; Hales and Furnivall, I, 119.

*   *   *   *   *

1 .   .   .   .   .   .

   'Ffor this same night att [Bucklesfeild-
     berry]
   Litle Musgreue is in bed with thy
     wife.'

2 'If it be trew, thou litle foote-page,
   This tale thou hast told to mee,
   Then all my lands in Buckle[s]feildberry
   I 'le freely giue to thee.

3 'But if this be a lye, thou little foot-
    page,
   This tale thou hast told to mee,
   Then on the highest tree in Buckles-
    feildberry
   All hanged that thou shalt bee.'

4 Saies, Vpp and rise, my merrymen all,
   And saddle me my good steede,
   For I must ride to Bucklesfeildberry;
   God wott I had neuer more need !

5 But some they whistled, and some thé
    sunge,
   And some they thus cold say,
   When euer as Lord Barnetts horne
    blowes,
   'Away, Musgreue, away !'

6 'Mie thinkes I heare the throstlecocke,
   Me thinkes I heare the iay,
   Me thinkes I heare Lord Barnetts horne,
   Away, Musgreue, away !'

7 'But lie still, lie still, Litle Musgreue,
   And huddle me from the cold,
   For it is but some sheaperds boy,
   Is whistling sheepe ore the mold.

8 'Is not thy hauke vpon a pearch,
   Thy horsse eating corne and hay ?
   And thou, a gay lady in thine armes,
   And yett thou wold goe away !'

9 By this time Lord Barnett was come to
    the dore,
   And light vpon a stone,

And he pulled out three silver kayes,
   And opened the dores euery one.

10 And first he puld the couering downe,
   And then puld downe the sheete;
   Saies, How now ? How now, Litle Mus-
    greue ?
   Dost find my gay lady sweet ?

11 'I find her sweete,' saies Litle Musgreue,
   'The more is my greefe and paine;'

.   .   .   .   .

*   *   *   *   *

12 .   .   .   .   .

   'Soe haue I done the fairest lady
   That euer wore womans weede.

13 'Soe haue I done a heathen child,
   Which ffull sore greiueth mee,
   For which Ile repent all the dayes of
    my life,
   And god be with them all three !'

82

THE BONNY BIRDY

Jamieson, in printing this ballad, gave the husband the name Lord Randal, made many changes, and introduced several stanzas, " to fill up chasms." But the chasms, such as they are, are easily leapt by the imagination, and Jamieson's interpolations are mere bridges of carpenter's work. The admirably effective burden is taken into the story at stanza 11.

The main part of the action is the same as in ' Little Musgrave' (No. 81). The superior lyrical quality of the Scottish ballad makes up for its inferiority as a story.

Jamieson-Brown MS., p. 42 ; Jamieson's Popular Ballads, I, 162.

1 THERE was a knight, in a summer's
    night,
   Was riding oer the lee,   diddle
  An there he saw a bonny birdy,
   Was singing upon a tree.   diddle
     O wow for day !   diddle
     An dear gin it were day!   diddle
     Gin it were day, an gin I were away!
     For I ha na lang time to stay.
          diddle

2 'Make hast, make hast, ye gentle knight,
    What keeps you here so late ?
Gin ye kent what was doing at hame,
    I fear you woud look blate.'

3 'O what needs I toil day an night,
    My fair body to kill,
Whan I hae knights at my comman,
    An ladys at my will ?'

4 'Ye lee, ye lee, ye gentle knight,
    Sa loud 's I hear you lee;
Your lady 's a knight in her arms twa
    That she lees far better nor the.'

5 'Ye lee, you lee, you bonny birdy,
    How you lee upo my sweet !
I will tak out my bonny bow,
    An in troth I will you sheet.'

6 'But afore ye hae your bow well bent,
    An a' your arrows yare,
I will flee till another tree,
    Whare I can better fare.'

7 'O whare was you gotten, and whare was ye clecked ?
    My bonny birdy, tell me:'
'O I was clecked in good green wood,
    Intill a holly tree;
A gentleman my nest herryed,
    An ga me to his lady.

8 'Wi good white bread an farrow-cow milk
    He bade her feed me aft,
An ga her a little wee simmer-dale wanny,
    To ding me sindle and saft.

9 'Wi good white bread an farrow-cow milk
    I wot she fed me nought,
But wi a little wee simmer-dale wanny
    She dang me sair an aft:
Gin she had deen as ye her bade,
    I woudna tell how she has wrought.'

10 The knight he rade, and the birdy flew,
    The live-lang simmer's night,
Till he came till his lady's bowr-door,
    Then even down he did light:
The birdy sat on the crap of a tree,
    An I wot it sang fu dight.

11 'O wow for day !   diddle
    An dear gin it were day !   diddle
Gin it were day, and gin I were away !
    For I ha na lang time to stay.'
                  diddle

12 'What needs ye lang for day,   diddle.
    An wish that you were away ?   diddle
Is no your hounds i my cellar,
    Eating white meal an gray ?   diddle
    O wow, etc.

13 'Is nae your steed in my stable,
    Eating good corn an hay ?
An is nae your hawk i my perch-tree,
    Just perching for his prey ?
An is nae yoursel i my arms twa ?
    Then how can ye lang for day ?'

14 'O wow for day !   diddle
    An dear gin it were day !   diddle
For he that 's in bed wi anither man's wife
    Has never lang time to stay.'   diddle

15 Then out the knight has drawn his sword,
    An straiked it oer a strae,
An thro and thro the fa'se knight's waste
    He gard cauld iron gae:
An I hope ilk ane sal sae be servd
    That treats ane honest man sae.

83

CHILD MAURICE

A is from the Percy MS. Of B Motherwell says (1827): "By testimony of a most unexceptionable description, but which it would be tedious here to detail, the editor can distinctly trace this ballad as existing in its present shape at least a century ago." The ballad was printed at Glasgow by Foulis in 1755 (and in an earlier edition, now lost), with considerable modern improvements. Hume's tragedy of Douglas, produced in Edinburgh in 1756, was founded upon the story, and the popularity of the play seems to have given vogue to the ballad. The sophisticated copy passed into recitation, and may very likely have more or less infected those which were repeated from earlier tradition. The poet Gray writes to Mason, June, 1757 (?) : "I have got the old Scottish ballad on which Douglas was

founded; it is divine, and as long as from here
[Cambridge] to Aston." He quotes the first
fifteen lines, substantially as in Foulis. Percy's
version in the Reliques, 1765 (III, 93), is that
of Foulis with further "improvements."

A

'Childe Maurice,' Percy MS., p. 346; Hales
and Furnivall, II, 502.

1 CHILDE MAURICE hunted ithe siluer
    wood,
  He hunted itt round about,
And noebodye *that* he ffound therin,
  Nor none there was with-out.

2 .   .   .   .   .   .

And he tooke his siluer combe in his
    hand,
  To kembe his yellow lockes.

3 He sayes, Come hither, thou litle ffoot-
    page,
That runneth lowlye by my knee,
Ffor thou shalt goe to Iohn Stewards
    wiffe
  And pray her speake with mee.

4 .   .   .   .   .   .

'I, and greete thou doe *that* ladye well,
  Euer soe well ffroe mee.

5 'And, as itt ffalls, as many times
  As knotts beene knitt on a kell,
Or marchant men gone to leeue London,
  Either to buy ware or sell.

6 'And, as itt ffalles, as many times
  As any hart can thinke,
Or schoole-masters are in any schoole-
    house,
  Writting with pen and inke:
Ffor if I might, as well as shee may,
  This night I wold with her speake.

7 'And heere I send her a mantle of
    greene,
  As greene as any grasse,
And bidd her come to the siluer wood,
  To hunt with Child Maurice.

8 'And there I send her a ring of gold,
  A ring of precyous stone,

And bidd her come to the siluer wood,
  Let ffor no kind of man.'

9 One while this litle boy he yode,
  Another while he ran,
Vntill he came to Iohn Stewards hall,
  I-wis he neuer blan.

10 And of nurture the child had good,
  Hee ran vp hall and bower ffree,
And when he came to this lady ffaire,
  Sayes, God you saue and see !

11 'I am come ffrom Ch[i]ld Maurice,
  A message vnto thee;
And Child Maurice, he greetes you well
  And euer soe well ffrom mee.

12 'And, as itt ffalls, as oftentimes
  As knotts beene knitt on a kell,
Or marchant-men gone to leeue London,
  Either ffor to buy ware or sell.

13 'And as oftentimes he greetes you well
  As any hart can thinke,
Or schoolemasters [are] in any schoole,
  Wryting with pen and inke.

14 'And heere he sends a mantle of greene,
  As greene as any grasse,
And he bidds you come to the siluer
    wood,
  To hunt with Child Maurice.

15 'And heere he sends you a ring of gold,
  A ring of the precyous stone;
He prayes you to come to the siluer
    wood,
  Let ffor no kind of man.'

16 'Now peace, now peace, thou litle ffoot-
    page,
  Ffor Christes sake, I pray thee !
Ffor if my lord heare one of these
    words,
  Thou must be hanged hye !'

17 Iohn Steward stood vnder the castle-
    wall,
  And he wrote the words euerye one,
.   .   .   .   .   .
.   .   .   .   .   .

18 And he called vnto his hors-keeper,
  'Make readye you my steede !'

I, and soe hee did to his chamber-
    laine,
' Make readye thou my weede ! '

19 And he cast a lease vpon his backe,
    And he rode to the siluer wood,
    And there he sought all about,
    About the siluer wood.

20 And there he ffound him Child Maurice
    Sitting vpon a blocke,
    With a siluer combe in his hand,
    Kembing his yellow locke[s].

*   *   *   *   *

21 But then stood vp him Child Maurice,
    And sayd these words trulye:
' I doe not know your ladye,' he said,
' If that I doe her see.'

22 He sayes, How now, how now, Child
    Maurice ?
    Alacke, how may this bee ?
    Ffor thou hast sent her loue-tokens,
    More now then two or three.

23 ' Ffor thou hast sent her a mantle of
    greene,
    As greene as any grasse,
    And bade her come to the siluer woode,
    To hunt with Child Maurice.

24 ' And thou [hast] sent her a ring of gold,
    A ring of precyous stone,
    And bade her come to the siluer wood,
    Let ffor noe kind of man.

25 ' And by my ffaith, now, Child Maurice,
    The tone of vs shall dye ! '
' Now be my troth,' sayd Child Maurice,
' And that shall not be I.'

26 But hee pulled forth a bright browne
    sword,
    And dryed itt on the grasse,
    And soe ffast he smote att Iohn Steward,
    I-wisse he neuer [did] rest.

27 Then hee pulled fforth his bright browne
    sword,
    And dryed itt on his sleeue,
    And the ffirst good stroke Iohn Stewart
    stroke,
    Child Maurice head he did cleeue.

28 And he pricked itt on his swords poynt,
    Went singing there beside,
    And he rode till he came to that ladye
    ffaire,
    Wheras this ladye lyed.

29 And sayes, Dost thou know Child
    Maurice head,
    If that thou dost itt see ?
    And lapp itt soft, and kisse itt offt,
    Ffor thou louedst him better than
    mee.

30 But when shee looked on Child Maurice
    head,
    Shee neuer spake words but three:
' I neuer beare no child but one,
    And you haue slaine him trulye.'

31 Sayes, Wicked be my merrymen all,
    I gaue meate, drinke, and clothe !
    But cold they not haue holden me
    When I was in all that wrath !

32 ' Ffor I haue slaine one of the cur-
    teousest knights
    That euer bestrode a steed,
    Soe haue I done one [of] the fairest
    ladyes
    That euer ware womans weede ! '

B

' Child Noryce,' Motherwell's MS., p. 255;
Motherwell's Minstrelsy, p. 282.   From the
singing of Widow McCormick, Paisley, January 19, 1825. Learned by her of an old
woman in Dumbarton: Motherwell's Note
Book, fol. 4.

1 CHILD NORYCE is a clever young man,
    He wavers wi the wind;
    His horse was silver-shod before,
    With the beaten gold behind.

2 He called to his little man John,
    Saying, You don't see what I see;
    O yonder I see the very first woman
    That ever loved me.

3 ' Here is a glove, a glove,' he said,
' Lined with the silver grey;
    You may tell her to come to the merry
    green-wood,
    To speak to Child Nory.

4 'Here is a ring, a ring,' he says,
    'It's all gold but the stane;
  You may tell her to come to the merry
        green-wood,
    And ask the leave o nane.'

5 'So well do I love your errand, my
        master,
    But far better do I love my life;
  O would you have me go to Lord Bar-
        nard's castle,
    To betray away his wife?'

6 'O do I not give you meat,' he says,
    'And do I not pay you fee?
  How dare you stop my errand?' he
        says;
    'My orders you must obey.'

7 O when he came to Lord Bernard's
        castle,
    He tinkled at the ring;
  Who was as ready as Lord Barnard
        himself
    To let this little boy in?

8 'Here is a glove, a glove,' he says,
    'Lined with the silver grey;
  You are bidden to come to the merry
        green-wood,
    To speak to Child Nory.

9 'Here is a ring, a ring,' he says,
    'It's all gold but the stane;
  You are bidden to come to the merry
        green-wood,
    And ask the leave o nane.'

10 Lord Barnard he was standing by,
    And an angry man was he:
  'O little did I think there was a lord in
        the world
    My lady loved but me!'

11 O he dressed himself in the holland
        smock,
    And garments that was gay,
  And he is away to the merry green-
        wood,
    To speak to Child Nory.

12 Child Noryce sits on yonder tree,
    He whistles and he sings:
  'O wae be to me,' says Child Noryce,
    'Yonder my mother comes!'

13 Child Noryce he came off the tree,
    His mother to take off the horse:
  'Och alace, alace,' says Child Noryce,
    'My mother was neer so gross!'

14 Lord Barnard he had a little small
        sword,
    Hung low down by his knee;
  He cut the head off Child Noryce,
    And put the body on a tree.

15 And when he came home to his castell,
    And to his ladie's hall,
  He threw the head into her lap,
    Saying, Lady, there's a ball!

16 She turned up the bloody head,
    She kissed it frae cheek to chin:
  'Far better do I love this bloody head
    Than all my royal kin.

17 'When I was in my father's castel,
    In my virginity,
  There came a lord into the North,
    Gat Child Noryce with me.'

18 'O wae be to thee, Lady Margaret,' he
        sayd,
    'An ill death may you die;
  For if you had told me he was your son,
    He should neer have been slain by me.'

D

'Gill Morice,' Motherwell's MS., p. 480, from
the recitation of Widow Michael, a very old
woman, as learned by her in Banffshire seventy
years before.   August, 1826.

1 GILL MORICE stood in stable-door,
    With red gold shined his weed;
  A bonnie boy him behind,
    Dressing a milk-white steed.

2 'Woe's me for you, maister,
    Your name it waxes wide;
  It is not for your rich, rich robes,
    Nor for your meikle pride,
  But all is for yon lord's ladie,
    She lives on Ithan side.'

3 'Here's to thee, my bonnie wee boy,
    That I pay meat and fee;
  You will run on to Ithan side
    An errand unto me.'

4 'If ye gar me that errand run,
  Sae sair against my will,
I 'll make a vow, and keep it true,
  I 'll do your errand ill.'

5 'I fear nae ill of thee, boy,
  I fear nae ill of thee;
I fearna ill of my bonnie boy,
  My sister's son are ye.

6 'Ye 'll tak here this green manteel,
  It 's lined with the frieze;
Ye 'll bid her come to gude green-wood,
  To talk with Gill Morice.

7 'Ye 'll tak here this sark o silk,
  Her ain hand sewed the sleeve;
Ye 'll bid her come to gude green-
  wood,
  And ask not Burnard's leave.'

8 When he gade to Ithan side
  They were hailing at the ba,
And four and twenty gay ladyes
  They lookd ower castle wa.

9 'God mak you safe, you ladies all,
  God mak you safe and sure;
But Burnard's lady amang you all,
  My errand is to her.

10 'Ye 'll tak here this green manteel,
   It 's a' lined wi the frieze;
Ye 're bidden come to gude green-wood
   And speak to Gill Morice.

11 'Ye 'll tak here this sark of silk,
   Your ain hand sewed the sleeve;
Ye 're bidden come to gude green-wood,
   And ask not Burnard's leave.'

12 Up it stood the little nurice,
   She winked with her ee:
'Welcome, welcome, bonnie boy,
   With luve-tidings to me.'

13 'Ye lie, ye lie, ye false nurice,
   Sae loud 's I hear ye lie;
It 's to the lady of the house,
   I 'm sure ye are not shee.'

14 Then out and spoke him bold Burnard,
   Behind the door stood he :
'I 'll go unto gude green-wood,
   And see what he may be.

15 'Come, bring to me the gowns of silk,
   Your petticoats so small,
And I 'll go on to gude green-wood,
   I 'll try with him a fall.'

16 Gill Morice stood in gude green-wood,
   He whistled and he sang:
'I think I see the woman come
   That I have loved lang.'

17 'What now, what now, ye Gill Mor-
   ice,
   What now, and how do ye ?
How lang hae ye my lady luved ?
   This day come tell to me.'

18 'First when I your lady loved,
   In green-wood amang the thyme,
I wot she was my first fair love
   Or ever she was thine.

19 'First when I your lady loved,
   In green-wood amang the flouirs,
I wot she was my first fair love
   Or ever she was yours.'

20 He 's taen out a lang, lang brand
   That he was used to wear,
And he 's taen aff Gill Morice head,
   And put it on a spear:
The soberest boy in a' the court
   Gill Morice head did bear.

21 He 's put it in a braid basin,
   And brocht it in the ha,
And laid it in his lady's lap;
   Said, Lady, tak a ba !

22 'Play ye, play ye, my lady,' he said,
   'Play ye frae ha to bower;
Play ye wi Gill Morice head,
   He was your paramour.'

23 'He was not my paramour,
   He was my son indeed;
I got him in my mother's bower,
   And in my maiden-weed.

24 'I got him in my mother's bower,
   Wi meikle sin and shame;
I brocht him up in good green-wood,
   Got mony a shower o rain.

25 'But I will kiss his bluidy head,
   And I will clap his chin;

I 'll make a vow, and keep it true,
    I 'll never kiss man again.

26 'Oftimes I by his cradle sat,
    And fond to see him sleep;
    But I may walk about his grave,
    The saut tears for to weep.'

27 'Bring cods, bring cods to my ladye,
    Her heart is full of wae;'
    'None of your cods, Burnet,' she says,
    'But lay me on the strae.'

28 'Pox on you, my lady fair,
    That wudna telled it me;
    If I had known he was your son,
    He had not been slain by me;
    And for ae penny ye wud hae gien
    I wud hae gien him three.'

29 'Keep weel your land, Burnet,' she said,
    'Your land and white monie;
    There 's land eneuch in Norroway
    Lies heirless I wot the day.'

30 The one was killed in the mornin air,
    His mother died at een,
    And or the mornin bells was rung
    The threesome were a' gane.

84

BONNY BARBARA ALLAN

Pepys makes this entry in his Diary, January 2, 1666 : "In perfect pleasure I was to hear her [Mrs Knipp, an actress] sing, and especially her little Scotch song of Barbary Allen." Goldsmith, in his third essay, 1765, p. 14, writes: "The music of the finest singer is dissonance to what I felt when our old dairy-maid sung me into tears with 'Johnny Armstrong's Last Good-night,' or 'The Cruelty of Barbara Allen.'"

A

a. 'Bonny Barbara Allan,' The Tea-Table Miscellany, IV, 46, ed. 1740; here from the London edition of 1750, p. 343. b. 'Sir John Grehme, and Barbara Allan,' Percy's Reliques, III, 131, ed. 1765, "with a few conjectural emendations from a written copy."

1 IT was in and about the Martinmas time,
    When the green leaves were a falling,
That Sir John Græme, in the Wes
    Country,
    Fell in love with Barbara Allan.

2 He sent his man down through the town
    To the place where she was dwelling
    'O haste and come to my master dear,
    Gin ye be Barbara Allan.'

3 O hooly, hooly rose she up,
    To the place where he was lying,
    And when she drew the curtain by,
    'Young man, I think you 're dying.'

4 'O it 's I 'm sick, and very, very sick,
    And 't is a' for Barbara Allan:'
    'O the better for me ye 's never be,
    Tho your heart's blood were a spill
    ing.'

5 'O dinna ye mind, young man,' sai
    she,
    'When ye was in the tavern a drink
    ing,
    That ye made the healths gae round an
    round,
    And slighted Barbara Allan ?'

6 He turnd his face unto the wall,
    And death was with him dealing:
    'Adieu, adieu, my dear friends all,
    And be kind to Barbara Allan.'

7 And slowly, slowly raise she up,
    And slowly, slowly left him,
    And sighing said, she coud not stay,
    Since death of life had reft him.

8 She had not gane a mile but twa,
    When she heard the dead-bell ringing
    And every jow that the dead-bell geid,
    It cry'd, Woe to Barbara Allan !

9 'O mother, mother, make my bed !
    O make it saft and narrow !
    Since my love died for me to-day,
    I 'll die for him to-morrow.'

B

a. 'Barbara Allen's Cruelty,' Roxburgh Ballads, II, 25; reprint of the Ballad Society III, 433. b. Roxburghe Ballads, III, 522 c. A broadside formerly belonging to Bisho Percy. d. Percy's Reliques, 1765, III, 125.

1 IN Scarlet Town, where I was bound,
   There was a fair maid dwelling,
   Whom I had chosen to be my own,
   And her name it was Barbara Allen.

2 All in the merry month of May,
   When green leaves they was spring-
      ing,
   This young man on his death-bed lay,
   For the love of Barbara Allen.

3 He sent his man unto her then,
   To the town where she was dwelling:
   'You must come to my master dear,
   If your name be Barbara Allen.

4 'For death is printed in his face,
   And sorrow 's in him dwelling,
   And you must come to my master dear,
   If your name be Barbara Allen.'

5 'If death be printed in his face,
   And sorrow 's in him dwelling,
   Then little better shall he be
   For bonny Barbara Allen.'

6 So slowly, slowly she got up,
   And so slowly she came to him,
   And all she said when she came there,
   Young man, I think you are a dying.

7 He turnd his face unto her then:
   'If you be Barbara Allen,
   My dear,' said he, 'come pitty me,
   As on my death-bed I am lying.'

8 'If on your death-bed you be lying,
   What is that to Barbara Allen?
   I cannot keep you from [your] death;
   So farewell,' said Barbara Allen.

9 He turnd his face unto the wall,
   And death came creeping to him:
   'Then adieu, adieu, and adieu to all,
   And adieu to Barbara Allen!'

10 And as she was walking on a day,
   She heard the bell a ringing,
   And it did seem to ring to her
   'Unworthy Barbara Allen.'

11 She turnd herself round about,
   And she spy'd the corps a coming:
   'Lay down, lay down the corps of clay,
   That I may look upon him.'

12 And all the while she looked on,
   So loudly she lay laughing,
   While all her friends cry'd [out] amain,
   'Unworthy Barbara Allen!'

13 When he was dead, and laid in grave,
   Then death came creeping to she:
   'O mother, mother, make my bed,
   For his death hath quite undone me.

14 'A hard-hearted creature that I was,
   To slight one that lovd me so dearly;
   I wish I had been more kinder to him,
   The time of his life when he was near
      me.'

15 So this maid she then did dye,
   And desired to be buried by him,
   And repented her self before she dy'd,
   That ever she did deny him.

85

LADY ALICE

This little ballad, which is said to be still
of the regular stock of the stalls, is a sort of
counterpart to 'Lord Lovel' (No. 75).

A

'Lady Alice.' a. Bell's Ancient Poems,
Ballads, and Songs of the Peasantry of England, p. 127, a stall copy. b. Edward Haw-
kins, in Notes and Queries, Second Series, I,
418. c. Notes and Queries, Second Series, I,
354, as heard sung forty years before 1856,
"Uneda," Philadelphia.

1 LADY ALICE was sitting in her bower-
      window,
   Mending her midnight quoif,
   And there she saw as fine a corpse
   As ever she saw in her life.

2 'What bear ye, what bear ye, ye six
      men tall?
   What bear ye on your shoulders?'
   'We bear the corpse of Giles Collins,
   An old and true lover of yours.'

3 'O lay him down gently, ye six men
      tall,
   All on the grass so green,

And tomorrow, when the sun goes
down,
Lady Alice a corpse shall be seen.

4 'And bury me in Saint Mary's church,
All for my love so true,
And make me a garland of marjoram,
And of lemon-thyme, and rue.'

5 Giles Collins was buried all in the east,
Lady Alice all in the west,
And the roses that grew on Giles Col-
lins's grave,
They reached Lady Alice's breast.

6 The priest of the parish he chanced to
pass,
And he severed those roses in twain;
Sure never were seen such true lovers
before,
Nor eer will there be again.

B

'Giles Collins and Proud Lady Anna,'
Gammer Gurton's Garland, p. 38, ed. 1810.

1 GILES COLLINS he said to his old mo-
ther,
Mother, come bind up my head,
And send to the parson of our parish,
For tomorrow I shall be dead.   dead,
For tomorrow I shall be dead.

2 His mother she made him some water-
gruel,
And stirrd it round with a spoon;
Giles Collins he ate up his water-gruel,
And died before 't was noon.

3 Lady Anna was sitting at her window,
Mending her night-robe and coif;
She saw the very prettiest corpse
She 'd seen in all her life.

4 'What bear ye there, ye six strong
men,
Upon your shoulders so high ?'
'We bear the body of Giles Collins,
Who for love of you did die.'

5 'Set him down, set him down,' Lady
Anna she cry'd,
'On the grass that grows so green;

Tomorrow, before the clock strikes
ten,
My body shall lye by hisn.'

6 Lady Anna was buried in the east,
Giles Collins was buried in the west;
There grew a lilly from Giles Collins
That touchd Lady Anna's breast.

7 There blew a cold north-easterly wind,
And cut this lilly in twain,
Which never there was seen before,
And it never will again.

C

'Giles Collin,' Miss M. H. Mason's Nursery
Rhymes and Country Songs, 1877, p. 46.

1 GILES COLLIN he said to his mother
one day,
Oh, mother, come bind up my head !
For tomorrow morning before it is day
I 'm sure I shall be dead.

2 'Oh, mother, oh, mother, if I should die,
And I am sure I shall,
I will not be buried in our churchyard,
But under Lady Alice's wall.'

3 His mother she made him some water-
gruel,
And stirred it up with a spoon;
Giles Collin he ate but one spoonful,
And died before it was noon.

4 Lady Alice was sitting in her window,
All dressed in her night-coif;
She saw as pretty a corpse go by
As ever she 'd seen in her life.

5 'What bear ye there, ye six tall men ?
What bear ye on your shourn ?'
'We bear the body of Giles Collin,
Who was a true lover of yourn.'

6 'Down with him, down with him, upon
the grass,
The grass that grows so green;
For tomorrow morning before it is day
My body shall lie by him.'

7 Her mother she made her some plum-
gruel,
With spices all of the best;

Lady Alice she ate but one spoonful,
    And the doctor he ate up the rest.

8 Giles Collin was laid in the lower
        chancel,
    Lady Alice all in the higher;
    There grew up a rose from Lady Alice's
        breast,
    And from Giles Collin's a briar.

9 And they grew, and they grew, to the
        very church-top,
    Until they could grow no higher,
    And twisted and twined in a true-lover's
        knot,
    Which made all the parish admire.

86

YOUNG BENJIE

Scott's version in the Border Minstrelsy,
1803, III, 251, contains the whole of A* except
the first stanza. It has about twice as many
verses as A*, and the other half might well
have been supplied by the editor. Scott's title
'Young Benjie' is here retained, and some of
the additional stanzas are given in the Notes.

A*

From Jean Scott. In the handwriting of
William Laidlaw. Scotch Ballads, Materials
for Border Minstrelsy, No. 29, Abbotsford.

1 FAIR Marjorie sat i her bower-door,
    Sewin her silken seam,
    When by then cam her false true-love,
    Gard a' his bridles ring.

2 'Open, open, my true-love,
    Open an let me in;'
    'I dare na, I dare na, my true-love,
    My brethren are within.'

3 'Ye lee, ye lee, my ain true-love,
    Sae loud I hear ye lee !
    For or I cam thrae Lothian banks
    They took fare-weel o me.'

4 The wind was loud, that maid was proud,
    An leath, leath to be dung,
    But or she wan the Lothian banks
    Her fair coulour was gane.

5 He took her up in his armis,
    An threw her in the lynn.

6 Up then spak her eldest brother,
    Said, What is yon I see ?
    Sure, youn is either a drowned ladie
    Or my sister Marjorie.

7 Up then spak her second brother,
    Said, How will we her ken ?
    Up then spak her . . . brother,
    There a hinnie-mark on her chin.

8 About the midle o the night
    The cock began to craw;
    About the middle o the night
    The corpse began to thraw.

9 'O whae has doon ye wrang, sister ?
    O whae has doon ye wrang ?'

10 'Young Boonjie was the ae first man
    I laid my love upon;
    He was sae proud an hardie
    He threw me oer the lynne.'

11 'O shall we Boonjie head, sister ?
    Or shall we Boonjie hang ?
    O shall we pyke out his twa grey
        eyes,
    An punish him or he gang ?'

12 'O ye sanna Boonjie head, brother,
    Ye sana Boonjie hang;
    But ye maun pyke out his twa grey
        eyes,
    An punish him or he gang.'

13 'The ae best man about your house
    Maun wait young Boonjie on.'

87

PRINCE ROBERT

There is a White Russian and a Ruthenian
ballad in which a mother prepares wholesome
drink for her son, poison for his wife; both son
and wife are poisoned. They are buried separately, one in the church, one in the graveyard. Trees from the graves join their tops.
There are other ballad-stories of a mother's
poisoning because of displeasure at a son's
match, but they do not demand comparison
with 'Prince Robert.'

A

'Prince Robert,' Scott's Minstrelsy, II, 124, ed. 1802; III, 269, ed. 1833: from the recitation of Miss Christian Rutherford.

1 PRINCE ROBERT has wedded a gay ladye,
    He has wedded her with a ring;
Prince Robert has wedded a gay ladye,
    But he daur na bring her hame.

2 'Your blessing, your blessing, my mother dear,
    Your blessing now grant to me!'
'Instead of a blessing ye sall have my curse,
    And you'll get nae blessing frae me.'

3 She has called upon her waiting-maid,
    To fill a glass of wine;
She has called upon her fause steward,
    To put rank poison in.

4 She has put it to her roudes lip,
    And to her roudes chin;
She has put it to her fause, fause mouth,
    But the never a drop gaed in.

5 He has put it to his bonny mouth,
    And to his bonny chin,
He's put it to his cherry lip,
    And sae fast the rank poison ran in.

6 'O ye hae poisoned your ae son, mother,
    Your ae son and your heir;
O ye hae poisoned your ae son, mother,
    And sons you'll never hae mair.

7 'O where will I get a little boy,
    That will win hose and shoon,
To rin sae fast to Darlinton,
    And bid Fair Eleanor come?'

8 Then up and spake a little boy,
    That wad win hose and shoon,
'O I'll away to Darlinton,
    And bid Fair Eleanor come.'

9 O he has run to Darlinton,
    And tirled at the pin;
And wha was sae ready as Eleanor's sell
    To let the bonny boy in?

10 'Your gude-mother has made ye a rare dinour,
    She's made it baith gude and fine;
Your gude-mother has made ye a gay dinour,
    And ye maun cum till her and dine.'

11 It's twenty lang miles to Sillertoun town,
    The langest that ever were gane;
But the steed it was wight, and the ladye was light,
    And she cam linkin in.

12 But when she came to Sillertoun town,
    And into Sillertoun ha,
The torches were burning, the ladies were mourning,
    And they were weeping a'.

13 'O where is now my wedded lord,
    And where now can he be?
O where is now my wedded lord?
    For him I canna see.'

14 'Your wedded lord is dead,' she says,
    'And just gane to be laid in the clay;
Your wedded lord is dead,' she says,
    'And just gane to be buried the day.

15 'Ye'se get nane o his gowd, ye'se get nane o his gear,
    Ye'se get nae thing frae me;
Ye'se na get an inch o his gude broad land,
    Tho your heart suld burst in three.'

16 'I want nane o his gowd, I want nane o his gear,
    I want nae land frae thee;
But I'll hae the ring that's on his finger,
    For them he did promise to me.'

17 'Ye'se na get the ring that's on his finger,
    Ye's na get them frae me;
Ye'se na get the ring that's on his finger,
    An your heart suld burst in three.'

18 She's turn'd her back unto the wa,
    And her face unto a rock,
And there, before the mother's face,
    Her very heart it broke.

19 The tane was buried in Marie's kirk,
    The tother in Marie's quair,
And out o the tane there sprang a birk,
    And out o the tother a brier.

20 And thae twa met, and thae twa plat,
    The birk but and the brier,
And by that ye may very weel ken
    They were twa lovers dear.

B

'Earl Robert,' Motherwell's MS., p. 149;
Motherwell's Minstrelsy, p. 200 : from the recitation of Mrs Thomson, Kilbarchan, a native of
Bonhill, Dumbartonshire, aged betwixt sixty
and seventy.

1 It's fifty miles to Sittingen's Rocks,
    As eer was ridden or gane;
And Earl Robert has wedded a wife,
    But he dare na bring her hame.
And Earl Robert has wedded a wife,
    But he dare na bring her hame.

2 His mother, she called to her waiting-
    maid,
    To bring her a pint o wine:
'For I dinna weel ken what hour of the
    day
    That my son Earl Robert shall dine.'

3 She's put it to her fause, fause cheek,
    But an her fause, fause chin;
She's put it to her fause, fause lips,
    But never a drap went in.

4 But he's put it to his bonny cheek,
    Aye and his bonny chin;
He's put it to his red rosy lips,
    And the poison went merrily doun.

5 'O where will I get a bonny boy,
    That will win hose and shoon,
That will gang quickly to Sittingen's
    Rocks,
    And bid my lady come?'

6 It's out then speaks a bonny boy,
    To Earl Robert was something akin:
'Many a time have I ran thy errand,
    But this day wi the tears I'll rin.'

7 Bat when he came to Sittingin's Rocks,
    To the middle of a' the ha,

There were bells a ringing, and music
    playing,
    And ladies dancing a'.

8 'What news, what news, my bonny boy?
    What news have ye to me?
Is Earl Robert in very good health,
    And the ladies of your countrie?'

9 'O Earl Robert's in very good health,
    And as weel as a man can be;
But his mother this night has a drink to
    be druken,
    And at it you must be.'

10 She called to her waiting-maid,
    To bring her a riding-weed,
And she called to her stable-groom,
    To saddle her milk-white steed.

11 But when she came to Earl Robert's
    bouir,
    To the middle of a' the ha,
There were bells a ringing, and sheets
    doun hinging,
    And ladies mourning a'.

12 'I've come for none of his gold,' she
    said,
    'Nor none of his white monie,
Excepting a ring of his smallest finger,
    If that you will grant me.'

13 'Thou'll not get none of his gold,' she
    said,
    'Nor none of his white monie;
Thou'll not get a ring of his smallest
    finger,
    Tho thy heart should break in three.'

14 She set her foot unto a stane,
    Her back unto a tree;
She set her foot unto a stane,
    And her heart did break in three.

15 The one was buried in Mary's kirk,
    The other in Mary's quire;
Out of the one there grew a birk,
    From the other a bonnie brier.

16 And these twa grew, and these twa
    threw,
    Till their twa craps drew near;
So all the warld may plainly see
    That they loved each other dear.

88

YOUNG JOHNSTONE

An explanation of Young Johnstone's motive for stabbing his lady was afforded by Motherwell's reciter: "The barbarous act was committed unwittingly, through Young Johnstone's suddenly waking from sleep, and, in that moment of confusion and alarm, unhappily mistaking his mistress for one of his pursuers." The apology may go for what it is worth. Awake or waking, Young Johnstone's first instinct is as duly to stab as a bull-dog's is to bite.

A

'The Cruel Knight,' Herd's Ancient and Modern Scots Songs, 1769, p. 305; I, 165, ed. 1776.

1 THE knight stands in the stable-door,
   As he was for to ryde,
When out then came his fair lady,
   Desiring him to byde.

2 'How can I byde? how dare I byde?
   How can I byde with thee?
Have I not killd thy ae brother?
   Thou hadst nae mair but he.'

3 'If you have killd my ae brother,
   Alas, and woe is me!
But if I save your fair body,
   The better you'll like me.'

4 She's tane him to her secret bower,
   Pinnd with a siller pin,
And she's up to her highest tower,
   To watch that none come in.

5 She had na well gane up the stair,
   And entered in her tower,
When four and twenty armed knights
   Came riding to the door.

6 'Now God you save, my fair lady,
   I pray you tell to me,
Saw you not a wounded knight
   Come riding by this way?'

7 'Yes, bloody, bloody was his sword,
   And bloody were his hands;
But if the steed he rides be good,
   He's past fair Scotland's strands.

8 'Light down, light down then, gentle men,
   And take some bread and wine;
The better you will him pursue
   When you shall lightly dine.'

9 'We thank you for your bread, lady,
   We thank you for your wine;
I would gie thrice three thousand pounds
   Your fair body was mine.'

10 Then she's gane to her secret bower,
    Her husband dear to meet;
But he drew out his bloody sword,
    And wounded her sae deep.

11 'What aileth thee now, good my lord?
    What aileth thee at me?
Have you not got my father's gold,
    But and my mother's fee?'

12 'Now live, now live, my fair lady,
    O live but half an hour,
There's neer a leech in fair Scotland
    But shall be at thy bower.'

13 'How can I live? how shall I live?
    How can I live for thee?
See you not where my red heart's blood
    Runs trickling down my knee?'

*   *   *   *   *

B

a. 'Young Johnstone,' Motherwell's Minstrelsy, p. 193, from the recitation of Mrs Gentles, Paisley. b. 'The Young Johnstone,' Finlay's Scottish Historical and Romantic Ballads, II, 71, from two recited copies.

1 YOUNG JOHNSTONE and the young Colnel
   Sat drinking at the wine:
'O gin ye wad marry my sister,
   It's I wad marry thine.'

2 'I wadna marry your sister
   For a' your houses and land;
But I'll keep her for my leman,
   When I come oer the strand.

3 'I wadna marry your sister
   For a' your gowd so gay;
But I'll keep her for my leman,
   When I come by the way.'

4 Young Johnstone had a little small
    sword,
  Hung low down by his gair,
And he stabbed it through the young
    Colnel,
  That word he neer spak mair.

5 But he 's awa to his sister's bower,
  He 's tirled at the pin:
' Whare hae ye been, my dear brither,
  Sae late a coming in ? '
' I hae been at the school, sister,
  Learning young clerks to sing.'

6 ' I 've dreamed a dreary dream this
    night,
  I wish it may be for good;
They were seeking you with hawks and
    hounds,
  And the young Colnel was dead.'

7 ' Hawks and hounds they may seek me,
  As I trow well they be;
For I have killed the young Colnel,
  And thy own true-love was he.'

8 ' If ye hae killed the young Colnel,
  O dule and wae is me !
But I wish ye may be hanged on a hie
    gallows,
  And hae nae power to flee.'

9 And he 's awa to his true-love's bower,
  He 's tirled at the pin:
' Whar hae ye been, my dear Johnstone,
  Sae late a coming in ? '
' It 's I hae been at the school,' he says,
  ' Learning young clerks to sing.'

10 ' I have dreamed a dreary dream,' she
    says,
  ' I wish it may be for good;
They were seeking you with hawks and
    hounds,
  And the young Colnel was dead.'

11 ' Hawks and hounds they may seek me,
  As I trow well they be;
For I hae killed the young Colnel,
  And thy ae brother was he.'

12 ' If ye hae killed the young Colnel,
  O dule and wae is me !
But I care the less for the young Colnel,
  If thy ain body be free.

13 ' Come in, come in, my dear Johnstone,
  Come in and take a sleep;
And I will go to my casement,
  And carefully I will thee keep.'

14 He had not weel been in her bower-door
  No not for half an hour,
When four and twenty belted knights
  Came riding to the bower.

15 ' Well may you sit and see, lady,
  Well may you sit and say;
Did you not see a bloody squire
  Come riding by this way ? '

16 ' What colour were his hawks ? ' she says,
  ' What colour were his hounds ?
What colour was the gallant steed,
  That bore him from the bounds ? '

17 ' Bloody, bloody were his hawks,
  And bloody were his hounds;
But milk-white was the gallant steed,
  That bore him from the bounds.'

18 ' Yes, bloody, bloody were his hawks,
  And bloody were his hounds;
And milk-white was the gallant steed,
  That bore him from the bounds.

19 ' Light down, light down now, gentle-
    men,
  And take some bread and wine;
And the steed be swift that he rides on
  He 's past the brig o Lyne.'

20 ' We thank you for your bread, fair lady,
  We thank you for your wine;
But I wad gie thrice three thousand
    pound
  That bloody knight was taen.'

21 ' Lie still, lie still, my dear Johnstone,
  Lie still and take a sleep;
For thy enemies are past and gone,
  And carefully I will thee keep.'

22 But Young Johnstone had a little wee
    sword,
  Hung low down by his gair,
And he stabbed it in fair Annet's breast,
  A deep wound and a sair.

23 ' What aileth thee now, dear Johnstone ?
  What aileth thee at me ?

Hast thou not got my father's gold
  Bot and my mither's fee?'

24 'Now live, now live, my dear ladye,
    Now live but half an hour,
    And there 's no a leech in a' Scotland
    But shall be in thy bower.'

25 'How can I live? how shall I live?
    Young Johnstone, do not you see
    The red, red drops o my bonny heart's
        blood
    Rin trinkling down my knee?

26 'But take thy harp into thy hand,
    And harp out owre yon plain,
    And neer think mair on thy true-love
    Than if she had never been.'

27 He hadna weel been out o the stable,
    And on his saddle set,
    Till four and twenty broad arrows
    Were thrilling in his heart.

89

FAUSE FOODRAGE

This ballad, though substantially genuine,
has come down to us in an enfeebled form.
The rebellion of the nobles in A is evidently a
corruption; it is a prosaic touch, and not at
all ballad-like. 'Fause Foodrage' is closely
related to the Scandinavian ballad of 'Svend
of Voldesløv' (Grundtvig-Olrik, No. 298).

A

'Fa'ase Footrage,' Alexander Fraser Tytler's Brown MS., No. 3.

1 KING EASTER has courted her for her
        gowd,
    King Wester for her fee,
  King Honor for her lands sae braid,
    And for her fair body.

2 They had not been four months married,
    As I have heard them tell,
  Until the nobles of the land
    Against them did rebel.

3 And they cast kaivles them amang,
    And kaivles them between,

And they cast kaivles them amang
  Wha shoud gae kill the king.

4 O some said yea, and some said nay,
    Their words did not agree;
  Till up it gat him Fa'se Footrage,
    And sware it shoud be he.

5 When bells were rung, and mass was
        sung,
    And a' man boon to bed,
  King Honor and his gay ladie
    In a hie chamer were laid.

6 Then up it raise him Fa'se Footrage,
    While a' were fast asleep,
  And slew the porter in his lodge,
    That watch and ward did keep.

7 O four and twenty silver keys
    Hang hie upon a pin,
  And ay as a door he did unlock,
    He has fastend it him behind.

8 Then up it raise him King Honor,
    Says, What means a' this din!
  Now what 's the matter, Fa'se Foot-
        rage?
    O wha was 't loot you in?

9 'O ye my errand well shall learn
    Before that I depart;'
  Then drew a knife baith lang and
        sharp
    And pierced him thro the heart.

10 Then up it got the Queen hersell,
    And fell low down on her knee:
  'O spare my life now, Fa'se Footrage!
    For I never injured thee.

11 'O spare my life now, Fa'se Footrage!
    Until I lighter be,
  And see gin it be lad or lass
    King Honor has left me wi.'

12 'O gin it be a lass,' he says,
    'Well nursed she shall be;
  But gin it be a lad-bairn,
    He shall be hanged hie.

13 'I winna spare his tender age,
    Nor yet his hie, hie kin;
  But as soon as eer he born is,
    He shall mount the gallows-pin.

4 O four and twenty valiant knights
   Were set the Queen to guard,
And four stood ay at her bower-door,
   To keep baith watch and ward.

5 But when the time drew till an end
   That she should lighter be,
She cast about to find a wile
   To set her body free.

6 O she has birled these merry young men
   Wi strong beer and wi wine,
Until she made them a' as drunk
   As any wallwood swine.

7 'O narrow, narrow is this window,
   And big, big am I grown!'
Yet thro the might of Our Ladie
   Out at it she has won.

18 She wanderd up, she wanderd down,
   She wanderd out and in,
And at last, into the very swines' stye,
   The Queen brought forth a son.

19 Then they cast kaivles them amang
   Wha should gae seek the Queen,
And the kaivle fell upon Wise William,
   And he 's sent his wife for him.

20 O when she saw Wise William's wife,
   The Queen fell on her knee;
'Win up, win up, madame,' she says,
   'What means this courtesie?'

21 'O out of this I winna rise
   Till a boon ye grant to me,
To change your lass for this lad-bairn
   King Honor left me wi.

22 'And ye maun learn my gay gose-hawke
   Well how to breast a steed,
And I shall learn your turtle-dow
   As well to write and read.

23 'And ye maun learn my gay gose-hawke
   To wield baith bow and brand,
And I shall learn your turtle-dow
   To lay gowd wi her hand.

24 'At kirk or market where we meet,
   We dare nae mair avow
But, Dame, how does my gay gose-
     hawk?
   Madame, how does my dow?'

25 When days were gane, and years came
     on,
   Wise William he thought long;
Out has he taen King Honor's son,
   A hunting for to gang.

26 It sae fell out at their hunting,
   Upon a summer's day,
That they cam by a fair castle,
   Stood on a sunny brae.

27 'O dinna ye see that bonny castle,
   Wi wa's and towers sae fair?
Gin ilka man had back his ain,
   Of it you shoud be heir.'

28 'How I shoud be heir of that castle
   In sooth I canna see,
When it belongs to Fa'se Footrage,
   And he 's nae kin to me.'

29 'O gin ye shoud kill him Fa'se Foot-
     rage,
   You woud do what is right;
For I wot he killd your father dear,
   Ere ever you saw the light.

30 'Gin ye should kill him Fa'se Foot-
     rage,
   There is nae man durst you blame;
For he keeps your mother a prisoner,
   And she dares no take you hame.'

31 The boy stared wild like a gray gose-
     hawke,
   Says, What may a' this mean!
'My boy, you are King Honor's son,
   And your mother 's our lawful queen.'

32 'O gin I be King Honor's son,
   By Our Ladie I swear,
This day I will that traytour slay
   And relieve my mother dear.'

33 He has set his bent bow till his breast,
   And lap the castle-wa,
And soon he 's siesed on Fa'se Footrage,
   Wha loud for help gan ca.

34 'O hold your tongue now, Fa'se Foot-
     rage,
   Frae me you shanno flee;'
Syne pierced him through the foul fa'se
     heart,
   And set his mother free.

35 And he has rewarded Wise William
    Wi the best half of his land,
And sae has he the turtle-dow
    Wi the truth of his right hand.

B

'The Eastmure King and the Westmure
King,' Motherwell's MS., p. 341.

1 THE Eastmure king, and the Westmure
        king,
    And the king of Onorie,
They have all courted a pretty maid,
    And guess wha she micht be.

2 The Eastmure king courted her for gold,
    And the Westmure king for fee,
The king of Onore for womanheid,
    And for her fair beautie.

3 The Eastmure king swore a solemn
        oath,
    He would keep it till May,
That he would murder the king of
        Onore,
    Upon his wedding day.

4 When bells was rung, and psalms was
        sung,
    And all men boune for sleep,
Up and started the Eastmure king
    At the king of Onore's head.

5 He has drawn the curtains by —
    Their sheets was made of dorn —
And he has murdered the king of Onore,
    As innocent as he was born.

6 This maid she awak'd in the middle of
        the night,
    Was in a drowsy dream;
She found her bride's-bed swim with
        blood,
    Bot and her good lord slain.

7 'What will the court and council say?
    What will they say to me?
What will the court and council say
    But this night I 've murderd thee?'

8 Out and speaks the Eastmure king:
    'Hold your tongue, my pretty may,
And come along with me, my dear,
    And that court ye 'll never see.'

9 He mounted her on a milk-white
        steed,
    Himself upon a gray;
She turnd her back against the court,
    And weeping rode away.

10 'Now if you be with child,' he says,
    'As I trew well you be,
If it be of a lassie-bairn,
    I 'll give her nurses three.

11 'If it be a lassie-bairn,
    If you please she 'll get five;
But if it be a bonnie boy,
    I will not let him live.'

12 Word is to the city gone,
    And word is to the town,
And word is to the city gone,
    She 's delivered of a son.

13 But a poor woman in the town
    In the same case does lye,
Wha gived to her her woman-child,
    Took awa her bonnie boy.

14 At kirk or market, whereer they met,
    They never durst avow,
But 'Thou be kind to my boy,' she
        says,
    'I 'll be kind to your bonnie dow.'

15 This boy was sixteen years of age,
    But he was nae seventeen,
When he is to the garden gone,
    To slay that Eastmure king.

16 'Be aware, be aware, thou Eastmure
        king,
    Be aware this day of me;
For I do swear and do declare
    Thy botcher I will be.'

17 'What aileth thee, my bonnie boy?
    What aileth thee at me?
I 'm sure I never did thee wrang;
    Thy face I neer did see.'

18 'Thou murdered my father dear,
    When scarse conceived was I;
Thou murdered my father dear,
    When scarse conceived was me:'
So then he slew that Eastmure king,
    Beneath that garden tree.

C

'Eastmuir King,' Harris MS., No. 18, fol. 22 : derived from Jannie Scott, an old Perthshire nurse, about 1790.

1 EASTMUIR king, and Wastmuir king,
   And king o Luve, a' three,
   It 's they coost kevils them amang,
   Aboot a gay ladie.

2 Eastmuir king he wan the gowd,
   An Wastmuir king the fee,
   But king o Luve, wi his lands sae broad,
   He 's won the fair ladie.

3 Thae twa kings, they made an aith,
   That, be it as it may,
   They wad slay him king o Luve,
   Upon his waddin day.

4 Eastmuir king he brak his aith,
   An sair penance did he;
   But Wastmuir king he made it oot,
   An an ill deid mat he dee !

90

JELLON GRAME

'Jellon Grame' may be regarded as a counterpart to 'Fause Foodrage' (No. 89). It has certainly suffered very much in transmission. There is a material difference in plot between the story furnished by A and what we learn from the three other copies (of which B is here printed).

A

a. 'Jellon Grame and Lillie Flower,' A. Fraser Tytler's Brown MS., No. 4. b. 'Jellon Grame,' Scott's Minstrelsy, II, 20, 1802.

1 O JELLON GRAME sat in Silver Wood,
   He whistled and he sang,
   And he has calld his little foot-page,
   His errand for to gang.

2 'Win up, my bonny boy,' he says,
   'As quick as eer you may;
   For ye maun gang for Lillie Flower,
   Before the break of day.'

3 The boy he 's buckled his belt about,
   And thro the green-wood ran,

And he came to the ladie's bower-door,
   Before the day did dawn.

4 'O sleep ye, or wake ye, Lillie Flower ?
   The red run 's i the rain:'
   'I sleep not aft, I wake right aft;
   Wha 's that that kens my name ? '

5 'Ye are bidden come to Silver Wood,
   But I fear you 'll never win hame;
   Ye are bidden come to Silver Wood,
   And speak wi Jellon Grame.'

6 'O I will gang to Silver Wood,
   Though I shoud never win hame;
   For the thing I most desire on earth
   Is to speak wi Jellon Grame.'

7 She had no ridden a mile, a mile,
   A mile but barely three,
   Ere she came to a new made grave,
   Beneath a green oak tree.

8 O then up started Jellon Grame,
   Out of a bush hard bye:
   'Light down, light down now, Lillie
      Flower,
   For it 's here that ye maun ly.'

9 She lighted aff her milk-white steed,
   And knelt upon her knee:
   'O mercy, mercy, Jellon Grame !
   For I 'm nae prepar'd to die.

10 'Your bairn, that stirs between my
      sides,
   Maun shortly see the light;
   But to see it weltring in my blude
   Woud be a piteous sight.'

11 'O shoud I spare your life,' he says,
   'Until that bairn be born,
   I ken fu well your stern father
   Woud hang me on the morn.'

12 'O spare my life now, Jellon Grame !
   My father ye neer need dread;
   I 'll keep my bairn i the good green
      wood,
   Or wi it I 'll beg my bread.'

13 He took nae pity on that ladie,
   Tho she for life did pray;
   But pierced her thro the fair body,
   As at his feet she lay.

14 He felt nae pity for that ladie,
    Tho she was lying dead;
    But he felt some for the bonny boy
    Lay weltring in her blude.

15 Up has he taen that bonny boy,
    Gien him to nurices nine,
    Three to wake, and three to sleep,
    And three to go between.

16 And he's brought up that bonny boy,
    Calld him his sister's son;
    He thought nae man would eer find
        out
    The deed that he had done.

17 But it sae fell out upon a time,
    As a hunting they did gay,
    That they rested them in Silver Wood,
    Upon a summer-day.

18 Then out it spake that bonny boy,
    While the tear stood in his eye,
    'O tell me this now, Jellon Grame,
    And I pray you dinna lie.

19 'The reason that my mother dear
    Does never take me hame?
    To keep me still in banishment
    Is baith a sin and shame.'

20 'You wonder that your mother dear
    Does never send for thee;
    Lo, there's the place I slew thy mother,
    Beneath that green oak tree.'

21 Wi that the boy has bent his bow,
    It was baith stout and lang,
    And through and thro him Jellon Grame
    He's gard an arrow gang.

22 Says, Lye you thare now, Jellon Grame,
    My mellison you wi;
    The place my mother lies buried in
    Is far too good for thee.

B

'Hind Henry,' Motherwell's MS., p. 443.

1 WORD has come to May Margerie,
    In her bower where she sat:
'You are bid come to good green-wood,
    To make your love a shirt.'

2 'I wonder much,' said May Margerie,
    'At this message to me;
    There is not a month gone of this year
    But I have made him three.'

3 Then out did speak her mother dear,
    A wise woman was she;
    Said, Stay at home, my daughter May,
    They seek to murder thee.

4 'O I'll cast off my gloves, mother,
    And hang them up, I say;
    If I come never back again,
    They will mind you on May.

5 'Go saddle my horseback,' she said,
    'It's quick as ever you may,
    And we will ride to good green-wood;
    It is a pleasant day.'

6 And when she came to good green-wood,
    It's through it they did ride;
    Then up did start him Hind Henry,
    Just at the lady's side.

7 Says, Stop, O stop, you May Margerie,
    Just stop I say to thee;
    The boy that leads your bridle reins
    Shall see you red and blue.

8 It's out he drew a long, long brand,
    And stroked it ower a strae,
    And through and through that lady's
        sides
    He made the cauld weapon gae.

9 Says, Take you that now, May Margerie,
    Just take you that from me,
    Because you love Brown Robin,
    And never would love me.

10 There was less pity for that lady,
    When she was lying dead,
    As was for her bony infant boy,
    Lay swathed amang her bleed.

11 The boy fled home with all his might,
    The tear into his ee:
'They have slain my lady in the wood,
    With fear I'm like to die.'

12 Her sister's ran into the wood,
    With greater grief and care,
    Sighing and sobbing all the way,
    Tearing her cloaths and hair.

3 Says, I'll take up that fair infant,
    And lull him on my sleeve;
  Altho his father should wish me woe,
    His mother to me was leeve.

4 Now she has taken the infant up,
    And she has brought him hame,
  And she has called him Brown Robin,
    That was his father's name.

5 And when he did grow up a bit,
    She put him to the lair,
  And of all the youths was at that school
    None could with him compare.

6 And it fell once upon a day
    A playtime it was come,
  And when the rest went from the school,
    Each one to their own home,

7 He hied him unto good green-wood,
    And leapt from tree to tree;
  It was to pull a hollin wand,
    To play his ownself wi.

8 And when he thus had passed his time,
    To go home he was fain,
  He chanced to meet him Hind Henry,
    Where his mother was slain.

19 'O how is this,' the youth cried out,
    'If it to you is known,
  How all this wood is growing grass,
    And on that small spot grows none?'

20 'Since you do wonder, bonnie boy,
    I shall tell you anon;
  That is indeed the very spot
    I killed your mother in.'

21 He catched hold of Henry's brand,
    And stroked it ower a strae,
  And thro and thro Hind Henry's sides
    He made the cauld metal gae.

22 Says, Take you that, O Hind Henry,
    O take you that from me,
  For killing of my mother dear,
    And her not hurting thee.

91

FAIR MARY OF WALLINGTON

'Fair Mary of Wallington' (A) was communicated to Bishop Percy, with other "old
Scots Songs," in 1775, by Roger Halt, and presumably in a copy of the garland from which
it is here printed. The story is well preserved
in this version. A Breton ballad, 'Pontplan-
coat' (Luzel, I, 382 ff.), exhibits such correspondences with the English and Scottish that
it may be assumed to have the same source.
The localization of A in Northumberland is
of no special significance.

A

'Fair Mary of Wallington,' Lovely Jenny's
Garland, three copies, as early as 1775, but
without place or date.

1 WHEN we were silly sisters seven,
    sisters were so fair,
  Five of us were brave knights' wives,
    and died in childbed lair.

2 Up then spake Fair Mary,
    marry woud she nane;
  If ever she came in man's bed,
    the same gate wad she gang.

3 'Make no vows, Fair Mary,
    for fear they broken be;
  Here's been the Knight of Walling-
      ton,
    asking good will of thee.'

4 'If here's been the knight, mother,
    asking good will of me,
  Within three quarters of a year
    you may come bury me.'

5 When she came to Wallington,
    and into Wallington hall,
  There she spy'd her mother dear,
    walking about the wall.

6 'You're welcome, daughter dear,
    to thy castle and thy bowers;'
  'I thank you kindly, mother,
    I hope they'll soon be yours.'

7 She had not been in Wallington
    three quarters and a day,
  Till upon the ground she could not
      walk,
    she was a weary prey.

8 She had not been in Wallington
    three quarters and a night,
  Till on the ground she coud not walk,
    she was a weary wight.

9 ' Is there neer a boy in this town,
　　who 'll win hose and shun,
That will run to fair Pudlington,
　　and bid my mother come ? '

10 Up then spake a little boy,
　　near unto a-kin;
' Full oft I have your errands gone,
　　but now I will it run.'

11 Then she calld her waiting-maid
　　to bring up bread and wine:
' Eat and drink, my bonny boy,
　　thou 'll neer eat more of mine.

12 ' Give my respects to my mother,
　　[as] she sits in her chair of stone,
And ask her how she likes the news,
　　of seven to have but one.

13 [' Give my respects to my mother,
　　as she sits in her chair of oak,
And bid her come to my sickening,
　　or my merry lake-wake.]

14 ' Give my love to my brother
　　William, Ralph, and John,
And to my sister Betty fair,
　　and to her white as bone.

15 ' And bid her keep her maidenhead,
　　be sure make much on 't,
For if eer she come in man's bed,
　　the same gate will she gang.'

16 Away this little boy is gone,
　　as fast as he could run;
When he came where brigs were
　　broke,
he lay down and swum.

17 When he saw the lady, he said,
　　Lord may your keeper be !
' What news, my pretty boy,
　　hast thou to tell to me ? '

18 ' Your daughter Mary orders me,
　　as you sit in a chair of stone,
To ask you how you like the news,
　　of seven to have but one.

19 ' Your daughter gives commands,
　　as you sit in a chair of oak,
And bids you come to her sickening,
　　or her merry lake-wake.

20 ' She gives command to her brother
　　William, Ralph, and John,
[And] to her sister Betty fair,
　　and to her white as bone.

21 ' She bids her keep her maidenhead,
　　be sure make much on 't,
For if eer she came in man's bed,
　　the same gate woud she gang.'

22 She kickt the table with her foot,
　　she kickt it with her knee,
The silver plate into the fire,
　　so far she made it flee.

23 Then she calld her waiting-maid
　　to bring her riding-hood,
So did she on her stable-groom
　　to bring her riding-steed.

24 ' Go saddle to me the black [the
　　black,]
go saddle to me the brown,
Go saddle to me the swiftest steed
　　that eer rid [to] Wallington.'

25 When they came to Wallington,
　　and into Wallington hall,
There she spy'd her son Fenwick,
　　walking about the wall.

26 ' God save you, dear son,
　　Lord may your keeper be !
Where is my daughter fair,
　　that used to walk with thee ? '

27 He turnd his head round about,
　　the tears did fill his ee:
' 'T is a month,' he said, ' since she
　　took her chambers from me.'

28 She went on　　.　　.　　.
　　and there were in the hall
Four and twenty ladies,
　　letting the tears down fall.

29 Her daughter had a scope
　　into her cheek and into her chin,
All to keep her life
　　till her dear mother came.

30 ' Come take the rings off my fingers,
　　the skin it is so white,
And give them to my mother dear,
　　for she was all the wite.

31 'Come take the rings off my fingers,
    the veins they are so red,
  Give them to Sir William Fenwick,
    I 'm sure his heart will bleed.'

32 She took out a razor
    that was both sharp and fine,
  And out of her left side has taken
    the heir of Wallington.

33 There is a race in Wallington,
    and that I rue full sare;
  Tho the cradle it be full spread up,
    the bride-bed is left bare.

C

'The Bonny Earl of Livingston,' Alexander
Fraser Tytler's Brown MS., No. 5.

1 'O we were sisters seven, Maisry,
    And five are dead wi child;
  There is nane but you and I, Maisry,
    And we 'll go maidens mild.'

2 She hardly had the word spoken,
    And turnd her round about,
  When the bonny Earl of Livingston
    Was calling Maisry out.

3 Upon a bonny milk-white steed,
    That drank out of the Tyne,
  And a' was for her Ladie Maisry,
    To take her hyne and hyne.

4 Upon a bonny milk-white steed,
    That drank out o the Tay,
  And a' was for her Lady Maisry,
    To carry her away.

5 She had not been at Livingston
    A twelve month and a day,
  Until she was as big wi bairn
    As any ladie coud gae.

6 She calld upon her little foot-page,
    Says, Ye maun run wi speed,
  And bid my mother come to me,
    For of her I 'll soon have need.

7 'See, there is the brootch frae my hause-
    bane,
    It is of gowd sae ried;
  Gin she winna come when I 'm alive,
    Bid her come when I am dead.'

8 But ere she wan to Livingston,
    As fast as she coud ride,
  The gaggs they were in Maisry's mouth,
    And the sharp sheers in her side.

9 Her good lord wrang his milk-white
    hands,
    Till the gowd rings flaw in three:
  'Let ha's and bowers and a' gae waste,
    My bonny love 's taen frae me!'

10 'O hold your tongue, Lord Livingston,
    Let a' your mourning be;
  For I bare the bird between my sides,
    Yet I maun thole her to die.'

11 Then out it spake her sister dear,
    As she sat at her head:
  'That man is not in Christendoom
    Shall gar me die sicken dead.'

12 'O hold your tongue, my ae daughter,
    Let a' your folly be,
  For ye shall be married ere this day
    week
  Tho the same death you should die.'

92

BONNY BEE HOM

The talisman in this ballad reminds one of
'Hind Horn' (No. 17); the vows, of 'Clerk
Saunders' (No. 69). Similar vows occur in a
song called 'The Lowlands of Holland' (see
the Notes).

A

'Bonny Bee Ho'm,' Alexander Fraser Tytler's
Brown MS., No. 6.

1 By Arthur's Dale as late I went
    I heard a heavy moan;
  I heard a ladie lammenting sair,
    And ay she cried Ohone!

2 'Ohon, alas! what shall I do,
    Tormented night and day!
  I never loved a love but ane,
    And now he 's gone away.

3 'But I will do for my true-love
    What ladies woud think sair;
  For seven year shall come and go
    Ere a kaim gang in my hair.

4 'There shall neither a shoe gang on my
    foot,
    Nor a kaim gang in my hair,
  Nor eer a coal nor candle-light
    Shine in my bower nae mair.'

5 She thought her love had been on the
    sea,
    Fast sailling to Bee Hom;
  But he was in a quiet chamer,
    Hearing his ladie's moan.

6 'Be husht, be husht, my ladie dear,
    I pray thee mourn not so;
  For I am deep sworn on a book
    To Bee Hom for to go.'

7 She has gien him a chain of the beaten
    gowd,
    And a ring with a ruby stone:
  'As lang as this chain your body
    binds,
    Your blude can never be drawn.

8 'But gin this ring shoud fade or fail,
    Or the stone shoud change its hue,
  Be sure your love is dead and gone,
    Or she has proved untrue.'

9 He had no been at Bonny Bee Hom
    A twelve month and a day,
  Till, looking on his gay gowd ring,
    The stone grew dark and gray.

10 'O ye take my riches to Bee Hom,
    And deal them presentlie,
  To the young that canna, the auld that
    maunna,
    And the blind that does not see.'

11 Now death has come into his bower,
    And split his heart in twain;
  So their twa souls flew up to heaven,
    And there shall ever remain.

93

LAMKIN

The versions are very numerous, — Professor Child prints twenty-six, including fragments,— but the story does not vary essentially.
Only three are given here. One of these (K)
is defective, but it is the oldest version, except
perhaps P, which is greatly inferior. The tale
has been localized in various places in Scotland.
The name Lamkin is probably an ironical designation for the bloody mason, the terror o
countless nurseries.

A

'Lamkin,' Jamieson's Popular Ballads, I, 176
communicated by Mrs Brown.

1 It's Lamkin was a mason good
    as ever built wi stane;
  He built Lord Wearie's castle,
    but payment got he nane.

2 'O pay me, Lord Wearie,
    come, pay me my fee:'
  'I canna pay you, Lamkin,
    for I maun gang oer the sea.'

3 'O pay me now, Lord Wearie,
    come, pay me out o hand:'
  'I canna pay you, Lamkin,
    unless I sell my land.'

4 'O gin ye winna pay me,
    I here sall mak a vow,
  Before that ye come hame again,
    ye sall hae cause to rue.'

5 Lord Wearie got a bonny ship,
    to sail the saut sea faem;
  Bade his lady weel the castle keep,
    ay till he should come hame.

6 But the nourice was a fause limmer
    as eer hung on a tree;
  She laid a plot wi Lamkin,
    whan her lord was oer the sea.

7 She laid a plot wi Lamkin,
    when the servants were awa,
  Loot him in at a little shot-window,
    and brought him to the ha.

8 'O whare's a' the men o this house,
    that ca me Lamkin?'
  'They're at the barn-well thrashing;
    't will be lang ere they come in.'

9 'And whare's the women o this house,
    that ca me Lamkin?'
  'They're at the far well washing;
    't will be lang ere they come in.'

10 ' And whare 's the bairns o this house,
    that ca me Lamkin ? '
' They 're at the school reading;
    't will be night or they come hame.'

11 ' O whare 's the lady o this house,
    that ca's me Lamkin ? '
' She 's up in her bower sewing,
    but we soon can bring her down.'

12 Then Lamkin 's tane a sharp knife,
    that hang down by his gaire,
And he has gien the bonny babe
    a deep wound and a sair.

13 Then Lamkin he rocked,
    and the fause nourice sang,
Till frae ilkae bore o the cradle
    the red blood out sprang.

14 Then out it spak the lady,
    as she stood on the stair:
' What ails my bairn, nourice,
    that he 's greeting sae sair ?

15 ' O still my bairn, nourice,
    O still him wi the pap ! '
' He winna still, lady,
    for this nor for that.'

16 ' O still my bairn, nourice,
    O still him wi the wand ! '
' He winna still, lady,
    for a' his father's land.'

17 ' O still my bairn, nourice,
    O still him wi the bell ! '
' He winna still, lady,
    till ye come down yoursel.'

18 O the firsten step she steppit,
    she steppit on a stane;
But the neisten step she steppit,
    she met him Lamkin.

19 ' O mercy, mercy, Lamkin,
    hae mercy upon me !
Though you 've taen my young son's
    life,
    ye may let mysel be.'

20 ' O sall I kill her, nourice,
    or sall I lat her be ? '
' O kill her, kill her, Lamkin,
    for she neer was good to me.'

21 ' O scour the bason, nourice,
    and mak it fair and clean,
For to keep this lady's heart's blood,
    for she 's come o noble kin.'

22 ' There need nae bason, Lamkin,
    lat it run through the floor;
What better is the heart's blood
    o the rich than o the poor ? '

23 But ere three months were at an end,
    Lord Wearie came again;
But dowie, dowie was his heart
    when first he came hame.

24 ' O wha's blood is this,' he says,
    ' that lies in the chamer ? '
' It is your lady's heart's blood;
    't is as clear as the lamer.'

25 ' And wha's blood is this,' he says,
    ' that lies in my ha ? '
' It is your young son's heart's blood;
    't is the clearest ava.'

26 O sweetly sang the black-bird
    that sat upon the tree;
But sairer grat Lamkin,
    when he was condemnd to die.

27 And bonny sang the mavis,
    out o the thorny brake;
But sairer grat the nourice,
    when she was tied to the stake.

B

' Lambert Linkin,' Motherwell's MS., p. 15;
from the recitation of Mrs Thomson, Kilbarchan, February 25, 1825.

1 BALANKIN was as gude a mason
    as eer picked a stane;
He built up Prime Castle,
    but payment gat nane.

2 The lord said to his lady,
    when he was going abroad,
O beware of Balankin,
    for he lyes in the wood.

3 The gates they were bolted,
    baith outside and in;
At the sma peep of a window
    Balankin crap in.

4 'Good morrow, good morrow,'
　　said Lambert Linkin:
'Good morrow to yoursell, sir,'
　　said the false nurse to him.

5 'O where is your good lord?
　　said Lambert Linkin:
'He's awa to New England,
　　to meet with his king.'

6 'O where is his auld son?'
　　said Lambert Linkin:
'He's awa to buy pearlings,
　　gin our lady lye in.'

7 'Then she'll never wear them,'
　　said Lambert Linkin:
'And that is nae pity,'
　　said the false nurse to him.

8 'O where is your lady?'
　　said Lambert Linkin:
'She's in her bower sleeping,'
　　said the false nurse to him.

9 'How can we get at her?'
　　said Lambert Linkin:
'Stab the babe to the heart,
　　wi a silver bokin.'

10 'That would be a pity,'
　　said Lambert Linkin:
'No pity, no pity,'
　　said the false nurse to him.

11 Balankin he rocked,
　　and the false nurse she sang,
Till all the tores of the cradle
　　wi the red blood down ran.

12 'O still my babe, nurice,
　　O still him wi the knife!'
'He'll no be still, lady,
　　tho I lay doun my life.'

13 'O still my babe, nurice,
　　O still him wi the kame!'
'He'll no be still, lady,
　　till his daddy come hame.'

14 'O still my babe, nurice,
　　O still him wi the bell!'
'He'll no be still, lady,
　　till ye come doun yoursell.'

15 'It's how can I come down,
　　this cauld winter nicht,
Without eer a coal,
　　or a clear candle-licht?'

16 'There's two smocks in your coffer,
　　as white as a swan;
Put one of them about you,
　　it will shew you licht down.'

17 She took ane o them about her,
　　and came tripping doun;
But as soon as she viewed,
　　Balankin was in.

18 'Good morrow, good morrow,'
　　said Lambert Linkin:
'Good morrow to yoursell, sir'
　　said the lady to him.

19 'O save my life, Balankin,
　　till my husband come back,
And I'll gie you as much red gold
　　as you'll hold in your hat.'

20 'I'll not save your life, lady,
　　till your husband come back,
Tho you would give me as much red
　　gold
　　as I could hold in a sack

21 'Will I kill her?' quo Balankin,
　　'will I kill her, or let her be?'
'You may kill her,' said the false nurse
　　'she was neer good to me;
And ye'll be laird of the castle,
　　and I'll be ladie.'

22 Then he cut aff her head
　　fram her lily breast-bane,
And he hung't up in the kitchen,
　　it made a' the ha shine.

23 The lord sat in England,
　　a drinking the wine:
'I wish a' may be weel
　　with my lady at hame;
For the rings of my fingers
　　the're now burst in twain!'

24 He saddled his horse,
　　and he came riding doun,
But as soon as he viewed,
　　Balankin was in.

25　He had na weel stepped
　　　　twa steps up the stair,
　　Till he saw his pretty young son
　　　　lying dead on the floor.

26　He had not weel stepped
　　　　other twa up the stair,
　　Till he saw his pretty lady
　　　　lying dead in despair.

27　He hanged Balankin
　　　　out over the gate,
　　And he burnt the fause nurice,
　　　　being under the grate.

K

'Long Longkin,' Percy Papers, communicated to Percy by Rev. P. Parsons, of Wye,
near Ashford, Kent, April 19, 1775.

1　MY lord said to my lady,
　　　　when he went from home,
　　Take care of Long Longkin,
　　　　he lies in the lone.

2　My lady said to my lord,
　　　　when he went abroad,
　　　·　　·　　·　　·

3　'I care not for Longkin,
　　　　nor none of his kin,
　　For my gate 's fast barrd,
　　　　and my windows shut in.'

4　My lord was not gone
　　　　many miles from the place,
　　Untill the false Longkin
　　　　came straight to the place.

　　*　　*　　*　　*　　*

5　'Pinch the bairn, nourry,
　　　　pinch it very sore,
　　Untill the mother
　　　　shall come down below.'

6　'Still the bairn, nury,
　　　　still it with the pap:'
　　'It wont be stilld, madam,
　　　　with neither this nor that.'

7　'Still the bairn, nury,
　　　　still it with a bell:'
　　'It wont be stilld, madam,
　　　　till you cum down yoursell.'

　　*　　*　　*　　*　　*

8　'Come down, Lady Betty,
　　　　the flower of all your kin,
　　And see your mother's heart's blood,
　　　　so freely running.

9　Down came Lady Betty,
　　　　her heart full of woe:
　　'Oh take my life, Longkin,
　　　　and let my mother go.'

10　'Come down, Lady Nelly,
　　　　the flower of all your kin,
　　And see your sister's heart's blood,
　　　　so freely running.'

11　Down came Lady Nelly,
　　　　her heart full of woe:
　　'Oh take my life, Longkin,
　　　　and let my sister go.'

12　'Come down, Lady Jenny, etc.

94

YOUNG WATERS

'Young Waters' was first printed in 1755;
Percy's text (Reliques, 1765, II, 172) agrees with
this edition except in half a dozen trivial points.
Motherwell says he had never met with any
traditionary version of this ballad. Buchan,
who may generally be relied upon to produce a
longer ballad than anybody else, has 'Young
Waters' in thirty-nine stanzas, "the only complete version which he had ever met." Everything in this copy which is not in the edition
of 1755 (itself a little worse for editing) is a
counterfeit of the lowest description.

It is possible, and Aytoun thinks highly
probable, that this ballad may have been
founded on some real event in Scottish history;
but Aytoun shows a commendable discretion in
his conclusion that, "though various conjectures have been hazarded as to its origin, none
appear sufficiently plausible to warrant their
adoption." A Scandinavian ballad (Grundtvig,
No. 178), historical to the extent that one version has historical names, exhibits the principal
incidents of the short story of 'Young Waters.'

Young Waters, an Ancient Scottish Poem,
never before printed. Glasgow, Printed and
sold by Robert and Andrew Foulis, 1755
Small 4°, 8 pages.

1 ABOUT Yule, when the wind blew cule,
 And the round tables began,
 A there is cum to our king's court
 Mony a well-favord man.

2 The queen luikt owre the castle-wa,
 Beheld baith dale and down,
 And there she saw Young Waters
 Cum riding to the town.

3 His footmen they did rin before,
 His horsemen rade behind;
 And mantel of the burning gowd
 Did keip him frae the wind.

4 Gowden-graithd his horse before,
 And siller-shod behind;
 The horse Young Waters rade upon
 Was fleeter than the wind.

5 Out then spack a wylie lord,
 Unto the queen said he,
 'O tell me wha's the fairest face
 Rides in the company?'

6 'I've sene lord, and I've sene laird,
 And knights of high degree,
 Bot a fairer face than Young Waters
 Mine eyne did never see.'

7 Out then spack the jealous king,
 And an angry man was he:
 'O if he had bin twice as fair,
 You micht have excepted me.'

8 'You're neither laird nor lord,' she
      says,
 'Bot the king that wears the crown,
 There is not a knight in fair Scotland
 But to thee maun bow down.'

9 For a' that she coud do or say,
 Appeasd he wad nae bee,
 Bot for the words which she had said,
 Young Waters he maun die.

10 They hae taen Young Waters,
 And put fetters to his feet;
 They hae taen Young Waters,
 And thrown him in dungeon deep.

11 'Aft I have ridden thro Stirling town
 In the wind bot and the weit;
 Bot I neir rade thro Stirling town
 Wi fetters at my feet.

12 'Aft I have ridden thro Stirling town
 In the wind bot and the rain;
 Bot I neir rade thro Stirling town
 Neir to return again.'

13 They hae taen to the heiding-hill
 His young son in his craddle,
 And they hae taen to the heiding-hill
 His horse bot and his saddle.

14 They hae taen to the heiding-hill
 His lady fair to see,
 And for the words the queen had spoke
 Young Waters he did die.

95

THE MAID FREED FROM THE GALLOWS

All the English versions are defective and distorted. In many others, both from northern and southern Europe, a young woman has fallen into the hands of corsairs; father, mother, brother, sister, refuse to pay ransom, but her lover, in one case husband, stickles at no price which may be necessary to retrieve her. The best ballad of the cycle is the Sicilian 'Scibilia Nobili' (Salomone-Marino, Leggende pop. siciliane in Poesia, No. 29). There are very numerous versions in Finnish and Esthonian, and numerous variations on the theme occur in Russia and elsewhere.

A

Percy Papers, communicated to Percy, April 7, 1770, by the Rev. P. Parsons, of Wye, from oral tradition.

*   *   *   *   *

1 'O GOOD Lord Judge, and sweet Lord
      Judge,
 Peace for a little while!
 Methinks I see my own father,
 Come riding by the stile.

2 'Oh father, oh father, a little of your
      gold,
 And likewise of your fee!
 To keep my body from yonder grave,
 And my neck from the gallows-tree.'

3 'None of my gold now you shall have,
 Nor likewise of my fee:

For I am come to see you hangd,
And hanged you shall be.'

4 ' Oh good Lord Judge, and sweet Lord
Judge,
Peace for a little while !
Methinks I see my own mother,
Come riding by the stile.

5 ' Oh mother, oh mother, a little of your
gold,
And likewise of your fee,
To keep my body from yonder grave,
And my neck from the gallows-tree !'

6 ' None of my gold now shall you
have,
Nor likewise of my fee;
For I am come to see you hangd,
And hanged you shall be.'

7 ' Oh good Lord Judge, and sweet Lord
Judge,
Peace for a little while !
Methinks I see my own brother,
Come riding by the stile.

8 ' Oh brother, oh brother, a little of your
gold,
And likewise of your fee,
To keep my body from yonder grave,
And my neck from the gallows-
tree !'

9 ' None of my gold now shall you have,
Nor likewise of my fee;
For I am come to see you hangd,
And hanged you shall be.'

10 ' Oh good Lord Judge, and sweet Lord
Judge,
Peace for a little while !
Methinks I see my own sister,
Come riding by the stile.

11 ' Oh sister, oh sister, a little of your
gold,
And likewise of your fee,
To keep my body from yonder grave,
And my neck from the gallows-tree !'

12 ' None of my gold now shall you have,
Nor likewise of my fee;
For I am come to see you hangd,
And hanged you shall be.'

13 ' Oh good Lord Judge, and sweet Lord
Judge,
Peace for a little while !
Methinks I see my own true-love,
Come riding by the stile.

14 ' Oh true-love, oh true-love, a little of
your gold,
And likewise of your fee,
To save my body from yonder grave,
And my neck from the gallows-tree.'

15 ' Some of my gold now you shall have,
And likewise of my fee,
For I am come to see you saved.
And saved you shall be.'

I

Scotch Ballads, Materials for Border Minstrelsy, No. 127, Abbotsford. Sent to John
Leyden, by whom and when does not appear.

1 'HOLD your hand, Lord Judge,' she
says,
' Yet hold it a little while;
Methinks I see my ain dear father
Coming wandering many a mile.

2 ' O have you brought me gold, father ?
Or have you brought me fee ?
Or are you come to save my life
From off this gallows-tree ?'

3 ' I have not brought you gold, daughter,
Nor have I brought you fee,
But I am come to see you hangd,
As you this day shall be.'

[" The verses run thus untill she has seen
her mother, her brother, and her sister likewise arrive, and then

Methinks I see my ain dear lover, etc."]

4 ' I have not brought you gold, true-love,
Nor yet have I brought fee,
But I am come to save thy life
From off this gallows-tree.'

5 ' Gae hame, gae hame, father,' she says,
' Gae hame and saw yer seed;
And I wish not a pickle of it may grow
up,
But the thistle and the weed.

6 'Gae hame, gae hame, gae hame, mother,
 Gae hame and brew yer yill;
 And I wish the girds may a' loup off,
 And the Deil spill a' yer yill.

7 'Gae hame, gae hame, gae hame, brother,
 Gae hame and lie with yer wife;
 And I wish that the first news I may hear
 That she has tane your life.

8 'Gae hame, gae hame, sister,' she says,
 'Gae hame and sew yer seam;
 I wish that the needle-point may break,
 And the craws pyke out yer een.'

96

THE GAY GOSHAWK

'The Gay Goshawk' first appeared in print
in the second volume of Scott's Minstrelsy, in
1802. Scott's copy was formed partly from
Mrs Brown's version (A) and partly from E*.
 A ballad widely known in France has the
central idea of 'The Gay Goshawk,' but in the
development of the story there is no likeness.
In a version of this ballad, 'Belle Isambourg,'
printed as early as 1607, the king wishes to
give Fair Isambourg a husband, but her heart
is fixed on a handsome knight, whom she loves
more than all her kin together, though he is
poor. The king shuts her up in a dark tower,
thinking that this treatment will bring about a
change, but it does not. Isambourg sees her
lover riding towards or by the tower at full
speed. She calls to him to stop, and says:

 Malade et morte m'y feray,
 Porter en terre m'y lairray,
 Pourtant morte je ne seray.

 Puis apres je vous prie amy,
 Qu'à ma chapelle à Sainct-Denis
 Ne m'y laissez pas enfouir.

Isambourg is now proclaimed to be dead, and
is carried to burial by three princes and a
knight. Her lover, hearing the knelling and
chanting, puts himself in the way and bids the
bearers stop. Since she has died for loving
him too well, he wishes to say a De Profundis.
He rips open a little of the shroud, and she
darts a loving smile at him. Everybody is astonished.
 In 'Willie's Lyke-Wake' (No. 25) a man
feigns death in order to capture a coy maid, or
a maid refused him by her parents.

A

'The Gay Goss Hawk,' Jamieson-Brown MS.,
No. 6, p. 15.

1 'O WELL 's me o my gay goss-hawk,
 That he can speak and flee;
 He 'll carry a letter to my love,
 Bring back another to me.'

2 'O how can I your true-love ken,
 Or how can I her know ?
 Whan frae her mouth I never **heard**
 couth,
 Nor wi my eyes her saw.'

3 'O well sal ye my true-love ken,
 As soon as you her see;
 For, of a' the flowrs in fair Englan,
 The fairest flowr is she.

4 'At even at my love's bowr-door
 There grows a bowing birk,
 An sit ye down and sing thereon,
 As she gangs to the kirk.

5 'An four-and-twenty ladies fair
 Will wash and go to kirk,
 But well shall ye my true-love ken,
 For she wears goud on her skirt.

6 'An four and twenty gay ladies
 Will to the mass repair,
 But well sal ye my true-love ken,
 For she wears goud on her hair.'

7 O even at that lady's bowr-door
 There grows a bowin birk,
 An he set down and sang thereon,
 As she ged to the kirk.

8 'O eet and drink, my marys a',
 The wine flows you among,
 Till I gang to my shot-window,
 An hear yon bonny bird's song.

9 'Sing on, sing on, my bonny bird,
 The song ye sang the streen,
 For I ken by your sweet singin
 You 're frae my true-love sen.'

10 O first he sang a merry song,
 An then he sang a grave,
 An then he peckd his feathers gray,
 To her the letter gave.

11 'Ha, there 's a letter frae your love,
  He says he sent you three;
  He canna wait your love langer,
  But for your sake he 'll die.

12 'He bids you write a letter to him;
  He says he 's sent you five;
  He canno wait your love langer,
  Tho you 're the fairest woman alive.'

13 'Ye bid him bake his bridal-bread,
  And brew his bridal-ale,
  An I 'll meet him in fair Scotlan
  Lang, lang or it be stale.'

14 She 's doen her to her father dear,
  Fa'n low down on her knee:
  'A boon, a boon, my father dear,
  I pray you, grant it me.'

15 'Ask on, ask on, my daughter,
  An granted it sal be;
  Except ae squire in fair Scotlan,
  An him you sall never see.'

16 'The only boon, my father dear,
  That I do crave of the,
  Is, gin I die in southin lands,
  In Scotland to bury me.

17 'An the firstin kirk that ye come till,
  Ye gar the bells be rung,
  An the nextin kirk that ye come till,
  Ye gar the mess be sung.

18 'An the thirdin kirk that ye come till,
  You deal gold for my sake,
  An the fourthin kirk that ye come till,
  You tarry there till night.'

19 She is doen her to her bigly bowr,
  As fast as she coud fare,
  An she has tane a sleepy draught,
  That she had mixed wi care.

20 She 's laid her down upon her bed,
  An soon she 's fa'n asleep,
  And soon oer every tender limb
  Cauld death began to creep.

21 Whan night was flown, an day was
    come,
  Nae ane that did her see
  But thought she was as surely dead
  As ony lady coud be.

22 Her father an her brothers dear
  Gard make to her a bier;
  The tae half was o guide red gold,
  The tither o silver clear.

23 Her mither an her sisters fair
  Gard work for her a sark;
  The tae half was o cambrick fine,
  The tither o needle wark.

24 The firstin kirk that they came till,
  They gard the bells be rung,
  An the nextin kirk that they came till,
  They gard the mess be sung.

25 The thirdin kirk that they came till,
  They dealt gold for her sake,
  An the fourthin kirk that they came till,
  Lo, there they met her make !

26 'Lay down, lay down the bigly bier,
  Lat me the dead look on;'
  Wi cherry cheeks and ruby lips
  She lay an smil'd on him.

27 'O ae sheave o your bread, true-love,
  An ae glass o your wine,
  For I hae fasted for your sake
  These fully days is nine.

28 'Gang hame, gang hame, my sever
    bold brothers,
  Gang hame and sound your horn;
  An ye may boast in southin lans
  Your sister 's playd you scorn.'

E*

Scotch Ballads, Materials for Border Min-strelsy, No. 146 a, Abbotsford.

1 'O WALY, waly, my gay goss-hawk,
  Gin your feathering be sheen !'
  'O waly, waly, my master dear,
  Gin ye look pale and lean !

2 'Whether is it for the gold sae rid,
  Or is it for the silver clear ?
  Or is it for the lass in southen land,
  That she cannot win here.'

3 'It is not for the gold sae rid,
  Nor is it for the silver clear,
  But it is for the lass in southen land,
  That she cannot win her[e].'

4 'Sit down, sit down, my master dear,
   Write a love-letter hastily,
And put it in under my feathern gray,
   And I 'll away to southen land as fast
      as I can flee.

5 'But how shall I your true-love ken?
   Or how shall I her know?
I bear the tongue never wi her spake,
   The eye that never her saw.'

6 'The red that is in my love's cheek
   Is like blood spilt amang the snaw;
The white that is on her breast-bone
   Is like the down on the white sea-
      maw.

7 'There 's one that stands at my love's
      gate
And opens the silver pin,
And there ye may safely set ye on
And sing a lovely song.

8 'First ye may sing it loud, loud, loud,
   And then ye may sing it clear,
And ay the oerword of the tune
   Is, Your love cannot win here.'

9 He has written a love-letter,
   Put it under his feathern gray,
And he 's awa to southen land,
   As fast as ever he may.

10 When he came to the lady's gate,
   There he lighted down,
And there he sat him on the pin
And sang a lovely song.

11 First he sang it loud, loud, loud,
   And then he sang it clear,
And ay the oerword of the tune
Was, Your love cannot win here.

12 'Hold your tongues, my merry maids all,
   And hold them a little while;
I hear some word from my true-love,
   That lives in Scotland's isle.'

13 Up she rose, to the door she goes,
   To hear what the bird woud say,
And he 's let the love-letter fall
   From under his feathern gray.

14 When she looked the letter on,
   The tear blinded her eye,

And when she read it oer and oer
   A loud laughter took she.

15 'Go hame, go hame, my bonny bird,
   And to your master tell,
If I be nae wi him at Martinmass,
   I shall be wi him at Yule.'

16 The lady 's to her chamber gane,
   And a sick woman grew she;
The lady 's taen a sudden brash,
   And nathing she 'll do but die.

17 'An asking, an asking, my father dear,
   An asking grant to me!
If that I die in southen land,
   In Scotland bury me.'

18 'Ask on, ask on, my daughter dear,
   That asking is granted thee;
If that you die in southen land,
   In Scotland I 'll bury thee.'

19 'Gar call to me my seven bretheren,
   To hew to me my bier,
The one half of the beaten gold,
   The other of the silver clear.

20 'Go call to me my seven sisters,
   To sew to me my caul;
Every needle-steik that they put in
   Put by a silver bell.'

21 The first Scots kirk that they came to,
   They heard the mavis sing;
The next Scots kirk that they came to,
   They heard the dead-bell ring.

22 The next Scots kirk that they came to,
   They were playing at the foot-ball,
And her true-love was them among,
   The chieftiar amangst them all.

23 'Set down, set down these corps,' said he,
   'Let me look them upon;'
As soon as he lookd the lady on,
   The blood sprang in her chin.

24 'One bite of your bread, my love,
   And one glass of your wine!
For I have fasted these five long days,
   All for your sake and mine.

25 'Go hame, go hame, my seven brothers,
   Go hame and blaw your horn,

And ye may tell thro southen land
  How I playd you the scorn.'

26 ' Woe to you, my sister dear,
    And ane ill death may you die !
  For we left father and mother at hame
    Breaking their heart for thee.'

97

BROWN ROBIN

The story undoubtedly stops at the right
point in A, with the escape of the two lovers
to the wood.

A

' Brown Robin.' a. Jamieson-Brown MS.,
p. 37. b. Abbotsford MS., Scottish Songs.

1 THE king but an his nobles a' }
    Sat birling at the wine;   } *bis*
  He would ha nane but his ae daughter
    To wait on them at dine.

2 She 's servd them butt, she 's servd them
    ben,
  Intill a gown of green,
  But her ee was ay on Brown Robin,
    That stood low under the rain.

3 She 's doen her to her bigly bowr,
    As fast as she coud gang,
  An there she 's drawn her shot-window,
    An she 's harped an she sang.

4 ' There sits a bird i my father's garden,
    An O but she sings sweet !
  I hope to live an see the day
    Whan wi my love I 'll meet.'

5 ' O gin that ye like me as well
    As your tongue tells to me,
  What hour o the night, my lady bright,
    At your bowr sal I be ? '

6 ' Whan my father an gay Gilbert
    Are baith set at the wine,
  O ready, ready I will be
    To lat my true-love in.'

7 O she has birld her father's porter
    Wi strong beer an wi wine,
  Untill he was as beastly drunk
    As ony wild-wood swine:

She 's stown the keys o her father's yates
  An latten her true-love in.

8 Whan night was gane, an day was come,
    An the sun shone on their feet,
  Then out it spake him Brown Robin,
    I 'll be discoverd yet.

9 Then out it spake that gay lady:
    My love, ye need na doubt;
  For wi ae wile I 've got you in,
    Wi anither I 'll bring you out.

10 She 's taen her to her father's cellar,
    As fast as she can fare;
  She 's drawn a cup o the gude red
    wine,
  Hung 't low down by her gare;
  An she met wi her father dear
    Just coming down the stair.

11 ' I woud na gi that cup, daughter,
    That ye hold i your han
  For a' the wines in my cellar,
    An gantrees whare the stan.'

12 ' O wae be to your wine, father,
    That ever 't came oer the sea;
  'T 'is pitten my head in sick a steer
    I my bowr I canna be.'

13 ' Gang out, gang out, my daughter dear,
    Gang out an tack the air;
  Gang out an walk i the good green wood,
    An a' your marys fair.'

14 Then out it spake the proud porter ---
    Our lady wishd him shame ---
  ' We 'll send the marys to the wood,
    But we 'll keep our lady at hame.'

15 ' There 's thirty marys i my bowr,
    There 's thirty o them an three;
  But there 's nae ane amo them a'
    Kens what flowr gains for me.'

16 She 's doen her to her bigly bowr,
    As fast as she could gang,
  An she has dresst him Brown Robin
    Like ony bowr-woman.

17 The gown she pat upon her love
    Was o the dainty green,
  His hose was o the saft, saft silk,
    His shoon o the cordwain fine.

18 She 's pitten his bow in her bosom,
        His arrow in her sleeve,
    His sturdy bran her body next,
        Because he was her love.

19 Then she is unto her bowr-door,
        As fast as she coud gang;
    But out it spake the proud porter —
        Our lady wishd him shame —
    'We 'll count our marys to the wood,
        An we 'll count them back again.'

20 The firsten mary she sent out
        Was Brown Robin by name;
    Then out it spake the king himsel,
        'This is a sturdy dame.'

21 O she went out in a May morning,
        In a May morning so gay,
    But she came never back again,
        Her auld father to see.

B

'Love Robbie,' Christie's Traditional Ballad
Airs, I, 136, from the recitation of an old woman in Buckie, Enzie, Banffshire.

1 'A FEATHERD fowl 's in your orchard,
        father,
        O dear, but it sings sweet !
    What would I give, my father dear,
        That bonnie bird to meet !'
        What would I give, etc.

2 'O hold your tongue, my daughter
        Mary,
        Let a' your folly be;
    There 's six Scots lords tomorrow, child,
        That will a' dine wi me,
    And ye maun serve them a', Mary,
        As 't were for meat and fee.'

3 She served them up, sae has she down,
        The footmen a' the same,
    But her mind was aye on Love Rob-
        bie,
        Stood out below the rain.

4 A hundred pun o pennies roun,
        Tied in a towel so sma,
    She has gien to him Love Robbie,
        Out oer the castle-wa;
    Says, Tak ye that, my love Robbie.
        And mysel ye may hae.

5 A hundred pun o pennies roun,
        Tied in a napkin white,
    She has gien to him Love Robbie,
        Out oer the garden-dyke;
    Says, Tak ye that, my Love Robbie,
        And mysel gin ye like.

6 'If this be true ye tell to me,
        As your tongue woudna lee,
    I shall be in your bigly bower
        Before the clock strike three;
    I shall be in your bigly bower,
        Dressd like a gay ladye.'

7 When bells were rung, and mass wa
        sung,
        And all men bound for bed,
    Love Robbie came to Mary's bower,
        Dressd like a comely maid.

8 They had not kissd nor love clappëd,
        As lovers when they meet,
    Till sighing said he Love Robbie,
        My life, my life I doubt.

9 'Your life, your life, you Love Robbie,
        Your life you needna doubt;
    For it was wiles brought in Robbie,
        And wiles will lat him out.'

10 Then in it came her father dear,
        And stood upon the floor,
    And she filld the cup of good red wine,
        Said, Father, will ye drink more ?

11 'O better I love the cup, Mary,
        The cup that 's in your hand,
    Than all my barrels full of wine,
        On the gantrees where they stand.'

12 'O woe be to your wine, father,
        It eer came oer the sea !
    If I getna the air o good greenwood
        O I will surely dee.'

13 'There 's seven maries in your bower,
        There 's seven o them and three,
    And I 'll send them to good green-
        wood,
        For flowers to shortsome thee.'

14 'There 's seven maries in my bower,
        There 's seven o them and three,
    But there 's nae a mary mang them a'
        Can pu flowers to shortsome me: '

'Then by my sooth,' said her father
    dear,
    'Let yoursel gang them wi.'

15 She dressd hersel in the royal red,
    Love Robbie was in dainty green;
    Love Robbie's brand was about his mid-
        dle,
    And he shone like ony queen.

16 The firsten ane that took the floor,
    Love Robbie was that ane:
    'Now by my sooth,' said the proud por-
        ter,
    'She is a sonsie dame;
    I would not care now very much
    To turn her in again.'

17 'I'd fain see any woman or man,
    Of high or low degree,
    Would turn a mary in again
    That once came out with me.'

18 They had not been in good greenwood,
    Pu'd a flower but only three,
    Till the porter stood behind a bush,
    And shot him Love Robbie.

19 Now word has come to her father
        dear,
    In the chamber where he lay,
    Lady Mary 's sick in good greenwood,
    And cannot come away.

20 He 's taen his mantle him about,
    His cane into his han,
    And he is on to good greenwood,
    As fast as he could gang.

21 'O want you fish out o the fleed,
    Or whale out o the sea?
    Or is there any one alive
    This day has angerd thee?'

22 'I want not fish out o the fleed,
    Nor whale out o the sea;
    But woe be to your proud porter,
    Sae sair 's he 's angerd me!
    He 's shot the fairest flower this day,
    That would hae comfort me.'

23 'O hold your tongue, my daughter Mary,
    Let a' your folly be;
    Tomorrow ere I eat or drink
    High hangëd shall he be.'

98

BROWN ADAM

'Brown Adam' was No. 14 of the fifteen ballads furnished William Tytler by Mrs Brown
in 1783. A Danish ballad (Grundtvig, No. 199)
has a remote likeness to 'Brown Adam'

A

'Brown Adam,' Jamieson-Brown MS., p.
17.

1 O WHA woud wish the win to blaw,
    Or the green leaves fa therewith?
    Or wha wad wish a leeler love
    Than Brown Adam the Smith?

2 His hammer 's o the beaten gold,
    His study 's o the steel,
    His fingers white are my delite,
    He blows his bellows well.

3 But they ha banishd him Brown Adam
    Frae father and frae mither,
    An they ha banishd him Brown Adam
    Frae sister and frae brither.

4 And they ha banishd Brown Adam
    Frae the flowr o a' his kin;
    An he 's biggit a bowr i the good green
        wood
    Betwen his lady an him.

5 O it fell once upon a day
    Brown Adam he thought lang,
    An he woud to the green wood gang,
    To hunt some venison.

6 He 's ta'en his bow his arm oer,
    His bran intill his han,
    And he is to the good green wood,
    As fast as he coud gang.

7 O he 's shot up, an he 's shot down,
    The bird upo the briar,
    An he 's sent it hame to his lady,
    Bade her be of good cheer.

8 O he 's shot up, an he 's shot down,
    The bird upo the thorn,
    And sent it hame to his lady,
    And hee 'd be hame the morn.

9 Whan he came till his lady's bowr-door
    He stood a little foreby,
And there he heard a fu fa'se knight
    Temptin his gay lady.

10 O he's taen out a gay gold ring,
    Had cost him mony a poun:
'O grant me love for love, lady,
    An this sal be your own.'

11 'I loo Brown Adam well,' she says,
    'I wot sae does he me;
An I woud na gi Brown Adam's love
    For nae fa'se knight I see.'

12 Out has he ta'en a purse of gold,
    Was a' fu to the string:
'Grant me but love for love, lady,
    An a' this sal be thine.'

13 'I loo Brown Adam well,' she says,
    'An I ken sae does he me;
An I woudna be your light leman
    For mair nor ye coud gie.'

14 Then out has he drawn his lang, lang
        bran,
    And he's flashd it in her een:
'Now grant me love for love, lady,
    Or thro you this sal gang!'

15 'O,' sighing said that gay lady,
    'Brown Adam tarrys lang!'
Then up it starts Brown Adam,
    Says, I'm just at your han.

16 He's gard him leave his bow, his bow,
    He's gard him leave his bran;
He's gard him leave a better pledge,
    Four fingers o his right han.

B

'Broun Edom,' Harris MS., fol. 27 b, No.
26.

1 .   .   .   .   .   .

For wha ere had a lealer luve
    Than Broun Edom the smith?

2 His studie was o the beaten gowd,
    His hammer o the pith;
His cords waur o the gude green silk,
    That blew his bellows with.

3 It fell out ance upon a time
    Broun Edom he thoucht lang,
That he wald gae to see his luve,
    By the le licht o the mune.

99

JOHNIE SCOT

A was No. 2 of the fifteen ballads in William
Tytler's lost Brown MS. The story of 'Willi
o Winsbury' (No. 100) has considerable re
semblance to that of 'Johnie Scot.' There i
also some resemblance to 'Child Maurice' (No
83).

A

'Jack, the Little Scot,' Jamieson-Brown MS
p. 5.

1 O JOHNEY was as brave a knight
    As ever saild the sea,
An he's done him to the English court
    To serve for meat and fee.

2 He had nae been in fair England
    But yet a little while,
Untill the kingis ae daughter
    To Johney proves wi chil.

3 O word's come to the king himsel,
    In his chair where he sat,
That his ae daughter was wi bairn
    To Jack, the Little Scott.

4 'Gin this be true that I do hear,
    As I trust well it be,
Ye pit her into prison strong,
    An starve her till she die.'

5 O Johney's on to fair Scotland,
    A wot he went wi speed,
An he has left the kingis court,
    A wot good was his need.

6 O it fell once upon a day
    That Johney he thought lang,
An he's gane to the good green wood,
    As fast as he coud gang.

7 'O whare will I get a bonny boy,
    To rin my errand soon,
That will rin into fair England,
    An haste him back again?'

8 O up it starts a bonny boy,
    Gold yallow was his hair,
I wish his mither meickle joy,
    His bonny love mieckle mair.

9 'O here am I, a bonny boy,
    Will rin your errand soon;
I will gang into fair England,
    An come right soon again.'

10 O whan he came to broken briggs,
    He bent his bow and swam;
An whan he came to the green grass
        growan,
    He slaikid his shoone an ran.

11 Whan he came to yon high castèl,
    He ran it roun about,
An there he saw the king's daughter,
    At the window looking out.

12 'O here's a sark o silk, lady,
    Your ain han sewd the sleeve;
You 'r bidden come to fair Scotlan,
    Speer nane o your parents leave.

13 'Ha, take this sark o silk, lady,
    Your ain han sewd the gare;
You 're bidden come to good green wood,
    Love Johney waits you there.'

14 She 's turnd her right and roun about,
    The tear was in her ee:
'How can I come to my true-love,
    Except I had wings to flee?

15 'Here am I kept wi bars and bolts,
    Most grievous to behold;
My breast-plate 's o the sturdy steel,
    Instead of the beaten gold.

16 'But tak this purse, my bonny boy,
    Ye well deserve a fee,
An bear this letter to my love,
    An tell him what you see.'

17 Then quickly ran the bonny boy
    Again to Scotlan fair,
An soon he reachd Pitnachton's towrs,
    An soon found Johney there.

18 He pat the letter in his han
    An taul him what he sa,
But eer he half the letter read,
    He loote the tears doun fa.

19 'O I will gae back to fair Englan,
    Tho death shoud me betide,
An I will relieve the damesel
    That lay last by my side.'

20 Then out it spake his father dear,
    My son, you are to blame;
An gin you 'r catchd on English groun,
    I fear you 'll neer win hame.

21 Then out it spake a valiant knight,
    Johny's best friend was he;
I can commaun five hunder men,
    An I 'll his surety be.

22 The firstin town that they came till,
    They gard the bells be rung;
An the nextin town that they came
        till,
    They gard the mess be sung.

23 The thirdin town that they came till,
    They gard the drums beat roun;
The king but an his nobles a'
    Was startld at the soun.

24 Whan they came to the king's palace
    They rade it roun about,
An there they saw the king himsel,
    At the window looking out.

25 'Is this the Duke o Albany,
    Or James, the Scottish king?
Or are ye some great foreign lord,
    That 's come a visiting?'

26 'I 'm nae the Duke of Albany,
    Nor James, the Scottish king;
But I 'm a valiant Scottish knight,
    Pitnachton is my name.'

27 'O if Pitnachton be your name,
    As I trust well it be,
The morn, or I tast meat or drink,
    You shall be hanged hi.'

28 Then out it spake the valiant knight
    That came brave Johney wi;
Behold five hunder bowmen bold,
    Will die to set him free.

29 Then out it spake the king again,
    An a scornfu laugh laugh he;
I have an Italian i my house
    Will fight you three by three.

30 'O grant me a boon,' brave Johney cried;
    'Bring your Italian here;
  Then if he fall beneath my sword,
    I 've won your daughter dear.'

31 Then out it came that Italian,
    An a gurious ghost was he;
  Upo the point o Johney's sword
    This Italian did die.

32 Out has he drawn his lang, lang bran,
    Struck it across the plain:
  'Is there any more o your English dogs
    That you want to be slain?'

33 'A clark, a clark,' the king then cried,
    'To write her tocher free;'
  'A priest, a priest,' says Love Johney,
    'To marry my love and me.

34 'I 'm seeking nane o your gold,' he says,
    'Nor of your silver clear;
  I only seek your daughter fair,
    Whose love has cost her dear.'

100

WILLIE O WINSBURY

The story of this ballad is similar to that of
'Johnie Scot' (No. 99), but Willie's extreme
beauty moves the king to offer his daughter to
him in marriage, without a combat.

A

'Willie o Winsbury,' Campbell MSS., ii, 38.

1 THE king he hath been a prisoner,
    A prisoner lang in Spain, O
  And Willie o the Winsbury
    Has lain lang wi his daughter at
    hame. O

2 'What aileth thee, my daughter Janet,
    Ye look so pale and wan?
  Have ye had any sore sickness,
    Or have ye been lying wi a man?
  Or is it for me, your father dear,
    And biding sae lang in Spain?'

3 'I have not had any sore sickness,
    Nor yet been lying wi a man;
  But it is for you, my father dear,
    In biding sae lang in Spain.'

4 'Cast ye off your berry-brown gown,
    Stand straight upon the stone,
  That I may ken ye by yere shape,
    Whether ye be a maiden or none.'

5 She 's coosten off her berry-brown gown,
    Stooden straight upo yon stone;
  Her apron was short, and her haunches
    were round,
    Her face it was pale and wan.

6 'Is it to a man o might, Janet?
    Or is it to a man of fame?
  Or is it to any of the rank robbers
    That 's lately come out o Spain?'

7 'It is not to a man of might,' she
    said,
    'Nor is it to a man of fame;
  But it is to William of Winsburry:
    I could lye nae langer my lane.'

8 The king 's called on his merry men
    all,
    By thirty and by three:
  'Go fetch me William of Winsburry,
    For hanged he shall be.'

9 But when he cam the king before,
    He was clad o the red silk;
  His hair was like to threeds o gold,
    And his skin was as white as milk.

10 'It is nae wonder,' said the king,
    'That my daughter's love ye did
    win;
  Had I been a woman, as I am a man,
    My bedfellow ye should hae been.

11 'Will ye marry my daughter Janet,
    By the truth of thy right hand?
  I 'll gie ye gold, I 'll gie ye money,
    And I 'll gie ye an earldom o land.'

12 'Yes, I 'll marry yere daughter Janet,
    By the truth of my right hand;
  But I 'll hae nane o yer gold, I 'll hae
    nane o yer money,
    Nor I winna hae an earldom o land.

13 'For I hae eighteen corn-mills,
    Runs all in water clear,
  And there 's as much corn in each o
    them
    As they can grind in a year.'

D

Percy Papers, communicated to Percy by the Rev. P. Parsons, of Wye, apparently in 1775. "This I had from the spinning-wheel."

1 THERE was a lady fine and gay,
　　She was so neat and trim;
　　She went unto her own garden-wall,
　　　To see her own ships come in.

2 And there she spied her daughter Jane,
　　Who lookd so pale and wan:
　'What, have you had some long sickness,
　　　Or lain with some young man?'

3 'No, I have had no long sickness,
　　Nor lain with no young man:'
　Her petticoats they were so short,
　　She was full nine months gone.

4 'Oh is it by some nobleman?
　　Or by some man of fame?
　Or is it by Johnny Barbary,
　　That's lately come from Spain?'

5 'No, it is by no nobleman,
　　Nor by no man of fame;
　But it is by Johnny Barbary,
　　That's lately come from Spain.'

6 Then she calld down her merry men,
　　By one, by two, by three;
　Johnny Barbary used to be the first,
　　But now the last came he.

7 'Oh will you take my daughter Jane,
　　And wed her out of hand?
　And you shall dine and sup with me,
　　And be heir of my land.'

8 'Yes, I will take your daughter Jane,
　　And wed her out of hand;
　And I will dine and sup with you,
　　But I do not want your land.'

9 Then she calld down her merry men,
　　With a shrill and a pleasant voice:
　'Come, let us all now mery be,
　　Since she has made such a happy choice.'

101

WILLIE O DOUGLAS DALE

A was among the fifteen ballads furnished by Mrs Brown to William Tytler in 1783. The first part of the story of this ballad, or down to the birth of the boy, is repeated in No. 102. This portion of the ballad also has resemblances to 'Leesome Brand' (No. 15).

A

'Willy o Douglass-dale,' Jamieson-Brown MS., p. 8.

1 O WILLY was as brave a lord
　　As ever saild the sea,
　And he has gane to the English court,
　　To serve for meat and fee.

2 He had nae been at the kingis court
　　A twelvemonth and a day,
　Till he longd for a sight o the king's daughter,
　　But ane he coud never see.

3 O it fell ance upon a day
　　To the green wood she has gane,
　An Willy he has followd her,
　　With the clear light o the moon.

4 He looted him low, by her did go,
　　Wi his hat intill his hand:
　'O what's your will wi me, Sir Knight?
　　I pray keep your hat on.'

5 'O I am not a knight, Madam,
　　Nor never thinks to be;
　For I am Willy o Douglassdale,
　　An I serve for meat and fee.'

6 'O I'll gang to my bowr,' she says,
　　'An sigh baith even an morn
　That ever I saw your face, Willy,
　　Or that ever ye was born.

7 'O I'll gang to my bowr,' she says,
　　'An I'll pray baith night an day,
　To keep me frae your tempting looks,
　　An frae your great beauty.'

8 O in a little after that
　　He keepit Dame Oliphant's bowr,

An the love that passd between this twa,
    It was like paramour.

9 'O narrow, narrow's my gown, Willy,
    That wont to be sae wide;
An short, short is my coats, Willy,
    That wont to be sae side;
An gane is a' my fair colour,
    An low laid is my pride.

10 'But an my father get word of this,
    He'll never drink again;
An gin my mother get word of this,
    In her ain bowr she'll go brain;
An gin my bold brothers get word o
        this,
    I fear, Willy, you'll be slain.'

11 'O will you leave your father's court,
    An go along wi me?
I'll carry you unto fair Scotland,
    And mak you a lady free.'

12 She pat her han in her pocket
    An gae him five hunder poun:
'An take you that now, Squire Willy,
    Till awa that we do won.'

13 Whan day was gane, and night was come,
    She lap the castle-wa;
But Willy kepit his gay lady,
    He was laith to let her fa.

14 Whan night was gane, an day come in,
    An lions gaed to their dens,
An ay the lady followd him,
    An the tears came hailing down.

15 'O want ye ribbons to your hair?
    Or roses to your shoone?
Or want ye as meickle dear bought love
    As your ain heart can contain?'

16 'I want nae ribbons to my hair,
    Nor roses till my shoone;
An Ohone, alas, for dear bought love!
    I have mair nor I can contain.'

17 O he's pu'd the oak in good green wood,
    An he's made to her a fire;
He coverd it oer wi withred leaves,
    An gard it burn thro ire.

18 He made a bed i the good green wood,
    An he's laid his lady down,
An he's coverd her oer wi fig-tree
        leaves,
    But an his ain night-gown.

19 'O had I a bunch o yon red roddins,
    That grows in yonder wood,
But an a drink o water clear,
    I think it woud do me good.'

20 He's pu'd her a bunch o yon red rod-
        dins,
    That grew beside yon thorn,
But an a drink o water clear,
    Intill his hunting-horn.

21 He's bent his bow, and shot the deer,
    An thro the green wood gane,
An ere that he came back again
    His lady took travailing.

22 'O up ye tak that horn,' she says,
    'An ye blaw a blast for me;
Gin my father be in good green wood,
    Sae seen's he'll come me ti.'

23 'O gin there be a man on earth
    That ye loo better nor me,
Ye blaw the horn yoursel,' he says,
    'For it's never be blawn by me.'

24 O he's bent his bow, an shot the
        deer,
    An thro the green wood has he gane,
An lang or he came back again
    His lady bare him a son.

25 O up has he tane his bonny young son,
    An washn him wi the milk,
An up has he tane his gay lady,
    An rowd her i the silk.

26 He's bent his bow, and shot the deer,
    An thro the green wood has he gane,
Till he met wi a well-fard may,
    Her father's flock feeding.

27 'Ye leave your father's flock feeding,
    An go along wi me;
I'll carry you to a lady fair,
    Will gi you both meat and fee.'

28 O whan she came the lady before,
    She's fa'n down on her knee:
'O what's your will wi me, my dame?
    An a dame you seem to be.'

29 'O I'm Dame Oliphant, the king's
    daughter,
  Nae doubt but ye've heard o me;
  Will you leave your father's flock feed-
    ing,
  An go to Scotlan wi me?

30 'An ye sal get a nouriship
  Intill an earldome,
  An I will gar provide for the
  To marry some brave Scotsman.'

31 The may she keepit the bonny boy,
  An Willy led his lady,
  Untill they took their fair shippin,
  Then quikly hame came they.

32 The win was fair, an the sea was clear,
  An they a' wan safe to lan;
  He's haild her lady of Douglassdale,
  Himsel the lord within.

102

WILLIE AND EARL RICHARD'S DAUGHTER

A was taken down from Mrs Brown's recitation by Jamieson in 1800, and published in
his collection in 1806, "without the alteration
of a single word." The first half of the story
in A, 1-9, is that of No. 101, A, 1-24. The
first part of B, 4-18, is a variety of the widespread tragic ballad of 'Leesome Brand' (No.
15). So, also, is the larger part of 'Willie
o Douglas Dale,' with the tragic features
dropped.

This ballad certainly does not belong to the
cycle of Robin Hood. The connection with
that hero was in all probability mediated by
the name Brown Robin (see No. 97).

A

'The Birth of Robin Hood,' Jamieson's Popular Ballads, II, 44, from Mrs Brown's recitation.

1 O WILLIE's large o limb and lith,
  And come o high degree,
  And he is gane to Earl Richard,
  To serve for meat and fee.

2 Earl Richard had but ae daughter,
  Fair as a lily-flower,

And they made up their love-contract
  Like proper paramour.

3 It fell upon a simmer's nicht,
  Whan the leaves were fair and green,
  That Willie met his gay ladie
  Intil the wood alane.

4 'O narrow is my gown, Willie,
  That wont to be sae wide;
  And gane is a' my fair colour,
  That wont to be my pride.

5 'But gin my father should get word
  What's past between us twa,
  Before that he should eat or drink,
  He'd hang you oer that wa.

6 'But ye'll come to my bower, Willie,
  Just as the sun gaes down,
  And kep me in your arms twa,
  And latna me fa down.'

7 O whan the sun was now gane down,
  He's doen him till her bower,
  And there, by the lee licht o the
    moon,
  Her window she lookit oer.

8 Intill a robe o red scarlet
  She lap, fearless o harm;
  And Willie was large o lith and limb,
  And keppit her in his arm.

9 And they've gane to the gude green
    wood,
  And, ere the night was deen,
  She's born to him a bonny young son,
  Amang the leaves sae green.

10 Whan night was gane, and day was
    come,
  And the sun began to peep,
  Up and raise the Earl Richard
  Out o his drowsy sleep.

11 He's ca'd upon his merry young men,
  By ane, by twa, and by three:
  'O what's come o my daughter dear,
  That she's nae come to me?

12 'I dreamt a dreary dream last night,
  God grant it come to gude!
  I dreamt I saw my daughter dear
  Drown in the saut sea flood.

13 'But gin my daughter be dead or sick,
      Or yet be stown awa,
   I mak a vow, and I 'll keep it true,
      I 'll hang ye ane and a' ! '

14 They sought her back, they sought her
      fore,
   They sought her up and down;
   They got her in the gude green wood,
      Nursing her bonny young son.

15 He took the bonny boy in his arms,
      And kist him tenderlie;
   Says, Though I would your father
      hang,
      Your mother 's dear to me.

16 He kist him oer and oer again:
      ' My grandson I thee claim,
   And Robin Hood in gude green wood,
      And that shall be your name.'

17 And mony ane sings o grass, o grass,
      And mony ane sings o corn,
   And mony ane sings o Robin Hood
      Kens little whare he was born.

18 It wasna in the ha, the ha,
      Nor in the painted bower,
   But it was in the gude green wood,
      Amang the lily-flower.

B

'The Birth of Robin Hood,' Buchan's Ballads of the North of Scotland, II, 1.

1 MONY ane talks o the grass, the grass,
      And mony ane o the corn,
   And mony ane talks o gude Robin Hood
      Kens little whar he was born.

2 He was gotten in a earl's ha,
      And in a lady's bower,
   And born into gude greenwood,
      Thro mony cauld winter's shower.

3 His father was the earl's own steward,
      Sprung frae sma pedigree;
   His mother, Earl Huntingdon's ae
      daughter,
      For he had nane else but she.

4 When nine months were near an end,
      And eight months they were gone,

The lady's cheeks wi tears were wet,
      And thus she made her moan:

5 ' What shall I say, my love Archibald,
      This day for you and me ?
   I will be laid in cauld irons,
      And ye 'll be hanged on tree.'

6 ' What aileth my love Clementina ?
      What gars you mourn sae sair ? '
   ' You know,' said she, ' I 'm with child
      to thee,
   These eight lang months and mair.

7 ' Will ye gae to my mother's bower,
      Stands on yon stately green ?
   Or will ye gae to the gude greenwood,
      Where ye will not be seen ? '

8 ' I winna gang to your mother's bower,
      Stands on yon stately green;
   But I will on to gude greenwood,
      For I will not be seen.'

9 He 's girt his sword down by his side,
      Took his lady by the hand,
   And they are on thro gude greenwood,
      As fast as they could gang.

10 With slowly steps these couple walkd,
      About miles scarcely three,
   When this lady, being sair wearied out,
      Lay down beneath a tree.

11 ' O for a few of yon junipers,
      To cheer my heart again,
   And likewise for a gude midwife,
      To ease me of my pain ! '

12 ' I 'll bring to you yon junipers,
      To cheer your heart again,
   And I 'll be to you a gude midwife,
      To ease you of your pain.'

13 ' Had far awa frae me, Archibald,
      For this will never dee;
   That 's nae the fashion o our land,
      And it 's nae be used by me.

14 ' Ye 'll take your small-sword by your
      side,
   Your buckler and your bow,
   And ye 'll gae down thro gude green-
      wood,
      And hunt the deer and roe.

15 'You will stay in gude greenwood,
    And with the chase go on,
    Until yon white hind pass you by,
    Then straight to me ye 'll come.'

16 He 's girt his sword then by his side,
    His buckler and his bow,
    And he is on thro gude greenwood,
    To hunt the deer and roe.

17 And in the greenwood he did stay,
    And with the chase gaed on,
    Until the white hind passd him by,
    Then to his love he came.

18 He girt his sword then by his side,
    Fast thro greenwood went he,
    And there he found his love lie dead,
    Beneath the green oak tree.

19 The sweet young babe that she had
        born
    Right lively seemed to be;
    'Ohon, alas !' said young Archibald,
    'A mournful scene to me !

20 'Altho my sweet babe is alive,
    This does increase my woe;
    How to nourish a motherless babe
    Is mair than I do know.'

21 He looked east, he looked west,
    To see what he could see,
    Then spied the Earl o Huntingdon,
    And mony a man him wi.

22 Then Archibald fled from the earl's
        face,
    Among the leaves sae green,
    That he might hear what might be said,
    And see, and nae be seen.

23 The earl straight thro the greenwood
        came,
    Unto the green oak tree,
    And there he saw his daughter dead,
    Her living child her wi.

24 Then he 's taen up the little boy,
    Rowed him in his gown-sleeve;
    Said, Tho your father 's to my loss,
    Your mother 's to me leave.

25 And if ye live until I die,
    My bowers and lands ye 'se heir;

You are my only daughter's child;
    But her I never had mair.

26 Ye 'se hae all kinds of nourishment,
    And likewise nurses three;
    If I knew where the fause knave were,
    High hanged should he be.

27 His daughter he buried in gude church-
        yard,
    All in a mournful mood,
    And brought the boy to church that day,
    And christend him Robin Hood.

28 This boy was bred in the earl's ha
    Till he became a man,
    But loved to hunt in gude greenwood,
    To raise his noble fame.

C

Kinloch MSS., v, 330 f., the last two stanzas
of 'Douglass Dale.'

1 MONY ane speaks o grass, o grass,
    And mony mare o corn,
    And mony ane sings o Robin Heed
    Kens little whare he was born.

2 He was born in good green wood,
    At the fut o yon olive tree;
    His father was a knight's ae son,
    And his mother a lady free.

103

ROSE THE RED AND WHITE LILY

A was one of the fifteen ballads written
down by Mrs Brown for William Tytler in
1783. The only part of the ballad which has
the stamp of indubitably ancient tradition is
the child-birth in the wood, and this scene is the
rightful and perhaps exclusive property of
'Leesome Brand' (No. 15). Several stanzas
of A are found again in No. 101, and the first
part of Nos. 101 and 102 is a variation of 'Leesome Brand.'

In B (Buchan's Ballads) the two maids, ill-
treated by their step-mother, betake themselves to the wood, where they meet, not Brown
Robin, but Robin Hood, and take service with
him. Rose and Lily change parts; Rose con-
sorting with Robin Hood and Lily with Little

John. It is not, however, Robin Hood and
Little John who turn out to be their lovers,
but "a lad in the company," and "another
youth among the company."

In the fragmentary C (Kinloch's Ballads)
the maids are daughters of a king. In consequence of the harshness of their stepmother,
these king's daughters go to the wood as
Nicholas and Rogee Roun, to seek Robin
Hood, and they are discovered to be maids by
a song which Rogee sings. Rogee is wedded
to Robin Hood, and Nicholas to Little John.

Robin Hood has no love-story in any ancient
ballad, though his name has been foisted into
modern love-ballads, as in 'Robin Hood and
the Tanner's Daughter.' Maid Marian is a
late accretion.

A

'Rose the Red and White Lilly,' Jamieson-
Brown MS., p. 1.

1 O Rose the Red and White Lilly,
  Their mother dear was dead,
  And their father married an ill woman,
  Wishd them twa little guede.

2 Yet she had twa as fu fair sons
  As eer brake manis bread,
  And the tane of them loed her White
    Lilly,
  An the tither lood Rose the Red.

3 O biggit ha they a bigly bowr,
  And strawn it oer wi san,
  And there was mair mirth i the ladies'
    bowr
  Than in a' their father's lan.

4 But out it spake their step-mother,
  Wha stood a little foreby:
  I hope to live and play the prank
  Sal gar your loud sang ly.

5 She's calld upon her eldest son:
  Come here, my son, to me;
  It fears me sair, my eldest son,
  That ye maun sail the sea.

6 'Gin it fear you sair, my mither dear,
  Your bidding I maun dee;
  But be never war to Rose the Red
  Than ye ha been to me.'

7 'O had your tongue, my eldest son,
  For sma sal be her part;

You'll nae get a kiss o her comely
    mouth
  Gin your very fair heart should break.'

8 She's calld upon her youngest son:
  Come here, my son, to me;
  It fears me sair, my youngest son,
  That ye maun sail the sea.

9 'Gin it fear you sair, my mither dear,
  Your bidding I maun dee;
  But be never war to White Lilly
  Than ye ha been to me.'

10 'O haud your tongue, my youngest son,
   For sma sall be her part;
   You'll neer get a kiss o her comely
     mouth
   Tho your very fair heart should break.'

11 When Rose the Red and White Lilly
   Saw their twa loves were gane,
   Then stopped ha they their loud, loud
     sang,
   And tane up the still mournin;
   And their step-mother stood listnin by,
   To hear the ladies' mean.

12 Then out it spake her White Lilly:
   My sister, we'll be gane;
   Why should we stay in Barnsdale,
   To waste our youth in pain?

13 Then cutted ha they their green cloath-
     ing
   A little below their knee,
   An sae ha they there yallow hair,
   A little aboon there bree;
   An they've doen them to haely chapel,
   Was christened by Our Lady.

14 There ha they chang'd their ain twa
     names,
   Sae far frae ony town,
   An the tane o them hight Sweet Willy,
   An the tither o them Roge the Roun.

15 Between this twa a vow was made,
   An they sware it to fulfil;
   That at three blasts o a bugle-horn,
   She'd come her sister till.

16 Now Sweet Willy's gane to the kingis
     court,
   Her true-love for to see,

An Roge the Roun to good green wood,
  Brown Robin's man to be.

17 As it fell out upon a day
  They a' did put the stane,
  Full seven foot ayont them a'
  She gard the puttin-stane gang.

18 She leand her back against an oak,
  And gae a loud Ohone !
  Then out it spake him Brown Robin,
  But that's a woman's moan !

19 'O ken ye by my red rose lip ?
  Or by my yallow hair ?
  Or ken ye by my milk-white breast ?
  For ye never saw it bare ? '

20 'I ken no by your red rose lip,
  Nor by your yallow hair;
  Nor ken I by your milk-white breast,
  For I never saw it bare;
  But come to your bowr whaever sae
    likes,
  Will find a lady there.'

21 'O gin ye come to my bowr within,
  Thro fraud, deceit, or guile,
  Wi this same bran that's in my han,
  I swear I will the kill.'

22 'But I will come thy bowr within,
  An spear nae leave,' quoth he;
  'An this same bran that's i my han
  I sall ware back on the.'

23 About the tenth hour of the night
  The ladie's bower-door was broken,
  An eer the first hour of the day
  The bonny knave-bairn was gotten.

24 When days were gane, and months were
    run,
  The lady took travailing,
  And sair she cry'd for a bowr-woman,
  For to wait her upon.

25 Then out it spake him Brown Robin:
  Now what needs a' this din ?
  For what coud any woman do
  But I coud do the same ?

26 ''T was never my mither's fashion,' she
    says,
  'Nor sall it ever be mine,

That belted knights shold eer remain
  Where ladies dreed their pine.

27 'But ye take up that bugle-horn,
  An blaw a blast for me;
  I ha a brother i the kingis court
  Will come me quickly ti.'

28 'O gin ye ha a brither on earth
  That ye love better nor me,
  Ye blaw the horn yoursel,' he says,
  'For ae blast I winna gie.'

29 She's set the horn till her mouth,
  And she's blawn three blasts sae
    shrill;
  Sweet Willy heard i the kingis court,
  And came her quickly till.

30 Then up it started Brown Robin,
  An an angry man was he:
  'There comes nae man this bowr within
  But first must fight wi me.'

31 O they hae fought that bowr within
  Till the sun was gaing down,
  Till drops o blude frae Rose the Red
  Came hailing to the groun.

32 She leand her back against the wa,
  Says, Robin, let a' be;
  For it is a lady born and bred
  That's foughten sae well wi thee.

33 O seven foot he lap a back;
  Says, Alas, and wae is me !
  I never wisht in a' my life,
  A woman's blude to see;
  An a' for the sake of ae fair maid
  Whose name was White Lilly.

34 Then out it spake her White Lilly,
  An a hearty laugh laugh she:
  She's lived wi you this year an mair,
  Tho ye kentna it was she.

35 Now word has gane thro a' the lan,
  Before a month was done,
  That Brown Robin's man, in good green
    wood,
  Had born a bonny young son.

36 The word has gane to the kingis
    court,
  An to the king himsel;

'Now, by my fay,' the king could say,
  'The like was never heard tell!'

37 Then out it spake him Bold Arthur,
    An a hearty laugh laugh he:
  I trow some may has playd the loun,
    And fled her ain country.

38 'Bring me my steed,' then cry'd the
      king,
    'My bow and arrows keen;
  I 'l ride mysel to good green wood,
    An see what 's to be seen.'

39 'An 't please your grace,' said Bold
      Arthur,
    'My liege, I 'll gang you wi,
  An try to fin a little foot-page,
    That 's strayd awa frae me.'

40 O they 've hunted i the good green
      wood
    The buck but an the rae,
  An they drew near Brown Robin's bowr,
    About the close of day.

41 Then out it spake the king in hast,
    Says, Arthur, look an see
  Gin that be no your little foot-page
    That leans against yon tree.

42 Then Arthur took his bugle-horn,
    An blew a blast sae shrill;
  Sweet Willy started at the sound,
    An ran him quickly till.

43 'O wanted ye your meat, Willy?
    Or wanted ye your fee?
  Or gat ye ever an angry word,
    That ye ran awa frae me?'

44 'I wanted nought, my master dear;
    To me ye ay was good;
  I came but to see my ae brother,
    That wons in this green wood.'

45 Then out it spake the king again,
    Says, Bonny boy, tell to me
  Wha lives into yon bigly bowr,
    Stands by yon green oak tree?

46 'O pardon me,' says Sweet Willy,
    'My liege, I dare no tell;
  An I pray you go no near that bowr,
    For fear they do you fell.'

47 'O haud your tongue, my bonny boy,
    For I winna be said nay;
  But I will gang that bowr within,
    Betide me weel or wae.'

48 They 've lighted off their milk-white
      steeds,
    An saftly enterd in,
  An there they saw her White Lilly,
    Nursing her bonny yong son.

49 'Now, by the rood,' the king coud say,
    'This is a comely sight;
  I trow, instead of a forrester's man,
    This is a lady bright!'

50 Then out it spake her Rose the Red,
    An fell low down on her knee:
  O pardon us, my gracious liege,
    An our story I 'll tell thee.

51 Our father was a wealthy lord,
    That wond in Barnsdale;
  But we had a wicked step-mother,
    That wrought us meickle bale.

52 Yet she had twa as fu fair sons
    As ever the sun did see,
  An the tane o them lood my sister
      dear,
    An the tither sayd he lood me.

53 Then out it spake him Bold Arthur,
    As by the king he stood:
  Now, by the faith o my body,
    This shoud be Rose the Red!

54 Then in it came him Brown Robin,
    Frae hunting o the deer,
  But whan he saw the king was there,
    He started back for fear.

55 The king has taen him by the hand,
    An bade him naithing dread;
  Says, Ye maun leave the good green
      wood,
    Come to the court wi speed.

56 Then up he took White Lilly's son,
    An set him on his knee;
  Says, Gin ye live to wiald a bran,
    My bowman ye sall bee.

57 The king he sent for robes of green,
    An girdles o shinning gold;

He gart the ladies be arrayd
  Most comely to behold.

8 They 've done them unto Mary Kirk,
  An there gat fair wedding,
An fan the news spread oer the lan,
  For joy the bells did ring.

9 Then out it spake her Rose the Red,
  An a hearty laugh laugh she:
I wonder what would our step-dame
    say,
  Gin she this sight did see !

104

PRINCE HEATHEN

The fragment A is partly explained by B,
which is no doubt some stall copy, reshaped
from tradition. Motherwell's copy was derived
from Buchan.

A

'The Disconsolate Lady,' The Jovial Rake's
Garland, n. d., p. 6, No. 4, Bodleian Library,
Douce PP, 164.

1 LADY MARGERY MAY sits in her bower,
  Sewing at her seem;
By there comes a heathen knight,
  From her her maidenhead has tane.

2 He has put her in a tower strong,
  With double locks on fifty doors:
'Lady Margery May, will you ga now ?'
  'O ye heathen knight, not yet for
    you.

3 'I am asking, you heathen knight;
  What I am asking will you grant to
    me ?
Will ye let one of your waitmen
  A drink of your well bring to me ?'

4 'Meat nor drink you shall never get,
  Nor out of that shall you never come,
Meat nor drink shall you never get,
  Until you bear to me daughter or son.'

5 Thus time drew on, and further on,
  For travail came this young lady to;
She travailed up, so did she down,
  But lighter could she never be.

6 'An asking, an asking, you heathen
    knight;
  An asking will you grant to me ?
Will you give me a scread of silk,
  For to row your young son wi ?'

7 He took the horse-sheet in his hand,
  The tears came twinkling down:
'Lady Margaret May, will ye ga now ?'
  'O ye heathen knight, not yet for
    you.'

8 'I 'll wash my young son with the milk,
  I will dry my young son with the silk;
For hearts will break, and bands will
    bow;
  So dear will I love my lady now !'

B

'Prince Heathen,' Buchan's MSS., I, 97;
Motherwell's MS., p. 665.

1 LADY MARGARET sat in her bower-door,
  Sewing at her silken seem,
When by it came Prince Heathen then,
  An gae to her a gay gold ring.

2 He turnd about, an gied a bow;
  She said, Begone, I love na you;
When he sware by his yellow hair
  That he woud gar her greet fu sair.

3 But she sware by her milk-white skin
  Prince Heathen shoud gar her greet
    nane:
'O bonny may, winna ye greet now ?'
  'Ye heathenish dog, nae yet for you.'

4 He 's taen her in his arms twa,
  Laid her between him an the wa,
An ere he let her free again,
  Her maidenhead frae her he 's taen.
'O bonny may, winna ye greet now ?'
  'Ye heathenish dog, nae yet for you.'

5 'I killd your father in his bed,
  And your gay mother by his side,
And your seven brothers, ane by ane,
  And they were seven pretty men.
O bonny may, winna ye greet now ?'
  'Ye heathenish dog, nae yet for you.

6 'I 'll put you in a vault o stone,
  Where five an thirty locks hing on;

Naebody there then shall you see,
For I will keep the keys wi me.
O bonny may, winna ye greet now?'
'Ye heathenish dog, nae yet for you.'

7   He's put her in a vault o stone,
Where five an thirty locks hing on;
Naebody there coud eer her see,
Prince Heathen kept the keys him wi.
But ae she cried, What shall I do!
The heathenish dog has gart me rue.

8   Prince Heathen from the mountains
came,
Attended by his armed men,
And he's gane to the bonny may,
And to the prison where she lay:
'O bonny may, what do you now?'
'Ye heathenish dog, dying for you.'

9   'I'll take you out upon the green,
Where women ye shall neer see ane,
But only me and my young men,
Till ye bring daughter hame or son.
O bonny may, what do you now?'
'Ye heathenish dog, dying for you.'

10 He's taen her out upon the green,
Where she saw women never ane,
But only him and's merry young men,
Till she brought hame a bonny young
son.
'O bonny may, what do you now?'
'Ye heathenish dog, dying for you.

11 'A drink, a drink, frae Prince Heathen's
hand,
Though it were frae yon cauld well
strong!'
'O neer a drap, Prince Heathen,' said
one,
'Till ye row up your bonny young son.'
'How can I row up my bonny young
son,
When I hae naething to row him in?'

12 'I will lend you my horse's sheet,
That will row him baith head and feet.'
As soon 's she took it in her han,
Tears oer her cheeks down rapping ran.
'O bonny may, ye do greet now:'
'Ye heathenish dog, but nae for you.

13 'But a' is for my bonny young son;
Your sheets are rough to row him in;

Ohon, alas, sair may I rue
That eer I saw such rogues as you!'

14 'Ye'll row my young son in the silk,
An ye will wash him wi the milk,
An lay my lady very saft,
That I may see her very aft.'
When hearts are broken, bands will bow;
Sae well 's he loved his lady now!

105

THE BAILIFF'S DAUGHTER OF ISLINGTON

This ballad is the counterpart of one found in other languages (and represented in English by Percy's cento 'The Friar of Orders Gray,' Reliques, i, 225, 1765), in which a man tells a woman that the object of her affection, lover, or more commonly husband, is dead. It is found in Italian, Spanish, Portuguese and Romaic.

'True Love Requited, or, The Bayliff's Daughter of Islington.' a. Printed for P. Brooksby, Roxburghe Ballads, ii, 457. b. Printed for J. Walter, Douce Ballads, ii, fol. 229. c. Printed for P. Brooksby, Pepys Ballads, iii, 258, No. 256. d. Printed for P. Brooksby, Roxburghe Ballads, iv, 56. e. Printed for P. Brooksby, Douce Ballads, ii, fol. 230. f. An Aldermary Churchyard copy.

1   THERE was a youth, and a well belovd
youth,
And he was a esquire's son,
He loved the bayliff's daughter dear,
That lived in Islington.

2   She was coy, and she would not believe
That he did love her so,
No, nor at any time she would
Any countenance to him show.

3   But when his friends did understand
His fond and foolish mind,
They sent him up to fair London,
An apprentice for to bind.

4   And when he had been seven long years,
And his love he had not seen,
'Many a tear have I shed for her
sake
When she little thought of me.'

5 All the maids of Islington
   Went forth to sport and play;
  All but the bayliff's daughter dear;
   She secretly stole away.

6 She put off her gown of gray,
   And put on her puggish attire;
  She 's up to fair London gone,
   Her true-love to require.

7 As she went along the road,
   The weather being hot and dry,
  There was she aware of her true-love,
   At length came riding by.

8 She stept to him, as red as any rose,
   And took him by the bridle-ring:
  'I pray you, kind sir, give me one penny,
   To ease my weary limb.'

9 'I prithee, sweetheart, canst thou tell me
   Where that thou wast born?'
  'At Islington, kind sir,' said she,
   'Where I have had many a scorn.'

10 'I prithee, sweetheart, canst thou tell me
   Whether thou dost know
  The bailiff's daughter of Islington?'
   'She 's dead, sir, long ago.'

11 'Then will I sell my goodly steed,
   My saddle and my bow;
  I will into some far countrey,
   Where no man doth me know.'

12 'O stay, O stay, thou goodly youth!
   She 's alive, she is not dead;
  Here she standeth by thy side,
   And is ready to be thy bride.'

13 'O farewel grief, and welcome joy,
   Ten thousand times and more!
  For now I have seen my own true-love,
   That I thought I should have seen no
    more.'

106

THE FAMOUS FLOWER OF SERVING–MEN

This ballad was given in Percy's Reliques, III, 87, 1765, "from a written copy, containing some improvements (perhaps modern ones)." These improvements are execrable in style and matter, so far as there is new matter, but not in so glaring contrast with the groundwork as literary emendations of traditional ballads. The Roxburghe copy is in the Ballad Society's edition, VI, 567.

a. Wood, E. 25, fol. 75, Bodleian Library. b. Pepys, III, 142, No. 140, Magdalene College Library, Cambridge. c. A Collection of Old Ballads, I, 216, 1723.

1 You beautious ladies, great and small,
   I write unto you one and all,
  Whereby that you may understand
   What I have suffered in this land.

2 I was by birth a lady fair,
   My father's chief and onely heir,
  But when my good old father dy'd,
   Then was I made a young knight's
    bride.

3 And then my love built me a bower,
   Bedeckt with many a fragrant flower;
  A braver bower you never did see
   Then my true-love did build for me.

4 But there came thieves late in the night,
   They rob'd my bower, and slew my
    knight,
  And after that my knight was slain,
   I could no longer there remain.

5 My servants all from me did flye,
   In the midst of my extremity,
  And left me by my self alone,
   With a heart more cold then any
    stone.

6 Yet, though my heart was full of care,
   Heaven would not suffer me to despair;
  Wherefore in hast I chang'd my name
   From Fair Elise to Sweet William.

7 And therewithal I cut my hair,
   And drest my self in man's attire,
  My doublet, hose, and bever-hat,
   And a golden band about my neck.

8 With a silver rapier by my side,
   So like a gallant I did ride;
  The thing that I delighted on,
   Was for to be a serving-man.

9 Thus in my sumptuous man's array
   I bravely rode along the way;

And at the last it chanced so
That I unto the king's court did go.

10 Then to the king I bowed full low,
My love and duty for to show,
And so much favour I did crave
That I a serving-man's place might
have.

11 'Stand up, brave youth,' the king replyd,
'Thy service shall not be denyd;
But tell me first what thou canst do;
Thou shalt be fitted thereunto.

12 'Wilt thou be usher of my hall,
To wait upon my nobles all?
Or wilt thou be taster of my wine,
To wait on me when I shall dine?

13 'Or wilt thou be my chamberlain,
To make my bed both soft and fine?
Or wilt thou be one of my guard?
And I will give thee thy reward.'

14 Sweet William, with a smiling face,
Said to the king, If 't please your
grace
To show such favour unto me,
Your chamberlain I fain would be.

15 The king then did the nobles call,
To ask the counsel of them all,
Who gave consent Sweet William he
The king's own chamberlain should be.

16 Now mark what strange things came to
pass:
As the king one day a hunting was,
With all his lords and noble train,
Sweet William did at home remain.

17 Sweet William had no company then
With him at home but an old man;
And when he saw the coast was clear,
He took a lute which he had there.

18 Upon the lute Sweet William plaid,
And to the same he sung and said,
With a pleasant and most noble voice,
Which made the old man to rejoyce:

19 'My father was as brave a lord
As ever Europe did afford;
My mother was a lady bright,
My husband was a valiant knight.

20 'And I my self a lady gay,
Bedeckt with gorgeous rich array;
The bravest lady in the land
Had not more pleasures to command.

21 'I had my musick every day,
Harmonious lessons for to play;
I had my virgins fair and free,
Continually to wait on me.

22 'But now, alas! my husband 's dead,
And all my friends are from me fled;
My former joys are past and gone,
For now I am a serving-man.'

23 At last the king from hunting came,
And presently upon the same
He called for the good old man,
And thus to speak the king began.

24 'What news, what news, old man?'
quod he;
'What news hast thou to tell to me?'
'Brave news,' the old man he did say;
'Sweet William is a lady gay.'

25 'If this be true thou tellest me
I 'le make thee a lord of high degree;
But if thy words do prove a lye,
Thou shalt be hanged up presently.'

26 But when the king the truth had found
His joys did more and more abound;
According as the old man did say,
Sweet William was a lady gay.

27 Therefore the king without delay
Put on her glorious rich array,
And upon her head a crown of gold,
Which was most famous to behold.

28 And then, for fear of further strife,
He took Sweet William for his wife;
The like before was never seen,
A serving-man to be a queen.

107

WILL STEWART AND JOHN

The first stanza of A furnishes a sort of general lyrical introduction, and does not belong to the story. A fragment in Campbell's MSS. (B) is simply a confused recollection of some part of the ballad.

A

'Will Stewart and Iohn,' Percy MS., p. 428;
ales and Furnivall, iii, 216.

1 ADLATTS parke is wyde and broad,
    And grasse growes greene in our
        countrye;
    Eche man can gett the loue of his ladye,
    But alas, I can gett none of mine !

2 Itt 's by two men I sing my song,
    Their names is William Stewart and
        Iohn;
    William he is the elder brother,
    But Iohn hee is the wiser man.

3 But William he is in care-bed layd,
    And for the loue of a ffaire ladye;
    If he haue not the loue of the Erle of
        Mar's daughter,
    In ffaith ffor loue *that* he must dye.

4 Then Iohn was sorry ffor his brother,
    To see him lye and languish soe:
    'What doe you mourne for, brother ?'
        he saies,
    'I pray you tell to me your woe.

5 'Doe [you] mourne for gold, brother ?'
        he saies,
    'Or doe you mourne ffor ffee ?
    'Or doe you mourne for a likesome
        ladye,
    You neuer saw her with your eye ?'

6 'I doe not mourne for gold,' he saies,
    'Nor I doe not mourne for any
        ffee;
    But I doe mourne for a likesome ladye,
    I neere blinke on her with mine
        eye.'

7 'But when haruest is gotten, my deere
        brother —
    All this is true *that* I tell thee —
    Gentlemen, they loue hunting well,
    And giue wight-men their cloth and
        ffee.

8 'Then I 'le goe a wooing ffor thy sake,
    In all the speed *that* I can gone,
    And for to see this likesome ladye,
    And hope to send thee good tydings
        home.'

9 Iohn Stewart is gone a wooing for his
        brother,
    Soe ffarr into ffaire Scottland,
    And left his brother in mikle ffeare,
    Vntill he heard the good tydand.

10 And when he came to the Erle of Mar's
        his house,
    Soe well he could his curtesye,
    And when he came before the erle,
    He kneeled low downe vpon his knee.

11 'O rise vp, rise vp, Iohn Steward,
    Rise vp, now, I doe bidd thee;
    How doth thy ffather, Iohn Stewart,
    And all the lords in his countrye ?'

12 'And itt please you, my lord, my ffather
        is dead;
    My brother and I cannott agree;
    My brother and I am ffallen att discord,
    And I am come to craue a service of
        thee.'

13 'O welcome, welcome, Iohn Stewart,
    A welcome man thou art to me;
    I 'le make thee chamberlaine to my
        daughter,
    And ffor to tend of *that* ladye soe
        ffree.

14 'And if thou wilt haue a better office,
    Aske, and thou shall haue itt of mee;
    And where I giue other men a penny of
        wage,
    Inffaith, Iohn, thou shalt haue three.'

15 And then bespake him Iohn Stewart,
    And these were the words said hee:
    There is no office in your court
    This day *that* better pleaseth mee.

16 The Ffryday is gone, the Sunday is
        come —
    All this is true *that* I doe say —
    And to the church that they be gone,
    Iohn Stewart and the lady gay.

17 And as they did come home againe —
    I-wis itt was a meeten mile —
    Iohn Stewart and the lady gay,
    They thought itt but a [little] while.

18 'I am a messenger, ladye,' he saies,
    'I am a messenger to thee·'

' O speake ffor thy selfe, Iohn Stewart,'
 shee saies,
' A welcome man *that* thou shalt bee.'

19 ' Nay, by my ffaith,' saies Iohn Stewart,
 ' Which euer, alas, *that* may not bee !
He hath a higher degree in honour,
 Allas, ladye, then euer I !

20 ' He is a lord now borne by birth,
 And an erle affter his ffather doth dye;
His haire is yellow, his eyes beene gray;
 All this is true *that* I tell yee.

21 ' He is ffine in the middle, and small in
 the wast,
 And pleasant in a woman's eye;
And more nor this, he dyes for your loue,
 Therefore, lady, show some pittye.'

22 ' If this be soe,' then saies the lady,
 ' If this be true *that* thou tells mee,
By my ffaith then, Iohn Stewart,
 I can loue him hartilye.

23 ' Bidd him meete me att St Patr[i]cke's
 Church
 On Sunday after St Andrew's day;
The fflower of Scottland will be there,
 And then begins our summer's play.

24 ' And bidd him bring with him a hundred
 gunners,
 And rawnke ryders lett them bee,
And lett them bee of the rankest ryders
 That be to be ffound in *that* countrye.

25 ' They best and worst, and all in like,
 Bidd him cloth them in one liuerye;
And ffor his men, greene is the best,
 And greene now lett their liueryes bee.

26 ' And clothe himselfe in scarlett redd,
 That is soe seemlye ffor to see;
Ffor scarlett is a ffaire coulour,
 And pleasant allwayes in a woman's
 eye.

27 ' He must play sixteene games att ball,
 Against the men of this countrye,
And if he winn the greater part,
 Then I shall love him more tenderlye.'

28 What the lady said, Iohn Stewart writt,
 And to Argyle Castle sent it hee;

And [when] Willie Steward saw the
 letter,
 Fforth of care-bed then lope hee.

29 Hee mustered together his merry men
 all,
 Hee mustered them soe louelilye;
Hee thought hee had had scarson halfe
 a hundred,
 Then had hee eleuen score and three.

30 He chose fforth a hundred of the best
 That were to be ffound in *that* coun-
 trye,
He cladd them all in one coulour,
 And greene i-wis their liueryes bee.

31 He cladd himselfe in scarlett redd,
 That is soe seemelye ffor to see;
Ffor scarlett is a ffaire coulor,
 And seemlye in a woman's eye.

32 And then towards Patricke Church he
 went,
 With all his men in braue array,
To gett a sight, if he might,
 And speake with his lady gay.

33 When they came to Patricke's churche,
 Shee kneeled downe by her mother
 trulye:
' O mother, if itt please you to giue me
 leaue,
 The Stewart's horsse ffaine wold I
 see.'

34 ' I 'le giue you leaue, my deere daughter,
 And I and my maide will goe with
 yee:'
The lady had rather haue gone her
 selfe
 Then haue had her mother's companye.

35 When they came before Willie Steward
 Soe well hee cold his curtesye:
' I wold kisse your daughter, ladye,' he
 said,
 ' And if your will *that* soe itt bee.'

36 The ladye's mother was content
 To doe a strannger *that* curtesye;
And when Willie had gotten a kisse,
 I-wis shee might haue teemed him
 three.

7 Sixteen games were plaid *that* day
    there —
  This is the truth as I doe say —
  Willie Stewart and his merry men,
  The carryed twelue of them away.

8 And when they games *that* they were
    done,
  And all they ffolkes away were gone
  But the Erle of Marr and Wil*liam*
    Stewart,
  The erle wold needs haue Wil*liam*
    home.

9 And when they came vnto the erle's
    howse,
  They walked to a garden greene;
  Ffor to confferr of their bussines,
  Into the garden they be gone.

0 'I loue *your* daughter,' saies Wil*liam*
    Stewart,
  ' But I cannott tell whether she loueth
    mee: '
  ' Marry, God defend,' saies the Erle of
    Mar,
  ' *That* euer soe *that* itt shold bee !

1 'I had rather a gallowes there was
    made,
  And hange thee ffor my daughter's
    sake;
  I had rather a ffyer were made att a
    stake,
  And burne thee ffor my daughter's
    sake !

2 ' To chamber, to chamber, gay ladye,'
    he saies,
  ' In the deuill's name now I bidd
    thee !
  And thou gett thee not to the chamber
    soone,
  I 'le beate thee before the Stewart's
    eye.'

3 And then bespake Wil*liam* Stewart,
  These were the words said hee:
  ' If thou beate thy daughter for my
    sake,
  Thou 'st beate a hundred men and
    mee.'

4 Then bespake Iohn Stewart —
  Lord ! an angry man was hee —

' O churle, if thou wouldest not haue
    macht with my brother,
  Thou might haue answerd him cur-
    teouslye.'

45 ' O hold thy peace, Iohn Stewart,
    And chamber thy words now, I bidd
    thee;
  If thou chamber not thy words soone,
    Thou 'st loose a good service; soe
    shalt thou doe me.'

46 ' Marry ! hang them *that* cares,' saies
    Iohn Stewart,
  ' Either ffor thy service or ffor thee;
  Services can I haue enoughe,
  But brethren wee must euer bee.'

47 Wil*liam* Stewart and his brother Iohn,
  To Argyle Castle gon they bee;
  And when Willye came to Argyle Castle,
  Into care-bedd then lope hee.

48 A parliament att Edenborrow was made,
  The *king* and his nobles all mett
    there;
  The sent ffor Wil*liam* Stewart and Iohn,
  To come amongst the other peeres.

49 Their clothing was of scarlett redd,
  That was soe seemelye ffor to see;
  Blacke hatts, white ffeathers plewed
    with gold,
  And sett all on their heads trulye.

50 Their stockings were of twisted silke,
  With garters ffringed about with
    gold;
  Their shoes were of the cordevine,
  And all was comelye to behold.

51 And when they came to Edenborrowe,
  They called ffor Iohn Stew*art* and
    Willie:
  ' I answer in a *lord*'s roome,' saies Will
    Stewart,
  ' But an erle I hope to bee.'

52 ' Come downe, come downe,' saies the
    Lord of Marr,
  ' I knew not what was thy degree : '
  ' O churle, if I might not haue macht
    with thy daughter,
  Itt had not beene long of my de-
    gree.

53 'My ffather, hee is the king his brother,
  And then the king is vuckle to me;
  O churle, if I might not haue macht
    with thy daughter,
  Itt had not beene long of my degree.'

54 'O hold your peace,' then sayd the king,
  'Cozen William, I doe bidd thee;
  Infaith, cozen William, he loues you the
    worsse
  Because you are a-kinn to mee.

55 'I 'le make thee an erle with a siluer
    wande,
  And adde more honors still to thee;
  Thy brother Ihon shall be a lord,
    Of the best att home in his countrye.

56 'Thy brother Kester shalbe a knight,
  Lands and liuings I will him giue,
  And still hee shall liue in court with mee,
  And I 'le maintaine him whilest he
    doth liue.'

57 And when the parlaiment was done,
  And all the ffolkes away were gone,
  Willye Stewart and Iohn his brother,
  To Argyle Castle they be gone.

58 But when they came to Argyle Castle,
  That was soe ffarr in that countrye,
  He thought soe much then of his loue
  That into care-bedd then lope hee.

59 Iohn Stewart did see his brother soe ill,
  Lord, in his heart that hee was woe !
  'I will goe wooing for thy sake
  Againe yonder gay ladye to.

60 'I 'le cloth my selfe in strange array,
  In a beggar's habbitt I will goe,
  That when I come before the Erle of
    Marr
    My clothing strange he shall not
    knowe.'

61 Iohn hee gott on a clouted cloake,
  Soe meete and low then by his knee,
  With four garters vpon one legg,
  Two aboue, and towe below trulye.

62 'But if thou be a beggar, brother,
  Thou art a beggar that is vnknowne;
  Ffor thou art one of the stoutest beggars
  That euer I saw since I was borne.

63 'Heere, geeue the lady this gay go
    ringe,
  A token to her that well is knowne;
  And if shee but aduise itt well,
    Shee 'le know some time itt was he
    owne.'

64 'Stay, by my ffaith, I goe not yett,'
  Iohn Stewart he can replye;
  'I 'le haue my bottle ffull of beere,
  The best that is in thy butterye.

65 'I 'le haue my sachell ffilld full of meat
  I am sure, brother, [it] will doe no
    harme;
  Ffor, before I come to the Erle of Marr
    his house,
    My lipps, I am sure, they will
    warme.'

66 And when he came to the Erle of Marr
    house,
  By chance itt was of the dole-day;
  But Iohn cold ffind no place to stand,
  Vntill he came to the ladye gaye.

67 But many a beggar he threw downe,
  And made them all with weepin
    say,
  He is the devill, hee is no beggar,
    That is come fforth of some strang
    countrye.

68 And now the dole that itt is delte,
  And all the beggars be gon away,
  Sauing Iohn Stewart, that seemed
    beggar,
  And the ladye that was soe gay.

69 'Lady,' sais Iohn, 'I am no beggar,
  As by my clothes you may think
    that I bee;
  I am your servant, Iohn Stewart,
  And I am sent a messenger to thee.'

70 'But if thou be Iohn Stewart,
  As I doe thinke that thou bee,
  Avayle thy capp, avayle thy hoode,
  And I will stand and speake to thee.

71 'How doth thy brother, Iohn Stewart,
  And all the lords in his countrye ?'
  'O ffye vpon thee, wicked woman !
    My brother he doth the worsse ffo
    thee.'

72 With *that* the teares stood in her eyes;
　　O lord, shee wept soe tenderlye !
　Sais, Ligg the blame vnto my ffather;
　　I pray you, Iohn Stew*art*, lay itt not
　　　to mee.

73 Comend me to my owne true-loue,
　　That liues soe farr in the North
　　　countrye,
　And bidd him meete me att Martings-
　　dale,
　　Ffullye w[i]thin these dayes three.

74 Hang them, sais the iady gay,
　　That letts their ffather witting bee !
　I 'le proue a ladye ffull of loue,
　　And be there by the sunn be a quar-
　　　ter highe.

75 And bidd him bring with him a hundred
　　gunners,
　　And ranke riders lett them bee;
　Lett them be of the rankest ryders
　　That be to be ffound in *that* countrye.

76 The best and worse, and all in like,
　　Bidd him clothe them in one liuerye;
　And for his men, greene is the best,
　　And greene now lett their lyueryes
　　　bee.

77 And cloth himselfe in scarlett redd,
　　That is soe seemelye for to see;
　For scarlett is a ffaire coulor,
　　And pleasant in a woman's eye.

78 What they lady sayd, Iohn Stewart
　　writt,
　　To Argyle Castle sent itt hee;
　His bagg and his dish and showing
　　horne,
　　Unto three beggars he gaue them all
　　　three.

79 And when Willie Stewart saw the let-
　　ter,
　　Fforth of care-bed then lope hee;
　He thought himselfe as lustye and sound
　　As any man in *that* countrye.

80 He mustered together his merrymen all,
　　He mustered them soe louinglye;
　He thought he had had scarce halfe a
　　hundred,
　　Then had hee eleuen score and three.

81 He chose fforth a hundred of the best
　　That were to be found in *that* com-
　　panye,
　And presentlye they tooke their horsse,
　　And to Martingsdale posted hee.

82 And when he came to Martingsdale,
　　He found his loue staying there trulye,
　For shee was a lady true of loue,
　　And was there by [the] sunn was a
　　qwarter highe.

83 Shee kisst Will*iam* Stewart and his
　　brother Iohn,
　　Soe did shee p*art* of his merry men :
　' If the churle, thy ffather, hee were
　　here,
　　He shold not haue thee backe againe.'

84 They sent ffor preist, they sent ffor
　　clarke,
　　And they were married there with
　　speede;
　Will*iam* tooke the lady home with him,
　　And they liued together long time
　　indeed.

85 And in twelue monthe soe they wrought,
　　The lady shee was great with childe;
　The sent Iohn Stewart to the Erle off
　　Marre,
　　To come and christen the barne soe
　　milde.

86 ' And if this be soe,' sayes the Erle of
　　Marre,
　　' Iohu Stewart, as thou tells mee,
　I hope in God you haue marryed my
　　daughter,
　　And put her bodye to honestye.'

87 ' Nay, by my ffaith,' then saies Iohn
　　Stewart,
　　' Ffor euer alas *that* shall not bee;
　Ffor now wee haue put her body to
　　shame,
　　Thou 'st haue her againe hame to
　　thee.'

88 ' I had rather make thee Erle of Marre,
　　And marry my daughter vnto thee;
　For by my ffaith,' sais the Erle of
　　Marr,
　　' Her marryage is marrd in our
　　countrye.'

89 ' If this be soe,' then sais Iohn Stewart,
   ' A marryage soone *that* thou shalt
      see;
   Ffor my brother William, my ffather's
      heyre,
   Shall marry thy daughter before thine
      eye.'

90 They sent ffor preist, thé sent ffor
      clarke,
   And married there they were with
      speed;
   And William Stewart is Erle of Marr,
   And his ffather-in-law dwells with
      him indeed.

108

CHRISTOPHER WHITE

This ballad is found in the Percy MS. only.

'Christopher White,' Percy MS., p. 513;
Hales and Furnivall, III, 494.

1 As I walked fforth one morninge,
   By one place *that* pleased mee,
   Wherin I heard a wandering wight,
   Sais, Christopher White is good com-
      panye.

2 I drew me neere, and very neere,
   Till I was as neere as neere cold bee;
   Loth I was her councell to discreene,
   Because I wanted companye.

3 ' Say on, say on, thou well faire mayd,
   Why makest thou moane soe heaui-
      lye ? '
   Sais, All is ffor one wandering wight,
   Is banished fforth of his owne coun-
      trye.

4 ' I am the burgesse of Edenburrow,
   Soe am I more of townes three;
   I haue money and gold great store,
   Come, sweet wench, and ligg thy loue
      on mee.'

5 The merchant pulled forth a bagg of
      gold
   Which had hundreds two or three;
   Sais, Euery day throughout the weeke
   I 'le comt as much downe on thy knee.

6 ' O merchant, take thy gold againe,
   A good liuing 't will purchase thee;
   If I be ffalse to Christopher White,
   Merchant, I cannott be true to thee.

7 Sais, I haue halls, soe haue I bowers,
   Sais, I haue shipps sayling on the sea
   I ame the burgess of Edenburrowe;
   Come, sweete wench, ligge thy lou
      on mee.

8 Come on, come, thou well faire mayde,
   Of our matters lett vs goe throughe,
   For to-morrowe I 'le marry thee,
   And thy dwelling shalbe in Edenbur
      rough.

9 The lady shee tooke this gold in he
      hand,
   The teares thé ffell ffast ffrom her eye
   Sais, Siluer and gold makes my hart t
      turne,
   And makes me leaue good companye

10 They had not beene marryed
   Not ouer monthes two or three,
   But tydings came to Edenburrowe
   That all the merchants must to th
      sea.

11 Then as this lady sate in a deske,
   Shee made a loue-letter ffull round;
   She mad a *lettre* to Christopher White,
   And in itt shee put a hundred pound

12 She lin'd the letter with gold soe red,
   And mony good store in itt was found
   Shee sent itt to Christopher White,
   That was soe ffar in the Scotts ground

13 Shee bade him then ffrankely spend,
   And looke *that* hee shold merry bee,
   And bid him come to Edenburrowe,
   Now all the merchants be to the sea.

14 But Christopher came to leeue London,
   And there he kneeled lowly downe,
   And there hee begd his pardon then,
   Of our noble king *that* ware th
      crowne.

15 But when he came to his true-loue
      house,
   Which was made both of lime an
      stone.

Shee tooke him by the lily-white hand,
　　Sais, True-loue, you are welcome
　　home !

6 Welcome, my honey, welcome, my ioy,
　　Welcome, my true-loue, home to mee !
　Ffor thou art hee *that* will lengthen my
　　dayes,
　　And I know thou art good companye.

7 Chr*istopher*, I am a merchant's wiffe;
　　Chr*istopher*, the more shall be yo*ur*
　　gaine;
　Siluer and gold you shall haue enough,
　　Of the merchant's gold *that* is in
　　Spaine.

8 ' But if you be a merchant's wiffe,
　　Something tó much you are to blame;
　I will thee reade a loue-lett*er*
　　Shall sture thy stumpes, thou noble
　　dame.'

9 ' Althoug I be a marchant's wiffe,
　　.　.　.　　shall　.　.　　mine
　.　and g　.　.　.　.　.
　　Into England I 'le goe w*i*th the.'

0 They packet vp both siluer and plate,
　　Siluer and gold soe great plentye,
　And they be gon into Litle England,
　　And the marchant must them neu*er*
　　see.

1 And when the merchants they came
　　home,
　　Their wiues to eche other can say,
　Heere hath beene good Chr*istopher* White,
　　And he hath tane thy wiffe away.

2 They haue packett vp spoone and plate,
　　Siluer and gold great plenty,
　And they be gon into Litle England,
　　And them againe thow must neu*er* see.

3 ' I care nott ffor my siluer and gold,
　　Nor for my plate soe great plentye,
　But I mourne for *that* like-some ladye
　　That Chr*istopher* White hath tane ffrom
　　mee.

4 ' But one thing I must needs confesse,
　　This lady shee did say to me,
　If shee were ffalse to Chr*istopher* White,
　　Shee cold neu*er* be true to mee.

25 ' All young men a warning take,
　　A warning, looke, you take by mee,
　Looke *that* you loue y*our* old loues best,
　　For infaith they are best companye.'

109

TOM POTTS

　Besides the copy in the Percy MS. there are
two broadside versions (B, C). All three are
of the seventeenth century, and the ballad need
not be put much beyond that date. Modernized editions, differing much, were issued in
the century following, perhaps earlier, some of
which have a Second Part, narrating the happy
married life of Tom Potts, Lord Arundel, and
Fair Rosamond. Unequal matches are common enough in ballads and romances, and very
naturally, since they are an easy expedient for
exciting interest, at least with those who belong
to the humbler party. We have other ballad-
examples of disparagement on the female side
in ' Richie Story' (No. 232) and ' The Kitchie-
Boy' (No. 252).

A

' Thomas of Potte,' Percy MS., p. 409 ; Hales
and Furnivall, iii, 135.

1 ALL you lords of Scottland ffaire,
　　And ladyes alsoe, bright of blee,
　There is a ladye amongst them all,
　　Of her report you shall heare of me.

2 Of her bewtye shee is soe bright,
　　And of her colour soe bright of blee;
　Shee is daughter to the Lord Arrndell,
　　His heyre apparrant ffor to bee.

3 ' I 'le see *that* bryde,' Lord Phenix sayes,
　　' *That* is a ladye of hye degree,
　And iff I like her countenance well,
　　The heyre of all my land shee'st bee.'

4 To *that* ladye ffayre Lord Phenix came,
　　And to *that* like-some dame said hee,
　Now God thee saue, my ladye ffaire,
　　The heyre of all my land tho'st bee.

5 ' Leaue of yo*ur* suite,' the ladye sayd;
　　' You are a lord of honor ffree;
　You may gett ladyes enowe att home,
　　And I haue a loue in mine owne
　　countrye.

6 ‘I haue a louer true of mine owne,
   A seruinge-man of a small degree;
Thomas a Pott, itt is his name,
   He is the ffirst loue *that* euer I had,
     and the last *that* hee shalbee.’

7 ‘Giue Thomas a Pott then be his name,
   I wott I ken him soe readilye;
I can spend forty pounds by weeke,
   And hee cannott spend pounds three.’

8 ‘God giue you good of your gold,’ said
     the ladye,
   ‘ And alsoe, sir, of your ffee !
Hee was the ffirst loue *that* euer I
     had,
   And the last, sir, shall hee bee.’

9 With *that* Lord Phenix was sore amoued;
   Vnto her ffather then went hee;
Hee told her ffather how itt was proued,
   How *that* his daughter’s mind was
     sett.

10 ‘Thou art my daughter,’ the Erle of
     Arrndell said,
   ‘ The heyre of all my land to bee;
Thou ’st be bryde to the Lord Phenix,
   Daughter, giue thou ’le be heyre to
     mee.’

11 For lacke of her loue this ladye must
     lose,
   Her foolish wooing lay all aside;
The day is appoynted, and ffreinds are
     agreede;
Shee is fforcte to be the Lord Phenix
     bryde.

12 With *that* the lady began to muse —
   A greened woman, God wott, was
     shee —
How shee might Lord Phenix beguile,
   And scape vnmarryed ffrom him *that*
     day.

13 Shee called to her her litle ffoote-page,
   To Iacke her boy, soe tenderlye;
Sayes, Come thou hither, thou litle ffoote-
     page,
For indeed I dare trust none but thee.

14 To Strawberry Castle, boy, thou must
     goe,
   To Thomas Pott there as hee can bee,

And giue him here this letter ffaire,
   And on Guilford Greene bidd him
     meete me.

15 Looke thou marke his contenance well,
   And his colour tell to mee;
And hye thee ffast, and come againe,
   And forty shillings I will giue thee.

16 For if he blush in his fface,
   Then in his hart hee ’se sorry bee;
Then lett my ffather say what hee will,
   For false to Potts I ’le neuer bee.

17 And giue hee smile then with his mouth,
   Then in his heart hee ’le merry be;
Then may hee gett him a loue where
     euer he can,
   For small of his companye my part
     shalbe.

18 Then one while *that* the boy hee went,
   Another while, God wott, rann hee,
And when hee came to Strawberry Cas
     tle,
   There Thomas Potts hee see.

19 Then he gaue him this letter ffaire,
   And when he began then for to reade
They boy had told him by word of mouth
   His loue must be the Lord Phenix
     bryde.

20 With *that*, Thomas a Pott began to
     blushe,
   The teares trickeled in his eye:
‘ Indeed this letter I cannot reede,
   Nor neuer a word to see or spye.

21 ‘ I pray thee, boy, to me thou ’le be trew
   And heer ’s fiue marke I will giue thee
And all these words thou must peruse,
   And tell thy lady this ffrom mee.

22 ‘Tell her by ffaith and troth shee is
     mine owne,
   By some part of promise, and soe itt ’s
     be found;
Lord Phenix shall neuer marry her, by
     night nor day,
   Without he can winn her with his
     hand.

23 ‘On Gilford Greene I will her meete,
   And bidd *that* ladye ffor mee pray;

For there I 'le loose my liffe soe sweete,
    Or else the wedding I will stay.'

24 Then backe againe the boy he went,
    As ffast againe as he cold hye;
    The ladye mett him fiue mile on the
        way:
    'Why hast thou stayd soe long?'
        saies shee.

25 'Boy,' said the ladye, 'thou art but
        younge;
    To please my mind thou 'le mocke
        and scorne;
    I will not beleeue thee on word of mouth,
    Vnlesse on this booke thou wilt be
        sworne.'

26 'Marry, by this booke,' the boy can say,
    'As Christ himselfe be true to mee,
    Thomas Pott cold not his letter reade
    For teares trickling in his eye.'

27 'If this be true,' the ladye sayd,
    'Thou bonny boy, thou tells to mee,
    Forty shillings I did thee promise,
    But heere 's ten pounds I 'le giue itt
        thee.

28 'All my maids,' the lady sayd,
    'That this day doe waite on mee,
    Wee will ffall downe vpon our knees,
    For Thomas Pott now pray will wee.

29 'If his ffortune be now ffor to winn —
    Wee will pray to Christ in Triny-
        tye —
    I 'le make him the fflower of all his
        kinn,
    Ffor they Lord of Arrundale he shal-
        be.'

30 Now lett vs leaue talking of this ladye
        faire,
    In her prayer good where shee can
        bee;
    And I 'le tell you hou Thomas Pott
    For ayd to his lord and master came
        hee.

31 And when hee came Lord Iockye before,
    He kneeled him low downe on his
        knee;
    Saies, Thou art welcome, Thomas Pott,
    Thou art allwayes full of thy curtesye.

32 Has thou slaine any of thy ffellowes,
    Or hast thou wrought me some vil-
        lanye?
    'Sir, none of my ffellowes I haue slaine,
    Nor I haue wrought you noe villanye.

33 'But I haue a loue in Scottland ffaire,
    I doubt I must lose her through pou-
        ertye;
    If you will not beleeue me by word of
        mouth,
    Behold the letter shee writt vnto mee.'

34 When Lord Iockye looked the letter
        vpon,
    The tender words in itt cold bee,
    'Thomas Pott, take thou no care,
    Thou 'st neuer loose her thronghe
        pouertye.

35 'Thou shalt have forty pounds a weeke,
    In gold and siluer thou shalt rowe,
    And Harbye towne I will thee allowe
    As longe as thou dost meane to
        wooe.

36 'Thou shalt haue fortye of thy ffellowes
        ffaire,
    And forty horsse to goe with thee,
    And forty speares of the best I haue,
    And I my-selfe in thy companye.'

37 'I thanke you, master,' sayd Thomas
        Pott,
    'Neither man nor boy shall goe with
        mee;
    I wold not ffor a thousand pounds
    Take one man in my companye.'

38 'Why then, God be with thee, Thomas
        Pott!
    Thou art well knowen and proued for
        a man;
    Looke thou shedd no guiltlesse bloode,
    Nor neuer confound no gentlman.

39 'But looke thou take with him some
        truce,
    Apoint a place of lybertye;
    Lett him prouide as well as hee cann,
    And as well prouided thou shalt bee.'

40 And when Thomas Pott came to Gil-
        ford Greene,
    And walked there a litle beside,

Then was hee ware of the Lord Phenix,
 And with him Ladye Rozamund his
  bryde.

41 Away by the bryde rode Thomas of Pott,
 But noe word to her *that* he did say;
 But when he came Lord Phenix before,
  He gaue him the right time of the
  day.

42 'O thou art welcome, Thomas a Potts,
 Thou serving-man, welcome to mee!
 How ffares they lord and master att
  home,
  And all the ladyes in thy cuntrye?'

43 'Sir, my lord and my master is in verry
  good health,
 I wott I ken itt soe readylye;
 I pray you, will you ryde to one outsyde,
  A word or towe to talke with mee.

44 'You are a nobleman,' sayd Thomas a
  Potts,
 'Yee are a borne lord in Scottland
  ffree;
 You may gett ladyes enowe att home;
 You shall neuer take my loue ffrom
  mee.'

45 'Away, away, thou Thomas a Potts!
 Thou seruing-man, stand thou a-side!
 I wott there's not a serving-man this
  day,
 I know, can hinder mee of my bryde.'

46 'If I be but a seruing-man,' sayd
  Thomas,
 'And you are a lord of honor ffree,
 A speare or two I'le with you runn,
 Before I'le loose her thus cowardlye.'

47 'On Gilford Greene,' Lord Phenix saies,
 'I'le thee meete;
 Neither man nor boy shall come hither
  with mee;'
 'And as I am a man,' said Thomas a
  Pott,
 'I'le haue as ffew in my companye.'

48 With *that* the wedding-day was stayd,
 The bryde went vnmarryed home
  againe;
 Then to her maydens ffast shee loughe,
 And in her hart shee was ffull ffaine.

49 'But all my mayds,' they ladye sayd,
 '*That* this day doe waite on mee,
 Wee will ffall downe againe vpon our
  knees,
 For Thomas a Potts now pray will
  wee.

50 'If his ffortune be ffor to winn —
 Wee'le pray to Christ in Trynitye —
 I'le make him the fflower of all his kinn,
 For the Lord of Arrundale he shalbe.'

51 Now let vs leaue talking of this lady
  fayre,
 In her prayers good where shee can
  bee;
 I'le tell you the troth how Thomas a Potts
 For aide to his lord againe came hee.

52 And when he came to Strawberry Castle,
 To try ffor his ladye he had but one
  weeke;
 Alacke, ffor sorrow hee cannott ffor-
  beare,
 For four dayes then he ffell sicke.

53 With *that* his lord and master to him
  came,
 Sayes, I pray thee, Thomas, tell mee
  without all doubt,
 Whether hast thou gotten the bonny
  ladye,
 Or thou man gange the ladye withoute.

54 'Marry, master, yett *that* matter is vn-
  tryde;
 Within two dayes tryed itt must bee;
 He is a lord, and I am but a seruing-
  man,
 I doubt I must loose her through
  pouertye.'
 'Why, Thomas a Pott, take thou no care:
 Thou'st neuer loose her through pou-
  ertye.

55 'Thou shalt haue halfe my land a yeere,
 And *that* will raise thee many a pound:
 Before thou shalt loose thy bonny ladye,
 Thou shalt drop angells with him to
  the ground.

56 'And thou shalt haue forty of thy ffellowes ffaire,
 And forty horsses to goe with thee,

And forty speres of the best I haue,
    And I my-selfe in thy companye.'

57 'I thanke you, master,' sayd Thomas a
        Potts,
    'But of one thinge, sir, I wold be
        ffaine;
    If I shold loose my bonny ladye,
    How shall I increase your goods
        againe ? '

58 'Why, if thou winn thy lady ffaire,
    Thou maye well fforth for to pay mee;
    If thou loose thy lady, thou hast losse
        enoughe;
    Not one penny I will aske thee.'

59 'Master, you haue thirty horsses in one
        hold,
    You keepe them ranke and royallye;
    There 's an old horsse — for him you
        doe not care —
    This day wold sett my lady ffree.

60 ' That is a white, with a cutt tayle,
    Ffull sixteen yeeres of age is hee;
    Giffe you wold lend me that old horsse,
    Then I shold gett her easilye.'

61 'Thou takes a ffoolish part,' the Lord
        Iockye sayd,
    ' And a ffoolish part thou takes on
        thee;
    Thou shalt haue a better then euer he
        was,
    That forty pounds cost more nor hee.'

62 'O master, those horsses beene wild and
        wicked,
    And litle they can skill of the old
        traine;
    Giffe I be out of my saddle cast,
    They beene soe wild they 'le neuer be
        tane againe.

63 ' Lett me haue age, sober and wise;
    Itt is a part of wisdome, you know itt
        plaine;
    If I be out of my sadle cast,
    Hee 'le either stand still or turne
        · againe.'

64 ' Thou shalt haue that horsse with all
        my hart,
    And my cote-plate of siluer ffree,

And a hundred men att thy backe,
    For to fight if neede shalbee.'

65 'I thanke you, master,' said Thomas a
        Potts,
    ' Neither man nor boy shall goe with
        mee;
    As you are a lord off honor borne,
    Let none of my ffellowes know this of
        mee.

66 'Ffor if they wott of my goinge,
    I wott behind me they will not bee;
    Without you keepe them vnder a locke,
    Vppon that greene I shall them see.'

67 And when Thomas came to Gilford
        Greene,
    And walked there some houres three,
    Then was he ware of the Lord Phenix,
    And four men in his companye.

68 'You haue broken your vow,' sayd
        Thomas a Pott,
    ' Your vowe that you made vnto mee;
    You said you wold come your selfe alone,
    And you haue brought more then two
        or three.'

69 'These are my waiting-men,' Lord Phe-
        nix sayd,
    ' That euery day doe waite on mee;
    Giffe any of these shold att vs stirr,
    My speare shold runn throwe his
        bodye.'

70 'I 'le runn noe race,' said Thomas Potts,
    ' Till that this othe heere made may
        bee:
    If the one of vs be slaine,
    The other fforgiuen that hee may bee.'

71 'I 'le make a vow,' Lord Phenix sayes,
    ' My men shall beare wittnesse with
        thee,
    Giffe thou slay mee att this time,
    Neuer the worsse beloued in Scottland
        thou shalt bee.'

72 Then they turned their horsses round
        about,
    To run the race more egarlye;
    Lord Phenix he was stiffe and stout,
    He has runn Thomas quite thorrow
        the thye.

73 And beere Thomas out of his saddle
ffaire;
Vpon the ground there did hee lye;
He saies, For my liffe I doe not care,
But ffor the loue of my ladye.

74 But shall I lose my ladye ffaire?
I thought shee shold haue beene my
wiffe;
I pray thee, Lord Phenix, ryde not away,
For with thee I will loose my liffe.

75 Tho Thomas a Potts was a seruing-man,
He was alsoe a phisityan good;
He clapt his hand vpon his wound,
With some kind of words he stauncht
the blood.

76 Then into his sadle againe hee leepe;
The blood in his body began to warme;
He mist Lord Phenix bodye there,
But he run him quite throw the brawne
of the arme.

77 And he bore him quite out of his saddle
ffaire;
Vpon the ground there did he lye;
He said, I pray thee, Lord Phenix, rise
and ffight,
Or else yeeld this ladye sweete to mee.

78 'To ffight with thee,' quoth Phenix, 'I
cannott stand,
Nor ffor to ffight, I cannott, sure;
Thou hast run me through the brawne of
the arme;
Noe longer of thy spere I cannott endure.

79 'Thou 'st haue that ladye with all my
hart,
Sith itt was like neuer better to proue.
Nor neuer a noble-man this day,
That will seeke to take a pore man's
loue.'

80 'Why then, be of good cheere,' saies
Thomas Pott,
'Indeed your bucher I 'le neuer bee,
For I 'le come and stanche your bloode,
Giff any thankes you 'le giue to mee.'

81 As he was stanching the Phenix blood,
These words Thomas a Pott cann to
him proue:

'I 'le neuer take a ladye of you thus,
But here I 'le giue you another choice.

82 'Heere is a lane of two miles longe;
Att either end sett wee will bee;
The ladye shall sitt vs betweene,
And soe will wee sett this ladye ffree.'

83 'If thou 'le doe soe,' Lord Phenix sayes,
'Thomas a Pott, as thou dost tell mee,
Whether I gett her or goe without her,
Heere 's forty pounds I 'le giue itt
thee.'

84 And when the ladye there can stand,
A woman's mind that day to proue,
'Now, by my ffaith,' said this ladye
ffaire,
'This day Thomas a Pott shall haue his
owne loue.'

85 Toward Thomas a Pott the lady shee
went,
To leape behind him hastilye;
'Nay, abyde a while,' sayd Lord Phenix,
'Ffor better yett proued thou shalt bee.

86 'Thou shalt stay heere with all thy
maids —
In number with thee thou hast but
three —
Thomas a Pott and I 'le goe beyond yonder wall,
There the one of vs shall dye.'

87 And when they came beyond the wall,
The one wold not the other nye;
Lord Phenix he had giuen his word
With Thomas a Pott neuer to ffight.

88 'Giue me a choice,' Lord Phenix sayes,
'Thomas a Pott, I doe pray thee;
Lett mee goe to yonder ladye ffaire,
To see whether shee be true to thee.'

89 And when hee came that ladye too,
Vnto that likesome dame sayd hee,
Now God thee saue, thou ladye ffaire,
The heyre of all my land thou 'st bee.

90 Ffor this Thomas a Potts I haue slaine;
He hath more then deadlye wounds
two or three;
Thou art mine owne ladye, he sayd,
And marryed together wee will bee.

91 The ladye said, If Thomas a Potts this
  day thou haue slaine,
    Thou hast slaine a better man than
      euer was thee;
  And I 'le sell all the state of my lande
    But thou 'st be hanged on a gallow-
      tree.

92 With that they lady shee ffell in a soone;
    A greeued woman, I wott, was shee;
  Lord Phenix hee was readye there,
    Tooke her in his armes most hastilye.

93 ' O Lord, sweete, and stand on thy ffeete,
    This day Thomas a Pott aliue can bee;
  I 'le send ffor thy father, the Lord of
      Arrundale,
    And marryed together I will you see:
  Giffe hee will not maintaine you well,
    Both gold and land you shall haue
      from me.'

94 ' I 'le see that wedding,' my Lord of
      Arrundale said,
    ' Of my daughter's loue that is soe
      ffaire;
  And sith itt will no better be,
    Of all my land Thomas a Pott shall
      be my heyre.'

95 ' Now all my maids,' the ladye said,
    ' And ladyes of England, faire and
      ffree,
  Looke you neuer change your old loue
      for no new,
    Nor neuer change for no pouertye.

96 ' Ffor I had a louer true of mine owne,
    A seruing-man of a small degree;
  Ffrom Thomas a Pott I 'le turne his
      name,
    And the Lord of Arrundale hee shall
      bee '

110

THE KNIGHT AND SHEP-
HERD'S DAUGHTER

The only English version of this ballad is a
broadside in the Roxburghe Collection. The
fifteenth stanza is quoted in Fletcher's comedy
of ' The Pilgrim,' 1621. Kinloch is fully justified in claiming for the Scottish ballad a
decided superiority. The humorous artifices
which the lady practises to maintain the character of a beggar's brat are, as he says, kept
up with great spirit and fancy.

Parts of this ballad inevitably suggest a
parallel with the tales belonging to the class of
the ' Marriage of Sir Gawain ' (No. 31), to which
Chaucer's Wife of Bath's Tale belongs. The
Danish ballad of ' Ebbe Galt ' (Grundtvig-
Olrik, No. 314) has also several features in
common with ' The Knight and Shepherd's
Daughter.' For a discussion of the whole mat-
ter, see G. H. Maynadier, The Wife of Bath's
Tale, 1901.

A

' The Beautifull Shepherdesse of Arcadia.'
a. Roxburghe Ballads, III, 160, 161. b. The
same, II, 30, 31.

1 THERE was a shepherd's daughter
    Came triping on the way,
  And there she met a courteous knight,
    Which caused her to stay.
  Sing trang dil do lee

2 ' Good morow to you, beautious maid,'
    These words pronounced he;
  ' O I shall dye this day,' he said,
    ' If I have not my will of thee.'

3 ' The Lord forbid,' the maid reply'd,
    ' That such a thing should be,
  That ever such a courteous yong knight
    Should dye for love of me.'

4 He took her by the middle so small,
    And laid her down on the plain,
  And after he had had his will,
    He took her up again.

5 ' Now you have had your wil, good sir
    And put my body thus to shame,
  Even as you are a courteous knight,
    Tel me what is your name.'

6 ' Some men do call me Jack, sweet
      heart,
    And some do call me John,
  But when I come to the king's [fair]
      court,
    They call me Sweet William.'

7 He set his foot in the stirrop,
    And away then did he ride;
  She tuckt her kirtle about her middle,
    And run close by his side.

8 But when she came to the broad water,
   She set her brest and swom,
And when she was got out again,
   She took her heels and run.

9 He never was the courteous knight
   To say, Fair maid, will you ride ?
Nor she never was so loving a maid
   To say, Sir Knight, abide.

10 But when she came to the king's fair
     court,
   She knocked at the ring;
So ready was the king himself
   To let this fair maid in.

11 ' O Christ you save, my gracious leige,
   Your body Christ save and see !
You have got a knight within your court
   This day hath robbed me.'

12 ' What hath he robbed thee of, fair
     maid ?
   Of purple or of pall ?
Or hath he took thy gay gold ring,
   From off thy finger small ? '

13 ' He hath not robbed me, my liege,
   Of purple nor of pall;
But he hath got my maidenhead,
   Which grieves me worst of all.'

14 ' Now if he be a batchelor,
   His body I 'le give to thee;
But if he be a married man,
   High hanged shall he be.'

15 He called down his merry men all,
   By one, by two, and by three;
Sweet William was us'd to be the first,
   But now the last comes hee.

16 He brought her down full forty pound,
   Ty'd up with[in] a glove:
' Fair maid, I give the same to the,
   And seek another love.'

17 ' O I 'le have none of your gold,' she
     said,
   ' Nor I 'le have none of your fee;
But I must have your fair body
   The king hath given me.'

18 Sweet William ran and fetcht her then
   Five hundred pound in gold,

Saying, Fair maid, take this unto thee;
   Thy fault will never be told.

19 ' 'T is not your gold that shall me tempt,'
   These words then answered she,
' But I must have your own body;
   So the king hath granted me.'

20 ' Would I had drank the fair water
   When I did drink the wine,
That ever any shepherd's daughter
   Should be a fair lady of mine !

21 ' Would I had drunk the puddle-water
   When I did drink the ale,
That ever any shepherd's daughter
   Should have told me such a tale ! '

22 ' A shepheard's daughter as I was,
   You might have let me be;
I 'd never come to the king's fair court
   To have craved any love of thee.'

23 He set her on a milk-white steed,
   And himselfe upon a gray;
He hung a bugle about his neck,
   And so they rode away.

24 But when they came unto the place
   Where marriage rites were done,
She provd her self a duke's daughter,
   And he but a squire's son.

25 ' Now you have married me, sir knight,
   Your pleasures may be free;
If you make me lady of one good town,
   I 'le make you lord of three.'

26 ' Accursed be the gold,' he said,
   ' If thou hadst not bin true,
That should have parted thee from me,
   To have chang'd thee for a new.'

27 Their hearts being then so linked fast,
   And joyning hand in hand,
He had both purse and person too,
   And all at his command.

B

' Shepherd's Dochter,' Kinloch MSS., v, 255,
in the handwriting of Mr Kinloch.

1 THERE was a shepherd's dochter
   Kept sheep upon yon hill,

And by cam a gay braw gentleman,
    And wad hae had his will.

2 He took her by the milk-white hand,
    And laid her on the ground,
    And whan he got his will o her
       He lift her up again.

3 'O syne ye 've got your will o me,
    Your will o me ye 've taen,
    'T is all I ask o you, kind sir,
      Is to tell to me your name.'

4 'Sometimes they call me Jack,' he said,
    'Sometimes they call me John,
    But whan I am in the king's court,
      My name is Wilfu Will.'

5 Then he loup on his milk-white steed,
    And straught away he rade,
    And she did kilt her petticoats,
      And after him she gaed.

6 He never was sae kind as say,
    O lassie, will ye ride ?
    Nor ever had she the courage to say,
      O laddie, will ye bide !

7 Until they cam to a wan water,
    Which was called Clyde,
    And then he turned about his horse,
      Said, Lassie, will ye ride ?

8 'I learned it in my father's hall,
    I learned it for my weel,
    That whan I come to deep water,
      I can swim as it were an eel.

9 'I learned it in my mother's bower,
    I learned it for my better,
    That whan I come to broad water,
      I can swim like ony otter.'

10 He plunged his steed into the ford,
    And straught way thro he rade,
    And she set in her lilly feet,
      And thro the water wade.

11 And whan she cam to the king's court,
    She tirled on the pin,
    And wha sae ready 's the king himsel
      To let the fair maid in ?

12 'What is your will wi me, fair maid ?
    What is your will wi me ? '

'There is a man into your court
    This day has robbed me.'

13 'O has he taen your gold,' he said,
    'Or has he taen your fee ?
    Or has he stown your maidenhead,
      The flower of your bodye ? '

14 'He has na taen my gold, kind sir,
    Nor as little has he taen my fee,
    But he has taen my maidenhead,
      The flower of my bodye.'

15 'O gif he be a married man,
    High hangit shall he be,
    But gif he be a bachelor,
      His body I 'll grant thee.'

16 'Sometimes they call him Jack,' she
      said,
    'Sometimes they call him John,
    But whan he 's in the king's court,
      His name is Sweet William.'

17 'There 's not a William in a' my court,
    Never a one but three,
    And one of them is the Queen's brother;
      I wad laugh gif it war he.'

18 The king called on his merry men,
    By thirty and by three;
    Sweet Willie, wha used to be foremost
      man,
      Was the hindmost a' but three.

19 O he cam cripple, and he cam blind,
    Cam twa-fald oer a tree:
    'O be he cripple, or be he blind,
      This very same man is he.'

20 'O whether will ye marry the bonny may,
    Or hang on the gallows-tree ? '
    'O I will rather marry the bonny may,
      Afore that I do die.'

21 But he took out a purse of gold,
    Weel locked in a glove:
    'O tak ye that, my bonny may,
      And seek anither love.'

22 'O I will hae none o your gold,' she
      says,
    'Nor as little ony of your fee,
    But I will hae your ain body,
      The king has granted me.'

23 O he took out a purse of gold,
    A purse of gold and store;
    'O tak ye that, fair may,' he said,
      ' Frae me ye 'll neer get mair.'

24 'O haud your tongue, young man,' she
      says,
    ' And I pray you let me be;
    For I will hae your ain body,
      The king has granted me.'

25 He mounted her on a bonny bay horse,
    Himsel on the silver grey;
    He drew his bonnet out oer his een,
    He whipt and rade away.

26 O whan they cam to yon nettle bush,
    The nettles they war spread:
    'O an my mither war but here,' she says,
      ' These nettles she wad sned.'

27 'O an I had drank the wan water
    Whan I did drink the wine,
    That eer a shepherd's dochter
      Should hae been a love o mine !

28 'O may be I 'm a shepherd's dochter,
    And may be I am nane;
    But you might hae ridden on your ways,
    And hae let me alane.'

29 O whan they cam unto yon mill,
    She heard the mill clap:

.   .   .   .   .

    .   .   .   .

30 'Clap on, clap on, thou bonny mill,
    Weel may thou, I say,
    For mony a time thou 's filled my pock
    Wi baith oat-meal and grey.'

31 'O an I had drank the wan water
    Whan I did drink the wine,
    That eer a shepherd's dochter
      Should hae been a love o mine ! '

32 'O may be I 'm a shepherd's dochter,
    And may be I am nane;
    But you might hae ridden on our ways,
    And hae let me alane.

33 'But yet I think a fitter match
    Could scarcely gang thegither
    Than the King of France's auld dochter
    And the Queen of Scotland's brither.'

111

CROW AND PIE

This is not a purely popular ballad, but rather of that kind which, for convenience, may be called the minstrel-ballad. It has, however, popular features, and markedly in stanzas 13, 14, for which see No. 50, sts. 5–7; No. 52, st. 6 ; No. 110, A, sts. 5, 6, B, sts. 3, 4, etc.

MS. Rawlinson, C. 813, fol. 56 b, beginning of the sixteenth century. Halliwell's Nugæ Poeticæ, p. 42.

1 THROUGHE a forest as I can ryde,
    To take my sporte yn on mornyng,
    I cast my eye on euery syde,
    I was ware of a bryde syngynge.

2 I sawe a faire mayde come rydyng;
    I speke to hur of loue, I trowe;
    She answered me all yn scornyng,
    And sayd, The crowe shall byte yow.

3 'I pray yow, damesell, scorne me nott;
    To wyn your loue ytt ys my wyll;
    For your loue I haue dere bought,
    And I wyll take good hede thertyll.'

4 ' Nay, for God, sir, that I nyll;
    I tell the, Jenken, as I trowe,
    Thow shalt nott fynde me suche a gyll;
    Therfore the crowe shall byte yow.'

5 He toke then owt a good golde ryng,
    A purse of velweytt, that was soo
      fyne :
    ' Haue ye thys, my dere swetyng,
    With that ye wylbe lemman myn.'

6 'Be Cryst, I dare nott, for my dame,
    To dele with hym þat I do nott
      knowe;
    For soo I myght dyspyse my name;
    Therfore the crow shall byte yow.'

7 He toke hur abowte the mydell small,
    That was soo faire of hyde and hewe;
    He kyssed hur cheke as whyte as whall,
    And prayed hur þat she wolde vpon
      hym rewe.

8 She scornyd hym, and callyd hym Hew:
    His loue was as a paynted blowe:

'To-day me, to-morowe a newe;
Therfore the crow shall byte yow.'

9 He toke hur abowte the mydell small,
And layd hur downe vpon the grene;
Twys or thrys he served hur soo with-
all,
He wolde nott stynt yet, as I wene.

10 'But sythe ye haue i-lyen me bye,
Ye wyll wedde me now, as I trowe:'
'I wyll be adusyed, Gyll,' sayd he,
'For now the pye hathe peckyd yow.'

11 'But sythe ye haue i-leyn me by,
And brought my body vnto shame,
Some of your good ye wyll part with
me,
Or elles, be Cryst, ye be to blame.'

12 'I wylbe adusyed,' he sayde;
'þe wynde ys wast þat thow doyst
blowe;
I haue a-noder þat most be payde;
Therfore the pye hathe pecked yow.'

13 'Now sythe ye haue i-leyn me bye,
A lyttle thyng ye wyll tell;
In case that I with chylde be,
What ys your name? Wher doo ye
dwell?'

14 'At Yorke, a[t] London, at Clerken-
well,
At Leycester, Cambryge, at myrye
Brystowe;
Some call me Rychard, Robart, Jacke,
and Wyll;
For now the pye hathe peckyd yow.

15 'But, all medans, be ware be rewe,
And lett no man downe yow throwe;
For and yow doo, ye wyll ytt rewe,
For then þe pye wyll pecke yow.'

16 'Farewell, corteor, ouer the medoo,
Pluke vp your helys, I yow beshrew!
Your trace, wher so euer ye ryde or
goo,
Crystes curse goo wythe yow!

17 'Thoughe a knave hathe by me leyne,
Yet am I noder dede nor slowe;
I trust to recouer my harte agayne,
And Crystes curse goo wythe yow!'

112

THE BAFFLED KNIGHT

Besides the version here printed there are
broadside copies, and others that have been
taken down from recitation. Percy inserted a
version of C (a broadside copy) abridged to
forty-five stanzas, in his Reliques, 1765, III,
238. A similar story occurs in many European
ballads.

A

a. Ravenscroft's Deuteromelia, or, The Second
Part of Musick's Melodie, or Melodious Musicke, etc., E 4, London, 1609. 'The Over Courteous Knight,' Ritson's Ancient Songs, 1790,
p. 159. b. Pills to Purge Melancholy, III, 37,
1719.

1 YONDER comes a courteous knight,
Lustely raking ouer the lay;
He was wel ware of a bonny lasse,
As she came wandring ouer the way.
Then she sang downe a downe, hey
downe derry (bis)

2 'Ioue you speed, fayre lady,' he said,
'Among the leaues that be so greene;
If I were a king, and wore a crowne,
Full soone, fair lady, shouldst thou be
a queen.

3 'Also Ioue saue you, faire lady,
Among the roses that be so red;
If I haue not my will of you,
Full soone, faire lady, shall I be dead.'

4 Then he lookt east, then hee lookt west,
Hee lookt north, so did he south;
He could not finde a priuy place,
For all lay in the diuel's mouth.

5 'If you will carry me, gentle sir,
A mayde vnto my father's hall,
Then you shall haue your will of me,
Vnder purple and vnder paule.'

6 He set her vp vpon a steed,
And him selfe vpon another,
And all the day he rode her by,
As though they had beene sister and
brother.

7 When she came to her father's hall,
It was well walled round about;

She yode in at the wicket-gate,
    And shut the foure-eard foole without.

8 'You had me,' quoth she, 'abroad in the
    field,
    Among the corne, amidst the hay,
Where you might had your will of mee,
    For, in good faith, sir, I neuer said
    nay.

9 'Ye had me also amid the field,
    Among the rushes that were so
    browne,
Where you might had your will of me,
    But you had not the face to lay me
    downe.'

10 He pulled out his nut-browne sword,
    And wipt the rust off with his sleeue,
And said, Ioue's curse come to his heart
    That any woman would beleeue !

11 When you haue your owne true-loue
    A mile or twaine out of the towne,
Spare not for her gay clothing,
    But lay her body flat on the ground.

113

THE GREAT SILKIE OF SULE
SKERRY

" Finns," as they are for the most part called,
denizens of a region below the depths of the
ocean, are able to ascend to the land above by
donning a seal-skin, which then they are wont to
lay off, and, having divested themselves of it,
they " act just like men and women." If this
integument be taken away from them, they
cannot pass through the sea again and return
to their proper abode, and they become subject
to the power of man, like the swan-maidens
and mer-wives of Scandinavian and German
tradition: Grimm's Mythologie, I, 354 f. Female Finns, under these circumstances, have
been fain to accept of human partners.

Proceedings of the Society of Antiquaries
of Scotland, I, 86, 1852. Communicated by
the late Captain F. W. L. Thomas, R. N.;
written down by him from the dictation of a
venerable lady of Snarra Voe, Shetland.

1 AN eartly nourris sits and sings,
    And aye she sings, Ba, lily wean !

Little ken I my bairnis father,
    Far less the land that he staps in.

2 Then ane arose at her bed-fit,
    An a grumly guest I 'm sure was he:
' Here am I, thy bairnis father,
    Although that I be not comelie.

3 ' I am a man, upo the lan,
    An I am a silkie in the sea;
And when I 'm far and far frae lan,
    My dwelling is in Sule Skerrie.'

4 ' It was na weel,' quo the maiden fair,
    ' It was na weel, indeed,' quo she,
' That the Great Silkie of Sule Skerrie
    Suld hae come and aught a bairn to
    me.'

5 Now he has taen a purse of goud,
    And he has pat it upo her knee,
Sayin, Gie to me my little young son,
    An tak thee up thy nourris-fee.

6 An it sall come to pass on a simmer's
    day,
    When the sin shines het on evera
    stane,
That I will tak my little young son,
    An teach him for to swim the faem.

7 An thu sall marry a proud gunner,
    An a proud gunner I 'm sure he 'll be,
An the very first schot that ere he
    schoots,
    He 'll schoot baith my young son and
    me.

114

JOHNIE COCK

The first notice in print of this precious
specimen of the unspoiled traditional ballad is
in Ritson's Scotish Song, 1794, I, xxxvi, note 25.
Before this, 1780, a lady of Carlisle had sent a
copy to Percy (A). Scott, 1802, was the first
to publish the ballad, selecting " the stanzas
of greatest merit " from several copies which
were in his hands.

A

Percy Papers, communicated to Percy by
Miss Fisher, of Carlisle, 1780, No. 5 of MS.

1 Johny he has risen up i the morn,
    Calls for water to wash his hands;
    But little knew he that his bloody hounds
    Were bound in iron bands. bands
    Were bound in iron bands

2 Johny's mother has gotten word o that,
    And care-bed she has taen:
    'O Johny, for my benison,
    I beg you 'l stay at hame;
    For the wine so red, and the well baken
        bread,
    My Johny shall want nane.

3 'There are seven forsters at Pickeram
        Side,
    At Pickeram where they dwell,
    And for a drop of thy heart's bluid
    They wad ride the fords of hell.'

4 Johny he 's gotten word of that,
    And he 's turnd wondrous keen;
    He 's put off the red scarlett,
    And he 's put on the Lincoln green.

5 With a sheaf of arrows by his side,
    And a bent bow in his hand,
    He 's mounted on a prancing steed,
    And he has ridden fast oer the strand.

6 He 's up i Braidhouplee, and down i
        Bradyslee,
    And under a buss o broom,
    And there he found a good dun deer,
    Feeding in a buss of ling.

7 Johny shot, and the dun deer lap,
    And she lap wondrous wide,
    Until they came to the wan water,
    And he stemd her of her pride.

8 He 'as taen out the little pen-knife,
    'T was full three quarters long,
    And he has taen out of that dun deer
    The liver bot and the tongue.

9 They eat of the flesh, and they drank of
        the blood,
    And the blood it was so sweet,
    Which caused Johny and his bloody
        hounds
    To fall in a deep sleep.

10 By then came an old palmer,
    And an ill death may he die !

For he 's away to Pickram Side,
    As fast as he can drie

11 'What news, what news?' says the
        Seven Forsters,
    'What news have ye brought to me?'
    'I have noe news,' the palmer said,
    'But what I saw with my eye.

12 'High up i Bradyslee, low down i Bra-
        disslee,
    And under a buss of scroggs,
    O there I spied a well-wight man,
    Sleeping among his dogs.

13 'His coat it was of light Lincoln,
    And his breeches of the same,
    His shoes of the American leather,
    And gold buckles tying them.'

14 Up bespake the Seven Forsters,
    Up bespake they ane and a':
    O that is Johny o Cockleys Well,
    And near him we will draw.

15 O the first y stroke that they gae him,
    They struck him off by the knee;
    Then up bespake his sister's son:
    'O the next 'll gar him die !'

16 'O some they count ye well-wight
        men,
    But I do count ye nane;
    For you might well ha wakend me,
    And askd gin I wad be taen.

17 'The wildest wolf in aw this wood
    Wad not ha done so by me;
    She 'd ha wet her foot ith wan water,
    And sprinkled it oer my brae,
    And if that wad not ha wakend me,
    She wad ha gone and let me be.

18 'O bows of yew, if ye be true,
    In London, where ye were bought,
    Fingers five, get up belive,
    Manhuid shall fail me nought.'

19 He has killd the Seven Forsters,
    He has killd them all but ane,
    And that wan scarce to Pickeram Side,
    To carry the bode-words hame.

20 'Is there never a boy in a' this wood
    That will tell what I can say;

That will go to Cockleys Well,
Tell my mither to fetch me away?'

21 There was a boy into that wood,
That carried the tidings away,
And many ae was the well-wight man
At the fetching o Johny away.

B

'Johnny Cock,' Pieces of Ancient Poetry
from Unpublished Manuscripts and Scarce
Books, Bristol, [John Fry,] 1814, p. 53.

1 FIFTEEN foresters in the Braid alow,
And they are wondrous fell;
To get a drop of Johnny's heart-bluid,
They would sink a' their souls to hell.

2 Johnny Cock has gotten word of this,
And he is wondrous keen;
He['s] custan off the red scarlet,
And on the Linkum green.

3 And he is ridden oer muir and muss,
And over mountains high,
Till he came to yon wan water,
And there Johnny Cock did lie.

4 They have ridden oer muir and muss,
And over mountains high,
Till they met wi an old palmer,
Was walking along the way.

5 ' What news, what news, old palmer?
What news have you to me?'
'Yonder is one of the proudest wed sons
That ever my eyes did see.'

* * * * *

6 He's taen out a horn from his side,
And he blew both loud and shrill,
Till a' the fifteen foresters
Heard Johnny Cock blaw his horn.

7 They have sworn a bluidy oath,
And they swore all in one,
That there was not a man among them a'
Would blaw such a blast as yon.

8 And they have ridden oer muir and
muss,
And over mountains high,
Till they came to yon wan water,
Where Johnny Cock did lie.

9 They have shotten little Johnny Cock,
A little above the ee:
. . . . . .
'For doing the like to me.

10 ' There's not a wolf in a' the wood
Woud ha done the like to me;
She'd ha dipped her foot in coll water,
And strinkled above my ee,
And if I would [not] have waked for
that,
She'd ha gane and let me be.

11 ' But fingers five, come here, [come here,]
And faint heart fail me nought,
And silver strings, value me sma things,
Till I get all this vengeance rowght!'

12 He ha[s] shot a' the fifteen foresters,
Left never a one but one,
And he broke the ribs a that ane's
side,
And let him take tiding home.

13 ' . . . a bird in a' the wood
Could sing as I could say,
It would go in to my mother's bower,
And bid her kiss me, and take me
away.'

C

'Johnny Cock,' Pieces of Ancient Poetry
from Unpublished Manuscripts and Scarce
Books, Bristol, 1814, p. 51.

1 JOHNNY COCK, in a May morning,
Sought water to wash his hands,
And he is awa to louse his dogs,
That's tied wi iron bans.
That's tied wi iron bans

2 His coat it is of the light Lincum green,
And his breiks are of the same;
His shoes are of the American leather,
Silver buckles tying them.

3 He hunted up, and so did he down,
Till he came to yon bush of scrogs,
And then to yon wan water,
Where he slept among his dogs.

* * * * *

4 Johnny Cock out-shot a' the foresters,
And out-shot a the three:

Out shot a' the foresters,
  Wounded Johnny aboun the bree.

5 ' Woe be to you, foresters,
    And an ill death may you die !
  For there would not a wolf in a' the wood
    Have done the liketo me.

6 ' For 't would ha' put its foot in the coll
    water
  And ha strinkled it on my bree,
  And gin that would not have done,
    Would have gane and lett me be.

7 ' I often took to my mother
    The dandoo and the roe,
  But now I 'l take to my mother
    Much sorrow and much woe.

8 ' I often took to my mother
    The dandoo and the hare,
  But now I 'l take to my mother
    Much sorrow and much care.

D

' Johnie of Cockerslee.' Kinloch's annotated
copy of his Ancient Scottish Ballads, p. 38 bis:
West-Country version.

1 Up Johnie raise in a May morning,
    Calld for water to wash his hands,
  And he has calld for his gude gray
    hunds,
  That lay bund in iron bands.   bands
    That lay bund in iron bands

2 ' Ye 'll busk, ye 'll busk my noble dogs,
    Ye 'll busk and mak them boun,
  For I 'm going to the Braidscaur hill,
    To ding the dun deer doun.'

3 Whan Johnie's mither gat word o that,
    On the very bed she lay,
  Says, Johnie, for my malison,
    I pray ye at hame to stay.

4 Your meat sall be of the very, very best,
    Your drink sall be the same,
  And ye will win your mither's benison,
    Gin ye wad stay at hame.

5 But Johnie has cast aff the black velvet,
    And put on the Lincolm twine,
  And he is on so gude greenwud,
    As fast as he could gang.

6 His mither's counsel he wad na tak,
    He 's aff, and left the toun,
  He 's aff unto the Braidscaur hill,
    To ding the dun deer doun.

7 Johnie lookit east, and Johnie lookit
    west,
  And he lookit aneath the sun,
  And there he spied the dun deer sleep-
    ing,
    Aneath a buss o whun.

8 Johnie shot, and the dun deer lap,
    And he 's scaithed him in the side,
  And atween the water and the wud
    He laid the dun deer's pride.

9 They ate sae meikle o the venison,
    And drank sae meikle o the blude,
  That Johnie and his twa gray hunds
    Fell asleep in yonder wud.

10 By there cam a silly auld man,
    And a silly auld man was he,
  And he 's aff to the proud foresters,
    As fast as he could dree.

11 ' What news, what news, my silly auld
    man ?
    What news ? come tell to me·'
  ' I heard na news, I speird na news
    But what my een did see.

12 ' As I cam in by Braidisbauks,
    And doun amang the whuns,
  The bonniest youngster eer I saw
    Lay sleepin amang his hunds.

13 ' His cheeks war like the roses red,
    His neck was like the snaw;
  His sark was o the holland fine,
    And his jerkin lac'd fu braw.'

14 Up bespak the first forester,
    The first forester of a':
  O this is Johnie o Cockerslee;
    Come draw, lads, we maun draw.

15 Up bespak the niest forester,
    The niest forester of a':
  An this be Johnie o Cockerslee,
    To him we winna draw.

16 The first shot that they did shoot,
    They woundit him on the bree;

Up bespak the uncle's son,
   The niest will gar him die.'

17 The second shot that eer they shot,
   It scaithd him near the heart;
'I only wauken,' Johnie cried,
   'Whan first I find the smart.

18 'Stand stout, stand stout, my noble dogs,
   Stand stout, and dinna flee;
Stand fast, stand fast, my gude gray
   hunds,
   And we will gar them die.'

19 He has killed six o the proud foresters,
   And wounded the seventh sair:
He laid his leg out owre his steed,
   Says, I will kill na mair.

20 'Oh wae befa thee, silly auld man,
   An ill death may thee dee!
Upon thy head be a' this blude,
   For mine, I ween, is free.'

K

Finlay's Scottish Ballads, I, xxxi.

'THERE's no a bird in a' this foreste
Will do as meikle for me
As dip its wing in the wan water
An straik it on my ee-bree.'

115

ROBYN AND GANDELEYN

Printed by Ritson, Ancient Songs, 1790, p. 48, and by Thomas Wright, Songs and Carols (selected from the Sloane MS.), No. x, London, 1836, and again in his edition of the whole MS. for the Warton Club, 1856, p. 42. The manuscript is put at about 1450.

Wright remarks on the similarity of the name Gandelyn to Gamelyn in the tale ascribed to the Cook in some manuscripts of the Canterbury Tales, and on the resemblance of the tale of Gamelyn to Robin Hood story. But he could hardly have wished to give the impression that Robin in this ballad is Robin Hood. This he no more is than John in the ballad of Johnie Cock is Little John; though Gandelyn is as true to his master as Little John is.

Sloane MS., 2593, fol. 14 b, British Museum.

1 I HERDE a carpyng of a clerk,
   Al at ȝone wodes ende,
Of gode Robyn and Gandeleyn;
   Was þer non oþer þynge.
Robynn lyth in grene wode bowndyn.

2 Stronge theuys wern þo chylderin non,
   But bowmen gode and hende;
He wentyn to wode to getyn hem fleych
   If God wold it hem sende.

3 Al day wentyn þo chylderin too,
   And fleych fowndyn he non,
Til it were a-geyn euyn;
   þe chylderin wold gon hom.

4 Half an honderid of fat falyf der
   He comyn a-ȝon,
And alle he wern fayr and fat i-now,
   But markyd was þer non:
'Be dere God,' seyde gode Robyn,
   'Here of we xul haue on.'

5 Robyn bent his joly bowe,
   þer in he set a flo;
þe fattest der of alle
   þe herte he clef a to.

6 He hadde not þe der i-flawe,
   Ne half out of þe hyde,
There cam a schrewde arwe out of þe west,
   þat felde Robertes pryde.

7 Gandeleyn lokyd hym est and west,
   Be euery syde:
'Hoo hat myn mayster slayin?
   Ho hat don þis dede?
Xal I neuer out of grene wode go
   Til I se [his] sydis blede.'

8 Gandeleyn lokyd hym est and lokyd
   west,
   And sowt vnder þe sunne;
He saw a lytil boy
   He clepyn Wrennok of Donne.

9 A good bowe in his hond,
   A brod arwe þer ine,
And fowre and twenti goode arwys,
   Trusyd in a þrumme:
'Be war þe, war þe, Gandeleyn,
   Her-of þu xalt han summe.

10 'Be war þe, war þe, Gandeleyn.
   Her of þu gyst plente:

'Euer on for an oper,' seyde Gandeleyn;
'Mysaunter haue he xal fle.

11 'Qwer-at xal our marke be?'
Seyde Gandeleyn:
'Eueryche at operis herte,'
Seyde Wrennok ageyn.

12 'Ho xal ʒeue þe ferste schote?'
Seyde Gandeleyn:
'And I xul ʒeue þe on be-forn,'
Seyde Wrennok ageyn.

13 Wrennok schette a ful good schote,
And he schet not to hye;
þrow þe sanchoþis of his bryk;
It towchyd neyþer thye.

14 'Now hast þu ʒouyn me on be-forn,'
Al þus to Wrennok seyde he,
'And þrow þe myʒt of our lady
A bettere I xal ʒeue þe.'

15 Gandeleyn bent his goode bowe,
And set þer in a flo;
He schet þrow his grene certyl,
His herte he clef on too.

16 'Now xalt þu neuer ʒelpe, Wrennok,
At ale ne at wyn,
þat þu hast slawe goode Robyn,
And his knaue Gandeleyn.

17 'Now xalt þu neuer ʒelpe, Wrennok,
At wyn ne at ale,
þat þu hast slawe goode Robyn,
And Gandeleyn his knaue.'

Robyn lyʒth in grene wode bowndyn

116

ADAM BELL, CLIM OF THE CLOUGH, AND WILLIAM OF CLOUDESLY

'Adam Bell' is licensed to John Kynge in the Stationers' Registers, 19 July, 1557-9 July, 1558. Again, among copies which were Sampson Awdeley's, to John Charlewood, 15 January, 1582; and, among copies which were John Charlwoode's, to James Robertes, 31 May, 1594. Seven reprints of the seventeenth century, later than d, are noted in Mr. W. C. Hazlitt's Handbook, p. 35.

The rescue of Robin Hood by Little John and Much in No. 119, sts. 61-82, has a general resemblance to the rescue of Cloudesly by Adam and Clim in this ballad, sts. 52 ff. The rescue of Will Stutly (No. 141) has also some slight similarity, sts. 26-33.

The shooting of an apple from a boy's head (sts. 151-162) is, as is well known, a trait in several German and Norse traditions, and these particular feats, as well as everything resembling them, have been a subject of eager discussion in connection with the apocryphal history of William Tell. The story is not remarkably widespread. The seven versions agree in two points: the shot is compulsory; the archer meditates revenge in case he harms the person on whose head the mark is placed. These features are wanting in the English ballad. William of Cloudesly offers of his own free motion to shoot an apple from his son's head, and this after the king had declared him the best archer he had ever seen, for splitting a hazel-rod at twenty score paces; so that the act was done purely for glory. To be sure, the king threatens him with death if he does not achieve what he has undertaken, as death is also threatened in four of the seven German-Scandinavian stories for refusal to try the shot or for missing; but the threats in sts. 154 f. of the English ballad are a revival of the vow in sts. 119 f. The shooting of the apple from the boy's head, isolated from any particular connection, is perhaps all of the German-Scandinavian story that was known to the English ballad-maker, and all minor resemblances may well be fortuitous.

If the shooting of an apple by somebody from somebody's head is to be regarded as the kernel of the story, its area may then be considerably extended. For various remoter parallels of this kind, see Child, III, 19 ff., where a full discussion will be found. Professor Child is opposed to the mythical explanation and takes particularly strong ground against making a sun-god out of William of Cloudesly. He sums up in the following sentence: "A story long current in Europe, a mythical story if you please, could certainly be taken up by an English ballad-maker without prejudice to the substantial and simply romantic character of his hero."

a. Two fragments, stanzas 113^4-128^2, 161^2-170, of an edition by John Byddell, London, 1536: Library of the University of Cambridge.
b. A fragment, stanzas 53^3-111^3, by a printer not identified: formerly in the possession of J. Payne Collier.
c. 'Adambel, Clym of the cloughe, and Wyllyam of cloudesle,' William Copeland, London [1548-68]: British Museum, C. 21. c. 64.

d. 'Adam Bell, Clim of the Clough, and William of Cloudesle,' James Roberts, London, 1605 : Bodleian Library, C. 39, Art. Selden.

e. Another edition with the same title-page : Bodleian Library, Malone, 299.

f. 'Adam Bell, Clime of the Cloug[he], and William off Cloudeslee,' Percy MS., p. 390: British Museum.   Hales and Furnivall, III, 76.

c. 1   MERY it was in grene forest,
  Amonge the leues grene,
  Where that men walke both east and west,
  Wyth bowes and arrowes kene,

2   To ryse the dere out of theyr denne;
  Suche sightes as hath ofte bene sene,
  As by th[r]e yemen of the north countrey,
  By them it is as I meane.

3   The one of them hight Adam Bel,
  The other Clym of the Clough,
  The thyrd was William of Cloudesly,
  An archer good ynough.

4   They were outlawed for venyson,
  These thre yemen euerechone;
  They swore them brethen vpon a day,
  To Englysshe-wood for to gone.

5   Now lith and lysten, gentylmen,
  And that of myrthes loueth to here:
  Two of them were single men,
  The third had a wedded fere.

6   Wyllyam was the wedded man,
  Muche more then was hys care:
  He sayde to hys brethen vpon a day,
  To Carelel he would fare,

7   For to speke with fayre Alse hys wife,
  And with hys chyldren thre:
  'By my trouth,' sayde Adam Bel,
  'Not by the counsell of me.

8   'For if ye go to Caerlel, brother,
  And from thys wylde wode wende,
  If the justice mai you take,
  Your lyfe were at an ende.'

9   'If that I come not to morowe, brother,
  By pryme to you agayne,
  Truste not els but that I am take,
  Or else that I am slayne.'

10   He toke hys leaue of hys brethen two,
  And to Carlel he is gone;
  There he knocked at hys owne wyndowe,
  Shortlye and anone.

11   'Wher be you, fayre Alyce, my wyfe,
  And my chyldren three ?
  Lyghtly let in thyne husbande,
  Wyllyam of Cloudesle.'

12   'Alas !' then sayde fayre Alyce,
  And syghed wonderous sore,
  'Thys place hath ben besette for you
  Thys halfe yere and more.'

13   'Now am I here,' sayde Cloudesle,
  'I woulde that I in were;
  Now feche vs meate and drynke ynoughe,
  And let vs make good chere.'

14   She feched him meat and drynke plenty,
  Lyke a true wedded wyfe,
  And pleased hym with that she had,
  Whome she loued as her lyfe.

15   There lay an old wyfe in that place,
  A lytle besyde the fyre,
  Whych Wyllyam had found, of cherytye,
  More then seuen yere.

16   Up she rose, and walked full styll,
  Euel mote she spede therefoore !
  For she had not set no fote on ground
  In seuen yere before.

17   She went vnto the justice hall,
  As fast as she could hye:
  'Thys nyght is come vn to thys town
  Wyllyam of Cloudesle.'

18   Thereof the iustice was full fayne,
  And so was the shirife also:
  'Thou shalt not trauaile hether, dame,
   for nought;
  Thy meed thou shalt haue or thou go.'

19   They gaue to her a ryght good goune,
  Of scarlat it was, as I heard say[n]e;
  She toke the gyft, and home she wente,
  And couched her doune agayne.

20   They rysed the towne of mery Carel,
  In all the hast that they can,

And came thronging to Wyllyames
  house,
  As fast [as] they might gone.

21 Theyr they besette that good yeman,
  Round about on euery syde;
  Wyllyam hearde great noyse of folkes,
  That heytherward they hyed.

22 Alyce opened a shot-wyndow,
  And loked all about;
  She was ware of the justice and the
    shrife bothe,
  Wyth a full great route.

23 'Alas! treason,' cryed Alyce,
  'Euer wo may thou be!
  Go into my chambre, my husband,' she
    sayd,
  'Swete Wyllyam of Cloudesle.'

24 He toke hys sweard and hys bucler,
  Hys bow and hy[s] chyldren thre,
  And wente into hys strongest chamber,
  Where he thought surest to be.

25 Fayre Alice folowed him as a louer
    true,
  With a pollaxe in her hande:
  'He shalbe deade that here cometh in
  Thys dore, whyle I may stand.'

26 Cloudesle bent a wel good bowe,
  That was of trusty tre,
  He smot the justise on the brest,
  That hys arrowe brest in thre.

27 'God's curse on his hartt,' saide William,
  'Thys day thy cote dyd on;
  If it had ben no better then myne,
  It had gone nere thy bone.'

28 'Yelde the, Cloudesle,' sayd the justise,
  'And thy bowe and thy arrowes the
    fro:'
  'Gods curse on hys hart,' sayde fair
    Al[i]ce,
  'That my husband councelleth so.'

29 'Set fyre on the house,' saide the
    sherife,
  'Syth it wyll no better be,
  And brenne we therin William,' he
    saide,
  'Hys wyfe and chyldren thre.'

30 They fyred the house in many a place,
  The fyre flew vpon hye;
  'Alas!' than cryed fayr Alice,
  'I se we shall here dy.'

31 William openyd hys backe wyndow,
  That was in hys chambre on hye,
  And wyth shetes let hys wyfe downe,
  And hys chyldren thre.

32 'Haue here my treasure,' sayde Wil-
    liam,
  'My wyfe and my chyldren thre;
  For Christes loue do them no harme,
  But wreke you all on me.'

33 Wyllyam shot so wonderous well,
  Tyll hys arrowes were all go,
  And the fyre so fast vpon hym fell,
  That hys bo[w]stryng brent in two.

34 The spercles brent and fell hym on,
  Good Wyllyam of Cloudesle;
  But than was he a wofull man, and
    sayde,
  Thys is a cowardes death to me.

35 'Leuer I had,' sayde Wyllyam,
  'With my sworde in the route to
    renne,
  Then here among myne ennemyes wode
  Thus cruelly to bren.'

36 He toke hys sweard and hys buckler,
  And among them all he ran;
  Where the people were most in prece,
  He smot downe many a man.

37 There myght no man stand hys stroke,
  So fersly on them he ran;
  Then they threw wyndowes and dores on
    him,
  And so toke that good yeman.

38 There they hym bounde both hand and
    fote,
  And in depe dongeon hym cast;
  'Now, Cloudesle,' sayde the hye justice,
  'Thou shalt be hanged in hast.'

39 'One vow shal I make,' sayde the
    sherife,
  'A payre of new galowes shall I for
  the make,

And al the gates of Caerlel shalbe
 shutte,
 There shall no man come in therat.

40 'Then shall not helpe Clim of the
 Cloughe,
 Nor yet Adam Bell,
 Though they came with a thousand
 mo,
 Nor all the deuels in hell.'

41 Early in the mornyng the justice vprose,
 To the gates fast gan he gon,
 And commaunded to be shut full cloce
 Lightile euerychone.

42 Then went he to the market-place,
 As fast as he coulde hye;
 A payre of new gallous there dyd he vp
 set,
 Besyde the pyllory.

43 A lytle boy stod them amonge,
 And asked what meaned that gallow-
 tre;
 They sayde, To hange a good yeaman,
 Called Wyllyam of Cloudesle.

44 That lytle boye was the towne swyne-
 heard,
 And kept fayre Alyce swyne;
 Full oft he had sene Cloudesle in the
 wodde,
 And geuen hym there to dyne.

45 He went out of a creues in the wall,
 And lightly to the woode dyd gone ;
 There met he with these wyght yonge
 men,
 Shortly and anone.

46 'Alas !' then sayde that lytle boye,
 'Ye tary here all to longe;
 Cloudesle is taken and dampned to
 death,
 All readye for to honge.'

47 'Alas !' then sayde good Adam Bell,
 'That euer we see thys daye !
 He myght her with vs haue dwelled,
 So ofte as we dyd him praye.

48 'He myght haue taryed in grene foreste,
 Under the shadowes sheene,

And haue kepte both hym and vs in
 reaste,
 Out of trouble and teene.'

49 Adam bent a ryght good bow,
 A great hart sone had he slayne;
 'Take that, chylde,' he sayde, 'to thy
 dynner,
 And bryng me myne arrowe agayne.'

50 'Now go we hence,' sayed these wight
 yong men,
 'Tary we no lenger here;
 We shall hym borowe, by Gods grace.
 Though we bye it full dere.'

51 To Caerlel went these good yemen,
 In a mery mornyng of Maye:
 Her is a fyt of Cloudesli,
 And another is for to saye.

52 And when they came to mery Caerlell,
 In a fayre mornyng-tyde,
 They founde the gates shut them vntyll,
 Round about on euery syde.

53 'Alas !' than sayd good Adam Bell,
 'That euer we were made men !
b. These gates be shyt so wonderly well,
 That we may not come here in.'

54 Than spake Clymme of the Cloughe:
 With a wyle we wyll vs in brynge;
 Let vs say we be messengers,
 Streyght comen from oure kynge.

55 Adam sayd, I haue a lettre wryten wele,
 Now let vs wysely werke;
 We wyll say we haue the kynges seale,
 I holde the porter no clerke.

56 Than Adam Bell bete on the gate,
 With strokës greate and stronge;
 The porter herde suche a noyse therate,
 And to the gate faste he thronge.

57 'Who is there nowe,' sayd the porter,
 'That maketh all this knockynge ?'
 'We be two messengers,' sayd Clymme
 of the Clo[ughe],
 'Be comen streyght frome oure
 kynge.'

58 'We haue a lettre,' sayd Adam Bell,
 'To the justyce we must it brynge;

Let vs in, oure message to do,
  That we were agayne to our kynge.'

59 'Here cometh no man in,' sayd the
    porter,
  'By hym that dyed on a tre,
Tyll a false thefe be hanged,
  Called Wyllyam of Clowdysle.'

60 Than spake that good [yeman Clym of
    the Cloughe,
  And swore by Mary fre,
If that we stande long wythout,
  Lyke a thefe hanged shalt thou be.]

61 [Lo here] we haue got the kynges seale;
  [What! l]ordane, arte thou wode ?
[The p]orter had wende it had been so,
  [And l]yghtly dyd of his hode.

62 '[Welco]me be my lordes seale,' sayd he,
  '[For] that shall ye come in:'
[He] opened the gate ryght shortly,
  [An] euyll openynge for hym !

63 '[N]owe we are in,' sayd Adam Bell,
  '[T]herof we are full fayne;
[But] Cryst knoweth that herowed hell,
  [H]ow we shall come oute agayne.'

64 '[Had] we the keys,' sayd Clym of the
    Clowgh,
  'Ryght well than sholde we spede;
[Than] myght we come out well ynough,
  [Whan] we se tyme and nede.'

65 [They] called the porter to a councell,
  [And] wronge hys necke in two,
[And] kest hym in a depe dongeon,
  [And] toke the keys hym fro.

66 '[N]ow am I porter,' sayd Adam Bell;
  '[Se], broder, the keys haue we here;
[The] worste porter to mery Carlell
  [That ye] had this hondreth yere.

67 '[Now] wyll we oure bowës bende,
  [Into the t]owne wyll we go,
[For to delyuer our dere] broder,
  [Where he lyeth in care and wo.'

68 Then they bent theyr good yew bowes,
  And loked theyr stringes were round;]
The market-place of mery Carlyll,
  They beset in that stounde.

69 And as they loked them besyde,
  A payre of newe galowes there they
    se,
And the iustyce, with a quest of swerers,
  That had iuged Clowdysle there
    hanged to be.

70 And Clowdysle hymselfe lay redy in a
    carte,
  Fast bounde bothe fote and hande,
And a strong rope aboute his necke,
  All redy for to be hangde.

71 The iustyce called to hym a ladde;
  Clowdysles clothes sholde he haue,
To take the mesure of that good yoman,
  And therafter to make his graue.

72 'I haue sene as greate a merueyll,' sayd
    Clowd[esle],
  'As bytwene this and pryme,
He that maketh thys graue for me,
  Hymselfe may lye therin.'

73 'Thou spekest proudely,' sayd the ius-
    tyce;
  'I shall hange the with my hande:'
Full well that herde his bretheren two,
  There styll as they dyd stande.

74 Than Clowdysle cast hys eyen asyde,
  And sawe hys bretheren stande,
At a corner of the market-place,
  With theyr good bowes bent in theyr
    hand,
Redy the iustyce for to chase.

75 'I se good comforte,' sayd Clowdysle,
  'Yet hope I well to fare;
If I myght haue my handes at wyll,
  [Ryght l]ytell wolde I care.'

76 [Than b]espake good Adam Bell,
  [To Clym]me of the Clowgh so fre;
[Broder], se ye marke the iustyce well;
  [Lo yon]der ye may him se.

77 [And at] the sheryf shote I wyll,
  [Stron]gly with an arowe kene;
[A better] shotte in mery Carlyll,
  [Thys se]uen yere was not sene.

78 [They lo]used theyr arowes bothe at
    ones,
  [Of no] man had they drede;

[The one] hyt the iustyce, the other the
    sheryf,
[That b]othe theyr sydes gan blede.

79 [All men] voyded, that them stode nye,
    [Whan] the iustyce fell to the
    grounde,
[And the] sheryf fell nyghe hym by;
[Eyther] had his dethës wounde.

80 [All the c]ytezeyns fast gan fle,
    [They du]rste no lenger abyde;
[There ly]ghtly they loused Clowdysle,
    [Where he] with ropes lay tyde.

81 [Wyllyam] sterte to an offycer of the
    towne,
[Hys axe] out his hande he wronge;
[On eche] syde he smote them downe,
    [Hym tho]ught he had taryed to
    longe.

82 [Wyllyam] sayd to his bretheren two,
    [Thys daye] let vs togyder lyue and
    deye;
[If euer you] haue nede as I haue
    nowe,
[The same] shall ye fynde by me.

83 [They] shyt so well in that tyde,
    For theyr strynges were of sylke full
    sure,
That they kepte the stretes on euery
    syde;
That batayll dyd longe endure.

84 They fought togyder as bretheren true,
    Lyke hardy men and bolde;
Many a man to the grounde they threwe,
    And made many an hertë colde.

85 But whan theyr arowes were all gone,
    Men presyd on them full fast;
They drewe theyr swerdës than anone,
    And theyr bowës from them caste.

86 They wente lyghtly on theyr waye,
    With swerdes and buckelers rounde;
By that it was the myddes of the daye,
    They had made many a wounde.

87 There was many an oute-horne in Carlyll
    blowen,
And the belles backwarde dyd they
    rynge;

Many a woman sayd alas,
    And many theyr handes dyd wrynge.

88 The mayre of Carlyll forth come was,
    And with hym a full grete route;
These thre yomen dredde hym full sore,
    For theyr lyuës stode in doubte.

89 The mayre came armed, a full greate
    pace,
With a polaxe in his hande;
Many a stronge man with hym was,
    There in that stoure to stande.

90 The mayre smote at Clowdysle with his
    byll,
His buckeler he brast in two;
Full many a yoman with grete yll,
    '[Al]as, treason!' they cryed for
    wo.
'[Ke]pe we the gates fast,' they bad,
    '[T]hat these traytours theroute not
    go.'

91 But all for nought was that they
    wrought,
For so fast they downe were layde
Tyll they all thre, that so manfully
    fought,
Were goten without at a brayde.

92 'Haue here your keys,' sayd Adam Bell,
    'Myne offyce I here forsake;
Yf ye do by my councell,
    A newë porter ye make.'

93 He threwe the keys there at theyr
    hedes,
And bad them evyll to thryue,
And all that letteth ony good yoman
    To come and comforte his wyue.

94 Thus be these good yomen gone to the
    wode,
As lyght as lefe on lynde;
They laughe and be mery in theyr mode,
    Theyr enemyes were farre behynde.

95 Whan they came to Inglyswode,
    Under theyr trysty-tre,
There they founde bowës full gode,
    And arowës greate plentë.

96 'So helpe me God,' sayd Adam Bell,
    And Clymme of the Clowgh so fre.

'I wolde we were nowe in mery Carlell,
[Be]fore that fayre meynë.'

97 They set them downe and made good
    chere,
    And eate au[d dr]anke full well:
Here is a fytte [of] these wyght yonge-
    men,
    And another I shall you tell.

98 As they sat in Inglyswode,
    Under theyr trysty-tre,
Them thought they herde a woman
    [wepe],
    But her they myght not se.

99 Sore syghed there fayre Alyce, and
    sayd,
    Alas that euer I se this daye !
For now is my dere husbonde slayne,
    Alas and welawaye !

100 Myght I haue spoken wyth hys dere
    breth[eren],
    With eyther of them twayne,
[To shew to them what him befell,]
    My herte were out of payne.

101 Clowdysle walked a lytell besyde,
    And loked vnder the grene wodde
    lynde;
He was ware of his wyfe and his chyl-
    dre[n thre],
    Full wo in herte and mynde.

102 'Welcome, wyfe,' than sayd Wyllyam,
    'Unto this trysty-tre;
I had wende yesterdaye, by swete
    Sai[nt John],
    Thou sholde me neuer haue se.'

103 'Now wele is me,' she sayd, 'that [ye
    be here],
    My herte is out of wo:'
'Dame,' he sayd, 'be mery and glad,
    And thanke my bretheren two.'

104 'Here of to speke,' sayd Ad[am]
    Bell,
    'I-wys it [is no bote];
The me[at that we must supp withall,
    It runneth yet fast on fote.'

105 Then went they down into a launde,
    These noble archares all thre,

Eche of the]m slewe a harte of grece,
    [The best t]hey coude there se.

106 '[Haue here the] best, Alyce my wyfe,'
    [Sayde Wyllya]m of Clowdysle,
'[By cause ye so] boldely stode me by
    [Whan I w]as slayne full nye.'

107 [Than they] wente to theyr souper,
    [Wyth suc]he mete as they had,
[And than]ked God of theyr fortune;
    [They we]re bothe mery and glad.

108 [And whan] they had souped well,
    [Certayne] withouten leace,
[Clowdysle] sayde, We wyll to oure
    kynge,
    [To get v]s a chartre of peace.

109 [Alyce shal] be at soiournynge,
    [In a nunry] here besyde;
[My tow sonn]es shall with her go,
    [And ther the]y shall abyde.

110 [Myne eldest so]ne shall go with me,
    [For hym haue I] no care,
[And he shall breng] you worde agayne
    [How that we do fare.

111 Thus be these wig]ht men to London
    gone,
    [As fast as they ma]ye hye,
    [Tyll they came to the kynges] palays,
c.   There they woulde nedës be.

112 And whan they came to the kyngës
    courte,
    Unto the pallace gate,
Of no man wold they aske leue,
    But boldly went in therat.

113 They preced prestly into the hall,
    Of no man had they dreade;
The porter came after and dyd them
    call,
a.   And with them began to [chyde.]

114 The vssher sayd, Yemen, what wolde
    ye haue ?
    I praye you tell me;
Ye myght thus make offycers shent:
    Good syrs, of whens be ye ?

115 'Syr, we be outlawes of the forest,
    Certayne withouten leace,

And hyther we be come to our kynge,
    To get vs a charter of peace.'

116 And whan they came before our kynge,
    As it was the lawe of the lande,
    They kneled downe without lettynge,
    And eche helde vp his hande.

117 They sayd, Lorde, we beseche you
        here,
    That ye wyll graunte vs grace,
    For we haue slayne your fatte falowe
        dere,
    In many a sondry place.

118 'What is your names?' than sayd our
        kynge,
    'Anone that you tell me:'
    They sayd, Adam Bell, Clym of the
        Clough,
    And Wylliam of Clowdesle.

119 'Be ye those theues,' than sayd our
        kynge,
    'That men haue tolde of to me?
    Here to God I make a vowe,
    Ye shall be hanged all thre.

120 'Ye shall be dead without mercy,
    As I am kynge of this lande:'
c.   He commanded his officers euerichone
    Fast on them to lay hand.

121 There they toke these good yemen,
    And arested them all thre:
    'So may I thryue,' sayd Adam Bell,
    'Thys game lyketh not me.

a. 122 'But, good lorde, we beseche you
        nowe,
    That ye wyll graunte vs grace,
    In so moche as we be to you com-
        men;
    Or elles that we may fro you passe,

123 'With suche weapons as we haue
        here,
    Tyll we be out of your place;
    And yf we lyue this hondred yere,
    We wyll aske you no grace.'

124 'Ye speke proudly,' sayd the kynge,
    'Ye shall be hanged all thre:'
    'That were great pity,' sayd the quene,
    'If any grace myght be.

125 'My lorde, whan I came fyrst in to
        this lande,
    To be your wedded wyfe,
    The fyrst bone that I wolde aske,
    Ye wolde graunte me belyfe.

126 'And I asked you neuer none tyll nowe,
    Therfore, good lorde, graunte it me:'
    'Nowe aske it, madame,' sayd the
        kynge,
    'And graunted shall it be.'

127 'Than, good lorde, I you beseche,
    The yemen graunte you me:'
    'Madame, ye myght haue asked a bone
    That sholde haue ben worthe them
        thre.

128 'Ye myght haue asked towres and
        towne[s],
    Parkes and forestes plentie:'
c.   'None so pleasaunt to mi pay,' she
        said,
    'Nor none so lefe to me.'

129 'Madame, sith it is your desyre,
    Your askyng graunted shalbe;
    But I had leuer haue geuen you
    Good market-townës thre.'

130 The quene was a glad woman,
    And sayd, Lord, gramarcy;
    I dare vndertake for them
    That true men shall they be.

131 But, good lord, speke som mery word,
    That comfort they may se:
    'I graunt you grace,' then said our king,
    'Wasshe, felos, and to meate go ye.'

132 They had not setten but a whyle,
    Certayne without lesynge,
    There came messengers out of the
        north,
    With letters to our kyng.

133 And whan the came before the kynge,
    The kneled downe vpon theyr kne,
    And sayd, Lord, your offycers grete
        you wel,
    Of Caerlel in the north cuntre.

134 'How fare[th] my justice,' sayd the
        kyng,
    'And my sherife also?'

'Syr, they be slayne, without leasynge,
And many an officer mo.'

135 'Who hath them slayne?' sayd the kyng,
'Anone thou tell me:'
'Adam Bel, and Clime of the Clough,
And Wyllyam of Cloudesle.'

136 'Alas for rewth!' then sayd our kynge,
'My hart is wonderous sore;
I had leuer [th]an a thousand pounde
I had knowne of thys before.

137 'For I haue y-graunted them grace,
And that forthynketh me;
But had I knowne all thys before,
They had ben hanged all thre.'

138 The kyng opened the letter anone,
Hym selfe he red it tho,
And founde how these thre outlawes had slaine
Thre hundred men and mo.

139 Fyrst the justice and the sheryfe,
And the mayre of Caerlel towne;
Of all the constables and catchipolles
Alyue were left not one.

140 The baylyes and the bedyls both,
And the sergeauntes of the law,
And forty fosters of the fe
These outlawes had y-slaw;

141 And broken his parks, and slaine his dere;
Ouer all they chose the best;
So perelous outlawes as they were
Walked not by easte nor west.

142 When the kynge this letter had red,
In hys harte he syghed sore;
'Take vp the table,' anone he bad,
'For I may eate no more.'

143 The kyng called hys best archars,
To the buttes with hym to go;
'I wyll se these felowes shote,' he sayd,
'That in the north haue wrought this wo.'

144 The kynges bowmen buske them blyue,
And the quenes archers also,

So dyd these thre wyght yemen,
Wyth them they thought to go.

145 There twyse or thryse they shote about,
For to assay theyr hande;
There was no shote these thre yemen shot
That any prycke might them stand.

146 Then spake Wyllyam of Cloudesle;
By God that for me dyed,
I hold hym neuer no good archar
That shuteth at buttes so wyde.

147 'Wherat?' then sayd our kyng,
'I pray thee tell me:'
'At suche a but, syr,' he sayd,
'As men vse in my countree.'

148 Wyllyam wente into a fyeld,
And his to brothren with him;
There they set vp to hasell roddes,
Twenty score paces betwene.

149 'I hold him an archar,' said Cloudesle,
'That yonder wande cleueth in two:'
'Here is none suche,' sayd the kyng,
'Nor none that can so do.'

150 'I shall assaye, syr,' sayd Cloudesle,
'Or that I farther go:'
Cloudesle, with a bearyng arow,
Claue the wand in to.

151 'Thou art the best archer,' then said the king,
'Forsothe that euer I se:'
And yet for your loue,' sayd Wylliam,
'I wyll do more maystry.

152 'I haue a sonne is seuen yere olde;
He is to me full deare;
I wyll hym tye to a stake,
All shall se that be here;

153 'And lay an apple vpon hys head,
And go syxe score paces hym fro,
And I my selfe, with a brode arow,
Shall cleue the apple in two.'

154 'Now hast the,' then sayd the kyng;
'By him that dyed on a tre,
But yf thou do not as thou hest sayde,
Hanged shalt thou be.

155 'And thou touche his head or gowne,
    In syght that men may se,
By all the sayntes that be in heaven,
    I shall hange you all thre.'

156 'That I haue promised,' said William,
    'I wyl it neuer forsake;'
And there euen before the kynge,
    In the earth he droue a stake;

157 And bound therto his eldest sonne,
    And bad hym stande styll therat,
And turned the childes face fro him,
    Because he shuld not sterte.

158 An apple vpon his head he set,
    And then his bowe he bent;
Syxe score paces they were outmet,
    And thether Cloudesle went.

159 There he drew out a fayr brode arrowe;
    Hys bowe was great and louge;
He set that arrowe in his bowe,
    That was both styffe and stronge.

160 He prayed the people that was there
    That they would styll stande;
'For he that shooteth for such a wager,
    Behoueth a stedfast hand.'

161 Muche people prayed for Cloudesle,
a.   That hys lyfe saued myght be,
And whan he made hym redy to shote,
    There was many a wepynge eye.

162 Thus Clowdesle clefte the apple in two,
    That many a man it se;
'Ouer goddes forbode,' sayd the kynge,
    'That thou sholdest shote at me!

163 'I gyue the .xviii. pens a daye,
    And my bowe shalte thou bere,
And ouer all the north countree
    I make the chefe rydere.'

164 'And I gyue the .xii. pens a day,' sayd the que[ne],
    'By God and by my faye;
Come fetche thy payment whan thou wylt,
    No man shall say the naye.

165 'Wyllyam, I make the gentylman
    Of clothynge and of fee,
And thy two brethren yemen of my chambr[e],
    For they are so semely to se.

166 'Your sone, for he is tendre of age,
    Of my wyne-seller shall he be,
And whan he commeth to mannës state,
    Better auaunced shall he be.

167 'And, Wylliam, brynge me your wyfe,'
    sayd th[e quene];
    'Me longeth sore here to se;
She shall be my chefe gentylwoman,
    And gouerne my nursery.'

168 The yemen thanked them full courteysly,
    And sayd, To Rome streyght wyll we wende,
[Of all the synnes that we haue done
    To be assoyled of his hand.

169 So forth]e be gone these good yemen,
    [As fast a]s they myght hye,
[And aft]er came and dwelled with the kynge,
    [And dye]d good men all thre.

170 [Thus e]ndeth the lyues of these good yemen,
    [God sen]de them eternall blysse,
[And all] that with hande-bowe shoteth,
    [That of] heuen they may neuer mysse!

117

A GEST OF ROBYN HODE

The best qualified judges are not agreed as to the typographical origin of a. The date of b may be anywhere from 1492 to 1534. Copland's edition was not earlier than 1548. The dates of the other texts are uncertain. a, b, f, g, are deficient at 7[1], 339[1], and misprinted at 49, 50, repeating, it may be, the faults of a prior impression. a appears, by internal evidence, to be an older text than b. Some obsolete words of the earlier copies have been modernized in f, g, and deficient lines have been supplied. A considerable number of Middle-English forms remain after those successive renovations of reciters and printers which are presumable in such cases. The Gest may have been compiled at a time when such forms had gone out of use, and these may be

relics of the ballads from which this little epic
was made up; or the whole poem may have
been put together as early as 1400, or before.
There are no firm grounds on which to base an
opinion.

No notice of Robin Hood has been recovered
earlier than that which was long ago pointed
out by Percy as occurring in Piers Plowman,
and this, according to Professor Skeat, cannot
be older than about 1377. Sloth, in that poem,
says in his shrift that he knows "rymes of
Robyn Hood and Randolf, erle of Chestre,"
though but imperfectly acquainted with his
paternoster. Thomas Robinhood is one of six
witnesses to a grant in 1380 or 1381 (Historical
MSS. Commission, Fifth Report, Appendix,
p. 511). References to Robin Hood are not
infrequent in the following century.

Thus it is evident that Robin Hood ballads
were popular for a century or more before the
time when the Gest was printed. Their popularity was fully established at the beginning
of this period, and unquestionably extended
back to a much earlier day. Of these ballads,
there have come down to us in a comparatively
ancient form the following: those from which
the Gest (printed, perhaps, before 1500) was
composed, being at least four, Robin Hood, the
Knight and the Monk, Robin Hood, Little
John and the Sheriff, Robin Hood and the
King, and Robin Hood's death (a fragment);
Robin Hood and the Monk (No. 119), more
properly Robin Hood rescued by Little John,
MS. of about 1450, but not for that older than
the ballads of the Gest; Robin Hood and Guy
of Gisborne (No. 118), Percy MS. ca. 1650;
Robin Hood's Death (No. 120), Percy MS. and
late garlands; Robin Hood and the Potter
(No. 121), MS. of about 1500, later perhaps than
any of the group. Besides these there are thirty-
two ballads (Nos. 122–153). About half a dozen
of these thirty-two have in them something of
the old popular quality; as many more not
the least trace of it. Fully a dozen are variations, sometimes wearisome, sometimes sickening, upon the theme 'Robin Hood met with
his match.' A considerable part of the Robin
Hood poetry looks like char-work done for the
petty press, and should be judged as such. The
earliest of these ballads, on the other hand, are
among the best of all ballads, and perhaps none
in English please so many and please so long.

Robin Hood is absolutely a creation of the
ballad-muse. The earliest mention we have
of him is as the subject of ballads. The only
two early historians who speak of him as a ballad hero (Bower, writing 1441–47, and Major,
born ca. 1450) pretend to have no information
about him except what they derive from ballads, and show that they have none other by the

description they give of him; this description
being in entire conformity with ballads in our
possession, one of which is found in a MS. as
old as the older of these two writers.

Robin Hood is a yeoman, outlawed for reasons not given, but easily surmised, "courteous
and free," religious in sentiment, and above all
reverent of the Virgin, for the love of whom
he is respectful to all women. He lives by
the king's deer (though he loves no man in the
world so much as his king) and by levies on
the superfluity of the higher orders, secular
and spiritual, bishops and archbishops, abbots,
bold barons, and knights, but harms no husbandman or yeoman, and is friendly to poor
men generally, imparting to them of what he
takes from the rich. Courtesy, good temper,
liberality, and manliness are his chief marks;
for courtesy and good temper he is a popular
Gawain. Yeoman as he is, he has a kind of
royal dignity, a princely grace, and a gentle-
man-like refinement of humor. This is the
Robin Hood of the Gest especially; the late
ballads debase this primary conception in various ways and degrees.

This is what Robin Hood is, and it is equally
important to observe what he is not. He has
no sort of political character, in the Gest or
any other ballad. This takes the ground from
under the feet of those who seek to assign him
a place in history. Nor has even a shadow
of a case been made out by those who would
equate Robin Hood with Odin or account for
him in accordance with the supposed principles
of comparative mythology.

The chief comrades of Robin Hood are in
'Robin Hood and the Monk,' Little John,
Scathlok (Scarlok, Scarlet), and Much; to
these the Gest adds Gilbert of the White Hand
and Reynold (292 f.). A friar is not a member
of his company in the older ballads. Maid
Marian is unknown to the genuine Robin Hood
tradition.

The Gest is a popular epic, composed from
several ballads by a poet of a thoroughly congenial spirit. No one of the ballads from which
it was made up is extant in a separate shape,
and some portions of the story may have been
of the compiler's own invention. The decoy-
ing of the sheriff into the wood, stanzas 181–
204, is of the same derivation as the last part
of Robin Hood and the Potter (No. 121), Little
John and Robin Hood exchanging parts; the
conclusion, 451–456, is of the same source as
Robin Hood's Death (No. 120). Though the
tale, as to all important considerations, is emi-
nently original, absolutely so as to the conception of Robin Hood, some traits and incidents,
as might be expected, are taken from what we
may call the general stock of mediæval fiction

The story is a three-ply web of the adventures of Robin Hood with a knight, with the sheriff of Nottingham, and with the king (the concluding stanzas, 451-456, being a mere epilogue), and may be decomposed accordingly. I. How Robin Hood relieved a knight, who had fallen into poverty, by lending him money on the security of Our Lady, the first fit, 1-81; how the knight recovered his lands, which had been pledged to Saint Mary Abbey, and set forth to repay the loan, the second fit, 82-143; how Robin Hood, having taken twice the sum lent from a monk of this abbey, declared that Our Lady had discharged the debt, and would receive nothing more from the knight, the fourth fit, 205-280. II. How Little John insidiously took service with Robin Hood's standing enemy, the sheriff of Nottingham, and put the sheriff into Robin Hood's hands, the third fit, 144-204; how the sheriff, who had sworn an oath to help and not to harm Robin Hood and his men, treacherously set upon the outlaws at a shooting-match, and they were fain to take refuge in the knight's castle; how, missing of Robin Hood, the sheriff made prisoner of the knight; and how Robin Hood slew the sheriff and rescued the knight, the fifth and sixth fit, 281-353. III. How the king, coming in person to apprehend Robin Hood and the knight, disguised himself as an abbot, was stopped by Robin Hood, feasted on his own deer, and entertained with an exhibition of archery, in the course of which he was recognized by Robin Hood, who asked his grace and received a promise thereof, on condition that he and his men should enter into the king's service; and how the king, for a jest, disguised himself and his company in the green of the outlaws, and going back to Nottingham caused a general flight of the people, which he stopped by making himself known; how he pardoned the knight; and how Robin Hood, after fifteen months in the king's court, heart-sick and deserted by all his men but John and Scathlock, obtained a week's leave of the king to go on a pilgrimage to Saint Mary Magdalen of Barnsdale, and would never come back in two-and-twenty years, the seventh and eighth fit, 354-450.

a. 'A Gest of Robyn Hode,' without printer's name, date, or place; the eleventh and last piece in a volume in the Advocates' Library, Edinburgh. Reprinted by David Laing, 1827, with nine pieces from the press of Walter Chepnan and Androw Myllar, Edinburgh, 1508, and one other, by a printer unknown, under the title of The Knightly Tale of Golagrus and Gawane, and other Ancient Poems.

b. 'A Lytell Geste of Robyn Hode,' etc.,

London, Wynken de Worde, n. d.: Library of the University of Cambridge.

c. Douce Fragment, No. 16: Bodleian Library.

d. Douce Fragment, No. 17: Bodleian Library.

e. Douce Fragment, No. 16: Bodleian Library.

f. 'A Mery Geste of Robyn Hoode,' etc., London, Wyllyam Copland, n. d.: British Museum, C. 21, c.

g. 'A Merry Iest of Robin Hood,' etc., London, printed for Edward White, n. d.: Bodleian Library, Z. 3, Art. Seld., and Mr Henry Huth's library.

a. 1 LYTHE and listin, gentilmen,
      That be of frebore blode;
    I shall you tel of a gode yeman,
      His name was Robyn Hode.

   2 Robyn was a prude outlaw,
      [Whyles he walked on grounde;
    So curteyse an outlawe] as he was one
      Was never non founde.

   3 Robyn stode in Bernesdale,
      And lenyd hym to a tre;
    And bi hym stode Litell Johnn,
      A gode yeman was he.

   4 And alsoo dyd gode Scarlok,
      And Much, the miller's son;
    There was none ynch of his bodi
      But it was worth a grome.

   5 Than bespake Lytell Johnn
      All vntoo Robyn Hode:
    Maister, and ye wolde dyne betyme
      It wolde doo you moche gode.

   6 Than bespake hym gode Robyn:
      To dyne haue I noo lust,
    Till that I haue som bolde baron,
      Or som vnkouth gest.

   7 .   .   .   .
      That may pay for the best,
    Or som knyght or [som] squyer,
      That dwelleth here bi west.

   8 A gode maner than had Robyn;
      In londe where that he were,
    Euery day or he wold dyne
      Thre messis wolde he here

9 The one in the worship of the Fader,
  And another of the Holy Gost,
  The thirde of Our derë Lady,
  That he loued allther moste.

10 Robyn loued Oure derë Lady;
   For dout of dydly synne,
   Wolde he neuer do compani harme
   That any woman was in.

11 'Maistar,' than sayde Lytil Johnn,
   'And we our borde shal sprede,
   Tel vs wheder that we shal go,
   And what life that we shall lede.

12 'Where we shall take, where we shall
     leue,
   Where we shall abide behynde;
   Where we shall robbe, where we shal
     reue,
   Where we shal bete and bynde.'

13 'Therof no force,' than sayde Robyn;
   'We shall do well inowe;
   But loke ye do no husbonde harme,
   That tilleth with his ploughe.

14 'No more ye shall no gode yeman
   That walketh by grenë-wode shawe;
   Ne no knyght ne no squyer
   That wol be a gode felawe.

15 'These bisshoppes and these arche-
     bishoppes,
   Ye shall them bete and bynde;
   The hyë sherif of Notyingham,
   Hym holde ye in your mynde.'

16 'This worde shalbe holde,' sayde Lytell
     Johnn,
   'And this lesson we shall lere;
   It is fer dayes; God sende vs a gest,
   That we were at oure dynere!'

17 'Take thy gode bowe in thy honde,'
     sayde Rob[yn];
   'Late Much wende with the;
   And so shal Willyam Scarlo[k],
   And no man abyde with me.

18 'And walke vp to the Saylis,
   And so to Watlinge Stret[e],
   And wayte after some vnkuth gest,
   Vp chaunce ye may them mete.

19 'Be he erle, or ani baron,
   Abbot, or ani knyght,
   Bringhe hym to lodge to me;
   His dyner shall be dight.'

20 They wente vp to the Saylis,
   These yeman all thre;
   They loked est, they loke[d] weest;
   They myght no man see.

21 But as they loked in to Bernysdale,
   Bi a dernë strete,
   Than came a knyght ridinghe;
   Full sone they gan hym mete.

22 All dreri was his semblaunce,
   And lytell was his pryde;
   His one fote in the styrop stode,
   That othere wauyd beside.

23 His hode hanged in his iyn two;
   He rode in symple aray;
   A soriar man than he was one
   Rode neuer in somer day.

24 Litell Johnn was full curteyes,
   And sette hym on his kne:
   'Welcom be ye, gentyll knyght,
   Welcom ar ye to me.

25 'Welcom be thou to grenë wode,
   Hendë knyght and fre;
   My maister hath abiden you fastinge,
   Syr, al these ourës thre.'

26 'Who is thy maister?' sayde the
     knyght;
   Johnn sayde, Robyn Hode;
   'He is [a] gode yoman,' sayde the
     knyght,
   'Of hym I haue herde moche gode.

27 'I graunte,' he sayde, 'with you to
     wende,
   My bretherne, all in fere;
   My purpos was to haue dyned to day
   At Blith or Dancastere.'

28 Furth than went this gentyl knight,
   With a carefull chere;
   The teris oute of his iyen ran,
   And fell downe by his lere.

29 They brought hym to the lodgë-dore;
   Whan Robyn hym gan see,

Full curtesly dyd of his hode
And sette hym on his knee.

30 'Welcome, sir knight,' than sayde
Robyn,
'Welcome art thou to me;
I haue abyden you fastinge, sir,
All these ouris thre.'

31 Than answered the gentyll knight,
With wordës fayre and fre;
God the saue, goode Robyn,
And all thy fayre meynë.

32 They wasshed togeder and wyped bothe,
And sette to theyr dynere;
Brede and wyne they had right ynoughe,
And noumbles of the dere.

33 Swannes and fessauntes they had full
gode,
And foules of the ryuere;
There fayled none so litell a birde
That euer was bred on bryre.

34 'Do gladly, sir knight,' sayde Robyn;
'Gramarcy, sir,' sayde he;
'Suche a dinere had I nat
Of all these wekys thre.

35 'If I come ageyne, Robyn,
Here by thys contrë,
As gode a dyner I shall the make
As that thou haest made to me.'

36 'Gramarcy, knyght,' sayde Robyn;
'My dyner whan that I it haue,
I was neuer so gredy, bi dere worthy
God,
My dyner for to craue.

37 'But pay or ye wende,' sayde Robyn;
'Me thynketh it is gode ryght;
It was neuer the maner, by dere worthi
God,
A yoman to pay for a knyhht.'

38 'I haue nought in my coffers,' saide the
knyght,
'That I may profer for shame: '
'Litell Johnn, go loke,' sayde Robyn,
'Ne let nat for no blame.

39 'Tel me truth,' than saide Robyn,
'So God haue parte of the: '

'I haue no more but ten shelynges,'
sayde the knyght,
'So God haue parte of me.'

40 'If thou hast no more,' sayde Robyn,
'I woll nat one peny;
And yf thou haue nede of any more,
More shall I lend the.

41 'Go nowe furth, Littell Johnn,
The truth tell thou me;
If there be no more but ten shelinges,
No peny that I se.'

42 Lyttell Johnn sprede downe hys mantel
Full fayre vpon the grounde,
And there he fonde in the knyghtës
cofer
But euen halfe [a] pounde.

43 Littell Johnn let it lye full styll,
And went to hys maysteer [full] lowe
'What tidyngës, Johnn ? ' sayde Robyn
'Sir, the knyght is true inowe.'

44 'Fyll of the best wine,' sayde Robyn,
'The knyght shall begynne;
Moche wonder thinketh me
Thy clot[h]ynge is so thin[n]e.

45 'Tell me [one] worde,' sayde Robyn,
'And counsel shal it be;
I trowe thou warte made a knyght or
force,
Or ellys of yemanry.

46 'Or ellys thou hast bene a sori husbande
And lyued in stroke and stryfe;
An okerer, or ellis a lechoure,' saydе
Robyn,
'Wyth wronge hast led thy lyfe.'

47 'I am none of those,' sayde the knyght,
'By God that madë me;
An hundred wynter here before
Myn auncetres knyghtes haue be.

48 'But oft it hath befal, Robyn,
A man hath be disgrate;
But God that sitteth in heuen aboue
May amende his state.

49 'Withyn this two yere, Robyne,' he
sayde,
'My neghbours well it knowe,

Foure hundred pounde of gode money
    Ful well than myght I spende.

50 'Nowe haue I no gode,' saide the knyght,
    'God hath shaped such an ende,
But my chyldren and my wyfe,
    Tyll God yt may amende.'

51 'In what maner,' than sayde Robyn,
    'Hast thou lorne thy rychesse ?'
'For my greatë foly,' he sayde,
    'And for my kynd[ë]nesse.

52 'I hade a sone, forsoth, Robyn,
    That shulde hau[e] ben myn ayre,
Whanne he was twenty wynter olde,
    In felde wolde iust full fayre.

53 'He slewe a knyght of Lancaster,
    And a squyer bolde;
For to saue hym in his ryght
    My godes both sette and solde.

54 'My londes both sette to wedde, Robyn,
    Vntyll a certayn day,
To a ryche abbot here besyde
    Of Seynt Mari Abbey.'

55 'What is the som ?' sayde Robyn;
    'Trouth than tell thou me;'
'Sir,' he sayde, 'foure hundred pounde;
    The abbot told it to me.'

56 'Nowe and thou lese thy lond,' sayde
    Robyn,
    'What woll fall of the ?'
'Hastely I wol me buske,' sayd the
    knyght,
    'Ouer the saltë see,

57 'And se w[h]ere Criste was quyke and
    dede,
    On the mount of Caluerë;
Fare wel, frende, and haue gode day;
    It may no better be.'

58 Teris fell out of hys iyen two ;
    He wolde haue gone hys way:
'Farewel, frende, and haue gode day;
    I ne haue no more to pay.'

59 'Where be thy frendës ?' sayde Robyn:
    'Syr, neuer one wol me knowe;
While I was ryche ynowe at home
    Great boste than wolde they blowe.

60 'And nowe they renne away fro me,
    As bestis on a rowe;
They take no more hede of me
    Thanne they had me neuer sawe.'

61 For ruthe thanne wept Litell Johnn,
    Scarlok and Muche in fere:
'Fyl of the best wyne,' sayde Robyn,
    'For here is a symple chere.

62 'Hast thou any frende,' sayde Robyn,
    'Thy borowe that woldë be ?'
'I haue none,' than sayde the knyght,
    'But God that dyed on tree.'

63 'Do away thy iapis,' than sayde Robyn,
    'Thereof wol I right none;
Wenest thou I wolde haue God to bor-
    owe,
    Peter, Poule, or Johnn ?

64 'Nay, by hym that me made,
    And shope both sonne and mone,
Fynde me a better borowe,' sayde Robyn,
    'Or money getest thou none.'

65 'I haue none other,' sayde the knyght,
    'The sothe for to say,
But yf yt be Our derë Lady;
    She fayled me neuer or thys day.'

66 'By dere worthy God,' sayde Robyn,
    'To seche all Englonde thorowe,
Yet fonde I neuer to my pay
    A moche better borowe.

67 'Come nowe furth, Litell Johnn,
    And go to my tresourë,
And bringe me foure hundered pound,
    And loke well tolde it be.'

68 Furth than went Litell Johnn,
    And Scarlok went before;
He tolde oute foure hundred pounde
    By eight and twenty score.

69 'Is thys well tolde ?' sayde [litell]
    Much;
Johnn sayde, 'What gre[ue]th the ?
It is almus to helpe a gentyll knyght,
    That is fal in pouertë.

70 'Master,' than sayde Lityll John,
    'His clothinge is full thynne;

Ye must gyue the knight a lyueray,
  To lappe his body therin.

71 'For ye haue scarlet and grene, mayster,
    And man[y] a riche aray;
  Ther is no marchaunt in mery Eng-
    lond
  So ryche, I dare well say.'

72 'Take hym thre yerdes of euery colour,
    And loke well mete that it be;'
  Lytell Johnn toke none other mesure
    But his bowë-tree.

'3 And at euery handfull that he met
    He lepëd footës three;
  'What deuyllës drapar,' sayid litell
    Muche,
  'Thynkest thou for to be?'

74 Scarlok stode full stil and loughe,
    And sayd, By God Almyght,
  Johnn may gyue hym gode mesure,
    For it costeth hym but lyght.

75 'Mayster,' than said Litell Johnn
    To gentill Robyn Hode,
  'Ye must giue the knig[h]t a hors,
    To lede home this gode.'

76 'Take hym a gray coursar,' sayde Robyn,
    'And a saydle newe;
  He is Oure Ladye's messangere;
    God graunt that he be true.'

77 'And a gode palfray,' sayde lytell Much,
    'To mayntene hym in his right;'
  'And a peyre of botës,' sayde Scarlock,
    'For he is a gentyll knight.'

78 'What shalt thou gyue hym, Litell
    John?' said Robyn;
  'Sir, a peyre of gilt sporis clene,
    To pray for all this company;
  God bringe hym oute of tene.'

79 'Whan shal mi day be,' said the knight,
    'Sir, and your wyll be?'
  'This day twelue moneth,' saide Robyn,
    'Vnder this grenë-wode tre.

80 'It were greate shamë,' sayde Robyn,
    'A knight alone to ryde,
  Withoutë squyre, yoman, or page,
    To walkë by his syde.

81 'I shall the lende Litell John, my
    man,
    For he shalbe thy knaue;
  In a yema[n]'s stede he may the stande
    If thou greate nedë haue.'

THE SECONDE FYTTE

82 Now is the knight gone on his way;
    This game hym thought full gode;
  Whanne he loked on Bernesdale
    He blessyd Robyn Hode.

83 And whanne he thought on Bernys-
    dale,
    On Scarlok, Much, and Johnn,
  He blyssyd them for the best com
    pany
b.   That euer he in come.

84 Then spake that gentyll knyght,
    To Lytel Johan gan he saye,
  To-morrowe I must to Yorke toune,
    To Saynt Mary abbay.

85 And to the abbot of that place
    Foure hondred pounde I must pay;
  And but I be there vpon this nyght
    My londe is lost for ay.

86 The abbot sayd to his couent,
    There he stode on grounde,
  This day twelfe moneth came there a
    knyght
  And borowed foure hondred pounde.

87 [He borowed foure hondred pounde,]
    Upon all his londë fre;
  But he come this ylkë day
    Dysheryte shall he be.

88 'It is full erely,' sayd the pryoure,
    'The day is not yet ferre gone;
  I had leuer to pay an hondred pounde,
    And lay downe anone.

89 'The knyght is ferre beyonde the see,
    In Englonde is his ryght,
  And suffreth honger and colde,
    And many a sory nyght.

90 'It were grete pytë,' said the pryoure,
    'So to haue his londe;
  And ye be so lyght of your consvence,
    Ye do to hym moch wronge.'

91 'Thou arte euer in my berde,' sayd the
    abbot,
  'By God and Saynt Rycharde;'
With that cam in a fat-heded monke,
    The heygh selerer.

92 'He is dede or hanged,' sayd the monke,
  'By God that bought me dere,
And we shall haue to spende in this place
    Foure hondred pounde by yere.'

93 The abbot and the hy selerer
    Sterte forthe full bolde,
The [hye] iustyce of Englonde
    The abbot there dyde holde.

94 The hyë iustyce and many mo
    Had take in to they[r] honde
Holy all the knyghtës det,
    To put that knyght to wronge.

95 They demed the knyght wonder sore,
    The abbot and his meynë:
'But he come this ylkë day
    Dysheryte shall he be.'

96 'He wyll not come yet,' sayd the ius-
    tyce,
  'I dare well vndertake;'
But in sorowe tymë for them all
    The knyght came to the gate.

97 Than bespake that gentyll knyght
    Untyll his meynë:
Now put on your symple wedes
    That ye brought fro the see.

98 [They put on their symple wedes,]
    They came to the gates anone;
The porter was redy hymselfe,
    And welcomed them euerychone.

99 'Welcome, syr knyght,' sayd the por-
    ter;
  'My lorde to mete is he,
And so is many a gentyll man,
    For the loue of the.'

100 The porter swore a full grete othe,
  'By God that madë me,
Here be the best coresed hors
    That euer yet sawe I me.

101 'Lede them in to the stable,' he sayd,
  'That eased myght they be;'

'They shall not come therin,' sayd the
    knyght,
  'By God that dyed on a tre.'

102 Lordës were to mete isette
    In that abbotes hall;
The knyght went forth and kneled
    downe,
    And salued them grete and small.

103 'Do gladly, syr abbot,' sayd the knyght,
  'I am come to holde my day:'
The fyrst word the abbot spake,
  'Hast thou brought my pay?'

104 'Not one peny,' sayd the knyght,
  'By God that maked me;'
'Thou art a shrewed dettour,' sayd the
    abbot;
  'Syr iustyce, drynke to me.

105 'What doost thou here,' sayd the abbot,
  'But thou haddest brought thy pay?'
'For God,' than sayd the knyght,
  'To pray of a lenger daye.'

106 'Thy daye is broke,' sayd the iustyce,
  'Londe getest thou none:'
'Now, good syr iustyce, be my frende,
    And fende me of my fone!'

107 'I am holde with the abbot,' sayd the
    iustyce,
  'Both with cloth and fee:'
'Now, good syr sheryf, be my frende!'
  'Nay, for God,' sayd he.

108 'Now, good syr abbot, be my frende,
    For thy curteysë,
And holde my londës in thy honde
    Tyll I haue made the gree!

109 'And I wyll be thy true seruaunte,
    And trewely seruë the,
Tyl ye haue foure hondred pounde
    Of money good and free.'

110 The abbot sware a full grete othe,
  'By God that dyed on a tree,
Get the londe where thou may,
    For thou getest none of me.'

111 'By dere worthy God,' then sayd the
    knyght,
  'That all this worlde wrought,

But I haue my londe agayne,
  Full dere it shall be bought.

112 ‘ God, that was of a mayden borne,
   Leue vs well to spede !
  For it is good to assay a frende
   Or that a man haue nede.’

113 The abbot lothely on hym gan loke,
   And vylaynesly hym gan call;
  ‘ Out,’ he sayd, ‘ thou falsë knyght,
   Spede the out of my hall ! ’

114 ‘ Thou lyest,’ then sayd the gentyll
    knyght,
   ‘ Abbot, in thy hal;
  False knyght was I neuer,
   By God that made vs all.’

115 Vp then stode that gentyll knyght,
   To the abbot sayd he,
  To suffre a knyght to knele so longe,
   Thou canst no curteysye.

116 ‘ In ioustës and in tournement
   Full ferre than haue I be,
  And put my selfe as ferre in prees
   As ony that euer I se.’

117 ‘ What wyll ye gyue more,’ sayd the
    iustice,
   ‘ And the knyght shall make a re-
    leyse ?
  And elles dare I safly swere
   Ye holde neuer your londe in pees.’

118 ‘ An hondred pounde,’ sayd the abbot;
   The justice sayd, Gyue hym two;
  ‘ Nay, be God,’ sayd the knyght,
a.   ‘ Yit gete ye it not so.

119 ‘ Though ye wolde gyue a thousand
    more,
   Yet were ye neuer the nere;
  Shall there neuer be myn heyre
   Abbot, iustice, ne frere.’

120 He stert hym to a borde anone,
   Tyll a table rounde,
  And there he shoke oute of a bagge
   Euen four hundred pound.

121 ‘ Haue here thi golde, sir abbot,’ saide
    the knight,
   ‘ Which that thou lentest me;

Had thou ben curtes at my comynge,
  Rewarded shuldest thou haue be.’

122 The abbot sat styll, and ete no more,
   For all his ryall fare;
  He cast his hede on his shulder,
   And fast began to stare.

123 ‘ Take me my golde agayne,’ saide the
    abbot,
   ‘ Sir iustice, that I toke the: ’
  ‘ Not a peni,’ said the iustice,
   ‘ Bi Go[d, that dy]ed on tree.’

124 ‘ Sir [abbot, and ye me]n of lawe,
b. Now haue I holde my daye;
  Now shall I haue my londe agayne,
   For ought that you can saye.’

125 The knyght stert out of the dore,
   Awaye was all his care,
  And on he put his good clothynge,
   The other he lefte there.

126 He wente hym forth full mery syng
    ynge,
   As men haue tolde in tale;
  His lady met hym at the gate,
   At home in Verysdale.

127 ‘ Welcome, my lorde,’ sayd his lady;
   ‘ Syr, lost is all your good ? ’
  ‘ Be mery, dame,’ sayd the knyght,
a.   ‘ And pray for Robyn Hode,

128 ‘ That euer his soulë be in blysse:
   He holpe me out of tene;
  Ne had be his kyndënesse,
   Beggers had we bene.

129 ‘ The abbot and I accorded ben,
   He is serued of his pay;
  The god yoman lent it me,
   As I cam by the way.’

130 This knight than dwelled fayre at
    home,
   The sothe for to saye,
  Tyll he had gete four hundred pound,
   Al redy for to pay.

131 He purueyed him an hundred bowes,
   The stryngës well ydyght,
  An hundred shefe of arowës gode,
   The hedys burneshed full bryght;

132 And euery arowe an ellë longe,
 With pecok wel idyght,
 Inocked all with whyte siluer;
 It was a semely syght.

133 He purueyed hym an [hondreth men],
 Well harness[ed in that stede],
b. And hym selfe in that same sete,
 And clothed in whyte and rede.

134 He bare a launsgay in his honde,
 And a man ledde his male,
 And reden with a lyght songe
 Vnto Bernysdale.

135 But as he went at a brydge ther was a
  wrastelyng,
 And there taryed was he,
 And there was all the best yemen
 Of all the west countree.

136 A full fayre game there was vp set,
 A whyte bulle vp i-pyght,
 A grete courser, with sadle and brydil,
a. With golde burnyssht full bryght.

137 A payre of gloues, a rede golde rynge,
 A pype of wyne, in fay;
 What man that bereth hym best i-wys
 The pryce shall bere away.

138 There was a yoman in that place,
 And best worthy was he,
 And for he was ferre and frembde
  bested,
 Slayne he shulde haue be.

139 The knight had ruthe of this yoman,
 In placë where he stode;
 He sayde that yoman shulde haue no
  harme,
 For loue of Robyn Hode.

140 The knyght presed in to the place,
 An hundreth folowed hym [free],
 With bowës bent and arowës sharpe,
 For to shende that companye.

141 They shulderd all and made hym rome,
 To wete what he wolde say;
 He toke the yeman bi the hande,
 And gaue hym al the play.

142 He gaue hym fyue marke for his wyne,
 There it lay on the molde,

And bad it shulde be set a broche,
 Drynkë who so wolde.

143 Thus longe taried this gentyll knyght,
 Tyll that play was done;
 So longe abode Robyn fastinge,
 Thre hourës after the none.

THE THIRDE FYTTE

144 Lyth and lystyn, gentilmen,
 All that nowe be here;
 Of Litell Johnn, that was the knightës
  man,
 Goode myrth ye shall here.

145 It was vpon a mery day
 That yonge men wolde go shete;
 Lytell Johnn fet his bowe anone,
 And sayde he wolde them mete.

146 Thre tymes Litell Johnn shet aboute,
 And alwey he slet the wande;
 The proudë sherif of Notingham
 By the markës can stande.

147 The sherif swore a full greate othe:
 'By hym that dyede on a tre,
 This man is the best arschére
 That euer yet sawe I [me.]

148 'Say me nowe, wight yonge man,
 What is nowe thy name?
 In what countre were thou borne,
 And where is thy wonynge wane?'

149 'In Holdernes, sir, I was borne,
 I-wys al of my dame;
 Men cal me Reynolde Grenëlef
 Whan I am at home.'

150 'Sey me, Reyno[l]de Grenëlefe,
 Wolde thou dwell with me?
 And euery yere I woll the gyue
 Twenty marke to thy fee.'

151 'I haue a maister,' sayde Litell Johnn,
 'A curteys knight is he;
 May ye leuë gete of hym,
 The better may it be.'

152 The sherif gate Litell John
 Twelue monethës of the knight;
 Therfore he gaue him right anone
 A gode hors and a wight.

153 Nowe is Litell John the sherifës man,
    God lende vs well to spede !
    But alwey thought Lytell John
    To quyte hym wele his mede.

154 'Nowe so God me helpë,' sayde Litell
        John,
    'And by my true leutye,
    I shall be the worst seruaunt to hym
    That euer yet had he.'

155 It fell vpon a Wednesday
    The sherif on huntynge was gone,
    And Litel Iohn lay in his bed,
    And was foriete at home.

156 Therfore he was fastinge
    Til it was past the none;
    'Gode sir stuarde, I pray to the,
    Gyue me my dynere,' saide Litell
        John.

157 'It is longe for Grenëlefe
    Fastinge thus for to be;
    Therfor I pray the, sir stuarde,
    Mi dyner gif me.'

158 'Shalt thou neuer ete ne drynke,' saide
        the stuarde,
    'Tyll my lorde be come to towne:'
    'I make myn auowe to God,' saide
        Litell John,
    'I had leuer to crake thy crowne.'

159 The boteler was full vncurteys,
    There he stode on flore;
    He start to the botery
    And shet fast the dore.

160 Lytell Johnn gaue the boteler suche a
        tap
    His backe went nere in two;
    Though he liued an hundred ier,
    The wors shuld he go.

161 He sporned the dore with his fote;
    It went open wel and fyne;
    And there he made large lyueray,
    Bothe of ale and of wyne.

162 'Sith ye wol nat dyne,' sayde Litell
        John,
    'I shall gyue you to drinke;
    And though ye lyue an hundred wynter,
    On Lytel Johnn ye shall thinke.'

163 Litell John ete, and Litel John drank,
    The whilë that he wolde;
    The sherife had in his kechyn a coke,
    A stoute man and a bolde.

164 'I make myn auowe to God,' saide
        the coke,
    'Thou arte a shrewde hynde
    In ani hous for to dwel,
    For to askë thus to dyne.'

165 And there he lent Litell John
        God[ë] strokis thre;
    'I make myn auowe to God,' sayde
        Lytell John,
    'These strokis lyked well me.

166 'Thou arte a bolde man and hardy,
    And so thinketh me;
    And or I pas fro this place
    Assayed better shalt thou be.'

167 Lytell Johnn drew a ful gode sworde,
    The coke toke another in hande;
    They thought no thynge for to fle,
    But stifly for to stande.

168 There they faught sore togedere
    Two mylë way and well more;
    Myght neyther other harme done,
    The mountnaunce of an owre.

169 'I make myn auowe to God,' sayde
        Litell Johnn,
    'And by my true lewtë,
    Thou art one of the best sworde-men
    That euer yit sawe I [me.]

170 'Cowdest thou shote as well in a
        bowe,
    To grenë wode thou shuldest with
        me,
    And two times in the yere thy clo-
        thinge
    Chaunged shuldë be;

171 'And euery yere of Robyn Hode
    Twenty merke to thy fe:'
    'Put vp thy swerde,' saide the coke,
    'And felowës woll we be.'

172 Thanne he fet to Lytell Johnn
    The nowmbles of a do,
    Gode brede, and full gode wyne;
    They ete and drank theretoo.

173 And when they had dronkyn well,
    Theyre trouthës togeder they plight
That they wo[l]de be with Robyn
    That ylkë samë nyght.

174 They dyd them to the tresoure-hows,
    As fast as they myght gone;
The lokkës, that were of full gode
    stele,
They brake them euerichone.

175 They toke away the siluer vessell,
    And all that thei mig[h]t get;
Pecis, masars, ne sponis,
    Wolde thei not forget.

176 Also [they] toke the godë pens,
    Thre hundred pounde and more,
And did them st[r]eyte to Robyn Hode,
    Under the grenë wode hore.

177 'God the saue, my derë mayster,
    And Criste the saue and se!'
And thanne sayde Robyn to Litell
    John,
Welcome myght thou be.

178 'Also be that fayre yeman
    Thou bryngest there with the;
What tydyngës fro Noty[n]gham?
    Lytill John, tell thou me.'

179 'Well the gretith the proudë sheryf,
    And sende[th] the here by me
His coke and his siluer vessell,
    And thre hundred pounde and thre.'

180 'I make myne avowe to God,' sayde
    Robyn,
'And to the Trenytë,
It was neuer by his gode wyll
    This gode is come to me.'

181 Lytyll John there hym bethought
    On a shrewde wyle;
Fyue myle in the forest he ran,
    Hym happed all his wyll.

182 Than he met the proudë sheref,
    Huntynge with houndes and horne;
Lytell John coude of curtesye,
    And knelyd hym beforne.

183 'God the saue, my derë mayster,
    And Criste the saue and se!'

'Reynolde Grenëlefe,' sayde the shryef,
    'Where hast thou nowe be?'

184 'I haue be in this forest;
    A fayre syght can I se;
It was one of the fayrest syghtes
    That euer yet sawe I me.

185 'Yonder I sawe a ryght fayre harte,
    His coloure is of grene;
Seuen score of dere vpon a herde
    Be with hym all bydene.

186 'Their tyndës are so sharpe, maister,
    Of sexty, and well mo,
That I durst not shote for drede,
    Lest they wolde me slo.'

187 'I make myn auowe to God,' sayde the
    shryef,
'That syght wolde I fayne se:'
'Buske you thyderwarde, mi derë
    mayster,
Anone, and wende with me.'

188 The sherif rode, and Litell John
    Of fote he was full smerte,
And whane they came before Robyn,
    'Lo, sir, here is the mayster-herte.'

189 Still stode the proudë sherief,
    A sory man was he;
'Wo the worthe, Raynolde Grenëlefe,
    Thou hast betrayed nowe me.'

190 'I make myn auowe to God,' sayde
    Litell John,
'Mayster, ye be to blame;
I was mysserued of my dynere
    Whan I was with you at home.'

191 Sone he was to souper sette,
    And serued well with siluer white,
And whan the sherif sawe his vessell,
    For sorowe he myght nat ete.

192 'Make glad chere,' sayde Robyn Hode,
    'Sherif, for charitë,
And for the loue of Litill John
    Thy lyfe I graunt to the.'

193 Whan they had souped well,
    The day was al gone;
Robyn commaunde[d] Litell John
    To drawe of his hosen and his shone

194 His kirtell, and his cote of pie,
  That was fured well and fine,
  And to[ke] hym a grene mantel,
  To lap his body theriu.

195 Robyn commaundyd his wight yonge
    men,
  Vnder the grenë-wode tree,
  They shulde lye in that same sute,
  That the sherif myght them see.

196 All nyght lay the proudë sherif
  In his breche a nd in his [s]chert;
  No wonder it was, in grenë wode,
  Though his sydës gan to smerte.

197 'Make glade chere, sayde Robyn Hode,
  'Sheref, for charitë;
  For this is our ordre i-wys,
  Vnder the grenë-wode tree.'

198 'This is harder order,' sayde the sherief,
  'Than any ankir or frere;
  For all the golde in mery Englonde
  I wolde nat longe dwell her.'

199 'All this twelue monthes,' sayde Robin,
  'Thou shalt dwell with me;
  I shall the techë, proudë sherif,
  An outlawë for to be.'

200 'Or I be here another nyght,' sayde
    the sherif,
  'Robyn, nowe pray I the,
  Smyte of mijn hede rather to-morowe,
  And I forgyue it the.

201 'Lat me go,' than sayde the sherif,
  'For sayntë charitë,
  And I woll be the best[ë] frende
  That euer yet had ye.'

202 'Thou shalt swere me an othe,' sayde
    Robyn,
  'On my bright bronde;
  Shalt thou neuer awayte me scathe,
  By water ne by lande.

203 'And if thou fynde any of my men,
  By nyght or [by] day,
  Vpon thyn othë thou shalt swere
  To helpe them tha[t] thou may.'

204 Nowe hathe the sherif sworne his othe,
  And home he began to gone;

He was as full of grenë wode
  As euer was hepe of stone.

205 The sherif dwelled in Notingham;
  He was fayne he was agone;
  And Robyn and his mery men
  Went to wode anone.

206 'Go we to dyner,' sayde Littell Johnn
    Robyn Hode sayde, Nay;
  For I drede Our Lady be wroth wit
    me,
  For she sent me nat my pay.'

207 'Haue no doute, maister,' sayde Litel
    Johnn;
  'Yet is nat the sonne at rest;
  For I dare say, and sauely swere,
  The knight is true and truste.'

208 'Take thy bowe in thy hande,' sayde
    Robyn,
  'Late Much wende with the,
b.   And so shal Wyllyam Scarlok,
    And no man abyde with me.

209 'And walke vp vnder the Sayles,
  And to Watlynge-strete,
  And wayte after some vnketh gest;
  Vp-chaunce ye may them mete.

210 'Whether he be messengere,
  Or a man that myrthës can,
  Of my good he shall haue some,
  Yf he be a porë man.'

211 Forth then stert Lytel Johan,
  Half in tray and tene,
  And gyrde hym with a full good
    swerde,
  Under a mantel of grene.

212 They went vp to the Sayles,
  These yemen all thre;
  They loked est, they loked west,
  They myght no man se.

213 But as [t]he[y] loked in Bernys-
    dale,
  By the hyë waye,
  Than were they ware of two blacke
    monkes,
  Eche on a good palferay.

214 Then bespake Lytell Johan,
 To Much he gan say,
I dare lay my lyfe to wedde,
 That [these] monkes haue brought
  our pay.

215 'Make glad chere,' sayd Lytell Johan,
 'And frese your bowes of ewe,
And loke your hertës be seker and sad,
 Your stryngës trusty and trewe.

216 'The monke hath two and fifty [men,]
 And seuen somers full strouge;
There rydeth no bysshop in this londe
 So ryally, I vnderstoud.

217 'Brethern,' sayd Lytell Johan,
 'Here are no more but we thre;
But we bryngë them to dyner,
 Our mayster dare we not se.

218 'Bende your bowes,' sayd Lytell Johan,
 'Make all yon prese to stonde;
The formost monke, his lyfe and his
  deth
 Is closed in my honde.

219 'Abyde, chorle monke,' sayd Lytell
  Johan,
 'No ferther that thou gone;
Yf thou doost, by dere worthy God,
 Thy deth is in my honde.

220 'And euyll thryfte on thy hede,' sayd
  Lytell Johan,
 'Ryght vnder thy hattës bonde;
For thou hast made our mayster wroth,
 He is fastynge so longe.'

221 'Who is your mayster?' sayd the
  monke;
 Lytell Johan sayd, Robyn Hode;
'He is a stronge thefe,' sayd the
  monke,
 'Of hym herd I neuer good.'

222 'Thou lyest,' than sayd Lytell Johan,
 'And that shall rewë the;
He is a yeman of the forest,
 To dyne he hath bodë the.'

223 Much was redy with a bolte,
 Redly and anone,
He set the monke to-fore the brest,
 To the grounde that he can gone.

224 Of two and fyfty wyght yonge ye-
  men
 There abode not one,
Saf a lytell page and a grome,
 To lede the somers with Lytel Johan.

225 They brought the monke to the lodgë-
  dore,
 Whether he were loth or lefe,
For to speke with Robyn Hode,
 Maugre in theyr tethe.

226 Robyn dyde adowne his hode,
 The monke whan that he se;
The monke was not so curtëyse,
 His hode then let he be.

227 'He is a chorle, mayster, by dere
  worthy God,'
 Than sayd Lytell Johan:
'Thereof no force,' sayd Robyn,
 'For curteysy can he none.

228 'How many men,' sayd Robyn,
 'Had this monke, Johan?'
'Fyfty and two whan that we met,
 But many of them be gone.'

229 'Let blowe a horne,' sayd Robyn,
 'That felaushyp may vs knowe;'
Seuen score of wyght yemen
 Came pryckynge on a rowe.

230 And euerych of them a good man-
  tell
 Of scarlet and of raye;
All they came to good Robyn,
 To wyte what he wolde say.

231 They made the monke to wasshe and
  wype,
 And syt at his denere,
Robyn Hode and Lytell Johan
 They serued him both in-fere.

232 'Do gladly, monke,' sayd Robyn.
 'Gramercy, syr,' sayd he.
'Where is your abbay, whan ye are at
  home,
 And who is your avowë?'

233 'Saynt Mary abbay,' sayd the monke,
 'Though I be symple here.'
'In what offyce?' sayd Robyn:
 'Syr, the hyë selerer.'

234 'Ye be the more welcome,' sayd
         Robyn,
    'So euer mote I the;
    Fyll of the best wyne,' sayd Robyn,
    'This monke shall drynke to me.

235 'But I haue grete meruayle,' sayd
         Robyn,
    'Of all this longë day;
    I drede Our Lady be wroth with me,
    She sent me not my pay.'

236 'Haue no doute, mayster,' sayd Lytell
         Johan,
    'Ye haue no nede, I saye;
    This monke it hath brought, I dare
         well swere,
    For he is of her abbay.'

237 'And she was a borowe,' sayd Robyn,
    'Betwene a knyght and me,
    Of a lytell money that I hym lent,
    Under the grenë-wode tree.

238 'And yf thou hast that syluer ibrought,
    I pray the let me se;
    And I shall helpë the eftsones,
    Yf thou haue nede to me.'

239 The monke swore a full grete othe,
    With a sory chere,
    'Of the borowehode thou spekest to
         me,
    Herde I neuer ere.'

240 'I make myn avowe to God,' sayd
         Robyn,
    'Monke, thou art to blame;
    For God is holde a ryghtwys man,
    And so is his dame.

241 'Thou toldest with thyn ownë tonge,
    Thou may not say nay,
    How thou arte her seruaunt,
    And seruest her euery day.

242 'And thou art made her messengere,
    My money for to pay;
    Therfore I cun the morë thanke
    Thou arte come at thy day.

243 'What is in your cofers?' sayd Robyn,
    'Trewe than tell thou me:'
    'Syr,' he sayd, 'twenty marke,
    Al so mote I the.'

244 'Yf there be no more,' sayd Robyn,
    'I wyll not one peny;
    Yf thou hast myster of ony more,
    Syr, more I shall lende to the.

245 'And yf I fiyndë [more,' sayd] Robyn,
    'I-wys thou shalte it for gone;
    For of thy spendynge-syluer, monke,
    Thereof wyll I ryght none.

246 'Go nowe forthe, Lytell Johan,
    And the trouth tell thou me;
    If there be no more but twenty marke,
    No peny that I se.'

247 Lytell Johan spred his mantell downe,
    As he had done before,
    And he tolde out of the monkës
         male
    Eyght [hondred] pounde and more.

248 Lytell Johan let it lye full styll,
    And went to his mayster in hast;
    'Syr,' he sayd, 'the monke is trewe
         ynowe,
    Our Lady hath doubled your cast.'

249 'I make myn avowe to God,' sayd
         Robyn —
    'Monke, what tolde I the? —
    Our Lady is the trewest woman
    That euer yet founde I me.

250 'By dere worthy God,' sayd Robyn,
    'To seche all Englond thorowe,
    Yet founde I neuer to my pay
    A moche better borowe.

251 'Fyll of the best wyne, and do hym
         drynke,' sayd Robyn,
    'And grete well thy lady hende,
    And yf she haue nede to Robyn Hode,
    A frende she shall hym fynde.

252 'And yf she nedeth ony more syluer,
    Come thou agayne to me,
    And, by this token she hath me sent,
    She shall haue such thre.'

253 The monke was goynge to London
         ward,
    There to holde grete mote,
    The knyght that rode so hye on
         hors,
    To brynge hym vnder fote.

254 ‘Whether be ye away ?’ sayd Robyn:
 ‘Syr, to maners in this londe,
Too reken with our reues,
 That haue done moch wronge.’

255 ‘Come now forth, Lytell Johan,
 And harken to my tale;
A better yemen I knowe none,
 To seke a monkës male.’

256 ‘How moch is in yonder other corser ?’
 sayd Robyn,
‘The soth must we see:’
‘By Our Lady,’ than sayd the monke,
 ‘That were no curteysye,

257 ‘To bydde a man to dyner,
 And syth hym bete and bynde.’
‘It is our oldë maner,’ sayd Robyn,
 ‘To leue but lytell behynde.’

258 The monke toke the hors with spore,
 Ne lenger wolde he abyde:
‘Askë to drynkë,’ than sayd Robyn,
 ‘Or that ye forther ryde.’

259 ‘Nay, for God,’ than sayd the monke,
 ‘Me reweth I cam so nere;
For better chepe I myght haue dyned
 In Blythe or in Dankestere.’

260 ‘Grete well your abbot,’ sayd Robyn,
 ‘And your pryour, I you pray,
And byd hym send me such a monke
 To dyner euery day.’

261 Now lete we that monke be styll,
 And speke we of that knyght:
Yet he came to holde his day,
 Whyle that it was lyght.

262 He dyde him streyt to Bernysdale,
 Under the grenë-wode tre,
And he founde there Robyn Hode,
 And all his mery meynë.

263 The knyght lyght doune of his good
 palfray;
Robyn whan he gan see,
So curteysly he dyde adoune his
 hode,
And set hym on his knee.

264 ‘God the sauë, Robyn Hode,
 And all this company:’

‘Welcome be thou, gentyll knyght,
 And ryght welcome to me.’

265 Than bespake hym Robyn Hode,
 To that knyght so fre:
What nedë dryueth the to grenë
 wode ?
I praye the, syr knyght, tell me.

266 ‘And welcome be thou, ge[n]tyll
 knyght,
Why hast thou be so longe ?’
‘For the abbot and the hyë iustyce
 Wolde haue had my londe.’

267 ‘Hast thou thy londe [a]gayne ?’ sayd
 Robyn;
‘Treuth than tell thou me :’
‘Ye, for God,’ sayd the knyght,
 And that thanke I God and the.

268 ‘But take not a grefe,’ sayd the knyght,
 ‘that I haue be so longe;
I came by a wrastelynge,
And there I holpe a porë yeman,
 With wronge was put behynde.’

269 ‘Nay, for God,’ sayd Robyn,
 ‘Syr knyght, that thanke I the;
What man that helpeth a good yeman,
 His frende than wyll I be.’

270 ‘Haue here foure hondred pounde,’
 than sayd the knyght,
‘The whiche ye lent to me;
And here is also twenty marke
 For your curteysy.’

271 ‘Nay, for God,’ than sayd Robyn,
 ‘Thou broke it well for ay;
For Our Lady, by her [hyë] selerer,
 Hath sent to me my pay.

272 ‘And yf I toke it i-twyse,
 A shame it were to me;
But trewely, gentyll knyght,
 Welcom arte thou to me.’

273 Whan Robyn had tolde his tale,
 He leugh and had good chere:
By my trouthe,’ then sayd the knyght,
 ‘Your money is redy here.’

274 ‘Broke it well,’ sayd Robyn,
 ‘Thou gentyll knyght so fre;

And welcome be thou, ge[n]tyll knyght,
Under my trystell-tre.

275 ' But what shall these bowës do ? ' sayd
    Robyn,
' And these arowës ifedred fre ? '
' By God,' than sayd the knyght,
' A porë present to the.'

276 ' Come now forth, Lytell Johan,
    And go to my treasurë,
And brynge me there foure hondred
    pounde;
The monke ouer-tolde it me.

277 ' Haue here foure hondred pounde,
    Thou gentyll knyght and trewe,
And bye hors and harnes good,
    And gylte thy spores all newe.

278 ' And yf thou fayle ony spendynge,
    Com to Robyn Hode,
And by my trouth thou shalt none fayle,
    The whyles I haue any good.

279 ' And broke well thy foure hondred
    pound,
Whiche I lent to the,
And make thy selfe no more so bare,
    By the counsell of me.'

280 Thus than holpe hym good Robyn,
    The knyght all of his care:
God, that syt in heuen hye,
    Graunte vs well to fare !

THE FYFTH FYTTE

281 Now hath the knyght his leue i-take,
    And wente hym on his way;
Robyn Hode and his mery men
    Dwelled styll full many a day.

282 Lyth and lysten, gentil men,
    And herken what I shall say,
How the proud[ë] sheryfe of Notyng-
    ham
Dyde crye a full fayre play;

283 That all the best archers of the north
    Sholde come vpon a day,
And [he] that shoteth allther best
    The game shall bere a way.

284 He that shoteth allther best,
    Furthest fayre and lowe,

At a payre of fynly buttes,
    Under the grenë-wode shawe,

285 A ryght good arowe he shall haue,
    The shaft of syluer whyte,
The hede and the feders of ryche rede
    golde,
In Englond is none lyke.

286 This than herde good Robyn,
    Under his trystell-tre:
' Make you redy, ye wyght yonge men;
    That shotynge wyll I se.

287 ' Buske you, my mery yonge men,
    Ye shall go with me;
And I wyll wete the shryuës fayth,
    Trewe and yf he be.'

288 Whan they had theyr bowes i-bent,
    Theyr takles fedred fre,
Seuen score of wyght yonge men
    Stode by Robyns kne.

289 Whan they cam to Notyngham,
    The buttes were fayre and longe;
Many was the bolde archere
    That shoted with bowës stronge.

290 ' There shall but syx shote with me;
    The other shal kepe my he[ue]de,
And standë with good bowës bent,
    That I be not desceyued.'

291 The fourth outlawe his bowe gan bende,
    And that was Robyn Hode,
And that behelde the proud[ë] sheryfe,
    All by the but [as] he stode.

292 Thryës Robyn shot about,
    And alway he slist the wand,
And so dyde good Gylberte
    Wyth the whytë hande.

293 Lytell Johan and good Scatheloke
    Were archers good and fre;
Lytell Much and good Reynolde,
    The worste wolde they not be.

294 Whan they had shot aboute,
    These archours fayre and good,
Euermore was the best,
    For soth, Robyn Hode.

295 Hym was delyuered the good arowe,
    For best worthy was he;

He toke the yeft so curteysly,
  To grenë wode wolde he.

296 They cryed out on Robyn Hode,
  And grete hornës gan they blowe:
  'Wo worth the, treason!' sayd Robyn,
  'Full euyl thou art to knowe.

297 'And wo be thou! thou proudë sheryf,
  Thus gladdynge thy gest;
  Other wyse thou behotë me
  In yonder wylde forest.

298 'But had I the in grenë wode,
  Under my trystell-tre,
  Thou sholdest leue me a better wedde
  Than thy trewe lewtë.'

299 Full many a bowë there was bent,
  And arowës let they glyde;
  Many a kyrtell there was rent,
  And hurt many a syde.

300 The outlawes shot was so stronge
  That no man myght them dryue,
  And the proud[ë] sheryfës men,
  They fled away full blyue.

301 Robyn sawe the busshement to-broke,
  In grene wode he wolde haue be;
  Many an arowe there was shot
  Amonge that company.

302 Lytell Johan was hurte full sore,
  With an arowe in his kne,
  That he myght neythor go nor ryde;
  It was full grete pytë.

303 'Mayster,' then sayd Lytell Johan,
  'If euer thou loue[d]st me,
  And for that ylkë lordës loue
  That dyed vpon a tre,

304 'And for the medes of my seruyce,
  That I haue serued the,
  Lete neuer the proudë sheryf
  Alyue now fyndë me.

305 'But take out thy brownë swerde,
  And smyte all of my hede,
  And gyue me woundës depe and wyde;
  No lyfe on me be lefte.'

306 'I wolde not that,' sayd Robyn,
  'Johan, that thou were slawe,

For all the golde in mery Englonde,
  Though it lay now on a rawe.'

307 'God forbede,' sayd Lytell Much,
  'That dyed on a tre,
  That thou sholdest, Lytell Johan,
  Parte our company.'

308 Up he toke hym on his backe,
  And bare hym well a myle;
  Many a tyme he layd hym downe,
  And shot another whyle.

309 Then was there a fayre castell,
  A lytell within the wode;
  Double-dyched it was about,
  And walled, by the rode.

310 And there dwelled that gentyll knyght,
  Syr Rychard at the Lee,
  That Robyn had lent his good,
  Under the grenë-wode tree.

311 In he toke good Robyn,
  And all his company:
  'Welcome be thou, Robyn Hode,
  Welcome arte thou to me;

312 And moche [I] thanke the of thy confort,
  And of thy curteysye,
  And of thy gretë kyndënesse,
  Under the grenë-wode tre.

313 'I loue no man in all this worlde
  So much as I do the;
  For all the proud[ë] sheryf of Notyng-
    ham,
  Ryght here shalt thou be.

314 'Shyt the gates, and drawe the brydge,
a. And let no man come in,
  And arme you well, and make you redy,
  And to the walles ye wynne.

315 'For one thynge, Robyn, I the behote;
  I swere by Saynt Quyntyne,
  These forty dayes thou wonnest with
    me,
  To soupe, ete, and dyne.'

316 Bordes were layde, and clothes were
    spredde,
  Redely and anone;
  Robyn Hode and his mery men
  To metë can they gone.

THE VI. FYTTE

317 Lythe and lysten, gentylmen,
    And herkyn to your songe;
    Howe the proudë shyref of Notyng-
        ham,
    And men of armys stronge,

318 Full fast cam to the hyë shyref,
    The contrë vp to route,
    And they besette the knyghtës castell,
    The wallës all aboute.

319 The proudë shyref loude gan crye,
    And sayde, Thou traytour knight,
    Thou kepest here the kynges enemys,
    Agaynst the lawe and right.

320 'Syr, I wyll auowe that I haue done,
    The dedys that here be dyght,
    Vpon all the landës that I haue,
    As I am a trewë knyght.

321 'Wende furth, sirs, on your way,
    And do no more to me
    Tyll ye wyt oure kyngës wille,
    What he wyll say to the.'

322 The shyref thus had his answere,
    Without any lesynge;
    [Fu]rth he yede to London towne,
    All for to tel our kinge.

323 Ther he telde him of that knight,
    And eke of Robyn Hode,
    And also of the bolde archars,
    That were soo noble and gode.

324 'He wyll auowe that he hath done,
    To mayntene the outlawes stronge;
    He wyll be lorde, and set you at
        nought,
    In all the northe londe.'

325 'I wil be at Notyngham,' saide our
        kynge,
    'Within this fourteenyght,
    And take I wyll Robyn Hode,
    And so I wyll that knight.

326 'Go nowe home, shyref,' sayde our
        kynge,
    'And do as I byd the;
    And ordeyn gode archers ynowe,
    Of all the wydë contrë.'

327 The shyref had his leue i-take,
    And went hym on his way,
    And Robyn Hode to grenë wode,
    Vpon a certen day.

328 And Lytel John was hole of the
        arowe
    That shot was in his kne,
    And dyd hym streyght to Robyn Hode,
    Vnder the grenë-wode tree.

329 Robyn Hode walked in the forest,
    Vnder the leuys grene;
    The proudë shyref of Notyngham
    Thereof he had grete tene.

330 The shyref there fayled of Robyn
        Hode,
    He myght not haue his pray;
    Than he awayted this gentyll knyght,
    Bothe by nyght and day.

331 Euer he wayted the gentyll knyght,
    Syr Richarde at the Lee,
    As he went on haukynge by the ryuer-
        syde,
    And lete [his] haukës flee.

332 Toke he there this gentyll knight,
    With men of armys stronge,
    And led hym to Notyngham warde,
    Bounde bothe fote and hande.

333 The sheref sware a full grete othe,
    Bi hym that dyed on rode,
    He had leuer than an hundred pound
    That he had Robyn Hode.

334 This harde the knyghtës wyfe,
    A fayr lady and a free;
    She set hir on a gode palfrey,
    To grenë wode anone rode she.

335 Whanne she cam in the forest,
    Vnder the grenë-wode tree,
    Fonde she there Robyn Hode,
    And al his fayre menë.

336 'God the sauë, godë Robyn,
    And all thy company;
    For Our derë Ladyes sake,
    A bonë graunte thou me.

337 'Late neuer my wedded lorde
    Shamefully slayne be;

He is fast bowne to Notingham warde,
  For the loue of the.'

338 Anone than saide goode Robyn
    To that lady so fre,
What man hath your lorde [i-]take ?

    .   .   .   .   .

339 .   .   .   .
    'For soth as I the say;
He is nat yet thre mylës
    Passed on his way.'

340 Vp than sterte gode Robyn,
    As man that had ben wode:
'Buske you, my mery men,
    For hym that dyed on rode.

341 'And he that this sorowe forsaketh,
    By hym that dyed on tre,
Shall he neuer in grenë wode
    No lenger dwel with me.'

342 Sone there were gode bowës bent,
    Mo than seuen score;
Hedge ne dyche spared they none
    That was them before.

343 'I make myn auowe to God,' sayde
    Robyn,
    'The sherif wolde I fayne see;
And if I may hym take,
    I-quyte shall it be.'

344 And whan they came to Notingham,
    They walked in the strete;
And with the proudë sherif i-wys
    Sonë can they mete.

345 'Abyde, thou proudë sherif,' he sayde,
    'Abyde, and speke with me;
Of some tidinges of oure kinge
    I wolde fayne here of the.

346 'This seuen yere, by dere worthy
    God,
    Ne yede I this fast on fote;
I make myn auowe to God, thou proudë
    sherif,
    It is nat for thy gode.'

347 Robyn bent a full goode bowe,
    An arrowe he drowe at wyll;
He hit so the proudë sherife
    Vpon the grounde he lay full still.

348 And or he myght vp aryse,
    On his fete to stonde,
He smote of the sherifs hede
    With his bright[ë] bronde.

349 'Lye thou there, thou proudë sherife,
    Euyll mote thou cheue !
There myght no man to the truste
b.   The whyles thou were a lyue.'

350 His men drewe out theyr brygbt
    swerdes,
    That were so sharpe and kene,
And layde on the sheryues men,
    And dryued them downe bydene.

351 Robyn stert to that knyght,
    And cut a two his bonde,
And toke hym in his hand a bowe,
    And bad hym by hym stonde.

352 'Leue thy hors the behynde,
    And lerne for to renne;
Thou shalt with me to grenë wode,
    Through myrë, mosse, and fenne.

353 'Thou shalt with me to grenë wode,
    Without ony leasynge,
Tyll that I haue gete vs grace
    Of Edwarde, our comly kynge.'

        THE VII. FYTTE

354 The kynge came to Notynghame,
    With knyghtës in grete araye,
For to take that gentyll knyght
    And Robyn Hode, and yf he may

355 He asked men of that countrë
    After Robyn Hode,
And after that gentyll knyght,
    That was so bolde and stout.

356 Whan they had tolde hym the case
    Our kynge vnderstode ther tale,
And seased in his honde
    The knyghtës londës all.

357 All the passe of Lancasshyre
    He went both ferre and nere,
Tyll he came to Plomton Parke;
    He faylyd many of his dere.

358 There our kynge was wont to se
    Herdës many one,

He coud vnneth fynde one dere,
 That bare ony good horne.

359 The kynge was wonder wroth with-
 all,
 And swore by the Trynytë,
'I wolde I had Robyn Hode,
 With eyen I myght hym se.

360 ' And he that wolde smyte of the
 knyghtës hede,
 And brynge it to me,
He shall haue the knyghtës londes,
 Syr Rycharde at the Le.

361 ' I gyue it hym with my charter,
 And sele it [with] my honde,
To haue and holde for euer more,
 In all mery Englonde.'

362 Than bespake a fayre olde knyght,
 That was treue in his fay:
' A, my leegë lorde the kynge,
 One worde I shall you say.

363 ' There is no man in this countrë
 May haue the knyghtës londes,
Whyle Robyn Hode may ryde or
 gone,
 And bere a bowe in his hondes,

364 ' That he ne shall lese his hede,
 That is the best ball in his hode:
Giue it no man, my lorde the kynge,
 That ye wyll any good.'

365 Half a yere dwelled our comly kynge
 In Notyngham, and well more;
Coude he not here of Robyn Hode,
 In what countrë that he were.

366 But alway went good Robyn
 By halke and eke by hyll,
And alway slewe the kyngës dere,
 And welt them at his wyll.

367 Than bespake a proude fostere,
 That stode by our kyngës kne:
' Yf ye wyll se good Robyn,
 Ye must do after me.

368 ' Take fyue of the best knyghtës
 That be in your lede,
And walke downe by yon abbay,
 And gete you monkës wede.

369 ' And I wyll be your ledës-man,
 And lede you the way,
And or ye come to Notyngham,
 Myn hede then dare I lay,

370 ' That ye shall mete with good Robyn,
 On lyue yf that he be;
Or ye come to Notyngham,
 With eyen ye shall hym se.'

371 Full hast[ë]ly our kynge was dyght,
 So were his knyghtës fyue,
Euerych of them in monkës wede,
 And hasted them thyder blyve.

372 Our kynge was grete aboue his cole,
 A brode hat on his crowne,
Ryght as he were abbot-lyke,
 They rode up in-to the towne.

373 Styf botës our kynge had on,
 Forsoth as I you say;
He rode syngynge to grenë wode,
 The couent was clothed in graye.

374 His male-hors and his gretë somers
 Folowed our kynge behynde,
Tyll they came to grenë wode,
 A myle vnder the lynde.

375 There they met with good Robyn,
 Stondynge on the waye,
And so dyde many a bolde archere,
 For soth as I you say.

376 Robyn toke the kyngës hors,
 Hastëly in that stede,
And sayd, ' Syr abbot, by your leue.
 A whyle ye must abyde.

377 ' We be yemen of this foreste,
 Vnder the grenë-wode tre;
We lyue by our kyngës dere,
 [Other shyft haue not wee.]

378 ' And ye haue chyrches and rentës
 both,
 And gold full grete plentë;
Gyue vs some of your spendynge,
 For saynt[ë] charytë.'

379 Than bespake our cumly kynge,
 Anone than sayd he;
' I brought no more to grenë wode
 But forty pounde with me.

380 'I haue layne at Notyngham
    This fourtynyght with our kynge,
    And spent I haue full moche good,
    On many a grete lordynge.'

381 'And I haue but forty pounde,
    No more than haue I me;
    But yf I had an hondred pounde,
    I wolde vouch it safe on the.'

382 Robyn toke the forty pounde,
    And departed it in two partye;
    Halfendell he gaue his mery men,
    And bad them mery to be.

383 Full curteysly Robyn gan say:
    'Syr, haue this for your spendyng;
    We shall mete another day;'
    'Gramercy,' than sayd our kynge.

384 'But well the greteth Edwarde, our
        kynge,
    And sent to the his seale,
    And byddeth the com to Notyngham,
    Both to mete and mele.'

385 He toke out the brodë targe,
    And sone he lete hym se;
    Robyn coud his courteysy,
    And set hym on his kne.

386 'I loue no man in all the worlde
    So well as I do my kynge;
    Welcome is my lordës seale;
    And, monke, for thy tydynge,

387 'Syr abbot, for thy tydynges,
    To day thou shalt dyne with me,
    For the loue of my kynge,
    Under my trystell-tre.'

388 Forth he lad our comly kynge,
    Full fayre by the honde;
    Many a dere there was slayne,
    And full fast dyghtande.

389 Robyn toke a full grete horne,
    And loude he gan blowe;
    Seuen score of wyght yonge men
    Came redy on a rowe.

390 All they kneled on theyr kne,
    Full fayre before Robyn:
    The kynge sayd hym selfe vntyll,
    And swore by Saynt Austyn,

391 'Here is a wonder semely syght;
    Me thynketh, by Goddës pyne,
    His men are more at his byddynge
    Then my men be at myn.'

392 Full hast[ë]ly was theyr dyner idyght,
    And therto gan they gone;
    They serued our kynge with al theyr
        myght,
    Both Robyn and Lytell Johan.

393 Anone before our kynge was set
    The fattë venyson,
    The good whyte brede, the good rede
        wyne,
    And therto the fyne ale and browne.

394 'Make good chere,' said Robyn,
    'Abbot, for charytë;
    And for this ylkë tydynge,
    Blyssed mote thou be.

395 'Now shalte thou se what lyfe we lede,
    Or thou hens wende;
    Than thou may enfourme our kynge,
    Whan ye togyder lende.'

396 Up they stertë all in hast,
    Theyr bowës were smartly bent;
    Our kynge was neuer so sore agast,
    He wende to haue be shente.

397 Two yerdës there were vp set,
    Thereto gan they gange;
    By fyfty pase, our kynge sayd,
    The merkës were to longe.

398 On euery syde a rose-garlonde,
    They shot vnder the lyne:
    'Who so fayleth of the rose-garlonde,'
        sayd Robyn,
    'His takyll he shall tyne,

399 'And yelde it to his mayster,
    Be it neuer so fyne;
    For no man wyll I spare,
    So drynke I ale or wyne:

400 'And bere a buffet on his hede,
    I-wys ryght all bare:'
    And all that fell in Robyns lote,
    He smote them wonder sare.

101 Twyse Robyn shot aboute,
    And euer he cleued the wande.

And so dyde good Gylberte
With the Whytë Hande.

402 Lytell Johan and good Scathelocke,
    For nothynge wolde they spare;
When they fayled of the garlonde,
    Robyn smote them full sore.

403 At the last shot that Robyn shot,
    For all his frendës fare,
Yet he fayled of the garlonde
    Thre fyngers and mare.

404 Than bespake good Gylberte,
    And thus he gan say;
'Mayster,' he sayd, 'your takyll is lost,
    Stande forth and take your pay.'

405 'If it be so,' sayd Robyn,
    'That may no better be,
Syr abbot, I delyuer the myn arowe,
    I pray the, syr, serue thou me.'

406 'It falleth not for myn ordre,' sayd
    our kynge,
    'Robyn, by thy leue,
For to smyte no good yeman,
    For doute I sholde hym greue.'

407 'Smyte on boldely,' sayd Robyn,
    'I giue the largë leue:'
Anone our kynge, with that worde,
    He folde vp his sleue,

408 And sych a buffet he gaue Robyn,
    To grounde he yede full nere:
'I make myn avowe to God,' sayd
    Robyn,
    'Thou arte a stalworthe frere.

409 'There is pith in thyn arme,' sayd
    Robyn,
    'I trowe thou canst well shete:'
Thus our kynge and Robyn Hode
    Togeder gan they mete.

410 Robyn behelde our comly kynge
    Wystly in the face,
So dyde Syr Rycharde at the Le,
    And kneled downe in that place.

411 And so dyde all the wylde outlawes,
    Whan they se them knele:
'My lorde the kynge of Englonde,
    Now I knowe you well.'

412 'Mercy then, Robyn,' sayd our kynge,
    'Vnder your trystyll-tre,
Of thy goodnesse and thy grace,
    For my men and me !'

413 'Yes, for God,' sayd Robyn,
    'And also God me saue,
I askë mercy, my lordë the kynge,
    And for my men I craue.'

414 'Yes, for God,' than sayd our kynge,
    'And therto sent I me,
With that thou leue the grenë wode,
    And all thy company;

415 'And come home, syr, to my courte,
    And there dwell with me.'
'I make myn avowe to God,' sayd
    Robyn,
    'And ryght so shall it be.

416 'I wyll come to your courte,
    Your seruyse for to se,
And brynge with me of my men
    Seuen score and thre.

417 'But me lykë well your seruyse,
    I [wyll] come agayne full soone,
And shote at the donnë dere,
    As I am wonte to done.'

THE VIII. FYTTE

418 'Haste thou ony grenë cloth,' sayd our
    kynge,
    'That thou wylte sell nowe to
    me ?'
'Ye, for God,' sayd Robyn,
    'Thyrty yerdës and thre.'

419 'Robyn,' sayd our kynge,
    'Now pray I the,
Sell me some of that cloth,
    To me and my meynë.'

420 'Yes, for God,' then sayd Robyn,
    'Or elles I were a fole;
Another day ye wyll me clothe,
    I trowe, ayenst the Yole.'

421 The kynge kest of his colë then,
    A grene garment he dyde on,
And euery knyght also, i-wys,
    Another had full sone.

422 Whan they were clothed in Lyncolne
grene,
They keste away theyr graye;
'Now we shall to Notyngham,'
All thus our kynge gan say.

423 They bente theyr bowes, and forth
they went,
Shotynge all in-fere,
Towarde the towne of Notyngham,
Outlawes as they were.

424 Our kynge and Robyn rode togyder,
For soth as I you say,
And they shote plucke-buffet,
As they went by the way.

425 And many a buffet our kynge wan
Of Robyn Hode that day,
And nothynge spared good Robyn
Our kynge in his pay.

426 'So God me helpë,' sayd our kynge,
'Thy game is nought to lere;
I sholde not get a shote of the,
Though I shote all this yere.'

427 All the people of Notyngham
They stode and behelde;
They sawe nothynge but mantels of
grene
That couered all the felde.

428 Than euery man to other gan say,
I drede our kynge be slone;
Comë Robyn Hode to the towne, i-
wys
On lyue he lefte neuer one.'

429 Full hast[ë]ly they began to fle,
Both yemen and knaues,
And olde wyues that myght euyll
goo,
They hypped on theyr staues.

430 The kynge l[o]ughe full fast,
And commaunded theym agayne;
When they se our comly kynge,
I-wys they were full fayne.

431 They ete and dranke, and made them
glad,
And sange with notës hye;
Than bespake our comly kynge
To Syr Rycharde at the Lee.

432 He gaue hym there his londe agayne,
A good man he bad hym be;
Robyn thanked our comly kynge,
And set hym on his kne.

433 Had Robyn dwelled in the kyngës
courte
But twelue monethes and thre,
That [he had] spent an hondred pounde,
And all his mennes fe.

434 In euery place where Robyn came
Euer more he layde downe,
Both for knyghtës and for squyres,
To gete hym grete renowne.

435 By than the yere was all agone
He had no man but twayne,
Lytell Johan and good Scathelocke,
With hym all for to gone.

436 Robyn sawe yonge men shote
Full fayre vpon a day;
'Alas!' than sayd good Robyn,
'My welthe is went away.

437 'Somtyme I was an archere good,
A styffe and eke a stronge;
I was compted the best archere
That was in mery Englonde.

438 'Alas!' then sayd good Robyn,
'Alas and well a woo!
Yf I dwele lenger with the kynge,
Sorowe wyll me sloo.'

439 Forth than went Robyn Hode
Tyll he came to our kynge:
'My lorde the kynge of Englonde,
Graunte me myn askynge.

440 'I made a chapell in Bernysdale,
That semely is to se,
It is of Mary Magdaleyne,
And thereto wolde I be.

441 'I myght neuer in this seuen nyght
No tyme to slepe ne wynke,
Nother all these seuen dayes
Nother ete ne drynke.

442 'Me longeth sore to Bernysdale,
I may not be therfro;
Barefote and wolwarde I haue hyght,
Thyder for to go.'

443 'Yf it be so,' than sayd our kynge,
   'It may no better be,
   Seuen nyght I gyue the leue,
    No lengre, to dwell fro me.'

444 'Gramercy, lorde,' then sayd Robyn,
   And set hym on his kne;
   He toke his leuë full courteysly,
    To grenë wode then went he

445 Whan he came to grenë wode,
   In a mery mornynge,
   There he herde the notës small
    Of byrdës mery syngynge.

446 'It is ferre gone,' sayd Robyn,
   'That I was last here;
   Me lyste a lytell for to shote
    At the donnë dere.'

447 Robyn slewe a full grete harte;
   His horne than gan he blow,
   That all the outlawes of that forest
    That horne coud they knowe,

448 And gadred them togyder,
   In a lytell throwe.
   Seuen score of wyght yonge men
    Came redy on a rowe,

449 And fayre dyde of theyr hodes,
   And set them on theyr kne:
   'Welcome,' they sayd, 'our [derë]
    mayster,
   Under this grenë-wode tre.'

450 Robyn dwelled in grenë wode
   Twenty yere and two;
   For all drede of Edwarde our kynge,
    Agayne wolde he not goo.

451 Yet he was begyled, i-wys,
   Through a wycked woman,
   The pryoresse of Kyrkësly,
    That nye was of hys kynne:

452 For the loue of a knyght,
   Syr Roger of Donkesly,
   That was her ownë speciall;
    Full euyll motë they the !

453 They toke togyder theyr counsell
   Robyn Hode for to sle,
   And how they myght best do that dede,
    His banis for to be.

454 Than bespake good Robyn,
   In place where as he stode,
   'To morow I muste to Kyrke[s]ly,
    Craftely to be leten blode.'

455 Syr Roger of Donkestere,
   By the pryoresse he lay,
   And there they betrayed good Robyn
    Hode,
   Through theyr falsë playe.

456 Cryst haue mercy on his soule,
   That dyed on the rode !
   For he was a good outlawe,
    And dyde pore men moch god.

118

ROBIN HOOD AND GUY OF GISBORNE

The beginning and perhaps the development of the story might have been more lucid but for verses lost at the very start. Robin Hood dreams of two yeomen that beat and bind him, and goes to seek them, "in green-wood where they be." Sir Guy being one, the other person pointed at must of course be the sheriff of Nottingham, in league with Sir Guy (a Yorkshireman, who has done many a curst turn) for the capture or slaying of Robin. The dream simply foreshadows danger from two quarters. But Robin Hood is nowhere informed, as we are, that the sheriff is out against him with seven score men, has attacked his camp, and taken John prisoner. He knows nothing of this so far on as stanza 45^3, where, after killing Guy, he says he will go to Barnsdale to see how his men are faring. Why then does he make his arrangements in stanzas 42–45^2, before he returns to Barnsdale, to pass himself off for Sir Guy ? Plainly this device is adopted with the knowledge that John is a prisoner, and as a means of delivering him; which all that follows shows. Our embarrassment is the greater because we cannot point out any place in the story at which the necessary information could have been conveyed. It will not be enough, therefore, to suppose that verses have been dropped out; there must also have been a considerable derangement of the story. The abrupt transition from the introductory verses is found in 'Adam Bell' (No. 116), and the like occurs in other ballads. A fragment of a dramatic piece founded on the ballad of 'Guy of Gisborne' has been preserved in a manuscript of the date of 1475 or earlier.

'Guye of Gisborne,' Percy MS., p. 262 ;
Hales and Furnivall, II. 227.

1 WHEN shawes beene sheene, and shradds
    full fayre,
  And leeues both large and longe,
  Itt is merry, walking in the fayre ffor-
    rest,
  To heare the small birds songe.

2 The woodweele sang, and wold not cease,
  Amongst the leaues a lyne :
  And it is by two wight yeomen,
  By deare God, *that* I meane.

    *   *   *   *   *

3 ' Me thought they did mee beate and
    binde,
  And tooke my bow mee froe ;
  If I bee Robin a-liue in this lande,
  I 'le be wrocken on both them towe.'

4 'Sweauens are swift, m*a*ster,' quoth Iohn,
  ' As the wind *that* blowes ore a hill ;
  Ffor if itt be neu*er* soe lowde this
    night,
  To-morrow it may be still.'

5 ' Buske yee, bowne yee, my merry men
    all,
  Ffor Iohn shall goe with mee ;
  For I 'le goe seeke yond wight yeomen
  In greenwood where the bee.'

6 Thé cast on their gowne of greene,
  A shooting gone are they,
  Vntill they came to the merry green-
    wood,
  Where they had gladdest bee ;
  There were the ware of [a] wight yeo-
    man,
  His body leaned to a tree.

7 A sword and a dagger he wore by his
    side,
  Had beene many a mans bane,
  And he was cladd in his capull-hyde,
  Topp, and tayle, and mayne.

8 ' Stand you still, m*a*ster,' quoth Litle
    Iohn,
  ' Vnder this trusty tree,
  And I will goe to yond wight yeoman,
  To know his meaning trulye.'

9 ' A, Iohn, by me thou setts noe store,
  And *that* 's a ffarley thinge ;
  How offt send I my men beffore,
  And tarry my-selfe behinde ?

10 ' It is noe cunning a knaue to ken,
  Aud a man but heare him speake ;
  And itt were not for bursting of my
    bowe,
  Iohn, I wold thy head breake.'

11 But often words they breeden bale,
  That parted Robin and Iohn ;
  Iohn is gone to Barn[e]sdale,
  The gates he knowes eche one.

12 And when hee came to Barnesdale,
  Great heauinesse there hee hadd ;
  He ffound two of his fellowes
  Were slaine both in a slade,

13 And Scarlett a ffoote flyinge was,
  Ou*er* stockes and stone,
  For the sheriffe with seuen score men
  Fast after him is gone.

14 ' Yett one shoote I 'le shoote,' sayes Little
    Iohn,
  ' With Crist his might and mayne ;
  I 'le make yond fellow *that* flyes soe fast
  To be both glad and ffaine.'

15 Iohn bent vp a good veiwe bow,
  And ffetteled him to shoote ;
  The bow was made of a tender boughe,
  And fell downe to his foote.

16 ' Woe worth thee, wicked wood,' say*d*
    Litle Iohn,
  ' *That* ere thou grew on a tree !
  Ffor this day thou art my bale,
  My boote when thou shold bee !'

17 This shoote it was but looselye shott,
  The arrowe flew in vaine,
  And it mett one of the sheriffes men ;
  Good W*illia*m a Trent was slaine.

18 It had beene better for W*illia*m a Trent
  To hange vpon a gallowe
  Then for to lye in the greenwoode,
  There slaine with an arrowe.

19 And it is sayd, when men be mett,
  Six can doe more then three :

And they haue tane Litle Iohn,
And bound him ffast to a tree.

20 'Thou shalt be drawen by dale and
  downe,' quoth the sheriffe,
  'And hanged hye on a hill:'
  'But thou may ffayle,' quoth Litle Iohn,
  'If itt be Christs owne will.'

21 Let vs leaue talking of Litle Iohn,
  For hee is bound fast to a tree,
  And talke of Guy and Robin Hood,
  In the green woode where they bee.

22 How these two yeomen together they
  mett,
  Vnder the leaues of lyne,
  To see what marchandise they made
  Euen at that same time.

23 'Good morrow, good fellow,' quoth Sir
  Guy;
  'Good morrow, good ffellow,' quoth
  hee;
  'Methinkes by this bow thou beares in
  thy hand,
  A good archer thou seems to bee.'

24 'I am wilfull of my way,' quoth Sir
  Guye,
  'And of my morning tyde:'
  'I 'le lead thee through the wood,' quoth
  Robin,
  'Good ffellow, I 'le be thy guide.'

25 'I seeke an outlaw,' quoth Sir Guye,
  'Men call him Robin Hood;
  I had rather meet with him vpon a day
  Then forty pound of golde.'

26 'If you tow mett, itt wold be seene
  whether were better
  Afore yee did part awaye;
  Let vs some other pastime find,
  Good ffellow, I thee pray.'

27 'Let vs some other masteryes make,
  And wee will walke in the woods euen;
  Wee may chance mee[t] with Robin
  Hoode
  Att some vnsett steven.'

28 They cutt them downe the summer
  shroggs
  Which grew both vnder a bryar,

And sett them three score rood in twinn,
To shoote the prickes full neare.

29 'Leade on, good ffellow,' sayd Sir Guye,
  'Lead on, I doe bidd thee :'
  'Nay, by my faith,' quoth Robin Hood,
  'The leader thou shalt bee.'

30 The first good shoot that Robin ledd
  Did not shoote an inch the pricke
  ffroe;
  Guy was an archer good enoughe,
  But he cold neere shoote soe.

31 The second shoote Sir Guy shott,
  He shott within the garlande;
  But Robin Hoode shott it better then
  hee,
  For he cloue the good pricke-wande.

32 'Gods blessing on thy heart!' sayes
  Guye,
  'Goode ffellow, thy shooting is goode;
  For an thy hart be as good as thy
  hands,
  Thou were better then Robin Hood.

33 'Tell me thy name, good ffellow,' quoth
  Guy,
  'Vnder the leaues of lyne:'
  'Nay, by my faith,' quoth good Robin,
  'Till thou haue told me thine.'

34 'I dwell by dale and downe,' quoth Guye,
  'And I haue done many a curst turne;
  And he that calles me by my right name
  Calles me Guye of good Gysborne.'

35 'My dwelling is in the wood,' sayes
  Robin,
  'By thee I set right nought;
  My name is Robin Hood of Barnesdale,
  A ffellow thou has long sought.'

36 He that had neither beene a kithe nor
  kin
  Might haue seene a full fayre sight,
  To see how together these yeomen went,
  With blades both browne and bright.

37 To haue seene how these yeomen to-
  gether foug[ht],
  Two howers of a summers day;
  Itt was neither Guy nor Robin Hood
  That ffettled them to flye away.

38 Robin was reacheles on a roote,
  And stumbled at *that* tyde,
  And Guy was quicke and nimble with-
    all,
  And hitt him ore the left side.

39 'Ah, deere Lady!' sayd Robin Hoode,
  'Thou art both mother and may!
  I thinke it was neu*er* mans destinye
  To dye before his day.'

40 Robin thought on Our Lady deere,
  And soone leapt vp againe,
  And thus he came w*i*th an awkwarde
    stroke;
  Good S*i*r Guy hee has slayne.

41 He tooke S*i*r Guys head by the hayre,
  And sticked itt on his bowes end:
  'Thou hast beene traytor all thy liffe,
  W*hi*ch thing must haue an ende.'

42 Robin pulled forth an Irish kniffe,
  And nicked S*i*r Guy in the ffácе,
  That hee was neuer on a woman borne
  Cold tell who S*i*r Guye was.

43 Saies, Lye there, lye there, good S*i*r
    Guye,
  And w*i*th me be not wrothe;
  If thou haue had the worse stroakes at
    my hand,
  Thou shalt haue the better cloathe.

44 Robin did off his gowne of greene,
  S*i*r Guye hee did it throwe;
  And hee put on *that* capull-hyde,
  That cladd him topp to toe.

45 'The bowe, the arrowes, and litle horne,
  And with me now I 'le beare;
  Ffor now I will goe to Barn[e]sdale,
  To see how my men doe ffare.'

46 Robin sett Guyes horne to his mouth,
  A lowd blast in it he did blow;
  That beheard the sheriffe of Notting-
    ham,
  As he leaned vnder a lowe.

47 'Hearken! hearken!' sayd the sheriffe,
  'I heard noe tydings but good;
  For yonder I heare S*i*r Guyes horne
    blowe,
  For he hath slaine Robin Hoode.

48 'For yonder I heare S*i*r Guyes horne
    blow,
  Itt blowes soe well in tyde,
  For yonder comes *that* wighty yeoman,
  Cladd in his capull-hyde.

49 'Come hither, thou good S*i*r Guy,
  Aske of mee what thou wilt haue:'
  'I 'le none of thy gold,' sayes Robin
    Hood,
  'Nor I 'le none of itt haue.

50 'But now I haue slaine the m*a*ster,' he
    sayd,
  'Let me goe strike the knaue;
  This is all the reward I aske,
  Nor noe other will I haue.'

51 'Thou art a madman,' said the shiriffe,
  'Thou sholdest haue had a knights
    ffee;
  Seeing thy asking [hath] beene soe badd,
  Well granted it shall be.'

52 But Litle Iohn heard his m*a*ster speake,
  Well he knew *that* was his steuen;
  'Now shall I be loset,' quoth Litle Iohn,
  'With Christs might in heauen.'

53 But Robin hee hyed him towards Litle
    Iohn,
  Hee thought hee wold loose him
    beliue;
  The sheriffe and all his companye
  Fast after him did driue.

54 'Stand abacke! stand abacke!' sayd
    Robin;
  'Why draw you mee soe neere?
  Itt was neu*er* the vse in our countrye
  One's shrift another shold heere.'

55 But Robin pulled forth an Irysh kniffe,
  And losed Iohn hand and ffoote,
  And gaue him S*i*r Guyes bow in his hand,
  And bade it be his boote.

56 But Iohn tooke Guyes bow in his hand —
  His arrowes were rawstye by the
    roote — ;
  The sherriffe saw Litle Iohn draw a bow
  And ffettle him to shoote.

57 Towards his house in Nottingam
  He ffled full fast away,

And soe did all his companye,
    Not one behind did stay.

58 But he cold neither soe fast goe,
        Nor away soe fast runn,
    But Litle Iohn, with an arrow broade,
        Did cleaue his heart in twinn.

119

ROBIN HOOD AND THE MONK

The gap at st. 30, l. 2, occurs between two
pages. Doubtless some one of Robin's many
friends carries the news of his capture to the
band. With this there must have come information that he was to await knowledge of
the King's pleasure. There is a general resemblance between the rescue of Robin in sts. 61–
81 and that of Cloudsly in 'Adam Bell' (No.
116), sts. 56–94. Robin Hood's devotion to the
Virgin (st. 34) is a feature which reappears in
Nos. 118, 121, 123, and above all in the Gest
(No. 117).

a. MS. of about 1450, Cambridge University Library, Ff. 5, 48, fol. 128 b. b. One leaf of
a MS. of the same age, containing stanzas 69³–
72, 77²–80², Bagford Ballads, vol. i, art. 6, British Museum.

1 In somer, when þe shawes be sheyne,
        And leves be large and long,
    Hit is full mery in feyre foreste
        To here þe foulys song:

2 To se þe dere draw to þe dale,
        And leve þe hilles hee,
    And shadow hem in þe levës grene,
        Vnder the grene-wode tre.

3 Hit befel on Whitsontide,
        Erly in a May mornyng,
    The son vp feyre can shyne,
        And the briddis mery can syng.

4 'This is a mery mornyng,' seid Litull
        John,
    'Be hym þat dyed on tre;
    A more mery man þen I am one
        Lyves not in Cristiantë.

5 'Pluk vp þi hert, my dere mayster,'
        Litull John can sey,
    'And thynk hit is a full fayre tyme
        In a mornyng of May.'

6 'Ȝe, on thyng greves me,' seid Robyn,
        'And does my hert mych woo;
    þat I may not no solem day
        To mas nor matyns goo.

7 'Hit is a fourtnet and more,' seid he,
        'Syn I my sauyour see;
    To day wil I to Notyngham,' seid Robyn,
        'With þe myght of mylde Marye.'

8 Than spake Moche, þe mylner sun,
        Euer more wel hym betyde !
    'Take twelue of þi wyght ȝemen,
        Well weppynd, be þi side.
    Such on wolde þi selfe slon,
        þat twelue dar not abyde.'

9 'Of all my mery men,' seid Robyn,
        'Be my feith I wil non haue,
    But Litull John shall beyre my bow,
        Til þat me list to drawe.'

10 'þou shall beyre þin own,' seid Litull
        Jon,
    'Maister, and I wyl beyre myne,
    And we well shete a peny,' seid Litull
        Jon,
    'Vnder þe grene-wode lyne.'

11 'I wil not shete a peny,' seyd Robyn
        Hode,
    'In feith, Litull John, with the,
    But euer for on as þou shetis,' seide
        Robyn,
    'In feith I holde þe thre.'

12 Thus shet þei forth, þese ȝemen too,
        Bothe at buske and brome,
    Til Litull John wan of his maister
        Fiue shillings to hose and shone.

13 A ferly strife fel þem betwene,
        As they went bi the wey;
    Litull John seid he had won fiue shil-
        lings,
    And Robyn Hode seid schortly nay.

14 With þat Robyn Hode lyed Litul Jon,
        And smote hym with his hande;
    Litul Jon waxed wroth þerwith,
        And pulled out his bright bronde.

15 'Were þou not my maister,' seid Litull
        John,
    'þou shuldis by hit ful sore;

Get þe a man wher þou w[ilt],
  For þou getis me no more.'

6 þen Robyn goes to Notyngham,
  Hym selfe mornyng allone,
  And Litull John to mery Scherwode,
  The pathes he knew ilkone.

7 Whan Robyn came to Notyngham,
  Sertenly withouten layn,
  He prayed to God and myld Mary
  To bryng hym out saue agayn.

18 He gos in to Seynt Mary chirch,
  And kneled down before the rode;
  Alle þat euer were þe church within
  Beheld wel Robyn Hode.

19 Beside hym stod a gret-hedid munke,
  I pray to God woo he be !
  Fful sone he knew gode Robyn,
  As sone as he hym se.

20 Out at þe durre he ran,
  Fful sone and anon;
  Alle þe ʒatis of Notyngham
  He made to be sparred euerychon.

21 ' Rise vp,' he seid, ' þou prowde schereff,
  Buske þe and make þe bowne;
  I haue spyed þe kynggis felon,
  Ffor sothe he is in þis town.

22 ' I haue spyed þe false felon,
  As he stondis at his masse;
  Hit is long of þe,' seide þe munke,
  ' And euer he fro vs passe.

23 ' þis traytur name is Robyn Hode,
  Vnder þe grene-wode lynde;
  He robbyt me onys of a hundred pound,
  Hit shalle neuer out of my mynde.'

24 Vp þen rose þis prowde shereff,
  And radly made hym ʒare;
  Many was þe moder son
  To þe kyrk with hym can fare.

25 In at þe durres þei throly thrast,
  With staves ful gode wone;
  ' Alas, alas ! ' seid Robyn Hode,
  ' Now mysse I Litull John.'

26 But Robyn toke out a too-hond sworde,
  þat hangit down be his kne;

þer as þe schereff and his men stode thyckust,
  The þurwarde wolde he.

27 Thryes thorowout þem he ran þen,
  For soþe as I yow sey,
  And woundyt mony a moder son,
  And twelue he slew þat day.

28 His sworde vpon þe schireff hed
  Sertanly he brake in too;
  ' þe smyth þat þe made,' seid Robyn,
  ' I pray to God wyrke hym woo !

29 ' Ffor now am I weppynlesse,' seid Robyn,
  ' Alasse ! agayn my wylle;
  But if I may fle þese traytors fro,
  I wot þei wil me kyll.'

30 Robyn in to the churchë ran,
  Throout hem euerilkon,

* * * * *

31 Sum fel in swonyng as þei were dede,
  And lay stil as any stone;
  Non of theym were in her mynde
  But only Litull Jon.

32 ' Let be your rule,' seid Litull Jon,
  ' Ffor his luf þat dyed on tre,
  Ʒe þat shulde be duʒty men;
  Het is gret shame to se.

33 ' Oure maister has bene hard bystode
  And ʒet scapyd away;
  Pluk vp your hertis, and leve þis mone,
  And harkyn what I shal say.

34 ' He has seruyd Oure Lady many a day,
  And ʒet wil, securly;
  þerfor I trust in hir specialy
  No wyckud deth shal he dye.

35 ' þerfor be glad,' seid Litul John,
  ' And let þis mournyng be;
  And I shal be þe munkis gyde,
  With þe myght of mylde Mary.

36 .   .   .   .   .   .
  ' We will go but we too;
  And I mete hym,' seid Litul John,

.   .   .   .   .

37 'Loke þat ʒe kepe wel owre tristil-tre,
　　Vnder þe levys smale,
　　And spare non of this venyson,
　　þat gose in thys vale.'

38 Fforþe þen went these ʒemen too,
　　Litul John and Moche on fere,
　　And lokid on Moch emys hows,
　　þe hye way lay full nere.

39 Litul John stode at a wyndow in þe
　　　　mornyng,
　　And lokid forþ at a stage;
　　He was war wher þe munke came
　　　　ridyng,
　　And with hym a litul page.

40 'Be my feith,' seid Litul John to Moch,
　　'I can þe tel tithyngus gode;
　　I se wher þe munke cumys rydyng,
　　I know hym be his wyde hode.'

41 They went in to the way, þese ʒemen
　　　　boþe,
　　As curtes men and hende;
　　þei spyrred tithyngus at þe munke,
　　As they hade bene his frende.

42 'Ffro whens come ʒe?' seid Litull
　　　　Jon,
　　'Tel vs tithyngus, I yow pray,
　　Off a false owtlay, [callid Robyn Hode,]
　　Was takyn ʒisterday.

43 'He robbyt me and my felowes boþe
　　Of twenti marke in serten;
　　If þat false owtlay be takyn,
　　Ffor soþe we wolde be fayn.'

44 'So did he me,' seid þe munke,
　　'Of a hundred pound and more ;
　　I layde furst hande hym apon,
　　ʒe may thonke me þerfore.'

45 'I pray God thanke you,' seid Litull
　　　　John,
　　'And we wil when we may;
　　We wil go with you, with your leve,
　　And bryng yow on your way.

46 'Ffor Robyn Hode hase many a wilde
　　　　felow,
　　I tell you in certen;
　　If þei wist ʒe rode þis way,
　　In feith ʒe shulde be slayn.'

47 As þei went talking be þe way,
　　The munke and Litull John,
　　John toke þe munkis horse be þe hede
　　Fful sone and anon.

48 Johne toke þe munkis horse be þe hed
　　Ffor soþe as I yow say;
　　So did Much þe litull page,
　　Ffor he shulde not scape away.

49 Be þe golett of þe hode
　　John pulled þe munke down;
　　John was nothyng of hym agast,
　　He lete hym falle on his crown.

50 Litull John was so[re] agrevyd,
　　And drew owt his swerde in hye;
　　This munke saw he shulde be ded,
　　Lowd mercy can he crye.

51 'He was my maister,' seid Litull John,
　　'þat þou hase browʒt in bale;
　　Shalle þou neuer cum at our kyng,
　　Ffor to telle hym tale.'

52 John smote of þe munkis hed,
　　No longer wolde he dwell;
　　So did Moch þe litull page,
　　Ffor ferd lest he wolde tell.

53 þer þei beryed hem boþe,
　　In nouþer mosse nor lyng,
　　And Litull John and Much infere
　　Bare þe letturs to oure kyng.

54 . 　　.　　.　　.　　.
　　He knelid down vpon his kne:
　　'God ʒow saue, my lege lorde,
　　Ihesus yow saue and se !

55 'God yow saue, my lege kyng !'
　　To speke John was full bolde;
　　He gaf hym þe letturs in his hond,
　　The kyng did hit vnfold.

56 þe kyng red þe letturs anon,
　　And seid, So mot I the,
　　þer was neuer ʒoman in mery Inglond
　　I longut so sore to se.

57 'Wher is þe munke þat þese shuld haue
　　　　brouʒt ?'
　　Oure kyng can say:
　　'Be my trouth,' seid Litull John,
　　'He dyed after þe way.'

8 Þe kyng gaf Moch and Litul Jon
　　Twenti pound in sertan,
　And made þeim ȝemen of þe crown,
　　And bade þeim go agayn.

9 He gaf John þe seel in hand,
　　The sheref for to bere,
　To bryng Robyn hym to,
　　And no man do hym dere.

0 John toke his leve at oure kyng,
　　Þe sothe as I yow say;
　Þe next way to Notyngham
　　To take, he ȝede þe way.

1 Whan John came to Notyngham
　　The ȝatis were sparred ychon;
　John callid vp þe porter,
　　He answerid sone anon.

2 'What is þe cause,' seid Litul Jon,
　　'Þou sparris þe ȝates so fast ?'
　'Because of Robyn Hode,' seid [þe]
　　　porter,
　'In depe prison is cast.

3 'John and Moch and Wyll Scathlok,
　　Ffor sothe as I yow say,
　þei slew oure men vpon our wallis,
　　And sawten vs euery day.'

4 Litull John spyrred after þe schereff,
　　And sone he hym fonde;
　He oppyned þe kyngus priue seell,
　　And gaf hym in his honde.

5 Whan þe scheref saw þe kyngus seell,
　　He did of his hode anon:
　'Wher is þe munke þat bare þe letturs ?'
　　He seid to Litull John.

6 'He is so fayn of hym,' seid Litul John,
　　'Ffor soþe as I yow say,
　He has made hym abot of Westmynster,
　　A lorde of þat abbay.'

7 The scheref made John gode chere,
　　And gaf hym wyne of the best;
　At nyȝt þei went to her bedde,
　　And euery man to his rest.

8 When þe scheref was on siepe,
　　Dronken of wyne and ale,
　Litul John and Moch for soþe
　　Toke þe way vnto þe jale.

69 Litul John callid vp þe jayler,
　　And bade hym rise anon;
　He seyd Robyn Hode had brokyn prison,
　　And out of hit was gon.

70 The porter rose anon sertan,
　　As sone as he herd John calle;
　Litul John was redy with a swerd,
　　And bare hym to þe walle.

71 'Now wil I be porter,' seid Litul John,
　　'And take þe keyes in honde :'
　He toke þe way to Robyn Hode,
　　And sone he hym vnbonde.

72 He gaf hym a gode swerd in his hond,
　　His hed [ther]with for to kepe,
　And ther as þe walle was lowyst
　　Anon down can þei lepe.

73 Be þat þe cok began to crow,
　　The day began to spryng;
　The scheref fond þe jaylier ded,
　　The comyn bell made he ryng.

74 He made a crye thoroout al þe tow[n],
　　Wheder he be ȝoman or knave,
　þat cowþe bryng hym Robyn Hode,
　　His warison he shuld haue.

75 'Ffor I dar neuer,' said þe scheref,
　　'Cum before oure kyng;
　Ffor if I do, I wot serten
　　Ffor soþe he wil me heng.'

76 The scheref made to seke Notyng-
　　　ham,
　　Bothe be strete and stye,
　And Robyn was in mery Scherwode,
　　As liȝt as lef on lynde.

77 Then bespake gode Litull John,
　　To Robyn Hode can he say,
　I haue done þe a gode turne for an
　　　euyll,
　Quyte þe whan þou may.

78 'I haue done þe a gode turne,' seid
　　　Litull John,
　　'Ffor sothe as I yow say;
　I haue brouȝt þe vnder grene-wode lyne:
　　Ffare wel, and haue gode day.'

79 'Nay, be my trouth,' seid Robyn Hode.
　　'So shall hit neuer be ;

I make þe maister,' seid Robyn Hode,
   ' Off alle my men and me.'

80 ' Nay, be my trouth,' seid Litull John,
   ' So shalle hit neuer be;
But lat me be a felow,' seid Litull John,
   ' No noder kepe I be.'

81 Thus John gate Robyn Hod out of prison,
   Sertan withoutyn layn;
Whan his men saw hym hol and sounde,
   Ffor sothe they were full fayne.

82 They filled in wyne, and made hem glad,
   Vnder þe levys smale,
And ȝete pastes of venyson,
   þat gode was with ale.

83 Than worde came to oure kyng
   How Robyn Hode was gon,
And how þe scheref of Notyngham
   Durst neuer loke hym vpon.

84 Then bespake oure cumly kyng,
   In an angur hye:
Litull John hase begyled þe schereff,
   In faith so hase he me.

85 Litul John has begyled vs bothe,
   And þat full wel I se;
Or ellis þe schereff of Notyngham
   Hye hongut shulde he be.

86 ' I made hem ȝemen of þe crowne,
   And gaf hem fee with my hond;
I gaf hem grith,' seid oure kyng,
   ' Thorowout all mery Inglond.

87 ' I gaf theym grith,' þen seid oure kyng;
   ' I say, so mot I the,
Ffor sothe soch a ȝeman as he is on
   In all Inglond ar not thre.

88 ' He is trew to his maister,' seid our kyng;
   ' I sey, be swete Seynt John,
He louys better Robyn Hode
   Then he dose vs ychon.

89 ' Robyn Hode is euer bond to hym,
   Bothe in strete and stalle;
Speke no more of this mater.' seid oure kyng,
   ' But John has begyled vs alle.'

90 Thus endys the talkyng of the munke
   And Robyn Hode i-wysse;
God, þat is euer a crowned kyng,
   Bryng vs all to his blisse !

120

ROBIN HOOD'S DEATH

A very interesting passage of the story is lost in A, owing to the tearing away of nine stanzas of the manuscript at st. 8. Robin Hood and John are on their way to Kirklees. They keep up their shooting all the way, until they come to a black water, crossed by a plank. On the plank an old woman is kneeling, and banning Robin Hood. Robin asks why the old woman is banning him, but the answer is lost, and it is not probable that we shall ever know: out of her proper malignity, surely, or because she is a hired witch, for Robin is the friend of lowly folk. But if this old woman is banning, others (no doubt women) are weeping, for somehow they have learned that he is to be let blood that day at the priory, and foresee that ill will come of it. At the middle of st. 18 nine stanzas are again wanting, and again in a place where we are not helped by the other version. John must call from the outside of the building, judging by what follows. An altercation seems to pass between Robin and Red Roger. Robin slips out of a shot-window, and as he does so is thrust through the side by Red Roger. Red Roger must be below, and John is certainly below. He would have seen to Red Roger had they both been within. But John must be under a window on a different side of the building from that whence Robin issues, for otherwise, again, he would have seen to Red Roger. We are driven to suppose that the words in st. 19 pass between Robin above and Roger below. The account of Robin Hood's death in the Gest agrees in the main with what we find in A. B, though found only in late garlands, is in the fine old strain.

A

' Robin Hoode his Death,' Percy MS., p. 21; Hales and Furnivall, i, 53.

1 ' I WILL neuer eate nor drinke,' Robin Hood said,
   ' Nor meate will doo me noe good,
Till I haue beene att merry Church-lees,
   My vaines for to let blood.'

2 'That I reade not,' said Will Scarllett,
  ' Master, by the assente of me,
Without halfe a hundred of your best
    bowmen
  You take to goe with yee.

3 'For there a good yeoman doth abide
  Will be sure to quarrell with thee,
And if thou haue need of vs, master,
  In faith we will not flee.'

4 'And thou be feard, thou William Scar-
    lett,
  Att home I read thee bee:'
' And you be wrothe, my deare master,
  You shall neuer heare more of mee.'

*   *   *   *   *

5 'For there shall noe man with me goe,
  Nor man with mee ryde,
And Litle Iohn shall be my man,
  And beare my benbow by my side.'

6 'You'st beare your bowe, master, your
    selfe,
  And shoote for a peny with mee:'
'To that I doe assent,' Robin Hood
    sayd,
  'And soe, Iohn, lett it bee.'

7 They two bolde children shotten to-
    gether,
  All day theire selfe in ranke,
Vntill they came to blacke water,
  And over it laid a planke.

8 Vpon it there kneeled an old woman,
  Was banning Robin Hoode;
' Why dost thou bann Robin Hoode?'
  said Robin,

.   .   .   .

*   *   *   *   *

9 .   .   .   .   .
  'To giue to Robin Hoode;
Wee weepen for his deare body,
  That this day must be lett bloode.'

10 'The dame prior is my aunts daughter,
  And nie vnto my kinne;
I know shee wold me noe harme this
    day,
  For all the world to winne.'

11 Forth then shotten these children two,
  And they did neuer lin,
Vntill they came to merry Churchlees,
  To merry Churchlee[s] with-in.

12 And when they came to merry Church-
    lees,
  They knoced vpon a pin;
Vpp then rose dame prioresse,
  And lett good Robin in.

13 Then Robin gaue to dame prioresse
  Twenty pound in gold,
And bad her spend while that wold
    last,
  And shee shold haue more when shee
    wold.

14 And downe then came dame prioresse,
  Downe she came in that ilke,
With a pair off blood-irons in her hands,
  Were wrapped all in silke.

15 'Sett a chaffing-dish to the fyer,' said
    dame prioresse,
  'And stripp thou vp thy sleeue:'
I hold him but an vnwise man
  That will noe warning leeue.

16 Shee laid the blood-irons to Robin Hoods
    vaine,
  Alacke, the more pitye !
And pearct the vaine, and let out the
    bloode,
  That full red was to see.

17 And first it bled, the thicke, thicke
    bloode,
  And afterwards the thinne,
And well then wist good Robin Hoode
  Treason there was within.

18 'What cheere my master?' said Litle
    Iohn;
  'In faith, Iohn, litle goode;'

.   .   .   .

*   *   *   *   *

19 'I haue upon a gowne of greene,
  Is cut short by my knee,
And in my hand a bright browne brand
  That will well bite of thee.'

20 But forth then of a shot-windowe
　　Good Robin Hood he could glide;
　Red Roger, with a grounden glaue,
　　Thrust him through the milke-white
　　　side.

21 But Robin was light and nimble of foote,
　　And thought to abate his pride,
　Ffor betwixt his head and his shoulders
　　He made a wound full wide.

22 Says, Ly there, ly there, Red Roger,
　　The doggs they must thee eate;
　'For I may haue my houzle,' he said,
　　'For I may both goe and speake.

23 'Now giue me mood,' Robin said to
　　　Litle Iohn,
　　'Giue me mood with thy hand;
　I trust to God in heauen soe hye
　　My houzle will me bestand.'

24 'Now giue me leaue, giue me leaue,
　　　master,' he said,
　　'For Christs loue giue leaue to me,
　To set a fier within this hall,
　　And to burne vp all Churchlee.'

25 'That I reade not,' said Robin Hoode
　　　then,
　　'Litle Iohn, for it may not be;
　If I shold doe any widow hurt, at my
　　　latter end,
　God,' he said, 'wold blame me;

26 'But take me vpon thy backe, Litle
　　　Iohn,
　　And beare me to yonder streete,
　And there make me a full fayre graue,
　　Of grauell and of greete.

27 'And sett my bright sword at my head,
　　Mine arrowes at my feete,
　And lay my vew-bow by my side,
　　My met-yard wi . . . .

B

'Robin Hood's Death and Burial.' a. The
English Archer, Paisley, printed by John Neil-
son for George Caldwell, Bookseller, near the
Cross, 1786, p. 81, No. 24. Bodleian Library,
Douce, F. F. 71 (6). b. The English Archer,
York, printed by N. Nickson, in Feasegate,
n. d., p. 70. Bodleian Library, Douce, F. F.
71 (4).

1 When Robin Hood and Little John
　　Down a down a down a down
　Went oer yon bank of broom,
　　Said Robin Hood bold to Littl
　　　John,
　We have shot for many a pound.
　　Hey, etc.

2 But I am not able to shoot one sho
　　　more,
　　My broad arrows will not flee;
　But I have a cousin lives down below,
　　Please God, she will bleed me.

3 Now Robin he is to fair Kirkly gone,
　　As fast as he can win;
　But before he came there, as we d
　　　hear,
　He was taken very ill.

4 And when he came to fair Kirkly-hall,
　　He knockd all at the ring,
　But none was so ready as his cousi
　　　herself
　For to let bold Robin in.

5 'Will you please to sit down, cousi
　　　Robin,' she said,
　　'And drink some beer with me ?
　'No, I will neither eat nor drink,
　　Till I am blooded by thee.'

6 'Well, I have a room, cousin Robin,
　　　she said,
　　'Which you did never see,
　And if you please to walk therein,
　　You blooded by me shall be.'

7 She took him by the lily-white hand,
　　And led him to a private room,
　And there she blooded bold Robin Hood
　　While one drop of blood would ru
　　　down.

8 She blooded him in a vein of the arm,
　　And locked him up in the room;
　Then did he bleed all the live-long
　　　day,
　Until the next day at noon.

9 He then bethought him of a casement
　　　there,
　　Thinking for to get down;
　But was so weak he could not leap,
　　He could not get him down.

10 He then bethought him of his bugle-
horn,
Which hung low down to his knee;
He set his horn unto his mouth,
And blew out weak blasts three.

11 Then Little John, when hearing him,
As he sat under a tree,
'I fear my master is now near dead,
He blows so wearily.'

12 Then Little John to fair Kirkly is gone,
As fast as he can dree;
But when he came to Kirkly-hall,
He broke locks two or three:

13 Until he came bold Robin to see,
Then he fell on his knee;
'A boon, a boon,' cries Little John,
'Master, I beg of thee.'

14 'What is that boon,' said Robin Hood,
'Little John, [thou] begs of me?'
'It is to burn fair Kirkly-hall,
And all their nunnery.'

15 'Now nay, now nay,' quoth Robin Hood,
'That boon I'll not grant thee;
I never hurt woman in all my life,
Nor men in woman's company.

16 'I never hurt fair maid in all my time,
Nor at mine end shall it be;
But give me my bent bow in my hand,
And a broad arrow I'll let flee
And where this arrow is taken up,
There shall my grave digged be.

17 'Lay me a green sod under my head,
And another at my feet;
And lay my bent bow by my side,
Which was my music sweet;
And make my grave of gravel and green,
Which is most right and meet.

18 'Let me have length and breadth
enough,
With a green sod under my head;
That they may say, when I am dead,
Here lies bold Robin Hood.'

19 These words they readily granted him,
Which did bold Robin please:
And there they buried bold Robin Hood,
Within the fair Kirkleys.

121

ROBIN HOOD AND THE POTTER

'Robin Hood and the Butcher' (No. 122)
repeats many of the incidents of the present
ballad. There are only too many variations of
the adventure in which Robin Hood unexpect-
edly meets his match in a hand-to-hand fight,
now with a pinder, then with a tanner, tinker,
shepherd, beggar, etc. His adversaries, after
proving their mettle, are sometimes invited
and induced to join his company: not so here.
In some broadside ballads of this description,
with an extravagance common enough in imitations, Robin Hood is very badly mauled, and
made all but contemptible. The Play of Robin
Hood, an imperfect copy of which is printed
at the end of Copland's and of White's edition
of the Gest, is founded on the present ballad
and on No. 123.

Library of the University of Cambridge, MS.
E e. 4. 35, fol. 14 b, of about 1500.

1 In schomer, when the leves spryng,
The bloschoms on euery bowe,
So merey doyt the berdys syng
Yn wodys merey now.

2 Herkens, god yemen,
Comley, corteys, and god,
On of the best þat yeuer bare bowe,
Hes name was Roben Hode.

3 Roben Hood was the yeman's name,
That was boyt corteys and ffre;
Ffor the loffe of owre ladey,
All wemen werschepyd he.

4 Bot as the god yeman stod on a day,
Among hes mery maney,
He was ware of a prowd potter,
Cam dryfyng owyr the ley.

5 'Yonder comet a prod potter,' seyde
Roben,
'That long hayt hantyd þis wey;
He was neuer so corteys a man
On peney of pawage to pay.'

6 'Y met hem bot at Went-breg,' seyde
Lytyll John,
'And therefore yeffell mot he the!
Seche thre strokes he me gafe,
Yet by my seydys cleffe þey.

7 'Y ley forty shillings,' seyde Lytyll
 John,
  'To pay het thes same day,
Ther ys nat a man among hus all
 A wed schall make hem ley.'

8 'Here ys forty shillings,' seyde Roben,
  'More, and thow dar say,
Þat y schall make þat prowde potter,
 A wed to me schall he ley.'

9 There thes money they leyde,
 They toke het a yeman to kepe;
Roben beffore the potter he breyde,
 A[nd] bad hem stond stell.

10 Handys apon hes hors he leyde,
 And bad the potter stonde foll stell;
The potter schorteley to hem seyde,
 Ffelow, what ys they well?

11 'All thes thre yer, and more, potter,' he
  seyde,
  'Thow hast hantyd thes wey,
Yet were tow neuer so cortys a man
 On peney of pauage to pay.'

12 'What ys they name,' seyde þe potter,
  'Ffor pauage thow aske of me?'
'Roben Hod ys mey name,
 A wed schall thow leffe me.'

13 'Wed well y non leffe,' seyde þe pot-
  ter,
  'Nor pavag well y non pay;
Awey they honde ffro mey hors!
 Y well the tene eyls, be mey ffay.'

14 The potter to hes cart he went,
 He was not to seke;
A god to-hande staffe þerowt he hent,
 Beffore Roben he leppyd.

15 Roben howt with a swerd bent,
 A bokeler en hes honde;
The potter to Roben he went,
 And seyde, Ffelow, let mey hors go.

16 Togeder then went thes to yemen,
 Het was a god seyt to se;
Thereof low Robyn hes men,
 There they stod onder a tre.

17 Leytell John to hes ffelowhe[s] seyde,
  'Yend potter well steffeley stonde:'

The potter, with a acward stroke,
 Smot the bokeler owt of hes honde.

18 A[nd] ar Roben meyt get het agen
 Hes bokeler at hes ffette,
The potter yn the neke hem toke,
 To the gronde sone he yede.

19 That saw Roben hes men,
 As thay stod onder a bow;
'Let vs helpe owre master,' seyde Lytell
  John,
  'Yonder potter,' seyde he, 'els well
  hem slo.'

20 Thes yemen went with a breyde,
 To ther mast[er] they cam.
Leytell John to hes mast[er] seyde,
 Ho haet the wager won?

21 'Schall y haffe yowre forty shillings,'
  seyde Lytl John,
  'Or ye, master, schall haffe myne?'
'Yeff they were a hundred,' seyde Roben,
  'Y ffeythe, they ben all theyne.'

22 'Het ys fol leytell cortesey,' seyde þe
  potter,
  'As y haffe harde weyse men saye,
Yeffe a pore yeman com drywyng on
  the wey,
 To let hem of hes gorney.'

23 'Be mey trowet, thow seys soyt,' seyde
  Roben,
  'Thow seys god yeme[n]rey;
And thow dreyffe fforthe yeuery day,
 Thow schalt neuer be let ffor me.

24 'Y well prey the, god potter,
 A ffelischepe well thow haffe?
Geffe me they clothyng, and þow schalt
  hafe myne;
 Y well go to Notynggam.'

25 'Y gra[n]t thereto,' seyde the potter,
  'Thow schalt ffeynde me a ffelow
  gode;
Bot thow can sell mey pottys well,
 Com ayen as thow yode.'

26 'Nay, be mey trowt,' seyde Roben,
  'And then y bescro mey hede.
Yeffe y bryng eny pottys ayen,
 And eney weyffe well hem chepe.'

27 Than spake Leytell John,
    And all hes ffelowhes heynd,
  'Master, be well ware of the screffe of
      Notynggam,
    Ffor he ys leytell howr ffrende.'

28 'Heyt war howte !' seyde Roben,
    'Ffelowhes, let me a lone;
  Thorow the helpe of Howr Ladey,
    To Notynggam well y gon.'

29 Robyn went to Notynggam,
    Thes pottys ffor to sell;
  The potter abode with Robens men,
    There he ffered not eylle.

30 Tho Roben droffe on hes wey,
    So merey ower the londe:
  Her es more, and affter ys to saye,
    The best ys beheynde.

31 When Roben cam to Notynggam,
    The soyt yef y scholde saye,
  He set op hes hors anon,
    And gaffe hem hotys and haye.

32 Yn the medys of the towne,
    There he schowed hes ware;
  'Pottys ! pottys !' he gan crey foll
      sone,
    'Haffe hansell ffor the mare ! '

33 Ffoll effen agenest the screffeys gate
    Schowed he hes chaffare;
  Weyffes and wedowes abowt hem
      drow,
    And chepyd ffast of hes ware.

34 Yet, 'Pottys, gret chepe !' creyed Robyn,
    'Y loffe yeffell thes to stonde; '
  And all that say hem sell
    Seyde he had be no potter long.

35 The pottys that were werthe pens ffeyffe,
    He solde tham ffor pens thre;
  Preveley seyde man and weyffe,
    'Ywnder potter schall neuer the.'

36 Thos Roben solde ffoll ffast,
    Tell he had pottys bot ffeyffe;
  Op he hem toke of hes care,
    And sende hem to the screffeys weyffe.

37 Thereof sche was ffoll ffayne,
    'Gereamarsey, ser,' than seyde sche;

  'When ye com to thes contre ayen,
    Y schall bey of the[y] pottys, so mot
      y the.'

38 'Ye schall haffe of the best,' seyde
      Roben,
    And sware be the Treneytë;
  Ffoll corteysley [sc]he gan hem call,
    'Com deyne with the screfe and
      me.'

39 'God amarsey,' seyde Roben,
    'Yowre bedyng schall be doyn; '
  A mayden yn the pottys gan bere,
    Roben and þe screffe weyffe ffolowed
      anon.

40 Whan Roben yn to the hall cam,
    The screffë sone he met;
  The potter cowed of corteysey,
    And sone the screffe he gret.

41 'Lo, ser, what thes potter hayt geffe yow
      and me;
    Ffeyffe pottys smalle and grete ! '
  'He ys ffoll wellcom,' seyd the screffe;
    'Let os was, and go to mete.'

42 As they sat at her methe,
    With a nobell chere,
  To of the screffes men gan speke
    Off a gret wager;

43 Off a schotyng, was god and ffeyne,
    Was made the thother daye,
  Off forty shillings, the soyt to saye,
    Who scholde thes wager wen.

44 Styll than sat thes prowde potter,
    Thos than thowt he;
  As y am a trow cerstyn man,
    Thes schotyng well y se.

45 Whan they had ffared of the best,
    With bred and ale and weyne,
  To the bottys the made them prest,
    With bowes and boltys ffoll ffeyne.

46 The screffes men schot ffoll ffast,
    As archares þat weren godde;
  There cam non ner ney the marke
    Bey halffe a god archares bowe.

47 Stell then stod the prowde potter,
    Thos than seyde he:

And y had a bow, be the rode,
 On schot scholde yow se.

48 'Thow schall haffe a bow,' seyde the screffe,
 'The best þat thow well cheys of thre;
Thou semyst a stalward and a stronge,
 Asay schall thow be.'

49 The screffe commandyd a yeman þat stod hem bey
 Affter bowhes to weynde;
 The best bow þat the yeman browthe
Roben set on a stryng.

50 'Now schall y wet and thow be god,
 And polle het op to they nere;'
'So god me helpe,' seyde the prowde potter,
 'þys ys bot ryȝt weke gere.'

51 To a quequer Roben went,
 A god bolt owthe he toke;
So ney on to the marke he went,
 He ffayled not a fothe.

52 All they schot abowthe agen,
 The screffes men and he;
Off the marke he welde not ffayle,
 He cleffcd the preke on thre.

53 The screffes men thowt gret schame
 The potter the mastry wan;
The screffë lowe and made god game,
 And seyde, Potter, thow art a man.

54 . . . . . .

 Thow art worthey to bere a bowe
 Yn what plas that þow goe.

55 'Yn mey cart y haffe a bowe,
 Ffor soyt,' he seyde, 'and that a godde;
Yn mey cart ys the bow
 That gaffe me Robyn Hode.'

56 'Knowest thow Robyn Hode?' seyde the screffe,
 'Potter, y prey the tell thow me;'
'A hundred torne y haffe schot with hem,
 Vnder hes tortyll-tre.'

57 'Y had leuer nar a hundred ponde,'
 seyde þe screffe,

'And sware be the Trenitë,
. . . . .
 þat the ffals outelawe stod be me.'

58 'And ye well do afftyr mey red,' seyde þe potter,
 'And boldeley go with me,
And to morow, or we het bred,
 Roben Hode well we se.'

59 'Y wel queyt the,' kod the screffe,
 'Y swere be God of meythe;'
Schetyng thay left, and hom þey went,
 Her soper was reddy deythe.

60 Vpon the morow, when het was day,
 He boskyd hem fforthe to reyde;
The potter hes cart fforthe gan ray,
 And wolde not leffe beheynde.

61 He toke leffe of the screffys wyrffe,
 And thankyd her of all thyng:
'Dam, ffor mey loffe and ye well þys were,
 Y geffe yow here a golde ryng.'

62 'Gramarsey,' seyde the weyffe,
 'Ser, god eylde het the;'
The screffes hart was neuer so leythe,
 The ffeyre fforeyst to se.

63 And when he cam yn to the fforeyst,
 Yonder the leffes grene,
Berdys there sange on bowhes prest,
 Het was gret goy to se.

64 'Here het ys merey to be,' seyde Roben,
 'Ffor a man that had hawt to spende;
Be mey horne I schall awet
 Yeff Roben Hode be here.'

65 Roben set hes horne to hes mowthe,
 And blow a blast þat was ffoll god;
þat herde hes men þat þere stode,
 Ffer downe yn the wodde.

66 'I her mey master blow,' seyde Leytell John,
. . . . .

 . . . . .
 They ran as thay were wode.

67 Whan thay to thar master cam,
 Leytell John wold not spare;

' Mast*er*, how haffe yow ffar*e* yn Notynggam ?
  How haffe yow solde yowr*e* war*e* ? '

68 ' Ye, be mey trowthe, Leyty[ll] John,
    Loke thow take no car*e*;
    Y haffe browt the screffe of Notynggam,
    Ffor all howr*e* chaffar*e*.'

69 ' He ys ffoll wellcom,' seyde Lytyll John,
    ' Thes tydyng ys ffoll godde;'
    The screffe had leuer nar a hundred
      ponde
    He had [neuer sene Roben Hode.]

70 ' [Had I] west þat befforen,
    At Notynggam when we wer*e*,
    Thow scholde not com yn ffeyr*e* fforest
    Of all thes thowsande eyr*e*.'

71 ' That wot y well,' seyde Roben,
    ' Y thanke God that ye be her*e*;
    Thereffore schall ye leffe yowr*e* hors
      with hos,
    And all yowr*e* hother ger*e*.'

72 ' That ffend I Godys fforbod,' kod the
      screffe,
    ' So to lese mey godde;
    .   .   .   .   .   .
    .   .   .   .   .   . ,

73 ' Hether ye cam on hors ffoll hey,
    And hom schall ye go on ffote;
    And gret well they weyffe at home,
    The woman ys ffoll godde.

74 ' Y schall her sende a wheyt palffrey,
    Het ambellet be mey ffey,
    .   .   .   .   .   .

75 ' Y schall her sende a wheyt palffrey,
    Het hambellet as the weynde;
    Ner*e* ffor the loffe of yowr*e* weyffe,
    Off mor*e* sorow scholde yow seyng.'

76 Thes parted Robyn Hode and the
      screffe;
    To Notynggam he toke the waye;
    Hes weyffe ffeyr*e* welcomed hem hom,
    And to hem gan sche saye:

77 Seyr, how haffe yow ffared yn gr*e*ne
      fforeyst ?
    Haffe ye browt Roben hom ?

' Dam, the deyell spede hem, bothe
    bodey and bon;
    Y haffe hade a ffoll gret skorne.

78 ' Of all the god that y haffe lade *to*
      grene wod,
    He hayt take het ffro me;
    All bot thes ffeyr*e* palffrey,
    That he hayt sende to the.'

79 With þat sche toke op a lowde lawhyng,
    And swhar*e* be hem þat deyed on tre,
    ' Now haffe yow payed ffor all þe pottys
    That Roben gaffe to me.

80 ' Now ye be com hom to Notynggam,
    Ye schall haffe god ynowe;'
    Now speke we of Roben Hode,
    And of the pottyr ondyr the grene
      bowhe.

81 ' Potter, what was they pottys worthe
    To Notynggam þat y ledde w*i*th me ?'
    ' They wer worthe to nobellys,' seyde he,
    ' So mot y treyffe or the;
    So cowde y [haffe] had ffor tham,
    And y had ther*e* be.'

82 ' Thow schalt hafe ten ponde,' seyde
      Roben,
    ' Of money ffeyr*e* and ffre;
    And yeuer whan thow comest to grene
      wod,
    Wellcom, pott*er*, to me.'

83 Thes p*a*rtyd Robyn, the screffe, and the
      pott*er*,
    Ondernethe the grene-wod tre;
    God haffe mersey on Roben Hodys solle
    And saffe all god yemanrey !

122

ROBIN HOOD AND THE BUTCHER

This story is a variation of ' Robin Hood
and the Potter ' (No. 121). There are three
considerable gaps in the manuscript of A; but
B enables us to complete the story. The passage in which the Sheriff is inveigled into
Robin's haunts has close affinity with the Gest,
sts. 181 ff. The first three stanzas of A apparently belong to some other ballad. B a is

signed T. R., as is No. 133 in two editions.
These appear to be the initials of the person
who wrote the story over with middle rhyme
in the third line of the stanza, a peculiarity
which distinguishes a group of ballads sung to
the tune of 'Robin Hood and the Stranger' (see
Introduction to No. 125).

A

'Robin Hood and the Butcher,' Percy MS.,
p. 7; Hales and Furnivall, I, 19.

1 But Robin he walkes in the g[reene]
    fforrest,
  As merry as bird on boughe,
  But he that feitches good Robins head,
    Hee 'le find him game enoughe.

2 But Robine he walkes in the greene
    fforrest,
  Vnder his trusty-tree;
  Sayes, Hearken, hearken, my merrymen
    all,
    What tydings is come to me.

3 The sheriffe he hath made a cry,
  Hee 'le have my head i-wis;
  But ere a tweluemonth come to an end
    I may chance to light on his.

4 Robin he marcht in the greene forrest,
  Vnder the greenwood scray,
  And there he was ware of a proud
    bucher,
    Came driuing flesh by the way.

5 The bucher he had a cut-taild dogg,
  And at Robins face he flew;
  But Robin he was a good sword,
    The bucher's dogg he slew.

6 'Why slayes thou my dogg?' sayes the
    bucher,
  'For he did none ill to thee;
  By all the saints that are in heaven
    Thou shalt haue buffetts three.'

7 He tooke his staffe then in his hand,
  And he turnd him round about:
  'Thou hast a litle wild blood in thy head,
  Good fellow, thou 'st haue it letten
    out.'

8 'He that does that deed,' sayes Robin,
  'I 'le count him for a man;

  But that while will I draw my sword,
    And fend it if I can.'

9 But Robin he stroke att the bloudy
    bucher,
  In place were he did stand,

     *   *   *   *   *

10 'I [am] a younge bucher,' sayes Robin,
  'You fine dames am I come amonge;
  But euer I beseech you, good Mrs Sher-
    iffe,
    You must see me take noe wronge.'

11 'Thou art verry welcome,' said Master
    Sherriff's wiffe,
  'Thy inne heere up [to] take;
  If any good ffellow come in thy com-
    panie,
    Hee 'st be welcome for thy sake.'

12 Robin called ffor ale, soe did he for
    wine,
  And for it he did pay:
  'I must to my markett goe,' says Robin,
  'For I hold time itt of the day.'

13 But Robin is to the markett gone,
  Soe quickly and beliue,
  He sold more flesh for one peny
    Then othe[r] buchers did for fiue.

14 The drew about the younge bucher,
  Like sheepe into a fold;
  Yea neuer a bucher had sold a bitt
    Till Robin he had all sold.

15 When Robin Hood had his markett
    made,
  His flesh was sold and gone;
  Yea he had receiued but a litle mony,
    But thirty pence and one.

16 Seauen buchers, the garded Robin Hood,
  Ffull many time and oft;
  Sayes, We must drinke with you, brother
    bucher,
    It 's custome of our crafte.

17 'If that be the custome of your crafte,
  As heere you tell to me,
  Att four of the clocke in the afternoone
    At the sheriffs hall I wilbe.'

     *   *   *   *   *

18 .   .   .   .   .   .
    ' If thou doe like it well;
    Yea heere is more by three hundred
       pound
    Then thou hast beasts to sell.'

19 Robyn sayd naught, the more he thought:
    ' Mony neere comes out of time;
    If once I catch thee in the greene fforest,
    That mony it shall be mine.'

20 But on the next day seuen butchers
    Came to guard the sheriffe that day;
    But Robin he was the whigh[t]est man,
    He led them all the way.

21 He led them into the greene fforest,
    Vnder the trusty tree;
    Yea, there were harts, and ther were
      hynds,
    And staggs with heads full high.

22 Yea, there were harts and there were
      hynds,
    And many a goodly ffawne;
    ' Now praised be God,' says bold Robin,
    ' All these they be my owne.

23 ' These are my horned beasts,' says Robin,
    ' Master Sherriffe, which must make
      the stake; '
    ' But euer alacke, now,' said the sheriffe,
    ' *That* tydings comes to late ! '

24 Robin sett a shrill horne to his mouth,
    And a loud blast he did blow,
    And then halfe a hundred bold archers
    Came rakeing on a row.

25 But when the came befor bold Robin,
    Even there the stood all bare:
    ' You are welcome, master, from Not-
      tingham:
    How haue you sold your ware ? '

     *   *   *   *   *

26 .   .   .   .   .
    .   .   .   .
    It proues bold Robin Hood.

27 ' Yea, he hath robbed me of all my
      gold
    And siluer *that* euer I had;

But that I had a verry good wife at home,
    I shold haue lost my head.

28 ' But I had a verry good wife at home,
    Which made him gentle cheere,
    And therfor, for my wifes sake,
    I shold haue better favor heere.

29 ' But such favor as he shewed me
    I might haue of the devills dam,
    That will rob a man of all he hath,
    And send him naked home.'

30 ' That is very well done,' then says his
      wiffe,
    ' Itt is well done, I say;
    You might haue tarryed att Nottingham,
    Soe fayre as I did you pray.'

31 ' I haue learned wisdome,' sayes the
      sherriffe,
    ' And, wife, I haue learned of thee;
    But if Robin walke easte, or he walke
      west,
    He shall neuer be sought for me.'

B

' Robin Hood and the Butcher.' **a.** Wood,
401, leaf 19 b. **b.** Garland of 1663, No. 6.
c. Garland of 1670, No. 5. **d.** Pepys, II, 102,
No. 89.

1 COME, all you brave gallants, and listen
    a while,
      With hey down, down, an a down
    That are in the bowers within;
    For of Robin Hood, that archer good,
    A song I intend for to sing.

2 Upon a time it chancëd so
    Bold Robin in forrest did spy
    A jolly butcher, with a bonny fine mare,
    With his flesh to the market did hye.

3 ' Good morrow, good fellow,' said jolly
      Robin,
    ' What food hast ? tell unto me;
    And thy trade to me tell, and where
      thou dost dwell,
    For I like well thy company.'

4 The butcher he answered jolly Robin:
    No matter where I dwell;
    For a butcher I am, and to Notingham
    I am going, my flesh to sell.

5 'What is [the] price of thy flesh?' said
    jolly Robin,
  'Come, tell it soon unto me;
And the price of thy mare, be she never
    so dear,
  For a butcher fain would I be.'

6 'The price of my flesh,' the butcher
    repli'd,
  'I soon will tell unto thee;
With my bonny mare, and they are not
    dear,
  Four mark thou must give unto me.'

7 'Four mark I will give thee,' saith jolly
    Robin,
  'Four mark it shall be thy fee;
Thy mony come count, and let me mount,
  For a butcher I fain would be.'

8 Now Robin he is to Notingham gone,
  His butcher's trade for to begin;
With good intent, to the sheriff he went,
  And there he took up his inn.

9 When other butchers they opened their
    meat,
  Bold Robin he then begun;
But how for to sell he knew not well,
  For a butcher he was but young.

10 When other butchers no meat could
    sell,
  Robin got both gold and fee;
For he sold more meat for one peny
  Than others could do for three.

11 But when he sold his meat so fast,
  No butcher by him could thrive;
For he sold more meat for one peny
  Than others could do for five.

12 Which made the butchers of Notingham
  To study as they did stand,
Saying, surely he was some prodigal,
  That had sold his father's land.

13 The butchers they stepped to jolly Robin,
  Acquainted with him for to be;
'Come, brother,' one said, 'we be all of
    one trade,
  Come, will you go dine with me?'

14 'Accurst of his heart,' said jolly Robin,
  'That a butcher doth deny;

I will go with you, my brethren true,
  And as fast as I can hie.'

15 But when to the sheriff's house they
    came,
  To dinner they hied apace,
And Robin he the man must be
  Before them all to say grace.

16 'Pray God bless us all,' said jolly Robin,
  'And our meat within this place;
A cup of sack so good will nourish our
    blood,
  And so I do end my grace.

17 'Come fill us more wine,' said jolly
    Robin,
  'Let us merry be while we do stay;
For wine and good cheer, be it never so
    dear,
  I vow I the reckning will pay.

18 'Come, brother[s], be merry,' said jolly
    Robin,
  'Let us drink, and never give ore;
For the shot I will pay, ere I go my
    way,
  If it cost me five pounds and more.'

19 'This is a mad blade,' the butchers then
    said;
  Saies the sheriff, He is some prodi-
    gal,
That some land has sold, for silver and
    gold,
  And now he doth mean to spend all.

20 'Hast thou any horn-beasts,' the sheriff
    repli'd,
  'Good fellow, to sell unto me?'
'Yes, that I have, good Master Sheriff,
  I have hundreds two or three.

21 'And a hundred aker of good free
    land,
  If you please it to see;
And I 'le make you as good assurance
    of it
  As ever my father made me.'

22 The sheriff he saddled a good palfrey,
  With three hundred pound in gold,
And away he went with bold Robin
    Hood,
  His horned beasts to behold.

23 Away then the sheriff and Robin did
    ride,
    To the forrest of merry Sherwood;
    Then the sheriff did say, God bless us
    this day
    From a man they call Robin Hood !

24 But when that a little further they
    came,
    Bold Robin he chancëd to spy
    A hundred head of good red deer,
    Come tripping the sheriff full nigh.

25 'How like you my hornd beasts, good
    Master Sheriff ?
    They be fat and fair for to see;'
    'I tell thee, good fellow, I would I were
    gone,
    For I like not thy company.'

26 Then Robin he set his horn to his
    mouth,
    And blew but blasts three;
    Then quickly anon there came Little
    John,
    And all his company.

27 'What is your will?' then said Little
    John,
    'Good master come tell it to me;'
    'I have brought hither the sheriff of
    Notingham,
    This day to dine with thee.'

28 'He is welcome to me,' then said Little
    John,
    'I hope he will honestly pay;
    I know he has gold, if it be but well
    told,
    Will serve us to drink a whole
    day.'

29 Then Robin took his mantle from his
    back,
    And laid it upon the ground,
    And out of the sheriffe['s] portmantle
    He told three hundred pound.

30 Then Robin he brought him thorow the
    wood,
    And set him on his dapple gray:
    'O have me commended to your wife
    at home;'
    So Robin went laughing away.

123

ROBIN HOOD AND THE CURTAL FRIAR

'Robin Hood and the Curtal Friar,' in both versions, is in a genuinely popular strain, and was made to sing, not to print. Verbal agreements show that A and B have an earlier ballad as their common source. Nearly, or quite, one half of A has been torn from the manuscript, but there is no reason to suppose the story differed much from that of B. The title of A in the manuscript is 'Robin Hood and Friar Tuck;' from which it follows that the copyist, or some predecessor, considered the stalwart friar of Fountains Abbey to be one with the jocular friar of the May-games and the morris-dance. But Friar Tuck, the wanton and the merry, like Maid Marian, owes his association with Robin Hood primarily to these popular sports, and not in the least to popular ballads. In the truly popular ballads Friar Tuck is never heard of, and in only two even of the broadside ballads (Nos. 145, 147) is he so much as named, and in both in conjunction with Maid Marian. The Play of Robin Hood (see p. 289, above), the first half of which is based on the present ballad, calls the friar Friar Tuck. So also the play founded on No. 118.

A

'Robine Hood and Ffryer Tucke,' Percy MS., p. 10; Hales and Furnivall, i, 26.

1 BUT how many merry monthes be in
    the yeere ?
    There are thirteen, I say ;
    The midsummer moone is the merryest
    of all,
    Next to the merry month of May.

2 In May, when mayds beene fast weep-
    and,
    Young men their hands done wringe,

    *   *   *   *   *

3 'I 'le . . pe . . . . .
    Over may noe man for villanie:'
    'I 'le never eate nor drinke,' Robin
    Hood sa[id],
    'Till I that cutted friar see.'

4 He builded his men in a brake of fearne,
    A litle from that nunery;
    Sayes, If you heare my litle horne blow
    Then looke you come to me.

5 When Robin came to Fontaines Abey,
    Wheras that fryer lay,
He was ware of the fryer where he
    stood,
    And to him thus can he say.

6 A payre of blacke breeches the yeoman
    had on,
    His coppe all shone of steele,
A fayre sword and a broad buckeler
    Beseemed him very weell.

7 'I am a wet weary man,' said Robin
    Hood,
    'Good fellow, as thou may see;
Wilt beare [me] over this wild water,
    Ffor sweete Saint Charity ? '

8 The fryer bethought him of a good deed;
    He had done none of long before;
He hent up Robin Hood on his backe,
    And over he did him beare.

9 But when he came over that wild water,
    A longe sword there he drew:
'Beare me backe againe, bold outlawe,
    Or of this thou shalt have enoughe.'

10 Then Robin Hood hent the fryer on his
    back,
    And neither sayd good nor ill;
Till he came ore that wild water,
    The yeoman he walked still.

11 Then Robin Hood wett his fayre greene
    hoze,
    A span aboue his knee;
S[ay]s, Beare me ore againe, thou cut-
    ted f[ryer]

    *   *   *   *

12 .   .   .   .   .   .

    .   .   .   . good bowmen
    [C]ame raking all on a rowe.

13 'I beshrew thy head,' said the cutted
    ffriar,
    'Thou thinkes I shall be shente;
I thought thou had but a man or two,
    And thou hast [a] whole conuent.

14 'I lett thee haue a blast on thy horne,
    Now giue me leaue to whistle an-
    other;

I cold not bidd thee noe better play
    And thou wert my owne borne bro-
    ther.'

15 'Now fute on, fute on, thou cutted fryar,
    I pray God thou neere be still;
It is not the futing in a fryers fist
    That can doe me any ill.'

16 The fryar sett his neave to his mouth,
    A loud blast he did blow;
Then halfe a hundred good bandoggs
    Came raking all on a rowe.

17 .   .   .   .   .

    .   .   .   .
    'Euery dogg to a man,' said the cutted
    fryar,
    'And I my selfe to Robin Hood.'

18 'Over God's forbott,' said Robin Hood,
    'That euer that soe shold bee;
I had rather be mached with three of
    the tikes
    Ere I wold be matched on thee.

19 'But stay thy tikes, thou fryar,' he said,
    'And freindshipp I 'le haue with thee;
But stay thy tikes, thou fryar,' he said,
    'And saue good yeomanry.'

20 The fryar he sett his neave to his mouth,
    A lowd blast he did blow;
The doggs the coucht downe euery one,
    They couched downe on a rowe.

21 'What is thy will, thou yeoman ? ' he
    said,
    'Haue done and tell it me;'
'If that thou will goe to merry green-
    wood,

    *   *   *   *   *

B

'The Famous Battel between Robin Hood
and the Curtal Fryer.' a. Garland of 1663,
No. 11. b. Pepys, I, 78, No. 37. c. Garland
of 1670, No. 10. d. Wood, 401, leaf 15 b. e.
Pepys, II, 99, No. 86. f. Douce, II, 184.

1 In summer time, when leaves grow
    green,
    And flowers are fresh and gay,
Robin Hood and his merry men
    Were disposed to play.

2 Then some would leap, and some would
    run,
  And some would use artillery:
' Which of you can a good bow draw,
  A good archer to be ?

3 ' Which of you can kill a buck ?
  Or who can kill a do ?
Or who can kill a hart of greece,
  Five hundred foot him fro ? '

4 Will Scadlock he killd a buck,
  And Midge he killd a do,
And Little John killd a hart of greece,
  Five hundred foot him fro.

5 ' God's blessing on thy heart,' said Robin
    Hood,
  ' That hath [shot] such a shot for me;
I would ride my horse an hundred miles,
  To finde one could match with thee.'

6 That causd Will Scadlock to laugh,
  He laughed full heartily:
' There lives a curtal frier in Fountains
    Abby
  Will beat both him and thee.

7 ' That curtal frier in Fountains Abby
  Well can a strong bow draw;
He will beat you and your yeomen,
  Set them all on a row.'

8 Robin Hood took a solemn oath,
  It was by Mary free,
That he would neither eat nor drink
  Till the frier he did see.

9 Robin Hood put on his harness good,
  And on his head a cap of steel,
Broad sword and buckler by his side,
  And they became him weel.

10 He took his bow into his hand,
  It was made of a trusty tree,
With a sheaf of arrows at his belt,
  To the Fountains Dale went he.

11 And comming unto Fountain[s] Dale,
  No further would he ride;
There was he aware of a curtal frier,
  Walking by the water-side.

12 The fryer had on a harniss good,
  And on his head a cap of steel,

Broad sword and buckler by his side,
  And they became him weel.

13 Robin Hood lighted off his horse,
  And tied him to a thorn:
' Carry me over the water, thou curtal
    frier,
  Or else thy life 's forlorn.'

14 The frier took Robin Hood on his back,
  Deep water he did bestride,
And spake neither good word nor bad,
  Till he came at the other side.

15 Lightly leapt Robin Hood off the friers
    back;
  The frier said to him again,
Carry me over this water, fine fellow,
  Or it shall breed thy pain.

16 Robin Hood took the frier on 's back,
  Deep water he did bestride,
And spake neither good word nor bad,
  Till he came at the other side.

17 Lightly leapt the fryer off Robin Hoods
    back;
  Robin Hood said to him again,
Carry me over this water, thou curtal
    frier,
  Or it shall breed thy pain.

18 The frier took Robin Hood on 's back
    again,
  And stept up to the knee;
Till he came at the middle stream,
  Neither good nor bad spake he.

19 And coming to the middle stream,
  There he threw Robin in :
' And chuse thee, chuse thee, fine fellow,
  Whether thou wilt sink or swim.'

20 Robin Hood swam to a bush of broom,
  The frier to a wicker wand;
Bold Robin Hood is gone to shore,
  And took his bow in hand.

21 One of his best arrows under his belt
  To the frier he let flye;
The curtal frier, with his steel buckler
  He put that arrow by.

22 ' Shoot on, shoot on, thou fine fellow,
  Shoot on as thou hast begun;

If thou shoot here a summers day,
Thy mark I will not shun.'

23 Robin Hood shot passing well,
Till his arrows all were gone;
They took their swords and steel buck-
lers,
And fought with might and maine;

24 From ten oth' clock that day,
Till four ith' afternoon;
Then Robin Hood came to his knees
Of the frier to beg a boon.

25 'A boon, a boon, thou curtal frier,
I beg it on my knee;
Give me leave to set my horn to my
mouth,
And to blow blasts three.'

26 'That will I do,' said the curtal frier,
'Of thy blasts I have no doubt;
I hope thou 'lt blow so passing well
Till both thy eyes fall out.'

27 Robin Hood set his horn to his mouth,
He blew but blasts three;
Half a hundred yeomen, with bows
bent,
Came raking over the lee.

28 'Whose men are these,' said the frier,
'That come so hastily?'
'These men are mine,' said Robin Hood;
'Frier, what is that to thee?'

29 'A boon, a boon,' said the curtal frier,
'The like I gave to thee;
Give me leave to set my fist to my
mouth,
And to whute whutes three.'

30 'That will I do,' said Robin Hood,
'Or else I were to blame;
Three whutes in a friers fist
Would make me glad and fain.'

31 The frier he set his fist to his mouth,
And whuted whutes three;
Half a hundred good ban-dogs
Came running the frier unto.

32 'Here 's for every man of thine a
dog,
And I my self for thee:'

'Nay, by my faith,' quoth Robin Hood,
'Frier, that may not be.'

33 Two dogs at once to Robin Hood did
go,
The one behind, the other before;
Robin Hoods mantle of Lincoln green
Off from his back they tore.

34 And whether his men shot east or
west,
Or they shot north or south,
The curtal dogs, so taught they were,
They kept their arrows in their
mouth.

35 'Take up thy dogs,' said Little John,
'Frier, at my bidding be;'
'Whose man art thou,' said the curtal
frier,
'Comes here to prate with me?'

36 'I am Little John, Robin Hoods man,
Frier, I will not lie;
If thou take not up thy dogs soon,
I 'le take up them and thee.'

37 Little John had a bow in his hand,
He shot with might and main;
Soon half a score of the friers dogs
Lay dead upon the plain.

38 'Hold thy hand, good fellow,' said the
curtal frier,
'Thy master and I will agree;
And we will have new orders taken
With all the haste that may be.'

39 'If thou wilt forsake fair Fountains
Dale,
And Fountains Abby free,
Every Sunday throughout the year,
A noble shall be thy fee.

40 'And every holy day throughout the
year,
Changed shall thy garment be,
If thou wilt go to fair Nottingham,
And there remain with me.'

41 This curtal frier had kept Fountains
Dale
Seven long years or more;
There was neither knight, lord, nor earl
Could make him yield before.

124

THE JOLLY PINDER OF WAKE-FIELD

This ballad is thoroughly lyrical, and therein like the old age, and was pretty well sung to pieces before it ever was printed. 'A ballett of Wakefylde and a grene' is entered in the Stationers' Register to Master John Wallye and Mistress Toye, 19 July, 1557 – 9 July, 1558. A snatch of 'The Jolly Pinder' is sung in each of the Robin Hood plays, Anthony Munday's Downfall of Robert Earl of Huntington, and Munday and Chettle's Death of Robert Earl of Huntington, both printed in 1601. Silence sings the line 'And Robin Hood, Scarlet, and John' in the Second Part of Henry IV (act v, scene 3), and there are other allusions to the ballad. The adventure of the ballad is naturally introduced into the play of George a Greene the Pinner of Wakefield, printed in 1599 (reprinted in Dodsley's Old Plays, and by Dyce among the works of Robert Greene). The scene in the play is found in the prose history of George a Green, London, 1706, of which a copy is known of the date 1632. The ballad is so imperfect that one might be in doubt whether the Pinder fights with Robin Hood, Scarlet, and John all together or successively. But we see from the History and from Greene's play that the Pinder must take them one after the other, and Robin the last of the three.

A

a. 'The Iolly Pinder of Wakefield,' Wood, 402, leaf 43. b. Garland of 1663, No. 4. c. Garland of 1670, No. 3. d. Pepys, II, 100, No. 87 a. e. Wood, 401, leaf 61 b.

1 IN Wakefield there lives a jolly pinder,
    In Wakefield, all on a green; (*bis*)

2 'There is neither knight nor squire,' said the pinder,
    'Nor baron that is so bold, (*bis*)
Dare make a trespasse to the town of Wakefield,
    But his pledge goes to the pinfold.' (*bis*)

3 All this beheard three witty young men,
    'T was Robin Hood, Scarlet, and John;
With that they spyed the jolly pinder,
    As he sate under a thorn.

4 'Now turn again, turn again,' said the pinder,
    'For a wrong way have you gone;
For you have forsaken the king his highway,
    And made a path over the corn.'

5 'O that were great shame,' said jolly Robin,
    'We being three, and thou but one:'
The pinder leapt back then thirty good foot,
    'T was thirty good foot and one.

6 He leaned his back fast unto a thorn,
    And his foot unto a stone,
And there he fought a long summer's day,
    A summer's day so long,
Till that their swords, on their broad bucklers,
    Were broken fast unto their hands.

*   *   *   *   *

7 'Hold thy hand, hold thy hand,' said Robin Hood,
    'And my merry men euery one;
For this is one of the best pinders
    That ever I try'd with sword.

8 'And wilt thou forsake thy pinder his craft,
    And live in [the] green wood with me?'

.   .   .   .   .

.   .   .   .   .

9 'At Michaelmas next my covnant comes out,
    When every man gathers his fee;
I 'le take my blew blade all in my hand,
    And plod to the green wood with thee.'

10 'Hast thou either meat or drink,' said Robin Hood,
    'For my merry men and me?

.   .   .   .   .

11 'I have both bread and beef,' said the pinder,
    'And good ale of the best;'
And that is meat good enough,' said Robin Hood,
    'For such unbidden guest.

12 'O wilt thou forsake the pinder his craft,
  And go to the green wood with me?
  Thou shalt have a livery twice in the
    year,
  The one green, the other brown [shall
    be].'

13 'If Michaelmas day were once come and
    gone
  And my master had paid me my
    fee,
  Then would I set as little by him
  As my master doth set by me.'

B

Percy MS., p. 15; Hales and Furnivall, i, 32.

*   *   *   *   *

1 'But hold y . . hold y . . . ' says Robin,
  'My merrymen, I bid yee,
  For this [is] one of the best pindars
  That euer I saw with mine eye.'

2 'But hast thou any meat, thou iolly
    pindar,
  For my merrymen and me?'
  .   .   .   .   .   .
  .   .   .   .   .   .

3 'But I haue bread and cheese,' sayes the
    pindar,
  'And ale all on the best:'
  'That's cheere good enoughe,' said
    Robin,
  'For any such vnbidden guest.

4 'But wilt be my man?' said good
    Robin,
  'And come and dwell with me?
  And twise in a yeere thy clothing [shall]
    be changed
  If my man thou wilt bee,
  The tone shall be of light Lincolne greene,
  The tother of Picklory.'

5 'Att Michallmas comes a well good time,
  When men haue gotten in their ffee;
  I'le sett as litle by my master
  As he now setts by me,
  I'le take my benbowe in my hande,
  And come into the grenwoode to
    thee.'

125

ROBIN HOOD AND LITTLE JOHN

There is a black-letter copy, printed by an
for W. Onley, in Lord Crawford's collection
No. 1320; the date put at 1680–85. A white-
letter copy is in Roxburghe, iii, 728 (see Ebsworth's Roxburghe Ballads, viii, 504). 'Robin
Hood and Little John' belongs to a set of ballads which have middle rhyme in the third line
of the stanza, and are directed to be sung to
one and the same tune. These are: 'Robin
Hood and the Bishop' (No. 143); 'Robin Hood
and the Beggar' (No. 133); 'Robin Hood and
the Tanner' (No. 126), to the tune of 'Robin
Hood and the Stranger;' 'Robin Hood and
the Butcher' (No. 122); 'Robin Hood's Chase'
(No. 146); 'Little John and the Four Beggars'
(No. 142 B), to the tune of 'Robin Hood and
the Beggar;' 'Robin Hood and Little John;'
'Robin Hood and the Ranger' (No. 131), to
the tune of 'Arthur a Bland' (that is, 'Robin
Hood and the Tanner'). There is no ballad
with the title 'Robin Hood and the Stranger.'
Ritson gave this title to a ballad which uni-
formly bears the title of 'Robin Hood Newly
Revived' (No. 128), but 'Robin Hood and Little John,' or rather some older version of it
(for the one we have is in rank seventeenth-
century style), is more likely to be meant. 'A
pastorall plesant commedie of Robin Hood and
Little John, etc.,' is entered to Edward White
in the Stationers' Registers, May 14, 1594, and
'Robin Hood and Little John' to Master Oul-
ton, April 22, 1640.

'Robin Hood and Little John.' a. A Collection of Old Ballads, 1723, i, 75. b. Aldermary Garland, by R. Marshall, n. d., No. 22.

1 When Robin Hood was about twenty
    years old,
    With a hey down down and a down
  He happend to meet Little John,
  A jolly brisk blade, right fit for th
    trade,
    For he was a lusty young man.

2 Tho he was calld Little, his limbs they
    were large,
    And his stature was seven foot
      high;
  Where-ever he came, they quak'd at his
    name,
    For soon he would make them to
      fly.

3 How they came acquainted, I 'll tell
    you in brief,
      If you will but listen a while;
  For this very jest, amongst all the rest,
      I think it may cause you to smile.

4 Bold Robin Hood said to his jolly bow-
    men,
      Pray tarry you here in this grove;
  And see that you all observe well my
    call,
      While thorough the forest I rove.

5 We have had no sport for these fourteen
    long days,
      Therefore now abroad will I go;
  Now should I be beat, and cannot re-
    treat,
      My horn I will presently blow.

6 Then did he shake hands with his merry
    men all,
      And bid them at present good b'w'ye;
  Then, as near a brook his journey he
    took,
      A stranger he chancd to espy.

7 They happend to meet on a long narrow
    bridge,
      And neither of them would give way;
  Quoth bold Robin Hood, and sturdily
    stood,
      I 'll show you right Nottingham play.

8 With that from his quiver an arrow he
    drew,
      A broad arrow with a goose-wing:
  The stranger reply'd, I 'll liquor thy
    hide,
      If thou offerst to touch the string.

9 Quoth bold Robin Hood, Thou dost
    prate like an ass,
      For were I to bend but my bow,
  I could send a dart quite thro thy proud
    heart,
      Before thou couldst strike me one
        blow.

10 'Thou talkst like a coward,' the stran-
     ger reply'd;
       'Well armd with a long bow you
         stand,
   To shoot at my breast, while I, I protest,
       Have nought but a staff in my hand.'

11 'The name of a coward,' quoth Robin,
     'I scorn,
       Wherefore my long bow I 'll lay by;
   And now, for thy sake, a staff will I take,
       The truth of thy manhood to try.'

12 Then Robin Hood stept to a thicket of
     trees,
       And chose him a staff of ground-oak;
   Now this being done, away he did run
       To the stranger, and merrily spoke:

13 'Lo ! see my staff, it is lusty and tough,
       Now here on the bridge we will play;
   Whoever falls in, the other shall win
       The battel, and so we 'll away.'

14 'With all my whole heart,' the stranger
     reply'd;
       'I scorn in the least to give out;'
   This said, they fell to 't without more
     dispute,
       And their staffs they did flourish
         about.

15 And first Robin he gave the stranger a
     bang,
       So hard that it made his bones ring:
   The stranger he said, This must be re-
     paid,
       I 'll give you as good as you bring.

16 So long as I 'm able to handle my staff,
       To die in your debt, friend, I scorn:
   Then to it each goes, and followd their
     blows,
       As if they had been threshing of corn.

17 The stranger gave Robin a crack on the
     crown,
       Which caused the blood to appear;
   Then Robin, enrag'd, more fiercely en-
     gag'd,
       And followd his blows more severe.

18 So thick and so fast did he lay it on him,
       With a passionate fury and ire,
   At every stroke, he made him to smoke,
       As if he had been all on fire.

19 O then into fury the stranger he grew,
       And gave him a damnable look,
   And with it a blow that laid him full
     low,
       And tumbld him into the brook.

20 'I prithee, good fellow, O where art
        thou now?'
    The stranger, in laughter, he cry'd;
    Quoth bold Robin Hood, Good faith, in
        the flood,
    And floating along with the tide.

21 I needs must acknowledge thou art a
        brave soul;
    With thee I 'll no longer contend;
    For needs must I say, thou hast got the
        day,
    Our battel shall be at an end.

22 Then unto the bank he did presently
        wade,
    And pulld himself out by a thorn;
    Which done, at the last, he blowd a loud
        blast
    Straitway on his fine bugle-horn.

23 The eccho of which through the vallies
        did fly,
    At which his stout bowmen appeard,
    All cloathed in green, most gay to be
        seen;
    So up to their master they steerd.

24 'O what 's the matter?' quoth William
        Stutely;
    'Good master, you are wet to the
        skin:'
    'No matter,' quoth he; 'the lad which
        you see,
    In fighting, hath tumbld me in.'

25 'He shall not go scot-free,' the others
        reply'd;
    So strait they were seizing him there,
    To duck him likewise; but Robin Hood
        cries,
    He is a stout fellow, forbear.

26 There 's no one shall wrong thee, friend,
        be not afraid;
    These bowmen upon me do wait;
    There 's threescore and nine; if thou
        wilt be mine,
    Thou shalt have my livery strait.

27 And other accoutrements fit for a
        man;
    Speak up, jolly blade, never fear;
    I 'll teach you also the use of the bow,
    To shoot at the fat fallow-deer.'

28 'O here is my hand,' the stranger re-
        ply'd,
    'I 'll serve you with all my whole
        heart;
    My name is John Little, a man of good
        mettle;
    Nere doubt me, for I 'll play my
        part.'

29 'His name shall be alterd,' quoth Wil-
        liam Stutely,
    'And I will his godfather be;
    Prepare then a feast, and none of the
        least,
    For we will be merry,' quoth he.

30 They presently fetchd in a brace of fat
        does,
    With humming strong liquor likewise;
    They lovd what was good; so, in the
        greenwood,
    This pretty sweet babe they baptize.

31 He was, I must tell you, but seven foot
        high,
    And, may be, an ell in the waste;
    A pretty sweet lad; much feasting they
        had;
    Bold Robin the christning grac'd,

32 With all his bowmen, which stood in a
        ring,
    And were of the Notti[n]gham breed;
    Brave Stutely comes then, with seven
        yeomen,
    And did in this manner proceed.

33 'This infant was called John Little,'
        quoth he,
    'Which name shall be changed anon;
    The words we 'll transpose, so where-
        ever he goes,
    His name shall be calld Little John.'

34 They all with a shout made the ele-
        ments ring,
    So soon as the office was ore;
    To feasting they went, with true merri-
        ment,
    And tippld strong liquor gillore.

35 Then Robin he took the pretty sweet
        babe,
    And cloathd him from top to the
        toe

In garments of green, most gay to be
   seen,
   And gave him a curious long bow.

36 'Thou shalt be an archer as well as the
   best,
     And range in the greenwood with
     us;
   Where we 'll not want gold nor silver,
     behold,
     While bishops have ought in their
     purse.

37 'We live here like squires, or lords of
   renown,
     Without ere a foot of free land;
   We feast on good cheer, with wine, ale,
     and beer,
     And evry thing at our command.'

38 Then musick and dancing did finish the
   day;
     At length, when the sun waxed low,
   Then all the whole train the grove did
     refrain,
     And unto their caves they did go.

39 And so ever after, as long as he livd,
     Altho he was proper and tall,
   Yet nevertheless, the truth to express,
     Still Little John they did him call.

126

ROBIN HOOD AND THE TANNER

The sturdy Arthur a Bland is well hit off,
and, bating the sixteenth and thirty-fifth stanzas, the ballad has a good popular ring.

'Robin Hood and the Tanner.' a. Wood,
401, leaf 9 b. b. Garland of 1663, No. 10.
c. Garland of 1670, No. 9. d. Pepys, ii, 111,
No. 98.

1 IN Nottingham there lives a jolly tan-
   ner,
     With a hey down down a down
     down
   His name is Arthur a Bland;
   There is nere a squire in Nottingham-
     shire
   Dare bid bold Arthur stand.

2 With a long pike-staff upon his shoulder,
     So well he can clear his way;
   By two and by three he makes them to
     flee,
     For he hath no list to stay.

3 And as he went forth, in a summer's
   morning,
     Into the forrest of merry Sherwood,
   To view the red deer, that range here
     and there,
     There met he with bold Robin Hood.

4 As soon as bold Robin Hood did him
   espy,
     He thought some sport he would
     make;
   Therefore out of hand he bid him to
     stand,
     And thus to him he spake:

5 Why, what art thou, thou bold fellow,
     That ranges so boldly here ?
   In sooth, to be brief, thou lookst like a
     thief,
     That comes to steal our king's deer.

6 For I am a keeper in this forrest;
     The king puts me in trust
   To look to his deer, that range here and
     there,
     Therefore stay thee I must.

7 'If thou beest a keeper in this forrest,
     And hast such a great command,
   Yet thou must have more partakers in
     store,
     Before thou make me to stand.'

8 'Nay, I have no more partakers in store,
     Or any that I do need;
   But I have a staff of another oke graff,
     I know it will do the deed.'

9 'For thy sword and thy bow I care not
     a straw,
     Nor all thine arrows to boot;
   If I get a knop upon thy bare scop,
     Thou canst as well shite as shoote.'

10 'Speak cleanly, good fellow,' said jolly
   Robin,
    'And give better terms to me;
   Else I 'le thee correct for thy neglect,
     And make thee more mannerly.'

11 'Marry gep with a wenion!' quoth
    Arthur a Bland,
   'Art thou such a goodly man?
I care not a fig for thy looking so big;
   Mend thou thyself where thou can.'

12 Then Robin Hood he unbuckled his belt,
   He laid down his bow so long;
He took up a staff of another oke graff,
   That was both stiff and strong.

13 'I 'le yield to thy weapon,' said jolly
    Robin,
   'Since thou wilt not yield to mine;
For I have a staff of another oke graff,
   Not half a foot longer then thine.

14 'But let me measure,' said jolly Robin,
   'Before we begin our fray;
For I 'le not have mine to be longer then
    thine,
For that will be called foul play.'

15 'I pass not for length,' bold Arthur
    reply'd,
   'My staff is of oke so free;
Eight foot and a half, it will knock down
    a calf,
And I hope it will knock down thee.'

16 Then Robin Hood could no longer for-
    bear;
   He gave him such a knock,
Quickly and soon the blood came down,
   Before it was ten a clock.

17 Then Arthur he soon recovered himself,
   And gave him such a knock on the
    crown,
That on every hair of bold Robin Hoods
    head,
   The blood came trickling down.

18 Then Robin Hood raged like a wild bore,
   As soon as he saw his own blood;
Then Bland was in hast, he laid on so
    fast,
   As though he had been staking of
    wood.

19 And about, and about, and about they
    went,
   Like two wild bores in a chase;
Striving to aim each other to maim,
   Leg, arm, or any other place.

20 And knock for knock they lustily dealt,
   Which held for two hours and more;
That all the wood rang at every bang,
   They ply'd their work so sore.

21 'Hold thy hand, hold thy hand,' said
    Robin Hood,
   'And let our quarrel fall;
For here we may thresh our bones into
    mesh,
   And get no coyn at all.

22 'And in the forrest of merry Sherwood
   Hereafter thou shalt be free:'
'God-a-mercy for naught, my freedom
    I bought,
   I may thank my good staff, and not
    thee.'

23 'What tradesman art thou?' said jolly
    Robin,
   'Good fellow, I prethee me show:
And also me tell in what place thou dost
    dwel,
For both these fain would I know.'

24 'I am a tanner,' bold Arthur reply'd,
   'In Nottingham long have I wrought;
And if thou 'lt come there, I vow and
    do swear
   I will tan thy hide for naught.'

25 'God a mercy, good fellow,' said jolly
    Robin,
   'Since thou art so kind to me;
And if thou wilt tan my hide for naught,
   I will do as much for thee.

26 'But if thou 'lt forsake thy tanners
    trade,
   And live in green wood with me,
My name 's Robin Hood, I swear by the
    rood
   I will give thee both gold and fee.'

27 'If thou be Robin Hood,' bold Arthur
    reply'd,
   'As I think well thou art,
Then here 's my hand, my name 's Ar-
    thur a Bland,
   We two will never depart.

28 'But tell me, O tell me, where is Little
    John?
   Of him fain would I hear;

For we are alide by the mothers side,
And he is my kinsman near.'

29 Then Robin Hood blew on the beaugle
horn,
He blew full lowd and shrill,
But quickly anon appeard Little John,
Come tripping down a green hill.

30 'O what is the matter?' then said Little
John,
'Master, I pray you tell;
Why do you stand with your staff in
your hand?
I fear all is not well.'

31 'O man, I do stand, and he makes me
to stand,
The tanner that stands thee beside;
He is a bonny blade, and master of his
trade,
For soundly he hath tand my hide.'

32 'He is to be commended,' then said
Little John,
'If such a feat he can do;
If he be so stout, we will have a bout,
And he shall tan my hide too.'

33 'Hold thy hand, hold thy hand,' said
Robin Hood,
'For as I do understand,
He 's a yeoman good, and of thine own
blood,
For his name is Arthur a Bland.'

34 Then Little John threw his staff away,
As far as he could it fling,
And ran out of hand to Arthur a Bland,
And about his neck did cling.

35 With loving respect, there was no neg-
lect,
They were neither nice nor coy,
Each other did face, with a lovely
grace,
And both did weep for joy.

36 Then Robin Hood took them both by
the hand,
And danc'd round about the oke
tree;
'For three merry men, and three merry
men,
And three merry men we be.

37 'And ever hereafter, as long as I live,
We three will be all one;
The wood shall ring, and the old wife
sing,
Of Robin Hood, Arthur, and John.'

127

ROBIN HOOD AND THE TINKER

In the Roxburghe collection, III, 22; not in
the Garland of 1663 or that of 1670. A mere
imitation of the poorest sort.

a. Wood, 401, leaf 17 b. b. Pepys, II, 107,
No. 94. c. Douce, III, 118 b.

1 IN summer time, when leaves grow
green,
Down a down a down
And birds sing on every tree,
Hey down a down a down

Robin Hood went to Nottingham,
Down a down a down
As fast as hee could dree.
Hey down a down a down

2 And as hee came to Nottingham
A Tinker he did meet,
And seeing him a lusty blade,
He did him kindly greet.

3 'Where dost thou live?' quoth Robin
Hood,
'I pray thee now mee tell;
Sad news I hear there is abroad,
I fear all is not well.'

4 'What is that news?' the Tinker said;
'Tell mee without delay;
I am a tinker by my trade,
And do live at Banbura.'

5 'As for the news,' quoth Robin Hood,
'It is but as I hear;
Two tinkers they were set ith' stocks,
For drinking ale and bear.'

6 'If that be all,' the Tinker said,
'As I may say to you,
Your news it is not worth a fart,
Since that they all bee true.

7 'For drinking of good ale and bear,
    You wil not lose your part:'
'No, by my faith,' quoth Robin Hood,
    'I love it with all my heart.

8 'What news abroad?' quoth Robin
    Hood;
'Tell mee what thou dost hear;
Being thou goest from town to town,
    Some news thou need not fear.'

9 'All the news,' the Tinker said,
    'I hear, it is for good;
It is to seek a bold outlaw,
    Which they call Robin Hood.

10 'I have a warrant from the king,
    To take him where I can;
If you can tell me where hee is,
    I will make you a man.

11 'The king will give a hundred pound
    That hee could but him see;
And if wee can but now him get,
    It will serve you and mee.'

12 'Let me see that warrant,' said Robin
    Hood;
'I 'le see if it bee right;
And I will do the best I can
    For to take him this night.'

13 'That will I not,' the Tinker said;
    'None with it I will trust;
And where hee is if you 'l not tell,
    Take him by force I must.'

14 But Robin Hood perceiving well
    How then the game would go,
'If you will go to Nottingham,
    Wee shall find him I know.'

15 The Tinker had a crab-tree staff,
    Which was both good and strong;
Robin hee had a good strong blade,
    So they went both along.

16 And when they came to Nottingham,
    There they both tooke one inn;
And they calld for ale and wine,
    To drink it was no sin.

17 But ale and wine they drank so fast
    That the Tinker hee forgot

What thing he was about to do;
    It fell so to his lot

18 That while the Tinker fell asleep,
    Hee made then haste away,
And left the Tinker in the lurch,
    For the great shot to pay.

19 But when the Tinker wakened,
    And saw that he was gone,
He calld then even for his host,
    And thus hee made his moan.

20 'I had a warrant from the king,
    Which might have done me good,
That is to take a bold outlaw,
    Some call him Robin Hood.

21 'But now my warrant and mony 's gone,
    Nothing I have to pay;
And he that promisd to be my friend,
    He is gone and fled away.'

22 'That friend you tell on,' said the
    host,
'They call him Robin Hood;
And when that first hee met with
    you,
He ment you little good.'

23 'Had I known it had been hee,
    When that I had him here,
Th' one of us should have tri'd our
    strength
Which should have paid full dear.

24 'In the mean time I must away;
    No longer here I 'le bide;
But I will go and seek him out,
    What ever do me betide.

25 'But one thing I would gladly know,
    What here I have to pay;'
'Ten shillings just,' then said the host;
    'I 'le pay without delay.

26 'Or elce take here my working-bag,
    And my good hammer too;
And if that I light but on the knave,
    I will then soon pay you.'

27 'The onely way,' then said the host,
    'And not to stand in fear,
Is to seek him among the parks,
    Killing of the kings deer.'

8 The Tinker hee then went with speed,
   And made then no delay,
   Till he had found then Robin Hood,
   That they might have a fray.

9 At last hee spy'd him in a park,
   Hunting then of the deer;
   ' What knave is that,' quoth Robin
      Hood,
   ' That doth come mee so near ? '

0 ' No knave, no knave,' the Tinker said,
   ' And that you soon shall know;
   Whether of us hath done most wrong,
   My crab-tree staff shall show.'

1 Then Robin drew his gallant blade,
   Made then of trusty steel;
   But the Tinker laid on him so fast
   That he made Robin reel.

2 Then Robins anger did arise;
   He fought full manfully,
   Vntil hee had made the Tinker
   Almost then fit to fly.

3 With that they had a bout again,
   They ply'd their weapons fast;
   The Tinker threshed his bones so sore
   He made him yeeld at last.

4 ' A boon, a boon,' Robin hee cryes,
   ' If thou wilt grant it mee;'
   ' Before I do it,' the Tinker said,
   ' I 'le hang thee on this tree.'

5 But the Tinker looking him about,
   Robin his horn did blow;
   Then came unto him Little John,
   And William Scadlock too.

6 ' What is the matter,' quoth Little John,
   ' You sit in th' highway side ? '
   ' Here is a Tinker that stands by,
   That hath paid well my hide.'

7 ' That Tinker,' then said Little John,
   ' Fain that blade I would see,
   And I would try what I could do,
   If hee 'l do as much for mee.'

8 But Robin hee then wishd them both
   They should the quarrel cease,
   ' That henceforth wee may bee as one,
   And ever live in peace.

39 ' And for the jovial Tinker's part,
   A hundred pound I 'le give,
   In th' year to maintain him on,
   As long as he doth live.

40 ' In manhood hee is a mettle man,
   And a mettle man by trade;
   I never thought that any man
   Should have made me so fraid.

41 ' And if hee will bee one of us,
   Wee will take all one fare,
   And whatsoever wee do get,
   He shall have his full share.'

42 So the Tinker was content
   With them to go along,
   And with them a part to take,
   And so I end my song.

128

ROBIN HOOD NEWLY REVIVED

The story seems to have been built up on a
portion of the ruins of the fine tale of Gamelyn.
(See Skeat's Chaucer, IV, 645 ff.).

' Robin Hood Newly Reviv'd.' a. Wood,
401, leaf 27 b. b. Roxburghe, III, 18, in the
Ballad Society's reprint, II, 426. c. Garland
of 1663, No. 3. d. Garland of 1670, No. 2.
e. Pepys, II, 101, No. 88.

1 COME listen a while, you gentlemen
      all,
   With a hey down down a down down
   That are in this bower within,
      For a story of gallant bold Robin
         Hood
   I purpose now to begin.

2 ' What time of the day ? ' quoth Robin
      Hood then;
   Quoth Little John, 'T is in the prime;
   ' Why then we will to the green wood
      gang,
   For we have no vittles to dine.'

3 As Robin Hood walkt the forrest along—
   It was in the mid of the day —
   There was he met of a deft young
      man
   As ever walkt on the way.

4 His doublet it was of silk, he said,
   His stockings like scarlet shone,
And he walkt on along the way,
   To Robin Hood then unknown.

5 A herd of deer was in the bend,
   All feeding before his face:
' Now the best of ye I 'le have to my
     dinner,
   And that in a little space.'

6 Now the stranger he made no mickle
     adoe,
   But he bends and a right good bow,
And the best buck in the herd he slew,
   Forty good yards him full froe.

7 ' Well shot, well shot,' quoth Robin
     Hood then,
   ' That shot it was shot in time;
And if thou wilt accept of the place,
   Thou shalt be a bold yeoman of mine.'

8 ' Go play the chiven,' the stranger said,
   ' Make haste and quickly go;
Or with my fist, be sure of this,
   I 'le give thee buffets store.'

9 ' Thou hadst not best buffet me,' quoth
     Robin Hood,
   ' For though I seem forlorn,
Yet I can have those that will take my
     part,
   If I but blow my horn.'

10 ' Thou wast not best wind thy horn,' the
     stranger said,
   ' Beest thou never so much in hast,
For I can draw out a good broad sword,
   And quickly cut the blast.'

11 Then Robin Hood bent a very good bow,
   To shoot, and that he would fain;
The stranger he bent a very good bow,
   To shoot at bold Robin again.

12 ' O hold thy hand, hold thy hand,' quoth
     Robin Hood,
   ' To shoot it would be in vain;
For if we should shoot the one at the
     other,
   The one of us may be slain.

13 ' But let 's take our swords and our
     broad bucklers,
   And gang under yonder tree: '

' As I hope to be sav'd,' the stranger said
   ' One foot I will not flee.'

14 Then Robin Hood lent the stranger
     blow
   Most scar'd him out of his wit;
' Thou never delt blow,' the stranger h
     said,
   ' That shall be better quit.'

15 The stranger he drew out a good broa
     sword,
   And hit Robin on the crown,
That from every haire of bold Robin
     head
   The blood ran trickling down.

16 ' God a mercy, good fellow ! ' quot
     Robin Hood then,
   ' And for this that thou hast done;
Tell me, good fellow, what thou art,
   Tell me where thou doest woon.'

17 The stranger then answered bold Robi
     Hood,
   I 'le tell thee where I did dwell;
In Maxfield was I bred and born,
   My name is Young Gamwell.

18 For killing of my own fathers steward
   I am forc'd to this English wood,
And for to seek an vncle of mine;
   Some call him Robin Hood.

19 ' But thou art a cousin of Robin Hood
     then ?
   The sooner we should have done:'
' As I hope to be sav'd,' the strange
     then said,
   ' I am his own sisters son.'

20 But, Lord ! what kissing and courtin
     was there,
   When these two cousins did greet !
And they went all that summers day,
   And Little John did meet.

21 But when they met with Little John,
   He there unto [him] did say,
O master, where have you been,
   You have tarried so long away ?

22 ' I met with a stranger,' quoth Robin
     Hood then,
   ' Full sore he hath beaten me: '

'Then I'le have a bout with him,' quoth
   Little John,
  'And try if he can beat me.'

23 'Oh [no], oh no,' quoth Robin Hood
   then,
   'Little John, it may [not] be so;
For he's my own dear sisters son,
   And cousins I have no mo.

24 'But he shall be a bold yeoman of mine,
   My chief man next to thee;
And I Robin Hood, and thou Little John,
   And Scarlet he shall be:

25 'And wee'l be three of the bravest out-
   laws
   That is in the North Country.'
If you will have any more of bold Robin
   Hood,
   In his second part it will be.

129

ROBIN HOOD AND THE PRINCE OF ARAGON

This is only a pseudo-chivalrous romance,
tagged to 'Robin Hood Newly Revived' as a
Second Part, with eight introductory stanzas.
Both parts are as vapid as possible.

'Robin Hood, Will. Scadlock and Little
John.' a. Roxburghe, I, 358, in the Ballad
Society's reprint, II, 431. b. Pepys, II, 120,
No. 106.

1 Now Robin Hood, Will Scadlock and
   Little John
   Are walking over the plain,
With a good fat buck which Will Scad-
   lock
   With his strong bow had slain.

2 'Jog on, jog on,' cries Robin Hood,
   'The day it runs full fast;
For though my nephew me a breakfast
   gave,
   I have not yet broke my fast.

3 'Then to yonder lodge let us take our
   way,
   I think it wondrous good,
Where my nephew by my bold yeomen
   Shall be welcomd unto the green wood.'

4 With that he took the bugle-horn,
   Full well he could it blow;
Streight from the woods came marching
   down
   One hundred tall fellows and mo.

5 'Stand, stand to your arms!' crys Will
   Scadlock,
   'Lo! the enemies are within ken:'
With that Robin Hood he laughd aloud,
   Crys, They are my bold yeomen.

6 Who, when they arriv'd and Robin es-
   py'd,
   Cry'd, Master, what is your will?
We thought you had in danger been,
   Your horn did sound so shrill.

7 'Now nay, now nay,' quoth Robin Hood,
   'The danger is past and gone;
I would have you to welcome my
   nephew here,
   That hath paid me two for one.'

8 In feasting and sporting they passed the
   day,
   Till Phœbus sunk into the deep;
Then each one to his quarters hy'd,
   His guard there for to keep.

9 Long had they not walked within the
   green wood,
   But Robin he was espy'd
Of a beautiful damsel all alone,
   That on a black palfrey did ride.

10 Her riding-suit was of sable hew
   black,
   Sypress over her face,
Through which her rose-like cheeks did
   blush,
   All with a comely grace.

11 'Come, tell me the cause, thou pritty
   one,'
   Quoth Robin, 'and tell me aright,
From whence thou comest, and whither
   thou goest,
   All in this mournful plight?'

12 'From London I came,' the damsel re-
   ply'd,
   'From London upon the Thames,
Which circled is, O grief to tell!
   Besieg'd with forraign arms.

13 ' By the proud Prince of Aragon,
    Who swears by his martial hand
To have the princess for his spouse,
    Or else to waste this land:

14 ' Except that champions can be found
    That dare fight three to three,
Against the prince and giants twain,
    Most horrid for to see:

15 ' Whose grisly looks, and eyes like
        brands,
    Strike terrour where they come,
With serpents hissing on their helms,
    Instead of feathered plume.

16 ' The princess shall be the victors prize,
    The king hath vowd and said,
And he that shall the conquest win
    Shall have her to his bride.

17 ' Now we are four damsels sent abroad,
    To the east, west, north, and south,
To try whose fortune is so good
    To find these champions forth.

18 ' But all in vaine we have sought
        about;
    Yet none so bold there are
That dare adventure life and blood,
    To free a lady fair.'

19 ' When is the day ? ' quoth Robin Hood,
    ' Tell me this and no more: '
' On Midsummer next,' the damsel said,
    ' Which is June the twenty-four.'

20 With that the teares trickled down her
        cheeks,
    And silent was her tongue;
With sighs and sobs she took her
        leave,
    Away her palfrey sprung.

21 This news struck Robin to the heart,
    He fell down on the grass;
His actions and his troubled mind
    Shewd he perplexed was.

22 ' Where lies your grief ? ' quoth Will
        Scadlock,
    ' O master, tell to me;
If the damsels eyes have pierced your
        heart,
    I 'll fetch her back to thee '

23 ' Now nay, now nay,' quoth Robin Hood
    ' She doth not cause my smart;
But it is the poor distressed princess
    That wounds me to the heart.

24 ' I will go fight the giants all
    To set the lady free: '
' The devil take my soul,' quoth Little
        John,
    ' If I part with thy company.'

25 ' Must I stay behind ? ' quoth Will
        Scadlock;
    ' No, no, that must not be;
I 'le make the third man in the fight,
    So we shall be three to three.'

26 These words cheerd Robin at the heart,
    Joy shone within his face;
Within his arms he huggd them both,
    And kindly did imbrace.

27 Quoth he, We 'll put on mothly gray,
    With long staves in our hands,
A scrip and bottle by our sides,
    As come from the Holy Land.

28 So may we pass along the high-way;
    None will ask from whence we came,
But take us pilgrims for to be,
    Or else some holy men.

29 Now they are on their journey gone,
    As fast as they may speed,
Yet for all haste, ere they arriv'd,
    The princess forth was led:

30 To be deliverd to the prince,
    Who in the list did stand,
Prepar'd to fight, or else receive
    His lady by the hand.

31 With that he walkt about the lists,
    With giants by his side:
' Bring forth,' said he, ' your champions,
    Or bring me forth my bride.

32 ' This is the four and twentieth day,
    The day prefixt upon;
Bring forth my bride, or London burns,
    I swear by Acaron.'

33 Then cries the king, and queen like-
        wise,
    Both weeping as they speak.

Lo ! we have brought our daughter dear,
　Whom we are forc'd to forsake.

34 With that stept out bold Robin Hood,
　　Crys, My liege, it must not be so;
　Such beauty as the fair princess
　　Is not for a tyrants mow.

35 The prince he then began to storm;
　　Crys, Fool, fanatick, baboon !
　How dares thou stop my valours prize ?
　　I 'll kill thee with a frown.

36 ' Thou tyrant Turk, thou infidel,'
　　Thus Robin began to reply,
　' Thy frowns I scorn; lo ! here 's my
　　　gage,
　　And thus I thee defie.

37 ' And for these two Goliahs there,
　　That stand on either side,
　Here are two little Davids by,
　　That soon can tame their pride.'

38 Then did the king for armour send,
　　For lances, swords, and shields:
　And thus all three in armour bright
　　Came marching to the field.

39 The trumpets began to sound a charge,
　　Each singled out his man;
　Their arms in pieces soon were hewd,
　　Blood sprang from every vain.

40 The prince he reacht Robin a blow —
　　He struck with might and main —
　Which forc'd him to reel about the
　　　field,
　　As though he had been slain.

41 'God-a-mercy,' quoth Robin, ' for that
　　　blow !
　The quarrel shall soon be try'd;
　This stroke shall shew a full divorce
　　Betwixt thee and thy bride.'

42 So from his shoulders he 's cut his head,
　　Which on the ground did fall,
　And grumbling sore at Robin Hood,
　　To be so dealt withal.

43 The giants then began to rage,
　　To see their prince lie dead:
　' Thou 's be the next,' quoth Little John,
　　' Unless thou well guard thy head.'

44 With that his faulchion he whirld
　　　about —
　　It was both keen and sharp —
　He clove the giant to the belt,
　　And cut in twain his heart.

45 Will Scadlock well had playd his part,
　　The giant he had brought to his
　　　knee;
　Quoth he, The devil cannot break his
　　　fast,
　　Unless he have you all three.

46 So with his faulchion he run him through,
　　A deep and gashly wound;
　Who damd and foamd, cursd and blas-
　　　phemd,
　　And then fell to the ground.

47 Now all the lists with cheers were filld,
　　The skies they did resound,
　Which brought the princess to herself,
　　Who was faln in a swound.

48 The king and queen and princess fair
　　Came walking to the place,
　And gave the champions many thanks,
　　And did them further grace.

49 ' Tell me,' quoth the king, ' whence you
　　　are,
　That thus disguised came,
　Whose valour speaks that noble blood
　　Doth run through every vain.'

50 ' A boon, a boon,' quoth Robin Hood,
　　' On my knees I beg and crave:'
　' By my crown,' quoth the king, ' I grant;
　　Ask what, and thou shalt have.'

51 ' Then pardon I beg for my merry
　　　men,
　　Which are within the green wood,
　For Little John, and Will Scadlock,
　　And for me, bold Robin Hood.'

52 ' Art thou Robin Hood ? ' then quoth
　　　the king;
　' For the valour you have shewn,
　Your pardons I doe freely grant,
　　And welcome every one.

53 ' The princess I promised the victors
　　　prize;
　　She cannot have you all three:'

'She shall chuse,' quoth Robin; saith
    Little John,
    Then little share falls to me.

54 Then did the princess view all three,
    With a comely lovely grace,
    Who took Will Scadlock by the hand,
    Quoth, Here I make my choice.

55 With that a noble lord stept forth,
    Of Maxfield earl was he,
    Who lookt Will Scadlock in the face,
    Then wept most bitterly.

56 Quoth he, I had a son like thee,
    Whom I lovd wondrous well;
    But he is gone, or rather dead;
    His name is Young Gamwell.

57 Then did Will Scadlock fall on his
    knees,
    Cries, Father ! father ! here,
    Here kneels your son, your Young Gam-
    well
    You said you lovd so dear.

58 But, lord ! what imbracing and kissing
    was there,
    When all these friends were met !
    They are gone to the wedding, and so
    to bedding,
    And so I bid you good night.

130

ROBIN HOOD AND THE SCOTCHMAN

A is simply the conclusion given to ' Robin
Hood Newly Revived ' (No. 128) in the broadsides, and has neither connection with that ballad nor coherence in itself, being on the face of
it the beginning and the end of an independent
ballad, with the break after the third stanza.
3 may possibly refer to the Scots giving up
Charles I to the parliamentary commissioners,
in 1647. In B, four stanzas appear to have
been added to the first three of A in order to
make out a story, — the too familiar one of
Robin being beaten in a fight with a fellow
whom he chances to meet, and consequently
enlisting the man as a recruit.

A

a. Wood, 401, leaf 27 b. b. Roxburghe,
III, 18, in the Ballad Society's reprint, II, 426.

c. Garland of 1663, No. 3. d. Garland of 1670,
No. 2. e. Pepys, II, 101, No. 88.

1 THEN bold Robin Hood to the north he
    would go,
    With a hey down down a down down
    With valour and mickle might,
    With sword by his side, which oft had
    been tri'd,
    To fight and recover his right.

2 The first that he met was a bony bold Scot,
    His servant he said he would be;
    ' No,' quoth Robin Hood, ' it cannot be
    good,
    For thou wilt prove false unto me.

3 ' Thou hast not bin true to sire nor cuz:'
    ' Nay, marry,' the Scot he said,
    ' As true as your heart, I 'le never part,
    Gude master, be not afraid.'

    *   *   *   *   *

4 Then Robin Hood turnd his face to the
    east;
    ' Fight on my merry men stout,
    Our cause is good,' quoth brave Robin
    Hood,
    ' And we shall not be beaten out.'

5 The battel grows hot on every side,
    The Scotchman made great moan;
    Quoth Jockey, Gude faith, they fight on
    each side;
    Would I were with my wife Ione !

6 The enemy compast brave Robin about,
    'T is long ere the battel ends;
    Ther 's neither will yeeld nor give up the
    field,
    For both are supplied with friends.

    *   *   *   *   *

7 This song it was made in Robin Hoods
    dayes;
    Let 's pray unto Iove above
    To give us true peace, that mischief may
    cease,
    And war may give place unto love.

B

Gutch's Robin Hood, II, 392, from an Irish
garland, printed at Monaghan, 1796.

1 Now bold Robin Hood to the north
would go,
With valour and mickle might,
With sword by his side, which oft had
been try'd,
To fight and recover his right.

2 The first that he met was a jolly stout
Scot,
His servant he said he would be;
'No,' quoth Robin Hood, 'it cannot be
good,
For thou wilt prove false unto me.

3 'Thou hast not been true to sire or cuz;'
'Nay, marry,' the Scot he said,
'As true as your heart, I never will part;
Good master, be not afraid.'

4 'But eer I employ you,' said bold Robin
Hood,
'With you I must have a bout;'
The Scotchman reply'd, Let the battle
be try'd,
For I know I will beat you out.

5 Thus saying, the contest did quickly
begin,
Which lasted two hours and more;
The blows Sawney gave bold Robin so
brave
The battle soon made him give oer.

6 'Have mercy, thou Scotchman,' bold
Robin Hood cry'd,
'Full dearly this boon have I bought;
We will both agree, and my man you
shall be,
For a stouter I never have fought.'

7 Then Sawny consented with Robin to
go,
To be of his bowmen so gay;
Thus ended the fight, and with mickle
delight
To Sherwood they hasted away.

131

ROBIN HOOD AND THE RANGER

'Robin Hood and the Ranger.' a. Robin
Hood's Garland. London, C. Dicey, in Bow

Church-Yard, n. d., but before 1741, p. 78.
b. R. H.'s Garland, London, W. & C. Dicey,
n. d. c. R. H.'s Garland, London, L. How,
in Peticoat Lane, n. d. d. The English Archer,
etc., York, N. Nickson, in Feasegate, n. d.
e. The English Archer, etc., Paisley, John
Neilson, 1786. f. R. H.'s Garland, York, T.
Wilson & R. Spence, n. d. (All in the Bodleian
Library.)

1 WHEN Phœbus had melted the sickles
of ice,
With a hey down, &c.
And likewise the mountains of snow,
Bold Robin Hood he would ramble to
see,
To frolick abroad with his bow.

2 He left all his merry men waiting behind,
Whilst through the green vallies he
passd;
There did he behold a forester bold,
Who cry'd out, Friend, whither so
fast?

3 'I 'm going,' quoth Robin, 'to kill a fat
buck,
For me and my merry men all;
Besides, eer I go, I 'll have a fat doe,
Or else it shall cost me a fall.'

4 'You 'd best have a care,' said the for-
ester then,
'For these are his majesty's deer;
Before you shall shoot, the thing I 'll
dispute,
For I am head-forester here.'

5 'These thirteen long summers,' quoth
Robin, 'I 'm sure,
My arrows I here have let fly,
Where freely I range; methinks it is
strange,
You should have more power than I.

6 'This forest,' quoth Robin, 'I think is
my own,
And so are the nimble deer too;
Therefore I declare, and solemnly swear,
I wont be affronted by you.'

7 The forester he had a long quarter-staff,
Likewise a broad sword by his side;
Without more ado, he presently drew,
Declaring the truth should be try'd.

8 Bold Robin Hood had a sword of the best,
   Thus, eer he would take any wrong,
His courage was flush, he 'd venture a
     brush,
   And thus they fell to it ding dong.

9 The very first blow that the forester gave,
   He made his broad weapon cry twang;
'T was over the head, he fell down for
     dead,
   O that was a damnable bang !

10 But Robin he soon did recover himself,
   And bravely fell to it again;
The very next stroke their weapons
     were broke,
   Yet never a man there was slain.

11 At quarter-staff then they resolved to
     play,
   Because they would have t'other bout;
And brave Robin Hood right valiantly
     stood,
   Unwilling he was to give out.

12 Bold Robin he gave him very hard blows,
   The other returnd them as fast;
At every stroke their jackets did smoke,
   Three hours the combat did last.

13 At length in a rage the bold forester
     grew,
   And cudgeld bold Robin so sore
That he could not stand, so shaking his
     hand,
   He said, Let us freely give oer.

14 Thou art a brave fellow, I needs must
     confess
   I never knew any so good;
Thou 'rt fitting to be a yeoman for me,
   And range in the merry green wood.

15 I 'll give thee this ring as a token of love,
   For bravely thou 'st acted thy part;
That man that can fight, in him I de-
     light,
   And love him with all my whole heart.

16 Then Robin Hood setting his horn to
     his mouth,
   A blast he merrily blows;
His yeomen did hear, and strait did ap-
     pear,
   A hundred, with trusty long bows.

17 Now Little John came at the head of
     them all,
   Cloathd in a rich mantle of green;
And likewise the rest were gloriously
     drest,
   A delicate sight to be seen.

18 'Lo, these are my yeomen,' said Robin
     Hood,
   ' And thou shalt be one of the train;
A mantle and bow, a quiver also,
   I give them whom I entertain.'

19 The forester willingly enterd the list,
   They were such a beautiful sight;
Then with a long bow they shot a fat
     doe,
   And made a rich supper that night.

20 What singing and dancing was in the
     green wood,
   For joy of another new mate !
With mirth and delight they spent the
     long night,
   And liv'd at a plentiful rate.

21 The forester neer was so merry before
   As then he was with these brave souls,
Who never would fail, in wine, beer or
     ale,
   To take off their cherishing bowls.

22 Then Robin Hood gave him a mantle
     of green,
   Broad arrows, and a curious long bow;
This done, the next day, so gallant and
     gay,
   He marched them all on a row.

23 Quoth he, My brave yeomen, be true to
     your trust,
   And then we may range the woods
     wide:
They all did declare, and solemnly swear,
   They 'd conquer, or die by his side.

132

THE BOLD PEDLAR AND ROBIN HOOD

" An aged female in Bermondsey, Surrey,
from whose oral recitation the editor took
down the present version, informed him, that

she had often heard her grandmother sing it,
and that it was never in print; but he has of
late met with several common stall copies."—
DIXON. This ballad is a traditional variation
of No. 128. A copy which varies but slightly
from that here printed is found in Captain
Delany's Garland [1775?], British Museum,
1346, m. 7 (9). It is given in Child, v, 240.

J. H. Dixon, Ancient Poems, Ballads, and
Songs of the Peasantry of England, p. 71, Percy
Society, vol. XVII, 1846.

1 THERE chanced to be a pedlar bold,
 A pedlar bold he chanced to be;
He rolled his pack all on his back,
 And he came tripping oer the lee.
  Down a down a down a down,
  Down a down a down

2 By chance he met two troublesome
  blades,
 Two troublesome blades they chanced
  to be;
The one of them was bold Robin Hood,
 And the other was Little John so
  free.

3 'O pedlar, pedlar, what is in thy pack?
 Come speedilie and tell to me:'
'I've several suits of the gay green silks,
 And silken bow-strings two or three.'

4 'If you have several suits of the gay
  green silk.
 And silken bow-strings two or three,
Then it's by my body,' cries Little
  John,
 'One half your pack shall belong to
  me.'

5 'O nay, o nay,' says the pedlar bold,
 'O nay, o nay, that never can be;
For there's never a man from fair Not-
  tingham
Can take one half my pack from
  me.'

6 Then the pedlar he pulled off his pack,
 And put it a little below his knee,
Saying, If you do move me one perch
  from this,
 My pack and all shall gang with
  thee.

7 Then Little John he drew his sword,
 The pedlar by his pack did stand;

They fought until they both did sweat,
 Till he cried, Pedlar, pray hold your
  hand!

8 Then Robin Hood he was standing by,
 And he did laugh most heartilie;
Saying, I could find a man, of a smaller
  scale,
 Could thrash the pedlar and also thee.

9 'Go you try, master,' says Little John,
 'Go you try, master, most speedilie,
Or by my body,' says Little John,
 'I am sure this night you will not
  know me.'

10 Then Robin Hood he drew his sword,
 And the pedlar by his pack did stand;
They fought till the blood in streams
  did flow,
 Till he cried, Pedlar, pray hold your
  hand!

11 Pedlar, pedlar, what is thy name?
 Come speedilie and tell to me:
'My name! my name I neer will tell,
 Till both your names you have told to
  me.'

12 'The one of us is bold Robin Hood,
 And the other Little John so free:'
'Now,' says the pedlar, 'it lays to my
  good will,
 Whether my name I chuse to tell to
  thee.

13 'I am Gamble Gold of the gay green
  woods,
 And travelled far beyond the sea;
For killing a man in my father's land
 From my country I was forced to
  flee.'

14 'If you are Gamble Gold of the gay
  green woods,
 And travelled far beyond the sea,
You are my mother's own sister's son;
 What nearer cousins then can we be?'

15 They sheathed their swords with friendly
  words,
 So merrilie they did agree;
They went to a tavern, and there they
  dined,
 And bottles cracked most merrilie.

133

ROBIN HOOD AND THE BEGGAR, I

There is a copy in the Roxburghe Collection, III, 20 (Ballad Society's ed., VIII, 517). The copy in the Wood and in the Roxburghe collections is signed T. R. like No. 122 B (see p. 294, above), and, like the latter ballad, this is a *rifacimento*, with middle rhyme in the third line. It is perhaps made up from two distinct stories; the Second Part, beginning at st. 20, from No. 140, and what precedes from a ballad resembling No. 134. But no seventeenth-century version of No. 134 is known, and it is more likely that we owe the fight between Robin Hood and the Beggar to the folly and bad taste of T. R.

'Robin Hood and the Beggar.' **a.** Wood, 401, leaf 23 b. **b.** Garland of 1663, No. 8. **c.** Garland of 1670, No. 7. **d.** Pepys, II, 116, No. 100.

1 COME light and listen, you gentlemen all,
    Hey down, down, and a down
That mirth do love for to hear,
And a story true I 'le tell unto you,
    If that you will but draw near.

2 In elder times, when merriment was,
    And archery was holden good,
There was an outlaw, as many did know,
    Which men called Robin Hood.

3 Vpon a time it chanced so
    Bold Robin was merry disposed,
His time to spend he did intend,
    Either with friends or foes.

4 Then he got vp on a gallant brave steed,
    The which was worth angels ten;
With a mantle of green, most brave to be seen,
    He left all his merry men.

5 And riding towards fair Nottingham,
    Some pastime for to spy,
There was he aware of a jolly beggar
    As ere he beheld with his eye.

6 An old patcht coat the beggar had on,
    Which he daily did vse for to wear;

And many a bag about him did wag,
    Which made Robin Hood to him repair.

7 'God speed, God speed,' said Robin Hood,
    'What countryman? tell to me:'
'I am Yorkshire, sir; but, ere you go far,
    Some charity give vnto me.'

8 'Why, what wouldst thou have?' said Robin Hood,
    'I pray thee tell vnto me:'
'No lands nor livings,' the beggar he said,
    'But a penny for charitie.'

9 'I have no money,' said Robin Hood then,
    'But, a ranger within the wood,
I am an outlaw, as many do know,
    My name it is Robin Hood.

10 'But yet I must tell thee, bonny beggar,
    That a bout with [thee] I must try;
Thy coat of gray, lay down I say,
    And my mantle of green shall lye by.'

11 'Content, content,' the beggar he cry'd,
    'Thy part it will be the worse;
For I hope this bout to give thee the rout,
    And then have at thy purse.'

12 The beggar he had a mickle long staffe,
    And Robin had a nut-brown sword;
So the beggar drew nigh, and at Robin let fly,
    But gave him never a word.

13 'Fight on, fight on,' said Robin Hood then,
    'This game well pleaseth me;'
For every blow that Robin did give,
    The beggar gave buffets three.

14 And fighting there full hard and sore,
    Not far from Nottingham town,
They never fled, till from Robin['s] head
    The blood came trickling down.

15 'O hold thy hand,' said Robin Hood then,
    'And thou and I will agree;'

'If that be true,' the beggar he said,
'Thy mantle come give vnto me.'

16 'Nay a change, a change,' cri'd Robin
Hood;
'Thy bags and coat give me,
And this mantle of mine I 'le to thee re-
sign,
My horse and my braverie.'

17 When Robin Hood had got the beggars
clothes,
He looked round about;
'Methinks,' said he, 'I seem to be
A beggar brave and stout.

18 'For now I have a bag for my bread,
So have I another for corn;
I have one for salt, and another for
malt,
And one for my little horn.

19 'And now I will a begging goe,
Some charitie for to find:'
And if any more of Robin you 'l know,
In this second part it 's behind.

20 Now Robin he is to Nottingham bound,
With his bags hanging down to his
knee,
His staff, and his coat, scarce worth a
groat,
Yet merrilie passed he.

21 As Robin he passed the streets along,
He heard a pittifull cry;
Three brethren deer, as he did hear,
Condemned were to dye.

22 Then Robin he highed to the sheriffs
[house],
Some reliefe for to seek;
He skipt, and leapt, and capored full
high,
As he went along the street.

23 But when to the sheriffs doore he came,
There a gentleman fine and brave,
'Thou beggar,' said he, 'come tell vnto
me
What is it that thou wouldest have?'

24 'No meat, nor drink,' said Robin Hood
then,
'That I come here to crave

But to beg the lives of yeomen three,
And that I fain would have.'

25 'That cannot be, thou bold beggar,
Their fact it is so cleer;
I tell to thee, hangd they must be,
For stealing of our kings deer.'

26 But when to the gallows they did come,
There was many a weeping eye;
'O hold your peace,' said Robin then,
'For certainly they shall not dye.'

27 Then Robin he set his horn to his mouth,
And he blew but blastes three,
Till a hundred bold archers brave
Came kneeling down to his knee.

28 'What is your will, master?' they said,
'We are here at your command:'
'Shoot east, shoot west,' said Robin
Hood then,
'And look that you spare no man.'

29 Then they shot east, and they shot
west;
Their arrows were so keen
The sheriffe he, and his companie,
No longer must be seen.

30 Then he stept to these brethren three,
And away he had them tane;
But the sheriff was crost, and many a
man lost,
That dead lay on the plain.

31 And away they went into the merry
green wood,
And sung with a merry glee,
And Robin took these brethren good
To be of his yeomandrie.

134

ROBIN HOOD AND THE BEGGAR, II

This tale is rightly called by Ritson a North
Country composition of some antiquity, "perhaps Scottish." Fragments of Robin Hood
ballads, Motherwell informs us, were traditionally extant in his day which had not (and have
not) found their way into printed collections,
and we know from very early testimony that
such ballads were current in Scotland. This is

by far the best of the Robin Hood ballads of
the secondary, so to speak cyclic, period. It
has plenty of homely humor, but the heroic
sentiment is gone. It does not belong to the
iron, the cast-iron, age of 'Robin Hood's Birth,
Breeding,' etc. (No. 149); but neither does it
belong to the golden age of 'Robin Hood and
the Monk,' or the Gest.

a. 'The History of Robin Hood and the Beggar,' Aberdeen, Printed by and for A. Keith:
Bodleian Library, Douce, HH 88, pasted between pp. 68, 69 of Robin Hood's Garland, London, C. Dicey. A. Keith of Aberdeen printed
from 1810 to 1835. b. 'A pretty dialogue betwixt Robin Hood and a Beggar,' Newcastle,
in Ritson's Robin Hood, 1795, I, 97.

1 LYTH and listen, gentlemen,
    That's come of high born blood;
    I'll tell you of a brave booting
    That befel Robin Hood.

2 Robin Hood upon a day,
    He went forth him alone,
    And as he came from Barnesdale
    Into a fair evening,

3 He met a beggar on the way,
    That sturdily could gang;
    He had a pike-staff in his hand,
    That was baith stark and strang.

4 A clouted cloak about him was,
    That held him from the cold;
    The thinnest bit of it, I guess,
    Was more than twenty fold.

5 His meal-pock hang about his neck,
    Into a leathern fang,
    Well fastened with a broad buckle,
    That was both stark and strang.

6 He had three hats upon his head,
    Together sticked fast;
    He cared neither for wind nor weet,
    In lands wherever he past.

7 Good Robin coost him in his way,
    To see what he might be;
    If any beggar had money,
    He thought some part had he.

8 'Tarry, tarry,' good Robin says,
    'Tarry, and speak with me;'
    He heard him as he heard [him] not,
    And fast his way can hie.

9 'It be's not so,' says good Robin,
    'Nay, thou must tarry still;'
    'By my troth,' says the bold beggar,
    'Of that I have no will.

10 'It is far to my lodging-house,
    And it is growing late;
    If they have supt ere I come in,
    I will look wondrous blate.'

11 'Now, by my troth,' says good Robin,
    'I see well by thy fare,
    If thou chear well to thy supper,
    Of mine thou takes no care;

12 'Who wants my dinner all the day,
    And wots not where to lie,
    And should I to the tavern go,
    I want money to buy.

13 'Sir, thou must lend me some money,
    Till we two meet again:'
    The beggar answerd cankerdly,
    I have no money to lend.

14 Thou art as young a man as I,
    And seems to be as sweer;
    If thou fast till thou get from me,
    Thou shalt eat none this year.

15 'Now, by my troth,' says good Robin,
    'Since we are sembled so,
    If thou have but a small farthing,
    I'll have it ere thou go.

16 'Therefore, lay down thy clouted cloak
    And do no longer stand,
    And loose the strings of all thy
        pocks;
    I'll ripe them with my hand.

17 'And now to thee I make a vow,
    If thou make any din,
    I shall see if a broad arrow
    Can pierce a beggar's skin.'

18 The beggar smil'd, and answer made:
    Far better let me be;
    Think not that I will be afraid
    For thy nip crooked tree.

19 Or that I fear thee any whit
    For thy curn nips of sticks;
    I know no use for them so meet
    As to be pudding-pricks.

20 Here I defy thee to do me ill,
    For all thy boistrous fare;
    Thou 's get nothing from me but ill,
    Would thou seek it evermair.

21 Good Robin bent his noble bow —
    He was an angry man —
    And in it set a broad arrow;
    Yet er 't was drawn a span,

22 The beggar, with his noble tree,
    Reacht him so round a rout
    That his bow and his broad arrow
    In flinders flew about.

23 Good Robin bound him to his brand,
    But that provd likewise vain;
    The beggar lighted on his hand
    With his pike-staff again.

24 I wot he might not draw a sword
    For forty days and more;
    Good Robin could not speak a word,
    His heart was never so sore.

25 He could not fight, he could not flee,
    He wist not what to do;
    The beggar, with his noble tree,
    Laid lusty flaps him to.

26 He paid good Robin back and side,
    And beft him up and down,
    And with his pike-staff still on laid
    Till he fell in a swoon.

27 'Fy! stand up, man,' the beggar
        said,
    ''T is shame to go to rest;
    Stay still till thou get thy mony [told],
    I think it were the best.

28 'And syne go to the tavern-house,
    And buy both wine and ale;
    Hereat thy friends will crack full crouse,
    Thou has been at a dale.'

29 Good Robin answerd never a word,
    But lay still as a stane;
    His cheeks were white as any clay,
    And closed were his eyne.

30 The beggar thought him dead but fail,
    And boldly bownd away;
    I would you had been at the dale,
    And gotten part of the play.

31 Now three of Robin's men, by chance,
    Came walking on the way,
    And found their master in a trance,
    On ground where he did lie.

32 Up have they taken good Robin,
    Making a piteous bier,
    Yet saw they no man there at whom
    They might the matter spear.

33 They looked him all round about,
    But wounds on him saw none,
    Yet at his mouth came bocking out
    The blood of a good vein.

34 Cold water they have taken syne,
    And cast into his face;
    Then he began to lift his eyne,
    And spake within short space.

35 'Tell us, dear master,' says his men,
    'How with you stands the case?'
    Good Robin sighd ere he began
    To tell of his disgrace.

36 'I have been watchman in this wood
    Near hand this forty year,
    Yet I was never so hard bestead
    As you have found me here.

37 'A beggar with a clouted cloak,
    In whom I feard no ill,
    Hath with a pike-staff clawd my
        back;
    I fear 't shall never be well.

38 'See, where he goes out oer yon hill,
    With hat upon his head;
    If ever you lovd your master well,
    Go now revenge this deed.

39 'And bring him back again to me,
    If it lie in your might,
    That I may see, before I die,
    Him punisht in my sight.

40 'And if you may not bring him back,
    Let him not go loose on;
    For to us all it were great shame
    If he escapt again.'

41 'One of us shall with you remain,
    Because you 're ill at ease;
    The other two shall bring him back,
    To use him as you please.'

42 'Now, by my troth,' says good Robin,
   'I trow there's enough said;
   If he get scouth to weild his tree,
   I fear you'll both be paid.'

43 'Be ye not feard, our good master,
   That we two can be dung
   With any blutter base beggar,
   That hath nought but a rung.

44 'His staff shall stand him in no stead;
   That you shall shortly see;
   But back again he shall be led,
   And fast bound shall he be,
   To see if you will have him slain,
   Or hanged on a tree.'

45 'But cast you slily in his way,
   Before he be aware,
   And on his pike-staff first lay hands;
   You'll speed the better far.'

46 Now leave we Robin with his man,
   Again to play the child,
   And learn himself to stand and gang
   By haulds, for all his eild.

47 Now pass we to the bold beggar,
   That raked oer the hill,
   Who never mended his pace no more
   Nor he had done no ill.

48 The young men knew the country well,
   So soon where he would be,
   And they have taken another way,
   Was nearer by miles three.

49 They rudely ran with all their might,
   Spar'd neither dub nor mire,
   They stirred neither at laigh nor hight,
   No travel made them tire,

50 Till they before the beggar wan,
   And coost them in his way;
   A little wood lay in a glen,
   And there they both did stay.

51 They stood up closely by a tree,
   In ilk side of the gate,
   Until the beggar came them to,
   That thought not of such fate.

52 And as he was betwixt them past,
   They leapt upon him baith;

The one his pike-staff gripped fast,
   They feared for its scaith.

53 The other he held in his sight
   A drawn dirk to his breast,
   And said, False carl, quit thy staff,
   Or I shall be thy priest.

54 His pike-staff they have taken him frae,
   And stuck it in the green;
   He was full leath to let [it] gae,
   If better might have been.

55 The beggar was the feardest man
   Of one that ever might be;
   To win away no way he can,
   Nor help him with his tree.

56 He wist not wherefore he was tane,
   Nor how many was there;
   He thought his life-days had been gone,
   And grew into despair.

57 'Grant me my life,' the beggar said,
   'For him that died on tree,
   And take away that ugly knife,
   Or then for fear I'll die.

58 'I grievd you never in all my life,
   By late nor yet by ayre;
   Ye have great sin, if ye should slay
   A silly poor beggar.'

59 'Thou lies, false lown,' they said again,
   'By all that may be sworn;
   Thou hast near slain the gentlest man
   That ever yet was born.

60 'And back again thou shalt be led,
   And fast bound shalt thou be,
   To see if he will have thee slain,
   Or hanged on a tree.'

61 The beggar then thought all was wrong;
   They were set for his wrack;
   He saw nothing appearing then
   But ill upon worse back.

62 Were he out of their hands, he thought,
   And had again his tree,
   He should not be had back for nought,
   With such as he did see.

63 Then he bethought him on a wile,
   If it could take effect,

How he the young men might beguile,
　And give them a begeck.

64 Thus for to do them shame or ill
　His beastly breast was bent;
　He found the wind grew something
　　shril,
　To further his intent.

65 He said, Brave gentlemen, be good,
　And let the poor man be;
　When ye have taken a beggar's blood,
　It helps you not a flee.

66 It was but in my own defence,
　If he hath gotten skaith;
　But I will make a recompence,
　Much better for your baith.

67 If ye will set me safe and free,
　And do me no danger,
　An hundred pounds I will you give,
　And much more good silver,

68 That I have gathered these many years,
　Under this clouted cloak,
　And hid up wonder privately,
　In bottom of my pock.

69 The young men to a council yeed,
　And let the beggar gae;
　They wist how well he had no speed
　From them to run away.

70 They thought they would the money
　　take,
　Come after what so may,
　And then they would not bring him
　　back,
　But in that part him slay.

71 By that good Robin would not know
　That they had gotten coin;
　It would content him for to show
　That there they had him slain.

72 They said, False carl, soon have done
　And tell forth that money;
　For the ill turn thou hast done
　'T is but a simple fee.

73 And yet we will not have thee back,
　Come after what so may,
　If thou will do that which thou spake,
　And make us present pay.

74 O then he loosd his clouted cloak,
　And spread it on the ground,
　And thereon laid he many a pock,
　Betwixt them and the wind.

75 He took a great bag from his hase;
　It was near full of meal;
　Two pecks in it at least there was,
　And more, I wot full well.

76 Upon his cloak he laid it down,
　The mouth he opend wide,
　To turn the same he made him bown,
　The young men ready spy'd.

77 In every hand he took a nook
　Of that great leathern meal,
　And with a fling the meal he shook
　Into their faces hail.

78 Wherewith he blinded them so close
　A stime they could not see;
　And then in heart he did rejoice,
　And clapt his lusty tree.

79 He thought, if he had done them wrong
　In mealing of their cloaths,
　For to strike off the meal again
　With his pike-staff he goes.

80 Or any one of them could red their
　　eyne,
　Or yet a glimmering could see,
　Ilk ane of them a dozen had,
　Well laid on with the tree.

81 The young men were right swift of foot,
　And boldly ran away;
　The beggar could them no more hit,
　For all the haste he may.

82 'What ails this haste?' the beggar said,
　'May ye not tarry still,
　Until your money be receivd?
　I 'll pay you with good will.

83 'The shaking of my pocks, I fear,
　Hath blown into your eyne;
　But I have a good pike-staff here
　Will ripe them out full clean.'

84 The young men answerd neer a word,
　They were dumb as a stane;
　In the thick wood the beggar fled,
　Eer they riped their eyne.

85 And syne the night became so late,
    To seek him was but vain:
  But judge ye, if they looked blate
    When they came home again.

86 Good Robin speard how they had sped;
    They answerd him, Full ill;
  'That cannot be,' good Robin says;
    'Ye have been at the mill.

87 'The mill it is a meatrif place,
    They may lick what they please;
  Most like ye have been at that art,
    Who would look to your cloaths.'

88 They hangd their heads, and droped
      down,
    A word they could not speak:
  Robin said, Because I fell a-swoon,
    I think you'll do the like.

89 Tell on the matter, less and more,
    And tell me what and how
  Ye have done with the bold beggar
    I sent you for right now.

90 And then they told him to an end,
    As I have said before,
  How that the beggar did them blind,
    What misters process more.

91 And how he lin'd their shoulders broad
    With his great trenchen tree,
  And how in the thick wood he fled,
    Eer they a stime could see,

92 And how they scarcely could win home,
    Their bones were beft so sore:
  Good Robin cry'd, Fy! out, for shame!
    We're sham'd for evermore.

93 Altho good Robin would full fain
    Of his wrong revenged be,
  He smil'd to see his merry young men
    Had gotten a taste of the tree.

135

ROBIN HOOD AND THE
SHEPHERD

It is but the natural course of exaggeration
that the shepherd, having beaten Robin Hood,
should beat Little John. This is descending
low enough, but we do not see the bottom of
this kind of balladry here.

a. Garland of 1663, No. 13. b. Garland
of 1670, No. 12. c. Wood, 401, leaf 13 b. d.
Pepys, II, 115, No. 102.

1 ALL gentlemen and yeomen good,
    Down a down a down a down
  I wish you to draw near;
  For a story of gallant brave Robin
      Hood
    Vnto you I wil declare.
      Down, etc.

2 As Robin Hood walkt the forrest along,
    Some pastime for to spie,
  There was he aware of a jolly shepherd,
    That on the ground did lie.

3 'Arise, arise,' cryed jolly Robin,
    'And now come let me see
  What is in thy bag and bottle, I say;
    Come tell it unto me.'

4 'What's that to thee, thou proud fel-
      low?
    Tell me as I do stand
  What thou hast to do with my bag and
      bottle?
    Let me see thy command.'

5 'My sword, which hangeth by my side,
    Is my command I know;
  Come, and let me taste of thy bottle,
    Or it may breed thee wo.'

6 'Tut, the devil a drop, thou proud fellow,
    Of my bottle thou shalt see,
  Untill thy valour here be tried,
    Whether thou wilt fight or flee.'

7 'What shall we fight for?' cries bold
      Robin Hood;
    'Come tell it soon to me;
  Here is twenty pounds in good red
      gold;
    Win it, and take it thee.'

8 The Shepherd stood all in a maze,
    And knew not what to say:
  'I have no money, thou proud fellow,
    But bag and bottle I'le lay.'

9 'I am content, thou shepherd-swain,
    Fling them down on the ground;
  But it will breed thee mickle pain,
    To win my twenty pound.'

10 'Come draw thy sword, thou proud fel-
    low,
  Thou stands too long to prate;
  This hook of mine shall let thee know
    A coward I do hate.'

11 So they fell to it, full hardy and sore;
  It was on a summers day;
  From ten till four in the afternoon
    The Shepherd held him play.

12 Robins buckler proved his chief defence,
  And saved him many a bang,
  For every blow the Shepherd gave
    Made Robins sword cry twang.

13 Many a sturdy blow the Shepherd gave,
  And that bold Robin found,
  Till the blood ran trickling from his
    head;
  Then he fell to the ground.

14 'Arise, arise, thou proud fellow,
  And thou shalt have fair play,
  If thou wilt yield, before thou go,
    That I have won the day.'

15 'A boon, a boon,' cried bold Robin;
  'If that a man thou be,
  Then let me take my beaugle-horn,
    And blow but blasts three.'

16 'To blow three times three,' the Shep-
    herd said,
  'I will not thee deny;
  For if thou shouldst blow till to-morrow
    morn,
  I scorn one foot to fly.'

17 Then Robin set his horn to his mouth,
  And he blew with mickle main,
  Until he espied Little John
    Come tripping over the plain.

18 'O who is yonder, thou proud fellow,
  That comes down yonder hill?'
  'Yonder is Little John, bold Robin
    Hoods man,
  Shall fight with thee thy fill.'

19 'What is the matter?' saies Little John,
  'Master, come tell to me:'
  'My case is great,' saies Robin Hood,
  'For the Shepherd hath conquered
    me.'

20 'I am glad of that,' cries Little John,
  'Shepherd, turn thou to me;
  For a bout with thee I mean to have,
    Either come fight or flee.'

21 'With all my heart, thou proud fellow,
  For it never shall be said
  That a shepherds hook of thy sturdy look
    Will one jot be dismaid.'

22 So they fell to it, full hardy and sore,
  Striving for victory;
  'I will know,' saies John, 'ere we give ore,
    Whether thou wilt fight or flye.'

23 The Shepherd gave John a sturdy blow,
  With his hook under the chin;
  'Beshrew thy heart,' said Little John,
    'Thou basely dost begin.'

24 'Nay, that's nothing,' said the Shepherd
  'Either yield to me the day,
  Or I will bang thee back and sides,
    Before thou goest thy way.

25 'What? dost thou think, thou proud
    fellow,
  That thou canst conquer me?
  Nay, thou shalt know, before thou go,
    I 'le fight before I 'le flee.'

26 With that to thrash Little John like mad
  The Shepherd he begun;
  'Hold, hold,' cryed bold Robin Hood,
    'And I 'le yield the wager won.'

27 'With all my heart,' said Little John,
  'To that I will agree;
  For he is the flower of shepherd-swains,
    The like I never did see.'

28 Thus have you heard of Robin Hood,
  Also of Little John,
  How a shepherd-swain did conquer them;
    The like did never none.

136

ROBIN HOOD'S DELIGHT

(ROBIN HOOD, JOHN, SCARLOCK, AND
THREE KEEPERS)

'The Bold Pedlar and Robin Hood,' No. 132,
a late traditional copy, shows traces of st. 20 of
this ballad in st. 12, where the Pedlar says it lies

with him whether he will tell his name, and again at the end, where Robin Hood, John, and the Pedlar drink friendship at the tavern. Robin Hood's antagonists are again foresters and keepers in Nos. 131 and 139. There are numerous agreements between this piece and No. 135.

'Robin Hood's Delight.' **a.** Wood, 401, leaf 41 b. **b.** Garland of 1663, No. 17. **c.** Garland of 1670, No. 16. **d.** Pepys, II, 112, No. 99.

1 THERE is some will talk of lords and knights,
  Doun a doun a doun a doun
And some of yeoman good,
  But I will tell you of Will Scarlock,
  Little John and Robin Hood.
  Doun a doun a doun a doun

2 They were outlaws, as 't is well known,
  And men of a noble blood;
And a many a time was their valour shown
  In the forrest of merry Sheerwood.

3 Vpon a time it chanced so,
  As Robin Hood would have it be,
They all three would a walking go,
  Some pastime for to see.

4 And as they walked the forest along,
  Upon a midsummer day,
There was they aware of three keepers,
  Clade all in green aray.

5 With brave long faucheons by their sides,
  And forest-bills in hand,
They calld aloud to those bold outlaws,
  And charged them to stand.

6 'Why, who are you,' cry'd bold Robin,
  'That speaks so boldly here?'
'We three belong to King Henry,
  And are keepers of his deer.'

7 'The devil thou art!' sayes Robin Hood,
  'I am sure that it is not so;
We be the keepers of this forest,
  And that you soon shall know.'

8 'Come, your coats of green lay on the ground,
  And so will we all three,
And take your swords and bucklers round,
  And try the victory.'

9 'We be content,' the keepers said,
  'We be three, and you no less;
Then why should we be of you afraid,
  And we never did transgress?'

10 'Why, if you be three keepers in this forest,
  Then we be three rangers good,
And we will make you to know, before you do go,
  You meet with bold Robin Hood.'

11 'We be content, thou bold outlaw,
  Our valour here to try,
And we will make you know, before we do go,
  We will fight before we will fly.'

12 'Then, come draw your swords, you bold outlaws,
  And no longer stand to prate,
But let us try it out with blows,
  For cowards we do hate.'

13 'Here is one of us for Will Scarlock,
  And another for Little John,
And I my self for Robin Hood,
  Because he is stout and strong.'

14 So they fell to it full hard and sore;
  It was on a midsummers day;
From eight a clock till two and past,
  They all shewed gallant play.

15 There Robin, and Will, and Little John,
  They fought most manfully,
Till all their winde was spent and gone,
  Then Robin aloud did cry:

16 'O hold, O hold,' cries bold Robin,
  'I see you be stout men;
Let me blow one blast on my bugle-horn,
  Then I 'le fight with you again.'

17 'That bargain's to make, bold Robin Hood,
  Therefore we it deny;
Though a blast upon thy bugle-horn
  Cannot make us fight nor fly.'

18 'Therefore fall on, or else be gone,
  And yield to us the day:
It shall never be said that we were afraid
  Of thee, nor thy yeomen gay.'

19 'If that be so,' cries bold Robin,
 'Let me but know your names,
 And in the forest of merry Sheerwood
 I shall extol your fames.'

20 'And with our names,' one of them
 said,
 'What hast thou here to do?
 Except that you will fight it out,
 Our names thou shalt not know.'

21 'We will fight no more,' sayes bold
 Robin,
 'You be men of valour stout;
 Come and go with me to Nottingham,
 And there we will fight it out.

22 'With a but of sack we will bang it out,
 To see who wins the day;
 And for the cost, make you no doubt
 I have gold and money to pay.

23 'And ever after, so long as we live,
 We all will brethren be;
 For I love those men with heart and
 hand
 That will fight, and never flee.'

24 So away they went to Nottingham,
 With sack to make amends;
 For three dayes space they wine did
 chase,
 And drank themselves good friends.

137

ROBIN HOOD AND THE PEDLARS

The manuscript in which this ballad occurs
contains a variety of matters, and, as the best
authority has declared, may in part have been
written as early as 1650, but all the ballads
are in a nineteenth-century hand, and some of
them are maintained to be forgeries. There is
no sufficient reason for regarding this particular piece as spurious; it may be a copy of a
broadside, or a copy of a copy. The story resembles that of 'Robin Hood's Delight' (No.
136), pedlars taking the place of keepers; but
Robin is reduced to an ignominy paralleled
only in the second ballad of 'Robin Hood and
the Beggar' (No. 134).

'Robinhood and the Peddlers,' the fourth
ballad in a MS. formerly in the possession of
J. Payne Collier, and now in the British Museum; previously printed in Gutch's Robin
Hood, II, 351.

1 WILL you heare a tale of Robin Hood,
 Will Scarlett, and Little John?
 Now listen awhile, it will make you
 smile,
 As before it hath many done.

2 They were archers three, of hie de-
 gree,
 As good as ever drewe bowe;
 Their arrowes were long and their armes
 were strong,
 As most had cause to knowe.

3 But one sommers day, as they toke their
 way
 Through the forrest of greene Sherwood,
 To kill the kings deare, you shall presently heare
 What befell these archers good.

4 They were ware on the roade of three
 peddlers with loade,
 Ffor each had his packe,
 Ffull of all wares for countrie faires,
 Trusst up upon his backe.

5 A good oke staffe, a yard and a halfe,
 Each one had in his hande;
 And they were all bound to Nottingham
 towne,
 As you shall understand.

6 'Yonder I see bolde peddlers three,'
 Said Robin to Scarlett and John;
 'We 'le search their packes upon their
 backes
 Before that they be gone.

7 'Holla, good fellowes!' quod Robin
 Hood,
 'Whither is it ye doe goe?
 Now stay and rest, for that is the best,
 'T is well ye should doe soe.'

8 'Noe rest we neede, on our roade we
 speede,
 Till to Nottingham we get:'
 'Thou tellst a lewde lye,' said Robin,
 'for I
 Can see that ye swinke and swet.'

9 The peddlers three crosst over the lee,
  They did not list to fight:
'I charge you tarrie,' quod Robin, 'for
    marry,
  This is my owne land by right.

10 'This is my mannor and this is my
    parke,
  I would have ye for to knowe;
Ye are bolde outlawes, I see by cause
  Ye are so prest to goe.'

11 The peddlers three turned round to see
  Who it might be they herd;
Then agen went on as they list to be
    gone,
  And never answered word.

12 Then toke Robin Hood an arrow so
    good,
  Which he did never lacke,
And drew his bowe, and the swift arrowe
  Went through the last peddlers packe.

13 Ffor him it was well on the packe it fell,
  Or his life had found an ende;
And it pierst the skin of his backe
    within,
  Though the packe did stand his frend.

14 Then downe they flung their packes
    eche one,
  And stayde till Robin came:
Quod Robin, I saide ye had better
    stayde;
  Good sooth, ye were to blame.

15 'And who art thou? by S. Crispin, I
    vowe
  I 'le quickly cracke thy head!'
Cried Robin, Come on, all three, or one;
  It is not so soone done as said.

16 My name, by the roode, is Robin Hood,
  And this is Scarlett and John;
It is three to three, ye may plainelie
    see,
  Soe now, brave fellowes, laye on.

17 The first peddlars blowe brake Robins
    bowe
  That he had in his hand;
And Scarlett and John, they eche had
    one
  That they unneath could stand.

18 'Now holde your handes,' cride Robin
    Hood,
  'Ffor ye have got oken staves;
But tarie till wee can get but three,
  And a fig for all your braves.'

19 Of the peddlers the first, his name Kit
    o Thirske,
  Said, We are all content;
Soe eche tooke a stake for his weapon,
    to make
  The peddlers to repent.

20 Soe to it they fell, and their blowes did
    ring well
  Uppon the others backes;
And gave the peddlers cause to wish
  They had not cast their packes.

21 Yet the peddlers three of their blowes
    were so free
  That Robin began for to rue;
And Scarlett and John had such loade
    laide on
  It made the sunne looke blue.

22 At last Kits oke caught Robin a stroke
  That made his head to sound;
He staggerd, and reelde, till he fell on
    the fielde,
  And the trees with him went round.

23 'Now holde your handes,' cride Little
    John,
  And soe said Scarlett eke;
'Our maister is slaine, I tell you plaine,
  He never more will speake.'

24 'Now, heaven forefend he come to that
    ende,'
  Said Kit, 'I love him well;
But lett him learne to be wise in turne,
  And not with pore peddlers mell.

25 'In my packe, God wot, I a balsame
    have got
  That soone his hurts will heale;'
And into Robin Hoods gaping mouth
  He presentlie powrde some deale.

26 'Now fare ye well, tis best not to
    tell
  How ye three peddlers met;
Or if ye doe, prithee tell alsoe
  How they made ye swinke and swett.'

27 Poore Robin in sound they left on the
     ground,
   And hied them to Nottingham,
   While Scarlett and John Robin tended
     on,
   Till at length his senses came.

28 Noe soone[r], in haste, did Robin
     Hood taste
   The balsame he had tane,
   Than he gan to spewe, and up he threwe
   The balsame all againe.

29 And Scarlett and John, who were look-
     ing on
   Their maister as he did lie,
   Had their faces besmeard, both eies and
     beard,
   Therewith most piteously.

30 Thus ended that fray ; soe beware
     alwaye
   How ye doe challenge foes;
   Looke well aboute they are not to stoute,
   Or you may have worst of the blowes.

138

ROBIN HOOD AND ALLEN A DALE

   This ballad, it will be observed, is first found
in broadside copies of the latter half of the
seventeenth century. The story is told of
Scarlock in the life of Robin Hood in Sloane MS.
780, 7, fol. 157, of the end of the sixteenth or
beginning of the seventeenth century ; Thoms,
Early Prose Romances, II, p. 39.

   a. ' Robin Hood and Allin of Dale,' Douce,
II, leaf 185. b. 'Robin Hood and Allin of
Dale,' Pepys, II, 110, No. 97. c. 'Robin Hood
and Allen a Dale,' Douce, III, 119 b.

1 COME listen to me, you gallants so free,
   All you that loves mirth for to hear,
   And I will you tell of a bold outlaw,
   That lived in Nottinghamshire. (bis.)

2 As Robin Hood in the forrest stood,
   All under the green-wood tree,
   There was he ware of a brave young
     man,
   As fine as fine might be.

3 The youngster was clothed in scarlet red,
   In scarlet fine and gay,
   And he did frisk it over the plain,
   And chanted a roundelay.

4 As Robin Hood next morning stood,
   Amongst the leaves so gay,
   There did he espy the same young man
   Come drooping along the way.

5 The scarlet he wore the day before,
   It was clean cast away;
   And every step he fetcht a sigh,
   ' Alack and a well a day ! '

6 Then stepped forth brave Little John,
   And Nick the millers son,
   Which made the young man bend his
     bow,
   When as he see them come.

7 ' Stand off, stand off,' the young man
     said,
   ' What is your will with me ? '
   ' You must come before our master
     straight,
   Vnder yon green-wood tree.'

8 And when he came bold Robin before,
   Robin askt him courteously,
   O hast thou any money to spare
   For my merry men and me ?

9 ' I have no money,' the young man said,
   ' But five shillings and a ring;
   And that I have kept this seven long
     years,
   To have it at my wedding.

10 ' Yesterday I should have married a
     maid,
   But she is now from me tane,
   And chosen to be an old knights delight,
   Whereby my poor heart is slain.'

11 ' What is thy name ? ' then said Robin
     Hood,
   ' Come tell me, without any fail : '
   ' By the faith of my body,' then said the
     young man,
   ' My name it is Allin a Dale.'

12 ' What wilt thou give me,' said Robin
     Hood,
   ' In ready gold or fee,

To help thee to thy true-love again,
And deliver her unto thee ?'

13 'I have no money,' then quoth the young
man,
'No ready gold nor fee,
But I will swear upon a book
Thy true servant for to be.'

14 'How many miles is it to thy true-love ?
Come tell me without any guile:'
'By the faith of my body,' then said the
young man,
'It is but five little mile.'

15 Then Robin he hasted over the plain,
He did neither stint nor lin,
Vntil he came unto the church
Where Allin should keep his wedding.

16 'What dost thou do here ?' the bishop
he said,
'I prethee now tell to me:'
'I am a bold harper,' quoth Robin Hood,
'And the best in the north countrey.'

17 'O welcome, O welcome,' the bishop he
said,
'That musick best pleaseth me;'
'You shall have no musick,' quoth Robin
Hood,
'Till the bride and the bridegroom I
see.'

18 With that came in a wealthy knight,
Which was both grave and old,
And after him a finikin lass,
Did shine like glistering gold.

19 'This is no fit match,' quoth bold Robin
Hood,
'That you do seem to make here;
For since we are come unto the church,
The bride she shall chuse her own
dear.'

20 Then Robin Hood put his horn to his
mouth,
And blew blasts two or three;
When four and twenty bowmen bold
Came leaping over the lee.

21 And when they came into the church-
yard,
Marching all on a row,

The first man was Allin a Dale,
To give bold Robin his bow.

22 'This is thy true-love,' Robin he said,
'Young Allin, as I hear say;
And you shall be married at this same
time,
Before we depart away.'

23 'That shall not be,' the bishop he
said,
'For thy word shall not stand;
They shall be three times askt in the
church,
As the law is of our land.'

24 Robin Hood pulld off the bishops coat,
And put it upon Little John;
'By the faith of my body,' then Robin
said,
'This cloath doth make thee a man.'

25 When Little John went into the quire,
The people began for to laugh;
He askt them seven times in the church,
Least three times should not be
enough.

26 'Who gives me this maid ?' then said
Little John;
Quoth Robin, That do I,
And he that doth take her from Allin a
Dale
Full dearly he shall her buy.

27 And thus having ended this merry wed-
ding,
The bride lookt as fresh as a queen,
And so they returnd to the merry green
wood,
Amongst the leaves so green.

139

ROBIN HOOD'S PROGRESS TO NOTTINGHAM

This is a comparatively late ballad, but has
not come down to us in its oldest form. The
story is told in the life of Robin Hood in
Sloane MS. 715, 7, fol. 157, written, as it seems,
towards the end of the sixteenth century. See
Thoms, Early Prose Romances, II, Robin Hood,
pp. 37 ff.

a. Wood, 402, leaf 14 b. b. Wood, 401, leaf 37 b. c. Garland of 1663, No. 2. d. Garland of 1670, No. 1. e. Pepys, II, 104, No. 92.

1 ROBIN HOOD hee was and a tall young man,
  Derry derry down
  And fifteen winters old,
  And Robin Hood he was a proper young man,
  Of courage stout and bold.
  Hey down derry derry down

2 Robin Hood he would and to fair Nottingham,
  With the general for to dine;
  There was he ware of fifteen forresters,
  And a drinking bear, ale, and wine.

3 'What news? What news?' said bold Robin Hood;
  'What news, fain wouldest thou know?
  Our king hath provided a shooting-match:'
  'And I 'm ready with my bow.'

4 'We hold it in scorn,' then said the forresters,
  'That ever a boy so young
  Should bear a bow before our king,
  That 's not able to draw one string.'

5 'I 'le hold you twenty marks,' said bold Robin Hood,
  'By the leave of Our Lady,
  That I 'le hit a mark a hundred rod,
  And I 'le cause a hart to dye.'

6 'We 'l hold you twenty mark,' then said the forresters,
  'By the leave of Our Lady,
  Thou hitst not the marke a hundred rod,
  Nor causest a hart to dye.'

7 Robin Hood he bent up a noble bow,
  And a broad arrow he let flye,
  He hit the mark a hundred rod,
  And he caused a hart to dy.

8 Some said hee brake ribs one or two,
  And some said hee brake three;

The arrow within the hart would not abide,
  But it glanced in two or three.

9 The hart did skip, and the hart did leap,
  And the hart lay on the ground;
  'The wager is mine,' said bold Robin Hood,
  'If 't were for a thousand pound.'

10 'The wager 's none of thine,' then said the forresters,
  'Although thou beest in haste;
  Take up thy bow, and get thee hence,
  Lest wee thy sides do baste.'

11 Robin Hood hee took up his noble bow,
  And his broad arrows all amain,
  And Robin Hood he laught, and begun to smile,
  As hee went over the plain.

12 Then Robin Hood hee bent his noble bow,
  And his broad arrows he let flye,
  Till fourteen of these fifteen forresters
  Vpon the ground did lye.

13 He that did this quarrel first begin
  Went tripping over the plain;
  But Robin Hood he bent his noble bow,
  And hee fetcht him back again.

14 'You said I was no archer,' said Robin Hood,
  'But say so now again;'
  With that he sent another arrow
  That split his head in twain.

15 'You have found mee an archer,' saith Robin Hood,
  'Which will make your wives for to wring,
  And wish that you had never spoke the word,
  That I could not draw one string.'

16 The people that lived in fair Nottingham
  Came runing out amain,
  Supposing to have taken bold Robin Hood,
  With the forresters that were slain.

17 Some lost legs, and some lost arms,
   And some did lose their blood,
   But Robin Hood hee took up his noble
      bow,
   And is gone to the merry green wood.

18 They carryed these forresters into fair
      Nottingham,
   As many there did know;
   They digd them graves in their church-
      yard,
   And they buried them all a row.

140

ROBIN HOOD RESCUING THREE SQUIRES

'Robin Hood and the Beggar,' I (No. 133),
from stanza 16, is another version of this ballad. There are passages in A and B which
are almost repetitions of 'Robin Hood and the
Curtal Friar' (No. 123). The rescue in the
ballad is introduced into Anthony Munday's
play of The Downfall of Robert, Earl of Huntington' (act ii, scene 2). For the disguise, cf.
'Hind Horn' (No. 17).

A

Percy MS., p. 5; Hales and Furnivall, i, 13;
Jamieson's Popular Ballads, ii, 49.

*   *   *   *   *

1 '.   .   .   .
   In faith thou shal[t] haue mine,
   And twenty pound in thy purse,
   To spend att ale and wine.'

2 'Though your clothes are of light Lin-
      colne green,
   And mine gray russett and torne,
   Yet it doth not you beseeme
   To doe an old man scorne.'

3 'I scorne thee not, old man,' says Robin,
   'By the faith of my body;
   Doe of thy clothes, thou shalt haue mine,
   For it may noe better bee.'

4 But Robin did on this old mans hose,
   The were torne in the wrist;
   'When I looke on my leggs,' said Robin,
   'Then for to laugh I list.'

5 But Robin did on the old mans shooes,
   And the were clutt full cleane;
   'Now, by my faith,' sayes Litle Iohn,
   'These are good for thornës keene.'

6 But Robin did on the old mans cloake,
   And it was torne in the necke;
   'Now, by my faith,' said William Scar-
      lett,
   'Heere shold be set a specke.'

7 But Robin did on this old mans hood,
   Itt gogled on his crowne;
   'When I come into Nottingham,' said
      Robin,
   'My hood it will lightly downe.'

8 'But yonder is an outwood,' said Robin,
   'An outwood all and a shade,
   And thither I reede you, my merry-
      men all,
   The ready way to take.

9 'And when you heare my litle horne
      blow,
   Come raking all on a rowte
   .   .   .   .   .   .

   .   .   .   .   .

*   *   *   *   *

10 But Robin he lope, and Robin he
      threw,
   He lope over stocke and stone;
   But those that saw Robin Hood run
   Said he was a liuer old man.

11 [Then Robin set his] horne to his mowth,
   A loud blast cold h[e] blow;
   Ffull three hundred bold yeomen
   Came rakinge all on a row.

12 But Robin cast downe his baggs of
      bread,
   Soe did he his staffe with a face,
   And in a doublet of red veluett
   This yeoman stood in his place.

13 'But bend your bowes, and stroke your
      strings,
   Set the gallow-tree aboute,
   And Christs cursse on his heart,' said
      Robin,
   'That spares the sheriffe and the ser-
      giant!'

14 When the sheriffe see gentle Robin wold
        shoote,
    He held vp both his hands;
    Sayes, Aske, good Robin, and thou shalt
        haue,
    Whether it be house or land.

15 'I will neither haue house nor land,'
        said Robin,
    'Nor gold, nor none of thy ffee,
    But I will haue those three squires
    To the greene fforest with me.

16 'Now marry, Gods forbott,' said the
        sheriffe,
    'That euer *that* shold bee;
    For why, they be the kings ffelons,
    They are all condemned to dye.'

17 'But grant me my askinge,' said Robin,
    'Or by the faith of my body
    Thou shalt be the first man
    Shall flower this gallow-tree.'

18 'But I wi[ll haue t]hose three squires
    .   .   .   .   .

B

a. 'Robin Hood rescuing the Widow's Three
Sons from the Sheriff, when going to be executed,' The English Archer, Robin Hood's Garland, York, N. Nickson, n. d., p. 65. b. The
English Archer, etc., Paisley, John Neilson,
1786. c. Adventures of . . . Robin Hood,
Falkirk, T. Johnston, 1808. All in the Bodleian Library, Douce, F. F. 71.

1 There are twelve months in all the
        year,
    As I hear many men say,
    But the merriest month in all the year
    Is the merry month of May.

2 Now Robin Hood is to Nottingham gone,
    With a link a down and a day,
    And there he met a silly old woman,
    Was weeping on the way.

3 'What news? what news, thou silly
        old woman?
    What news hast thou for me?'
    Said she, There's three squires in Not-
        tingham town
    To-day is condemned to die.

4 'O have they parishes burnt?' he said,
    'Or have they ministers slain?
    Or have they robbed any virgin,
    Or with other men's wives have lain?'

5 'They have no parishes burnt, good
        sir,
    Nor yet have ministers slain,
    Nor have they robbed any virgin,
    Nor with other men's wives have lain.'

6 'O what have they done?' said bold
        Robin Hood,
    'I pray thee tell to me:'
    'It's for slaying of the king's fallow
        deer,
    Bearing their long bows with thee.'

7 'Dost thou not mind, old woman,' he
        said,
    'Since thou made me sup and dine?
    By the truth of my body,' quoth bold
        Robin Hood,
    You could not tell it in better time.'

8 Now Robin Hood is to Nottingham
        gone,
    With a link a down and a day,
    And there he met with a silly old palmer,
    Was walking along the highway.

9 'What news? what news, thou silly old
        man?
    What news, I do thee pray?'
    Said he, Three squires in Nottingham
        town
    Are condemnd to die this day.

10 'Come change thy apparel with me, old
        man,
    Come change thy apparel for mine;
    Here is forty shillings in good silver,
    Go drink it in beer or wine.'

11 'O thine apparel is good,' he said,
    'And mine is ragged and torn;
    Whereever you go, wherever you ride,
    Laugh neer an old man to scorn.'

12 'Come change thy apparel with me, old
        churl,
    Come change thy apparel with mine;
    Here are twenty pieces of good broad
        gold,
    Go feast thy brethren with wine.'

13 Then he put on the old man's hat,
    It stood full high on the crown:
'The first bold bargain that I come at,
    It shall make thee come down.'

14 Then he put on the old man's cloak,
    Was patchd black, blew, and red;
He thought no shame all the day long
    To wear the bags of bread.

15 Then he put on the old man's breeks,
    Was patchd from ballup to side;
'By the truth of my body,' bold Robin
    can say,
    'This man lovd little pride.'

16 Then he put on the old man's hose,
    Were patchd from knee to wrist;
'By the truth of my body,' said bold
    Robin Hood,
    'I'd laugh if I had any list.'

17 Then he put on the old man's shoes,
    Were patchd both beneath and aboon;
Then Robin Hood swore a solemn oath,
    It's good habit that makes a man.

18 Now Robin Hood is to Nottingham gone,
    With a link a down and a down,
And there he met with the proud sheriff,
    Was walking along the town.

19 'O save, O save, O sheriff,' he said,
    'O save, and you may see!
And what will you give to a silly old man
    To-day will your hangman be?'

20 'Some suits, some suits,' the sheriff he
    said,
    'Some suits I'll give to thee;
Some suits, some suits, and pence thir-
    teen
    To-day's a hangman's fee.'

21 Then Robin he turns him round about,
    And jumps from stock to stone;
'By the truth of my body,' the sheriff he
    said,
    'That's well jumpt, thou nimble old
    man.'

22 'I was neer a hangman in all my life,
    Nor yet intends to trade;
But curst be he,' said bold Robin,
    'That first a hangman was made.

23 'I've a bag for meal, and a bag for
    malt,
    And a bag for barley and corn;
A bag for bread, and a bag for beef,
    And a bag for my little small horn.

24 'I have a horn in my pocket,
    I got it from Robin Hood,
And still when I set it to my mouth,
    For thee it blows little good.'

25 'O wind thy horn, thou proud fellow,
    Of thee I have no doubt;
I wish that thou give such a blast
    Till both thy eyes fall out.'

26 The first loud blast that he did blow,
    He blew both loud and shrill;
A hundred and fifty of Robin Hood's men
    Came riding over the hill.

27 The next loud blast that he did give,
    He blew both loud and amain,
And quickly sixty of Robin Hood's men
    Came shining over the plain.

28 'O who are yon,' the sheriff he said,
    'Come tripping over the lee?'
'The're my attendants,' brave Robin did
    say,
    'They'll pay a visit to thee.'

29 They took the gallows from the slack,
    They set it in the glen,
They hangd the proud sheriff on that,
    Releasd their own three men.

141

ROBIN HOOD RESCUING
WILL STUTLY

This ballad probably occurs in all the large
collections of broadsides. It was made for
print and has little of the traditional in the
matter and nothing in the style. It may be
considered as an imitation of the Rescue of the
Three Squires (No. 140), whence the ambush
in st. 9 and the palmer 'fair' in 10.

'Robin Hood his rescuing Will Stutly,' etc.
a. Wood, 401, leaf 35 b. **b.** Garland of 1663,
No. 7. **c.** Garland of 1670, No. 6. **d.** Pepys,
II, 106, No. 93.

1 WHEN Robin Hood in the green-wood
    livd,
      Derry derry down
    Vnder the green-wood tree,
    Tidings there came to him with speed,
    Tidings for certainty,
      Hey down derry derry down

2 That Will Stutly surprized was,
    And eke in prison lay;
    Three varlets that the sheriff had hired
    Did likely him betray.

3 I, and to-morrow hanged must be,
    To-morrow as soon as it is day;
    But before they could this victory get,
    Two of them did Stutly slay.

4 When Robin Hood he heard this news,
    Lord! he was grieved sore,
    I, and unto his merry men [said],
    Who altogether swore,

5 That Will Stutly should rescued be,
    And be brought safe again;
    Or else should many a gallant wight
    For his sake there be slain.

6 He cloathed himself in scarlet then,
    His men were all in green;
    A finer show, throughout the world,
    In no place could be seen.

7 Good lord! it was a gallant sight
    To see them all on a row;
    With every man a good broad sword,
    And eke a good yew bow.

8 Forth of the green wood are they gone,
    Yea, all couragiously,
    Resolving to bring Stutly home,
    Or every man to die.

9 And when they came the castle neer
    Whereas Will Stutly lay,
    'I hold it good,' saith Robin Hood,
    ' Wee here in ambush stay,

10 ' And send one forth some news to hear,
    To yonder palmer fair,
    That stands under the castle-wall;
    Some news he may declare.'

11 With that steps forth a brave young man,
    Which was of courage bold;

Thus hee did say to the old man:
    I pray thee, palmer old,

12 Tell me, if that thou rightly ken,
    When must Will Stutly die,
    Who is one of bold Robins men,
    And here doth prisoner lie?

13 ' Alack, alass,' the palmer said,
    ' And for ever wo is me!
    Will Stutly hanged must be this day,
    On yonder gallows-tree.

14 ' O had his noble master known,
    Hee would some succour send;
    A few of his bold yeomandree
    Full soon would fetch him hence.'

15 ' I, that is true,' the young man said;
    ' I, that is true,' said hee;
    ' Or, if they were neer to this place,
    They soon would set him free.

16 ' But fare thou well, thou good old man,
    Farewell, and thanks to thee;
    If Stutly hanged be this day,
    Revengd his death will be.'

17 He was no sooner from the palmer
    gone,
    But the gates was opened wide,
    And out of the castle Will Stutly came,
    Guarded on every side.

18 When hee was forth from the castle
    come,
    And saw no help was nigh,
    Thus he did say unto the sheriff,
    Thus he said gallantly:

19 Now seeing that I needs must die,
    Grant me one boon, says he;
    For my noble master nere had man
    That yet was hangd on the tree.

20 Give me a sword all in my hand,
    And let mee be unbound,
    And with thee and thy men I 'le fight,
    Vntill I lie dead on the ground.

21 But his desire he would not grant,
    His wishes were in vain;
    For the sheriff had sworn he hanged
    should be,
    And not by the sword be slain.

22 'Do but unbind my hands,' he saies,
    'I will no weapons crave,
And if I hanged be this day,
    Damnation let me have.'

23 'O no, O no,' the sheriff he said,
    'Thou shalt on the gallows die,
I, and so shall thy master too,
    If ever in me it lie.'

24 'O dastard coward !' Stutly cries,
    'Thou faint-heart pesant slave !
If ever my master do thee meet,
    Thou shalt thy paiment have.

25 'My noble master thee doth scorn,
    And all thy cowardly crew;
Such silly imps unable are
    Bold Robin to subdue.'

26 But when he was to the gallows come,
    And ready to bid adiew,
Out of a bush leaps Little John,
    And steps Will Stutly to.

27 'I pray thee, Will, before thou die,
    Of thy dear friends take leave;
I needs must borrow him a while,
    How say you, master sheriff ? '

28 'Now, as I live,' the sheriff he said,
    'That varlet will I know;
Some sturdy rebell is that same,
    Therefore let him not go.'

29 With that Little John so hastily
    Away cut Stutly's bands,
And from one of the sheriff his men,
    A sword twicht from his hands.

30 'Here, Will, here, take thou this same,
    Thou canst it better sway;
And here defend thy self a while,
    For aid will come straight way.'

31 And there they turnd them back to back,
    In the middle of them that day,
Till Robin Hood approached neer,
    With many an archer gay.

32 With that an arrow by them flew,
    I wist from Robin Hood;
'Make haste, make haste,' the sheriff
    he said,
    'Make haste, for it is good.'

33 The sheriff is gone; his doughty men
    Thought it no boot to stay,
But, as their master had them taught,
    They run full fast away.

34 'O stay, O stay,' Will Stutly said,
    'Take leave ere you depart;
You nere will catch bold Robin Hood
    Vnless you dare him meet.'

35 'O ill betide you,' quoth Robin Hood,
    'That you so soon are gone;
My sword may in the scabbord rest,
    For here our work is done.'

36 'I little thought when I came here,
    When I came to this place,
For to have met with Little John,
    Or seen my masters face.'

37 Thus Stutly was at liberty set,
    And safe brought from his foe;
'O thanks, O thanks to my master,
    Since here it was not so.'

38 'And once again, my fellows,
    We shall in the green woods meet,
Where we will make our bow-strings
    twang,
    Musick for us most sweet.'

142

LITTLE JOHN A BEGGING

The beginning of A is very like that of No.
140 A ; but the disguise is for a different
object. We are reminded again of 'Hind
Horn ' (No. 17). B is also in the Roxburghe
collection, III, 10 (Ballad Society's ed., VIII,
497).

A

Percy MS., p. 20; Hales and Furnivall, I, 47.

*   *   *   *   *

1 .   .   .   .   .   .

    .   .   .   beggar,' he sayes,
    'With none such fellows as thee.'

2 'I am not in iest,' said Litle Iohn,
    'I sweare all by the roode;
Change with mee,' said Little Iohn,
    'And I will giue thee some boote.'

3 But he has gotten on this old mans
    gowne,
    It reacht not to his wrist;
  'Christ's curse on's hart,' said Litle
    Iohn,
  'That thinkes my gowne amisse.'

4 But he has gotten on this old mans
    shoes,
    Are clouted nine fold about;
  'Beshrew his hart,' says Litle Iohn,
  'That bryer or thorne does doubt.

5 'Wilt teach me some phrase of thy beg-
    ing?' says Iohn;
  'I pray thee, tell it mee,
  How I may be as beggar-like
    As any in my companie.'

6 'Thou must goe two foote on a staffe,
    The third vpon a tree;
  Full loud that thou must cry and
    fare,
    When nothing ayleth thee.'

7 But Iohn he walket the hills soe high,
    Soe did [he] the hills soe browne;
  The ready way that he cold take
    Was towards Nottingham towne.

8 But as he was on the hills soe high,
    He mett with palmers three;
  Sayes, God you saue, my brethren
    all,
    Now God you saue and see!

9 This seuen yeere I haue you sought;
    Before I cold neuer you see!
  Said they, Wee had leuer such a cankred
    carle
    Were neuer in our companie.

10 But one of them tooke Litle Iohn on
    his head,
    The blood ran over his eye;
  Little Iohn turned him twise about

   .   .   .   .   .

   *   *   *   *   *

11 'If I   .   .   .   .   .
    As I haue beene but one day,
    I shold haue purcchased three of the
    best churches
    That stands by any highway.'

B

'Little John and the Four Beggers.' **a.**
Wood, 401, leaf 33 b. **b.** Garland of 1663, No.
16. **c.** Garland of 1670, No. 15. **d.** Pepys, II,
119, No. 105.

1 ALL you that delight to spend some time
    With a hey down down a down down
    A merry song for to sing,
  Vnto me draw neer, and you shall hear
    How Little John went a begging.

2 As Robin Hood walked the forrest along,
    And all his yeomandree,
  Sayes Robin, Some of you must a beg-
    ging go,
    And, Little John, it must be thee.

3 Sayes John, If I must a begging go,
    I will have a palmers weed,
  With a staff and a coat, and bags of all
    sort,
    The better then I shall speed.

4 Come, give me now a bag for my bread,
    And another for my cheese,
  And one for a peny, when as I get any,
    That nothing I may leese.

5 Now little John he is a begging gone,
    Seeking for some relief;
  But of all the beggers he met on the
    way,
    Little John he was the chief.

6 But as he was walking himself alone,
    Four beggers he chanced to spy,
  Some deaf, and some blind, and some
    came behind;
    Says John, Here's brave company!

7 'Good-morrow,' said John, 'my breth-
    ren dear,
    Good fortune I had you to see;
  Which way do you go? pray let me
    know,
    For I want some company.

8 'O what is here to do?' then said Little
    John,
  'Why rings all these bells?' said he;
  'What dog is a hanging? come, let us
    be ganging,
    That we the truth may see.'

9 'Here is no dog a hanging,' then one of
   them said,
   'Good fellow, we tell unto thee;
But here is one dead wil give us cheese
   and bred,
   And it may be one single peny.'

10 'We have brethren in London,' another
   he said,
   'So have we in Coventry,
In Barwick and Dover, and all the
   world over,
   But nere a crookt carril like thee.

11 'Therefore stand thee back, thou crooked
   carel,
   And take that knock on the crown;'
'Nay,' said Little John, 'I 'le not yet
   be gone,
   For a bout will I have with you round.

12 'Now have at you all,' then said Little
   John,
   'If you be so full of your blows;
Fight on, all four, and nere give ore,
   Whether you be friends or foes.'

13 John nipped the dumb, and made him
   to rore,
   And the blind that could not see,
And he that a cripple had been seven
   years,
   He made him run faster then he.

14 And flinging them all against the wall,
   With many a sturdie bang,
It made John sing, to hear the gold ring,
   Which against the walls cryed twang.

15 Then he got out of the beggers cloak
   Three hundred pound in gold;
'Good fortune had I,' then said Little
   John,
   'Such a good sight to behold.'

16 But what found he in a beggers bag,
   But three hundred pound and three?
'If I drink water while this doth last,
   Then an ill death may I dye!

17 'And my begging-trade I will now give
   ore,
   My fortune hath bin so good;
Therefore I 'le not stay, but I will away
   To the forrest of merry Sherwood.'

18 And when to the forrest of Sherwood he
   came,
   He quickly there did see
His master good, bold Robin Hood,
   And all his company.

19 'What news? What news?' then said
   Robin Hood,
   'Come, Little John, tell unto me;
How hast thou sped with thy beggers
   trade?
   For that I fain would see.'

20 'No news but good,' then said Little
   John,
   'With begging ful wel I have sped;
Six hundred and three I have here for
   thee,
   In silver and gold so red.'

21 Then Robin took Little John by the
   hand,
   And danced about the oak-tree:
'If we drink water while this doth last,
   Then an il death may we die!'

22 So to conclude my merry new song,
   All you that delight it to sing,
'T is of Robin Hood, that archer good,
   And how Little John went a begging.

143

ROBIN HOOD AND THE BISHOP

This ballad and the following are variations
upon the theme of Robin Hood and the Monk,
in the Gest. The disguise as a woman occurs
in other outlaw stories; as in Eustace the
Monk, Michel, p. 43. Also in Blind Harry's
Wallace, ed. Moir, book i, 239, and book iv,
764, pp. 9, 72: in the first case Wallace has a
rock and sits spinning (see also No. 157). We
hear again of the forced mass (st. 23) in No.
145, A 31, B 40; and of money borrowed
against the bishop's will, in A 32 of the same.
It is the Bishop of Hereford who suffers (see
No. 144).

'Robin Hood and the Bishop.' a. Wood,
401, leaf 11 b. b. Garland of 1663, No. 5.
c. Garland of 1670, No. 4. d. Pepys, ii, 109,
No. 96. e. Roxburghe, i, 362, in the Ballad
Society's reprint, ii. 448.

1 COME, gentlemen all, and listen a while,
　　Hey down down an a down
　And a story I 'le to you unfold;
　I 'le tell you how Robin Hood served
　　the Bishop,
　　When he robbed him of his gold.

2 As it fell out on a sun-shining day,
　　When Phebus was in his prime,
　Then Robin Hood, that archer good,
　　In mirth would spend some time.

3 And as he walkd the forrest along,
　　Some pastime for to spy,
　There was he aware of a proud bishop,
　　And all his company.

4 'O what shall I do ?' said Robin Hood
　　then,
　'If the Bishop he doth take me,
　No mercy he 'l show unto me, I know,
　　But hanged I shall be.'

5 Then Robin was stout, and turnd him
　　about,
　And a little house there he did spy;
　And to an old wife, for to save his life,
　　He loud began for to cry.

6 'Why, who art thou ?' said the old
　　woman,
　'Come tell it to me for good:'
　'I am an out-law, as many do know,
　　My name it is Robin Hood.

7 'And yonder 's the Bishop and all his
　　men,
　And if that I taken be,
　Then day and night he 'l work me
　　spight,
　　And hanged I shall be.'

8 'If thou be Robin Hood,' said the old
　　wife,
　'As thou dost seem to be,
　I 'le for thee provide, and thee I will
　　hide
　　From the Bishop and his company.

9 'For I well remember, one Saturday
　　night
　Thou bought me both shoos and hose;
　Therefore I 'le provide thy person to
　　hide,
　　And keep thee from thy foes.'

10 'Then give me soon thy coat of gray,
　　And take thou my mantle of green;
　Thy spindle and twine unto me resign,
　　And take thou my arrows so keen.'

11 And when that Robin Hood was so araid,
　　He went straight to his company;
　With his spindle and twine, he oft lookt
　　behind
　　For the Bishop and his company.

12 'O who is yonder,' quoth Little John,
　　'That now comes over the lee ?
　An arrow I will at her let flie,
　　So like an old witch looks she.'

13 'O hold thy hand, hold thy hand,' said
　　Robin then,
　'And shoot not thy arrows so keen;
　I am Robin Hood, thy master good,
　　And quickly it shall be seen.'

14 The Bishop he came to the old womans
　　house,
　And he called with furious mood,
　'Come let me soon see, and bring unto
　　me,
　　That traitor Robin Hood.'

15 The old woman he set on a milk-white
　　steed,
　Himselfe on a dapple-gray,
　And for joy he had got Robin Hood,
　　He went laughing all the way.

16 But as they were riding the forrest
　　along,
　The Bishop he chanc'd for to see
　A hundred brave bow-men bold
　　Stand under the green-wood tree.

17 'O who is yonder,' the Bishop then said,
　　'That 's ranging within yonder wood ?'
　'Marry,' says the old woman, 'I think
　　it to be
　　A man calld Robin Hood.'

18 'Why, who art thou,' the Bishop he said,
　　'Which I have here with me ?'
　'Why, I am an old woman, thou cuck-
　　oldly bishop;
　　Lift up my leg and see.'

19 'Then woe is me,' the Bishop he said,
　　'That ever I saw this day !'

He turnd him about, but Robin so stout
  Calld him, and bid him stay.

20 Then Robin took hold of the Bishops
    horse,
  And ty'd him fast to a tree;
Then Little John smil'd his master upon,
  For joy of that company.

21 Robin Hood took his mantle from 's
    back,
  And spread it upon the ground,
And out of the Bishops portmantle he
  Soon told five hundred pound.

22 'So now let him go,' said Robin Hood;
  Said Little John, That may not be;
For I vow and protest he shall sing us a
    mass
  Before that he goe from me.

23 Then Robin Hood took the Bishop by
    the hand,
  And bound him fast to a tree,
And made him sing a mass, God wot,
  To him and his yeomandree.

24 And then they brought him through the
    wood,
  And set him on his dapple-gray,
And gave the tail within his hand,
  And bade him for Robin Hood pray.

144

ROBIN HOOD AND THE BISHOP OF HEREFORD

The conclusion of this ballad is to the same
effect as that of the preceding, and was probably suggested by the Gest. No copy has
been found in print or writing earlier than the
eighteenth century; a fact of no special importance. Whenever written, if written it was,
it is far superior to most of the seventeenth-
century broadsides.

A

a. Robin Hood's Garland, London, J. Marshall & Co., Aldermary Churchyard, No. 23.
b. 'Robin Hood and the Bishop of Hereford,'
Douce Ballads, III, 123 b, London, C. Sheppard,
1791. c. Chappell's Popular Music of the
Olden Time, p. 395, from a broadside printed
for Daniel Wright, next the Sun Tavern in

Holborn. d. Robin Hood's Garland, without
place, 1749, No. 23, p. 98.

1 SOME they will talk of bold Robin
    Hood,
  And some of barons bold,
But I 'll tell you how he servd the
    Bishop of Hereford,
  When he robbd him of his gold.

2 As it befel in merry Barnsdale,
  And under the green-wood tree,
The Bishop of Hereford was to come by,
  With all his company.

3 'Come, kill a venson,' said bold Robin
    Hood,
  'Come, kill me a good fat deer;
The Bishop of Hereford is to dine with
    me to-day,
  And he shall pay well for his cheer.

4 'We 'll kill a fat venson,' said bold
    Robin Hood,
  'And dress it by the highway-side;
And we will watch the Bishop narrowly,
  Lest some other way he should ride.'

5 Robin Hood dressd himself in shep-
    herd's attire,
  With six of his men also;
And, when the Bishop of Hereford
    came by,
  They about the fire did go.

6 'O what is the matter ?' then said the
    Bishop,
  'Or for whom do you make this a-do ?
Or why do you kill the king's venson,
  When your company is so few ?'

7 'We are shepherds,' said bold Robin
    Hood,
  'And we keep sheep all the year,
And we are disposed to be merry this
    day,
  And to kill of the king's fat deer.'

8 'You are brave fellows !' said the
    Bishop,
  'And the king of your doings shall
    know;
Therefore make haste and come along
    with me,
  For before the king you shall go.'

9 'O pardon, O pardon,' said bold Robin
Hood,
'O pardon, I thee pray!
For it becomes not your lordship's coat
To take so many lives away.'

10 'No pardon, no pardon,' says the Bishop,
'No pardon I thee owe;
Therefore make haste, and come along
with me,
For before the king you shall go.'

11 Then Robin set his back against a tree,
And his foot against a thorn,
And from underneath his shepherd's
coat
He pulld out a bugle-horn.

12 He put the little end to his mouth,
And a loud blast did he blow,
Till threescore and ten of bold Robin's
men
Came running all on a row;

13 All making obeysance to bold Robin
Hood;
'T was a comely sight for to see:
'What is the matter, master,' said Little
John,
'That you blow so hastily?'

14 'O here is the Bishop of Hereford,
And no pardon we shall have:'
'Cut off his head, master,' said Little
John,
'And throw him into his grave.'

15 'O pardon, O pardon,' said the Bishop,
'O pardon, I thee pray!
For if I had known it had been you,
I'd have gone some other way.'

16 'No pardon, no pardon,' said Robin
Hood,
'No pardon I thee owe;
Therefore make haste and come along
with me,
For to merry Barnsdale you shall go.'

17 Then Robin he took the Bishop by the
hand,
And led him to merry Barnsdale;
He made him to stay and sup with him
that night,
And to drink wine, beer, and ale.

18 'Call in the reckoning,' said the Bishop,
'For methinks it grows wondrous
high:'
'Lend me your purse, Bishop,' said
Little John,
'And I'll tell you bye and bye.'

19 Then Little John took the bishop's
cloak,
And spread it upon the ground,
And out of the bishop's portmantua
He told three hundred pound.

20 'Here's money enough, master,' said
Little John,
'And a comely sight 't is to see;
It makes me in charity with the Bishop,
Tho he heartily loveth not me.'

21 Robin Hood took the Bishop by the
hand,
And he caused the music to play,
And he made the Bishop to dance in his
boots,
And glad he could so get away.

145

ROBIN HOOD AND QUEEN KATHERINE

About half of A is lost, and the particulars
of the outlaws' exploits are wanting in that
version. Robin Hood has made Queen Katherine his friend by presenting her with a sum
of gold which he has taken from the king's
harbingers. The king has offered a heavy
wager that his archers cannot be excelled, and
the queen may have her choice of all other
bowmen in England. She summons Robin
Hood and his men, who are to come to London
under feigned names. No. 146 is a sequel to
this ballad. For the adventure of the Bishop
of Hereford cf. No. 144.

A

'Robin Hoode and Quene Kath[erine],'
Percy MS., p. 15; Hales and Furnivall, I, 37.

1 Now list you, lithe you, gentlemen,
A while for a litle space,
And I shall tell you how Queene Kat-
terine
Gott Robin Hood his grace.

2 Gold taken from the kings harben-
    gers
    Seldome times hath beene seene,

.   .   .   .   .   .
    .   .   .   .   .   .

    *   *   *   *   *

3 .   .   .   .   .   .
    ' Queene Katherine, I say to thee;'
    ' That's a princly wager,' quoth Queene
      Katherine,
    ' Betweene your grace and me.

4 ' Where must I haue mine archers?'
    says Queene Katherine;
    ' You haue the flower of archery:'
    ' Now take your choice, dame,' he sayes,
    ' Thorow out all England free.

5 ' Yea from North Wales to Westchester,
    And also to Couentry;
    And when you haue chosen the best you
      can,
    The wager must goe with mee.'

6 ' If that prooue,' says Queene Kathe-
    rine,
    ' Soone that wilbe tride and knowne;
    Many a man counts of another mans
      pursse,
    And after looseth his owne.'

7 The queene is to her palace gone,
    To her page thus shee can say:
    Come hither to me, Dicke Patrinton,
    Trusty and trew this day.

8 Thou must bring me the names of my
    archers all,
    All strangers must they bee,
    Yea from North Wales to West Ches-
    ter,
    And alsoe to Couentrie.

9 Commend me to Robin Hood, says
    Queene Katherine,
    And alsoe to Litle John,
    And specially to Will Scarlett,
    Ffryar Tucke and Maid Marryan.

10 Robin Hood we must call Loxly,
    And Little John the Millers sonne;
    Thus wee then must change their names,
    They must be strangers euery one.

11 Commend mee to Robin Hood, sayes
    Queene Katherine,
    And marke, page, what I say;
    In London they must be with me
    [Vpon St Georges day.]

    *   *   *   *   *

12 .   .   .   .   .   .
    ' These words hath sent by me;
    Att London you must be with her
    Vpon St Georg[e]s day.

13 ' Vpon St Georg[e]s day att noone
    Att London needs must you bee;
    Shee wold not misse your companie
    For all the gold in Cristinty.

14 ' Shee hath tane a shooting for your
    sake,
    The greatest in Christentie,
    And her part you must needs take
    Against her prince, Henery.

15 ' Shee sends you heere her gay gold ring
    A trew token for to bee;
    And, as you are [a] banisht man,
    Shee trusts to sett you free.'

16 ' And I loose that wager,' says bold
    Robin Hoode,
    ' I 'le bring mony to pay for me;
    And wether that I win or loose,
    On my queenes part I will be.'

17 In sommer time when leaues grow
    greene,
    And flowers are fresh and gay,
    Then Robin Hood he deckt his men
    Eche one in braue array.

18 He deckt his men in Lincolne greene,
    Himselfe in scarlett red;
    Fayre of theire brest then was it seene
    When his siluer armes were spread.

19 With hattis white and fethers blacke,
    And bowes and arrowes keene,
    And thus he ietted towards louly London,
    To present Queene Katherine.

20 But when they cam to louly London,
    They kneeled vpon their knee;
    Sayes, God you saue, Queene Katherine,
    And all your dignitie !

*   *   *   *   *

21 . . . . . . of my guard,'
    Thus can King Henry say,
  'And those that wilbe of Queene Kate-
    rines side,
  They are welcome to me this day.'

22 'Then come hither to me, Sir Richard
    Lee,
  Thou art a knight full good;
  Well it is knowen ffrom thy pedygree
  Thou came from Gawiins blood.

23 'Come hither, Bishopp of Hereford,'
    quoth Queene Katherine —
  A good preacher I watt was hee —
  'And stand thou heere vpon a odd
    side,
  On my side for to bee.'

24 'I like not that,' sayes the bishopp then,
  'By faikine of my body,
  For if I might haue my owne will,
  On the kings I wold bee.'

25 'What will thou be[t] against vs,' says
    Loxly then,
  'And stake it on the ground?'
  'That will I doe, fine fellow,' he says,
  'And it drawes to fiue hundreth pound.'

26 'There is a bett,' says Loxly then;
  'Wee 'le stake it merrily;'
  But Loxly knew full well in his mind
  And whose that gold shold bee.

27 Then the queenes archers they shot
    about
  Till it was three and three;
  Then the lady's gaue a merry shout,
  Sayes, Woodcocke, beware thine eye!

28 'Well, gam and gam,' then quoth our
    king,
  'The third three payes for all;'
  Then Robine rounded with our queene,
  Says, The kings part shall be small.

29 Loxly puld forth a broad arrowe,
  He shott it vnder hand,
  .   .   . s vnto .   .
  .   .   .   .   .

30 .   .   .   .   .   .
  'For once he vndidd mee;
  If I had thought it had beene bold Robin
    Hoode,
  I wold not haue betted one peny.

31 'Is this Robin Hood?' says the bishopp
    againe;
  'Once I knew him to soone;
  He made me say a masse against my will,
  Att two a clocke in the afternoone.

32 'He bound me fast vnto a tree,
  Soe did he my merry men;
  He borrowed ten pound against my will,
  But he neuer paid me againe.'

33 'What and if I did?' says bold Robin
    Hood,
  'Of that masse I was full faine;
  In recompence, befor king and queene
  Take halfe of thy gold againe.'

34 'I thanke thee for nothing,' says the
    bishopp,
  'Thy large gift to well is knowne,
  That will borrow a mans mony against
    his will,
  And pay him againe with his owne.'

35 'What if he did soe?' says King Henery,
  'For that I loue him neuer the worsse;
  Take vp thy gold againe, bold Robin
    Hood,
  And put [it] in thy pursse.

36 'If thou woldest leaue thy bold outlawes,
  And come and dwell with me,
  Then I wold say thou art welcome, bold
    Robin Hood,
  The flower of archery.'

37 'I will not leaue my bold outlawes
  For all the gold in Christentie;
  In merry Sherwood I 'le take my end,
  Vnder my trusty tree.

38 'And gett your shooters, my leeig[e],
    where you will,
  For in faith you shall haue none of me;
  And when Queene Katherine puts up her
    f[inger]
  Att her Graces commandement I 'le
    bee.'

*   *   *   *   *

B

'Renowned Robin Hood,' etc. **a.** Wood, 402, leaf 10. **b.** Roxburghe, I, 356, in the Ballad Society's reprint, II, 419. **c.** Garland of 1663, No. 9. **d.** Garland of 1670, No. 8. **e.** Wood, 401, leaf 31 b. **f.** Pepys, II, 103, No. 90.

1 GOLD tane from the kings harbengers,
  Down a down a down
As seldome hath been seen,
  Down a down a down
And carried by bold Robin Hood
  For a present to the queen.
  Down a down a down

2 'If that I live a year to an end,'
  Thus gan Queen Katherin say,
'Bold Robin Hood, I will be thy friend,
  And all thy yeomen gay.'

3 The queen is to her chamber gone,
  As fast as she can wen;
She cals unto her her lovely page,
  His name was Richard Patringten.

4 'Come hither to mee, thou lovely page,
  Come thou hither to mee;
For thou must post to Notingham,
  As fast as thou canst dree.

5 'And as thou goest to Notingham,
  Search all those English wood;
Enquire of one good yeoman or another
  That can tell thee of Robin Hood.'

6 Sometimes he went, sometimes hee ran,
  As fast as he could win;
And when hee came to Notingham,
  There he took up his inne.

7 And when he came to Notingham,
  And had took up his inne,
He calls for a pottle of Renish wine,
  And drank a health to his queen.

8 There sat a yeoman by his side;
  'Tell mee, sweet page,' said hee,
'What is thy business or the cause,
  So far in the North Country?'

9 'This is my business and the cause,
  Sir, I 'le tell it you for good,
To inquire of one good yeoman or another
  To tell mee of Robin Hood.'

10 'I 'le get my horse betime in the morn,
  By it be break of day,
And I will shew thee bold Robin Hood,
  And all his yeomen gay.'

11 When that he came at Robin Hoods place,
  Hee fell down on his knee:
'Queen Katherine she doth greet you well,
  She greets you well by mee.

12 'She bids you post to fair London court,
  Not fearing any thing;
For there shall be a little sport,
  And she hath sent you her ring.'

13 Robin took his mantle from his back —
  It was of the Lincoln green —
And sent it by this lovely page,
  For a present unto the queen.

14 In summer time, when leaves grow green,
  It is a seemly sight to see
How Robin Hood himself had drest,
  And all his yeomandry.

15 He cloathed his men in Lincoln green,
  And himself in scarlet red,
Black hats, white feathers, all alike;
  Now bold Robin Hood is rid.

16 And when he came at Londons court,
  Hee fell downe on his knee:
'Thou art welcome, Locksly,' said the queen,
  'And all thy good yeomendree.'

17 The king is into Finsbury field,
  Marching in battel ray,
And after follows bold Robin Hood,
  And all his yeomen gay.

18 'Come hither, Tepus,' said the king,
  'Bow-bearer after mee,
Come measure mee out with this line
  How long our mark shall be.'

19 'What is the wager?' said the queen,
  'That must I now know here:'
'Three hundred tun of Renish wine,
  Three hundred tun of beer.

20 'Three hundred of the fattest harts
  That run on Dallom lee;

That 's a princely wager,' said the
king,
  ' That needs must I tell thee.'

21 With that bespake one Clifton then,
  Full quickly and full soon;
  ' Measure no mark for us, most soveraign
leige,
  Wee 'l shoot at sun and moon.'

22 ' Ful fifteen score your mark shall be,
  Ful fifteen score shall stand;'
  ' I 'le lay my bow,' said Clifton then,
  ' I 'le cleave the willow wand.'

23 With that the kings archers led about,
  While it was three and none;
  With that the ladies began to shout,
  Madam, your game is gone !

24 ' A boon, a boon,' Queen Katherine
cries,
  ' I crave on my bare knee;
  Is there any knight of your privy counsel
  Of Queen Katherines part will be ?

25 ' Come hither to mee, Sir Richard Lee,
  Thou art a knight full good;
  For I do know by thy pedigree
  Thou springst from Goweres blood.

26 ' Come hither to me, thou Bishop of
Herefordshire ' —
  For a noble priest was he —
  ' By my silver miter,' said the bishop
then,
  ' I 'le not bet one peny.

27 ' The king hath archers of his own,
  Full ready and full light,
  And these be strangers every one,
  No man knows what they height.'

28 ' What wilt thou bet,' said Robin Hood,
  ' Thou seest our game the worse ? '
  ' By my silver miter,' said the bishop
then,
  ' All the mony within my purse.'

29 ' What is in thy purse ? ' said Robin
Hood,
  ' Throw it down on the ground;'
  ' Fifteen score nobles,' said the bishop
then,
  ' It 's neer an hundred pound.'

30 Robin Hood took his bagge from his side,
  And threw it down on the green;
  William Scadlocke went smiling away,
  ' I know who this mony must win.'

31 With that the queens archers led about,
  While it was three and three;
  With that the ladies gave a shout,
  ' Woodcock, beware thyn ee ! '

32 ' It is three and three, now,' said the
king,
  ' The next three pays for all;'
  Robin Hood went and whispered to the
queen,
  ' The kings part shall be but small.'

33 Robin Hood he led about,
  He shot it under hand,
  And Clifton, with a bearing arrow,
  He clave the willow wand.

34 And little Midge, the Miller's son,
  Hee shot not much the worse;
  He shot within a finger of the prick;
  ' Now, bishop, beware thy purse ! '

35 ' A boon, a boon,' Queen Katherine cries,
  ' I crave on my bare knee, —
  That you will angry be with none
  That is of my party.'

36 ' They shall have forty days to come,
  And forty days to go,
  And three times forty to sport and play;
  Then welcome friend or fo.'

37 ' Then thou art welcome, Robin Hood,'
  said the queen,
  ' And so is Little John,
  So is Midge, the Miller's son;
  Thrice welcome every one.'

38 ' Is this Robin Hood ? ' the king now
said;
  ' For it was told to mee
  That he was slain in the pallace-gate,
  So far in the North Country.'

39 ' Is this Robin Hood,' said the bishop
then,
  ' As I see well to be ?
  Had I knowne that had been that bold
outlaw,
  I would not have bet one peny.

40 'Hee took me late one Saturday at night,
    And bound mee fast to a tree,
    And made mee sing a mass, God wot,
    To him and his yeomendree."

41 'What and if I did?' says Robin Hood,
    'Of that mass I was full fain;
    For recompense to thee,' he says,
    'Here's half thy gold again.'

42 'Now nay, now nay,' saies Little John,
    'Master, that shall not be;
    We must give gifts to the kings officers;
    That gold will serve thee and mee.'

146

ROBIN HOOD'S CHASE

'Robin Hood's Chase' is a sequel to 'Robin Hood and Queen Katherine' (No. 145), and begins with a summary of that story. It is a well-conceived ballad, and only needs to be older. Edition c is signed by T. R. (see p. 294, above).

'Robin Hood's Chase.' a. Garland of 1663, No. 15. b. Garland of 1670, No. 14. c. Wood, 401, leaf 29 b. d. Pepys, II, 104, No. 91.

1 COME you gallants all, to you I do call,
        With a hey down down a down down
    That now is within this place,
    For a song I will sing of Henry the king,
    How he did Robin Hood chase.

2 Queen Katherine she a match then did make,
        As plainly doth appear,
    For three hundred tun of good red wine,
    And three hundred tun of beer.

3 But yet her archers she had to seek,
        With their bows and arrows so good;
    But her mind it was bent, with a good intent,
    To send for bold Robin Hood.

4 But when bold Robin Hood he came there,
        Queen Katherine she did say,
    Thou art welcome, Locksley, said the queen,
    And all thy yeomen gay.

5 For a match at shooting I have made,
        And thou my part must be:
    'If I miss the mark, be it light or dark,
    Then hanged I will be.'

6 But when the game came to be playd,
        Bold Robin he then drew nigh;
    With his mantle of green, most brave to be seen,
    He let his arrows fly.

7 And when the game it ended was,
        Bold Robin wan it with a grace,
    But after, the king was angry with him,
    And vowed he would him chase.

8 What though his pardon granted was
        While he with them did stay,
    But yet the king was vexed at him
    When as he was gone his way.

9 Soon after the king from the court did hie,
        In a furious angry mood,
    And often enquire, both far and near,
    After bold Robin Hood.

10 But when the king to Nottingham came,
        Bold Robin was then in the wood;
    'O come now,' said he, 'and let me see
    Who can find me bold Robin Hood.'

11 But when that Robin Hood he did hear
        The king had him in chase,
    Then said Little John, 'T is time to be gone,
    And go to some other place.

12 Then away they went from merry Sherwood,
        And into Yorkshire he did hie,
    And the king did follow, with a hoop and a hallow,
    But could not come him nigh.

13 Yet jolly Robin he passed along,
        He [went] straight to Newcastle town,
    And there stayed he hours two or three,
    And then he for Berwick was gone.

14 When the king he did see how Robin did flee,
        He was vexed wondrous sore;

With a hoop and a hallow he vowed to
follow,
And take him, or never give ore.

15 'Come now, let 's away,' then cries
Little John,
'Let any man follow that dare;
To Carlile wee 'l hie with our company,
And so then to Lancaster.'

16 From Lancaster then to Chester they
went,
And so did king Henery;
But Robin away, for he durst not stay,
For fear of some treachery.

17 Saies Robin, Come, let us to London go,
To see our noble queens face;
It may be she wants our company,
Which makes the king so us chase.

18 When Robin he came Queen Katherine
before,
He fell upon his knee:
'If it please your Grace, I am come to
this place,
To speak with king Henery.'

19 Queen Katherine she answered bold
Robin again,
The king is gone to merry Sherwood;
And when he went he to me did say
He would go seek Robin Hood.

20 'Then fare you well, my gracious queen,
For to Sherwood I will hie apace;
For fain would I see what he would
with me,
If I could but meet with his Grace.'

21 But when King Henery he came home,
Full weary, and vexed in mind,
When he did hear Robin had been
there,
He blamed Dame Fortune unkind.

22 'You are welcome home,' Queen Kath-
erine cried,
'Henry, my soveraign liege;
Bold Robin Hood, that archer good,
Your person hath been to seek.'

23 But when King Henry he did hear
That Robin had been there him to
seek,

This answer he gave, He 's a cunning
knave,
For I have sought him this whole
three weeks.

24 'A boon! a boon!' Queen Katherine
cried,
'I beg it here on your Grace,
To pardon his life, and seek no more
strife:'
And so endeth Robin Hoods chase.

147

ROBIN HOOD'S GOLDEN PRIZE

Edition a seems to be signed L. P., probably the initials of the versifier. The kernel of
the story is an old tale, found, for example, in
Pauli's Schimpf und Ernst, 1533 (Oesterley,
Anhang, No. 14).

'Robin Hoods Golden Prize.' **a.** Wood,
401, leaf 39 b. **b.** Garland of 1663, No. 14.
c. Garland of 1670, No. 13. **d.** Pepys, II, 144,
No. 101.

1 I HAVE heard talk of bold Robin Hood,
  Derry derry down
And of brave Little John,
Of Fryer Tuck, and Will Scarlet,
Loxley, and Maid Marion.
  Hey down derry derry down

2 But such a tale as this before
I think there was never none;
For Robin Hood disguised himself,
And to the wood is gone.

3 Like to a fryer, bold Robin Hood
Was accoutered in his array;
With hood, gown, beads and crucifix,
He past upon the way.

4 He had not gone [past] miles two or
three,
But it was his chance to spy
Two lusty priests, clad all in black,
Come riding gallantly.

5 'Benedicete,' then said Robin Hood,
'Some pitty on me take;
Cross you my hand with a silver groat,
For Our dear Ladies sake.

6 'For I have been wandring all this day,
  And nothing could I get;
Not so much as one poor cup of drink,
  Nor bit of bread to eat.'

7 'Now, by my holydame,' the priests
    repli'd,
  'We never a peny have;
For we this morning have been robd,
  And could no mony save.'

8 'I am much afraid,' said bold Robin
    Hood,
  'That you both do tell a lye;
And now before that you go hence,
  I am resolvd to try.'

9 When as the priests heard him say so,
  Then they rode away amain;
But Robin Hood betook him to his
    heels,
  And soon overtook them again.

10 Then Robin Hood laid hold of them
    both,
  And pulld them down from their
    horse:
'O spare us, fryer!' the priests cry'd
    out,
  'On us have some remorse!'

11 'You said you had no mony,' quoth he,
  'Wherefore, without delay,
We three will fall down on our knees,
  And for mony we will pray.'

12 The priests they could not him gainsay,
  But down they kneeled with speed;
'Send us, O send us,' then quoth they,
  'Some mony to serve our need.'

13 The priests did pray with mournful
    chear,
  Sometimes their hands did wring,
Sometimes they wept and cried aloud,
  Whilst Robin did merrily sing.

14 When they had been praying an hours
    space,
  The priests did still lament;
Then quoth bold Robin, Now let 's see
  What mony heaven hath us sent.

15 We will be sharers now all alike
  Of the mony that we have;

And there is never a one of us
  That his fellows shall deceive.

16 The priests their hands in their pockets
    put,
  But mony would find none:
'We 'l search our selves,' said Robin
    Hood,
  'Each other, one by one.'

17 Then Robin Hood took pains to search
    them both,
  And he found good store of gold;
Five hundred peeces presently
  Vpon the grass was told.

18 'Here is a brave show,' said Robin Hood,
  'Such store of gold to see,
And you shall each one have a part,
  Cause you prayed so heartily.'

19 He gave them fifty pound a-peece,
  And the rest for himself did keep;
The priests durst not speak one word,
  But they sighed wondrous deep.

20 With that the priests rose up from their
    knees,
  Thinking to have parted so;
'Nay, stay,' said Robin Hood, 'one
    thing more
  I have to say ere you go.

21 'You shall be sworn,' said bold Robin
    Hood.
  'Vpon this holy grass,
That you will never tell lies again,
  Which way soever you pass.

22 'The second oath that you here must
    take,
  All the days of your lives
You never shall tempt maids to sin,
  Nor lye with other mens wives.

23 'The last oath you shall take, it is this,
  Be charitable to the poor;
Say you have met with a holy fryer,
  And I desire no more.'

24 He set them upon their horses again,
  And away then they did ride;
And hee returnd to the merry green-
    wood,
  With great joy, mirth and pride.

148

THE NOBLE FISHERMAN, OR ROBIN HOOD'S PREFERMENT

Robin Hood is here made to try his fortunes on the sea, like Eustace the Monk and Wallace. ' The Noble Ffisherman, or, Robin Hoods great Prize ' is receipted for to Francis Coules in the Stationers' Registers, June 13, 1631.

'The Noble Fisher-man, or, Robin Hoods Preferment.' **a.** Wood, 402, p. 18. **b.** Wood, 401, leaf 25 b. **c.** Garland of 1663, No. 12. **d.** Garland of 1670, No. 11. **e.** Rawlinson, 566. **f.** Pepys, II, 108, No. 95. **g.** Pepys, II, 123, No. 108.

1 IN summer time, when leaves grow green,
    When they doe grow both green and long,
  Of a bould outlaw, calld Robin Hood,
    It is of him I sing this song.

2 When the lilly leafe and the elephant
    Doth bud and spring with a merry good cheere,
  This outlaw was weary of the wood-side,
    And chasing of the fallow deere.

3 ' The fishermen brave more mony have
    Then any merchant, two or three;
  Therefore I will to Scarborough goe,
    That I a fisherman brave may be.'

4 This outlaw calld his merry men all,
    As they sate under the green-wood tree:
  ' If any of you have gold to spend,
    I pray you heartily spend it with me.

5 ' Now,' quoth Robin, ' I 'le to Scarborough goe,
    It seemes to be a very faire day;'
  Who tooke up his inne at a widdow-womans house,
    Hard by upon the water gray.

6 Who asked of him, Where wert thou borne ?
    Or tell to me, where dost thou fare ?
  ' I am a poore fisherman,' saith he then,
    ' This day intrapped all in care.'

7 ' What is thy name, thou fine fellow ?
    I pray thee heartily tell to me;'
  ' In mine own country where I was borne,
    Men called me Simon over the Lee.'

8 ' Simon, Simon,' said the good wife,
    ' I wish thou maist well brook thy name;'
  The outlaw was ware of her courtesie,
    And rejoycd he had got such a dame.

9 ' Simon, wilt thou be my man ?
    And good round wages I 'le give thee;
  I have as good a ship of mine owne
    As any sayle upon the sea.

10 ' Anchors and planks thou shalt want none,
    Masts and ropes that are so long;'
  ' And if that you thus furnish me,'
    Said Simon, ' nothing shall goe wrong.'

11 They pluckt up anchor, and away did sayle,
    More of a day then two or three;
  When others cast in their baited hooks,
    The bare lines into the sea cast he.

12 ' It will be long,' said the master then,
    ' Ere this great lubber do thrive on the sea;
  I 'le assure you he shall have no part of our fish,
    For in truth he is of no part worthy.'

13 ' O woe is me,' said Simon then,
    ' This day that ever I came here !
  I wish I were in Plomton Parke,
    In chasing of the fallow deere.

14 ' For every clowne laughs me to scorne,
    And they by me set nought at all;
  If I had them in Plomton Park,
    I would set as little by them all.'

15 They pluckt up anchor, and away did sayle,
    More of a day then two or three;
  But Simon spied a ship of warre,
    That sayld towards them most valourously.

16 'O woe is me,' said the master then,
  'This day that ever I was borne !
For all our fish we have got to-day
  Is every bit lost and forlorne.

17 'For your French robbers on the sea,
  They will not spare of us one man,
But carry us to the coast of France,
  And ligge us in the prison strong.'

18 But Simon said, Doe not feare them,
  Neither, master, take you no care;
Give me my bent bow in my hand,
  And never a Frenchman will I spare.

19 'Hold thy peace, thou long lubber,
  For thou art nought but braggs and
      boast ;
If I should cast the over-board,
  There were nothing but a lubber lost.'

20 Simon grew angry at these words,
  And so angry then was he
That he tooke his bent bow in his hand,
  And to the ship-hatch goe doth he.

21 'Master, tye me to the mast,' saith he,
  'That at my mark I may stand fair,
And give me my bended bow in my
      hand,
  And never a Frenchman will I spare.'

22 He drew his arrow to the very head,
  And drew it with all might and maine,
And straightway, in the twinkling of an
      eye,
  Doth the Frenchmans heart the arow
      gain.

23 The Frenchman fell downe on the ship-
      hatch,
  And under the hatches down below;
Another Frenchman that him espy'd
  The dead corps into the sea doth
      throw.

24 'O master, loose me from the mast,' he
      said,
  'And for them all take you no care,
And give me my bent bow in my hand,
  And never a Frenchman will I spare.'

25 Then streight [they] did board the
      Frenchmans ship,
  They lying all dead in their sight;

They found within the ship of warre
  Twelve thousand pound of money
      bright.

26 'The one halfe of the ship,' said Simon
      then,
  'I 'le give to my dame and children
      small;
The other halfe of the ship I 'le bestow
  On you that are my fellowes all.'

27 But now bespake the master then,
  For so, Simon, it shall not be;
For you have won her with your own
      hand,
  And the owner of it you shall bee.

28 'It shall be so, as I have said;
  And, with this gold, for the opprest
An habitation I will build,
  Where they shall live in peace and
      rest.'

149

ROBIN HOOD'S BIRTH, BREED–ING, VALOR, AND MARRIAGE

The jocular author of this ballad, who would certainly have been diverted by any one's supposing him to write under the restraints of tradition, brings Adam Bell, Clim, and Cloudesly into company with Robin Hood's father. He makes Robin Hood's mother niece to Guy of Warwick, and sister to Gamwel of Gamwel Hall. In No. 128 Young Gamwell is Robin Hood's sister's son. The author knows nothing of the Earl of Huntington and Matilda Fitzwater, but represents Robin Hood as the son of a forester. In everything except keeping Robin a yeoman, he writes "as the world were now but to begin, antiquity forgot, custom not known; " but poets in his day, to quote the editor of the ballad collection of 1723, "were looked upon like other Englishmen, born to live and write with freedom."

a. 'A new ballad of bold Robin Hood, shewing his Birth, Breeding, Valour and Marriage, at Titbury Bull-running : calculated for the meridian of Staffordshire, but may serve for Derbyshire or Kent.' Roxburghe, I, 360, in the Ballad Society's reprint, II, 440. b. Pepys, II, 116, No. 103. c. Pepys, II, 118, No. 104.

1 KIND gentlemen, will you be patient
      awhile ?
  Ay, and then you shall hear anon

A very good ballad of bold Robin Hood,
  And of his man, brave Little John.

2 In Locksly town, in Nottinghamshire,
    In merry sweet Locksly town,
  There bold Robin Hood he was born
    and was bred,
  Bold Robin of famous renown.

3 The father of Robin a forrester was,
    And he shot in a lusty long bow,
  Two north country miles and an inch at
    a shot,
  As the Pinder of Wakefield does
    know.

4 For he brought Adam Bell, and Clim
    or the Clugh,
    And William a Clowdesle
  To shoot with our forrester for forty
    mark,
  And the forrester beat them all three.

5 His mother was neece to the Coventry
    knight,
    Which Warwickshire men call Sir
    Guy;
  For he slew the blue bore that hangs up
    at the gate,
  Or mine host of The Bull tells a lye.

6 Her brother was Gamwel, of Great
    Gamwel Hall,
    And a noble house-keeper was he,
  Ay, as ever broke bread in sweet Not-
    tinghamshire,
  And a squire of famous degree.

7 The mother of Robin said to her hus-
    band,
    My honey, my love, and my dear,
  Let Robin and I ride this morning to
    Gamwel,
  To taste of my brothers good cheer.

8 And he said, I grant thee thy boon,
    gentle Joan,
    Take one of my horses, I pray;
  The sun is a rising, and therefore make
    haste,
  For to-morrow is Christmas-day.

9 Then Robin Hoods fathers grey geld-
    ing was brought,
    And sadled and bridled was he;

God wot, a blew bonnet, his new suit of
    cloaths,
    And a cloak that did reach to his
    knee.

10 She got on her holiday kirtle and gown,
    They were of a light Lincoln green;
  The cloath was homespun, but for colour
    and make
  It might a beseemed our queen.

11 And then Robin got on his basket-hilt
    sword,
    And his dagger on his tother side,
  And said, My dear mother, let's haste
    to be gone,
  We have forty long miles to ride.

12 When Robin had mounted his gelding
    so grey,
    His father, without any trouble,
  Set her up behind him, and bad her not
    fear,
  For his gelding had oft carried double.

13 And when she was settled, they rode to
    their neighbours,
    And drank and shook hands with
    them all;
  And then Robin gallopt, and never gave
    ore,
  Till they lighted at Gamwel Hall.

14 And now you may think the right wor-
    shipful squire
    Was joyful his sister to see;
  For he kist her and kist her, and swore
    a great oath,
  Thou art welcome, kind sister, to me.

15 To-morrow, when mass had been said
    in the chappel,
    Six tables were coverd in the hall,
  And in comes the squire, and makes a
    short speech,
  It was, Neighbours, you're welcome
    all.

16 But not a man here shall taste my
    March beer,
    Till a Christmas carrol he sing:
  Then all clapt their hands, and they
    shouted and sung,
  Till the hall and the parlour did
    ring.

17 Now mustard and braun, roast beef and
       plumb pies,
   Were set upon every table:
   And noble George Gamwel said, Eat
       and be merry,
   And drink too, as long as you 're
       able.

18 When dinner was ended, his chaplain
       said grace,
   And, ' Be merry, my friends,' said
       the squire;
   ' It rains, and it blows, but call for more
       ale,
   And lay some more wood on the
       fire.

19 ' And now call ye Little John hither to
       me,
   For Little John is a fine lad
   At gambols and juggling, and twenty
       such tricks
   As shall make you merry and glad.'

20 When Little John came, to gambols
       they went,
   Both gentleman, yeoman and clown;
   And what do you think ? Why, as
       true as I live,
   Bold Robin Hood put them all down.

21 And now you may think the right wor-
       shipful squire
   Was joyful this sight for to see;
   For he said, Cousin Robin, thou 'st go
       no more home,
   But tarry and dwell here with me.

22 Thou shalt have my land when I dye,
       and till then
   Thou shalt be the staff of my age;
   ' Then grant me my boon, dear uncle,'
       said Robin,
   ' That Little John may be my page.'

23 And he said, Kind cousin, I grant thee
       thy boon;
   With all my heart, so let it be;
   ' Then come hither, Little John,' said
       Robin Hood,
   ' Come hither, my page, unto me.

24 ' Go fetch me my bow, my longest long
       bow,
   And broad arrows, one, two, or three;

For when it is fair weather we 'll into
       Sherwood,
   Some merry pastime to see.'

25 When Robin Hood came into merry
       Sherwood,
   He winded his bugle so clear,
   And twice five and twenty good yeomen
       and bold
   Before Robin Hood did appear.

26 ' Where are your companions all ? ' said
       Robin Hood,
   ' For still I want forty and three; '
   Then said a bold yeoman, Lo, yonder
       they stand,
   All under a green-wood tree.

27 As that word was spoke, Clorinda came
       by;
   The queen of the shepherds was she;
   And her gown was of velvet as green
       as the grass,
   And her buskin did reach to her knee.

28 Her gait it was graceful, her body was
       straight,
   And her countenance free from pride;
   A bow in her hand, and quiver and arrows
   Hung dangling by her sweet side.

29 Her eye-brows were black, ay, and so
       was her hair,
   And her skin was as smooth as glass;
   Her visage spoke wisdom, and modesty
       too;
   Sets with Robin Hood such a lass !

30 Said Robin Hood, Lady fair, whither
       away ?
   O whither, fair lady, away ?
   And she made him answer, To kill a fat
       buck;
   For to-morrow is Titbury day.

31 Said Robin Hood, Lady fair, wander
       with me
   A little to yonder green bower;
   There sit down to rest you, and you
       shall be sure
   Of a brace or a lease in an hour.

32 And as we were going towards the green
       bower,
   Two hundred good bucks we espy'd :

She chose out the fattest that was in
    the herd,
    And she shot him through side and
      side.

33 'By the faith of my body,' said bold
    Robin Hood,
    'I never saw woman like thee;
    And comst thou from east, ay, or comst
      thou from west,
    Thou needst not beg venison of me.

34 'However, along to my bower you shall
    go,
    And taste of a forresters meat:'
    And when we come thither, we found as
      good cheer
    As any man needs for to eat.

35 For there was hot venison, and warden
    pies cold,
    Cream clouted, with honey-combs
      plenty;
    And the sarvitors they were, beside
      Little John,
    Good yeomen at least four and twenty.

36 Clorinda said, Tell me your name, gen-
    tle sir;
    And he said, 'T is bold Robin Hood:
    Squire Gamwel's my uncle, but all my
      delight
    Is to dwell in the merry Sherwood.

37 For 't is a fine life, and 't is void of all
    strife.
    'So 't is, sir,' Clorinda reply'd;
    'But oh,' said bold Robin, 'how sweet
      would it be,
    If Clorinda would be my bride!'

38 She blusht at the motion; yet, after a
    pause
    Said, Yes, sir, and with all my heart;
    'Then let 's send for a priest,' said
      Robin Hood,
    'And be married before we do part.'

39 But she said, It may not be so, gentle
    sir,
    For I must be at Titbury feast;
    And if Robin Hood will go thither with
      me,
    I 'll make him the most welcome
      guest.

40 Said Robin Hood, Reach me that buck,
    Little John,
    For I 'll go along with my dear;
    Go bid my yeomen kill six brace of
      bucks,
    And meet me to-morrow just here.

41 Before we had ridden five Staffordshire
    miles,
    Eight yeomen, that were too bold,
    Bid Robin Hood stand, and deliver his
      buck;
    A truer tale never was told.

42 'I will not, faith!' said bold Robin:
    'come, John,
    Stand to me, and we 'll beat em all:'
    Then both drew their swords, an so cut
      em and slasht em
    That five of them did fall.

43 The three that remaind calld to Robin
    for quarter,
    And pitiful John beggd their lives;
    When John's boon was granted, he gave
      them good counsel,
    And so sent them home to their wives.

44 This battle was fought near to Titbury
    town,
    When the bagpipes bated the bull;
    I am king of the fidlers, and sware 't is
      a truth,
    And I call him that doubts it a gull.

45 For I saw them fighting, and fidld the
    while,
    And Clorinda sung, Hey derry down!
    The bumpkins are beaten, put up thy
      sword, Bob,
    And now let 's dance into the town.

46 Before we came to it, we heard a strange
    shouting,
    And all that were in it lookd madly;
    For some were a bull-back, some dan-
      cing a morris,
    And some singing Arthur-a-Bradly.

47 And there we see Thomas, our justices
    clerk,
    And Mary, to whom he was kind;
    For Tom rode before her, and calld
      Mary, Madam,
    And kist her full sweetly behind.

48 And so may your worships. But we
   went to dinner,
   With Thomas and Mary and Nan;
   They all drank a health to Clorinda,
   and told her
   Bold Robin Hood was a fine man.

19 When dinner was ended, Sir Roger, the
   parson
   Of Dubbridge, was sent for in haste;
   He brought his mass-book, and he bade
   them take hands,
   And he joynd them in marriage full
   fast.

50 And then, as bold Robin Hood and his
   sweet bride
   Went hand in hand to the green
   bower,
   The birds sung with pleasure in merry
   Sherwood,
   And 't was a most joyful hour.

51 And when Robin came in the sight of
   the bower,
   ' Where are my yeomen ? ' said he;
   And Little John answered, Lo, yonder
   they stand,
   All under the green-wood tree.

52 Then a garland they brought her, by
   two and by two,
   And plac'd them upon the bride's
   head;
   The music struck up, and we all fell to
   dance,
   Till the bride and the groom were
   a-bed.

53 And what they did there must be coun-
   sel to me,
   Because they lay long the next day,
   And I had haste home, but I got a good
   piece
   Of the bride-cake, and so came away.

54 Now out, alas ! I had forgotten to tell ye
   That marryd they were with a ring;
   And so will Nan Knight, or be buried
   a maiden,
   And now let us pray for the king:

55 That he may get children, and they
   may get more,
   To govern and do us some good;

And then I 'll make ballads in Robin
   Hood's bower,
   And sing em in merry Sherwood.

150

ROBIN HOOD AND MAID MARIAN

Though Maid Marian and Robin Hood had
perhaps been paired in popular sports, no one
thought of putting more of her than her name
into a ballad, until one S. S. (so the broadside is signed) composed this foolish ditty.
The bare name of Maid Marian occurs in No.
145 A, st. 9, and in No. 147, st. 1. Even in Bar-
clay's fourth eclogue, written not long after
1500, where, according to Ritson, the earliest
notice of Maid Marian occurs, and where, he
says, " she is evidently connected with Robin
Hood." the two are really kept distinct; for the
lusty Codrus in that eclogue wishes to hear
" some mery fit of Maid Marion, or els of Robin
Hood." In Munday's play of The Downfall of
Robert Earl of Huntington, Matilda, otherwise
Marian, daughter to Lord Lacy, accompanies
Earl Robert to Sherwood, upon his being outlawed for debt on the very day of their troth-
plight. There. she lives a spotless maiden,
awaiting the time when the outlawry shall be
repealed and Robin may legally take her to
wife. Neither the author of the play nor that
of the ballad was, so far as is known, repeating
any popular tradition. The ordinary partner
of Maid Marian is Friar Tuck, not Robin
Hood.

' A Famous Battle between Robin Hood and
Maid Marian, declaring their Love, Life, and
Liberty,' Wood, 401, leaf 21 b.

1 A BONNY fine maid of a noble degree,
      With a hey down down a down
      down
   Maid Marian calld by name,
   Did live in the North, of excellent
   worth,
      For she was a gallant dame.

2 For favour and face, and beauty most
   rare,
      Queen Hellen shee did excell;
   For Marian then was praisd of all
   men
      That did in the country dwell.

3 'T was neither Rosamond nor Jane
    Shore,
    Whose beauty was clear and bright,
  That could surpass this country lass,
    Beloved of lord and knight.

4 The Earl of Huntington, nobly born,
    That came of noble blood,
  To Marian went, with a good intent,
    By the name of Robin Hood.

5 With kisses sweet their red lips meet,
    For shee and the earl did agree;
  In every place, they kindly imbrace,
    With love and sweet unity.

6 But fortune bearing these lovers a
    spight,
    That soon they were forced to part,
  To the merry green wood then went
    Robin Hood,
    With a sad and sorrowfull heart.

7 And Marian, poor soul, was troubled
    in mind,
    For the absence of her friend;
  With finger in eye, shee often did cry,
    And his person did much comend.

8 Perplexed and vexed, and troubled in
    mind,
    Shee drest her self like a page,
  And ranged the wood to find Robin
    Hood,
    The bravest of men in that age.

9 With quiver and bow, sword, buckler,
    and all,
    Thus armed was Marian most bold,
  Still wandering about to find Robin out,
    Whose person was better then gold.

10 But Robin Hood, hee himself had dis-
    guisd,
    And Marian was strangly attir'd,
  That they provd foes, and so fell to
    blowes,
    Whose vallour bold Robin admir'd.

11 They drew out their swords, and to cut-
    ting they went,
    At least an hour or more,
  That the blood ran apace from bold
    Robins face,
    And Marian was wounded sore.

12 'O hold thy hand, hold thy hand,' said
    Robin Hood,
    'And thou shalt be one of my string,
  To range in the wood with bold Robin
    Hood,
    To hear the sweet nightingall sing.'

13 When Marian did hear the voice of her
    love,
    Her self shee did quickly discover,
  And with kisses sweet she did him
    greet,
    Like to a most loyall lover.

14 When bold Robin Hood his Marian did
    see,
    Good lord, what clipping was there !
  With kind imbraces, and jobbing of
    faces,
    Providing of gallant cheer.

15 For Little John took his bow in his
    hand,
    And wandring in the wood,
  To kill the deer, and make good chear,
    For Marian and Robin Hood.

16 A stately banquet the[y] had full soon,
    All in a shaded bower,
  Where venison sweet they had to eat,
    And were merry that present hour.

17 Great flaggons of wine were set on the
    board,
    And merrily they drunk round
  Their boules of sack, to strengthen the
    back,
    Whilst their knees did touch the
    ground.

18 First Robin Hood began a health
    To Marian his onely dear,
  And his yeomen all, both comly and tall,
    Did quickly bring up the rear.

19 For in a brave veine they tost off the[ir]
    bouls,
    Whilst thus they did remain,
  And every cup, as they drunk up,
    They filled with speed again.

20 At last they ended their merryment,
    And went to walk in the wood,
  Where Little John and Maid Marian
    Attended on bold Robin Hood.

21 In sollid content together they livd,
    With all their yeomen gay;
  They livd by their hands, without any
        lands,
    And so they did many a day.

22 But now to conclude, an end I will
        make
    In time, as I think it good,
  For the people that dwell in the North
        can tell
    Of Marian and bold Robin Hood.

151

THE KING'S DISGUISE, AND FRIENDSHIP WITH ROBIN HOOD

The story, as far as st. 38, is a loose para-
phrase, with omissions, of the seventh and
eighth fits of the Gest, and seems, like Nos.
152, 153, " to have been written by some mis-
erable retainer to the press, merely to eke out
the book ; being in fact, a most contemptible
performance " (Ritson). The two concluding
lines are intended to serve as a link with
' Robin Hood and the Valiant Knight' (No.
153), which, however, does not succeed in the
garlands, ' Robin Hood and the Golden Arrow '
(No. 152) being interposed.

' The King's Disguise, and Friendship with
Robin Hood.' a. Robin Hood's Garland, London, W. & C. Dicey, in St Mary Aldermary
Church Yard, Bow Lane, Cheapside, n. d. (but
not older than 1753), p. 76, No. 25. b. Robin
Hood's Garland, London. Printed by L. How,
in Peticoat Lane, n. d. c. 'The King's Disguise and True Friendship with Robin Hood,'
London, Printed by L. How, in Petticoat Lane,
Douce Ballads, III, 113 b (not black letter).
d. Robin Hood's Garland, London, R. Marshall,
in Aldermary Church-Yard, Bow-Lane, n. d.,
p. 80, No. 25.

1 KING RICHARD hearing of the pranks
    Of Robin Hood and his men,
  He much admir'd, and more desir'd,
    To see both him and them.

2 Then with a dozen of his lords
    To Nottingham he rode;
  When he came there, he made good
        cheer,
    And took up his abode.

3 He having staid there some time,
    But had no hopes to speed,
  He and his lords, with [free] accord,
    All put on monk's weeds.

4 From Fountain-abby they did ride,
    Down to Barnsdale;
  Where Robin Hood prepared stood
    All company to assail.

5 The king was higher then the rest,
    And Robin thought he had
  An abbot been whom he did spleen;
    To rob him he was glad.

6 He took the king's horse by the head,
    ' Abbot,' says he, 'abide;
  I am bound to rue such knaves as you,
    That live in pomp and pride.'

7 ' But we are messengers from the king,
    The king himself did say;
  ' Near to this place his royal Grace
    To speak with thee does stay.'

8 ' God save the king,' said Robin Hood,
    ' And all that wish him well;
  He that does deny his sovereignty,
    I wish he was in hell.'

9 ' O thyself thou curses,' says the king,
    ' For thou a traitor art: '
  ' Nay, but that you are his messenger,
    I swear you lie in heart.

10 ' For I never yet hurt any man
    That honest is and true;
  But those that give their minds to live
    Upon other men's due.

11 ' I never hurt the husbandman,
    That use to till the ground;
  Nor spill their blood that range the
        wood
    To follow hawk or hound.

12 ' My chiefest spite to clergy is,
    Who in these days bear a great
        sway;
  With fryars and monks, with their fine
        sprunks,
    I make my chiefest prey.

13 ' But I am very glad.' says Robin Hood
    ' That I have met you here;

Come, before we end, you shall, my
   friend,
   Taste of our green-wood cheer.'

14 The king did then marvel much,
   And so did all his men;
   They thought with fear, what kind of
      cheer
   Robin would provide for them.

15 Robin took the king's horse by the head,
   And led him to the tent;
   'Thou would not be so usd,' quoth he,
   'But that my king thee sent.

16 'Nay, more than that,' said Robin Hood,
   'For good king Richard's sake,
   If you had as much gold as ever I
      told,
   I would not one penny take.'

17 Then Robin set his horn to his mouth,
   And a loud blast he did blow,
   Till a hundred and ten of Robin Hood's
      men
   Came marching all of a row.

18 And when they came bold Robin before,
   Each man did bend his knee;
   'O,' thought the king, ''t is a gallant
      thing,
   And a seemly sight to see.'

19 Within himself the king did say,
   These men of Robin Hood's
   More humble be than mine to me;
   So the court may learn of the woods.

20 So then they all to dinner went,
   Upon a carpet green;
   Black, yellow, red, finely minglëd,
   Most curious to be seen.

21 Venison and fowls were plenty there,
   With fish out of the river:
   King Richard swore, on sea or shore,
   He neer was feasted better.

22 Then Robin takes a can of ale:
   'Come, let us now begin;
   Come, every man shall have his can;
   Here 's a health unto the king.'

23 The king himself drank to the king,
   So round about it went;

Two barrels of ale, both stout and stale,
   To pledge that health were spent.

24 And after that, a bowl of wine
   In his hand took Robin Hood;
   'Until I die, I 'll drink wine,' said he,
   'While I live in the green-wood.

25 'Bend all your bows,' said Robin Hood,
   'And with the grey goose wing
   Such sport now shew as you would do
   In the presence of the king.'

26 They shewd such brave archery,
   By cleaving sticks and wauds,
   That the king did say, Such men as
      they
   Live not in many lands.

27 'Well, Robin Hood,' then says the king,
   'If I could thy pardon get,
   To serve the king in every thing
   Wouldst thou thy mind firm set ?

28 'Yes, with all my heart,' bold Robin
      said,
   So they flung off their hoods;
   To serve the king in every thing,
   They swore they would spend their
      bloods.

29 'For a clergyman was first my bane,
   Which makes me hate them all;
   But if you 'll be so kind to me,
   Love them again I shall.'

30 The king no longer could forbear,
   For he was movd with ruth;
   ['Robin,' said he, 'I now tell thee
   The very naked truth.]

31 'I am the king, thy sovereign king,
   That appears before you all;'
   When Robin see that it was he,
   Strait then he down did fall.

32 'Stand up again,' then said the king,
   'I 'll thee thy pardon give;
   Stand up, my friend; who can contend,
   When I give leave to live ? '

33 So they are all gone to Nottingham,
   All shouting as they came;
   But when the people them did see,
   They thought the king was slain,

34 And for that cause the outlaws were
      come,
   To rule all as they list;
   And for to shun, which way to run
      The people did not wist.

35 The plowman left the plow in the
      fields,
   The smith ran from his shop;
   Old folks also, that scarce could go,
      Over their sticks did hop.

36 The king soon let them understand
   He had been in the green wood,
   And from that day, for evermore,
   He 'd forgiven Robin Hood.

37 When the people they did hear, ·
   And the truth was known,
   They all did sing, 'God save the king !
   Hang care, the town 's our own !'

38 'What 's that Robin Hood ?' then said
      the sheriff;
   'That varlet I do hate;
   Both me and mine he causd to dine,
   And servd us all with one plate.'

39 'Ho, ho,' said Robin, 'I know what you
      mean;
   Come, take your gold again;
   Be friends with me, and I with thee,
   And so with every man.

40 'Now, master sheriff, you are paid,
   And since you are beginner,
   As well as you give me my due;
   For you neer paid for that dinner.

41 'But if that it should please the king
   So much your house to grace
   To sup with you, for to speak true,
   [I] know you neer was base.'

42 The sheriff could not [that] gain say,
   For a trick was put upon him;
   A supper was drest, the king was
      guest,
   But he thought 't would have undone
      him.

43 They are all gone to London court,
   Robin Hood, with all his train;
   He once was there a noble peer,
   And now he 's there again.

44 Many such pranks brave Robin playd
      While he lived in the green wood:
   Now, my friends, attend, and hear an
      end
   Of honest Robin Hood.

152

ROBIN HOOD AND THE
GOLDEN ARROW

   The first twenty-three stanzas are based
upon the Gest, sts. 282–95. The remainder is
mostly taken up with John's astute device for
sending information to the sheriff. The two
concluding lines are for connection with 'Robin
Hood and the Valiant Knight,' which follows
in some garlands, as here. (See Introduction
to No. 151.)

   a. Robin Hood's Garland, London, W. and
C. Dicey, St Mary Aldermary Church-Yard,
Bow-Lane, n. d., p. 80, No. 26.   b. Robin
Hood's Garland, London, R. Marshall, in Alder-
mary Church-yard, Bow-Lane, n. d., p. 84,
No. 26.   c. Robin Hood's Garland, Preston,
Printed and sold by W. Sergent, n. d.

1 WHEN as the sheriff of Nottingham
      Was come, with mickle grief,
   He talkd no good of Robin Hood,
      That strong and sturdy thief.
         Fal lal dal de

2 So unto London-road he past,
      His losses to unfold
   To King Richard, who did regard
      The tale that he had told.

3 'Why,' quoth the king, 'what shall I
      do ?
   Art thou not sheriff for me ?
   The law is in force, go take thy course
      Of them that injure thee.

4 'Go get thee gone, and by thyself
      Devise some tricking game
   For to enthral yon rebels all;
      Go take thy course with them.'

5 So away the sheriff he returnd,
      And by the way he thought
   Of the words of the king, and how the
      thing
      To pass might well be brought.

6 For within his mind he imagined
   That when such matches were,
   Those outlaws stout, without [all]
     doubt,
   Would be the bowmen there.

7 So an arrow with a golden head
   And shaft of silver white,
   Who won the day should bear away
   For his own proper right.

8 Tidings came to brave Robin Hood,
   Under the green-wood tree:
   'Come prepare you then, my merry
     men,
   We 'll go yon sport to see.'

9 With that stept forth a brave young
     man,
   David of Doncaster:
   'Master,' said he, 'be ruld by me,
   From the green-wood we 'll not stir.

10 'To tell the truth, I 'm well informed
    Yon match is a wile;
    The sheriff, I wiss, devises this
    Us archers to beguile.'

11 'O thou smells of a coward,' said Robin
    Hood,
    'Thy words does not please me;
    Come on 't what will, I 'll try my skill
    At yon brave archery.'

12 O then bespoke brave Little John:
    Come, let us thither gang;
    Come listen to me, how it shall be
    That we need not be kend.

13 Our mantles, all of Lincoln green,
    Behind us we will leave;
    We 'll dress us all so several
    They shall not us perceive.

14 One shall wear white, another red,
    One yellow, another blue;
    Thus in disguise, to the exercise
    We 'll gang, whatee ensue.

15 Forth from the green-wood they are
      gone,
    With hearts all firm and stout,
    Resolving [then] with the sheriff's men
    To have a hearty bout.

16 So themselves they mixed with the rest,
    To prevent all suspicion;
    For if they should together hold
    They thought [it] no discretion.

17 So the sheriff looking round about,
    Amongst eight hundred men,
    But could not see the sight that he
    Had long expected then.

18 Some said, If Robin Hood was here,
    And all his men to boot,
    Sure none of them could pass these men,
    So bravely they do shoot.

19 'Ay,' quoth the sheriff, and scratchd
      his head,
    'I thought he would have been here;
    I thought he would, but, tho he 's bold,
    He durst not now appear.'

20 O that word grieved Robin Hood to the
      heart;
    He vexëd in his blood;
    Eer long, thought he, thou shalt well
      see
    That here was Robin Hood.

21 Some cried, Blue jacket! another cried,
      Brown!
    And the third cried, Brave Yellow!
    But the fourth man said, Yon man in
      red
    In this place has no fellow.

22 For that was Robin Hood himself,
    For he was cloathd in red;
    At every shot the prize he got,
    For he was both sure and dead.

23 So the arrow with the golden head
    And shaft of silver white
    Brave Robin Hood won, and bore with
      him
    For his own proper right.

24 These outlaws there, that very day,
    To shun all kind of doubt,
    By three or four, no less no more,
    As they went in came out.

25 Until they all assembled were
    Under the green-wood shade,
    Where they report, in pleasant sport,
    What brave pastime they made

26 Says Robin Hood, All my care is,
   How that yon sheriff may
   Know certainly that it was I
   That bore his arrow away.

27 Says Little John, My counsel good
   Did take effect before,
   So therefore now, if you 'll allow,
   I will advise once more.

28 'Speak on, speak on,' said Robin Hood,
   'Thy wit 's both quick and sound;
   [I know no man amongst us can
   For wit like thee be found.']

29 'This I advise,' said Little John,
   'That a letter shall be pend,
   And when it is done, to Nottingham
   You to the sheriff shall send.'

30 'That is well advised,' said Robin Hood,
   'But how must it be sent ? '
   'Pugh ! when you please, it 's done with
      ease,
   Master, be you content.

31 'I 'll stick it on my arrow's head,
   And shoot it into the town;
   The mark shall show where it must go,
   When ever it lights down.'

32 The project it was full performd;
   The sheriff that letter had;
   Which when he read, he scratchd his
      head,
   And rav'd like one that 's mad.

33 So we 'll leave him chafing in his grease,
   Which will do him no good;
   Now, my friends, attend, and hear the
      end
   Of honest Robin Hood.

153

ROBIN HOOD AND THE VAL-
IANT KNIGHT

Written, perhaps, because it was thought
that authority should in the end be vindicated
against outlaws, which may explain why this
piece surpasses in platitude everything that
goes before. (See Introduction to Nos. 151,
152.)

'Robin Hood and the Valiant Knight.' **a.**
Robin Hood's Garland, London, C. Dicey, Bow
Church Yard, n. d., but before 1741, p. 88,
Bodleian Library, Douce H H, 88. **b.** Robin
Hood's Garland, 1749, without place or printer,
p. 101, No. 24. **c.** Robin Hood's Garland, Lon-
don, R. Marshall, in Aldermary Church-Yard,
Bow-Lane, n. d., p. 87, No. 27.

1 WHEN Robin Hood, and his merry men
      all,
         Derry, etc.
   Had reigned many years,
   The king was then told they had been
      too bold
   To his bishops and noble peers.
         Hey, etc.

2 Therefore they called a council of state,
   To know what was best to be done
   For to quell their pride, or else, they
      reply'd,
   The land would be over-run.

3 Having consulted a whole summers day,
   At length it was agreed
   That one should be sent to try the event,
   And fetch him away with speed.

4 Therefore a trusty and worthy knight
   The king was pleasd to call,
   Sir William by name; when to him he
      came,
   He told him his pleasure all.

5 'Go you from hence to bold Robin
      Hood,
   And bid him, without more a-do,
   Surrender himself, or else the proud elf
   Shall suffer with all his crew.

6 ' Take here a hundred bowmen brave,
   All chosen men of might,
   Of excellent art for to take thy part,
   In glittering armour bright.'

7 Then said the knight, My sovereign
      liege,
   By me they shall be led;
   I 'll venture my blood against bold
      Robin Hood,
   And bring him alive or dead.

8 One hundred men were chosen straight,
   As proper as eer men saw;

On Midsummer-day they marched away,
To conquer that brave outlaw.

9 With long yew bows and shining spears,
They marchd in mickle pride,
And never delayd, or halted, or stayd,
Till they came to the greenwood-side.

10 Said he to his archers, Tarry here;
Your bows make ready all,
That, if need should be, you may follow
me,
And see you observe my call.

11 'I'll go in person first,' he cry'd,
'With the letters of my good king,
Both signd and seald, and if he will
yield,
We need not draw one string.'

12 He wanderd about till at length he came
To the tent of Robin Hood;
The letter he shews; bold Robin arose,
And there on his guard he stood.

13 'They'd have me surrender,' quoth bold
Robin Hood,
'And lie at their mercy then;
But tell them from me, that never shall
be,
While I have full seven-score men.'

14 Sir William the knight, both hardy and
bold,
Did offer to seize him there,
Which William Locksly by fortune did
see,
And bid him that trick forbear.

15 Then Robin Hood set his horn to his
mouth,
And blew a blast or twain,
And so did the knight, at which there
in sight
The archers came all amain.

16 Sir William with care he drew up his
men,
And plac'd them in battle array;
Bold Robin, we find, he was not behind;
Now this was a bloody fray.

17 The archers on both sides bent their
bows,
And the clouds of arrows flew;

The very first flight, that honoured
knight
Did there bid the world adieu.

18 Yet nevertheless their fight did last
From morning till almost noon;
Both parties were stout, and loath to
give out;
This was on the last [day] of June.

19 At length they went off; one part they
went
To London with right good will;
And Robin Hood he to the green-wood
tree,
And there he was taken ill.

20 He sent for a monk, who let him blood,
And took his life away;
Now this being done, his archers they
run,
It was not a time to stay.

21 Some got on board and crossd the seas,
To Flanders, France, and Spain,
And others to Rome, for fear of their
doom,
But soon returnd again.

22 Thus he that never feard bow nor
spear
Was murdered by letting of blood;
And so, loving friends, the story doth
end
Of valiant bold Robin Hood.

23 There's nothing remains but his epitaph
now,
Which, reader, here you have;
To this very day, and read it you may,
As it was upon his grave.

Robin Hood's Epitaph,
Set on his tomb
By the Prioress of Birkslay Monastery,
in Yorkshire.

Robin, Earl of Huntington,
Lies under this little stone.
No archer was like him so good;
His wildness nam'd him Robin Hood.
Full thirteen years, and something more,
These northern parts he vexed sore.
Such outlaws as he and his men
May England never know again!

154

A TRUE TALE OF ROBIN HOOD

Martin Parker's True Tale of Robin Hood was entered to Francis Grove in the Stationers' Registers on the 29th of February, 1632. A copy in the British Museum, which is here reprinted, is thought to be of this first edition. The title of this copy is: 'A True Tale of Robbin [Hood], or, A briefe touch of the life and death o[f that] Renowned Outlaw, Robert Earle of Huntin[gton] vulgarly called Robbin Hood, who lived and died in [A. D.] 1198, being the 9. yeare of the reigne of King Ric[hard] the first, commonly called Richard Cuer de Lyon. Carefully collected out of the truest Writers of our English C[hroni]cles. And published for the satisfaction of those who desire to s[ee] Truth purged from falsehood. By Martin Parker. Printed at London for T. Cotes, and are to be sold by F. Grove dwellin[g] upon Snow-hill, neare the Saracen[s head].'

Martin Parker professes in st. 117 to follow chronicles, not "fained tales." Perhaps he regards broadside-ballads with historical names in them as chronicles: at any rate, though he reports some things which are found in Grafton, and in Major as cited by Grafton, much the larger part of his True Tale is now to be found only in ballads. When he does not agree with ballads which have come down to us, he may have used earlier copies, or he may have invented. The story of the abbot in sts. 23-26 is at least from the same source as 'Robin Hood and the Bishop' (No. 143); the plundering of King Richard's receivers in st. 33 is evidently the same event as that referred to in the second stanza of 'Robin Hood and Queen Katherine' (No. 145); Robin Hood is said to have built eight almshouses in 71, and one in the last stanza of 'The Noble Fisherman' (No. 148). The Gest could hardly have been unknown to Parker. Sts. 3-9, concerning Robin's rank, prodigality, and outlawry, may have been based upon Munday's play; but nothing is said of Maid Marian. Sts. 44-50 and 56-65 may report the substance of some lost broadside. Perhaps Parker calls his compilation a True Tale because a tale of Robin Hood was a proverb for an incredible story : "Tales of Robin Hood are good for fools."

1 BOTH gentlemen, or yoemen bould,
  Or whatsoever you are,
    To have a stately story tould,
      Attention now prepare.

2 It is a tale of Robin Hood,
    Which I to you will tell,
  Which being rightly understood,
    I know will please you well.

3 This Robbin, so much talked on,
    Was once a man of fame,
  Instiled Earle of Huntington,
    Lord Robert Hood by name.

4 In courtship and magnificence,
    His carriage won him prayse,
  And greater favour with his prince
    Than any in his dayes.

5 In bounteous liberality
    He too much did excell,
  And loved men of quality
    More than exceeding well.

6 His great revennues all he sould
    For wine and costly cheere;
  He kept three hundred bowmen bold,
    He shooting lovd so deare.

7 No archer living in his time
    With him might well compare;
  He practisd all his youthfull prime
    That exercise most rare.

8 At last, by his profuse expence,
    He had consumd his wealth,
  And being outlawed by his prince,
    In woods he livd by stealth.

9 The abbot of Saint Maries rich,
    To whom he mony ought,
  His hatred to this earle was such
    That he his downefall wrought.

10 So being outlawed, as 't is told,
    He with a crew went forth
  Of lusty cutters, stout and bold,
    And robbed in the North.

11 Among the rest, one Little John,
    A yeoman bold and free,
  Who could, if it stood him upon,
    With ease encounter three.

12 One hundred men in all he got,
    With whom, the story sayes,
  Three hundred common men durst
      not
    Hold combate any wayes.

13 They Yorkshire woods frequented much,
   And Lancashire also,
Wherein their practises were such
   That they wrought mickle woe.

14 None rich durst travell to and fro,
   Though nere so strongly armd,
But by these theeves, so strong in show,
   They still were robd and harmd.

15 His chiefest spight to the clergie was,
   That lived in monstrous pride;
No one of them he would let passe
   Along the high-way side,

16 But first they must to dinner goe,
   And afterwards to shrift:
Full many a one he served so,
   Thus while he livd by theft.

17 No monkes nor fryers he would let goe,
   Without paying their fees:
If they thought much to be usd so,
   Their stones he made them leese.

18 For such as they the country filld
   With bastards in those dayes;
Which to prevent, these sparkes did geld
   All that came by their wayes.

19 But Robbin Hood so gentle was,
   And bore so brave a minde,
If any in distresse did passe,
   To them he was so kinde

20 That he would give and lend to them,
   To helpe them at their neede:
This made all poore men pray for him,
   And wish he well might speede.

21 The widdow and the fatherlesse
   He would send meanes unto,
And those whom famine did oppresse
   Found him a friendly foe.

22 Nor would he doe a woman wrong,
   But see her safe conveid;
He would protect with power strong
   All those who crav'd his ayde.

23 The abbot of Saint Maries then,
   Who him undid before,
Was riding with two hundred men,
   And gold and silver store.

24 But Robbin Hood upon him set
   With his couragious sparkes,
And all the coyne perforce did get,
   Which was twelve thousand markes.

25 He bound the abbot to a tree,
   And would not let him passe
Before that to his men and he
   His lordship had sayd masse.

26 Which being done, upon his horse
   He set him fast astride,
And with his face towards his ar—
   He forced him to ride.

27 His men were faine to be his guide,
   For he rode backward home;
The abbot, being thus villifide,
   Did sorely chafe and fume.

28 Thus Robbin Hood did vindicate
   His former wrongs receivd;
For 't was this covetous prelate
   That him of land bereavd.

29 The abbot he rode to the king
   With all the haste he could,
And to his Grace he every thing
   Exactly did unfold.

30 And sayd if that no course were tane,
   By force or stratagem,
To take this rebell and his traine,
   No man should passe for them.

31 The king protested by and by
   Unto the abbot then
That Robbin Hood with speed should dye,
   With all his merry men.

32 But ere the king did any send,
   He did another feate,
Which did his Grace much more offend;
   The fact indeed was great.

33 For in a short time after that,
   The kings receivers went
Towards London with the coyne they got,
   For 's Highnesse northerne rent.

34 Bold Robbin Hood and Little John,
   With the rest of their traine,
Not dreading law, set them upon,
   And did their gold obtaine.

35 The king much moved at the same,
    And the abbots talke also,
  In this his anger did proclaime,
    And sent word to and fro,

36 That whosoere, alive or dead,
    Could bring him Robbin Hood,
  Should have one thousand markes, well payd
    In gold and silver good.

37 This promise of the king did make
    Full many yeomen bold
  Attempt stout Robbin Hood to take,
    With all the force they could.

38 But still when any came to him,
    Within the gay greene wood,
  He entertainement gave to them,
    With venison fat and good.

39 And shewd to them such martiall sport,
    With his long bow and arrow,
  That they of him did give report,
    How that it was great sorow,

40 That such a worthy man as he
    Should thus be put to shift,
  Being late a lord of high degree,
    Of living quite bereft.

41 The king, to take him, more and more
    Sent men of mickle might,
  But he and his still beate them sore,
    And conquered them in fight.

42 Or else, with love and courtesie,
    To him he won their hearts:
  Thus still he lived by robbery,
    Throughout the northerne parts.

43 And all the country stood in dread
    Of Robbin Hood and 's men;
  For stouter lads nere livd by bread,
    In those dayes nor since then.

44 The abbot which before I nam'd
    Sought all the meanes he could
  To have by force this rebell tane,
    And his adherents bold.

45 Therefore he armd five hundred men,
    With furniture compleate,
  But the outlawes slew halfe of them,
    And made the rest retreate.

46 The long bow and the arrow keene
    They were so usd unto
  That still they kept the forest greene,
    In spight o th' proudest foe.

47 Twelve of the abbots men he tooke,
    Who came him to have tane,
  When all the rest the field forsooke;
    These he did entertaine

48 With banquetting and merriment,
    And, having usd them well,
  He to their lord them safely sent,
    And willd them him to tell

49 That if he would be pleasd at last
    To beg of our good king
  That he might pardon what was past,
    And him to favour bring,

50 He would surrender backe agen
    The money which before
  Was taken by him and his men,
    From him and many more.

51 Poore men might safely passe by him,
    And some that way would chuse,
  For well they knew that to helpe them
    He evermore did use.

52 But where he knew a miser rich,
    That did the poore oppresse,
  To feele his coyne his hand did itch;
    Hee 'de have it, more or lesse.

53 And sometimes, when the high-way fayld,
    Then he his courage rouses;
  He and his men have oft assayld
    Such rich men in their houses.

54 So that, through dread of Robbin then
    And his adventurous crew,
  The mizers kept great store of men,
    Which else maintaynd but few.

55 King Richard, of that name the first,
    Sirnamed Cuer de Lyon,
  Went to defeate the Pagans curst,
    Who kept the coasts of Syon.

56 The Bishop of Ely, chancelor,
    Was left as vice-roy here,
  Who like a potent emperor
    Did proudly domminere.

57 Our chronicles of him report
   That commonly he rode
With a thousand horse from court to
   court,
   Where he would make abode.

58 He, riding downe towards the north,
   With his aforesayd traine,
Robbin and his did issue forth,
   Them all to entertaine.

59 And, with the gallant gray-goose wing,
   They shewed to them such play,
That made their horses kickle and fling,
   And downe their riders lay.

60 Full glad and faine the bishop was,
   For all his thousand men,
To seeke what meanes he could to passe
   From out of Robbins ken.

61 Two hundred of his men were kil'd,
   And fourescore horses good;
Thirty, who did as captives yeeld,
   Were carryed to the greene wood.

62 Which afterwards were ransomed,
   For twenty markes a man;
The rest set spurres to horse, and fled
   To th' town of Warrington.

63 The bishop, sore enraged then,
   Did, in King Richards name,
Muster a power of northerne men,
   These outlawes bold to tame.

64 But Robbin, with his courtesie,
   So wonne the meaner sort,
That they were loath on him to try
   What rigor did import.

65 So that bold Robbin and his traine
   Did live unhurt of them,
Vntill King Richard came againe
   From faire Jerusalem.

66 And then the talke of Robbin Hood
   His royall eares did fill;
His Grace admir'd that ith' greene wood
   He thus continued still.

67 So that the country farre and neare
   Did give him great applause;
For none of them neede stand in feare,
   But such as broke the lawes.

68 He wished well unto the king,
   And prayed still for his health,
And never practised any thing
   Against the common wealth.

69 Onely, because he was undone
   By th' crewell clergie then,
All meanes that he could thinke upon
   To vexe such kinde of men

70 He enterprized, with hatefull spleene;
   For which he was to blame,
For fault of some, to wreeke his teene
   On all that by him came.

71 With wealth which he by robbery got
   Eight almes-houses he built,
Thinking thereby to purge the blot
   Of blood which he had spilt.

72 Such was their blinde devotion then,
   Depending on their workes;
Which, if 't were true, we Christian
   men
   Inferiour were to Turkes.

73 But, to speake true of Robbin Hood,
   And wrong him not a iot,
He never would shed any mans blood
   That him invaded not.

74 Nor would he iniure husbandmen,
   That toyld at cart and plough;
For well he knew, were 't not for them,
   To live no man knew how.

75 The king in person, with some lords,
   To Notingham did ride,
To try what strength and skill affords
   To crush these outlawes pride.

76 And, as he once before had done,
   He did againe proclaime,
That whosoere would take upon
   To bring to Notingham,

77 Or any place within the land,
   Rebellious Robbin Hood,
Should be preferd in place to stand
   With those of noble blood.

78 When Robbin Hood heard of the same,
   Within a little space,
Into the towne of Notingham
   A letter to his Grace

79 He shot upon an arrow-head,
   One evening cunningly;
Which was brought to the king, and read
   Before his Maiestie.

80 The tennour of this letter was
   That Robbin would submit,
And be true leigeman to his Grace,
   In any thing that 's fit,

81 So that his Highnesse would forgive
   Him and his merry men all;
If not, he must i th' greene wood live,
   And take what chance did fall.

82 The king would faine have pardoned him,
   But that some lords did say,
This president will much condemne
   Your Grace another day.

83 While that the king and iords did stay
   Debating on this thing,
Some of these outlawes fled away
   Unto the Scottish king.

84 For they supposd, if he were tane,
   Or to the king did yeeld,
By th' commons all the rest on 's traine
   Full quickely would be quelld.

85 Of more than full a hundred men
   But forty tarryed still,
Who were resolvd to sticke to him,
   Let fortune worke her will.

86 If none had fled, all for his sake
   Had got their pardon free;
The king to favour meant to take
   His merry men and he.

87 But ere the pardon to him came,
   This famous archer dy'd:
His death, and manner of the same,
   I 'le presently describe.

88 For, being vext to thinke upon
   His followers revolt,
In melancholly passion
   He did recount their fault.

89 'Perfideous traytors!' sayd he then,
   'In all your dangers past

Have I you guarded as my men
   To leave me thus at last?'

90 This sad perplexity did cause
   A fever, as some say,
Which him unto confusion drawes,
   Though by a stranger way.

91 This deadly danger to prevent,
   He hide him with all speede
Vnto a nunnery, with intent
   For his healths sake to bleede.

92 A faithlesse fryer did pretend
   In love to let him blood;
But he by falshood wrought the end
   Of famous Robbin Hood.

93 The fryer, as some say, did this
   To vindicate the wrong
Which to the clergie he and his
   Had done by power strong.

94 Thus dyed he by trechery,
   That could not dye by force;
Had he livd longer, certainely,
   King Richard, in remorse,

95 Had unto favour him receavd;
   He brave men elevated;
'T is pitty he was of life bereavd
   By one which he so hated.

96 A treacherous leech this fryer was,
   To let him bleed to death;
And Robbin was, me thinkes, an asse,
   To trust him with his breath.

97 His corpes the priores of the place,
   The next day that he dy'd,
Caused to be buried, in mean case,
   Close by the high-way side.

98 And over him she caused a stone
   To be fixed on the ground;
An epitaph was set thereon,
   Wherein his name was found.

99 The date o th' yeare, and day also,
   Shee made to be set there,
That all who by the way did goe
   Might see it plaine appeare

100 That such a man as Robbin Hood
   Was buried in that place;

And how he lived in the greene wood,
And robd there for a space.

101 It seemes that though the clergie he
Had put to mickle woe,
He should not quite forgotten be,
Although he was their foe.

102 This woman, though she did him hate,
Yet loved his memory;
And thought it wondrous pitty that
His fame should with him dye.

103 This epitaph, as records tell,
Within this hundred yeares
By many was discerned well,
But time all things outweares.

104 His followers, when he was dead,
Were some received to grace;
The rest to forraigne countries fled,
And left their native place.

105 Although his funerall was but meane,
This woman had in minde
Least his fame should be buried cleane
From those that came behind.

106 For certainely, before nor since,
No man ere understood,
Vnder the reigne of any prince,
Of one like Robbin Hood.

107 Full thirteene yeares, and something more,
These outlawes lived thus,
Feared of the rich, loved of the poore,
A thing most marvelous.

108 A thing unpossible to us
This story seemes to be;
None dares be now so venturous;
But times are chang'd, we see.

109 We that live in these latter dayes
Of civill government,
If neede be, have a hundred wayes
Such outlawes to prevent.

110 In those dayes men more barbarous were,
And lived lesse in awe;
Now, God be thanked ! people feare
More to offend the law.

111 No roaring guns were then in use,
They dreampt of no such thing;
Our English men in fight did chuse
The gallant gray-goose wing.

112 In which activity these men,
Through practise, were so good,
That in those dayes non equald them,
Specially Robbin Hood.

113 So that, it seemes, keeping in caves,
In woods and forrests thicke,
Thei 'd beate a multitude with staves,
Their arrowes did so pricke.

114 And none durst neare unto them come,
Unlesse in courtesie;
All such he bravely would send home,
With mirth and iollity.

115 Which courtesie won him such love,
As I before have told;
'T was the cheefe cause that he did prove
More prosperous than he could.

116 Let us be thankefull for these times
Of plenty, truth and peace,
And leave out great and horrid crimes,
Least they cause this to cease-

117 I know there 's many fained tales
Of Robbin Hood and 's crew;
But chronicles, which seldome fayles,
Reports this to be true.

118 Let none then thinke this a lye,
For, if 't were put to th' worst,
They may the truth of all discry
I th' raigne of Richard the first.

119 If any reader please to try,
As I direction show,
The truth of this brave history,
Hee 'l finde it true I know.

120 And I shall thinke my labour well
Bestowed, to purpose good,
When 't shall be sayd that I did tell
True tales of Robbin Hood.

The Epitaph which the Prioresse of the Monastery of Kirkes Lay in Yorke-shire set over Robbin Hood, which, as is before mentioned, was to bee reade within these hundreth

yeares, though in old broken English, much
to the same sence and meaning.
Decembris quarto die, 1198: anno regni Ri-
chardii Primi 9.

> Robert Earle of Huntington
> Lies under this little stone.
> No archer was like him so good:
> His wildnesse named him Robbin Hood.
> Full thirteene yeares, and something
>   more,
> These northerne parts he vexed sore.
> Such out-lawes as he and his men
> May England never know agen.

Some other superstitious words were in it,
which I thought fit to leave out.

155

SIR HUGH, OR, THE JEW'S DAUGHTER

The twenty-one versions of this ballad (so
far as they are not mere fragments) agree in
the outline of the story and in many of the details. In N, a singular copy obtained in New
York, the boy's name is corrupted to Harry
Hughes, and the Jew's daughter becomes the
Duke's daughter.

The story of Hugh of Lincoln is told in the
Annals of Waverley, under the year 1255, by a
contemporary writer, to this effect. A boy in
Lincoln, named Hugh, was crucified by the
Jews in contempt of Christ with various preliminary tortures. To conceal the act from
Christians, the body, when taken from the
cross, was thrown into a running stream; but
the water would not endure the wrong done
its maker, and immediately ejected it upon
dry land. The body was then buried in the
earth, but was found above ground the next
day. The guilty parties were now very much
frightened and quite at their wits' end; as a
last resort they threw the corpse into a well.
Thereupon the whole place was filled with so
brilliant a light and so sweet an odor that it
was clear to everybody that there must be
something holy and prodigious in the well.
The body was seen floating on the water, and,
upon its being drawn up, the hands and feet
were found to be pierced, the head had, as it
were, a crown of bloody points, and there were
various other wounds: from all which it was
plain that this was the work of the Jews. A
blind woman, touching the bier on which the
blessed martyr's corpse was carrying to the

church, received her sight, and many other
miracles followed. Eighteen Jews, convicted
of the crime, and confessing it with their own
mouth, were hanged. Matthew Paris, also
writing contemporaneously, supplies additional
circumstances, one of which, the mother's finding of the child, is prominent in the ballad.
The Annals of Burton give a long report of
this case, which is perhaps contemporary,
though the manuscript is mostly of the next
century.

An Anglo-French ballad, which also appears to be contemporary with the event, agrees
in many particulars with the account given in
the Annals of Burton and adds new details.

The English ballads, the oldest of which
were recovered about the middle of the eighteenth century, must, in the course of five
hundred years of tradition, have departed
considerably from the early form. The occurrence of Our Lady's draw-well, in A, is due to
a mixing, to this extent, of the story of Hugh
with that of the young devotee of the Virgin
who is celebrated in Chaucer's Prioresses Tale.

Murders like that of Hugh of Lincoln have
been imputed to the Jews for at least seven
hundred and fifty years, and the charge, which
there is reason to suppose may still from time
to time be renewed, has brought upon the
accused every calamity that the hand of man
can inflict, pillage, confiscation, banishment,
torture, and death, and this in huge propor-
tions. The process of these murders has often
been described as a parody of the crucifixion
of Jesus. The motive most commonly alleged,
in addition to the contempt for Christianity, has
been the obtaining of blood for use in the Pas-
chal rites, — a most unhappily devised slander,
in stark contradiction with Jewish precept and
practice. That no Christian child was ever
killed by a Jew, that there never even was so
much truth as that (setting aside the object) in a
single case of these particular criminations, is
what no Christian or Jew would undertake to
assert; but of these charges in the mass it may
safely be said, as it has been said, that they are
as credible as the miracles which, in a great
number of cases, are asserted to have been
worked by the reliques of the young saints,
and as well substantiated as the absurd sacri-
lege of stabbing, baking, or boiling the Host,
or the enormity of poisoning springs, with
which the Jews have equally been taxed. And
these pretended child-murders, with their
horrible consequences, are only a part of a per-
secution which, with all moderation, may be
rubricated as the most disgraceful chapter in
the history of the human race.

Several cases of such murders in England
are reported from the twelfth and thirteenth

centuries. The oldest is that of William of Norwich, 1144, given in the Anglo-Saxon Chronicle under 1137 (ed. Plummer, I, 265). See The Life and Miracles of Saint William, edited by Jessopp and James, 1897.

A

'Hugh of Lincoln,' Jamieson's Popular Ballads, I, 151, as taken down by the editor from Mrs Brown's recitation.

1 FOUR and twenty bonny boys
  Were playing at the ba,
And by it came him sweet Sir Hugh,
  And he playd oer them a'.

2 He kicked the ba with his right foot,
  And catchd it wi his knee,
And throuch-and-thro the Jew's window
  He gard the bonny ba flee.

3 He 's doen him to the Jew's castell,
  And walkd it round about;
And there he saw the Jew's daughter,
  At the window looking out.

4 'Throw down the ba, ye Jew's daughter,
  Throw down the ba to me!'
'Never a bit,' says the Jew's daughter,
  'Till up to me come ye.'

5 'How will I come up? How can I come up?
  How can I come to thee?
For as ye did to my auld father.
  The same ye'll do to me.'

6 She 's gane till her father's garden,
  And pu'd an apple red and green;
'T was a' to wyle him sweet Sir Hugh,
  And to entice him in.

7 She 's led him in through ae dark door,
  And sae has she thro nine;
She 's laid him on a dressing-table,
  And stickit him like a swine.

8 And first came out the thick, thick blood,
  And syne came out the thin,
And syne came out the bonny heart's blood;
  There was nae mair within.

9 She 's rowd him in a cake o lead,
  Bade him lie still and sleep;
She 's thrown him in Our Lady's draw-well,
  Was fifty fathom deep.

10 When bells were rung, and mass was sung,
   And a' the bairns came hame,
When every lady gat hame her son,
   The Lady Maisry gat nane.

11 She 's taen her mantle her about,
   Her coffer by the hand,
And she 's gane out to seek her son,
   And wanderd oer the land.

12 She 's doen her to the Jew's castell,
   Where a' were fast asleep:
'Gin ye be there, my sweet Sir Hugh,
   I pray you to me speak.'

13 She 's doen her to the Jew's garden,
   Thought he had been gathering fruit:
'Gin ye be there, my sweet Sir Hugh,
   I pray you to me speak.'

14 She neard Our Lady's deep draw-well,
   Was fifty fathom deep:
'Whareer ye be, my sweet Sir Hugh,
   I pray you to me speak.'

15 'Gae hame, gae hame, my mither dear,
   Prepare my winding sheet,
And at the back o merry Lincoln
   The morn I will you meet.'

16 Now Lady Maisry is gane hame,
   Made him a winding sheet,
And at the back o merry Lincoln
   The dead corpse did her meet.

17 And a' the bells o merry Lincoln
   Without men's hands were rung,
And a' the books o merry Lincoln
   Were read without man's tongue,
And neer was such a burial
   Sin Adam's days begun.

B

'The Jew's Daughter,' Percy's Reliques, I, 32, 1765; from a manuscript copy sent from Scotland.

1 THE rain rins doun through Mirry-land
      toune,
    Sae dois it doune the Pa;
    Sae dois the lads of Mirry-land toune,
      Whan they play at the ba.

2 Than out and cam the Jewis dochter,
      Said, Will ye cum in and dine?
    'I winnae cum in, I cannae cum in,
      Without my play-feres nine.'

3 Scho powd an apple reid and white,
      To intice the yong thing in:
    Scho powd an apple white and reid,
      And that the sweit bairne did win.

4 And scho has taine out a little pen-
      knife,
    And low down by her gair;
    Scho has twin'd the yong thing and
      his life,
    A word he nevir spak mair.

5 And out and cam the thick, thick
      bluid,
    And out and cam the thin,
    And out and cam the bonny herts bluid;
      Thair was nae life left in.

6 Scho laid him on a dressing-borde,
      And drest him like a swine,
    And laughing said, Gae nou and pley
      With your sweit play-feres nine.

7 Scho rowd him in a cake of lead,
      Bade him lie stil and sleip;
    Scho cast him in a deip draw-well,
      Was fifty fadom deip.

8 Whan bells wer rung, and mass was
      sung,
    And every lady went hame,
    Than ilka lady had her yong sonne,
      Bot Lady Helen had nane.

9 Scho rowd hir mantil hir about,
      And sair, sair gan she weip,
    And she ran into the Jewis castel,
      Whan they wer all asleip.

10 'My bonny Sir Hew, my pretty Sir
       Hew,
     I pray thee to me speik:'
    'O lady, rinn to the deip draw-well,
       Gin ye your sonne wad seik.'

11 Lady Helen ran to the deip draw-well,
      And knelt upon her kne:
    'My bonny Sir Hew, an ye be here,
      I pray thee speik to me.'

12 'The lead is wondrous heavy, mither,
      The well is wondrous deip;
    A keen pen-knife sticks in my hert,
      A word I dounae speik.

13 'Gae hame, gae hame, my mither deir,
      Fetch me my windling sheet,
    And at the back o Mirry-land toun,
      It's thair we twa sall meet.'

C

'The Jewis Daughter,' Percy papers; communicated to Percy by Paton, in 1768 or 1769,
and derived from a friend of Paton's.

1 FOUR and twenty bonny boys
      War playing at the ba;
    Then up and started sweet Sir Hew,
      The flower amang them a'.

2 He hit the ba a kick wi 's fit,
      And kept it wi his knee,
    That up into the Jew's window
      He gart the bonny ba flee.

3 'Cast doun the ba to me, fair maid,
      Cast doun the ba to me;'
    'O neer a bit o the ba ye get
      Till ye cum up to me.

4 'Cum up, sweet Hew, cum up, dear
       Hew,
      Cum up and get the ba;'
    'I canna cum, I darna cum,
      Without my play-feres twa.'

5 'Cum up, sweet Hew, cum up, dear
       Hew,
      Cum up and play wi me;'
    'I canna cum, I darna cum,
      Without my play-feres three.'

6 She's gane into the Jew's garden,
      Where the grass grew lang and green;
    She powd an apple red and white,
      To wyle the young thing in.

7 She wyl'd him into ae chamber,
      She wyl'd him into twa,

She wyl'd him to her ain chamber,
The fairest o them a'.

8 She laid him on a dressing-board,
Where she did sometimes dine;
She put a penknife in his heart,
And dressed him like a swine.

9 Then out and cam the thick, thick
blude,
Then out and cam the thin;
Then out and cam the bonny heart's
blude,
Where a' the life lay in.

10 She rowd him in a cake of lead,
Bad him lie still and sleep;
She cast him in the Jew's draw-well,
Was fifty fadom deep.

11 She 's tane her mantle about her head,
Her pike-staff in her hand,
And prayed Heaven to be her guide
Unto some uncouth land.

12 His mither she cam to the Jew's castle,
And there ran thryse about:
'O sweet Sir Hew, gif ye be here,
I pray ye to me speak.'

13 She cam into the Jew's garden,
And there ran thryse about:
'O sweet Sir Hew, gif ye be here,
I pray ye to me speak.'

14 She cam unto the Jew's draw-well,
And there ran thryse about:
'O sweet Sir Hew, gif ye be here,
I pray ye to me speak.'

15 ' How can I speak, how dare I speak,
How can I speak to thee ?
The Jew's penknife sticks in my heart,
I canna speak to thee.

16 ' Gang hame, gang hame, O mither dear,
And shape my winding sheet,
And at the birks of Mirryland town
There you and I shall meet.'

17 Whan bells war rung, and mass was
sung,
And a' men bound for bed,
Every mither had her son,
But sweet Sir Hew was dead.

N

'Little Harry Hughes and the Duke's Daughter,' Newell's Games and Songs of American Children, 1883, p. 75, as sung by a little girl in New York : derived, through her mother, from a grandmother born in Ireland.

1 IT was on a May, on a midsummer's
day,
When it rained, it did rain small;
And little Harry Hughes and his play-
fellows all
Went out to play the ball.

2 He knocked it up, and he knocked it
down,
He knocked it oer and oer;
The very first kick little Harry gave the
ball,
He broke the duke's windows all.

3 She came down, the youngest duke's
daughter,
She was dressed in green:
'Come back, come back, my pretty little
boy,
And play the ball again.'

4 'I wont come back, and I daren't come
back,
Without my playfellows all;
And if my mother she should come in,
She 'd make it the bloody ball.'

5 She took an apple out of her pocket,
And rolled it along the plain;
Little Harry Hughes picked up the
apple,
And sorely rued the day.

6 She takes him by the lily-white hand,
And leads him from hall to hall,
Until she came to a little dark room,
That no one could hear him call.

7 She sat herself on a golden chair,
Him on another close by,
And there 's where she pulled out her
little penknife,
That was both sharp and fine.

8 Little Harry Hughes had to pray for his
soul,
For his days were at an end;

She stuck her penknife in little Harry's
heart,
   And first the blood came very thick,
and then came very thin.

9 She rolled him in a quire of tin,
   That was in so many a fold;
She rolled him from that to a little
draw-well,
   That was fifty fathoms deep.

10 'Lie there, lie there, little Harry,' she
cried,
   'And God forbid you to swim,
If you be a disgrace to me,
   Or to any of my friends.'

11 The day passed by, and the night came
on,
   And every scholar was home,
And every mother had her own child,
   But poor Harry's mother had none.

12 She walked up and down the street,
   With a little sally rod in her hand,
And God directed her to the little draw-
well,
   That was fifty fathoms deep.

13 'If you be there, little Harry,' she
said,
   'And God forbid you to be,
Speak one word to your own dear
mother,
   That is looking all over for thee.'

14 'This I am, dear mother,' he cried,
   'And lying in great pain,
With a little penknife lying close to my
heart,
   And the duke's daughter she has me
slain.

15 'Give my blessing to my schoolfellows,
all,
   And tell them to be at the church,
And make my grave both large and
deep,
   And my coffin of hazel and green
birch.

16 'Put my Bible at my head,
   My busker (?) at my feet,
My little prayer-book at my right side,
   And sound will be my sleep.'

156

QUEEN ELEANOR'S CONFESSION

This ballad seems first to have got into print
in the latter part of the seventeenth century,
but was no doubt circulating orally some time
before that, for it is in the truly popular tone.
The fact that *two* friars hear the confession
would militate against a much earlier date.
Eleanor of Aquitaine was married to Henry
II of England in 1152, a few weeks after her
divorce from Louis VII of France, she being
then about thirty and Henry nineteen years of
age. "It is needless to observe," says Percy,
"that the following ballad is altogether fabu-
lous; whatever gallantries Eleanor encouraged
in the time of her first husband, none are imputed to her in that of her second." In Peele's
play of Edward I (1593) the story is absurdly
transferred to Edward Longshanks and that
model of women and wives, Eleanor of Castile.
There are several sets of tales in which a husband takes a shrift-father's place and hears
his wife's confession. Such are the fabliau
"Du Chevalier qui fist sa femme confesse"
(Montaiglon, No. 16); Les Cent Nouvelles Nouvelles, 1432, No. 78; Boccaccio, vii, 5.

A

a. 'Queen Eleanor's Confession,' a broad-
side, London, Printed for C. Bates, at the Sun
& Bible in Gilt-spur-street, near Pye-corner,
Bagford Ballads, II, No. 26, 1685? British
Museum. b. A broadside, Printed for C.
Bates, in Pye-corner, Bagford Ballads, I, No.
33, 1685? c. Another copy of b, reprinted in
Utterson's Little Book of Ballads, p. 22. d.
A Collection of Old Ballads, 1723, I, 18.

1 Queen Elenor was a sick woman,
   And afraid that she should dye;
Then she sent for two fryars of France,
   For to speak with them speedily.

2 The King calld down his nobles all,
   By one, by two, and by three,
And sent away for Earl Martial,
   For to speak with him speedily.

3 When that he came before the King,
   He fell on his bended knee;
'A boon, a boon! our gracious king,
   That you sent so hastily.'

4 'I 'll pawn my living and my lands,
  My septer and my crown,
That whatever Queen Elenor says,
  I will not write it down.

5 'Do you put on one fryar's coat,
  And I 'll put on another,
And we will to Queen Elenor go,
  One fryar like another.'

6 Thus both attired then they go;
  When they came to Whitehall,
The bells they did ring, and the quiris-
    ters sing,
  And the torches did light them all.

7 When that they came before the Queen,
  They fell on their bended knee :
'A boon, a boon ! our gracious queen,
  That you sent so hastily.'

8 'Are you two fryars of France ? ' she
    said,
  'Which I suppose you be;
But if you are two English fryars,
  Then hanged shall you be.'

9 'We are two fryars of France,' they
    said,
  'As you suppose we be;
We have not been at any mass
  Since we came from the sea.'

10 'The first vile thing that ere I did
  I will to you unfold;
Earl Martial had my maidenhead,
  Underneath this cloath of gold.'

11 'That is a vile sin,' then said the king,
  'God may forgive it thee ! '
'Amen ! Amen ! ' quoth Earl Martial,
  With a heavy heart then spoke he.

12 'The next vile thing that ere I did
  To you I 'll not deny;
I made a box of poyson strong,
  To poyson King Henry.'

13 'That is a vile sin,' then said the King,
  'God may forgive it thee ! '
'Amen ! Amen ! ' quoth Earl Martial,
  'And I wish it so may be.'

14 'The next vile thing that ere I did
  To you I will discover;

I poysoned Fair Rosamond,
  All in fair Woodstock bower.'

15 'That is a vile sin,' then said the King,
  'God may forgive it thee ! '
'Amen ! Amen ! ' quoth Earl Martial,
  'And I wish it so may be.'

16 'Do you see yonders little boy,
  A tossing of that ball ?
That is Earl Martial['s] eldest son,
  And I love him the best of all.

17 'Do you see yonders little boy,
  A catching of the ball ?
That is King Henry's son,' she said,
  'And I love him the worst of all.

18 'His head is like unto a bull,
  His nose is like a boar;'
'No matter for that,' King Henry said,
  'I love him the better therefore.'

19 The King pulld of his fryar's coat,
  And appeard all in red;
She shriekd and she cry'd, she wrong
    her hands,
  And said she was betrayd.

20 The King lookd over his left shoulder,
  And a grim look looked he,
And said, Earl Martial, but for my
    oath,
  Then hanged shouldst thou be.

B

" The Old Lady's Collection," MS., No. 6.

1 OUR quin 's seek, an very seek,
  She 's seek an leak to dee,
An she has sent for the friears of
    France,
  To speak we her spedely.

2 'Ye 'll pit on a frier's robe,
  An I 'll put one anether,
An we 'll goo to madam the Quin,
  Leak frayers bath together.'

3 'God forbid,' sayes Earl Marchel!,
  'That ever the leak sud be,
That I sud begule madam the Quin;
  I wad be hangëd hei.'

4 .   .   .   .   .   .

> The King suar by the croun an the septer
> roun
> Eearl Marchell sudne dei.

5 The king pat one a frier's rob,
> Eearl Marchell on anether,
> The 'r on to the Quin,
> Like frayers bath together.

6 'Gin ye be the frayers of France,' she
> says,
> 'As I trust wiell ye be,
> Bat an ye be ony eather men
> Ye sall be hangëd he.'

7 The king he turned him roun,
> An by his troth suare he,
> 'We ha na sung masse
> San we came fra the sea.'

8 'The first sin ever I did,
> An a very grat sin it was tee,
> I gaa my medenhead to Earl Marchell,
> Belou a green-wood tree.'

9 'That was a sin, an a very grate sin,
> Bat pardoned it man be;'
> 'We menement,' said Earl Marchell,
> Bat a heavë, heavë heart had he.

10 'The nist sin ever I did,
> An a grat sin it was tee,
> I pusned Lady Rosomon,
> Ar the King's darling was she.'

11 'That was a sin, an a grat sin,
> Bat pardoned it may be;'
> 'We menement,' said King Henry,
> Bat a heavë, heavë heart had he.

12 'The nist sin I ever did,
> An a grat sin it was tee,
> I keepet pusin in my bosom seven
> year
> To pusin him King Henre.'

13 'That was a sin, an a grat sin,
> Bat pardoned it may be;'
> 'We menement,' sa[i]d King Henrie,
> Bat a heavë, heavë heart had he.

14 'O see ye na yon bony boys,
> As they play att the baa?

> An see ye na Earl Merchal's son?
> I lee him best of all.

15 'But see ye na King Henry's son?
> He is headed leak a bull an baked leak
> a bore,
> I leak him warst of a':'
> 'An, by my soth,' says him King Henry
> 'I leak him best of the twa.'

16 The king he turned him roun,
> Pat on the coat of goud,
> The Quin turned her roun,
> The king to behald.

17 '.   .   .   .   .   .
>
> Gin I had na sworn by the croun an the
> septer roun,
> Eearl Marchell sud ben gared dee.'

157

GUDE WALLACE

Blind Harry's Wallace (of about 1460, earlier than 1488) is clearly the source of this ballad. A–F are derived from vv. 1080–1119 of the Fifth Book. Here Wallace, on his way to the hostelry with a comrade, met a woman who counselled them to pass by, if Scots, for Southrons were there, drinking and talking of Wallace; twenty are there, making great din but no man of fence. "Wallace went in and bad *Benedicite*." The Captain said, "Thou art a Scot, the devil thy nation quell." Wallace drew and ran the captain through; "fifteen he straik and fifteen has he slayn;" his comrade killed the other five. G prefixes to the story of the other versions another adventure of Wallace, taken from the Fourth Book of Blind Harry, vv. 704–87. The first half of G is plainly a late piece of work, very possibly of the nineteenth century, much later than the other, which itself need not be very old. But the portions of Blind Harry's poem out of which these ballads were made were perhaps themselves composed from older ballads, and the restitution of the lyrical form may have given us something not altogether unlike what was sung in the fifteenth, or even the fourteenth century.

A

'On an honourable Achievement of Sir William Wallace, near Falkirk,' a chap-book of Four New Songs and a Prophecy, 1745

The Scots Musical Museum, 1853, D. Laing's
additions, IV, 458*; Maidment, Scotish Ballads and Songs, 1859, p. 83.

1 'HAD we a king,' said Wallace then,
　'That our kind Scots might live by
　　their own !
　But betwixt me and the English blood
　I think there is an ill seed sown.'

2 Wallace him over a river lap,
　He lookd low down to a linn;
　He was war of a gay lady
　Was even at the well washing.

3 'Well mot ye fare, fair madam,' he
　　said,
　' And ay well mot ye fare and see !
　Have ye any tidings me to tell,
　I pray you 'll show them unto me.'

4 'I have no tidings you to tell,
　Nor yet no tidings you to ken;
　But into that hostler's house
　There 's fifteen of your Englishmen.

5 ' And they are seeking Wallace there,
　For they 've ordained him to be slain: '
　' O God forbid !' said Wallace then,
　' For he 's oer good a kind Scotsman.

6 ' But had I money me upon,
　And evn this day, as I have none,
　Then would I to that hostler's house,
　And evn as fast as I could gang.'

7 She put her hand in her pocket,
　She told him twenty shillings oer her
　　knee;
　Then he took off both hat and hood,
　And thankd the lady most reverently.

8 ' If eer I come this way again,
　Well paid [your] money it shall be; '
　Then he took off both hat and hood,
　And he thankd the lady most rever-
　　ently.

9 He leand him twofold oer a staff,
　So did he threefold oer a tree,
　And he 's away to the hostler's house,
　Even as fast as he might dree.

10 When he came to the hostler's house,
　He said, Good-ben be here ! quoth he:

An English captain, being deep load,
　He asked him right cankerdly,

11 Where was you born, thou crooked
　　carle,
　And in what place, and what country?
　' 'T is I was born in fair Scotland,
　A crooked carle although I be.'

12 The English captain swore by th' rood,
　' We are Scotsmen as well as thee,
　And we are seeking Wallace; then
　　To have him merry we should be.'

13 'The man,' said Wallace, ' ye 're look-
　　ing for,
　I seed him within these days three;
　And he has slain an English captain,
　And ay the fearder the rest may be.'

14 ' I 'd give twenty shillings,' said the cap-
　　tain,
　' To such a crooked carle as thee,
　If you would take me to the place
　　Where that I might proud Wallace
　　see.'

15 'Hold out your hand,' said Wallace
　　then,
　' And show your money and be free,
　For tho you 'd bid an hundred pound,
　I never bade a better bode' [, said
　　he].

16 He struck the captain oer the chafts,
　Till that he never chewed more;
　He stickd the rest about the board,
　And left them all a sprawling there.

17 'Rise up, goodwife,' said Wallace then,
　' And give me something for to eat;
　For it 's near two days to an end
　Since I tasted one bit of meat.'

18 His board was scarce well covered,
　Nor yet his dine well scantly dight,
　Till fifteen other Englishmen
　Down all about the door did light.

19 ' Come out, come out,' said they, ' Wal-
　　lace !' then,
　' For the day is come that ye must
　　die; '
　And they thought so little of his might,
　But ay the fearder they might be.

20 The wife ran but, the gudeman ran ben,
     It put them all into a fever;
   Then five he sticked where they stood,
     And five he trampled in the gutter.

21 And five he chased to yon green wood,
     He hanged them all out-oer a grain;
   And gainst the morn at twelve o'clock,
     He dined with his kind Scottish men.

G

'Sir William Wallace,' The Thistle of Scotland, Alexander Laing, p. 100, from the repetition of an old gentlewoman in Aberdeenshire. Also Motherwell's MS., p. 487, communicated by Peter Buchan of Peterhead, "who had it from an old woman in that neighborhood."

1 Woud ye hear of William Wallace,
     An sek him as he goes,
   Into the lan of Lanark,
     Amang his mortel faes?

2 There was fyften English sogers
     Unto his ladie cam,
   Said, Gie us William Wallace,
     That we may have him slain.

3 Woud ye gie William Wallace,
     That we may have him slain,
   And ye's be wedded to a lord,
     The best in Christendeem.

4 'This verra nicht at seven,
     Brave Wallace will come in,
   And he'll come to my chamber-door,
     Without or dread or din.'

5 The fyften English sogers
     Around the house did wait,
   And four brave southron foragers
     Stood hie upon the gait.

6 That verra nicht at seven
     Brave Wallace he came in,
   And he came to his ladie's bouir,
     Withouten dread or din.

7 When she beheld him Wallace,
     She star'd him in the face;
   'Ohon, alas!' said that ladie,
     'This is a woful case.

8 'For I this nicht have sold you,
     This nicht you must be taen,

And I'm to be wedded to a lord,
     The best in Christendeem.'

9 'Do you repent,' said Wallace,
     'The ill you've dane to me?'
   Ay, that I do,' said that ladie,
     'And will do till I die.

10 'Ay, that I do,' said that ladie,
     'And will do ever still,
   And for the ill I've dane to you,
     Let me burn upon a hill.'

11 'Now God forfend,' says brave Wallace,
     'I shoud be so unkind;
   Whatever I am to Scotland's faes,
     I'm aye a woman's friend.

12 'Will ye gie me your gown, your gown,
     Your gown but and your kirtle,
   Your petticoat of bonny brown,
     And belt about my middle?

13 'I'll take a pitcher in ilka hand,
     And do me to the well;
   They'll think I'm one of your maidens,
     Or think it is yoursell.'

14 She has gien him her gown, her gown,
     Her petticoat and kirtle,
   Her broadest belt, wi silver clasp,
     To bind about his middle.

15 He's taen a pitcher in ilka hand,
     And dane him to the well;
   They thought him one of her maidens,
     They kend it was nae hersell.

16 Said one of the southron foragers,
     See ye yon lusty dame?
   I woud nae gie muckle to thee, neebor,
     To bring her back agen.

17 Then all the southrons followd him,
     And sure they were but four;
   But he has drawn his trusty brand,
     And slew them pair by pair.

18 He threw the pitchers frae his hands,
     And to the hills fled he,
   Until he cam to a fair may,
     Was washin on yon lea.

19 'What news, what news, ye weel-far'd may?
     What news hae ye to gie?'

'Ill news, ill news,' the fair may said,
  'Ill news I hae to thee.

20 'There is fyften English sogers
    Into that thatched inn,
  Seeking Sir William Wallace;
    I fear that he is slain.'

21 'Have ye any money in your pocket?
    Pray lend it unto me,
  And when I come this way again,
    Repaid ye weel shall be.'

22 She['s] put her hand in her pocket,
    And taen out shillings three;
  He turnd him right and 'round about,
    And thankd the weel-far'd may.

23 He had not gone a long rig length,
    A rig length and a span,
  Until he met a bold beggar,
    As sturdy as coud gang.

24 'What news, what news, ye bold beggar?
    What news hae ye to gie?'
  'O heavy news,' the beggar said,
    'I hae to tell to thee.

25 'There is fyften English sogers,
    I heard them in yon inn,
  Vowing to kill him Wallace;
    I fear the chief is slain.'

26 'Will ye change apparell wi me, auld
      man?
    Change your apparell for mine?
  And when I come this way again,
    Ye'll be my ain poor man.'

27 When he got on the beggar's coat,
    The pike-staff in his hand,
  He's dane him down to yon tavern,
    Where they were drinking wine.

28 'What news, what news, ye staff-beg-
      gar?
    What news hae ye to gie?'
  'I hae nae news, I heard nae news,
    As few I'll hae frae thee.'

29 'I think your coat is ragged, auld
      man;
    But woud you wages win,
  And tell where William Wallace is,
    We'll lay gold in your hand.'

30 'Tell down, tell down your good red
      gold,
    Upon the table-head,
  And ye sall William Wallace see,
    Wi the down-come of Robin Hood.'

31 They had nae tauld the money down,
    And laid it on his knee,
  When candles, lamps, and candlesticks,
    He on the floor gard flee.

32 And he has drawn his trusty brand,
    And slew them one by one,
  Then sat down at the table-head,
    And called for some wine.

33 The goodwife she ran but, ran but,
    The goodman he ran ben,
  The verra bairns about the fire
    Were a' like to gang brain.

34 'Now if there be a Scotsman here,
    He'll come and drink wi me;
  But if there be an English loun,
    It is his time to flee.'

35 The goodman was an Englishman,
    And to the hills he ran;
  The goodwife was a Scots woman,
    And she came to his hand.

158

HUGH SPENCER'S FEATS IN FRANCE

Of the many Hugh Spensers if we select the younger of the favorites of Edward II, his exploits, had they any foundation in reality, would necessarily fall between 1322, when Charles IV came to the French throne, and 1326, when the Spensers, father and son, ended their career. The French king says in B 8 that Spenser had sunk his ships and slain his men. Hugh Spenser the younger was engaged in piracy in 1321. The quarrel between Edward II and Charles IV, touching the English possessions in France, was temporarily arranged in 1325, but not through the mediation of the younger Spenser, who never was sent on an embassy to France. Another Sir Hugh Spenser was a commander in the Earl of Arundel's fleet in the operations against the French in Charles VI's time, 1387, and was taken prisoner in consequence of his ship grounding.

This ballad is after the fashion of Russian
bylinas, and especially the bylina of Dobrynja
and Vasilij Kazimirović. In this very fine ballad, Vladimir is in arrears with his tribute to
a Saracen king, and appoints Vasilij his envoy,
to make payment. Vasilij asks that he may
have Dobrynja go with him, and Dobrynja
asks for Ivanuška's company. Dobrynja beats
the king at chess and at the bow (which corresponds to the justing in the English ballad);
then follows a great fight, the result of which
is that the Saracen king is fain to pay tribute
himself. See Wollner, Volksepik der Gross-
russen, pp. 123–5.

A

'Hugh Spencer,' Percy MS., p. 281; Hales
and Furnivall, II, 290.

1 THE court is kept att leeue London,
   And euermore shall be itt;
   The King sent for a bold embassador,
   And Sir Hugh Spencer that he hight.

2 'Come hither, Spencer,' saith our kinge,
   'And come thou hither vnto mee;
   I must make thee an embassadour
   Betweene the king of Ffrance and
   mee.

3 'Thou must comend me to the king of
   Ffrance,
   And tell him thus and now ffrom mee,
   I wold know whether there shold be
   peace in his land,
   Or open warr kept still must bee.

4 'Thou'st haue thy shipp at thy co-
   mande,
   Thou'st neither want for gold nor
   ffee;
   Thou'st haue a hundred armed men,
   All att thy bidding ffor to bee.'

5 The wind itt serued, and they sayled,
   And towards Ffrance thus they be
   gone;
   The wind did bring them safe to shore,
   And safelye landed euerye one.

6 The Ffrenchman lay on the castle-wall,
   The English souldiers to behold:
   'You are welcome, traitors, out of Eng-
   land;
   The heads of you are bought and
   sold.'

7 With that spake proud Spencer:
   My leege, soe itt may not bee;
   I am sent an embassador
   Ffrom our English king to yee.

8 The king of England greetes you well,
   And hath sent this word by mee;
   He wold know whether there shold be
   peace in your land,
   Or open warres kept still must bee.

9 'Comend me to the English kinge,
   And tell this now ffrom mee;
   There shall neuer peace be kept in my
   land
   While open warres kept there may
   bee.'

10 With that came downe the queene of
   Ffrance,
   And an angry woman then was shee;
   Saies, Itt had beene as ffitt now for a
   king
   To be in his chamber with his ladye,
   Then to be pleading with traitors out
   of England,
   Kneeling low vppon their knee.

11 But then bespake him proud Spencer,
   For noe man else durst speake but
   hee:
   You haue not wiped your mouth, madam,
   Since I heard you tell a lye.

12 'O hold thy tounge, Spencer!' shee said,
   'I doe not come to plead with thee;
   Darest thou ryde a course of warr
   With a knight that I shall put to
   thee?'

13 'But euer alacke!' then Spencer sayd,
   'I thinke I haue deserued Gods
   cursse;
   Ffor I haue not any armour heere,
   Nor yett I haue noe iusting-horsse.'

14 'Thy shankes,' quoth shee, 'beneath
   the knee
   Are verry small aboue the shinne
   Ffor to doe any such honourablle deeds
   As the Englishmen say thou has done.

15 'Thy shankes beene small aboue thy
   shoone,
   And soe the beene aboue thy knee;

Thou art to slender euery way
   Any good iuster ffor to bee.'

16 'But euer alacke,' said Spencer then,
   'For one steed of the English coun-
     trye!'
   With that bespake and one Ffrench
     knight,
   This day thou'st haue the choyce of
     three.

17 The first steed he ffeiched out,
   I-wis he was milke-white;
   The ffirst ffoot Spencer in stirropp sett,
   His backe did from his belly tyte.

18 The second steed that he ffeitcht out,
   I-wis that hee was verry browne;
   The second ffoot Spencer in stirropp
     sett,
   That horsse and man and all ffell
     downe.

19 The third steed that hee ffeitched out,
   I-wis that he was verry blacke;
   The third ffoote Spencer into the stir-
     ropp sett,
   He leaped on to the geldings backe.

20 'But euer alacke,' said Spencer then,
   'For one good steed of the English
     countrye!
   Goe ffeitch me hither my old hacneye,
   That I brought with me hither be-
     yond the sea.'

21 But when his hackney there was
     brought,
   Spencer a merry man there was hee;
   Saies, With the grace of God and St
     George of England,
   The ffeild this day shall goe with
     mee.

22 'I haue not fforgotten,' Spencer sayd,
   'Since there was ffeild foughten att
     Walsingam,
   When the horsse did heare the trum-
     petts sound,
   He did beare ore both horsse and
     man.'

23 The day was sett, and togetther they
     mett,
   With great mirth and melodye,

With minstrells playing, and trumpetts
     soundinge,
   With drumes striking loud and hye.

24 The ffirst race that Spencer run,
   I-wis hee run itt wonderous sore;
   He [hitt] the knight vpon his brest,
   But his speare itt burst, and wold
     touch noe more.

25 'But euer alacke,' said Spencer then,
   'For one staffe of the English coun-
     trye!
   Without you'le bind me three together,'
   Quoth hee, 'they'le be to weake ffor
     mee.'

26 With that bespake him the Ffrench
     knight,
   Sayes, Bind him together the whole
     thirtye,
   For I haue more strenght in my to
     hands
   Then is in all Spencers bodye.

27 'But proue att parting,' Spencer sayes,
   'Ffrench knight, here I tell itt thee;
   For I will lay thee five to four
   The bigger man I proue to bee.'

28 But the day was sett, and together they
     mett,
   With great mirth and melodye,
   With minstrells playing, and trumpetts
     soundinge,
   With drummes strikeing loud and
     hye.

29 The second race that Spencer run,
   I-wis hee ridd itt in much pride,
   And he hitt the knight vpon the brest,
   And draue him ore his horsse beside.

30 But he run thorrow the Ffrench campe;
   Such a race was neuer run beffore;
   He killed of King Charles his men
   Att hand of thirteen or fourteen
     score.

31 But he came backe againe to the K[ing],
   And kneeled him downe vpon his
     knee;
   Saies, A knight I haue slaine, and a
     steed I haue woone,
   The best that is in this countrye.

32 'But nay, by my faith,' then said the
    King,
    'Spencer, soe itt shall not bee;
I 'le haue *that* traitors head of thine,
    To enter plea att my iollye.'

33 But Spencer looket him once about,
    He had true bretheren left but four;
He killed ther of the Kings gard
    About twelve or thirteen score.

34 'But hold thy hands,' the King doth
    say,
    'Spencer, now I doe pray thee;
And I will goe into litle England,
    Vnto *that* cruell kinge with thee.'

35 'Nay, by my ffaith,' Spencer sayd,
    'My leege, for soe itt shall not bee;
For an you sett ffoot on English ground,
    You shall be hanged vpon a tree.'

36 'Why then, comend [me] to *that* Eng-
    lishe kinge,
    And tell him thus now ffrom mee,
That there shall neu*er* be open warres
    kept in my land
    Whilest peace kept *that* there may
    bee.'

B

'Hugh Spencer,' Percy Papers: communicated by the Duchess Dowager of Portland.

1 OUR king lay at Westminster,
    as oft times he had done,
And he sent for Hugh Spencer,
    to come to him anon.

2 Then in came Hugh Spencer,
    low kneeling on his knee:
'What 's the matter, my liege,
    you sent so speedily for me ?'

3 'Why you must go ambassadour
    to France now, to see
Whether peace shall be taken,
    aye, or open wars must be.'

4 'Who shall go with me ?'
    says Hugh Spencer, he:
'That shall Hugh Willoughby
    and John of Atherly.'
'O then,' says Hugh Spencer,
    ' we 'll be a merry company.'

5 When they came before the French
    king,
    they kneeled low on the knee:
'O rise up, and stand up,
    whose men soer you be.'

6 The first that made answer
    Was Hugh Spencer, he:
'We are English ambassad*ours*,
    come hither to see
Whether peace shall be taken,
    aye, or open wars must be.'

7 Then spoke the French king,
    and he spoke courteously:
The last time peace was broken,
    it was neer along of me.

8 For you sunk my ships, slew my
    men,
    and thus did ye;
And the last time peace was broken,
    it was neer along of me.

9 Then in came Queen Maude,
    and full as ill was she:
'A chamber of presence
    is better for thee,
Then amongst English shepherds,
    low bending on the knee.'

10 The first that made answer
    was Hugh Spencer, he:
'We are no English shepherds,
    Queen Maude, I tell thee,
But we 're knights, and knights fel-
    lows,
    the worst man in our company.'

11 O then spoke Queen Maude,
    and full as ill was she:
Thou shouldst be Hugh Spencer,
    thou talkst so boldly.

12 And if thou beest Hugh Spencer,
    as well thou seemst to be,
I 've oft heard of thy justling,
    and some of it would fain see.

13 I have a steed in my stable
    that thou canst not ride;
I have a spear in my keeping
    that thou canst not guide;
And I have a knight in my realm
    that thou darest not abide.

14 Then Spencer askd Willoughby
    and John of Atherly
  Whether he should take this justling in
    hand,
    aye, or let it be.

15 O then spoke Hugh Willoughby
    and John of Atherly:
  If you won't take it [in] hand,
    why turn it unto we.

16 'It shall neer be said in England,'
    says Hugh Spencer, he,
  'That I refused a good justling
    and turned it to ye.

17 'Alas,' says Hugh Spencer,
    'full sore may I moan,
  I have nought here but an ambler,
    my good steed's at home.'

18 Then spoke a French knight,
    and he spoke courteously:
  I have thirty steeds in my stables,
    the best of them take to thee.

19 'Gramercy,' says Spencer,
    'aye, and gramercy;
  If eer thou comest to England,
    well rewarded shalt thou be.'

20 The first steed they brought him,
    he was a milk-white:
  'Take that away,' says Spencer,
    'for I do not him like.'

21 The next steed they brought him,
    he was a good dun:
  'Take that away,' says Spencer,
    'for he's not for my turn.'

22 The next steed they brought him,
    he was a dapple-grey:
  'Take that away,' says Spencer,
    'for he is not used to the way.'

23 The next steed they brought him,
    he was a coal-black;
  His eyes burnt in his head,
    as if fire were in flax;
  'Come saddle me that horse,' says
    Spencer,
    'for I'll have none but that.'

24 When that horse was saddled,
    aud Spencer got on,
  With his spear at his foot,
    O he was portly man!

25 'Now I am on that steede-back
    that I could not ride,
  That spear in my keeping
    that I could not guide,
  Come shew me that French knight
    that I dare not abide.'

26 'It is a sign by thy sharp shin,
    ay, and thy cropped knee,
  That you are no fit match
    to justle with me:'
  'Why it makes no matter,' says Spencer
    'you hear no brags of me.'

27 The first time they rode together,
    Now Sir Hugh and he,
  He turnd him in his saddle
    like an apple on a tree.

28 The next time they rode together,
    now Sir Hugh and he,
  He lit upon his breast-plate,
    and he broke his spear in three.

29 'A spear now,' says Spencer,
    'a spear now get me:'
  'Thou shalt have one,' says Willoughby,
    'if in France one there be.'

30 'O tye two together,
    and the stronger they'l be,
  For the French is the better,
    and the better shall be:'
  'Why it makes no matter,' says Spencer,
    'you hear no brags of me.'

31 The next time they rode together,
    now Sir Hugh and he,
  He threw him fifteen foot from his
    saddle,
    and he broke his back in three:
  'Now I have slain thy justler,
    Queen Maude, I tell thee.'

32 O then spoke Queen Maude,
    and full as ill was she:
  If thou'st slain my justler,
    by the Kings laws thou'st dye.

33 ' It shall neer be said in England,'
   says Hugh Spencer, he;
 ' It shall neer be said in England,'
   says Hugh Willoughby;

34 ' It shall neer be said in England,'
   says John of Atherly,
 ' That a queen of another nation
   eer had her will of we.'

35 They laid their heads together,
   and their backs to the wall;
 There were four score of the Queen's
   guards,
   and they slew them all.

36 Then spoke the French king,
   and he spoke courteously:
 O hold thy hand, Spencer,
   I dearly pray thee.

37 Thou art sharp as thy spear,
   and as fierce as thy steed,
 And the stour of thy lilly-white hand
   makes my heart bleed.

38 Thou hadst twenty ships hither,
   thou 'st have twenty away;
 Then hold thy hand, Spencer,
   I dearly thee pray.

159

DURHAM FIELD

While Edward Third was absent in France, and for the time engaged with the siege of Calais, David Bruce, the young king of Scotland, at the instance of Philip of Valois, but also because he " yearned to see fighting," invaded England with a large army. Having taken by storm the Border castle of Liddel, he was advised by William of Douglas to turn back, which, it was represented by Douglas, he could do with credit after this success. Other lords said that Douglas had filled his bags, but theirs were toom, and that the way lay open to London, for there were no men left in England but souters, skinners, and traders. The Scots moved on to Durham, and encamped in a park not far from the town, in a bad position. In the mean while a powerful force had been collected by the northern nobility and the English churchmen, without the knowledge of the Scots. William of Douglas, going out to forage, rode straight to the ground where his foes lay, and in the attempt to retreat lost five hundred of his men. King David drew up his army in three divisions: one under his own command, another under the Earl of Murray and William Douglas, the third under the Steward of Scotland and the Earl of March. The operations of the Scots were impeded by the ditches and fences that traversed the ground on which they stood, and their situation made them almost helpless, a mark for the ten thousand archers of the English army. Murray's men were completely routed by a charge of cavalry, and their leader killed. The English then fell upon the King's division, which, after a desperate fight, was " vanquished utterly." David, who had received two wounds from arrows, was taken prisoner by John Copland, " by force, not yolden," after knocking out two of the Englishman's teeth with a knife. Wyntoun's Cronykil, ed. Laing, II, 470 ff. ; Scotichronicon, ed. Goodall, II, 339 ff. The battle was fought on the 17th of October, 1346.

' Durham ffeilde,' Percy MS., p. 245; Hales and Furnivall, II, 190.

1 LORDINGES, listen, and hold you still;
   Hearken to me a litle;
 I shall you tell of the fairest battell
   That euer in England beffell.

2 For as it befell in Edward the Thirds
   dayes,
 In England, where he ware the
   crowne,
 Then all the cheefe chiualry of England
   They busked and made them bowne.

3 They chosen all the best archers
   That in England might be found,
 And all was to fight with the k*in*g of
   Ffrance,
 *Wi*thin a litle stounde.

4 And when our k*in*g was ou*er* the water,
   And on the salt sea gone,
 Then tydings into Scotland came
   That all England was gone.

5 Bowes and arrowes they were all forth,
   At home was not left a man
 But shepards and millers both,
   And preists with shauen crownes.

6 Then the k*in*g of Scotts in a study stood,
   As he was a man of great might;

He sware he wold hold his parlam*ent* in
   leeue London,
If he cold ryde there right.

7 Then bespake a sq*uier*, of Scottland
   borne,
   And sayd, My leege, apace,
Before you come to leeue London,
   Full sore you 'le rue *that* race.

8 Ther beene bold yeomen in merry Eng-
   land,
   Husbandmen stiffe and strong;
Sharpe swords they done weare,
   Bearen bowes and arrowes longe.

9 The K*ing* was angrye at that word;
   A long sword out hee drew,
And there befor his royall companye
   His owne squier hee slew.

10 Hard hansell had the Scottes *that* day,
   That wrought them woe enoughe,
For then durst not a Scott speake a word
   Ffor hanging att a boughe.

11 'The Earle of Anguish, where art thou?
   In my coate-armor thou shalt bee,
And thou shalt lead the forward
   Thorrow the English countrye.

12 'Take thee Yorke,' then sayd the K*ing*,
   'In stead wheras it doth stand;
I 'le make thy eldest sonne after thee
   Heyre of all Northumberland.

13 'The Earle of Vaughan, where be yee?
   In my coate-armor thou shalt bee;
The high Peak and Darbyshire
   I giue it thee to thy fee.'

14 Then came in famous Douglas,
   Saies, What shall my meede bee?
And I 'le lead the vawward, lord,
   Thorow the English countrye.

15 'Take thee Worster,' sayd the K*ing*,
   'Tuxburye, Killingworth, Burton vpon
   Trent;
Doe thou not say another day
   But I haue giuen thee lands and rent.

16 'Sir Rich*ard* of Edenborrow, where are
   yee?
   A wise man in this warr!

I 'le giue thee Bristow and the shire
   The time *that* wee come there.

17 'My lo*rd* Nevill, where beene yee?
   You must in this warres bee;
I 'le giue thee Shrewsburye,' saies the
   K*ing*,
   'And Couentrye faire and free.

18 'My lo*rd* of Hambleton, where art thou?
   Thou art of my kin full nye;
I 'le giue thee Lincolne and Lincolne-
   shire,
   And *that* 's enouge for thee.'

19 By then came in W*illi*am Douglas,
   As breeme as any bore;
He kneeled him downe vpon his knees,
   In his hart he sighed sore.

20 Saies, I haue serued you, my louelye
   leege,
   This thirty winters and four,
And in the Marches betweene England
   and Scottland
   I haue beene wounded and beaten
   sore.

21 For all the good service *that* I haue done,
   What shall my meed bee?
And I will lead the vanward
   Thorrow the English countrye.

22 'Aske on, Douglas,' said the king,
   'And granted it shall bee:'
'Why then, I aske litle London,' saies
   W*illi*am Douglas,
   'Gotten giff *that* it bee.'

23 The K*ing* was wrath, and rose away,
   Saies, Nay, *that* cannot bee!
For *that* I will keepe for my cheefe
   chamber,
   Gotten if it bee.

24 But take thee North Wales and Wes-
   chaster,
   The cuntrye all round about,
And rewarded thou shalt bee,
   Of *that* take thou noe doubt.

25 Fiue score k*nigh*ts he made on a day,
   And dubbd them w*ith* his hands;
Rewarded them right worthilye
   W*ith* the townes in merry England.

26 And when the fresh knights they were
        made,
    To battell the buske them bowne;
  Iames Douglas went before,
        And he thought to haue wonnen him
        shoone.

27 But the were mett in a morning of May
        With the comminaltye of litle Eng-
        land;
    But there scaped neuer a man away,
        Through the might of Christës hand.

28 But all onely Iames Douglas;
        In Durham in the ffeild
    An arrow stroke him in the thye;
        Fast flinge[s he] towards the King.

29 The King looked toward litle Durham,
        Saies, All things is not well!
    For Iames Dowglas beares an arrow in
        his thye,
        The head of it is of steele.

30 'How now Iames?' then said the King,
        'How now, how may this bee?
    And where beene all thy merrymen
        That thou tooke hence with thee?'

31 'But cease, my king,' saies Iames Doug-
        las,
        'Aliue is not left a man!'
    'Now by my faith,' saies the king of
        Scottes,
        'That gate was euill gone.

32 'But I 'le reuenge thy quarrell well,
        And of that thou may be faine;
    For one Scott will beate fiue English-
        men,
        If the meeten them on the plaine.'

33 'Now hold your tounge,' saies Iames
        Douglas,
        'For in faith that is not soe;
    For one English man is worth fiue Scotts,
        When they meeten together thoe.

34 'For they are as egar men to fight
        As a faulcon vpon a pray;
    Alas! if euer the winne the vanward,
        There scapes noe man away.'

35 'O peace thy talking,' said the King,
        'They bee but English knaues,

But shepards and millers both,
        And preists with their staues.'

36 The King sent forth one of his heralds
        of armes
        To vew the Englishmen:
    'Be of good cheere,' the herald said,
        'For against one wee bee ten.'

37 'Who leades those ladds?' said the
        king of Scottes,
        'Thou heraid, tell thou mee:'
    The herald said, The Bishopp of Dur-
        ham
        Is captaine of that companye.

38 'For the Bishopp hath spred the King's
        banner,
        And to battell he buskes him bowne;'
    'I sweare by St Andrewes bones,' saies
        the King,
        'I 'le rapp that preist on the crowne.'

39 The King looked towards litle Durham,
        And that hee well beheld,
    That the Earle Percy was well armed,
        With his battell-axe entred the feild.

40 The King looket againe towards litle
        Durham,
        Four ancyents there see hee;
    There were to standards, six in a valley,
        He cold not see them with his eye.

41 My Lord of Yorke was one of them,
        My Lord of Carlile was the other,
    And my Lord Fltuwilliams,
        The one came with the other.

42 The Bishopp of Durham commanded
        his men,
        And shortlye he them bade,
    That neuer a man shold goe to the feild
        to fight
        Till he had serued his God.

43 Fiue hundred preists said masse that
        day
        In Durham in the feild,
    And afterwards, as I hard say,
        They bare both speare and sheeld.

44 The Bishopp of Durham orders him
        selfe to fight,
        With his battell-axe in his hand;

He said, This day now I will fight
  As long as I can stand !

45 'And soe will I,' sayd my Lord of Car-
    lile,
  'In this faire morning gay;'
  'And soe will I,' said my Lord Ffluwil-
    liams,
  'For Mary, that myld may.'

46 Our English archers bent their bowes
  Shortlye and anon;
  They shott ouer the Scottish oast
  And scantlye toucht a man.

47 'Hold downe your hands,' sayd the Bish-
    opp of Durham,
  'My archers good and true:'
  The second shoote that the shott,
  Full sore the Scottes itt rue.

48 The Bishopp of Durham spoke on hye,
  That both partyes might heare:
  'Be of good cheere, my merrymen
    all,
  The Scotts flyen, and changen there
    cheere.'

49 But as the saidden, soe the didden,
  They fell on heapës hye;
  Our Englishmen laid on with their
    bowes,
  As fast as they might dree.

50 The king of Scotts in a studye stood
  Amongst his companye;
  An arrow stoke him thorrow the nose,
  And thorrow his armorye.

51 The King went to a marsh-side
  And light beside his steede;
  He leaned him downe on his sword-
    hilts,
  To let his nose bleede.

52 There followed him a yeaman of merry
    England,
  His name was Iohn of Coplande:
  'Yeeld thee, traytor !' saies Coplande
    then,
  'Thy liffe lyes in my hand.'

53 'How shold I yeeld me,' sayes the
    King,
  'And thou art noe gentleman ?'

'Noe, by my troth,' sayes Copland there,
  'I am but a poore yeaman.

54 'What art thou better then I, Sir King ?
  Tell me if that thou can !
  What art thou better then I, Sir King,
  Now we be but man to man ?'

55 The King smote angerly at Copland
    then,
  Angerly in that stonde;
  And then Copland was a bold yeaman,
  And bore the King to the ground.

56 He sett the King upon a palfrey,
  Himselfe upon a steede;
  He tooke him by the bridle-rayne,
  Towards London he can him lead.

57 And when to London that he came,
  The King from Ffrance was new come
    home,
  And there unto the king of Scottes
  He sayd these words anon.

58 'How like you my shepards and my
    millers ?
  My priests with shaven crownes ?'
  'By my fayth, they are the sorest fight-
    ing men
  That ever I mett on the ground.

59 'There was never a yeaman in merry
    England
  But he was worth a Scottish knight:'
  'I, by my troth,' said King Edward,
    and laughe,
  'For you fought all against the right.'

60 But now the prince of merry England,
  Worthilye under his sheelde,
  Hath taken the king of Ffrance,
  At Poytiers in the ffeelde.

61 The prince did present his father with
    that food,
  The louely king off Ffrance,
  And fforward of his iourney he is gone:
  God send us all good chance !

62 'You are welcome, brother !' sayd the
    king of Scotts, to the king of Ffrance,
  'For I am come hither to soone:
  Christ leeve that I had taken my way
  Unto the court of Roome !'

63 ‘ And soe wold I,’ said the king of
    Ffrance,
    ‘ When I came over the streame,
    That I had taken my iourney
      Unto Ierusalem ! ’

64 Thus ends the battell of ffaire Durham,
    In one morning of May,
    The battell of Cressey, and the battle of
    Potyers,
      All within one monthës day.

65 Then was welthe and welfare in mery
    England,
    Solaces, game, and glee.
And every man loved other well,
    And the King loved good yeomanrye.

66 But God that made the grasse to growe,
    And leaves on greenwoode tree,
Now save and keepe our noble king,
    And maintaine good yeomanry !

160

THE KNIGHT OF LIDDESDALE

William Douglas, the Knight of Liddesdale, who figures in the foregoing ballad (No. 159) was assassinated in 1353, while hunting in Ettrick forest, by his kinsman and godson, William Lord Douglas. According to the Scotichronicon, the motive was said to be revenge for the death by starvation of Alexander Ramsay and the murder of Sir David Berkeley. Hume of Godscroft considers the motive assigned to be quite unnatural, and at best a pretence. A ballad known to him gave a different account. “ The Lord of Liddesdale, being at his pastime, hunting in Attrick forest, is beset by William Earle of Douglas, and such as hee had ordained for that purpose, and there assailed, wounded, and slain, beside Galsewood, in the year 1353 ; upon a jealousie that the Earle had conceived of him with his lady, as the report goeth, for so says the old song.” After citing the stanza which follows, Hume goes on to say: “ The song also declareth how shee did write her love-letters to Liddisdale, to disswade him from that hunting. It tells likewise the manner of the taking of his men, and his owne killing at Galsewood, and how hee was carried the first night to Lindin Kirk, a mile from Selkirk, and was buried within the Abbacie of Melrose.”

“ The sole basis for this statement of Hume’s,” says Sir William Fraser (The Douglas

Book, 1, 223 f., 1885), “ seems to be the anonymous Border ballad, part of which he quotes, to which he adds the tradition that the lady wrote to her lover to dissuade him from that hunting. Apart from the fact that this tradition is opposed to contemporary history, which states that Sir William was wholly unsuspicious of danger, the story told by Godscroft is otherwise erroneous. . . . Douglas was not created earl until 26th January, 1357–8, and there was therefore no ‘ Countess of Douglas ’ to wail for the Knight of Liddesdale. Douglas’s only wife was Lady Margaret of Mar, who survived him. Douglass had no countess of the family of March in 1353, while it is doubtful if at that date he was married. Popular tradition is therefore at fault in assigning matrimonial jealousy as a motive for killing the Knight of Liddesdale.”

Hume of Godscroft, History of the Houses of Douglas and Angus, 1644, p. 77.

The Countesse of Douglas out of her boure
    she came,
    And loudly there that she did call:
‘ It is for the Lord of Liddesdale
    That I let all these teares downe fall.’

161

THE BATTLE OF OTTERBURN

The Battle of Otterburn was fought on August 19th, 1388. The most circumstantial account may be found in Froissart’s Chronicles. His narrative is, as usual, highly felicitous, and is based on the authority of knights and squires actually present, both English and Scots, and also French. That a Scots ballad of Otterburn was popular in the sixteenth century appears from The Complaynte of Scotlande, 1549, where a line is cited, “ The Perssee and the Mongumrye met ” (p. 65, ed. Murray). Motherwell maintains that the ballad which passes as English (A) is the Scots song altered to please the other party ; but his argument is far from conclusive. There is no reason to doubt that a Scots ballad once existed, much better than the two inferior, and partly suspicious, things which were printed by Herd and Scott ; but there is no evidence, positive or probable, that A was adapted from the Scots song made of Otterburn. Rather are we to infer that the few verses of B and C which repeat or resemble the text of A were borrowed from A.

A, in the shape in which it has come down to us, must have a date long subsequent to the battle, but is likely to have been modernized from a ballad current as early as 1400. Scott's version (C) of the Scottish ballad in the second edition of the Minstrelsy is put together, for the most part, from two copies sent him by James Hogg. These copies are here printed as C*, and Scott's text is given in the Notes.

A

a. Cotton MS. Cleopatra, C. iv, leaf 64, of about 1550. b. Harleian MS. 293, leaf 52. Both in the British Museum.

1 Yt fell abowght the Lamasse tyde,
   Whan husbondes wynnes ther haye,
The dowghtye Dowglasse bowynd hym
    to ryde,
   In Ynglond to take a praye.

2 The yerlle of Fyffe, wythowghten stryffe,
   He bowynd hym over Sulway;
The grete wolde ever to-gether ryde;
   That raysse they may rewe for aye.

3 Over Hoppertope hyll they cam in,
   And so down by Rodclyffe crage;
Vpon Grene Lynton they lyghted dowyn,
   Styrande many a stage.

4 And boldely brente Northomberlond,
   And haryed many a towyn;
They dyd owr Ynglyssh men grete
    wrange,
   To batell that were not bowyn.

5 Than spake a berne vpon the bent,
   Of comforte that was not colde,
And sayd, We haue brente Northomber-
    lond,
   We haue all welth in holde.

6 Now we haue haryed all Bamborowe
    schyre,
   All the welth in the worlde haue wee,
I rede we ryde to Newe Castell,
   So styll and stalworthlye.

7 Vpon the morowe, when it was day,
   The standerds schone full bryght;
To the Newe Castell the toke the waye,
   And thether they cam full ryght.

8 Syr Henry Perssy laye at the New Castell,
   I tell yow wythowtten drede;

He had byn a march-man all hys dayes,
   And kepte Barwyke vpon Twede.

9 To the Newe Castell when they cam,
   The Skottes they cryde on hyght.
'Syr Hary Perssy, and thou byste within,
   Com to the fylde, and fyght.

10 'For we haue brente Northomberlonde,
   Thy erytage good and ryght,
And syne my logeyng I haue take
   Wyth my brande dubbyd many a
    knyght.'

11 Syr Harry Perssy cam to the walles,
   The Skottyssch oste for to se,
And sayd, And thou hast brente North-
    omberlond,
   Full sore it rewyth me.

12 Yf thou hast haryed all Bamborowe
    schyre,
   Thow hast done me grete envye;
For the trespasse thow hast me done,
   The tone of vs schall dye.

13 'Where schall I byde the?' sayd the
    Dowglas,
   'Or where wylte thow com to me?'
'At Otterborne, in the hygh way,
   [T]her mast thow well logeed be.

14 '[T]he roo full rekeles ther sche rinnes,
   [T]o make the game a[nd] glee;
[T]he fawken and the fesaunt both,
   Among the holtes on hye.

15 'Ther mast thow haue thy welth at wyll,
   Well looged ther mast be;
Yt schall not be long or I com the
    tyll,'
   Sayd Syr Harry Perssye.

16 'Ther schall I byde the,' sayd the Dowg-
    las,
   'By the fayth of my bodye:'
'Thether schall I com,' sayd Syr Harry
    Perssy,
   'My trowth I plyght to the.'

17 A pype of wyne he gaue them over the
    walles,
   For soth as I yow saye;
Ther he mayd the Dowglasse drynke,
   And all hys ost that daye.

18 The Dowglas turnyd hym homewarde
    agayne,
For soth wit*h*owghten naye;
He toke hys logeyng at Oterborne,
    Vpon a Wedynsday.

19 And ther he pyght hys standerd dowyn,
    Hys gettyng more and lesse,
And syne he warned hys men to goo
    To chose ther geldyng*es* gresse.

20 A Skottysshe knyght hoved vpon the
    bent,
A wache I dare well saye;
So was he ware on the noble Perssy,
    In the dawnyng of the daye.

21 He prycked to hys pavyleon-dore,
    As faste as he myght ronne;
'Awaken, Dowglas,' cryed the knyght,
    'For hys love that syttes in trone.

22 'Awaken, Dowglas,' cryed the knyght,
    'For thow maste waken wyth wynne;
Yender haue I spyed the prowde Perssye,
    And seven stondardes wyth hym.'

23 'Nay by my trowth,' the Dowglas sayed,
    'It ys but a fayned taylle;
He durst not loke on my brede banner
    For all Ynglonde so haylle.

24 'Was I not yesterdaye at the Newe Cas-
    tell,
That stond*es* so fayre on Tyne ?
For all the men the Perssy had,
    He coude not garre me ones to
    dyne.'

25 He stepped owt at his pavelyon-dore,
    To loke and it were lesse:
'Araye yow, lordyng*es*, one and all,
    For here bygynnes no peysse.

26 'The yerle of Mentaye, thow arte my
    eme,
The fowarde I gyve to the:
The yerlle of Huntlay, cawte and kene,
    He schall be w*yth* the.

27 'The lorde of Bowghan, in armure
    bryght,
On the other hand he schall be;
Lord Jhonsto*u*ne and Lorde Maxwell,
    They to schall be w*yth* me.

28 'Swynton, fayre fylde vpon your pryde !
    To batell make yow bowen
Syr Davy Skotte, Syr Water Stewarde,
    Syr Jhon of Agurstone !'

29 The Perssy cam byfore hys oste,
    Wych was ever a gentyll knyght;
Vpon the Dowglas lowde can he crye,
    'I wyll holde that I haue hyght.

30 'For thou haste brente Northomber-
    londe,
And done me grete envye;
For thys trespasse thou hast me done,
    The tone of vs schall dye.'

31 The Dowglas answerde hym agayne,
    W*yth* grett wurd*es* vpon hye,
And sayd, I haue twenty agaynst thy one,
    Byholde, and thou maste see.

32 Wyth that the Perssy was grevyd sore,
    For soth as I yow saye;
He lyghted dowyn vpon his foote,
    And schoote hys horsse clene awaye.

33 Euery man sawe that he dyd soo,
    That ryall was euer in rowght;
Euery man schoote hys horsse hym froo,
    And lyght hym rowynde abowght.

34 Thus Syr Hary Perssye toke the fylde,
    For soth as I yow saye;
Jh*esu* Cryste in hevyn on hyght
    Dyd helpe hym well that daye.

35 But nyne thowzand, ther was no moo,
    The cronykle wyll not layne;
Forty thowsande of Skottes and fowre
    That day fowght them agayne.

36 But when the batell byganne to ioyne,
    In hast ther cam a knyght;
The letters fayre furth hath he tayne,
    And thus he sayd full ryght:

37 'My lorde your father he gretes yow
    well,
Wyth many a noble knyght;
He desyres yow to byde
    That he may see thys fyght.

38 'The Baron of Grastoke ys com out of
    the west,
Wyth hym a noble companye;

All they loge at your fathers thys nyght,
And the batell fayne wolde they see.'

39 'For Jhesus love,' sayd Syr Harye
Perssy,
'That dyed for yow and me,
Wende to my lorde my father agayne,
And saye thow sawe me not wyth yee.

40 'My trowth ys plyght to yonne Skot-
tysh knyght,
It nedes me not to layne,
That I schulde byde hym vpon thys
bent,
And I haue hys trowth agayne.

41 'And if that I w[e]ynde of thys grow-
ende,
For soth, onfowghten awaye,
He wolde me call but a kowarde knyght
In hys londe another daye.

42 'Yet had I lever to be rynde and rente,
By Mary, that mykkel maye,
Then ever my manhood schulde be re-
provyd
Wyth a Skotte another day.

43 'Wherfore schote, archars, for my
sake,
And let scharpe arowes flee;
Mynstrells, playe vp for your waryson,
And well quyt it schall bee.

44 'Euery man thynke on hys trewe-love,
And marke hym to the Trenite;
For to God I make myne avowe
Thys day wyll I not flee.'

45 The blodye harte in the Dowglas armes,
Hys standerde stode on hye,
That euery man myght full well knowe;
By syde stode starrës thre.

46 The whyte lyon on the Ynglyssh perte,
For soth as I yow sayne,
The lucettes and the cressawntes both;
The Skottes favght them agayne.

47 Vpon Sent Androwe lowde can they
crye,
And thrysse they schowte on hyght,
And syne merked them one owr Yn-
glysshe men,
As I haue tolde yow ryght.

48 Sent George the bryght, owr ladyes
knyght,
To name they were full fayne;
Owr Ynglyssh men they cryde on hyght,
And thrysse the schowtte agayne.

49 Wyth that scharpe arowes bygan to flee,
I tell yow in sertayne;
Men of armes byganne to joyne,
Many a dowghty man was ther slayne.

50 The Perssy and the Dowglas mette,
That ether of other was fayne;
They swapped together whyll that the
swette,
Wyth swordes of fyne collayne:

51 Tyll the bloode from ther bassonnettes
ranne,
As the roke doth in the rayne;
'Yelde the to me,' sayd the Dowglas,
'Or elles thow schalt be slayne.

52 'For I see by thy bryght bassonet,
Thow arte sum man of myght;
And so I do by thy burnysshed brande;
Thow arte an yerle, or elles a knyght.'

53 'By my good faythe,' sayd the noble
Perssye,
'Now haste thow rede full ryght;
Yet wyll I never yelde me to the,
Whyll I may stonde and fyght.'

54 They swapped together whyll that they
swette,
Wyth swordës scharpe and long;
Ych on other so faste thee beette,
Tyll ther helmes cam in peyses
dowyn.

55 The Perssy was a man of strenghth,
I tell yow in thys stounde;
He smote the Dowglas at the swordës
length
That he felle to the growynde.

56 The sworde was scharpe, and sore can
byte,
I tell yow in sertayne;
To the harte he cowde hym smyte,
Thus was the Dowglas slayne.

57 The stonderdes stode styll on eke a syde,
Wyth many a grevous grone;

Ther the fowght the day, and all the
   nyght,
   And many a dowghty man was slayne.

58 Ther was no freke that ther wolde flye,
   But styffely in stowre can stond,
   Ychoue hewyng on other whyll they
    myght drye,
   Wyth many a bayllefull bronde.

59 Ther was slayne vpon the Skottës syde,
   For soth and sertenly,
   Syr James a Dowglas ther was slayne,
   That day that he cowde dye.

60 The yerlle of Mentaye he was slayne,
   Grysely groned vpon the growynd;
   Syr Davy Skotte, Syr Water Stewarde,
   Syr Jhon of Agurstoune.

61 Syr Charllës Morrey in that place,
   That never a fote wold flee;
   Syr Hewe Maxwell, a lorde he was,
   Wyth the Dowglas dyd he dye.

62 Ther was slayne vpon the Skottës syde,
   For soth as I yow saye,
   Of fowre and forty thowsande Scottes
   Went but eyghtene awaye.

63 Ther was slayne vpon the Ynglysshe
   syde,
   For soth and sertenlye,
   A gentell knyght, Syr Jhon Fechewe,
   Yt was the more pety.

64 Syr James Hardbotell ther was slayne,
   For hym ther hartes were sore;
   The gentyll Lovell ther was slayne,
   That the Perssys standerd bore.

65 Ther was slayne vpon the Ynglyssh
   perte,
   For soth as I yow saye,
   Of nyne thowsand Ynglyssh men
   Fyve hondert cam awaye.

66 The other were slayne in the fylde;
   Cryste kepe ther sowlles from wo!
   Seyng ther was so fewe fryndes
   Agaynst so many a foo.

67 Then on the morne they mayde them
   beerys
   Of byrch and haysell graye;

Many a wydowe, wyth wepyng teyres,
   Ther makes they fette awaye.

68 Thys fraye bygan at Otterborne,
   Bytwene the nyght and the day;
   Ther the Dowglas lost hys lyffe,
   And the Perssy was lede awaye.

69 Then was ther a Scottysh prisoner tayne,
   Syr Hewe Mongomery was hys name;
   For soth as I yow saye,
   He borowed the Perssy home agayne.

70 Now let vs all for the Perssy praye
   To Jhesu most of myght,
   To bryng hys sowlle to the blysse of
   heven,
   For he was a gentyll knyght.

B

a. Herd's MS., I, 149, II, 30; Herd's Scottish
Songs, 1776, I, 153. b. Scott's Minstrelsy, I, 31,
1802, "corrected" from Herd, 1776, "by a
MS. copy."

1 IT fell and about the Lammas time,
   When husbandmen do win their hay,
   Earl Douglass is to the English woods,
   And a' with him to fetch a prey.

2 He has chosen the Lindsays light,
   With them the gallant Gordons gay,
   And the Earl of Fyfe, withouten strife,
   And Sir Hugh Montgomery upon a
   grey.

3 They have taken Northumberland,
   And sae hae they the north shire,
   And the Otter Dale, they hae burnt it
   hale,
   And set it a' into fire.

4 Out then spake a bonny boy,
   That servd ane o Earl Douglass kin;
   Methinks I see an English host,
   A-coming branken us upon

5 'If this be true, my little boy,
   And it be troth that thou tells me,
   The brawest bower in Otterburn
   This day shall be thy morning-fee.

6 'But if it be fase, my little boy,
   But and a lie that thou tells me,

On the highest tree that 's in Otterburn
    With my ain hands I 'll hing thee
        high.'

7 The boy 's taen out his little penknife,
    That hanget low down by his gare,
    And he gaed Earl Douglass a deadly
        wound,
        Alack ! a deep wound and a sare.

8 Earl Douglas said to Sir Hugh Mont-
        gomery,
    Take thou the vanguard o the three,
    And bury me at yon braken-bush,
        That stands upon yon lilly lee.

9 Then Percy and Montgomery met,
    And weel a wot they warna fain;
    They swaped swords, and they twa swat,
        And ay the blood ran down between.

10 'O yield thee, yield thee, Percy,' he said,
    'Or else I vow I 'll lay thee low;'
    'Whom to shall I yield,' said Earl Percy,
        'Now that I see it maun be so ?'

11 'O yield thee to yon braken-bush,
    That grows upon yon lilly lee;
        .   .   .   .   .   .
        .   .   .   .   .   .

12 'I winna yield to a braken-bush,
    Nor yet will I unto a brier;
    But I would yield to Earl Douglass,
        Or Sir Hugh Montgomery, if he was
        here.'

13 As soon as he knew it was Montgomery,
    He stuck his sword's point in the
        ground,
    And Sir Hugh Montgomery was a cour-
        teous knight,
    And he quickly broght him by the
        hand.

14 This deed was done at Otterburn,
    About the breaking of the day;
    Earl Douglass was buried at the braken-
        bush,
    And Percy led captive away.

C*

Scotch Ballads, Materials for Border Minstrelsy, No. 132, Abbotsford, stanzas 1–24,
35–38, 40; the same, No. 5, stanzas 25–34, 39.

Communicated to Scott, in a letter, by James
Hogg.

1 It fell about the Lammas time,
    When the muir-men won their hay,
    That the doughty Earl Douglas went
        Into England to catch a prey.

2 He chose the Gordons and the Graemes,
    With the Lindsays light and gay;
    But the Jardines wadna wi him ride,
        And they rued it to this day.

3 And he has burnt the dales o Tine
    And part of Almonshire,
    And three good towers on Roxburgh fells
        He left them all on fire.

4 Then he marchd up to Newcastle,
    And rode it round about:
    'O whae 's the lord of this castle,
        Or whae 's the lady o 't ?'

5 But up spake proud Lord Piercy then,
    And O but he spak hie !
    I am the lord of this castle,
        And my wife 's the lady gaye.

6 'If you are lord of this castle,
    Sae weel it pleases me;
    For ere I cross the border again
        The ane of us shall die.'

7 He took a lang speir in his hand,
    Was made of the metal free,
    And for to meet the Douglas then
        He rode most furiously.

8 But O how pale his lady lookd,
    Frae off the castle wa,
    When down before the Scottish spear
        She saw brave Piercy fa !

9 How pale and wan his lady lookd,
    Frae off the castle hieght,
    When she beheld her Piercy yield
        To doughty Douglas' might !

10 'Had we twa been upon the green,
    And never an eye to see,
    I should have had ye flesh and fell;
        But your sword shall gae wi me.'

11 'But gae you up to Otterburn,
    And there wait dayes three.

And if I come not ere three days' end
  A fause lord ca ye me.'

12 'The Otterburn 's a bonny burn,
  'T is pleasant there to be,
But there is naught at Otterburn
  To feed my men and me.

13 'The deer rins wild owr hill and dale,
  The birds fly wild frae tree to tree,
And there is neither bread nor kale
  To fend my men and me.

14 'But I will stay at Otterburn,
  Where you shall welcome be;
And if ye come not ere three days' end
  A coward I 'll ca thee.'

15 'Then gae your ways to Otterburn,
  And there wait dayes three;
And if I come not ere three days' end
  A coward ye 's ca me.'

16 They lighted high on Otterburn,
  Upon the bent so brown,
They lighted high on Otterburn,
  And threw their pallions down.

17 And he that had a bonny boy
  Sent his horses to grass,
And he that had not a bonny boy
  His ain servant he was.

18 But up then spak a little page,
  Before the peep of the dawn;
'O waken ye, waken ye, my good lord,
  For Piercy 's hard at hand!'

19 'Ye lie, ye lie, ye loud liar,
  Sae loud I hear ye lie !
The Piercy hadna men yestreen
  To dight my men and me.

20 'But I have seen a dreary dream,
  Beyond the isle o Sky;
I saw a dead man won the fight,
  And I think that man was I.'

21 He belted on his good broad-sword
  And to the field he ran,
Where he met wi the proud Piercy,
  And a' his goodly train.

22 When Piercy wi the Douglas met,
  I wat he was right keen;

They swakked their swords till sair they
    swat,
  And the blood ran them between.

23 But Piercy wi his good broad-sword,
  Was made o the metal free,
Has wounded Douglas on the brow
  Till backward he did flee.

24 Then he calld on his little page,
  And said, Run speedily,
And bring my ain dear sister's son,
  Sir Hugh Montgomery.

25 [Who, when he saw the Douglas bleed,
  His heart was wonder wae:
'Now, by my sword, that haughty
    lord
Shall rue before he gae.'

26 'My nephew bauld,' the Douglas said,
  'What boots the death of ane ?
Last night I dreamd a dreary dream,
  And I ken the day 's thy ain.

27 'I dreamd I saw a battle fought
  Beyond the isle o Sky,
When lo, a dead man wan the field,
  And I thought that man was I.

28 'My wound is deep, I fain wad sleep,
  Nae mair I 'll fighting see;
Gae lay me in the breaken bush
  That grows on yonder lee.

29 'But tell na ane of my brave men
  That I lye bleeding wan,
But let the name of Douglas still
  Be shouted in the van.

30 'And bury me here on this lee,
  Beneath the blooming brier,
And never let a mortal ken
  A kindly Scot lyes here.'

31 He liftit up that noble lord,
  Wi the saut tear in his ee,
And hid him in the breaken bush,
  On yonder lily lee.

32 The moon was clear, the day drew
    near,
  The spears in flinters flew,
But mony gallant Englishman
  Ere day the Scotsmen slew.

33 Sir Hugh Montgomery he rode
    Thro all the field in sight,
  And loud the name of Douglas still
    He urgd wi a' his might.

34 The Gordons good, in English blood
    They steepd their hose and shoon,
  The Lindsays flew like fire about,
    Till a' the fray was doon.]

35 When stout Sir Hugh wi Piercy met,
    I wat he was right fain;
  They swakked their swords till sair they
      swat,
    And the blood ran down like rain.

36 'O yield thee, Piercy,' said Sir Hugh,
    'O yield, or ye shall die!'
  'Fain wad I yield,' proud Piercy said,
    'But neer to loun like thee.'

37 'Thou shalt not yield to knave nor loun,
    Nor shalt thou yield to me;
  But yield thee to the breaken bush
    That grows on yonder lee.'

38 'I will not yield to bush or brier,
    Nor will I yield to thee;
  But I will yield to Lord Douglas,
    Or Sir Hugh Montgomery.'

39 [When Piercy knew it was Sir Hugh,
    He fell low on his knee,
  But soon he raisd him up again,
    Wi mickle courtesy.]

40 He left not an Englishman on the field
   .   .   .   .   .
  That he hadna either killd or taen
    Ere his heart's blood was cauld.

162

THE HUNTING OF THE CHEVIOT

The 'Hunttis of Chevet' is among the "sangis of natural music of the antiquite" mentioned as sung by the "shepherds" in The Complaynte of Scotlande, 1549. It was an old and a popular song at the middle of the sixteenth century. A, the copy in the Ashmolean manuscript, is subscribed 'Expliceth. quod Rychard Sheale,' upon which ground Sheale has been held to be the author, and not, as Percy and Ritson assumed, simply the transcriber, of the ballad. Sheale describes himself as a minstrel living at Tamworth, whose business was to 'sing and talk,' or to chant ballads and tell stories. He was the author of four pieces of verse in the same manuscript, one of which is of the date 1559. This and another piece, in which he tells how he was robbed of above threescore pound, give a sufficient idea of his dialect and style and a measure of his ability. This ballad was of course part of his stock as minstrel; the supposition that he was the author is preposterous in the extreme.

'The Battle of Otterburn' (No. 161) and 'The Hunting of the Cheviot' appear to be founded upon the same occurrence, 'The Hunting of the Cheviot' being the later of the two, and following in part its own tradition, though repeating some portions of the older ballad. The grammatical forms of A are, however, earlier than those of the particular copy of 'The Battle of Otterburn' which has been preserved. Sidney's well-known words may apply either to 'Otterburn' or to the present ballad: "Certainly I must confesse my own barbarousnes, I never heard the olde song of Percy and Duglas, that I found not my heart mooued more then with a Trumpet," etc. (Apologie for Poetrie, ed. Arber, p. 46).

B is a striking but by no means a solitary example of the impairment which an old ballad would suffer when written over for the broadside press. This very seriously enfeebled edition was in circulation throughout the seventeenth century, and much sung (says Chappell) despite its length. It is declared by Addison, in his appreciative and tasteful critique (Spectator, Nos. 70, 74, 1711), to be the favorite ballad of the common people of England. Addison, who knew no other version, informs us that Ben Jonson used to say that he had rather have been the author of Chevy Chase than of all his works. The broadside copy may possibly have been the only one known to Jonson also, but in all probability the traditional ballad was still sung in the streets in Jonson's youth, if not later.

A

MS. Ashmole, 48, Bodleian Library, in Skeat's Specimens of English Literature, 1394–1579, third edition, 1880, p. 67.

1 THE Persë owt off Northombarlonde,
    and avowe to God mayd he
  That he wold hunte in the mowntayns
    off Chyviat within days thre,
  In the magger of doughtë Dogles,
    and all that euer with him be.

2 The fattiste hart*es* in all Cheviat
  he sayd he wold kyll, and cary them
    away:
  ' Be my feth,' sayd *th*e dougheti Doglas
    agayn,
  ' I wyll let *that* hontyng yf *that* I
    may.'

3 The[n] *th*e Persë owt off Banborowe cam,
  w*ith* him a myghtee meany,
  W*ith* fifteen hondrith archar*es* bold off
    blood and bone;
  *th*e wear chosen owt of shyars thre.

4 This begane on a Monday at morn,
  in Cheviat the hillys so he;
  The chylde may rue that ys vn-born,
  it wos the mor pittë.

5 The dryvars thorowe the wood*es* went,
  for to reas the dear;
  Bomen byckarte vppone the bent
  w*ith* ther browd aros cleare.

6 Then the wyld thorowe the wood*es* went,
  on eu*er*y sydë shear;
  Greahond*es* thorowe the grevis glent,
  for to kyll thear dear.

7 *Th*is begane in Chyviat *th*e hyls abone,
  yerly on a Monnyn-day;
  Be *that* it drewe to the oware off none,
  a hondrith fat hart*es* ded *the*r lay.

8 The blewe a mort vppone *th*e bent,
  *th*e semblyde on sydis shear;
  To the quyrry then the Persë went,
  to se the bryttlynge off the deare.

9 He sayd, It was the Duglas promys
  this day to met me hear;
  But I wyste he wolde faylle, verament;
  a great oth *th*e Persë swear.

10 At the laste a squyar off Northomber-
    londe
  lokyde at his hand full ny;
  He was war a the doughetie Doglas
    commynge,
  with him a myghttë meany.

11 Both with spear, bylle, and brande,
  yt was a myghtti sight to se;
  Hardyar men, both off hart nor hande,
  wear not in Cristiantë.

12 The wear twenti hondrith spear-men
    good,
  withoute any feale;
  The wear borne along be the watt*er* a
    Twyde,
  yth bownd*es* of Tividale.

13 ' Leave of the brytlyng of the dear,' he
    sayd,
  ' and to your boÿs lock ye tayk good
    hede;
  For neu*er* sithe ye wear on your mothars
    borne
  had ye neu*er* so mickle nede.'

14 The dougheti Dogglas on a stede,
  he rode all*e* his men beforne;
  His armor glytteryde as dyd a glede;
  a boldar barne was nev*er* born.

15 ' Tell me whos men ye ar,' he says,
  ' o*r* whos men that ye be:
  Who gave youe leave to hunte in this
    Chyviat chays,
  in *th*e spyt of myn and of me.'

16 The first mane that ev*er* him an answear
    mayd,
  yt was *th*e good lord Persë:
  ' We wyll not tell the whoys men we ar,'
    he says,
  ' nor whos men *that* we be;
  But we wyll hounte hear in this chays,
  in the spyt of thyne and of the.

17 ' *Th*e fattiste hart*es* in all Chyviat
  we haue kyld, and cast to carry them
    away: '
  ' Be my troth,' sayd *th*e doughetë Dog-
    glas agay[n],
  ' *the*rfor the ton of vs shall de this day.'

18 Then sayd the doughtë Doglas
  unto the lord Persë:
  ' To kyll all*e* thes giltles men,
  alas, it wear great pittë !

19 ' But, Persë, thowe art a lord of lande,
  I am a yerle callyd w*ith*in my contrë;
  Let all our men vppone a p*ar*ti stande,
  and do the battell off the and of me.'

20 ' Nowe Crist*es* cors on his crowne,' sayd
    the lorde Persë,
  ' who-so-euer *the*r-to says nay !

Be my troth, doughttë Doglas,' he
    says,
  'thow shalt neuer se that day.

21 'Nethar in Ynglonde, Skottlonde, nar
      France,
    nor for no man of a woman born,
  But, and fortune be my chance,
    I dar met him, on man for on.'

22 Then bespayke a squyar off Northom-
      barlonde,
    Richard Wytharyngton was his nam;
  'It shall neuer be told in Sothe-Yn-
      glonde,' he says,
  'To Kyng Herry the Fourth for
      sham.

23 'I wat youe byn great lordës twaw,
    I am a poor squyar of lande;
  I wylle neuer se my captayne fyght on
      a fylde,
    and stande my selffe and loocke on,
  But whylle I may my weppone welde,
    I wylle not [fayle] both hart and
      hande.'

24 That day, that day, that dredfull day !
      the first fit here I fynde;
  And youe wyll here any mor a the
      hountynge a the Chyviat,
    yet ys ther mor behynde.

25 The Yngglyshe men hade ther bowys
      yebent,
    ther hartes wer good yenoughe;
  The first off arros that the shote off,
    seven skore spear-men the sloughe.

26 Yet byddys the yerle Doglas vppon the
      bent,
    a captayne good yenoughe,
  And that was sene verament,
    for he wrought hom both woo and
      wouche.

27 The Dogglas partyd his ost in thre,
    lyk a cheffe cheften off pryde;
  With suar spears off myghttë tre,
    the cum in on euery syde;

28 Thrughe our Yngglyshe archery
      gave many a wounde fulle wyde;
  Many a doughetë the garde to dy,
    which ganyde them no pryde.

29 The Ynglyshe men let ther boys be,
      and pulde owt brandes that wer
        brighte;
    It was a hevy syght to se
      bryght swordes on basnites lyght.

30 Thorowe ryche male and myneyeple,
      many sterne the strocke done streght;
    Many a freyke that was fulle fre,
      ther vndar foot dyd lyght.

31 At last the Duglas and the Persë met,
      lyk to captayns of myght and of
        mayne;
    The swapte togethar tylle the both
        swat,
      with swordes that wear of fyn myllan.

32 Thes worthë freckys for to fyght,
      ther-to the wear fulle fayne,
    Tylle the bloode owte off thear basnetes
        sprente,
      as euer dyd heal or ra[y]n.

33 'Yelde the, Persë,' sayde the Doglas,
      'and i feth I shalle the brynge
    Wher thowe shalte haue a yerls wagis
      of Jamy our Skottish kynge.

34 'Thoue shalte haue thy ransom fre,
      I hight the hear this thinge;
    For the manfullyste man yet art thowe
      that euer I conqueryd in filde fight-
        tynge.'

35 'Nay,' sayd the lord Persë,
      'I tolde it the beforne,
    That I wolde neuer yeldyde be
      to no man of a woman born.'

36 With that ther cam an arrowe hastely,
      forthe off a myghttë wane;
    Hit hathe strekene the yerle Duglas
      in at the brest-bane.

37 Thorowe lyvar and longës bathe
      the sharpe arrowe ys gane,
    That neuer after in all his lyffe-days
      he spayke mo wordës but ane:
    That was, Fyghte ye, my myrry men,
      whyllys ye may,
      for my lyff-days ben gan.

38 The Persë leanyde on his brande,
      and sawe the Duglas de;

He tooke the dede mane by the hande,
  and sayd, Wo ys me for the !

39 'To haue savyde thy lyffe, I wolde haue
    partyde with
  my landes for years thre,
  For a better man, of hart nare of hande,
    was nat in all the north contrë.'

40 Off all that se a Skottishe knyght,
    was callyd Ser Hewe the Monggom-
    byrry;
  He sawe the Duglas to the deth was
    dyght,
  he spendyd a spear, a trusti tre.

41 He rod vppone a corsiare
    throughe a hondrith archery:
  He neuer stynttyde, nar neuer blane,
  tylle he cam to the good lord Persë.

42 He set vppone the lorde Persë
    a dynte that was full soare;
  With a suar spear of a myghttë tre
  clean thorow the body he the Persë
    ber,

43 A the tothar syde that a man myght se
    a large cloth-yard and mare:
  Towe bettar captayns wear nat in Cris-
    tiantë
  then that day slan wear ther.

44 An archar off Northomberlonde
    say slean was the lord Persë;
  He bar a bende bowe in his hand,
    was made off trusti tre.

45 An arow that a cloth-yarde was lang
    to the harde stele halyde he;
  A dynt that was both sad and soar
  he sat on Ser Hewe the Monggom-
    byrry.

46 The dynt yt was both sad and sar
    that he of Monggomberry sete;
  The swane-fethars that his arrowe bar
  with his hart-blood the wear wete.

47 Ther was neuer a freake wone foot wolde
    fle,
  but still in stour dyd stand,
  Heawyng on yche othar, whylle the
    myghte dre,
  with many a balfull brande.

48 This battell begane in Chyviat
    an owar befor the none,
  And when even-songe bell was rang,
    the battell was nat half done.

49 The tocke . . on ethar hande
    be the lyght off the mone;
  Many hade no strenght for to stande,
    in Chyviat the hillys abon.

50 Of fifteen hondrith archars of Ynglonde
    went away but seuenti and thre;
  Of twenti hondrith spear-men of Skot-
    londe,
    but even five and fifti.

51 But all wear slayne Cheviat within;
    the hade no streng[th]e to stand on
    by;
  The chylde may rue that ys vnborne,
    it was the mor pittë.

52 Thear was slayne, withe the lord Persë,
    Ser Johan of Agerstone,
  Ser Rogar, the hinde Hartly,
    Ser Wyllyam, the bolde Hearone.

53 Ser Jorg, the worthë Loumle,
    a knyghte of great renowen,
  Ser Raff, the ryche Rugbe,
    with dyntes wear beaten dowene.

54 For Wetharryngton my harte was wo,
    that euer he slayne shulde be;
  For when both his leggis wear hewyne
    in to,
    yet he knyled and fought on hys
    kny.

55 Ther was slayne, with the dougheti
    Duglas,
    Ser Hewe the Monggombyrry,
  Ser Dauy Lwdale, that worthë was,
    his sistars son was he.

56 Ser Charls a Murrë in that place,
    that neuer a foot wolde fle;
  Ser Hewe Maxwelle, a lorde he was,
    with the Doglas dyd he dey.

57 So on the morrowe the mayde them
    byears
    off birch and hasell so g[r]ay;
  Many wedous, with wepyng tears,
    cam to fache ther makys away.

58 Tivydale may carpe off care,
   Northombarlond may mayk great mon,
For towe such captayns as slayne wear
      thear
      on the March-parti shall neuer be
   non.

59 Word ys commen to Eddenburrowe,
      to Jamy the Skottishe kynge,
That dougheti Duglas, lyff-tenant of the
      Marches,
      he lay slean Chyviot within.

60 His handdës dyd he weal and wryng,
      he sayd, Alas, and woe ys me !
Such an othar captayn Skotland within,
      he sayd, ye-feth shuld neuer be.

61 Worde ys commyn to lovly Londone,
      till the fourth Harry our kynge,
That lord Persë, leyff-tenante of the
      Marchis,
      he lay slayne Chyviat within.

62 'God haue merci on his solle,' sayde
      Kyng Harry,
   'good lord, yf thy will it be !
I haue a hondrith captayns in Yng-
      londe,' he sayd,
   'as good as euer was he:
But, Persë, and I brook my lyffe,
      thy deth well quyte shall be.'

63 As our noble kynge mayd his avowe,
      lyke a noble prince of renowen,
For the deth of the lord Persë
      he dyde the battell of Hombyll-
      down;

64 Wher syx and thrittë Skottishe knyghtes
      on a day wear beaten down;
Glendale glytteryde on ther armor
      bryght,
      over castille, towar, and town.

65 This was the hontynge off the Cheviat,
      that tear begane this spurn;
Old men that knowen the grownde well
      yenoughe
   call it the battell of Otterburn.

66 At Otterburn begane this spurne,
      vppone a Monnynday;
Ther was the doughtë Doglas slean,
      the Persë neuer went away.

67 Ther was neuer a tym on the Marche-
      partës
      sen the Doglas and the Persë met,
But yt ys mervele and the rede blude
      ronne not,
      as the reane doys in the stret.

68 Ihesue Crist our balys bete,
      and to the blys vs brynge !
Thus was the hountynge of the Chivyat:
   God send vs alle good endyng !

B

   a. 'Chevy Chase,' Percy MS., p. 188, Hales
and Furnivall, II, 7.   b. Pepys Ballads, I, 92,
No. 45, Magdalene College, Cambridge, broadside, London, printed for M. G.   c. Douce Ballads, fol. 27ᵇ, and Roxburghe Ballads, III, 66,
broadside, printed for F. Coles, T. Vere, and J.
Wright.   d. Wood's Ballads, 401, 48, broadside, printed for F. Coles, T. Vere, and W.
Gilbertson.   e. Bagford Ballads, I, No. 32,
broadside, printed by and for W. Onley.   f. A
Scottish copy, without printer, Harvard College Library.

1 GOD prosper long our noble king,
      our liffes and saftyes all !
A woefull hunting once there did
   in Cheuy Chase befall.

2 To driue the deere with hound and
      horne
      Erle Pearcy took the way:
The child may rue that is vnborne
   the hunting of that day !

3 The stout Erle of Northumberland
      a vow to God did make
His pleasure in the Scottish woods
   three sommers days to take,

4 The cheefest harts in Cheuy C[h]ase
      to kill and beare away:
These tydings to Erle Douglas came
   in Scottland, where he lay.

5 Who sent Erle Pearcy present word
      he wold prevent his sport;
The English erle, not fearing that,
   did to the woods resort,

6 With fifteen hundred bowmen bold,
   all chosen men of might,

Who knew ffull well in time of neede
    to ayme their shafts arright.

7 The gallant greyhound[s] swiftly ran
    to chase the fallow deere;
On Munday they began to hunt,
    ere daylight did appeare.

8 And long before high noone the had
    a hundred fat buckes slaine;
Then hauing dined, the drouyers went
    to rouze the deare againe.

9 The bowmen mustered on the hills,
    well able to endure;
Theire backsids all with speciall care
    that day were guarded sure.

10 The hounds ran swiftly through the
        woods
    the nimble deere to take,
That with their cryes the hills and
        dales
    an eccho shrill did make.

11 Lord Pearcy to the querry went
    to veiw the tender deere;
Quoth he, Erle Douglas promised once
    this day to meete me heere;

12 But if I thought he wold not come,
    noe longer wold I stay.
With that a braue younge gentlman
    thus to the erle did say:

13 'Loe, yonder doth Erle Douglas come,
    hys men in armour bright;
Full twenty hundred Scottish speres
    all marching in our sight.

14 'All men of pleasant Tiuydale,
    fast by the riuer Tweede:'
'O ceaze your sportts!' Erle Pearcy
        said,
    'and take your bowes with speede.

15 'And now with me, my countrymen,
    your courage forth advance!
For there was neuer champion yett,
    in Scottland nor in Ffrance,

16 'That euer did on horsbacke come,
    [but], and if my hap it were,
I durst encounter man for man,
    with him to breake a spere.'

17 Erle Douglas on his milke-white steede,
    most like a baron bold,
Rode formost of his company,
    whose armor shone like gold.

18 'Shew me,' sayd hee, 'whose men you
        bee
    that hunt soe boldly heere,
That without my consent doe chase
    and kill my fallow deere.'

19 The first man that did answer make
    was noble Pearcy hee,
Who sayd, Wee list not to declare
    nor shew whose men wee bee;

20 Yett wee will spend our deerest blood
    thy cheefest harts to slay.
Then Douglas swore a solempne oathe,
    and thus in rage did say:

21 'Ere thus I will outbraued bee,
    one of vs tow shall dye;
I know thee well, an erle thou art;
    Lord Pearcy, soe am I.

22 'But trust me, Pearcye, pittye it were,
    and great offence, to kill
Then any of these our guiltlesse men,
    for they haue done none ill.

23 'Let thou and I the battell trye,
    and set our men aside:'
'Accurst bee [he!]' Erle Pearcye sayd,
    'by whome it is denyed.'

24 Then stept a gallant squire forth —
    Witherington was his name —
Who said, 'I wold not haue it told
    to Henery our king, for shame,

25 'That ere my captaine fought on foote,
    and I stand looking on.
You bee two Erles,' quoth Witherington,
    'and I a squier alone;

26 'I 'le doe the best that doe I may,
    while I haue power to stand;
While I haue power to weeld my sword,
    I 'le fight with hart and hand.'

27 Our English archers bent their bowes:
    their harts were good and trew;
Att the first flight of arrowes sent,
    full foure score Scotts the slew.

28 To driue the deere with hound and horne,
  Dauglas bade on the bent;
  Two captaines moued with mickle might,
  their speres to shiuers went.

29 They closed full fast on euerye side,
  noe slacknes there was found,
  But many a gallant gentleman
  lay gasping on the ground.

30 O Christ ! it was great greeue to see
  how eche man chose his spere,
  And how the blood out of their brests
  did gush like water cleare.

31 At last these two stout erles did meet,
  like captaines of great might;
  Like lyons woode they layd on lode;
  the made a cruell fight.

32 The fought vntill they both did sweat,
  with swords of tempered steele,
  Till blood downe their cheekes like raine
  the trickling downe did feele.

33 ' O yeeld thee, Pearcye ! ' Douglas
    sayd,
  ' And in faith I will thee bringe
  Where thou shall high advanced bee
  by Iames our Scottish king.

34 ' Thy ransome I will freely giue,
  and this report of thee,
  Thou art the most couragious knight
  [that ever I did see.] '

35 ' Noe, Douglas ! ' quoth Erle Percy then,
  ' thy profer I doe scorne;
  I will not yeelde to any Scott
  that euer yett was borne ! '

36 With that there came an arrow keene,
  out of an English bow,
  Which stroke Erle Douglas on the brest
  a deepe and deadlye blow.

37 Who neuer sayd more words then these;
  Fight on, my merry men all !
  For why, my life is att [an] end,
  lord Pearcy sees my fall.

38 Then leauing liffe, Erle Pearcy tooke
  the dead man by the hand;
  Who said, ' Erle Dowglas, for thy life,
  wold I had lost my land !

39 ' O Christ ! my verry hart doth bleed
  for sorrow for thy sake,
  For sure, a more redoubted knight
  mischance cold neuer take.'

40 A knight amongst the Scotts there
    was
  which saw Erle Douglas dye,
  Who streight in hart did vow revenge
  vpon the Lord Pearcye.

41 Sir Hugh Mountgomerye was he called,
  who, with a spere full bright,
  Well mounted on a gallant steed,
  ran feircly through the fight,

42 And past the English archers all,
  without all dread or feare,
  And through Erle Percyes body then
  he thrust his hatfull spere.

43 With such a vehement force and might
  his body he did gore,
  The staff ran through the other side
  a large cloth-yard and more.

44 Thus did both those nobles dye,
  whose courage none cold staine;
  An English archer then perceiued
  the noble erle was slaine.

45 He had [a] good bow in his hand,
  made of a trusty tree;
  An arrow of a cloth-yard long
  to the hard head haled hee.

46 Against Sir Hugh Mountgomerye
  his shaft full right he sett;
  The grey-goose-winge that was there-on
  in his harts bloode was wett.

47 This fight from breake of day did last
  till setting of the sun,
  For when the rung the euening-bell
  the battele scarse was done.

48 With stout Erle Percy there was slaine
  Sir Iohn of Egerton,
  Sir Robert Harcliffe and Sir William,
  Sir Iames, that bold barron.

49 And with Sir George and Sir Iames,
  both knights of good account,
  Good Sir Raphe Rebbye there was slaine,
  whose prowesse did surmount.

50 For Witherington needs must I wayle
    as one in dolefull dumpes,
For when his leggs were smitten of,
    he fought vpon his stumpes.

51 And with Erle Dowglas there was slaine
    Sir Hugh Mountgomerye,
And Sir Charles Morrell, *that* from
    feelde
one foote wold neu*er* flee;

52 Sir Roger Heuer of Harcliffe tow,
    his sisters sonne was hee;
Sir David Lambwell, well esteemed,
    but saved he cold not bee.

53 And the Lor*d* Maxwell, in like case,
    with Douglas he did dye;
Of twenty hundred Scottish speeres,
    scarce fifty-fiue did flye.

54 Of fifteen hundred Englishmen
    went home but fifty-three;
The rest in Cheuy Chase were slaine,
    vnder the greenwoode tree.

55 Next day did many widdowes come
    their husbands to bewayle;
They washt their wounds in brinish
    teares,
but all wold not prevayle.

56 Theyr bodyes, bathed in purple blood,
    the bore with them away;
They kist them dead a thousand times
    ere the were cladd in clay.

57 The newes was brought to Eddenborrow,
    where Scottlands king did rayne,
That braue Erle Douglas soddainlye
    was with an arrow slaine.

58 'O heauy newes!' King Iames can say;
    'Scottland may wittenesse bee
I haue not any capt*aine* more
    of such account as hee.'

59 Like tydings to King Henery came,
    within as short a space,
That Pearcy of Northumberland
    was slaine in Cheuy Chase.

60 'Now God be with him!' said our
    king,
    'sith it will noe better bee;

I trust I haue within my realme
    fiue hundred as good as hee.

61 'Yett shall not Scotts nor Scottland say
    but I will vengeance take,
And be revenged on them all
    for braue Erle Percyes sake.'

62 This vow the king did well performe
    after on Humble-downe;
In one day fifty knights were slayne,
    with lords of great renowne.

63 And of the rest, of small account,
    did many hundreds dye:
Thus endeth the hunting in Cheuy Chase,
    made by the Erle Pearcye.

64 God saue our king, and blesse this land
    with plentye, ioy, and peace,
And grant henceforth *that* foule debate
    twixt noble men may ceaze!

163

THE BATTLE OF HARLAW

The Battle of Harlaw was fought on the 24th July, 1411. Donald of the Isles, to maintain his claim to the Earldom of Ross, invaded the country south of the mountains with ten thousand islanders and men of Ross in the hope of sacking Aberdeen, and reducing to his power the country as far as the Tay. He was met at Harlaw, eighteen miles northwest of Aberdeen, by Alexander Stewart, Earl of Mar, and Alexander Ogilby, sheriff of Angus, with the forces of Mar, Garioch, Angus, and The Mearns, and his further progress was stayed. The Celts lost more than nine hundred, the Lowlanders five hundred, including nearly all the gentry of Buchan. This defeat was in the interest of civilization against savagery, and was felt, says Burton, "as a more memorable deliverance even than that of Bannockburn."

As might be expected, the Lowlanders made a ballad about this hard fight. 'The battel of the Hayrlau' is noted among other popular songs, in immediate connection with 'The Hunttis of Chevet,' by the author of The Complaynt of Scotland, 1549, but most unfortunately this ancient song, unlike Chevy Chase, has been lost. There is a well-known poem upon the battle, printed by Ramsay, in his Ever Green, 1724, but it is not in the least of a popular character.

A

a. Communicated by Charles Elphinstone Dalrymple, Esq., of Kinaldie, Aberdeenshire, in 1888, as obtained from the country people by himself and his brother fifty years before. b. Notes and Queries. Third Series, VII, 393, communicated by A. Ferguson.

1 As I cam in by Dunidier,
　　An doun by Netherha,
　　There was fifty thousand Hielanmen
　　　A-marching to Harlaw.
　　Wi a dree dree dradie drumtie dree.

2 As I cam on, an farther on,
　　An doun an by Balquhain,
　　Oh there I met Sir James the Rose,
　　　Wi him Sir John the Gryme.

3 'O cam ye frae the Hielans, man?
　　An cam ye a' the wey?
　　Saw ye Macdonell an his men,
　　　As they cam frae the Skee?'

4 'Yes, me cam frae ta Hielans, man,
　　An me cam a' ta wey,
　　An she saw Macdonell an his men,
　　　As they cam frae ta Skee.'

5 'Oh was ye near Macdonell's men?
　　Did ye their numbers see?
　　Come, tell to me, John Hielanman,
　　　What micht their numbers be?'

6 'Yes, me was near, an near eneuch,
　　An me their numbers saw;
　　There was fifty thousan Hielanmen
　　　A-marchin to Harlaw.'

7 'Gin that be true,' says James the Rose,
　　'We'll no come meikle speed;
　　We'll cry upo our merry men,
　　　And lichtly mount our steed.'

8 'Oh no, oh no,' says John the Gryme,
　　'That thing maun never be;
　　The gallant Grymes were never bate,
　　　We'll try phat we can dee.'

9 As I cam on, an farther on,
　　An doun an by Harlaw,
　　They fell fu close on ilka side;
　　　Sic fun ye never saw.

10 They fell fu close on ilka side,
　　Sic fun ye never saw;
　　For Hielan swords gied clash for clash,
　　　At the battle o Harlaw.

11 The Hielanmen, wi their lang swords,
　　They laid on us fu sair,
　　An they drave back our merry men
　　　Three acres breadth an mair.

12 Brave Forbes to his brither did say,
　　Noo brither, dinna ye see?
　　They beat us back on ilka side,
　　　An we'se be forced to flee.

13 'Oh no, oh no, my brither dear,
　　That thing maun never be;
　　Tak ye your good sword in your hand,
　　　An come your wa's wi me.'

14 'Oh no, oh no, my brither dear,
　　The clans they are ower strang,
　　An they drive back our merry men,
　　　Wi swords baith sharp an lang.'

15 Brave Forbes drew his men aside,
　　Said, Tak your rest a while,
　　Until I to Drumminnor send,
　　　To fess my coat o mail.

16 The servan he did ride,
　　An his horse it did na fail,
　　For in twa hours an a quarter
　　　He brocht the coat o mail.

17 Then back to back the brithers twa
　　Gaed in amo the thrang,
　　An they hewed doun the Hielanmen,
　　　Wi swords baith sharp an lang.

18 Macdonell, he was young an stout,
　　Had on his coat o mail,
　　An he has gane oot throw them a',
　　　To try his han himsell.

19 The first ae straik that Forbes strack,
　　He garrt Macdonell reel,
　　An the neist ae straik that Forbes strack,
　　　The great Macdonell fell.

20 An siccan a lierachie
　　I'm sure ye never saw
　　As wis amo the Hielanmen,
　　　When they saw Macdonell fa.

21 An whan they saw that he was deid,
 They turnd an ran awa,
An they buried him in Leggett's Den,
 A large mile frae Harlaw.

22 They rade, they ran, an some did gang,
 They were o sma record;
But Forbës an his merry men,
 They slew them a' the road.

23 On Monanday, at mornin,
 The battle it began,
On Saturday, at gloamin,
 Ye 'd scarce kent wha had wan.

24 An sic a weary buryin
 I 'm sure ye never saw
As wis the Sunday after that,
 On the muirs aneath Harlaw.

25 Gin ony body speer at you
 For them ye took awa,
Ye may tell their wives and bairnies
 They 're sleepin at Harlaw.

B

The Thistle of Scotland, 1823, p. 92.

1 As I cam thro the Garrioch land,
 And in by Over Ha,
There was sixty thousan Highland men
 Marching to Harlaw.

11 The Highland men, with their broad
  sword,
 Pushd on wi might and power,
Till they bore back the red-coat lads
 Three furlongs long, and more.

15 Lord Forbës calld his men aside,
 Says, Take your breath awhile,
Until I send my servant now
 To bring my coat o mail.

164

KING HENRY FIFTH'S CON-
QUEST OF FRANCE

All the known copies are of recent date, and the ballad may probably have first been published in the second quarter of the eighteenth century. The broadside is in a popular manner, but has no mark of antiquity. It may, however, represent an older ballad disfigured by some purveyor for the Aldermary press. The recited versions probably had their ultimate source in print. Another and much more circumstantial ballad on Agincourt, written from the chronicles, was current in the seventeenth century. It may be seen in the Percy Manuscript (Hales and Furnivall, II, 166).

a–d. Broadsides. a. Among Percy's papers. b. Roxburghe Ballads, III, 358. c. Jewitt's Ballads and Songs of Derbyshire, p. 1. d. Chetham's Library, Manchester, in Hales and Furnivall, Percy's Folio MS., II, 597. e. Percy Papers, " taken down from memory." f. Nicolas, History of the Battle of Agincourt, 1832, Appendix, p. 78, from the recitation of a very aged person. g. The same, p. 80, source not mentioned. h. Tyler, Henry of Monmouth, II, 197, apparently from memory. i. Percy Society, XVII, Dixon, Ancient Poems, etc., from singing. j. Skene MS., p. 42. k. Macmath MS., p. 27, from tradition. l, m. Buchan's MSS., I, 176, II, 124, probably broadside or stall copies. n. C. K. Sharpe's " first collection," MS., p. 29.

1 As our king lay musing on his bed,
 He bethought himself upon a time
Of a tribute that was due from France,
 Had not been paid for so long a time.
  Fal, lal, etc.

2 He called for his lovely page,
 His lovely page then called he,
Saying, You must go to the king of
  France,
To the king of France, sir, ride
  speedily.

3 O then went away this lovely page,
 This lovely page then away went he;
And when he came to the king of France,
 Low he fell down on his bended knee.

4 ' My master greets you, worthy sir;
 Ten ton of gold that is due to he,
That you will send him his tribute home,
 Or in French land you soon will him
  see.'

5 ' Your master 's young and of tender
  years,
 Not fit to come into my degree,
And I will send him three tennis-balls,
 That with them he may learn to
  play.'

6 O then returned this lovely page,
   This lovely page then returned he,
   And when he came to our gracious
      king,
   Low he fell down on his bended knee.

7 'What news, what news, my trusty
      page ?
   What is the news you have brought to
      me ? '
   ' I have brought such news from the king
     of France
   That you and he will never agree.

8 'He says you 're young and of tender
     years,
   Not fit to come into his degree,
   And he will send you three tennis-balls,
   That with them you may learn to
     play.'

9 'Recruit me Cheshire and Lancashire,
   And Derby Hills that are so free;
   No marryd man nor no widow's son;
   For no widow's curse shall go with
     me.'

10 They recruited Cheshire and Lanca-
     shire,
   And Derby Hills that are so free;
   No marryd man, nor no widow's son;
   Yet there was a jovial bold company.

11 O then we marchd into the French land,
   With drums and trumpets so merrily;
   And then bespoke the king of France,
   ' Lo, yonder comes proud King
     Henry.'

12 The first shot that the Frenchmen gave,
   They killd our Englishmen so free;
   We killd ten thousand of the French,
   And the rest of them they ran away.

13 And then we marched to Paris gates,
   With drums and trumpets so merrily:
   O then bespoke the king of France,
   ' The Lord have mercy on my men
     and me !

14 'O I will send him his tribute home,
   Ten ton of gold that is due to he,
   And the finest flower that is in all France
   To the Rose of England I will give
     free.'

165

SIR JOHN BUTLER

The subject of this ballad is the murder of
a Sir John Butler at Bewsey Hall, near Warrington, Lancashire. The person meant died
in 1463, and there is no evidence that he was
murdered, though the ballad and a parallel tradition so assert. His wife afterwards married
for her third husband Henry Lord Grey of
Codnor (cf. st. 25).

'Sir Iohn Butler,' Percy MS., p. 427; Hales
and Furnivall, III, 205.

1 BUT word is come to Warrington,
   And Busye Hall is laid about;
   Sir Iohn Butler and his merry men
   Stand in ffull great doubt.

2 When they came to Busye Hall
   Itt was the merke midnight,
   And all the bridges were vp drawen,
   And neuer a candle-light.

3 There they made them one good
     boate,
   All of one good bull skinn;
   William Sauage was one of the ffirst
   That euer came itt within.

4 Hee sayled ore his merrymen,
   By two and two together,
   And said itt was as good a bote
   As ere was made of lether.

5 ' Waken you, waken you, deare ffather !
   God waken you within !
   For heere is your vnckle Standlye
   Come your hall within.'

6 'If *that* be true, Ellen Butler,
   These tydings you tell mee,
   A hundred pound in good redd gold
   This night will not borrow mee.'

7 Then came downe Ellen Butler
   And into her ffathers hall,
   And then came downe Ellen Butler,
   And shee was laced in pall.

8 'Where is thy ffather, Ellen Butler ?
   Haue done, and tell itt mee:'
   ' My ffather is now to London ridden,
   As Christ shall haue *part* of mee.'

9 'Now nay, now nay, Ellen Butler,
　Ffor soe itt must not bee;
　Ffor ere I goe fforth of this hall,
　　Your ffather I must see.'

10 The sought *that* hall then vp and downe
　Theras Iohn Butler lay;
　The sought *that* hall then vp and downe
　Theras Iohn Butler lay.

11 Ffaire him ffall, litle Holcrofft !
　Soe merrilye he kept the dore,
　Till *that* his head ffrom his shoulders
　Came tumbling downe the ffloore.

12 'Yeeld thee, yeelde thee, Iohn Butler !
　Yeelde thee now to mee !'
　'I will yeelde me to my vnckle Stanlye,
　And neere to ffalse Peeter Lee.'

13 'A preist, a preist,' saies Ellen Butler,
　'To housle and to shriue !
　A preist, a preist,' sais Ellen Butler,
　'While *that* my father is a man aliue !'

14 Then bespake him Will*iam* Sauage,
　A shames death may hee dye !
　Sayes, He shall haue no other preist
　But my bright sword and mee.

15 The Ladye Butler is to London rydden,
　Shee had better haue beene att home;
　Shee might haue beggd her owne mar-
　　ryed lo*rd*
　Att her good brother Iohn.

16 And as shee lay in leeue London,
　And as shee lay in her bedd,
　Shee dreamed her owne marryed lo*rd*
　Was swiminnge in blood soe red.

17 Shee called vp her merry men all,
　Long ere itt was day;
　Saies, Wee must ryde to Busye Hall,
　With all speed *that* wee may.

18 Shee mett with three Kendall men,
　Were ryding by the way:
　'Tydings, tydings, Kendall men,
　I pray you tell itt mee !'

19 'Heauy tydings, deare madam;
　Ffrom you wee will not leane;
　The worthyest k*night* in merry England,
　Iohn Butler, Lord ! hee is slaine !'

20 'Ffarewell, ffarwell, Iohn Butler !
　Ffor thee I must neuer see:
　Ffarewell, ffarwell, Busiye Hall !
　For thee I will neu*er* come nye.'

21 Now Ladye Butler is to London againe,
　In all the speed might bee,
　And when shee came before her prince,
　Shee kneeled low downe on her knee.

22 'A boone, a boone, my leege !' shee
　　sayes,
　　'Ffor Gods loue grant itt mee !'
　'What is thy boone, Lady Butler ?
　Or what wold thou haue of mee ?

23 'What is thy boone, Lady Butler ?
　Or what wold thou haue of mee ?'
　'*That* ffalse Peeres of Lee, and my bro-
　　ther Stanley,
　And Will*iam* Sauage, and all, may
　　dye.'

24 'Come you hither, Lady Butler,
　Come you ower this stone;
　Wold you haue three men ffor to dye,
　All ffor the losse off one ?

25 'Come you hither, Lady Butler,
　With all the speed you may;
　If thou wilt come to London, La*dy* But-
　　ler,
　Thou shalt goe home Lady Gray.'

166

THE ROSE OF ENGLAND

The title of this ballad is quoted in Fletcher's *Monsieur Thomas* (printed in 1639), act iii, scene 3. The subject is the winning of the crown of England from Richard III by Henry VII, and the parties on both sides, though some of them are sometimes called by their proper names, are mostly indicated by their badges or cognizances.

The red rose of Lancaster was rooted up by a boar, Richard, who was generally believed to have murdered Henry VI and his son Edward, the Prince of Wales ; but the seed of the rose, the Earl of Richmond, afterwards wore the crown. The sixth stanza gives us to understand that the young Earl of Richmond was under the protection of Lord Stanley at Lathom before his uncle, the Earl of Pembroke, fled with him to Brittany, in 1471; but this does not appear in the histories. The Earl of Richmond came back to claim his right (in 1485), and brought with him the blue boar, the Earl of Oxford, to encounter with Richard, the white boar. Richmond sends a messenger to the old eagle, Lord Stanley, his stepfather, to announce his arrival; Stanley thanks God, and hopes that the rose shall flourish again. The Welshmen rise in a mass under Rice ap Thomas and shog on to Shrewsbury. Master Mitton, bailiff of Shrewsbury, refuses first to let Richmond enter, but, upon receiving letters from Sir William Stanley of Holt Castle, opens the gates. Richmond moves on to Newport, and then has a private meeting at Atherstone with Lord Stanley, who makes great moan because the young eagle, Lord Strange, his eldest son, is a hostage in the hands of the white boar (Richard). At the battle Oxford (the blue boar) has the van; Lord Stanley follows fast. The Talbot-dog (Sir Gilbert Talbot) bites sore; the unicorn (Sir John Savage) quits himself well; then comes in the hart's head (Sir William Stanley), the field is fought, the white boar slain, and the young eagle saved as by fire.

'The Rose of Englande,' Percy MS., p. 423; Hales and Furnivall, III, 187.

1 THROUGHOUT a garden greene and gay,
    A seemlye sight itt was to see
How fflowers did flourish fresh and gay,
    And birds doe sing melodiouslye.

2 In the midst of a garden there sprange
    a tree,
    Which tree was of a mickle price,
And there vppon sprang the rose soe
    redd,
    The goodlyest that euer sprange on
    rise.

3 This rose was ffaire, ffresh to behold,
    Springing with many a royall lance;
A crowned king, with a crowne of gold,
    Ouer England, Ireland, and of
    Ffrance.

4 Then came in a beast men call a bore,
    And he rooted this garden vpp and
    downe;
By the seede of the rose he sett noe
    store,
    But afterwards itt wore the crowne

5 Hee tooke the branches of this rose away,
    And all in sunder did them teare,

And he buryed them vnder a clodd of
    clay,
    Swore they shold neuer bloome nor
    beare.

6 Then came in an egle gleaming gay,
    Of all ffaire birds well worth the best;
He took the branche of the rose away,
    And bore itt to Latham to his nest.

7 But now is this rose out of England ex-
    iled,
    This certaine truth I will not laine;
But if itt please you to sitt a while,
    I 'le tell you how the rose came in
    againe.

8 Att Milford Hauen he entered in,
    To claime his right, was his delight;
He brought the blew bore in with him,
    To encounter with the bore soe white.

9 The[n] a messenger the rose did send
    To the egles nest, and bidd him hye:
' To my ffather, the old egle, I doe [me]
    comend,
    His aide and helpe I craue speedylye.'

10 Saies, I desire my father att my com-
    inge
    Of men and mony att my need,
And alsoe my mother of her deer bless-
    ing;
    The better then I hope to speede.

11 And when the messenger came before
    thold egle,
    He kneeled him downe vpon his knee;
Saith, Well greeteth you my lord the
    rose,
    He hath sent you greetings here by me.

12 Safe ffrom the seas Christ hath him
    sent,
    Now he is entered England within:
' Let vs thanke God,' the old egle did
    say,
    ' He shall be the fflower of all his kine.

13 ' Wend away, messenger, with might
    and maine;
    Itt 's hard to know who a man may
    trust;
I hope the rose shall fflourish againe,
    And haue all things att his owne lust.'

14 Then Sir Rice ap Thomas drawes Wales
       with him;
     A worthy sight itt was to see,
   How the Welchmen rose wholy with him,
     And shogged them to Shrewsburye.

15 Att *that* time was baylye in Shrews-
       burye
     One M*aste*r Mitton, in the towne;
   The gates were strong, and he mad
       them ffast,
     And the portcullis he lett downe.

16 And throug a garrett of the walls,
     Ouer Severne these words said hee;
   'Att these gates no man enter shall;'
     But he kept him out a night and a day.

17 These words Mitton did Erle Richmond
       tell
     (I am sure the chronicles of this will
       not lye);
   But when l*ett*res came from S*ir* W*illia*m
       Stanley of the Holt castle,
     Then the gates were opened present-
       lye.

18 Then entred this towne the noble lord,
     The Erle Richmond, the rose soe
       redd;
   The Erle of Oxford, with a sword,
     Wold haue smitt of the bailiffes head.

19 'But hold yo*ur* hand,' saies Erle Rich-
       mond,
     'Ffor his loue *that* dyed vpon a tree!
   Ffor if wee begin to head so soone,
     In England wee shall beare no de-
       gree.'

20 'What offence haue I made thee,' sayd
       Erle Richmonde,
     'That thou kept me out of my
       towne?'
   'I know no king,' sayd Mitton then,
     'But Rich*ard* now, *that* weares the
       crowne.'

21 'Why, what wilt tho*u* say,' said Erle
       Richmonde,
     'When I haue put K*in*g Richard
       downe?'
   'Why, then Ile be as true to you, my
       l*or*d,
     After the time *tha*t I am sworne.'

22 'Were itt not great pitty,' sayd Erle
       Richmond,
     'That such a man as this shold dye,
   Such loyall service by him done?
     (The cronickles of this will not lye.)

23 'Thou shalt not be harmed in any
       case;'
     He p*ar*done[d] him p*re*sentlye;
   They stayd not past a night and a day,
     But towards Newp*or*t did they hye.

24 But [at] Attherston these lords did
       meete;
     A worthy sight itt was to see,
   How Erle Richmond tooke his hatt in
       his hand,
     And said, Cheshire and Lancashire,
       welcome to me!

25 But now is a bird of the egle taken;
     Ffrom the white bore he cannot fflee;
   Therfore the old egle makes great
       moane,
     And prayes to God most certainly.

26 'O stedfast God, verament,' he did say,
     'Thre p*er*sons in one god in Trinytye,
   Saue my sonne, the young egle, this
       day
     Ffrom all ffalse craft and trecherye!'

27 Then the blew bore the vanward had;
     He was both warry and wise of witt;
   The right hand of them he tooke,
     The sunn and wind of them to gett.

28 Then the egle ffollowed fast vpon his
       pray,
     With sore dints he did them smyte;
   The talbott he bitt wonderous sore,
     Soe well the vnicorne did him quite.

29 And then came in the harts head;
     A worthy sight itt was to see,
   The iacketts *that* were of white and
       redd,
     How they laid about them lustilye.

30 But now is the ffeirce ffeeld foughten
       and ended,
     And the white bore there lyeth
       slaine,
   And the young egle is p*re*serued,
     And come to his nest againe.

31 But now this garden fflourishes ffreshly
     and gay,
   With ffragrant fflowers comely of
     hew,
  And gardners itt doth maintaine;
  I hope they will proue iust and true.

32 Our k*ing*, he is the rose soe redd,
    That now does fflourish ffresh and
     gay :
   Confound his ffoes, L*ord*, wee beseeche,
   And loue His Grace both night and
     day !

167

SIR ANDREW BARTON

  Andrew Barton had letters of reprisal from
the king of Scotland against the Portuguese
in consequence of the seizure of a ship commanded by his father. There is some reason
to believe that he abused this privilege, and in
1511 Sir Thomas and Sir Edward Howard, with
the consent of Henry VIII, set out with two
ships against him. There was a hard fight.
Barton was killed, and his ship, The Lion, was
captured. The king of Scotland demanded redress, which was refused on the ground that
Barton was a pirate.
  A version of this ballad from a sixteenth-
century manuscript in York Minster Library
is much like A. Some of the more interesting variations are given in the Notes. B is a
broadside version, and is here omitted.

A

'Sir Andrew Bartton,' Percy MS., p. 490;
Hales and Furnivall, iii, 399.

1 As itt beffell in m[i]dsumer-time,
   When burds singe sweetlye on euery
     tree,
  Our noble k*ing*, K*ing* Henery the Eighth,
  Ouer the riuer of Thames past hee.

2 Hee was no sooner ouer the riuer,
   Downe in a fforrest to take the ayre,
  But eighty merchants of London cittye
  Came kneeling before K*ing* Henery
     there.

3 'O yee are welcome, rich merchants,
   [Good saylers, welcome vnto me !']

They swore by the rood the were saylers
     good,
  But rich merchants they cold not bee.

4 'To Ffrance nor Fflanders dare we nott
     passe,
   Nor Burdeaux voyage wee dare not
     ffare,
  And all ffor a ffalse robber *that* lyes on
     the seas,
   And robb[s] vs of our merchants-
     ware.'

5 K*ing* Henery was stout, and he turned
     him about,
   And swore by the Lord *that* was
     mickle of might,
  'I thought he had not beene in the
     world throughout
    That durst haue wrought England
     such vnright.'

6 But euer they sighed, and said, alas !
   Vnto K*ing* Harry this answere againe:
  'He is a proud Scott *that* will robb vs
     all
   If wee were twenty shipps and hee
     but one.'

7 The *king* looket ouer his left shoulder,
   Amongst his lords and barrons soe
     ffree:
  'Haue I neuer l*ord* in all my realme
   Will ffeitch yond traitor vnto mee ?'

8 'Yes, *that* dare I !' sayes my l*ord*
     Chareles Howard,
   Neere to the k*ing* wheras hee did
     stand;
  'If *that* Your Grace will giue me leaue,
   My selfe wilbe the only man.'

9 'Thou shalt haue six hundred men,'
     saith our k*ing*,
   'And chuse them out of my realme
     soe ffree;
  Besids marriners and boyes,
   To guide the great shipp on the sea.'

10 'I 'le goe speake with Sir Andrew,' sais
     Charles, my l*ord* Haward;
   'Vpon the sea, if hee be there;
  I will bring him and his shipp to shore,
   Or before my prince I will neu*er*
     come neere.

11 The ffirst of all my lord did call,
   A noble gunner hee was one;
  This man was three score yeeres and
    ten,
   And Peeter Simon was his name.

12 'Peeter,' sais hee, 'I must sayle to the
    sea,
   To seeke out an enemye; God be my
    speed !
  Before all others I haue chosen thee;
   Of a hundred guners thoust be my
    head.'

13 'My lord,' sais hee, 'if you haue chosen
    mee
  Of a hundred gunners to be the head,
  Hange me att your maine-mast tree
   If I misse my marke past three pence
    bread.'

14 The next of all my lord he did call,
   A noble bowman hee was one;
  In Yorekshire was this gentleman
    borne,
   And William Horsley was his name.

15 'Horsley,' sayes hee, 'I must sayle to
    the sea,
   To seeke out an enemye; God be my
    speede !
  Before all others I haue chosen thee;
   Of a hundred bowemen thoust be my
    head.'

16 'My lord,' sais hee, 'if you haue chosen
    mee
  Of a hundred bowemen to be the head,
  Hang me att your mainemast-tree
   If I misse my marke past twelue
    pence bread.'

17 With pikes, and gunnes, and bowemen
    bold,
   This noble Howard is gone to the sea
  On the day before midsummer-euen,
   And out att Thames mouth sayled
    they.

18 They had not sayled dayes three
   Vpon their iourney they tooke in
    hand,
  But there they mett with a noble shipp,
   And stoutely made itt both stay and
    stand.

19 'Thou must tell me thy name,' sais
   Charles, my lord Haward,
    'Or who thou art, or ffrom whence
    thou came,
  Yea, and where thy dwelling is,
   To whom and where thy shipp does
    belong.'

20 'My name,' sayes hee, 'is Henery Hunt,
   With a pure hart and a penitent mind;
  I and my shipp they doe belong
   Vnto the New-castle that stands vpon
    Tine.'

21 'Now thou must tell me, Harry Hunt,
   As thou hast sayled by day and by
    night,
  Hast thou not heard of a stout robber ?
   Men calls him Sir Andrew Bartton,
    knight.'

22 But euer he sighed, and sayd, Alas !
   Ffull well, my lord, I know that
    wight;
  He robd me of my merchants ware,
   And I was his prisoner but yester-
    night.

23 As I was sayling vppon the sea,
   And [a] Burdeaux voyage as I did
    ffare,
  He clasped me to his archborde,
   And robd me of all my merchants-
    ware.

24 And I am a man both poore and bare,
   And euery man will haue his owne of
    me,
  And I am bound towards London to
    ffare,
   To complaine to my prince Henerye.

25 'That shall not need,' sais my lord
   Haward;
    'If thou canst lett me this robber
    see,
  Ffor euery peny he hath taken thee
    ffroe,
   Thou shalt be rewarded a shilling,'
    quoth hee.

26 'Now God fforefend,' saies Henery
   Hunt,
    'My lord, you shold worke soe ffarr
    amisse !

God keepe you out of *that* traitors
   hands !
For you wott ffull litle what a man
   hee is.

27 ' Hee is brasse *within*, and steele *without*,
   And beames hee beares in his top-
      castle stronge;
His shipp hath ordinance cleane round
   about;
   Besids, my lord, hee is verry well
      mand.

28 ' He hath a pinnace, is deerlye dight,
   Saint Andrews crosse, *that* is his
      guide;
His pinnace beares nine score men and
   more,
   Besids fifteen cannons on euery side.

29 ' If you were twenty shippes, and he
   but one,
   Either in archbord or in hall,
He wold ouercome you euerye one,
   And if his beames they doe downe
      ffall.'

30 ' This is cold comfort,' sais my Lord
   Haward,
   ' To wellcome a stranger thus to the sea;
I 'le bring him and his shipp to shore,
   Or else into Scottland hee shall carrye
      mee.'

31 ' Then you must gett a noble gunner,
   my lord,
   That can sett well with his eye,
And sinke his pinnace into the sea,
   And soone then ouercome will hee be.

32 ' And when *that* you haue done this,
   If you chance Sir Andrew for to bord,
Lett no man to his topcastle goe;
   And I will giue you a glasse, my lord,

33 ' And then you need to ffeare no Scott,
   Whether you sayle by day or by
      night;
And to-morrow, by seuen of the clocke,
   You shall meete with Sir Andrew
      Bartton; knight.

34 ' I was his prisoner but yester night,
   And he hath taken mee sworne,' quoth
      hee;

' I trust my L[ord] God will me fforgiue
   And if *that* oath then broken bee.

35 ' You must lend me sixe peeces, my
   lord,' quoth hee,
   ' Into my shipp, to sayle the sea,
And to-morrow, by nine of the clocke,
   Your Honour againe then will I see.'

*   *   *   *   *

36 And the hache-bord where Sir Andrew
   lay
   Is hached with gold deerlye dight:
' Now by my ffaith,' sais Charles, my
   lord Haward,
   ' Then yonder Scott is a worthye
      wight !

37 ' Take in your ancyents and your stand-
   ards,
   Yea *that* no man shall them see,
And put me fforth a white willow wand,
   As merchants vse to sayle the sea.'

38 But they stirred neither top nor mast,
   But Sir Andrew they passed by:
' Whatt English are yonder,' said Sir
   Andrew,
   ' *That* can so litle curtesye ?

39 ' I haue beene admirall ouer the sea
   More then these yeeres three;
There is neuer an English dog, nor
   Portingall,
   Can passe this way without leaue of
      mee.

40 ' But now yonder pedlers, they are past,
   Which is no litle greffe to me:
Ffeich them backe,' sayes Sir Andrew
   Bartton,
   ' They shall all hang att my maine-
      mast tree.'

41 With *that* the pinnace itt shott of,
   That my Lord Haward might itt well
      ken;
Itt stroke downe my lords fforemast,
   And killed fourteen of my lord his
      men.

42 ' Come hither, Simon ! ' sayes my lord
   Haward,
   ' Looke *that* thy words be true thou
      sayd;

I 'le hang thee att my maine-mast tree
    If thou misse thy marke past twelue
        pence bread.'

43 Simon was old, but his hart itt was
      bold;
    Hee tooke downe a peece, and layd
      itt ffull lowe;
He put in chaine yeards nine,
    Besids other great shott lesse and
      more.

44 With *that* hee lett his gun-shott goe;
    Soe well hee settled itt with his eye,
The ffirst sight *that* Sir Andrew sawe,
    Hee see his pinnace sunke in the
      sea.

45 When hee saw his pinace sunke,
    Lord ! in his hart hee was not well:
'Cutt my ropes ! itt is time to be gon !
    I 'le goe ffeitch yond pedlers backe
      my selfe !'

46 When my lord Haward saw Sir An-
      drew loose,
    Lord ! in his hart *that* hee was ffaine:
'Strike on your drummes ! spread out
    your ancyents !
    Sound out your trumpetts ! sound
      out amaine !'

47 'Ffight on, my men !' sais Sir Andrew
      Bartton;
    'Weate, howsoeuer this geere will
      sway,
Itt is my lord Adm[i]rall of England
    Is come to seeke mee on the sea.'

48 Simon had a sonne; with shott of a
      gunn —
    Well Sir Andrew might itt ken —
He shott itt in att a priuye place,
    And killed sixty more of Sir An-
      drews men.

49 Harry Hunt came in att the other syde,
    And att Sir Andrew hee shott then;
He droue downe his fformast-tree,
    And killed eighty more of Sir An-
      driwes men.

50 'I haue done a good turne,' sayes
      Harry Hunt;
    'Sir Androw is not our kings ffreind;

He hoped to haue vndone me yester-
      night,
    But I hope I haue quitt him well in
      the end.'

51 'Euer alas !' sayd Sir Andrew Barton,
    'What shold a man either thinke or
      say ?
Yonder ffalse theeffe is my strongest
      enemye,
    Who was my prisoner but yesterday.

52 'Come hither to me, thou Gourden
      good,
    And be thou readye att my call,
And I will giue thee three hundred
      pound
    If thou wilt lett my beames downe
      ffall.'

53 With *that* hee swarued the maine-mast
      tree,
    Soe did he itt with might and maine;
Horseley, with a bearing arrow,
    Stroke the Gourden through the
      braine.

54 And he ffell into the haches againe,
    And sore of this wound *that* he did
      bleed;
Then word went throug Sir Andrews
      men,
    That the Gourden hee was dead.

55 'Come hither to me, Iames Hambliton,
    Thou art my sisters sonne, I haue no
      more ;
I will giue [thee] six hundred pound
    If thou will lett my beames downe
      ffall.'

56 With *that* hee swarued the maine-mast
      tree,
    Soe did hee itt with might and
      maine:
Horseley, with another broad arrow,
    Strake the yeaman through the
      braine.

57 *That* hee ffell downe to the haches
      againe;
    Sore of his wound *that* hee did bleed;
Couetousness getts no gaine,
    Itt is verry true, as the Welchman
      sayd.

58 But when hee saw his sisters sonne
        slaine,
    Lord ! in his heart hee was not well:
  ' Goe ffeitch me downe my armour of
        proue,
    Ffor I will to the topcastle my-selfe.

59 ' Goe ffeitch me downe my armour of
        prooffe,
    For itt is guilded with gold soe
        cleere;
    God be with my brother, Iohn of Bart-
        ton !
    Amongst the Portingalls hee did itt
        weare.'

60 But when hee had his armour of
        prooffe,
    And on his body hee had itt on,
    Euery man that looked att him
    Sayd, Gunn nor arrow hee neede
        feare none.

61 ' Come hither, Horsley ! ' sayes my lord
        Haward,
    ' And looke your shaft that itt goe
        right;
    Shoot a good shoote in the time of
        need,
    And ffor thy shooting thoust be made
        a knight.'

62 ' I 'le doe my best,' sayes Horslay then,
    ' Your Honor shall see beffore I
        goe ;
    If I shold be hanged att your maine-
        mast,
    I haue in my shipp but arrowes tow.'

63 But att Sir Andrew hee shott then;
    Hee made sure to hitt his marke;
    Vnder the spole of his right arme
    Hee smote Sir Andrew quite throw
        the hart.

64 Yett ffrom the tree hee wold not start,
    But hee clinged to itt with might
        and maine;
    Vnder the coller then of his iacke,
    He stroke Sir Andrew thorrow the
        braine.

65 ' Ffight on my men,' sayes Sir Andrew
        Bartton,
    ' I am hurt, but I am not slaine;

    I 'le lay mee downe and bleed a-while,
    And then I 'le rise and ffight againe.

66 ' Ffight on my men,' sayes Sir Andrew
        Bartton,
    ' These English doggs they bite soe
        lowe;
    Ffight on ffor Scottland and Saint An-
        drew
    Till you heare my whistle blowe ! '

67 But when the cold not heare his whistle
        blow,
    Sayes Harry Hunt, I 'le lay my head
    You may bord yonder noble shipp, my
        lord,
    For I know Sir Andrew hee is dead.

68 With that they borded this noble shipp,
    Soe did they itt with might and
        maine;
    The ffound eighteen score Scotts aliue,
    Besids the rest were maimed and
        slaine.

69 My lord Haward tooke a sword in his
        hand,
    And smote of Sir Andrews head;
    The Scotts stood by did weepe and
        mourne,
    But neuer a word durst speake or say.

70 He caused his body to be taken downe,
    And ouer the hatch-bord cast into
        the sea,
    And about his middle three hundred
        crownes:
    ' Whersoeuer thou lands, itt will bury
        thee.'

71 With his head they sayled into Eng-
        land againe,
    With right good will, and fforce and
        main,
    And the day beffore Newyeeres euen
    Into Thames mouth they came
        againe.

72 My lord Haward wrote to King Hene-
        ryes grace,
    With all the newes hee cold him
        bring:
    ' Such a Newyeeres gifft I haue brought
        to your Gr[ace]
    As neuer did subiect to any king.

73 'Ffor merchandyes and manhood,
    The like is nott to be ffound;
  The sight of these wold doe you good,
    Ffor you haue not the like in your
      English ground.'

74 But when hee heard tell *that* they were
      come,
    Full royally hee welcomed them
      home;
  Sir Andrews shipp was the kings New-
      yeeres guifft;
    A brauer shipp you neuer saw none.

75 Now hath our king Sir Andrews shipp,
    Besett with pearles and precyous
      stones;
  Now hath England two shipps of warr,
    Two shipps of warr, before but one.

76 'Who holpe to this ?' sayes King Hene-
      rye,
    'That I may reward him ffor his
      paine:'
  'Harry Hunt, and Peeter Simon,
    William Horseleay, and I the same.'

77 'Harry Hunt shall haue his whistle and
      chaine,
    And all his iewells, whatsoeuer they
      bee,
  And other rich giffts *that* I will not
      name,
    For his good service he hath done
      mee.

78 'Horslay, right thoust be a knight,
    Lands and liuings thou shalt haue
      store;
  Howard shalbe erle of Nottingham,
    And soe was neuer Haward before.

79 'Now, Peeter Simon, thou art old;
    I will maintaine thee and thy sonne;
  Thou shalt haue fiue hundred pound all
      in gold
    Ffor the good service *that* thou hast
      done.'

80 Then King Henerye shiffted his roome;
    In came the Queene and ladyes
      bright;
  Other arrands they had none
    But to see Sir Andrew Bartton,
      knight.

81 But when they see his deadly fface,
    His eyes were hollow in his head;
  'I wold giue a hundred pound,' sais
    King Henerye,
  'The man were aliue as hee is dead !

82 'Yett ffor the manfull part *that* hee
      hath playd,
    Both heere and beyond the sea,
  His men shall haue halfe a crowne a day
    To bring them to my brother, King
      Iamye.'

168

FLODDEN FIELD

"A booke called Jack of Newberry" was entered to Thomas Millington, March 7, 1597 (Arber, Stationers' Registers, III, 81). The edition of 1633, the earliest which Mr Halliwell-Phillipps had met with, was the ninth, published by Cuthbert Wright. The author has introduced several pieces of verse into his tale, two of them popular ballads, 'The Fair Flower of Northumberland' and this of Flodden, of which Deloney says, "in disgrace of the Scots, and in remembrance of the famous atchieved historie, the commons of England made this song, which to this day is not forgotten of many" (p. 47). The Field of Flodden was fought September 9, 1513. For other pieces (not ballads) on Flodden, see Percy MS., Hales and Furnivall, I, 199 ff., 313 ff.; Robson, Chetham Miscellanies, 1855; The Battle of Flodden Field, edited by Henry Weber, 1808; Child, III, 353 ff.

From Deloney's Pleasant History of John Winchcomb, in his younger yeares called Jacke of Newberie, etc., London, 1633; reprinted by J. O. Halliwell, London, 1859, p. 48.

1 KING JAMIE hath made a vow,
    Keepe it well if he may !
  That he will be at lovely London
    Upon Saint James his day.

2 'Upon Saint James his day at noone,
    At faire London will I be,
  And all the lords in merrie Scotland,
    They shall dine there with me.'

3 Then bespake good Queene Margaret,
    The teares fell from her eye:
  'Leave off these warres, most noble king,
    Keepe your fidelitie.

4 'The water runnes swift and wondrous
        deepe,
    From bottome unto the brimme;
My brother Henry hath men good
        enough;
    England is hard to winne.'

5 'Away,' quoth he, ' with this silly
        foole!
    In prison fast let her lie:
For she is come of the English bloud,
    And for these words she shall dye.'

6 With that bespake Lord Thomas How-
        ard,
    The queenes chamberlaine that day:
'If that you put Queene Margaret to
        death,
    Scotland shall rue it alway.'

7 Then in a rage King Jamie did say,
    'Away with this foolish mome!
He shall be hanged, and the other be
        burned,
    So soone as I come home.'

8 At Flodden Field the Scots came in,
    Which made our English men faine;
At Bramstone Greene this battaile was
        seene,
    There was King Jamie slaine.

9 Then presently the Scots did flie,
    Their cannons they left behind;
Their ensignes gay were won all away,
    Our souldiers did beate them blinde.

10 To tell you plaine, twelve thousand were
        slaine
    That to the fight did stand,
And many prisoners tooke that day,
    The best in all Scotland.

11 That day made many [a] fatherlesse
        child,
    And many a widow poore,
And many a Scottish gay lady
    Sate weeping in her bower.

12 Jack with a feather was lapt all in
        leather,
    His boastings were all in vaine;
He had such a chance, with a new mor-
        rice-dance,
    He never went home againe.

169

JOHNIE ARMSTRONG

'Ihonne Ermistrangis dance' is mentioned in The Complaynt of Scotland, 1549 (ed. Murray, p. 66). The ballad is known in two forms, — one represented by A and B, the other by C. It was an early favorite of Goldsmith's: "The music of the finest singer is dissonance to what I felt when our old dairy-maid sung me into tears with Johnny Armstrong's Last Good-Night, or the Cruelty of Barbara Allen" (Essays, 1765, p. 14).

The Armstrongs were people of consideration in Liddesdale from the end, or perhaps from the middle, of the fourteenth century, and by the sixteenth had become the most important sept, as to numbers, in that region, not only extending themselves over a large part of the Debateable Land, but spreading also into Eskdale, Ewesdale, Wauchopedale, and Annandale. The Earl of Northumberland, in 1528, puts the power of the Armstrongs, with their adherents, above three thousand horsemen. Mangerton, in Liddesdale, on the east bank of the Liddel, a little north of its junction with the Kersope, was the seat of the chief. John Armstrong, known later as Gilnockie, a brother of Thomas, laird of Mangerton, is first heard of in 1525. Removing from Liddesdale early in the century, as it is thought, he settled on the church lands of Canonby, and at a place called The Hollows, on the west side of the Esk, built a tower, which still remains. The Armstrongs, if nominally Scots, were so far from being "in due obeysaunce" that, at a conference of commissioners of both realms in November of the year 1528, the representatives of the Scottish king could not undertake to oblige them to make a redress for injuries done the English, though a peace depended upon this condition. Both the English and the Scottish border suffered from their forays. Other measures having failed, King James V, in 1530, took the pacifying of his borders into his own hand, and for this purpose levied an army of from eight to twelve thousand men. Among the reivers who suffered death was John Armstrong of Gilnockie, the hero of the present ballad. It appears from various accounts that his capture was not effected by honorable means. There is no record of a trial, and the execution was probably as summary as the arrest was perfidious.

A

a. 'A Northern Ballet,' Wit Restord in severall Select Poems not formerly publisht

London, 1658, p. 30, in Facetiæ, London, 1817,
I, 132. **b.** 'A Northern Ballad,' Wit and
Drollery, London, 1682, p. 57.

1 THERE dwelt a man in faire Westmer-
    land,
    Ionnë Armestrong men did him call,
  He had nither lands nor rents coming
    in,
    Yet he kept eight score men in his
    hall.

2 He had horse and harness for them all,
    Goodly steeds were all milke-white;
  O the golden bands an about their
    necks,
    And their weapons, they were all
    alike.

3 Newes then was brought unto the king
    That there was sicke a won as hee,
  That livëd lyke a bold out-law,
    And robbëd all the north country.

4 The king he writt an a letter then,
    A letter which was large and long;
  He signëd it with his owne hand,
    And he promised to doe him no
    wrong.

5 When this letter came Ionnë untill,
    His heart it was as blythe as birds
    on the tree:
  ' Never was I sent for before any king,
    My father, my grandfather, nor none
    but mee.

6 ' And if wee goe the king before,
    I would we went most orderly;
  Every man of you shall have his scar-
    let cloak,
    Laced with silver laces three.

7 ' Every won of you shall have his vel-
    vett coat,
    Laced with sillver lace so white;
  O the golden bands an about your necks,
    Black hatts, white feathers, all alyke.'

8 By the morrow morninge at ten of the
    clock,
    Towards Edenburough gon was hee,
  And with him all his eight score men;
    Good lord, it was a goodly sight for
    to see !

9 When Ionnë came befower the king,
    He fell downe on his knee;
  ' O pardon, my soveraine leige,' he
    said,
    ' O pardon my eight score men and
    mee ! '

10 ' Thou shalt have no pardon, thou traytor
    strong,
    For thy eight score men nor thee;
  For to-morrow morning by ten of the
    clock,
    Both thou and them shall hang on
    the gallow-tree.'

11 But Ionnë looke'd over his left shoulder,
    Good Lord, what a grevious look
    looked hee !
  Saying, Asking grace of a graceles
    face —
    Why there is none for you nor me.

12 But Ionnë had a bright sword by his
    side,
    And it was made of the mettle so free,
  That had not the king stept his foot
    aside,
    He had smitten his head from his
    faire boddë.

13 Saying, Fight on, my merry men all,
    And see that none of you be taine;
  For rather then men shall say we were
    hange'd,
    Let them report how we were slaine.

14 Then, God wott, faire Eddenburrough
    rose,
    And so besett poore Ionnë rounde,
  That fowerscore and tenn of Ionnës best
    men
    Lay gasping all upon the ground.

15 Then like a mad man Ionnë laide about,
    And like a mad man then fought hee,
  Untill a falce Scot came Ionnë behinde,
    And runn him through the faire
    boddee.

16 Saying, Fight on, my merry men all,
    And see that none of you be taine;
  For I will stand by and bleed but
    awhile,
    And then will I come and fight
    againe.

17 Newes then was brought to young
Ionnë Armestrong,
As he stood by his nurses knee,
Who vowed if ere he live'd for to be a man,
O the treacherous Scots revengd hee'd
be.

B

a. 'John Arm-strong's last Good-Night,' etc.,
Wood, 401, fol. 93 b, London, printed for Francis Grove (1620–55 ?). **b.** Pepys, II, 133, No.
117, London, printed for W. Thackeray and
T. Passenger (1660–82 ?). **c.** 'Johnny Armstrongs last Good-Night,' A Collection of Old
Ballads, 1723, I, 170.

1 Is there never a man in all Scotland,
From the highest state to the lowest
degree,
That can shew himself now before the
king ?
Scotland is so full of their traitery.

2 Yes, there is a man in Westmerland,
And John Armstrong some do him
call;
He has no lands nor rents coming in,
Yet he keeps eightscore men within
his hall.

3 He has horse and harness for them all,
And goodly steeds that be milk-white,
With their goodly belts about their necks,
With hats and feathers all alike.

4 The king he writ a lovely letter,
With his own hand so tenderly,
And has sent it unto John Armstrong,
To come and speak with him speedily.

5 When John he looked the letter upon,
Then, Lord ! he was as blithe as a
bird in a tree:
'I was never before no king in my life,
My father, my grandfather, nor none
of us three.

6 'But seeing we must [go] before the king,
Lord ! we will go most valiantly;
You shall every one have a velvet coat,
Laid down with golden laces three.

7 'And you shall every one have a scarlet
cloak,
Laid down with silver laces five,

With your golden belts about your necks,
With hats [and] brave feathers all
alike.'

8 But when John he went from Guiltknock
Hall !
The wind it blew hard, and full sore it
did rain:
'Now fare you well, brave Guiltknock
Hall !
I fear I shall never see thee again.'

9 Now John he is to Edenborough gone,
And his eightscore men so gallantly,
And every one of them on a milk-white
steed,
With their bucklers and swords hang-
ing down to the knee.

10 But when John he came the king before,
With his eightscore men so gallant to
see,
The king he moved his bonnet to him;
He thought he had been a king as well
as he.

11 'O pardon, pardon, my soveraign leige,
Pardon for my eightscore men and
me !
For my name it is John Armstrong,
And a subject of yours, my leige,' said
he.

12 'Away with thee, thou false traitor !
No pardon I will grant to thee,
But, to-morrow before eight of the clock,
I will hang thy eightscore men and
thee.'

13 O how John looked over his left shoul-
der !
And to his merry men thus said he:
I have asked grace of a graceless face,
No pardon here is for you nor me.

14 Then John pulld out a nut-brown
sword,
And it was made of mettle so free;
Had not the king moved his foot as he
did,
John had taken his head from his
body.

15 'Come, follow me, my merry men all,
We will scorn one foot away to fly;

It never shall be said we were hung
like doggs;
No, wee 'l fight it out most manfully.'

16 Then they fought on like champions
bold —
For their hearts was sturdy, stout,
and free —
Till they had killed all the kings good
guard;
There was none left alive but onely
three.

17 But then rise up all Edenborough,
They rise up by thousands three;
Then a cowardly Scot came John be-
hind,
And run him thorow the fair body.

18 Said John, Fight on, my merry men all,
I am a little hurt, but I am not slain;
I will lay me down for to bleed a while,
Then I 'le rise and fight with you
again.

19 Then they fought on like mad men all,
Till many a man lay dead on the plain;
For they were resolved, before they
would yield,
That every man would there be slain.

20 So there they fought couragiously,
'Till most of them lay dead there and
slain,
But little Musgrave, that was his foot-
page,
With his bonny grissell got away un-
tain.

21 But when he came up to Guiltknock Hall,
The lady spyed him presently:
'What news, what news, thou little
foot-page?
What news from thy master and his
company?'

22 'My news is bad, lady,' he said,
'Which I do bring, as you may see;
My master, John Armstrong, he is slain,
And all his gallant company.

23 'Yet thou are welcome home, my bonny
grisel !
Full oft thou hast fed at the corn and
hay,

But now thou shalt be fed with bread an
wine,
And thy sides shall be spurred n
more, I say.'

24 O then bespoke his little son,
As he was set on his nurses knee:
'If ever I live for to be a man,
My fathers blood revenged shall be.

C

'Johnie Armstrang,' Allan Ramsay, The
Ever Green, 1724, II, 190, "copied from a gen
tleman's mouth of the name of Armstrang, wh
is the 6th generation from this John."

1 Sum speiks of lords, sum speiks of lairds
And siclyke men of hie degrie;
Of a gentleman I sing a sang,
Sumtyme calld Laird of Gilnockie.

2 The king he wrytes a luving letter,
With his ain hand sae tenderly:
And he hath sent it to Johny Armstrang
To cum and speik with him speidily.

3 The Eliots and Armstrangs did con-
vene,
They were a gallant company:
'We 'ill ryde and meit our lawful king,
And bring him safe to Gilnockie.

4 'Make kinnen and capon ready, then,
And venison in great plenty;
We 'ill welcome hame our royal king;
I hope he 'ill dyne at Gilnockie !'

5 They ran their horse on the Langum
howm,
And brake their speirs with mekle
main;
The ladys lukit frae their loft-windows,
'God bring our men weil back again !'

6 When Johny came before the king,
With all his men sae brave to see,
The king he movit his bonnet to him;
He weind he was a king as well as he.

7 'May I find grace, my sovereign liege,
Grace for my loyal men and me?
For my name it is Johny Armstrang,
And subject of yours, my liege,' said
he.

8 ' Away, away, thou traytor, strang !
    Out of my sicht thou mayst sune be !
  I grantit nevir a traytors lyfe,
    And now I 'll not begin with thee.'

9 ' Grant me my lyfe, my liege, my king,
    And a bony gift I will give to thee;
  Full four-and-twenty milk-whyt steids,
    Were a' foald in a yeir to me.

10 ' I 'll gie thee all these milk-whyt steids,
    That prance and nicher at a speir,
  With as mekle gude Inglis gilt
    As four of their braid backs dow beir.'

11 ' Away, away, thou traytor strang !
    Out o' my sicht thou mayst sune be !
  I grantit nevir a traytors lyfe,
    And now I 'll not begin with thee.'

12 ' Grant me my lyfe, my liege, my king,
    And a bony gift I 'll gie to thee;
  Gude four-and-twenty ganging mills,
    That gang throw a' the yeir to me.

13 ' These four-and-twenty mills complete
    Sall gang for thee throw all the yeir,
  And as mekle of gude reid wheit
    As all their happers dow to bear.'

14 ' Away, away, thou traytor, strang !
    Out of my sicht thou mayst sune be !
  I grantit nevir a traytors lyfe,
    And now I 'll not begin with thee.'

15 ' Grant me my lyfe, my liege, my king,
    And a great gift I 'll gie to thee;
  Bauld four-and-twenty sisters sons,
    Sall for the fecht, tho all sould flee.'

16 ' Away, away, thou traytor, strang!
    Out of my sicht thou mayst sune be !
  I grantit nevir a traytors lyfe,
    And now I 'll not begin with thee.'

17 ' Grant me my lyfe, my liege, my king,
    And a brave gift I 'll gie to thee;
  All betwene heir and Newcastle town
    Sall pay thair yeirly rent to thee.'

18 ' Away, away, thou traytor, strang !
    Out of my sicht thou mayst sune
      be !
  I grantit nevir a traytors lyfe,
    And now I 'll not begin with thee.'

19 ' Ye lied, ye lied, now, king,' he says,
    ' Althocht a king and prince ye be,
  For I luid naithing in all my lyfe,
    I dare well say it, but honesty;

20 ' But a fat horse, and a fair woman,
    Twa bony dogs to kill a deir:
  But Ingland suld haif found me meil
      and malt,
    Gif I had livd this hundred yeir !

21 ' Scho suld haif found me meil and malt,
    And beif and mutton in all plentie;
  But neir a Scots wyfe could haif said
    That eir I skaithd her a pure flie.

22 ' To seik het water beneth cauld yce,
    Surely it is a great folie;
  I haif asked grace at a graceless face,
    But there is nane for my men and me.

23 ' But had I kend, or I came frae hame,
    How thou unkynd wadst bene to me,
  I wad haif kept the border-syde,
    In spyte of all thy force and thee.

24 ' Wist Englands king that I was tane,
    O gin a blyth man wald he be !
  For anes I slew his sisters son,
    And on his breist-bane brak a tree.'

25 John wore a girdle about his midle,
    Imbroiderd owre with burning gold,
  Bespangled with the same mettle,
    Maist beautifull was to behold.

26 Ther hang nine targats at Johnys hat,
    And ilk an worth three hundred
      pound:
  ' What wants that knave that a king
      suld haif,
    But the sword of honour and the
      crown !

27 ' O whair gat thou these targats, Johnie,
    That blink sae brawly abune thy
      brie ? '
  I gat them in the field fechting,
    Wher, cruel king, thou durst not be.

28 ' Had I my horse, and my harness gude,
    And ryding as I wont to be,
  It sould haif bene tald this hundred
      yeir
    The meiting of my king and me.

29 ' God be withee, Kirsty, my brither,
    Lang live thou Laird of Mangertoun!
  Lang mayst thou live on the border-
     syde
  Or thou se thy brither ryde up and
    doun.

30 ' And God be withee, Kirsty, my son,
    Whair thou sits on thy nurses knee!
  But and thou live this hundred yeir,
    Thy fathers better thoult never be.

31 ' Farweil, my bonny Gilnock-Hall,
    Whair on Esk-syde thou standest
     stout!
  Gif I had lived but seven yeirs mair,
    I wald haif gilt thee round about.'

32 John murdred was at Carlinrigg,
    And all his galant companie:
  But Scotlands heart was never sae wae,
    To see sae mony brave men die.

33 Because they savd their country deir
    Frae Englishmen ; nane were sae
     bauld,
  Whyle Johnie livd on the border-syde,
    Nane of them durst cum neir his
    hald.

170

THE DEATH OF QUEEN JANE

Jane Seymour gave birth to Prince Edward
October 12, 1537, and by a natural process,
but, in consequence of imprudent manage-
ment, died twelve days after. There was a
belief that severe surgery had been required,
under which the queen sank.

A

Percy Papers, communicated to Percy by
the Dean of Derry, as written from memory by
his mother, Mrs Bernard, February, 1776.

1 QUEEN JANE was in labour full six
    weeks and more,
  And the women were weary, and fain
    would give oer:
  ' O women, O women, as women ye be,
    Rip open my two sides, and save my
    baby!'

2 ' O royal Queen Jane, that thing may
    not be;
    We 'll send for King Henry to come
     unto thee.'
  King Henry came to her, and sate on
    her bed:
    ' What ails my dear lady, her eyes
    look so red ? '

3 ' O royal King Henry, do one thing for
    me:
    Rip open my two sides, and save my
    baby ! '
  ' O royal Queen Jane, that thing will
    not do ;
    If I lose your fair body, I 'll lose
    your baby too.'

4 She wept and she waild, and she wrung
    her hands sore;
    O the flour of England must flurish
    no more !
  She wept and she waild till she fell in a
    swoond,
    They opend her two sides, and the
    baby was found.

5 The baby was christened with joy and
    much mirth,
    Whilst poor Queen Jane's body lay
    cold under earth:
  There was ringing and singing and
    mourning all day,
    The princess Eliz[abeth] went weep-
    ing away.

6 The trumpets in mourning so sadly did
    sound,
    And the pikes and the muskets did
    trail on the ground.

  .   .   .   .   .
    .   .   .   .

B

' Queen Jeanie,' Kinloch's Ancient Scottish
Ballads, p. 116.

1 QUEEN JEANIE, Queen Jeanie, traveld
    six weeks and more,
    Till women and midwives had quite
    gien her oer:
  ' O if ye were women as women should be,
    Ye would send for a doctor, a doctor
    to me.'

2 The doctor was called for and set by her
    bedside:
    ' What aileth thee, my ladie, thine
      eyes seem so red ? '
    ' O doctor, O doctor, will ye do this for me,
      To rip up my two sides, and save my
      babie ? '

3 ' Queen Jeanie, Queen Jeanie, that 's
    the thing I 'll neer do,
    To rip up your two sides to save your
      babie : '
    Queen Jeanie, Queen Jeanie, traveld six
      weeks and more,
    Till midwives and doctors had quite
      gien her oer.

4 ' O if ye were doctors as doctors should be,
    Ye would send for King Henry, King
      Henry to me '
    King Henry was called for, and sat by
      her bedside,
    ' What aileth thee, Jeanie ? what ail-
      eth my bride ? '

5 ' King Henry, King Henry, will ye do
    this for me,
    To rip up my two sides, and save my
      babie ? '
    ' Queen Jeanie, Queen Jeanie, that 's
    what I 'll never do,
    To rip up your two sides to save your
      babie.'

6 But with sighing and sobbing she 's
    fallen in a swoon,
    Her side it was ript up, and her babie
      was found ;
    At this bonie babie's christning there
      was meikle joy and mirth,
    But bonnie Queen Jeanie lies cold in
      the earth.

7 Six and six coaches, and six and six more,
    And royal King Henry went mourn-
      ing before ;
    O two and two gentlemen carried her
      away,
    But royal King Henry went weeping
      away.

8 O black were their stockings, and black
    were their bands,
    And black were the weapons they
      held in their hands ;

    O black were their mufflers, and black
      were their shoes,
    And black were the cheverons they
      drew on their luves.

9 They mourned in the kitchen, and they
    mournd in the ha,
    But royal King Henry mournd lang-
      est of a' :
    Farewell to fair England, farewell for
      evermore !
    For the fair flower of England will
      never shine more.

171

THOMAS CROMWELL

June 10, 1540, Thomas Lord Cromwell,
"when he least expected it," was arrested at
the council-table by the Duke of Norfolk for
high-treason, and on the 28th of July following he was executed. Cromwell, says Lord
Herbert of Cherbury, judged " his perdition
more certain that the duke was uncle to the
Lady Katherine Howard, whom the king began now to affect." Later writers have asserted that Katherine Howard exerted herself
to procure Cromwell's death, and we can understand nobody else but her to be doing this
in the third stanza of this fragment ; nevertheless there is no authority for such a repre-
sentation. The king had no personal interview
with the minister whom he so suddenly struck
down, but he did send the Duke of Norfolk and
two others to visit Cromwell in prison, for the
purpose of extracting confessions pertaining to
Anne of Cleves. Cromwell wrote two letters
to the king, imploring the mercy which, as well
as confession, he refuses in stanza five. (See
Merriman, Life and Letters of Thomas Cromwell, 1902.)

Percy MS., p. 55 ; Hales and Furnivall, I, 129.

    *   *   *   *   *

1 .   .   .   .   .
    ' Ffor if your boone be askeable,
      Soone granted it shalbe :

2 ' If it be not touching my crowne,' he said,
    ' Nor hurting poore comminaltye.'
    ' Nay, it is not touching your crowne,'
      shee sayes,
      Nor hurting poore cominaltye,

3 'But I begg the death of Thomas Crom-
    well,
    For a false traitor to you is hee.'
    'Then feitch me hither the Earle of
    Darby
    And the Earle of Shrewsbury,

4 'And bidde them bring Thomas Croma-
    well;
    Let's see what he can say to mee;'
    For Thomas had woont to haue carryed
    his head vp,
    But now he hanges it vppon his knee.

5 'How now ? How now ? ' the king did
    say,
    'Thomas, how is it with thee ? '
    'Hanging and drawing, O king !' he
    saide;
    'You shall neuer gett more from
    mee.'

172

MUSSELBURGH FIELD

The Protector Somerset, to overcome or to
punish the opposition of the Scots to the marriage of Mary Stuart with Edward VI, invaded
Scotland at the end of the summer of 1547 with
eighteen thousand men, supported by a fleet.
The Scots mustered at Musselburgh, a town on
the water five or six miles east of Edinburgh.
The northern army abandoned an impregnable
position, and their superior, but ill-managed
and partly ill-composed force, after successfully
resisting a cavalry charge, was put to flight by
the English, who had an advantage in cannon
and cavalry as well as generalship. A hideous
slaughter followed ; it is said that, in the chase
and battle, there were slain above ten thousand
Scots. The battle is known also by the name
of Pinkie or Pinkie Cleuch, appellations of an
estate, a burn and a hill, near or within the field
of operations.

The ballad is perhaps quoted by Sir Toby,
in Twelfth Night, act ii, scene 3: "O, the
twelfth day of December!"

'Musleboorrowe ffeild,' Percy MS., p. 54;
Hales and Furnivall, i, 123.

1 On the tenth day of December,
    And the fourth yeere of King Edwards
    raigne,

Att Musleboorrowe, as I remember,
    Two goodly hosts there mett on a
    plaine.

2 All that night they camped there,
    Soe did the Scotts, both stout and
    stubborne;
    But "wellaway," it was their song,
    For wee haue taken them in their
    owne turne.

3 Over night they carded for our English
    mens coates ;
    They fished before their netts were
    spunn;
    A white for sixpence, a red for two
    groates;
    Now wisdome wold haue stayed till
    they had been woone.

4 Wee feared not but that they wold
    fight,
    Yett itt was turned vnto their owne
    paine;
    Thoe against one of vs that they were
    eight,
    Yett with their owne weapons wee
    did them beat.

5 On the twelfth day in the morne
    The made a face as the wold fight,
    But many a proud Scott there was downe
    borne,
    And many a ranke coward was put to
    flight.

6 But when they heard our great gunnes
    cracke,
    Then was their harts turned into their
    hose;
    They cast down their weapons, and
    turned their backes,
    They ran soe fast that the fell on their
    nose.

7 The Lord Huntley, wee had him there;
    With him hee brought ten thousand
    men,
    Yett, God bee thanked, wee made them
    such a banquett
    That none of them returned againe.

8 Wee chased them to D[alkeith]

*   *   *   *   *

173

MARY HAMILTON

When Mary Stuart was sent to France in 1548, being then between five and six, she had four companions " sundry gentlewomen and noblemen's sons and daughters, almost of her own age, of the which there were four in special of whom every one of them bore the same name of Mary, being of four sundry honorable houses, to wit, Fleming, Livingston, Seton, and Beaton of Creich ; who remained all four with the queen in France during her residence there, and returned again in Scotland with her Majesty in the year of our Lord 1561." Lesley, History of Scotland, 1830, p. 209.

This ballad purports to relate the tragic history of one of the queen's Maries. In some of the versions her lover is said to be the king (Darnley). The ballad seems to have taken its rise in an incident which occurred at Mary's court in 1563, which involved the queen's apothecary and " a French woman that served in the queen's chamber." There is also a striking coincidence between the ballad and the fate of a Miss Hamilton who, in the reign of Peter the Great, was one of the attendants of the Russian Empress. The subject is fully discussed by Professor Child, Ballads, III. 381 ff., v, 298 f., and Mr Andrew Lang, Blackwood's Magazine, September, 1895, pp. 381 ff.

A

a. 'Marie Hamilton,' Sharpe's Ballad Book, 1824, p. 18. b. Communicated by the late John Francis Campbell, as learned from his father about 1840. c. Aungervyle Society's publications, No. v, p. 5 (First Series, p. 85) ; " taken down early in the present century from the lips of an old lady in Annandale."

1 WORD 's gane to the kitchen,
    And word 's gane to the ha,
That Marie Hamilton gangs wi bairn
    To the hichest Stewart of a'.

2 He 's courted her in the kitchen,
    He 's courted her in the ha,
He 's courted her in the laigh cellar,
    And that was warst of a'.

3 She 's tyed it in her apron
    And she 's thrown it in the sea;
Says, Sink ye, swim ye, bonny wee babe !
    You 'l neer get mair o me.

4 Down then cam the auld queen,
    Goud tassels tying her hair:
'O Marie, where 's the bonny wee babe
    That I heard greet sae sair ? '

5 ' There was never a babe intill my room,
    As little designs to be;
It was but a touch o my sair side,
    Come oer my fair bodie.'

6 'O Marie, put on your robes o black,
    Or else your robes o brown,
For ye maun gang wi me the night,
    To see fair Edinbro town.'

7 ' I winna put on my robes o black,
    Nor yet my robes o brown;
But I 'll put on my robes o white,
    To shine through Edinbro town.'

8 When she gaed up the Cannogate,
    She laughd loud laughters three;
But whan she cam down the Cannogate
    The tear blinded her ee.

9 When she gaed up the Parliament stair,
    The heel cam aff her shee;
And lang or she cam down again
    She was condemnd to dee.

10 When she cam down the Cannogate,
    The Cannogate sae free,
Many a ladie lookd oer her window,
    Weeping for this ladie.

11 'Ye need nae weep for me,' she says,
    ' Ye need nae weep for me;
For had I not slain mine own sweet babe,
    This death I wadna dee.

12 'Bring me a bottle of wine,' she says,
    ' The best that eer ye hae,
That I may drink to my weil-wishers,
    And they may drink to me.

13 'Here 's a health to the jolly sailors,
    That sail upon the main ;
Let them never let on to my father and mother
    But what I 'm coming hame.

14 'Here 's a health to the jolly sailors,
    That sail upon the sea;
Let them never let on to my father and mother
    That I cam here to dee.

15 'Oh little did my mother think,
   The day she cradled me,
What lands I was to travel through,
   What death I was to dee.

16 'Oh little did my father think,
   The day he held up me,
What lands I was to travel through,
   What death I was to dee.

17 'Last night I washd the queen's feet,
   And gently laid her down;
And a' the thanks I've gotten the nicht
   To be hangd in Edinbro town!

18 'Last nicht there was four Maries,
   The nicht there 'l be but three;
There was Marie Seton, and Marie
      Beton,
   And Marie Carmichael, and me.'

B

'Mary Hamilton,' Motherwell's MS., p. 337.

1 THERE were ladies, they lived in a bower,
   And oh but they were fair!
The youngest o them is to the king's court,
   To learn some unco lair.

2 She hadna been in the king's court
   A twelve month and a day,
Till of her they could get na wark,
   For wantonness and play.

3 Word is to the kitchen gane,
   And word is to the ha,
And word is up to Madame the Queen,
   And that is warst of a',
That Mary Hamilton has born a bairn,
   To the hichest Stewart of a'.

4 'O rise, O rise, Mary Hamilton,
   O rise, and tell to me
What thou did with thy sweet babe
   We sair heard weep by thee.'

5 'Hold your tongue, madame,' she said,
   'And let your folly be;
It was a shouir o sad sickness
   Made me weep sae bitterlie.'

6 'O rise, O rise, Mary Hamilton,
   O rise, and tell to me

What thou did with thy sweet babe
   We sair heard weep by thee.'

7 'I put it in a piner-pig,
   And set it on the sea;
I bade it sink, or it might swim,
   It should neer come hame to me.'

8 'O rise, O rise, Mary Hamilton,
   Arise, and go with me;
There is a wedding in Glasgow town
   This day we 'll go and see.'

9 She put not on her black clothing,
   She put not on her brown,
But she put on the glistering gold,
   To shine thro Edinburgh town.

10 As they came into Edinburgh town,
   The city for to see,
The bailie's wife and the provost's wif
   Said, Och an alace for thee!

11 'Gie never alace for me,' she said,
   'Gie never alace for me;
It 's all for the sake of my poor babe,
   This death that I maun die.'

12 As they gaed up the Tolbuith stair,
   The stair it was sae hie,
The bailie's son and the provost's son
   Said, Och an alace for thee!

13 'Gie never alace for me,' she said,
   'Gie never alace for me!
It 's all for the sake of my puir babe,
   This death that I maun die.

14 'But bring to me a cup,' she says,
   'A cup bot and a can,
And I will drink to all my friends,
   And they 'll drink to me again.

15 'Here 's to you all, travellers,
   Who travels by land or sea;
Let na wit to my father nor mother
   The death that I must die.

16 'Here 's to you all, travellers,
   That travels on dry land;
Let na wit to my father nor mother
   But I am coming hame.

17 'Little did my mother think,
   First time she cradled me,

What land I was to travel on,
Or what death I would die.

18 'Little did my mother think,
First time she tied my head,
What land I was to tread upon,
Or whare I would win my bread.

19 'Yestreen Queen Mary had four Maries,
This night she 'll hae but three;
She had Mary Seaton, and Mary Beaton,
And Mary Carmichael, and me.

20 'Yestreen I wush Queen Mary's feet,
And bore her till her bed;
This day she 's given me my reward,
This gallows-tree to tread.

21 'Cast off, cast off my goun,' she said,
'But let my petticoat be,
And tye a napkin on my face,
For that gallows I downa see.'

22 By and cum the king himsell,
Lookd up with a pitiful ee:
'Come down, come down, Mary Hamil-
ton,
This day thou wilt dine with me.'

23 'Hold your tongue, my sovereign leige,
And let your folly be;
An ye had a mind to save my life,
Ye should na shamed me here.'

174

EARL BOTHWELL

This ballad represents the murder of Darnley as done in revenge for his complicity in the murder of Riccio. The Regent Murray is described as " banishing " Queen Mary, whereupon she fled to England. Mary escaped from Lochleven Castle on the second of May, 1568, and took refuge in England on the sixteenth. We must suppose the ballad to have been made not long after.

'Earle Bodwell,' Percy MS., p. 272; Hales and Furnivall, II, 260.

1 WOE worth thee, woe worth thee, false
Scottlande !
Ffor thou hast euer wrought by a
sleight;

For the worthyest prince *that* euer was
borne,
You hanged vnder a cloud by night.

2 The Queene of France a letter wrote,
And sealed itt with hart and ringe,
And bade him come Scottland within,
And shee wold marry him and crowne
him king.

3 To be a king, itt is a pleasant thing,
To bee a prince vnto a peere;
But you haue heard, and so haue I too,
A man may well by gold to deere.

4 There was an Italyan in that place,
Was as wel beloued as euer was hee;
Lord David was his name,
Chamberlaine vnto the queene was hee.

5 Ffor if the king had risen forth of his
place,
He wold haue sitt him downe in the
cheare,
And tho itt beseemed him not soe well,
Altho the king had beene present
there.

6 Some lords in Scottland waxed wonder-
ous wroth,
And quarrelld with him for the nonce;
I shall you tell how itt beffell;
Twelue daggers were in him all att
once.

7 When this queene see the chamberlaine
was slaine,
For him her cheeks shee did weete,
And made a vow for a twelue month
and a day
The king and shee wold not come in
one sheete.

8 Then some of the lords of Scottland
waxed wrothe,
And made their vow vehementlye,
'For death of the queenes chamber-
laine
The king himselfe he shall dye.'

9 They strowed his chamber ouer with gun-
powder,
And layd greene rushes in his way;
Ffor the traitors thought *that* night
The worthy king for to betray.

10 To bedd the worthy king made him
    bowne,
  To take his rest, *that* was his desire;
He was noe sooner cast on sleepe,
  But his chamber was on a blasing fyer.

11 Vp he lope, and a glasse window broke,
  He had thirty foote for to ffall;
Lord Bodwell kept a priuy wach
  Vnderneath his castle-wall:
' Who haue wee heere ? ' sayd Lord Bod-
  well;
' Answer me, now I doe call.'

12 ' King Henery the Eighth my vnckle
  was;
Some pitty show for his sweet sake !
Ah, Lord Bodwell, I know thee well;
  Some pitty on me I pray thee take ! '

13 ' I 'le pitty thee as much,' he sayd,
  ' And as much favor I 'le show to
  thee
As thou had on the queene's chamber-
  laine
  That day thou deemedst him to dye.'

14 Through halls and towers this king they
  ledd,
  Through castles and towers that were
  hye,
Through an arbor into an orchard,
  And there hanged him in a peare tree.

15 When the gouernor of Scottland he
  heard tell
  That the worthye king he was slaine,
He hath banished the queene soe bit-
  terlye
  That in Scottland shee dare not remaine.

16 But shee is ffled into merry England,
  And Scottland to a side hath laine,
And through the Queene of Englands
  good grace
Now in England shee doth remaine.

175

THE RISING IN THE NORTH

The ballad, which is the work of a loyal but
not unsympathetic minstrel, gives a cursory and
imperfect account of the rebellion of the Earls
of Northumberland and Westmoreland in 1569.

' Risinge in the Northe,' Percy MS., p. 256;
Hales and Furnivall, II, 210.

1 LISTEN, liuely lordings all,
  And all that beene this place within:
If you 'le giue eare vnto my songe,
  I will tell you how this geere did
  begin.

2 It was the good Erle of Westmorlande,
  A noble erle was callëd hee,
And he wrought treason against the
  crowne;
  Alas, itt was the more pittye !

3 And soe itt was the Erle of Northum-
  berland,
  Another good noble erle was hee;
They tooken both vpon one part,
  Against the crowne they wolden bee.

4 Earle Pearcy is into his garden gone,
  And after walkes his awne ladye:
' I heare a bird sing in my eare
  That I must either flight or fflee.'

5 ' God fforbidd,' shee sayd, ' good my
  lord,
  That euer soe that it shalbee !
But goe to London to the court,
  And faire ffall truth and honestye ! '

6 ' But nay, now nay, my ladye gay,
  That euer it shold soe bee;
My treason is knowen well enoughe;
  Att the court I must not bee.'

7 ' But goe to the court yet, good my lord,
  Take men enowe with thee;
If any man will doe you wronge,
  Your warrant they may bee.'

8 ' But nay, now nay, my lady gay,
  For soe itt must not bee;
If I goe to the court, ladye,
  Death will strike me, and I must dye.'

9 ' But goe to the court yett, [good] my
  lord,
  I my-selfe will ryde with thee;
If any man will doe you wronge,
  Your borrow I shalbee.'

10 'But nay, now nay, my lady gay,
  For soe it must not bee;
  For if I goe to the court, ladye,
    Thou must me neuer see.

11 'But come hither, thou litle foot-page,
  Come thou hither vnto mee,
  For thou shalt goe a message to Master
    Norton,
    In all the hast *that* euer may bee.

12 'Comend me to *that* gentleman;
  Bring him here this letter from mee,
  And say, I pray him earnestlye
    That hee will ryde in my companye.'

13 But one while the foote-page went,
  Another while he rann;
  Vntill he came to Master Norton,
    The ffoot-page neuer blanne.

14 And when he came to Master Nortton,
  He kneeled on his knee,
  And tooke the letter betwixt his hands,
    And lett the gentleman it see.

15 And when the letter itt was reade,
  Affore all his companye,
  I-wis, if you wold know the truth,
    There was many a weeping eye.

16 He said, Come hither, Kester Nortton,
  A ffine ffellow thou seemes to bee;
  Some good councell, Kester Nortton,
    This day doe thou giue to mee.

17 'Marry, I 'le giue you councell, ffather,
  If you 'le take councell att me,
  That if you haue spoken the word,
    father,
    That backe againe you doe not flee.'

18 'God a mercy ! Christopher Nortton,
  I say, God a mercye !
  If I doe liue and scape with liffe,
    Well advanced shalt thou bee.

19 'But come you hither, my nine good
    sonnes,
  In mens estate I thinke you bee;
  How many of you, my children deare,
    On my part *that* wilbe ? '

20 But eight of them did answer soone,
  And spake ffull hastilye;

Sayes, We wilbe on your part, ffather,
  Till the day *that* we doe dye.

21 'But God a mercy ! my children deare,
  And euer I say God a mercy !
  And yett my blessing you shall haue,
    Whether-soeuer I liue or dye.

22 'But what sayst thou, thou Ffrancis
    Nortton,
  Mine eldest sonne and mine heyre
    trulye ?
  Some good councell, Ffrancis Nortton,
    This day thou giue to me.'

23 'But I will giue you councell, ffather,
  If you will take councell att mee;
  For if you wold take my councell, father,
    Against the crowne you shold not bee.'

24 'But ffye vpon thee, Ffrancis Nortton
  I say ffye vpon thee !
  When thou was younge and tender of
    age
    I made ffull much of thee.'

25 'But your head is white, ffather,' he
    sayes,
  'And your beard is wonderous gray;
  Itt were shame ffor your countrye
    If you shold rise and fflee away.'

26 'But ffye vpon thee, thou coward Ffran-
    cis !
  Thou neuer tookest *that* of mee !
  When thou was younge and tender of
    age
    I made too much of thee.'

27 'But I will goe with you, father,' quoth
    hee;
  'Like a naked man will I bee;
  He *that* strikes the first stroake against
    the crowne,
    An ill death may hee dye !'

28 But then rose vpp Master Nortton, *that*
    esquier,
  With him a ffull great companye;
  And then the erles they comen downe
    To ryde in his companye.

29 Att Whethersbye the mustered their
    men,
  Vpon a ffull fayre day;

Thirteen thousand there were seene
   To stand in battel ray.

30 The Erle of Westmoreland, he had in
     his ancyent
   The dunn bull in sight most hye,
And three doggs with golden collers
   Were sett out royallye.

31 The Erle of Northumberland, he had in
     his ancyent
   The halfe moone in sight soe hye,
As the Lord was crucifyed on the crosse,
   And set forthe pleasantlye.

32 And after them did rise good Sir George
     Bowes,
   After them a spoyle to make;
The erles returned backe againe,
   Thought euer that knight to take.

33 This barron did take a castle then,
   Was made of lime and stone;
The vttermost walls were ese to be
     woon;
   The erles haue woon them anon.

34 But tho they woone the vttermost walls,
   Quickly and anon,
The innermust walles the cold not winn;
   The were made of a rocke of stone.

35 But newes itt came to leeue London,
   In all the speede that euer might bee;
And word it came to our royall queene
   Of all the rebells in the north coun-
     trye.

36 Shee turned her grace then once about,
   And like a royall queene shee sware;
Sayes, I will ordaine them such a breake-
     fast
   As was not in the north this thousand
     yeere !

37 Shee caused thirty thousand men to be
     made,
   With horsse and harneis all quicklye;
And shee caused thirty thousand men
     to be made,
   To take the rebells in the north coun-
     trye.

38 They tooke with them the false Erle of
     Warwicke;
   Soe did they many another man;

Vntill they came to Yorke castle,
   I-wis they neuer stinted nor blan.

   *   *   *   *   *

39 .   .   .   .   .   .

   ' Spread thy ancyent, Erle of Westmore-
     land !
   The halfe-moone ffaine wold wee see !'

40 But the halfe-moone is fled and gone,
   And the dun bull vanished awaye;
And Ffrancis Nortton and his eight
     sonnes
   Are ffled away most cowardlye.

41 Ladds with mony are counted men,
   Men without mony are counted none;
But hold your tounge ! why say you soe?
   Men wilbe men when mony is gone.

176

NORTHUMBERLAND BETRAYED BY DOUGLAS

The Earl of Northumberland, after the failure of the Rising in the North, took refuge in
Liddesdale, but was soon given up to the
Regent Murray, and confined in the castle of
Lochleven. Here he remained, in the custody
of Douglas of Lochleven, from January, 1570,
to June, 1572. The Countess of Northumberland had offered Douglas two thousand pounds
for her husband ; but, as the result of diplo-
matic negotiations, the same amount was paid
by Lord Hunsdon, Queen Elizabeth's representative, and the Earl was put into his hands.
The ballad-minstrel acquaints us with circumstances concerning this surrender which are
unknown to the historians.

' Northumberland betrayd by Dowglas,'
Percy MS., p. 259 ; Hales and Furnivall, II, 217.

1 Now list and lithe, you gentlemen,
   And I 'st tell you the veretye,
How they haue dealt with a banished
     man,
   Driuen out of his countrye.

2 When as hee came on Scottish ground,
   As woe and wonder be them amonge !
Ffull much was there traitorye
   The wrought the Erle of Northum-
     berland.

3 When they were att the supper sett,
Beffore many goodly gentlemen,
The ffell a fflouting and mocking both,
And said to the Erle of Northumber-
land:

4 'What makes you be soe sad, my lord,
And in your mind soe sorrowffullye?
In the north of Scottland to-morrow
there's a shooting,
And thither thou'st goe, my Lord
Percye.

5 'The buttes are sett, and the shooting
is made,
And there is like to be great royaltye,
And I am sworne into my bill
Thither to bring my Lord Pearcy.'

6 'I'le giue thee my hand, Douglas,' he
sayes,
'And be the faith in my bodye,
If that thou wilt ryde to the worlds end,
I'le ryde in thy companye.'

7 And then bespake the good ladye,
Marry a Douglas was her name:
'You shall byde here, good English
lord;
My brother is a traiterous man.

8 'He is a traitor stout and stronge,
As I'st tell you the veretye;
For he hath tane liuerance of the Erle,
And into England he will liuor thee.'

9 'Now hold thy tounge, thou goodlye
ladye,
And let all this talking bee;
Ffor all the gold that's in Loug Leuen,
William wold not liuor mee.

10 'It wold breake truce betweene Eng-
land and Scottland,
And freinds againe they wold neuer
bee,
If he shold liuor a bani[s]ht erle,
Was driuen out of his owne countrye.'

11 'Hold your tounge, my lord,' shee sayes,
'There is much ffalsehood them
amonge;
When you are dead, then they are done,
Soone they will part them freinds
againe.

12 'If you will giue me any trust, my
lord,
I'le tell you how you best may bee;
You'st lett my brother ryde his wayes,
And tell those English lords, trulye,

13 'How that you cannot with them ryde,
Because you are in an ile of the sea;
Then, ere my brother come againe,
To Edenborrow castle I'le carry thee.

14 'I'le liuor you vnto the Lord Hume.
And you know a trew Scothe lord is
hee,
For he hath lost both land and goods
In ayding of your good bodye.'

15 'Marry, I am woe, woman,' he sayes,
'That any freind fares worse for
mee;
For where one saith it is a true tale,
Then two will say it is a lye.

16 'When I was att home in my [realme],
Amonge my tennants all trulye,
In my time of losse, wherin my need
stoode,
They came to ayd me honestlye.

17 'Therfore I left a many a child ffather-
lese,
And many a widdow to looke wanne;
And therfore blame nothing, ladye,
But the woeffull warres which I be-
gan.'

18 'If you will giue me noe trust, my
lord,
Nor noe credence you will give mee,
And you'le come hither to my right
hand,
Indeed, my lorid, I'le lett you see.'

19 Saies, I neuer loued noe witchcraft,
Nor neuer dealt with treacherye,
But euermore held the hye way;
Alas, that may be seene by mee!

20 'If you will not come your selfe, my
lord,
You'le lett your chamberlaine goe
with mee,
Three words that I may to him speake,
And soone he shall come againe to
thee.'

21 When Iames Swynard came *that* lady
    before,
    Shee let him see thorrow the weme
    of her ring
    How many there was of English lords
    To wayte there for his m*aster* and
    him.

22 'But who beene yonder, my good ladye,
    That walkes soe royallye on yonder
    greene?'
    'Yonder is Lord Huusden, Iamye,' she
    saye[d],
    'Alas, hee'le doe you both tree and
    teene!'

23 'And who beene yonder, thou gay
    ladye,
    That walkes soe royallye him be-
    side?'
    'Yond is Sir W*illia*m Drurye, Iamy,'
    shee sayd,
    'And a keene cap*tain* hee is, and
    tryde.'

24 'How many miles is itt, thou good
    ladye,
    Betwixt yond English lord and mee?'
    'Marry, thrise fifty mile, Iamy,' shee
    sayd,
    'And euen to seale and by the sea.

25 'I neuer was on English ground,
    Nor neuer see itt with mine eye,
    But as my witt and wisedome serues,
    And as [the] booke it telleth mee.'

26 'My mother, shee was a witch woman,
    And p*ar*t of itt shee learned mee;
    Shee wold let me see out of Lough
    Leuen
    What they dyd in London cytye.'

27 'But who is yonde, thou good laydye,
    That comes yonder w*it*h an osterne
    fface?'
    'Yond's Sir Iohn Forster, Ia*m*ye,' shee
    sayd;
    'Methinkes thou sholdest better
    know him then I.'
    'Euen soe I doe, my goodlye ladye,
    And eu*er* alas, soe woe am I!'

28 He pulled his hatt ouer his eyes,
    And, Lord, he wept soe tenderlye!

He is gone to his m*aster* againe,
    And euen to tell him the veretye.

29 'Now hast thou beene with Marry,
    Iamy,' he sayd,
    'Euen as thy tounge will tell to mee;
    But if thou trust in any womans words,
    Thou must refraine good companye.'

30 'It is noe words, my lord,' he sayes;
    'Yonder the men shee letts me see,
    How many English lords there is
    Is wayting there for you and mee.

31 'Yonder I see the Lord Hunsden,
    And hee and you is of the third de-
    gree;
    A greater enemye, indeed, my Lord,
    In England none haue yee.'

32 'And I haue beene in Lough Leven
    The most part of these yeeres three:
    Yett had I neuer noe out-rake,
    Nor good games *that* I cold see.

33 'And I am thus bidden to yonder shoot-
    ing
    By William Douglas all trulye;
    Therfore speake neu*er* a word out of
    thy mouth
    That thou thinkes will hinder mee.'

34 Then he writhe the gold ring of his
    ffingar
    And gaue itt to *that* ladye gay;
    Sayes, *That* was a legacye left vnto
    mee
    In Harley woods where I cold bee.'

35 'Then ffarewell hart, and farewell hand,
    And ffarwell all good companye!
    That woman shall neuer beare a sonne
    Shall know soe much of your priui-
    tye.'

36 'Now hold thy tounge, ladye,' hee sayde,
    'And make not all this dole for mee,
    For I may well drinke, but I'st neuer
    eate,
    Till againe in Lough Leuen I bee.'

37 He tooke his boate att the Lough Leuen,
    For to sayle now ouer the sea,
    And he hath cast vpp a siluer wand,
    Saies, Fare thou well, my good ladye!

The ladye looked ouer her left sholder ;
 In a dead swoone there fell shee.

38 ' Goe backe againe, Douglas ! ' he sayd,
 ' And I will goe in thy companye,
For sudden sicknesse yonder lady has
  tane,
 And euer, alas, shee will but dye !

39 ' If ought come to yonder ladye but
  good,
 Then blamed sore *that* I shall bee,
Because a banished man I am,
 And driuen out of my owne countrye.'

40 ' Come on, come on, my lord,' he sayes,
 ' And lett all such talking bee;
There 's ladyes enow in Lough Leuen
 And for to cheere yonder gay ladye.'

41 ' And you will not goe your selfe, my
  lord,
 You will lett my chamberlaine go
  with mee;
Wee shall now take our boate againe,
 And soone wee shall ouertake thee.'

42 ' Come on, come on, my lord,' he
  sayes,
 ' And lett now all this talking bee;
Ffor my sister is craftye enoughe
 For to beguile thousands such as you
  and mee.'

43 When they had sayled fifty myle,
 Now fifty mile vpon the sea,
Hee had fforgotten a message *that*
  hee
 Shold doe in Lough Leuen trulye:
Hee asked, how ffarr it was to *that* shoot-
  ing
 That William Douglas promised mee.

44 ' Now faire words makes fooles faine,
 And *that* may be seene by thy master
  and thee;
Ffor you may happen think itt soone
  enoughe
 When-euer you *that* shooting see.'

45 Iamye pulled his hatt now ouer his
  browe,
 I wott the teares fell in his eye;
And he is to his master againe,
 And ffor to tell him the veretye.

46 ' He sayes fayre words makes focles
  faine,
 And *that* may be seene by you and
  mee,
Ffor wee may happen thinke itt soone
  enoughe
 When-euer wee *that* shooting see.

47 ' Hold vpp thy head, Iamye,' the erle
  sayd,
 ' And neuer lett thy hart fayle thee;
He did itt but to proue thee *with*,
 And see how thow wold take with
  death trulye.'

48 When they had sayled other fifty mile,
 Other fifty mile vpon the sea,
Lord Peercy called to him, himselfe,
 And sayd, Douglas, what wilt thou
  doe with mee ?

49 ' Looke *that* your brydle be wight, my
  lord,
 That you may goe as a shipp att sea;
Looke *that* your spurres be bright and
  sharpe,
 That you may pricke her while shee 'le
  awaye.'

50 ' What needeth this, Douglas,' he sayth,
 ' *That* thou needest to ffloute mee ?
For I was counted a horsseman good
 Before *that* euer I mett with thee.

51 ' A ffalse Hector hath my horsse,
 And euer an euill death may hee dye !
And Willye Armestronge hath my
  spurres
 And all the geere belongs to mee.'

52 When the had sayled other fifty mile,
 Other fifty mile vpon the sea,
The landed low by Barwicke-side;
 A deputed lord landed Lord Percye.

177

THE EARL OF WESTMORE-LAND

The first thirteen stanzas have an historical substratum, though details are inaccurate. They give a brief account of what happened to the Earl of Westmoreland (Charles Neville) from

the failure of the Rising in the North to his
embarkation for Flanders in 1570.   What follows is an imitation of old romance, very
possibly of Libeaus Desconus (see Schofield,
Studies on the Libeaus Desconus, p. 242).

'Earle of Westmorlande,' Percy MS., p. 112;
Hales and Furnivall, I, 292.

1 'How long shall fortune faile me now,
    And keepe me heare in deadlye
        dreade ?
    How long shall I in bale abide,
    In misery my life to leade ?

2 'To ffall from my rose, it was my
        chance;
    Such was the Queene of England free;
    I tooke a lake, and turned my backe,
    On Bramaball More shee caused me
        flye.

3 'One gentle Armstrong *that* I doe ken,
    Alas, *with* thee I dare not mocke !
    Thou dwellest soe far on the west bor-
        der,
    Thy name is called the Lord Iocke.'

4 Now hath Armstrong taken noble Nevill,
    And as one Martinfield did *profecye*;
    He hath taken the Lord Dakers,
    A lords sonne of great degree.

5 He hath taken old Master Nortton,
    And sonnes four in his companye;
    Hee hath taken another gentleman,
    Called Iohn of Carnabie.

6 Then bespake him Charles Nevill;
    To all his men, I wott, sayd hee,
    Sayes, I must into Scottland fare;
    Soe nie the borders is noe biding for
        me.

7 When he came to Humes Castle,
    And all his noble companye;
    The Lord Hume halched them right
        soone,
    Saying, Banished men, welcome to
        mee !

8 They had not beene in Humes Castle
    Not a month and dayes three,
    But the regent of Scottland and he got
        witt
    That banished men there shold be.

9 'I 'le write a letter,' sayd the regent then,
    'And send to Humes Castle hastilye,
    To see whether Lord Hume wilbe soe
        good
    To bring the banished men vnto mee.

10 '*That* lord and I haue beene att deadlye
        fuyde,
    And hee and I cold neu*er* agree;
    Writting a letter, *that* will not serue;
    The banished men must not speake
        with me.

11 'But I will send for the garrison of
        Barwicke,
    That they will come all *with* speede,
    And *with* them will come a noble cap-
        taine,
    Which is called Cap*tain* Reade.'

12 Then the Lord Hume he got witt
    They wold seeke vnto Nevill, where
        he did lye;
    He tooke them out of the castle of
        Hume,
    And brought them into the castle of
        Camelye.

13 Then bespake him Charles Nevill,
    To all his men, I wott, spoke hee,
    Sayes, I must goe take a noble shippe,
    And wee 'le be marriners vpon the sea.

14 I 'le seeke out fortune where it doth
        lye;
    In Scottland there is noe byding for
        mee;
    Then the tooke leaue *with* fayre Scott-
        land,
    For they are sealing vpon the sea.

15 They had not sayled vpon the sea
    Not one day and monthes three,
    But they were ware of a noble shippe,
    That fiue topps bare all soe hye.

16 Then Nevill called to Martinfeeld,
    Sayd, Martinffeeld, come hither to
        mee;
    Some good councell, Martinfeeld,
    I pray thee giue it vnto mee.

17 Thou told me when I was in England
        fayre,
    Before *that* I did take the sea,

Thou neu*er* sawst noe banner borne
  But thou wold ken it with thine eye.

18 Thou neu*er* saw noe man in the face,
  Iff thou had seene before w*i*th thine
    eye,
  [But] thou coldest haue kend thy freind
    by thy foe,
  And then haue told it vnto mee.

19 Thou neu*er* heard noe speeche spoken,
  Neither in Greeke nor Hebrewe,
  [But] thou coldest haue answered them
    in any language,
  And then haue told it vnto mee.

20 'M*a*ster, m*a*ster, see you yonder faire
    ancyent ?
  Yonder is the serpent and the ser-
    pents head,
  The mould-warpe in the middest of itt,
  And itt all shines w*i*th gold soe redde.

21 'Yonder is Duke Iohn of Austria,
  A noble warryour on the sea,
  Whose dwelling is in Ciuill land,
  And many men, God wot, hath hee.'

22 Then bespake him Martinfeelde,
  To all his fellowes, I wot, said hee,
  Turne our noble shipp about,
  And *that*'s a token *that* wee will flee.

23 'Thy councell is not good, Martinfeeld;
  Itt falleth not out fitting for mee;
  I rue the last time I turnd my backe;
  I did displease my prince and the
    countrye.'

24 Then bespake him noble Nevill,
  To all his men, I wott, sayd hee,
  Sett me vp my faire Dun Bull,
  W*i*th gilden hornes hee beares all soe
    hye.

25 And I will passe yonder noble Duke,
  By the leaue of mild Marye;
  For yonder is the Duke of Austria,
  That trauells now vpon the sea.

26 And then bespake this noble Duke,
  Vnto his men then sayd hee,
  Yonder is sure some nobleman,
  Or else some youth *that* will not
    flee.

27 I will put out a pinace fayre,
  A harold of armes vpon the sea,
  And goe thy way to yonder noble shippe,
  And bring the m*a*sters name to mee.

28 When the herald of armes came before
    noble Nevill,
  He fell downe low vpon his knee:
  'You must tell me true what is your
    name,
  And in what countrye your dwelling
    may bee.'

29 'That will I not doe,' sayd noble Nevill,
  'By Mary mild, *that* mayden ffree,
  Except I first know thy m*a*sters name,
  And in what country his dwelling may
    bee.'

30 Then bespake the herald of armes,
  O *that* he spoke soe curteouslye !
  Duke Iohn of Austria is my m*a*sters
    name,
  He will neu*er* lene it vpon the sea.

31 He hath beene in the citye of Rome,
  His dwelling is in Ciuillee:
  'Then wee are poore Brittons,' the Nevill
    can say,
  'Where wee trauell vpon the sea.

32 'And Charles Nevill itt is my name,
  I will neu*er* lene it vpon the sea;
  When I was att home in England faire,
  I was the Erle of Westmoreland,'
    sayd hee.

33 Then backe is gone this herald of armes
  Whereas this noble duke did lye;
  'Loe, yonder are poore Brittons,' can he
    say,
  'Where the trauell vpon the sea.

34 'And Charles Nevill is their m*a*sters
    name,
  He will neu*er* lene it vpon the sea;
  When he was at home in England fayre,
  He was the Erle of Westmoreland,
    said hee.'

35 Then bespake this noble duke,
  And euer he spake soe hastilye,
  And said, Goe backe to yonder noble-
    man,
  And bid him come and speake w*i*th me.

36 For I haue read in the Booke of Mable,
  There shold a Brittaine come ouer
    the sea,
  Charles Nevill with a childs voice:
  I pray God that it may be hee.

37 When these two nobles they didden
    meete,
  They halched eche other right cur-
    teouslye;
  Yett Nevill halched Iohn the sooner
  Because a banished man, alas ! was
    hee.

38 'Call in your men,' sayd this noble duke,
  'Faine your men that I wold see;'
  'Euer alas !' said noble Nevill,
  'They are but a litle small companye.'

39 First he called in Martinfield,
  That Martinffeeld that cold prophe-
    cye;
  He call[ed] in then Lord Dakers,
  A lords sonne of high degree.

40 Then called he in old Master Nortton,
  And sonnes four in his companye;
  He called in one other gentleman,
  Called Iohn of Carnabye.

41 'Loe ! these be all my men,' said noble
    Nevill,
  'And all that's in my companye;
  When we were att home in England
    fayre,
  Our prince and wee cold not agree.'

42 Then bespake this noble duke:
  To try your manhood on the sea,
  Old Master Nortton shall goe ouer into
    France,
  And his sonnes four in his companye.

43 And my lord Dakers shall goe over into
    Ffrance,
  There a captaine ffor to bee;
  And those two other gentlemen wold
    goe with him,
  And for to fare in his companye.

44 And you your-selfe shall goe into Ciuill
    land,
  And Marttinffeild that can prophecye;
  'That will I not doe,' sayd noble Nevill,
  'By Mary mild, that mayden free.

45 'For the haue knowen me in wele and
    woe,
  In neede, scar[s]nesse and pouertye;
  Before I 'le part with the worst of them,
  I 'le rather part with my liffe,' sayd
    hee.

46 And then bespake this noble duke,
  And euer he spake soe curteouslye;
  Says, You shall part with none of
    them,
  There is soe much manhood in your
    bodye.

47 Then these two noblemen labored to-
    gether,
  Pleasantlye vpon the sea;
  Their landing was in Ciuill land,
  In Ciuilee that ffaire citye.

48 Three nights att this dukes Nevill did
    lye,
  And serued like a nobleman was hee;
  Then the duke made a supplication,
  And sent it to the queene of Ciuilee.

49 Saying, Such a man is your citye within,
  I mett him pleasantlye vpon the sea;
  He seemes to be a noble man,
  And captaine to your Grace he faine
    wold bee.

50 Then the queene sent for [these] noble
    men
  For to come into her companye;
  When Nevill came before the queene,
  Hee kneeled downe vpon his knee.

51 Shee tooke him vp by the lilly-white
    hand,
  Said, Welcome, my lord, hither to
    me;
  You must first tell me your name,
  And in what countrye thy dwelling
    may bee.

52 He said, Charles Nevill is my name;
  I will neuer lene it in noe countrye;
  When I was att home in England fayre,
  I was the Erle of Westmorland trulye.

53 The queene made him captaine ouer
    forty thousand,
  Watch and ward within Ciuill land
    to keepe,

And for to warr against the heathen
   soldan,
   And for to helpe her in her neede.

54 When the heathen soldan he gott witt,
   In Barbarye where he did lye,
   Sainge, Such a man is in yonder citye
    within,
   And a bold venturer by sea is hee,

55 Then the heathen soldan made a letter,
   And sent it to the queene instantlye,
   And all that heard this letter reade
   Where it was rehersed in Ciuillee.

56 Saying, Haue you any man your land
    within
   Man to man dare fight with mee ?
   And both our lands shalbe ioyned in
    one,
   And cristened lands they both shalbe.

57 Shee said, I haue noe man my land
    within
   Man to man dare fight with thee;
   But euery day thou shalt haue a battell,
   If it be for these weekes three.

58 All beheard him Charles Nevill,
   In his bedd where he did lye,
   And when he came the queene before,
   He fell downe low vpon his knee.

59 ' Grant me a boone, my noble dame,
   For Chrissts loue that dyed on tree;
   Ffor I will goe fight with yond heathen
    soldan,
   If you will bestowe the manhood on
    mee.'

60 Then bespake this curteous queene,
   And euer shee spoke soe curteouslye:
   Though you be a banished man out of
    your realme,
   It is great pitye that thou shold dye.

61 Then bespake this noble duke,
   As hee stood hard by the queenes
    knee:
   As I haue read in the Booke of Mable,
   There shall a Brittone come ouer the
    sea,

62 And Charles Nevill shold be his name;
   But a childs voyce, I wott, hath hee,

And if he be in Christendome;
   For hart and hand this man hath hee.

63 Then the queenes councell cast their
    heads together,
   .   .   .   .   .
   That Nevill shold fight with the heathen
    soldan
   That dwelt in the citye of Barbarye.

64 The battell and place appointed was
   In a fayre greene, hard by the sea,
   And they shood meete att the Headless
    Crosse,
   And there to fight right manfullye.

65 Then Nevill cald for the queenes an-
    cient,
   And faine that ancient he wold see;
   The brought him forth the broken sword,
   With bloodye hands therein trulye.

66 The brought him forth the headless
    crosse,
   In that ancyent it was seene;
   ' O this is a token,' sayd Martinfeeld,
    ' That sore ouerthrowen this prince
    hath beene.

67 ' O sett me vp my fayre Dun Bull,
   And trumpetts blow me farr and nee,
   Vntill I come within a mile of the Head-
    lesse Crosse,
   That the Headlesse Crosse I may see.'

68 Then lighted downe noble Nevill,
   And sayd, Marttinffeeld, come hither
    to me;
   Heere I make thee choice captain over
    my host
   Vntill againe I may thee see.

69 Then Nevill rode to the Headless Crosse,
   Which stands soe fayre vpon the sea;
   There was he ware of the heathen soldan,
   Both fowle and vglye for to see.

70 Then the soldan began for to call;
   Twise he called lowd and hye,
   And sayd, What is this ? Some kitchin
    boy
   That comes hither to fight with mee ?

71 Then bespake him Charles Nevill,
   But a childs voice, I wott, had hee:

' Thou spekest soe litle of Gods might,
   Much more lesse I doe care for thee.'

72 Att the first meeting *that* these two mett,
   The heathen soldan and the christen
      man,
   The broke their speares quite in sunder,
   And after *that* on foote did stand.

73 The next meeting *that* these two mett,
   The swapt together w*i*th swords soe
      fine;
   The fought together till they both swett,
   Of blowes *that* were both derf and
      dire.

74 They fought an houre in battell strong;
   The soldan marke[d] Nevill w*i*th his
      eye;
   ' There shall neuer man me ouercome
      Except it be Charles Nevill,' sayd hee.

75 Then Nevill he waxed bold,
   And cunning in fight, I wott, was hee;
   Euen att the gorgett of the soldans iacke
   He stroke his head of p*r*esentlye.

76 Then kneeled downe noble Nevill,
   And thanked God for his great grace,
   That he shold come soe farr into a
      strang[e] land,
   To ouercome the soldan in place.

77 Hee tooke the head vpon his sword-
      poynt,
   And carryed it amongst his host soe
      fayre;
   When the saw the soldans head,
   They thanked God on their knees
      there.

78 Seuen miles from the citye the queene
      him mett,
   With p*r*ocession *that* was soe fayre;
   Shee tooke the crowne beside her heade,
   And wold haue crowned him k*in*g
      there.

79 ' Now nay ! Now nay ! my noble dame,
      For soe, I wott, itt cannott bee;
   I haue a ladye in England fayre,
      And wedded againe I wold not bee.'

80 The queene shee called for her penman,
   I wot shee called him lowd and hye,

Saying, ' Write him downe a hundred
      pound a day,
   To keepe his men more merrylye.'

81 ' I thanke your Grace,' sayd noble Nevill,
   ' For this worthy gift you haue giuen
      to me;
   If euer your Grace doe stand in neede,
      Champion to your Highnesse again
      I 'le bee.'

178

CAPTAIN CAR, OR, EDOM O GORDON

During the three wretched and bloody years which followed the assassination of the Regent Murray, the Catholic Earl of Huntly, George Gordon, was one of the most eminent and active of the partisans of the queen. Mary created him her lieutenant-governor, and his brother, Adam Gordon, a remarkably gallant and able soldier, whether so created or not, is sometimes called the queen's deputy-lieutenant in the north. Our ballad is concerned with a minor incident of the hostilities in Aberdeenshire between the Gordons and the Forbeses, a rival but much less powerful clan, who supported the Reformed faith and the regency or king's party. In November, 1571, Captain Thomas Ker was sent by Adam Gordon to reduce the house of Towie, belonging to Alexander (or John) Forbes, who was absent, or, perhaps, to conduct a general harrying against the Forbeses. The lady refused to surrender the place, and it was burnt, with all the household. The details are somewhat in dispute ; but there must have been something quite beyond the common in Captain Ker's proceedings, for they are denounced even in those days as infamous, and the name of Adam Gordon is said to have been made odious by them. It is not certain how far Gordon was responsible for the outrage.

A

Cotton MS. Vespasian, A. xxv, No. 67, fol. 187, of the last quarter of the 16th century; Ritson's Ancient Songs, 1790, p. 137 ; Furnivall, in Transactions of the New Shakspere Society, 1880–86, Appendix, p. 52†.

1 It befell at Martynmas,
      When wether waxed colde,
   Captaine Care said to his me*n*,
      We must go take a holde.

Syck, sike, and to-towe sike,
　And sike and like to die;
The sikest nighte that euer I abode,
　God lord haue mercy on me!

2 'Haille, master, and wether you will,
　And wether ye like it best;'
　'To the castle of Creerynbroghe,
　And there we will take our reste.'

3 'I knowe wher is a gay castle,
　Is builded of lyme and stone;
Within their is a gay ladie,
　Her lord is riden and gone.'

4 The ladie she lend on her castle-walle,
　She loked vpp and downe;
There was she ware of an host of men,
　Come riding to the towne.

5 'Se yow, my meri men all,
　And se yow what I see?
Yonder I see an host of men,
　I muse who they bee.'

6 She thought he had ben her wed lord,
　As he comd riding home;
Then was it traitur Captaine Care,
　The lord of Ester-towne.

7 They wer no soner at supper sett,
　Then after said the grace,
Or Captaine Care and all his men
　Wer lighte aboute the place.

8 'Gyue ouer thi howsse, thou lady gay,
　And I will make the a bande;
To-nighte thou shall ly within my armes,
　To-morrowe thou shall ere my lande.'

9 Then bespacke the eldest sonne,
　That was both whitt and redde:
O mother dere, geue ouer your howsse,
　Or elles we shalbe deade.

10 'I will not geue ouer my hous,' she saithe,
　'Not for feare of my lyffe;
It shalbe talked throughout the land,
　The slaughter of a wyffe.

11 'Fetch me my pestilett,
　And charge me my gonne,
That I may shott at yonder bloddy
　butcher,
　The lord of Easter-towne.'

12 Styfly vpon her wall she stode,
　And lett the pellettes flee;
But then she myst the blody bucher,
　And she slew other three.

13 '[I will] not geue ouer my hous,' she
　saithe,
　'Netheir for lord nor lowne;
Nor yet for traitour Captaine Care,
　The lord of Easter-towne.

14 'I desire of Captine Care,
　And all his bloddye band,
That he would saue my eldest sonne,
　The eare of all my lande.'

15 'Lap him in a shete,' he sayth,
　'And let him downe to me,
And I shall take him in my armes,
　His waran shall I be.'

16 The captayne sayd vnto him selfe:
　Wyth sped, before the rest,
He cut his tonge out of his head,
　His hart out of his brest.

17 He lapt them in a handkerchef,
　And knet it of knotes three,
And cast them ouer the castell-wall,
　At that gay ladye.

18 'Fye vpon the, Captayne Care,
　And all thy bloddy band!
For thou hast slayne my eldest sonne,
　The ayre of all my land.'

19 Then bespake the yongest sonne,
　That sat on the nurses knee,
Sayth, Mother gay, geue ouer your
　house;
　It smoldereth me.

20 'I wold geue my gold,' she saith,
　'And so I wolde my ffee,
For a blaste of the westryn wind,
　To dryue the smoke from thee.

21 'Fy vpon the, John Hamleton,
　That euer I paid the hyre!
For thou hast broken my castle-wall,
　And kyndled in the ffyre.'

22 The lady gate to her close parler,
　The fire fell aboute her head:

She toke vp her children thre,
    Seth, Babes, we are all dead.

23 Then bespake the hye steward,
    That is of hye degree;
Saith, Ladie gay, you are in close,
    Wether ye fighte or flee.

24 Lord Hamleton dremd in his dream,
    In Caruall where he laye,
His halle were all of fyre,
    His ladie slayne or daye.

25 'Busk and bowne, my mery men all,
    Even and go ye with me;
For I dremd that my haal was on fyre,
    My lady slayne or day.'

26 He buskt him and bownd hym,
    And like a worthi knighte;
And when he saw his hall burning,
    His harte was no dele lighte.

27 He sett a trumpett till his mouth,
    He blew as it plesd his grace;
Twenty score of Hamlentons
    Was light aboute the place.

28 'Had I knowne as much yesternighte
    As I do to-daye,
Captaine Care and all his men
    Should not haue gone so quite.

29 'Fye vpon the, Captaine Care,
    And all thy blody bande!
Thou haste slayne my lady gay,
    More wurth then all thy lande.

30 'If thou had ought eny ill will,' he saith,
    'Thou shoulde haue taken my lyffe,
And haue saved my children thre,
    All and my louesome wyffe.'

B

Percy MS., p. 34; Hales and Furnivall, 1, 79.

1 'Ffaith, master, whither you will,
    Whereas you like the best;
Vnto the castle of Bittons-borrow,
    And there to take your rest.'

2 'But yonder stands a castle faire,
    Is made of lyme and stone;
Yonder is in it a fayre lady,
    Her lord is ridden and gone.'

3 The lady stood on her castle-wall,
    She looked vpp and downe;
She was ware of an hoast of men,
    Came rydinge towards the towne.

4 'See you not, my merry men all,
    And see you not what I doe see?
Methinks I see a hoast of men;
    I muse who they shold be.'

5 She thought it had beene her louly lord,
    He had come ryding home;
It was the traitor, Captaine Carre,
    The lord of Westerton-towne.

6 They had noe sooner super sett,
    And after said the grace,
But the traitor, Captaine Carre,
    Was light about the place.

7 'Giue over thy house, thou lady gay,
    I will make thee a band;
All night with-in mine armes thou'st lye,
    To-morrow be the heyre of my land.'

8 'I'le not giue over my house,' shee said,
    'Neither for ladds nor man,
Nor yet for traitor Captaine Carre,
    Vntill my lord come home.

9 'But reach me my pistoll pe[c]e,
    And charge you well my gunne;
I'le shoote at the bloody bucher,
    The lord of Westerton.'

10 She stood vppon her castle-wall
    And let the bulletts flee,
And where shee mist   .   .
    .   .   .   .

11 But then bespake the litle child,
    That sate on the nurses knee;
Saies, Mother deere, giue ore this house,
    For the smoake it smoothers me.

12 'I wold giue all my gold, my childe,
    Soe wold I doe all my fee,
For one blast of the westerne wind
    To blow the smoke from thee.'

13 But when shee saw the fier
    Came flaming ore her head,
Shee tooke then vpp her children two,
    Sayes, Babes, we all beene dead!

14 But Adam then he fired the house,
    A sorrowfull sight to see;
Now hath he burned this lady faire
    And eke her children three.

15 Then Captaine Carre he rode away,
    He staid noe longer at that tide;
He thought that place it was to warme
    Soe neere for to abide.

16 He calld vnto his merry men all,
    Bidd them make hast away;
'For we haue slaine his children three,
    All and his lady gay.'

17 Worde came to louly London,
    To London wheras her lord lay,
His castle and his hall was burned,
    All and his lady gay.

18 Soe hath he done his children three,
    More dearer vnto him
Then either the siluer or the gold,
    That men soe faine wold win.

19 But when he looket this writing on,
    Lord, in is hart he was woe !
Saies, I will find thee, Captaine Carre,
    Wether thou ryde or goe !

20 Buske yee, bowne yee, my merrymen all,
    With tempered swords of steele,
For till I haue found out Captaine
    Carre,
    My hart it is nothing weele.

21 But when he came to Dractons-borrow,
    Soe long ere it was day,
And ther he found him Captaine Carre;
    That night he ment to stay.

*   *   *   *   *

F

The New Statistical Account of Scotland, v,
846, 1845, Parish of Loudoun, by Rev. Norman
Macleod : " known among the peasantry from
time immemorial ; " 'Loudoun Castle,' The
Ballads and Songs of Ayrshire, J. Paterson
and C. Gray, 1st Series, p. 74, Ayr, 1846.

1 It fell about the Martinmas time,
    When the wind blew snell and cauld,
That Adam o Gordon said to his men,
    Where will we get a hold ?

2 See [ye] not where yonder fair castle
    Stands on yon lily lee ?
The laird and I hae a deadly feud,
    The lady fain would I see.

3 As she was up on the househead,
    Behold, on looking down,
She saw Adam o Gordon and his men,
    Coming riding to the town.

4 The dinner was not well set down,
    Nor the grace was scarcely said,
Till Adam o Gordon and his men
    About the walls were laid.

5 'It's fause now fa thee, Jock my man !
    Thou might a let me be;
Yon man has lifted the pavement-stone,
    An let in the low unto me.'

6 'Seven years I served thee, fair ladie,
    You gave me meat and fee;
But now I am Adam o Gordon's man,
    An maun either do it or die.'

7 'Come down, come down, my lady Lou-
    doun,
    Come down thou unto me !
I'll wrap thee on a feather-bed,
    Thy warrand I shall be.'

8 'I'll no come down, I'll no come down,
    For neither laird no[r] loun;
Nor yet for any bloody butcher
    That lives in Altringham town.

9 'I would give the black,' she says,
    'And so would I the brown,
If that Thomas, my only son,
    Could charge to me a gun.'

10 Out then spake the lady Margaret,
    As she stood on the stair;
The fire was at her goud garters,
    The lowe was at her hair.

11 'I would give the black,' she says,
    'And so would I the brown,
For a drink of yon water,
    That runs by Galston Town.'

12 Out then spake fair Annie,
    She was baith jimp and sma:
'O row me in a pair o sheets,
    And tow me down the wa !'

13 'O hold thy tongue, thou fair Annie,
    And let thy talkin be;
  For thou must stay in this fair castle,
    And bear thy death with me.'

14 'O mother,' spoke the lord Thomas,
    As he sat on the nurse's knee,
  'O mother, give up this fair castle,
    Or the reek will worrie me.'

15 'I would rather be burnt to ashes
    sma,
  And be cast on yon sea-foam,
  Before I 'd give up this fair castle,
    And my lord so far from home.

16 'My good lord has an army strong,
    He 's now gone oer the sea;
  He bad me keep this gay castle,
    As long as it would keep me.

17 'I 've four-and-twenty brave milk kye,
    Gangs on yon lily lee;
  I 'd give them a' for a blast of wind,
    To blaw the reek from me.'

18 O pittie on yon fair castle,
    That 's built with stone and lime !
  But far mair pittie on Lady Loudoun,
    And all her children nine !

H

Scotch Ballads, Materials for Border Min-
strelsy, No. 75, Abbotsford. Communicated to
Scott November 6, 1803, by Bruce Campbell,
Sornbeg, Galston, Ayrshire, through David
Boyle, Advocate, afterwards Lord Justice Gen-
eral of Scotland.

1 IT fell about the Martinmass time,
    When the wind blew shill and cald,
  That Adam McGordon said to his
    men,
  Where will we get a hall ?

2 'There is a hall here near by,
    Well built with lime and stone;
  There is a lady there within
    As white as the . . bone.'

3 'Seven year and more this lord and I
    Has had a deadly feud,
  And now, since her good lord 's frae
    hame,
  His place to me she 'll yield.'

4 She looked oer her castle-wall,
    And so she looked down,
  And saw Adam McGordon and his
    men
  Approaching the wood-end.

5 'Steik up, steik up my yett,' she says,
    'And let my draw-bridge fall;
  There is meickle treachery
    Walking about my wall.'

6 She had not the sentence past,
    Nor yet the word well said,
  When Adam McGordon and his men
    About the walls were laid.

7 She looked out at her window,
    And then she looked down,
  And then she saw Jack, her own man,
    Lifting the pavement-stane.

8 'Awa, awa, Jack my man !
    Seven year I paid you meat and fee,
  And now you lift the pavement-stane
    To let in the low to me.'

9 'I yield, I yield, O lady fair,
    Seven year ye paid me meat and
      fee;
  But now I am Adam McGordon's man,
    I must either do or die.'

10 'If ye be Adam McGordon's man,
    As I true well ye be,
  Prove true unto your own master,
    And work your will to me.'

11 'Come down, come down, my lady
      Campbell,
  Come down into my hand;
  Ye shall lye all night by my side,
    And the morn at my command.'

12 'I winna come down,' this lady says,
    'For neither laird nor lown,
  Nor to no bloody butcher's son,
    The Laird of Auchindown.

13 'I wald give all my kine,' she says,
    'So wald I fifty pound,
  That Andrew Watty he were here;
    He would charge me my gun.

14 'He would charge me my gun,
    And put in bullets three,

That I might shoot that cruel traitor
   That works his wills on me.'

15 He shot in, and [s]he shot out,
   The value of an hour,
Until the hall Craigie North
   Was like to be blawn in the air.

16 He fired in, and she fired out,
   The value of hours three,
Until the hall Craigie North
   The reik went to the sea.

17 ' O the frost, and ae the frost,
   The frost that freezes fell!
I cannot stay within my bower,
   The powder it blaws sae bald.'

18 But then spake her oldest son,
   He was both white and red;
' O mither dear, yield up your house !
   We 'll all be burnt to deed.'

19 Out then spake the second son,
   He was both red and fair;
' O brother dear, would you yield up
     your house,
And you your father's heir ! '

20 Out then spake the little babe,
   Stood at the nurse's knee;
' O mither dear, yield up your house !
   The reik will worry me.'

21 Out then speaks the little nurse,
   The babe upon her knee;
' O lady, take from me your child !
   I 'll never crave my fee.'

22 ' Hold thy tongue, thou little nurse,
   Of thy prating let me bee;
For be it death or be it life,
   Thou shall take share with me.

23 ' I wald give a' my sheep,' she says,
   ' T[hat] . . yon . . s[ha],
I had a drink of that wan water
   That runs down by my wa.'

179

ROOKHOPE RYDE

The date of this ryde, or raid, may be precisely ascertained from the ballad itself; it is shown by 13⁴, 11 to be December 6, 1569. The thieves of Thirlwall (Northumberland) and Williehaver, or Willeva (Cumberland), avail themselves of the confusion incident to the Rising in the North and of the absence of a part of the fencible men (some of whom were with the earls, others with Bowes in Barnard castle) to make a foray into Rookhope, in Weardale, Durham. Rookhope is the name of a valley, about five miles in length, at the termination of which Rookhope burn empties itself into the river Wear.

The Bishopric Garland, or Durham Minstrel, [edited by Joseph Ritson,] 2d ed., Newcastle, 1792; here, from the reprint by Joseph Haslewood, 1809, p. 54, in Northern Garlands, London, 1810. " Taken down from the chanting of George Collingood the elder, late of Boltsburn, in the neighborhood of Ryhope," who died in 1785.

1 ROOKHOPE stands in a pleasant place,
   If the false thieves wad let it be;
But away they steal our goods apace,
   And ever an ill death may they die !

2 And so is the men of Thirlwa 'nd Willie-
     haver,
And all their companies thereabout,
That is minded to do mischief,
   And at their stealing stands not out.

3 But yet we will not slander them all,
   For there is of them good enough;
It is a sore consumed tree
   That on it bears not one fresh bough.

4 Lord God ! is not this a pitful case,
   That men dare not drive their goods
     to t' fell,
But limmer thieves drives them away,
   That fears neither heaven nor hell ?

5 Lord, send us peace into the realm,
   That every man may live on his own !
I trust to God, if it be his will,
   That Weardale men may never be
     overthrown.

6 For great troubles they 've had in
     hand,
With borderers pricking hither and
     thither,
But the greatest fray that eer they had
   Was with the ' men ' of Thirlwa 'nd
     Williehaver.

7 They gatherd together so royally,
    The stoutest men and the best in gear,
And he that rade not on a horse,
    I wat he rade on a weil-fed mear.

8 So in the morning, before they came
        out,
    So well, I wot, they broke their fast;
In the [forenoon they came] unto a bye
        fell,
    Where some of them did eat their
        last.

9 When they had eaten aye and done,
    They sayd some captains here needs
        must be:
Then they choosed forth Harry Corbyl,
    And 'Symon Fell,' and Martin Rid-
        ley.

10 Then oer the moss, where as they came,
    With many a brank and whew,
One of them could to another say,
    'I think this day we are men enew.'

11 'For Weardale men is a journey taen;
    They are so far out-oer yon fell
That some of them's with the two earls,
    And others fast in Barnard castell.

12 'There we shal get gear enough,
    For there is nane but women at hame;
The sorrowful fend that they can make
    Is loudly cries as they were slain.'

13 Then in at Rookhope-head they came,
    And there they thought tul a had their
        prey,
But they were spy'd coming over the
        Dry Rig,
    Soon upon Saint Nicholas' day.

14 Then in at Rookhope-head they came,
    They ran the forest but a mile;
They gatherd together in four hours
    Six hundred sheep within a while.

15 And horses I trow they gat
    But either ane or twa,
And they gat them all but ane
    That belanged to great Rowley.

16 That Rowley was the first man that did
        them spy;
    With that he raised a mighty cry;

The cry it came down Rookhope burn,
    And spread through Weardale has-
        teyly.

17 Then word came to the bailif's house,
    At the East Gate, where he did dwell;
He was walkd out to the Smale Burns,
    Which stands above the Hanging
        Well.

18 His wife was wae when she heard tell,
    So well she wist her husband wanted
        gear;
She gard saddle him his horse in haste,
    And neither forgot sword, jack, nor
        spear.

19 The bailif got wit before his gear came
    That such news was in the land;
He was sore troubled in his heart,
    That on no earth that he could stand.

20 His brother was hurt three days before,
    With limmer thieves that did him
        prick;
Nineteen bloody wounds lay him upon;
    What ferly was 't that he lay sick?

21 But yet the bailif shrinked nought,
    But fast after them he did hye,
And so did all his neighbours near,
    That went to bear him company.

22 But when the bailiff was gathered,
    And all his company,
They were numberd to never a man
    But forty [or] under fifty.

23 The thieves was numberd a hundred men,
    I wat they were not of the worst
That could be choosed out of Thirlwa
    'nd Williehaver,
    .   .   .   .   .

24 But all that was in Rookhope-head,
    And all that was i Nuketon Cleugh,
Where Weardale men oertook the
        thieves,
    And there they gave them fighting
        eneugh.

25 So sore they made them fain to flee,
    As many was 'a'' out of hand,
And, for tul have been at home again,
    They would have been in iron bands;

26 And for the space of long seven years,
   As sore they mighten a had their
      lives;
   But there was never one of them
   That ever thought to have seen their
      'wives.'

27 About the time the fray began,
   I trow it lasted but an hour,
   Till many a man lay weaponless,
   And was sore wounded in that stour.

28 Also before that hour was done,
   Four of the thieves were slain,
   Besides all those that wounded were,
   And eleven prisoners there was taen.

29 George Carrick and his brother Edie,
   Them two, I wot, they were both
      slain;
   Harry Corbyl and Lennie Carrick
   Bore them company in their pain.

30 One of our Weardale men was slain,
   Rowland Emerson his name hight;
   I trust to God his soul is well,
   Because he 'fought' unto the right.

31 But thus they sayd: 'We'll not depart
   While we have one; speed back
      again!'
   And when they came amongst the dead
      men,
   There they found George Carrick
      slain.

32 And when they found George Carrick
      slain,
   I wot it went well near their 'heart;'
   Lord, let them never make a better end
   That comes to play them sicken a
      'part!'

33 I trust to God, no more they shal,
   Except it be one for a great chance;
   For God wil punish all those
   With a great heavy pestilence.

34 Thir limmer thieves, they have good
      hearts,
   They nevir think to be oerthrown;
   Three banners against Weardale men
      they bare,
   As if the world had been all their
      own.

35 Thir Weardale men, they have good
      hearts,
   They are as stif as any tree;
   For, if they'd every one been slain,
   Never a foot back man would flee.

36 And such a storm amongst them fell
   As I think you never heard the like,
   For he that bears his head so high,
   He oft-times falls into the dyke.

37 And now I do entreat you all,
   As many as are present here,
   To pray for [the] singer of this song,
   For he sings to make blithe your
      cheer.

180

KING JAMES AND BROWN

   This ballad must of course not be regarded
as historical, but there are correspondences between the story and the proceedings by which
the Earl of Morton, in April, 1578, after his
resignation of the regency, obtained possession
of the person of the young king James VI and
virtually reëstablished himself in power. The
citizens of Edinburgh rose in arms against Morton (cf. sts. 21, 22), and large forces collected
from other parts of Scotland for the liberation
of James. The Douglas of the ballad is clearly
William Douglas of Lochleven, who was a par-
tisan of Morton.

   'Kinge James and Browne,' Percy MS., p.
58; Hales and Furnivall, I, 135.

1 As I did walke my selfe alone,
     And by one garden greene,
   I heard a yonge prince make great
      moane,
     Which did turne my hart to teene.

2 'O Lord!' he then said vntou me,
   'Why haue I liued soe long?
   For yonder comes a cruell Scott,'
     Quoth hee, 'that will doe me some
      ronge.'

3 And then came traitor Douglas there,
     He came for to betray his king;
   Some they brought bills, and some they
      brought bowes,
     And some the brought other things.

4 The king was aboue in a gallery,
   With a heauy heart;
   Vnto his body was sett about
     With swords and speares soe sharpe.

5 'Be you the lordes of Scotland,' he said,
   '*That* hither for councell seeke to
     me ?
   Or bee yoe traitors to my crowne,
     My blood *that* you wold see ? '

6 'Wee are the lords of Scottland,' they
     said,
   'Nothing we come to craue of thee;
   But wee be traitors to thy crowne,
     Thy blood that wee will see.'

7 'O fye vpon you, you false Scotts !
   For you neuer all trew wilbe;
   My grandfather you haue slaine,
     And caused my mother to flee.

8 'My grandfather you haue slaine,
   And my owne father you hanged on a
     tree;
   And now,' quoth he, 'the like treason
     You haue now wrought for me.

9 'Ffarwell hart, and farwell hand !
   Farwell all pleasures alsoe !
   Farwell th .   . my head
   .   .   .   .

10 .   .   .   .   .
   'If thou wilt .   .   .
     And soe goe away with mee.'

11 'Goe marry thy daughter to whome
     thou wilt,'
   Quoth Browne; 'thou marrys none to
     me;
   For I 'le not be a traitor,' quoth Browne,
     'For all the gold that euer I see.'

12 This Douglas, hearing Browne soe say,
   Began to flee away full fast;
   'But tarry a while,' saies lusty Browne,
   'I 'le make you to pay before you
     passe.'

13 He hath taken the Douglas prisoner,
   And hath brought him before the king;
   He kneeled low vpon his knee,
     For pardon there prainge.

14 'How shold I pardon thee,' saith the
     king,
   'And thou 'le remaine a traitor still ?
   For euer since that I was borne,'
     Quoth he, 'thou hast sought my blood
     to spill.'

15 'For if you will grant me my pardon,'
     he said,
   'Out of this place soe free,
   I wilbe sworne before your Grace
     A trew subiect to bee.'

16 'God for-gaue his death,' said the king,
   'When he was nayled vpon a tree;
   And as free as euer God forgaue his
     death,
   Douglas,' quoth he, 'I 'le forgiue thee.

17 'And all the traitors in Scottland,'
   Quoth he, 'both great and small;
   As free as euer God forgaue his death,
     Soe free I will forgiue them all.'

18 'I thanke you for your pardon, king,
   That you haue granted forth soe
     plaine;
   If I liue a twelue month to an end,
     You shall not aliue remaine.

19 'Tomorrow yet, or ere I dine,
   I meane to doo thee one good turne;
   For Edenborrow, that is thine owne,'
     Quoth he, 'I will both h[arry] and
     [burne].'

20 Thus Douglas hied towards Edenborrow,
   And many of his men were gone
     beffore,
   And after him on euery side,
     With him there went some twenty
     score.

21 But when that they did see him come,
   They cryed lowd with voices, saying,
   'Yonder comes a false traitor,
     That wold haue slaine our king.'

22 They chaynd vp the gates of Edenbor-
     row,
   And there the made them wonderous
     fast,
   And there Browne sett on Douglas
     againe,
     And quicklye did him ouer cast.

23 But worde came backe againe to the king,
    With all the speed that euer might
    bee,
    That traitor Douglas there was taken,
    And his body was there to see.

24 'Bring me his taker,' quoth the king,
    'Come, quickly bring him vnto me!
    I 'le giue a thousand pound a yeere,
    What man soeuer he bee.'

25 But then they called lusty Browne;
    Sayes, 'Browne, come thou hither to
    mee.
    How oft hast thou foughten for my sake,
    And alwayes woone the victory?'

26 'The first time that I fought for you,
    It was in Edenborrow, king;
    If there I had not stoutly stood,
    My leege, you neuer had beene king.

27 'The second time I fought for you,
    Here I will tell you in this place;
    I killd the sheriffs sonne of Carlile,'
    Quoth he, 'that wold haue slaine your
    Grace.

28 'The third time *that* I fought for you,
    Here for to let you vnderstand,
    I slew the Bishopp of St Andrew[s],'
    Quoth he, 'with a possat in [his
    hand].'

29 .   .   . quoth hee,
    '*That* euer my manhood I did trye;
    I 'le make a vow for Englands sake
    That I will neuer battell flee.'

30 'God amercy, Browne,' then said the
    king,
    'And God amercy heartilye!
    Before I made thee but a knight,
    But now an earle I will make thee.

31 'God saue the queene of England,' he
    said,
    'For her blood is verry neshe;
    As neere vnto her I am
    As a colloppe shorne from the fleshe.'

32 'If I be false to England,' he said,
    'Either in earnest or in iest,
    I might be likened to a bird,'
    Quoth he, 'that did defile it nest.'

181

THE BONNY EARL OF MURRAY

James Stewart, son of Sir James Stewart of Doune, became Earl of Murray in consequence of his marriage with the oldest daughter and heiress of the Regent Murray. "He was a comely personage, of a great stature, and strong of body like a kemp." There was a violent hostility between Murray and the Earl of Huntly. According to Spottiswood (History of the Church of Scotland, 1655, p. 387), after his assault on Holyrood House in December (or September), 1591, "Bothwell went into the north, looking to be supplied by the Earl of Murray, his cousin-german; which the king suspecting, Andrew Lord Ochiltrie was sent to bring Murray unto the south, of purpose to work a reconcilement betwixt him and Huntly. But a rumor being raised in the mean while that the Earl of Murray was seen in the palace with Bothwell on the night of the enterprise, the same was entertained by Huntly (who waited then at court) to make him suspected of the king, and prevailed so far as he did purchase a commission to apprehend and bring Murray to his trial. The nobleman, not fearing that any such course should be used, was come to Donibristle, a house situated on the north side of Forth, and belonging to his mother the Lady Doune. Huntly, being advertised of his coming, and how he lay there secure, accompanied only with the Sheriff of Murray and a few of his own retinue, went thither and beset the house, requiring him to render. The Earl of Murray refusing to put himself in the hands of his enemy, after some defence made, wherein the sheriff was killed, fire was set to the house, and they within forced by the violence of the smoke and flame to come forth. The earl staid a great space after the rest, and, the night falling down, ventured among his enemies, and, breaking through the midst of them, did so far outrun them all as they supposed he was escaped; yet searching him among the rocks, he was discovered by the tip of his head-piece, which had taken fire before he left the house, and unmercifully slain." This outrage was done in the month of February, 1592. Huntly sheltered himself under the king's commission, and was not punished.

A

'The Bonny Earl of Murray,' Ramsay's Tea-Table Miscellany, 11th ed., London, 1750, p. 356 (vol. iv).

1 Ye Highlands, and ye Lawlands,
   Oh where have you been ?
They have slain the Earl of Murray,
   And they layd him on the green.

2 ' Now wae be to thee, Huntly!
   And wherefore did you sae ?
I bade you bring him wi you,
   But forbade you him to slay.'

3 He was a braw gallant,
   And he rid at the ring;
And the bonny Earl of Murray,
   Oh he might have been a king !

4 He was a braw gallant,
   And he playd at the ba;
And the bonny Earl of Murray
   Was the flower amang them a'.

5 He was a braw gallant,
   And he playd at the glove;
And the bonny Earl of Murray,
   Oh he was the Queen's love !

6 Oh lang will his lady
   Look oer the castle Down,
Eer she see the Earl of Murray
   Come sounding thro the town !
   Eer she, etc.

B

' The Bonnie Earl o Murray,' Finlay's Scottish Ballads, ii, 11 ; from recitation.

1 ' Open the gates,
   and let him come in;
He is my brother Huntly,
   he 'll do him nae harm.'

2 The gates they were opent,
   they let him come in,
But fause traitor Huntly,
   he did him great harm.

3 He 's ben and ben,
   And ben to his bed,
And with a sharp rapier
   he stabbed him dead.

4 The lady came down the stair,
   wringing her hands:
' He has slain the Earl o Murray,
   the flower o Scotland.'

5 But Huntly lap on his horse,
   rade to the king:
' Ye 're welcome hame, Huntly,
   and whare hae ye been ?

6 ' Whare hae ye been ?
   and how hae ye sped ? '
' I 've killed the Earl o Murray,
   dead in his bed.'

7 ' Foul fa you, Huntly !
   and why did ye so ?
You might have taen the Earl o Murray,
   and saved his life too.'

8 ' Her bread it 's to bake,
   her yill is to brew;
My sister 's a widow,
   and sair do I rue.

9 ' Her corn grows ripe,
   her meadows grow green,
But in bonny Dinnibristle
   I darena be seen.'

182

THE LAIRD O LOGIE

Francis Stewart, Earl of Bothwell, a madcap cousin of James VI. had been guilty of a violent assault upon Holyrood House in December (or September), 1591, and in June, 1592, had " conspired the apprehension of the king's person " while James was residing at Falkland. A confederate, Wemyss of Logie, was arrested and " ordained to be tried by an assize and executed to the death. But the same night that he was examined, he escaped out by the means of a gentlewoman whom he loved, a Dane, who conveyed him out of his keepers' hands, through the queen's chamber, where his Majesty and the queen were lying in their beds, to a window in the backside of the place, where he went down upon a tow [rope], and shot three pistols in token of his onlouping [mounting his horse] where some of his servants, with the laird of Niddry, were awaiting him." (Moysie's Memoirs, p. 95.) According to another account, the gentlewoman got Logie out of his keepers' hands by pretending that the king wished to speak with him, and they, " suspecting nothing, for they knew her to be the principal maid in the chamber, conveyed him to the door of the bedchamber " and waited there while she was letting him down at a window. Though the queen had no hand in the freeing of Young Logie, she stood by her Danish attendant, and appears to have pacified the king. Logie was pardoned and married the gentlewoman. Her name was really Margaret, as in the ballad.

A*

'The Laird of Logie.' Scotch Ballads, Materials for Border Minstrelsy, No. 3 a, Abbotsford. Sent to Scott September 11, 1802, by William Laidlaw; received by him from Mr Bartram of Biggar.

1 I WILL sing, if ye will harken,
      An ye wad listen unto me;
    I 'll tell ye of a merry passage
      Of the wanton laird of Young Logie.

2 Young Logie 's laid in Edinborough chapel,
      Carmichaell 's keeper of the key;
    I heard a may lamenting sair,
      All for the laird of Young Logie.

3 'Lament, lament na, May Margret,
      And o your weeping let me be;
    For ye maun to the king your sell,
      And ask the life of Young Logie.'

4 May Margaret has kilted her green cleeding,
      And she 's currld back her yellow hair,
    And she 's away to the king hersell,
      And adieu to Scotland for ever mair !

5 When she came before the king,
      She fell low down on her knee:
    'It 's what 's your will wi me, May Margret,
      And what makes all this courtesey ?'
    'Naething, naething, my sovreign liege,
      But grant me the life of Young Logie.'

6 'O no, O no, May Margret,
      No, in sooth it maun na be;
    For the morn, or I taste meat or drink,
      Hee hanged shall Young Logie be.'

7 She has stolen the king's reeding-comb,
      But an the queen her wedding-knife,
    And she has sent it to Carmichaell,
      To cause Young Logie come by life.

8 She sent him a purse of the red gold,
      Another of the white money,
    And sent him a pistol into each hand,
      And bade him shoot when he got fra.

9 When he came to the Tolbooth stair,
      There he loot his volley flee,
    Which made the king in his chamber start,
      Even in the chamber where he lay.

10 'Gae out, gae out, my merrie men,
      And gar Carmichael come speake wi me,
    For I 'll lay my life the pledge of that,
      That yon 's the volley of Young Logie.'

11 When Carmichael came before the king,
      He fell low down on his knee;
    The very first word that the king spake,
      'How dois the laird o Young Logie ?'

12 Carmichael turnd him round about,
      A wait the salt tear blint his eye:
    'There came a tacken frae the king
      Has tean the laird awa frae me.'

13 'Hast thou playd me that, Carmichael ?
      Hast thou playd me that ?' quo he;
    'The morn the Justice Court 's to stand,
      And Logie's place ye maun supply.'

14 Carmichal 's awa to May Margr[e]t's bower,
      Een as fast as he may dree :
    'It 's if Young Logie be within,
      Tell him to come speak to me.'

15 May Margret's turnd her round about,
      A wait a loud laughter gae she:
    'The egg is cheeped and the bird is flown,
      And seek ye the laird of Young Logie.'

16 The one is sheppd at the pier o Leith,
      The other at the Queen's Ferry,
    And she has gotten a father to her bairn,
      The wanton laird of Young [Logie].

B

a. 'The young Laird of Ochiltrie,' Herd, The Ancient and Modern Scots Songs, 1769, p. 240; ed. 1776, I, 21. b. 'The Winsome Laird of

Young Logie,' Scotch Ballads, Materials for
Border Minstrelsy, No. 137 a, Abbotsford,
"sung by Lady A. Lindsay."

1 O LISTEN, gude peopell, to my tale,
    Listen to what I tel to thee;
  The king has taiken a poor prisoner,
    The wanton laird of Ochiltrie.

2 When news came to our guidly queen,
    Sche sicht, and said right mournfullie,
  'O what will cum of Lady Margret!
    Wha beirs sick luve to Ochiltrie.'

3 Lady Margret tore hir yellow hair
    When as the queen tald hir the saim:
  'I wis that I had neir bin born,
    Nor neir had knawn Ochiltrie's naim!'

4 'Fie, na!' quoth the queen, 'that maunna
    be;
  Fie, na! that maunna be;
  I'll fynd ye out a better way
    To saif the lyfe of Ochiltrie.'

5 The queen sche trippit up the stair,
    And lowlie knielt upon hir knie:
  'The first boon which I cum to craive
    Is the life of gentel Ochiltrie.'

6 'O iff you had askd me castels or
    towirs,
  I wad hae gin thaim, twa or thrie;
  Bot a' the monie in fair Scotland
    Winna buy the lyfe of Ochiltrie.'

7 The queen sche trippit down the stair,
    And down she gade richt mournfullie:
  'It's a' the monie in fair Scotland
    Winna buy the lyfe of Ochiltrie!'

8 Lady Margaret tore her yellow hair
    When as the queen tald hir the saim:
  'I'll tak a knife and end my lyfe,
    And be in the grave as soon as him!'

9 'Ah, na! Fie, na!' quoth the queen,
    'Fie, na! Fie, na! this maunna be;
  I'll set ye on a better way
    To loose and set Ochiltrie frie.'

10 The queen sche slippit up the stair,
    And sche gaid up richt privatlie,
  And sche has stoun the prison-keys,
    And gane and set Ochiltrie frie.

11 And sche's gien him a purse of gowd,
    And another of whyt monie;
  Sche's gien him twa pistoles by's syde,
    Saying to him, Shute, when ye win
    frie.

12 And when he cam to the queen's window,
    Whaten a joyfou shute gae he!
  'Peace be to our royal queen,
    And peace be in hir companie!'

13 'O whaten a voyce is that?' quoth the
    king,
  'Whaten a voyce is that?' quoth he;
  'Whaten a voyce is that?' quoth the
    king;
    'I think it's the voyce of Ochiltrie.

14 'Call to me a' my gaolours,
    Call thaim by thirtie and by thrie;
  Whairfoir the morn, at twelve a clock,
    It's hangit schall they ilk ane be.'

15 'O didna ye send your keyis to us?
    Ye sent thaim be thirtie and be thrie,
  And wi thaim sent a strait command
    To set at lairge young Ochiltrie.'

16 'Ah, na! Fie, na!' quoth the queen,
    'Fie, my dear luve, this maunna be!
  And iff ye're gawn to hang thaim a',
    Indeed ye maun begin wi me.'

17 The tane was schippit at the pier of
    Leith,
  The ither at the Queen's Ferrie,
  And now the lady has gotten hir luve,
    The winsom laird of Ochiltrie.

183

WILLIE MACINTOSH

The murder of the "Bonny Earl of Murray"
(see No. 181) was the occasion of serious com-
motions in the North Highlands. Towards the
end of the year 1592, the Macintoshes of the
Clan Chattan, who of all the faction of Murray
"most eagerly endeavored to revenge his
death," invaded the estates of the Earl of
Huntly, and killed four gentlemen of the surname of Gordon. Huntly retaliated, "and
rade into Pettie (which was then in the possession of the Clan Chattan), where he wasted
and spoiled all the Clan Chattan's lands, and

killed divers of them. But as the Earl of Huntly had returned home from Pettie, he was advertised that William Macintosh with eight hundred of Clan Chattan were spoiling his lands of Cabrach: whereupon Huntly and his uncle Sir Patrick Gordon of Auchindown, with some few horsemen, made speed towards the enemy, desiring the rest of his company to follow him with all possible diligence. . . . Huntly overtook the Clan Chattan before they left the bounds of Cabrach, upon the head of a hill called Stapliegate, where, without staying for the rest of his men, he invaded them with those few he then had. After a sharp conflict he overthrew them, chased them, killed sixty of their ablest men, and hurt William Macintosh with divers others of his company."

Two William Macintoshes are confounded in the ballad. The burning of Auchindown is attributed, rightly or wrongly, to an earlier William, captain of the clan, who, in August, 1500, was formally convicted of conspiracy against the life of the Earl of Huntly, then lieutenant in the north, sentenced to lose his life and lands, and, despite a pledge to the contrary, executed shortly after by the Countess of Huntly.

A

'Burning of Auchindown.' **a.** The Thistle of Scotland, p. 106, 1823. **b.** Whitelaw, The Book of Scottish Ballads, p. 248; from an Aberdeen newspaper of about 1815.

1 'TURN, Willie Macintosh,
　　Turn, I bid you;
　Gin ye burn Auchindown,
　　Huntly will head you.'

2 'Head me or hang me,
　　That canna fley me;
　I 'll burn Auchendown
　　Ere the life lea me.'

3 Coming down Deeside,
　　In a clear morning,
　Auchindown was in flame,
　　Ere the cock-crawing.

4 But coming oer Cairn Croom,
　　And looking down, man,
　I saw Willie Macintosh
　　Burn Auchindown, man.

5 'Bonny Willie Macintosh,
　　Whare left ye your men?'
　'I left them in the Stapler,
　　But they 'll never come hame.'

6 'Bonny Willie Macintosh,
　　Whare now is your men?'
　'I left them in the Stapler,
　　Sleeping in their sheen.'

B

'Willie Mackintosh,' Finlay's Scottish Ballads, II, 89, 1808, as recollected by a lady and communicated by Walter Scott.

1 As I came in by Fiddich-side,
　　In a May morning,
　I met Willie Mackintosh,
　　An hour before the dawning.

2 'Turn again, turn again,
　　Turn again, I bid ye;
　If ye burn Auchindown,
　　Huntly he will head ye.'

3 'Head me, hang me,
　　That sall never fear me;
　I 'll burn Auchindown
　　Before the life leaves me.'

4 As I came in by Auchindown,
　　In a May morning,
　Auchindown was in a bleeze,
　　An hour before the dawning.

*　　*　　*　　*　　*

5 Crawing, crawing,
　　For my crowse crawing,
　I lost the best feather i my wing
　　For my crowse crawing.

184

THE LADS OF WAMPHRAY

" The following song celebrates the skirmish, in 1593, betwixt the Johnstones and Crichtons, which led to the revival of the ancient quarrel betwixt Johnstone and Maxwell, and finally to the battle of Dryffe Sands, in which the latter lost his life. Wamphray is the name of a parish in Annandale. Lethenhall was the abode of Johnstone of Wamphray, and continued to be so till of late years. William Johnstone of Wamphray, called the Galliard, was a noted freebooter. A place near the head of Teviotdale retains the name of the Galliard's Faulds (folds), being a valley where he used to secrete and divide his spoil with his Liddesdale and

Eskdale associates. His *nom de guerre* seems to have been derived from the dance called the galliard. The word is still used in Scotland to express an active, gay, dissipated character. Willie of Kirkhill, nephew to the Galliard, and his avenger, was also a noted Border robber." (Minstrelsy, I, 208, ed. 1802.)

It is hard to determine whether the first eight stanzas of the ballad are anything more than a prelude, and whether sts. 5, 7 note the customary practice of the Lads of Wamphray, or anticipate, as is done in st. 3, certain points in the story which follows.

'Lads of Wamphray, ane old ballad, sometimes called The Galiard,' Glenriddell MSS., XI, 34, 1791.

1 TWIXT the Girthhead and Langwood-end
Livd the Galiard and Galiard's men.

2 It is the lads of Lethenha,
The greatest rogues among them a'.

3 It is the lads of Leverhay,
That drove the Crichtons' gier away.

4 It is the lads o the Kirkhill,
The gay Galiard and Will o Kirkhill,

5 But and the lads o Stefenbiggin,
They broke the house in at the riggin.

6 The lads o Fingland and Hellbackhill,
They were neer for good, but aye for ill.

7 Twixt the Staywood Buss and Langside Hill,
They stelld the broked cow and branded bull.

8 It is the lads o the Girthhead,
The diel's in them for pride and greed.

9 .   .   .   .   .
  .   .   .   .   .

10 The Galiard is to the stable gane;
Instead o the Dun, the Blind he's taen.

11 'Come out now, Simmy o the Side,
Come out and see a Johnston ride!

12 'Here's the boniest horse in a' Nithside,
And a gentle Johnston aboon his hide.'

13 Simmy Crichton's mounted then,
And Crichtons has raised mony a ane.

14 The Galiard thought his horse had been fleet,
But they did outstrip him quite out o sight.

15 As soon as the Galiard the Crichton he saw,
Beyond the saugh-bush he did draw.

16 The Crichtons there the Galiard hae taen,
And nane wi him but Willy alane.

17 'O Simmy, Simmy, now let me gang,
And I vow I'll neer do a Crichton wrang!

18 'O Simmy, Simmy, now let me be,
And a peck o goud I'll gie to thee!

19 'O Simmy, Simmy, let me gang,
And my wife shall heap it wi her hand!'

20 But the Crichtons wadna let Willy bee,
But they hanged him high upon a tree.

21 O think then Will he was right wae,
When he saw his uncle guided sae.

22 'But if ever I live Wamphray to see,
My uncle's death revenged shall be!'

23 Back to Wamphray Willy's gane,
And riders has raised mony a ane.

24 Saying, My lads, if ye'll be true,
Ye's a' be clad in the noble blue.

25 Back to Nidsdale they are gane,
And away the Crichtons' nout they hae taen.

26 As they came out at the Wallpath-head,
The Crichtons bad them light and lead.

27 And when they came to the Biddess-burn,
The Crichtons bad them stand and turn.

28 And when they came to the Biddess-strand,
The Crichtons they were hard at hand.

29 But when they cam to the Biddess-law,
   The Johnstons bad them stand and
      draw.

30 Out then spake then Willy Kirkhill:
   'Of fighting, lads, ye 's hae your fill.'

.31 Then off his horse Willy he lap,
   And a burnishd brand in his hand he
      took.

32 And through the Crichtons Willy he ran,
   And dang them down both horse and
      man.

33 O but these lads were wondrous rude,
   When the Biddess-burn ran three days
      blood !

34 'I think, my lads, we 've done a noble
      deed;
   We have revengd the Galiard's blood.

35 'For every finger o the Galiard's hand,
   I vow this day I 've killed a man.'

36 And hame for Wamphray they are
      gane,
   And away the Crichtons' nout they 've
      taen.

37 'Sin we 've done na hurt, nor we 'll
            take na wrang,
   But back to Wamphray we will gang.'

38 As they came in at Evanhead,
   At Reaklaw-holm they spred abroad.

39 'Drive on, my lads, it will be late;
   We 'll have a pint at Wamphray Gate.

40 'For where eer I gang, or eer I ride,
   The lads o Wamphr[a]y 's on my side.

41 'For of a' the lads that I do ken,
   The lads o Wamphr[a]y 's king o men.'

185

DICK O THE COW

a seems to have been communicated to Percy
by Roger Halt in 1775. b was contributed to
Caw's Museum by John Elliot of Reidheugh,
a gentleman, says Scott, well skilled in the
antiquities of the western border. c was taken
down "from the singing and recitation of a
Liddesdale-man, namely, Robert Shortreed,
sheriff-substitute of Roxburghshire, in the au-
tumn of 1816 ;" but it differs from b in no
important respect except the omission of thirteen stanzas, 17, 18, 24, 32, 35–38, 51, 52, 56–
58. The ballad was popular before the end of
the sixteenth century, as is shown by a passage
in Nashe's Have with you to Saffron Walden,
1596 : " Dick of the Cow, that mad demi-lance
northren borderer, who plaied his prizes with
the lord Jockey so bravely " (Grosart's Nashe,
III, 6). In a list of books printed for and
sold by P. Brooksby, 1688, occurs " Dick-a-
the-Cow, containing north-country songs." The
Cow in Dick's name can have no reference to
cattle, for then his style would have been ' Dick
o the Kye.' It may possibly denote the hut in
which he lived ; or brush, or broom.

a. ' An excelent old song cald Dick of the
Cow.' Percy Papers, 1775. b. Caw's Poetical
Museum, p. 22, 1784. c. Campbell, Albyn's
Anthology, II, 31, 1818.

1 Now Liddisdale has lain long in,
         Fa la
   There is no rideing there a ta;
         Fa la
   Their horse is growing so lidder and fatt
   That are lazie in the sta.
         Fa la la didle

2 Then Johnë Armstrang to Willie can say,
   Billie, a rideing then will we;
   England and us has been long at a feed;
   Perhaps we may hitt of some bootie.

3 Then they 'r comd on to Hutton Hall,
   They rade that proper place about;
   But the laird he was the wiser man,
   For he had left nae gear without.

4 Then he had left nae gear to steal,
      Except six sheep upon a lee;
   Says Johnie, I 'de rather in England
      die
   Before their six sheep good to Liddis-
      dale with me.

5 'But how cald they the man we last
      with mett,
   Billie, as we came over the know ? '
   'That same he is an innocent fool,
      And some men calls him Dick o the
      Cow.'

6 ' That fool has three as good kyne of his
          own
        As is in a' Cumberland, billie,' quoth
          he:
    ' Betide my life, betide my death,
        These three kyne shal go to Liddis-
          daile with me.'

7 Then they 're comd on to the poor fool's
          house,
        And they have broken his wals so wide;
    They have loosd out Dick o the Cow's
          kyne three,
        And tane three coerlets off his wife's
          bed.

8 Then on the morn, when the day grew
          light,
        The shouts and crys rose loud and
          high:
    ' Hold thy tongue, my wife,' he says,
        ' And of thy crying let me bee.

9 ' Hald thy tongue, my wife,' he says,
        ' And of thy crying let me bee,
    And ay that where thou wants a kow,
        Good sooth that I shal bring the three.'

10 Then Dick 's comd on to lord and master,
        And I wate a drerie fool [was] he :
    ' Hald thy tongue, my fool,' he says,
        ' For I may not stand to jest with
          thee.'

11 ' Shame speed a your jesting, my lord,'
          quo Dickie,
        ' For nae such jesting grees with me;
    Liddesdaile has been in my house this
          last night,
        And they have tane my three kyne
          from me.

12 ' But I may nae langer in Cumberland
          dwel,
        To be your poor fool and your leel,
    Unless ye give me leave, my lord,
        To go to Liddisdale and steal.'

13 ' To give thee leave, my fool,' he says,
        ' Thou speaks against mine honour
          and me;
    Unless thou give me thy trouth and thy
          right hand
        Thou 'l steal frae nane but them that
          sta from thee.'

14 ' There is my trouth and my right hand;
        My head shal hing on Hairibie,
    I 'le never crose Carlele sands again,
        If I steal frae a man but them that
          sta frae me.'

15 Dickie has tane leave at lord and mas-
          ter,
        And I wate a merrie fool was he;
    He has bought a bridle and a pair of
          new spurs,
        And has packed them up in his breek-
          thigh.

16 Then Dickie 's come on for Puddin-
          burn,
        Even as fast as he may drie;
    Dickie 's come on for Puddinburn,
        Where there was thirty Armstrongs
          and three.

17 ' What 's this comd on me ! ' quo Dickë,
        ' What meakle wae 's this happend on
          me,' quo he,
    ' Where here is but ae innocent fool,
        And there is thirty Armstrongs and
          three ! '

18 Yet he 's comd up to the hall among
          them all;
        So wel he became his courtisie:
    ' Well may ye be, my good Laird's Jock !
        But the deil bless all your companie.

19 ' I 'm come to plain of your man Fair
          Johnie Armstrong,
        And syne his billie Willie,' quo he;
    ' How they have been in my house this
          last night,
        And they have tane my three ky frae
          me.'

20 Quo Johnie Armstrong, We 'll him hang;
        ' Nay,' thain quo Willie, ' we 'll him
          slae;'
    But up bespake another young man,
        We 'le nit him in a four-nooked sheet,
        Give him his burden of batts, and lett
          him gae.

21 Then up bespake the good Laird's Jock.
        The best falla in the companie:
    Sitt thy way down a little while, Dickë,
        And a peice of thine own cow's hough
          I 'l give to thee.

22 But Dicki's heart it grew so great
    That never a bitt of it he dought to eat;
  But Dickie was warr of ane auld peat-
    house,
    Where there al the night he thought
    for to sleep.

23 Then Dickie was warr of that auld peat-
    house,
    Where there al the night he thought
    for to ly;
  And a' the prayers the poor fool prayd
    was,
    ' I wish I had a mense for my own
    three kye ! '

24 Then it was the use of Puddinburn,
    And the house of Mangertoun, all haile!
  These that came not at the first call
    They gott no more meat till the next
    meall.

25 The lads, that hungry and aevery was,
    Above the door-head they flang the
    key;
  Dickie took good notice to that;
    Says, There's a bootie younder for me.

26 Then Dickie's gane into the stable,
    Where there stood thirty horse and
    three;
  He has ty'd them a' with St Mary knot,
    All these horse but barely three.

27 He has ty'd them a' with St Mary knott,
    All these horse but barely three;
  He has loupen on one, taken another in
    his hand,
    And out at the door and gane is Dickie.

28 Then on the morn, when the day grew
    light,
    The shouts and cryes rose loud and
    high;
  ' What's that theife ? ' quo the good
    Laird's Jock;
    ' Tel me the truth and the verity.

29 ' What's that theife ? ' quo the good
    Laird's Jock;
    ' See unto me ye do not lie: '
  ' Dick o the Cow has been in the stable
    this last night,
    And has my brother's horse and mine
    frae me '

30 ' Ye wad never be teld it,' quo the Laird's
    Jock;
    ' Have ye not found my tales fu leel ?
  Ye wade never out of England bide,
    Till crooked and blind and a' wad
    steal.'

31 ' But will thou lend me thy bay ? ' Fair
    Johnë Armstrong can say,
    ' There's nae mae horse loose in the
    stable but he;
  And I 'le either bring ye Dick o the
    Kow again,
    Or the day is come that he must die.'

32 ' To lend thee my bay,' the Laird's Jock
    can say,
    ' He's both worth gold and good
    monie;
  Dick o the Kow has away twa horse,
    I wish no thou should no make him
    three.'

33 He has tane the Laird's jack on his back,
    The twa-handed sword that hang
    lieugh by his thigh;
  He has tane the steel cap on his head,
    And on is he to follow Dickie.

34 Then Dickie was not a mile off the town,
    I wate a mile but barely three,
  Till John Armstrang has oertane Dick
    o the Kow,
    Hand for hand on Cannobei lee.

35 ' Abide th[e], bide now, Dickie than,
    The day is come that thow must die ; '
  Dickie looked oer his left shoulder;
    ' Johnie, has thow any mo in thy com-
    pany ?

36 ' There is a preacher in owr chapell,
    And a' the lee-lang day teaches he;
  When day is gane, and night is come,
    There's never a word I mark but
    three.

37 ' The first and second 's Faith and Con-
    science;
    The third is, Johnie, Take head of
    thee;
  But what faith and conscience had thow,
    traitor,
    When thou took my three kye frae
    me ?

38 'And when thou had tane my three kye,
  Thou thought in thy heart thou was
    no wel sped;
  But thou sent thi billie Willie oer the
    know,
  And he took three coerlets of my
    wife's bed.'

39 Then Johne lett a spear fa leaugh by
    his thigh,
  Thought well to run the innocent
    through;
  But the powers above was more than his,
  He ran but the poor fool's jerkin
    through.

40 Together they ran or ever they blan —
  This was Dickie, the fool, and hee —
  Dickie could not win to him with the
    blade of the sword,
  But he feld [him] with the plummet
    under the eye.

41 Now Dickie has [feld] Fair Johnë Arm-
    strong,
  The prettiest man in the south coun-
    trey;
  'Gramercie,' then can Dickie say,
  'I had twa horse, thou has made me
    three.'

42 He has tane the laird's jack off his back,
  The twa-handed sword that hang
    leiugh by his thigh;
  He has tane the steel cape off his head:
  'Johnie, I 'le tel my master I met with
    thee.'

43 When Johnë wakend out of his dream,
  I wate a dreiry man was he:
  'Is thou gane now, Dickie, than ?
  The shame gae in thy company !

44 'Is thou gane now, Dickie, than ?
  The shame go in thy companie !
  For if I should live this hundred year,
  I shal never fight with a fool after
    thee.'

45 Then Dickie comed home to lord and
    master,
  Even as fast as he may driee:
  'Now Dickie, I shal neither eat meat
    nor drink
  Till high hanged that thou shall be !'

46 'The shame speed the liars, my lord !'
    quo Dickie,
  'That was no the promise ye made to
    me;
  For I 'd never gane to Liddesdale to steal
  Till that I sought my leave at thee.'

47 'But what gart thow steal the Laird's-
    Jock's horse ?
  And, limmer, what gart thou steal
    him ?' quo he;
  'For lang might thow in Cumberland
    dwelt
  Or the Laird's Jock had stoln ought
    frae thee.'

48 'Indeed I wate ye leed, my lord,
  And even so loud as I hear ye lie;
  I wan him frae his man, Fair Johnë
    Armstrong,
  Hand for hand on Cannobie lee.

49 'There 's the jack was on his back,
  The twa-handed sword that hung
    lewgh by his thigh;
  There 's the steel cap was on his head;
  I have a' these takens to lett you see.'

50 'If that be true thou to me tels —
  I trow thou dare not tel a lie —
  I 'le give thee twenty pound for the
    good horse,
  Wel teld in thy cloke-lap shall be.

51 'And I 'le give thee one of my best
    milk-kye,
  To maintain thy wife and children
    three;
  [And that may be as good, I think,
  As ony twa o thine might be.']

52 'The shame speed the liars, my lord !'
    quo Dicke,
  'Trow ye ay to make a fool of me ?
  I 'le either have thirty pound for the
    good horse,
  Or els he 's gae to Mattan fair wi me.'

53 Then he has given him thirty pound for
    the good horse,
  All in gold and good monie;
  He has given him one of his best milk-
    kye,
  To maintain his wife and children
    three.

54 Then Dickie's come down through Car-
       lile town,
   Even as fast as he may drie:
   The first of men that he with mett
       Was my lord's brother, Bailife Gla-
       zenberrie.

55 'Well may ye be, my good Ralph
       Scrupe!'
       'Welcome, my brother's fool!' quo
       he;
   'Where did thou gett Fair Johnie Arm-
       strong's horse?'
       'Where did I get him but steall him,'
       quo he.

56 'But will thou sell me Fair Johnie Arm-
       strong['s] horse?
       And, billie, will thou sel him to me?'
       quo he:
   'Ay, and tel me the monie on my cloke-
       lap,
       For there's not one fathing I 'le trust
       thee.'

57 'I 'le give thee fifteen pound for the
       good horse,
       Wel teld on thy cloke-lap shal be;
   And I 'le give [thee] one of my best
       milk-kye,
       To maintain thy wife and thy chil-
       dren three.'

58 'The shame speed the liars, my lord!'
       quo Dickë,
       'Trow ye ay to make a fool of me?'
       quo he:
   'I 'le either have thirty pound for the
       good horse,
       Or else he's to Mattan Fair with me.'

59 He has given him thirty pound for the
       good horse,
       All in gold and good monie;
   He has given him one of his best milk-
       kye,
       To maintain his wife and children
       three.

60 Then Dickie lap a loup on high,
       And I wate a loud laughter leugh he:
   'I wish the neck of the third horse were
       browken,
       For I have a better of my own, and
       onie better can be.'

61 Then Dickie comd hame to his wife
       again;
   Judge ye how the poor fool he sped;
   He has given her three score of English
       pounds
       For the three auld coerlets was tane
       of her bed.

62 'Hae, take thee there twa as good
       kye,
       I trow, as al thy three might be;
   And yet here is a white-footed naigg;
       I think he 'le carry booth thee and
       me.'

63 'But I may no langer in Cumberland
       dwell;
       The Armstrongs the 'le hang me high:'
   But Dickie has tane leave at lord and
       master,
       And Burgh under Stanemuir there
       dwels Dickie.

186

KINMONT WILLIE

This ballad celebrates a bold and masterly
exploit of Sir Walter Scott of Branxholm, laird
of Buccleuch, April 13, 1596, which is fully
narrated by a contemporary, Archbishop Spot-
iswood, in his History of the Church of Scotland, ed. 1655, pp. 413 ff. Kinmont Willie was
"one William Armstrong, commonly called
Will of Kinmouth, against whom the English
had a quarrel for many wrongs he had committed, as he was indeed a notorious thief."
Sir Walter Scott, who alone preserves the ballad, says that it had been "much mangled by
reciters" and that "some conjectural emendations [were] absolutely necessary to render it
intelligible." Probably a great deal more
emendation was done than this observation
would indicate. One would like, for example,
to see sts. 10–12 and 31 in their mangled condition.

Minstrelsy of the Scottish Border, i, 111,
1802; ii, 32, 1833.

1 O HAVE ye na heard o the fause Sakelde?
   O have ye na heard o the keen Lord
       Scroop?
   How they hae taen bauld Kinmont
       Willie,
   On Hairibee to hang him up?

2 Had Willie had but twenty men,
    But twenty men as stout as he,
  Fause Sakelde had never the Kinmont
      taen,
    Wi eight score in his companie.

3 They band his legs beneath the steed,
    They tied his hands behind his back;
  They guarded him, fivesome on each
      side,
    And they brought him ower the Lid-
      del-rack.

4 They led him thro the Liddel-rack,
    And also thro the Carlisle sands;
  They brought him to Carlisle castell,
    To be at my Lord Scroope's com-
      mands.

5 'My hands are tied, but my tongue is
      free,
    And whae will dare this deed avow?
  Or answer by the border law?
    Or answer to the bauld Buccleuch?'

6 'Now haud thy tongue, thou rank reiver!
    There's never a Scot shall set ye free;
  Before ye cross my castle-yate,
    I trow ye shall take farewell o me.'

7 'Fear na ye that, my lord,' quo Willie;
    'By the faith o my bodie, Lord
      Scroop,' he said,
  'I never yet lodged in a hostelrie
    But I paid my lawing before I gaed.'

8 Now word is gane to the bauld Keeper,
    In Branksome Ha where that he lay,
  That Lord Scroope has taen the Kin-
      mont Willie,
    Between the hours of night and day.

9 He has taen the table wi his hand,
    He garrd the red wine spring on
      hie;
  'Now Christ's curse on my head,' he
      said,
  'But avenged of Lord Scroop I'll be!

10 'O is my basnet a widow's curch?
    Or my lance a wand of the willow-
      tree?
  Or my arm a ladye's lilye hand?
    That an English lord should lightly
      me.

11 'And have they taen him Kinmont Wil-
      lie,
    Against the truce of Border tide,
  And forgotten that the bauld Bacleuch
    Is keeper here on the Scottish side?

12 'And have they een taen him Kinmont
      Willie,
    Withouten either dread or fear,
  And forgotten that the bauld Bacleuch
    Can back a steed, or shake a spear?

13 'O were there war between the lands,
    As well I wot that there is none,
  I would slight Carlisle castell high,
    Tho it were builded of marble-stone.

14 'I would set that castell in a low,
    And sloken it with English blood;
  There's nevir a man in Cumberland
    Should ken where Carlisle castell
      stood.

15 'But since nae war's between the lands,
    And there is peace, and peace should
      be,
  I'll neither harm English lad or lass,
    And yet the Kinmont freed shall
      be!'

16 He has calld him forty marchmen
      bauld,
    I trow they were of his ain name,
  Except Sir Gilbert Elliot, calld
    The Laird of Stobs, I mean the same.

17 He has calld him forty marchmen
      bauld,
    Were kinsmen to the bauld Buc-
      cleuch,
  With spur on heel, and splent on spauld,
    And gleuves of green, and feathers
      blue.

18 There were five and five before them a',
    Wi hunting-horns and bugles bright;
  And five and five came wi Buccleuch,
    Like Warden's men, arrayed for fight.

19 And five and five like a mason-gang,
    That carried the ladders lang and
      hie;
  And five and five like broken men;
    And so they reached the Woodhouse-
      lee.

20 And as we crossd the Bateable Land,
    When to the English side we held,
  The first o men that we met wi,
    Whae sould it be but fause Sakelde!

21 'Where be ye gaun, ye hunters keen?'
    Quo fause Sakelde; 'come tell to me!'
  'We go to hunt an English stag,
    Has trespassd on the Scots countrie.'

22 'Where be ye gaun, ye marshal-men?'
    Quo fause Sakelde; 'come tell me
      true!'
  'We go to catch a rank reiver,
    Has broken faith wi the bauld Buc-
      cleuch.'

23 'Where are ye gaun, ye mason-lads,
    Wi a' your ladders lang and hie?'
  'We gang to herry a corbie's nest,
    That wons not far frae Woodhouse-
      lee.'

24 'Where be ye gaun, ye broken men?'
    Quo fause Sakelde; 'come tell to me!'
  Now Dickie of Dryhope led that band,
    And the never a word o lear had he.

25 'Why trespass ye on the English side?
    Row-footed outlaws, stand!' quo he;
  The neer a word had Dickie to say,
    Sae he thrust the lance thro his fause
      bodie.

26 Then on we held for Carlisle toun,
    And at Staneshaw-bank the Eden we
      crossd;
  The water was great, and meikle of
      spait,
    But the nevir a horse nor man we
      lost.

27 And when we reachd the Staneshaw-
      bank,
    The wind was rising loud and hie;
  And there the laird garrd leave our
      steeds,
    For fear that they should stamp and
      nie.

28 And when we left the Staneshaw-bank,
    The wind began full loud to blaw;
  But 't was wind and weet, and fire and
      sleet,
    When we came beneath the castel-wa.

29 We crept on knees, and held our breath,
    Till we placed the ladders against the
      wa;
  And sae ready was Buccleuch himsell
    To mount the first before us a'.

30 He has taen the watchman by the
      throat,
    He flung him down upon the lead:
  'Had there not been peace between our
      lands,
    Upon the other side thou hadst gaed.

31 'Now sound out, trumpets!' quo Buc-
      cleuch;
    'Let's waken Lord Scroope right
      merrilie!'
  Then loud the Warden's trumpets
      blew
    'O whae dare meddle wi me?'

32 Then speedilie to wark we gaed,
    And raised the slogan ane and a',
  And cut a hole thro a sheet of lead,
    And so we wan to the castel-ha.

33 They thought King James and a' his
      men
    Had won the house wi bow and speir:
  It was but twenty Scots and ten
    That put a thousand in sic a stear!

34 Wi coulters and wi forehammers,
    We garrd the bars bang merrilie,
  Untill we came to the inner prison,
    Where Willie o Kinmont he did lie.

35 And when we cam to the lower prison,
    Where Willie o Kinmont he did lie,
  'O sleep ye, wake ye, Kinmont Willie,
    Upon the morn that thou's to die?'

36 'O I sleep saft, and I wake aft,
    It's lang since sleeping was fleyd frae
      me;
  Gie my service back to my wyfe and
      bairns,
    And a' gude fellows that speer for
      me.'

37 Then Red Rowan has hente him up,
    The starkest men in Teviotdale:
  'Abide, abide now, Red Rowan,
    Till of my Lord Scroope I take fare
      well.

38 'Farewell, farewell, my gude Lord
    Scroope !
  My gude Lord Scroope, farewell ! ' he
    cried;
  ' I 'll pay you for my lodging-maill
    When first we meet on the border-
    side.'

39 Then shoulder high, with shout and cry,
    We bore him down the ladder lang;
  At every stride Red Rowan made,
    I wot the Kinmont's airns playd
    clang.

40 'O mony a time,' quo Kinmont Willie,
    ' I have ridden horse baith wild and
    wood;
  But a rougher beast than Red Rowan
    I ween my legs have neer bestrode.

41 'And mony a time,' quo Kinmont Willie,
    ' I 've pricked a horse out oure the
    furs;
  But since the day I backed a steed
    I nevir wore sic cumbrous spurs.'

42 We scarce had won the Staneshaw-
    bank,
    When a' the Carlisle bells were rung,
  And a thousand men, in horse and foot,
    Cam wi the keen Lord Scroope along.

43 Buccleuch has turned to Eden Water,
    Even where it flowd frae bank to
    brim,
  And he has plunged in wi a' his band,
    And safely swam them thro the
    stream.

44 He turned him on the other side,
    And at Lord Scroope his glove flung
    he:
  ' If ye like na my visit in merry Eng-
    land,
    In fair Scotland come visit me ! '

45 All sore astonished stood Lord Scroope,
    He stood as still as rock of stane;
  He scarcely dared to trew his eyes
    When thro the water they had gane.

46 ' He is either himsell a devil frae hell,
    Or else his mother a witch maun be;
  I wad na have ridden that wan water
    For a' the gowd in Christentie.'

187

JOCK O THE SIDE

The earliest appearance of John o the Side is,
perhaps, in the list of the marauders against
whom complaint was made to the Bishop of
Carlisle " presently after " Queen Mary Stuart's
departure for France ; not far, therefore, from
1550 : "John of the Side (Gleed John)." The
earls of Northumberland and Westmoreland,
after the failure of the Rising in the North,
fled first to Liddesdale, and thence " to one
of the Armstrongs," in the Debateable Land.
The Liddesdale men stole the Countess of
Northumberland's horses, and the earls, contin-
uing their flight, left her " on foot, at John of
the Syde's house, a cottage not to be compared
to any dog-kennel in England." At his de-
parting, " my lord of Westmoreland changed
his coat of plate and sword with John of the
Syde, to be the more unknown " (Sussex to
Cecil, December 22, 1569, printed in Sharp's
Memorials of the Rebellion, p. 114 f.).

This ballad is one of the best in the world,
and enough to make a moss-trooper of any
young borderer, had he lacked the impulse.
In deference to history, it is put after Kinmont
Willie, for it may be a free version of his
story. Scott's version (Minstrelsy, 1802, I,
154) is B b, with the insertion of three stanzas
(6, 7 23) from B a.

A

' John a Side,' Percy MS., p. 254 ; Hales and
Furnivall, II, 203.

*   *   *   *   *

1 PEETER a Whifeild he hath slaine,
    And Iohn a Side, he is tane,
  And Iohn is bound both hand and foote,
    And to the New-castle he is gone.

2 But tydinges came to the Sybill o the
    Side,
    By the water-side as shee rann;
  Shee tooke her kirtle by the hem,
    And fast shee runn to Mangerton.

3 .   .   .   .   .
    The lord was sett downe at his meate;
  When these tydings shee did him tell,
    Neuer a morsell might he eate.

4 But lords, the wrunge their fingars white,
    Ladyes did pull themselues by the
    haire.

Crying, Alas and weladay !
  For Iohn o the Side wee shall neu*er*
    see more.

5 ' But wee 'le goe sell our droues of kine,
    And after them our oxen sell,
  And after them our troopes of sheepe,
    But wee will loose him out of the
      New Castell.'

6 But then bespake him Hobby Noble,
    And spoke these words wonderous
      hye;
  Says, Giue me fiue men to my selfe,
    And I 'le feitch Iohn o the Side to
      thee.

7 ' Yea, thou 'st haue fiue, Hobby Noble,
    Of the best *that* are in this countrye;
  I 'le giue thee fiue thousand, Hobby
      Noble,
    That walke in Tyuidale trulye.'

8 ' Nay, I 'le haue but fiue,' saies Hobby
      Noble,
    ' *That* shall walke away with mee;
  Wee will ryde like noe men of warr;
    But like poore badgers wee wilbe.'

9 They stuffet vp all their baggs with
      straw,
    And their steeds barefoot must bee;
  ' Come on, my bretheren,' sayes Hobby
      Noble,
    ' Come on your wayes, and goe with
      mee.'

10 And when they came to Culerton ford,
    The water was vp, they cold it not
      goe;
  And then they were ware of a good old
      man,
    How his boy and hee were at the
      plowe.

11 ' But stand you still,' sayes Hobby Noble,
    ' Stand you still heere at this shore,
  And I will ryde to yonder old man,
    And see w[h]ere the gate it lyes ore.

12 ' But Christ you saue, father ! ' quoth
      hee,
    ' Crist both you saue and see !
  Where is the way ou*er* this fford ?
    For Christ's sake tell itt mee ! '

13 ' But I haue dwelled heere three score
      yeere,
    Soe haue I done three score and three;
  I neu*er* sawe man nor horsse goe ore,
    Except itt were a horse of tree.'

14 ' But fare thou well, thou good old man !
    The devill in hell I leave with thee,
  Noe better comfort heere this night
    Thow giues my bretheren heere and
      me.'

15 But when he came to his brether againe,
    And told this tydings full of woe,
  And then they found a well good gate
    They might ryde ore by two and two.

16 And when they were come ou*er* the
      fforde,
    All safe gotten att the last,
  ' Thankes be to God ! ' sayes Hobby
      Nobble,
    ' The worst of our perill is past.'

17 And then they came into Howbrame
      wood,
    And there then they found a tree,
  And cutt itt downe then by the roote;
    The lenght was thirty ffoote and three.

18 And four of them did take the planke,
    As light as it had beene a fflee,
  And carryed itt to the New Castle,
    Where as Iohn a Side did lye.

19 And some did climbe vp by the walls,
    And some did climbe vp by the tree,
  Vntill they came vpp to the top of the
      castle,
    Where Iohn made his moane trulye.

20 He sayd, God be with thee, Sybill o the
      Side !
    My owne mother thou art, quoth hee;
  If thou knew this night I were here,
    A woe woman then woldest thou bee.

21 And fare you well, Lord Mangerton !
    And eu*er* I say God be with thee !
  For if you knew this night I were heere,
    You wold sell your land for to loose
      mee.

22 And fare thou well, Much, Millers sonne!
    Much, Millars sonne, I say;

Thou has beene better att merke mid-
     night
Then euer thou was att noone o the
     day.

23 And fare thou well, my good Lord
     Clough !
Thou art thy ffathers sonne and heire;
Thou neuer saw him in all thy liffe
But with him durst thou breake a
     speare.

24 Wee are brothers childer nine or ten,
     And sisters children ten or eleven.
We neuer came to the feild to fight,
     But the worst of us was counted a
     man.

25 But then bespake him Hoby Noble,
     And spake these words vnto him;
Saies, Sleepest thou, wakest thou, Iohn
     o the Side,
     Or art thou this castle within ?

26 'But who is there,' quoth Iohn oth Side,
     ' That knowes my name soe right and
     free ? '
' I am a bastard-brother of thine;
     This night I am comen for to loose
     thee.'

27 'Now nay, now nay,' quoth Iohn o the
     Side;
' Itt ffeares me sore that will not bee;
Ffor a pecke of gold and silver,' Iohn
     sayd,
     ' In faith this night will not loose mee.'

28 But then bespake him Hobby Noble,
     And till his brother thus sayd hee;
Sayes, Four shall take this matter in
     hand,
     And two shall tent our geldings ffree.

29 Four did breake one dore without,
     Then Iohn brake fiue himsell;
But when they came to the iron dore,
     It smote twelue vpon the bell.

30 'Itt ffeares me sore,' sayd Much, the
     Miller,
     ' That heere taken wee all shalbee;'
' But goe away, bretheren,' sayd Iohn a
     Side,
     ' For euer alas ! this will not bee.'

31 'But ffye vpon thee ! ' sayd Hobby
     Noble;
' Much, the Miller, fye vpon thee !
It sore feares me,' said Hobby Noble,
     ' Man that thou wilt neuer bee.'

32 But then he had Fflanders files two or
     three,
And hee fyled downe that iron dore,
And tooke Iohn out of the New Castle,
     And sayd, Looke thou neuer come
     heere more !

33 When he had him fforth of the New
     Castle,
     ' Away with me, Iohn, thou shalt
     ryde: '
But euer alas ! itt cold not bee;
     For Iohn cold neither sitt nor stryde.

34 But then he had sheets two or three,
     And bound Iohns boults fast to his
     ffeete,
And sett him on a well good steede,
     Himselfe on another by him seete.

35 Then Hobby Noble smiled and loug[h]e,
     And spoke these worde in mickle
     pryde:
Thou sitts soe finely on thy geldinge
     That, Iohn, thou rydes like a bryde.

36 And when they came thorrow How-
     brame towne,
     Iohns horsse there stumbled at a
     stone;
' Out and alas ! ' cryed Much, the Miller,
     ' Iohn, thou 'le make vs all be tane.'

37 'But fye vpon thee ! ' saies Hobby
     Noble,
     ' Much, the Millar, fye on thee !
I know full well,' sayes Hobby Noble,
     ' Man that thou wilt neuer bee.'

38 And when the came into Howbrame
     wood,
He had Fflanders files two or three
To file Iohns bolts beside his ffeete,
     That hee might ryde more easilye.

39 Sayes, 'Iohn, now leape ouer a steede ! '
     And Iohn then hee lope ouer fiue:
' I know well,' sayes Hobby Noble,
     ' Iohn, thy ffellow is not aliue.'

40 Then he brought him home to Manger-
 ton;
  The lord then he was att his meate;
 But when Iohn o the Side he there did
  see,
  For faine hee cold noe more eate.

41 He sayes, Blest be thou, Hobby Noble,
  That euer thou wast man borne !
 Thou hast feitched vs home good Iohn
  oth Side,
  That was now cleane ffrom vs gone.

B

'Jock o the Side.' a. Caw's Poetical Museum, 1784, p. 145 ; "from an old manuscript
copy." b. Campbell's Albyn's Anthology, II,
28, 1818 ; "taken down from the recitation of
Mr Thomas Shortreed," of Jedburgh, "who
learnt it from his father."

1 'Now Liddisdale has ridden a raid,
  But I wat they had better staid at
  hame;
 For Mitchel o Winfield he is dead,
  And my son Johnie is prisner tane.'
   With my fa ding diddle, la la dow
   diddle.

2 For Mangerton House auld Downie is
  gane;
  Her coats she has kilted up to her
  knee,
 And down the water wi speed she
  rins,
  While tears in spaits fa fast frae her
  eie.

3 Then up and bespake the lord Mangerton:
  'What news, what news, sister Downie, to me ? '
 'Bad news, bad news, my lord Mangerton;
  Mitchel is killd, and tane they hae
  my son Johnie.'

4 'Neer fear, sister Downie,' quo Mangerton;
  'I hae yokes of oxen four and twentie,
 My barns, my byres, and my faulds, a'
  weel filld,
  And I 'll part wi them a' ere Johnie
  shall die.

5 'Three men I 'll take to set him free,
  Weel harnessd a' wi best o steel;
 The English rogues may hear, and drie
  The weight o their braid swords to
  feel.

6 'The Laird's Jock ane, the Laird's Wat
  twa,
  Oh, Hobie Noble, thou ane maun
  be ;
 Thy coat is blue, thou has been true,
  Since England banishd thee, to me.'

7 Now Hobie was an English man,
  In Bewcastle-dale was bred and born;
 But his misdeeds they were sae great,
  They banishd him neer to return.

8 Lord Mangerton them orders gave,
  'Your horses the wrang way maun a'
  be shod;
 Like gentlemen ye must not seem,
  But look like corn-caugers gawn ae
  road.

9 'Your armour gude ye maunna shaw,
  Nor ance appear like men o weir;
 As country lads be all arrayd,
  Wi branks and brecham on ilk mare.'

10 Sae now a' their horses are shod the
  wrang way,
  And Hobie has mounted his grey sae
  fine,
 Jock his lively bay, Wat 's on his white
  horse behind,
  And on they rode for the water o
  Tyne.

11 At the Choler-ford they a' light down,
  And there, wi the help o the light o
  the moon,
 A tree they cut, wi fifteen naggs upo
  ilk side,
  To climb up the wa o Newcastle town.

12 But when they cam to Newcastle town,
  And were alighted at the wa,
 They fand their tree three ells oer laigh,
  They fand their stick baith short and
  sma.

13 Then up and spake the Laird's ain Jock,
  'There 's naething for 't, the gates
  we maun force;'

But when they cam the gates unto,
  A proud porter withstood baith men
    and horse.

14 His neck in twa I wat they hae wrung,
    Wi hand or foot he neer playd paw;
  His life and his keys at anes they hae
    tane,
    And cast his body ahind the wa.

15 Now soon they reach Newcastle jail,
    And to the prisner thus they call:
  'Sleips thou, wakes thou, Jock o the
    Side?
  Or is thou wearied o thy thrall?'

16 Jock answers thus, wi dolefu tone:
    Aft, aft I wake, I seldom sleip;
  But wha's this kens my name sae weel,
    And thus to hear my waes do[e]s
    seik?

17 Then up and spake the good Laird's
    Jock,
  'Neer fear ye now, my billie,' quo he;
  'For here's the Laird's Jock, the
    Laird's Wat,
  And Hobie Noble, come to set thee
    free.'

18 'Oh, had thy tongue, and speak nae
    mair,
  And o thy tawk now let me be!
  For if a' Liddisdale were here the night,
    The morn's the day that I maun die.

19 'Full fifteen stane o Spanish iron
    They hae laid a' right sair on me;
  Wi locks and keys I am fast bound
    Into this dungeon mirk and drearie.'

20 'Fear ye no that,' quo the Laird's Jock;
  'A faint heart neer wan a fair ladie;
  Work thou within, we'll work without,
    And I'll be bound we set thee free.'

21 The first strong dore that they came at,
    They loosed it without a key;
  The next chaind dore that they cam at,
    They gard it a' in flinders flee.

22 The prisner now, upo his back,
    The Laird's Jock's gotten up fu hie;
  And down the stair him, irons and a',
    Wi nae sma speed and joy brings he.

23 'Now, Jock, I wat,' quo Hobie Noble,
    'Part o the weight ye may lay on me;'
  'I wat weel no,' quo the Laird's Jock,
    'I count him lighter than a flee.'

24 Sae out at the gates they a' are gane,
    The prisner's set on horseback hie;
  And now wi speed they've tane the
    gate,
    While ilk ane jokes fu wantonlie.

25 'O Jock, sae winsomely's ye ride,
    Wi baith your feet upo ae side!
  Sae weel's ye're harnessd, and sae trig!
    In troth ye sit like ony bride.'

26 The night, tho wat, they didna mind,
    But hied them on fu mirrilie,
  Until they cam to Cholerford brae,
    Where the water ran like mountains
    hie.

27 But when they came to Cholerford,
    There they met with an auld man;
  Says, Honest man, will the water ride?
    Tell us in haste, if that ye can.

28 'I wat weel no,' quo the good auld man;
    'Here I hae livd this threty yeirs and
    three,
  And I neer yet saw the Tyne sae big,
    Nor rinning ance sae like a sea.'

29 Then up and spake the Laird's saft Wat,
    The greatest coward in the company;
  'Now halt, now halt, we needna try 't;
    The day is comd we a' maun die!'

30 'Poor faint-hearted thief!' quo the
    Laird's Jock,
  'There'll nae man die but he that's
    fie;
  I'll lead ye a' right safely through;
    Lift ye the prisner on ahint me.'

31 Sae now the water they a' hae tane,
    By anes and twas they a' swam
    through;
  'Here are we a' safe,' says the Laird's
    Jock,
  'And, poor faint Wat, what think ye
    now?'

32 They scarce the ither side had won,
    When twenty men they saw pursue;

Frae Newcastle town they had been sent,
    A' English lads, right good and true.

33 But when the land-sergeant the water
        saw,
    'It winna ride, my lads,' quo he;
    Then out he cries, Ye the prisner may
        take,
    But leave the irons, I pray, to me.

34 'I wat weel no,' cryd the Laird's Jock,
    'I 'll keep them a', shoon to my mare
        they 'll be;
    My good grey mare, for I am sure,
    She 's bought them a' fu dear frae
        thee.'

35 Sae now they 're away for Liddisdale,
    Een as fast as they coud them hie;
    The prisner 's brought to his ain fireside,
    And there o 's airns they make him
        free.

36 'Now, Jock, my billie,' quo a' the three,
    'The day was comd thou was to die;
    But thou 's as weel at thy ain fire-side,
    Now sitting, I think, tween thee and
        me.'

37 They hae gard fill up ae punch-bowl,
    And after it they maun hae anither,
    And thus the night they a' hae spent,
    Just as they had been brither and
        brither.

188

ARCHIE O CAWFIELD

This ballad is in all of the salient features a
repetition of 'Jock o the Side' (No. 187), Halls
playing the parts of Armstrongs. The Halls are
several times complained of for reif and away-
taking of ky, oxen, etc., in 1579. B a was printed
by Scott in the first edition of his Minstrelsy,
with certain changes, besides Scotticising of the
spelling. The later edition of the same contains ten stanzas from another version preserved
in Abbotsford MS. (see Child, IV, 516) and omits
some stanzas of B a. The new stanzas are given
in the Notes as they stand in the manuscript.

A

'Archie of the Cawfield,' Percy Papers.
communicated to Percy by Miss Fisher of
Carlisle, 1780.

1 LATE in an evening forth as I went,
    'T was on the dawning of the day;
    I heard two brothers make their moan,
    I listend well what they did say.

2 .   .   .   .   .   .
    .   .   .   .   .
    We were three born brethren,
    There[s] one of us condemnd to die.

3 Then up bespake Jock the laird:
    'If I had but a hundre men,
    A hundred o th best i Christenty,
    I wad go on to fair Dumfries, I wad
    loose my brother and set him free.'

4 So up bespak then Dicky Ha,
    He was the wisest o the three:
    'A hundre men we 'll never get,
    Neither for gold nor fee,
    But some of them will us betray;
    They 'l neither fight for gold nor fee.

5 'Had I but ten well-wight men,
    Ten o the best i Christenty,
    I wad gae on to fair Dumfries,
    I wad loose my brother and set him
        free.

6 'Jocky Ha, our cousin, 's be the first
        man '
        (For leugh o Liddesdale cracked he);
    'An ever we come till a pinch,
    He 'll be as good as ony three.'

7 They mounted ten well-wight men,
    Ten o the best i Christenty;
    .   .   .   .   .
    .   .   .   .   .

8 There was horsing and horsing of haste,
    And cracking o whips out oer the
        lee,
    Till they came to fair Barngliss,
    And they ca'd the smith right quietly.

9 He has shod them a' their horse,
    He 's shod them siccer and honestly,
    And he as turnd the cawkers backwards
        oer,
    Where foremost they were wont to be.

10 And there was horsing, horsing of haste,
    And cracking of whips out oer the
        lee,

Until they came to the Bonshaw wood,
    Where they held their council pri-
        vately.

11 Some says, We 'll gang the Annan road,
    It is the better road, said they;
Up bespak then Dicky Ha,
    The wisest of that company.

12 ' Annan road 's a publick road,
    It 's no the road that makes for me;
But we will through at Hoddam ford,
    It is the better road,' said he.

13 And there was horsing, horsing o haste,
    And cracking of whips out oer the lea,
Until they came to fair Dumfries,
    And it was newly strucken three.

14 Up bespake then Jocky Ha,
    For leugh o Liddesdale cracked he:
' I have a mare, they ca her Meg,
    She is the best i Christenty;
An ever we come till a pinch,
    She 'll bring awa both thee and me.'

15 ' But five we 'll leave to had our horse,
    And five will watch, guard for to be;
Who is the man,' said Dicky then,
    ' To the prison-door will go with me ? '

16 Up bespak then Jocky Ha,
    For leugh o Liddesdale cracked he:
' I am the man,' said Jocky than,
    ' To the prison-door I 'll go with thee.'

17 They are up the jail-stair,
    They stepped it right soberly,
Until they came to the jail-door;
    They ca'd the prisoner quietly.

18 ' O sleeps thou, wakest thou, Archie, my
    billy ?
    O sleeps thou, wakes thou, dear
        billy ? '
' Sometimes I sleep, sometimes I wake;
    But who 's that knows my name so
        well ? ' [said he.]
' I am thy brother Dicky,' he says;
    ' This night I 'm come to borrow thee.'

19 But up bespake the prisoner then,
    And O but he spake woefully !
' Today has been a justice-court,

   .   .   .   .

And a' Liddesdale were here the night,
    The morn 's the day at I 'se to die.'

20 ' What is thy crime, Archie, my billy ?
    What is the crime they lay to thee ? '
I brake a spear i the warden's breast,
    For saving my master's land,' said he.

21 ' If that be a' the crime they lay to thee,
    Archie, my billy,
If that be the crime they lay to thee,
Work thou within, and me without,
    And thro good strength I 'll borrow
        thee.'

22 ' I cannot work, billy,' he says,
    ' I cannot work, billy, with thee,
For fifteen stone of Spanish iron
    Lyes fast to me with lock and key.'

23 When Dicky he heard that,
    ' Away, thou crabby chiel !' cried he;
He 's taen the door aye with his foot,
    And fast he followd it with his knee.
Till a' the bolts the door hung on,
    O th' prison-floor he made them flee.

24 ' Thou 's welcome, welcome, Archy, my
    billy,
    Thou 's aye right dear welcome to
        me ;
There shall be straiks this day,' he said,
    ' This day or thou be taen from me.'

25 He 's got the prisoner on o his back,
    He 's gotten him irons and aw,

   .   .   .   .

26 Up bespake then Jocky Ha,
    ' Let some o th' prisoner lean on me;'
' The diel o there,' quo Dicky than,
    ' He 's no the wightdom of a flea.'

27 They are on o that gray mare,
    And they are on o her aw three,
And they linked the irons about her
    neck,
    And galloped the street right wan-
        tonly.

28 ' To horse, to horse,' then, ' all,' he says,
    ' Horse ye with all the might ye may,
For the jailor he will waken next;
    And the prisoners had a' wan away.'

29 There was horsing, horsing of haste,
    And cracking o whips out oer the lea,
Until they came to the Bonshaw Shield;
    There they held their council pri-
      vately.

30 Some says, 'We 'll gang the Annan
    road ;
It is the better road,' said they;
But up bespak than Dicky Ha,
    The wisest of that company:

31 'Annan road 's a publick road,
    It 's not the road that makes for me;
But we will through at Annan Holme,
    It is the better road,' said he;
' An we were in at Wamfrey Gate,
    The Johnstones they will a' help me.'

32 But Dicky lookd oer his left shoulder,
    I wait a wiley look gave he;
He spied the leiutenant coming,
    And a hundre men of his company.

33 'So horse ye, horse ye, lads !' he said,
    'O horse ye, sure and siccerly !
For yonder is the lieutenant,
    With a hundred men of his company.'

34 There was horsing, horsing of haste,
    And cracking o whips out oer the lea,
Until they came to Annan Holme,
    And it was running like a sea.

35 But up bespake the lieutenant,
    Until a bonny lad said he,
' Who is the man,' said the leiutenant,
    'Rides foremost of yon company ?'

36 Then up bespake the bonny lad,
    Until the lieutenant said he,
'Some men do ca him Dicky Ha,
    Rides foremost of yon company.'

37 'O haste ye, haste ye !' said the leiu-
    tenant,
    'Pursue with a' the might ye may !
For the man had needs to be well
    saint
    That comes thro the hands o Dicky
    Ha.'

38 But up bespak Jock the laird,
    'This has been a dearsome night to
    me;

I 've a colt of four years old,
    I wait he wannelld like the wind:
If ever he come to the deep,
    He will plump down, leave me be-
    hind.'

39 ' Wae light o thee and thy horse baith,
    Jock,
    And even so thy horse and thee !
Take thou mine, and I 'll take thine,
    Foul fa the warst horse i th' com-
    pany !
I 'll cast the prisoner me behind;
    There 'll no man die but him that 's
    fee.'

40 There they 've a' taen the flood,
    And they have taen it hastily;
Dicky was the hindmost took the flood,
    And foremost on the land stood he.

41 Dicky 's turnd his horse about,
    And he has turnd it hastily:
'Come through, come thro, my lieuten-
    ant,
    Come thro this day, and drink wi me,
And thy dinner 's be dressd in Annan
    Holme,
    It sall not cost thee one penny.'

42 'I think some witch has bore the, Dicky,
    Or some devil in hell been thy daddy;
I woud not swum that wan water double-
    horsed,
    For a' the gold in Christenty.

43 ' But throw me thro my irons, Dicky,
    I wait they cost me full dear;'
'O devil be there,' quo Jocky Hall,
    'They 'l be good shoon to my gray
    mare.'

44 O up bespoke then Jock the laird,
    'This has been a dearsome night to
    me;
For yesternight the Cawfield was my
    ain,
    Landsman again I neer sall be.'

45 'Now wae light o thee and thy lands
    baith, Jock,
    And even so baith the land and thee !
For gear will come and gear will gang,
    But three brothers again we never
    were to be '

B

'Archie of Cafield' (miswritten 'Capeld'),
Glenriddell MSS., xi, 14, 1791, "an old West
Border ballad;" Scott's Minstrelsy, 1802, i, 177.

1 As I was walking mine alane,
    It was by the dawning o the day,
I heard twa brothers make their maine,
    And I listned well what they did say.

2 The eldest to the youngest said,
    'O dear brother, how can this be !
There was three brethren of us born,
    And one of us is condemnd to die.'

3 'O chuse ye out a hundred men,
    A hundred men in Christ[e]udie,
And we 'll away to Dumfries town,
    And set our billie Archie free.'

4 'A hundred men you cannot get,
    Nor yet sixteen in Christendie;
For some of them will us betray,
    And other some will work for fee.

5 'But chuse ye out eleven men,
    And we ourselves thirteen will be,
And we 'ill away to Dumfries town,
    And borrow bony billie Archie.'

6 There was horsing, horsing in haste,
    And there was marching upon the lee,
Untill they came to the Murraywhat,
    And they lighted a' right speedylie.

7 'A smith, a smith !' Dickie he crys,
    'A smith, a smith, right speedily,
To turn back the cakers of our horses
        feet !
    For it is forward we woud be.'

8 There was a horsing, horsing in haste,
    There was marching on the lee,
Untill they came to Dumfries port,
    And there they lighted right man-
        fulie.

9 'There six of us will hold the horse,
    And other five watchmen will be;
But who is the man among you a'
    Will go to the Tolbooth door wi me ?'

10 O up then spake Jokie Hall
    (Fra the laigh of Tiviotdale was he),

'If it should cost my life this very night,
    I 'll ga to the Tollbooth door wi thee.'

11 'O sleepst thou, wakest thow, Archie
        laddie ?
    O sleepst thou, wakest thow, dear
        billie ?'
'I sleep but saft, I waken oft,
    For the morn 's the day that I man
        die.'

12 'Be o good cheer now, Archie lad,
    Be o good cheer now, dear billie;
Work thow within and I without,
    And the morn thou 's dine at Cafield
        wi me.'

13 'O work, O work, Archie ?' he cries,
    'O work, O work ? ther 's na work-
        ing for me;
For ther 's fifteen stane o Spanish iron,
    And it lys fow sair on my body.'

14 O Jokie Hall stept to the door,
    And he bended it back upon his knee,
And he made the bolts that the door
        hang on
    Jump to the wa right wantonlie.

15 He took the prisoner on his back,
    And down the Tollbooth stairs came
        he;
Out then spak Dickie and said,
    Let some o the weight fa on me;
'O shame a ma !' co Jokie Ha,
    'For he 's no the weight of a poor flee.

16 The gray mare stands at the door,
    And I wat neer a foot stirt she,
Till they laid the links out oer her neck,
    And her girth was the gold-twist to be.

17 And they came down thro Dumfries
        town,
    And O but they came bonily !
Untill they came to Lochmaben port,
    And they leugh a' the night manfulie.

18 There was horsing, horsing in haste,
    And there was marching on the lee,
Untill they came to the Murraywhat,
    And they lighted a' right speedilie.

19 'A smith, a smith !' Dickie he cries,
    'A smith, a smith, right speedilie,

To file off the shakles fra my dear bro-
     ther!
   For it is forward we wad be.'

20 They had not filtt a shakle of iron,
     A shakle of iron but barely three,
   Till out then spake young Simon brave,
     'Ye do na see what I do see.

21 'Lo yonder comes Liewtenant Gordon,
     And a hundred men in his company:'
   'O wo is me!' then Archie cries,
     'For I'm the prisoner, and I must
     die.'

22 O there was horsing, horsing in haste,
     And there was marching upon the lee,
   Untill they came to Annan side,
     And it was flowing like the sea.

23 'I have a colt, and he's four years old,
     And he can amble like the wind,
   But when he comes to the belly deep,
     He lays himself down on the ground.'

24 'But I have a mare, and they call her
     Meg,
     And she's the best in Christendie;
   Set ye the prisoner me behind;
     Ther'll na man die but he that's
     fae!'

25 Now they did swim that wan water,
     And O but they swam bonihe!
   Untill they came to the other side,
     And they wrang their cloathes right
     drunk[i]lie.

26 'Come through, come through, Lieu-
     tenant Gordon!
     Come through, and drink some wine
     wi me!
   For ther's a ale-house neer hard by,
     And it shall not cost thee one penny.'

27 'Throw me my irons, Dickie!' he cries,
     'For I wat they cost me right dear;'
   'O shame a ma!' cries Jokie Ha,
     'For they'll be good shoon to my
     gray mare.'

28 'Surely thy minnie has been some witch,
     Or thy dad some warlock has been;
   Else thow had never attempted such,
     Or to the bottom thow had gone.

29 'Throw me my irons, Dickie!' he cries,
     'For I wot they cost me dear enough;'
   'O shame a ma!' cries Jokie Ha,
     'They'll be good shakles to my
     plough.'

30 'Come through, come through, Liew-
     tenant Gordon!
     Come throw, and drink some wine wi
     me!
   For yesterday I was your prisoner,
     But now the night I am set free.'

189

HOBIE NOBLE

Hobie Noble, though banished from Bewcastle for his irregularities, will always command the hearty liking of those who live too
late to suffer from them, on account of his gallant bearing in the rescue of Jock o the Side
(No. 187); see especially **A**, of which Hobie
is the hero. All that we know of him is so
much as we are told in that ballad and in this.

a. Caw's Poetical Museum, p. 193. b. 'Hobie
Noble,' Percy Papers, apparently from Roger
Halt, 1775.

1 FOUL fa the breast first treason bred in!
     That Liddisdale may safely say,
   For in it there was baith meat and drink,
     And corn unto our geldings gay.
       Fala la diddle, etc.

2 We were stout-hearted men and true,
     As England it did often say;
   But now we may turn our backs and fly,
     Since brave Noble is seld away.

3 Now Hobie he was an English man,
     And born into Bewcastle dale,
   But his misdeeds they were sae great,
     They banishd him to Liddisdale.

4 At Kershope-foot the tryst was set,
     Kershope of the lily lee;
   And there was traitour Sim o the Mains,
     With him a private companie.

5 Then Hobie has graithd his body weel,
     I wat it was wi baith good iron and
     steel:

And he has pulld out his fringed grey,
    And there, brave Noble, he rade him
    weel.

6 Then Hobie is down the water gane,
    Een as fast as he may drie;
Tho they shoud a' brusten and broken
    their hearts,
    Frae that tryst Noble he would not be.

7 'Weel may ye be, my feiries five !
    And aye, what is your wills wi me ?'
Then they cryd a' wi ae consent,
    Thou 'rt welcome here, brave Noble.
    to me.

8 Wilt thou with us in England ride ?
    And thy safe-warrand we will be,
If we get a horse worth a hundred
    punds,
    Upon his back that thou shalt be.

9 'I dare not with you into England ride,
    The land-sergeant has me at feid;
I know not what evil may betide
    For Peter of Whitfield his brother 's
    dead.

10 'And Anton Shiel, he loves not me,
    For I gat twa drifts of his sheep;
The great Earl of Whitfield loves me
    not,
    For nae gear frae me he eer coud
    keep.

11 'But will ye stay till the day gae down,
    Until the night come oer the grund,
And I 'll be a guide worth ony twa
    That may in Liddisdale be fund.

12 'Tho dark the night as pick and tar,
    I 'll guide ye oer yon hills fu hie,
And bring ye a' in safety back,
    If you 'll be true and follow me.'

13 He 's guided them oer moss and muir,
    Oer hill and houp, and mony ae down,
Til they came to the Foulbogshiel,
    And there brave Noble he lighted
    down.

14 Then word is gane to the land-sergeant,
    In Askirton where that he lay:
'The deer that ye hae hunted lang
    Is seen into the Waste this day.'

15 'Then Hobie Noble is that deer;
    I wat he carries the styie fu hie !
Aft has he beat your slough-hounds
    back,
    And set yourselves at little eie.

16 'Gar warn the bows of Hartlie-burn,
    See they shaft their arrows on the wa !
Warn Willeva and Spear Edom,
    And see the morn they meet me a'.

17 'Gar meet me on the Rodrie-haugh,
    And see it be by break o day;
And we will on to Conscowthart Green,
    For there, I think, w 'll get our
    prey.'

18 Then Hobie Noble has dreamd a dream,
    In the Foulbogshiel where that he lay;
He thought his horse was neath him
    shot,
    And he himself got hard away.

19 The cocks could crow, and the day
    could dawn,
    And I wat so even down fell the
    rain ;
If Hobie had no wakend at that time,
    In the Foulbogshiel he had been tane
    or slain.

20 'Get up, get up, my feiries five —
    For I wat here makes a fu ill day —
And the warst clock of this companie
    I hope shall cross the Waste this
    day.'

21 Now Hobie thought the gates were
    clear,
    But, ever alas ! it was not sae;
They were beset wi cruel men and keen,
    That away brave Noble could not gae.

22 'Yet follow me, my feiries five,
    And see of me ye keep good ray,
And the worst clock of this companie
    I hope shall cross the Waste this
    day.'

23 There was heaps of men now Hobie
    before,
    And other heaps was him behind,
That had he been as wight as Wallace
    was
    Away brave Noble he could not win.

24 Then Hobie he had but a laddies sword,
     But he did more than a laddies deed;
   In the midst of Conscouthart Green,
     He brake it oer Jers a Wigham's
       head.

25 Now they have tane brave Hobie Noble,
     Wi his ain bowstring they band him
       sae;
   And I wat his heart was neer sae sair
     As when his ain five band him on the
       brae.

26 They have tane him [on] for West Car-
       lisle;
     They askd him if he knew the way;
   Whateer he thought, yet little he said;
     He knew the way as well as they.

27 They hae tane him up the Ricker-gate;
     The wives they cast their windows
       wide,
   And ilka wife to anither can say,
     That's the man loosd Jock o the
       Side !

28 'Fy on ye, women ! why ca ye me man ?
     For it 's nae man that I 'm usd like;
   I 'm but like a forfoughen hound,
     Has been fighting in a dirty syke.'

29 Then they hae tane him up thro Car-
       lisle town,
     And set him by the chimney-fire;
   They gave brave Noble a wheat loaf to
       eat,
     And that was little his desire.

30 Then they gave him a wheat loaf to eat
     And after that a can o beer;
   Then they cried a', wi ae consent,
     Eat, brave Noble, and make good
       cheer !

31 Confess my lord's horse, Hobie, they
       say,
     And the morn in Carlisle thou 's no
       die;
   'How shall I confess them ?' Hobie
       says,
   'For I never saw them with mine eye.'

32 Then Hobie has sworn a fu great aith,
     By the day that he was gotten or
       born,

He never had onything o my lord's
  That either eat him grass or corn.

33 'Now fare thee weel, sweet Mangerton !
     For I think again I 'll neer thee see;
   I wad betray nae lad alive,
     For a' the goud in Christentie.

34 'And fare thee well now, Liddisdale,
     Baith the hie land and the law !
   Keep ye weel frae traitor Mains !
     For goud and gear he 'll sell ye a'.

35 'I 'd rather be ca'd Hobie Noble,
     In Carlisle, where he suffers for his
       faut,
   Before I were ca'd traitor Mains,
     That eats and drinks of meal and
       maut.'

190

JAMIE TELFER IN THE FAIR DODHEAD

A* is from a manuscript written about the beginning of the nineteenth century and now in the possession of Mr William Macmath. Scott's copy (Minstrelsy, 1802, I, 80) has a few more stanzas than A, and attributes the honor of the rescue to the Scotts of Teviotdale, but it resembles A closely, even in details of phraseology. Scott's title, 'Jamie Telfer of the Fair Dodhead,' makes Jamie proprietor of the estate, whereas 'in' signifies, according to Scottish usage, that he was a tenant simply. The situation of the Dodhead is uncertain.

A*

'Jamie Telfer in the Fair Dodhead,' C. K. Sharpe's papers.

1 IT fell about the Martinmas,
     When steads were fed wi corn and
       hay,
   The Captain of Bewcastle said to his
       lads,
     We 'll into Tiviotdale and seek a prey.

2 The first ae guide that they met with
     Was high up in Hardhaugh swire,
   The second guide that they met with
     Was laigh down in Borthick water.

3 'What tidings, what tidings, my bonny
        guide?'
    'Nae tidings, nae tidings I hae to
        thee;
    But if ye 'll gae to the Fair Dodhead
    Mony a cow's calf I 'll let ye see.'

4 When they came to the Fair Dodhead,
    Right hastily they clam the peel,
    They loosd the nolt out, ane and a',
    And ranshakled the house right weel.

5 Now Jamie's heart it was right sair,
    The tear ay rowing in his eye;
    He pled wi the Captain to hae his gear,
    Or else revengëd he would be.

6 Bat the Captain turnd himsel about,
    Said, Man, there's naething in thy
        house
    But an auld sword without a scabbard,
    That scarcely now would fell a mouse.

7 The moon was up and the sun was down,
    'T was the gryming of a new-fa'n
        snaw;
    Jamie Telfer has run eight miles bare-
        foot
    Between Dodhead and Branxholm
        Ha.

8 And when he came to Branxholm Ha
    He shouted loud and cry'd weel he,
    Till up bespake then auld Buccleugh,
    'Whae's this that brings the fray to
        me?'

9 'It 's I, Jamie Telfer i the Fair Dod-
        head,
    And a harried man I think I be;
    There 's naething left i the Fair Dod-
        head
    But only wife and children three.'

10 'Gae seek your succour frae Martin El-
        liot,
    For succour ye 's get nane frae me;
    Gae seek your succour where ye paid
        blackmail,
    For, man, ye never paid money to me.'

11 Jamie he 's turnd him round about,
    And ay the tear blinded his eye:
    'I 'se never pay mail to Scott again,
    Nor the Fair Dodhead I 'll ever see.'

12 Now Jamie is up the water-gate,
    Een as fast as he can drie,
    Till he came to the Coultart Cleugh,
    And there he shouted and cry'd weel
        he.

13 Then up bespake him auld Jock Grieve,
    'Whae's this that bring[s] the fray
        to me?'
    'It 's I, Jamie Telfer i the Fair Dod-
        head,
    And a harried man I think I be.

14 'There 's naething left i the Fair Dod
        head
    But only wife and children three,
    And sax poor calves stand i the sta,
    A' routing loud for their minnie.'

15 'Alack, wae 's me!' co auld Jock Grieve,
    'Alack, alack, and wae is me!
    For ye was married t' the auld sister,
    And I t' the younges[t] o the three.'

16 Then he 's taen out a bonny black,
    It was weel fed wi corn and hay,
    And set Jamie Telfer on his back,
    To the Catlock hill to take the fray.

17 When he came to the Catlock hill,
    He shouted loud and cry'd weel he;
    Whae 's that, whae 's that?' co Mar-
        tin's Hab,
    'Whae 's this that brings the fray to
        me?'

18 'It 's I, Jamie Telfer i the Fair Dod-
        head,
    And a harried man I think I be;
    There 's neathing left i the Fair Dod-
        head
    But only wife and children three.'

19 'Alack, wae 's me!' co Martin's Hab,
    'Alack, awae, my heart is sair!
    I never came bye the Fair Dodhead
    That ever I faund thy basket bare.'

20 Then he 's taen out a bonny black,
    It was weel fed wi corn and hay,
    And set Jamie Telfer on his back
    To the Pricken haugh to take the fray.

21 When he came to the Pricken haugh,
    He shouted loud and cry'd weel he;

Up then bespake auld Martin Elliot,
  'Whae 's this that brings the fray to
    me ?'

22 'It 's I, Jamie Telfer i the Fair Dod-
      head,
    And a harried man I think I be;
    There 's naething left i the Fair Dod-
      head
    But only wife and children three.'

23 'Ever alack !' can Martin say,
    'And ay my heart is sair for thee !
    But fy, gar ca on Simmy my son,
    And see that he come hastily.

24 'Fy, gar warn the water-side,
    Gar warn it soon and hastily;
    Them that winna ride for Telfer's kye,
    Let them never look i the face o me.

25 'Gar warn the water, braid and wide,
    And warn the Currers i the shaw;
    When ye come in at the Hermitage slack,
    Warn doughty Willie o Gorrenberry.'

26 The gear was driven the Frostily up,
    From the Frostily into the plain;
    When Simmie lookëd him afore,
    He saw the kye right fast driving.

27 'Whae drives the kye,' then Simmy can
      say,
    'To make an outspeckle o me ?'
    'It 's I, the Captain o Bewcastle, Sim-
      my,
    I winna lain my name frae thee.'

28 'O will ye let the gear gae back ?
    Or will ye do ony thing for me ?'
    'I winna let the gear gae back,
    Nor naething, Simmy, I 'll do for
      the[e].

29 'But I 'll drive Jamie Telfer's kye
    In spite o Jamie Telfer's teeth and
      thee;'
    'Then by my sooth,' can Simmy say,
    'I 'll ware my dame's calfskin on
      thee.

30 'Fa on them, lads !' can Simmy say,
    'Fy, fa on them cruelly !
    For or they win to the Ritter ford
    Mony toom saddle there shall be.'

31 But Simmy was striken oer the head,
    And thro the napskape it is gane,
    And Moscrop made a dolefull rage
    When Simmy on the ground lay slain.

32 'Fy, lay on them !' co Martin Elliot,
    'Fy, lay on them cruelly !
    For ere they win to the Kershop ford
    Mony toom saddle there shall be.'

33 John o Biggam he was slain,
    And John o Barlow, as I heard say,
    And fifteen o the Captain's men
    Lay bleeding on the ground that
      day.

34 The Captain was shot through the head,
    And also through the left ba-stane;
    Tho he had livd this hundred years,
    He 'd neer been loed by woman again.

35 The word is gane unto his bride,
    Een in the bower where she lay,
    That her good lord was in 's enemy's
      land
    Since into Tiviotdale he led the way.

36 'I loord a had a winding sheed
    And helpd to put it oer his head,
    Or he 'd been taen in 's enemy's lands,
    Since he oer Liddle his men did
      lead.'

37 There was a man in our company,
    And his name was Willie Wudëspurs:
    'There is a house in the Stanegarside,
    If any man will ride with us.'

38 When they came to the Stanegarside,
    They bangd wi trees and brake the
      door,
    They loosd the kye out, ane and a',
    And set them furth our lads before.

39 There was an auld wif ayont the fire,
    A wee bit o the Captain's kin:
    'Whae loo[s]es out the Captain's kye,
    And sae mony o the Captain's men
      wi[t]hin ?'

40 'I, Willie Wudëspurs, let out the kye,
    I winna lain my name frae thee,
    And I 'll loose out the Captain's kye
    In spite o the Captain's teeth and
      thee.'

41 Now on they came to the Fair Dodhead,
      They were a welcome sight to see,
    And instead of his ain ten milk-kye
      Jamie Telfer's gotten thirty and
        three.

191

HUGHIE GRAME

Scott's copy in the Minstrelsy (1803, III, 85)
is from C*, a version procured for him by William Laidlaw, with the insertion of some
stanzas from Ritson's Ancient Songs. Ritson's
version is A a, collated with another copy.
Scott conjectures that Hugh Graham may have
been one of more than four hundred borderers
against whom complaints were exhibited to the
Lord Bishop of Carlisle in 1548.

A

'The Life and Death of Sir Hugh of the
Grime.' **a.** Roxburghe Ballads, II, 294. **b.**
Douce Ballads, II, 204 b. **c.** Rawlinson Ballads, 566, fol. 9. All printed for P. Brooksby:
1672–95 (?). **d.** Pills to purge Melancholy, VI,
289, 17. **e.** Roxburghe Ballads, III, 344.

1 As it befell upon one time,
      About mid-summer of the year,
    Every man was taxt of his crime,
      For stealing the good Lord Bishop's
        mare.

2 The good Lord Screw he sadled a horse,
      And rid after this same scrime;
    Before he did get over the moss,
      There was he aware of Sir Hugh of
        the Grime.

3 'Turn, O turn, thou false traytor,
      Turn, and yield thyself unto me;
    Thou hast stolen the Lord Bishops mare,
      And now thou thinkest away to flee.'

4 'No, soft, Lord Screw, that may not be !
      Here is a broad sword by my side,
    And if that thou canst conquer me,
      The victory will soon be try'd.'

5 'I ner was afraid of a traytor bold,
      Although thy name be Hugh in the
        Grime,
    I 'le make thee repent thy speeches foul,
      If day and life but give me time.'

6 'Then do thy worst, good Lord Screw,
      And deal your blows as fast as you
        can;
    It will be try'd between me and you
      Which of us two shall be the best
        man.'

7 Thus as they dealt their blows so free,
      And both so bloody at that time,
    Over the moss ten yeomen they see,
      Come for to take Sir Hugh in the
        Grime.

8 Sir Hugh set his back against a tree,
      And then the men encompast him
        round;
    His mickle sword from his hand did
        flee,
      And then they brought Sir Hugh to
        the ground.

9 Sir Hugh of the Grime now taken is
      And brought back to Garlard town;
    [Then cry'd] the good wives all in Gar-
        lard town,
      'Sir Hugh in the Grime, thou 'st ner
        gang down.'

10 The good Lord Bishop is come to the
        town,
      And on the bench is set so high;
    And every man was taxt to his crime,
      At length he called Sir Hugh in the
        Grime.

11 'Here am I, thou false bishop,
      Thy humours all to fulfill;
    I do not think my fact so great
      But thou mayst put it into thy own
        will.'

12 The quest of jury-men was calld,
      The best that was in Garlard town;
    Eleven of them spoke all in a breast,
      'Sir Hugh in the Grime, thou 'st ner
        gang down.'

13 Then another questry-men was calld,
      The best that was in Rumary;
    Twelve of them spoke all in a breast,
      'Sir Hugh in the Grime, thou 'st now
        guilty.'

14 Then came down my good Lord Boles,
      Falling down upon his knee:

'Five hundred pieces of gold would I
give,
To grant Sir Hugh in the Grime to
me.'

15 'Peace, peace, my good Lord Boles,
And of your speeches set them by !
If there be eleven Grimes all of a name,
Then by my own honour they all
should dye.'

16 Then came down my good Lady Ward,
Falling low upon her knee:
'Five hundred measures of gold I'le give,
To grant Sir Hugh of the Grime to
me.'

17 'Peace, peace, my good Lady Ward,
None of your proffers shall him buy !
For if there be twelve Grimes all of a
name,
By my own honour they all should dye.'

18 Sir Hugh of the Grime 's condemnd to
dye,
And of his friends he had no lack;
Fourteen foot he leapt in his ward,
His hands bound fast upon his back.

19 Then he lookt over his left shoulder,
To see whom he could see or spy;
Then was he aware of his father dear,
Came tearing his hair most pittifully.

20 'Peace, peace, my father dear,
And of your speeches set them by !
Though they have bereavd me of my life,
They cannot bereave me of heaven so
high.'

21 He lookt over his right shoulder,
To see whom he could see or spye;
There was he aware of his mother dear,
Came tearing her hair most pittifully.

22 'Pray have me remembred to Peggy,
my wife;
As she and I walkt over the moor,
She was the cause of [the loss of] my life,
And with the old bishop she plaid the
whore.

23 'Here, Johnny Armstrong, take thou
my sword,
That is made of the mettle so fine,

And when thou comst to the border-side,
Remember the death of Sir Hugh of
the Grime.'

C*

Scotch Ballads, Materials for Border Minstrelsy, No. 87, Abbotsford ; in the handwriting of William Laidlaw. "From Robert
Laidlaw."

1 GUDE Lord Scroop 's to the huntin gane;
He 's ridden oer monie a moss an
muir,
An he has grippit Hughie the Græme,
For stealin o the bishop's mare.

2 An they hae grippit Hughie the Græme,
An brought him up thro Carlisle
town;
The lasses an lads they stood by the
wa's,
Cryin, Hughie the Græme, thou 's no
gae down !

3 They ha chosen a jury o men,
The best that were i Coventry,
An fifteen o them out a' at anse,
'Hughie the Græme, thou art guil-
tie.'

4 Than up bespak him gude Lord Hume,
As he sat at the judge's knee;
'Twentie white ousen, my gude lord,
If ye 'll grant Hughie the Græme to
me.'

5 'O no, no, no, my gude Lord Hume,
For sooth an so it mauna be;
For war there but twae Græms o the
name,
They sould be hangit a' for me.'

6 'T was up than spak her gude Lady
Hume,
As she sat by the judge's knee;
'A peck o white pennies, my gude lord,
If ye 'll grant Hughie the Greame to
me.'

7 'O no, O no, my gude Lady Hume,
For sooth an so it sal na be;
For war there but twae Greames of the
name,
They soud be hangit a' for me.'

8 'If I be guilty,' said Hughie the
          Græme,
    'Of me my friends sal hae nae lack;'
  An he has luppen fifteen feet an three,
    An his hands they war tyed ahint his
          back.

9 He's lookit oer his left shouther,
    To see what he coud see,
  An there he saw his auld father com-
          min,
    An he was weepin bitterlie.

10 'O had yer tongue, my father,' he
          says,
    'An see that ye dinna weep for me,
  For they may ravish me o my life,
    But they canna banish me thrae the
          heavens hie.

11 'Fare ye weel, Maggie, my wife;
    The last time I came oer the muir,
  It was you berievt me o my life,
    An wi the bishop playd the w[hore].'

192

THE LOCHMABEN HARPER

Scott's version of this ballad (Minstrelsy,
1802, I, 65) is that in the Glenriddell MSS., with
some changes.

A

a. 'The Blind Harper of Lochmaben,' Glenriddell MSS., XI, 42, 1791; "from a MS. collection of Mr Henderson." b. 'The Blind Harper,' Johnson's Museum, No. 579, VI, 598, 1803,
communicated by Burns. c. 'The Lochmaben Harper,' Minstrelsy of the Scottish Border, 1802, I, 65; 1833, I, 422.

1 HEARD ye eer of the silly blind harper,
    That long livd in Lochmaben town,
  How he wad gang to fair England,
      To steal King Henry's Wanton
          Brown?
          Sing, Faden dilly and faden dilly
          Sing, Faden dilly and deedle dan

2 But first he gaed to his gude wife,
    Wi a' the speed that he coud thole;
  'This wark,' quo he, 'will never work
    Without a mare that has a foal.'

3 Quo she, Thou has a gude gray mare,
    That'al rin oer hills baith law and
          hie;
  Gae tak the gray mare in thy hand,
    And leave the foal at hame wi me.

4 'And tak a halter in thy hose,
    And o thy purpose dinna fail;
  But wap it oer the Wanton's nose,
    And tie her to the gray mare's tail.

5 'Syne ca her out at yon back geate,
    Oer moss and muir and ilka dale;
  For she'll neer let the Wanton bite
    Till she come hame to her ain foal.'

6 So he is up to England gane,
    Even as fast as he can hie,
  Till he came to King Henry's geate;
    And wha was there but King Henry?

7 'Come in,' quo he, 'thou silly blind
          harper,
    And of thy harping let me hear;'
  'O, by my sooth,' quo the silly blind
          harper,
    'I'd rather hae stabling for my
          mare.'

8 The king he looks oer his left shoul-
          der,
    And says unto his stable-groom,
  Gae tak the silly poor harper's mare,
    And tie her side my Wanton Brown.

9 And ay he harpit, and ay he carpit,
    Till a' the lords had fitted the floor;
  They thought the music was sae sweet,
    And they forgot the stable-door.

10 And ay he harpit, and ay he carpit,
    Till a' the nobles were sound asleep;
  Then quietly he took aff his shoon,
    And safly down the stair did creep.

11 Syne to the stable-door he hies,
    Wi tread as light as light coud be,
  And when he opned and gaed in,
    There he fand thirty gude steads and
          three.

12 He took the halter frae his hose,
    And of his purpose did na fail;
  He slipt it oer the Wanton's nose,
    And tied it [to] his gray mare's tail.

13 He ca'd her out at yon back geate,
    Oer moss and muir and ilka dale,
  And she loot neer the Wanton bite,
    But held her still gaun at her tail.

14 The gray mare was right swift o fit,
    And did na fail to find the way,
  For she was at Lochmaben geate
    Fu lang three hours ere 't was day.

15 When she came to the harper's door,
    There she gave mony a nicher and
    sneer;
  ' Rise,' quo the wife, 'thou lazey lass,
    Let in thy master and his mare.'

16 Then up she rose, pat on her claes,
    And lookit out through the lock-hole;
  ' O, by my sooth,' then quoth the lass,
    ' Our mare has gotten a braw big
    foal !'

17 ' Come had thy peace, thou foolish
    lass,
    The moon 's but glancing in thy eye;
  I 'll wad my hail fee against a groat,
    It 's bigger than eer our foal will
    be.'

18 The neighbours too that heard the
    noise
    Cried to the wife to put hir in;
  ' By my sooth,' then quo the wife,
    ' She 's better than ever he rade on.'

19 But on the morn, at fair day light,
    Whan they had ended a' thier chear,
  King Henry's Wanton Brown was
    stawn,
    And eke the poor old harper's mare.

20 ' Allace ! allace !' says the silly blind
    harper,
  ' Allace, allace, that I came here !
  In Scotland I 've tint a braw cowte-
    foal,
    In England they 've stawn my gude
    gray mare.'

21 ' Come had thy tongue, thou silly blind
    harper,
    And of thy allacing let me be;
  For thou shalt get a better mare,
    And weel paid shall thy cowte-foal
    be.'

193

THE DEATH OF PARCY REED

Mr Robert White records a tradition in Redesdale, Northumberland, which accords in almost every particular with this ballad. He thinks that the story is not to be dated later than the sixteenth century (Richardson's Borderer's Table Book, VII, 361).

A

' A song of Parcy Reed and the Three False Halls,' the late Robert White's papers ; " Woodburn, December 1, 1829, Thomas Hedley, Bridge End, Corsonside Parish."

1 THE Liddesdale Crosiers hae ridden a
    race,
    And they had far better staid at hame,
  For they have lost a gallant gay,
    Young Whinton Crosier it was his
    name.

2 For Parcy Reed he has him taen,
    And he 's delivered him to law,
  But auld Crosier has made answer
    That he 'll gar the house of the Trough-
    end fa.

3 So as it happened on a day
    That Parcy Reed is a hunting gane,
  And the three false Halls of Girsons-
    field
    They all along with him are gane.

4 They hunted up and they hunted down,
    They hunted all Reedwater round,
  Till weariness has on him seized;
    At the Batinghope he 's fallen asleep.

5 O some they stole his powder-horn,
    And some put water in his lang gun:
  ' O waken, waken, Parcy Reed !
    For we do doubt thou sleeps too
    sound.

6 ' O waken, O waken, Parcy Reed !
    For we do doubt thou sleeps too long;
  For yonder 's the five Crosiers coming,
    They 're coming by the Hingin Stane.'

7 ' If they be five men, we are four,
    If ye will all stand true to me;

Now every one of you may take one,
    And two of them ye may leave to
    me.'

8 'We will not stay, nor we dare not
    stay,
    O Parcy Reed, for to fight with thee;
For thou wilt find, O Parcy Reed,
    That they will slay both us and thee.'

9 'O stay, O stay, O Tommy Hall,
    O stay, O man, and fight with me!
If we see the Troughend again,
    My good black mare I will give thee.'

10 'I will not stay, nor I dare not stay,
    O Parcy Reed, to fight for thee;
For thou wilt find, O Parcy Reed,
    That they will slay both me and thee.'

11 'O stay, O stay, O Johnnie Hall,
    O stay, O man, and fight for me!
If I see the Troughend again,
    Five yoke of oxen I will give thee.'

12 'I will not stay, nor I dare not stay,
    O Parcy Reed, for to fight with thee;
For thou wilt find, O Parcy Reed,
    That they will slay both me and thee.'

13 'O stay, O stay, O Willie Hall,
    O stay, O man, and fight for me!
If we see the Troughend again,
    The half of my land I will give thee.'

14 'I will not stay, nor I dare not stay,
    O Parcy Reed, for to fight with thee;
For thou wilt find, O Parcy Reed,
    That they will slay both me and thee.'

15 'Now foul fa ye, ye traitors all,
    That ever ye should in England won!
You have left me in a fair field standin,
    And in my hand an uncharged gun.

16 'O fare thee well, my wedded wife!
    O fare you well, my children five!
And fare thee well, my daughter Jane,
    That I love best that's born alive!

17 'O fare thee well, my brother Tom!
    And fare you well his children five!
If you had been with me this day,
    I surely had been man alive.

18 'Farewell all friends! as for my foes,
    To distant lands may they be tane,
And the three false Halls of Girsonsfield,
    They'll never be trusted nor trowed
    again.'

194

THE LAIRD OF WARISTON

John Kincaid of Wariston was murdered in 1600 by Robert Weir, at the instigation of Kincaid's wife, Jean Livingston, who was incensed by his brutal treatment of her. Jean Livingston's nurse, Janet Murdo, was an agent in the affair, summoning Weir, who had been a servant of the wife's father. All three were executed. Both Kincaid and his wife belonged to houses of some note, and the case attracted much attention.

A

'The Laird of Waristoun,' Jamieson's Popular Ballads, I, 109, as taken down by Sir Walter Scott from the recitation of his mother.

1 DOWN by yon garden green
    Sae merrily as she gaes;
She has twa weel-made feet,
    And she trips upon her taes.

2 She has twa weel-made feet,
    Far better is her hand;
She's as jimp in the middle
    As ony willow-wand.

3 'Gif ye will do my bidding,
    At my bidding for to be,
It's I will make you lady
    Of a' the lands you see.'

    *   *   *   *   *

4 He spak a word in jest;
    Her answer wasna good;
He threw a plate at her face,
    Made it a' gush out o blood.

5 She wasna frae her chamber
    A step but barely three,
When up and at her richt hand
    There stood Man's Enemy.

6 'Gif ye will do my bidding,
    At my bidding for to be,

I 'll learn you a wile
　Avenged for to be.'

7 The Foul Thief knotted the tether,
　　She lifted his head on hie,
　The nourice drew the knot
　　That gard lord Waristoun die.

8 Then word is gane to Leith,
　　Also to Edinburgh town,
　That the lady had killd the laird,
　　The laird o Waristoun.

*　　*　　*　　*　　*

9 'Tak aff, tak aff my hood,
　　But lat my petticoat be;
　Put my mantle oer my head,
　　For the fire I downa see.

10 'Now, a' ye gentle maids,
　　Tak warning now by me,
　And never marry ane
　　But wha pleases your ee.

11 'For he married me for love,
　　But I married him for fee;
　And sae brak out the feud
　　That gard my dearie die.'

B

' Laird o Waristoun,' Kinloch MSS., vii, 217 ;
from the recitation of Jenny Watson ; Kinloch's
Ancient Scottish Ballads, p. 49.

1 It was at dinner as they sat,
　　And whan they drank the wine,
　How happy war the laird and lady
　　Of bonnie Wariston !

2 The lady spak but ae word,
　　The matter to conclude;
　The laird strak her on the mouth,
　　Till she spat out o blude.

3 She did not know the way
　　Her mind to satisfy,
　Till evil cam into [her] head
　　All by the Enemy.

*　　*　　*　　*　　*

4 'At evening when ye sit,
　　And whan ye drink the wine,

See that ye fill the glass weill up
　To the laird o Wariston.'

5 So at table whan they sat,
　　And whan they drank the wine,
　She made the glass aft gae round
　　To the laird o Wariston.

6 The nurice she knet the knot,
　　And O she knet it sicker !
　The lady did gie it a twig,
　　Till it began to wicker.

7 But word 's gane doun to Leith,
　　And up to Embro toun,
　That the lady she has slain the laird,
　　The laird o Waristoun.

8 Word has gane to her father, the grit
　　　　Dunipace,
　　And an angry man was he;
　Cries, Gar mak a barrel o pikes,
　　And row her down some lea !

9 She said, Wae be to ye, Wariston,
　　I wish ye may sink for sin !
　For I have been your wife
　　These nine years, running ten;
　And I never loved ye sae well
　　As now whan ye 're lying slain.

10 'But tak aff this gowd brocade,
　　And let my petticoat stay,
　And tie a handkerchief round my face,
　　That the people may not see.'

195

LORD MAXWELL'S LAST GOODNIGHT

John, ninth Lord Maxwell, killed Sir James
Johnstone, with whom he had an old feud,
in 1608. Maxwell fled the country, but was
sentenced to death in his absence. Return-
ing after four years, he was betrayed into the
power of the government by a kinsman, and
was beheaded at Edinburgh, May 21, 1613.
Lord Byron, in the preface to Childe Harold,
says that " the good-night in the beginning of
the first canto was suggested by Lord Maxwell's Goodnight in the Border Minstrelsy."
Scott's text (Minstrelsy, 1802, i, 194) is based
on B.

A

'Lord Maxwell's Last Goodnight,' communicated to Percy by G. Paton, Edinburgh, December 4, 1778.

1 'GOOD lord of the land, will you stay
      thane
    About my faither's house,
  And walk into these gardines green,
      In my arms I'll the embraice.

2 'Ten thousand times I'll kiss thy face;
      Make sport. and let's be mery:'
  'I thank you, lady, fore your kindness;
      Trust me, I may not stay with the.

3 'For I have kil'd the laird Johnston;
      I vallow not the feed;
  My wiked heart did still incline;
      He was my faither's dead.

4 'Both night and day I did proced,
      And a' on him revainged to be;
  But now have I gotten what I long
      sowght,
    Trust me, I may not stay with the.

5 'Adue, Dumfriese, that proper place!
      Fair well, Carlaurike faire!
  Adue the castle of the Trive,
      And all my buldings there!

6 'Adue, Lochmaben gaits so faire,
      And the Langhm shank, where birks
      bobs bony!
    Adue, my leady and only joy!
      Trust me, I may not stay with the.

7 'Adue, fair Eskdale, up and doun,
      Wher my poor frends do duell!
  The bangisters will beat them doun,
      And will them sore compell.

8 'I'll reveinge the cause mysell,
      Again when I come over the sea;
  Adue, my leady and only joy!
      Fore, trust me, I may not stay with
      the.

9 'Adue, Dumlanark! fals was ay,
      And Closburn! in a band;
  The laird of the Lag from my faither
      fled
    When the Jhohnstones struek of his
      haud.

10 'They wer three brethren in a band:
      I pray they may never be merry;
  Adue, my leady and only joy!
      Trust me, I may not stay with the.

11 'Adue, madam my mother dear,
      But and my sister[s] two!
  Fair well, Robin in the Orchet!
      Fore the my heart is wo.

12 'Adue, the lillie, and fair well, rose,
      And the primros, spreads fair and
      bony!
    Adue, my leady and only joy!
      Fore, trust me, I may not stay with the.'

13 He took out a good gold ring,
      Where at hang sygnets three:
  'Take thou that, my own kind thing,
      And ay have mind of me.

14 'Do not mary another lord
      Agan or I come over the sea;
  Adue, my leady and only joy!
      For, trust me, I may not stay with
      the.'

15 The wind was fair, and the ship was
      clare,
    And the good lord went away;
  The most part of his frends was there,
      Giving him a fair convoy.

16 They drank the wine, they did not spare,
      Presentting in that good lord's sight;
  Now he is over the floods so gray;
      Lord Maxwell has te'n his last good-
      night.

B

Glenriddell MSS., xi, 18, 1791.

1 'ADIEW, madam my mother dear,
      But and my sisters two!
  Adiew, fair Robert of Oarchyardtoan!
      For thee my heart is woe.

2 'Adiew, the lilly and the rose,
      The primrose, sweet to see!
  Adiew, my lady and only joy!
      For I manna stay with thee.

3 'Tho I have killed the laird Johnston,
      What care I for his feed?

My noble mind dis still incline;
He was my father's dead.

4 'Both night and day I laboured oft
   Of him revenged to be,
And now I 've got what I long sought;
   But I manna stay with thee.

5 'Adiew, Drumlanrig ! false was ay,
   And Cloesburn ! in a band,
Where the laird of Lagg fra my father
   fled
When the Johnston struck off his
   hand.

6 'They were three brethren in a band;
   Joy may they never see !
But now I 've got what I long sought,
   And I maunna stay with thee.

7 'Adiew, Dumfries, my proper place,
   But and Carlaverock fair,
Adiew, the castle of the Thrieve,
   And all my buildings there !

8 'Adiew, Lochmaben's gates so fair,
   The Langholm shank, where birks
   they be !
Adiew, my lady and only joy !
   And, trust me, I maunna stay with
   thee.

9 'Adiew, fair Eskdale, up and down,
   Where my poor friends do dwell !
The bangisters will ding them down,
   And will them sore compel.

10 'But I 'll revenge that feed mysell
   When I come ou'r the sea;
Adiew, my lady and only joy !
   For I maunna stay with thee.'

11 'Lord of the land, will you go then
   Unto my father's place,
And walk into their gardens green,
   And I will you embrace.

12 'Ten thousand times I 'll kiss your face,
   And sport, and make you merry;'
'I thank thee, my lady, for thy kindness,
   But, trust me, I maunna stay with
   thee.'

13 Then he took off a great gold ring,
   Where at hang signets three:

'Hae, take thee that, my ain dear
   thing,
   And still hae mind of me.

14 'But if thow marry another lord
   Ere I come ou'r the sea —
Adiew, my lady and only joy !
   For I maunna stay with thee.'

15 The wind was fair, the ship was close,
   That good lord went away,
And most part of his friends were there,
   To give him a fair convay.

16 They drank thair wine, they did not
   spare,
   Even in the good lord's sight;
Now he is oer the floods so gray,
   And Lord Maxwell has taen his good-
   night.

196

THE FIRE OF FRENDRAUGHT

James Crichton of Frendraught in Aberdeenshire and William Gordon of Rothiemay in Banffshire (a neighboring estate on the opposite side of the Deveron) had a fierce dispute about fishing-rights. This resulted in private warfare, in the course of which Rothiemay was killed. The feud was settled by the mediation of the Marquis of Huntly; but friends of the parties were soon embroiled, and Frendraught went to Huntly and begged him to make peace. Huntly, fearing for Frendraught's safety, kept him two days at the Bog of Gight, and then, hearing that the Leslies were lying in wait, sent his own son, John Gordon (Viscount Aboyne), and the young laird of Rothiemay, to protect him on the way home. Arrived there, the laird and his lady begged these young gentlemen to remain over night, "and did their best, with all demonstration of love and kindness, to entertain them, thinking themselves happy now to have purchased such friends who had formerly been their foes." At about two in the morning the tower of Frendraught house, in which these guests lay, took fire, and they with four of their servants were burnt to death. This occurred in October, 1630. The ballad lays the blame on the Frendraughts (especially on Lady Frendraught). The matter was never cleared up, but the evidence tends to show that the fire was an accident.

A

a. 'Fire of Frendraught,' Motherwell's Minstrelsy, p. 161, from a MS. of Charles Kirkpatrick Sharpe. b. 'Burning of Frendraught,' Maidment's North Countrie Garland, p. 4; "long preserved by tradition in Aberdeenshire, and procured from an intelligent individual resident in that part of Scotland."

1 THE eighteenth of October,
    A dismal tale to hear
  How good Lord John and Rothiemay
    Was both burnt in the fire.

2 When steeds was saddled and well
      bridled,
    And ready for to ride,
  Then out it came her false Frendraught,
    Inviting them to bide.

3 Said, 'Stay this night untill we sup,
    The morn untill we dine;
  'T will be a token of good greement
    'Twixt your good lord and mine.'

4 'We 'll turn again,' said good Lord
      John;
    'But no,' said Rothiemay,
  'My steed 's trapand, my bridle 's bro-
      ken,
    I fear the day I 'm fey.'

5 When mass was sung, and bells was
      rung,
    And all men bound for bed,
  Then good Lord John and Rothiemay
    In one chamber was laid.

6 They had not long cast off their cloaths,
    And were but now asleep,
  When the weary smoke began to rise,
    Likewise the scorching heat.

7 'O waken, waken, Rothiemay!
    O waken, brother dear!
  And turn you to our Saviour;
    There is strong treason here.'

8 When they were dressed in their cloaths,
    And ready for to boun,
  The doors and windows was all secur'd,
    The roof-tree burning down.

9 He did him to the wire-window,
    As fast as he could gang;

Says, Wae to the hands put in the
      stancheons!
    For out we 'll never win.

10 When he stood at the wire-window,
      Most doleful to be seen,
    He did espy her Lady Frendraught,
      Who stood upon the green.

11 Cried, Mercy, mercy, Lady Frend-
      raught!
    Will ye not sink with sin?
    For first your husband killed my father,
      And now you burn his son.

12 O then out spoke her Lady Frendraught,
      And loudly did she cry;
    'It were great pity for good Lord
      John,
      But none for Rothiemay;
    But the keys are casten in the deep
      draw-well,
      Ye cannot get away.'

13 While he stood in this dreadful plight,
      Most piteous to be seen,
    There called out his servant Gordon,
      As he had frantic been:

14 'O loup, O loup, my dear master!
      O loup and come to me!
    I 'll catch you in my arms two,
      One foot I will not flee.

15 'O loup, O loup, my dear master!
      O loup and come away!
    I 'll catch you in my arms two,
      But Rothiemay may lie.'

16 'The fish shall never swim in the
      flood,
      Nor corn grow through the clay,
    Nor the fiercest fire that ever was kin-
      dled
      Twin me and Rothiemay.

17 'But I cannot loup, I cannot come,
      I cannot win to thee;
    My head 's fast in the wire-window,
      My feet burning from me.

18 'My eyes are seething in my head,
      My flesh roasting also,
    My bowels are boiling with my blood;
      Is not that a woeful woe?

19 'Take here the rings from my white
       fingers,
    That are so long and small,
    And give them to my lady fair,
    Where she sits in her hall.

20 'So I cannot loup, I cannot come,
       I cannot loup to thee;
    My earthly part is all consumed,
       My spirit but speaks to thee.'

21 Wringing her hands, tearing her hair,
       His lady she was seen,
    And thus addressed his servant Gordon,
       Where he stood on the green.

22 'O wae be to you, George Gordon!
       An ill death may you die!
    So safe and sound as you stand there,
       And my lord bereaved from me.'

23 'I bad him loup, I bad him come,
       I bad him loup to me;
    I 'd catch him in my arms two,
       A foot I should not flee.   &c.

24 'He threw me the rings from his white
       fingers,
    Which were so long and small,
    To give to you, his lady fair,
       Where you sat in your hall.'   &c.

25 Sophia Hay, Sophia Hay,
       O bonny Sophia was her name,
    Her waiting maid put on her cloaths,
       But I wot she tore them off again.

26 And aft she cried, Ohon! alas! alas!
       A sair heart 's ill to win;
    I wan a sair heart when I married him,
       And the day it 's well returnd again.

C

'The Fire of Frendraught,' from a note-
book of Dr Joseph Robertson: "procured in
the parish of Forgue by A. Scott; communicated to me by Mr John Stuart, Aberdeen, 11
October, 1832."

1 IT was in October the woe began —
       It lasts for now and aye, —
    The burning o the bonny house o fause
       Frendraught,
    Lord John and Rothiemay.

2 When they were in their saddles set,
       And ready to ride away,
    The lady sat down on her bare knees,
       Beseeching them to stay.

3 'Ye 's hae a firlot o the gude red gowd,
       Well straiket wi a wan;
    And if that winna please you well,
       I 'll heap it wi my han.'

4 Then out it spake the gude Lord John,
       And said to Rothiemay,
    'It is a woman that we 're come o,
       And a woman we 'll obey.'

5 When a' man was well drunken,
       And a' man bound for bed,
    The doors were lockd, the windows
       shut,
    And the keys were casten by.

6 When a' man was well drunken,
       And a' man bound for sleep,
    The dowy reek began to rise,
       And the joists began to crack.

7 He 's deen him to the wire-window,
       And ruefu strack and dang;
    But they would neither bow nor brack,
       The staunchions were so strang.

8 He 's deen him back and back again,
       And back to Rothiemay;
    Says, Waken, waken, brother dear!
       Waken, Rothiemay!

9 'Come let us praise the Lord our God,
       The fiftieth psalm and three;
    For the reek and smoke are us about,
       And there 's fause treason tee.

10 'O mercy, mercy, Lady Frendraught!
       As ye walk on the green:'
    'The keys are in the deep draw-well,
       The doors were lockt the streen.'

11 'O woe be to you, Lady Frendraught
       An ill death may you die!
    For think na ye this a sad torment
       Your own flesh for to burn?'

12 George Chalmers was a bonny boy;
       He leapt the stanks so deep,
    And he is on to Rothiemay,
       His master for to help.

13 Colin Irving was a bonny boy,
    And leapt the stanks so deep:
'Come down, come down, my master
    dear !
    In my arms I 'll thee kep.'

14 'Come down ? come down ? how can I
    come ?
    How can I come to thee ?
My flesh is burning me about,
    And yet my spirit speaks to thee.'

15 He 's taen a purse o the gude red
    gowd,
    And threw it oer the wa:
'It 's ye 'll deal that among the poor,
    Bid them pray for our souls a'.'

16 He 's taen the rings off his fingers,
    And threw them oer the wa;
Says, Ye 'll gie that to my lady dear,
    From me she 'll na get more.

17 'Bid her make her bed well to the
    length,
    But no more to the breadth,
For the day will never dawn
    That I 'll sleep by her side.'

18 Lady Rothiemay came on the morn,
    She kneeled it roun and roun:
'Restore your lodgers, fause Frend-
    raught,
    That ye burnd here the streen.

19 'O were I like yon turtle-dove,
    Had I wings for to flie,
I 'd fly about fause Frendraught
    Crying vengeance till I die.

20 'Frendraught fause, all thro the ha's,
    Both back and every side;
For ye 've betrayd the gay Gordons,
    And lands wherein they ride.

21 'Frendraught fause, all thro the ha's;
    I wish you 'd sink for sin;
For first you killd my own good lord,
    And now you 've burnd my son.'

22 'I caredna sae muckle for my good
    lord
    I saw him in battle slain,
But a' is for my own son dear,
    The heir o a' my lan.

23 'I caredna sae muckle for my good
    lord
    I saw him laid in clay,
But a' is for my own son dear,
    The heir o Rothiemay.'

197

JAMES GRANT

There was an implacable feud between the
Grants of Ballindalloch and the Grants of Carron, for as much as ninety years after 1550.
This fragment has to do with the later stage
of their enmity. In 1628, John Grant of Ballindalloch killed John Grant of Carron. James
Grant of Carron, uncle of the slain man, burnt
all the corn, barns, and byres of Ballindalloch
young and old, and took to the hills (1630).
The Ballindallochs complained to Murray, the
lieutenant, and he set the Clanchattan upon
James Grant. They laid siege to a house
where he was with a party of his men; he
made his way out, was pursued, and was taken
after receiving eleven arrow-wounds. When
he was well enough to travel, he was sent to
Edinburgh, and, as everybody supposed, to his
death ; but after a confinement of more than a
year he broke ward. Large sums were offered
for him, alive or dead, but in 1633 he began
to appear again in the north. A gang of the
McGregors, who had been brought into the
country by Ballindalloch to act against James
Grant, beset him in a small house in Carron
where he was visiting his wife, having only
his son and one other man with him; but he
defended himself with the spirit of another
Cloudesly, shot the captain, and got off to the
bog with his men. In 1636 "some of the
Marquis of Huntly's followers and servants
did invade the rebel James Grant and some
of his associates, hard by Strathbogy. They
burnt the house wherein he was, but, the night
being dark and windy, he and his brother,
Robert Grant, escaped." (Sir Robert Gordon,
History of the Earldom of Sutherland, pp.
481, 460.) This last escapade of James Grant
may perhaps be the one to which this fragment has reference, though Ballindalloch was
not personally engaged in the assault on the
house.

a. Motherwell's MS., p. 470, communicated
apparently by Buchan; 'The Gordons and the
Grants,' Buchan's Ballads of the North of
Scotland, ii, 220. b. C. K. Sharpe's "second
collection," MS.

1 'AWAY with you, away with you, James
        de Grant !
    And, Douglas, ye 'll be slain;
    For Baddindalloch 's at your gates,
        With many brave Highland men.'

2 'Baddindalloch has no feud at me,
        And I have none at him;
    Cast up my gates baith broad and wide,
        Let Baddindalloch in.'

3 'James de Grant has made a vaunt,
        And leaped the castle-wa;
    But, if he comes this way again,
        He 'll no win sae well awa.

4 'Take him, take him, brave Gordons,
        O take him, fine fellows a' !
    If he wins but ae mile to the Highland
        hills,
    He 'll defy you Gordons a'.'

198

BONNY JOHN SETON

The ballad is accurate as to the date, not
commonly a good sign for such things. On
Tuesday, the eighteenth of June, 1639, Montrose began an attack on the bridge of Dee,
which had been fortified and manned by the
royalists of Aberdeen to stop his advance on
the city. The bridge was bravely defended
that day and part of the next by Lieutenant-
Colonel Johnston (not Middleton; Middleton
was of the assailants). The young Lord of
Aboyne, just made the king's lieutenant in the
north, had a small body of horse on the north
side of the river. Montrose's cavalry were
sent up the south side as if to cross (though
there was no ford), and Aboyne's were moved
along the opposite bank to resist a passage.
This exposed the latter to Montrose's cannon,
and the Covenanters let fly some shot at them,
one of which killed "a gallant gentleman,
John Seton of Pitmeddin." Johnston's leg was
crushed by stones and he had to be carried off.
The loss of their commander and the disap-
pearance of Aboyne's horse discouraged the
now small party who were holding the bridge,
and they abandoned it. Aboyne rode off, and
left Aberdeen to shift for itself.

A

a. 'Bonny John Seton,' Maidment's North
Countrie Garland, p. 15 ; Buchan's Gleanings,
p. 161; Maidment's Scotish Ballads and Songs,
Historical and Traditionary, i, 280. b. MS.
of C. K. Sharpe ; North Country Ballads,
Miscellanea Curiosa, MS., Abbotsford.

1 UPON the eighteenth day of June,
    A dreary day to see,
    The southern lords did pitch their camp
        Just at the bridge of Dee.

2 Bonny John Seton of Pitmeddin,
    A bold baron was he,
    He made his testament ere he went
        out,
    The wiser man was he.

3 He left his land to his young son,
    His lady her dowry,
    A thousand crowns to his daughter Jean,
    Yet on the nurse's knee

4 Then out came his lady fair,
    A tear into her ee;
    Says, Stay at home, my own good lord,
    O stay at home with me !

5 He looked over his left shoulder,
    Cried, Souldiers, follow me !
    O then she looked in his face,
    An angry woman was she:
    'God send me back my steed again,
    But neer let me see thee !'

6 His name was Major Middleton
    That manned the bridge of Dee,
    His name was Colonel Henderson
    That let the cannons flee.

7 His name was Major Middleton
    That manned the bridge of Dee,
    And his name was Colonel Henderson
    That dung Pitmeddin in three.

8 Some rode on the black and grey,
    And some rode on the brown,
    But the bonny John Seton
    Lay gasping on the ground.

9 Then bye there comes a false Forbes,
    Was riding from Driminere;
    Says, Here there lies a proud Seton;
    This day they ride the rear.

10 Cragievar said to his men,
    'You may play on your shield;

For the proudest Seton in all the lan
This day lies on the field.'

11 'O spoil him ! spoil him !' cried Cra-
gievar,
  'Him spoiled let me see;
For on my word,' said Cragievar,
  'He had no good will at me.'

12 They took from him his armour clear,
His sword, likewise his shield;
Yea, they have left him naked there,
Upon the open field.

13 The Highland men, they 're clever men
At handling sword and shield,
But yet they are too naked men
To stay in battle field.

14 The Highland men are clever men
At handling sword or gun,
But yet they are too naked men
To bear the cannon's rung.

15 For a cannon's roar in a summer night
Is like thunder in the air;
There 's not a man in Highland dress
Can face the cannon's fire.

199

THE BONNIE HOUSE O AIRLIE

The Committee cf Estates, June 12, 1640,
gave commission to the Earl of Argyle to rise
in arms against certain people, among whom
was the Earl of Airlie, as enemies to religion
and unnatural to their country, and to pursue
them with fire and sword until they should be
brought to their duty or else be utterly rooted
out. The Earl of Airlie had gone to England
and had left his house to the keeping of his
eldest son, Lord Ogilvie. Montrose, who had
signed the commission as one of the Committee,
but was not inclined to so strenuous proceedings, invested Airlie, forced a surrender, and
put a garrison in the place to hold it for the
"public." Argyle did not interpret his commission in this mild way. He took Airlie in
hand in the beginning of July, and caused both
this house and that of Forthar, belonging to
Lord Ogilvie, to be pillaged, burned, and de-
molished. The earliest copy of this ballad
hitherto found is a broadside of 1790, used by
Finlay in forming the text in his Ballads, II,
25.

A

a. A small MS. volume with the title "Songs"
on the cover, entirely in C. K. Sharpe's handwriting, p. 22 ; Sharpe's Ballad Book, p. 59,
No. 20, 1823 (with some " improvements ").
b. ' The Bonnie House o Airly,' Finlay's Ballads, II, 25, 1808, from two recited copies and
" one printed about twenty years ago on a
single sheet." c. The Old Lady's Collection,
MS., No. 1 ; Skene MS., pp. 28, 54 ; from recitation in the north of Scotland, 1802–3. d.
' The Bonny House of Airly,' Campbell MSS.,
II, 113, probably from a stall-copy. e, f. Aberdeen stall copies, " printed for the booksellers."
g. Hogg's Jacobite Relics, II, 152, No. 76, " Cromek and a street ballad collated, 1821." h.
Kinloch MSS., VI, 5, one stanza, taken down
from an old woman's recitation by J. Robertson.

1 It fell on a day, and a bonny summer
day,
  When corn grew green and yellow,
That there fell out a great dispute
  Between Argyll and Airly.

2 Argyll has raisd an hundred men,
  An hundred men, and so many,
And he is away by the back of Dunkeld,
  For to plunder the bonny house of
  Airly.

3 Lady Margaret looks oer her bower-
window,
  And O but she looks weary !
And there she spied the great Argyll,
  Coming to plunder the bonny house
  of Airly.

4 'Come down, come down, Lady Margret,'
he said,
  'Come down, and kiss me fairly:'
' O I will not kiss the great Argyll,
  If he should not leave a standing stone
  in Airly.'

5 He hath taken her by the left shoulder,
  Says, Lady, where lyes thy dowry ?
' It 's up and it 's down by the bonny
bank-side,
  Amongst the planting of Airly.'

6 They have sought it up, they have
sought it down,
  They have sought it both late and
  early,

And they have found it in the bonny
    plumb-tree
  That shines on the bowling-green of
    Airly.

7 He hath taken her by the middle so
    small,
    And O but she lookd weary !
  He hath laid her down by the bonny
    burn-side,
    Till he hath plundered the bonny
    house of Airly.

8 'If my good lord were at home this
    night,
    As he is with Prince Charly,
  Nouther you nor no Scottish lord
    Durst have set a foot on the bowling-
    green of Airly.

9 'Ten bonny sons I have born unto him,
    The eleventh neer saw his daddy;
  Although I had an hundred more,
    I would give them all to Prince
    Charly.'

200

THE GYPSY LADDIE

The earliest edition of the ballad styles the
gypsy Johny Faa, but gives no clew to the fair
lady. Johnny Faa was a prominent and frequent name among the gypsies. Johnnë Faw's
right and title as lord and earl of Little Egypt
were recognized by James V in 1540. But in
the next year Egyptians were ordered to quit
the realm within thirty days on pain of death.
The gypsies were formally expelled from Scotland by act of Parliament in 1609. Johnnë,
alias Willie, Faa, with three others of the name,
remained notwithstanding, and were sentenced
to be hanged, 1611. In 1616, July 24, Johnnë
Faa, Egyptian, his son, and two others were
condemned to be hanged for contemptuous repairing to the country and abiding therein.
Finally, in 1624, January 24, Captain Johnnë
Faa and seven others were sentenced to be
hanged for the same offence. The execution
of the notorious Egyptian and chieftain Johnny
Faa must have made a considerable impression,
and it is presumable that this ballad may have
arisen not long after. Whether this were so or
not, Johnny Faa acquired popular fame, and
became a personage to whom any adventure
might plausibly be imputed.

Toward the end of the eighteenth century
we begin to hear that the people in Ayrshire
make the wife of the Earl of Cassilis the heroine of the ballad; but there is positive evidence
that this lady (who died in 1642) had never done
anything to alienate her husband's affections.

The Scottish ballad appears to have been first
printed in the fourth volume of the Tea-Table
Miscellany, 1740, but no copy of that edition
has been recovered. The English version (G),
though derived from the Scottish ballad, may
perhaps have been printed earlier; it is found
in a broadside in the Roxburghe collection,
III, 685.

A

'Johny Faa, the Gypsy Laddie,' Ramsay's
Tea-Table Miscellany, vol. IV, 1740. Here from
the London edition of 1763, p. 427.

1 THE gypsies came to our good lord's
    gate,
    And wow but they sang sweetly !
  They sang sae sweet and sae very com-
    pleat
    That down came the fair lady.

2 And she came tripping down the stair,
    And a' her maids before her;
  As soon as they saw her well-far'd face,
    They coost the glamer oer her.

3 'Gae tak frae me this gay mantile,
    And bring to me a plaidie;
  For if kith and kin and a' had sworn,
    I 'll follow the gypsie laddie.

4 'Yestreen I lay in a well-made bed,
    And my good lord beside me;
  This night I 'll ly in a tenant's barn,
    Whatever shall betide me.'

5 'Come to your bed,' says Johny Faa,
    'Oh come to your bed, my deary;
  For I vow and I swear, by the hilt of
    my sword,
    That your lord shall nae mair come
    near ye.'

6 'I 'll go to bed to my Johny Faa,
    I 'll go to bed to my deary;
  For I vow and I swear, by what past
    yestreen,
    That my lord shall nae mair come
    near me.

7 'I 'll mak a hap to my Johnny Faa,
    And I 'll mak a hap to my deary;
And he 's get a' the coat gaes round,
    And my lord shall nae mair come near
    me.'

8 And when our lord came hame at een,
    And speir'd for his fair lady,
The tane she cry'd, and the other re-
    ply'd,
    'She 's away with the gypsie laddie.'

9 'Gae saddle to me the black, black
    steed,
    Gae saddle and make him ready;
Before that I either eat or sleep,
    I 'll gae seek my fair lady.'

10 And we were fifteen well-made men,
    Altho we were nae bonny;
And we were a' put down for ane,
    A fair young wanton lady.

B

a. C. K. Sharpe's papers, " written from recitation in Nithisdale, November, 1814; " The
Edinburgh Magazine and Literary Miscellany,
being a new series of the Scots Magazine (vol.
LXXX of the entire work), November, 1817,
p. 309, communicated by Sharpe. b. A fragment recited by Miss Fanny Walker, of Mount
Pleasant, near Newburgh-on-Tay, as communicated by Mr Alexander Laing, 1873.

1 THE gypsies they came to my lord Cas-
    silis' yett,
    And O but they sang bonnie !
They sang so sweet and so complete
    Till down came our fair ladie.

2 She came tripping down the stairs,
    And all her maids before her;
As soon as they saw her weel-far'd
    face,
    They cast their glamourie owre her.

3 She gave them the good wheat bread,
    And they give her the ginger;
But she give them a far better thing,
    The gold rings of her fingers.

4 'Will you go with me, my hinny and
    my heart ?
    Will you go with me, my dearie ?

And I will swear, by the hilt of my
    spear,
    That your lord shall no more come
    near thee.'

5 'Gar take from me my silk manteel,
    And bring to me a plaidie,
For I will travel the world owre
    Along with the gypsie laddie.

6 'I could sail the seas with my Jackie
    Faa,
    I could sail the seas with my dearie;
I could sail the seas with my Jackie
    Faa,
    And with pleasure could drown with
    my dearie.'

7 They wandred high, they wandred low,
    They wandred late and early,
Untill they came to an old farmer's
    barn,
    And by this time she was weary.

8 'Last night I lay in a weel-made bed,
    And my noble lord beside me,
And now I most ly in an old farmer's
    barn,
    And the black crae glowring owre
    me.'

9 'Hold your tongue, my hinny and my
    heart,
    Hold your tongue, my dearie,
For I will swear, by the moon and the
    stars,
    That thy lord shall no more come
    near thee.'

10 They wandred high, they wandred low,
    They wandred late and early,
Untill they came to that on water,
    And by this time she was wearie.

11 'Many a time have I rode that on wa-
    ter,
    And my lord Cassilis beside me,
And now I most set in my white feet
    and wade,
    And carry the gypsie laddie.'

12 By and by came home this noble lord,
    And asking for his ladie,
The one did cry, the other did reply,
    'She is gone with the gypsie laddie.'

13 'Go saddle to me the black,' he says,
  'The brown rides never so speedie,
  And I will neither eat nor drink
  Till I bring home my ladie.'

14 He wandred high, he wandred low,
  He wandred late and early,
  Untill he came to that on water,
  And there he spied his ladie.

15 'O wilt thou go home, my hinny and my
    heart,
  O wilt thou go home, my dearie?
  And I'll close thee in a close room,
  Where no man shall come near thee.'

16 'I will not go home, my hinny and my
    heart,
  I will not go home, my dearie;
  If I have brewn good beer, I will drink
    of the same,
  And my lord shall no more come near
    me.

17 'But I will swear, by the moon and the
    stars,
  And the sun that shines so clearly,
  That I am as free of the gypsie gang
  As the hour my mother bore me.'

18 They were fifteen valiant men,
  Black, but very bonny,
  They lost all their lives for one,
  The Earl of Cassillis' ladie.

201

BESSY BELL AND MARY GRAY

This little ballad, or song, was very well known in the last years of the seventeenth century. The first stanza was made by Ramsay the beginning of a song of his own (Poems, Edinburgh, 1721, p. 80). The most important document relating to Bessy Bell and Mary Gray is a letter written June, 1781, by Major Barry, then proprietor of Lednock, and printed in the Transactions of the Society of Antiquaries of Scotland, II, 108, 1822. "When I came first to Lednock," says Major Barry, "I was shewn in a part of my ground (called the Dranoch-haugh) an heap of stones almost covered with briers, thorns and fern, which they assured me was the burial place of Bessie Bell and Mary Gray. The tradition of the country relating to these ladys is, that Mary

Gray's father was laird of Lednock and Bessie Bell's of Kinvaid, a place in this neighbourhood; that they were both very handsome, and an intimate friendship subsisted between them; that while Miss Bell was on a visit to Miss Gray, the plague broke out, in the year 1666; in order to avoid which they built themselves a bower about three quarters of a mile west from Lednock House, in a very retired and romantic place called Burn-braes, on the side of Beauchieburn. Here they lived for some time; but the plague raging with great fury, they caught the infection, it is said, from a young gentleman who was in love with them both. He used to bring them their provision. They died in this bower, and were buried in the Dranoch-haugh, at the foot of a brae of the same name, and near to the bank of the river Almond. The burial-place lies about half a mile west from the present house of Lednock."

Major Barry's date of 1666 should be put back twenty years. Perth and the neighborhood (Lednock is seven miles distant) were fearfully ravaged by the plague in 1645 and a year or two following. Three thousand people are said to have perished. Scotland escaped the pestilence of 1665–66.

Bessy Bell was made into a nursery-rhyme in England (see Halliwell's Nursery Rhymes, 1874, No. 484).

a. Sharpe's Ballad Book, 1823, p. 62. b. Lyle's Ancient Ballads and Songs, 1827, p. 160, "collated from the singing of two aged persons, one them a native of Perthshire." c. Scott's Minstrelsy, 1830, I, 39, 1833, I, 45, two stanzas, (1, 3).

1 O Bessie Bell and Mary Gray,
  They war twa bonnie lasses;
  They bigget a bower on yon burn-brae,
  And theekit it oer wi rashes.

2 They theekit it oer wi rashes green,
  They theekit it oer wi heather;
  But the pest cam frae the burrows-town,
  And slew them baith thegither.

3 They thought to lye in Methven kirk-
    yard,
  Amang their noble kin;
  But they maun lye in Stronach haugh,
  To biek forenent the sin.

4 And Bessy Bell and Mary Gray,
  They war twa bonnie lasses;
  They biggit a bower on yon burn-brae,
  And theekit it oer wi rashes.

202

THE BATTLE OF PHILIP-HAUGH

After six brilliant victories, gained in less than a year, September 1, 1644 – August 15, 1645, Montrose was surprised by David Leslie at Philiphaugh, September 13 following, and his army cut to pieces or dispersed. This army, consisting of only five hundred Irish foot and twelve hundred Scottish horse, was lying at Philiphaugh, a meadow on the west side of the Ettrick, and at Selkirk, on and above the opposite bank. Leslie came down from the north with four thousand cavalry and some infantry, was less than four miles from Selkirk the night of the twelfth, and on the morrow, favored by a heavy mist, had advanced to about half a mile's distance before his approach was reported. A hundred and fifty of Montrose's horse received and repulsed two charges of greatly superior numbers ; the rest stood off and presently took to flight. The foot remained firm. Two thousand of Leslie's horse crossed the river and got into Montrose's rear, and made resistance vain. Montrose and a few friends hewed their way through the enemy.

Minstrelsy of the Scottish Border, III, 153, 1803, II, 166, 1833, " preserved by tradition in Selkirkshire."

1 On Philiphaugh a fray began,
    At Hairheadwood it ended;
The Scots outoer the Græmes they ran,
    Sae merrily they bended.

2 Sir David frae the Border came,
    Wi heart an hand came he;
Wi him three thousand bonny Scots,
    To bear him company.

3 Wi him three thousand valiant men,
    A noble sight to see !
A cloud o mist them weel conceald,
    As close as eer might be.

4 When they came to the Shaw burn,
    Said he, Sae weel we frame,
I think it is convenient
    That we should sing a psalm.

5 When they came to the Lingly burn,
    As daylight did appear,
They spy'd an aged father,
    And he did draw them near.

6 ' Come hither, aged father,'
    Sir David he did cry,
' And tell me where Montrose lies,
    With all his great army.'

7 ' But first you must come tell to me,
    If friends or foes you be;
I fear you are Montrose's men,
    Come frae the north country.'

8 ' No, we are nane o Montrose's men,
    Nor eer intend to be;
I am Sir David Lesly,
    That 's speaking unto thee.'

9 ' If you 're Sir David Lesly,
    As I think weel ye be,
I am sorry ye hae brought so few
    Into your company.

10 ' There 's fifteen thousand armed men
    Encamped on yon lee;
Ye 'll never be a bite to them,
    For aught that I can see.

11 ' But halve your men in equal parts,
    Your purpose to fulfill;
Let ae half keep the water-side,
    The rest gae round the hill.

12 ' Your nether party fire must,
    Then beat a flying drum;
And then they 'll think the day 's their ain,
    And frae the trench they 'll come.

13 ' Then, those that are behind them maun
    Gie shot, baith grit and sma;
And so, between your armies twa,
    Ye may make them to fa.'

14 ' O were ye ever a soldier ? '
    Sir David Lesly said;
' O yes; I was at Solway Flow,
    Where we were all betrayd.

15 ' Again I was at curst Dunbar,
    And was a prisner taen,
And many weary night and day
    In prison I hae lien.'

16 ' If ye will lead these men aright,
    Rewarded shall ye be;
But, if that ye a traitor prove,
    I 'll hang thee on a tree.'

17 'Sir, I will not a traitor prove;
    Montrose has plunderd me;
    I 'll do my best to banish him
    Away frae this country.'

18 He halvd his men in equal parts,
    His purpose to fulfill;
    The one part kept the water-side,
    The other gaed round the hill.

19 The nether party fired brisk,
    Then turnd and seemd to rin;
    And then they a' came frae the trench,
    And cry'd, The day's our ain !

20 The rest then ran into the trench,
    And loosd their cannons a':
    And thus, between his armies twa,
    He made them fast to fa.

21 Now let us a' for Lesly pray,
    And his brave company,
    For they hae vanquishd great Montrose,
    Our cruel enemy.

203

THE BARON OF BRACKLEY

At least two events are probably confounded in this ballad : (1) the murder of the Baron of Brackley, in 1592, by Highland caterans whom he had hospitably entertained, and (2) an affray occurring in 1666 between John Gordon of Brackley and John Farquharson of Inverey. Other tragedies in the troubled history of the Brackley family may also have contributed to the tradition.

A

a. 'The Baronne of Braikley,' Scarce Ancient Ballads [Alexander Laing], Aberdeen, 1822, p. 9. **b.** 'The Baron of Braikley,' Buchan's Gleanings, 1825, p. 68. **c.** The New Deeside Guide, by James Brown (i. e. Joseph Robertson), Aberdeen, [1832,] p. 46.

1 INVEREY cam doun Deeside, whistlin and playin,
    He was at brave Braikley's yett ere it was dawin.

2 He rappit fu loudly an wi a great roar,
    Cried, Cum doun, cum doun, Braikley, and open the door.

3 'Are ye sleepin, Baronne, or are ye wakin ?
    There's sharpe swords at your yett, will gar your blood spin.

4 'Open the yett, Braikley, and lat us within,
    Till we on the green turf gar your bluid rin.'

5 Out spak the brave baronne, owre the castell-wa:
    'Are ye cum to spulyie and plunder mi ha ?

6 'But gin ye be gentlemen, licht and cum in:
    Gin ye drink o my wine, ye 'll nae gar my bluid spin.

7 'Gin ye be hir'd widifus, ye may gang by,
    Ye may gang to the lawlands and steal their fat ky.

8 'Ther spulyie like rievers o wyld kettrin clan,
    Who plunder unsparing baith houses and lan.

9 'Gin ye be gentlemen, licht an cum [in],
    Ther's meat an drink i my ha for every man.

10 'Gin ye be hir'd widifus, ye may gang by,
    Gang doun to the lawlands, and steal horse and ky.'

11 Up spak his ladie, at his bak where she lay,
    'Get up, get up, Braikley, and be not afraid;
    The 'r but young hir'd widifus wi belted plaids.'

12 'Cum kiss me, mi Peggy, I 'le nae langer stay,
    For I will go out and meet Inverey.

13 'But haud your tongue, Peggy, and mak nae sic din,
    For yon same hir'd widifus will prove themselves men.'

14 She called on her marys, they cam to her
          hand;
    Cries, Bring me your rocks, lassies, we
          will them command.

15 ' Get up, get up, Braikley, and turn bak
          your ky,
    Or me an mi women will them defy.

16 ' Cum forth then, mi maidens, and show
          them some play;
    We 'll ficht them, and shortly the cow-
          ards will fly.

17 ' Gin I had a husband, whereas I hae
          nane,
    He woud nae ly i his bed and see his ky
          taen.

18 ' Ther 's   four-and-twenty   milk-whit
          calves, twal o them ky,
    In the woods o Glentanner, it 's ther
          thei a' ly.

19 ' Ther 's goat i the Etnach, and sheep o
          the brae,
    An a' will be plunderd by young In-
          verey.'

20 ' Now haud your tongue, Peggy, and gie
          me a gun,
    Ye 'll see me gae furth, but I 'll never
          cum in.

21 ' Call mi brother William, mi unkl also,
    Mi cousin James Gordon; we 'll mount
          and we 'll go.'

22 When Braikley was ready and stood i
          the closs,
    He was the bravest baronne that eer
          mounted horse.

23 Whan all wer assembld o the castell
          green,
    No man like brave Braikley was ther to
          be seen.

24 .   .   .   .   .   .
    ' Turn bak, brother William, ye are a
          bridegroom;

25 ' Wi bonnie Jean Gordon, the maid o
          the mill;
    O sichin and sobbin she 'll soon get her fill.'

26 ' I 'm no coward, brother, 't is kend
          I 'm a man;
    I 'll ficht i your quarral as lang 's I can
          stand.

27 ' I 'll ficht, my dear brother, wi heart
          and gude will,
    And so will young Harry that lives at
          the mill.

28 ' But turn, mi dear brother, and nae
          langer stay:
    What 'll cum o your ladie, gin Braikley
          thei slay ?

29 ' What 'll cum o your ladie and bonnie
          young son ?
    O what 'll cum o them when Braikley is
          gone ? '

30 ' I never will turn: do you think I will
          fly ?
    But here I will ficht, and here I will
          die.'

31 ' Strik dogs,' crys Inverey, ' and ficht
          till ye 're slayn,
    For we are four hundered, ye are but
          four men.

32 ' Strik, strik, ye proud boaster, your
          honour is gone,
    Your lands we will plunder, your cas-
          tell we 'll burn.'

33 At the head o the Etnach the battel
          began,
    At Little Auchoilzie thei killd the first
          man.

34 First thei killd ane, and soon they killd
          twa,
    Thei killd gallant Braikley, the flour o
          them a'.

35 Thei killd William Gordon, and James
          o the Knox,
    And brave Alexander, the flour o Glen-
          muick.

36 What sichin and moaning was heard i
          the glen,
    For the Baronne o Braikley, who basely
          was slayn !

37   Cam ye bi the castell, and was ye in
there?
Saw ye pretty Peggy tearing her hair?'

38   'Yes, I cam by Braikley, and I gaed in
there,
And there [saw] his ladie braiding her
hair.

39   She was rantin, and dancin, and singin
for joy,
And vowin that nicht she woud feest
Inverey.

40   'She eat wi him, drank wi him, welcomd
him in,
Was kind to the man that had slayn her
baronne.'

41   Up spake the son on the nourice's knee,
'Gin I live to be a man, revenged I'll
be.'

42   Ther's dool i the kitchin, and mirth i
the ha,
The Baronne o Braikley is dead and
awa.

B

'The Baron of Brackley,' Kinloch MSS., v,
379, in the handwriting of John Hill Burton.

1   'Baron of Brackley, are ye in there?
The 're sharp swords at yer yetts, winna
ye spear.'

2   'If they be gentlemen, lat them cum
in;
But if they be reavers, we'll gar them
be taen.'

3   'It is na gentlemen, nor yet pretty lads,
But a curn hir'd widdifus, wears belted
plaids.'

4   She called on her women and bade them
come in:
'Tack a' yer rocks, lasses, and we'll
them coman.

5   'We'll fecht them, we'll slight them,
we'll do what we can,
And I vow we will shoot them altho
we shod bang.

6   'Rise up, John,' she said, 'and turn in
yer kye,
For they'll hae them to the Hielands,
and you they'l defie.'

7   'Had your still, Catharine, and still yer
young son,
For ye'll get me out, but I'll never cum
in.'

8   'If I had a man, as I hae na nane,
He wudna lye in his bed and see his kye
tane.'

9   'Ye'll cum kiss me, my Peggy, and
bring me my gun,
For I'm gaing out, but I'll never cum in.'

10   There was twenty wi Invery, twenty
and ten;
There was nane wi the baron but his
brother and him.

11   At the head of Reneeten the battle began;
Ere they wan Auchoilzie, they killed
mony a man.

12   They killed Harry Gordon and Harry
of the Knock,
The mullertd's four sons up at Glen-
muick.

13   They killed Harry Gordon and Harry
of the Knock,
And they made the brave baron like
kail to a pot.

14   First they killed ane, and then they
killed twa,
Then they killed the brave baron, the
flower o them a'.

15   Then up came Craigievar, and a party
wi him;
If he had come an hour sooner, Brackley had not been slain.

16   'Came ye by Brackley? and was ye in
there?
Or say ye his lady, was making great
care?'

17   'I came by Brackley, and I was in there,
But I saw his lady no makin great care.

18 ' For she eat wi them, drank wi them,
  welcomed them in;
 She drank to the villain that killed her
  guid man.

19 ' Woe to ye, Kate Fraser! sorry may
  yer heart be,
 To see yer brave baron's blood cum to
  yer knee.'

20 There is dule in the kitchen, and mirth
  i the ha,
 But the Baron o B[r]ackley is dead and
  awa.

204

JAMIE DOUGLAS

Lady Barbara Erskine, eldest daughter of
John, Earl of Mar, was married to James, second Marquis of Douglas, near the end of the
year 1670. The marriage did not prove to be
happy, and the parties were formally separated
in 1681. The blame of the alienation of Douglas from his wife is imputed by tradition to
William Lawrie, the marquis's principal chamberlain or factor, who was appointed to that
place in 1670, the year of the marriage. Lawrie married Marion Weir, of the family of
Blackwood, then a widow. He is often styled
the laird of Blackwood, a title which belonged
to his son by this marriage, his own proper
designation being, after the birth of his son,
the Tutor of Blackwood.

The ballad first appeared in print in the second edition of Herd's Scottish Songs, 1776, but
only as a fragment of five stanzas. Most of
the versions have from one stanza to four of a
beautiful song, known from the first quarter of
the eighteenth century, and printed fifty years
earlier than any copy of the ballad (see Notes).

A

' Lord Douglas,' or, ' The Laird of Blackwood,' Kinloch MSS., i, 93; from the recitation
of Mary Barr, Lesmahago, Lanarkshire, May,
1827, and learned by her about sixty years before from an old dey at Douglas Castle.

1 I WAS a lady of high renown
  As lived in the north countrie;
 I was a lady of high renown
  Whan Earl Douglas loved me.

2 Whan we cam through Glasgow toun,
  We war a comely sight to see;

 My gude lord in velvet green,
  And I mysel in cramasie.

3 Whan we cam to Douglas toun,
  We war a fine sight to behold;
 My gude lord in cramasie,
  And I myself in shining gold.

4 Whan that my auld son was born,
  And set upon the nurse's knee,
 I was as happy a woman as eer was
  born,
 And my gude lord he loved me.

5 But oh, an my young son was born,
  And set upon the nurse's knee,
 And I mysel war dead and gane,
  For a maid again I 'll never be!

6 There cam a man into this house,
  And Jamie Lockhart was his name,
 And it was told to my gude lord
  That I was in the bed wi him.

7 There cam anither to this house,
  And a bad friend he was to me;
 He put Jamie's shoon below my bed-
  stock,
 And bade my gude lord come and see.

8 O wae be unto thee, Blackwood,
  And ae an ill death may ye dee!
 For ye was the first and the foremost
  man
 That parted my gude lord and me.

9 Whan my gude lord cam in my room,
  This grit falsehood for to see,
 He turnd about, and, wi a gloom,
  He straucht did tak farewell o me.

10 ' O fare thee well, my once lovely maid!
  O fare thee well, once dear to me!
 O fare thee well, my once lovely maid!
  For wi me again ye sall never be.'

11 ' Sit doun, sit doun, Jamie Douglas,
  Sit thee doun and dine wi me,
 And I 'll set thee on a chair of gold,
  And a silver towel on thy knee.'

12 ' Whan cockle-shells turn silver bells,
  And mussels they bud on a tree,
 Whan frost and snaw turns fire to burn,
  Then I 'll sit down and dine wi thee.'

13 O wae be unto thee, Blackwood,
    And ae an ill death may ye dee !
Ye war the first and the foremost man
    That parted my gude lord and me.

14 Whan my father he heard word
    That my gude lord had forsaken
        me,
He sent fifty o his brisk dragoons
    To fesh me hame to my ain countrie.

15 That morning before I did go,
    My bonny palace for to leave,
I went into my gude lord's room,
    But alas ! he wad na speak to me.

16 'Fare thee well, Jamie Douglas !
    Fare thee well, my ever dear to me !
Fare thee well, Jamie Douglas !
    Be kind to the three babes I 've born
        to thee.'

205

LOUDON HILL, OR, DRUM–
CLOG

This ballad gives an account of the fight at
Drumclog, near Loudon Hill on the borders
of the shires of Ayr and Lanark, June 1, 1679,
between the " Gospel-lads " or Covenanters and
Claverhouse. The Covenanters were commanded by Robert Hamilton, with whom were
associated John Balfour of Kinloch, called
Burly, and others.

'The Battle of Loudon Hill,' Minstrelsy of
the Scottish Border, III, 188, 1803; II, 206,
1833.

1 You 'l marvel when I tell ye o
    Our noble Burly and his train,
When last he marchd up through the
        land,
    Wi sax-and-twenty westland men.

2 Than they I neer o braver heard,
    For they had a' baith wit and skill;
They proved right well, as I heard tell,
    As they cam up oer Loudoun Hill.

3 Weel prosper a' the gospel-lads
    That are into the west countrie
Ay wicked Claverse to demean,
    And ay an ill dead may he die !

4 For he 's drawn up i battle rank,
    An that baith soon an hastilie;
But they wha live till simmer come,
    Some bludie days for this will see.

5 But up spak cruel Claverse then,
    Wi hastie wit an wicked skill,
'Gae fire on yon westlan men;
    I think it is my sovreign's will.'

6 But up bespake his cornet then,
    'It 's be wi nae consent o me;
I ken I 'll neer come back again,
    An mony mae as weel as me.

7 'There is not ane of a' yon men
    But wha is worthy other three;
There is na ane amang them a'
    That in his cause will stap to die.

8 'An as for Burly, him I knaw;
    He 's a man of honour, birth, an fame;
Gie him a sword into his hand,
    He 'll fight thysel an other ten.'

9 But up spake wicked Claverse then —
    I wat his heart it raise fu hie —
And he has cry'd, that a' might hear,
    'Man, ye hae sair deceived me.

10 'I never kend the like afore,
    Na, never since I came frae hame,
That you sae cowardly here suld prove,
    An yet come of a noble Græme.'

11 But up bespake his cornet then,
    'Since that it is your honour's will,
Mysel shall be the foremost man
    That shall gie fire on Loudoun Hill.

12 'At your command I 'll lead them on,
    But yet wi nae consent o me;
For weel I ken I 'll neer return,
    And mony mae as weel as me.'

13 Then up he drew in battle rank —
    I wat he had a bonny train —
But the first time that bullets flew
    Ay he lost twenty o his men.

14 Then back he came the way he gaed,
    I wat right soon an suddenly;
He gave command amang his men,
    And sent them back, and bade them
        flee.

15 Then up came Burly, bauld an stout,
    Wi 's little train o westland men,
Wha mair than either aince or twice
    In Edinburgh confind had been.

16 They hae been up to London sent,
    An yet they 're a' come safely down;
Sax troop o horsemen they hae beat,
    And chased them into Glasgow town.

206

BOTHWELL BRIDGE

The report of the success of the Covenanters at Drumclog (see No. 205) brought four or five thousand malcontents into the rising. They established their camp on June 19, 1679, at Hamilton, on the south side of the Clyde, near the point where the river is crossed by Bothwell Bridge. The king named the Duke of Monmouth to command his army in Scotland. The royal forces were at Bothwell Muir on June 22d, and their advanced guards within a quarter of a mile of the bridge. The duke marched his army to an eminence opposite the main body of the enemy, who lay on the moor (st. 10). The defenders of the bridge maintained themselves until their powder was exhausted, and then unwillingly withdrew to the main body. The bridge was cleared of obstructions, and the royal army crossed and advanced against the rebels on the moor. The first fire made the Covenanters' horse wheel about, and their retreat threw the nearest foot into disorder; in consequence of which the whole army fell into confusion. Twelve hundred surrendered without resistance, the rest fled, and several hundred were killed in the pursuit.

Minstrelsy of the Scottish Border, III, 209, 1803; II, 226, 1833. From recitation.

1 'O BILLIE, billie, bonny billie,
    Will ye go to the wood wi me ?
We 'll ca our horse hame masterless,
    An gar them trow slain men are we.'

2 'O no, O no !' says Earlstoun,
    'For that 's the thing that mauna be;
For I am sworn to Bothwell Hill,
    Where I maun either gae or die.'

3 So Earlstoun rose in the morning,
    An mounted by the break o day,
An he has joind our Scottish lads,
    As they were marching out the way.

4 'Now, farewell, father ! and farewell, mother !
    An fare ye weel, my sisters three !
An fare ye well, my Earlstoun !
    For thee again I 'll never see.'

5 So they 're awa to Bothwell Hill,
    An waly, they rode bonnily !
When the Duke o Monmouth saw them comin,
    He went to view their company.

6 'Ye 're welcome, lads,' then Monmouth said,
    'Ye 're welcome, brave Scots lads, to me;
And sae are you, brave Earlstoun,
    The foremost o your company.

7 'But yield your weapons ane an a',
    O yield your weapons, lads, to me;
For, gin ye 'll yield your weapons up,
    Ye 'se a' gae hame to your country.'

8 Out then spak a Lennox lad,
    And waly, but he spoke bonnily !
'I winna yield my weapons up,
    To you nor nae man that I see.'

9 Then he set up the flag o red,
    A' set about wi bonny blue:
'Since ye 'll no cease, and be at peace,
    See that ye stand by ither true.'

10 They stelld their cannons on the height,
    And showrd their shot down in the how,
An beat our Scots lads even down;
    Thick they lay slain on every know.

11 As eer you saw the rain down fa,
    Or yet the arrow frae the bow,
Sae our Scottish lads fell even down,
    An they lay slain on every know.

12 'O hold your hand,' then Monmouth cry'd,
    'Gie quarters to yon men for me;'
But wicked Claverhouse swore an oath
    His cornet's death revengd sud be.

13 'O hold your hand,' then Monmouth
　　　cry'd,
　　　'If ony thing you 'll do for me;
　　Hold up your hand, you cursed Græme,
　　　Else a rebel to our king ye 'll be.'

14 Then wicked Claverhouse turnd about—
　　　I wot an angry man was he—
　　And he has lifted up his hat,
　　　And cry'd, God bless his Majesty!

15 Than he 's awa to London town,
　　　Ay een as fast as he can dree;
　　Fause witnesses he has wi him taen,
　　　An taen Monmouth's head frae his
　　　body.

16 Alang the brae beyond the brig,
　　　Mony brave man lies cauld and still;
　　But lang we 'll mind, and sair we 'll rue,
　　　The bloody battle of Bothwell Hill.

207

LORD DELAMERE

　　The duel in this ballad is on a par for historical verity with that in 'Johnie Scot' (No.
99). If there was to be a duel, Devonshire
(Earl, he was not created Duke till 1694, the
last year of Delamere's life) was well chosen
for the nonce. He had fought with Lord
Mohun, in 1676, and was credited with chal-
lenging Count Königsmark, in 1682. What is
true in the ballad is that Delamere was a
strenuous and uncompromising advocate of
constitutional government, and that he and
Devonshire were political and personal friends.
Both were particularly active in bringing in
the Prince of Orange; and so was Lord Danby,
with whom, according to the title of B (not here
printed), Devonshire was fighting the duel the
year before the revolution.

A

　'The Long-armed Duke,' taken down from
recitation in Derbyshire, and first printed, about
1843, in a periodical called The Story Teller;
afterwards in Notes and Queries, First Series,
v, 243, 1852, by C. W. G.

1 GOOD people, give attention, a story you
　　　shall hear,
　　It is of the king and my lord Dela-
　　　mere;

The quarrel it arose in the Parliament
　　　House,
Concerning some taxations going to be
　　　put in force.
　　　Ri toora loora la.

2 Says my lord Delamere to his Majesty
　　　soon,
　　'If it please you, my liege, of you I 'll
　　　soon beg a boon.'
　　'Then what is your boon? let me it
　　　understand:'
　　'It 's to have all the poor men you have
　　　in your land.

3 'And I 'll take them to Cheshire, and
　　　there I will sow
　　Both hempseed and flaxseed, and [hang]
　　　them all in a row.
　　Why, they 'd better be hanged, and
　　　stopped soon their breath,
　　If it please you, my liege, than to starve
　　　them to death.'

4 Then up starts a French lord, as we do
　　　hear,
　　Saying, 'Thou art a proud Jack,' to my
　　　lord Delamere;
　　'Thou oughtest to be stabbed'—then
　　　he turnd him about—
　　'For affronting the king in the Parlia-
　　　ment House.'

5 Then up starts his grace, the Duke of
　　　Devonshire,
　　Saying, I 'll fight in defence of my lord
　　　Delamere.
　　Then a stage was erected, to battle they
　　　went,
　　To kill or to be killed was our noble
　　　duke's intent.

6 The very first push, as we do under-
　　　stand,
　　The duke's sword he bended it back
　　　into his hand.
　　He waited a while, but nothing he
　　　spoke,
　　Till on the king's armour his rapier he
　　　broke.

7 An English lord, who by that stage did
　　　stand,
　　Threw Devonshire another, and he got
　　　it in his hand:

'Play low for your life, brave Devonshire,' said he,
'Play low for your life, or a dead man
   you will be.'

8 Devonshire dropped on his knee, and
   gave him his death-wound;
O then that French lord fell dead upon
   the ground.
The king called his guards, and he unto
   them did say,
'Bring Devonshire down, and take the
   dead man away.'

9 'No, if it please you, my liege, no! I 've
   slain him like a man;
I 'm resolved to see what clothing he 's
   got on.
Oh, fie upon your treachery, your
   treachery!' said he,
'Oh, king, 't was your intention to
   have took my life away.

10 'For he fought in your armour, whilst
   I have fought in bare;
The same thou shalt win, king, before
   thou does it wear.'
Then they all turned back to the Par-
   liament House,
And the nobles made obesiance with
   their hands to their mouths.

11 'God bless all the nobles we have in our
   land,
And send the Church of England may
   flourish still and stand;
For I 've injured no king, no kingdom,
   nor no crown,
But I wish that every honest man might
   enjoy his own.'

208

LORD DERWENTWATER

James Ratcliffe, Earl of Derwentwater, being suspected or known to be engaged in
concerting a rising in the north of England
in behalf of the Pretender, a warrant was
issued by the Secretary of State for his apprehension, towards the end of September, 1715.
Hereupon he took arms, and he was one of the
fifteen hundred English and Scots who were
forced to an inglorious surrender at Preston,
November 14. Derwentwater was impeached
of high treason, and pleaded guilty, in January,
1716; was sentenced to death February 9, and
was executed February 24.

A

'Lord Dunwaters,' Motherwell's MS., p.
331, July 19. 1825, "from the recitation of
Agnes Lile, Kilbarchan, a woman verging on
fifty; " learned from her father, who died fourteen years before, at the age of eighty. 'Lord
Derwentwater,' Motherwell's Minstrelsy, p.
349.

1 OUR king has wrote a lang letter,
   And sealed it owre with gold;
He sent it to my lord Dunwaters,
   To read it if he could.

2 He has not sent it with a boy, with a
   boy,
   Nor with anie Scotch lord;
But he 's sent it with the noblest knight
   Eer Scotland could afford.

3 The very first line that my lord did read,
   He gave a smirkling smile;
Before he had the half o 't read,
   The tears from his eyes did fall.

4 'Come saddle to me my horse,' he said,
   'Come saddle to me with speed;
For I must away to fair London town,
   For me was neer more need.'

5 Out and spoke his lady gay,
   In child-bed where she lay:
'I would have you make your will, my
   lord Dunwaters,
   Before you go away.'

6 'I leave to you, my eldest son,
   My houses and my land;
I leave to you, my second son,
   Ten thousand pounds in hand.

7 'I leave to you, my lady gay —
   You are my wedded wife —
I leave to you, the third of my estate;
   That 'll keep you in a lady's life.'

8 They had not rode a mile but one,
   Till his horse fell owre a stane:
'It 's warning gude eneuch,' my lord
   Dunwaters said,
   'Alive I 'll neer come hame.'

9 When they came into fair London town,
   Into the courtiers' hall,
   The lords and knichts in fair London
      town
   Did him a traitor call.

10 'A traitor! a traitor!' says my lord,
   'A traitor! how can that be,
   An it was na for the keeping of five
      thousand men
   To fight for King Jamie?

11 'O all you lords and knichts in fair Lon-
      don town,
   Come out and see me die;
   O all you lords and knichts into fair
      London town,
   Be kind to my ladie.

12 'There's fifty pounds in my richt
      pocket,
   Divide it to the poor;
   There's other fifty pounds in my left
      pocket,
   Divide it from door to door.'

D

'Lord Derntwater,' Kinloch MSS., i, 323.

1 THE king has written a braid letter,
   And seald it up wi gowd,
   And sent it to Lord Derntwater,
   To read it if he coud.

2 The first lines o 't that he read,
   A blythe, blythe man was he;
   But ere he had it half read through,
   The tear blinded his ee.

3 'Go saddle to me my milk-white horse,
   Go saddle it with speed;
   For I maun ride to Lun[n]on town,
   To answer for my head.'

4 'Your will, your will, my lord Dernt-
      water,
   Your will before ye go;
   For you will leave three dochters fair,
   And a wife to wail and woe.'

5 'My will, my will, my lady Derntwater?
   Ye are my wedded wife;
   Be kind, be kind to my dochters dear,
   If I should lose my life.'

6 He set his ae fit on the grund,
   The tither on the steed;
   The ring upon his finger burst,
   And his nose began to bleed.

7 He rode till he cam to Lunnon town,
   To a place they ca Whiteha;
   And a' the lords o merry England
   A traitor him gan ca.

8 'A traitor! a traitor! O what means
      this?
   A traitor! what mean ye?'
   'It's a' for the keeping o five hundred
      men
   To fecht for bonny Jamie.'

9 Then up started a gray-headed man,
   Wi a braid axe in his hand:
   'Your life, your life, my lord Dernt-
      water,
   Your life's at my command.'

10 'My life, my life, ye old gray-headed
      man,
   My life I'll freely gie;
   But before ye tak my life awa
   Let me speak twa words or three.

11 'I've fifty pounds in ae pocket,
   Go deal it frae door to door;
   I've fifty five i the other pocket,
   Go gie it to the poor.

12 'The velvet coat that I hae on,
   Ye may tak it for your fee;
   And a' ye lords o merry Scotland
   Be kind to my ladie!'

209

GEORDIE

Kinloch and others incline to take Geordie
to be George Gordon, fourth earl of Huntly,
who incurred the Queen Regent's displeasure
for failing to execute a commission against a
Highland robber in 1554. Huntly was committed to Edinburgh Castle, and some of his
many enemies urged that he should be put to
death. The Earl of Cassilis, though a foe to
Huntly, resisted these measures on grounds of
patriotism, and proposed that he should be de-
prived of certain honors and offices and fined.
A fine was exacted, and the places which had

been taken from him were restored. With regard to this hypothesis, it may at least be said that, if it should be accepted, the ballad would be quite as faithful to history as many others.

A

'Geordie,' Johnson's Musical Museum, No. 346, p. 357, 1792; communicated by Robert Burns.

1 THERE was a battle in the north,
    And nobles there was many,
And they hae killd Sir Charlie Hay,
    And they laid the wyte on Geordie.

2 O he has written a lang letter,
    He sent it to his lady:
'Ye maun cum up to Enbrugh town,
    To see what word 's o Geordie.'

3 When first she lookd the letter on,
    She was baith red and rosy;
But she had na read a word but twa
    Till she wallowt like a lily.

4 'Gar get to me my gude grey steed,
    My menyie a' gae wi me,
For I shall neither eat nor drink
    Till Enbrugh town shall see me.'

5 And she has mountit her gude grey steed,
    Her menyie a' gaed wi her,
And she did neither eat nor drink
    Till Enbrugh town did see her.

6 And first appeard the fatal block,
    And syne the aix to head him,
And Geordie cumin down the stair,
    And bands o airn upon him.

7 But tho he was chaind in fetters strang,
    O airn and steel sae heavy,
There was na ane in a' the court
    Sae bra a man as Geordie.

8 O she 's down on her bended knee,
    I wat she 's pale and weary:
'O pardon, pardon, noble king,
    And gie me back my dearie !

9 'I hae born seven sons to my Geordie dear,
    The seventh neer saw his daddie·
O pardon, pardon, noble king,
    Pity a waefu lady !'

10 'Gar bid the headin-man mak haste,'
    Our king reply'd fu lordly:
'O noble king, tak a' that 's mine,
    But gie me back my Geordie !'

11 The Gordons cam, and the Gordons ran,
    And they were stark and steady,
And ay the word amang them a'
    Was, Gordons, keep you ready !

12 An aged lord at the king's right hand
    Says, Noble king, but hear me;
Gar her tell down five thousand pound,
    And gie her back her dearie.

13 Some gae her marks, some gae her crowns,
    Some gae her dollars many,
And she 's telld down five thousand pound,
    And she 's gotten again her dearie.

14 She blinkit blythe in her Geordie's face,
    Says, Dear I 've bought thee, Geordie;
But there sud been bluidy bouks on the green
    Or I had tint my laddie.

15 He claspit her by the middle sma,
    And he kist her lips sae rosy:
'The fairest flower o woman-kind
    Is my sweet, bonie lady !'

D

'The Laird of Gigh, or Gae,' Scotch Ballads, Materials for Border Minstrelsy, No. 64, MS. of Thomas Wilkie, 1813–15, p. 50, Abbotsford. "I took this down from the recitation of Janet Scott, Bowden, who sung it to a beautiful plaintive old air."

1 THERE was a battle i the north
    Among the nobles many,
The Laird of Gigh he 's killd a man,
    The brother of his lady.

2 'Where will I get a man or boy,
    That will win both goud and money,
That will run into the north,
    And fetch to me my lady ?'

3 Up then spake a bonny boy,
    He was both blythe and merry;

'O I will run into the north,
　And fetch to you your lady.'

4 'You may tell her to sew me a gude
　　side shirt,
　She 'll no need to sew me mony;
　Tell her to bring me a gude side shirt,
　It will be the last of any.'

5 He has written a broad letter,
　And he 's sealed it sad and sorry;
　He 's gaen it to that bonny boy,
　To take to his fair lady.

6 Away the bonny boy he 's gaen,
　He was both blythe and merrie;
　He 's to that fair lady gane,
　And taen her word frae Geordie.

7 When she looked the letter on,
　She was both sad and sorrie:
　'O I 'll away to fair Edinburgh town
　Myself and see my Geordie.'

8 'Gar saddle to me the black,' she says,
　'The brown was neer sae bonny;
　And I 'll straight to Edinburgh
　Myself and see my Geordie.'

9 When she came to that wan water,
　The boats was not yet ready;
　She wheeld her horse's head around,
　And swimd at the Queen's Ferry.

10 When she came to the Parliament
　　Close,
　Amang the poor folks many,
　She dealt the crowns with duckatoons,
　And bade them pray for Geordy.

11 When she came to the Parliament
　　House,
　Among the nobles many,
　The rest sat all wi hat on head,
　But hat in hand sat Geordie.

12 Up bespake an English lord,
　And he spake blythe and merrie;
　'Was Geordie's head upon the block,
　I am sure I would have his lady.'

13 Up bespake that lady fair,
　And O but she was sorrie !
　'If Geordie's head were on the block,
　There 's never a man gain his lady.

14 'I have land into the north,
　And I have white rigs many,
　And I could gie them a' to you
　To save the life of Geordie.

15 'I have seven children in the north,
　And they seem very bonnie,
　And I could bear them a' over again
　For to win the life o Geordie.'

16 Up bespake the gude Argyle;
　He has befriended many;
　'If ye 'll tell down ten hundred crowns,
　Ye 's win the life o Geordie.'

17 Some gaed her shillings, and some her
　　crowns,
　And some gaed her guineas many,
　And she 's telld down ten hundred
　　crowns,
　And she 's wone the life o Geordie.

18 When she came down through Edin-
　　borough,
　And Geordie in her hand, O,
　'Where will I get a writer's [house],
　A writer's house so ready,
　That I may write into the north
　I have wone the life o Geordie ' ?

210

BONNIE JAMES CAMPBELL

The James Campbell of this ballad cannot
be identified. C, like many things in the Scotish Minstrel, has passed through editorial hands.

A

Herd's MSS., I, 40, II, 184.

1 O IT 's up in the Highlands,
　　and along the sweet Tay,
　Did bonie James Campbell
　　ride monie a day.

2 Sadled and bridled,
　　and bonie rode he;
　Hame came horse, hame came sadle,
　　but neer hame cam he.

3 And doun cam his sweet sisters,
　　greeting sae sair,

And down cam his bonie wife,
    tearing her hair.

4 'My house is unbigged,
    my barn's unbeen,
My corn's unshorn,
    my meadow grows green.'

*   *   *   *   *

B

Finlay's Scottish Ballads, 1808, I, xxxiii.

1 SADDLED and briddled
    and booted rade he;
Toom hame cam the saddle,
    but never cam he.

2 Down cam his auld mither,
    greetin fu sair,
And down cam his bonny wife,
    wringin her hair.

3 Saddled and briddled
    and booted rade he;
Toom hame cam the saddle,
    but never cam he.

C

'Bonnie George Campbell,' Smith's Scotish Minstrel, v, 42.

1 HIE upon Hielands,
    and laigh upon Tay,
Bonnie George Campbell
    rode out on a day.

2 He saddled, he bridled,
    and gallant rode he,
And hame cam his guid horse,
    but never cam he.

3 Out cam his mother dear,
    greeting fu sair,
And out cam his bonnie bryde,
    riving her hair.

4 'The meadow lies green,
    the corn is unshorn,
But bonnie George Campbell
    will never return.'

5 Saddled and bridled
    and booted rode he,
A plume in his helmet,
    A sword at his knee.

6 But toom cam his saddle,
    all bloody to see,
Oh, hame cam his guid horse,
    but never cam he !

D

Cunningham's Songs of Scotland, III, 2, communicated by Mr Yellowlees.

1 HIGH upon Highlands,
    and low upon Tay,
Bonnie George Campbell
    rode out on a day.

2 'My meadow lies green,
    and my corn is unshorn,
My barn is to build,
    and my babe is unborn.'

211

BEWICK AND GRAHAM

There was no doubt an older and better copy of this ballad than those which are extant, the earliest of which is of the eighteenth century. The story is so well composed, proportion is so well kept, on the whole, that it is reasonable to suppose that certain passages may have suffered some injury. But it is a fine-spirited ballad as it stands.

a. 'The Song of Bewick and Grahame,' a stall-copy, in octavo, British Museum, 11621. e. 1. (4.) b. 'A Remarkable and Memorable Song of Sir Robert Bewick and the Laird Graham,' broadside, Roxburghe Ballads, III, 624. c. 'A Remarkable and Memorable Song of Sir Robert Bewick and the Laird Graham,' broadside, Percy Papers. d. 'Bewick and Graham's Garland,' M. Angus and Son, Newcastle, Bell Ballads, Abbotsford Library, P. 5, vol. I, No. 60. e. Broadside, in "A Jolly Book of Garlands collected by John Bell in Newcastle," No. 29, Abbotsford Library, E. 1. f. 'Bewick and Graham,' chapbook, Newcastle, W. Fordyce. g. Scotch Ballads, Materials for Border Minstrelsy, No. 145, Abbotsford. h. 'Chirstie Græme,' the same, No. 89.

1 OLD Grahame [he] is to Carlisle gone,
   Where Sir Robert Bewick there met
   he;
   In arms to the wine they are gone,
   And drank till they were both merry.

2 Old Grahame he took up the cup,
   And said, 'Brother Bewick, here 's to
   thee;
   And here 's to our two sons at home,
   For they live best in our country.'

3 'Nay, were thy son as good as mine,
   And of some books he could but read,
   With sword and buckler by his side,
   To see how he could save his head,

4 'They might have been calld two bold
   brethren
   Where ever they did go or ride;
   They might [have] been calld two bold
   brethren,
   They might have crackd the Border-
   side.

5 'Thy son is bad, and is but a lad,
   And bully to my son cannot be;
   For my son Bewick can both write and
   read,
   And sure I am that cannot he.'

6 'I put him to school, but he would not
   learn,
   I bought him books, but he would not
   read;
   But my blessing he 's never have
   Till I see how his hand can save his
   head.'

7 Old Grahame called for an account,
   And he askd what was for to pay;
   There he paid a crown, so it went round,
   Which was all for good wine and hay.

8 Old Grahame is into the stable gone,
   Where stood thirty good steeds and
   three;
   He 's taken his own steed by the head,
   And home rode he right wantonly.

9 When he came home, there did he espy,
   A loving sight to spy or see,
   There did he espy his own three sons,
   Young Christy Grahame, the fore-
   most was he.

10 There did he espy his own three sons,
    Young Christy Grahame, the fore-
    most was he:
    'Where have you been all day, father,
    That no counsel you would take by
    me ?'

11 'Nay, I have been in Carlisle town,
    Where Sir Robert Bewick there met
    me;
    He said thou was bad, and calld thee a
    lad,
    And a baffled man by thou I be.

12 'He said thou was bad, and calld thee
    a lad,
    And bully to his son cannot be;
    For his son Bewick can both write and
    read,
    And sure I am that cannot thee.

13 'I put thee to school, but thou would
    not learn,
    I bought thee books, but thou would
    not read;
    But my blessing thou 's never have
    Till I see with Bewick thou can save
    thy head.'

14 'Oh, pray forbear, my father dear;
    That ever such a thing should be !
    Shall I venture my body in field to fight
    With a man that 's faith and troth to
    me ?'

15 'What 's that thou sayst, thou limmer
    loon ?
    Or how dare thou stand to speak to
    me ?
    If thou do not end this quarrel soon,
    Here is my glove thou shalt fight me.'

16 Christy stoopd low unto the ground,
    Unto the ground, as you 'll under-
    stand:
    'O father, put on your glove again,
    The wind hath blown it from your
    hand.'

17 'What 's that thou sayst, thou limmer
    loon ?
    Or how dare thou stand to speak to
    me ?
    If thou do not end this quarrel soon,
    Here is my hand thou shalt fight me.'

18 Christy Grahame is to his chamber gone,
    And for to study, as well might be,
  Whether to fight with his father dear,
    Or with his bully Bewick he.

19 'If it be [my] fortune my bully to
    kill,
    As you shall boldly understand,
  In every town that I ride through,
    They 'll say, There rides a brother-
        less man !

20 'Nay, for to kill my bully dear,
    I think it will be a deadly sin;
  And for to kill my father dear,
    The blessing of heaven I neer shall
        win.

21 'O give me your blessing, father,' he
    said,
    'And pray well for me for to thrive;
  If it be my fortune my bully to kill,
    I swear I 'll neer come home alive.'

22 He put on his back a good plate-jack,
    And on his head a cap of steel,
  With sword and buckler by his side;
    O gin he did not become them
        well !

23 'O fare thee well, my father dear !
    And fare thee well, thou Carlisle
        town !
  If it be my fortune my bully to kill,
    I swear I 'll neer eat bread again.'

24 Now we 'll leave talking of Christy
    Grahame,
    And talk of him again belive;
  But we will talk of bonny Bewick,
    Where he was teaching his scholars
        five.

25 Now when he had learnd them well to
    fence,
    To handle their swords without any
        doubt,
  He 's taken his own sword under his
        arm,
    And walkd his father's close about.

26 He lookd between him and the sun,
    To see what farleys he coud see;
  There he spy'd a man with armour on,
    As he came riding over the lee.

27 'I wonder much what man you be
    That so boldly this way does come;
  I think it is my nighest friend,
    I think it is my bully Grahame.

28 'O welcome, O welcome, bully Grahame !
    O man, thou art my dear, welcome !
  O man, thou art my dear, welcome !
    For I love thee best in Christendom.'

29 'Away, away, O bully Bewick,
    And of thy bullyship let me be !
  The day is come I never thought on;
    Bully, I 'm come here to fight with
        thee.'

30 'O no ! not so, O bully Grahame !
    That eer such a word should spoken
        be !
  I was thy master, thou was my scholar:
    So well as I have learnëd thee.'

31 'My father he was in Carlisle town,
    Where thy father Bewick there met
        he;
  He said I was bad, and he calld me a
        lad,
    And a baffled man by thou I be.'

32 'Away, away, O bully Grahame,
    And of all that talk, man, let us
        be !
  We 'll take three men of either side
    To see if we can our fathers agree.'

33 'Away, away, O bully Bewick,
    And of thy bullyship let me be !
  But if thou be a man, as I trow thou
        art,
    Come over this ditch and fight with
        me.'

34 'O no ! not so, my bully Grahame !
    That eer such a word should spoken
        be !
  Shall I venture my body in field to fight
    With a man that 's faith and troth to
        me ?'

35 'Away, away, O bully Bewick,
    And of all that care, man, let us
        be !
  If thou be a man, as I trow thou art,
    Come over this ditch and fight with
        me.'

36 'Now, if it be my fortune thee, Grahame, to kill,
  As God's will 's, man, it all must
  be;
 But if it be my fortune thee, Grahame,
  to kill,
  'T is home again I 'll never gae.'

37 'Thou art of my mind then, bully Be-
 wick,
  And sworn-brethren will we be;
 If thou be a man, as I trow thou art,
  Come over this ditch and fight with
  me.'

38 He flang his cloak from [off] his shoul-
 ders,
  His psalm-book out of his hand flang
  he,
 He clapd his hand upon the hedge,
  And oer lap he right wantonly.

39 When Grahame did see his bully come,
  The salt tear stood long in his eye:
 'Now needs must I say that thou art a
  man,
  That dare venture thy body to fight
  with me.

40 'Now I have a harness on my back;
  I know that thou hath none on thine;
 But as little as thou hath on thy back,
  Sure as little shall there be on mine.'

41 He flang his jack from off his back,
  His steel cap from his head flang
  he;
 He 's taken his sword into his hand,
  He 's tyed his horse unto a tree.

42 Now they fell to it with two broa[d
 swords],
  For two long hours fought Bewick
  [and he];
 Much sweat was to be seen on them
  both,
  But never a drop of blood to see.

43 Now Grahame gave Bewick an ackward
 stroke,
  An ackward stroke surely struck he;
 He struck him now under the left
  breast,
  Then down to the ground as dead fell
  he.

44 'Arise, arise, O bully Bewick,
  Arise, and speak three words to me!
 Whether this be thy deadly wound,
  Or God and good surgeons will mend
  thee.'

45 'O horse, O horse, O bully Grahame,
  And pray do get thee far from me!
 Thy sword is sharp, it hath wounded my
  heart,
  And so no further can I gae.

46 'O horse, O horse, O bully Grahame,
  And get thee far from me with speed!
 And get thee out of this country quite!
  That none may know who 's done the
  deed.'

47 'O if this be true, my bully dear,
  The words that thou dost tell to
  me,
 The vow I made, and the vow I 'll keep;
  I swear I 'll be the first that die.'

48 Then he stuck his sword in a moody-
 hill,
  Where he lap thirty good foot and
  three;
 First he bequeathed his soul to God,
  And upon his own sword-point lap he.

49 Now Grahame he was the first that died,
  And then came Robin Bewick to
  see;
 'Arise, arise, O son!' he said,
  'For I see thou 's won the victory.

50 'Arise, arise, O son!' he said,
  'For I see thou 's won the victory:'
 '[Father, co]uld ye not drunk your wine
  at home,
  [And le]tten me and my brother be?

51 'Nay, dig a grave both low and wide,
  And in it us two pray bury;
 But bury my bully Grahame on the sun-
  side,
  For I 'm sure he 's won the victory.'

52 Now we 'll leave talking of these two
 brethren,
  In Carlisle town where they lie slain,
 And talk of these two good old men,
  Where they were making a pitiful
  moan.

53 With that bespoke now Robin Bewick:
   'O man, was I not much to blame?
I have lost one of the liveliest lads
   That ever was bred unto my name.'

54 With that bespoke my good lord Gra-
   hame:
   'O man, I have lost the better block;
I have lost my comfort and my joy,
   I have lost my key, I have lost my
   lock.

55 'Had I gone through all Ladderdale,
   And forty horse had set on me,
Had Christy Grahame been at my back,
   So well as he woud guarded me.'

56 I have no more of my song to sing,
   But two or three words to you I 'll
   name;
But 't will be talk'd in Carlisle town
   That these two [old] men were all
   the blame

212

THE DUKE OF ATHOLE'S NURSE

The 'new-come darling' of the Duke of
Athole offers the duke's nurse a ring if she
will carry a word to her leman. This leman
had previously been the nurse's lover, and
comes to tell her that another has now possession of his heart. The nurse plans revenge,
but dissimulates; she tells the faithless fellow
to go for the night to an ale-house, and she
will meet him there in the morning. But instead of the nurse he sees a band of men, her
seven brothers (nine brothers, F), coming towards the house, and easily divines that they
are coming to slay him. He appeals to the
landlady to save him; she dresses him in
woman's clothes and sets him to her baking.
The seven brothers ask the landlady if she had
a lodger last night; they are come to pay his
reckoning. A lodger had been there, but he
did not stay till morning. They search the
house and stab the beds, often passing the sham
baking-maid without detecting the disguise.
C–F have nothing about the 'new-come darling,' but begin at once with the nurse, who
longs for her lover, and would give her half
year's fee to see him. He appears, and avows
to her that another woman has gained his heart.
Compare 'Sir James the Rose' (No. 213).

A

Cromek's Select Scotish Songs, 1810, II,
196, 194; sent, with other fragments, by Robert Burns to William Tytler, August, 1790;
stanzas 2–6.

* * * * *

1 'WHERE shall I gang, my ain true
      love?
   Where shall I gang to hide me?
For weel ye ken i yere father's bowr
   It wad be death to find me.'

2 'O go you to yon tavern-house,
      An there count owre your lawin,
An, if I be a woman true,
   I 'll meet you in the dawin.'

3 O he 's gone to yon tavern-house,
      An ay he counted his lawin,
An ay he drank to her guid health
   Was to meet him in the dawin.

4 O he 's gone to yon tavern-house,
      An counted owre his lawin,
When in there cam three armed men,
   To meet him in the dawin.

5 'O woe be unto woman's wit!
      It has beguiled many;
She promised to come hersel,
   But she sent three men to slay me.'

B

Skene MS., p. 10; taken down in the north
of Scotland, 1802–3.

1 'YE are the Duke of Athol's nurse,
      And I 'm the new-come darling;
I 'll gie you my gay gold rings
   To get ae word of my leman.'

2 'I am the Duke of Athol's nurse,
      And ye 're the new-come darling;
Keep well your gay gold rings,
   Ye sall get twa words o your leman.'

3 He leand oure his saddle-bow,
      It was not for to kiss her:
'Anither woman has my heart,
   And I but come here to see ye.'

4 'If anither woman has your heart,
      O dear, but I am sorry!

Ye hie you down to yon ale-house,
  And stay untill 't be dawing,
And if I be a woman true
  I 'll meet you in the dawing.'

5 He did him down to yon ale-house,
  And drank untill 't was dawing;
He drank the bonnie lassie's health
  That was to clear his lawing.

6 He lookit out of a shot-window,
  To see if she was coming,
And there he seed her seven brithers,
  So fast as they were running!

7 He went up and down the house,
  Says, 'Landlady, can you save me?
For yonder comes her seven brithers,
  And they are coming to slay me.'

8 So quick she minded her on a wile
  How she might protect him!
She dressd him in a suit of woman's
    attire
  And set him to her baking.

9 'Had you a quarterer here last night,
  Or staid he to the dawing?
Shew us the room the squire lay in,
  We are come to clear his lawing.'

10 'I had a quarterer here last night,
  But he staid not to the dawing;
He called for a pint, and paid as he
    went,
You have nothing to do with his law-
    ing.'

11 They searchd the house baith up and
    down,
The curtains they spaird not to rive
    em,
And twenty times they passd
  The squire at his baking.

213

SIR JAMES THE ROSE

There are some resemblances between 'Sir James the Rose' and No. 212. 'Sir James the Ross,' composed by Michael Bruce (d. 1767) upon the story of the present ballad, has perhaps enjoyed more favor than the original.

'Sir James the Rose.' a. From a stall-tract of about 1780, Abbotsford library, P. 6. b. Motherwell's Minstrelsy, p. 321. c. Sir James the Rose's Garland, one of a volume of the like from Heber's library. d. Motherwell's MS., p. 281; from the recitation of Mrs Gentles, of Paisley. e. Herd's MSS., I, 82. f. The same, II, 42. g. 'Sir James the Rose,' Pinkerton's Scottish Tragic Ballads, 1781, p. 61.

1 O HEARD ye of Sir James the Rose,
  The young heir of Buleighen?
For he has killd a gallant squire,
  An 's friends are out to take him.

2 Now he 's gone to the House of Marr,
  Where the nourice was his leman;
To see his dear he did repair,
  Thinking she would befriend him.

3 'Where are you going, Sir James?' she
    says,
  'Or where now are you riding?'
'O I am bound to a foreign land,
  For now I 'm under hiding.

4 'Where shall I go? Where shall I
    run?
Where shall I go to hide me?
For I have killd a gallant squire,
  And they 're seeking to slay me.'

5 'O go ye down to yon ale-house,
  And I 'll pay there your lawing;
And, if I be a woman true,
  I 'll meet you in the dawing.'

6 'I 'll not go down to yon ale-house,
  For you to pay my lawing;
There 's forty shillings for one supper,
  I 'll stay in 't till the dawing.'

7 He 's turnd him right and round about
  And rowd him in his brechan,
And he has gone to take a sleep,
  In the lowlands of Buleighen.

8 He was not well gone out of sight,
  Nor was he past Milstrethen,
Till four and twenty belted knights
  Came riding oer the Leathen.

9 'O have you seen Sir James the Rose,
  The young heir of Buleighen?
For he has killd a gallant squire,
  And we 're sent out to take him.'

10 ‘ O I have seen Sir James,’ she says,
    ‘ For he past here on Monday;
If the steed be swift that he rides on,
    He ’s past the gates of London.’

11 But as they were going away,
    Then she calld out behind them;
‘ If you do seek Sir James,’ she says,
    ‘ I ’ll tell you where you ’ll find him.

12 ‘ You ’ll seek the bank above the mill,
    In the lowlands of Buleighen,
And there you ’ll find Sir James the
    Rose,
Lying sleeping in his brechan.

13 ‘ You must not wake him out of sleep,
    Nor yet must you affright him,
Till you run a dart quite thro his heart,
    And thro the body pierce him.’

14 They sought the bank above the mill,
    In the lowlands of Buleighan,
And there they found Sir James the
    Rose,
A sleeping in his brechan.

15 Then out bespoke Sir John the Græme,
    Who had the charge a keeping;
‘ It ’s neer be said, dear gentlemen,
    We ’ll kill him when he ’s sleeping.’

16 They seizd his broadsword and his
    targe,
And closely him surrounded;
But when he wak’d out of his sleep,
    His senses were confounded.

17 ‘ O pardon, pardon, gentlemen !
    Have mercy now upon me !’
‘ Such as you gave, such you shall have,
    And so we ’ll fall upon thee.’

18 ‘ Donald my man, wait me upon,
    And I ’ll give you my brechan,
And, if you stay here till I die,
    You ’ll get my trews of tartan.

19 ‘ There is fifty pounds in my pocket,
    Besides my trews and brechan;
You ’ll get my watch and diamond ring;
    And take me to Loch Largon.’

20 Now they have taken out his heart
    And stuck it on a spear,

Then took it to the House of Marr,
    And gave it to his dear.

21 But when she saw his bleeding heart
    She was like one distracted;
She smote her breast, and wrung her
    hands,
Crying, ‘ What now have I acted !

22 ‘ Sir James the Rose, now for thy sake
    O but my heart ’s a breaking !
Curst be the day I did thee betray,
    Thou brave knight of Buleighen.’

23 Then up she rose, and forth she goes,
    All in that fatal hour,
And bodily was born away,
    And never was seen more.

24 But where she went was never kend,
    And so, to end the matter,
A traitor’s end, you may depend,
    Can be expect’d no better.

214

THE BRAES O YARROW

First published in Minstrelsy of the Scottish
Border, 1803, principally from E. A had been
somewhat edited before it was communicated
to Percy; the places were, however, indicated
by commas. There is no basis for an identification of the story with any historical event.
The facts must have occurred often enough,
and there is a similar story in other ballads,
as the Scandinavian ‘ Herr Helmer.’ ‘ The
Braes of Yarrow ’ (‘ Busk ye, busk ye, my
bonny, bonny bride ’), by William Hamilton of
Bangour, was suggested by the present ballad.

A

‘ The Braes of Yarrow,’ communicated to
Percy by Dr William Robertson, Principal of
Edinburgh.

1 ‘ I DREAMED a dreary dream this night,
    That fills my heart wi sorrow;
I dreamed I was pouing the heather
    green
Upon the braes of Yarrow.

2 ‘ O true-luve mine, stay still and dine,
    As ye ha done before, O:’

'O I 'll be hame by hours nine,
  And frae the braes of Yarrow.'

3 I dreamed a dreary dream this night,
  That fills my heart wi sorrow;
  I dreamed my luve came headless
    hame,
  O frae the braes of Yarrow !

4 'O true-luve mine, stay still and dine,
  As ye ha done before, O;'
  'O I 'll be hame by hours nine,
  And frae the braes of Yarrow.'

5 'O are ye going to hawke,' she says,
  'As ye ha done before, O ?
  Or are ye going to weild your brand,
  Upon the braes of Yarrow ? '

6 'O I am not going to hawke,' he says,
  'As I have done before, O,
  But for to meet your brother Jhon,
  Upon the braes of Yarrow.'

7 As he gade down yon dowy den,
  Sorrow went him before, O;
  Nine well-wight men lay waiting him,
  Upon the braes of Yarrow.

8 'I have your sister to my wife,
  'Ye' think me an unmeet marrow;
  But yet one foot will I never flee
  Now frae the braes of Yarrow.'

9 'Than' four he killd and five did
    wound,
  That was an unmeet marrow !
  'And he had weel nigh wan the day
  Upon the braes of Yarrow.'

10 'Bot' a cowardly 'loon' came him be-
    hind,
  Our Lady lend him sorrow !
  And wi a rappier pierced his heart,
  And laid him low on Yarrow.

11 'Now Douglas' to his sister 's gane,
  Wi meikle dule and sorrow:
  'Gae to your luve, sister,' he says,
  'He 's sleeping sound on Yarrow.'

12 As she went down yon dowy den,
  Sorrow went her before, O;
  She saw her true-love lying slain
  Upon the braes of Yarrow.

13 'She swoond thrice upon his breist
  That was her dearest marrow;
  Said, Ever alace and wae the day
  Thou wentst frae me to Yarrow ! '

14 She kist his mouth, she kaimed his hair,
  As she had done before, O;
  She 'wiped' the blood that trickled doun
  Upon the braes of Yarrow.

15 Her hair it was three quarters lang,
  It hang baith side and yellow;
  She tied it round 'her' white hause-bane,
  'And tint her life on Yarrow.'

E

  a. 'The Dowy Houms o Yarrow,' in the
handwriting of James Hogg, the Ettrick Shepherd, about 1801 ; now in a volume with the
title Scotch Ballads, Materials for Border Minstrelsy, No. 136, Abbotsford. **b.** 'The Dowie
Dens of Yarrow,' Scott's Minstrelsy, III, 72,
1803, III, 143, 1833.

1 LATE at een, drinkin the wine,
  Or early in a mornin,
  The set a combat them between,
  To fight it in the dawnin.

2 'O stay at hame, my noble lord !
  O stay at hame, my marrow !
  My cruel brother will you betray,
  On the dowy houms o Yarrow.'

3 'O fare ye weel, my lady gaye !
  O fare ye weel, my Sarah !
  For I maun gae, tho I neer return
  Frae the dowy banks o Yarrow.'

4 She kissd his cheek, she kaimd his
    hair,
  As she had done before, O;
  She belted on his noble brand,
  An he 's awa to Yarrow.

5 O he 's gane up yon high, high hill —
  I wat he gaed wi sorrow —
  An in a den spied nine armd men,
  I the dowy houms o Yarrow.

6 'O ir ye come to drink the wine,
  As ye hae doon before, O ?
  Or ir ye come to wield the brand,
  On the bonny banks o Yarrow ? '

7 'I im no come to drink the wine,
    As I hae doon before, O,
But I im come to wield the brand,
    On the dowy houms o Yarrow.'

8 Four he hurt, an five he slew,
    On the dowy houms o Yarrow,
Till that stubborn knight came him be-
        hind,
    An ran his body thorrow.

9 'Gae hame, gae hame, good-brother
        John,
    An tell your sister Sarah
To come an lift her noble lord,
    Who 's sleepin sound on Yarrow.'

10 'Yestreen I dreamd a dolefu dream;
    I kend there wad be sorrow;
I dreamd I pu'd the heather green,
    On the dowy banks o Yarrow.'

11 She gaed up yon high, high hill —
    I wat she gaed wi sorrow —
An in a den spy'd nine dead men,
    On the dowy houms o Yarrow.

12 She kissd his cheek, she kaimd his hair,
    As oft she did before, O;
She drank the red blood frae him ran,
    On the dowy houms o Yarrow.

13 'O haud your tongue, my douchter dear,
    For what needs a' this sorrow?
I 'll wed you on a better lord
    Than him you lost on Yarrow.'

14 'O haud your tongue, my father dear,
    An dinna grieve your Sarah;
A better lord was never born
    Than him I lost on Yarrow.

15 'Tak hame your ousen, tak hame your
        kye,
    For they hae bred our sorrow;
I wiss that they had a' gane mad
    Whan they cam first to Yarrow.'

215

RARE WILLIE DROWNED IN YARROW, OR, THE WATER O GAMRIE

Willie is drowned in Yarrow according to the older (southern) tradition, A; also B, C. In the northern copies, D, E, F, with which G, H, agree, the scene is transferred to Gamrie, on the coast of the Moray Frith, where "there is no water that Willie could have been drowned in but the sea, on his way along the sands to the old kirk." In No. 216, a western variety of the same story, Willie is drowned in the Clyde.

A

'Willy 's rare and Willy 's fair,' Thomson's Orpheus Caledonius, II, 110, 1733.

1 'WILLY 's rare, and Willy 's fair,
    And Willy 's wondrous bony,
And Willy heght to marry me,
    Gin eer he marryd ony.

2 'Yestreen I made my bed fu brade,
    The night I 'll make it narrow,
For a' the live-long winter's night
    I lie twin'd of my marrow.

3 'O came you by yon water-side?
    Pu'd you the rose or lilly?
Or came you by yon meadow green?
    Or saw you my sweet Willy?'

4 She sought him east, she sought him
        west,
    She sought him brade and narrow;
Sine, in the clifting of a craig,
    She found him drownd in Yarrow.

B

a. Cromek's Select Scotish Songs, 1810, II, 196; eighth and ninth stanzas of a fragment sent William Tytler by Burns in 1790. b. Stenhouse's edition of the Musical Museum, 1853, IV, 464.

1 SHE sought him east, she sought him
        west,
    She sought him braid and narrow,
Till in the clintin of a craig
    She found him drownd in Yarrow.

2 She 's taen three links of her yellow
        hair,
    That hung down lang and yellow,
And she 's tied it about sweet Willie's
        waist,
    An drawn him out o Yarrow.

D*

'The Water of Gamry,' The Old Lady's Collection, MS., No. 10.

1 'WILLIE is fair, an Willë's rair,
      An Willë's wondres bonny,
   An Willë has promised to marey me,
      Gin ever he marred ony.'

2 'Ye's gett Jeamie, or ye's gett Jonny,
      Or ye's get bonny Piter;
   Ye's gett the walle of a' my sins,
      Bat live to me Willë the writter.'

3 'I winnë ha Jamie, I winnë ha Jonny,
      Nor will I ha bonny Peter;
   I winnë ha ony of yer sins,
      In I gett na Willie the writter.'

4 Ther was three score an ten brisk young
         men
      Was boun to brid-stell we him.

5 'Ride on, ride on, my merry men a',
      I forget some thing behine me;
   I [ha] forgetten my mider's blissing,
      To boun to bridstell we me.'

6 'God's blissing an mine gae we ye, my
         son Willie,
      A' the blissings of God ga we ye;
   For y'er na an hour but bare ninten,
      Fan y'er gain to meet yer Meggey.'

7 They road on, an forder on,
      Till they came to the water of Gamry;
   An they all wen safe throu,
      Unless it was Suet Willie.

8 For the first an step att Willie's hors
         steped,
      He steped to the bridel;
   The nixt an step att Wellie's hors steped,
      Toom grue Willë's sadle.

9 They rod on, an forder on,
      Till they came to the kirk of Gamry,
   .   .   .   .   .
   .   .   .   .   .

10 .   .   .   .   .
      'A rounin, a rouning,' she says,
      'An fat means a' this rouning?'

11 Out spak the bonny bried,
      Just att the kirk of Gamrie;
   'Far is the man that was to gee me his
         han
      This day att the kirk of Gamry?'

12 Out spak his breder John,
      An O bat he was sorry!
   'It fears me sair, my bonny brid,
      He slipes our sune in Gaamry.'

13 The ribbons they wer on her hare,
      They wer thik an mony;
   She rive them a', late them doun faa,
      An is on to the water of Gamry.

14 She sought it up, she sought it doun,
      She sought it braid an narrou,
   An the depest pot in a' Gamry,
      Ther she got Suit Willie.

15 She has kissed his comly mouth,
      As she had don befor, O:
   'Baith our miders sall be alike sory,
      For we's baith slep soun in Gamry.'

216

THE MOTHER'S MALISON, OR, CLYDE'S WATER

The passage in A 10-16, in which the mother, pretending to be her daughter, repels the lover, and the daughter, who has dreamed that her lover had come and had been refused admittance, is told by her mother that this had actually happened, and sets off in pursuit of her lover, seems to have been adopted from No. 76. A very popular Italian ballad (Nigra, No. 23) has some of the traits of 'The Mother's Malison,' parts being exchanged and the girl drowned.

A*

'Clide's Water,' The Old Lady's Collection, MS., No. 11.

1 'YE gie corn to my hors,
      An meatt to my man,
   For I will gai to my true-love's gates
      This night, gin I can wine.'

2 'O stay att home, my son Willie,
      This a bare night we me;
   The best bed in a' my house
      Sall be well made to the.'

3 'I care na for your beds, mider,
    I care na a pin;
  For I ill gae to my love's gates
    This night, gin I can wine.'

4 'O stay, my son Willie,
    This night we me;
  The best hen in a' mey reast
    Sall be well made ready for the.'

5 'I care na for your heans, midder,
    I care na a pin;
  For I ull gae to my love's gates
    This night, gin I can wine.'

6 'Gin ye winnë stay, my son Willie,
    This a bare night we me,
  Gin Claid's water be dip an fue of flud,
    My maliceen droun ye in.'

7 He road up yon high hill,
    An doun yon douë den;
  The roring of Clid's water
    Wod ha flied ten thousand men.

8 'O spair me, Claid's water,
    Spare me as I gaa !
  Make me yer wrak as I come back,
    Bat spare me as I gaa !'

9 He raid in, an forder in,
    Till he came to the chin;
  An he raid in, an forder in,
    Till he came to dray lan.

10 An fan he came to his love's gates
    He tirled att the pin:
  'Open yer gates, May Meggie,
    Open yer gates to me,
  For my bets is fue of Claid's water,
    An the rain rins our my chine.'

11 'I ha ne loves therout,' she says,
    'I haa ne love theren;
  My true-love is in my arms tua,
    An nean will I latt in.'

12 'Open yer gates, Meggie,
    This night to me,
  For Clide's water is full of flood,
    An my mider's mallison will droun
      me in.'

13 'An of my chambers is full of corn,'
    she says,
  'Anether is full of hay,

The other is full of gentlemen,
    An they winnë remove till day.'

14 Out waked her May Meggie,
    Out of her drussie dream:
  'I dreamed a dream nou san the streen,
    God read a' dreams to gued !
  That my true-love Willie
    Was staning att my bed-feet.'

15 'Nou lay still, my a dather,
    An keep my back fraa the call;
  It's na the space of haf an hour
    Sayn he gade fra your hall.'

16 'Hey, Willie ! an hou, Willie !
    An Willie, winnë ye turn agen ?'
  But ay the louder that she crayed
    He read agenst the wind.

17 He raid up yon high hill,
    An doun yon douë den,
  An the roring that was in Clid's water
    Wad ha fleed ten thousand men.

18 He raid in
    Tell he came to the chine,
  An he raid forder in,
    Bat never mare came out agen.

19 She sought him up, she sought him
      doun,
  She sought him braid an narrou;
  In the depest pot in a' Claid's water,
    Ther she gat Suit Willie.

20 She has kissed his comly mouth,
    As she had den afore:
  'Baith our midders sall be alike sorry,
    For we's bath slipe soun in Clide's
      water.'

21 Ther was na mare seen of that gued lord
    Bat his hat frae his head;
  There was na mare seen of that gued
      lady
  Bat her keem an her sneed.

22 Ther mideers went up an doun the water,
    Saying, Clayd's water din us wrong !

B

'Willie and May Margaret,' Jamieson's Popular Ballads, I, 135 ; from Mrs Brown's recitation, apparently in 1800.

1 'GIE corn to my horse, mither,
  Gie meat unto my man,
  For I maun gang to Margaret's bower
  Before the nicht comes on.'

2 'O stay at hame now, my son Willie,
  The wind blaws cald and sour;
  The nicht will be baith mirk and late
  Before ye reach her bower.'

3 'O tho the nicht were ever sae dark,
  Or the wind blew never sae cald,
  I will be in my Margaret's bower
  Before twa hours be tald.'

4 'O gin ye gang to May Margaret,
  Without the leave of me,
  Clyde's water 's wide and deep enough,
  My malison drown thee!'

5 He mounted on his coal-black steed,
  And fast he rade awa,
  But ere he came to Clyde's water
  Fu loud the wind did blaw.

6 As he rode oer yon hich, hich hill,
  And down yon dowie den,
  There was a roar in Clyde's water
  Wad feard a hunder men.

7 His heart was warm, his pride was up;
  Sweet Willie kentna fear;
  But yet his mither's malison
  Ay sounded in his ear.

8 O he has swam through Clyde's water,
  Tho it was wide and deep,
  And he came to May Margaret's door,
  When a' were fast asleep.

9 O he 's gane round and round about,
  And tirled at the pin;
  But doors were steekd, and windows
      barrd,
  And nane wad let him in.

10 'O open the door to me, Margaret!
   O open and lat me in!
   For my boots are full o Clyde's water
   And frozen to the brim.'

11 'I darena open the door to you,
   Nor darena lat you in,
   For my mither she is fast asleep,
   And I darena mak nae din.'

12 'O gin ye winna open the door,
   Nor yet be kind to me,
   Now tell me o some out-chamber
   Where I this nicht may be.'

13 'Ye canna win in this nicht, Willie,
   Nor here ye canna be;
   For I 've nae chambers out nor in,
   Nae ane but barely three.

14 'The tane o them is fu o corn,
   The tither is fu o hay;
   The tither is fu o merry young men;
   They winna remove till day.'

15 'O fare ye weel, then, May Margaret,
   Sin better manna be;
   I 've win my mither's malison,
   Coming this nicht to thee.'

16 He 's mounted on his coal-black steed,
   O but his heart was wae!
   But, ere he came to Clyde's water,
   'T was half up oer the brae.

*   *   *   *   *

17 .   .   .   .   .   .

   .   .   .   he plunged in,
   But never raise again.

217

THE BROOM OF COWDEN-
KNOWS

This ballad was widely diffused in Scotland. "It would be useless," says Motherwell, "to enumerate the titles of the different versions which are common among reciters." The earliest known copies are of the second half of the eighteenth century. There is an English "ditty" (not a traditional ballad) of a northern lass who got harm while milking her father's ewes, which was printed in the first half of the seventeenth century. This ditty is "to a pleasant Scotch tune called The broom of Cowden Knowes," and the burden is:

With, O the broome, the bonny broome,
   The broome of Cowden Knowes!
Fain would I be in the North Countrey,
   To milk my dadyes ewes.

The tune was remarkably popular, and the burden is found, variously modified, in connection with several songs.

There is very little story to the English ditty,
far too little to have served as a basis for the
Scottish ballad. On the other hand, the English
author seems to have known only the burden
of the Scottish ballad and to have built his very
slight tale on that.

'Malfred og Sadelmand,' Kristensen, I, 258,
No. 99, is an independent ballad, but has some
of the traits of this: the maid, who is treated
with great violence, asks the knight's name,
as in two versions of 'The Broom of Cowdenknows;' he comes back to marry her, after she
has borne twins.

Cowdenknowes is on the east bank of Leader,
near Earlston, and some four or five miles from
Melrose.

A

'The Laird of Knotington,' Percy Papers;
communicated to Percy by R. Lambe, of Norham, August 17, 1768, and dated May, 1768.

1 THERE was a troop of merry gentlemen
  Was riding atween twa knows,
And they heard the voice of a bonny lass,
  In a bught milking her ews.

2 There 's ane o them lighted frae off his
    steed,
  And has ty'd him to a tree,
And he 's gane away to yon ew-bught,
  To hear what it might be.

3 'O pity me, fair maid,' he said,
  'Take pity upon me;
O pity me, and my milk-white steed
  That 's trembling at yon tree.'

4 'As for your steed, he shall not want
  The best of corn and hay;
But as to you yoursel, kind sir,
  I 've naething for to say.'

5 He 's taen her by the milk-white hand,
  And by the green gown-sleeve,
And he as led her into the ew-bught,
  Of her friends he speerd nae leave.

6 He as put his hand in his pocket,
  And given her guineas three:
'If I dinna come back in half a year,
  Then luke nae mair for me.

7 'Now show to me the king's hie street,
  Now show to me the way;
Now show to me the king's hie street,
  And the fair water of Tay.'

8 She showd to him the king's hie street,
  She showd to him the way;
She showd him the way that he was to go,
  By the fair water of Tay.

9 When she came hame, her father said,
  'Come, tell to me right plain;
I doubt you 've met some in the way,
  You have not been your lain.'

10 'The night it is baith mist and mirk,
  You may gan out and see;
The night is mirk and misty too,
  There 's nae body been wi me.

11 'There was a tod came to your flock,
  The like I neer did see;
When he spake, he lifted his hat,
  He had a bonny twinkling eee.'

12 When fifteen weeks were past and gane,
  Full fifteen weeks and three,
Then she began to think it lang
  For the man wi the twinkling eee.

13 It fell out on a certain day,
  When she cawd out her father's ky,
There was a troop of gentlemen
  Came merrily riding by.

14 'Weel may ye sigh and sob,' says ane,
  'Weel may you sigh and see;
Weel may you sigh, and say, fair maid,
  Wha 's gotten this bairn wi thee?'

15 She turned her sel then quickly about,
  And thinking meikle shame,
O no, kind sir, it is na sae,
  For it has a dad at hame.'

16 'O hawd your tongue, my bonny lass,
  Sae loud as I hear you lee!
For dinna you mind that summer night
  I was in the bught wi thee?'

17 He lighted off his milk-white steed,
  And set this fair maid on;
'Now caw out your ky, good father,' he
    said,
  'She 'll neer caw them out again.

18 'I am the laird of Knottington,
  I 've fifty plows and three;
I 've gotten now the bonniest lass
  That is in the hale country.'

B

'Bonny May.' **a.** Herd's Ancient and Modern Scots Songs, 1769, p. 308; 1776, i, 98. **b.** Johnson's Museum, No. 110, p. 113.

1 It was on an evning sae saft and sae
　　　clear
　　A bonny lass was milking the kye,
　　And by came a troup of gentlemen,
　　　And rode the bonny lassie by.

2 Then one of them said unto her,
　　'Bonny lass, prythee shew me the
　　　way:'
　　'O if I do sae, it may breed me wae,
　　　For langer I dare nae stay.'

```
*       *       *       *       *
```

3 But dark and misty was the night
　　Before the bonny lass came hame :
　　'Now where hae you been, my ae daughter?
　　I am sure you was nae your lane.'

4 'O father, a tod has come oer your lamb,
　　A gentleman of high degree,
　　And ay whan he spake he lifted his hat,
　　　And bonny, bonny blinkit his ee.'

5 Or eer six months were past and gane,
　　Six months but and other three,
　　The lassie begud for to fret and to frown,
　　　And think lang for his blinkin ee.

6 'O wae be to my father's shepherd,
　　An ill death may he die !
　　He bigged the bughts sae far frae hame,
　　　And trysted a gentleman to me !'

7 It fell upon another fair evening
　　The bonny lassie was milking her ky,
　　And by came the troop of gentlemen,
　　　And rode the bonny lassie by.

8 Then one of them stopt, and said to her,
　　'Whae's aught that baby ye are wi ?'
　　The lassie began for to blush, and think,
　　　To a father as good as ye.

9 'O had your tongue, my bonny may,
　　Sae loud I hear you lie !
　　O dinnae you mind the misty night
　　　I was in the bught with thee?'

10 Now he's come aff his milk-white steed,
　　And he has taen her hame:
　　'Now let your father bring hame the
　　　ky,
　　You neer mair shall ca them agen.

11 'I am a lord of castles and towers,
　　With fifty ploughs of land and three,
　　And I have gotten the bonniest lass
　　　That is in this countrie.'

218

THE FALSE LOVER WON BACK

Two pretty stanzas in **A** (4, 5) seem not to belong to the story. The inconstant youth would have been only too glad to have the faithful maid look to other men, and gives her all liberty to do so. These two stanzas are first found in Herd's MSS., i, 53, and in Herd's Ancient and Modern Scottish Songs, 1776, ii, 6, as follows :

> False luve, and hae ye played me this,
> 　In the simmer, mid the flowers?
> I sall repay ye back agen,
> 　In the winter, mid the showers.
>
> Bot again, dear luve, and again, dear luve,
> 　Will ye not turn again?
> As ye look to ither women,
> 　Sall I to ither men.

A

'The Fause Lover,' Buchan's MSS., i, 114; Buchan's Ballads of the North of Scotland, i, 268.

1 A fair maid sat in her bower-door,
　　Wringing her lily hands,
　　And by it came a sprightly youth,
　　　Fast tripping oer the strands.

2 'Where gang ye, young John,' she
　　　says,
　　'Sae early in the day?
　　It gars me think, by your fast trip,
　　　Your journey's far away.'

3 He turnd about wi surly look,
　　And said, What's that to thee?
　　I'm gaen to see a lovely maid,
　　　Mair fairer far than ye.

4 'Now hae ye playd me this, fause
    love,
  In simmer, mid the flowers?
I shall repay ye back again,
  In winter, mid the showers.

5 'But again, dear love, and again, dear
    love,
  Will ye not turn again?
For as ye look to other women,
  I shall to other men.'

6 'Make your choice of whom you please,
  For I my choice will have;
I've chosen a maid more fair than
    thee,
  I never will deceive.'

7 But she's kilt up her claithing fine,
  And after him gaed she;
But aye he said, Ye'll turn again,
  Nae farder gae wi me.

8 'But again, dear love, and again, dear
    love,
  Will ye never love me again?
Alas for loving you sae well,
  And you nae me again!'

9 The first an town that they came till,
  He bought her brooch and ring;
And aye he bade her turn again,
  And gang nae farder wi him.

10 'But again, dear love, and again, dear
    love,
  Will ye never love me again?
Alas for loving you sae well,
  And you nae me again!'

11 The next an town that they came till,
  He bought her muff and gloves;
But aye he bade her turn again,
  And choose some other loves.

12 'But again, dear love, and again, dear
    love,
  Will ye never love me again?
Alas for loving you sae well,
  And you nae me again!'

13 The next an town that they came till,
  His heart it grew mair fain,
And he was as deep in love wi her
  As she was ower again.

14 The next an town that they came till,
  He bought her wedding gown,
And made her lady of ha's and bowers,
  Into sweet Berwick town.

B

'The place where my love Johnny dwells,'
Christie's Traditional Ballad Airs, I, 144; from
the recitation of a woman born in Buchan.

1 THE sun shines high on yonder hill,
    And low on yonder town;
  In the place where my love Johnny
    dwells,
  The sun gaes never down

2 'O when will ye be back, bonny lad,
    O when will ye be hame?'
  'When heather-hills are nine times
    brunt,
    And a' grown green again.'

3 'O that's ower lang awa, bonny lad,
    O that's ower lang frae hame;
  For I'll be dead and in my grave
    Ere ye come back again.'

4 He put his foot into the stirrup
    And said he maun go ride,
  But she kilted up her green claithing
    And said she woudna bide.

5 The firsten town that they came to,
    He bought her hose and sheen,
  And bade her rue and return again,
    And gang nae farther wi him.

6 'Ye likena me at a', bonny lad,
    Ye likena me at a';'
  'It's sair for you likes me sae weel
    And me nae you at a'.'

7 The nexten town that they came to,
    He bought her a braw new gown,
  And bade her rue and return again,
    And gang nae farther wi him.

8 The nexten town that they came to,
    He bought her a wedding ring,
  And bade her dry her rosy cheeks,
    And he would tak her wi him.

9 'O wae be to your bonny face,
    And your twa blinkin een!

And wae be to your rosy cheeks !
They 've stown this heart o mine.

10 'There 's comfort for the comfortless,
There 's honey for the bee;
There 's comfort for the comfortless,
There 's nane but you for me.'

219

THE GARDENER

The Gardener is in Five Excellent New
Songs, Edinburgh, Printed and sold by William Forrest, 1766; but the copy is considerably
corrupted and is not given here (see Child, v,
258). A 7 is found substantially in the preceding ballad, and perhaps belonged originally to
neither.

A

Kinloch MSS., v, 47, in the handwriting of
James Beattie; from the recitation of his aunt,
Miss Elizabeth Beattie.

1 THE gardener stands in his bower-door,
With a primrose in his hand,
And by there came a leal maiden,
As jimp 's a willow wand.
And by, etc.

2 'O lady, can you fancy me,
For to be my bride,
You 'll get a' the flowers in my garden,
To be to you a weed.

3 'The lily white shall be your smock;
Becomes your body neat;
And your head shall be deckd with
jelly-flower,
And the primrose in your breast.

4 'Your gown shall be o the sweet-william,
Your coat o camovine,
And your apron o the sallads neat,
That taste baith sweet and fine.

5 'Your stockings shall be o the broad
kail-blade,
That is baith broad and long;
And narrow, narrow at the coot,
And broad, broad at the brawn.

6 'Your gloves shall be the marygold,
All glittering to your hand,

Well spread oer wi the blue blaewort,
That grows in corn-land.'

7 'O fare you well, young man,' she says,
'Farewell, and I bid adieu;
Since you 've provided a weed for me,
Among the summer flowers,
Then I 'll provide another for you,
Among the winter showers.

8 'The new-fallen snow to be your smock;
Becomes your body neat;
And your head shall be deckd with the
eastern wind,
And the cold rain on your breast.'

220

THE BONNY LASS OF
ANGLESEY

There is a resemblance, remarkable as far as
it goes, to the Scandinavian ballad of 'Little
Kirstin's Dance' (Grundtvig, No. 263). In the
Danish ballad (A), a king's son, to induce Little
Kirstin to dance before him, promises a succession of gifts, none of which avail until he
plights his honor and troth. The remainder
of the story is like the conclusion of 'Gil Brenton' (No. 5).

A

'The Bonny Lass of Anglesey,' Herd's MSS.,
I, 148; Herd's Ancient and Modern Scottish
Songs, 1776, II, 231.

1 OUR king he has a secret to tell,
And ay well keepit it must be:
The English lords are coming down
To dance and win the victory.

2 Our king has cry'd a noble cry,
And ay well keepit it must be:
Gar saddle ye, and bring to me
The bonny lass of Anglesey.'

3 Up she starts, as white as the milk,
Between him and his company:
'What is the thing I hae to ask,
If I sould win the victory?'

4 'Fifteen ploughs but and a mill
I gie thee till the day thou die,
And the fairest knight in a' my court
To chuse thy husband for to be.'

5 She 's taen the fifteen lord[s] by the
        hand,
      Saying, ' Will ye come dance with
        me ? '
  But on the morn at ten o'clock
      They gave it oer most shamefully.

6 Up then rais the fifteenth lord —
      I wat an angry man was he —
  Laid by frae him his belt and sword,
      And to the floor gaed manfully.

7 He said, ' My feet shall be my dead
      Before she win the victory; '
  But before 't was ten o'clock at night
      He gaed it oer as shamefully.

B

' The Bonny Lass o Englessie's Dance,' Buchan's Ballads of the North of Scotland, II, 63.

1 WORD has gane thro a' this land,
      And O well noticed it maun be !
  The English lords are coming down
      To dance and gain the victorie.

2 The king has made a noble cry,
      And well attended it maun be:
  ' Come saddle ye, and bring to me
      The bonny lass o Englessie.'

3 She started up, a' dress'd in white,
      Between him and his companie;
  Said, What will ye gie, my royal liege,
      If I will dance this dance for thee ?

4 ' Five good ploughs but and a mill
      I 'll give you till the day ye die;
  The bravest knight in all my court,
      I 'll give, your husband for to be.'

5 She 's taen the first lord by the hand,
      Says, ' Ye 'll rise up and dance wi me; '
  But she made a' these lords fifeteen
      To gie it up right shamefullie.

6 Then out it speaks a younger lord,
      Says, ' Fye for shame ! how can this
        be ? '
  He loosd his brand frae aff his side,
      Likewise his buckler frae his knee.

7 He sware his feet should be his dead
      Before he lost the victorie;
  He danc'd full fast, but tired at last,
      And gae it up as shamefullie.

221

KATHARINE JAFFRAY

  The ballad was first published by Sir Walter
Scott, under the title ' The Laird of Lamington,' in the first edition of the Minstrelsy, 1802,
I, 216.   This copy was fashioned by the editor
from A and B.   Scott's later copy (Minstrelsy,
1803, I, 238 ; 1833, III, 122) is chiefly made up
from A, B, and C.   ' Lochinvar,' in the fifth
canto of Marmion, was modelled on ' Katharine Jaffray.'   The lover is called Lochinvar
in several versions of the ballad.   Another
ballad, much later and inferior, in which a
lover carries off a bride on her wedding-day
is No. 254.

A

' Katharine Jaffray.' a. Herd's MSS., I, 61,
II, 56. b. The Aldine edition of Burns's
Poems, by Sir Harris Nicolas, 1839, III, 181,
from Burns's autograph.

1 THERE livd a lass in yonder dale,
      And doun in yonder glen, O
  And Kathrine Jaffray was her name,
      Well known by many men. O

2 Out came the Laird of Lauderdale,
      Out frae the South Countrie,
  All for to court this pretty maid,
      Her bridegroom for to be.

3 He has teld her father and mither baith,
      And a' the rest o her kin,
  And has teld the lass hersell,
      And her consent has win.

4 Then came the Laird of Lochinton,
      Out frae the English border,
  All for to court this pretty maid,
      Well mounted in good order.

5 He 's teld her father and mither baith,
      As I hear sindry say,
  But he has nae teld the lass her sell,
      Till on her wedding day.

6 When day was set, and friends were
        met,
      And married to be,
  Lord Lauderdale came to the place,
      The bridal for to see.

7 ' O are you came for sport, young man ?
      Or are you come for play ?

Or are you come for a sight o our bride,
　　Just on her wedding day ? '

8 ' I 'm nouther come for sport,' he says,
　　' Nor am I come for play;
　But if I had one sight o your bride,
　　I 'll mount and ride away.'

9 There was a glass of the red wine
　　Filld up them atween,
　And ay she drank to Lauderdale,
　　Wha her true-love had been.

10 Then he took her by the milk-white
　　hand,
　And by the grass-green sleeve,
　And he mounted her high behind him
　　there,
　At the bridegroom he askt nae leive.

11 Then the blude run down by the Cow-
　　den Banks,
　And down by Cowden Braes,
　And ay she gard the trumpet sound,
　　' O this is foul, foul play ! '

12 Now a' ye that in England are,
　　Or are in England born,
　Come nere to Scotland to court a lass,
　　Or else ye 'l get the scorn.

13 They haik ye up and settle ye by,
　　Till on your wedding day,
　And gie ye frogs instead o fish,
　　And play ye foul, foul play.

B

' The Laird of Laminton,' Herd's MSS., i,
164, ii, 58.

1 THE gallant laird of Lamington
　　Cam frae the North Countree
　To court a gallant gay lady,
　　And wi presents entered he.

2 He neither stood for gould nor gear —
　　For she was a well-fared may —
　And whan he got her friends' consent
　　He set the wedding-day.

3 She 's sent unto her first fere love,
　　Gin he would come to see,
　And he has sent word back again
　　Weel answered should she be.

4 He has sent a messenger
　　Right quietly throe the land,
　Wi mony armed men,
　　To be at his command.

5 The bridegroom looked out at a high
　　window,
　Beheld baith dool and doon,
　And there he spied her first fere love,
　　Come riding to the toun.

6 She scoffed and she scorned him,
　　Upo the wedding-day,
　And said it had been the Fairy Court
　　That he had seen in array.

7 But as he sat at yon table-head,
　　Amo yon gentlemen,
　And he began to speak some words
　　That na ane there could ken.

8 ' There is a lass into this town —
　　She is a weel-far'd may —
　She is another man's bride today,
　　But she 'll play him foul play.'

9 Up did start the bonny bridegroom,
　　His hat into his hand,
　.　　.　　.　　.　　.　　.
　　.　　.　　.　　.　　.

10 ' O cam you here, young man, to fight ?
　　Or came you here to flee ?
　Or cam you here to drink good wine,
　　And be good company ? '

11 They filled a cup o good red wine,
　　Drunk out between them twa:
　' For one dance wi your bonny bride,
　　I shall gae hame my wa.'

12 He 's taen her by the milk-white hand,
　　And by the grass-green sleeve,
　He 's mounted her high behind himself,
　　At her kin 's speired nae leave.

13 Now　　.　　.　　.
　　And swords flew in the skies,
　And droop and drowsie was the blood
　　Ran our yon lilly braes.

14 The blood ran our the lilly bank,
　　And our the lilly brae,
　And sighing said the bonny bride,
　　' A, wae 's me for foul play ! '

15 'My blessing on your heart, sweet thing,
   Wae to your wilfu will !
So many a gallant gentleman's blood
   This day as ye 've garred spill.

16 'But a' you that is norland men,
   If you be norland born,
Come never south to wed a bryde,
   For they 'll play you the scorn.

17 'They will play you the scorn
   Upo your wedding-day,
And gie you frogs instead o fish,
   And do you foul, foul play.'

C

'Katherine Jaffarie,' Scotch Ballads, Materials for Border Minstrelsy, No. 30, Abbotsford. Sent Scott by William Laidlaw, in September, 1802; obtained by him from Jean Scott.

1 THERE leeft a may, an a weel-far'd may,
   High, high up in yon glen; O
Her name was Katarine Janfarie,
   She was courtit by monie men.   O

2 Up then cam Lord Lauderdale,
   Up thrae the Lawland border,
And he has come to court this may,
   A' mountit in gude order.

3 He 's telld her father, he 's telld her mother,
   An a' the lave o her kin,
An he has telld the bonnie lass hersel,
   An has her favour win.

4 Out then cam Lord Faughanwood,
   Out frae the English border,
An for to court this well-far'd may,
   A' mountit in gude order.

5 He telld her father, he telld her mother,
   An a' the rest o her kin,
But he neer telld the bonnie lass hersell
   Till on her waddin-een.

6 When they war a' at denner set,
   Drinkin the bluid-red wine,
'T was up then cam Lord Lauderdale,
   The bridegroom soud hae been.

7 Up then spak Lord Faughanwood,
   An he spak very slee:
'O are ye come for sport ?' he says,
   'Or are ye come for play ?
Or are ye come for a kiss o our bride,
   An the morn her waddin-day ?'

8 'O I 'm no come for ought,' he says,
   'But for some sport or play;
An ae word o yer bonnie bride,
   Than I 'll horse an ride away.'

9 She filld a cup o the gude red wine,
   She filld it to the ee:
'Here 's a health to you, Lord Lauderdale,
   An a' your companie.'

10 She filld a cup o the gude red wine,
   She filld it to the brim:
'Here 's a health to you, Lord Lauderdale,
   My bridegroom should hae been.'

11 He 's taen her by the milk-white hand,
   And by the gars-green sleeve,
An he has mountit her behind him,
   O the bridegroom spierd nae leave.

12 'It '[s] now take yer bride, Lord Faughanwood,
   Now take her an ye may;
But if ye take yer bride again
   We will ca it foul play.'

13 There war four a twenty bonnie boys,
   A' clad i the simple grey;
They said the wad take their bride again,
   By the strang hand an the may.

14 Some o them were fu willin men,
   But they war na willin a';
Sae four an twentie ladies gay
   Bade them ride on their way.

15 The bluid ran down by the Cadan bank,
   An in by the Cadan brae,
An ther the gard the piper play
   It was a' for foul, foul play.

16 A' ye lords in fair England
   That live by the English border,
Gang never to Scotland to seek a wife,
   Or than ye 'll get the scorn.

17 They 'll keep ye up i temper guid
   Untill yer wadin-day,
They 'll thraw ye frogs instead o fish,
   An steal your bride away.

222

BONNY BABY LIVINGSTON

A is the only version of this ballad that
ends well. The others give the story a tragical
catastrophe. The kidnapping of women for a
compulsory marriage was a practice which prevailed for hundreds of years, and down to a
late date, and, of course, not only in Great
Britain. Other Scottish ballads celebrating similar abductions are Nos. 223, 224, 225.

A

'Bonny Baby Livingston.' a. Jamieson-
Brown MS., Appendix, p. xii, sent by Mrs
Brown to Jamieson, in a letter dated September 15, 1800. b. Jamieson's Popular Ballads,
ii, 135, as taken from Mrs Brown's recitation
a short time before a was written down.

1 O bonny Baby Livingston
   Went forth to view the hay,
And by it came him Glenlion,
   Sta bonny Baby away.

2 O first he 's taen her silken coat,
   And neest her satten gown,
Syne rowd her in a tartan plaid,
   And hapd her round and rown.

3 He has set her upon his steed
   And roundly rode away,
And neer loot her look back again
   The live-long summer's day.

4 He 's carried her oer hills and muirs
   Till they came to a Highland glen,
And there he 's met his brother John,
   With twenty armed men.

5 O there were cows, and there were ewes,
   And lasses milking there,
But Baby neer anse lookd about,
   Her heart was filld wi care.

6 Glenlion took her in his arms,
   And kissd her, cheek and chin;
Says, I 'd gie a' these cows and ewes
   But ae kind look to win.

7 'O ae kind look ye neer shall get,
   Nor win a smile frae me,
Unless to me you 'll favour shew,
   And take me to Dundee.'

8 'Dundee, Baby? Dundee, Baby?
   Dundee you neer shall see
Till I 've carried you to Glenlion
   And have my bride made thee.

9 'We 'll stay a while at Auchingour,
   And get sweet milk and cheese,
And syne we 'll gang to Glenlion,
   And there live at our ease.'

10 'I winna stay at Auchingour,
   Nor eat sweet milk and cheese,
Nor go with thee to Glenlion,
   For there I 'll neer find ease.'

11 Than out it spake his brother John,
   'O were I in your place,
I 'd take that lady hame again,
   For a' her bonny face.

12 'Commend me to the lass that 's kind,
   Tho na so gently born;
And, gin her heart I coudna gain,
   To take her hand I 'd scorn.'

13 'O had your tongue now, John,' he
      says,
   'You wis na what you say;
For I 've lood that bonny face
   This twelve month and a day.

14 'And tho I 've lood her lang and sair
   A smile I neer coud win;
Yet what I 've got anse in my power
   To keep I think nae sin.'

15 When they came to Glenlion castle,
   They lighted at the yate,
And out it came his sisters three,
   Wha did them kindly greet.

16 O they 've taen Baby by the hands
   And led her oer the green,
And ilka lady spake a word,
   But bonny Baby spake nane.

17 Then out it spake her bonny Jean,
   The youngest o the three,
'O lady, dinna look sae sad,
   But tell your grief to me.'

18 'O wherefore should I tell my grief,
    Since lax I canna find ?
I 'm stown frae a' my kin and friends,
    And my love I left behind.

19 'But had I paper, pen, and ink,
    Before that it were day,
I yet might get a letter sent
    In time to Johny Hay.'

20 O she 's got paper, pen, and ink,
    And candle that she might see,
And she has written a broad letter
    To Johny at Dundee.

21 And she has gotten a bonny boy,
    That was baith swift and strang,
Wi philabeg and bonnet blue,
    Her errand for to gang.

22 'O boy, gin ye 'd my blessing win
    And help me in my need,
Run wi this letter to my love,
    And bid him come wi speed.

23 'And here 's a chain of good red gowd,
    And gowdn guineas three,
And when you 've well your errand
    done,
    You 'll get them for your fee.'

24 The boy he ran oer hill and dale,
    Fast as a bird coud flee,
And eer the sun was twa hours height
    The boy was at Dundee.

25 And when he came to Johny's door
    He knocked loud and sair;
Then Johny to the window came,
    And loudly cry'd, 'Wha 's there ?'

26 'O here 's a letter I have brought,
    Which ye maun quickly read,
And, gin ye woud your lady save,
    Gang back wi me wi speed.'

27 O when he had the letter read,
    An angry man was he;
He says, Glenlion, thou shalt rue
    This deed of villany !

28 'O saddle to me the black, the black,
    O saddle to me the brown,
O saddle to me the swiftest steed
    That eer rade frae the town.

29 'And arm ye well, my merry men a',
    And follow me to the glen,
For I vow I 'll neither eat nor sleep
    Till I get my love again.'

30 He 's mounted on a milk-white steed,
    The boy upon a gray,
And they got to Glenlion's castle
    About the close of day.

31 As Baby at her window stood,
    The west wind saft did bla;
She heard her Johny's well-kent voice
    Beneath the castle wa.

32 'O Baby, haste, the window jump !
    I 'll kep you in my arm;
My merry men a' are at the yate,
    To rescue you frae harm.'

33 She to the window fixt her sheets
    And slipped safely down,
And Johny catchd her in his arms,
    Neer loot her touch the ground.

34 When mounted on her Johny's horse,
    Fou blithely did she say,
'Glenlion, you hae lost your bride !
    She 's aff wi Johny Hay.'

35 Glenlion and his brother John
    Were birling in the ha,
When they heard Johny's bridle ring,
    As first he rade awa.

36 'Rise, Jock, gang out and meet the
    priest,
    I hear his bridle ring;
My Baby now shall be my wife
    Before the laverocks sing.'

37 'O brother, this is not the priest;
    I fear he 'll come oer late;
For armed men with shining brands
    Stand at the castle-yate.'

38 'Haste Donald, Duncan, Dugald, Hugh!
    Haste, take your sword and spier !
We 'll gar these traytors rue the hour
    That eer they ventured here.'

39 The Highland men drew their claymores,
    And gae a warlike shout,
But Johny's merry men kept the yate,
    Nae ane durst venture out.

40 The lovers rade the live-lang night,
And safe gat on their way,
And bonny Baby Livingston
Has gotten Johny Hay.

41 'Awa, Glenlion ! fy for shame !
Gae hide ye in some den !
You've lettn your bride be stown frae
you,
For a' your armed men.'

C

Motherwell's MS., p. 375, from the recitation
of Agnes Lyle of Kilbarchan; 'Barbara Livingston,' Motherwell's Minstrelsy, p. 304.

1 FOUR-AND-TWENTY ladies fair
Was playing at the ba,
And out cam Barbra Livingston,
The flower amang them a'.

2 Out cam Barbra Livingston,
The flower amang them a';
The lusty laird of Linlyon
Has stown her clean awa.

3 'The Hielands is no for me, kind sir,
The Hielands is no for me;
But, if you wud my favour win,
You'll tak me to Dundee.'

4 'The Hielands 'll be for thee, my dear,
The Hielands will be for thee;
To the lusty laird o Linlyon
A-married ye shall be.'

5 When they came to Linlyon's yetts,
And lichted on the green,
Every ane spak Earse to her,
The tears cam trinkling down.

6 When they went to bed at nicht,
To Linlyon she did say,
'Och and alace, a weary nicht !
Oh, but it's lang till day !'

7 'Your father's steed in my stable,
He's eating corn and hay,
And you're lying in my twa arms;
What need you long for day ?'

8 'If I had paper, pen, and ink,
And candle for to see,
I wud write a lang letter
To my love in Dundee.'

9 They brocht her paper, pen, and ink,
And candle for to see,
And she did write a lang letter
To her love in Dundee.

10 When he cam to Linlyon's yetts,
And lichtit on the green,
But lang or he wan up the stair
His love was dead and gane.

11 'Woe be to thee, Linlyon,
An ill death may thou die !
Thou micht hae taen anither woman,
And let my lady be.'

223

EPPIE MORRIE

· This ballad," says Maidment, "is probably
much more than a century old, though the circumstances which have given rise to it were
unfortunately too common to preclude the possibility of its being of a later date." He does
not tell us where the ballad came from; but a
copy has been found among Sharpe's papers.

a. 'Eppie Morrie,' Maidment's North Countrie Garland, p. 40, 18. **b.** MS. of C. K.
Sharpe; also a copy of the same pieces, North
Country Ballads, in Miscellanea Curiosa, Abbotsford Library.

1 FOUR-AND-TWENTY Highland men
Came a' from Carrie side
To steal awa Eppie Morrie,
Cause she would not be a bride.

2 Out it's came her mother,
It was a moonlight night,
She could not see her daughter,
Their swords they shin'd so bright.

3 'Haud far awa frae me, mother,
Haud far awa frae me;
There's not a man in a' Strathdon
Shall wedded be with me.'

4 They have taken Eppie Morrie,
And horse back bound her on, .
And then awa to the minister,
As fast as horse could gang.

5 He's taken out a pistol,
And set it to the minister's breast:

'Marry me, marry me, minister,
　Or else I'll be your priest.'

6 'Haud far awa frae me, good sir,
　Haud far awa frae me;
　For there's not a man in all Strathdon
　That shall married be with me.'

7 'Haud far awa frae me, Willie,
　Haud far awa frae me;
　For I darna avow to marry you,
　Except she's as willing as ye.'

8 They have taken Eppie Morrie,
　Since better could nae be,
　And they're awa to Carrie side,
　As fast as horse could flee.

9 When mass was sung, and bells were rung,
　And all were bound for bed,
　Then Willie an Eppie Morrie
　In one bed they were laid.

10 'Haud far awa frae me, Willie,
　Haud far awa frae me;
　Before I'll lose my maidenhead,
　I'll try my strength with thee.'

11 She took the cap from off her head
　And threw it to the way;
　Said, Ere I lose my maidenhead,
　I'll fight with you till day.

12 Then early in the morning,
　Before her clothes were on,
　In came the maiden of Scalletter,
　Gown and shirt alone.

13 'Get up, get up, young woman,
　And drink the wine wi me;'
　'You might have called me maiden,
　I'm sure as leal as thee.'

14 'Wally fa you, Willie,
　That ye could nae prove a man
　And taen the lassie's maidenhead!
　She would have hired your han.'

15 'Haud far awa frae me, lady,
　Haud far awa frae me;
　There's not a man in a' Strathdon
　The day shall wed wi me.'

16 Soon in there came Belbordlane,
　With a pistol on every side:

'Come awa hame, Eppie Morrie,
　And there you'll be my bride.'

17 'Go get to me a horse, Willie,
　And get it like a man,
　And send me back to my mother
　A maiden as I cam.

18 'The sun shines oer the westlin hills;
　By the light lamp of the moon,
　Just saddle your horse, young John Forsyth,
　And whistle, and I'll come soon.'

224

THE LADY OF ARNGOSK

The subject of this ballad is the carrying off of Miss Margaret Gibb by a Mr Graham about 1736. Full particulars are given in a letter from a daughter of the lady's waiting-maid to Sharpe, printed by Child, IV, 241 ff.

Sharpe's Ballad Book, 1823, p. 99.

1 THE Highlandmen hae a' come down,
　They 've a' come down almost,
　They 've stowen away the bonny lass,
　The Lady of Arngosk.

2 They hae put on her petticoat,
　Likewise her silken gown;
　The Highland man he drew his sword,
　Said, Follow me ye's come.

3 Behind her back they 've tied her hands,
　An then they set her on;
　'I winna gang wi you,' she said,
　'Nor ony Highland loon.'

225

ROB ROY

The hero of this ballad was the youngest of the five sons of the Rob Roy who has been immortalized by Sir Walter Scott, and was known as Robert Oig, i. e. 'young,' or 'junior.' In 1750, with the aid of his brothers James and Duncan, he carried off Jean Key, a young widow of means, whom he constrained to marry him. Rob Oig was apprehended, and was executed in 1754. The ballad adheres to fact rather closely.

A*

The Old Lady's Collection, MS., No. 9; north of Scotland; copied in Skene's MS., p. 41, with a few slight changes.

1 ROB ROY, frae the high Highlands,
   Came to the Lawlan border;
  It was to steel a lady away,
   To keep his Highland house in or-
     der.

2 As he came in by White House,
   He sent nae ane before him;
  Or she wad hae secured the house,
   For she did ay abhor him.

3 Twenty men serundad the house, an
   twenty they went in,
  They found her wi her mither;
  Wi sighs an cries an watery eyes
   They parted fra each other.

4 'O will ye be my dear?' he says,
   'Or will ye be my bonnie?
  O will ye be my wedded wife?
   I lee you best of ony.'

5 'I winna be your dear,' [she says,]
   'Nor will I be your bonnie,
  Nor will I be your wedded wife;
   Ye lee me for my money.'

6 .   .   .   .   by the way,
   This lady aftimes fainted;
  Says, Woe be to my cursed gold,
   This road to me has invented!

7 He gave her no time for to dress
   Like ladies when they're ridin,
  But set her on hie horseback,
   Himsell beside her.

8 Whan they came by Black House,
   And at Stirling tarried,
  There he bought her coat an gown,
   But she would not be married.

9 Four men held her to the priest,
   An four they did her bed,
  Wi sighs an cries an watery eyes
   Whan she by him was laid.

10 'Be content, [be content,]
   Be content wi me, lady;

Now ye are my wedded wife
   Untill the day ye die, lady.

11 'My father was a Highlan laird,
   McGrigor was his name, [lady];
  A' the country roun about
   They dreadit his great fame, lady.

12 'He kept a hedge about his land,
   A prickle for his foes, [lady,]
  Every ane that did him wrang,
   He took them by the nose, lady.

13 'My father delights in nout and goats,
   [An] me in horse and sheep, lady;
  You an twenty thousan pound
   Makes me a man complete, lady.

14 'Y'er welcome to this Highlan lan,
   It is my native plain, lady;
  Think nae mair of gauin back,
   But tak it for your hame, lady.

15 'I'm gauin, [I'm gauin,]
   I'm gauin to France, lady;
  Whan I come back
   I'll learn ye a dance, lady.

16 'Set your foot, [set your foot,]
   Set your foot to mine, lady;
  Think nae mair of gauin back,
   But tak it for your hame, lady.'

B

'Rob Roy,' Kinloch MSS., I, 343.

1 ROB ROY frae the Hielands cam
   Unto the Lawland border,
  And he has stown a ladie fair,
   To haud his house in order.

2 He guarded the house round about,
   Himsel went in and found her out,
  She hung close by her mither;
  Wi dolefu cries and watery eyes
   They parted frae each ither.

3 'Gang wi me, my dear,' he says,
   'Gang and be my honey;
  Gang and be my wedded wife,
   I loe ye best o onie.'

4 'I winna gang wi you,' she says,
   'I winna be your honey;

I winna be your wedded wife;
 Ye loe me for my money.'

5 He gied na her na time to dress
 As ladies whan they 're brides,
But hurried her awa wi speed,
 And rowd her in his plaids.

6 He gat her up upon a horse,
 Himsel lap on ahind her;
And they 're awa to the Hieland hills;
 Her friends they canna find her.

7 As they gaed oure the Hieland hills,
 This lady aften fainted,
Saying, Wae be to my cursed gowd,
 This road to me invented !

8 As they gaed oure the Hieland hills,
 And at Buchanan tarried,
He bought to her baith cloak and goun,
 Yet she wadna be married.

9 Six held her up afore the priest,
 Four laid her in a bed, O;
Maist mournfully she wept and cried
 Whan she bye him was laid, O.

10 ' O be content, be content,
 Be content to stay, ladie;
For now ye are my wedded wife
 Unto your dying day, ladie.

11 ' Rob Roy was my father calld,
 M'Gregor was his name, ladie;
And in a' the country whare he dwalt
 He exceeded ae in fame, ladie.

12 ' He was a hedge unto his friends,
 A heckle to his faes. ladie;
And ilka ane that did him wrang,
 He beat him on the neis, ladie.

13 ' I 'm as bold, I am as bold
 As my father was afore, ladie;
Ilka ane that does me wrang
 Sall feel my gude claymore, ladie.

14 ' There neer was frae Lochlomond west
 That eer I did him fear, ladie;
For, if his person did escape,
 I seizd upon his gear, ladie.

15 ' My father delights in horse and kye,
 In sheep and goats and a', ladie,

And thee wi me and thirty merks
 Will mak me a man fu braw, ladie.

16 ' I hae been in foreign lands,
 And servd the king o France, ladie;
We will get the bagpipes,
 And we 'll hae a dance, ladie.'

226

LIZIE LINDSAY

In his preface to B, Kinloch remarks that the ballad is very popular in the North, " and few milk-maids in that quarter but can chaunt it, to a very pleasing tune. Lizie Lindsay," he adds, " according to the tradition of Mearns-shire, is said to have been a daughter of Lind-say of Edzell ; but I have searched in vain for genealogical confirmation of the tradition."

A

' Lizie Lindsay.' a. Jamieson-Brown MS., Appendix, p. ii, as sent Jamieson by Professor Scott of Aberdeen, June 9, 1805. b. Jamie-son's Popular Ballads, 1806, ii, 149, " trans-mitted to the editor by Professor Scott of Aberdeen, as it was taken down from the reci-tation of an old woman," but " corrected " from Jamieson's recollection in two or three passages.

*   *   *   *   *

1 OUT it spake Lizee Linzee,
 The tear blinket in her ee;
How can I leave father and mother,
 Along with young Donald to gae !

2 Out spoke Lizee's young handmaid,
 A bonny young lassie was she;
Said, Were I heress to a kingdom,
 Along with young Donald I 'd ga.

3 ' O say ye so to me, Nelly ?
 O say ye so to me ?
Must I leave Edinburgh city,
 To the high Highland to gae ? '

4 Out spoke Lizie's own mother,
 A good old lady was she;
If you speak such a word to my dochter,
 I 'll gar hang [you] hi.

5 ' Keep well your dochter from me, madam,
 Keep well your dochter fa me;

For I care as little for your dochter
  As ye can care for me.'

6 The road grew wetty and dubby,
    And Lizee began to think lang;
  Said, I wish had staid with my mother,
    And nae wi young Donald had gane.

7 'You 'r welcome hame, Sir Donald,
    You 'r thrice welcome to me;
  You 'r welcome hame, Sir Donald,
    And your young lady you wi.'

8 .   .   .   .   .

  'Ye cali na me Sir Donald,
    But ca me Donald your son.'

9 'Rise up, Lizee Linzee,
    You [have] lain too long in the day;
  Ye might have helped my mother
    To milch her goats and her kie.'

10 Out it spake Lizee Linzee,
    The tear blinket in her eye;
  'The ladys of Edinburgh city,
    They neither milch goats nor kie.'

B

'Donald of the Isles,' Kinloch MSS., i, 237,
from Miss Catherine Beattie, Mearnsshire.
Aytoun's Ballads of Scotland, 1859, i, 277.

1 It 's of a young lord o the Hielands,
    A bonnie braw castle had he,
  And he says to his lady mither,
    'My boon ye will grant to me:
  Sall I gae to Edinbruch city,
    And fesh hame a lady wi me ? '

2 'Ye may gae to Edinbruch city,
    And fesh hame a lady wi thee,
  But see that ye bring her but flattrie,
    And court her in grit povertie.'

3 'My coat, mither, sall be o the plaiden,
    A tartan kilt oure my knee,
  Wi hosens and brogues and the bonnet;
    I 'll court her wi nae flattrie.'

4 Whan he cam to Edinbruch city,
    He playd at the ring and the ba,
  And saw monie a bonnie young ladie,
    But Lizie Lindsay was first o them a'.

5 Syne, dressd in his Hieland grey plaiden,
    His bonnet abune his ee-bree,
  He called on fair Lizie Lindsay;
    Says, Lizie, will ye fancy me ?

6 'And gae to the Hielands, my lassie,
    And gae, gae wi me ?
  O gae to the Hielands, Lizie Lindsay,
    I 'll feed ye on curds and green whey.

7 'And ye 'se get a bed o green bracken,
    My plaidie will hap thee and me;
  Ye 'se lie in my arms, bonnie Lizie,
    If ye 'll gae to the Hielands wi me.'

8 'O how can I gae to the Hielands,
    Or how can I gae wi thee,
  Whan I dinna ken whare I 'm gaing,
    Nor wha I hae to gae wi ? '

9 'My father, he is an auld shepherd,
    My mither, she is an auld dey;
  My name it is Donald Macdonald,
    My name I 'll never deny.'

10 'O Donald, I 'll gie ye five guineas
    To sit ae hour in my room,
  Till I tak aff your ruddy picture;
    Whan I hae 't, I 'll never think lang.'

11 'I dinna care for your five guineas;
    It 's ye that 's the jewel to me;
  I 've plenty o kye in the Hielands,
    To feed ye wi curds and green whey.

12 'And ye 'se get a bonnie blue plaidie,
    Wi red and green strips thro it a';
  And I 'll be the lord o your dwalling,
    And that 's the best picture ava.

13 'And I am laird o a' my possessions;
    The king canna boast o na mair;
  And ye 'se hae my true heart in keeping,
    There 'll be na ither een hae a share.

14 'Sae gae to the Hielands, my lassie,
    O gae awa happy wi me;
  O gae to the Hielands, Lizie Lindsay,
    And hird the wee lammies wi me.'

15 'O how can I gae wi a stranger,
    Oure hills and oure glens frae my
      hame ? '
  'I tell ye I am Donald Macdonald;
    I 'll ever be proud o my name.'

16 Doun cam Lizie Lindsay's ain father,
      A knicht o a noble degree;
    Says, If ye do steal my dear daughter,
      It 's hangit ye quickly sall be.

17 On his heel he turnd round wi a bouncie,
      And a licht lauch he did gie:
    'There 's nae law in Edinbruch city
      This day that can dare to hang me.'

18 Then up bespak Lizie's best woman,
      And a bonnie young lass was she;
    'Had I but a mark in my pouchie,
      It 's Donald that I wad gae wi.'

19 'O Helen, wad ye leave your coffer,
      And a' your silk kirtles sae braw,
    And gang wi a bare-houghd puir laddie,
      And leave father, mither, and a' ?

20 'But I think he 's a witch or a war-
        lock,
      Or something o that fell degree,
    For I 'll gae awa wi young Donald,
      Whatever my fortune may be.'

21 Then Lizie laid doun her silk mantle,
      And put on her waiting-maid's goun,
    And aff and awa to the Hielands
      She 's gane wi this young shepherd
        loun.

22 Thro glens and oure mountains they
        wanderd,
      Till Lizie had scantlie a shoe;
    'Alas and ohone !' says fair Lizie,
      'Sad was the first day I saw you !
    I wish I war in Edinbruch city;
      Fu sair, sair this pastime I rue.'

23 'O haud your tongue now, bonnie Lizie,
      For yonder 's the shieling, my hame;
    And there 's my guid auld honest mither,
      That 's coming to meet ye her lane.'

24 'O ye 're welcome, ye 're welcome, Sir
        Donald,
      Ye 're welcome hame to your ain.'
    'O ca me na young Sir Donald,
      But ca me Donald my son;'
    And this they hae spoken in Erse,
      That Lizie micht not understand.

25 The day being weetie and daggie,
      They lay till 't was lang o the day:

'Win up, win up, bonnie Lizie,
      And help at the milking the kye.'

26 O slowly raise up Lizie Lindsay,
      The saut tear blindit her ee:
    'O, war I in Edinbruch city,
      The Hielands shoud never see me !'

27 He led her up to a hie mountain
      And bade her look out far and wide:
    'I 'm lord o thae isles and thae moun-
        tains,
      And ye 're now my beautiful bride.

28 'Sae rue na ye 've come to the Hielands,
      Sae rue na ye 've come aff wi me,
    For ye 're great Macdonald's braw lady,
      And will be to the day that ye dee.'

227

BONNY LIZIE BAILLIE

"The heroine of this song," says Sharpe,
"was a daughter of Baillie of Castle Carey, and
sister, as it is said, to the wife of Macfarlane
of Gartartan." The Baillies, as Maidment has
shown, acquired Castle Cary "at a comparatively recent date," and that editor must be
nearly, or quite, right in declaring the ballad
to be not older than the commencement of the
eighteenth century.

The broadside which contains a may probably have been printed at the beginning of the
eighteenth century, at Edinburgh.

a. 'Bonny Lizie Balie, A New Song very
much in Request,' Laing broadsides, No. 46;
no date or place. b. 'Bonny Lizzie Bailie,'
Maidment's Scotish Ballads and Songs, 1859,
p. 13. c. 'My bonny Lizzie Baillie,' Johnson's Museum, ed. 1853, IV, *451. d. 'Lizae
Baillie,' Herd's MSS., I, 101, and, in part, II,
121. e. 'Lizie Baillie,' Campbell MSS., I, 98.
f. 'Lizzie Bailie,' Smith's Scotish Minstrel, IV,
90. g. 'Lizie Baillie,' Buchan's Ballads of the
North of Scotland, II, 173. h. Old Lady's MS.

1 It fell about the Lammbass tide,
      When the leaves were fresh and green,
    Lizie Bailie is to Gartartain [gane],
      To see her sister Jean.

2 She had not been in Gartartain
      Even but a little while
    Till luck and fortune happend her,
      And she went to the Isle.

3 And when she went into the Isle
   She met with Duncan Grahame;
So bravely as he courted her !
   And he convoyd her hame.

4 ' My bonny Lizie Bailie,
   I 'll row thee in my pladie,
If thou will go along with me
   And be my Highland lady.'

5 ' If I would go along with thee,
   I think I were not wise;
For I cannot milk cow nor ewe,
   Nor yet can I speak Erse.'

6 ' Hold thy tongue, bonny Lizie Bailie,
   And hold thy tongue,' said he;
' For any thing that thou does lack,
   My dear, I 'll learn thee.'

7 She would not have a Lowland laird,
   He wears the high-heeld shoes;
She will marry Duncan Grahame,
   For Duncan wears his trews.

8 She would not have a gentleman,
   A farmer in Kilsyth,
But she would have the Highland man,
   He lives into Monteith.

9 She would not have the Lowland man,
   Nor yet the English laddie,
But she would have the Highland man,
   To row her in his pladie.

10 He took her by the milk-white hand,
   And he convoyd her hame,
And still she thought, both night and
   day,
   On bonny Duncan Grahame.

11 ' O bonny Duncan Grahame,
   Why should ye me miscarry ?
For, if you have a love for me,
   We 'll meet a[t] Castle Carry.

12 ' As I came in by Dennie bridge,
   And by the holland-bush,
My mother took from me my cloaths,
   My rings, ay and my purse.

13 ' Hold your tongue, my mother dear,
   For that I do not care;
For I will go with Duncan Grahame
   Tho I should ner get mair.

14 ' For first when I met Duncan Grahame
   I met with meikle joy,
And many pretty Highland men
   Was there at my convoy.'

15 And now he is gone through the muir,
   And she is through the glen:
' O bonny Lizie Bailie,
   When will we meet again !'

16 Shame light on these logerheads
   That lives in Castle Carry,
That led away the bonny lass
   The Highland man to marry !

17 ' O bonny Lizie, stay at home !
   Thy mother cannot want thee;
For any thing that thou does lack,
   My dear, I 'll cause get thee.'

18 ' I would not give my Duncan Grahame
   For all my father's land,
Altho he had three lairdships more,
   And all at my command.'

19 Now she 's cast off her silken gowns,
   That she weard in the Lowland,
And she 's up to the Highland hills,
   To wear [the] gowns of tartain.

20 And she 's cast off her high - heeld
   shoes,
   Was made of the gilded leather,
And she 's up to Gillecrankie,
   To go among the heather.

21 And she 's cast off her high-heeld shoes,
   And put on a pair of laigh ones,
And she 's away with Duncan Grahame,
   To go among the brachans.

22 ' O my bonny Lizie Bailie,
   Thy mother cannot want thee;
And if thou go with Duncan Grahame
   Thou 'll be a Gilliecrankie.'

23 ' Hold your tongue, my mother dear,
   And folly let thee be;
Should not I fancie Duncan Grahame
   When Duncan fancies me ?

24 ' Hold your tongue, my father dear,
   And folly let thee be;
For I will go with Duncan Grahame
   Fore all the men I see.'

25 'Who is it that's done this turn ?
   Who has done this deed ? '
   ' A minister it 's, father,' she says,
   ' Lives at the Rughburn bridge.'

26 ' A minister, daughter ? ' he says,
   ' A minister for mister ! '
   ' O hold your tongue, my father dear,
   He married first my sister.'

27 ' O fare you well, my daughter dear,
   So dearly as I lovd thee !
   Since thou wilt go to Duncan Grahame,
   My bonny Lizie Bailie.'

28 ' O fare you well, my father dear,
   Also my sister Betty;
   O fare you well, my mother dear,
   I leave you all compleatly.'

228

GLASGOW PEGGIE

Sharpe printed **A**, with a few slight changes, in his Ballad Book, p. 40.

A*

From a MS. among C. K. Sharpe's relics, having 1819 in the water-mark ; in two hands, sts. 1–6, 8, 9¹ in one, 7 (inserted in the margin) and the rest in another.

1 ' As I cam in by boney Glasggow town,
   The Highland troops were a' before me,
   And the bon[ey]est lass that ere I saw,
   She lives in Glasgow, tha ca her Peggy.

2 ' I wad gie my boney black horse,
   So wad I my good gray nagie,
   If I were a hundred miles in the North,
   And nan wee me but my boney Peggy.'

3 Up then spoke her father dear,
   Dear vow ! but he was wondrous sorey;
   ' Weel may yea steel a cow or a ewe,
   But ye darna steel my boney Peggy.'

4 Up then spoke her mother dear,
   Dear vow ! but she spoke wondrious sorey;

' Now, since I 've brought ye up this length,
   Wod ye gang awa wee a Highland fellow ? '

5 He set her on his boney black horse,
   He set himsel on his good gray nagy;
   They have riden over hill[s] and dales,
   Now he is awa wee his boney Peggy.

6 They are riden or hills and dales,
   They have riden or mountains maney,
   Untill that thay com to a low, low glen,
   And there he 's lain down wee his boney Peggy.

7 Up then spoke the Earll o Argyle,
   Dear vow ! bet he spoke wondrous sorry;
   ' The bonniest lass in a' Scotland
   Is af an awa wi [a] Highland fellow!'

8 There bed was of the boney green grass,
   There blankets was o the hay sa boney;
   He falded his philabeg below her head,
   Now he 's lawing down wee his boney Peggy.

9 Up then spoke the boney Lawland lass,
   And oh, but she spoke wondrous sorry;
   ' A 's warruant my mother would hae a gae soir heart
   To see me lian here wi you, my Willie !'

10 ' In my father's house there 's feather-beds,
   Feather-beds an blankets many;
   The 're a' mine, an the 'll shoon be thine,
   An what needs your mother be sae sorry, Peggie ?

11 ' Dinna you see yon nine score o kye,
   Feding on yon hill sae boney ?
   The 're a' mine, an the 'll shoon be thine,
   An what needs your mother be sorry, Peggie ?

12 ' Dinna you see yon nine score o sheep,
   Feeding on yon brae sae bonny ?
   The 're a' mine, an the 'll shoon be thine,
   An what needs your mother be sorry for you ?

13 ' Dinna you see yon bonny white house,
    Shining on yon brae sae bonny ?
An I am the earl o the Isle o Sky,
    And surely my Peggie will be calle[d]
    a lady.'

229

EARL CRAWFORD

The late Earl of Crawford recognized in some of the details of this story an agreement with facts of his family history in the second half of the sixteenth century.

A

'Earl Crawford.' **a.** Christie's Traditional Ballad Airs, i, 290, as taken down 1867–73, from the recitation of Mrs. Mary Robertson, wife of James Robertson, shoemaker, Bogmoor, near Fochabers. **b.** Obtained by Mr Macmath, March 25, 1890, from the daughter of Mrs Robertson, Mrs Mary Thomson, wife of James Thomson, gardener at Gordon Castle gardens, Fochabers.

1 O WE were sisters, sisters seven,
    We were a comely crew to see,
And some got lairds, and some got lords,
    And some got knichts o hie degree;
And I mysel got the Earl o Crawford,
    And wasna that a great match for me !

2 It was at fifteen that I was married,
    And at sixteen I had a son;
And wasna that an age ower tender
    For a lady to hae her first-born !
    And wasna, etc.

3 But it fell ance upon a day
    I gaed into the garden green,
And naebody was therein walking
    But Earl Crawford and his young son.

4 ' I wonder at you, ye Earl Crawford,
    I wonder at you wi your young son;
Ye daut your young son mair than your
    Lillie;
    [I 'm sure you got na him your lane.']

5 [He turned about upon his heel,
    I wite an angry man was he;
Says, If I got nae my young son my
    lane,
    Bring me here the one that helpet me.]

6 ['O hold your tongue, my Earl Craw-
    ford,
    And a' my folly lat it be;
There was nane at the gettin o oor son,
    Nae body only but you and me.']

7 He set her on a milk-white steed,
    Her little young son her before;
Says, Ye maun gae to bonny Stobha,
    For ye will enter my yates no more.

8 When she cam to her father's bowers,
    She lichtit low down on the stane,
And wha sae ready as her auld father
    To welcome Lady Lillie in ?

9 ' O how 's a' wi you, my daughter Lillie,
    That ye come here sae hastilie ?
And how 's a' wi' the Earl o Crawford,
    That he didna send a boy wi thee ?'

10 ' O haud your tongue now, my old
    father,
    And ye 'll lat a' your folly be;
For ae word that my merry mou spak
    Has parted my good lord and me.'

11 ' O haud your tongue, my daughter Lillie,
    And a' your follies lat them be;
I 'll double your portion ten times ower,
    And a better match I 'll get for thee.'

12 ' O haud your tongue now, my old father,
    And a' your folly lat it be;
I wouldna gie ae kiss o Crawford
    For a' the goud that ye can gie.

13 ' Whare will I get a bonny boy,
    That 's willin to win meat and fee,
Wha will gae on to Earl Crawford
    An see an 's heart be fawn to me ?'

14 When he cam to the yates o Crawford,
    They were a' sitting down to dine:
' How comes it now, ye Earl Craw-
    ford,
    Ye arena takin Lady Lillie hame ?'

15 ' Ye may gae tell her Lady Lillie,
    And ye maun neither lee nor len,
She may stay in her father's bowers,
    For she 'll not enter my yates again.'

16 When he cam back to her father's yates,
    He lichtit low down on his knee:

'What news, what news, my bonny boy?
    What news, what news hae ye to me?'

17 'I 'm bidden tell you, Lady Lillie —
    I 'm bidden neither to lee nor len —
    She may stay in her father's bowers,
    For she 'll not enter my yates again.'

18 She stretched out her lily hand,
    Says, 'Adieu, adieu to ane and a!
    Adieu, adieu to Earl Crawford!'
    Wi that her sair heart brak in twa.

19 Then dowie, dowie her father raise up,
    And dowie, dowie the black put on,
    And dowie, dowie he mounted the brown,
    And dowie, dowie sat thereon.

20 And dowie rade to the yates o Craw-
        ford,
    And when to Crawford's yates he
        came,
    They were a' dressd in the robes o scar-
        let,
    Just gaun to tak Lady Lillie hame.

21 'Ye may cast aff your robes o scarlet —
    I wyte they set you wondrous weel —
    And now put on the black sae dowie,
    And come and bury your Lady Lill.'

22 He took his hat into his hand,
    And laid it low down by his knee:
    'An it be true that Lillie 's dead,
    The sun shall nae mair shine on me.'

230

THE SLAUGHTER OF THE LAIRD OF MELLERSTAIN

This fragment tells of the murder of John Haitlie, of Mellerstain, in 1603. Mellerstain stands on a rising ground near the right bank of the Eden. The lady of stanza 1 was Marion Lumsden, Haitlie's wife.

In a folio volume with the title "Miscellanies," the last piece in the volume, Abbotsford.

1 .   .   .   .
    As they came in by the Eden side,
    They heard a lady lamenting sair,
    Bewailing the time she was a bride.

2 .   .   .   .
    A stately youth of blude and bane,
    .   .   .   .   .   .
    John Hately, the laird of Meller-
        stain.

3 'Cowdenknows, had ye nae lack?
    And Earlstoun, had ye nae shame?
    Ye took him away behind my back,
    But ye never saw to bring him hame.'

4 And she has lookit to Fieldiesha,
    So has she through Yirdandstane;
    She lookit to Earlstoun, and she saw the
        Fans,
    But he 's coming hame by West Gor-
        don.

5 And she staggerd and she stood,
    .   .   .   .   .   .
    .   .   .   .   .   .

6 '.   .   .   .   .   wude;
    How can I keep in my wits,
    When I look on my husband's blood?'

7 'Had we been men as we are women,
    And been at his back when he was
        slain,
    It should a been tauld for mony a lang
        year,
    The slaughter o the laird of Meller-
        stain.'

231

THE EARL OF ERROL

Sir Gilbert Hay, tenth Earl of Errol, was married to Lady Catherine Carnegy, younger daughter of James, second Earl of Southesk, January 7, 1658, and had no children by her. He died in 1674. The ballad, says the person who communicated A b to the Edinburgh Miscellany, was "founded, it would seem, on some attempt to withhold from the Earl of Errol his consort's portion." It will be observed that the father proposes a beguiling to his daughter, and that she is ready to assent, in A, 12, 13. It appears from a letter cited by Sharpe in his Ballad Book that the matters treated in the ballad were agitating, and had even "come to public hearing," in February, 1659.

A

a. 'Kate Carnegie,' Campbell MSS., ii, 94.
b. The Edinburgh Magazine, or Literary Miscellany, June, 1803, p. 458.

1 THERE was a jury sat at Perth,
　In the merry month of May,
Betwixt the noble Duke of Perth
　But and Sir Gilbert Hay.

2 My lord Kingside has two daughters,
　They are proper, straight and tall;
But my lord Carnegie he has two
　That far excells them all.

3 Then Errol he has dressd him,
　As very well he could;
I 'm sure there was not one cloth-yard
　But what was trimmd with gold.

4 'Ane asking, ane asking, my lord Carnegie,
　Ane asking I 've to thee;
I 'm come to court your daughter Jean,
　My wedded wife to be.'

5 'My daughter Jean was wed yestreen,
　To one of high degree,
But where Jean got one guinea of gold
　With Kate I 'll give thee three.

6 'Full fifteen hundred pounds
　Had Jean Carnegie,
But three fifteen hundred pounds
　With Kate I 'll gie to thee.'

7 Then Errol he has wed her,
　And fairly brought her hame;
There was nae peace between them twa
　Till they sundered oer again.

8 When bells were rung, and mess was sung,
　And a' man bound to bed,
The Earl of Errol and his countess
　In one chamber was laid.

9 Early in the morning
　My lord Carnegie rose,
The Earl of Errol and his countess,
　And they 've put on their clothes.

10 Up spake my lord Carnegie;
　'Kate, is your toucher won?'

'Ye may ask the Earl of Errol,
　If he be your good-son.

11 'What need I wash my petticoat
　And hing it on a pin?
For I am as leal a maid yet
　As yestreen when I lay down.

12 'What need I wash my apron
　And hing it on the door?
It 's baith side and wide enough,
　Hangs even down before.'

13 Up spake my lord Carnegie;
　'O Kate, what do ye think?
We 'll beguile the Earl of Errol
　As lang as he 's in drink.'

14 'O what will ye beguile him wi?
　Or what will ye do than?
I 'll swear before a justice-court
　That he 's no a sufficient man.'

15 Then Errol he cam down the stair,
　As bold as oney rae:
'Go saddle to me my Irish coach,
　To Edinbro I 'll go.'

16 When he came to Edinbro,
　He lighted on the green;
There were four-and-twenty maidens
　A' dancing in a ring.

17 There were four-and-twenty maidens
　A' dancing in a row;
The fatest and the fairest
　To bed wi him must go.

18 He 's taen his Peggy by the hand,
　And he led her thro the green,
And twenty times he kissd her there,
　Before his ain wife's een.

19 He 's taen his Peggy by the hand,
　And he 's led her thro the hall,
And twenty times he 's kissd her there,
　Before his nobles all.

20 'Look up, look up, my Peggy lass,
　Look up, and think nae shame;
Ten hundred pounds I 'll gie to you
　To bear to me a son.'

21 He 's keepit his Peggy in his room
　Three quarter of a year,

And just at the nine months' end
    She a son to him did bear.

22 'Now if ye be Kate Carnegie,
    And I Sir Gilbert Hay,
  I 'll make your father sell his lands
    Your toucher for to pay.'

23 'To make my father sell his lands,
    It wad be a great sin,
  To toucher oney John Sheephead
    That canna toucher win.'

24 'Now hold your tongue, ye whorish
    bitch,
    Sae loud as I hear ye lie !
  For yonder sits Lord Errol's son,
    Upon his mother's knee;
  For yonder sits Lord Errol's son,
    Altho he 's no by thee.'

25 'You may take hame your daughter
    Kate,
    And set her on the glen;
  For Errol canna please her,
    Nor nane o Errol's men;
  For Errol canna please her,
    Nor twenty of his men.'

26 The ranting and the roving,
    The thing we a' do ken,
  The lady lost her right that night,
    The first night she lay down;
  And the thing we ca the ranting o 't,
    The lady lies her lane.

232

RICHIE STORY

" Lillias Fleming, a daughter of John, third
Earl of Wigton by his wife Jane Drummond,
did elope with and marry one of her father's
servants, named Richard Storry. In 1673, she,
with consent of her husband, resigned her portion, consisting of the five-merk land of Smyth-
son, etc., in the barony of Lenzie, into the hands
of her brother, Lieutenant-Colonel Fleming.
The Fleming family afterwards procured for
Richie a situation in the Custom-House." Hunter, Biggar and the House of Fleming, p. 555.

The well-known song of 'Huntingtower'
(' When ye gang awa, Jamie ') is founded on
this ballad. It has been often printed ; as, for
example, in G. F. Graham's Popular Songs of
Scotland, revised by J. Muir Wood, Glasgow,
1887, p. 152.

A

' Ritchie Storie,' Motherwell's MS., p. 426 ;
from the recitation of Mrs ——, of Kilbarchan,
January 3, 1826.

1 THE Earl of Wigton had three daugh-
    ters,
  Oh and a waly, but they were unco
    bonnie !
  The eldest of them had the far brawest
    house,
  But she 's fallen in love with her foot-
    man-laddie.

2 As she was a walking doun by yon river-
    side,
  Oh and a wally, but she was unco
    bonnie !
  There she espied her own footman,
  With ribbons hanging over his shoul-
    ders sae bonnie.

3 'Here 's a letter to you, madame,
    Here 's a letter to you, madame;
  The Earl of Hume is waiting on,
  And he has his service to you, ma-
    dame.'

4 'I 'll have none of his service,' says she,
    'I 'll have none of his service,' says
    she,
  'For I 've made a vow, and I 'll keep it
    true,
    That I'll marry none but you, Ritchie.'

5 'O say not so again, madame,
    O say not so again, madame;
  For I have neither lands nor rents
    For to keep you on, madam.'

6 'I 'll live where eer you please, Ritchie,
  I 'll live where eer you please,
    [Ritchie,]
  And I 'll be ready at your ca',
    Either late or early, Ritchie.'

7 As they went in by Stirling toun,
  Oh and a wally, but she was unco
    bonnie !
  A' her silks were sailing on the ground,
  But few of them knew of Ritchie
    Story.

8 As they went in by the Parliament Close,
   O and a wally, but she was unco
     bonnie !
   All the nobles took her by the hand,
     But few of them knew she was
     Ritchie's lady.

9 As they came in by her goodmother's
     yetts,
   O and a wally, but she was unco
     bonnie !
   Her goodmother bade her kilt her coats,
     And muck the byre with Ritchie
     Storie.

10 'Oh, may not ye be sorry, madame,
    Oh, may not ye be sorry, madame,
   To leave a' your lands at bonnie Cum-
     bernaud,
     And follow home your footman-lad-
     die ?'

11 'What need I be sorry ?' says she,
    'What need I be sorry ?' says she,
   'For I 've gotten my lot and my heart's
     desire,
     And what Providence has ordered for
     me.'

B*

"The Old Lady's Collection," No. 21.

1 COMARNAD it is a very bonny place,
   An ther is ladys three, madam,
   Bat the farest an rarest of them a'
   Has marred Richerd Storry.

2 'O hear is a letter to ye, madam,
   Hear is a letter to ye, madam;
   The Earl of Hume, that galant knight,
   Is faln in love we you, madam.

3 'Ther is a letter to you, madam,
   [Ther is a letter to you, madam;]
   The Eearl of Hume, that galant knight,
   Disers to be yer servant trou, madam.'

4 'I ill haa nan of his letters, Richerd,
   I ill hae nane of his letters, [Richerd,]
   I have voued, an I ill keep it trou,
   I ill marry nane bat ye, Richie.'

5 'Say na saa to me, lady,
   Sai na saie to me, lady,

For I ha nether lands nor rents
For to manten ye on, lady.'

6 'Hunten Tour an Tillebarn,
   The house of Athell is mine, Richë,
   An ye sall haa them a',
   Fan ever ye inclen, Richë.

7 'For we will gaa to sea, Richë,
   I ill sit on the deak, Richë,
   I ill be yer servant air an lait,
   Att any houre ye laek, [Richë.]'

8 'O manie ye be sad, sister,
   An mennie ye be sorry, Nelly,
   To live the has of bony Comernid,
   An follou Richert Storry ?'

9 'O fatt neads I be sad, sister,
   Or fou cane I be sorry, Anna ?
   A bony lad is my delit,
   An my lot has been laid afore me.'

10 As she wen[t] up the Parliment Closs,
   We her lassed shene so fine,
   Monny an bad the lady good day,
     But fue thought she was Richert's
     lady.

11 As she went up the Parliment Closs,
   We her laised shon so fine,
   Monny an halled that gay lady,
     But fue halled Richerd Storry.

233

ANDREW LAMMIE

Jamieson, in his preface, 1806, says that this
ballad was current in the Border counties within
a few years, and that A was taken down by
Leyden from the recitation of a young lady
who learned it in Teviotdale.

"Bonny Andrew Lammie" was a well-known
personage at the beginning of the eighteenth
century, for, as Jamieson has pointed out, he is
mentioned in a way that implies this by Allan
Ramsay, in the second of his two cantos in
continuation of Christ's Kirk on the Green,
written, as Ramsay says, in 1718. Mill of Tiftie is, or was, a farmhouse on the side of a
glen about half a mile northeast of the castle
of Fyvie, and in view of its turrets. Annie
was Agnes Smith, Nannie being among her
people an affectionate form for Agnes. An in-

scription on her gravestone makes Agnes Smith
to have died January 19, 1673.

A

'The Trumpeter of Fyvie,' Jamieson's Popular Ballads, I, 126; "taken down by Dr Leyden from the recitation of a young lady, Miss
Robson, of Edinburgh, who learned it in Teviotdale."

1 ' AT Fyvie's yetts there grows a flower,
     It grows baith braid and bonny;
   There 's a daisie in the midst o it,
     And it 's ca'd by Andrew Lammie.

2 ' O gin that flower war in my breast,
     For the love I bear the laddie !
   I wad kiss it, and I wad clap it,
     And daut it for Andrew Lammie.

3 ' The first time me and my love met
     Was in the woods of Fyvie;
   He kissed my lips five thousand times,
     And ay he ca'd me bonny,
   And a' the answer he gat frae me,
     Was, My bonny Andrew Lammie ! '

4 ' Love, I maun gang to Edinburgh;
     Love, I maun gang and leave thee ! '
   ' I sighed right sair, and said nae mair
     But, O gin I were wi ye ! '

5 ' But true and trusty will I be,
     As I am Andrew Lammie;
   I 'll never kiss a woman's mouth
     Till I come back and see thee.'

6 ' And true and trusty will I be,
     As I am Tiftie's Annie;
   I 'll never kiss a man again
     Till ye come back and see me.'

7 Syne he 's come back frae Edinburgh
     To the bonny hows o Fyvie,
   And ay his face to the nor-east,
     To look for Tiftie's Annie.

8 ' I hae a love in Edinburgh,
     Sae hae I intill Leith, man;
   I hae a love intill Montrose,
     Sae hae I in Dalkeith, man.

9 ' And east and west, whereer I go,
     My love she 's always wi me;
   For east and west, whereer I go,
     My love she dwells in Fyvie.

10 ' My love possesses a' my heart,
     Nae pen can eer indite her;
   She 's ay sae stately as she goes
     That I see nae mae like her.

11 ' But Tiftie winna gie consent
     His dochter me to marry,
   Because she has five thousand marks,
     And I have not a penny.

12 ' Love pines away, love dwines away,
     Love, love decays the body;
   For love o thee, oh I must die;
     Adieu, my bonny Annie ! '

13 Her mither raise out o her bed,
     And ca'd on baith her women:
   ' What ails ye, Annie, my dochter dear ?
     O Annie, was ye dreamin ?

14 ' What dule disturbd my dochter's
     sleep ?
   O tell to me, my Annie ! '
   She sighed right sair, and said nae mair
     But, O for Andrew Lammie !

15 Her father beat her cruellie,
     Sae also did her mother;
   Her sisters sair did scoff at her;
     But wae betide her brother !

16 Her brother beat her cruellie,
     Till his straiks they werena canny;
   He brak her back, and he beat her sides,
     For the sake o Andrew Lammie.

17 ' O fie, O fie, my brother dear !
     The gentlemen 'll shame ye;
   The Laird o Fyvie he 's gaun by,
     And he 'll come in and see me.

18 ' And he 'll kiss me, and he 'll clap me,
     And he will speer what ails me;
   And I will answer him again,
     It 's a' for Andrew Lammie.'

19 Her sisters they stood in the door,
     Sair grievd her wi their folly:
   ' O sister dear, come to the door,
     Your cow is lowin on you.'

20 ' O fie, O fie, my sister dear !
     Grieve me not wi your folly.
   I 'd rather hear the trumpet sound
     Than a' the kye o Fyvie.

21 ' Love pines away, love dwines away,
    Love, love decays the body;
    For love o thee now I maun die;
    Adieu to Andrew Lammie ! '

22 But Tiftie 's wrote a braid letter,
    And sent it into Fyvie,
    Saying his daughter was bewitchd
    By bonny Andrew Lammie.

23 ' Now, Tiftie, ye maun gie consent,
    And lat the lassie marry ; '
    ' I 'll never, never gie consent
    To the trumpeter of Fyvie.'

24 When Fyvie looked the letter on,
    He was baith sad and sorry :
    Says, The bonniest lass o the country-
        side
    Has died for Andrew Lammie.

25 O Andrew 's gane to the house-top
    O the bonny house o Fyvie,
    He 's blawn his horn baith loud and
        shill
    Oer the lawland leas o Fyvie.

26 ' Mony a time hae I walkd a' night,
    And never yet was weary ;
    But now I may walk wae my lane,
    For I 'll never see my deary.

27 ' Love pines away, love dwines away,
    Love, love decays the body ;
    For the love o thee now I maun die ;
    I come, my bonny Annie ! '

234

CHARLIE MACPHERSON

Buchan's version (B) in his Ballads of the
North of Scotland, I, 85, completes the story,
but very tamely, for we expect a collision, and
judging by A, st. 8, there was one. For the
pertinent stanzas see Notes.

A

' Charlie MacPherson,' Harris MS., fol. 23 b ;
from Mrs Harris's singing.

1 CHARLIE MACPHERSON, that braw Hie-
        land lad[die],
    On Valentine's even cam doun to Kinal-
        tie,

Courtit Burd Hellen, baith wakin an
    sleepin :
' Oh, fair fa them has my love in keep-
    in ! '

2 Charlie MacPherson cam doun the dyke-
        side,
    Baith Milton an Muirton an a' bein his
        guide ;
    Baith Milton an Muirton an auld Water
        Nairn,
    A' gaed wi him, for to be his warn.

3 Whan he cam to the hoose o Kinaltie,
    'Open your yetts, mistress, an lat us
        come in !
    Open your yetts, mistress, an lat us
        come in !
    For here 's a commission come frae your
        gude-son.

4 ' Madam,' says Charlie, ' whare [i]s your
        dochter ?
    Mony time have I come to Kinatie an
        socht her ;
    Noo maun she goe wi me mony a mile,
    Because I 've brocht mony men frae the
        West Isle.'

5 ' As for my dochter, she has gane abroad,
    You 'll no get her for her tocher
        gude ;
    She 's on to Whitehouse, to marry auld
        Gairn :
    Oh, fair fa them that wait on my bairn ! '

6 Charlie MacPherson gaed up the dyke-
        side,
    Baith Muirtoun an Milton an a' bein his
        guide ;
    Baith Muirton an Milton an auld Water
        Nairn,
    A' gaed wi him, for to be his warn.

7 Whan he cam to the hoose in Braemar,
    Sae weel as he kent that his Nellie was
        there !
    An Nellie was sittin upon the bed-side,
    An every one there was ca'ing her,
        bride.

8 The canles gaed oot, they waurna weel
        licht,
    Swords an spears they glancet fou
        bricht ;

Sae laith as she was her true-love to be-
guile,
Because he brocht mony men frae the
West Isle.

*   *   *   *   *

235

THE EARL OF ABOYNE

Charles, first Earl of Aboyne, married for his
first wife Margaret Irvine of Drum, who died
in 1662. The story of the ballad, so far as is
known, is an absolute fiction.

A

'The Earl of Aboyne,' Kinloch MSS., v, 351;
in the handwriting of John Hill Burton.

1 THE Earl of Aboyne he 's courteous and
kind,
He 's kind to every woman,
And the Earl of Aboyne he 's courteous
and kind,
But he stays ower lang in London.

2 The ladie she stood on her stair-head,
Beholding his grooms a coming;
She knew by their livery and raiment so
rare
That their last voyage was from Lon-
don.

3 'My groms all, ye 'll be well in call,
Hold all the stables shining;
With a bretther o degs ye 'll clear up my
nags,
Sin my gude Lord Aboyne is a coming.

4 'My minstrels all, be well in call,
Hold all my galleries ringing;
With music springs ye 'll try well your
strings,
Sin my gude lord 's a coming.

5 'My cooks all, be well in call,
Wi pots and spits well ranked;
And nothing shall ye want that ye call
for,
Sin my gude Lord Aboyne 's a coming.

6 'My chamber-maids, ye 'll dress up my
beds,
Hold all my rooms in shining;

With Dantzic waters ye 'll sprinkle my
walls,
Sin my good lord 's a coming.'

7 Her shoes was of the small cordain,
Her stockings silken twisting;
Cambrick so clear was the pretty lady's
smock,
And her stays o the braided sattin.

8 Her coat was of the white sarsenent,
Set out wi silver quiltin,
And her gown was o the silk damask,
Set about wi red gold walting.

9 Her hair was like the threads o gold,
Wi the silk and sarsanet shining,
Wi her fingers sae white, and the gold
rings sae grite,
To welcome her lord from London.

10 Sae stately she steppet down the stair,
And walket to meet him coming;
Said, O ye 'r welcome, my bonny lord,
Ye 'r thrice welcome home from Lon-
don !

11 'If this be so that ye let me know,
Ye 'll come kiss me for my coming,
For the morn should hae been my bonny
wedding-day
Had I stayed the night in London.'

12 Then she turned her about wi an angry
look,
O for such an a sorry woman !
'If this be so that ye let me know,
Gang kiss your ladies in London.'

13 Then he looked ower his left shoulder
To the worthie companie wi him;
Says he, Isna this an unworthy welcome
The we 've got, comin from London !

14 'Get yer horse in call, my nobles all,
And I 'm sorry for yer coming,
But we 'll horse, and awa to the bonny
Bog o Gight,
And then we 'll go on to London.'

15 'If this be Thomas, as they call you,
You 'll see if he 'll hae me with him;
And nothing shall he be troubled with
me
But myself and my waiting-woman.'

16 'I've asked it already, lady,' he says,
  'And your humble servant, madam;
  But one single mile he winna lat you
    ride
  Wi his company and him to London.'

17 A year and mare she lived in care,
  And docters wi her dealin,
  And with a crack her sweet heart brack,
  And the letters is on to London.

18 When the letters he got, they were all
    sealed in black,
  And he fell in a grievous weeping;
  He said, She is dead whom I loved
    best
  If I had but her heart in keepin.

19 Then fifteen o the finest lords
  That London could afford him,
  From their hose to their hat, they were
    all clad in black,
  For the sake of her corpse, Margaret
    Irvine.

20 The furder he gaed, the sorer he wept,
  Come keping her corpse, Margaret
    Irvine,
  Until that he came to the yetts of
    Aboyne,
  Where the corpse of his lady was
    lying.

236

THE LAIRD O DRUM

Alexander Irvine, the young laird of Drum (ten miles west of Aberdeen), was married to the lady Mary Gordon in 1643. Lady Mary Gordon was fourth daughter to George the second Marquis of Huntly, and niece to the Marquis of Argyll. The Laird of Drum suffered extremely in his worldly fortunes through his fidelity to the cause of the Stuarts. This would have been a natural reason for his declining a peerage offered him at the Restoration, and for his marrying, the second time, to win and not to spend. He took for his second wife Margaret Coutts (A 9), "a woman of inferior birth and manners, which step gave great offence to his relations" (Kinloch). He died in 1687. After the death of Irvine of Drum, Margaret Coutts married Irvine of Cults. She died in 1710, at the age of only forty-five.

A

a. Kinloch MSS., v, 9, in the handwriting of James Beattie. b. 'Laird of Drum,' Kinloch's Ancient Scottish Ballads, p. 199; "from recitation."

1 O IT fell out upon a day,
  When Drums was going to ride, O
  And there he met with a well-far'd
    may,
  Keeping her flocks on yon side. O

2 'O fair may, O rare may,
  Can not you fancy me?
  Of a' the lasses here about
  I like nane so well as thee.'

3 'Set your love on another, kind sir,
  Set it not on me,
  For I'm not fit to be your bride,
  And your whore I'll never be.'

4 Drums is to her father gane,
  Keeping his flocks on yon hill,
  And he has gotten his consent,
  And the maid was at his will.

5 'My daughter can neither read nor
    write,
  She was neer brought up at school;
  But well can she milk cow and ewe,
  And make a kebbuck well.

6 'She'll winn in your barn at bear-seed
    time,
  Cast out your muck at Yule;
  She'll saddle your steed in time o need,
  Draw aff your boots hersell.'

7 'Have not I no clergymen?
  Pay I no clergy fee?
  I'll school her as I think fit,
  And as I think fit to be.'

8 Drums is to the Highlands gane
  For to be made ready,
  And a' the gentry thereabout
  Says, Yonder comes Drums and his
    lady.

9 'Peggy Coutts is a very bonnie bride,
  And Drums is a wealthy laddie;
  But Drums might hae chosen a higher
    match
  Than any shepherd's daughter.'

10 Then up bespake his brother John,
   Says, Brother you 've done us wrong;
   You 've married ane below our degree,
   A stain to a' our kin.

11 'Hold your tongue, my brother John,
   I have done you no wrong;
   For I 've married ane to wirk and win,
   And ye 've married ane to spend.

12 'The last time that I had a wife,
   She was above my degree;
   I durst not come in her presence
   But with my hat on my knee.'

13 There was four-and-twenty gentlemen
   Stood at the yetts o Drum;
   There was na ane amang them a'
   That welcomd his lady in.

14 He 's taen her by the milk-white hand
   And led her in himsell,
   And in thro ha's and in thro bowers,
   'And you 're welcome, Lady o Drum.'

15 Thrice he kissd her cherry cheek,
   And thrice her cherry chin,
   And twenty times her comely mouth,
   'And you 're welcome, Lady o Drum.'

16 'Ye shall be cook in my kitchen,
   Butler in my ha;
   Ye shall be lady at my command
   When I ride far awa.'

17 'But what will I do when auld Drum
   dies,
   When auld Drum dies and leaves me ?
   Then I 'll tak back my word again,
   And the Coutts will come and see me.'

*   *   *   *   *

237

THE DUKE OF GORDON'S DAUGHTER

Nothing in the story of the ballad is known
to have even a shadow of foundation in fact.

a. 'The Duke of Gordon's Daughter,' The
Duke of Gordon's Garland, Percy Papers, and
another edition in a volume of garlands for-
merly in Heber's library. **b.** 'The Duke of
Gordon's Daughters,' a stall-copy, printed for
John Sinclair, Dumfries. **c.** 'The Duke of
Gordon's Daughters,' Stirling, printed by M.
Randall. **d.** 'The Duke of Gordon's Three
Daughters,' Peterhead, printed by P. Buchan.
e. 'The Duke of Gordon's Three Daughters,'
Kinloch MSS., I, 125. **f.** 'The Duke o Gordon's Daughters,' Murison MS., p. 90, Aberdeenshire. **g.** 'The Duke o Gordon's Daughter,' Gibb MS., p. 13, No. 3, from the recitation
of Mrs Gibb, senior. **h.** 'The Duke of Gordon's Three Daughters,' Macmath MS., p. 31,
a fragment recited by Mrs Macmath, senior, in
1874, and learned by her fifty years before. **i.**
Copy in a collection of folio sheet ballads, British Museum, 1346, m. 8, September, 1775.

1 THE Duke of Gordon has three daugh-
   ters,
   Elizabeth, Margaret, and Jean;
   They would not stay in bonny Castle
   Gordon,
   But they would go to bonny Aber-
   deen.

2 They had not been in Aberdeen
   A twelvemonth and a day
   Till Lady Jean fell in love with Captain
   Ogilvie,
   And away with him she would gae.

3 Word came to the Duke of Gordon,
   In the chamber where he lay,
   Lady Jean has fell in love with Captain
   Ogilvie,
   And away with him she would gae.

4 'Go saddle me the black horse,
   And you 'll ride on the grey,
   And I will ride to bonny Aberdeen,
   Where I have been many a day.'

5 They were not a mile from Aberdeen,
   A mile but only three,
   Till he met with his two daughters walk-
   ing,
   But away was Lady Jean.

6 'Where is your sister, maidens ?
   Where is your sister now ?
   Where is your sister, maidens,
   That she is not walking with you ? '

7 'O pardon us, honoured father,
   O pardon us,' they did say;
   'Lady Jean is with Captain Ogilvie,
   And away with him she will gae.'

8 When he came to Aberdeen,
  And down upon the green,
  There did he see Captain Ogilvie,
  Training up his men.

9 'O wo to you, Captain Ogilvie,
  And an ill death thou shalt die;
  For taking to thee my daughter,
  Hangëd thou shalt be.'

10 Duke Gordon has wrote a broad letter,
   And sent it to the king,
   To cause hang Captain Ogilvie
   If ever he hanged a man.

11 'I will not hang Captain Ogilvie,
   For no lord that I see;
   But I 'll cause him to put off the lace
     and scarlet,
   And put on the single livery.'

12 Word came to Captain Ogilvie,
   In the chamber where he lay,
   To cast off the gold lace and scarlet,
   And put on the single livery.

13 'If this be for bonny Jeany Gordon,
   This pennance I 'll take wi;
   If this be for bonny Jeany Gordon,
   All this I will dree.'

14 Lady Jean had not been married,
   Not a year but three,
   Till she had a babe in every arm,
   Another upon her knee.

15 'O but I 'm weary of wandering !
   O but my fortune is bad !
   It sets not the Duke of Gordon's daugh-
     ter
   To follow a soldier-lad.

16 'O but I 'm weary of wandering !
   O but I think lang !
   It sets not the Duke of Gordon's daugh-
     ter
   To follow a single man.'

17 When they came to the Highland hills,
   Cold was the frost and snow;
   Lady Jean's shoes they were all torn,
   No farther could she go.

18 'O wo to the hills and the mountains !
   Wo to the wind and the rain !

My feet is sore with going barefoot,
   No further am I able to gang.

19 'Wo to the hills and the mountains !
   Wo to the frost and the snow !
   My feet is sore with going barefoot,
   No farther am I able for to go.

20 'O if I were at the glens of Foudlen,
   Where hunting I have been,
   I would find the way to bonny Castle
     Gordon,
   Without either stockings or shoon.'

21 When she came to Castle Gordon,
   And down upon the green,
   The porter gave out a loud shout,
   'O yonder comes Lady Jean !'

22 'O you are welcome, bonny Jeany Gor-
     don,
   You are dear welcome to me;
   You are welcome, dear Jeany Gordon,
   But away with your Captain Ogilvie.'

23 Now over seas went the captain,
   As a soldier under command;
   A message soon followed after
   To come and heir his brother's land.

24 'Come home, you pretty Captain Ogil-
     vie,
   And heir your brother's land;
   Come home, ye pretty Captain Ogilvie,
   Be Earl of Northumberland.'

25 'O what does this mean ? ' says the cap-
     tain;
   'Where's my brother's children
     three ? '
   'They are dead and buried,
   And the lands they are ready for
     thee.'

26 'Then hoist up your sails, brave cap-
     tain,
   Let 's be jovial and free;
   I 'll to Northumberland and heir my
     estate,
   Then my dear Jeany I 'll see.'

27 He soon came to Castle Gordon,
   And down upon the green;
   The porter gave out with a loud shout,
   'Here comes Captain Ogilvie !'

28 'You 're welcome, pretty Captain Ogilvie,
    Your fortune 's advanced I hear;
No stranger can come unto my gates
    That I do love so dear.'

29 'Sir, the last time I was at your gates,
    You would not let me in;
I 'm come for my wife and children,
    No friendship else I claim.'

30 'Come in, pretty Captain Ogilvie,
    And drink of the beer and the wine;
And thou shalt have gold and silver
    To count till the clock strike nine.'

31 'I 'll have none of your gold or silver,
    Nor none of your white-money;
But I 'll have bonny Jeany Gordon,
    And she shall go now with me.'

32 Then she came tripping down the stair,
    With the tear into her eye;
One babe was at her foot,
    Another upon her knee.

33 'You 're welcome, bonny Jeany Gordon,
    With my young family;
Mount and go to Northumberland,
    There a countess thou shall be.'

238

GLENLOGIE, OR, JEAN O BETHELNIE

The earliest copy taken down is among the
Percy Papers (F), and was communicated to
Percy by R. Lambe, 1768, but it is not unvar-
nished tradition.

A

Skene MS., p. 13 ; taken down from recitation in the north of Scotland, 1802–3.

1 FOUR an twenty noblemen they rode
    thro Banchory fair,
But bonnie Glenlogie was flower [of a']
    that was there.

2 Four and twenty noblemen rode from
    Banchory ha,
But bonnie Glenlogie he was flower of
    them a'.

3 'O bonnie Glenlogie, be constant and
    kind,
An, bonnie Glenlogie, I 'll tell you my
    mind.

4 .   .   .   .   so frank and so
    free,
    .   .   .   and I get na Glenlogie,
    I 'll die.'

5 'O bonnie Jeanie, your portion 's but
    sma
To lay your love on me, that 's promist
    awa.'

6 Her cherry cheeks grew pale an wan;
    with the tear in her ee,
'Gin I get na Glenlogie, I surely will
    die.'

7 Ben came her father, steps to her bowr:
'Dear Jeanie, you 'r acting the part of
    a [whore].

8 'You 're seeking ane that cares na for
    thee;
Ye 's get Lord William, let Glenlogie
    be.'

9 'O had you still, father, let your folly
    be;
Gin I get na Glenlogie, I surely will
    die.'

10 Ben came her mother, steps on the floor:
'Dear daughter Jeanie, you 're acting
    the [whore],

11 'Seeking of ane that cares na for
    thee;
For ye 'll get Lord William, let Glen-
    logie be.'

12 'O had your tongue, mother, and let me
    be;
An I get na Glenlogie, I surely will die.'

13 O ben came her father's chaplain, a man
    of great skill,
And he has written a broad letter, and
    he has pennd it well.

14 H 'as pennd it well, an sent it awa
To bonnie Glenlogie, the flower of them
    a'.

15 When he got the letter, his tears did
        down fa ;
  'She's laid her love on me, that was
        promist awa.'

16 He calld on his servant wi speed, and
        bade him saddle his horses, and bri-
        dle them a':
  'For she has laid her love on me, altho
        I was promist awa.'

17 The horses were saddled wi speed, but
        ere they came he was four mile awa,
  To Jean of Bethelny, the flowr of them a'.

18 But when he came to her bowr she was
        pale and wan,
  But she grew red and ruddy when Glen-
        logie came in.

19 'Cheer up, bonnie Jeannie, ye are flowr
        o them a';
  I have laid my love on you, altho I was
        promist awa.'

20 Her beauty was charming, her tocher
        down tauld;
  Bonnie Jean of Bethelny was scarce fif-
        teen year auld.

B

'Glenlogie,' Sharpe's Ballad Book, p. 37, 1823.

1 FOUR and twenty nobles sits in the king's
        ha,
  Bonnie Glenlogie is the flower among
        them a'.

2 In came Lady Jean, skipping on the floor,
  And she has chosen Glenlogie 'mong a'
        that was there.

3 She turned to his footman, and thus she
        did say:
  Oh, what is his name ? and where does
        he stay ?

4 'His name is Glenlogie, when he is from
        home ;
  He is of the gay Gordons, his name it is
        John.'

5 'Glenlogie, Glenlogie, an you will prove
        kind,
  My love is laid on you ; I am telling my
        mind.'

6 He turned about lightly, as the Gordons
        does a':
  'I thank you, Lady Jean, my loves is
        promised awa.'

7 She called on her maidens her bed for
        to make,
  Her rings and her jewels all from her
        to take.

8 In came Jeanie's father, a wae man was
        he ;
  Says, I'll wed you to Drumfendrich, he
        has mair gold than he.

9 Her father's own chaplain, being a man
        of great skill,
  He wrote him a letter, and indited it
        well.

10 The first lines he looked at, a light laugh
        laughed he;
  But ere he read through it the tears
        blinded his ee.

11 Oh, pale and wan looked she when Glen-
        logie cam in,
  But even rosy grew she when Glenlogie
        sat down.

12 'Turn round, Jeanie Melville, turn round
        to this side,
  And I'll be the bridegroom, and you'll
        be the bride.'

13 Oh, 't was a merry wedding, and the por-
        tion down told,
  Of bonnie Jeanie Melville, who was scarce
        sixteen years old.

239

LORD SALTOUN AND
AUCHANACHIE

There can hardly be a doubt that this is one
of five ballads mentioned by Mrs. Brown in a
letter of Dec. 23, 1800, and called by her 'The
Lass o Philorth.' Philorth is the seat of the
Frasers of Saltoun, near Fraserburg, in the extreme northeast corner of Aberdeenshire.

A

'Lord Salton and Auchanachie.' a. Buchan's Ballads of the North of Scotland, II,

133, 1828. **b.** Maidment's North Countrie Garland, p. 10, 1824; Buchan's Gleanings, p. 161, 1825.

1 'AUCHANACHIE GORDON is bonny and braw,
  He would tempt any woman that ever he saw;
  He would tempt any woman, so has he tempted me,
  And I 'll die if I getna my love Auchanachie.'

2 In came her father, tripping on the floor,
  Says, Jeanie, ye 're trying the tricks o a whore;
  Ye 're caring for them that cares little for thee;
  Ye must marry Salton, leave Auchanachie.

3 'Auchanachie Gordon, he is but a man;
  Altho he be pretty, where lies his free land?
  Salton's lands they lie broad, his towers they stand hie,
  Ye must marry Salton, leave Auchanachie.

4 .   .   .   .   .   .
  .   .   .   .   .   .
  'Salton will gar you wear silk gowns fring'd to thy knee,
  But ye 'll never wear that wi your love Auchanachie.'

5 'Wi Auchanachie Gordon I would beg my bread
  Before that wi Salton I 'd wear gowd on my head,
  Wear gowd on my head, or gowns fring'd to the knee;
  And I 'll die if I getna my love Auchanachie.

6 'O Salton's [a] valley lies low by the sea,
  He 's bowed on the back, and thrawin on the knee;'

  .   .   .   .   .
  .   .   .   .   .

7 'O Salton's a valley lies low by the sea;
  Though he 's bowed on the back and thrawin on the knee,

Though he 's bowed on the back and thrawin on the knee,
  The bonny rigs of Salton they 're nae thrawin tee.'

8 'O you that are my parents to church may me bring,
  But unto young Salton I 'll never bear a son;
  For son or for daughter, I 'll ne'er bow my knee,
  And I 'll die if I getna my love Auchanachie.'

9 When Jeanie was married, from church was brought hame,
  When she wi her maidens sae merry shoud hae been,
  When she wi her maidens sae merry shoud hae been,
  She 's called for a chamber, to weep there her lane.

10 'Come to your bed, Jeanie, my honey and my sweet,
  For to stile you mistress I do not think it meet:'
  'Mistress or Jeanie, it is a' ane to me,
  It 's in your bed, Salton, I never will be.'

11 Then out spake her father, he spake wi renown;
  Some of you that are maidens, ye 'll loose aff her gown;
  Some of you that are maidens, ye 'll loose aff her gown,
  And I 'll mend the marriage wi ten thousand crowns.

12 Then ane of her maidens they loosed aff her gown,
  But bonny Jeanie Gordon she fell in a swoon;
  She fell in a swoon low down by their knee;
  Says, Look on, I die for my love Auchanachie!

13 That very same day Miss Jeanie did die,
  And hame came Auchanachie, hame frae the sea;
  Her father and mither welcomd him at the gate;
  He said, Where 's Miss Jeanie, that she 's nae here yet?

14 Then forth came her maidens, all wringing their hands,
Saying, Alas for your staying sae lang
frae the land !
Sae lang frae the land, and sae lang on
the fleed !
They 've wedded your Jeanie, and now
she is dead.

15 'Some of you, her maidens, take me by
the hand,
And show me the chamber Miss Jeanie
died in;'
He kissd her cold lips, which were colder
than stane,
And he died in the chamber that Jeanie
died in.

240

THE RANTIN LADDIE

The ' rantin' laddie ' turns out to be the Earl
of Aboyne, who is also celebrated in No. 235.

A

a. 'The Rantin Laddie,' Johnson's Musical
Museum, No. 462, p. 474, communicated by
Robert Burns; 1797. b. 'Lord Aboyne,' Buchan's Ballads of the North of Scotland, II, 66,
1828.

1 'AFTEN hae I playd at the cards and
the dice,
For the love of a bonie rantin laddie,
But now I maun sit in my father's
kitchen-neuk
And balow a bastard babie.

2 ' For my father he will not me own,
And my mother she neglects me,
And a' my friends hae lightlyed me,
And their servants they do slight
me.

3 ' But had I a servant at my command,
As aft times I 've had many,
That wad rin wi a letter to bonie Glens-
wood,
Wi a letter to my rantin laddie ! '

4 ' O is he either a laird or a lord,
Or is he but a cadie,
That ye do him ca sae aften by name
Your bonie, bonie rantin laddie ? '

5 'Indeed he is baith a laird and a lord,
And he never was a cadie,
But he is the Earl o bonie Aboyne,
And he is my rantin laddie.'

6 'O ye 'se get a servant at your com-
mand,
As aft times ye 've had many,
That sall rin wi a letter to bonie Glens-
wood,
A letter to your rantin laddie.'

7 When Lord Aboyne did the letter get,
O but he blinket bonie !
But or he had read three lines of it
I think his heart was sorry.

8 'O wha is [this] daur be sae bauld
Sae cruelly to use my lassie ?

. . . . . .

. . . . .

9 'For her father he will not her know,
And her mother she does slight her,
And a' her friends hae lightlied her,
And their servants they neglect her.

10 'Go raise to me my five hundred men,
Make haste and make them ready,
With a milk-white steed under every
ane,
For to bring hame my lady.'

11 As they cam in thro Buchanshire,
They were a company bonie,
With a gude claymor in every hand,
And O but they shin'd bonie !

241

THE BARON O LEYS

This ballad purports to relate an escapade
of one of the Burnetts of Leys, Kincardine-
shire.

A

Skene MS., p. 20; taken down in the north
of Scotland, 1802-3.

1 THE Laird of Leys is on to Edinbrugh,
To shaw a fit o his follie;
He drest himsel in the crimson-brown,
An he provd a rantin laddie.

2 Ben came a weel-faird lass,
　　Says, Laddie, how do they ca ye ?
　‘ They ca me this, an they ca me that,
　　Ye wudna ken fat they ca me ;
　But whan I 'm at home on bonnie Dee-
　　side
　　They ca me The Rantin Laddie.’

3 They sought her up, they sought her
　　down,
　　They sought her in the parlour ;
　She coudna be got but whar she was,
　　In the bed wi The Rantin Laddie.

4 ‘ Tell me, tell me, Baron of Leys,
　　Ye tell me how they ca ye !
　Your gentle blood moves in my side,
　　An I dinna ken how they ca ye.’

5 ‘ They ca me this, an they ca me that,
　　Ye couldna ken how they ca me ;
　But whan I 'm at home on bonnie Dee-
　　side
　　They ca me The Rantin Laddie.’

6 ‘ Tell me, tell me, Baron of Leys,
　　Ye tell me how they ca ye !
　Your gentle blood moves in my side,
　　An I dinna ken how to ca ye.’

7 ‘ Baron of Leys, it is my stile,
　　Alexander Burnett they ca me ;
　Whan I 'm at hame on bonnie Deeside
　　My name is The Rantin Laddie.’

8 ‘ Gin your name be Alexander Burnett,
　　Alas that ever I saw ye !
　For ye hae a wife and bairns at hame,
　　An alas for lyin sae near ye !

9 ‘ But I 'se gar ye be headit or hangt,
　　Or marry me the morn,
　Or else pay down ten thousand crowns
　　For giein o me the scorn.’

10 ‘ For my head, I canna want ;
　　I love my lady dearly ;
　But some o my lands I maun lose in the
　　case,
　　Alas for lyin sae near ye !’

11 Word has gane to the Lady of Leys
　　That the laird he had a bairn ;
　The warst word she said to that was,
　　‘ I wish I had it in my arms.

12 ‘ For I will sell my jointure-lands —
　　I am broken an I 'm sorry —
　An I 'll sell a', to my silk gowns,
　　An get hame my rantin laddie.’

242

THE COBLE O CARGILL

Stobhall is on the left bank of the Tay, eight miles above Perth, in Cargill parish, and Cargill is a little farther up. Balathy is opposite Cargill, and Kercock is higher up the river on the right bank. The local tradition, as given by Motherwell in his manuscript and his book, is that the butler of Stobhall had a leman both at Kercock and at Balathy. Upon an occasion when the butler had gone to Kercock, the lass of Balathy scuttled the coble, which he had left below, "and waited his return, deeming that her suspicions of his infidelity would be well founded if he took the boat without visiting her in passing." The butler took the boat without stopping at Balathy, and in her sight the weary coble sank. Local tradition in such cases seldom means more than a theory which people have formed to explain a preëxisting ballad.

‘ The Coble o Cargill,’ Motherwell's MS., p. 80 ; ‘ The Weary Coble o Cargill,’ Motherwell's Minstrelsy, p. 230. Communicated to Motherwell by William George, tenant in Cambus Michael, Perthshire, who took it from the recitation of an old woman.

1 DAVID DRUMMOND'S destinie,
　　Gude man o appearance o Cargill ;
　I wat his blude rins in the flude,
　　Sae sair against his parents' will.

2 She was the lass of Balathy toun,
　　And he the butler o Stobhall,
　And mony a time she wauked late
　　To bore the coble o Cargill.

3 His bed was made in Kercock ha,
　　Of gude clean sheets and of [the]
　　hay ;
　He wudna rest ae nicht therein,
　　But on the prude waters he wud gae.

4 His bed was made in Balathy toun,
　　Of the clean sheets and of the strae ;
　But I wat it was far better made
　　Into the bottom o bonnie Tay.

5 She bored the coble in seven pairts,
   I wat her heart might hae been fu
      sair;
   For there she got the bonnie lad lost
      Wi the curly locks and the yellow
      hair.

6 He put his foot into the boat,
   He little thocht o ony ill;
   But before that he was mid-waters,
      The weary coble began to fill.

7 'Woe be to the lass o Balathy toun,
   I wat an ill death may she die!
   For she bored the coble in seven pairts,
      And let the waters perish me.

8 'Oh, help, oh help, I can get nane,
   Nae help o man can to me come!'
   This was about his dying words,
      When he was choaked up to the
      chin.

9 'Gae tell my father and my mother
   It was naebody did me this ill;
   I was a-going my ain errands,
      Lost at the coble o bonnie Cargill.'

10 She bored the boat in seven pairts,
   I wat she bored it wi gude will;
   And there they got the bonnie lad's
      corpse,
   In the kirk-shot o bonnie Cargill.

11 Oh a' the keys o bonnie Stobha
   I wat they at his belt did hing;
   But a' the keys of bonnie Stobha
      They now ly low into the stream.

12 A braver page into his age
   Neer set a foot upon the plain;
   His father to his mother said,
   'Oh, sae soon as we've wanted him!

13 'I wat they had mair luve than this
   When they were young and at the
      scule;
   But for his sake she wauked late,
      And bored the coble o bonnie Cargill.'

14 'There's neer a clean sark gae on my
      back,
   Nor yet a kame gae in my hair;
   There's neither coal nor candle-licht
      Shall shine in my bouir for evir mair.

15 'At kirk nor market I'se neer be at,
   Nor yet a blythe blink in my ee;
   There's neer a ane shall say to anither,
      That's the lassie gard the young man
      die.

16 'Between the yates o bonnie Stobha
   And the kirk-style o bonnie Cargill,
   There is mony a man and mother's son
      That was at my love's burial.'

243

JAMES HARRIS
(THE DÆMON LOVER)

There are several copies of the broadside
version (A); that in the Pepys collection was
printed for Thackeray and Passenger, and the
ballad is No. 71 in Thackeray's list, printed
1685. 'The Dæmon Lover' was first published
in Scott's Minstrelsy, 5th edition, 1812 (F).
William Laidlaw, who furnished the copy, inserted four stanzas of his own (here omitted).
D (probably by the fortunate accident of being
a fragment) leaves us to put our own construction upon the weird seaman; and though it retains the homely ship-carpenter, is on the whole
the most satisfactory of all the versions.

A

A Warning for Married Women, being an
example of Mrs Jane Reynolds (a West-country
woman), born near Plymouth, who, having
plighted her troth to a Seaman, was afterwards
married to a Carpenter, and at last carried
away by a Spirit, the manner how shall presently be recited. To a West-country tune
called 'The Fair Maid of Bristol,' 'Bateman,'
or 'John True.' Pepys Ballads, IV, 101.

1 THERE dwelt a fair maid in the West,
   Of worthy birth and fame,
   Neer unto Plimouth, stately town,
      Jane Reynolds was her name.

2 This damsel dearly was belovd
   By many a proper youth,
   And what of her is to be said
      Is known for very truth.

3 Among the rest a seaman brave
   Unto her a wooing came;
   A comely proper youth he was,
      James Harris calld by name.

4 The maid and young man was agreed,
    As time did them allow,
And to each other secretly
    They made a solemn vow,

5 That they would ever faithfull be
    Whilst Heaven afforded life;
He was to be her husband kind,
    And she his faithfull wife.

6 A day appointed was also
    When they was to be married;
But before these things were brought to pass
Matters were strangely carried.

7 All you that faithfull lovers be
    Give ear and hearken well,
And what of them became at last
    I will directly tell.

8 The young man he was prest to sea,
    And forcèd was to go;
His sweet-heart she must stay behind,
    Whether she would or no.

9 And after he was from her gone
    She three years for him staid,
Expecting of his comeing home,
    And kept herself a maid.

10 At last news came that he was dead
    Within a forraign land,
And how that he was buried
    She well did understand,

11 For whose sweet sake the maiden she
    Lamented many a day,
And never was she known at all
    The wanton for to play.

12 A carpenter that livd hard by,
    When he heard of the same,
Like as the other had done before,
    To her a wooing came.

13 But when that he had gained her love
    They married were with speed,
And four years space, being man and wife,
    They loveingly agreed.

14 Three pritty children in this time
    This loving couple had,

Which made their father's heart rejoyce,
    And mother wondrous glad.

15 But as occasion servd, one time
    The good man took his way
Some three days journey from his home,
    Intending not to stay.

16 But, whilst that he was gone away,
    A spirit in the night
Came to the window of his wife,
    And did her sorely fright.

17 Which spirit spake like to a man,
    And unto her did say,
'My dear and onely love,' quoth he,
    'Prepare and come away.

18 'James Harris is my name,' quoth he,
    'Whom thou didst love so dear,
And I have traveld for thy sake
    At least this seven year.

19 'And now I am returnd again,
    To take thee to my wife,
And thou with me shalt go to sea,
    To end all further strife.'

20 'O tempt me not, sweet James,' quoth she,
    'With thee away to go;
If I should leave my children small,
    Alas! what would they do?

21 'My husband is a carpenter,
    A carpenter of great fame;
I would not for five hundred pounds
    That he should know the same.'

22 'I might have had a king's daughter,
    And she would have married me;
But I forsook her golden crown,
    And for the love of thee.

23 'Therefore, if thou 'lt thy husband forsake,
    And thy children three also,
I will forgive the[e] what is past,
    If thou wilt with me go.'

24 'If I forsake my husband and
    My little children three,
What means hast thou to bring me to,
    If I should go with thee?'

25 'I have seven ships upon the sea;
      When they are come to land,
   Both marriners and marchandize
      Shall be at thy command.

26 'The ship wherein my love shall sail
      Is glorious to behold;
   The sails shall be of finest silk,
      And the mast of shining gold.'

27 When he had told her these fair tales,
      To love him she began,
   Because he was in human shape,
      Much like unto a man.

28 And so together away they went
      From off the English shore,
   And since that time the woman-kind
      Was never seen no more.

29 But when her husband he come home
      And found his wife was gone,
   And left her three sweet pretty babes
      Within the house alone,

30 He beat his breast, he tore his hair,
      The tears fell from his eyes,
   And in the open streets he run
      With heavy doleful cries.

31 And in this sad distracted case
      He hangd himself for woe
   Upon a tree near to the place;
      The truth of all is so.

32 The children now are fatherless,
      And left without a guide,
   But yet no doubt the heavenly powers
      Will for them well provide.

D

'The Carpenter's Wife,' Kinloch MSS., I,
297; from the recitation of T. Kinnear, Stone-
haven.

1 'O WHARE hae ye been, my dearest dear,
      These seven lang years and more ?'
   'O I am come to seek my former vows,
      That ye promisd me before.'

2 'Awa wi your former vows,' she says,
      'Or else ye will breed strife;
   Awa wi your former vows,' she says,
      'For I 'm become a wife.

3 'I am married to a ship-carpenter,
      A ship-carpenter he 's bound;
   I wadna he kend my mind this nicht
      For twice five hundred pound.'

*   *   *   *   *

4 She has put her foot on gude ship-board,
      And on ship-board she 's gane,
   And the veil that hung oure her face
      Was a' wi gowd begane.

5 She had na sailed a league, a league,
      A league but barely twa,
   Till she did mind on the husband she left,
      And her wee young son alsua.

6 'O haud your tongue, my dearest dear,
      Let all your follies abee;
   I 'll show whare the white lillies grow,
      On the banks of Italie.'

7 She had na sailed a league, a league,
      A league but barely three,
   Till grim, grim grew his countenance,
      And gurly grew the sea.

8 'O haud your tongue, my dearest dear,
      Let all your follies abee;
   I 'll show whare the white lillies grow,
      In the bottom of the sea.'

9 He 's tane her by the milk-white hand,
      And he 's thrown her in the main;
   And full five-and-twenty hundred ships
      Perishd all on the coast of Spain.

F

'The Dæmon Lover,' Minstrelsy of the Scottish Border, 5th edition, 1812, II, 427; taken
down from the recitation of Walter Grieve by
William Laidlaw.

1 'O WHERE have you been, my long, long
      love,
      This long seven years and mair ?'
   'O I 'm come to seek my former vows
      Ye granted me before.'

2 'O hold your tongue of your former
      vows,
      For they will breed sad strife;
   O hold your tongue of your former
      vows,
      For I am become a wife.'

3 He turned him right and round about,
 And the tear blinded his ee:
'I wad never hae trodden on Irish
  ground,
  If it had not been for thee.'

4 'I might hae had a king's daughter,
 Far, far beyond the sea;
I might have had a king's daughter,
 Had it not been for love o thee.'

5 'If ye might have had a king's daughter,
 Yer sel ye had to blame;
Ye might have taken the king's daugh·
  ter,
  For ye kend that I was nane.

6 'If I was to leave my husband dear,
 And my two babes also,
O what have you to take me to,
 If with you I should go?'

7 'I hae seven ships upon the sea —
 The eighth brought me to land —
With four-and-twenty bold mariners,
 And music on every hand.'

8 She has taken up her two little babes,
 Kissd them baith cheek and chin:
'O fair ye weel, my ain two babes,
 For I 'll never see you again.'

9 She set her foot upon the ship,
 No mariners could she behold;
But the sails were o the taffetie,
 And the masts o the beaten gold.

10 She had not sailed a league, a league,
 A league but barely three,
When dismal grew his countenance,
 And drumlie grew his ee.

11 They had not saild a league, a league,
 A league but barely three,
Until she espied his cloven foot,
 And she wept right bitterlie.

12 'O hold your tongue of your weeping,'
  says he,
'Of your weeping now let me be;
I will shew you how the lilies grow
 On the banks of Italy.'

13 'O what hills are yon, yon pleasant hills,
 That the sun shines sweetly on?'

'O yon are the hills of heaven,' he said,
 'Where you will never win.'

14 'O whaten a mountain is yon,' she said,
 'All so dreary wi frost and snow?'
'O yon is the mountain of hell,' he cried,
 'Where you and I will go.'

15 He strack the tap-mast wi his hand,
 The fore-mast wi his knee,
And he brake that gallant ship in twain,
 And sank her in the sea.

244

JAMES HATLEY

In a version in Motherwell's MS. (C), Fenwick becomes Phenix and James Hatley becomes Jamie O'Lee.

A

a. Scotch Ballads, Materials for Border Minstrelsy, No. 35, MS. of Thomas Wilkie, p. 6,
Abbotsford; "from Betty Hoyl, who learned
it from her mother." Gattonside. b. 'James
Hatley,' Campbell MSS., II, 289. c. 'James
Hatelie,' R. Chambers, The Romantic Scottish
Ballads, etc., 1859, p. 37; "taken down many
years ago from the singing of an old man in the
south of Scotland."

1 IT happened once upon a time,
 When the king he was from home,
Sir Fenwick he has stolen his jewels,
 And laid the blame on James Hatley.

2 James Hatley was in prison strong,
 A wait he was condemned to die;
There was not one in all the court
 To speak one word for James Hatley.

3 No one but the king's daughter,
 A wait she loved him tenderlie;
She 's stolen the keys from her father's
  head,
 And gaed and conversed wi James
  Hatley.

4 'Come, tell to me now, James,' she said,
 'Come, tell to me if thou hast them
  stolen,
And I 'll make a vow, and I 'll keep it
  true,
 Ye shall never be the worse of me.'

5 'I have not stolen them, lady,' he said,
 'Nor as little it was intended by me;
Sir Fenwick he has stolen them himself;
 A wait he has laid the blame on me.'

6 'One asking, one asking, father dear,
 One asking, one asking grant to me,
For I never asked one in my life;
 I am sure you cannot but grant it to
  me.'

7 'Weel ask it, weel ask it, daughter dear,
 Ask it, and it granted shall be;
If it should be my hale estate,
 Naesaid, naesaid, it shall not be.'

8 'I want none of your gold, father,
 And I want none of your fee;
All that I ask, father dear,
 It is the life of James Hatley.'

9 'Weel ask it, weel ask it, daughter dear,
 Weel ask it, and it answerëd shall
  be;
For I'll make a vow, and I'll keep it
  true,
James Hatley shall never hangëd be.'

10 'Another asking, father dear,
 Another asking grant to me;
Let Fenwick and Hatley go [to] the
  sword,
And let them try their verity.'

11 ''T is weel askëd, daughter dear,
 'T is weel asked, and it granted shall
  be;
For eer the morn or twelve o'clock
 They both at the point of the sword
  shall be.'

12 James Hatley was fifteen years old,
 Sir Fenwick he was thirty three;
But James lap about, and he struck about,
 Till he's gaen Sir Fenwick wounds
  three.

13 'Hold up, hold up, James Hatley,' he
  cry'd,
'And let my breath go out and in;
For I have stolen them myself,
 More shame and disgrace it is to me.'

14 Up and spake an English lord,
 And O but he spake haughtily !

'I would reather given my whole estates
 Before ye had not hanged James Hatley.'

15 But up and spake a Scottish lord,
 And O but he spake boldly !
'I would reather hae foughten among
  blood to the knees
Before ye had hanged James Hatley.'

16 Up and spake the king's eldest son,
 'Come hame, James Hatley, and dine
  wi me;
For I've made a vow, I'll keep it true.
 Ye's be my captain by land and by
  sea.'

17 Up and spake the king's daughter,
 'Come hame, James Hatley, and dine
  wi me;
For I've made a vow, I'll keep it true,
 I'll never marry a man but thee.'

245

YOUNG ALLAN

This ballad is mixed with 'Sir Patrick Spens'
(No. 58). By far the most interesting feature
in it is Allan's addressing his ship and the ship's
intelligent behavior. Such ships are known
elsewhere in popular tradition. In one of the
best of the Danish ballads (Grundtvig, No. 50),
the Ox, when sailed by St Olav, responds to his
commands as if fully endowed with conscious-
ness ; he thwacks it in the side and over the
eye, and it goes faster and faster ; but it is ani-
mate only for the nonce. The Phæacian ships
have neither helmsman nor he'm, and know
men's minds and the way to all cities : Odyssey,
viii, 557 ff. There is a magical self-moving
ship in Marie de France's Guigemar, and elsewhere.

A*

The Old Lady's Collection, MS., No. 4.

1 Aa the skippers of bonny Lothen,
 As they sat att the wine,
Ther fell a rosin them among,
 An it was in an unhappy time.

2 Some of them roused ther haks,
 An some of them ther hounds,
An some of them ther gay ladys,
 Trood neat on the plain:

Young Allan he roused his comely
    coug,
  That lay upon the strand.

3 'I haa as good a ship this day
    As ever sailled our seas,
  Except it be the Burges Black,
    Bat an the Small Cordvine,
  The comly coug of Dornisdall;
    We sall lay that three bay in time.'

4 Out spak a littel boy,
    Just att Young Allan's knee,
  'Ye lie, ye lie, ye Young Allan,
    Sae loud as I hear ye lie.

5 'For my master has a littel boat
    Will sail thris as well as thin;
  For she 'll come in att your formast
    An gee out att yer forlee,
  An nine times in a winter night
    She 'll take the wine fra the.

6 'O fatt will ye wade, ye Young Allan,
    Or fatt will ye wad we me ?'
  'I ill wad my head agenst yer land,
    Till I gett more monie.'

7 They hed na sailed a legg, [a legg,]
    A legg bat bairly three,
  Till throug an throu ther bonny ship
    They saa the green wall sea.

8 They had na sailled a leag, [a leag,]
    A leag bat barly fave,
  Till through en throu ther bonny ship
    They saa the green wall wave.

9 He gied up to the tapmast,
    To see fat he coud see,
  An ther he saa the Burges Black,
    Bat an the Small Cordvine,
  The comly coug of Dornasdell;
    The three was rent in nine.

10 Young Allan he grat, an he wrang his
    hans,
  An he kent na fat till dee:
  'The win is loud, an the waves is prood,
    An we will a' sink in the sea.

11 'Bat gin I cod gett a bonny boy
    To tak my healm in han,
  . . . . that wad bring
    My bonny ship safe to lan,

12 'He sud gett the tua part of my
    goud,
    An the therd part of my lan,
  An gin we wine safe to shor
    He sud gett my daughter Ann.'

13 'Hear am I, a bonny boy
    That will take yer helm in han,
  . . . . an will bring
    Your bonny ship safe to land.

14 'Ye take four-an-twenty fether-beds,
    An ye lay the bonny ship roun,
  An as much of the good cannis
    As make her hell an soun.'

15 They took four-an-tuenty fether-beds,
    An laid the bonny ship roun,
  An as much of the good canies
    As made her hell an soun.

16 'Spring up, my bony ship,
    An goud sall be yer hair !'
  Fan the bonny ship hard of that,
    Att goud sud be her hire,
  She sprang as fast fra the sate water
    As the spark dis frae the fire.

17 'Spring up, my bonny ship,
    An goud sall be yer fee !'
  An fan the bonny ship hard of that,
    Goud was to be her fee,
  She sprang as fast fra the sat water
    As the life dos fra the tree.

18 The salors stans on the shore-sid,
    We ther ill-bukled shen:
  'Thanks to God an our gued mas-
    ter
    That ever we came to land !'

19 'Far is the bonny boy
    That took my healm in hand ?
  . . . that brought
    My bonny ship safe to land ?

20 'He 's gett the twa part of my goud,
    The therd part of my lan,
  An since we ha wone safe to shore
    He 's gett my doughter Ann.'

21 'Hear am I, the bonny boy
    That took yer healm in han,
  That brought yer bonny ship,
    An brought her safe to lan.

22 ‘ I winnë ha the tua part of yer goud,
   Nor the therd part of yer lan,
   Bat since we ha wine safe to shor
   I will wed yer daugter Ann.’

23 Fortey ships went to the sea,
   Forty ships an five,
   An ther came never on back
   Bat Young Allan alive.

246

REDESDALE AND WISE WILLIAM

This ballad may be an offshoot from a widely
spread story which is tediously told further on
in ‘ The Twa Knights ’ (No. 268). A, sts. 1, 2, 5,
are substantially a repetition of No. 245, A, 1,
2, 6, etc.

A

‘ Reedisdale and Wise William,’ Buchan’s
Ballads of the North of Scotland, ii, 701, written down from memory by Mr Nicol, Strichen,
as learned in his earlier years from old people ;
Motherwell’s MS., p. 452 ; Motherwell’s Minstrelsy, p. 298.

1 WHEN Reedisdale and Wise William
   Were drinking at the wine,
   There fell a roosing them amang,
   On an unruly time.

2 For some o them hae roosd their hawks,
   And other some their hounds,
   And other some their ladies fair,
   And their bowers whare they walkd in.

3 When out it spake him Reedisdale,
   And a rash word spake he ;
   Says, There is not a lady fair,
   In bower wherever she be,
   But I could aye her favour win
   Wi ae blink o my ee.

4 Then out it spake him Wise William,
   And a rash word spake he ;
   Says, I have a sister of my own,
   In bower where ever she be,
   And ye will not her favour win
   With three blinks of your ee.

5 ‘ What will ye wager, Wise William ?
   My lands I ’ll wad with thee ; ’

‘ I ’ll wad my head against your land,
   Till I get more monie.’

6 Then Reedisdale took Wise William,
   Laid him in prison strang,
   That he might neither gang nor ride,
   Nor ae word to her send.

7 But he has written a braid letter,
   Between the night and day,
   And sent it to his own sister
   By dun feather and gray.

8 When she had read Wise William’s
   letter,
   She smilëd and she leugh ;
   Said, Very well, my dear brother,
   Of this I have eneuch.

9 She looked out at her west window
   To see what she could see,
   And there she spied him Reedisdale
   Come riding ower the lea.

10 Says, Come to me, my maidens all,
   Come hitherward to me ;
   For here it comes him Reedisdale,
   Who comes a-courting me.

11 ‘ Come down, come down, my lady
   fair,
   A sight of you give me ; ’
   ‘ Go from my yetts now, Reedisdale,
   For me you will not see.’

12 ‘ Come down, come down, my lady
   fair,
   A sight of you give me ;
   And bonny are the gowns of silk
   That I will give to thee.’

13 ‘ If you have bonny gowns of silk,
   O mine is bonny tee ;
   Go from my yetts now, Reedisdale,
   For me you shall not see.’

14 ‘ Come down, come down, my lady fair,
   A sight of you I ’ll see ;
   And bonny jewels, brooches and rings
   I will give unto thee.’

15 ‘ If you have bonny brooches and rings,
   O mine are bonny tee ;
   Go from my yetts now, Reedisdale,
   For me you shall not see.’

16 'Come down, come down, my lady
        fair,
    One sight of you I 'll see;
    And bonny are the ha's and bowers
        That I will give to thee.'

17 'If you have bonny ha's and bowers,
        O mine are bonny tee;
    Go from my yetts now, Reedisdale,
        For me you shall not see.'

18 'Come down, come down, my lady fair,
        A sight of you I 'll see;
    And bonny are my lands so broad
        That I will give to thee.'

19 'If you have bonny lands so broad,
        O mine are bonny tee;
    Go from my yetts now, Reedisdale,
        For me ye will not see.'

20 'Come down, come down, my lady fair,
        A sight of you I 'll see;
    And bonny are the bags of gold
        That I will give to thee.'

21 'If you have bonny bags of gold,
        I have bags of the same;
    Go from my yetts now, Reedisdale,
        For down I will not come.'

22 'Come down, come down, my lady fair,
        One sight of you I 'll see;
    Or else I 'll set your house on fire,
        If better cannot be.'

23 Then he has set the house on fire,
        And all the rest it tuke;
    He turned his wight horse head about,
        Said, Alas, they 'll ne'er get out!

24 'Look out, look out, my maidens fair,
        And see what I do see,
    How Reedisdale has fired our house,
        And now rides oer the sea.

25 'Come hitherwards, my maidens fair,
        Come hither unto me;
    For thro this reek, and thro this smeek,
        O thro it we must be!'

26 They took wet mantles them about,
        Their coffers by the band,
    And thro the reek, and thro the flame,
        Alive they all have wan.

27 When they had got out thro the fire,
        And able all to stand,
    She sent a maid to Wise William,
        To bruik Reedisdale's land.

28 'Your lands is mine now, Reedisdale,
        For I have won them free;'
    'If there is a gude woman in the world,
        Your one sister is she.'

247

LADY ELSPAT

This ballad was No. 10 of the fifteen of Mrs
Brown's which were obtained by William
Tytler from Professor Thomas Gordon in 1783.

'Lady Elspat.' a. Jamieson-Brown MS., p.
19. Printed in Jamieson's Popular Ballads, II,
191. b. Scottish Songs, MS., fol. 30, Abbotsford Library, N. 3, in the handwriting of Walter
Scott, about 1795.

1 'How brent is your brow, my Lady
        Elspat!
    How golden yallow is your hair!
    Of all the maids of fair Scotland,
        There 's nane like Lady Elspat fair.'

2 'Perform your vows, Sweet William,'
        she says,
    'The vows which ye ha made to
        me,
    An at the back o my mother's castle
        This night I 'll surely meet wi thee'

3 But wae be to her brother's page,
        Who heard the words this twa did
        say!
    He 's told them to her lady mother,
        Who wrought Sweet William mieckle
        wae.

4 For she has taen him Sweet William,
        An she 's gard bind him wi his bow
        string
    Till the red bluide o his fair body
        Frae ilka nail o his hand did spring.

5 O it fell once upon a time
        That the Lord Justice came to town
    Out has she taen him Sweet William,
        Brought him before Lord Justice
        boun.

6 'An what is the crime, now, madame,'
    he says,
    'Has been committed by this young
        man?'
  'O he has broken my bonny castel,
    That was well biggit wi lime an stane.

7 'An he has broken my bonny coffers,
    That was well banded wi aiken ban,
  An he has stoln my rich jewels;
    I wot he has them every one.'

8 Then out it spake her Lady Elspat,
    As she sat by Lord Justice knee;
  'Now ye hae taul your tale, mother,
    I pray, Lord Justice, you'l now hear
        me.

9 'He has na broken her bonny castel,
    That was well biggit wi lime an stane,
  Nor has he stoln her rich jewels,
    For I wot she has them every one.

10 'But tho he was my first true love,
    An tho I had sworn to be his bride,
  Cause he had not a great estate,
    She would this way our loves divide.'

11 An out it spake the Lord Justice,
    I wot the tear was in his ee;
  'I see nae fault in this young man,
    Sae loose his bans, an set him free.

12 'Take back your love, now, Lady Els-
        pat,
    An my best blessing you baith upon!
  For gin he be your first true love,
    He is my eldest sister's son.

13 'There is a steed in my stable
    Cost me baith gold and white money;
  Ye's get as mieckle o my free lan
    As he'll ride about in a summer's
        day.'

248

THE GREY COCK, OR, SAW
YOU MY FATHER?

This piece is a variety of the *aube* (concerning which species see Jeanroy, Les Origines de
la Poésie lyrique en France, chapter 3), but is
none the less quite modern.   There are French
and Italian ballads of the same general description.   The treacherous or troublesome
bird is in French the lark, in one case the cock;
in Italian the swallow.

a. 'The Grey Cock,' Herd's Ancient and
Modern Scots Songs, 1769, p. 324; Herd's
MSS., I, 4; Herd's Ancient and Modern Scot-
tish Songs, 1776, II, 208. b. 'Saw you my
father?' Chappell's Popular Music of the
Olden Time, p. 731.

1 'O SAW ye my father? or saw ye my
        mother?
    Or saw ye my true-love John?'
  'I saw not your father, I saw not your
        mother,
    But I saw your true-love John.

2 'It's now ten at night, and the stars gie
        nae light,
    And the bells they ring ding, dang;
  He's met wi some delay that causeth
        him to stay,
    But he will be here ere lang.'

3 The surly auld carl did naething but
        snarl,
    And Johny's face it grew red;
  Yet, tho he often sighd, he neer a word
        replied
    Till all were asleep in bed.

4 Up Johny rose, and to the door he goes,
    And gently tirlëd the pin;
  The lassie taking tent unto the door she
        went,
    And she opend and let him in.

5 'And are ye come at last? and do I
        hold ye fast?
    And is my Johny true?'
  'I hae nae time to tell, but sae lang's
        I like mysell
    Sae lang will I love you.'

6 'Flee, flee up, my bonny grey cock,
    And craw whan it is day;
  Your neck shall be like the bonny beaten
        gold,
    And your wings of the silver grey.'

7 The cock prov'd false, and untrue he was,
    For he crew an hour oer soon;
  The lassie thought it day when she sent
        her love away,
    And it was but a blink of the moon.

249

AULD MATRONS

This piece was made by some one who had acquaintance with the first fit of 'Adam Bell.' The anonymous 'old wife' becomes 'auld Matrons;' Inglewood, Ringlewood. The conclusion is in imitation of the rescues in Robin Hood ballads.

'Auld Matrons,' Buchan's Ballads of the North of Scotland, II, 238; Motherwell's MS., p. 585, with the title 'Love Annie.'

1 MY love she is a gentlewoman,
    Has her living by the seam;
I kenna how she is provided
    This night for me and my foot-
        groom.

2 He is gane to Annie's bower-door,
    And gently tirled at the pin:
'Ye sleep, ye wake, my love Annie,
    Ye 'll rise and lat your true-love
        in.'

3 Wi her white fingers lang and sma
    She gently lifted up the pin;
Wi her arms lang and bent
    She kindly caught sweet Willie in.

4 'O will ye go to cards or dice?
    Or will ye go to play?
Or will ye go to a well made bed,
    And sleep a while till day?'

5 'I winna gang to cards nor dice,
    Nor yet will I to play;
But I will gang to a well made bed,
    And sleep a while till day.

6 'My love Annie, my dear Annie,
    I would be at your desire;
But wae mat fa the auld Matrons,
    As she sits by the kitchen fire!'

7 'Keep up your heart, Willie,' she said,
    'Keep up your heart, dinna fear;
It 's seven years, and some guid mair,
    Sin her foot did file the flear.'

8 They hadna kissd nor love clapped,
    As lovers when they meet,
Till up it raise the auld Matrons,
    Sae well 's she spread her feet.

9 O wae mat fa the auld Matrons,
    Sae clever 's she took the gate!
And she 's gaen ower yon lang, lang hill,
    Knockd at the sheriff's yate.

10 'Ye sleep, ye wake, my lord?' she said;
    'Are ye not your bower within?
There 's a knight in bed wi your daugh-
        ter,
    I fear she 's gotten wrang.'

11 'Ye 'll do ye down thro Kelso town,
    Waken my wall-wight men;
And gin ye hae your wark well dune
    I 'll be there at command.'

12 She 's done her down thro Kelso town,
    Wakend his wall-wight men;
But gin she had her wark well done
    He was there at command.

13 He had his horse wi corn fodderd,
    His men armd in mail;
He gae the Matrons half a merk
    To show them ower the hill.

14 Willie sleepd, but Annie waked
    Till she heard their bridles ring;
Then tapped on her love's shoulder,
    And said, Ye 've sleepit lang.

15 'O save me, save me, my blessd lady,
    Till I 've on my shooting-gear;
I dinna fear the king himsell,
    Tho he an 's men were here.'

16 Then they shot in, and Willie out,
    The arrows graz'd his brow;
The maid she wept and tore her hair,
    Says, This can never do.

17 Then they shot in, and he shot out,
    The bow brunt Willie's hand;
But aye he kissd her ruby lips,
    Said, My dear, thinkna lang.

18 He set his horn to his mouth,
    And has blawn loud and shrill,
And he 's calld on his brother John,
    In Ringlewood he lay still.

19 The first an shot that Lord John shot,
    He wound fifty and fifteen;
The next an shot that Lord John shot,
    He ca'd out the sheriff's een.

20 'O some o you lend me an arm,
  Some o you lend me twa;
And they that came for strife this day,
  Take horse, ride fast awa.

21 'But wae mat fa you, auld Matrons,
  An ill death mat ye die !
I 'll burn you on yon high hill-head,
  Blaw your ashes in the sea.'

250

HENRY MARTYN

This ballad must have sprung from the ashes
of 'Sir Andrew Barton' (No. 167). E comes
nearer than the others to the original, but sts.
11–13 are derived from No. 287, sts. 8, 10.
Only one copy (A a) preserves the trait of Barton's death, an incident not quite in keeping
with the rest of the story of the new ballad.

A

'Henry Martyn,' taken down by the Rev.
S. Baring-Gould. a. From Matthew Baker,
an old cripple, Lew Down, Devon. b. From
Roger Luxton, an old man at Halwell, North
Devon.

1 In merry Scotland, in merry Scotland
    There lived brothers three;
  They all did cast lots which of them
      should go
  A robbing upon the salt sea.

2 The lot it fell on Henry Martyn,
    The youngest of the three;
  That he should go rob on the salt, salt
      sea,
  To maintain his brothers and he.

3 He had not a sailed a long winter's
      night,
    Nor yet a short winter's day,
  Before that he met with a lofty old ship,
    Come sailing along that way.

4 O when she came by Henry Martyn,
    'I prithee now, let us go !'
  'O no ! God wot, that, that will I not,
    O that will I never do.

5 'Stand off ! stand off !' said Henry
      Martyn,
    'For you shall not pass by me;

For I am a robber all on the salt seas,
  To maintain us brothers three.

6 'How far, how far,' cries Henry Martyn,
    'How far do you make it ?' said he;
  'For I am a robber all on the salt seas,
    To maintain us brothers three.'

7 For three long hours they merrily
      fought,
    For hours they fought full three;
  At last a deep wound got Henry Martyn,
    And down by the mast fell he.

8 'T was broadside to a broadside then,
    And a rain and hail of blows,
  But the salt sea ran in, ran in, ran in,
    To the bottom then she goes.

9 Bad news, bad news for old England,
    Bad news has come to the town,
  For a rich merchant's vessel is cast
      away,
    And all her brave seamen drown.

10 Bad news, bad news through London
      street,
    Bad news has come to the king,
  For all the brave lives of the mariners
      lost,
    That are sunk in the watery main.

E

'Andrew Bartin,' communicated by Miss
Louise Porter Haskell as derived from Gen.
E. P. Alexander of South Carolina, and de-
rived by him from the singing of a cadet at
West Point Military Academy in the winter of
1856–7. Two or three slight corrections have
been made by Mrs A. C. Haskell, sister of
Gen. Alexander.

1 Three bold brothers of merrie Scot-
      land,
    And three bold brothers were they,
  And they cast lots the one with the
      other,
    To see who should go robbing all oer
      the salt sea;
  And they cast lots the one with the
      other,
    To see who should go robbing all oer
      the salt sea.

2 The lot it fell on Andrew Bartin,
    The youngest of the three,

That he should go robbing all oer the
    salt sea,
        To maintain his two brothers and
        he.

3 He had not sailed but one long summer
        night,
    When daylight did appear;
He saw a ship sailing far off and far
    round,
    At last she came sailing quite near.

4 'Who art? who art?' says Andrew
        Bartin,
    'Who art thee comes sailing so
    nigh?'
'We are the rich merchants of merrie
    England,
    Just please for to let us pass by.'

5 'Pass by? pass by?' says Andrew
        Bartin,
    'No, no, that never can be;
Your ship and your cargo I will take
    away,
    And your brave men drown in the
    sea.'

6 Now when this news reached merrie
        England —
    King George he wore the crown —
That his ship and his cargo were taken
    away,
    And his brave men they were all
    drowned.

7 'Go build me a ship,' says Captain
        Charles Stewart,
    'A ship both stout and sure,
And if I dont fetch this Andrew Bartin,
    My life shall no longer endure.'

8 He had not sailed but one long summer
        night,
    When daylight did appear,
He saw a ship sailing far off and far
    round,
    And then she came sailing quite near.

9 'Who art? who art?' says Captain
        Charles Stewart,
    'Who art comes sailing so nigh?'
'We are the bold brothers of merrie
    Scotland,
    Just please for to let us pass by.'

10 'Pass by? pass by?' says Captain
        Charles Stewart,
    'No, no, that never can be;
Your ship and your cargo I will take
    away,
    And your brave men carry with
    me.'

11 'Come on! come on!' says Andrew
        Bartin,
    'I value you not one pin;
And though you are lined with good
    brass without,
    I'll show you I've fine steel within.'

12 Then they drew up a full broadside
    And each at other let pour;
They had not fought for four hours or
    more,
    When Captain Charles Stewart gave
    oer.

13 'Go home! go home!' says Andrew
        Bartin,
    'And tell your king for me,
That he may reign king of the merry
    dryland,
    But that I will be king of the sea.'

251

LANG JOHNNY MORE

'Lang Johnny More' should be compared
with 'Johnie Scot' (No. 99). It is perhaps an
imitation. and in fact almost a parody of that
ballad. There John is the little Scot; here he
is the muckle Scot, stanza 6 (Gaelic *mor* = big),
and his helpmates, as well as he, are of gigan-
tic size. Except this and one other particular,
the stories are materially the same.

'Lang Johnny Moir,' Buchan's Ballads of
the North of Scotland,' i, 248.

1 THERE lives a man in Rynie's land,
    Anither in Auchindore,
The bravest lad amo them a'
    Was lang Johnny Moir.

2 Young Johnny was an airy blade,
    Fu sturdy, stout, and strang;
The sword that hang by Johnny's
    side
    Was just full ten feet lang

3 Young Johnny was a clever youth,
　　Fu sturdy, stout, and wight,
　Just full three yards around the waist,
　　And fourteen feet in hight.

4 But if a' be true they tell me now,
　　And a' be true I hear,
　Young Johnny 's on to Lundan gane,
　　The king's banner to bear.

5 He hadna been in fair Lundan
　　But twalmonths twa or three
　Till the fairest lady in a' Lundan
　　Fell in love wi young Johnny.

6 This news did sound thro Lundan town,
　　Till it came to the king
　That the muckle Scot had fa'in in love
　　Wi his daughter, Lady Jean.

7 Whan the king got word o that,
　　A solemn oath sware he,
　This weighty Scot sall strait a rope,
　　And hanged he shall be.

8 When Johnny heard the sentence past,
　　A light laugh then gae he:
　'While I hae strength to wield my blade,
　　Ye darena a' hang me.'

9 The English dogs were cunning rogues;
　　About him they did creep,
　And gae him draps o lodomy
　　That laid him fast asleep.

10 Whan Johnny wakend frae his sleep
　　A sorry heart had he;
　His jaws and hands in iron bands,
　　His feet in fetters three.

11 'O whar will I get a little wee boy
　　Will work for meat and fee,
　That will rin on to my uncle,
　　At the foot of Benachie?'

12 'Here am I, a little wee boy
　　Will work for meat and fee,
　That will rin on to your uncle,
　　At the foot of Benachie.'

13 'Whan ye come whar grass grows green,
　　Slack your shoes and rin;
　And whan ye come whar water's strong,
　　Ye 'll bend your bow and swim.

14 'And whan ye come to Benachie
　　Ye 'll neither chap nor ca;
　Sae well 's ye 'll ken auld Johnny there,
　　Three feet abeen them a'.

15 'Ye 'll gie to him this braid letter,
　　Seald wi my faith and troth,
　And ye 'll bid him bring alang wi him
　　The body Jock o Noth.'

16 Whan he came whar grass grew green,
　　He slackt his shoes and ran;
　And whan he came whar water 's strong
　　He bent his bow and swam.

17 And whan he came to Benachie
　　Did neither chap nor ca;
　Sae well 's he kent auld Johnny there,
　　Three feet abeen them a'.

18 'What news, what news, my little wee
　　　boy?
　　Ye never were here before;'
　'Nae news, nae news, but a letter from
　　Your nephew, Johnny Moir.

19 'Ye 'll take here this braid letter,
　　Seald wi his faith and troth,
　And ye 're bidden bring alang wi you
　　The body Jock o Noth.'

20 Benachie lyes very low,
　　The tap o Noth lyes high;
　For a' the distance that 's between,
　　He heard auld Johnny cry.

21 Whan on the plain these champions
　　　met,
　　Twa grizly ghosts to see,
　There were three feet between their
　　　brows,
　　And shoulders were yards three.

22 These men they ran ower hills and dales,
　　And ower mountains high,
　Till they came on to Lundan town,
　　At the dawn o the third day.

23 And whan they came to Lundan town
　　The yetts were lockit wi bands,
　And wha were there but a trumpeter,
　　Wi trumpet in his hands?

24 'What is the matter, ye keepers all?
　　Or what 's the matter within

That the drums do beat and bells do
    ring,
  And make sic dolefu din ? '

25 'There 's naething the matter,' the
    keeper said,
  'There 's naething the matter to thee,
But a weighty Scot to strait the rope,
  And the morn he maun die.'

26 'O open the yetts, ye proud keepers,
    Ye 'll open without delay;'
The trembling keeper, smiling, said,
  'O I hae not the key.'

27 'Ye 'll open the yetts, ye proud keepers,
    Ye 'll open without delay,
Or here is a body at my back
  Frae Scotland has brought the key.'

28 'Ye 'll open the yetts,' says Jock o Noth,
    'Ye 'll open them at my call;'
Then wi his foot he has drove in
  Three yards braid o the wall.

29 As they gaed in by Drury Lane,
    And down by the town's hall,
And there they saw young Johnny Moir
  Stand on their English wall.

30 'Ye 're welcome here, my uncle dear,
    Ye 're welcome unto me;
Ye 'll loose the knot, and slack the
    rope,
  And set me frae the tree.'

31 'Is it for murder, or for theft ?
    Or is it for robberie ?
If it is for ony heinous crime,
  There 's nae remeid for thee.'

32 'It 's nae for murder, nor for theft,
    Nor yet for robberie;
A' is for the loving a gay lady
  They 're gaun to gar me die.'

33 'O whar 's thy sword,' says Jock o Noth,
    'Ye brought frae Scotland wi thee ?
I never saw a Scotsman yet
  But coud wield a sword or tree.'

34 'A pox upo their lodomy,
    On me had sic a sway
Four o their men, the bravest four,
  They bore my blade away.'

35 'Bring back his blade,' says Jock o Noth,
    'And freely to him it gie,
Or I hae sworn a black Scot's oath
  I 'll gar five million die.

36 'Now whar 's the lady ?' says Jock o
    Noth,
  'Sae fain I woud her see;'
'She 's lockd up in her ain chamber,
  The king he keeps the key.'

37 So they hae gane before the king,
    With courage bauld and free;
Their armour bright cast sic a light
  That almost dim'd his ee.

38 'O whar 's the lady ?' says Jock o Noth
    'Sae fain as I woud her see;
For we are come to her wedding,
  Frae the foot o Benachie.'

39 'O take the lady,' said the king,
    'Ye welcome are for me;
I never thought to see sic men,
  Frae the foot o Benachie.'

40 'If I had kend,' said Jock o Noth,
    'Ye 'd wonderd sae muckle at me,
I woud hae brought ane larger far
  By sizes three times three.

41 'Likewise if I had thought I 'd been
    Sic a great fright to thee,
I 'd brought Sir John o Erskine Park;
  He 's thretty feet and three.'

42 'Wae to the little boy,' said the king,
    'Brought tidings unto thee !
Let all England say what they will,
  High hangëd shall he be.'

43 'O if ye hang the little wee boy
    Brought tidings unto me,
We shall attend his burial,
  And rewarded ye shall be.'

44 'O take the lady,' said the king,
    'And the boy shall be free;'
'A priest, a priest,' then Johnny cried,
  'To join my love and me.'

45 'A clerk, a clerk,' the king replied,
    'To seal her tocher wi thee;'
Out it speaks auld Johnny then,
  These words pronounced he:

46 'I want nae lands and rents at hame,
       I 'll ask nae gowd frae thee;
    I am possessd o riches great,
       Hae fifty ploughs and three;
    Likewise fa's heir to ane estate
       At the foot o Benachie.

47 'Hae ye ony masons in this place,
       Or ony at your call,
    That ye may now send some o them
       To build your broken wall ? '

48 'Yes, there are masons in this place,
       And plenty at my call;
    But ye may gang frae whence ye
         came,
       Never mind my broken wall.'

49 They 've taen the lady by the hand
       And set her prison-free;
    Wi drums beating, and fifes playing,
       They spent the night wi glee.

50 Now auld Johnny Moir, and young
         Johnny Moir,
       And Jock o Noth, a' three,
    The English lady, and little wee boy,
       Went a' to Benachie.

252

THE KITCHIE–BOY

This ballad is a modern adaptation of 'King
Horn' (No. 17), from which some stanzas are
taken outright.

A*

The Old Lady's Collection, MS., No. 20.

1 THER was a lady fair an rear,
       A lady of birth an fame,
    She loyed her father's kittchen-boy,
       The greater was her shame.

2 She coud never her love revell,
       Nor to him take,
    Bat in the forestes weed an brade,
       Far they wer wont to wake.

3 It fell ance apon a day
       Her father went fra home,
    An she sent for the kitchë-boy
       Into her room.

4 'Canna ye fancë me, Willie ?
       Cannie ye fancë me ?
    By a' the lords I ever seed,
       Ther is nane I cane loie bat ye.'

5 'O latt ne this be kent, lady,
       O lat ne this be knouen,
    For in yer father got word of this,
       I vou he wad gare me die.'

6 'Yer life sall na be tane, Willie,
       Yer life sall na be tean;
    I rader loss my ain heart-blead
       Or thy body gat wrang.'

7 We her mony fair spiches
       She made the boy bold,
    Till he began to kiss an clap,
       An on his love lay hold.

8 They hadne kissed an love-clapet,
       As lovers fan they meatt,

        .   .

9 'The master-cook he will on me call,
       An ansured he man be;
    In it war kent I war in bour we the,
       I fear they woud gar me diei.'

10 'The master-cook may on ye call,
       But ansured he will never be,
    For I haa thrie coffers fue of goud,
       Yer eyen did never see.

11 'An I will buld a bony ship for my
         love,
       An sett her to the seea,
    An saill she east, or saill she west,
       The ship sall be fair to see.'

12 She has buld a bonny ship,
       An sett her to the sea;
    The top-masts was of the read goud,
       The saill of taffety.

13 She gaie him a gay gold ring,

        .   .

    To mind him on a gay lady
       That ance bair love to him.

14 The day was fair, the ship was rair,
       Fan that suan sett to sea;
    Fan that day tuall-month came an gade,
       Att London landed he.

15 A lady louked our castell-wa,
    Beheld the day gaa doun,
    An she beheld that bonny ship,
    Came halling to the toun.

16 'Come hear, come hear, my mairës a',
    Ye see na fat I see;
    The bonnest ship is coming to land
    Yer eyen did ever see.

17 'Ye busk ye, busk ye, my marrës a',
    Ye busk ye unco fine,
    Till I gaa doun to yon shore-side
    To invite yon squar to dine.

18 'O ye come up, ye gay young squar,
    An take we me a dine;
    Ye sall eatt of the gued white lofe,
    An drink the claret wine.'

19 'I thank ye for yer bread,
    I thank ye for yer wine,
    I thank ye for yer courticë,
    Bat indeed I hanna time.'

20 'Canna ye fancë me?' she says,
    'Cannie ye fancë me?
    Bay a' the lords an lairds I see,
    Ther is nane I fancë bat ye.'

21 'They are farr awa fra me,' he says,
    'The 'r farr ayont the sea,
    That has my heart an hand,
    An my love ay sall be.'

22 'Hear is a gued gould ring,
    .   .   .   .
    It will mind ye on a gay lady
    That ance bare love to ye.'

23 'I haa a ring on my finger
    I lee thrice as well as thine,
    Tho yours war of the gued read goud,
    An mine bat simpell tin.'

24 The day was fair, the ship was rair,
    Fan that squar sett to sea;
    Fan that day tuall-month came an gaid,
    Att hame again landed he.

25 The lady's father louked ouer castell-
        wa,
    Beheld the day gaa doun,
    An he beheld that bonny ship
    Come halling to the toun.

26 'Come hear, my a dother,
    Ye see na fat I see;
    The bonnest ship is coming to land
    My eyen did ever see.

27 'Ye busk ye, my dother,
    Ye busk ye unco fine,
    An I ill gai doun to yon shore-side
    An invite yon squer to dine:
    I wad gie a' my reants
    To haa ye marrëd to him.'

28 'They ar farr awa fra me,' she says,
    'The 'r far ayont the sea,
    That has my heart an hand,
    An my love ay sall be.'

29 'O will ye come, ye gay hine squar,
    An take we me a dine?
    Ye sall eat of the gued fait bread
    An drink the claret wine.'

30 'I thank ye for yer bread,
    I thank ye for your wine,
    I thank ye for your courtisy,
    For indeed I haa na grait time.'

31 'O cannie ye fancë me?' [he says,
    'Cannie ye fancë me?]
    By a' the ladys I eair did see,
    Ther is nain I lue bat ye.'

32 'They are farr awa fra me,' she sayes,
    'They are farr ayont the sea,
    That has my heart an han,
    An my love ay sall be.'

33 'Hear it is, a gay goud ring,
    .   .   .   .
    It will mind ye on a gay hin chill
    That ance bare love to ye.'

34 'O gatt ye that ring on the sea sal-
        ing?
    Or gat ye it on the sand?
    Or gat ye it on the shore laying,
    On a drouned man's hand?'

35 'I got na it on the sea saling,
    I got na it on the sand,
    Bat I gat it on the shore laying,
    On a drouned man's hand.

36 'O bonny was his chike,
    And lovely was his face!'

'Alass' says she, 'it is my true-love
    Willie,

.   .   .   .   .

37 He turned him rond about,
    An suitly could he smill;
  She turned her round, says, My love
    Willie,
    Hou could ye me biggeall?

38 'A prist, a prist,' the old man crayed,
    'Latt this tua marrëd be:'
  Bat lettel did the old man keen
    It was his ain kittchen-boy.

253

THOMAS O YONDERDALE

This looks like a recent piece, fabricated, with a certain amount of cheap mortar, from recollections of Nos. 62, 73, and 53.

a. Buchan's Ballads of the North of Scotland, I, 221. **b.** Christie's Traditional Ballad Airs, I, 96.

1 LADY MAISRY lives intill a bower,
    She never wore but what she would;
  Her gowns were o the silks sae fine,
    Her coats stood up wi bolts o gold.

2 Mony a knight there courted her,
    And gentlemen o high degree,
  But it was Thomas o Yonderdale
    That gaind the love o this ladie.

3 Now he has hunted her till her bower,
    Baith late at night and the mid day,
  But when he stole her virgin rose
    Nae mair this maid he would come
    nigh.

4 But it fell ance upon a time
    Thomas her bower he walkëd by;
  There he saw her Lady Maisry,
    Nursing her young son on her knee.

5 ' O seal on you, my bonny babe,
    And lang may ye my comfort be !
  Your father passes by our bower,
    And now minds neither you nor me.'

6 Now when Thomas heard her speak,
    The saut tear trinkled frae his ee;

To Lady Maisry's bower he went,
    Says, Now I 'm come to comfort thee.

7 ' Is this the promise ye did make
    Last when I was in your companie ?
  You said before nine months were gane
    Your wedded wife that I should be.'

8 ' If Saturday be a bonny day,
    Then, my love, I maun sail the sea;
  But if I live for to return,
    O then, my love, I 'll marry thee.'

9 ' I wish Saturday a stormy day,
    High and stormy be the sea,
  Ships may not sail, nor boats row,
    But gar true Thomas stay wi me.'

10 Saturday was a bonny day,
    Fair and leesome blew the wind;
  Ships did sail, and boats did row,
    Which had true Thomas to unco
    ground.

11 He hadna been on unco ground
    A month, a month but barely three,
  Till he has courted anither maid,
    And quite forgotten Lady Maisry.

12 Ae night as he lay on his bed,
    In a dreary dream dreamed he
  That Maisry stood by his bedside,
    Upbraiding him for 's inconstancie.

13 He 's calld upon his little boy,
    Says, Bring me candle, that I see;
  And ye maun gang this night, [my]
    boy,
    Wi a letter to a gay ladie.

14 ' It is my duty you to serve,
    And bring you coal and candle-light,
  And I would rin your errand, master,
    If 't were to Lady Maisry bright.

15 ' Tho my legs were sair I coudna gang,
    Tho the night were dark I coudna
    see,
  Tho I should creep on hands and feet,
    I woud gae to Lady Maisry.'

16 ' Win up, win up, my bonny boy,
    And at my bidding for to be;
  For ye maun quickly my errand rin,
    For it is to Lady Maisry.

17 'Ye 'll bid her dress in the gowns o silk,
   Likewise in the coats o cramasie;
Ye 'll bid her come alang wi you,
   True Thomas's wedding for to see.

18 'Ye 'll bid her shoe her steed before,
   And a' gowd graithing him behind;
On ilka tip o her horse mane,
   Twa bonny bells to loudly ring.

19 'And on the tor o her saddle
   A courtly bird to sweetly sing;
Her bridle-reins o silver fine,
   And stirrups by her side to hing.'

20 She dressd her in the finest silk,
   Her coats were o the cramasie,
And she 's awa to unco land,
   True Thomas's wedding for to see.

21 At ilka tippet o her horse mane,
   Twa bonny bells did loudly ring,
And on the tor o her saddle
   A courtly bird did sweetly sing.

22 The bells they rang, the bird he sang,
   As they rode in yon pleasant plain;
Then soon she met true Thomas's bride,
   Wi a' her maidens and young men.

23 The bride she gazed round about,
   'I wonder,' said she, 'who this may be?
It surely is our Scottish queen,
   Come here our wedding for to see.'

24 Out it speaks true Thomas's boy,
   'She maunna lift her head sae hie;
But it 's true Thomas's first love,
   Come here your wedding for to see.'

25 Then out bespake true Thomas's bride,
   I wyte the tear did blind her ee;
If this be Thomas's first true-love,
   I 'm sair afraid he 'll neer hae me.

26 Then in it came her Lady Maisry,
   And aye as she trips in the fleer,
'What is your will, Thomas?' she said,
   'This day, ye know, ye calld me here.'

27 'Come hither by me, ye lily flower,
   Come hither and set ye down by me,
For ye 're the ane I 've call'd upon,
   And ye my wedded wife maun be.'

28 Then in it came true Thomas's bride,
   And aye as she trippd on the stane,
'What is your will, Thomas?' she said,
   'This day, ye know, ye calld me hame.'

29 'Ye hae come on hired horseback,
   But ye 'se gae hame in coach sae free;
For here 's the flower into my bower
   I mean my wedded wife shall be.'

30 'O ye will break your lands, Thomas,
   And part them in divisions three;
Gie twa o them to your ae brother,
   And cause your brother marry me.'

31 'I winna break my lands,' he said,
   'For ony woman that I see;
My brother 's a knight o wealth and might,
   He 'll wed nane but he will for me.'

254

LORD WILLIAM, OR, LORD LUNDY

For the story, compare 'Katharine Jaffray,' No. 221. In Buchan's version the lady's father is "Lord Lundie."

A

Motherwell's MS., p. 361; from the recitation of Agnes Lyle, an old woman of Kilbarchan. 'Sweet William,' Motherwell's Minstrelsy, p. 307.

1 SWEET WILLIAM 's gone over seas,
   Some unco lair to learn,
And our gude Bailie's ae dochter
   Is awa to learn the same.

2 In one broad buke they learned baith,
   In one broad bed they lay;
But when her father came to know
   He gart her come away.

3 'It 's you must marry that Southland lord,
   His lady for to be;
It 's ye maun marry that Southland lord,
   Or nocht ye 'll get frae me.'

4 'I must marry that Southland lord,
   Father, an it be your will;

But I rather it were my burial-day,
  My grave for to fill.'

5 She walked up, she walked down,
  Had none to make her moan,
Nothing but the pretty bird
  Sat on the causey-stone.

6 'If thou could speak, wee bird,' she says,
  'As weell as thou can flee,
I would write a long letter
  To Will ayont the sea.'

7 'What thou wants wi Will,' it says,
  'Thou 'll seal it with thy ring,
Tak a thread o silk and anither o twine,
  About my neck will hing.'

8 What she wanted wi Willie
  She sealed it wi a ring,
Took a thread of silk, another o twine,
  About its neck did hing.

9 This bird flew high, this bird flew low,
  This bird flew owre the sea,
Until it entered the same room
  Wherein was Sweet Willie.

10 This bird flew high, this bird flew low,
  Poor bird, it was mistaen !
It let the letter fa on Baldie's breist,
  Instead of Sweet William.

11 'Here 's a letter, William,' he says,
  I 'm sure it 's not to me;
And gin the morn gin twelve o'clock
  Your love shall married be.'

12 'Come saddle to me my horse,' he said,
  'The brown and a' that 's speedie,
And I 'll awa to Old England,
  To bring home my ladie.'

13 Awa he gaed, awa he rade,
  Awa wi mickle speed;
He lichtit at every twa miles' end,
  Lichtit and changed his steed.

14 When she entered the church-style,
  The tear was in her ee;
But when she entered the church-door
  A blythe sicht did she see.

15 'O hold your hand, you minister,
  Hold it a little wee,

Till I speak wi the bonnie bride,
  For she 's a friend to me.

16 'Stand off, stand off, you braw bride-
    groom,
  Stand off a little wee;
Stand off, stand off, you braw bride-
    groom,
  For the bride shall join wi me.'

17 Up and spak the bride's father,
  And an angry man was he;
'If I had pistol, powther and lead,
  And all at my command,
I would shoot thee stiff and dead
  In the place where thou dost stand.'

18 Up and spoke then Sweet William,
  And a blithe blink from his ee;
'If ye neer be shot till I shoot you,
  Ye 'se neer be shot for me.

19 'Come out, come out, my foremost
    man,
  And lift my lady on;
Commend me all to my good-mother,
  At night when ye gang home.'

255

WILLIE'S FATAL VISIT

The first half of this piece is a medley of
'Sweet William's Ghost' (No. 77), 'Clerk Saun-
ders' (No. 69) and 'The Grey Cock' (No. 248).
St. 13 is caught, or taken from 'Clyde's Water'
(No. 216), A 7.

Buchan's Ballads of the North of Scotland,
II, 259.

1 'T WAS on an evening fair I went to take
    the air,
  I heard a maid making her moan;
Said, Saw ye my father ? Or saw ye my
    mother ?
  Or saw ye my brother John ?
Or saw ye the lad that I love best,
  And his name it is Sweet William ?

2 'I saw not your father, I saw not your
    mother,
  Nor saw I your brother John;
But I saw the lad that ye love best,
  And his name it is Sweet William.'

3 'O was my love riding? or was he
    running?
  Or was he walking alone?
  Or says he that he will be here this
    night?
  O dear, but he tarries long!'

4 'Your love was not riding, nor yet was
    he running,
  But fast was he walking alone;
  He says that he will be here this night
    to thee,
  And forbids you to think long.'

5 Then Willie he has gane to his love's
    door,
  And gently tirled the pin:
  'O sleep ye, wake ye, my bonny Meggie,
  Ye'll rise, lat your true love in.'

6 The lassie being swack ran to the door
    fu snack,
  And gently she lifted the pin,
  Then into her arms sae large and sae
    lang
  She embraced her bonny love in.

7 'O will ye gang to the cards or the dice,
  Or to a table o wine?
  Or will ye gang to a well-made bed,
  Well coverd wi blankets fine?'

8 'O I winna gang to the cards nor the
    dice,
  Nor yet to a table o wine;
  But I'll rather gang to a well-made bed,
  Well coverd wi blankets fine.'

9 'My braw little cock, sits on the house
    tap,
  Ye'll craw not till it be day,
  And your kame shall be o the gude red
    gowd,
  And your wings o the siller grey.'

10 The cock being fause untrue he was,
   And he crew an hour ower seen;
  They thought it was the gude day-light,
  But it was but the light o the meen.

11 'Ohon, alas!' says bonny Meggie then,
   'This night we hae sleeped ower lang!'
  'O what is the matter?' then Willie re-
    plied,
  'The faster then I must gang.'

12 Then Sweet Willie raise, and put on his
    claise,
  And drew till him stockings and sheen,
  And took by his side his berry-brown
    sword,
  And ower yon lang hill he's gane.

13 As he gaed ower yon high, high hill,
   And down yon dowie den,
  Great and grievous was the ghost he
    saw,
  Would fear ten thousand men.

14 As he gaed in by Mary kirk,
   And in by Mary stile,
  Wan and weary was the ghost
  Upon sweet Willie did smile.

15 'Aft hae ye travelld this road, Willie,
  Aft hae ye travelld in sin;
  Ye neer said sae muckle for your saul
  As My Maker bring me hame!'

16 'Aft hae ye travelld this road, Willie,
  Your bonny love to see;
  But ye'll never travel this road again
  Till ye leave a token wi me.'

17 Then she has taen him Sweet Willie,
  Riven him frae gair to gair,
  And on ilka seat o Mary's kirk
  O Willie she hang a share;
  Even abeen his love Meggie's dice,
  Hang's head and yellow hair.

18 His father made moan, his mother made
    moan,
  But Meggie made muckle mair;
  His father made moan, his mother made
    moan,
  But Meggie reave her yellow hair.

256

ALISON AND WILLIE

a. 'My luve she lives in Lincolnshire.' Harris MS., fol. 18 b; Mrs Harris. b. 'Alison,'
Buchan's MSS., I, 231.

1 'My luve she lives in Lincolnshire,
  I wat she's neither black nor broun,
  But her hair is like the thread o gowd,
  Aye an it waur weel kaimëd doun.'

2 She 's pued the black mask owre her
  face,
  An blinkit gaily wi her ee:
'O will you to my weddin come,
  An will you bear me gude companie ?'

3 'I winna to your weddin come,
  Nor [will] I bear you gude companie,
Unless you be the bride yoursell,
  An me the bridegroom to be.'

4 'For me to be the bride mysel,
  An you the bonnie bridegroom to be —
Cheer up your heart, Sweet Willie,' she
  said,
  'For that 's the day you 'll never see.

5 'Gin you waur on your saiddle set,
  An gaily ridin on the way,
You 'll hae nae mair mind o Alison
  Than she waur dead an laid in clay.'

6 When he was on his saiddle set,
  An slowly ridin on the way,
He had mair mind o Alison
  Than he had o the licht o day.

7 He saw a hart draw near a hare,
  An aye that hare drew near a toun,
An that same hart did get a hare,
  But the gentle knicht got neer a toun.

8 He leant him owre his saiddle-bow,
  An his heart did brak in pieces three;
Wi sighen said him Sweet Willie,
  'The pains o luve hae taen hald o me.'

9 . . . . . .

There cam a white horse an a letter,
  That stopped the weddin speidilie.

10 She leant her back on her bed-side,
  An her heart did brak in pieces three;
She was buried an bemoaned,
  But the birds waur Willie's companie.

257

BURD ISABEL AND EARL
PATRICK

B (Buchan's Ballads) has nearly the same
story as A, with additional circumstances.

Patrick wishes that eleven devils may attend
his last day should he wed another woman.
When he goes to inquire how Isabel came to
refuse the request he had made through his
aunt, he takes the opportunity to make over to
her child the third part of his land. She has
two clerks, her cousins, at her call, who see to
the legal formalities pertaining to this trans-
fer; she commits the boy to one of these, and
herself goes to an unco land to drive love out
of her mind. We hear of nothing worse hap-
pening to Earl Patrick for selling his precious
soul than his never getting further ben than
the church door. C (Motherwell's MS.) is a
variety of B, but not half so long.

A

'Burd Bell,' Kinloch MSS., i, 211; "obtained in the North Country, from the recitation of Mrs Charles."

1 THERE is a stane in yon water,
  It 's lang or it grow green;
It 's a maid that maks her ain for-
  tune,
  It 'll never end its leen.

2 Burd Bell was na full fyfteen
  Till to service she did gae;
Burd Bell was na full sixteen
  Till big wi bairn was scho.

 * * * * *

3 'Burd Bell she is a gude woman,
  She bides at hame wi me;
She never seeks to gang to church,
  But bides at hame wi me.'

4 It fell ance upon a day
  She fell in travail-pain;
He is gane to the stair-head
  Some ladies to call in.

5 'O gin ye hae a lass-bairn, Burd Bell,
  A lass-bairn though it be,
Twenty ploughs bot and a mill
  Will mak ye lady free.

6 'But gin ye hae a son, Burd Bell,
  Ye 'se be my wedded wife,

 . . . . .

7 The knichts they knack their white fingers,
  The ladies sat and sang,

'T was a' to cheer bonnie Burd Bell,
   She was far sunk in pain.

*   *   *   *   *

8 Earl Patrick is to his mither gane,
   As fast as he could hie:
'An askin, an askin, dear mither,
   An askin I want frae thee.

9 'Burd Bell has born to me a son;
   What sall I do her wi?'
'Gie her what ye like, Patrick,
   Mak na her your ladie.'

10 He has gane to bonnie Burd Bell,
   Hir heart was pressd wi care:
.   .   .   .   .

11 'My father will dee, bonnie Burd Bell,
   My mither will do the same,
And whan ye hear that they are gane
   It 's then I 'll bring ye hame.'

12 Earl Patrick 's bigget to her a bour,
   And strawn it round wi sand;
He coverd it wi silver on the outside,
   Wi the red gowd within.

13 It happened ance upon a day
   She was kaiming his yellow hair,
.   .   .   .   .

14 'Your father is dead, Earl Patrick,
   Your mither is the same;
And what is the reason, Earl Patrick,
   Ye winna tak me hame?'

15 'I 've bigget to you a bonnie bour,
   I 've strawn it round wi sand;
I 've coverd it wi silver on the out-
   side,
Wi gude red gowd within.

16 'If eer I marry anither woman,
   Or bring anither hame,
I wish a hundred evils may enter me,
   And may I fa oure the brim!'

17 It was na very lang after this
   That a duke's dochter he 's wed,

Wi a waggon fu of gowd
.   .   .   .   .

18 Burd Bell lookit oure her castle-wa,
   And spied baith dale and down,
And there she saw Earl Patrick's aunt
   Come riding to the town.

19 'What want ye here, Earl Patrick's
   aunt?
What want ye here wi me?'
'I want Earl Patrick's bonnie young
   son;
His bride fain wad him see.'

20 'I wad like to see that woman or man,
   Of high or low degree,
That wad tak the bairn frae my foot
   That I ance for bowd my knee.'

*   *   *   *   *

21 'Burd Bell, she 's the bauldest woman
   That ever I did see:'
'It 's I 'll gang to bonnie Burd Bell,
   She was never bauld to me.'

22 Burd Bell lookit oure her castle-wa,
   Behauding brave dale and down,
And there she spied him Earl Patrick
   Slowly riding to the town.

23 'What said ye to my great-grand-aunt
.   .   .   .   .
.   .   .   .   .'

24 'I said nathing to your great-grand-aunt
   But I will say to thee:
I wad like to see the woman or man,
   Of high or low degree,
That wad tak the bairn frae my foot
   I ance for bowd my knee.

25 'O dinna ye mind, Earl Patrick,
   The vows ye made to me,
That a hundred evils wad enter you
   If ye provd fause to me?'

26 He 's turnd him richt and round about,
   His horse head to the wind,
The hundred evils enterd him,
   And he fell oure the brim.

258

BROUGHTY WA'S

A young woman is carried off from Broughty
Castle, near Dundee, by a body of armed
Highlanders. Her lover, who is making her a
visit at the time, is either taken along with
her — an unnecessary incumbrance, one would
think — or follows her. The pair go out to
take the air; she throws herself into a river;
her lover leaps in after her and is drowned.
She kilts up her clothes and makes her way to
Dundee, congratulating herself that she had
learned to swim for liberty.

a. 'Helen,' Buchan's MSS., I, 233. **b.** 'Burd
Hellen,' or 'Browghty Wa's,' Harris MS., fol.
17 b, from Mrs Harris.

1 BURD HELEN was her mother's dear,
　　Her father's heir to be;
　He was the laird of Broughty Walls,
　　And the provost o Dundee.

2 Burd Helen she was much admired
　　By all that were round about;
　Unto Hazelan she was betrothed,
　　Her virgin days were out.

3 Glenhazlen was a comely youth,
　　And virtuous were his friends;
　He left the schools o bonny Dundee
　　And on to Aberdeen.

4 It fell upon a Christmas Day
　　Burd Helen was left alone
　For to keep her father's towers;
　　They stand two miles from town.

5 Glenhazlen 's on to Broughty Walls,
　　Was thinking to win in;
　But the wind it blew, and the rain dang on
　　And wat him to the skin.

6 He was very well entertaind,
　　Baith for his bed and board,
　Till a band o men surrounded them,
　　Well armd wi spear and sword.

7 They hurried her along wi them,
　　Lockd up her maids behind;
　They threw the keys out-ower the walls,
　　That none the plot might find.

8 They hurried her along wi them,
　　Ower mony a rock and glen,

But, all that they could say or do,
　　From weeping would not refrain.

9 'The Hiland hills are hie, hie hills,
　　The Hiland hills are hie;
　They are no like the banks o Tay,
　　Or bonny town o Dundee.'

10 It fell out ance upon a day
　　They went to take the air;
　She threw hersell upon the stream,
　　Against wind and despair.

11 It was sae deep he coudna wide,
　　Boats werna to be found,
　But he leapt in after himsell,
　　And sunk down like a stone.

12 She kilted up her green claiding
　　A little below her knee,
　And never rest nor was undrest
　　Till she reachd again Dundee.

13 'I learned this at Broughty Walls,
　　At Broughty near Dundee,
　That if water were my prison strong
　　I would swim for libertie.'

259

LORD THOMAS STUART

Lord Thomas Stuart has married a young
countess, and has given her Strathbegie and
Aboyne for a morning-gift. The lady has a
desire to see these places. As they are on
their way thither (from Edinburgh), her husband is attacked with a pain which obliges
him to turn back; he tells her to ride on, and
she seems so to do. The pain proves to be beyond the skill of leeches. Lord Thomas begs
his father to see that his wife gets what he has
given her. He dies; the horses turn wild in
the stables, the hounds howl on the leash.
Lady Stuart has the usual dream (No. 74, **A** 8,
B 11, etc.). She comes back wringing her
hands; she knows by the horses that are standing about the house that the burial is preparing.

Maidment's North Countrie Garland, p. 1.

1 THOMAS STUART was a lord,
　　A lord of mickle land;
　He used to wear a coat of gold,
　　But now his grave is green.

2 Now he has wooed the young countess,
　　The Countess of Balquhin,
　An given her for a morning-gift
　　Strathboggie and Aboyne.

3 But women's wit is aye willful,
　　Alas that ever it was sae !
　She longed to see the morning-gift
　　That her gude lord to her gae.

4 When steeds were saddled an weel
　　bridled,
　An ready for to ride,
　There came a pain on that gude lord,
　　His back, likewise his side.

5 He said, Ride on, my lady fair,
　　May goodness be your guide !
　For I 'm sae sick an weary that
　　No farther can I ride.

6 Now ben did come his father dear,
　　Wearing a golden band;
　Says, Is there nae leech in Edinburgh
　　Can cure my son from wrang ?

7 'O leech is come, an leech is gane,
　　Yet, father, I 'm aye waur;
　There 's not a leech in Edinbro
　　Can death from me debar.

8 'But be a friend to my wife, father,
　　Restore to her her own;
　Restore to her my morning-gift,
　　Strathboggie and Aboyne.

9 'It had been gude for my wife, father,
　　To me she 'd born a son;
　He would have got my land an rents,
　　Where they lie out an in.

10 'It had been gude for my wife, father,
　　To me she 'd born an heir;
　He would have got my land an rents,
　　Where they lie fine an fair.'

11 The steeds they strave into their stables,
　　The boys could'nt get them bound;
　The hounds lay howling on the leech,
　　Cause their master was behind.

12 'I dreamed a dream since late yestreen,
　　I wish it may be good,
　That our chamber was full of swine,
　　An our bed full of blood.'

13 I saw a woman come from the West,
　　Full sore wringing her hands,
　And aye she cried, Ohon, alas !
　　My good lord 's broken bands.

14 As she came by my good lord's bower,
　　Saw mony black steeds an brown:
　'I 'm feared it be mony unco lords
　　Havin my love from town !'

15 As she came by my gude lord's bower,
　　Saw mony black steeds an grey :
　'I 'm feared it 's mony unco lords
　　Havin my love to the clay !'

260

LORD THOMAS AND LADY MARGARET

Christie, who gives B, "epitomized and slightly changed," under the title ' Clerk Tamas and Fair Annie,' Traditional Ballad Airs, II, 12, says that he can trace the ballad, traditionally, far into the eighteenth century.

A

a. ' Lord Thomas,' Motherwell's MS., p. 407; from the recitation of Mrs Parkhill, Maxweltown, 28 September, 1825 (with variations, furnished by another person of the same neighborhood, interlined). b. ' Lord Thomas and Lady Margaret,' Motherwell's MS., p. 71 ; from Miss ——, Glasgow.

1 LORD THOMAS is to the hunting gone,
　　To hunt the fallow deer;
　Lady Margaret 's to the greenwood shaw,
　　To see her lover hunt there.

2 He has looked over his left shoulder,
　　To see what might be seen,
　And there he saw Lady Margaret,
　　As she was riding her lane.

3 He called on his servants all,
　　By one, by two, by three:
　'Go hunt, go hunt that wild woman,
　　Go hunt her far from me !'

4 They hunted her high, they hunted her low,
　　They hunted her over the plain,

And the red scarlet robes Lady Margaret had on
Would never be mended again.

5 They hunted her high, they hunted her
 low,
 They hunted her over the plain,
Till at last she spy'd a tall young man,
 As he was riding alane.

6 'Some relief, some relief, thou tall
 young man !
 Some relief I pray thee grant me !
For I am a lady deep wronged in love,
 And chased from my own countrie.'

7 ' No relief, no relief, thou lady fair,
 No relief will I grant unto thee
Till once thou renounce all the men in
 the world
 My wedded wife for to be.'

8 Then he set her on a milk-white steed,
 Himself upon a gray,
And he has drawn his hat over his face,
 And chearfully they rode away.

9 Lady Margaret was at her bower-
 window,
 Sewing her silken seam,
And there she spy'd, like a wandering
 bodie,
 Lord Thomas begging alane.

10 ' Some relief, some relief, thou lady
 fair !
 Some relief, I pray thee grant me !
For I am a puir auld doited carle,
 And banishd from my ain countrie.'

11 ' No relief, no relief, thou perjured man,
 No relief will I grant unto thee;
For oh, if I had thee within my bower,
 There hanged dead thou would be.'

12 ' No such thing, Lady Margaret,' he said,
 ' Such a thing would never be;
For with my broadsword I would kill
 thy wedded lord,
 And carry thee far off with me.'

13 ' Oh no, no ! Lord Thomas,' she said,
 ' Oh, no such things must be;
For I have wine in my cellars,
 And you must drink with me.'

14 Lady Margaret then called her servants
 all,
 By one, by two, by three:
' Go fetch me the bottles of blude-red
 wine,
 That Lord Thomas may drink with
 me.'

15 They brought her the bottles of blude-
 red wine,
 By one, by two, by three,
And with her fingers long and small
 She poisond them all three.

16 She took the cup in her lilly-white hand,
 Betwixt her finger and her thumb,
She put it to her red rosy lips,
 But never a drop went down.

17 Then he took the cup in his manly hand,
 Betwixt his finger and his thumb,
He put it to his red rosy lips,
 And so merrily it ran down.

18 ' Oh, I am wearied drinking with thee,
 Margaret !
 I am wearied drinking with thee ! '
' And so was I,' Lady Margaret said,
 ' When thou hunted thy hounds after
 me.'

19 ' But I will bury thee, Lord Thomas,'
 she said,
 ' Just as if thou wert one of my own;
And when that my good lord comes
 home
 I will say thou 's my sister's son.'

261

LADY ISABEL

Sts. 20, 21 are a commonplace. St. 24, in
various forms, not always well adapted to the
particular circumstances, ends several ballads :
as ' Lord Ingram and Chiel Wyet ' (No. 66),
A 29 (in this case it occurs shortly before the
end) ; ' Glasgerion ' (No. 67), B, etc.

' Lady Isabel,' Buchan's Ballads of the North
of Scotland, I, 129.

1 'T WAS early on a May morning
 Lady Isabel combd her hair;
But little kent she, or the morn
 She woud never comb it mair.

2 'T was early on a May morning
　　Lady Isabel rang the keys;
　But little kent she, or the morn
　　A fey woman she was.

3 Ben it came her step-mother,
　　As white 's the lily flower:
　' It 's tauld me this day, Isabel,
　　You are your father's whore.'

4 'O them that tauld you that, mother,
　　I wish they neer drink wine;
　For if I be the same woman
　　My ain sell drees the pine.

5 'And them that 's tauld you that, mother,
　　I wish they neer drink ale;
　For if I be the same woman
　　My ain sell drees the dail.'

6 'It may be very well seen, Isabel,
　　It may be very well seen;
　He buys to you the damask gowns,
　　To me the dowie green.'

7 'Ye are of age and I am young,
　　And young amo my flowers;
　The fairer that my claithing be,
　　The mair honour is yours.

8 'I hae a love beyond the sea,
　　And far ayont the faem;
　For ilka gown my father buys me,
　　My ain luve sends me ten.'

9 'Come ben, come ben now, Lady Isa-
　　bel,
　　And drink the wine wi me;
　I hae twa jewels in ae coffer,
　　And ane o them I 'll gie [ye].'

10 'Stay still, stay still, my mother dear,
　　Stay still a little while,
　Till I gang into Marykirk;
　　It 's but a little mile.'

11 When she gaed on to Marykirk,
　　And into Mary's quire,
　There she saw her ain mother
　　Sit in a gowden chair.

12 'O will I leave the lands, mother?
　　Or shall I sail the sea?
　Or shall I drink this dowie drink
　　That is prepar'd for me ?'

13 'Ye winna leave the lands, daugh-
　　ter,
　　Nor will ye sail the sea,
　But ye will drink this dowie drink
　　This woman 's prepar'd for thee.

14 'Your bed is made in a better place
　　Than ever hers will be,
　And ere ye 're cauld into the room
　　Ye will be there wi me.'

15 'Come in, come in now, Lady Isabel,
　　And drink the wine wi me;
　I hae twa jewels in ae coffer,
　　And ane o them I 'll gie [ye].'

16 'Stay still, stay still, my mother dear,
　　Stay still a little wee,
　Till I gang to yon garden green,
　　My Maries a' to see.'

17 To some she gae the broach, the broach,
　　To some she gae a ring;
　But wae befa her step-mother !
　　To her she gae nae thing.

18 'Come in, come in now, Lady Isabel,
　　And drink the wine wi me;
　I hae twa jewels in ae coffer,
　　And ane o them I 'll gie [ye].'

19 Slowly to the bower she came,
　　And slowly enterd in,
　And being full o courtesie,
　　Says, Begin, mother, begin.

20 She put it till her cheek, her cheek,
　　Sae did she till her chin,
　Sae did she till her fu fause lips,
　　But never a drap gaed in.

21 Lady Isabel put it till her cheek,
　　Sae did she till her chin,
　Sae did she till her rosy lips,
　　And the rank poison gaed in.

22 'O take this cup frae me, mother,
　　O take this cup frae me;
　My bed is made in a better place
　　Than ever yours will be.

23 'My bed is in the heavens high,
　　Amang the angels fine;
　But yours is in the lowest hell,
　　To drie torment and pine.'

24 Nae moan was made for Lady Isabel
　　In bower where she lay dead,
　But a' was for that ill woman,
　　In the fields mad she gaed.

262

LORD LIVINGSTON

As far as can be made out, Livingston and Seaton engage themselves to play against one another at some game, the victor expecting to stand the better in the eyes of a lady. They then proceed to Edinburgh castle, where a lady, whose ' gowns seem like green,' marshals the company in pairs, and chooses Livingston for her own partner. This preference enrages Seaton, who challenges Livingston to fight with him the next day. Up to this point the pairing may have been for a dance, or what not, but now we are told that Livingston and the fair dame are laid in the same bed, and further on that they were wedded that same night. In the morning Livingston arms himself for his fight; he declines to let his lady dress herself in man's clothes and fight in his stead. On his way ' to plain fields' a witch warns him that she has had the dream which Sweet William dreams in No. 74, and others elsewhere. Livingston is ' slain,' but for all that stands presently bleeding by his lady's knee. She begs him to hold out but half an hour, and every leech in Edinburgh shall come to him (see No. 88, A 12, etc.). He orders his lands to be dealt as in ' Bonny Bee Hom ' (No. 92). The lady will now do for his sake what other ladies would not be equal to (what nevertheless many other ballad-ladies have undertaken, as in No. 69 and elsewhere). When seven years are near an end her heart breaks. This ballad, or something like it, was known at the end of the eighteenth century.

' Lord Livingston,' Buchan's Ballads of the North of Scotland, II, 39.

1 It fell about the Lammas time,
　　When wightsmen won their hay,
　A' the squires in merry Linkum
　　Went a' forth till a play.

2 They playd until the evening tide,
　　The sun was gaeing down;
　A lady thro plain fields was bound,
　　A lily leesome thing.

3 Two squires that for this lady pledged,
　　In hopes for a renown,
　The one was calld the proud Seaton,
　　The other Livingston.

4 ' When will ye, Michaell o Livingston,
　　Wad for this lady gay ? '
　' To-morrow, to-morrow,' said Livingston,
　　' To-morrow, if you may.'

5 Then they hae wadded their wagers,
　　And laid their pledges down;
　To the high castle o Edinbro
　　They made them ready boun.

6 The chamber that they did gang in,
　　There it was daily dight;
　The kipples were like the gude red gowd,
　　As they stood up in hight,
　And the roof-tree like the siller white,
　　And shin'd like candles bright.

7 The lady fair into that ha
　　Was comely to be seen;
　Her kirtle was made o the pa,
　　Her gowns seemd o the green.

8 Her gowns seemd like green, like green,
　　Her kirtle o the pa;
　A siller wand intill her hand,
　　She marshalld ower them a'.

9 She gae every knight a lady bright,
　　And every squire a may;
　Her own sell chose him Livingston,
　　They were a comely tway.

10 Then Seaton started till his foot,
　　The fierce flame in his ee:
　' On the next day, wi sword in hand,
　　On plain fields meet ye me.'

11 When bells were rung, and mass was sung,
　　And a' man bound for bed,
　Lord Livingston and his fair dame
　　In bed were sweetly laid.

12 The bed, the bed where they lay in
　　Was coverd wi the pa;
　A covering o the gude red gowd
　　Lay nightly ower the twa.

13 So they lay there, till on the morn
　　The sun shone on their feet;
　Then up it raise him Livingston
　　To draw to him a weed.

14 The first an weed that he drew on
　　Was o the linen clear;

The next an weed that he drew on,
It was a weed o weir.

15 The niest an weed that he drew on
Was gude iron and steel;
Twa gloves o plate, a gowden helmet,
Became that hind chiel weel.

16 Then out it speaks that lady gay —
A little forbye stood she —
'I 'll dress mysell in men's array,
Gae to the fields for thee.'

17 'O God forbid,' said Livingston,
'That eer I dree the shame;
My lady slain in plain fields,
And I coward knight at hame!'

18 He scarcely travelled frae the town
A mile but barely twa
Till he met wi a witch-woman,
I pray to send her wae!

19 'This is too gude a day, my lord,
To gang sae far frae town;
This is too gude a day, my lord,
On field to make you boun.

20 'I dreamd a dream concerning thee,
O read ill dreams to guid!
Your bower was full o milk-white
swans,
Your bride's bed full o bluid.'

21 'O bluid is gude,' said Livingston,
'To bide it whoso may;
If I be frae yon plain fields,
Nane knew the plight I lay.'

22 Then he rade on to plain fields
As swift 's his horse coud hie,
And there he met the proud Seaton,
Come boldly ower the lee.

23 'Come on to me now, Livingston,
Or then take foot and flee;
This is the day that we must try
Who gains the victorie.'

24 Then they fought with sword in hand
Till they were bluidy men;
But on the point o Seaton's sword
Brave Livingston was slain.

25 His lady lay ower castle-wa,
Beholding dale and down,

When Blenchant brave, his gallant steed,
Came prancing to the town.

26 'O where is now my ain gude lord
He stays sae far frae me?'
'O dinna ye see your ain gude lord
Stand bleeding by your knee?'

27 'O live, O live, Lord Livingston,
The space o ae half hour,
There 's nae a leech in Edinbro town
But I 'll bring to your door.'

28 'Awa wi your leeches, lady,' he said,
'Of them I 'll be the waur;
There 's nae a leech in Edinbro town
That can strong death debar.

29 'Ye 'll take the lands o Livingston
And deal them liberallie,
To the auld that may not, the young
that cannot,
And blind that does na see,
And help young maidens' marriages,
That has nae gear to gie.'

30 'My mother got it in a book,
The first night I was born,
I woud be wedded till a knight,
And him slain on the morn.

31 'But I will do for my love's sake
What ladies woudna thole;
Ere seven years shall hae an end,
Nae shoe 's gang on my sole.

32 'There 's never lint gang on my head,
Nor kame gang in my hair,
Nor ever coal nor candle-light
Shine in my bower mair.'

33 When seven years were near an end,
The lady she thought lang,
And wi a crack her heart did brake,
And sae this ends my sang.

263

THE NEW–SLAIN KNIGHT

A large part of this piece is imitated or taken outright from very well known ballads (Nos. 76, 88, etc.). The ninth stanza is pretty, but not quite artless.

'The New-Slain Knight,' Buchan's Ballads of the North of Scotland, I, 197.

1 My heart is lighter than the poll;
  My folly made me glad,
As on my rambles I went out,
  Near by a garden-side.

2 I walked on, and farther on,
  Love did my heart engage;
There I spied a well-faird maid,
  Lay sleeping near a hedge.

3 Then I kissd her with my lips
  And stroked her with my hand:
'Win up, win up, ye well-faird maid,
  This day ye sleep oer lang.'

4 'This dreary sight that I hae seen
  Unto my heart gives pain;
At the south side o your father's garden,
  I see a knight lies slain.'

5 'O what like was his hawk, his hawk?
  Or what like was his hound?
And what like was the trusty brand
  This new-slain knight had on?'

6 'His hawk and hound were from him
    gone,
  His steed tied to a tree;
A bloody brand beneath his head,
  And on the ground lies he.'

7 'O what like was his hose, his hose?
  And what like were his shoon?
And what like was the gay clothing
  This new-slain knight had on?'

8 'His coat was of the red scarlet,
  His waistcoat of the same;
His hose were of the bonny black,
  And shoon laced with cordin.

9 'Bonny was his yellow hair,
  For it was new combd down;'
Then, sighing sair, said the lady fair,
  'I combd it late yestreen.

10 'O wha will shoe my fu fair foot?
   Or wha will glove my hand?
Or wha will father my dear bairn,
   Since my love 's dead and gane?'

11 'O I will shoe your fu fair foot,
   And I will glove your hand;
And I 'll be father to your bairn,
   Since your love 's dead and gane.'

12 'I winna father my bairn,' she said,
   'Upon an unkent man;
I 'll father it on the King of Heaven,
   Since my love 's dead and gane.'

13 The knight he knackd his white fingers,
   The lady tore her hair;
He 's drawn the mask from off his face,
   Says, Lady, mourn nae mair.

14 'For ye are mine, and I am thine,
   I see your love is true;
And if I live and brook my life
   Ye 'se never hae cause to rue.'

264

THE WHITE FISHER

To make this story hang together at all, we must suppose that the third and fourth stanzas are tropical, and that Willie was the priest; or else that they are sarcastic, and are uttered in bitter resentment of Willie's suspicion, or affected suspicion.

'The White Fisher,' Buchan's Ballads of the North of Scotland, 1, 200.

1 'It is a month, and isna mair,
  Love, sin I was at thee,
But find a stirring in your side;
  Who may the father be?

2 'Is it to a lord of might,
  Or baron of high degree?
Or is it to the little wee page
  That rode along wi me?'

3 'It is not to a man of might,
  Nor baron of high degree,
But it is to a popish priest;
  My lord, I winna lie.

4 'He got me in my bower alone,
  As I sat pensively;
He vowed he would forgive my sins,
  If I would him obey.'

5 Now it fell ance upon a day
  This young lord went from home,
And great and heavy were the pains
  That came this lady on.

6 Then word has gane to her gude lord,
  As he sat at the wine,

And when the tidings he did hear
   Then he came singing hame.

7 When he came to his own bower-door,
      He tirled at the pin:
   'Sleep ye, wake ye, my gay lady,
      Ye 'll let your gude lord in.'

8 Huly, huly raise she up,
      And slowly put she on,
   And slowly came she to the door;
      She was a weary woman.

9 'Ye 'll take up my son, Willie,
      That ye see here wi me,
   And hae him down to yon shore-side,
      And throw him in the sea.

10 'Gin he sink, ye 'll let him sink,
      Gin he swim, ye 'll let him swim;
   And never let him return again
      Till white fish he bring hame.'

11 Then he 's taen up his little young son,
      And rowd him in a band,
   And he is on to his mother,
      As fast as he could gang.

12 'Ye 'll open the door, my mother dear,
      Ye 'll open, let me come in;
   My young son is in my arms twa,
      And shivering at the chin.'

13 'I tauld you true, my son Willie,
      When ye was gaun to ride,
   That lady was an ill woman
      That ye chose for your bride.'

14 'O hold your tongue, my mother dear,
      Let a' your folly be;
   I wat she is a king's daughter
      That 's sent this son to thee.

15 'I wat she was a king's daughter
      I loved beyond the sea,
   And if my lady hear of this
      Right angry will she be.'

16 'If that be true, my son Willie —
      Your ain tongue winna lie —
   Nae waur to your son will be done
      Than what was done to thee.'

17 He 's gane hame to his lady,
      And sair mourning was she:

'What ails you now, my lady gay,
      Ye weep sa bitterlie ?'

18 'O bonny was the white fisher
      That I sent to the sea:
   But lang, lang will I look for fish
      Ere white fish he bring me !

19 'O bonny was the white fisher
      That ye kiest in the faem;
   But lang, lang will I look for fish
      Ere white fish he fetch hame !

20 'I fell a slumbering on my bed
      That time ye went frae me,
   And dreamd my young son filld my arms,
      But when waked, he 's in the sea.'

21 'O hold your tongue, my gay lady,
      Let a' your mourning be,
   And I 'll gie you some fine cordial,
      My love, to comfort thee.'

22 'I value not your fine cordial,
      Nor aught that ye can gie;
   Who could hae drownd my bonny young
         son
      Could as well poison me.'

23 'Cheer up your heart, my lily flower,
      Think nae sic ill o me;
   Your young son 's in my mother's bower,
      Set on the nourice knee.

24 'Now, if ye 'll be a gude woman,
      I 'll neer mind this to thee;
   Nae waur is done to your young son
      Than what was done to me.'

25 'Well fells me now, my ain gude lord;
      These words do cherish me;
   If it hadna come o yourself, my lord,
      'T would neer hae come o me.'

265

THE KNIGHT'S GHOST

The piece has not a perceptible globule of
old blood in it, yet it has had the distinction
of being more than once translated as a specimen of Scottish popular ballads.

'The Knight's Ghost,' Buchan's Ballads of
the North of Scotland, I, 227.

1 ' THERE is a fashion in this land,
 And even come to this country,
That every lady should meet her lord
 When he is newly come frae sea:

2 'Some wi hawks, and some wi hounds,
 And other some wi gay monie;
But I will gae myself alone,
 And set his young son on his knee.'

3 She 's taen her young son in her arms,
 And nimbly walkd by yon sea-strand,
And there she spy'd her father's ship,
 As she was sailing to dry land.

4 'Where hae ye put my ain gude lord,
 This day he stays sae far frae me ? '
'If ye be wanting your ain gude lord,
 A sight o him ye 'll never see.'

5 ' Was he brunt ? or was he shot ?
 Or was he drowned in the sea ?
Or what 's become o my ain gude lord,
 That he will neer appear to me ? '

6 'He wasna brunt, nor was he shot,
 Nor was he drowned in the sea;
He was slain in Dumfermling,
 A fatal day to you and me.'

7 'Come in, come in, my merry young
  men,
 Come in and drink the wine wi me;
And a' the better ye shall fare
 For this gude news ye tell to me.'

8 She 's brought them down to yon cellar,
 She brought them fifty steps and
  three;
She birled wi them the beer and wine,
 Till they were as drunk as drunk
  could be.

9 Then she has lockd her cellar-door,
 For there were fifty steps and three:
' Lie there, wi my sad malison,
 For this bad news ye 've tauld to me.

10 She 's taen the keys intill her hand
 And threw them deep, deep in the sea:
' Lie there, wi my sad malison,
 Till my gude lord return to me.'

11 Then she sat down in her own room,
 And sorrow lulld her fast asleep,

And up it starts her own gude lord,
 And even at that lady's feet.

12 ' Take here the keys, Janet,' he says,
 ' That ye threw deep, deep in the sea;
And ye 'll relieve my merry young men,
 For they 've nane o the swick o me.

13 ' They shot the shot, and drew the stroke,
 And wad in red bluid to the knee;
Nae sailors mair for their lord coud do
 Nor my young men they did for me.'

14 ' I hae a question at you to ask,
 Before that ye depart frae me;
You 'll tell to me what day I 'll die,
 And what day will my burial be ? '

15 ' I hae nae mair o God's power
 Than he has granted unto me;
But come to heaven when ye will,
 There porter to you I will be.

16 ' But ye 'll be wed to a finer knight
 Than ever was in my degree;
Unto him ye 'll hae children nine,
 And six o them will be ladies free.

17 ' The other three will be bold young men,
 To fight for king and countrie;
The ane a duke, the second a knight,
 And third a laird o lands sae free.'

266

JOHN THOMSON AND THE TURK

This ridiculous ballad is a seedling from the ancient and widespread story of King Solomon and his wife. A typical version, preserved in a Russian prose tale, may be summarized as follows : The wife of Solomon is stolen from him by his brother Kitovras, through the agency of a magician, who, in the character of a merchant, excites Solomon's admiration for a magnificent purple robe. Solomon buys the robe, and invites the seeming merchant to his table. During the repast the magician envelops the king and his people in darkness, brings a heavy slumber upon the queen and her people, and carries her off in his arms to his ship. Solomon proceeds against Kitovras with an army, which he orders to come to his help when they shall hear his horn sound the third time

Clad as an old pilgrim or beggar, he enters
Kitovras's garden, where he comes upon a girl
with a gold cup, who is about to draw water.
He asks to drink from the king's cup. The
girl objects, but the gift of a gold ring induces
her to consent. The queen sees the ring on
the girl's hand, and asks who gave it to her.
'An old pilgrim,' she replies. 'No pilgrim,'
says the queen, 'but my husband, Solomon.'
Solomon is brought before the queen, and
asked what he has come for. 'To take off
your head,' he answers. 'To your own death!'
rejoins the queen. 'You shall be hanged.'
Kitovras is sent for, and pronounces this doom.
Solomon reminds Kitovras that they are brothers, and asks that he may die in regal style ;
that Kitovras and the queen shall attend the
execution, with all the people of the city ; and
that there shall be ample provision of food and
drink : all which is granted. At the gallows
he finds a noose of bast ; he begs that two other
nooses may be provided, one of red silk, one
of yellow, so that he may have a choice, and
this whim is complied with. Always urging
their brotherhood, Solomon, at three successive stages, asks the privilege of blowing his
horn. The army is at hand upon the third blast,
and is ordered to kill everybody. Kitovras and
the queen are hanged in the silken nooses, the
magician in the bast. (Jagić, Archiv für
slavische Philologie, I, 107 f. ; Vesselofsky, the
same, VI, 406.)

Other versions of the Solomon story are
found in the old German poems of Salman und
Morolf, Salomon und Morolf, and König Rother,
in the Cligès of Crestien de Troies, in the romance of Li Bastars de Buillon, in the Portuguese legend of Don Ramiro, and elsewhere.

Two versions of the Scottish ballad are
known, A and B, the latter a fragment of four
stanzas. Leyden, to whom we owe B, says that
he "had heard the whole song when very
young."

A

'John Thomson and the Turk,' Buchan's
Ballads of the North of Scotland, II. 159 ; Mo-
therwell's MS., p. 615 ; Motherwell's Minstrelsy,
Appendix, p. ix.

1 JOHN THOMSON fought against the
        Turks
    Three years into a far country,
    And all that time, and something more,
    Was absent from his gay lady.

2 But it fell ance upon a time,
    As this young chieftain sat alane,
    He spied his lady in rich array,
    As she walkd oer a rural plain.

3 'What brought you here, my lady gay,
        So far awa from your own coun-
        try ?
    I 've thought lang, and very lang,
    And all for your fair face to see.'

4 For some days she did with him stay,
    Till it fell ance upon a day,
    'Farewell for a time,' she said,
    'For now I must bound home away.'

5 He 's gien to her a jewel fine,
    Was set with pearl and precious stone ;
    Says, My love, beware of these savages
        bold,
    That 's on your way as ye go home.

6 Ye 'll take the road, my lady fair,
    That leads you faer across the lee ;
    That keeps you from wild Hind Soldan,
    And likewise from base Violentrie.

7 With heavy heart these two did part,
    And minted as she would go home ;
    Hind Soldan by the Greeks was slain,
    But to base Violentrie she 's gone.

8 When a twelvemonth had expired,
        John Thomson he thought wondrous
        lang,
    And he has written a broad letter,
    And seald it well with his own hand.

9 He sent it along with a small vessel
        That there was quickly going to
        sea,
    And sent it on to fair Scotland,
    To see about his gay ladie.

10 But the answer he received again,
        The lines did grieve his heart right
        sair ;
    None of her friends there had her seen
    For a twelvemonth and something
        mair.

11 Then he put on a palmer's weed,
    And took a pikestaff in his hand ;
    To Violentrie's castle he hied,
    But slowly, slowly he did gang.

12 When within the hall he came,
    He joukd and couchd out-oer his tree :
    'If ye be lady of this hall,
    Some of your good bountieth give me.'

13 'What news, what news, palmer?' she
    said,
    'And from what countrie came ye?'
'I'm lately come from Grecian plains,
    Where lys some of the Scots army.'

14 'If ye be come from Grecian plains,
    Some more news I will ask of thee;
Of one of the chieftains that lies there,
    If he have lately seen his gay ladie.'

15 'It is twelve months and something
    more
    Since we did part in yonder plain;
And now this knight has begun to fear
    One of his foes he has her taen.'

16 'He has not taen me by force nor
    might,
    It was all by my own free will;
He may tarry in the fight,
    For here I mean to tarry still.

17 'And if John Thomson ye do see,
    Tell him I wish him silent sleep;
His head was not so cozelie
    Nor yet so well as lies at my feet.'

18 With that he threw [aff] his strange dis-
    guise,
    Laid by the mask that he had on;
Said, Hide me now, my ladie fair,
    For Violentrie will soon be home.

19 'For the love I bare thee once,
    I'll strive to hide you if I can;'
Then put him down to a dark cellar,
    Where there lay mony a new slain
    man.

20 But he hadna in the cellar been
    Not an hour but barely three,
Till hideous was the sound he heard;
    Then in at the gates came Violentrie.

21 Says, I wish you well, my lady fair,
    It's time for us to sit and dine;
Come, serve me with the good white
    bread,
    And likewise with the claret wine.

22 'That Scots chieftain, our mortal foe,
    So oft from field has made us flee,
Ten thousand sequins this day I'd give
    That I his face could only see.'

23 'Of that same gift would ye give me,
    If I could bring him unto thee?
I fairly hold you at your word;
    Come ben, John Thomson, to my lord.'

24 Then from the vault John Thomson
    came,
    Wringing his hands most piteouslie;
'What would ye do,' the Turk he cried,
    'If ye had me, as I have thee?'

25 'If I had you, as ye have me,
    I'll tell you what I'd do to thee;
I'd hang you up in good greenwood,
    And cause your own hand wile the
    tree.

26 'I meant to stick you with my knife,
    For kissing my beloved wife;'
'But that same weed ye've shaped for
    me,
    It quickly shall be sewed for thee.'

27 Then to the wood they both are gone,
    John Thomson clamb from tree to
    tree;
And aye he sighd, and said, Ohon!
    Here comes the day that I must die!

28 He tied a ribbon on every branch,
    Put up a flag his men might see;
But little did his false foe ken
    He meant them any injurie.

29 He set his horn to his mouth,
    And he has blawn baith loud and
    shrill;
And then three thousand armed men
    Came tripping all out-oer the hill.

30 'Deliver us our chief!' they all did cry,
    'It's by our hand that ye must die!'
'Here is your chief,' the Turk replied,
    With that fell on his bended knee.

31 'O mercy, mercy, good fellows all,
    Mercy I pray you'll grant to me!'
'Such mercy as ye meant to give,
    Such mercy we shall give to thee.'

32 This Turk they in his castle burnt,
    That stood upon yon hill so hie;
John Thomson's gay lady they took,
    And hangd her on yon greenwood
    tree.

B

Leyden's Glossary to The Complaynt of Scotland, p. 371.

1 O CAM ye in by the House o Rodes,
    Or cam ye there away ?
  Or have [ye] seen Johne Tamson ?
    They say his wife has run away.

        *   *   *   *   *

2 'O what wad ye do, Johne Tamson,
    Gin ye had me as I hae thee ?'
  'I wad tak ye to the gude green-wood,
    And gar your ain hand weil the tree.'

        *   *   *   *   *

3 Johne Tamson peeped and poorly spake
    Untill he did his ain men see;
  'O by my sooth,' quo Johne Tamson,
    ' Methinks I see a coming tree.'

        *   *   *   *   *

4 And they hae hanged that grim Soudan
    For a' his mirth and meikle pride,
  And sae hae they that ill woman,
    Upon a scrogg-bush him beside.

267

THE HEIR OF LINNE

Percy, Reliques, 1765, II, 309 (1794, II, 128),
revised and completed A by " the insertion of
supplemental stanzas," " suggested by a modern
ballad on a similar subject." In fact, Percy
made a new ballad, and a very good one, which
since his day has passed for ' The Heir of
Linne.' The modern ballad on a similar subject used by Percy was ' The Drunkard's Legacy,' an inexpressibly pitiable ditty, from which
Percy did not and could not take a line, but
only, as he says, a suggestion for the improvement of the story.

There are several Oriental stories which
closely resemble that of ' The Drunkard's Legacy,' or of Percy's ' Heir of Linne.' Such are
the tale of Sinadab (Gueulette, Contes Tartares,
Cabinet des Fées, XXI, 66 ff., 89 ff.) ; The Forty
Vezirs, Gibb, p. 244 ; Arabian Nights. Habicht,
von der Hagen u. Schall, 1840, XIV, 65 ff.,
etc. Cf. also the Greek Anthology, IX, 44, 45
(translated by Ausonius, Epigrammata, 22, 23) ;
Giraldi Cinthio, Hecatommithi, 1565, II, 563 ;
the Greek Syntipas, Æsop. ed. Coray, p. 246,
No. 384 : Anvar-i Suhailf, Eastwick, p. 74.

A

' The Heir of Lin,' Percy MS., p. 71 ; Hales
and Furnivall, I, 174.

1 OFF all the lords in faire Scottland
    A song I will begin;
  Amongst them all there dweld a lord
    Which was the vnthrifty lord of Linne.

2 His father and mother were dead him
      froe,
    And soe was the head of all his
      kinne;
  To the cards and dice that he did run
    He did neither cease nor bl[i]nne.

3 To drinke the wine that was soe cleere,
    With euery man he wold make merry;
  And then bespake him Iohn of the
      Scales,
    Vnto the heire of Linne sayd hee.

4 Sayes, How dost thou, Lord of Linne ?
    Doest either want gold or fee ?
  Wilt thou not sell thy lands soe brode
    To such a good fellow as me ?

5 'Ffor . . I . .' he said,
    ' My land, take it vnto thee;'
  'I draw you to record, my lord[ë]s
      all;'
    With that he cast him a god's peny.

6 He told him the gold vpon the bord,
    It wanted neuer a bare penny:
  ' That gold is thine, the land is mine,
    The heire of Linne I wilbee.'

7 ' Heere 's gold inoughe,' saithe the heire
      of Linne,
    ' Both for me and my company:'
  He drunke the wine that was soe cleere,
    And with euery man he made merry.

8 With-in three quarters of a yeere
    His gold and fee it waxed thinne,
  His merry men were from him gone,
    And left him himselfe all alone.

9 He had neuer a penny left in his pursse,
    Neuer a penny [left] but three,
  And one was brasse, and another was
      lead,
    And another was white mony.

10 'Now well-aday!' said the heire of
    Linne,
  'Now welladay, and woe is mee!
  For when I was the lord of Linne,
  I neither wanted gold nor fee.

11 'For I haue sold my lands soe broad,
  And haue not left me one penny;
  I must goe now and take some read
  Vnto Edenborrow, and begg my
  bread.'

12 He had not beene in Edenborrow
  Not three qwarters of a yeere,
  But some did giue him, and some said nay,
  And some bid 'to the deele gang yee!

13 'For if we shold hang any landles feer,
  The first we wold begin with thee.'
  'Now welladay!' said the heire of Linne,
  'No[w] welladay, and woe is mee!

14 'For now I have sold my lands soe
    broad,
  That mery man is irke with mee;
  But when that I was the lord of Linne,
  Then on my land I liued merrily.

15 'And now I have sold my land soe
    broade
  That I haue not left me one pennye!
  God be with my father!' he said,
  'On his land he liued merrily.'

16 Still in a study there as he stood,
  He vnbethought him of [a] bill;
  He vnbethought him of [a] bill
  Which his father had left with him.

17 Bade him he shold neuer on it looke
  Till he was in extreame neede,
  'And by my faith,' said the heire of
    Linne,
  'Then now I had neuer more neede.'

18 He tooke the bill, and looked it on,
  Good comfort that he found there;
  Itt told him of a castle wall
  Where there stood three chests in
    feare.

19 Two were full of the beaten gold,
  The third was full of white mony;
  He turned then downe his baggs of bread,
  And filled them full of gold soe red.

20 Then he did neuer cease nor blinne
  Till Iohn of the Scales house he did
    winne.
  When that he came to Iohn of the Scales,
  Vpp at the speere he looked then.

21 There sate three lords vpon a rowe,
  And Iohn o the Scales sate at the
    bord's head,
  And Iohn o the Scales sate at the bord's
    head,
  Because he was the lord of Linne.

22 And then bespake the heire of Linne,
  To Iohn o the Scales' wiffe thus sayd
    hee:
  Sayd, Dame, wilt thou not trust me one
    shott
  That I may sitt downe in this com-
    pany?

23 'Now, Christ's curse on my head,' shee
    said,
  'If I doe trust thee one pennye;'
  Then be-spake a good fellowe,
  Which sate by Iohn o the Scales his
    knee.

24 Said, Haue thou here, thou heire of
    Linne,
  Forty pence I will lend thee;
  Some time a good fellow thou hast
    beene;
  And other forty if neede bee.

25 The dru[n]ken wine that was soe cleere,
  And euery man the made merry;
  And then bespake him Iohn o the Scales,
  Vnto the lord of Linne said hee.

26 Said, How doest thou, heire of Linne,
  Since I did buy thy lands of thee?
  I will sell it to thee twenty pound better
    cheepe
  Nor euer I did buy it of thee.

27 'I draw you to recorde, lord[ë]s all,'
  With that he cast him [a] god's penny;
  Then he tooke to his baggs of bread,
  And they were full of the gold soe
    redd.

28 He told him the gold then over the
    borde,
  It wanted neuer a broad pennye:

'*That* gold is thine, the land is mine,
    And the heire of Linne againe I wil-
        bee.'

29 'Now welladay!' said Iohn o the Scales'
        wife,
    'Welladay, and woe is me!
    Yesterday I was the lady of Linne,
        And now I am but Iohn o the Scales'
            wiffe!'

30 Saies, Haue thou heere, thou good fel-
        low,
    Forty pence thou did lend me,
    Forty pence thou did lend me,
        And forty pound I will giue thee.

31 'Ile make thee keep*er* of my forrest
    Both of the wild deere and the
        tame,'

.   .   .   .   .

32 But then bespake the heire of Linne,
    These were the words, and thus said
        hee,
    Christs curse light vpon my crowne
        If ere my land stand in any ieopardye!

B

a. 'The Heir of Linne,' Buchan's MSS., I,
40; Motherwell's MS., p. 630; Dixon, Scottish
Traditional Versions of Ancient Ballads, p. 30,
Percy Society, vol. XVII. **b.** 'The Weary Heir
of Linne,' Buchan's MSS., II, 114. **c.** 'The
Laird o Linne,' Christie's Traditional Ballad
Airs, I, 112.

1 'THE bonny heir, and the well-faird
        heir,
    And the weary heir o Linne,
    Yonder he stands at his father's yetts,
        And naebody bids him come in.

2 'O see for he gangs, an see for he
        stands,
    The weary heir o Linne!
    O see for he stands on the cauld
        casey,
    And nae an bids him come in!

3 'But if he had been his father's heir,
        Or yet the heir o Linne,
    He wadna stand on the cauld casey,
        Some an woud taen him in.'

4 'Sing ower again that sang, nourice,
        The sang ye sung just now;'
    'I never sung a sang in my life
        But I woud sing ower to you.

5 'O see for he gangs, an see for he
        stands,
    The weary heir o Linne!
    O see for he stands on the cauld casey,
        An nae an bids him come in!

6 'But if he had been his father's heir,
        Or yet the heir o Linne,
    He woudna stand on the cauld casye.
        Some an woud taen him in.

7 'When his father's lands a selling were,
        His claise lay well in fauld,
    But now he wanders on the shore,
        Baith hungry, weet, and cauld.'

8 As Willie he gaed down the town,
        The gentlemen were drinking;
    Some bade gie Willie a glass, a glass,
        And some bade him gie nane,
    Some bade gie Willie a glass, a glass,
        The weary heir o Linne.

9 As Willie he came up the town,
        The fishers were a' sitting;
    Some bade gie Willie a fish, a fish,
        Some bade gie him a fin,
    Some bade gie him a fish, a fish,
        And lat the palmer gang.

10 He turned him right and round about,
        As will as a woman's son,
    And taen his cane into his hand,
        And on his way to Linne.

11 His nourice at her window lookd,
        Beholding dale and down,
    And she beheld this distressd young man
        Come walking to the town.

12 'Come here, come here, Willie,' she
        said,
    'And rest yoursel wi me;
    I hae seen you in better days,
        And in jovial companie.'

13 'Gie me a sheave o your bread, nourice,
        And a bottle o your wine,
    And I'll pay you it a' ower again,
        When I'm the laird o Linne.'

14 'Ye 'se get a sheave o my bread, Willie,
    And a bottle o my wine,
But ye 'll pay me when the seas gang
    dry,
    For ye 'll neer be heir o Linne.'

15 Then he turnd him right and round
    about,
    As will as woman's son,
And aff he set, and bent his way,
    And straightway came to Linne.

16 But when he came to that castle,
    They were set down to dine;
A score o nobles there he saw,
    Sat drinking at the wine.

17 Then some bade gie him beef, the beef,
    And some bade gie him the bane;
And some bade gie him naething at a',
    But lat the palmer gang.

18 Then out it speaks the new-come laird,
    A saucy word spake hee;
'Put round the cup, gie my rival a sup,
    Let him fare on his way.'

19 Then out it speaks Sir Ned Magnew,
    Ane o young Willie's kin;
'This youth was ance a sprightly boy
    As ever lived in Linne.'

20 He turned him right and round about,
    As will as woman's son,
Then minded him on a little wee key,
    That his mother left to him.

21 His mother left [him] this little wee
    key
    A little before she died;
And bade him keep this little wee key
    Till he was in maist need.

22 Then forth he went, these nobles left,
    All drinkin' in the room,
Wi walking rod intill his hand,
    He walked the castle roun.

23 There he found out a little door,
    For there the key slipped in,
And there [he] got as muckle red gowd
    As freed the lands o Linne.

24 Back through the nobles then he went,
    A saucy man was then:

'I 'll take the cup frae this new-come
    laird,
    For he neer bade me sit down.'

25 Then out it speaks the new-come laird,
    He spake wi mock an jeer;
'I 'd gie a seat to the laird o Linne,
    Sae be that he were here.

26 'When the lands o Linne a selling were,
    A' men said they were free;
This lad shall hae them frae me this
    day,
    If he 'll gie the third pennie.'

27 'I take ye witness, nobles a',
    Guide witnesses ye 'll be;
I 'm promisd the lands o Linne this
    day,
    If I gie the third pennie.'

28 'Ye 've taen us witness, Willie,' they
    said,
    'Guide witnesses we 'll be;'
'Buy the lands o Linne who likes,
    They 'll neer be bought by thee.'

29 He 's done him to a gaming-table,
    For it stood fair and clean;
There he tauld down as much rich gowd
    As freed the lands o Linne.

30 Thus having done, he turnd about,
    A saucy man was he;
'Take up your monie, my lad,' he says,
    'Take up your third pennie.

31 'Aft hae I gane wi barefeet cauld,
    Likewise wi legs full bare,
An mony days walkd at these yetts
    Wi muckle dool and care.

32 'But now my sorrow 's past and gane,
    And joy 's returned to me,
And here I 've gowd enough forbye,
    Ahin this third pennie.'

33 As Willie he gaed down the town,
    There he crawd wonderous crouse;
He calld the may afore them a',
    The nourice o the house,

34 'Come here, come here, my nurse,' he
    says,
    'I 'll pay your bread and wine;

Seas ebb and flow [as] they wont to do,
  Yet I 'm the laird o Linne.'

35 As he gaed up the Gallowgate port,
  His hose abeen his sheen;
But lang ere he came down again
  Was convoyed by lords fifeteen.

268

THE TWA KNIGHTS

  This ballad can have had no currency in Scotland, and perhaps was known only through print. A similar one is strictly traditional in Greece, and widely dispersed, both on the mainland and among the islands. There are numerous tales in which a man wagers heavily upon a woman's (generally his wife's) constancy, and, upon plausible evidence, which in the end proves to be nugatory, is adjudged to have lost. Such are the Old French Roman de la Violette and Flore et Jehane; Decameron, ii, 9 (repeated in Shakspere's Cymbeline), etc. Only a small section of these stories, however, has the distinctive traits of the Scottish and Romaic ballads. Examples are the thirteenth - century rhymed tale 'Von zwein Kaufmannen' (von der Hagen, Gesammtabenteuer, III, 357) and the Welsh tale of 'Taliesin' in the so-called Mabinogian.

Buchan's Ballads of the North of Scotland, II, 271.

1 THERE were twa knights in fair Scotland,
  And they were brothers sworn;
They made a vow to be as true
  As if they 'd been brothers born.

2 The one he was a wealthy knight,
  Had lands and buildings free;
The other was a young hynde squire,
  In rank of lower degree.

3 But it fell ance upon a day
  These squires they walkd alone,
And to each other they did talk
  About the fair women.

4 'O wed a may,' the knight did say,
  'For your credit and fame;
Lay never your love on lemanry,
  Bring nae gude woman to shame.'

5 'There 's nae gude women,' the squire did say,
  'Into this place but nine;'
'O well falls me,' the knight replied,
  'For ane o them is mine.'

6 'Ye say your lady 's a gude woman,
  But I say she is nane;
I think that I could gain her love
  Ere six months they are gane.

7 'If ye will gang six months away,
  And sail upon the faem,
Then I will gain your lady's love
  Before that ye come hame.'

8 'O I 'll gang till a far countrie,
  And far beyond the faem,
And ye winna gain my lady's love
  Whan nine lang months are gane.'

9 When the evening sun did set,
  And day came to an end,
In then came the lady's gude lord,
  Just in at yon town's end.

10 'O comely are ye, my lady gay,
  Sae fair and rare to see;
I wish whan I am gane away
  Ye keep your mind to me.'

11 She gae 'm a bason to wash in,
  It shin'd thro a' the ha;
But aye as she gaed but and ben
  She loot the saut tears fa.

12 'I wonder what ails my gude lord
  He has sic jealousie;
Never when we parted before,
  He spak sic words to me.'

13 When cocks did craw, and day did daw,
  This knight was fair at sea;
Then in it came the young hynde squire,
  To work him villanie.

14 'I hae a coffer o gude red gowd,
  Another o white monie;
I woud gie you 't a', my gay lady,
  To lye this night wi me.'

15 'If ye warna my lord's brother,
  And him sae far frae hame,
Even before my ain bower-door
  I 'd gar hang you on a pin.'

16 He 's gane frae the lady's bower,
    Wi the saut tear in his ee,
  And he is to his foster-mother
    As fast as gang coud he.

17 'There is a fancy in my head
    That I 'll reveal to thee,
  And your assistance I will crave
    If ye will grant it me.

18 'I 've fifty guineas in my pocket,
    I 've fifty o them and three,
  And if ye 'll grant what I request
    Ye 'se hae them for your fee.'

19 'Speak on, speak on, ye gude hynde
    squire,
    What may your asking be ?
  I kenna wha woud be sae base
    As nae serve for sic a fee.'

20 'O I hae wagerd wi my brother,
    When he went to the faem,
  That I woud gain his lady's love
    Ere six months they were gane.

21 'To me he laid his lands at stake
    Tho he were on the faem,
  I wudna gain his lady's love
    Whan nine lang months were gane.

22 'Now I hae tried to gain her love,
    But finds it winna do;
  And here I 'm come, as ye her know,
    To seek some help frae you.

23 'For I did lay my life at stake,
    Whan my brother went frae hame,
  That I woud gain his lady's love
    Whan he was on the faem.'

24 But when the evening sun was set,
    And day came to an end,
  In it came that fause carline,
    Just in at yon town's end.

25 'O comely are ye, my gay lady,
    Your lord is on the faem;
  Yon unco squire will gain your love,
    Before that he come hame.'

26 'Forbid it,' said the lady fair,
    'That eer the like shoud be,
  That I woud wrang my ain gude lord,
    And him sae far at sea.'

27 'O comely are ye, my gay lady,
    Stately is your fair bodie;
  Your lovely visage is far chang'd,
    That is best known to me.

28 'You 're sair dune out for want o sleep
    Sin your lord went to sea;
  Unless that ye do cease your grief,
    It will your ruin be.

29 'You 'll send your maids unto the hay,
    Your young men unto the corn;
  I 'll gar ye sleep as soun a sleep
    As the night that ye were born.'

30 She sent her maids to ted the hay,
    Her men to shear the corn,
  And she gard her sleep as soun a sleep
    As the night that she was born.

31 She rowd that lady in the silk,
    Laid her on holland sheets;
  Wi fine enchanting melodie
    She lulld her fast asleep.

32 She lockd the yetts o that castle
    Wi thirty locks and three,
  Then went to meet the young hynde
    squire,
    To him the keys gae she.

33 He 's opend the locks o that castle,
    Were thirty and were three,
  And he 's gane where that lady lay,
    And thus to her said he.

34 'O wake, O wake, ye gay lady,
    O wake and speak to me;
  I hae it fully in my power
    To come to bed to thee.'

35 'For to defile my husband's bed,
    I woud think that a sin;
  As soon as this lang day is gane,
    Then I shall come to thine.'

36 Then she has calld her niece Maisry,
    Says, An asking ye 'll grant me,
  For to gang to yon unco squire
    And sleep this night for me.

37 'The gude red gowd shall be your hire,
    And siller 's be your fee;
  Five hundred pounds o pennies round,
    Your tocher it shall be.'

38 She turnd her right and round about,
    And thus to her did say;
O there was never a time on earth
    So fain's I woud say nay.

39 But when the evening sun was set,
    And day drawn to an end,
Then Lady Maisry she is gane,
    Fair out at yon town-end.

40 Then she is to yon hynde squire's yates,
    And tirled at the pin;
Wha was sae busy as the hynde squire
    To lat that lady in !

41 He's taen her in his arms twa,
    He was a joyfu man;
He neither bade her meat nor drink,
    But to the bed he ran.

42 When he had got his will o her,
    His will as he lang sought,
Her ring but and her ring-finger
    Away frae her he brought.

43 With discontent straight home she went
    And thus lamented she;
Says, Wae be to yon young hynde squire !
    Sae ill as he's used me.

44 When the maids came frae the hay,
    The young men frae the corn,
Ben it came that lady gay,
    Who thought lang for their return.

45 'Where hae ye been, my maidens a',
    Sae far awa frae me ?
My foster-mother and lord's brother
    Thought to hae beguiled me.

46 'Had not she been my foster-mother,
    I suckd at her breast-bane,
Even before my ain bower-door,
    She in a gleed shoud burn.

47 'The squire he thought to gain my
    love,
He's got but Lady Maisry;
He's cutted her ring and her ring-finger,
    A love-token for to be.

48 'I'll tie my finger in the dark,
    Where nae ane shall me see;
I hope to loose it in the light,
    Amang gude companie.'

49 When night was gane, and birds did sing,
    And day began to peep,
The hynde squire walkd alang the shore,
    His brother for to meet.

50 'Ye are welcome, welcome, landless
    lord,
To my ha's and my bowers;
Ye are welcome hame, ye landless lord,
    To my lady white like flowers.'

51 'Ye say I am a landless lord,
    But I think I am nane,
Without ye show some love-token
    Awa frae her ye've tane.'

52 He drew the strings then o his purse,
    And they were a' bludie;
The ring but and the ring-finger
    Sae soon as he lat him see.

53 'O wae be to you, fause hynde squire,
    Ane ill death mat ye dee !
It was too sair a love-token
    To take frae my ladie.

54 'But ae asking of you, hynde squire,
    In your won bowers to dine;'
'With a' my heart, my brother dear,
    Tho ye had asked nine.'

55 Then he is to his lady's father,
    And a sorrow man was he:
'O judge, O judge, my father dear,
    This judgment pass for me.

56 'What is the thing that shoud be done
    Unto that gay lady
Who woud gar her lord gae landless,
    And children bastards to be ?'

57 'She shoud be brunt upon a hill,
    Or hangd upon a tree,
That woud gar her lord gang landless
    And children bastards be.'

58 'Your judgment is too rash, father;
    Your ain daughter is she
That this day has made me landless;
    Your squire gaind it frae me.

59 'Yet nevertheless, my parents dear,
    Ae favour ye'll grant me,
And gang alang to my lost ha's,
    And take your dine wi me.'

60 He threw the charters ower the table,
   And kissd the yates o tree;
Says, Fare ye well, my lady gay,
   Your face I 'll never see.

61 Then his lady calld out to him,
   ' Come here, my lord, and dine;
There 's nae a smith in a' the land
   That can ae finger join.

62 ' I tied my finger in the dark,
   Whan nae ane did me see;
But now I 'll loose it in the light,
   Amang gude companie.

63 ' Even my niece, Lady Maisry,
   The same woman was she;
The gude red gowd shall be her hire,
   And likeways white monie.

64 ' Five hundred pounds o pennies round
   Her tocher then shall be,
Because she did my wills obey,
   Beguild the squire for me.'

65 Then they did call this young hynde
     squire
   To come right speedilie,
Likeways they calld young Lady Maisry
   To pay her down her fee.

66 Then they laid down to Lady Maisry
   The brand but and the ring;
It was to stick him wi the brand,
   .Or wed him wi the ring.

67 Thrice she minted to the brand,
   But she took up the ring;
And a' the ladies who heard o it
   Said she was a wise woman.

269

LADY DIAMOND

The source of this ballad is Boccaccio's tale
of Guiscardo and Ghismonda in the Decameron, iv, 1. Guiscardo has sunk to the rank
of kitchen-boy. An echo of Guismonda's name
is heard in *Dysmal*, *Diamond*, the name of
the heroine in C, D; in A she is called Daisy;
in B, Dayesie; in E, Dysie. Boccaccio's story
belongs to a large and complicated group of
popular and romantic fictions (see Child, v,
29 ff.).

A

' Lady Daisy,' Aytoun's Ballads of Scotland,
II, 173, 1859, from the recollection of a lady
residing at Kirkaldy.

1 THERE was a king, and a very great king,
   And a king of meikle fame;
He had not a child in the world but ane,
   Lady Daisy was her name.

2 He had a very bonnie kitchen-boy,
   And William was his name;
He never lay out o Lady Daisy's bower,
   Till he brought her body to shame.

3 When een-birds sung, and een-bells rung,
   And a' men were boune to rest,
The king went on to Lady Daisy's bower,
   Just like a wandering ghaist.

4 He has drawn the curtains round and
     round,
   And there he has sat him down;
' To whom is this, Lady Daisy,' he says,
   ' That now you go sae round ?

5 ' Is it to a laird ? or is it to a lord ?
   Or a baron of high degree ?
Or is it William, my bonnie kitchen-boy?
   Tell now the truth to me.'

6 ' It 's no to a laird, and it 's no to a lord,
   Nor a baron of high degree:
But it 's to William, your bonnie kitchen-
     boy:
   What cause hae I to lee ? '

7 ' O where is all my merry, merry men,
   That I pay meat and fee,
That they will not take out this kitchen-
     boy,
   And kill him presentlie ? '

8 They hae taen out this bonnie kitchen-
     boy,
   And killd him on the plain;
His hair was like the threads o gold,
   His een like crystal stane;
His hair was like the threads o gold,
   His teeth like ivory bane.

9 They hae taen out this bonnie boy's heart,
   Put it in a cup o gold;
' Take that to Lady Daisy,' he said,
   ' For she 's impudent and bold;'

And she washd it with the tears that ran
    from her eye
    Into the cup of gold.

10 'Now fare ye weel, my father the king!
    You hae taen my earthly joy;
    Since he's died for me, I'll die for him,
    My bonnie kitchen-boy.'

11 'O where is all my merry, merry men,
    That I pay meat and wage,
    That they could not withold my cruel
    hand,
    When I was mad with rage?

12 'I think nae wonder, Lady Daisy,' he
    said,
    'That he brought your body to shame;
    For there never was man of woman born
    Sae fair as him that is slain.'

270

THE EARL OF MAR'S DAUGHTER

The lover in bird-shape is a very familiar
trait in fiction, particularly in popular tales.
So in Marie de France's Lai d'Yonec, and in the
Scandinavian ballad 'Ridderen i Fugleham'
(Grundtvig, No. 68).

'The Earl of Mar's Daughter,' Buchan's
Ballads of the North of Scotland, I, 49; Motherwell's MS., p. 565.

1 IT was intill a pleasant time,
    Upon a simmer's day,
    The noble Earl of Mar's daughter
    Went forth to sport and play.

2 As thus she did amuse hersell,
    Below a green aik tree,
    There she saw a sprightly doo
    Set on a tower sae hie.

3 'O Cow-me-doo, my love sae true,
    If ye'll come down to me,
    Ye'se hae a cage o guid red gowd
    Instead o simple tree:

4 'I'll put gowd hingers roun your cage,
    And siller roun your wa;
    I'll gar ye shine as fair a bird
    As ony o them a'.'

5 But she hadnae these words well spoke,
    Nor yet these words well said,
    Till Cow-me-doo flew frae the tower
    And lighted on her head.

6 Then she has brought this pretty bird
    Hame to her bowers and ha,
    And made him shine as fair a bird
    As ony o them a'.

7 When day was gane, and night was come,
    About the evening tide,
    This lady spied a sprightly youth
    Stand straight up by her side.

8 'From whence came ye, young man?'
    she said;
    'That does surprise me sair;
    My door was bolted right secure,
    What way hae ye come here?'

9 'O had your tongue, ye lady fair,
    Lat a' your folly be;
    Mind ye not on your turtle-doo
    Last day ye brought wi thee?'

10 'O tell me mair, young man,' she said,
    'This does surprise me now;
    What country hae ye come frae?
    What pedigree are you?'

11 'My mither lives on foreign isles,
    She has nae mair but me;
    She is a queen o wealth and state,
    And birth and high degree.

12 'Likewise well skilld in magic spells,
    As ye may plainly see,
    And she transformd me to yon shape,
    To charm such maids as thee.

13 'I am a doo the live-lang day,
    A sprightly youth at night;
    This aye gars me appear mair fair
    In a fair maiden's sight.

14 'And it was but this verra day
    That I came ower the sea;
    Your lovely face did me enchant;
    I'll live and dee wi thee.'

15 'O Cow-me-doo, my luve sae true,
    Nae mair frae me ye'se gae;'
    That's never my intent, my luve,
    As ye said, it shall be sae.'

16 'O Cow-me-doo, my luve sae true,
    It's time to gae to bed;'
  'Wi a' my heart, my dear marrow,
    It's be as ye hae said.'

17 Then he has staid in bower wi her
    For sax lang years and ane,
  Till sax young sons to him she bare,
    And the seventh she's brought hame.

18 But aye as ever a child was born
    He carried them away,
  And brought them to his mither's
    care,
    As fast as he coud fly.

19 Thus he has staid in bower wi her
    For twenty years and three;
  There came a lord o high renown
    To court this fair ladie.

20 But still his proffer she refused,
    And a' his presents too;
  Says, I'm content to live alane
    Wi my bird, Cow-me-doo.

21 Her father sware a solemn oath
    Amang the nobles all,
  'The morn, or ere I eat or drink,
    This bird I will gar kill.'

22 The bird was sitting in his cage,
    And heard what they did say;
  And when he found they were dismist,
    Says, Wae's me for this day!

23 'Before that I do langer stay,
    And thus to be forlorn,
  I'll gang unto my mither's bower,
    Where I was bred and born.'

24 Then Cow-me-doo took flight and flew
    Beyond the raging sea,
  And lighted near his mither's castle,
    On a tower o gowd sae hie.

25 As his mither was wauking out,
    To see what she coud see,
  And there she saw her little son,
    Set on the tower sae hie.

26 'Get dancers here to dance,' she said,
    'And minstrells for to play;
  For here's my young son, Florentine,
    Come here wi me to stay.'

27 'Get nae dancers to dance, mither,
    Nor minstrells for to play,
  For the mither o my seven sons,
    The morn's her wedding-day.'

28 'O tell me, tell me, Florentine,
    Tell me, and tell me true,
  Tell me this day without a flaw,
    What I will do for you.'

29 'Instead of dancers to dance, mither,
    Or minstrells for to play,
  Turn four-and-twenty wall-wight men
    Like storks in feathers gray;

30 'My seven sons in seven swans,
    Aboon their heads to flee;
  And I mysell a gay gos-hawk,
    A bird o high degree.'

31 Then sichin said the queen hersell,
    'That thing's too high for me;'
  But she applied to an auld woman,
    Who had mair skill than she.

32 Instead o dancers to dance a dance,
    Or minstrells for to play,
  Four-and-twenty wall-wight men
    Turnd birds o feathers gray;

33 Her seven sons in seven swans,
    Aboon their heads to flee;
  And he himsell a gay gos-hawk,
    A bird o high degree.

34 This flock o birds took flight and flew
    Beyond the raging sea,
  And landed near the Earl Mar's castle,
    Took shelter in every tree.

35 They were a flock o pretty birds,
    Right comely to be seen;
  The people viewd them wi surprise,
    As they danced on the green.

36 These birds ascended frae the tree
    And lighted on the ha,
  And at the last wi force did flee
    Amang the nobles a'.

37 The storks there seized some o the men,
    They coud neither fight nor flee;
  The swans they bound the bride's best
    man
    Below a green aik tree.

38 They lighted next on maidens fair,
　　Then on the bride's own head,
　And wi the twinkling o an ee
　　The bride and them were fled.

39 There's ancient men at weddings been
　　For sixty years or more,
　But sic a curious wedding-day
　　They never saw before.

40 For naething coud the companie do,
　　Nor naething coud they say
　But they saw a flock o pretty birds
　　That took their bride away.

41 When that Earl Mar he came to know
　　Where his dochter did stay,
　He signd a bond o unity,
　　And visits now they pay.

271

THE LORD OF LORN AND THE FALSE STEWARD

'The Lord of Lorne and the false Steward' was entered in the Stationers' Registers, with two other ballads, to Master Walley, 6 October, 1580; 'Lord of Lorne' to Master Pavier and others (among 128 pieces), 14 December, 1624. There are several broadsides of the second half of the seventeenth century, affording version B, which is an abridgement of an old copy. The story of B is the same as that of A in all material particulars.

'The Lord of Lorn' is apparently founded on the romance of Roswall and Lillian, which itself belongs with a well-known group of popular tales, represented by the Grimms' 'Goose-girl' (No. 89).

A

'Lord of Learne,' Percy MS., p. 73; Hales and Furnivall, i, 180.

1 It was the worthy Lord of Learen,
　　He was a lord of a hie degree;
　He had noe more children but one sonne,
　　He sett him to schoole to learne cur-
　　　tesie.

2 Lear[n]ing did soe proceed with that
　　　child,
　　I tell you all in veretie,
　He learned more vpon one day
　　Then other children did on three,

3 And then bespake the schoole-master,
　　Vnto the Lord of Learne said hee,
　I thinke thou be some stranger borne,
　　For the holy gost remaines with thee.

4 He said, I am noe stranger borne,
　　Forsooth, master, I tell it to thee;
　It is a gift of Almighty God
　　Which he hath giuen vnto mee.

5 The schoole-master turnd him round
　　　about,
　　His angry mind he thought to asswage,
　For the child cold answer him soe
　　　quicklie,
　　And was of soe tender yeere of age.

6 The child he caused a steed to be
　　　brought,
　　A golden bridle done him vpon;
　He tooke his leaue of his schoolfellows,
　　And home the child that he is gone.

7 And when he came before his father,
　　He ffell low downe vpon his knee:
　'My blessing, father, I wold aske,
　　If Christ wold grant you wold giue
　　　it me.'

8 'Now God thee blesse, my sonne and
　　　my heire,
　　His servant in heauen that thou may
　　　bee!
　What tydings hast thou brought me,
　　　child,
　　Thou art comen home so soone to
　　　mee?'

9 'Good tydings, father, I haue you
　　　brought,
　　Goo[d tydings] I hope it is to thee;
　The booke is not in all S[c]ottlande
　　But I can reade it before your eye.'

10 A ioyed man his father was,
　　　Euen the worthy Lord of Learne:
　'Thou shalt goe into Ffrance, my child,
　　The speeches of all strange lands to
　　　learne.'

11 But then bespake the child his mother,
　　The Lady of Learne and then was shee;
　Saies, Who must be his well good guide,
　　When he goes into that strange coun-
　　　try?

12 And then bespake that bonnie child,
    Vntill his father tenderlie;
  Saies, Father, I 'le haue the hend stew-
    ard,
    For he hath beene true to you and
      mee.

13 The lady to concell the steward did
    take,
    And counted downe a hundred pound
      there;
  Saies, Steward, be true to my sonne and
    my heire,
    And I will giue thee mickle mere.

14 'If I be not true to my *master*,' he said,
    'Christ himselfe be not trew to mee!
  If I be not true to my lord and *master*,
    An ill death *that* I may die!'

15 The L*o*rd of Learne did apparell his child
    With bruche, and ringe, and many a
      thinge;
  The apparrell he had his body vppon,
    Thé say was worth a squier's liuinge.

16 The parting of the younge L*o*rd of
    Learne
    With his ffather, his mother, his ffel-
      lows deere,
  Wold haue made a manis hart for to
    change,
    If a Iew borne that he were.

17 The wind did serue, and thé did sayle
    Over the sea into Ffrance land;
  He vsed the child soe hardlie,
    He wold let him haue neuer a penny
      to spend.

18 And meate he wold let the child haue
    none,
    Nor mony to buy none, trulie;
  The boy was hungry and thirsty both;
    Alas! it was the more pitty.

19 He laid him downe to drinke the water
    That was soe low beneathe the brime;
  He [that] was wont to haue drunke both
    ale and wine
    Then was faine of the water soe
      thinne.

20 And as he was drinking of the water
    That ran soe low beneath the brime,

  Soe ready was the false steward
    To drowne the bonny boy therin.

21 'Haue mercy on me, worthy steward!
    My life,' he said, 'lend it to mee,
  And all *that* I am heire vpon,'
    Saies, 'I will giue vnto thee.'

22 Mercy to him the steward did take,
    And pulld the child out of the brime;
  Euer alacke, the more pittye!
    He tooke his clothes euen from him.

23 Saies, 'Doe thou me of that veluett
    gowne,
    The crimson hose beneath thy knee,
  And doe me of thy cordiuant shoone,
    Are buckled with the gold soe free.

24 'Doe thou me off thy sattin doublett,
    Thy shirtband wrought with glister-
      ing gold,
  And doe mee off thy golden chaine,
    About thy necke soe many a fold.

25 'Doe thou me off thy veluett hat,
    With fether in *that* is soe ffine;
  All vnto thy silken shirt,
    That's wrought with many a golden
      seam.'

26 The child before him naked stood,
    With skin as white as lilly flower;
  For [t]his worthy lords bewtie
    He might haue beene a ladye's para-
      moure.

27 He put vpon him a lether cote,
    And breeches of the same beneath
      the knee,
  And sent that bony child him froe,
    Service for to craue, truly.

28 He pulld then forth a naked sword
    That hange full low then by his
      side;
  'Turne thy name, thou villaine,' he said,
    'Or else this sword shall be thy
      guide.'

29 'What must be my name, worthy stew-
    ard?
    I pray thee now tell it me:'
  'Thy name shalbe Pore Disaware,
    To tend sheepe on a lonelye lee.'

30 The bonny child he went him froe,
  And looked to himselfe, truly;
  Saw his apparrell soe simple vppon;
  O Lord ! he weeped tenderlye.

31 Vnto a shepard's house that childe did goe,
  And said, Sir, God you saue and see !
  Doe you not want a servant-boy,
  To tend your sheepe on a lonelie lee ?

32 'Where was thou borne ?' the shepard said,
  'Where, my boy, or in what country ?'
  'Sir,' he said, 'I was borne in fayre Scottland,
  That is soe farr beyond the sea.'

33 'I haue noe child,' the shepard sayd;
  'My boy, thoust tarry and dwell with mee;
  My liuinge,' he sayd, 'and all my goods,
  I 'le make thee heire [of] after mee.'

34 And then bespake the shepard's wife,
  To the Lord of Learne thus did she say;
  'Goe thy way to our sheepe,' she said,
  'And tend them well both night and day.'

35 It was a sore office, O Lord, for him
  That was a lord borne of a great degree !
  As he was tending his sheepe alone,
  Neither sport nor play cold hee.

36 Let vs leaue talking of the Lord of Learne,
  And let all such talking goe;
  Let vs talke more of the false steward,
  That caused the child all this woe.

37 He sold this Lord of Learne's his clothes
  For fiue hundred pound to his pay [there],
  And bought himselfe a suite of apparrell
  Might well beseeme a lord to weare.

38 When he that gorgeous apparrell bought,
  That did soe finelie his body vppon,
  He laughed the bony child to scorne
  That was the bonny Lord of Learne.

39 He laughed that bonny boy to scorne;
  Lord ! pitty it was to heare;

I haue herd them say, and soe haue you too,
  That a man may buy gold to deere.

40 When that he had all that gorgeous apparrell,
  That did soe finelie his body vpon,
  He went a woing to the Duke's daughter of France,
  And called himselfe the Lord of Learne.

41 The Duke of Ffrance heard tell of this,
  To his place that worthy lord was come, truly;
  He entertaind him with a quart of red Renish wi[ne],
  Saies, Lord of Learne, thou art welcome to me.

42 Then to supper that they were sett,
  Lords and ladyes in their degree;
  The steward was sett next the Duke of France;
  An vnseemlye sight it was to see.

43 Then bespake the Duke of Ffrance,
  Vnto the Lord of Leearne said hee there,
  Sayes, Lord of Learne, if thou 'le marry my daught[er],
  I 'le mend thy liuing fiue hundred pound a yeere.

44 Then bespake that lady fayre,
  Answered her ffather soe alone,
  That shee would be his marryed wiffe
  If he wold make her lady of Learne.

45 Then hand in hand the steward her he tooke,
  And plight that lady his troth alone,
  That she shold be his marryed wiffe,
  And he wold make her the ladie of Learne.

46 Thus that night it was gone,
  The other day was come, truly;
  The lady wold see the robucke run,
  Vp hills and dales and forrest free.

47 Then shee was ware of the younge Lord of Learne
  Tending sheepe vnder a bryar, trulye.

. . . . . .

. . . . . .

48 And thus shee called vnto her maids,
  And held her hands vp thus an hie;
  Sayes, Feitch me youd shepard's boy,
  I 'le know why he doth mourne, trulye.

49 When he came before *that* lady fayer,
  He fell downe vpon his knee;
  He had beene so well brought vpp
  He needed not to learne curtesie.

50 'Where wast thou borne, thou bonny
    boy ?
  Where or in what countrye ? '
  'Madam, I was borne in faire Scott-
    land,
  That is soe farr beyond the sea.'

51 'What is thy name, thou bonny boy ?
  I pray thee tell it vnto mee;'
  'My name,' he sayes, 'is Poore Disa-
    ware,
  That tends sheepe on a lonely lee.'

52 'One thing thou must tell mee, bonny
    boy,
  Which I must needs aske of thee,
  Dost not thou know the young Lord of
    Learne ?
  He is comen a woing into France to
    me.'

53 'Yes, *that* I doe, madam,' he said,
  And then he wept most tenderlie;
  'The Lord of Learne is a worthy lord,
  If he were at home in his oune coun-
    try.'

54 'What ayles thee to weepe, my bonny
    boy ?
  Tell me or ere I part thee froe:'
  'Nothing but for a freind, madam,
  That's dead from me many a yeere
    agoe.'

55 A loud laughter the ladie lought,
  O Lord ! shee smiled wonderous hie:
  'I haue dwelled in France since I was
    borne;
  Such a shepard's boy I did neuer see.

56 'Wilt thou not leaue thy sheepe, my
    child,
  And come vnto service vnto mee ?
  And I will giue thee meate and fee,
  And my chamberlaine thou shalt bee.'

57 'Then I will leaue my sheepe, madam,'
    he sayd,
  'And come into service vnto thee,
  If you will giue me meate and fee,
  Your chamberlaine *that* I may bee.'

58 When the lady came before her father,
  Shee fell low downe vpon her knee;
  'Grant me, father,' the lady said,
  'This boy my chamberlaine to be.'

59 'But O nay, nay,' the duke did say,
  'Soe my daughter it may not bee;
  The lord *that* is come a woing to you
  Will be offended with you and mee.'

60 Then came downe the false steward,
    Which called himselfe the Lord of
    Learne, trulie;
  When he looked that bonny boy vpon,
  An angry man i-wis was hee.

61 'Where was thou borne, thou vagabond ?
  Where ? ' he sayd, 'and in what coun-
    try ? '
  Says, I was borne in fayre Scotland,
  That is soe far beyond the sea.

62 'What is thy name, thou vagabond ?
  Haue done qu[i]cklie, and tell it to
    me;'
  'My name,' he sayes, 'is Poore Disa-
    ware,
  I tend sheep on the lonelie lee.'

63 'Thou art a theefe,' the steward said,
  'And soe in the end I will prooue thee;'
  . . . . . .
  . . . .

64 Then be-spake the ladie fayre,
  'Peace, Lord of Learne ! I doe pray
    thee;
  Ffor if noe loue you show this child,
  Noe favor can you haue of mee.'

65 'Will you beleeue me, lady faire,
  When the truth I doe tell yee ?
  Att Aberdonie, beyond the sea,
  His father he robbed a hundred three.'

66 But then bespake the Duke of France
  Vnto the boy soe tenderlie;
  Saies, Boy, if thou loue harsses well,
  My stable-groome I will make thee.

67 And thus *that that* did passe vppon
    Till the twelve monthes did draw to
      an ende;
    The boy applyed his office soe well
    Euery man became his freind.

68 He went forth earlye one morning
    To water a gelding at the water soe free;
    The gelding vp, and with his head
    He hitt the child aboue his eye.

69 'Woe be to thee, thou gelding,' he sayd,
    'And to the mare *that* foled thee !
    Thou hast striken the Lord of Learne
    A litle tinye aboue the eye.

70 'First night after I was borne, a lord I
      was,
    An earle after my father doth die;
    My father is the worthy Lord of Learne,
    And child he hath noe more but mee;
    He sent me over the sea with the false
      steward,
    And thus that he hath beguiled mee.'

71 The lady [wa]s in her garden greene,
    Walking with her mayds, trulye,
    And heard the boy this mourning make,
    And went to weeping, trulie.

72 'Sing on thy song, thou stable groome,
    I pray thee doe not let for mee,
    And as I am a true ladie
    I wilbe trew vnto thee.'

73 'But nay, now nay, madam !' he sayd,
    'Soe *that* it may not bee;
    I am tane sworne vpon a booke,
    And forsworne I will not bee.'

74 'Sing on thy song to thy gelding,
    And thou doest not sing to mee;
    And as I am a true ladie
    I will euer be true vnto thee.'

75 He sayd, Woe be to thee, gelding,
    And to the mare *that* foled thee !
    For thou hast strucken the Lord of
      Learne
    A litle aboue mine eye.

76 First night I was borne, a lord I was,
    An earle after my father doth dye;
    My father is the good Lord of Learne,
    And child he hath noe other but mee;

My father sent me over [the sea] with
    the false steward,
    And thus *that* he hath beguiled mee.

77 'Woe be to the steward, lady,' he sayd,
    'Woe be to him verrily !
    He hath beene about this twelve mouths
      day
    For to deceiue both thee and mee.

78 'If you doe not my councell keepe,
    That I haue told you with good in-
      tent,
    And if you doe it not well keepe,
    Ffarwell ! my life is at an ende.'

79 'I wil be true to thee, Lord of Learne,
    Or else Christ be not soe vnto me;
    And as I am a trew ladye,
    I le neuer marry none but thee.'

80 Shee sent in for her father, the Duke,
    In all the speed *that* ere might bee;
    'Put of my wedding, father,' shee said,
    'For the loue of God, this monthes
      three.

81 'Sicke I am,' the ladye said,
    'O sicke, and verry like to die !
    Put of my wedding, father Duke,
    Ffor the loue of God, this monthes
      three.'

82 The Duke of France put of this wedding
    Of the steward and the lady monthes
      three,
    For the ladie sicke shee was,
    Sicke, sicke, and like to die.

83 Shee wrote a letter with her owne hand,
    In all the speede *that* euer might bee;
    Shee sent [it] over into Scottland,
    That is soe ffarr beyond the sea.

84 When the messenger came beffore the
    old Lord of Learne,
    He kneeled low downe on his knee,
    And he deliuered the letter vnto him,
    In all the speed *that* euer might bee.

85 [The] first looke he looked the letter
    vpon,
    Lo ! he wept full bitterly;
    The second looke he looked it vpon,
    Said, False steward, woe be to thee!

86 When the Ladye of Learne these tyd-
    ings heard,
      O Lord ! shee wept soe biterlye:
  'I told you of this, now good my lord,
    When I sent my child into that wild
    country.'

87 'Peace, Lady of Learne,' the lord did
    say,
    'For Christ his loue I doe pray thee;
  And as I am a christian man,
    Wroken vpon him *that* I wilbe.'

88 He wrote a letter with his owne hand,
    In all the speede *that* ere might
    bee;
  He sent it into the lords in Scottland,
    That were borne of a great degree.

89 He sent for lords, he sent for k*night*s,
    The best that were in the countrye,
  To go with him into the land of France,
    To seeke his sonne in *that* strange
    country.

90 The wind was good, and they did sayle,
    Fiue hundred men into France land,
  There to seeke *that* bonny boy
    That was the worthy Lord of Learne.

91 They sought the country through and
    through,
    Soe farr to the Duke's place of Ffrance
    land;
  There they were ware of *that* bonny
    boy,
    Standing with a porter's staffe in his
    hand.

92 Then the worshippfull, thé did bowe,
    The serving-men fell on their knee,
  They cast their hatts vp into the ayre
    For ioy *that* boy *that* they had seene.

93 The Lord of Learne then he light downe,
    And kist his child both cheeke and
    chinne,
  And said, God blesse thee, my sonne and
    my heire !
    The blisse of heauen *that* thou may
    winne !

94 The false steward and the Duke of
    France
    Were in a castle-topp, trulie;

'What fooles are yond,' says the false
    steward,
  'To the porter makes soe lowe curte-
    sie ?'

95 Then bespake the Duke of Ffrance,
    Calling my Lord of Learne, trulie;
  He sayd, I doubt the day be come
    That either you or I must die.

96 Thé sett the castle round about,
    A swallow cold not haue flone away;
  And there thé tooke the false steward
    That the Lord of Learne did betray.

97 And when they had taken the false
    steward,
    He fell lowe downe vpon his knee,
  And craued mercy of the Lord of
    Learne
    For the villanous dedd he had done,
    trulye.

98 'Thou shalt haue mercy,' said the Lord
    of Learne,
    'Thou vile traitor, I tell to thee,
  As the lawes of the realme they will
    thee beare,
    Wether it bee for thee to liue or
    dye.'

99 A quest of lords *that* there was chosen,
    To goe vppon his death, trulie;
  There thé iudged the false steward,
    Whether he was guiltie, and for to
    dye.

100 The forman of the iury he came in,
    He spake his words full lowd and hie;
  Said, Make thee ready, thou false stew-
    ard,
    For now thy death it drawes full nie.

101 Sayd he, If my death it doth draw nie,
    God forgiue me all I haue done
    amisse !
  Where is *that* lady I haue loued soe
    longe ?
    Before my death to giue me a kisse.

102 'Away, thou traitor !' the lady said,
    'Auoyd out of my company !
  For thy vild treason thou hast wrought,
    Thou had need to cry to God for mer-
    cye.'

103 First they tooke him and h[a]ngd him
        halfe,
    And let him downe before he was
        dead,
    And quartered him in quarters many,
    And sodde him in a boyling lead.

104 And then they tooke him out againe,
    And cutten all his ioynts in sunder,
    And burnte him eke vpon a hyll;
    I-wis thé did him curstlye cumber.

105 A loud laughter the lady laught,
        O Lord ! she smiled merrylie;
    She sayd, I may praise my heauenly
        king
    That euer I seene this vile traytor die.

106 Then bespake the Duke of France,
    Vnto the right Lord of Learne sayd
        he there;
    Says, Lord of Learne, if thou wilt marry
        my daught[er]
    I 'le mend thy liuing fiue hundred a
        yeere.

107 But then bespake *that* bonie boy,
    And answered the Duke quicklie,
    I had rather marry *your* daughter *with*
        a ring of go[ld]
    Then all the gold *that* ere I blinket on
        with mine eye.

108 But then bespake the old Lord of
        Learne,
    To the Duke of France thus he did
        say,
    Seeing our children doe soe well agree,
    They shalbe marryed ere wee goe
        away.

109 The Lady of Learne shee was sent for
    Throughout Scottland soe speedilie,
    To see these two children sett vpp
    In their seats of gold full royallye.

272

THE SUFFOLK MIRACLE

This ballad is, in a blurred, enfeebled, and
disfigured shape, the representative in England
of one of the most remarkable tales and one of
the most impressive and beautiful ballads of the

European continent. The relationship is put
beyond doubt by the existence of a story in
Cornwall which comes much nearer to the Con-
tinental tale.

Long, long ago, Frank, a farmer's son, was
in love with Nancy, a very attractive girl, who
lived in the condition of a superior servant in
his mother's house. Frank's parents opposed
their matching, and sent the girl home to her
mother; but the young pair continued to meet,
and they bound themselves to each other for
life or for death. To part them effectually,
Frank was shipped for an India voyage. He
could not write, and nothing was heard of him
for nearly three years. On All-hallows-Eve
Nancy went out with two companions to sow
hemp-seed. Nancy began the rite, saying:

Hemp-seed, I sow thee,
Hemp-seed, grow thee !
And he who will my true-love be
Come after me
And shaw thee.

This she said three times, and then, looking
back over her left shoulder, she saw Frank indeed, but he looked so angry that she shrieked,
and so broke the spell. One night in November a ship was wrecked on the coast, and
Frank was cast ashore, with just enough life
in him to ask that he might be married to
Nancy before he died, a wish which was not to
be fulfilled. On the night of his funeral, as
Nancy was about to lock the house-door, a
horseman rode up. His face was deadly pale,
but Nancy knew him to be her lover. He told
her that he had just arrived home, and had
come to fetch her and make her his bride.
Nancy was easily induced to spring on the horse
behind him. When she clasped Frank's waist,
her arm became stiff as ice. The horse went
at a furious pace; the moon came out in full
splendor. Nancy saw that the rider was in
grave-clothes. She had lost the power of
speech, but, passing a blacksmith's shop, where
the smith was still at work, she recovered voice
and cried, Save me ! with all her might. The
smith ran out with a hot iron in his hand, and,
as the horse was rushing by, caught the girl's
dress and pulled her to the ground. But the
rider held on to the gown, and both Nancy and
the smith were dragged on till they came near
the churchyard. There the horse stopped for
a moment, and the smith seized his chance to
burn away the gown with his iron and free the
girl. The horseman passed over the wall of
the churchyard, and vanished at the grave in
which the young man had been laid a few hours
before. A piece of Nancy's dress was found
on the grave. Nancy died before morning. It
was said that one or two of the sailors who
survived the wreck testified that Frank, on

Halloween, was like one mad, and, after great excitement, lay for hours as if dead, and that when he came to himself he declared that if he ever married the woman who had cast the spell, he would make her suffer for drawing his soul out of his body. (Popular Romances of the West of England, collected and edited by Robert Hunt, First Series, pp. 265–72, dating from about 1830.) A tale of a dead man coming on horseback to his inconsolable love, and carrying her to his grave, is widely spread among the Slavic people and the Austrian Germans, was well known a century ago among the northern Germans, and has lately been recovered in the Netherlands, Denmark, Iceland, and Brittany. Besides the tale in its integrity, certain verses which occur in it, and which are of a kind sure to impress the memory, are very frequent, and these give evidence of a very extensive distribution. The verses are to this effect:

> The moon shines bright in the lift,
> The dead, they ride so swift,
> Love, art thou not afraid?

to which the lovelorn maid answers,

> How fear, when I am with thee?

A portion (or portions) of a Low German tale of this class, the verses and a little more, was the basis of Bürger's 'Lenore,' composed in 1773. There are also ballads with the same story, one in German, several in Slavic, but these have not so original a stamp as the tale, and have perhaps sprung from it.

In marked and pleasing contrast with most of the versions of this tale, in so many copies grotesque and ferocious, is a dignified and tender ballad, in which the lovers are replaced by brother and sister. This ballad is found among the Servians, Bulgarians, Greeks, Albanians, and Roumanians. Professor Schischmánov (Indogermanische Forschungen, IV, 412–48, 1894) makes out a very strong probability of the derivation of all the ballads of 'The Dead Brother' from the Greek.

'The Suffolk Miracle,' broadsides. a. Wood, E. 25, fol. 83 [1689]. b. Roxburghe, II, 240; Moore's Pictorial Book of Ancient Ballad Poetry, p. 463.

1 A WONDER stranger ne'r was known
Then what I now shall treat upon.
In Suffolk there did lately dwell
A farmer rich and known full well.

2 He had a daughter fair and bright,
On whom he plac'd his chief delight·
Her beauty was beyond compare,
She was both virtuous and fair.

3 A young man there was living by,
Who was so charmëd with her eye
That he could never be at rest,
He was with love so much possest.

4 He made address to her, and she
Did grant him love immediately;
Which when her father came to hear,
He parted her and her poor dear.

5 Forty miles distant was she sent,
Unto his brother's, with intent
That she should there so long remain
Till she had chang'd her mind again.

6 Hereat this young man sadly grievd,
But knew not how to be relievd;
He sighd and sobd continually
That his true love he could not see.

7 She by no means could to him send
Who was her heart's espousëd friend;
He sighd, she grievd, but all in vain,
For she confin'd must still remain.

8 He mournd so much that doctor's art
Could give no ease unto his heart;
Who was so strang[e]ly terrified,
That in short time for love he dyed.

9 She that from him was sent away
Knew nothing of his dying-day,
But constant still she did remain;
To love the dead was then in vain.

10 After he had in grave been laid
A month or more, unto this maid
He comes about middle of the night,
Who joyd to see her heart's delight.

11 Her father's horse, which well she knew,
Her mother's hood and safeguard too,
He brought with him to testifie
Her parents' order he came by.

12 Which when her unckle understood,
He hop't it would be for her good,
And gave consent to her straightway
That with him she should come away.

13 When she was got her love behind,
They passd as swift as any wind,
That in two hours, or little more,
He brought her to her father's door.

14 But as they did this great haste make,
   He did complain his head did ake;
Her handkerchief she then took out,
   And tyed the same his head about.

15 And unto him she thus did say:
   'Thou art as cold as any clay;
When we come home, a fire wee 'l have;'
   But little dreamt he went to grave.

16 Soon were they at her father's door,
   And after she ne'r see him more;
'I 'le set the horse up,' then he said,
   And there he left this harmless maid.

17 She knockt, and strait a man he cryed,
   'Who's there?' ''T is I,' she then re-
     plyed;
Who wondred much her voice to hear,
   And was possest with dread and fear.

18 Her father he did tell, and then
   He stared like an affrighted man:
Down stairs he ran, and when he see
    her,
Cry'd out, My child, how cam'st thou
    here?

19 'Pray, sir, did you not send for me,
   By such a messenger?' said she:
Which made his hair stare on his head,
   As knowing well that he was dead.

20 'Where is he?' then to her he said;
   'He's in the stable,' quoth the maid.
'Go in,' said he, 'and go to bed;
   I 'le see the horse well littered.'

21 He stared about, and there could hee
   No shape of any mankind see,
But found his horse all on a sweat;
   Which made him in a deadly fret.

22 His daughter he said nothing to,
   Nor no one else, though well they knew
That he was dead a month before,
   For fear of grieving her full sore.

23 Her father to his father went
   Who was deceasd, with this intent,
To tell him what his daughter said;
   So both came back unto this maid.

24 They askd her, and she still did say
   'T was he that then brought her away;

Which when they heard they were amaz'd,
   And on each other strang[e]ly gaz'd.

25 A handkerchief she said she tyed
   About his head, and that they tryed;
The sexton they did speak unto,
   That he the grave would then undo.

26 Affrighted then they did behold
   His body turning into mould,
And though he had a month been dead,
   This kercheif was about his head.

27 This thing unto her then they told,
   And the whole truth they did unfold;
She was thereat so terrified
   And grievd, she quickly after dyed.

28 Part not true love, you rich men, then;
   But, if they be right honest men
Your daughters love, give them their
    way,
For force oft breeds their lives' decay.

273

KING EDWARD THE FOURTH AND A TANNER OF TAMWORTH

In the Stationers' Registers, Oct. 6, 1600, there was entered by William White, by the consent of Widow Danter, 'A merye, pleasant and delectable history betwene Kinge Edward the IIIJ[th] and a Tanner of Tamworthe,' and, by like consent of the Widow Danter, "the bal-[l]ad of the same matter that was printed by her husband John Danter." Arber, III, 173. The ballad mentioned in this entry is unquestionably our ballad, or an earlier form of it. No copy from the first half of the seventeenth century is known to be preserved. The "delectable history" entered under the same date is extant in an edition of 1596, printed by John Danter, and in one of 1613, printed by William White (both edited in Child, v, 81 ff.). The ballad, as we have it, was made by abridging the fifty-six stanzas of the history to thirty-nine, with other changes. The history itself has its undoubted original in 'The King and the Barker' (printed in Child, v, 78 ff.), between which and the history, though the former has come down to us in a sadly mutilated condition, and has been freely treated in the remoulding, there still remain a few verbal correspondences. Several good points are added in the history, and one or two dropped.

Other similar rhymed tales in English are John the Reeve (Percy MS.), Rauf Coilyear, King Edward III and the Shepherd (Hartshorne's Ancient Metrical Tales), King Henry II and the Miller of Mansfield (Child, v, 84 ff.), etc.

a. Wood, 401, fol. 44. **b.** Douce, i, 109. **c.** Roxburghe, i, 176, 177; Chappell, Roxburghe Ballads, i, 529.

1 IN summer time, when leaves grew
        green,
    and birds were singing on every tree,
King Edward would a hunting ride,
    some pastime for to see.

2 Our king he would a hunting ride,
    by eight a clock of the day,
And well was he ware of a bold tanner,
    came riding on the way.

3 A good russet coat the tanner had on,
    fast buttoned under his chin,
And under him a good cow-hide,
    and a mare of four shilling.

4 ' Now stand you here, my good lords all,
    under this trusty tree,
And I will wend to yonder fellow,
    to know from whence came he.

5 'God speed, God speed,' then said our
        king;
    ' thou art welcome, good fellow,' quoth
        he;
    ' Which is the way to Drayton Basset
    I pray thee shew to me.'

6 ' The ready way to Drayton Basset,
    from this place as thou dost stand,
The next pair of gallows thou comst to
    thou must turn up [on] thy right
    hand.'

7 ' That is not the way,' then said our king,
    ' the ready way I pray thee shew me;'
    ' Whether thou be thief or true man,'
        quoth the tanner,
    ' I 'm weary of thy company.

8 ' Away, with a vengeance,' quoth the
        tanner,
    ' I hold thee out of thy wit,
For all this day have I ridden and gone,
And I am fasting yet.'

9 ' Go with me to Drayton Basset,' said
        our king,
    ' no daintyes we will lack;
We 'l have meat and drink of the
        best,
    And I will pay the shot.'

10 ' Godamercy for nothing,' said the tanner,
    ' thou shalt pay for no dinner of
        mine;
I have more groats and nobles in my
        purse
    then thou hast pence in thine.'

11 ' God save your goods,' then said the
        king,
    ' and send them well to thee ! '
    ' Be thou thief or true man,' quoth the
        tanner,
    ' I am weary of thy company.

12 ' Away, with a vengeance,' quoth the
        tanner,
    ' of thee I stand in fear;
The aparrell thou wearst on thy back
May seem a good lord to wear.'

13 ' I never stole them,' said our king,
    ' I swear to thee by the rood;'
    ' Thou art some ruffian of the country,
    thou rid'st in the midst of thy good.'

14 ' What news dost thou hear ? ' then said
        our king,
    ' I pray what news do you hear ? '
    ' I hear no news,' answered the tanner,
    ' but that cow-hides be dear.'

15 ' Cow-hides ? cow-hides ? ' then said our
        king,
    ' I marvell what they be;'
    ' Why, art thou a fool ? ' quoth the
        tanner,
    ' look, I have one under me.'

16 ' Yet one thing now I would thee pray,
    so that thou wouldst not be strange;
If thy mare be better then my steed,
    I pray thee let us change.'

17 ' But if you needs with me will change,
    As change full well may ye,
By the faith of my body,' quoth the
        tanner,
    ' I look to have boot of thee.'

18 'What boot wilt thou ask?' then said
 our king,
  'what boot dost thou ask on this
  ground?'
 'No pence nor half-pence,' said the tanner,
  'but a noble in gold so round.'

19 'Here's twenty good groats,' then said
 the king,
  'so well paid see you be;'
 'I love thee better then I did before,
  I thought thou hadst nere a peny.

20 'But if so be we needs must change,
 as change thou must abide,
 Though thou hast gotten Brock my
  mare,
  thou shalt not have my cow-hide.'

21 The tanner took the good cow-hide,
 that of the cow was hilt,
 And threw it upon the king's saddle,
  that was so fairly guilt.

22 'Now help me, help me,' quoth the tanner,
  'Full quickly that I were gone,
 For when I come home to Gillian my
  wife
  she'l say I'm a gentleman.'

23 The king took the tanner by the leg,
 he girded a fart so round;
 'You'r very homely,' said the king,
  'were I aware, I'd laid you o th'
  ground.'

24 But when the tanner was in the king's
 saddle
  astonëd then he was;
 He knew not the stirrops that he did
  wear,
  whether they were gold or brass.

25 But when the steed saw the black cow-
 tale wag,
  for and the black cow-horn,
 The steed began to run away,
  as the divel the tanner had born.

26 Untill he came unto a nook,
 a little beside an ash;
 The steed gave the tanner such a fall
  his neck was almost brast.

27 'Take thy horse again, with a vengeance,' he said,
  'with me he shall not abide;'
 'It is no marvell,' said the king, and
  laught,
  'he knew not your cow-hide.

28 'But if that we needs now must change,
 as change that well we mought,
 I'le swear to you plain, if you have
  your mare,
  I look to have some boot.'

29 'What boot will you ask?' quoth the
 tanner,
  'What boot will you ask on this
  ground?'
 'No pence nor half-pence,' said our king,
  'but a noble in gold so round.'

30 'Here's twenty [good] groats,' said the
 tanner,
  'and twenty more I have of thine;
 I have ten groats more in my purse,
  we'l drink five of them at the wine.'

31 The king set a bugle-horne to his
 mouth,
  that blew both loud and shrill,
 And five hundred lords and knights
  came riding over a hill.

32 'Away, with a vengeance,' quoth the
 tanner,
  'with thee I 'le no longer abide;
 Thou art a strong thief, yonder be thy
  fellows,
  they will steal away my cow-hide.'

33 'No, I protest,' then said our king,
 'for so it may not be;
 They be the lords of Drayton Basset,
  come out of the North Country.'

34 But when they came before the king
 full low they fell on their knee;
 The tanner had rather then a thousand
  pound
  he had been out of his company.

35 'A coller! a coller!' then said the king,
 'a coller!' then did he cry;
 Then would he have given a thousand
  pound
  he had not been so nigh.

36 'A coller? a coller?' then quoth the
      tanner,
   'it is a thing which will breed sorrow;
   For after a coller commeth a halter,
      and I shall be hanged tomorrow.'

37 'No, do not fear,' the king did say;
   'for pastime thou hast shown me,
   No coller nor halter thou shalt have,
      but I will give thee a fee.

38 'For Plompton Park I will give thee,
      with tenements three beside,
   Which is worth three hundred pound a
      year,
      to maintain thy good cow-hide.'

39 'Godamercy, Godamercy,' quoth the
      tanner;
   'for this good deed thou hast done,
   If ever thou comest to merry Tamworth,
      thou shalt have clouting-leather for
      thy shone.'

274

OUR GOODMAN

B is a broadside version which has had an
interesting history on the Continent. It was
translated into German by Friedrich Wilhelm
Meyer, in 1789, in very happy style, with a
dénoûment in which the man gives his wife a
beating and explains his cuffs as caresses which
her mother has sent her. Meyer's ballad was
printed in 1790. It had great and immediate
success, was circulated as a broadside, and was
taken up by the people, in whose mouth it un-
derwent the usual treatment of ballads traditionally propagated. From Germany it spread
into Scandinavia and Hungary, and perhaps
elsewhere.

A similar ballad, 'Marion' or 'Le Jaloux,'
is common in France, especially in the south.
For a serious ballad exhibiting similar questions and evasions, see 'Clerk Saunders' (No.
69 F).

A

Herd's MSS., i, 140; Herd's Ancient and
Modern Scottish Songs, 1776, ii, 172.

1 HAME came our goodman,
      And hame came he.
   And then he saw a saddle-horse,
      Where nae horse should be.

2 'What's this now, goodwife?
      What's this I see?
   How came this horse here,
      Without the leave o me?'

   Recitative.   'A horse?' quo she.
      'Ay, a horse,' quo he.

3 'Shame fa your cuckold face,
      Ill mat ye see!
   'T is naething but a broad sow,
      My minnie sent to me.'

   'A broad sow?' quo he.
      'Ay, a sow,' quo shee.

4 'Far hae I ridden,
      And farer hae I gane,
   But a sadle on a sow's back
      I never saw nane.'

5 Hame came our goodman,
      And hame came he;
   He spy'd a pair of jack-boots,
      Where nae boots should be.

6 'What's this now, goodwife?
      What's this I see?
   How came these boots here,
      Without the leave o me?'

   'Boots?' quo she.
      'Ay, boots,' quo he.

7 'Shame fa your cuckold face,
      And ill mat ye see!
   It's but a pair of water-stoups,
      My minnie sent to me.'

   'Water-stoups?' quo he.
      'Ay, water-stoups,' quo she.

8 'Far hae I ridden,
      And farer hae I gane,
   But siller spurs on water-stoups
      I saw never nane.'

9 Hame came our goodman,
      And hame came he,
   And he saw a sword,
      Whare a sword should na be

10 'What's this now, goodwife?
      What's this I see?
   How came this sword here,
      Without the leave o me?'

'A sword ?' quo she.
'Ay, a sword,' quo he.

11 'Shame fa your cuckold face,
    Ill mat ye see !
  It 's but a porridge-spurtle,
    My minnie sent to me.'

'A spurtle ?' quo he.
'Ay, a spurtle,' quo she.

12 'Far hae I ridden,
    And farer hae I gane,
  But siller-handed spurtles
    I saw never nane.'

13 Hame came our goodman,
    And hame came he;
  There he spy'd a powderd wig,
    Where nae wig shoud be.

14 'What 's this now, goodwife ?
    What 's this I see ?
  How came this wig here,
    Without the leave o me ?'

'A wig ?' quo she.
'Ay, a wig,' quo he.

15 'Shame fa your cuckold face,
    And ill mat you see !
  'T is naething but a clocken-hen,
    My minnie sent to me.'

'Clocken hen ?' quo he.
'Ay, clocken hen,' quo she.

16 'Far hae I ridden,
    And farer hae I gane,
  But powder on a clocken-hen
    I saw never nane.'

17 Hame came our goodman,
    And hame came he,
  And there he saw a muckle coat,
    Where nae coat shoud be.

18 'What 's this now, goodwife ?
    What 's this I see ?
  How came this coat here,
    Without the leave o me ?'

'A coat ?' quo she.
'Ay, a coat,' quo he.

19 'Shame fa your cuckold face,
    Ill mat ye see !
  It 's but a pair o blankets,
    My minnie sent to me.'

'Blankets ?' quo he.
'Ay, blankets,' quo she.

20 'Far hae I ridden,
    And farer hae I gane,
  But buttons upon blankets
    I saw never nane.'

21 Ben went our goodman,
    And ben went he,
  And there he spy'd a sturdy man,
    Where nae man shoud be.

22 'What 's this now, goodwife ?
    What 's this I see ?
  How came this man here,
    Without the leave o me ?'

'A man ?' quo she.
'Ay, a man,' quo he.

23 'Poor blind body,
    And blinder mat ye be !
  It 's a new milking-maid,
    My mither sent to me.'

'A maid ?' quo he.
'Ay, a maid,' quo she.

24 'Far hae I ridden,
    And farer hae I gane,
  But lang-bearded maidens
    I saw never nane.'

B

'The Merry Cuckold and Kind Wife,' a
broadside : Printed and Sold at the Printing-
Office in Bow Church-Yard, London.

1 O I WENT into the stable,
    and there for to see,
  And there I saw three horses stand,
    by one, by two, and by three.

2 O I calld to my loving wife,
    and 'Anon, kind sir !' quoth she:
  'O what do these three horses here,
    without the leave of me ?'

3 'Why, you old cuckold, blind cuckold,
    can't you very well see ?

These are three milking-cows,
  my mother sent to me.'

4 'Heyday! Godzounds! Milking-cows
    with bridles and saddles on!
  the like was never known!'
Old Wichet a cuckold went out,
  and a cuckold he came home.

5 O I went into the kitchen,
  and there for to see,
And there I saw three swords hang,
  by one, by two, and by three.

6 O I calld to my loving wife,
  and 'Anon, kind sir!' quoth she:
'O what do these three swords do here,
  without the leave of me?'

7 'Why, you old cuckold, blind cuckold,
  can't you very well see?
They are three roasting-spits,
  my mother sent to me.'

8 'Heyday! Godzounds! Roasting spits
    with scabbards on!
  the like was never known!'
Old Wichet a cuckold went out,
  and a cuckold he came home.

9 O I went into the parlour,
  and there for to see,
And there I saw three cloaks hang,
  by one, by two, and by three.

10 O I calld to my loving wife,
  and 'Anon, kind sir!' quoth she:
'O what do these three cloaks do here,
  without the leave of me?'

11 'Why, you old cuckold, blind cuckold,
  can't you very well see?
These are three mantuas,
  my mother sent to me.'

12 'Heyday! Godzounds! Mantuas with
    capes on!
  the like was never known!'
Old Wichet a cuckold went out,
  and a cuckold he came home.

13 I went into the pantry,
  and there for to see,
And there I saw three pair of boots hang,
  by one, by two, and by three.

14 O I called to my loving wife,
  and 'Anon, kind sir!' quoth she:
'O what do these three pair of boots do
  here,
  without the leave of me?'

15 'Why, you old cuckold, blind cuckold,
  can't you very well see?
These are three pudding-bags,
  my mother sent to me.'

16 'Heyday! Godzounds! Pudding-bags
    with spurs on!
  the like was never known!'
Old Wichet a cuckold went out,
  and a cuckold he came home.

17 I went into my closet,
  and there for to see,
And there I saw three pair of breeches
  lie,
  by one, by two, and by three.

18 O I calld to my loving wife,
  and 'Anon, kind sir!' quoth she:
'O what do these three pair of breeches
  do here,
  without the leave of me?'

19 'Why, you old cuckold, blind cuckold,
  can't you very well see?
These are three petticoats,
  my mother sent to me.'

20 'Heyday! Godzounds! Petticoats with
    waistbands on!
  the like was never known!'
Old Wichet a cuckold went out,
  and a cuckold he came home.

21 I went into the dairy,
  and there for to see,
And there I saw three hats hang,
  by one, by two, and by three.

22 I calld to my loving wife,
  and 'Anon, kind sir!' quoth she:
'Pray what do these three hats do
  here,
  without the leave of me?'

23 'Why, you old cuckold, blind cuckold,
  can't you very well see?
They are three skimming-dishes,
  my mother sent to me.'

24 'Heyday ; Godzounds! Skimming-
        dishes with hat-bands on !
    the like was never known ! '
    Old Wichet a cuckold went out,
        and a cuckold he came home.

25 I went into the chamber,
        and there for to see,
    And there I saw three men in bed lie,
        by one, by two, and by three.

26 I called to my loving wife,
        and ' Anon, kind sir ! ' quoth she :
    ' O what do these three men in bed,
        without the leave of me ? '

27 ' Why, you old cuckold, blind cuckold,
        don't you very well see ?
    They are three milking-maids,
        my mother sent to me.'

28 'Heyday ! Godzounds ! Milking-maids
        with beards on !
    the like was never known ! '
    Old Wichet a cuckold went out,
        and a cuckold he came home.

275

GET UP AND BAR THE DOOR

This tale is one of a group which may or
may not have had a single archetype. Of the
varieties, that which comes nearest is the first
story in Straparola's Eighth Day. The story
is well known in the East (see, for example,
Forty Vezirs, Gibb, p. 171) and elsewhere (see
Crane, Italian Popular Tales, p. 284).

A

a. Herd, ' Get up and bar the Door,' The
Ancient and Modern Scots Songs, 1769, p. 330 ;
Ancient and Modern Scottish Songs, 1776, ii,
159. b. [Pinkerton], Select Scotish Ballads,
1783, ii, 150.   •

1 It fell about the Martinmas time,
        And a gay time it was then,
    When our goodwife got puddings to make,
        And she 's boild them in the pan.

2 The wind sae cauld blew south and north,
        And blew into the floor ;
    Quoth our goodman to our goodwife,
        ' Gae out and bar the door.'

3 ' My hand is in my hussyfskap,
        Goodman, as ye may see ;
    An it shoud nae be barrd this hundred
            year,
        It 's no be barrd for me.'

4 They made a paction tween them twa,
        They made it firm and sure,
    That the first word whaeer shoud speak,
        Shoud rise and bar the door.

5 Then by there came two gentlemen,
        At twelve o clock at night,
    And they could neither see house nor
            hall,
        Nor coal nor candle-light.

6 ' Now whether is this a rich man's house,
        Or whether is it a poor ? '
    But neer a word wad ane o them speak,
        For barring of the door.

7 And first they ate the white puddings,
        And then they ate the black ;
    Tho muckle thought the goodwife to
            hersel,
        Yet neer a word she spake.

8 Then said the one unto the other,
        ' Here, man, tak ye my knife ;
    Do ye tak aff the auld man's beard,
        And I 'll kiss the goodwife.'

9 ' But there 's nae water in the house,
        And what shall we do than ? '
    ' What ails ye at the pudding-broo,
        That boils into the pan ? '

10 O up then started our goodman,
        An angry man was he :
    ' Will ye kiss my wife before my een,
        And scad me wi pudding-bree ? '

11 Then up and started our goodwife,
        Gied three skips on the floor :
    ' Goodman, you 've spoken the foremost
            word,
        Get up and bar the door.'

B

' John Blunt,' Macmath MS., p. 74. " From
the singing of Miss Jane Webster, 15th October, 1886, and 20th August, 1887, who learned
it at Airds of Kells, Kirkcudbrightshire, many
years ago, from James McJannet."

1 THERE leeved a wee man at the fit o
    yon hill,
  John Blunt it was his name, O
And he selld liquor and ale o the best,
  And bears a wondrous fame. O
Tal lara ta lilt, tal lare a lilt,
Tal lara ta lilt, tal lara

2 The win it blew frae north to south,
    It blew into the floor;
Says auld John Blunt to Janet the wife,
    Ye maun rise up and bar the door.

3 'My hans are in my husseyskep,
    I canna weel get them free,
And if ye dinna bar it yersel
    It 'll never be barred by me.'

4 They made it up atween them twa,
    They made it unco sure,
That the ane that spoke the foremost word
    Was to rise and bar the door.

5 There was twa travellers travelling late,
    Was travelling cross the muir,
And they cam unto wee John Blunt's,
    Just by the light o the door.

6 'O whether is this a rich man's house,
    Or whether is it a puir?'
But never a word would the auld bodies
    speak,
For the barring o the door.

7 First they bad good een to them,
    And syne they bad good morrow;
But never a word would the auld bodies
    speak,
For the barring o the door, O.

8 First they ate the white puddin,
    And syne they ate the black,
And aye the auld wife said to hersel,
    May the deil slip doun wi that!

9 And next they drank o the liquor sae
    strong,
    And syne they drank o the yill:
'Now since we hae got a house o our ain
    I'm sure we may tak our fill.'

10 It 's says the ane unto the ither,
    Here, man, tak ye my knife,
An ye 'll scrape aff the auld man's beard,
    While I kiss the gudewife.

11 'Ye hae eaten my meat, ye hae drucken
    my drink,
  Ye 'd make my auld wife a whore!'
'John Blunt, ye hae spoken the fore-
    most word,
  Ye maun rise up and bar the door.'

276

THE FRIAR IN THE WELL

A reference of Skelton's in his Colyn Cloute
(vv. 879 ff.) carries the story, and almost certainly the ballad, back to the first quarter of
the sixteenth century. The Scottish ballad (B)
is an improvement on the English. The tale
appears to be of Oriental origin. It is also represented in English by 'The Wright's Chaste
Wife,' by Adam of Cobsam.

A

a. 'The Fryer well fitted,' etc., Rawlinson
Ballads, 566, fol. 63, 4°. **b.** 'The Fryer well
fitted,' etc., Roxburghe Ballads, II, 172; Ebs-
worth, Roxburghe Ballads, VII, 222. **c.** 'The
Fryer and the Maid,' D'Urfey's Pills to purge
Melancholy, ed. 1719, III, 325.

1 As I lay musing all alone,
    fa, la, la, la, la
A pretty jeast I thought upon;
    fa, la, la, la, la
Then listen a while, and I will you tell
Of a fryer that loved a bonny lass well,
    fa, la, la, la, la
    fa, la, la, lang-tre-down-dilly

2 He came to the maid when she went to
    bed,
Desiring to have her maidenhead,
But she denyëd his desire,
And told him that she feard hell-fire.

3 'Tush,' quoth the fryer, 'thou needst
    not doubt
If thou wert in hell I could sing thee
    out:'
'Then,' quoth the maid, 'thou shalt have
    thy request;'
The fryer was glad as a fox in his nest.

4 'But one thing,' quoth she, 'I do desire,
Before you have what you require;
Before that you shall do the thing,
An angel of mony thou shalt me bring.'

5 'Tush,' quoth the fryer, 'we shall agree,
No mony shall part my love and me;
Before that I will see thee lack,
I 'le pawn the grey gown from my back.'

6 The maid bethought her of a wile
How she the fryer might beguile;
While he was gone, the truth to tell,
She hung a cloth before the well.

7 The fryer came, as his covenant was,
With money to his bonny lass;
'Good morrow, fair maid!' 'Good
morrow!' quoth she.
'Here is the mony I promised thee.'

8 She thankt the man, and she took his
mony:
'Now let us go to 't,' quoth he, 'sweet
hony:'
'O stay,' quoth she, 'some respite make,
My father comes, he will me take.'

9 'Alas!' quoth the fryer, 'where shall I
run,
To hide me till that he be gone?'
'Behinde the cloath run thou,' quoth she,
'And there my father cannot thee see.'

10 Behind the cloath the fryer crept,
And into the well on the sudden he
leapt;
'Alas,' quoth he, 'I am in the well!'
'No matter,' quoth she, 'if thou wert in
hell.

11 'Thou sayst thou couldst sing me out of
hell,
Now prithee sing thy self out of the
well:'
The fryer sung with a pittiful sound,
Oh help me out, or I shall be dround!

12 'I trow,' quoth she, 'your courage is
coold.'
Quoth the fryer, I was never so foold,
I never was servëd so before.
'Then take heed,' quoth she, 'thou
comst there no more.'

13 Quoth he, For sweet Saint Francis sake
On his disciple some pitty take:
Quoth she, Saint Francis never taught
His scholars to tempt young maids to
naught.

14 The fryer did entreat her still
That she should help him out of the well;
She heard him make such pittious moan
She helpd him out, and bid him be gone.

15 Quoth he, Shall I have my mony again,
Which thou from me hast beforehand
tane?
Good sir,' said she, 'there 's no such
matter;
I 'le make you pay for fouling my
water.'

16 The fryer went all along the street,
Droping wet, like a new-washd sheep;
Both old and young commended the
maid
That such a witty prank had plaid.

B

a. 'The Friar and Fair Maid,' Buchan's
MSS., II, 351.   b. 'The Friar,' Kinloch MSS.,
VI, 97, in Kinloch's handwriting.   c. Kinloch
MSS., V, 60, in the handwriting of James Beat-
tie.

1 O HEARKEN and hear, and I will you tell
Sing, Faldidae, faldidadi
Of a friar that loved a fair maiden well.
Sing, Faldi dadi di di (bis)

2 The friar he came to this maiden's bed-
side,
And asking for her maidenhead.

3 'O I would grant you your desire,
If 't werena for fear o hell's burning fire.'

4 'O hell's burning fire ye need have no
doubt;
Altho you were in, I could whistle you
out.'

5 'O if I grant to you this thing,
Some money you unto me must bring.'

6 He brought her the money, and did it
down tell;
She had a white cloth spread over the
well.

7 Then the fair maid cried out that her
master was come;
'O,' said the friar, 'then where shall I
run?'

8 'O ye will go in behind yon screen,
    And then by my master ye winna be seen.'

9 Then in behind the screen she him sent,
    But he fell into the well by accident.

10 Then the friar cried out with a piteous
    moan,
    O help ! O help me ! or else I am gone.

11 'Ye said ye wad whistle me out o hell;
    Now whistle your ain sel out o the well.'

12 She helped him out and bade him be gone;
    The friar he asked his money again.

13 'As for your money, there is no much
    matter
    To make you pay more for jumbling our
    water.'

14 Then all who hear it commend this fair
    maid
    For the nimble trick to the friar she
    played.

15 The friar he walked on the street,
    And shaking his lugs like a well-washen
    sheep.

277

THE WIFE WRAPT IN WETHER'S SKIN

The story of the ballad was in all likelihood
traditionally derived from the good old tale of
the Wife Lapped in Morrel's Skin (Hazlitt's
Early Popular Poetry, IV, 179). Here a husband, who has put up with a great deal from
an excessively restive wife, flays his old horse
Morrell and salts the hide, takes the shrew down
cellar, and, after a sharp contest for mastery,
beats her with birchen rods till she swoons,
then wraps her in the salted hide : by which
process the woman is perfectly reformed.

A

a. 'Sweet Robin,' Jamieson's Popular Ballads, I, 319. "From the recitation of a friend
of the editor's in Morayshire."

1 SHE wadna bake, she wadna brew
    Hollin, green hollin
    For spoiling o her comely hue.
    Bend your bow, Robin

2 She wadna wash, she wadna wring,
    For spoiling o her gay goud ring.

3 Robin he 's gane to the fald
    And catched a weather by the spauld.

4 And he has killed his weather black
    And laid the skin upon her back.

5 'I darena pay you, for your kin,
    But I can pay my weather's skin.

6 'I darena pay my lady's back,
    But I can pay my weather black.'

7 'O Robin, Robin, lat me be,
    And I 'll a good wife be to thee.

8 'It 's I will wash, and I will wring,
    And never mind my gay goud ring.

9 'It 's I will bake, and I will brew,
    And never mind my comely hue.

10 'And gin ye thinkna that eneugh,
    I 'se tak the goad and I 'se ca the pleugh

11 'Gin ye ca for mair whan that is doon,
    I 'll sit i the neuk and I 'll dight your
    shoon.'

B

'Robin he 's gane to the wude,' Harris MS.,
fol. 26 b, No. 25, from Miss Harris.

1 ROBIN he 's gane to the wast,
    Hollin, green hollin
    He 's waled a wife amang the warst.
    Bend your bows, Robin

2 She could neither bake nor brew,
    For spoilin o her bonnie hue.

3 She could neither spin nor caird,
    But fill the cup, an sair the laird.

4 She could neither wash nor wring,
    For spoilin o her gay goud ring.

5 Robin 's sworn by the rude
    That he wald mak an ill wife gude.

6 Robin he 's gaun to the fauld,
    An taen his blaik [wither] by the
    spauld.

7 He 's taen aff his wither's skin
 An he has preened his ain wife in.

8 'I daurna beat my wife, for a' her kin,
 But I may beat my wither's skin.'

9 'I can baith bake an brew;
 What care I for my bonnie hue ?

10 'I can baith wash an wring;
 What care I for my gay gowd ring ?

11 'I can baith spin an caird;
 Lat onybodie sair the laird.'

12 Robin 's sworn by the rude
 That he has made an ill wife gude.

D

Jamieson-Brown MS., Appendix, p. iii, letter of R. Scott to Jamieson, June 9, 1805.

1 THERE livd a laird down into Fife,
 Riftly, raftly, now, now, now
An he has married a bonny young wife.
 Hey Jock Simpleton, Jenny['s] white petticoat,
 Robin a Rashes, now, now, now

2 He courted her and he brought her hame,
 An thought she would prove a thrifty dame.

3 She could neither spin nor caird,
 But sit in her chair and dawt the laird.

4 She wadna bake and she wadna brew,
 An a' was for spoiling her delicate hue.

5 She wadna wash nor wad she wring,
 For spoiling o her gay goud ring.

6 But he has taen him to his sheep-fauld,
 An taen the best weather by the spauld.

7 Aff o the weather he took the skin,
 An rowt his bonny lady in.

8 'I dare na thump you, for your proud kin,
 But well sall I lay to my ain weather's skin.'

 * * * * *

F

From the recitation of Miss Lydia R. Nichols, Salem, Massachusetts, as heard in the early years of the nineteenth century; sung by a New England country fellow on ship-board : Journal of American Folk-Lore, VII, 253 ff., 1894.

1 SWEET WILLIAM he married a wife,
 Gentle Jenny cried rosemaree
To be the sweet comfort of his life.
 As the dew flies over the mulberry tree.

2 Jenny couldnt in the kitchen to go,
 For fear of dirting her white-heeled shoes.

3 Jenny couldnt wash, and Jenny couldnt bake,
 For fear of dirting her white apurn tape.

4 Jenny couldnt card, and Jenny couldnt spin,
 For fear of hurting her gay gold ring.

5 Sweet William came whistling in from plaow,
 Says, 'O my dear wife, is my dinner ready naow ? '

6 She called him a dirty paltry whelp:
 'If you want any dinner, go get it yourself.'

7 Sweet William went aout unto the sheep-fold,
 And aout a fat wether he did pull.

8 And daown on his knees he began for to stick,
 And quicklie its skin he thereof did strip.

9 He took the skin and laid on his wife's back,
 And with a good stick went whikety whack.

10 'I 'll tell my father and all my kin
 How still a quarrel you 've begun.'

11 'You may tell your father and all your kin
 How I have thrashed my fat wether's skin.'

12 Sweet William came whistling in from
     plaow,
     Says, 'O my dear wife, is my dinner
     ready naow?'

13 She drew her table and spread her board,
     And, 'Oh my dear husband,' was every
     word.

14 And naow they live free from all care
     and strife,
     And naow she makes William a very
     good wife.

278

THE FARMER'S CURST WIFE

A curst wife who was a terror to demons is
a feature in a widely spread and highly humorous tale, Oriental and European. See Benfey,
Pantschatantra, i, 519–34; and, for a variety
which is, at the beginning, quite close to our
ballad, Ralston, Russian Folk-Tales, p. 39.

A

'The Farmer's Old Wife,' Dixon, Ancient
Poems, Ballads, and Songs, p. 210, Percy Society, vol. XVII.

1 THERE was an old farmer in Sussex did
     dwell,
         (*Chorus of whistlers*)
     There was an old farmer in Sussex did
     dwell,
     And he had a bad wife, as many knew
     well.
         (*Chorus of whistlers*)

2 Then Satan came to the old man at the
     plough:
     'One of your family I must have now.

3 'It is not your eldest son that I crave,
     But it is your old wife, and she I will
     have.'

4 'O welcome, good Satan, with all my
     heart!
     I hope you and she will never more part.'

5 Now Satan has got the old wife on his
     back,
     And he lugged her along, like a pedlar's
     pack.

6 He trudged away till they came to his
     hall-gate;
     Says he, Here, take in an old Sussex
     chap's mate.

7 O then she did kick the young imps
     about;
     Says one to the other, Let's try turn
     her out.

8 She spied thirteen imps all dancing in
     chains,
     She up with her pattens and beat out
     their brains.

9 She knocked the old Satan against the
     wall:
     'Let's turn her out, or she'll murder
     us all.'

10 Now he's bundled her up on his back
     amain,
     And to her old husband he took her again.

11 'I have been a tormentor the whole of
     my life,
     But I neer was tormented so as with
     your wife.'

B

Macmath MS., p. 96. Taken down by Mr
Macmath from the recitation of his aunt, Miss
Jane Webster, Crossmichael, Kirkcudbright-
shire, August 27th, 1892; learned many years
ago, at Airds of Kells, from the singing of
Samuel Galloway.

1 THE auld Deil cam to the man at the
     pleugh,
         Rumchy ae de aidie
     Saying, I wish ye gude luck at the mak-
     ing o yer sheugh.
         Mushy toorin an ant tan aira.

2 'It's neither your oxen nor you that I
     crave;
     It's that old scolding woman, it's her
     I must have.'

3 'Ye're welcome to her wi a' my gude
     heart;
     I wish you and her it's never may part.'

4 She jumpet on to the auld Deil's back,
     And he carried her awa like a pedlar's
     pack.

5 He carried her on till he cam to hell's
     door,
  He gaed her a kick till she landed in
     the floor.

6 She saw seven wee deils a' sitting in a
     raw,
  She took up a mell and she murdered
     them a'.

7 A wee reekit deil lookit owre the wa:
  ' O tak her awa, or she 'll ruin us a'.'

8 ' O what to do wi her I canna weel tell;
  She 's no fit for heaven, and she 'll no
     bide in hell.'

    *   *   *   *   *

9 She jumpit on to the auld Deil's back,
  And he carried her back like a pedlar's
     pack.

    *   *   *   *   *

10 She was seven year gaun, and seven
     year comin,
  And she cried for the sowens she left in
     the pot.

280

THE BEGGAR–LADDIE

This resembles the well-known rhymed tale
of The Gaberlunyie-Man, but has a romantic
conclusion, resembling that of ' Lizie Lindsay '
(No. 226).

A

' The Shiperd Boy,' Old Lady's Collection,
No. 35 ; north of Scotland.

1 SHIPERD-BOY, what is yer trade ?
  Or what way do ye wine yer bread ?
  Or what way do ye wine yer bread,
    Fan the kipeng nout gies over ?

2 ' Spindels an forls it is my trade,
  An bits of sticks to them who nead,
  Whelk is a gentell trade indeed;
    Bony lassie, cane ye lea me ? '

3 ' I lea you as I supos
  Rachell loued Jacob of old,
  As Jason loied his flice of gould,
    Sae dearly do I lea ye.

4 ' Ye cast off yer clouty coat,
  An ye pitt one my scarlett cloke,
  An I will follou you just att the back,
    Becass ye are a bonny laddie.'

5 He cust off his cloutty coat,
  An he patt on her scarlet cloke,
  An she folloued him just att the back,
    Becaus he was a bonny laddie.

6 They gaed on, an forder on,
  Till they came to yon borrous-toun;
  She bought a loaf an they both satt
     doun,
    Bat she ate no we her laddie.

7 They gaed on, an forder one,
  Till they came to the nest borrous-toun;
  I wat the lassie louked doun,
    For the following of her laddie.

8 ' O if I wer on the head of yon hill,
  There I wad greet my fill,
    For the following of my laddie.'

9 ' O had yer toung, my dearest dear,
  I ill ha ye back as I brought ye hear,
    For I canna bear yer morning.'

10 ' O had yer toung, my dearest dear,
  I will gae throu the warld baith far an
     near,
    Becaus ye 'r a bonny ladie.'

11 They gad on, an forder on,
  Till they came to his father's haa,
    An he knoked ther fue loudly.

12 ' O had yer hand, my dear[est] dear,
  An dou not knoke sae loudly,
    For fear they sud be angry.'

13 Four-an-tuenty gentilmen
  They conved the beager ben,
    An as mony gay ladës
      Conved the beager's lassie.

14 His brother lead her throu the haa:
  ' I wis, brother, we had beagged a',
    For sick a bonny lassie.'

15 That same night she was bedded,
  An the nist morning she was wedded;
  She came to gued by grait misgiding,
    By the following of her laddie.

282

JOCK THE LEG AND THE MERRY MERCHANT

This piece, but for names (and Jock the Leg is only a thin shrouding for Little John), might have gone with the Robin Hood ballads. It was composed, probably, in the last half of the eighteenth century, and for hawker's purposes, but it is a better ballad, imitation as it is, than some of the seventeenth-century broadsides of the same class (which is indeed saying very little). The fight for the pack we have in 'The Bold Pedlar and Robin Hood' (No. 132); the "asking" of a blast on the horn and the scornful reply, in 'Robin Hood and the Shepherd' (No. 135).

Buchan's Ballads of the North of Scotland, II, 165.

1 As Jock the Leg and the merry merchant
    Came from yon borrow's town,
  They took their budgets on their backs,
    And fieldert they were boun.

2 But they came to a tavern-house,
    Where chapmen used to be:
  'Provide, provide,' said Jock the Leg,
    'A good supper for me.

3 'For the merry merchant shall pay it a',
    Tho it were good merks three;'
  'But never a penny,' said the merry
        merchant,
    'But shot, as it fa's me.

4 'A bed, a bed,' said the merry merchant,
    'It's time to go to rest;'
  'And that ye shall,' said the good good-
        wife,
    'And your covrings o the best.'

5 Then Jock the Leg in one chamber was
        laid,
    The merchant in another,
  And lockfast door atween them twa,
    That the one might not see the other.

6 But the merchant was not well lain down,
    Nor yet well fa'en asleep,
  Till up it starts him Jock the Leg,
    Just at the merchant's feet.

7 'Win up, win up,' said Jock the Leg,
    'We might hae been miles three;'

'But never a foot,' said the merry mer-
        chant,
    'Till day that I do see.

8 'For I cannot go by Barnisdale,
    Nor yet by Coventry;
  For Jock the Leg, that common thief,
    Would take my pack from me.'

9 'I'll hae you in by Barnisdale,
    And down by Coventry,
  And I'll guard you frae Jock the Leg
    Till day that ye do see.'

10 When they were in by Barnisdale,
    And in by Coventry,
  'Repeat, repeat,' said Jock the Leg,
    'The words ye ance tauld me.'

11 'I never said aught behind your back
    But what I'll say to thee;
  Are ye that robber, Jock the Leg,
    Will take my pack frae me?'

12 'O by my sooth,' said Jock the Leg,
    'You'll find that man I be;
  Surrender that pack that's on your back,
    Or then be slain by me.'

13 He's ta'en his pack down frae his back,
    Set it below yon tree;
  Says, I will fight for my good pack
    Till day that I may see.

14 Then they fought there in good green-
        wood
    Till they were bloody men;
  The robber on his knees did fall,
    Said, Merchant, hold your hand.

15 'An asking, asking,' said Jock the Leg,
    'An asking ye'll grant me;'
  'Ask on, ask on,' said the merry mer-
        chant,
    'For men to asking are free.'

16 'I've dune little harm to you,' he said,
    'More than you'd been my brother;
  Give me a blast o my little wee horn,
    And I'll give you another.'

17 'A blast o your little wee horn,' he said,
    'Of this I take no doubt;
  I hope you will take such a blast
    Ere both your eyes fly out.'

18 He set his horn to his mouth,
   And he blew loud and shrill,
   And four-and-twenty bauld bowmen
   Came Jock the Leg until.

19 'Ohon, alas!' said the merry merchant,
   'Alas! and woe is me!
   Sae many, a party o common thiefs,
   But nane to party me!

20 'Ye'll wile out six o your best bowmen,
   Yourself the seventh to be,
   And, put me one foot frae my pack,
   My pack ye shall have free.'

21 He wiled six o his best bowmen,
   Himself the seventh to be,
   But [him] frae his pack they couldna get,
   For all that they could dee.

22 He's taen his pack into one hand,
   His broadsword in the other,
   And he slew five o the best bowmen,
   And the sixth he has dung over.

23 Then all the rest they gae a shout,
   As they stood by the tree;
   Some said they would this merchant head,
   Some said they'd let him be.

24 But Jock the Leg he then replied,
   To this I'll not agree;
   He is the boldest broadsword-man
   That ever I fought wi.

25 'If ye could wield the bow, the bow
   As ye can do the brand,
   I would hae you to good greenwood,
   To be my master's man.'

26 'Tho I could wield the bow, the bow
   As I can do the brand,
   I would not gang to good greenwood,
   To join a robber-band.'

27 'O give me some of your fine linen,
   To cleathe my men and me,
   And ye'se hae some of my dun deers'
   skins,
   Below yon greenwood-tree.'

28 'Ye'se hae nane o my fine linen,
   To cleathe your men and thee,
   And I'll hae nane o your stown deers'
   skins,
   Below yon greenwood-tree.'

29 'Ye'll take your pack upon your back,
   And travel by land or sea;
   In brough or land, wherever we meet,
   Good billies we shall be.'

30 'I'll take my pack upon my back,
   And go by land or sea;
   In brough or land, wherever we meet,
   A rank thief I'll call thee.'

283

THE CRAFTY FARMER

This very ordinary ballad has enjoyed great popularity, and is given for that reason and as a specimen of its class.

a. 'The Crafty Farmer,' Logan, A Pedlar's Pack, p. 126, from a chap-book of 1796; 'The Crafty Miller,' Maidment, Scotish Ballads and Songs, 1859, p. 208, from a Glasgow stall-copy; a stall-copy, printed by M. Randall, Stirling.

1 THE song that I'm going to sing,
   I hope it will give you content,
   Concerning a silly old man,
   That was going to pay his rent.

2 As he was riding along,
   Along all on the highway,
   A gentleman-thief overtook him,
   And thus to him did say.

3 'Well overtaken!' said the thief,
   'Well overtaken!' said he;
   And 'Well overtaken!' said the old
   man,
   'If thou be good company.'

4 'How far are you going this way?'
   Which made the old man for to smile;
   'By my faith,' said the old man,
   'I'm just going two mile.

5 'I am a poor farmer,' he said,
   'And I farm a piece of ground,
   And my half-year's rent, kind sir,
   Just comes to forty pound.

6 'And my landlord has not been at home
   I've not seen him this twelvemonth or
   more,
   Which makes my rent be large;
   I've to pay him just fourscore.'

7 'Thou shouldst not have told any body,
   For thieves there's ganging many;
   If any should light on thee,
   They'll rob thee of thy money.'

8 'O never mind,' said the old man,
   'Thieves I fear on no side,
   For the money is safe in my bags,
   On the saddle on which I ride.'

9 As they were riding along,
   The old man was thinking no ill,
   The thief he pulled out a pistol
   And bid the old man stand still.

10 But the old man provd crafty,
   As in the world there's many;
   He threw his saddle oer the hedge,
   Saying, Fetch it, if thou 'lt have any.

11 The thief got off his horse,
   With courage stout and bold,
   To search for the old man's bag,
   And gave him his horse to hold.

12 The old man put's foot i the stirrup
   And he got on astride;
   To its side he clapt his spur up,
   You need not bid the old man ride.

13 'O stay!' said the thief, 'O stay!
   And half the share thou shalt have;'
   'Nay, by my faith,' said the old man,
   'For once I have bitten a knave.'

14 The thief he was not content,
   But he thought there must be bags;
   He out with his rusty old sword
   And chopt the old saddle in rags.

15 When he came to the landlord's house,
   This old man he was almost spent;
   Saying, Come, show me a private room
   And I'll pay you a whole year's rent.

16 'I ve met a fond fool by the way,
   I swapt horses and gave him no boot;
   But never mind,' said the old man,
   'For I got the fond fool by the foot.'

17 He opend this rogue's portmantle,
   It was glorious to behold;
   There were three hundred pounds in
   silver,
   And three hundred pounds in gold.

18 And as he was riding home,
   And down a narrow lane,
   He espied his mare tied to a hedge,
   Saying, Prithee, Tib, wilt thou gang
   hame?

19 When he got home to his wife
   And told her what he had done,
   Up she rose and put on her clothes,
   And about the house did run.

20 She sung, and she sung, and she sung,
   She sung with a merry devotion,
   Saying, If ever our daughter gets wed,
   It will help to enlarge her portion.

284

JOHN DORY

This ballad had a remarkable popularity in the seventeenth century, as is evinced by the numerous cases of its being cited which Chappell has collected (Popular Music, p. 67 f.). As to the history of the transactions set forth in the ballad, an account of them was given by Carew in his Survey of Cornwall, 1602, p. 135, an account which is likely to have been taken from the ballad, with the specification from tradition that Nicholl was "son to a widow near Foy." The king in the ballad would be John II, the Good, who was taken prisoner at Poitiers, and died in 1364. No John Doria is mentioned as being in his service.

Ravenscroft's Deuteromelia, London, 1609; No. 1 of Freemen's Songs, sig. B.

1 As it fell on a holy-day,
   And vpon an holy-tide-a,
   Iohn Dory bought him an ambling nag,
   To Paris for to ride-a.

2 And when John Dory to Paris was come,
   A little before the gate-a,
   John Dory was fitted, the porter was
   witted
   To let him in thereat-a.

3 The first man that John Dory did meet
   Was good king John of France-a;
   John Dory could well of his courtesie,
   But fell downe in a trance-a.

4 'A pardon, a pardon, my liege and my
   king,
   For my merie men and for me-a,

And all the churles in merie England,
  I 'le bring them all bound to thee-a.'

5 And Nicholl was then a Cornish man,
  A little beside Bohide-a,
And he mande forth a good blacke barke,
  With fiftie good oares on a side-a.

6 'Run vp, my boy, vnto the maine top,
  And looke what thou canst spie-a:'
'Who ho! who ho! a goodly ship I do
  see,
  I trow it be John Dory[-a].'

7 They hoist their sailes, both top and
  top,
The meisseine and all was tride-a,
And euery man stood to his lot,
  What euer should betide-a.

8 The roring cannons then were plide,
  And dub-a-dub went the drumme-a;
The braying trumpets lowde they cride
  To courage both all and some-a.

9 The grappling-hooks were brought at
  length,
The browne bill and the sword-a,
John Dory at length, for all his strength,
  Was clapt fast vnder board-a.

285

THE GEORGE ALOE AND THE SWEEPSTAKE

In 1611 there were entered to Richard Jones, "Captayne Jennings his songe, which he made in the Marshalsey," etc., and "the second parte of the George Aloo and the Swiftestake, beinge both ballades" (Arber, III, 456). The second part of the George Aloo must needs mean a second ballad, not the printers' second half (which begins in c with st. 14). In The Two Noble Kinsmen, printed in 1634, or earlier, the Jailer's Daughter sings:

The George Alow came from the south,
  From the coast of Barbary-a,
And there he met with brave gallants of war,
  By one, by two, by three-a.

Well haild, well haild, you jolly gallants,
  And whither now are you bound-a?
Oh, let me have your company
  Till [I] come to the sound-a.

These verses certainly seem to belong to another ballad. 'The Swepstacke' was a king's ship in 1545, and 'The Sweepstakes' apparently again in 1666.

a. Percy Papers, "from an ancient blackletter copy in Ballard's collection." b. Rawlinson, 566, fol. 183, 4°. c. Roxburghe, III, 204, in Ebsworth, Roxburghe Ballads, VI, 408.

1 THE George Aloe and the Sweepstakes
  too,
  With hey, with ho, for and a nony no
They were two merchant-men, a sailing
  for Safee.
  And along the course of Barbary

2 [The George Aloe to anchor came,
But the jolly Sweepstake kept on her
  way.]

3 They had not sayled leagues two or
  three
Before they spyed a sail upon the sea.

4 'O hail, O hail, you lusty gallants,
From whence is your good ship, and
  whither is she bound?'

5 'O we are some merchant-men, sailing
  for Safee:'
'And we be French rebels, a roving on
  the sea.

6 'O hail, O hail, you English dogs,
  [hail!]'
'The[n] come aboard, you French dogs,
  and strike down your sail''

7 'Amain, amain, you gallant Englishmen!'
'Come, you French swades, and strike
  down your sails!'

8 They laid us aboard on the starboard
  side,
And they overthrew us into the sea so
  wide.

9 When tidings to the George Aloe came
That the jolly Sweepstakes by a Frenchman was tane,

10 'To top, to top, thou little ship-boy,
And see if this French man-of-war thou
  canst descry.'

11 'A sail, a sail, under your lee,
  Yea, and another under her bough.'

12 'Weigh anchor, weigh anchor, O jolly
    boatswain,
  We will take this Frenchman if we can.'

13 We had not sailed leagues two or three
  But we met the French man-of-war
    upon the sea.

14 'All hail, all hail, you lusty gallants,
  Of whence is your fair ship, and whither
    is she bound?'

15 'O we are merchant-men, and bound
    for Safee;'
  'And we are Frenchmen, roving upon
    the sea.

16 'Amain, amain, you English dogs!'
  'Come aboard, you French rogues, and
    strike your sails!'

17 The first good shot the George Aloe shot,
  It made the Frenchmen's hearts sore
    afraid.

18 The second shot the George Aloe did
    afford,
  He struck the main-mast over the board.

19 'Have mercy, have mercy, you brave
    English[men].'
  'O what have you done with our brethren
    on [shore]?'
  As they sail[ed].

20 'We laid them aboard on the starboard
    side,
  And we threw them into the sea so wide.'

21 'Such mercy as you have shewed unto
    them,
  Even the like mercy shall you have
    again.'

22 We laid them aboard on the larboard
    side,
  And we threw them into the sea so
    wide.

23 Lord, how it grieved our hearts full sore
  To see the drowned Frenchmen float
    along the shore!

24 Now, gallant seamen all, adieu,
  With hey, with ho, for and a nony no
  This is the last news that I can write
    to you.
  To England's coast from Barbary

286

THE SWEET TRINITY (THE GOLDEN VANITY)

B is probably a traditional variation of the
broadside A. The conclusion of the broadside is sufficiently inadequate to impel almost
any singer to attempt an improvement, and a
rather more effective catastrophe is the only
signal difference besides names. It is, however, not quite impossible that the ultimate
source of the traditional copies may be as old
as the broadside.

A

'Sir Walter Raleigh sailing in the Lowlands,' etc., Pepys Ballads, IV, 196, No. 189
(1682–85).

1 SIR WALTER RAWLEIGH has built a ship,
    In the Neatherlands
  Sir Walter Rawleigh has built a ship,
    In the Neather-lands
  And it is called The Sweet Trinity,
  And was taken by the false gallaly.
    Sailing in the Low-lands

2 'Is there never a seaman bold
    In the Neather-lands
  Is there never a seaman bold
    In the Neather-lands
  That will go take this false gallaly,
  And to redeem The Sweet Trinity?'
    Sailing, etc.

3 Then spoke the little ship-boy;
    In the Neather-lands
  Then spoke the little ship-boy;
    In the Neather-lands
  'Master, master, what will you give me
  And I will take this false gallaly,
  And release The Sweet Trinity?'
    Sailing, etc.

4 'I'll give thee gold, and I'le give thee
    fee,
    In the Neather-lands
  I'll give thee gold and I'le give thee fee,
    In the Neather-lands

And my eldest daughter thy wife shall
   be.'
   Sailing, etc.

5 He set his breast, and away he did swim,
   Until he came to the false gallaly.

6 He had an augor fit for the [n]once,
   The which will bore fifteen good holes at
      once.

7 Some ware at cards, and some at dice,
   Until the salt water flashd in their eyes.

8 Some cut their hats, and some cut their
      caps,
   For to stop the salt-water gaps.

9 He set his breast, and away did swim,
   Until he came to his own ship again.

10 'I have done the work I promised to do,
   For I have sunk the false gallaly,
   And released The Sweet Trinity.

11 'You promised me gold, and you pro-
      mised me fee,
   Your eldest daughter my wife she must
      be.'

12 'You shall have gold, and you shall have
      fee,
   But my eldest daughter your wife shall
      never be.'
   For sailing, etc.

13 'Then fare you well, you cozening lord,
   Seeing you are not so good as your word.'
   For sailing, etc.

14 And thus I shall conclude my song,
   Of the sailing in the Low-lands
   Wishing all happiness to all seamen both
      old and young.
   In their sailing in the Low-lands

B

a. 'The Goulden Vanitie,' Logan's Pedlar's
Pack, p. 42, as sung about 1840 by Mr P. S.
Fraser, of Edinburgh, and obtained by him
orally. b. As sung by Mr George Du Maurier
to Mr J. R. Lowell, 1884. c. 'The French Gal-
ley,' Motherwell's MS., p. 420; from Mr John
Cleland, marble-cutter, Glasgow, who had it of
Mr Forrester, Stirling. d. Communicated by
Mrs Moncrieff, as taught to a relative of hers by
an old Scottish lady about 1830. e. 'The Low-
lands Low,' Findlay MSS., I, 161, "from Strang,
Divinity Student, 1868." f. Sharpe's Ballad
Book, 1880, p. 160, note by Sir Walter Scott.

1 THERE was a gallant ship, and a gallant
      ship was she
   Eck iddle du, and the Lowlands low
   And she was called The Goulden Vanitie.
   As she sailed to the Lowlands low

2 She had not sailed a league, a league
      but only three,
   Eck, etc.
   When she came up with a French gallee.
   As she sailed, etc.

3 Out spoke the little cabin-boy, out spoke
      he;
   'What will you give me if I sink that
      French gallee?'
   As ye sail, etc.

4 Out spoke the captain, out spoke he;
   'We'll gie ye an estate in the North
      Countrie.'
   As we sail, etc.

5 'Then row me up ticht in a black bull's
      skin,
   And throw me oer deck-buird, sink I or
      swim.'
   As ye sail, etc.

6 So they've rowed him up ticht in a black
      bull's skin,
   And have thrown him oer deck-buird,
      sink he or soom.
   As they sail, etc.

7 About, and about, and about went he,
   Until he cam up with the French gallee.
   As they sailed, etc.

8 O some were playing cards, and some
      were playing dice,
   When he took out an instrument, bored
      thirty holes at twice.
   As they sailed, etc.

9 Then some they ran with cloaks, and
      some they ran with caps,
   To try if they could stap the saut-water
      draps.
   As they sailed, etc.

10 About, and about, and about went he,
    Until he cam back to The Goulden Van-
        itie.
    As they sailed, etc.

11 'Now throw me oer a rope and pu me
        up on buird,
    And prove unto me as guid as your
        word.
    As ye sail, etc.

12 'We 'll no throw you oer a rope, nor pu
        you up on buird,
    Nor prove unto you as guid as our
        word.'
    As we sail, etc.

13 Out spoke the little cabin-boy, out spoke
        he;
    Then hang me, I 'll sink ye as I sunk the
        French gallee.
    As ye sail, etc.

14 But they 've thrown him oer a rope, and
        have pu'd him up on buird,
    And have proved unto him far better
        than their word.
    As they sailed, etc.

287

CAPTAIN WARD AND THE RAINBOW

The Rainbow was the name of one of Drake's
four ships in his expedition against Cadiz in
1587; it is mentioned very often from 1589.
John Ward, an Englishman of Kent, is said to
have commenced 'rover' about 1604, by indu-
cing the crew of a king's ship in which he had
some place to turn pirates under his command.
His race, though eventful, was, naturally
enough, not long. He seems not to be heard of
after 1609, in which year Ward and his col-
league, Dansekar, are spoken of as the "two
late famous pirates." (See Mr Ebsworth's preface in Bagford Ballads, Ballad Society, vi,
423 ff.) George Clifford (Earl of Cumberland),
Charles Blount (Lord Mountjoy), and Robert
Devereux (Earl of Essex), died, respectively,
in 1605, 1606, and 1601.

'The Famous Sea-Fight between Captain
Ward and the Rainbow,' London, Printed by
and for W. Onley. Bagford Ballads, i, 65.
Date, 1680 at the earliest.

1 STRIKE up, you lusty gallants, with
        musick and sound of drum,
    For we have descryed a rover, upon the
        sea is come;
    His name is Captain Ward, right well
        it doth appear,
    There has not been such a rover found
        out this thousand year.

2 For he hath sent unto our king, the sixth
        of January,
    Desiring that he might come in, with all
        his company:
    'And if your king will let me come till
        I my tale have told,
    I will bestow for my ransome full thirty
        tun of gold.'

3 'O nay! O nay!' then said our king,
        'O nay! this may not be,
    To yield to such a rover my self will
        not agree;
    He hath deceivd the French-man, like-
        wise the King of Spain,
    And how can he be true to me that hath
        been false to twain?'

4 With that our king provided a ship of
        worthy fame,
    Rainbow she is called, if you would
        know her name;
    Now the gallant Rainbow she rowes
        upon the sea,
    Five hundred gallant seamen to bear her
        company.

5 The Dutch-man and the Spaniard she
        made them for to flye,
    Also the bonny French-man, as she met
        him on the sea:
    When as this gallant Rainbow did come
        where Ward did lye,
    'Where is the captain of this ship?'
        this gallant Rainbow did cry.

6 'O that am I,' says Captain Ward,
        'there 's no man bids me lye,
    And if thou art the king's fair ship, thou
        art welcome unto me:'
    'I 'le tell thee what,' says Rainbow,
        'our king is in great grief
    That thou shouldst lye upon the sea and
        play the arrant thief,

7 'And will not let our merchants ships
    pass as they did before;
Such tydings to our king is come, which
    grieves his heart full sore.'
With that this gallant Rainbow she shot,
    out of her pride,
Full fifty gallant brass pieces, charged
    on every side.

8 And yet these gallant shooters prevailed
    not a pin,
Though they were brass on the out-side,
    brave Ward was steel within;
'Shoot on, shoot on,' says Captain Ward,
    'your sport well pleaseth me,
And he that first gives over shall yield
    unto the sea.

9 'I never wrongd an English ship, but
    Turk and King of Spain,
For and the jovial Dutch-man as I met
    on the main.
If I had known your king but one two
    years before,
I would have savd brave Essex life,
    whose death did grieve me sore.

10 'Go tell the King of England, go tell
    him thus from me,
If he reign king of all the land, I will
    reign king at sea.'
With that the gallant Rainbow shot,
    and shot, and shot in vain,
And left the rover's company, and re-
    turnd home again.

11 'Our royal king of England, your ship's
    returnd again,
For Ward's ship is so strong it never
    will be tane:'
'O everlasting!' says our king, 'I have
    lost jewels three,
Which would have gone unto the seas
    and brought proud Ward to me.

12 'The first was Lord Clifford, Earl of
    Cumberland;
The second was the lord Mountjoy, as
    you shall understand;
The third was brave Essex, from field
    would never flee;
Which would a gone unto the seas and
    brought proud Ward to me.'

288

THE YOUNG EARL OF ESSEX'S VICTORY OVER THE EMPEROR OF GERMANY

This ballad belongs undoubtedly to the eighteenth century, when High Germany had become familiar to the humble English. The ballad-maker's independence, in fact unconsciousness, of history and common sense, beginning with the title, in which young Essex is made Queen Elizabeth's champion, is amusing and not unpleasing. A version (B) from recitation begins with a prologue which must be derived from some other ballad or song.

A

Queen Elizabeth's Champion, or, Great Britain's Glory,' etc. a. Douce Ballads, III, fol. 80 b. b. Roxburghe, III, 416, in Ebsworth's Roxburghe Ballads, VI, 405.

1 COME, sound up your trumpets and beat
    up your drums,
And let's go to sea with a valiant
    good cheer,
In search of a mighty vast navy of
    ships,
The like has not been for these fifty
    long year.
    Raderer two, tandaro te,
    Raderer, tandorer, tan do re.

2 The queen she provided a navy of ships,
    With sweet flying streamers, so glorious to see,
Rich top and top-gallants, captains and
    lieutenants,
    Some forty, some fifty, brass-pieces
    and three.

3 They had not saild past a week on the
    seas,
    Not passing a week and days two or
    three,
But they were aware of the proud emperor,
    Both him and all his proud company.

4 When he beheld our powerful fleet,
    Sailing along in their glory and pride,
He was amazed at their valour and
    fame,
    Then to his warlike command[er]s he
    cry'd.

5 These were the words of the old emperor:
   Pray who is this that is sailing to me ?
If he be king that weareth a crown,
   Yet I am a better man than he.

6 ' It is not a king, nor lord of a crown,
   Which now to the seas with his navy
     is come,
But the young Earl of Essex, the Queen's
   lieutenant,
Who fears no foes in Christendom.'

7 ' Oh ! is that lord then come to the seas ?
   Let us tack about and be steering
     away;
I have heard so much of his father
   before
That I will not fight with young Essex
   today.'

8 O then bespoke the emperor's son,
   As they were tacking and steering
     away,
' Give me, royal father, this navy of
   s[h]ips,
And I will go fight with Essex today.'

9 ' Take them with all my heart, loving
   son,
Most of them are of a capital size;
But should he do as his father has done,
   Farewel thine honour and mine like-
     wise.'

10 With cannons hot and thundering shot,
   These two gallants fought on the
     main,
And as it was young Essex's lot,
   The emperor's son by him was taen.

11 ' Give me my son,' the emperor cry'd,
   ' Who you this day have taken from
     me,
And I 'll give to the[e] three keys of
   gold,
The one shall be of High Germany.'

12 ' I care not for thy three keys of gold,
   Which thou hast profferd to set him
     free,
But thy son he shall to England sail,
   And go before the queen with me.'

13 ' Then have I fifty good ships of the best,
   As good as ever were sent to the sea,

And eer my son into England sail,
   They shall go all for good company.'

14 They had not fought this famous battle,
   They had not fought it hours three,
But some lost legs, and some lost arms,
   And some lay tumbling in the sea.

15 Essex he got this battle likewise,
   Tho 't was the hotest that ever was
     seen;
Home he returnd with a wonderful prize,
   And brought the emperor's son to the
     queen.

16 O then bespoke the prentices all,
   Living in London, both proper and tall,
In a kind letter, sent straight to the
   queen,
For Essex's sake they would fight all.

289

THE MERMAID

This is the ballad referred to under ' Sir
Patrick Spens ' (No. 58). It is still common as
a broadside.

A

' The Seamen's Distress,' the second piece in
The Glasgow Lasses Garland, British Museum,
11621, c. 3 (68). " Newcastle, 1765 ? "

1 As we lay musing in our beds,
   So well and so warm at ease,
I thought upon those lodging-beds
   Poor seamen have at seas.

2 Last Easter day, in the morning fair,
   We was not far from land,
Where we spied a mermaid on the rock,
   With comb and glass in hand.

3 The first came up the mate of our ship,
   With lead and line in hand,
To sound and see how deep we was
   From any rock or sand.

4 The next came up the boatswain of our
   ship,
   With courage stout and bold:
' Stand fast, stand fast, my brave lively
   lads,
   Stand fast, my brave hearts of gold !'

5 Our gallant ship is gone to wreck,
   Which was so lately trimmd;
   The raging seas has sprung a leak,
   And the salt water does run in.

6 Our gold and silver, and all our cloths,
   And all that ever we had,
   We forced was to heave them overboard,
   Thinking our lives to save.

7 In all, the number that was on board
   Was five hundred and sixty-four,
   And all that ever came alive on shore
   There was but poor ninety-five.

8 The first bespoke the captain of our ship,
   And a well-spoke man was he;
   'I have a wife in fair Plymouth town,
   And a widow I fear she must be.'

9 The next bespoke the mate of our ship,
   And a well-bespoke man was he;
   'I have a wife in fair Portsmouth,
   And a widow I fear she must be.'

10 The next bespoke the boatswain of our
   ship,
   And a well-bespoke man was he;
   'I have a wife in fair Exeter,
   And a widow I fear she must be.'

11 The next bespoke the little cabbin-boy,
   And a well-bespoke boy was he;
   'I am as sorry for my mother dear
   As you are for your wives all three.'

12 'Last night, when the moon shin'd
   bright,
   My mother had sons five,
   But now she may look in the salt seas
   And find but one alive.'

13 'Call a boat, call a boat, you little Plymouth boys,
   Don't you hear how the trumpet[s]
   sound ?
   [For] the want of our boat our gallant
   ship is lost,
   And the most of our merry men is
   drownd.'

14 Whilst the raging seas do roar,
   And the lofty winds do blow,
   And we poor seamen do lie on the top,
   Whilst the landmen lies below.

B

a. 'The stormy winds do blow,' Chappell's
Popular Music of the Olden Time, p. 742.   b.
The same, p. 743, one stanza and the burden,
contributed by Mr Charles Sloman, in 1840.
c. Notes and Queries, 6th Series, VII, 276, communicated from memory by Mr Thomas Bayne,
Helensburgh, N. B., stanzas 1, 6.

1 ONE Friday morn when we set sail,
   Not very far from land,
   We there did espy a fair pretty maid
   With a comb and a glass in her hand,
   her hand, her hand,
   With a comb and a glass in her hand.
   While the raging seas did roar,
   And the stormy winds did blow,
   While we jolly sailor-boys were up
   into the top,
   And the land-lubbers lying down
   below, below, below,
   And the land-lubbers lying down
   below.

2 Then up starts the captain of our gallant
   ship,
   And a brave young man was he:
   'I 've a wife and a child in fair Bristol
   town,
   But a widow I fear she will be.'
   For the raging seas, etc.

3 Then up starts the mate of our gallant
   ship,
   And a bold young man was he:
   'Oh ! I have a wife in fair Portsmouth
   town,
   But a widow I fear she will be.'
   For the raging seas, etc.

4 Then up starts the cook of our gallant
   ship,
   And a gruff old soul was he:
   Oh ! I have a wife in fair Plymouth town,
   But a widow I fear she will be.'

5 And then up spoke the little cabin-boy,
   And a pretty little boy was he;
   'Oh ! I am more grievd for my daddy
   and my mammy
   Than you for your wives all three.'

6 Then three times round went our gallant ship,
   And three times round went she:

For the want of a life-boat they all went
   down,
   And she sank to the bottom of the sea.

291

CHILD OWLET

The chain of gold in the first stanza and the
penknife below the bed in the fourth have a
false ring.   The ballad seems at best to be a
late one, and is perhaps mere imitation, but,
for an imitation, the last two stanzas are unusually successful.

'Childe Owlet,' Buchan's Ballads of the
North of Scotland, I, 27; Motherwell's MS.,
p. 572.

1   LADY ERSKINE sits in her chamber,
      Sewing at her silken seam,
   A chain of gold for Childe Owlet,
      As he goes out and in.

2   But it fell ance upon a day
      She unto him did say,
   Ye must cuckold Lord Ronald,
      For a' his lands and ley.

3   'O cease ! forbid, madam,' he says,
      'That this shoud eer be done !
   How would I cuckold Lord Ronald,
      And me his sister's son ?'

4   Then she 's ta'en out a little penknife,
      That lay below her bed,
   Put it below her green stay's cord,
      Which made her body bleed.

5   Then in it came him Lord Ronald,
      Hearing his lady's moan;
   'What blood is this, my dear,' he says,
      'That sparks on the fire-stone ?'

6   'Young Childe Owlet, your sister's son,
      Is now gane frae my bower;
   If I hadna been a good woman,
      I 'd been Childe Owlet's whore.'

7   Then he has taen him Childe Owlet,
      Laid him in prison strong,
   And all his men a council held
      How they woud work him wrong.

8   Some said they woud Childe Owlet hang,
      Some said they woud him burn;

Some said they woud have Childe Owlet
      Between wild horses torn.

9   'There are horses in your stables stand
      Can run right speedilie,
   And ye will to your stable go,
      And wile out four for me.'

10 They put a foal to ilka foot,
      And ane to ilka hand,
   And sent them down to Darling muir,
      As fast as they coud gang.

11 There was not a kow in Darling muir,
      Nor ae piece o a rind,
   But drappit o Childe Owlet's blude
      And pieces o his skin.

12 There was not a kow in Darling muir,
      Nor ae piece o a rash,
   But drappit o Childe Owlet's blude
      And pieces o his flesh.

292

THE WEST–COUNTRY DAMO-
SEL'S COMPLAINT

The first eleven stanzas are in a fairly popular tone.   It will be observed that the first
and third verses rhyme in 12–24, but not in 1–
11.   The whole may be one man's work, who
may have thought that an elegy should properly be more artificial, both in form and in
style, than a story, but it is more likely that
the lament is a later attachment.

   a. Douce Ballads, II, fol. 254; Roxburghe
Ballads, II, 499, Ebsworth, VI, 635.   b. Douce
Ballads, II, 245 b.   All three, Printed for P.
Brooksby (1672–95).

1   'WHEN will you marry me, William,
      And make me your wedded wife ?
   Or take you your keen bright sword
      And rid me out of my life.'

2   'Say no more so then, lady,
      Say you no more then so,
   For you shall into the wild forrest,
      And amongst the buck and doe.

3   'Where thou shalt eat of the hips and
      haws,
      And the roots that are so sweet,

And thou shalt drink of the cold water,
   That runs underneath [thy] feet.'

4 Now she had not been in the wild forrest
   Passing three months and a day
But with hunger and cold she had her
     fill,
   Till she was quite worn away.

5 At last she saw a fair tyl'd-house,
   And there she swore by the rood
That she would to that fair tyl'd-house,
   There for to get her some food.

6 But when she came unto the gates,
   Aloud, aloud she cry'd,
An alms, an alms, my own sister!
   I ask you for no pride.

7 Her sister calld up her merry men all,
   By one, by two, and by three,
And bid them hunt away that wild doe,
   As far as ere they could see.

8 They hunted her ore hill and dale,
   And they hunted her so sore
That they hunted her into the forrest,
   Where her sorrows grew more and
     more.

9 She laid a stone all at her head,
   And another all at her feet,
And down she lay between these two,
   Till death had lulld her asleep.

10 When sweet Will came and stood at
     her head,
   And likewise stood at her feet,
A thousand times he kist he[r] cold lips,
   Her body being fast asleep.

11 Yea, seaven times he stood at her feet,
   And seaven times at her head,
A thousand times he shook her hand,
   Although her body was dead.

12 'Ah wretched me!' he loudly cry'd,
   'What is it that I have done?
O woud to the powers above I 'de dy'd,
   When thus I left her alone!

13 'Come, come, you gentle red-breast now,
   And prepare for us a tomb,
Whilst unto cruel Death I bow,
   And sing like a swan my doom.

14 'Why could I ever cruel be
   Unto so fair a creature?
Alas! she dy'd for love of me,
   The loveliest she in nature!

15 'For me she left her home so fair
   To wander in this wild grove,
And there with sighs and pensive care
   She ended her life for love.

16 'O constancy, in her thou 'rt lost!
   Now let women boast no more;
She 's fled unto the Elizium coast,
   And with her carryd the store.

17 'O break, my heart, with sorrow filld,
   Come, swell, you strong tides of grief
You that my dear love have killd,
   Come, yield in death to me relief.

18 'Cruel her sister, was 't for me
   That to her she was unkind?
Her husband I will never be,
   But with this my love be joynd.

19 'Grim Death shall tye the marriage-
     bands,
   Which jealousie shan't divide;
Together shall tye our cold hands,
   Whilst here we lye side by side.

20 'Witness, ye groves, and chrystial
     streams,
   How faithless I late have been,
But do repent with dying leaves
   Of that my ungrateful sin;

21 'And wish a thousand times that I
   Had been but to her more kind,
And not have let a virgin dye
   Whose equal there 's none can find.

22 'Now heaps of sorrow press my soul;
   Now, now 't is she takes her way;
I come, my love, without controule,
   Nor from thee will longer stay.'

23 With that he fetchd a heavy groan
   Which rent his tender breast,
And then by her he laid him down,
   When as death did give him rest.

24 Whilst mournful birds, with leavy
     boughs,
   To them a kind burial gave,

And warbled out their love-sick vows,
Whilst they both slept in their grave.

293

JOHN OF HAZELGREEN

Upon the first stanza of E was built Scott's
'Jock of Hazeldean,' first printed in Campbell's Albyn's Anthology, 1816, i, 18.

A

Elizabeth Cochrane's MS., p. 126.

1 INTO a sweet May morning,
    As the sun clearly shone,
I heard a propper damsell
    Making a heavy moan;
Making a heavy moan,
    I marvelled what she did mean,
And it was for a gentleman,
    Sir John of Hasillgreen.

2 'What aileth thee now, bony maid,
    To mourn so sore into the tide?
O happy were the man,' he sayes,
    'That had thee to his bride,
To ly down by his side;
    Then he were not to mean;'
But still she let the tears down fall
    For pleasant Hasilgreen.

3 'Oh what for a man is Hasillgreen?
    Sweet heart, pray tell to me.'
'He is a propper gentleman,
    Dwels in the South Countrie;
With shoulders broad and arms long,
    And comely to be seen;
His hairs are like the threeds of gold,
    My pleasant Hasilgreen.'

4 'Now Hasilgreen is married,
    Let all this talking be.'
'If Hasilgreen be married,
    This day then woe to me;
For I may sigh and sob no more,
    But close my weeping een,
And hold my peace and cry no more,
    But dy for Hasilgreen.'

5 'Will you let Hasilgreen alone,
    And go along with me?
I 'll marry you on my eldest son,
    Make you a gay lady.'

'Make me a gay lady?' she sayes,
    'I am a maid too mean;
I 'll rather stay at home,' she cries,
    'And dy for Hasilgreen.'

6 He takes this pretty maid him behind
    And fast he spurred the horse,
And they 're away to Bigger toun,
    Then in to Biggar Cross.
Their lodging was far sought,
    And so was it foreseen;
But still she let the tears doun fall
    For pleasant Hasillgreen.

7 He 's ta'en this pretty maid by the hand,
    And he is doun the toun;
He bought for her a pettycoat,
    Yea, and a trailing goun;
A silken kell fitt for her head,
    Laid oer with silver sheen;
But still she let the tears doun fall
    For pleasant Hasilgreen.

8 He 's taen this bony mey him behind,
    And he is to the Place,
Where there was mirth and merryness,
    And ladyes fair of face;
And ladyes fair of face,
    Right seemly to be seen,
But still she let the tears doun fall
    For pleasant Hasilgreen.

9 Young Hasilgreen ran hastilie
    To welcome his father dear;
He 's ta'en that pretty maid in his arms,
    And kist off her falling tear:
'O bony mey, now for thy sake
    I would be rent and rien;
I would give all my father's lands
    To have thee in Hasilgreen.'

10 'O hold your tongue now, son,' he sayes,
    'Let no more talking be;
This maid has come right far from home
    This day to visit thee.
This day should been your wedding-
        day,
    It shall be thy bridall-een,
And thou 's get all thy father's lands,
    And dwell in Hasillgreen.'

E

a. "Got in the South County by Mr Pringle:" Kinloch's MSS., i, 321. b. Kinloch's
MSS., VII, 2.

1 'WHY weep ye by the tide, ladye?
    Why weep ye by the tide?
  I 'll wed ye to my youngest son,
    And ye sall be his bride.
  And ye sall be his bride, ladye,
    Sae comely to be seen;'
  But aye she loot the tears down fa
    For John o Hazelgreen.

2 'O whaten a man is Hazelgreen?
    I pray thee tell to me.'
  'O there 's not a handsomer gentleman
    In a' the South Countrie.
  His arms are long, his shoulders broad,
    Sae comely to be seen!'
  And aye she loot the tears down fa
    For John o Hazelgreen.

294

DUGALL QUIN

B, though corrupted at the end, removes the chief verbal difficulties of A. The conclusion of B is borrowed mostly from 'The Gypsy Laddie' (No. 200).

'Dugall Quin,' The Old Lady's MS. Collection, No. 27.

1 DUGALL QUIN came to the toun,
    An he 's ben lang awaa,
  An he is one to Lissie's bed,
    Tartan-trues, an a'.

2 'Hou wad ye leak me, Lisie,' he says,
    'Gin that I war yer ain,
  We raged cot apon my back,
    An singel-soled sheen,
  A littel we bonnet on my head,
    An tua merry wenking ean?'

3 'Well wad I leak ye, Dugall,' she says,
    'Gin that ye war my ain,
  We ragged coat upon yer back,
    An singel-soled sheen,
  A littel we bonnet on yer head,
    An tua merry wenking eyn.

4 'Hou wad ye leak me, Dugall,' she says,
    'Gin I wer yer ain,
  We silken sneed upon my head,
    An gold fann in my hand,
  An madins ning, a' clead in green,
    To be att my comand?'

5 'Well wad I leak ye, Lisie,' he says,
    'Gin ye wer my ain,
  We silken sneed upon yer head,
    An a goud fan in yer hand,
  An madins nine, a' clad in green,
    To be att yer command.

6 'Follou me nou, Lisie,' he says,
    'Follou me throu Farie,
  An reap the boddoms of my pakets,
    An ye 'll gett tempeng chiss of farei.'

7 Outspak her father, says,
    Lissie, I widna wish ye,
  For gin ye gay we this young man
    They will say I ha bat lost ye.

8 'O had yer toung, my father dear,
    For a' that winne brake me;
  For I will gaa we this young man,
    Since it 's his will to take me.'

9 'Follou me nou, Lissë,' he says,
    'An follou me throu Farie,
  An reap the boddom of my poket,
    An ye 'll gett tempeng chess of farie.'

10 Wea matt worth yer well-fared face,
    Alas that ever I saa ye!
  The first an thing that ever ye gaa to me
    Was the tempen chess of farie.'

11 Dugall Quin read doun the toun,
    Upon Dumfarling's horses,
  An Lisie Meanes folloued him,
    For a' her father's forces.

12 'Follou me nou, Lisie,' he says,
    'An follou me our Boggie;
  I ill make ye lady of ning mills,
    An lady of bonny Garlogë.'

13 She has folloued her trou-love
    [An folloued him] our Boggie,
  An she has marred Dugall Quin,
    An lives belou Strathbogy.

B

'Donald M'Queen's Flight wi Lizie Menzie,' Buchan's Ballads of the North of Scotland, II, 117.

1 DONALD, he 's come to this town,
    And he 's been lang awa,

And he is on to Lizie's bedside,
Wi his tartan trews and a'.

2 'How woud you like me, Lizie,' he said,
  'An I ware a' your ain,
  Wi tartan coat upo my back,
  And single-soled sheen,
  A blue bonnetie on my head,
  And my twa winking een?'

3 'Weel woud I like you, Donald,' she said,
  'An ye ware a' my ain,
  Wi tartan coat upon your back,
  And single-soled sheen,
  And little blue bonnetie on your head,
  And blessings on your een.

4 'But how woud ye like me, Donald,' she
    said,
  'An I ware a' your ain,
  Wi a siller snood into my head,
  A gowd fan in my hand,
  And maidens clad in green satins,
  To be at my command?'

5 'Weal would I like you, Lizie,' he said,
  'And ye ware a' my ain,
  Wi a siller snood into your head,
  A gowd fan in your hand,
  But nane o your maidens clad in green,
  To be at your command.'

6 Then but it speaks her mither dear,
  Says, 'Lizie, I maun cross you;
  To gang alang wi this young man,
  We'd think we had but lost you.'

7 'O had your tongue, my mither dear,
  And dinna think to break me,
  For I will gang wi this young man,
  If it is his will to take me.'

8 Donald M'Queen rade up the green,
  On ane o Dumfermline's horses,
  And Lizie Menzie followed him,
  Thro a' her father's forces.

9 'O follow me, Lizie, my heart's delight,
  And follow me for you please;
  Rype well the grounds o my pouches,
  And ye'll get tempting cheese.'

10 'O wae mat worth you, Donald M'Queen!
   Alas, that ever I saw thee!
   The first love-token ye gae me
   Was the tempting cheese o Fyvie.

11 'O wae be to the tempting cheese,
   The tempting cheese o Fyvie,
   Gart me forsake my ain gudeman
   And follow a footman-laddie!

12 'But lat me drink a hearty browst,
   Just sic as I did brew!
   On Seton brave I turnd my back,
   A' for the sake o you.'

13 She didna wear the silken gowns
   Were made into Dumbarton,
   But she is to the Highlands gane,
   To wear the weeds o tartan.

14 She's casten aff the high-heeld sheen,
   Made o the Turkey leather,
   And she's put on the single brogues,
   To skip amo the heather.

15 Well can Donald hunt the buck,
   And well can Lizie sew;
   Whan ither trades begin to fail,
   They can take their bowies and brew.

295

THE BROWN GIRL

This little ballad recalls Nos. 69, 73, 77, 78, 84, and has something of them all. Still it is not deliberately and mechanically patched together, and in the point of the proud and unrelenting character of the Brown Girl it is original.

A

'The bonny Brown Girl,' 'The Brown Girl,' The Brown Girl's Garland, British Museum 11621. c. 3 (10), n. d., before 1788.

1 'I AM as brown as brown can be,
  My eyes as black as a sloe;
  I am as brisk as a nightingale,
  And as wilde as any doe.

2 'My love has sent me a love-letter,
  Not far from yonder town,
  That he could not fancy me,
  Because I was so brown.

3 'I sent him his letter back again,
  For his love I valu'd not,
  Whether that he could fancy me
  Or whether he could not.

4 'He sent me his letter back again,
    That he lay dangerous sick,
  That I might then go speedily
    To give him up his faith.'

5 Now you shall hear what love she had
    Then for this love-sick man;
  She was a whole long summer's day
    In a mile a going on.

6 When she came to her love's bed-side,
    Where he lay dangerous sick,
  She could not for laughing stand
    Upright upon her feet.

7 She had a white wand all in her hand,
    And smoothd it all on his breast;
  'In faith and troth come pardon me,
    I hope your soul's at rest.

8 'I 'll do as much for my true-love
    As other maidens may;
  I 'll dance and sing on my love's grave
    A whole twelvemonth and a day.'

B

Taken down about 1894 by the Rev. S. Baring-
Gould from a blacksmith, parish of Thrushle-
ton, Devon.

1 'I AM as brown as brown can be,
    And my eyes as black as sloe;
  I am as brisk as brisk can be,
    And wild as forest doe.

2 'My love he was so high and proud,
    His fortune too so high,
  He for another fair pretty maid
    Me left and passed me by.

3 'Me did he send a love-letter,
    He sent it from the town,
  Saying no more he loved me,
    For that I was so brown.

4 'I sent his letter back again,
    Saying his love I valued not,
  Whether that he would fancy me,
    Whether that he would not.

5 'When that six months were overpassd,
    Were overpassd and gone,
  Then did my lover, once so bold,
    Lie on his bed and groan.

6 'When that six months were overpassd,
    Were gone and overpassd,
  O then my lover, once so bold,
    With love was sick at last.

7 'First sent he for the doctor-man :
    'You, doctor, me must cure;
  The pains that now do torture me
    I can not long endure.'

8 'Next did he send from out the town,
    O next did send for me;
  He sent for me, the brown, brown girl
    Who once his wife should be.

9 'O neer a bit the doctor-man
    His sufferings could relieve;
  O never an one but the brown, brown
        girl
    Who could his life reprieve.'

10 Now you shall hear what love she had
    For this poor love-sick man,
  How all one day, a summer's day,
    She walked and never ran.

11 When that she came to his bedside,
    Where he lay sick and weak,
  O then for laughing she could not stand
    Upright upon her feet.

12 'You flouted me, you scouted me,
    And many another one;
  Now the reward is come at last,
    For all that you have done.'

13 The rings she took from off her hands,
    The rings by two and three:
  'O take, O take these golden rings,
    By them remember me.'

14 She had a white wand in her hand,
    She strake him on the breast:
  'My faith and troth I give back to thee,
    So may thy soul have rest.'

15 'Prithee,' said he, 'forget, forget,
    Prithee forget, forgive;
  O grant me yet a little space,
    That I may be well and live.'

16 'O never will I forget, forgive,
    So long as I have breath;
  I 'll dance above your green, green grave
    Where you do lie beneath.'

296

WALTER LESLY

A late, but life-like and spirited ballad.

'Walter Lesly,' Buchan's Ballads of the North of Scotland, II, 139.

1 On the second of October, a Monday at noon,
   In came Walter Lesly, to see his proper one;
   He set a chair down by her side, and gently sat her by,
   Says, Will ye go to Conland, this winter-time to lye?

2 He's taen a glass into his hand, inviting her to drink,
   But little knew she his meaning, or what the rogue did think;
   Nor what the rogue did think, to steal the maid away;
   'Will ye go to Conland, this winter-time to lye?'

3 When they had taen a glass or two, and all were making merry,
   In came Geordy Lesly, and forth he did her carry;
   Then upon high horseback sae hard's he did her tye,
   'Will ye go to Conland, this winter-time to lye?'

4 Her mother she came to the door, the saut tears on her cheek,
   She coudna see her daughter, it was for dust and reek;
   It was for dust and reek, the swords they glanced sae high;
   'And will ye go to Conland, this winter-time to lye?'

5 When they came to the ale-house, the people there were busy;
   A bridal-bed it was well made, and supper well made ready;
   When the supper down was set, baith plum-pudding and pie,
   'And will ye go to Conland, this winter-time to lye?'

6 When they had eaten and well drunken, and a' man bound for bed,

The laddie and the lassie in ae chamber were laid;
He quickly stript her to the smock, and gently laid her bye,
Says, Will ye go to Conland, this winter-time to lye?

7 But Walter being weary, he fell fast asleep,
   And then the lassie thought it fit to start up till her feet;
   To start up till her feet, and her petti-coats to tye,
   'We'll go no more to Conland, the winter-time to lye.'

8 Then over moss and over muir sae cleverly she ran,
   And over hill and over dale, without stockings or shoon;
   The men pursued her full fast, wi mony shout and cry,
   Says, Will ye go to Conland, the winter-time to lye.

9 'Wae to the dubs o Duffus land, that eer they were sae deep;
   They've trachled a' our horsemen and gart our captain sleep;
   And gart our captain sleep, and the lassie win away,
   And she'll go no more to Conland, the winter-time to lye.'

10 'I'd rather be in Duffus land, selling at the ale,
   Before I was wi Lesly, for a' his auld meal;
   For a' his auld meal, and sae mony comes to buy;
   I'll go no more to Conland the winter-time to lye.

11 'I'd rather be in Duffus land, dragging at the ware,
   Before I was wi Lesly, for a' his yellow hair;
   For a' his yellow hair, and sae well's he can it tye;
   I'll go no more to Conland, this winter-time to lye.'

12 It was not for her beauty, nor yet her gentle bluid,
   But for her mither's dollars, of them he had great need;

Of them he had great need, now he maun
    do them by,
For she 'll go no more to Conland, this
    winter-time to lye.

297

EARL ROTHES

'Earl Rothes,' Kinloch MSS., i, 333.

1 'O Earl Rothes, an thou wert mine,
    And I were to be thy ladie,
I wad drink at the beer, and tipple at
    the wine,
    And be my bottle with any.'

2 'Hold thy tongue, sister Ann,' he says,
    'Thy words they are too many;
What wad ye do wi sae noble a lord,
    When he has so noble a ladie?

3 'O I 'll pay you your tocher, Lady Ann,
    Both in gear and money,
If ye 'll forsake Earl Rothes's companie,
    And mind that he has a ladie.'

4 'I do not value your gold,' she says,
    'Your gear it 's no sae readie;
I 'll neer forsake Earl Rothes's companie,
    And I don't gie a fig for his ladie.'

5 'I 'll keep ye i the castle, Lady Ann,
    O servants ye shall hae monie;
I 'll keep ye till ye 're safely brocht to
    bed,
    And I 'll mak you a marquis's ladie.'

6 'I do not value your castle,' she says,
    'Your servants are no sae readie;
Earl Rothes will keep me till I 'm brocht
    to bed,
    And he 'll mak me a marquis's ladie.'

7 'Woe be to thee, Earl Rothes,' he says,
    'And the mark o the judge be upon
    thee,
For the using o this poor thing sae,
    For the using my sister so badly.

8 'When I 'm come to the years of a man,
    And able a sword to carry,
I 'll thrust it thro Earl Rothes' bodie
    For the using my sister sae basely.

9 'Fare thee well, Lady Ann,' he says,
    'No longer will I tarry;
You and I will never meet again,
    Till we meet at the bonny town o
    Torry.'

298

YOUNG PEGGY

'Young Peggy,' Kinloch's Ancient Scottish
Ballads, p. 153.

1 'O whare hae ye been, Peggy?
    O whare hae ye been?'
'I the garden amang the gilly-flowrs,
    Atween twal hours and een.'

2 'Ye 've na been there your leen, Peggy,
    Ye 've na been there your leen;
Your father saw you in Jamie's arms,
    Atween twal hours and een.'

3 'Tho my father saw me in Jamie's arms,
    He 'll see me there again;
For I will sleep in Jamie's arms
    When his grave 's growin green.'

4 'Your Jamie is a rogue, Peggy,
    Your Jamie is a loun,
For trysting out our ae dochter,
    And her sae very young.'

5 'Lay no the wyte on Jamie, mither,
    The blame a' lies on me;
For I will sleep in Jamie's arms
    When your een winna see.'

6 Now she has to her ain bouer gane;
    He was waiting there him leen:
'I 'm blythe to see ye, Jamie, here,
    For we maunna meet again.'

7 She 's tane the wine-glass in her hand,
    Pourd out the wine sae clear;
Says, Here 's your health and mine, Jamie,
    And we maun meet na mair.

8 She has tane him in her arms twa,
    And gien him kisses five;
Says, Here 's your health and mine, Jamie,
    I wish weel mote ye thrive.

9 'Your father has a bonnie cock,
    Divides the nicht and day,

And at the middle watch o the nicht
    In greenwud ye 'll meet me.'

10 Whan bells war rung, and mass was sung,
    And a' men boun for bed,
    She 's kilted up her green claithing,
    And met Jamie in the wud.

11 Whan bells war rung, and mass was sung
    About the hour o twa,
    It 's up bespak her auld father,
    Says, Peggy is awa !

12 'Ga saddle to me the black, the black,
    Ga saddle to me the grey;'
    But ere they wan to the tap o the hill
    The wedding was a' bye.

300

BLANCHEFLOUR AND JELLYFLORICE

Buchan suspects that some " poetaster " has remodelled the story of the romance of Florice and Blancheflour, " modernizing it to suit the climate of his time," that is, perhaps, turning a princess into a sempstress.   The only thing in the romance that is even remotely like what we find in the ballad is that Florice saves Blancheflour from the death which his father had contrived for her in order to part the lovers, and this passage does not occur in the English versions of the romance.

'Blancheflour and Jellyflorice,' Buchan's Ballads of the North of Scotland, i, 125 ; Motherwell's MS., p. 588.

1 THERE was a maid, richly arrayd,
    In robes were rare to see,
    For seven years and something mair
    She servd a gay ladie.

2 But being fond o a higher place,
    In service she thought lang;
    She took her mantle her about,
    Her coffer by the band.

3 And as she walkd by the shore-side,
    As blythe 's a bird on tree,
    Yet still she gaz'd her round about,
    To see what she could see.

4 At last she spied a little castle,
    That stood near by the sea;
    She spied it far and drew it near,
    To that castle went she.

5 And when she came to that castle
    She tirled at the pin,
    And ready stood a little wee boy
    To lat this fair maid in.

6 'O who 's the owner of this place,
    O porter-boy, tell me;'
    'This place belongs unto a queen
    O birth and high degree.'

7 She put her hand in her pocket,
    And gae him shillings three:
    'O porter, bear my message well
    Unto the queen frae me.'

8 The porter 's gane before the queen,
    Fell low down on his knee:
    'Win up, win up, my porter-boy,
    What makes this courtesie ?'

9 'I hae been porter at your yetts,
    My dame, these years full three,
    But see a ladie at your yetts
    The fairest my eyes did see.'

10 'Cast up my yetts baith wide **and**
        braid,
    Lat her come in to me,
    And I 'll know by her courtesie
    Lord's daughter if she be.'

11 When she came in before the queen,
    Fell low down on her knee:
    'Service frae you, my dame the queen,
    I pray you grant it me.'

12 'If that service ye now do want,
    What station will ye be ?
    Can ye card wool, or spin, fair maid,
    Or milk the cows to me ?'

13 'No, I can neither card nor spin,
    Nor cows I canno milk,
    But sit into a lady's bower
    And sew the seams o silk.'

14 'What is your name, ye comely dame ?
    Pray tell this unto me:'
    'O Blancheflour, that is my name,
    Born in a strange countrie.'

15 'O keep ye well frae Jellyflorice —
    My ain dear son is he —
    When other ladies get a gift,
    O that ye shall get three.'

16 It wasna tald into the bower
      Till it went thro the ha,
    That Jellyflorice and Blancheflour
      Were grown ower great witha.

17 When the queen's maids their visits paid,
      Upo the gude Yule-day,
    When other ladies got horse to ride,
      She boud take foot and gae.

18 The queen she calld her stable-groom,
      To come to her right seen;
    Says, 'Ye'll take out yon wild waith steed
      And bring him to the green.

19 'Ye'll take the bridle frae his head,
      The lighters frae his een;
    Ere she ride three times roun the cross,
      Her weel-days will be dune.'

20 Jellyflorice his true-love spy'd
      As she rade roun the cross,
    And thrice he kissd her lovely lips,
      And took her frae her horse.

21 'Gang to your bower, my lily-flower,
      For a' my mother's spite;
    There's nae other amang her maids,
      In whom I take delight.

22 'Ye are my jewel, and only ane,
      Nane's do you injury;
    For ere this-day-month come and gang
      My wedded wife ye 'se be.'

301

THE QUEEN OF SCOTLAND

On the resemblance of this ballad to the story
of Caradoc and his love, see Miss C. A. Harper's
article in Modern Language Notes, XIII, 417,
and cf. G. Paris, Romania, XXVIII, 214.

'The Queen of Scotland,' Buchan's Ballads
of the North of Scotland, I, 46; Motherwell's
MS., p. 577.

1 'O TROY MUIR, my lily-flower,
     An asking I'll ask thee;
   Will ye come to my bigley bower
     And drink the wine wi me?'

2 'My dame, this is too much honour
     You have conferrd on me;

  I'm sure it's mair than I've deservd
  Frae sic a one as thee.'

3 'In Reekie's towers I hae a bower,
     And pictures round it set;
   There is a bed that is well made,
     Where you and I shall sleep.'

4 'O God forbid,' this youth then said,
     'That ever I drie sic blame
   As ever to touch the queen's bodie,
     Altho the king's frae hame.'

5 When that he had these words spoken,
     She secretly did say,
   Some evil I shall work this man,
     Before that it be day.

6 Whan a' her maids were gane to bed,
     And knights were gane frae hame,
   She calld upon young Troy Muir,
     To put fire in her room.

7 'An asking, asking, Troy Muir,
     An asking ye'll grant me;'
   'O, if it be a lawful thing,
     My dame it's granted be.'

8 'There is a stane in yon garden,
     Nae ane lifts it for me;
   But if that ye woud lift the same,
     A brave man I'll ca thee.

9 'Under yon stane there is a pit,
     Most dreary for to see,
   And in it there's as much red gowd
     As buy a dukedom to thee.'

10 'O if I had ae sleep in bed,
     And saw the morning sun,
   As soon 's I rise and see the skies,
     Your will it shall be done.'

11 When birds did sing, and sun did rise,
     And sweetly sang the lark,
   Troy Muir to the garden went,
     To work this dreary wark.

12 He's taen the stane then by a ring,
     And lifted manfullie;
   A serpent that lang wanted meat
     Round Troy Muir's middle did flee.

13 'How shall I get rid o this foul beast?
     It's by it I must dee;

I never thought the queen, my friend,
 Woud work this mischief to me.'

14 But by there came a weelfaird may,
 As Troy Muir did tauk,
 The serpent's furious rage to lay,
 Cut aff her fair white pap.

15 As soon as she the same had done,
 Young Troy Muir was set free,
 And in ane hour the wound was heald,
 That nae mair pain had she.

16 Says Troy Muir, My lily-flower,
 Ye hae releasëd me;
 But before I see another day,
 My wedded wife ye 'se be.

17 He married her on that same day,
 Brought her to his ain hame;
 A lovely son to him she bare,
 When full nine months were gane.

18 As heaven was pleasd, in a short time,
 To ease her first sad pain,
 Sae was it pleasd, when she 'd a son,
 To hae a pap again.

302

YOUNG BEARWELL

This is one of half a dozen pieces sent Buchan by Mr Nicol of Strichen, "who wrote them from memory as he had learned them in his earlier years from old people." It is also one of not a few flimsy and unjointed ballads found in Buchan's volumes, the like of which is hardly to be found elsewhere, that require a respectable voucher, such as Mr Nicol undoubtedly was, for the other five pieces communicated by him were all above suspicion, and have a considerable value. It will not, however, help the ballad much that it was not palmed off on Buchan in jest or otherwise, or even if it was learned from an old person by Mr Nicol in his youth. The intrinsic character of the ballad remains, and old people have sometimes burdened their memory with worthless things.

'Young Bearwell,' Buchan's Ballads of the North of Scotland, II, 75; Motherwell's MS., p. 456, derived from Buchan; Motherwell's Minstrelsy, p. 345.

1 WHEN two lovers love each other well,
 Great sin it were them to twinn;

And this I speak from Young Bearwell;
 He loved a lady young,
 The Mayor's daughter of Birktoun-brae,
 That lovely, leesome thing.

2 One day when she was looking out,
 When washing her milk-white hands,
 That she beheld him Young Bearwell,
 As he came in the sands.

3 Says, Wae 's me for you, Young Bearwell,
 Such tales of you are tauld;
 They 'll cause you sail the salt sea so far
 As beyond Yorkisfauld.

4 . . . .
 . . . .
 'O shall I bide in good greenwood,
 Or stay in bower with thee?'

5 'The leaves are thick in good greenwood,
 Would hold you from the rain;
 And if you stay in bower with me
 You will be taken and slain.

6 'But I caused build a ship for you
 Upon Saint Innocent's day;
 I 'll bid Saint Innocent be your guide,
 And Our Lady, that meikle may.
 You are a lady's first true-love,
 God carry you well away!'

7 Then he sailed east, and he sailed west,
 By many a comely strand;
 At length a puff of northern wind
 Did blow him to the land.

8 When he did see the king and court,
 Were playing at the ba;
 Gave him a harp into his hand,
 Says, Stay, Bearwell, and play.

9 He had not been in the king's court
 A twelvemonth and a day,
 Till there came lairds and lords anew
 To court that lady gay.

10 They wooed her with brooch and ring,
 They nothing could keep back;
 The very charters of their lands
 Into her hands they pat.

11 She 's done her down to Heyvalin,
 With the light of the moon;

Says, ' Will ye do this deed for me,
  And will ye do it soon ?

12 ' Will ye go seek him Young Bearwell,
  On seas wherever he be ?
And if I live and bruik my life
  Rewarded ye shall be.'

13 ' Alas, I am too young a skipper,
  So far to sail the faem;
But if I live and bruik my life
  I 'll strive to bring him hame.'

14 So he has saild east and then saild west,
  By many a comely strand,
Till there came a blast of northern wind
  And blew him to the land.

15 And there the king and all his court
  Were playing at the ba;
Gave him a harp into his hand,
  Says, Stay, Heyvalin, and play.

16 He has tane up the harp in hand,
  And unto play went he,
And Young Bearwell was the first man
  In all that companie.

*   *   *   *

303

THE HOLY NUNNERY

'The Holy Nunnery,' Buchan's Ballads of
the North of Scotland, I, 193.

1 FAIR ANNIE had a costly bower,
  Well built wi lime and stane,
And Willie came to visit her,
  Wi the light o the meen.

2 When he came to Annie's bower-door,
  He tirled at the pin:
' Ye sleep, ye wake, ye Fair Annie,
  Ye 'll open, lat me come in.'

3 ' O never a fit,' says Fair Annie,
  ' Till I your errand ken;'
' My father 's vowd a vow, Annie,
  I 'll tell you when I 'm in.

4 ' My father 's vowed a rash vow,
  I darena marry thee;
My mither 's vowed anither vow,
  My bride ye 'se never be.'

5 ' If ye had tauld me that, Willie,
  When we began to woo,
There was naithing in this warld wide
  Shoud drawn my love to you.

6 ' A nun, a nun,' said Fair Annie,
  ' A nun will I be then;'
' A priest, a priest,' said Sweet Willie,
  ' A priest will I be syne.'

7 She is gane to her father,
  For mither she had nane;
And she is on to her father,
  To see if she 'd be a nun.

8 ' An asking, asking, father dear,
  An asking ye 'll grant me;
That 's to get to the holy nunnery,
  And there to live or die.'

9 ' Your asking 's nae sae great, daugh-
  ter,
  But granted it shall be;
For ye 'se won to the holy nunnery,
  There to live or die.'

10 Then they gaed on, and farther on,
  Till they came to the yate;
And there they spied a maiden porter,
  Wi gowd upon her hat.

11 ' An asking, asking, maiden porter,
  An asking ye 'll grant me;
If I 'll won to the holy nunnery,
  There to live or die.'

12 ' Your asking 's nae sae great, lady,
  But granted it shall be;
For ye 'se won to the holy nunnery,
  There to live or die.

13 ' But ye maun vow a vow, lady,
  Before that ye seek in;
Never to kiss a young man's mouth
  That goes upon the grun.

14 ' And ye must vow anither vow,
  Severely ye must work;
The well-warst vow that ye 're to vow,
  Is never to gang to kirk.'

15 ' I will vow a vow,' she said,
  ' Before that I seek in;
I neer shall kiss a young man's mouth
  That goes upon the grun.

16 'And I will vow anither vow,
 Severely I will work ;
The well-warst vow that I 'm to vow
 Is never to gang to kirk.'

17 For seven years now Fair Annie,
 In the holy nunnery lay she,
And seven years Sweet Willie lay,
 In languish like to die.

18 'Is there nae duke nor lord's daughter,
 My son, can comfort thee,
And save thee frae the gates o death ?
 Is there nae remedie ? '

19 'There is nae duke nor lord's daughter,
 Mother, can comfort me,
Except it be my love, Annie,
 In the holy nunnery lies she.'

20 They 've dressd Sweet Willie up in silk,
 Wi gowd his gown did shine,
And nane coud ken by his pale face
 But he was a lady fine.

21 So they gaed on, and farther on,
 Till they came to the yate,
And there they spied a maiden porter,
 Wi gowd upon her hat.

22 'An asking, an asking, maiden porter,
 An asking ye 'll grant me;
For to win in to the holy nunnery,
 Fair Annie for to see.'

23 'Your asking 's nae sae great, lady,
 But granted it shall be;
Ye 'se won into the holy nunnery,
 Fair Annie for to see.

24 'Be she duke's or lord's daughter,
 It 's lang sin she came here:'
Fair Annie kent her true love's face;
 Says, Come up, my sister dear.

25 Sweet Willie went to kiss her lips,
 As he had wont to do;
But she softly whispered him,
 I darena this avow.

304
YOUNG RONALD

Professor Child observes: "If any lover of ballads should feel his understanding insulted by the presentation of such a piece as this, I can have no quarrel with him. There is certainly much in it that is exasperating, — the greeters in the school, the lifting of the hat, and, most of all, perhaps, the mint in meadows. These are, however, the writer's own property ; the nicking with nay and the giant are borrowed from romances. In this and not a very few other cases, I have suppressed disgust, and admitted an actually worthless and a manifestly — at least in part — spurious ballad, because of a remote possibility that it might contain relics, or be a debased representative, of something genuine and better. Such was the advice of my lamented friend, Grundtvig, in more instances than those in which I have brought myself to defer to his judgment."

Buchan's Ballads of the North of Scotland, II, 282; Motherwell's MS., p. 601, derived from Buchan.

1 IT fell upon the Lammas time,
 When flowers were fresh and green,
And craig and cleugh was covered ower
 With cloathing that was clean.

2 'T was at that time a noble squire,
 Sprung from an ancient line,
Laid his love on a lady fair,
 The king's daughter o Linne.

3 When cocks did craw, and day did daw,
 And mint in meadows sprang,
Young Ronald and his little wee boy
 They rode the way alang.

4 So they rode on, and farther on,
 To yonder pleasant green,
And there he spied that lady fair,
 In her garden alane.

5 These two together lang they stood,
 And love's tale there they taul;
The glancing o her fair color
 Did Ronald's own impale.

6 He lifted 's hat, and thus he spake;
 O pity have on me !
For I could pledge what is my right,
 All for the sake of thee.

7 'Ye 're young amo your mirth, kind sir,
 And fair o your dull hours;
There 's nae a lady in a' London
 But might be your paramour.

8 'But I 'm too young to wed, kind sir,
    You must not take it ill;
Whate'er my father bids me do,
    I maun be at his will.'

9 He kissd her then and took his leave,
    His heart was all in pride,
And he is on to Windsor gone,
    And his boy by his side.

10 And when he unto Windsor came,
    And lighted on the green,
There he spied his mother dear,
    Was walking there alane.

11 'Where have ye been, my son, Ronald,
    From gude school-house, this day ?'
'I hae been at Linne, mother,
    Seeing yon bonny may.'

12 'O wae 's me for you now, Ronald,
    For she will not you hae;
For mony a knight and bauld baron
    She 's nickd them a' wi nae.'

13 Young Ronald 's done him to his bower,
    And he took bed and lay;
Nae woman could come in his sight,
    For the thoughts o this well-fard may.

14 Then in it came his father dear,
    Well belted in a brand;
The tears ran frae his twa gray eyes,
    All for his lovely son.

15 Then Ronald calld his stable-groom
    To come right speedilie;
Says, Ye 'll gang to yon stable, boy
    And saddle a steed for me.

16 'His saddle o the guid red gowd,
    His bits be o the steel,
His bridle o a glittering hue;
    See that ye saddle him weel.

17 'For I 've heard greeters at your school-
        house,
    Near thirty in a day;
But for to hear an auld man greet,
    It passes bairns' play.'

18 When cocks did craw, and day did daw,
    And mint in meadows sprang,
Young Ronald and his little wee boy
    The way they rode alang.

19 So they rode on, and further on,
    To yonder pleasant green,
And there they saw that lady fair,
    In her garden alane.

20 And twenty times before he ceasd
    He kissd her lips sae clear,
And said, Dear lady, for your sake,
    I 'll fight fell lang and sair.

21 'Full haste, nae speed, for me, kind
        sir,'
    Replied the lady clear;
'Far better bucklings ye maun bide
    Or ye gain my love by weir.

22 'King Honour is my father's name,
    The morn to war maun fare,
And that 's to fight a proud giant,
    That 's wrought him muckle care.

23 'Along wi him he is to take
    Baith noble knights and squires;
I woud wish you as well-dressd a knight
    As ony will be there.

24 'And I 'll gie you a thousand crowns,
    To part amang your men;
A robe upon your ain body,
    Weel sewd wi my ain hand.

25 'Likewise a ring, a royal thing,
    The virtue it is gude;
If ony o your men be hurt,
    It soon will stem their blude.

26 'Another ring, a royal thing,
    Whose virtue is well known;
As lang 's this ring your body 's on,
    Your bluid shall neer be drawn.'

27 He kissd her then, and took his leave,
    His heart was all in pride,
And he is on to Windsor gone,
    And his boy by his side.

28 And when he unto Windsor came,
    And lighted on the green,
There he saw his auld father,
    Was walking him alane.

29 'Where hae ye been, my son, Ronald,
    From gude school-house the day ?'
'O I hae been at Linne, father,
    Seeking yon bonny may.'

30 'O wae 's me for you now, Ronald,
　　For she will not you hae;
　Mony a' knight and bauld baron
　　She 's nickd them a' wi nay.'

31 'O had your tongue, my father dear,
　　Lat a your folly be;
　The last words that I wi her spake,
　　Her love was granted me.

32 'King Honour is her father's name,
　　The morn to war maun fare,
　And that 's to fight a proud giant,
　　That 's wrought him muckle care.

33 'Alang wi him he means to take
　　Baith knights and noble squires;
　And she wishes me as well drest a
　　　knight
　As ony will be there.

34 'And she 's gaen me a thousand crowns,
　　To part amang my men;
　A robe upon my ain body,
　　Weel sewd wi her ain hand.

35 'Likewise a ring, a royal thing,
　　The virtue it is gude;
　If ony o my men be hurt,
　　It soon will stem their blude.

36 'Another ring, a royal thing,
　　Whose virtue is unknown;
　As lang 's this ring my body 's on,
　　My blude will neer be drawn.'

37 'If that be true, my son, Ronald,
　　That ye hae tauld to me,
　I 'll gie to you an hundred men,
　　To bear you companie.

38 'Besides as muckle gude harness
　　As carry them on the lee;
　It is a company gude enough
　　For sic a squire as thee.'

39 When cocks did craw, and day did daw,
　　And mint in meadows spread,
　Young Ronald and his merry young men
　　Were ready for to ride.

40 So they rode on, and farther on,
　　To yonder pleasant green,
　And there they spied that lady fair,
　　In her garden, sair mourning.

41 These twa together lang they stood,
　　And love's tale there they taul,
　Till her father and his merry young men
　　Had ridden seven mile.

42 He kissd her then, and took his leave,
　　His heart was all in pride,
　And then he sprang alang the road
　　As sparks do frae the gleed.

43 Then to his great steed he set spur;
　　He being swift o feet,
　They soon arrived on the plain,
　　Where all the rest did meet.

44 Then flew the foul thief frae the west,
　　His make was never seen;
　He had three heads upon ae hause,
　　Three heads on ae breast-bane.

45 He bauldly stept up to the king,
　　Seiz'd 's steed in his right hand;
　Says, Here I am, a valiant man,
　　Fight me now if ye can.

46 'Where is the man in a' my train
　　Will take this deed in hand?
　And he shall hae my daughter dear,
　　And third part o my land.'

47 'O here am I,' said young Ronald,
　　'Will take the deed in hand;
　And ye 'll gie me your daughter dear,
　　I 'll seek nane o your land.'

48 'I woudna for my life, Ronald,
　　This day I left you here;
　Remember ye yon lady gay
　　For you shed mony a tear.'

49 Fan he did mind on that lady
　　That he left him behind,
　He hadna mair fear to fight
　　Nor a lion frae a chain.

50 Then he cut aff the giant's heads
　　Wi ae sweep o his hand,
　Gaed hame and married that lady,
　　And heird her father's land.

305

THE OUTLAW MURRAY

This ballad was known before 1700; how
much earlier it is to be put cannot be ascer

tained. There is, however, nothing in the language of the piece as it stands which obliges
us to assign it a much higher antiquity. It
is here given according to the copy in Herd's
MSS. (**A** a), which he received in 1795 from
Andrew Plummer. Scott's version in the Minstrelsy agrees substantially, except for his interpolations. B (from Glenriddell's MSS.) is defective and corrupt, and C (from an Abbotsford MS.) is a fragment. Various attempts
have been made to find an historical foundation for 'The Outlaw Murray,' but the ballad
corresponds to nothing that is known, or even
probably surmised, in the relations between the
Murrays and the Scottish kings.

A

a. 'The Song of the Outlaw Murray,' Herd's
MSS., II, fol. 76; 'The Outlaw Murray,' I, 255,
1795. **b**. 'The Song of the Outlaw Murray,'
Minstrelsy of the Scottish Border, 1803, I, 1;
principally from a copy found among the
papers of the late Mrs. Cockburn, of Edinburgh. **c**. 'The Song of the Outlaw Murray,'
Aytoun's Ballads of Scotland, 1859, II, 131;
"from an old manuscript in the Philiphaugh
charter-chest," now not accessible. **d**. 'The
Sang of the Outlaw Murray,' a copy among
the Philiphaugh papers, transcribed not earlier
than 1848.

1 ETRICK forest is a fair foreste,
    In it grows manie a semelie trie;
  The hart, the hynd, the dae, the rae,
    And of a' [wylde] beastis grete plen-
      tie.

2 There's a castell biggit with lime and
      stane,
    O gin it stands not pleasantlie !
  In the fore front o that castell fair
    Twa unicorns are bra to see.

3 There's the picture of a knight and a
      ladye bright,
    And the grene hollin aboon their brie;
  There an Outlaw keepis five hundred
      men,
    He keepis a royalle companie.

4 His merrie men are in [ae] liverie clad,
    Of the Lincoln grene so fair to see;
  He and his ladie in purple clad,
    O if they live not royallie !

5 Word is gane to our nobell king,
    In Edinburgh where that he lay,

That there was an Outlaw in Etterick
    forest
  Counted him nought and all his cour-
    trie gay.

6 'I mak a vowe,' then the goode king said,
    ' Unto the man that dear bought me,
  I 'se either be king of Etrick forest,
    Or king of Scotland that Outlaw's bee.'

7 Then spak the erle hight Hamilton,
    And to the noble king said he;
  My sovereign prince, sum counsell tak,
    First of your nobles, syne of me.

8 'I redd you send yon bra Outlaw till
    And see gif your man cum will he;
  Desire him cum and be your man,
    And hald of you yon forest frie.

9 'And gif he refuses to do that,
    We 'll conquess both his lands and he,
  Or else we 'll throw his castell down,
    And mak a widowe of his gaye ladie.'

10 The king called on a gentleman,
    James Boyd, Erle of Arran, his brother
      was he;
  When James he came before the king
    He fell before him on his knie.

11 ' Welcum, James Boyd,' said our nobil
      king,
    ' A message ye maun gang for me;
  Ye maun hie to Etrick forrest,
    To yon Outlaw, where dwelleth he.

12 ' Ask hym of quhom he haldis his lands,
    Or, man, wha may his master be;
  Desyre him come and be my man,
    And hald of me yon forrest frie.

13 ' To Edinburgh to cum and gang
    His safe-warrand I sall be;
  And, gif he refuses to do that,
    We 'll conquess baith his lands and he.

14 'Thou mayst vow I'll cast his castell doun,
    And mak a widow of his gay ladie;
  I 'll hang his merrie men pair by pair
    In ony frith where I may them see.'

15 James Boyd took his leave of the nobill
      king,
    To Etrick forrest fair came he:

Down Birkendale brae when that he cam,
  He saw the fair forest with his ee.

16 Baith dae and rae and hart and hynd,
     And of all wylde beastis grete plentie;
   He heard the bows that bauldly ring,
     And arrows whidderand near him by.

17 Of the fair castell he got a sight,
     The like he nere saw with his ee;
   On the fore front of that castell
     Twa unicorns were bra to see.

18 The picture of a knight and a ladie bright,
     And the grene hollin aboon their brie;
   Thereat he spy'd five hundred men,
     Shuting with bows upon the lee.

19 They a' were in ae liverie clad,
     Of the Lincoln grene, sae fair to see;
   The knight and his ladye in purple clad;
     O gif they lived right royallie !
   Therefore he kend he was master-man,
     And served him in his ain degree.

20 'God mot thee save, brave Outlaw Mur-
     ray,
     Thy ladie and a' thy chivalrie !'
   'Marry, thou 's wellcum, gentleman,
     Sum king's-messenger thou seems to
     be.'

21 'The King of Scotland sent me hier,
     And, gude Outlaw, I'm sent to thee;
   I wad wat of whom ye hald your lands,
     Or, man, wha may thy master be.'

22 'Thir landis are mine,' the Outlaw said,
     'I own na king in Christentie;
   Frae Soudron I this forest wan,
     When the king nor 's knights were not
     to see.'

23 'He desires you 'l come to Edinburgh,
     And hald of him this forest frie;
   And gif you refuse to do this,
     He 'll conquess both thy landis and
     thee;
   He has vowd to cast thy castell down,
     And make a widow of thy gaye ladie.

24 'He 'll hang thy merrie men pair by pair,
     In ony frith where he may them finde;'
   'Aye, by my troth,' the Outlaw said,
     'Then wad I think me far behinde.

25 'Eere the king my fair countrie get,
     This land that 's nativest to me,
   Mony of his nobils sall be cauld,
     Their ladies sall be right wearie.'

26 Then spak his ladye fair of face,
     She said, Without consent of me
   That an outlaw shuld come before the
     king:
     I am right rad of treasonrie.

27 'Bid him be gude to his lordis at hame,
     For Edinburgh my lord sall never see:'
   James tuke his leave of the Outlaw keene
     To Edinburgh boun is he.

28 And when he came before the king,
     He fell before him on his knie:
   'Wellcum, James Boyd,' said the nobil
     king,
     'What foreste is Etrick forest frie ?'

29 'Etrick forest is the fairest forest
     That ever man saw with his ee;
   There 's the dae, the rae, the hart, the
     hynde,
     And of all wild beastis great plentie.

30 'There 's a prittie castell of lime and
     stone,
     O gif it stands not pleasauntlie !
   There 's on the fore side of that castell
     Twa unicorns sae bra to see.

31 'There 's the picture of a knight and [a]
     ladie bright,
     And the grene hollin aboon their brie;
   There the Outlaw keepis five hundred
     men,
     O gif they live not royallie !

32 'His merry men in [ae] liverie clad,
     O the Lincoln grene, so fair to see;
   He and his ladye in purple clad,
     O gif they live not royallie !

33 'He says yon forest is his ain,
     He wan it from the Soudronie;
   Sae as he won it, sae will he keep it,
     Contrair all kings in Christentie.'

34 'Gar ray my horse,' said the nobil king,
     'To Etrick [forest] hie will I me;'
   Then he gard graith five thousand men,
     And sent them on for the forest frie

35 Then word is gane the Outlaw till,
    In Etrick forest where dwelleth he,
  That the king was cumand to his cuntrie,
    To conquess baith his lands and he.

36 'I mak a vow,' the Outlaw said,
    'I mak a vow, and that trulie,
  Were there but three men to tak my part,
    Yon king's cuming full deir suld be.'

37 Then messengers he called forth,
    And bade them haste them speedilie:
  'Ane of you go to Halliday,
    The laird of the Corehead is he.

38 'He certain is my sister's son,
    Bid him cum quick and succour me;
  Tell Halliday with thee to cum,
    And shaw him a' the veritie.'

39 'What news? what news,' said Halli-
    day,
    'Man, frae thy master unto me?'
  'Not as ye wad; seeking your aid;
    The king's his mortal enemie.'

40 'Aye, by my troth,' quoth Halliday,
    'Even for that it repenteth me;
  For, gif he lose fair Ettrick forest,
    He'll take fair Moffatdale frae me.

41 'I'll meet him wi five hundred men,
    And surely mae, if mae may be:'
  [The Outlaw calld a messenger,
    And bid him hie him speedily.]

42 'To Andrew Murray of Cockpool,
    That man's a deir cousin to me;
  Desire him cum and make me aid,
    With all the power that he may be.

43 'The king has vowd to cast my castell
    down,
    And mak a widow of my gay ladye;
  He'll hang my merry men pair by pair
    I[n] ony place where he may them see.'

44 'It stands me hard,' quoth Andrew Mur-
    ray,
    'Judge if it stands not hard with me,
  To enter against a king with crown,
    And put my lands in jeopardie.

45 'Yet, gif I cum not on the daye,
    Surelie at night he sall me see:'

To Sir James Murray, laird of Traquair,
    A message came right speedilie.

46 'What news? what news,' James Mur-
    ray said,
    'Man, frae thy master unto me?'
  'What needs I tell? for well ye ken
    The king's his mortal enemie.

47 'He desires ye'll cum and make him
    aid,
    With all the powers that ye may be:'
  'And, by my troth,' James Murray said,
    'With that Outlaw I'll live and die.

48 'The king has gifted my lands lang
    syne,
    It can not be nae war with me;'
    .   .   .   .   .   .
    .   .   .   .   .   .

49 The king was cumand thro Cadden ford,
    And fiftene thousand men was he;
  They saw the forest them before,
    They thought it awsom for to see.

50 Then spak the erle hight Hamilton,
    And to the nobil king said he,
  My sovereign prince, sum counsell take,
    First at your nobles, syne at me.

51 'Desyre him meet you at Penman's
    Core,
    And bring four in his cumpanie;
  Fyve erles sall gang yoursell before,
    Gude cause that you suld honord be.

52 'And, if he refuses to do that,
    Wi fire and sword we'll follow thee;
  There sall never a Murray after him
    Have land in Etrick forest frie.'

53 The king then called a gentleman,
    Royal-banner-bearer then was he,
  James Hope Pringle of Torsonse by
    name;
    He came and knelit upon his knie.

54 'Welcum, James Pringle of Torsonse;
    Ye man a message gae for me;
  Ye man gae to yon Outlaw Murray,
    Surely where bauldly bideth he.

55 'Bid him meet me at Penman's Core,
    And bring four of his companie;

Five erles sall cum wi mysell,
   Gude reason I suld honord be.

56 'And if he refuses to do that,
   Bid him look for nae gude o me;
There sall never a Murray after him
Have land in Etric forest frie.'

57 James came before the Outlaw keene,
   And served him in his ain degree:
'Wellcum, James Pringle of Torsonse,
   What tidings frae the king to me ?'

58 'He bids you meet him at Penman's
   Core,
And bring four of your companie;
Five erles will cum with the king,
   Nae more in number will he be.

59 'And gif you refuse to do that,
   I freely here upgive with thee,
There will never a Murray after thee
   Have land in Etrick forest frie.

60 'He 'll cast your bonny castell down,
   And make a widow of your gay ladie,
He 'll hang your merry men pair by
   pair
In ony place where he may them see.'

61 'It stands me hard,' the Outlaw said,
   'Judge if it stands not hard with me;
I reck not of losing of mysell,
   But all my offspring after me.

62 'Auld Haliday, young Haliday,
   Ye sall be twa to gang wi me;
Andrew Murray and Sir James Murray,
   We 'll be nae mae in cumpanie.'

63 When that they came before the king,
   They fell before him on their knee:
'Grant mercy, mercy, royal king,
   Een for his sake who died on tre !'

64 'Sicken-like mercy sall ye have,
   On gallows ye sall hangit be;'
'God forbid !' quo the Outlaw then,
   'I hope your Grace will better be.

65 'These lands of Etrick forest fair,
   I wan them frae the enemie;
Like as I wan them, sae will I keep
   them,
Contrair all kings in Christentie.'

66 All the nobilis said, the king about,
   Pitye it were to see him die:
'Yet graunt me mercye, sovereign
   prince,
Extend your favour unto me !

67 'I 'll give you the keys of my castell,
   With the blessing of my fair ladie;
Mak me the sheriff of the forest,
   And all my offspring after me.'

68 'Wilt thou give me the keys of thy cas-
   tell,
With the blessing of thy fair ladye ?
I 'll mak the[e] shiryff of the forest,
   Surely while upwards grows the trie;
If you be not traytour to the king,
   Forfaulted sall ye never be.'

69 'But, prince, what sall cum o my men?
   When I go back, traitour they 'll ca
   me;
I had rather lose my life and land,
   Eer my merry men rebukëd me.'

70 'Will your merry men amend their
   lives
And all their pardouns I grant thee:
Now name thy landes whe'ere they be,
   And here I render them to thee.'

71 'Fair Philiphaugh, prince, is my awin,
   I biggit it wi lime and stane;
The Tinnies and the Hangingshaw,
   My leige, are native steeds of mine.

72 '.   .   .   .   .   .
  .   .   .   .   .
I have mony steeds in the forest shaw,
   But them by name I dinna knaw.'

73 The keys of the castell he gave the
   king,
With the blessing of his fair ladye;
He was made sheryff of Etrick forest,
   Surely while upward grows the trie;
And, if he was not traytour to the
   king,
Forfaulted he suld never be.

74 Wha ever heard, in ony tymes,
   Sicken an outlaw in his degree
Sic favour get before a king
   As did the Outlaw Murray of the for
   est frie ?

FRAGMENTS

"DISPERSED thro Shakspere's plays are innumerable little fragments of ancient ballads, the entire copies of which could not be recovered," says Bishop Percy in his preface to 'The Friar of Orders Gray.' What he says of Shakspere is equally true of Beaumont and Fletcher, but it is not true, in either case, that there are many fragments of popular traditional ballads. Portions of ballads of one kind or another, and still more of songs, are introduced into the plays of these authors, though not so frequently as one would suppose from Percy's words. Ten of the twenty-eight stanzas of 'The Friar of Orders Gray' are taken, mostly in part only, from Shakspere and Fletcher,[1] but the original verses are from songs, not properly from ballads. It is not, however, always easy to say whether an isolated stanza belonged to a ballad or a song. Some snatches from familiar ballads, which occur in Beaumont and Fletcher, have already been given at the proper places. A few bits from unknown pieces, which occur in Shakspere, or Beaumont and Fletcher (strictly, perhaps, Fletcher), will be given here. It is surprising that other dramatists have not furnished something.

A very meagre gathering of fragments from other sources follows those which have been gleaned from the dramatists, but it must be once more said that there is not an absolute certainty that all of these belong to ballads.

Some popular tales are interspersed with verses of a ballad character, and one or two cases have been incidentally noted already. Examples are 'The Paddo,' Chambers's Popular Rhymes of Scotland, 1870, p. 87;[2] 'The Red Etin,' ib. p. 89; 'The Black Bull of Norroway,' ib. p. 95; 'Child Rowland and Burd Ellen,' Illustrations of Northern Antiquities, p. 397;[3] 'The Golden Ball,' see No. 95, H, Child, II, 353–55.

[1] Stanza 1[1],[2] of Percy's ballad is from The Taming of the Shrew, iv, 1; 3, 5, 7, are, wholly or in part, from Hamlet, iv, 5; 12, 13, from Fletcher's Queen of Corinth, iii, 2; 15 from Hamlet, as before; 17, 18, from Much Ado about Nothing, ii, 3; one line of 22 from King Lear, iii, 4.

[2] The verses from this tale are printed separately in Buchan's Ballads of the North of Scotland, I, 117, 'The Maid and Fairy.'

[3] But Jamieson confesses: "Of the verses which have been introduced I cannot answer for the exactness of any, except the stanza put into the mouth of the king of Elfland, which was indelibly impressed upon my memory [though J. was only seven or eight years old] long before I knew anything of Shakspere." The stanza is: [in came the king of Elfland,]

> ' With fi, fi, fo and fum !
>   I smell the blood of a Christian man ;
> Be he dead, be he living, wi my brand
>   I 'll clash his harns frae his harn-pan.'

SHAKSPERE

From King Lear, Act iii, sc. 4, printed 1608.

Child Rowland to the darke tower came.
His word was still, Fy, fo, and fumme !
  I smell the bloud of a British man.

1. *So* 1623 : *both quartos*, darke towne come.

Act iii, sc. 6.

Sleepest or wakest thou, jolly shepheard ?
  Thy sheepe bee in the corne;
And for one blast of thy minikin mouth
  Thy sheepe shall take no harme.

From The Taming of the Shrew, Act iv, sc. 1, printed 1623, I, 221.

> It was the friar of orders gray,
>   As he forth walked on his way.

BEAUMONT AND FLETCHER

From The Knight of the Burning Pestle, produced apparently in 1611, Act ii, sc. 8; Dyce, II, 173.

She cares not for her daddy,
  Nor she cares not for her mammy,
For she is, she is, she is, she is
  My lord of Lowgave's lassy.

(*Perhaps only a song.*)

Give him flowers enow, palmer, give him flowers enow,
Give him red and white, and blue, green, and yellow.

Act v, sc. 3 ; Dyce, p. 226.

With that came out his paramour,
She was as white as the lily-flower.
  Hey, troul, troly, loly

With that came out her own dear knight,
He was as true as ever did fight.

From Bonduca, produced before March, 1619 : Act v, sc. 2, Dyce, v, 88.

It was an old tale, ten thousand times told,
Of a young lady was turnd into mould,
Her life it was lovely, her death it was bold.

From The Two Noble Kinsmen, printed in 1634, Act iii, sc. 4; Dyce, xi, 383.

For I 'll cut my green coat a foot above my
  knee,
And I 'll clip my yellow locks an inch below
  mine ee.
    Hey, nonny, nonny, nonny

He 's buy me a white cut, forth for to ride,
And I 'll go seek him through the world
  that is so wide.
    Hey, nonny, nonny, nonny

The Complaynt of Scotland, 1549, gives two lines of a song on the murder, in 1517, of the Sieur de la Bastie, a distinguished knight in the service of the Regent, Duke of Albany. The song may, or may not, have been a ballad.

God sen the Duc hed byddin in France,
And Delabautë hed neuyr cum hame.
            Ed. Leyden, p. 100.

The History of the Houses of Douglas and Angus, written by Master David Hume of Godscroft, p. 155, Edinburgh, 1644.

Of the treacherous execution of William, sixth Earl of Douglas, at the castle of Edinburgh, in 1440, Hume of Godscroft says: "It is sure the people did abhorre it, execrating the very place where it was done ; in detestation of the fact of which the memory remaineth yet in our dayes in these words." Since Hume mentions no ballad, it is not likely that he knew of more than this single stanza, or that more existed. (Sir Walter Scott, however, confidently assumes that there was a ballad. Minstrelsy, 1833, i, 221 f.)

Edinburgh castle, towne, and tower,
  God grant thou sinke for sinne !
And that even for the black dinner
  Earle Douglas got therein.

Written on the fly-leaf of a little volume printed at Edinburgh about 1670 (Quevedo's Novels), Laing MSS., University of Edinburgh, Div. ii, 358. (Communicated by Mr Macmath.)

' He steps full statly on yᵉ stre[et],
  He hads yᵉ charters of him sell,
In to his cloathing he is compl[ete],
  In Craford's mure he bears yᵉ bell.

' I wish I had died my own fai[r] death,
  In tender age, qⁿ I was young;

I would never have broke my heart
  For yᵉ love of any churl's son.

' Wo be to my parents all,
  Yᵗ lives so farr beyond yᵉ sea !
I might have lived a noble life,
  And wedded in my own countrë.'

Finlay's Scottish Ballads, i, xxxii.

A "romantic ballad, of which, unfortunately, one stanza only has been preserved. The tradition bears that a young lady was carried away by the fairies, and that, although invisible to her friends who were in search of her, she was sometimes heard by them lamenting her destiny in a pathetic song, of which the stanza just mentioned runs nearly thus : " —

O Alva hills is bonny,
  Dalycoutry hills is fair,
But to think on the braes of Menstrie
  It maks my heart fu sair.

The following variant was communicated (with a story of a wife carried off by fairies) by J. C. to The Scottish Journal, ii, 275, 1848 (Macmath) : —

O Alva woods are bonnie,
  Tillycoultry hills are fair,
But when I think on the braes o Menstrie
  It maks my heart aye sair.

KING EDELBRODE

Sent by Motherwell to C. K. Sharpe, with a letter dated October 8, 1825. Also entered in Motherwell's Note-Book, p. 53 (excepting the second line of the first stanza).

King Edelbrode cam owre the sea,
    Fa la lilly
All for to marry a gay ladye.
    Fa la lilly.

(Then follows the description of a queen, jimp and sma, not remembered.)

Her lilly hands, sae white and sma,
    Fa la lilly
Wi gouden rings were buskit braw.
    Fa la lilly

" I cannot get any precise account of its subject, but it related somehow to a most magnificent marriage. The old lady who sung it died some years ago." (Letter to Sharpe.)

"It may be the same ballad as the scrap I have, with something of a similar chorus." (Note-Book, where the "chorus" is Fa fa lilly.)

The reference seems to be to 'The Whummil Bore,' No. 27.

———◆———

C. K. Sharpe's Letters, ed. Allardyce, II, 106 (1813).

'O come you from the earth?' she said,
'Or come you from the skye?'
'Oh, I am from yonder churchyard,
Where my crumbling relicks lie.'

Sharpe somewhere asks, Where does this belong?
Possibly in some version of 'Proud Lady Margaret,' No. 47.

———◆———

MS. of Thomas Wilkie, p. 80, Scotch Ballads, Materials for Border Minstrelsy, No. 73 C, Abbotsford.

The great bull of Bendy-law
Has broken his band and run awa,
And the king and a' his court
Canna turn that bull about.

———◆———

Scotch Ballads, Materials for Border Minstrelsy, No. 86 a, Abbotsford, in the handwriting of Thomas Wilkie.

Red-Cap he was there,
And he was there indeed,
And he was standing by,
With a red cap on his head.

———◆———

Scotch Ballads, Materials for Border Minstrelsy, No. 73a; MS. of Thomas Wilkie, Abbotsford, derived by Wilkie from his father, "who heard a Lady Brigs sing this when he was a boy."

He took a sword in every hand
And on the house did venture,
And swore if they wad not gee her up
He would make all their doors play clatter.

Her angry father, when he saw this,
That he would lose his ae daughter,
He swore if he had not been gude at the sword
He durst not come to make his doors clatter.

NOTES

NOTES

[The references are to page, stanza, and verse.]

1

Six versions.

2. *A a* was "printed for F. Coles, T. Vere, I. Wright, and I. Clarke;" *b* "for W. Thackeray, E. M. and A. M.;" *c* "by Tho. Norris."

2. *A* 5¹. *a, b, c, d* read *youngest*.

2

Nineteen versions (some of them fragmentary).

3. *A* 3². *B* reads: Yea, and the knight in my arms niest [i. e. next].

3. *A* 9. *C* (Kinloch's Ballads) adds:—

And ye maun wash it in yon cistran,
Whare water never stood nor ran.

And ye maun dry it on yon hawthorn,
Whare the sun neer shon sin man was born.

3. *A* 9¹. The broadside reads : needle and sheerless. But cf. *C*: knife-, sheer-less.

4. *A* 11². Atween the saut sea and the sand *C*.

4. *A* 12². Some versions have "with one peppercorn"; *F* (Kinloch MSS.) reads "with ae peck o corn."

4. Sts. 18–19 are not appropriate. They perhaps belong to some lost ballad, of which sts. 1–4 may also have formed a part. Cf. No. 4.

3

Two versions and a fragment.

4

Nine versions.

6. *H* 1. Defective in the MS. A related version (*C*) begins thus (Herd's MSS., I, 166) :—

False Sir John a wooing came
To a maid of beauty fair;
May Colven was this lady's name,
Her father's only heir.

7. *H* 15. A related version (*C*) has:—

'O hold your tongue, my pretty parrot,
Lay not the blame upon me;
Your cup shall be of the flowered gold,
Your cage of the root of the tree.'

Up then spake the king himself,
In the bed-chamber where he lay :
'What ails the pretty parrot,
That prattles so long or day?'

'There came a cat to my cage door,
It almost a worried me,
And I was calling on May Colven
To take the cat from me.'

5

Eight versions and a fragment.

7. *A* 8, 9. Sir Walter Scott's version (*B*) has :—

And she was clad in the finest pall,
But aye she let the tears down fall.

'O is your saddle set awrye?
Or rides your steed for you owre high?'

8. 24. In a Galloway version (*C*) the "Billie Blin" (cf. Nos. 6, 30, 53) plays an important part. Contrary to the page's warning, the bride sits down in the magic chair before she is bidden :—

Out then spake the lord's mother;
Says, 'This is not a maiden fair.

'In that chair nae leal maiden
Eer sits down till they be bidden.'

The Billie Blin then outspake he,
As he stood by the fair ladie.

'The bonnie may is tired wi riding,
Gaurd her sit down ere she was bidden.'

The lady persuades her waiting-maid to play the part of bride for her; and when

Childe Branton and the waiting-maid
Into the bridal bed were laid,

Childe Branton says :—

'Now tell to me, ye Billie Blin,
If this fair dame be a leal maiden.'

'I wat she is as leal a wight
As the moon shines on in a simmer night.

'I wat she is as leal a may
As the sun shines on in a simmer day.

'But your bonnie bride's in her bower,
Dreeing the mither's trying hour.'

6

One version.

10. 33. Between sts. 33 and 34, *b* has eight verses which narrate the carrying out of the Belly Blind's directions : "He did him to the market place," etc. They are, of course, practically a repetition of sts. 30–33.

7

Eleven versions.

11. 1. The name Earl o Bran (otherwise, Earl Bran or Brand) is probably a modification of the *Hildebrand* found in several Danish versions.

11. 2. This stanza can hardly be the right

ful property of ' Earl Brand.' Something very similar is met with in ' Leesome Brand ' (No. 15) and is not much in place there.

11. 7. Version *A* has : —

Until they meet with old Carl Hood ;
He comes for ill, but never for good.

11. 13². *A* has *Winchester.*

12. 18. In *A* : —

' Ha, ha, ha ! ye are a' mistaen :
Gae count your maidens oer again.'

8

Three versions.

15. *A** 14⁴. Another copy reads : ' I 'll serve you till my days be near.'

15. *B* 1². If *A** be right, gross injustice is done to the father by changing ' I trow he 's weird her ' into ' An he wad wed her.' One of the two is a singular corruption.

9

Seven versions.

16. 1. The burden varies. Thus in *B* (Kinloch MSS.) we have : —

The provost's daughter went out a walking,
A may's love whiles is easy won
She heard a poor prisoner making his moan,
And she was the fair flower of Northumberland.

18. *B* has a more elaborate ending. The lady's father reproves her, but —

Her mother she gently on her did smile,
O that her love was so easy won !
' She is not the first that the Scotts have beguild,
But she 's still the fair flower of Northumberland.

' She shanna want gold, she shanna want fee,
Altho that her love was so easy won,
She shanna want gold to gain a man wi,
And she 's still the fair flower of Northumberland.'

10

Twenty-seven versions.

19. 10. There are three strings made from the girl's hair in the two Icelandic versions, and in the English version *B*, and the three tets or links in five of the English versions were no doubt taken to make three strings originally. Corresponding to this are three enunciations of the instrument in some of the English and in some of the Scandinavian versions. In those English copies in which the instrument speaks but once, it expresses a desire for vengeance. This is found in no Norse ballad, neither is it found in the earliest English versions. These, and the better forms of the Norse, reveal the awful secret, directly or indirectly, and, in the latter case, sometimes note the effect on the bride. Most impressive of all, with its terse, short lines, is an Icelandic version taken down in the seventeenth century (Grundtvig and Sigurðsson, Íslenzk Fornkvæði, No. 13) : —

The first string made response :
' The bride was my sister once.'

The bride on the bench, she spake :
' The harp much trouble doth make.'

The second string answered the other :
' She is parting me and my lover.'

Answered the bride, red as gore :
' The harp is vexing us sore.'

The canny third string replied :
' I owe my death to the bride.'

He made all the harp-strings clang ;
The bride's heart burst with the pang.

19. *B* 1. The ' Binnorie ' burden, which Scott says was " the most common and popular," runs as follows in his version (*C*) : —

There were two sisters sat in a bour ;
Binnorie, O Binnorie
There came a knight to be their wooer.
By the bonny mill-dams of Binnorie.

11

Fifteen versions.

21. 26. The cause of the bride's enmity for her brother's wife is, in true ballad style, left to be inferred by the hearer.

22. 15, 16. Cf. ' Gil Brenton ' (No. 5), *A* 9–11.

12

Twenty-five versions.

23. 7. For the testament, see ' The Cruel Brother ' (No. 11) ; ' Edward ' (No. 13).

13

Three versions (one a fragment).

25. 7. Alexander Laing's MS., 1829, p. 25, has the following stanza (*C*) : —

' O what did the fray begin about ?
My son, come tell to me : '
' It began about the breaking o the bonny hazel wand,
And a penny wad hae bought the tree.'

25. 10. For the testament, see ' The Cruel Brother ' (No. 11), ' Lord Randal ' (No. 12).

25. *B.* Initial *qu* for *w* and *z* for *y* have been changed throughout to *w* and *y.*

14

Six versions.

26. 1. The burden differs in different versions. In *B* (Herd's MSS.) the stanza runs : —

There wond three ladies in a bower,
Annet and Margret and Marjorie
And they have gane out to pu a flower.
And the dew it lyes on the wood, gay ladie.

In *C* (Motherwell's MS.) it is as follows : —

There were three sisters on a road,
Gilly flower gentle rosemary
And there they met a banished lord.
And the dew it hings over the mulberry tree.

26. 2. In some of the versions the three sisters go to the wood separately. Thus in *D* (Motherwell's MS.) : —

The oldest of them she's to the wood gane,
To seek a braw leaf and to bring it hame.

There she met with an outlyer bold,
Lies many long nights in the woods so cold.

15

Two versions.

28. *A.* The mixture of four-line with two-line stanzas of course comes from different ballads having been blended, but for all that, these ballads might have had the same theme. Sts. 33–35, however, are such as we meet with in ballads of the 'Earl Brand' class (No. 7), but not in those of the class to which 'Leesome Brand' belongs, and st. 4 of 'Leesome Brand' closely resembles st. 2 of 'Earl Brand,' *A**.

28. 1. The "unco land" is at least a reminiscence of the paradise depicted in the beginning of many of the versions of the Danish 'Ribold and Guldborg' (Grundtvig, No. 82): see p. 11, above.

28. 28–30. The white hind is met with in no other ballad of this class.

29. 36–41. Stanzas similar to these (and to *B* 12–16) occur in 'Sheath and Knife' (No. 16), to which they are especially suited by their riddling character. Probably that is where they belong. It is worthy of remark, too, that there is a *hind* in another ballad, closely related to No. 16 ('The Bonny Hind,' No. 50), and that the hind in 'Leesome Brand' may have come from this.

29. 44–47. These are in no kind of keeping with what goes before, since they speak of the "young son" as having been brought home at some previous time.

29. 3. The "auld son" here, like the first bringing home of the young son in *A* 45, 47, shows how completely the proper story has been lost sight of. There should be no son of any description at the point at which this stanza comes in. The best we can do, to make sense of st. 3, is to put it after st. 8, with the understanding that woman and child are carried off for burial; though really there is no need to move them on that account. The shooting of the child is unintelligible in the mutilated state of the ballad. It is apparently meant to be an accident. Nothing of the kind occurs in other ballads of the class, and the divergence is probably a simple corruption.

16

Six versions.

30. 3, 4. Cf. 'Robin Hood's Death,' No. 120, *B* 16.

30. 6. *F* inserts this stanza : —

It was nae wonder his heart was sair,
When he shooled the mools on her yellow hair.

30. 8. Cf. 'Leesome Brand' (No. 15), sts. 36–41, and 'The Squire of Low Degree,' vv. 117 ff., Percy Folio, Hales and Furnivall, III, 267.

17

Nine versions.

31. 3. *B* and *F* have "three singing lav-rocks" (i. e. larks). These are to be taken as curiosities of art. Such birds are often mentioned (Liebrecht, Zur Volkskunde, p. 85 f.).

31. 6. The king's daughter was faithful to Horn, and they were marrying her against her will. The contingency seems not to have been foreseen when the ring was given; but it was better for the ring to change, to the temporary clouding of the lady's character, than to have Horn stay away and the forced marriage go on.

18

Six versions.

34. 1. For the burden, cf. a song of the time of Henry VIII (see Flügel, Anglia, XII, 238).

19

37. The history of the romance is discussed by Kittredge, American Journal of Philology, VII, 176 ff.; Bugge, Arkiv för nordisk Filologi, VII, 97 ff. (especially with reference to its relation to the Danish ballad of 'The Might of the Harp'), and Hertz, Spielmannsbuch, 2d ed., pp. 356 ff.

37. 1. The burden is Scandinavian and was perhaps no more intelligible to the singer than "Hey non nonny" is to us. For the first line the Danish "Skoven årle grön (Early green's the wood)" has been suggested by Grundtvig; for the second "Hvor hjorten han går årlig (where the hart goes yearly)." Dr. Axel Olrik prefers "Skoven [er] herlig grön (The wood is magnificently green)" or "Skoven herlig grönnes (The wood grows splendidly green); " and "Hvor urten hun grönnes herlig (Where the plants grow splendidly green)."

20

Nineteen versions.

37. The Danish ballad is thus translated by Professor Child, Ballads, I, 219, from Kristensen, Jydske Folkeviser, I, 329.

Little Kirsten took with her the bower-women five,
And with them she went to the wood belive.

She spread her cloak down on the earth,
And on it to two little twins gave birth.

She laid them under a turf so green,
Nor suffered for them a sorrow unseen.

She laid them under so broad a stone,
Suffered sorrow nor harm for what she had done.

Eight years it was, and the children twain
Would fain go home to their mother again.

They went and before Our Lord they stood:
'Might we go home to our mother, we would.'

'Ye may go to your mother, if ye will,
But ye may not contrive any ill.'

They knocked at the door, they made no din:
'Rise up, our mother, and let us in.'

By life and by death hath she cursed and sworn,
That never a child in the world hath she borne.

'Stop, stop, dear mother, and swear not so fast,
We shall recount to you what has passed.

'You took with you the bower-women five,
And with them went to the wood belive.

'You spread your cloak down on the earth,
And on it to two little twins gave birth.

'You laid us under a turf so green,
Nor suffered for us a sorrow unseen.

'You laid us under so broad a stone,
Suffered sorrow nor harm for what you had done.'

'Nay, my dear bairns, but stay with me;
And four barrels of gold shall be your fee.'

'You may give us four, or five, if you choose,
But not for all that, heaven will we lose.

'You may give us eight, you may give us nine,
But not for all these, heaven will we tine.

'Our seat is made ready in heavenly light,
But for you a seat in hell is dight.'

39. 23–25. These three stanzas are of course an addition of the broadside hack writer.

21

Two versions.

23

41. The MS. is not divided into stanzas. At the end of vv. 8, 25, 30, the MS. has .íí. This appears to indicate that this line is to be repeated, and we have so printed the text. It will be observed that this makes the stanzas regular throughout.
42. 15[1]. The insertion of *frek* ('man') is suggested by Skeat. The MS. has a blank.

24

Three versions.
42. 2. *A* may exhibit the original plot; but it is just as likely that the captain was substituted for a passenger, under the influence of 'Brown Robyn's Confession' (No. 57). A third version, from South Devon, agrees with *A* in this point.

25

Six versions.
44. 1. A preceding stanza may be supplied from *B* (Buchan's Ballads of the North of Scotland, I, 185) :—

'O Willie my son, what makes you sae sad?'
    As the sun shines over the valley
'I lye sarely sick for the love of a maid.'
    Amang the blue flowers and the yellow

Four versions have this stanza.

26

Two versions.
45. 1. Another version begins —

As I cam by yon auld house end,
I saw twa corbies sittin thereon.

29

48. 28–30. There is something like this in the Gaelic ballad. When MacReith's wife tried

on the mantle, it fitted her "as far as the tips of her little fingers and toes." She explains this failure of the mantle to cover her completely: "I once had a kiss in secret from O'Duibhne's son Diarmaid; the mantel would reach the ground, were it not for that."
48. 37[2]. Perhaps, as Percy suggested, two lines have dropped out after this, and the two which follow belong with the next stanza.

30

51. 31[2]. The rub-chadler for *thrub chadler* of the MS. The fiend is certainly closed under a barrel or tub, probably a rubbish barrel or tub.
52. 43[2]. The MS. has : of the trubchandler.
54. 69. In the part that is lost, the Burlow-beanie explains the use of the powder in blowing the horn.

31

55. 3. What is lost between sts. 3 and 4 may fortunately be supplied from Arthur's narrative in sts. 9–13.
57. 32. Sir Banier is perhaps a mistake for Beduer (Bedivere), Arthur's constable. Sir Bore and Sir Garrett are Sir Bors de Gauves, brother of Lionel, and Gareth (Gaheriet), the younger brother of Gawain.

32

58. 1[4]. And fu o courtesey (Scott).
58. 4. For this Scott has :—

He's taen him to his hunting ha,
    For to make buirly cheir;
When loud the wind was heard to sound,
    And an earthquake rocked the floor.

And darkness covered a' the hall,
    Where they sat at their meat;
The gray dogs, youling, left their food,
    And crept to Henrie's feet.

And louder houled the rising wind
    And burst the fastned door;
And in there came a griesly ghost,
    Stood stamping on the floor.

59. 14. Not in the MS. Here given from Jamieson, II, 94, who may have obtained it from Mrs Brown. Scott has it, with some verbal variation.
59. 15. Between vv. 2 and 3 Scott has :—

And what's the bed i this house, ladye,
    That ye're nae wellcum tee?

59. 15[3]. O ye maun pu the green heather (Scott).
59. 20. Scott has :—

For I was witched to a ghastly shape,
    All by my stepdame's skill,
Till I should meet wi a courteous knight
    Wad gie me a' my will.

34

Three versions.
60. 2[4]. A variant is "craig of sea."

61. 18⁴. Scott's version adds : —

And sighing said that weary wight,
I doubt that day I 'll never see.

36

63. 3. Maisry's services in washing and combing are more conceivable when rendered by a maid in her proper shape, as in ' Allison Gross ' (No. 35), than when attributed to a machrel of the sea ; and it is likely that the machrel returned to her own figure every Saturday, and that this is one of the points lost from the story. It is said here, as in ' Allison Gross ' (No. 35), that Maisry kames the laily head on her knee.

37

Five versions.
64. 7. Stands as 15 in the MS.
64. 11², ³ are 11³, ² in the MS. The order of words is still not simple enough for a ballad.

38

Seven versions.

39

Fifteen versions.
67. 3¹. The Museum text reads *has belted*.
67. 7. After this, in *L* (MS. at Abbotsford) : —

He 's tean her by the milk-white hand,
And by the grass-green sleeve,
And laid her lo at the foot of the tree,
At her he askt no leave.

68. 17. Before this, in *L* : —

There grows a flower in Charters Woods,
It grows on gravel greay,
It ould destroy the boney young bern
That ye got in your pley.

68. 20. After this, in *L* : —

If it were to an earthly man,
As [it is] to an elphan knight,
I ould walk [wake?] for my true-love's sake
All the long winter's night.'

68. 23 ff. Cf. *D* (Motherwell's MS.) : —

But it fell once upon a day,
As hunting I did ride,
As I rode east and west yon hill
There woe did me betide.

O drowsy, drowsy as I was !
Dead sleep upon me fell ;
The Queen of Fairies she was there,
And took me to hersell.

Cf. *L* : —

When I was a boy of eleven years old,
And much was made of me,
I went out to my father's garden,
Fell asleep at yon aple tree :
The queen of Elphan [she] came by,
And laid on her hands on me.

68. 26. *B* (Glenriddell's MSS.) is simpler and more genuine : —

The night it is gude Halloween,
The fairie folk do ride.

69. 34. Cf. *B* 34 : —

First dip me in a stand o milk,
And then a stand o water ;
Haud me fast, let me na gae,
I 'll be your bairnie's father.

The well-water has an occult and very important significance which modern reciters had completely lost knowledge of, as appears by the disorder into which the stanzas have fallen. Immersion in a liquid, generally water, but sometimes milk, is a process requisite for passing from a non-human shape, produced by enchantment or original. Judging by analogy, the naked man should issue from the bath of milk or water, into which he should have gone in one of his non-human shapes, a dove, swan, or snake ; but *A* is the only version which has preserved an essentially correct process : Tam Lin, when a burning gleed, is to be thrown into well-water, from which he will step forth a naked knight.

69. 34². Johnson's Museum has *burning lead*.
69. 41, 42. Cf. *B* 40, 41 : —

' Had I kend, Thomas,' she says,
' A lady wad hae borrowd thee,
I wad hae taen out thy twa grey een,
Put in twa een o tree.

' Had I but kend, Thomas,' she says,
' Before I came frae hame,
I had taen out that heart o flesh,
Put in a heart o stane.'

41

Three versions.
71. 1. Cf. ' Lady Isabel and the Elf-Knight ' (No. 4), st. 1. *Elmond* is perhaps a corruption of *Elf-man*.
71. 3. With this and the following stanzas cf. ' Tam Lin ' (No. 39), *A* 5-7. A rose, as in Tam Lin, would be more ballad-like for Margaret to be plucking.
71. 6. *Akin* is a corruption for *Etin*, i.e. " giant." Version *B* has *Etin*.
71. 15. The lines about the cupbearer are absurd. Etin was no cupbearer and he is not meant to lie to his son. The " misty night," however, may be significant. In one version there is a magic mist (a common phenomenon) which facilitates the lady's abduction.
73. 1³. *Nuts* is clearly a mistake for the elfin *note* of *A* 1.
74. 11. Version *C* (in Buchan's Ballads) has :

And seven bairns, fair and fine,
There has she born to him,
And never was in gude church-door,
Nor ever got gude kirking.

Ance she took harp into her hand,
And harped them a' asleep,
Then she sat down at their couch-side,
And bitterly did weep.

Said, Seven bairns hae I born now
To my lord in the ha ;
I wish they were seven greedy rats,
To run upon the wa,
And I mysel a great grey cat,
To eat them ane and a'.

Cf. ' Fair Annie ' (No. 62), *A* 23.

42

Three versions.

74. 1. *Colvill* (as in *B*) is the correct form and *Colven* a vulgarized one.

75. 14. *C* (from Forfarshire) has these stanzas which do not occur in *A* or *B*: —

> He wasna weel laid in his bed,
>   Nor yet well fa'en asleep,
> When up an started the mermaiden,
>   Just at Clerk Colin's feet.

> 'Will ye lie there an die, Clerk Colin,
>   Will ye lie there an die?
> Or will ye gang to Clyde's water,
>   To fish in flood wi me?'

> 'I will lie here an die,' he said,
>   'I will lie here an die;
> In spite o a' the deils in hell
>   I will lie here and die.'

43

Six versions.

76. 8. St. 8 of *C* (Buchan's version) throws light on the magic means employed. The witch-wife says: —

> Ye 'll pu the bloom frae aff the broom,
>   Strew 't at his head and feet,
> And aye the thicker that ye do strew,
>   The sounder he will sleep.

76. 13–14. These are in no other version, like "Hive Hill" in st. 8. Kinloch's version (*D*), however, ends savagely with a stanza (addressed to the hawk) which has some resemblance to st. 13: —

> Then be it sae, my wager gane,
>   'T will skaith frae meikle ill,
> For gif I had found her in bonnie broom-fields,
>   O her heart's blude ye 'd drunken your fill.

C has a similar, but more cynical, stanza.

77. 1. In all versions except *A* the tryst is the result of a wager. *F*, a broadside version, is distinctly jocular.

77. 2. The gap after this stanza may be filled from *D* 3–5; or from *E* (Robertson's Note-Book) as follows: —

> But when she cam to the bonnie green bower,
>   Her true-love was fast asleep;
> Sumtimes she kist his rosie, rosie lips,
>   And his breath was wondrous sweet.

77. 4. In *C* there are similar questions, addressed to hound, hawk, and merry men; in *D*, to hound and hawk; in *E*, to merry men and hawk; in *F*, to hawk, hound, and serving-man.

45

Two versions.

80. 25–27. Of the Egyptian questions only one is at all like the English. "The king proceeded: 'How much does the sun earn each day by his work for each son of Adam?' [The potter] replied, 'One qīrāt; for the day-laborer who works from sunrise to sunset receives that amount.'"

46

Three versions.

84. 8. For two of the three dishes cf. the following song, from a MS. assigned to the fifteenth century (Sloane MS. 2593, British Museum), — Wright's Songs and Carols, 1836, No. 8; as printed for the Warton Club, 1856, No. 29, p. 33: —

> I have a ჳong suster fer beჳondyn the se,
> Many be the drowryis that che sente me.

> Che sente me the cherye withoutyn ony ston;
> And so che dede [the] dowe withoutyn ony bon;

> Che sente me the brere withoutyn ony rynde,
> Sche bad me love my lemman withoute longgyng.

> How xuld ony cherye be withoute ston?
> And how xuld ony dowe ben withoute bon?

> How xuld ony brere ben withoute rynde?
> How xuld y love myn lemman without longyng?

> Quan the cherye was a flour, than hadde it non ston;

> Quan the dowe was an ey, than hadde it non bon;

> Quan the brere was onbred, than hadde it non rynd;

> Quan the maydyn haჳt that che lovit, che is without longyng.

47

Five versions.

87. 6. Cf. *C*, st. 6 (Buchan's MSS.): —

> 'An asking, asking, sir,' she said,
>   'An asking ye 'll grant me:'
> 'Ask on, ask on, lady,' he said,
>   'What may your asking be?'

87. 7–8. Version *D* (Harris MS.) has the following: —

> 'What gaes in a speal?' she said,
>   'What in a horn green?
> An what gaes on a lady's head,
>   Whan it is washen clean?'

> 'Ale gaes in a speal,' he said,
>   'Wine in a horn green;
> An silk gaes on a lady's head,
>   Whan it is washen clean.'

87. 9. In *C* there is a third question in this stanza, and a third answer in the next: —

> 'Or what is the finest thing,' she says,
>   'That king or queen can wile?'

> 'And yellow gold is the finest thing,' etc.

87. 10–11. Cf. *C* 9–10: —

> 'You have asked many questions, lady,
>   I 've you as many told;'
> 'But how many pennies round
>   Make a hundred pounds in gold?

> 'How many small fishes
>   Do swim the salt seas round?
> Or what 's the seemliest sight you 'll see
>   Into a May morning?'

49

Nine versions.

91. 1. Cf. *D* (Jamieson) 1–2: —

> 'O will ye gae to the school, brother?
>   Or will ye gae to the ba?
> Or will ye gae to the wood a-warslin,
>   To see whilk o 's maun fa?'

> 'It 's I winna gae to the school, brother,
>   Nor will I gae to the ba;
> But I will gae to the wood a-warslin,
>   And it is you maun fa.'

91. 6 ff. *D* reads : —

Ye 'll lift me up upon your back
  Tak me to Kirkland fair ;
Ye 'll mak my greaf baith braid and lang,
  And lay my body there.

Ye 'll lay my arrows at my head,
  My bent bow at my feet,
My sword and buckler at my side,
  As I was wont to sleep.

Whan ye gae hame to your father,
  He 'll speer for his son John :
Say, ye left him into Kirkland fair,
  Learning the school alone.

When ye gae hame to my sister,
  She 'll speer for her brother John :
Ye 'll say, ye left him in Kirkland fair,
  The green grass growin aboon.

Whan ye gae hame to my true-love,
  She 'll speer for her lord John :
Ye 'll say, ye left him in Kirkland fair,
  But hame ye fear he 'll never come.

91. 10. Some versions supplement the story with more or less of the ballad of ' Edward ' (No. 13).

50

92. 3². Should be ' It 's not for you a weed ' (Motherwell).

92. 5–7. A commonplace that may be expected to recur under the same or analogous circumstances, as it does in ' Tam Lin ' (No. 39) *D*, ' The Knight and Shepherd's Daughter ' (No. 110), ' Crow and Pie ' (No. 111), and in one version of ' The Broom of Cowdenknows ' (No. 217). These are much less serious ballads, and the tone of st. 5, which so ill befits the distressful situation, is perhaps owing to that stanza's having been transferred from some copy of one of these. It might well change places with this, from ' The Knight and Shepherd's Daughter,' *A :* —

Now you have had your wil, good sir,
  And put my body thus to shame,
Even as you are a courteous knight,
  Tel me what is your name.

Much better with this in ' Ebbe Galt,' *Danske Viser*, No. 63, 8 : —

Now you have had your will of me,
  To both of us small gain,
By the God that is above all things,
  I beg you tell your name.

51

Two versions.
94. 11–12. Cf. the conclusion of No. 49, *A*.

52

Four versions.
94. 4. Cf. *B* (Motherwell's MS.), st. 4 : —

' How dare ye shake the leaves ? ' he said,
  ' How dare ye break the tree ?
How dare ye pluck the nuts,' he said,
  ' Without the leave of me ? '

Cf. also ' Tam Lin ' (No. 39), *A* 6.

95. 18. *C* (Buchan's Ballads) has the following stanza after this : —

' Win up, and see your ae brother,
  That 's new come ower the sea ; '
' Ohon, alas ! ' says fair Annie,
  ' He spake ower soon wi me.'

53

Fifteen versions.
95. 5. The hero's name is mostly *Beichan*, with slight modifications like *Bekie, Bichan, Bichet, Brechin. Bateman* and *Bondwell* also occur. The heroine is usually *Susan Pye*.
95. 2⁴. *B* (Glenriddell MSS.) reads : Which horse and owsn were wont to drie.
96. 9. The following stanzas are from *F* (Pitcairn's MSS.) : —

O she 's gaen murning up and down,
  And she 's gaen murnin to the sea,
Then to her father she has gane in,
  Wha spak to her right angrily.

' O do ye mourn for the goud, daughter,
  Or do ye mourn for the whyte monie ?
Or do ye mourn for the English squire ?
  I wat I will gar hang him hie.'

' I neither mourn for the goud, father,
  Nor do I for the whyte monie,
Nor do I for the English squire ;
  And I care na tho ye hang him hie.

' But I hae promised an errand to go,
  Seven lang miles ayont the sea,
And blythe and merry I never will be
  Untill that errand you let me.'

' That errand, daughter, you may gang,
  Seven long miles beyond the sea,
Since blythe and merry you 'll neer be
  Untill that errand I 'll let thee.'

O she has built a bonny ship,
  And she has set it in the sea,
And she has built a bonny ship,
  It 's all for to tak her a long journie.

96. 16. Cf. *F*, st. 21 : —

I hae been porter at your yett,
  I 'm sure this therty lang years and three,
But the fairest lady stands thereat
  That evir my twa eyes did see.

96. 17. The next stanzas in *F* are : —

' She bids you send a bite of bread,
  It 's and a glass of your gude red wine,
Nor to forget the lady's love
  That let you out of prison strong.'

It 's up and spak the bride's mother,
  A weight of goud hung at her chin :
' There is no one so fair without
  But there are, I wat, as fair within.'

It ' s up and spak the bride herself,
  As she sat by the gude lord's knee :
' Awa, awa, ye proud porter,
  This day ye might hae excepted me.'

96. 3. " The prisoner's mane " in *H* (Kinloch's Ballads) is as follows (st. 9) : —

My hounds they all go masterless,
  My hawks they flee frae tree to tree,
My youngest brother will heir my lands,
  My native land I 'll never see.

97. 14. The important figure of the Billy Blin is lacking in all other versions except *M* (Buchan's MSS.), which substitutes " a woman clad in green," obviously a fairy. On the Billy Blin, see note to No. 8 (p. 641, above).

54

98. 3. The tree is a palm in the apocryphal Gospel. In England it is always a cherry, as in the fifteenth of the so-called Coventry Mysteries.

99. *B* 9–13. These sometimes occur, with variations and additions, as an independent carol, 'Joseph and the Angel.' See Chappell's Christmas Carols, ed. by Rimbault, p. 22, where for st. 11 we have : —

> He neither shall be clothed
> in purple nor in pall,
> But in the fair white linen
> that usen babies all.

100. 18. This suspiciously modern stanza is wanting in *b*, *c*, *d*.

55

100. 2². Sure all the world will turn, *b*.
101. 20³,⁴.

> And made a lowly reverence
> To Jesus Christ his grace. *b*.

56

Two versions.
102. 1. The rich man's name is *Diverus* in a version (*B*) in Notes and Queries, 4th Ser., III, 76.
102. 13. In *B* (with which *A b* practically agrees): —

> Rise up, rise up, brother Diverus,
> And come along with me ;
> There is a place prepared in hell,
> For to sit upon a serpent's knee.

58

Eighteen versions, several of them small fragments.
104. 11¹. So in *C* (*Aberdour* also in *F*). The water at St Johnston's wall *B* ; Nore-east, nore-west frae Aberdeen *D* ; There 's a brig at the back o Sanct John's toun *E* ; It 's forty miles to Aberdeen, And fifty fathoms deep *G* ; O forty miles off Aberdeen *H* ; It 's even ower by Aberdour *I* ; It 's och, och owre to Aberdour *J* ; Atween Leith an Aberdeen *K* ; Down below Dunbarton castle *P*. We may fairly say, — somewhere off the coast of Aberdeen. The southern Aberdour, in the Firth of Forth, cannot be meant.
104. 10. In *C* and *E* (both in Motherwell's MS.), Sir Patrick sends the boy aloft and sticks to the rudder himself. Thus in *C* : —

> ' Wha will come,' the captain says,
> ' And take my helm in hand ?
> Or wha 'll gae up to my topmast,
> And look for some dry land ?

> ' Mount up, mount up, my pretty boy,
> See what you can spy ;
> Mount up, mount up, my pretty boy,
> See if any land we 're nigh.'

> ' We 're fifty miles from shore to shore,
> And fifty banks of sand ;
> And we have all that for to sail
> Or we come to dry land.'

> ' Come down, come down, my pretty boy,
> I think you tarry long ;
> For the saut sea 's in at our coat-neck
> And out at our left arm.

> ' Come down, come down, my pretty boy,
> I fear we here maun die ;
> For thro and thro my goodly ship
> I see the green-waved sea.'

105. *G*. Scott's version, *H* (in the Border Minstrelsy, ed. 1803, III, 64), was made up from two versions, the better of which was *G*, and five stanzas recited by Mr. Hamilton, sheriff of Lanarkshire, who is said to have got them from an old nurse in the middle of the eighteenth century. These are the stanzas : —

> ' O where will I get a gude sailor,
> To take my helm in hand,
> Till I get up to the tall topmast,
> To see if I can spy land ?'

> ' O here am I, a sailor gude,
> To take the helm in hand,
> Till you go up to the tall topmast ;
> But I fear you 'll neer spy land.'

> He hadna gane a step, a step,
> A step but barely ane,
> When a bout flew out of our goodly ship,
> And the salt sea it came in.

> ' Gae fetch a web o the silken claith,
> Another o the twine,
> And wap them into our ship's side,
> And letna the sea come in.'

> They fetched a web o the silken claith,
> Another o the twine,
> And they wapped them roun that gude ship's side
> But still the sea came in.

105. 3. *H* gives the letter as follows : —

> To Noroway, to Noroway,
> To Noroway oer the faem ;
> The king's daughter of Noroway,
> 'T is thou maun bring her hame.

Cf. *I* (Buchan's Ballads), st. 9 : —

> But I maun sail the seas, the morn,
> And likewise sae maun you ;
> To Noroway, wi our king's daughter,
> A chosen queen she 's now.

And the first stanza of *J* (Harris MS.) : —

> Hie sits oor king in Dumfermline,
> Sits birlin at the wine ;
> Says, Whare will I get a bonnie boy
> That will sail the saut seas fine ?
> That will hie owre to Norraway,
> To bring my dear dochter hame ?

105. 12. In *J* a mermaid appears (st. 18) : —

> Then up it raise the mermaiden,
> Wi the comb an glass in her hand :
> ' Here 's a health to you, my merrie young men,
> For you never will see dry land.'

So in some other versions. Cf. 'The Mermaid,' No. 289.

105. 14. Cf. *J*, st. 20 : —

> There was Saturday, an Sabbath day,
> And Monnonday at morn,
> That feather-beds an silken sheets
> Cam floatin to Kinghorn.

59

Three versions.

106. 1. *Ravengaard, Röngård*, and *Ronnegaar*, — found, with variations, in the Scandinavian ballads, — and *Rodingar (Roddyngar)* — found in Anglo-Latin texts of the story of Gunhild — are the forerunners of the English *Sir Aldingar* (for *Sir Raldingar*) and *Rodingham*.

107. 12. The lady is *Gunild* in Scandinavian. The English *Elinor* is probably a later substitution. She may have been meant for the wife of the English King Henry II, less probably for the wife of Henry III.

107. 28. The diminutive size of the champion is emphasized in Scandinavian as well as in the story of Gunild in a thirteenth-century French metrical life of Edward the Confessor (Luard, Lives of Edward, p. 39 f., VII). In the latter he is called *Mimecan* (in the Scandinavian ballad, *Memering*). There is perhaps a trace of his dwarfishness in the tale of the Lombard queen Gundeberg.

60

113. 42². On tow good renish (Percy).

114. 59³, 60¹. The words printed in smaller type are acknowledged changes or additions of Percy's.

114. 63. "Some liberties have been taken in the following stanzas " (Percy).

61

115. The first two stanzas in the MS. have been omitted as belonging to another ballad. They are as follows : —

> Jesus, lord, mickle of might,
> *That* dyed ffor vs on the roode,
> To maintaine vs in all our right
> *That* loues true English blood.
>
> Ffor by a k*night* I say my song,
> Was bold and ffull hardye ;
> Sir Robert Briuse wold fforth to fflight,
> In-to Ireland ouer the sea.

116. 29. This unintelligible stanza seems to preserve a trace of an adventure lost in our defective text.

62

Ten versions.

118. 11. The name Lord Thomas was probably suggested by 'Lord Thomas and Fair Annet ' (No. 73). The first line of st. 12 reads in *D* (Herd's fragment, which supplied Scott with sts. 2–6, 12, 17, 19) : 'You 're welcome to your house, master.'

63

Eleven versions.

124. 1. *C* (Kinloch's MSS.) begins thus : —

> ' The corn is turning ripe, Lord John,
> The nuts are growing fu,
> And ye are bound for your ain countrie,
> Fain wad I go wi you.'
>
> ' Wi me, Margret, wi me, Margret,
> What wad ye do wi me ?
> I 've mair need o a pretty little boy,
> To wait upon my steed.'
>
> ' It 's I will be your pretty little boy,
> To wait upon your steed ;
> And ilka town that we come to,
> A pack of hounds I 'll lead.'
>
> ' My hounds will eat o the bread o wheat,
> And ye of the bread of bran ;
> And then you will sit and sigh,
> That eer ye loed a man.'

124. 11. *C* has the following stanzas (sts. 10–15) : —

> It 's whan she cam to the other side,
> She sat doun on a stane ;
> Says, Them that made me, help me now,
> For I am far frae hame.
>
> ' How far is it frae your mither's bouer,
> Gude Lord John tell to me ? '
> ' It 's therty miles, Lady Margaret,
> It 's therty miles and three :
> And yese be wed to ane o her serving men,
> For yese get na mair o me.'
>
> Then up bespak the wylie parrot,
> As it sat on the tree,
> ' Ye lee, ye lee, Lord John,' it said,
> ' Sae loud as I hear ye lee.
>
> ' Ye say it 's therty miles frae your mither's
> bouer,
> Whan it 's but barely three ;
> And she 'll neer be wed to a serving man,
> For she 'll be your ain ladie.'
>
> [' O dinna ye see yon bonnie castle,
> Lies on yon sunny lea ?
> And yese get ane o my mither's men,
> For yese get na mair o me.']
>
> [' Well see I yon bonnie castle,
> Lies on yon sunny lea,
> But Ise neer hae nane o your mither's men,
> Tho I never gat mair o thee.']

The stanzas bracketed are inserted by Kinloch in his later copy. In *H* (Motherwell's MS.) there is a corresponding passage (sts. 2–6, in which Lord John informs his love that he has ' a wife and seven bairns ' and is contradicted by a ' wild parrot.') *G* (Buchan's MSS.) has a stanza (10) similar to *C* 14.

124. 14.

> Atho there be a ladie there,
> Should sunder you and me,
> Betide my life, betide my death,
> I will go thither and see. *B b.*

125. 26.

> He has looked oer his left shoulder,
> And a loud laugh laughed he ;
> Says, He 's a squire's ae dear son,
> I got in the north countrie. *B b.*

125. 28²⁻⁴.

And the corn in her right hand,
And she's hied her to the stable-door,
As fast as she could gang. *B b.*

125. 30¹, ².

She has leand her to the manger side
And gien a grievous groan. *B b.*

125. 31, 32. One stanza in *b* : —

Then out it spake Lord John's mother,
As she stood on the stair,
'I think I hear a woman groan,
And a bairn greeting sair.'

125. 34. Two stanzas in *b* : —

'Now open the door, Bird Ellen,' he says,
'O open and let me in,
Or baith the door and the door cheeks
Into the floor I'll fling.'

He is struck the door wi his right foot,
And pushd it wi his knee,
Till iron bolts and iron bars
In flinders he has gard flee :
'Be not afraid, Bird Ellen,' he says,
'For there's nane win in but me.'

Then follows in *b* : —

The never a word spake that ladie,
As on the floor she lay,
But hushd her young son in her arms
And turnd his face away.

125. 36. Two stanzas in *b* : —

'And smile on me now, Bird Ellen,
And cast awa your care,
For I'll make you ladie of a' my lands,
And your son shall be my heir.'

'Blessd be the day,' sayd Bird Ellen,
'That I followd you frae the town,
For I'd rather far be your foot-page
Than the queen that wears the crown.'

64

Eight versions.

126. *A* is confused at the beginning. The following stanzas from a MS. at Abbotsford (Child, IV, 464) are clearer : —

Young Janet sits in her garden,
Makin a heavie maen,
Whan by cam her father dear,
Walkin himself alane.

'It's telld me in my bower, Janet,
It's telld me in my bed,
That ye're in love wi Sweet Willie ;
But a French lord ye maun wed.'

'In it be telld ye in yer bower, father,
In it be telld ye in your bed,
That me an Willie bears a love,
Yet a French lord I maun wed,
But here I mak a leel, leel vow
He's neer come in my bed.

'An for to please my father dear
A French lord I will wed ;
But I hae sworn a solemn oth
He's neer come in my bed.'

Young Janet's away to her bower-door,
As fast as she can hie,
An Willie he has followd her,
He's followd speedilie.

An whan he cam to her bowr-door
He tirld at the pin :
'O open, open, Janet love,
Open an let me in.'

'It was never my mother's custm, Willie,
It never sal be mine,
For a man to come the bower within
When a woman's travelin.

'Gae yer ways to my sisters' bower,
Crie, Meg, Marion an Jean,
Ye maun come to yer sister Janet,
For fear that she be gane.'

127. 30. See No. 7 for the plants from graves. The version mentioned in the first note (above) adds : —

Thae twae met, an thae twae plaet,
An ay they knitit near,
An ilka ane that cam thereby
Said, There lies twa lovers dear.

128. 13-14. Cf. *E* (Kinloch MSS.), sts. 9-10 : —

'Now chuse, now chuse now, Fair Janet,
What man you'll ride behind :'
'O wha sae fitting as Sweet Willie ?
He'll fit my saddle fine.'

O they rode on, and they rode on,
Till they cam to Merrytown green ;
But Sweet Willie and Fair Janet
Cam aye hoolie ahin.

The version mentioned in the first note above has (sts. 14-18) : —

'But I hae sorn a solemn oath,
Afore a companie,
That ye sal ride this day, Janet,
This day an ye soud die.

'Whae'll horse ye to the kirk, Janet ?
An whae will horse ye best ?'
'Whae but Willie, my true-love ?
He kens my mister best.'

'Whae'll horse ye to the kirk, Janet ?
An whae will horse ye there ?'
'Whae but Willie, my true-love ?
He neer will doo'd nae maer.

'Ye may saddle a steed, Willie,
An see that ye saddle 't soft ;
Ye may saddle a steed, Willie,
For ye winna saddle 't oft.

'Ye may saddle a steed, Willie,
An see that ye saddle 't side ;
Ye may saddle a steed, Willie,
But I thought to have been yer bride.'

65

Eleven versions.

130. 25. *K* (from a MS. at Abbotsford) adds : —

He's burstit the black unto the slack,
The grey unto the brae,
An ay the page that ran before
Cried, 'Ride, sir. an ye may.'

130. 29. In *G*, Margery (as she is called) blesses her lover most touchingly, with almost her last words (st. 13) : —

She turned her head on her left shoulder,
Saw her girdle hang on the tree :
'O God bless them that gave me that !
They'll never give more to me.'

66

Five versions.
131. 1⁴. Sharpe's MS. has *their bonneur*.
133. 26. In *D* (Kinloch MSS.) and *E* (Buchan) one of the brothers (Childe Vyet *E*) gives the other a choice of swords : —

> ' There 's two swords in one scabbard,
>   They cost me many a pound ;
> Take you the best, leave me the worst,
>   We 's fight till they be done.' *D*.

Cf. ' Little Musgrave ' (No. 81), *A* 22.
133. 28–31. There is a confusion of two accounts : in one, Lady Maisery does penance by begging ; in the other she goes mad (probably a later modification). With st. 28 cf., for example, No. 70, *B* 25.

67

Three versions.
137. 5. In *C* (Kinloch's MSS.) : —

> He harpit i the king's palace,
>   He harpit them a' asleep,
> Unless it were Burd Bell alone,
>   And she stud on her feet.

138. 25.

> Ye shall na hae to say, Glenkindie,
>   When you sit at the wine,
> That once you loved a queen's daughter,
>   And she was your footman's quean. *C*.

68

Eleven versions.
139. 1⁸. *Garlick's Wells*. Scott (*J*) has *Garlioch Wells*.
139. 8. Scott has : —

> thy clattering toung,
>   That trattles in thy head.

139. 15. Before this Scott has the following stanzas : —

> She hadna crossd a rigg o land,
>   A rigg but barely ane,
> When she met wi his auld father,
>   Came riding all alane.

> ' Where hae ye been, now, ladye fair,
>   Where hae ye been sae late ?
> We hae been seeking Erl Richard,
>   But him we canna get.'

> ' Erl Richard kens a' the fords in Clyde,
>   He 'll ride them ane by ane ;
> And though the night was neer sae mirk,
>   Erl Richard will be hame.'

140. 19. Before this Scott has : —

> ' Gar douk, gar douk,' the king he cried,
>   ' Gar douk for gold and fee ;
> O wha will douk for Erl Richard's sake,
>   Or wha will douk for me ? '

141. 10. *D* (Motherwell's MSS.) has : —

> They turnd down his yellow hair,
>   Turnd up his milk-white feet ;
> ' Lye thou there, Earl Richard,' she said,
>   ' Till the blood seep from thy bane ;
> That fairer maid than ten of me
>   Will look lang or thou come hame.'

141. 23. Scott's copy (*J*) has : —

> The maiden touchd the clay-cauld corpse,
>   A drop it never bled ;
> The ladye laid her hand on him,
>   And soon the ground was red.

Cf. *B* (Kinloch's MSS.) : —

> O white, white war his wounds washen,
>   As white as a linen clout ;
> But as the traitor she cam near,
>   His wounds they gushit out.

> ' It 's surely been my bouer-woman,
>   O ill may her betide !
> I neer wad slain him Young Redin,
>   And thrown him in the Clyde.'

69

Eight versions.
143. 26. *D* (Motherwell's MS.) ends as follows : —

> It 's I will do for my love's sake
>   What many ladies would think lang ;
> Seven years shall come and go
>   Before a glove go on my hand.

> And I will do for my love's sake
>   What many ladies would not do ;
> Seven years shall come and go
>   Before I wear stocking or shoe.

> There 'll neer a shirt go on my back,
>   There 'll neer a kame go in my hair,
> There 'll never coal nor candle-light
>   Shine in my bower nae mair.

Cf. note to p. 173, 29, and see No. 92, *A* 3, 4.

70

Two versions.

71

149. 25, 26. These stanzas are remarkably like *F* 3, 5 of ' Earl Brand ' (No. 7), the Percy copy, and may have served in some Scottish version of ' The Douglas Tragedy.'
150. 36–41. These stanzas are borrowed from ' The Knight and Shepherd's Daughter ' (No. 110). Folly could not go further than in making the mother clip her locks and kilt her clothes, as in 36 ; unless it be in making a boat of a coat and a topmast of a cane, as in 3, 4.

72

Four versions.
151. *A*, as sung, had a sequel of six stanzas, which is found separately and belongs with ' The Wife of Usher's Well ' (No. 79) ; see p. 168, version *B*.

73

Ten versions.
153. 25. In some versions of the Scandinavian ballad, little Kerstin, the forsaken mistress, sets fire to the bride-house : —

> Sir Peter awakes, but he wakes not ere
> The flame is playing in the young bride's hair.

> Sir Peter springs from his bed, oer late ;
> He saw Little Kersti go out through the gate.

'Ah, dear Little Kersti, now help thou me!
Another time shall I help thee.'

And it was Little Kersti, her laugh he heard :
'I wot how well you keep your word.'

74

Four versions.
157. The fragments in The Knight of the
Burning Pestle are : —

When it was grown to dark midnight,
And all were fast asleep,
In came Margaret's grimly ghost,
And stood at Wlliam's feet.   (Act ii, sc. 8.)

You are no love for me, Margaret,
I am no love for you.   (Act iii, sc. 5.)

157. 14. The brown girl, characteristic of
No. 73, has slipped in from that ballad.

75

Ten versions.

76

Thirteen versions.
163. 3-4. In E (A. Fraser Tytler's Brown
MS.), these stanzas are in the direct discourse : —

Your father will shoe your fu fair foot,
Your mother will glove your hand ;
Your sister will lace your middle jimp
Wi the new made London band.

Your brother will kaim your yellow hair,
Wi the new made silver kaim ;
And the king of heaven will father your bairn,
Till Love Gregor come haim.

164. 28 ff. E ends as follows : —
The wind blew loud, the sea grew rough,
And dashd the boat on shore ;
Fair Annie floats on the raging sea,
But her young son raise no more.

Love Gregor tare his yellow hair,
And made a heavy moan ;
Fair Annie's corpse lay at his feet,
But his bonny young son was gone.

O cherry, cherry was her cheek,
And gowden was her hair,
But clay cold were her rosey lips,
Nae spark of life was there.

And first he 's kissd her cherry cheek,
And neist he 's kissed her chin ;
And saftly pressd her rosey lips,
But there was nae breath within.

'O wae betide my cruel mother,
And an ill dead may she die !
For she turnd my true-love frae my door,
When she came sae far to me.'

77

Seven versions.
165. 8. In three versions (B D E) Margaret
will not give William back his faith and troth
unless he resolves certain questions about the
state of the dead. Thus in D (from Dr Joseph
Robertson's Note-Book) : —

'Yere faith and troth ye 'se never get,
Till ye tell me this ane ;
Till ye tell me where the women go
That hang themsell for sin.'

'O they gang till the low, low hell,
Just by the devil's knee ;
It 's a' clad ower wi burnin pitch,
A dreadfu sicht to see.'

'But your faith and troth ye 'se never get,
Till ye tell me again ;
Till ye tell me where the children go
That die without a name.'

'O they gang till the high, high heaven,
Just by our Saviour's knee,
And it 's a' clad ower wi roses red,
A lovelie sicht to see.'

'But gie me my faith and troth, Margrat,
And let me pass on my way ;
For the psalms o heaven will be sung,
An I 'll be mist away.'

'But your faith and troth yese never get,
Till ye tell me again ;
Till ye tell me where the women go
That die in child-beddin.'

'O they gang till the hie, hie heaven,
Just by our Saviour's knee,
And every day at twal o'clock
They 're dipped ower the head.'

165. 11. In C (Motherwell's MS.) there is
an impressive scene at the grave : —

She followed him high, she followed him low,
Till she came to yon church-yard ;
O there the grave did open up,
And young William he lay down.

'What three things are these, Sweet William,' she
says,
'That stands here at your head ? '
'It 's three maidens, Marjorie,' he says,
'That I promised once to wed.'

'What three things are these, Sweet William,' she
says,
'That stands here at your side ? '
'It 's three babes, Marjorie,' he says,
'That these three maidens had.'

'What three things are these, Sweet William,' she
says,
'That stands here at your feet ? '
'It is three hell-hounds, Marjorie,' he says,
'That 's waiting my soul to keep.'

She took up her white, white hand,
And she struck him in the breast,
Saying, Have there again your faith and troth,
And I wish your soul good rest.

165. 15, 16. These are clearly modern, but
very likely represent original stanzas not remembered in form.

166. 8. C (Motherwell's MS.) has : —
'The cocks they are crowing, Marjory,' he says,
'The cocks they are crawing again ;
It 's time the deid should part the quick,
Marjorie, I must be gane.'

166. F. The first part of this version was
evidently derived from No. 47.

78

Eight versions.
167. 1. Version C (from Suffolk) reads : —

Cold blows the wind oer my true-love,
Cold blow the drops of rain ;
I never, never had but one sweetheart,
In the greenwood he was slain.

Similarly in some other versions. A fragment (C. K. Sharpe's papers) is: —

> O wet and weary is the night,
> And evendown pours the rain,
> And he that was sae true to me
> Lies in the greenwood slain.

167. 3. A stanza in *H* expresses the common belief that the tears of the living wet the shroud of the dead : —

> What is it that you want of me
> And will not let me sleep?
> Your salten tears they trickle down
> And wet my winding-sheet.

167. 5. After this the ghost says, in *H* : —

> If you were not my own sweet-heart,
> As now I know you be,
> I 'd tear you as the withered leaves
> That grew on yonder tree.

79

Four versions.
168. 4². *Fashes* is Scott's emendation for *fishes* of the MS. ; Aytoun reads *freshes*.
168. *B*. This version, as sung, formed the conclusion of No. 72 *A*.
169. *C* should be compared with *D*. It is given in order that no text may be omitted which can throw light on this ballad.
170. 4³. Perhaps *lovely;* the MS. is not clear.
170. 9⁴. Read, probably, "They wet our winding sheet." Cf. No. 78, *A* 3.

80

171. 15². *Cooke* seems wrongly repeated.
171. 26¹. For *light* read *fayre* (?).

81

Fifteen versions.
172. 8. In *C* and several other versions the lovers try a bribe, a threat, or both, to make the page keep counsel.
173. 29. *L* (Buchan's MSS.) ends with a vow of penance (cf. note to p. 143, 26).

> Ye 'll darken my windows up secure,
> Wi staunchions round about,
> And there is not a living man
> Shall eer see me walk out.
>
> Nae mair fine clothes my body deck,
> Nor kame gang in my hair,
> Nor burning coal nor candle light
> Shine in my bower mair.

Cf. note to p. 143, 26, and see No. 92, *A* 3, 4.

83

Seven versions.
177. 1. *C* (Motherwell's MS.) reads: —

> Bob Norice is to the grein-wude gane,
> He is awa wi the wind.

178. 6.

> 'Do I nae pay you gowd?' he said,
> 'Do I nae pay you fee?
> How daur you stand my bidding, Sir,
> Whan I bid you to flee?' *C*.

178. 7. These stanzas follow in *C:* —

> 'What news, what news, my bonnie wee boy?
> What news hae ye to me?'
> 'Nae news, nae news, Lord Barnet,' he said,
> 'But your ladie I fain would see.
>
> 'Here is a pair o gluves to her,
> Thay 'r o the silver gray;
> And tell her to cum to the merrie green-wud,
> And speik to Bob Norice.
>
> 'Here is a gay gowd ring to her,
> It 's aw gowd but the stane;
> And she maun cum to the merrie green-wud,
> And speir the leive o nane.
>
> 'Here is a gay manteil to her,
> It 's aw silk but the sleive;
> And she maun cum to the merrie grein-wud,
> And ask not bauld Barnet's leive.'
>
> Then out bespack the yellow nurse,
> Wi the babie on her knee,
> Sayand, Gif thay be cum frae Bob Norice,
> They are welcum to me.
>
> 'O haud your tung, ye yellow nurse,
> Aloud an I heir ye lie;
> For they 're to Lord Barnet's lady,
> I trew that this be she.'
>
> Lord Barnet 's to a dressing-room,
> And buskit him in woman's array,
> And he 's awa to the merrie green-wud,
> To speik to Bob Norrice.

84

Three versions.
180. *B a* was "printed for P. Brooksby, J. Deacon, J. Blare, J. Back."

85

Five versions.

86

Three versions.
183. Scott's version (*A*) begins with the following stanzas, which are intended to extenuate young Benjie's guilt: —

> Of a' the maids o fair Scotland
> The fairest was Marjorie,
> And Young Benjie was her ae true-love,
> And a dear true-love was he.
>
> And wow! but they were lovers dear,
> And loved fu constantlie;
> But ay the mair, when they fell out,
> The sairer was their plea.
>
> And they hae quarrelled on a day,
> Till Marjorie's heart grew wae,
> And she said she 'd chuse another luve
> And let Young Benjie gae.
>
> And he was stout, and proud-hearted,
> And thought o 't bitterlie,
> And he 's gaen by the wan moon-light
> To meet his Marjorie.

183. 5. St. 4 should probably follow st. 5. Scott has: —

> Then saft she smiled, and said to him,
> O what ill hae I done?
> He took her in his armis twa,
> And threw her oer the linn.

183. 8. Scott's copy introduces this stanza with the following: —

Then they've taen up the comely corpse,
    And laid it on the grund:
'O wha has killed our ae sister,
    And how can he be found?

'The night it is her low lykewake,
    The morn her burial day,
And we maun watch at mirk midnight,
    And hear what she will say.'

Wi doors ajar, and candle-light,
    And torches burning clear,
The streikit corpse, till still midnight,
    They waked, but naething hear.

183. 9. In Scott's copy —

O wha has done the wrang, sister,
    Or dared the deadly sin?
Wha was sae stout, and feared nae dout,
    As thraw ye oer the linn?

183. 13. Scott's version ends: —

Tie a green gravat round his neck,
    And lead him out and in,
And the best ae servant about your house
    To wait Young Benjie on.

And ay, at every seven year's end,
    Ye'll tak him to the linn;
For that's the penance he maun drie,
    To scug his deadly sin.

Cf. Buchan's version (*B*): —

'Ye winna Bondsey head, brothers,
    Nor will ye Bondsey hang;
But ye'll take out his twa grey een,
    Make Bondsey blind to gang.

'Ye'll put to the gate a chain o gold,
    A rose garland gar make,
And ye'll put that in Bondsey's head,
    A' for your sister's sake.'

87

Four versions.

184. 2. The defective version *D* (Harris MS.) contains the following mutilated stanza: —

It is the fashion in oor countrie, mither,
    I dinna ken what it is here,
To like your wife better than your mither,
    That . . . bought you sae dear.

88

Six versions.

186. *Introduction.* A similar turn is given to the act in *E* (Buchan's Ballads): —

Ohon, alas, my lady gay,
    To come sae hastilie!
I thought it was my deadly foe,
    Ye had trysted into me.

But *E* seems to be *A* altered, or imperfectly remembered, with the addition of a few stanzas.

89

Three versions.

190. 4⁴. In the MS. *feet* is corrected to *head*, but *sleep* is not changed to *bed*. Clearly we should read either *sleep* and *feet*, or *bed* and *head*.

90

Four versions and a variant.

191. 1. Cf. 'Child Maurice,' No. 83, *A* 1.

193. 15³⁴. A faint trace of an old feature that comes out clearly in *C* (Buchan's Ballads):

Then brought to the next borough's town,
    And gae him nurses three;
He grew as big in ae year auld
    As some boys would in three.

Then he was sent to guid squeel-house,
    To learn how to thrive;
He learnd as muckle in ae year's time
    As some boys would in five.

This extraordinary growth of heroes is a widespread idea, and examples occur in the popular literature of many peoples.

91

Seven versions.

193. 6². Read, perhaps, *towers*.

193. 2-4. Cf. *B* (Herd's MSS.): —

But there came knights, and there came squiers
    An knights of high degree;
She pleased hersel in Levieston,
    Thay wear a comly twa.

He has bought her rings for her fingers,
    And garlands for her hair,
The brooshis till her bosome braid;
    What wad my love ha mair?
And he has brought her on to Livingston,
    And made her lady thear.

194. 19⁴. Read, perhaps, *weary* for *merry*.

92

Two versions.

195. The following stanzas of 'The Lowlands of Holland' occur in Herd's MSS. and are all that here concern us: —

'My love hath built a bony ship, and set her on
    the sea,
With seven score good mariners to bear her company;
There's three score is sunk, and three score dead
    at sea,
And the Lowlands of Holland has twin'd my love
    and me.

'My love he built another ship, and set her on
    the main,
And nane but twenty mariners for to bring her
    hame;
But the weary wind began to rise, and the sea
    began to rout,
My love then and his bonny ship turnd wither-
    shins about.

'Then shall neither coif come on my head nor
    comb come in my hair;
Then shall neither coal nor candle-light shine in
    my bower mair;
Nor will I love another one until the day I die,
For I never lovd a love but one, and he's drowned
    in the sea.'

'O had your tongue, my daughter dear, be still
    and be content;
There are mair lads in Galloway, ye neen nae
    sair lament:'

'O there is none in Gallow, there 's none at a' for
me,
For I never lovd a love but one, and he 's drowned
in the sea.'

195. *A* 3, 4. See note to p. 173, 29.
196. 5². *Bahome* in *B* (Buchan's Ballads.)

93

Twenty-six versions (including fragments).

94

200. 3³. *And* is corrected to *Ane* in the
second edition of Percy's Reliques.

95

Thirteen versions.
200. One version of this ballad has become
a children's game (Notes and Queries, 6th Ser.,
VI, 476). In others the verses are set in a popular tale, and a characteristic explanation is
furnished of the heroine's danger : she has lost
a golden key, or a golden ball, which had been
entrusted to her.

96

Eight versions.
203. 21. In some versions hot lead or gold
is dropped on the maiden to make sure whether
she is really dead. Thus in *C* (Motherwell's
MS.) : —

Then down as dead that lady drapd,
 Beside her mother's knee ;
Then out it spoke an auld witch-wife,
 By the fire-side sat she.

Says, Drap the hot lead on her cheek,
 And drop it on her chin,
And drop it on her rose-red lips,
 And she will speak again :
For much a lady young will do,
 To her true-love to win.

They drapd the het lead on her cheek,
 So did they on her chin ;
They drapt it on her red-rose lips,
 But they breathed none again.

97

Three versions.
205. *C* (Buchan's Ballads) has a feeble sequel intended to complicate the plot. It is not
beyond the invention of the blind beggar who
collected ballads for Buchan.

98

Three versions.

99

Twenty versions.
209. 15. Cf. *B* (Glenriddell MSS.) : —

The fetters they are on my feet,
 And O but they are cauld !
My bracelets they are sturdy steel,
 Instead of beaten gold.

But I will write a lang letter,
 And seal it tenderlie,
And I will send to my true-love,
 Before that I do die.

209. 26⁴. *McNauchtan* in *C* (Motherwell's
MS.). Other versions give other names.
209. 29³. In *B* I have a champion in my
court.
210. 31². In *H* (Kinloch MSS.) the champion is described as a "greecy [frightful]
ghost ; " in *L* (Campbell MSS.) he is a "fear-
some sight," with three women's spans between
his brows and three yards between his shoulders ;
in *R* (MS. at Abbotsford) he is "a gurrly fellow, with twa lang sclasps between his eyes,"
and so on. These points are probably taken
from another and a later ballad, which is perhaps an imitation, and might almost be called
a parody of Johnie Scot, 'Lang Johnny More'
(No. 251).
210. 31. Cf. *B*, sts. 24, 25 : —

The king but and his nobles a'
 Went out into the plain,
The queen but and her maidens a',
 To see young Johnny slain.

The first wound that Johnny gae the champion
 Was a deep wound and sair ;
The next wound that he gae the champion,
 He never spak mair.

In *D* (Motherwell's MS.) we have : —

Lords and ladies flocked all,
 They flocked all amain,
They flocked all to the green wood,
 To see poor Johnnie slain.

This Talliant he could find no way
 To be poor Johnnie's dead,
But, like unto a swallow swift,
 He jumped oer Johnnie's head.

But Johnnie was a clever man,
 Cunning and crafty withal,
And up on the top of his braid sword
 He made this Talliant fall.

This fatal jump of the Italian occurs in some
other versions.

100

Eleven versions.
210. 13. *C* (Kinloch MSS.) ends thus : —

He 's mounted her on a milk-white steed,
 Himself on a dapple-grey,
And made her a lady of as much land
 She could ride in a whole summer day.

211. 6. This stanza occurs in No. 110, *A* 15.

101

Four versions.
211. 1. *B*, *C*, and *D* have a more elaborate
beginning. Thus in *B* (Buchan MSS.) : —

Willie was an earl's ae son,
 And an earl's ae son was he,
But he thought his father lack to sair,
 And his mother of low degree.

But he is on to fair England,
 To sair for meat an fee,
And all was for Dame Oliphant,
 A woman of great beauty.

He hadna been in fair England
  A month but barely ane,
Ere he dreamd that fair Dame Oliphant
  Gied him a gay gold ring.

He had not been in fair England
  A month but barely four,
Ere he dreamd that fair Dame Oliphant
  Gied him a red rose flower,
Well set about with white lillies,
  Like to the paramour.

212. 9. A popular passage the like of which is found in many of our ballads: as No. 63, *A* 2, 3; No. 102, *A* 4; also in many foreign ballads.

212. 13, 14. Cf. *B* (Buchan MSS.):—

But she's taen a web of the scarlet,
  And she tare it fine an sma,
And even into Willie's arms
  She leapt the castle-wa:
And Willie was wight and well able,
  And he keept her frae a fa.

But the cocks they crew, and the horns blew,
  And the lions took the hill,
And Willie's ladie followed him,
  And the tears did twinkle still.

Cf. also *C* (Kinloch MSS.):—

The cocks do craw, and the day does daw,
  And the wild fowl bodes on hill;
The lassie she followed her Sweet William,
  And let the tears down fall.

102

Three versions.
214. 3. The Earl of Huntingdon has no place in the ancient traditional ballads of Robin Hood, but is of later literary invention. *A* 17, *B* 1, and *C* 1, may, however, very well have belonged to some Robin Hood ballad.

103

Three versions.
219. 59. The concluding stanza of *C* (Kinloch's Ballads) shows how No. 103 was fitted to the *dramatis personae* of the Robin Hood cycle:—

The tane was wedded to Robin Hood,
  And the tither to Little John;
And it was a' owing to their stepmother,
  That garrd them leave their hame.

104

Two versions.

105

220. Brooksby printed 1672–95; J. Walter, 1690–1720 (Chappell).

106

221. *a* was "printed for J. Hose" (1660–75); *b* for "W. Thackeray [1660–89] and T. Passinger [1670–82]."
221. 4. The Dean of Derry communicated to Percy in 1776 the following stanzas, which he wrote down from the recitation of his mother, Mrs Barnard, wife of the Bishop of Derry:—

My mother showd me a deadly spight;
She sent three thieves at darksome night;
They put my servants all to flight,
They robd my bower, and they slew my knight

They could not do me much more harm,
But they slew my baby on my arm;
They left me nothing to wrap it in
But the bloody, bloody sheet that it lay in.

They left me nothing to make a grave
But the bloody sword that slew my babe;
All alone the grave I made,
And all alone salt tears I shed.

All alone the bell I rung,
And all alone sweet psalms I sung;
I leant my head against a block,
And there I cut my lovely locks.

I cut my locks, and chang'd my name
From Fair Eleanore to Sweet William.

Scott inserted in his Border Minstrelsy, III, 80, 1803, seven stanzas under the title of ' The Lament of the Border Widow,' which show broader traces of the sheet-ballad and agreements with ' The Three Ravens' (No. 26). This fragment was given to Scott by the Ettrick Shepherd. It is here given from the MS. at Abbotsford.

My love he built me a bonny bowr,
  An cled it a' wi lily-flowr;
A brawer bowr ye neer did see
  Than my true-love he built to me.

There came a man by middle day,
  He spy'd his sport an went away,
An brought the king that very night,
  Who brak my bowr, an slew my knight.

He slew my knight, to me sae dear;
  He slew my knight, an poind his gear;
My servants all for life did flee,
  An left me in extremity.

I sewd his sheet, making my moan;
  I watchd the corpse, mysel alone;
I watchd his body night and day;
  No living creature came that way.

I took the corpse then on my back,
  And whiles I gaed, and whiles I sat;
I digd a grave, and laid him in,
  And hapd him wi the sod sae green.

But thinkna ye my heart was sair
  When I laid the mool on his yellow hair?
O thinkna ye my heart was wae
  When I turnd about, away to gae?

Nae langer there I could remain
  Since that my lovely knight was slain;
· · · · · · · ·
· · · · · · · ·

107

Two versions.

109

Three versions.
230. 6. In *B* (broadside of 1677):—

For I have a lover true of mine own,
  A serving-man of low degree,
One Tommy Pots it is his name,
  My first love and last that ever shall be.

230. 12. In B : —

With that the lady began to weep;
  She knew not well then what to say,
How she might Lord Phenix deny,
  And escape from marriage quite away.

232. 54. Two stanzas in B : —

'O master, yet it is unknown;
  Within these two days well try'd it must be;
He is a lord, I am but a serving-man,
  I fear I shall lose her with poverty.'

'I prethee, Tom Potts, get thee on thy feet;
  My former promises kept shall be;
As I am a lord in Scotland fair,
  Thou 'st never lose her with poverty.'

110

Sixteen versions.

235. a was "printed for William Gilbertson" (1640–63); b "for A. M[ilbourne], W. O[nley], and T. Thackeray" about 1680.

237. 1^3. C (Kinloch's MSS.) has: a knicht frae the High College.

237. 10. C has: —

'Jump on behind, ye weill-faurd may,
  Or do ye chuse to ride?'
'No, thank ye, sir,' the lady said,
  'I rather chuse to wade;'
And afore that he was mid-water,
  She was at the ither side.

'Turn back, turn back, ye weill-faurd may,
  My heart will brak in three:'
'And sae did mine in yon bonny hill-side,
  Whan ye wad [na] lat me be.'

'Whare gat ye that gay claithing
  This day I see on thee?'
My mither was a gude milk-nurse,
  And a gude nourice was she;
She nursd the Earl of Stockford's daughter,
  And gat aw this to me.'

237. 17. C has: —

Then out bespak the queen hersel,
  Wha sat by the king's knee:
There 's na a knicht in aw our court
  Wad hae dune that to thee,
Unless it war my brither, Earl Richard,
  And forbid it it war he!

Wad ye ken your love,
  Amang a hunder men?
'I wad,' said the bonnie ladie,
  'Amang five hunder and ten.'

238. 26. C has: —

Whan she cam to yon nettle-dyke,
  . . . .
'An my auld mither she was here,
  Sae weill as she wad ye pu.

'She wad boil ye weill, and butter ye weill,
  And sup till she war fu,
And lay her head upon her dish-doup,
  And sleep like onie sow.'

238. 29, 30. C lacks the mill, but has the following: —

Whan she cam to Earl Richard's house,
  The sheets war holland fine:
'O haud awa thae linen sheets,
  And bring to me the linsey clouts
I hae been best used in.

'Awa, awa wi your siller spoons,
  Haud them awa frae me;
It would set me better to feed my flocks
  Wi the brose-cap on my knee:
Sae bring to me the gude ram's horn,
  The spoons I 've been used wi.'

238. 33. In C and some other versions, as in Chaucer, the bridegroom is unwilling to turn about and make much of his wife. Cf. C, sts. 29–30: —

'Ye 'll turn about, Earl Richard,
  And mak some mair o me;
An ye mak me lady o ae puir plow,
  I can mak ye laird o three.'

'If ye be the Earl of Stockford's dochter,
  As I 've taen some thouchts ye be,
Aft hae I waited at your father's yett,
  But your face I coud never see.'

In F (Buchan's Ballads) and some other versions, the Billy Blin (see note on p. 8, st. 24) reveals the lady's parentage (sts. 60, 61): —

It 's out then spake the Billy-Blin,
  Says, I speak nane out of time;
If ye make her lady o nine cities,
  She 'll make you lord o ten.

Out it spake the Billy-Blin,
  Says, The one may serve the other;
The King of Gosford's ae daughter,
  And the Queen of Scotland's brother.

112

Five versions.

114

Thirteen versions.

241. 19. Cf. G (Harris MS.), st. 11: —

The firsten shot that Johnnie shot,
  He shot them a' but ane,
An he flang him owre a milk-white steed,
  Bade him bear tidings hame.

241. 20. *Boy* is evidently a corruption of *bird*. Cf. B 13, and note, and K.

242. 13. Cf. F (Scott's compounded version), sts. 19, 20: —

'O is there na a bonnie bird
  Can sing as I can say,
Could flee away to my mother's bower,
  And tell to fetch Johnie away?'

The starling flew to his mother's window-stane,
  It whistled and it sang,
And aye the ower-word o the tune
  Was, Johnie tarries lang!

In L, a fragment of one stanza from the Harris MS., information is given in a different way: —

But aye at ilka ae mile's end
  She fand a cat o clay,
An written upon the back o it
  'Tak your son Johnie Brod away.'

244. 19. Evidently corrupt. See note on A 19.

116

246. The text is made up as follows: 1–53² from c; 53³–111³ from b; 111⁴–113³ from c; 113⁴–120² from a; 120³–121 from c; 122–128² from a;

128³–161¹ from c; 161²–170 from a. That is, a and b are used for that part of the ballad which they contain and the rest is taken from c. Minor defects in a and b are supplied (within brackets) from c, except 100³, which is from d, e. Full collations will be found in Professor Child's collection. For 'The Second Part of Adam Bell,' which is not a traditional ballad, see Child, III, 34.

117

256. The text is made up as follows: 1–83³ from a; 83⁴–118³ from b; 118⁴–124¹ from a; 124²–127³ from b; 127⁴–133² from a; 133³–136³ from b; 136⁴–208³ from a; 208⁴–314¹ from b; 314²–349³ from a; 349⁴–456 from b. Minor deficiencies in a are in general supplied from b; in c, from other copies. A full collation will be found in Child.

273. 338⁴. The proude shirife than sayd she. f.

119

282. 1, 2. Cf. the beginning of Nos. 116, 121, 148.

283. 30¹. Skeat's reading. The line is almost illegible, but the first word is *Robyn*.

283. 30². A gap here between two pages, and there are commonly six stanzas to a page.

285. 77⁴. b has *Quit me* (perhaps better).

120

286, 287. 1–7. Cf. No. 119, sts. 6–12.

287. 4³, ⁴. This probably means that Scarlet, seeing his master is wroth, will say no more. It might mean something stronger, but it is unlikely that Will is so touchy as to throw up fealty for a testy word from a sick man.

288. 23¹. For 'give me mood' Child suggests 'give me my God,' i. e. the host.

289. 14². In b: thou begs.

289. 19. In a two poor stanzas follow, to introduce the epitaph, which, however, does not follow; b has two different stanzas (quite as bad) and the epitaph. For the epitaph, see p. 361. The transitional stanzas in a are as follows: —

> Thus he that never feard bow nor spear
>   Was murderd by letting blood;
> And so, loving friends, the story it ends
>   Of valiant Robin Hood.
>
> There's nothing remains but his epitaph now,
>   Which, reader, here you have,
> To this very day which read you may,
>   As it is upon his grave.
> Hey down a derry derry down

121

290. 25. St. 29 is wrongly put here in the MS.

291. 28. The order of lines in the MS. is 3, 2, 1, 4.

291. 37². In the MS.: Gere amarsey seyde sche *ser*(?) than.

292. 50². And [thow]? The scribe may have meant *potte* (i.e. put) rather than *polle*.

292. 55³, ⁴. In the MS.: You mey cart ys the bow Þat Robyn gaffe me.

293. 74¹, ². Ought perhaps to be dropped. The scribe, having got the second verse wrong, may have begun the stanza again.

122

294. 9². Half a page gone, as also after st. 17 and st. 25.

296. B a was "printed for F. Grove" (1620–55); d "for I. Clarke, W. Thackeray, and T. Passenger" (1670–86?).

123

297. 1, 2. Cf. the opening verses of Nos. 116, 118, 119, and others. St. 1 has been corrupted, and st. 2 also, one would think, as there is no apparent reason for maids weeping and young men wringing hands in the merry month of May. In 1³ the MS. has: 13 in May. In 1³, ⁴ *month* might be changed to *moon*, to justify *thirteen* in the second, and to accord with *moon* in the third. For *in May* in l. 2, we may read *I say* or *many say*. Cf. No. 140, B 1.

297. 3⁴. *Cutted* can mean only 'short-frocked,' which would make the friar a Franciscan. Fountains Abbey was a Cistercian monastery. The friar in the play has a "long cote." *Curtal* in B seems to be the proper word. It appears to be simply *curtilarius* (Eng. *curtiler*), and to be applied to the friar and the dogs because they had the care and keeping of the vegetable garden (*curtile*) of the monastery.

298. 7¹. For *wet weary* read probably *wel weary*.

298. 21. Cf. B, sts. 38–40. We must infer that Robin's offer is accepted; but the Curtal Friar plays no part in Robin Hood story out of his own ballad.

298. B b was "printed at London for H. Gosson" (1607–41); d was "printed for F. Coles, T. Vere, W. Gilbertson" (1640–80?); e was "printed for W. Thackeray, J. Millet, and A. Milbourn" (1680–97?); f was "printed for F. Coles, T. Vere, and J. Wright" (1655–80).

124

301. A a was "printed for F. Coles, T. Vere, and W. G[i]llbertson" (F. Coles, 1646–74; T. Vere, 1648–80; W. Gilbertson, 1640–63); d was "printed by and for Alex. Milbourn" (1670–97).

301. 1. Thus quoted in Munday and Chettle's Life and Death of Robert Earl of Huntington: —

> O there dwelleth a jolly pinder
>   At Wakefield all on the green.

301. 3. *Witty* is a corruption for *wight*.

301. 9. Thus quoted in Munday's Downfall of Robert Earl of Huntington: —

At Michaelmas cometh my covenant out,
My master gives me my fee;
Then, Robin, I'll wear thy Kendall green,
And wend to the greenwood with thee.

126

305. *A* and *b* were " printed for W. Gilbertson " (1640–63); *d* " for J. Wright, J. Clarke, W.
Thackeray, and T. Passenger " (1670–82 ?).
305. 8³. *Another* seems to be corrupt (cf.
12³). In 13³ the word makes sense.

127

307. *a* was " printed for F. Grove, dwelling
on Snowhill " (1620–55); *b* " for I. Clarke, W.
Thackeray, and T. Passenger " (1670–86 ?); *c*
" by J. Hodges," not in black letter.

128

309. *a* and *b* were " printed for Richard Burton " (1641–74); *e* " for J. Clarke, W. Thackeray,
and T. Passenger " (1670–82 ?).
311. 25. Followed in all the copies by seven
stanzas which belong to another ballad (No. 130
A).

129

311. *a* was " printed by and for W. O[nley] "
(1650–1702); *b* " for A. M[ilbourne], W. O[nley],
and T. Thackeray " (1670–89 ?).

130

Two versions.
314. *A*. For the printer, etc., see note to
No. 128.

132

Two versions.

133

318. *a* was printed at London, " for Francis
Grove " (1620–55); *d* was " printed for I. Clarke,
W. Thackeray, and T. Passinger " (1670–86).

135

324. *c* was " printed for John Andrews "
(1660); *d* " for William Thackeray " (1689).

136

326. *a* was " printed for John Andrews "
(1660); *d* " for William Thackeray " (1689).

138

329. *a* was " printed for F. Cole, T. Vere,
J. Wright and J. Clarke " (Cole, Vere, and
Wright, 1655–80; J. Clarke, 1650–82); *b* " for
Alex. Milbourn " (1670–97).

139

331. *a* was " printed for Fran. Grove " (1620–
55); *b* " for F. Coles, T. Vere, and J. Wright "
(1655–80); *e* " for J. Clarke, W. Thackeray, and
T. Passenger " (1670–82 ?).

140

Three versions.
333. *B* 3. In *C* the squires are expressly
said to be the three sons of the lady (so she is
called, and not " a silly old woman "). *C* occurs
in several editions of Robin Hood's Garland
(*C a* was printed about 1753).
334. *B* 19 ff. *C* ends thus: —

' One boon, one boon,' says jolly Robin,
'One boon I beg on my knee;
That, as for the deaths of these three squires,
Their hangman I may be.'

' Soon granted, soon granted,' says great master
sheriff,
'Soon granted unto thee;
And you shall have all their gay cloathing,
Aye, and all their white money.'

' O I will have none of their gay cloathing,
Nor none of their white money,
But I 'll have three blasts on my bugle-horn,
That their souls to heaven may flee.'

Then Robin Hood mounted the gallows so high,
Where he blew loud and shrill,
Till an hundred and ten of Robin Hood's men
They came marching all down the green hill.

' Whose men are they all these?' says great
master sheriff,
'Whose men are they? tell unto me:'
' O they are mine, but none of thine,
And they 're come for the squires all three.'

' O take them, O take them,' says great master
sheriff,
'O take them along with thee;
For there 's never a man in all Nottingham
Can do the like of thee.'

141

334. *a* was " printed for F. Grove " (1620–
55); *d* " for J. Clarke, W. Thackeray, and T.
Passenger " (1670–86 ?).

142

Two versions.
337. *B a* was " printed for William Gil-
ber[t]son " (1640–63); *B d* " for J. Wright, J.
Clarke, W. Thackeray, and T. Passenger "
(1670–86 ?).

43

338. *a* was " printed for F. Grove " (1620–
55); *e* " by and for W. O[nley] " (1650–1702).

144

Two versions.
340. *A b* was " published April 7th, 1791, by
C. Sheppard," London.

145

Three versions.

343. *A* 22. Sir Richard Lee is known to us already in the Gest.

344. *B a* was "printed for F. Grove" (1620–55); *b* "for Francis Grove"; *e* "for F. Coles, T. Vere & J. Wright" (1655–80); *f* "for J. W[right], J. C[larke], W. T[hackeray], and T. P[assinger]" (1670–86?).

146

346. *d* was "printed for William Thackeray" (1689).

147

347. *a* was "printed for F. Grove" (whose dates, according to Chappell, were 1620–55). Ritson says that the ballad was entered in the Stationers' book by Francis Grove, 2d June, 1656. *d* was "printed for William Thackeray" (1689).

148

349. *a* was "printed for F. Coles" (1631?); *b* "for F. Coles, T. Vere, and W. Gilbertson" (1648–63?); *e* "for F. Coles, T. Vere, J. Wright, and J. Clarke" (1650–80?); *f* "for Alex. Milbourn, Will. Ownley, Tho. Thackeray" (after 1670); *g* "for I. Wright, I. Clarke, W. Thackeray, and T. Passinger" (1670–86?).

149

350. *a* was "printed for W. O[nley]" (1650–1702); *b* "for I. Wright, I. Clarke, W. Thackeray, and T. Passenger" (1670–86?); *c* "by and for Alex. Milbourn" (1670–97).

351. 2. Robin Hood assumes the name of Loxley (Locksley) in No. 145. It appears that there is a Loxley Chase in Yorkshire, and a Loxley River too (Gutch, Robin Hood, I, 75).

353. 46. Arthur a Bradley is printed by Ritson, Robin Hood, 1795, II, 210.

151

357. 29. By "the clergyman" is meant the Prior of York, who in Munday's play, The Downfall of Robert Earl of Huntington, procures his outlawry. The forcing of the sheriff to give the king a supper may be the beggarly author's own invention.

357. 30³, ⁴. Supplied from Robin Hood's Garland, York, Thomas Wilson & Son, 1811. The lines are wanting in *a b c d*.

152

360. 28³, ⁴. Supplied from the garland just mentioned; wanting in *a b c*.

153

361. 18⁴. *day* is found in *b*, wanting in *a c*.

154

362. The mutilated parts of the title are supplied, to a slight extent, from a copy in the Bodleian Library (L. 78, Art., 5th tract); the rest from an edition printed for J. Clark, W. Thackeray, and T. Passinger, 1686.

155

Twenty-one versions.

369. *A* 7. *E* (Motherwell's Minstrelsy) has:

> She laid him on a dressing-table,
>   She dressd him like a swine;
> Says, Lie ye there, my bonnie Sir Hugh,
>   Wi yere apples red and green!

369. *A* 9. *E* has next: —

> A schoolboy walking in the garden
>   Did grievously hear him moan;
> He ran away to the deep draw-well,
>   And fell down on his knee.
>
> Says, Bonnie Sir Hugh, and pretty Sir Hugh,
>   I pray you speak to me!
> If you speak to any body in this world,
>   I pray you speak to me.

369. *A* 14. In *E* this stanza precedes, spoken by Sir Hugh's schoolfellow: —

> 'Lady Helen, if ye want your son,
>   I'll tell ye where to seek;
> Lady Helen, if ye want your son,
>   He's in the well sae deep.'

370. *B* 1. *Mirry-land toune* is probably a corruption of *merry Lincoln* (*A* 16, 17).

370. *B* 12. After this *E* has: —

> 'But lift me out o this deep draw-well,
>   And bury me in yon churchyard;
> . . . .
>
> 'Put a Bible at my head,' he says,
>   'And a Testament at my feet,
> And pen and ink at every side,
>   And I'll lie still and sleep.
>
> 'And go to the back of Maitland town,
>   Bring me my winding sheet;
> For it's at the back of Maitland town
>   That you and I shall meet.'
>
> O the broom, the bonny, bonny broom,
>   The broom that makes full sore,
> A woman's mercy is very little,
>   But a man's mercy is more.

A request like that in *E* 20 occurs in some other versions.

156

Seven versions.

373. 8. *E* (Kinloch's Ballads) has: —

> 'O fathers, O fathers, I'm very, very sick,
>   I'm sick, and like to dee;
> Some ghostly comfort to my poor soul
>   O tell if ye can gie!'
>
> 'Confess, confess,' Earl Marshall cried,
>   'And you shall pardoned be;'
> 'Confess, confess,' the King replied,
>   'And we shall comfort gie.'

374. *B* 4. In *G* (MS. at Abbotsford) and some other versions, Earl Marshal gets an oath of immunity. Thus in *G* : —

> But I will swear by my septer and crown,
>   And by the seas so free,
> I will swear by my septer and crown,
>   Earl Marshall, thow's no dee.

157

Nine versions.

375. 2³. In *D* (Kinloch's papers), a pretty, pretty maid ; in *F* (Buchan's Gleanings), a well-fared maid.

158

Three versions.

378. 1. In *C*, from Aberdeenshire, Hugh is naturally turned into a Scotsman : —

> It fell about the Martinmas time
>   The wind blew loud and cauld,
> And all the knichts of fair Scotland
>   They drew them to sum hald.
>
> Unless it was him young Sir Hugh,
>   And he beet to sail the sea,
> Wi a letter between twa kings, to see an they wald
>   let down the wars,
>   And live and lat them be.

381. 23. In *C* : —

> The nexten steed that he drew out
>   He was the raven-black ;
> His een was glancin in his head
>   Like wild-fire in a slack ;
> ' Get here a boy,' says young Sir Hugh,
>   ' Cast on the saddle on that.'

159

383. 11. The Earl of Angus was really on the other side.

383. 13. *Vaughan :* i. e. Baughan or Buchan. It is very doubtful whether there was an Earl of Buchan in 1346.

386. 64. Crécy was fought 26 Aug., 1346 ; Poitiers, 19 Sept., 1356.

161

Six versions.

387. 3. Hoppertope hyll, says Percy, is a corruption for Ottercap Hill (now Ottercaps Hill) in the parish of Kirk Whelpington, Tynedale Ward, Northumberland. Rodclyffe Cragge (now Rothley Crags) is a cliff near Rodeley, a small village in the parish of Hartburn, in Morpeth Ward, south-east of Ottercap ; and Green Leyton, corruptly Green Lynton, is another small village, south-east of Rodeley, in the same parish.

387. 3⁴. Percy's emendation. The MSS. have " Many a styrande (stirande) stage."

388. 26. *Mentaye :* Menteith. The earldom of Huntley was created in 1449.

391. 11. In *b* (Scott's copy) : —

> Thou shalt not yield to lord nor loun,
>   Nor yet shalt thou yield to me ;
> But yield thee to the bracken-bush,
>   That grows upon yon lilye lee.

391. 12, 13. *B* agrees with Froissart in making a Montgomery the captor of Percy, whereas *A* represents that Montgomery was taken prisoner and exchanged for Percy. In No. 162 Sir Hugh Montgomery kills Percy, and in return is shot by a Northumberland archer.

391. 14. Douglas was buried at Melrose Abbey, where his tomb may still be seen.

391. *C*.* Scott's text (*C*) is given below as it stands in the Minstrelsy, 1833, I, 345. There are a few slight variations from the form in which Scott first printed it (in the second edition, 1803, I, 27). Hogg's two copies, which furnished the greater part of *C*, were complementary, — the first copy containing twenty-nine stanzas (1–24, 35–38, 40), the second copy, eleven (25–34, 39).

> 1 IT fell about the Lammas tide,
>   When the muir-men win their hay,
>   The doughty Douglas bound him to ride
>   Into England, to drive a prey.
>
> 2 He chose the Gordons and the Græmes,
>   With them the Lindesays, light and gay;
>   But the Jardines wald not with him ride,
>   And they rue it to this day.
>
> 3 And he has burnd the dales of Tyne,
>   And part of Bambrough shire,
>   And three good towers on Reidswire fells,
>   He left them all on fire.
>
> 4 And he marchd up to Newcastle,
>   And rode it round about :
>   ' O wha's the lord of this castle ?
>   Or wha's the lady o't?'
>
> 5 But up spake proud Lord Percy then,
>   And O but he spake hie !
>   I am the lord of this castle,
>   My wife's the lady gay.
>
> 6 ' If thou 'rt the lord of this castle,
>   Sae weel it pleases me,
>   For, ere I cross the Border fells,
>   The tane of us shall die.'
>
> 7 He took a lang spear in his hand,
>   Shod with the metal free,
>   And for to meet the Douglas there
>   He rode right furiouslie.
>
> 8 But O how pale his lady lookd,
>   Frae aff the castle-wa,
>   When down before the Scottish spear
>   She saw proud Percy fa.
>
> 9 ' Had we twa been upon the green,
>   And never an eye to see,
>   I wad hae had you, flesh and fell ;
>   But your sword sall gae wi me.'
>
> 10 ' But gae ye up to Otterbourne,
>   And, wait there dayis three,
>   And, if I come not ere three dayis end,
>   A fause knight ca ye me.'
>
> 11 ' The Otterbourne 's a bonnie burn ;
>   'T is pleasant there to be ;
>   But there is nought at Otterbourne
>   To feed my men and me.
>
> 12 ' The deer rins wild on hill and dale,
>   The birds fly wild from tree to tree ;
>   But there is neither bread nor kale
>   To fend my men and me.
>
> 13 ' Yet I will stay at Otterbourne,
>   Where you shall welcome be ;

And, if ye come not at three dayis end,
A fause lord I 'll ca thee.'

14 'Thither will I come,' proud Percy said,
  'By the might of Our Ladye;'
  'There will I bide thee,' said the Douglas,
  'My troth I plight to thee.'

15 They lighted high on Otterbourne,
  Upon the bent sae brown;
  They lighted high on Otterbourne,
  And threw their pallions down.

16 And he that had a bonnie boy,
  Sent out his horse to grass;
  And he that had not a bonnie boy,
  His ain servant he was.

17 But up then spake a little page,
  Before the peep of dawn:
  'O waken ye, waken ye, my good lord,
  For Percy 's hard at hand.'

18 'Ye lie, ye lie, ye liar loud!
  Sae loud I hear ye lie:
  For Percy had not men yestreen
  To dight my men and me.

19 'But I have dreamd a dreary dream,
  Beyond the Isle of Sky;
  I saw a dead man win a fight,
  And I think that man was I.'

20 He belted on his guid braid sword,
  And to the field he ran,
  But he forgot the helmet good,
  That should have kept his brain.

21 When Percy wi the Douglas met,
  I wat he was fu fain;
  They swakked their swords, till sair they
  swat,
  And the blood ran down like rain.

22 But Percy with his good broad sword,
  That could so sharply wound,
  Has wounded Douglas on the brow,
  Till he fell to the ground.

23 Then he calld on his little foot-page,
  And said, Run speedilie,
  And fetch my ain dear sister's son,
  Sir Hugh Montgomery.

24 'My nephew good,' the Douglas said,
  'What recks the death of ane!
  Last night I dreamd a dreary dream,
  And I ken the day 's thy ain.

25 'My wound is deep; I fain would sleep;
  Take thou the vanguard of the three,
  And hide me by the braken-bush,
  That grows on yonder lilye lee.

26 'O bury me by the braken-bush,
  Beneath the blooming brier;
  Let never living mortal ken
  That ere a kindly Scot lies here.'

27 He lifted up that noble lord,
  Wi the saut tear in his ee;
  He hid him in the braken-bush,
  That his merrie men might not see.

28 The moon was clear, the day drew near,
  The spears in flinders flew,
  But mony a gallant Englishman
  Ere day the Scotsmen slew.

29 The Gordons good, in English blood
  They steepd their hose and shoon;
  The Lindsays flew like fire about,
  Till all the fray was done.

30 The Percy and Montgomery met,
  That either of other were fain;
  They swapped swords, and they twa swat,
  And aye the blood ran down between.

31 'Now yield thee, yield thee, Percy,' he said,
  'Or else I vow I 'll lay thee low!'
  'To whom must I yield,' quoth Earl Percy,
  'Now that I see it must be so?'

32 'Thou shalt not yield to lord nor loun,
  Nor yet shalt thou yield to me;
  But yield thee to the braken-bush,
  That grows upon yon lilye lee.'

33 'I will not yield to a braken-bush,
  Nor yet will I yield to a brier;
  But I would yield to Earl Douglas,
  Or Sir Hugh the Montgomery, if he were
  here.'

34 As soon as he knew it was Montgomery,
  He struck his sword's point in the gronde;
  The Montgomery was a courteous knight,
  And quickly took him by the honde.

35 This deed was done at the Otterbourne,
  About the breaking of the day;
  Earl Douglas was buried at the braken-bush,
  And the Percy led captive away.

162

Two versions.
394. 15. *Cheviot Chase* becomes *Chevy Chace* by the same process by which *Teviotdale* becomes *Tividale*.

397. 65[2]. Doubtless corrupt. Skeat's suggestion of a proverb, meaning "That tear, or pull, brought about this kick" is improbable. Perhaps a lamentation: "That ear (ever) begane this spurn!" or possibly *that tear* is for *that there*, meaning simply 'there.'

397. *B b* was "printed for M. G.," perhaps an error for H. G., i.e. Henry Gosson (1607–41); *c* was "printed for F. Coles, T. Vere and J. Wright" (1655–80?); *d* "for F. Coles, T. Vere and W. Gilbertson" (1648–61?); *e* "by and for W. Onley" (1650–1702?); *f* was probably printed about the beginning of the 18th century.

163

Two versions.
401. 7[3, 4]. In *b*: —

So we 'd best cry in our merry men,
And turn our horses' heeds.

164

402. 2. Here *g* has: —

O then calld he his lovely page,
His lovely page then called he,
Who, when he came before the king,
Lo, he fell down on his bended knee.

'Welcome, welcome, thou lovely page,
Welcome. welcome art thou here;
Go sped thee now to the king of France,
And greet us well to him so dear.'

'And when thou comst to the king of France
And hast greeted us to him so dear,
Thou then shall ask for the tribute due,
That has not been paid for many a year.'

403. 8. After this *g* has : —

O then in wroth rose our noble king,
In anger great then up rose he :
'I 'll send such balls to the king in France
As Frenchmen ne'er before did see.'

167

Three versions.

407. The variants noted below are from a sixteenth-century MS. in York Minster Library (see Child, IV, 502 ff.). There are many other differences.

407. *A* 1.

It fell against a midsomer moneth,
When birds soonge well in every tree,
Our worthē prence, Kinge Henrye,
He roode untoe a chelvellrye.

407. *A* 3.

'Ye are welcome home, my rich merchantes,
The best salers in Christentie !'
'We thanke yowe ; by the rood, we are salers good,
But rich merchantes we cannot be.'

3² is pared away in the Percy MS. The line in the text is from the Reliques.

407. *A* 6.

The merchantes answered, soore they sight,
With a woefull harte to the kinge againe,
'He is one that robes us of our right,
Were we twentie shippes and he but one.'

407. *A* 7⁴.

Der take yon robber upon the sea !

409. *A* 35.

'Will yowe lend me sexe peece of ordenance, my lord,
To carye into my shippe with mee ?
Toe morrowe by seven a clocke, and souner,
In the morne yowe shall Sir Andrewe see.

'Fore I will set yowe a glasse, my lord,
That yowe shall saille forth all this night :
Toe morrowe be seven a clocke, and souner,
Yow 's se Sir Andrewe Barton, knight.'

Nowe will we leave talkinge of Harry Hunt ;
The worthye Howwarde tooke to the sea ;
By the morne, by seven a clocke, and souner,
My lord hee did Sir Andrewe see.

A larborde, wher Sir Andrewe laye,
They saide he tould his gold in the light ;
'Nowe, by my faith,' saide my lord Charlles Howwarde,
'I se yonne Scootte, a worthē wight !

'All our greatt ordienance wee 'll take in ;
Fetch downe my streemers,' then saide hee,
'And hange me forth a white willowe-wande,
As a marchante-man that sailles by the sea.'

409. *A* 39. After this : —

Once I met with the Portingaills,
Yea, I met with them, ye, I indeed
I salted thirtie of ther heades,
And sent them home to eate with breade.

410. *A* 51. After this : —

'Yet feare no English dogges,' said Sir Andrew Barton,
'Nor fore ther forse stand ye [in] no awe ;
My hands shall hange them all my selfe,
Froe once I let my beames downe fawe.'

168

413. 12. 'Jack with a feather' is said in contempt of the Scottish king's levity or foolhardiness. Dead bodies were sometimes sewn up in a hide before (or instead of) being "lapped in lead."

169

Three versions.

415. *B a* and *b* are signed "T. R."

416. *C.* The substance, or at least the hint of *C* 21³, ⁴, 17³, ⁴, 26, 15, 22³, ⁴, 23, 24¹, ², is to be found in the narrative of Lindsay of Pitscottie, Chronicles of Scotland, ed. Dalyell, II, 341 ff.

170

Nine versions.

419. 3¹, 5³. *do* is to be pronounced *dee*.

172

420. 2⁴. *horne* may be the reading of the MS., instead of *turne*.

173

Twenty-eight versions (including fragments).

421. 1. Cf. *U* (MS. at Abbotsford) : —

But word is up, and word is down,
Amang the ladyes a',
That Marie 's born a babe sin yestreen,
That babe it is awa.

421. 3. Before this some versions have a stanza corresponding to the following (*D*, Motherwell's MS.) : —

She 's gane to the garden gay
To pu of the savin tree ;
But for a' that she could say or do,
The babie it would not die.

In *U*, the corresponding stanza (st. 13) mentions an apothecary as Mary's lover : —

My love he was a pottinger,
Mony drink he gae me,
And a' to put back that bonnie babe,
But alas ! it wad na do.

421. 7. *U* has : —

Slowly, slowly, gat she up,
And slowly put she on,
And slowly went she to that milk-steed,
To ride to Edinburgh town.

421. 13, 14. *C* (Motherwell's MS.) has : —

'O all you gallant sailors,
That sail upon the sea,
Let neither my father nor mother know
The death I am to die !

'O all you gallant sailors,
That sail upon the faem,
Let neither my father nor mother know
But I am coming hame.'

422. 16. *C* has : —

Little did my father know,
When he held up my head,
What lands I was to travel in,
What was to be my deid.

422. 18. The best-known form of this famous stanza is the following, which it bears in Scott's version (*I*) and several others: —

Yestreen the queen had four Maries,
  The night she 'll hae but three;
There was Marie Seaton, and Marie Beaton,
  And Marie Carmichael, and me.

422. 1, 2. *C* begins: —

There lived a lord into the west,
  And he had dochters three,
And the youngest o them is to the king's court,
  To learn some courtesie.

She was not in the king's court
  A twelvemonth and a day,
Till she was neither able to sit nor gang,
  Wi the gaining o some play.

U reads: —

My father was the Duke of York,
  My mother a gay ladye,
And I myself a daintie dame;
  The queen she sent for me.
  (And the king desired me. *P*)

But the queen's meat it was sae sweet,
  And her clothing was sae rare,
It made me long for a young man's bed,
  And I rued it evermair.

Cf. *J* (Harris MS.), st. 2: —

Queen Marie's bread it was sae sweet,
  An her wine it was sae fine,
That I hae lien in a young man's arms,
  An I rued it aye synsyne.

422. 17. *V* (MS. at Abbotsford) ends: —

O if my father now but kend
  The death that I 'm to die,
O muckle, muckle wad be the red gowd
  That he wad gie for me.

An if my brothers kend the death
  That I am now to die,
O muckle, muckle wad be the red blood
  That wad be shed for me.

423. Scott's composite version of No. 173 (*I*) is here printed (Minstrelsy, 1833, III, 294): —

1 Marie Hamilton 's to the kirk gane,
    Wi ribbons in her hair;
  The king thought mair o Marie Hamilton
    Than ony that were there.

2 Marie Hamilton 's to the kirk gane,
    Wi ribbons on her breast;
  The king thought mair o Marie Hamilton
    Then he listend to the priest.

3 Marie Hamilton 's to the kirk gane,
    Wi gloves upon her hands;
  The king thought mair o Marie Hamilton,
    Than the queen and a' her lands.

4 She hadna been about the king's court
    A month, but barely one,
  Till she was beloved by a' the king's court,
    And the king the only man.

5 She hadna been about the king's court
    A month, but barely three,
  Till frae the king's court Marie Hamilton,
    Marie Hamilton durstna be.

6 The king is to the Abbey gane,
    To pu the Abbey-tree,
  To scale the babe frae Marie's heart,
    But the thing it wadna be.

7 O she has rowd it in her apron,
    And set it on the sea:
  'Gae sink ye, or swim ye, bonny babe!
    Ye 's get nae mair o me.'

8 Word is to the kitchen gane,
    And word is to the ha,
  And word is to the noble room,
    Amang the ladyes a',
  That Marie Hamilton 's brought to bed,
    And the bonny babe 's mist and awa.

9 Scarcely had she lain down again,
    And scarcely fa'en asleep,
  When up then started our gude queen,
    Just at her bed-feet,
  Saying, Marie Hamilton, where 's your babe?
    For I am sure I heard it greet.

10 'O no, O no, my noble queen,
    Think no such thing to be!
  'T was but a stitch into my side,
    And sair it troubles me.'

11 'Get up, get up, Marie Hamilton,
    Get up and follow me;
  For I am going to Edinburgh town,
    A rich wedding for to see.'

12 O slowly, slowly raise she up,
    And slowly put she on,
  And slowly rode she out the way,
    Wi mony a weary groan.

13 The queen was clad in scarlet,
    Her merry maids all in green,
  And every town that they cam to,
    They took Marie for the queen.

14 'Ride hooly, hooly, gentlemen,
    Ride hooly now wi me!
  For never, I am sure, a wearier burd
    Rade in your cumpanie.'

15 But little wist Marie Hamilton,
    When she rade on the brown,
  That she was gaen to Edinburgh town,
    And a' to be put down.

16 'Why weep ye so, ye burgess-wives,
    Why look ye so on me?
  O I am going to Edinburgh town
    A rich wedding for to see!'

17 When she gaed up the Tolbooth stairs,
    The corks frae her heels did flee;
  And lang or eer she cam down again
    She was condemnd to die.

18 When she cam to the Netherbow Port,
    She laughed loud laughters three:
  But when she cam to the gallows-foot,
    The tears blinded her ee.

19 'Yestreen the queen had four Maries,
    The night she 'll hae but three;
  There was Marie Seaton, and Marie Beaton,
    And Marie Carmichael, and me.

20 'O often have I dressd my queen,
    And put gold upon her hair;
  But now I 've gotten for my reward
    The gallows to be my share.

21 'Often have I dressd my queen,
    And often made her bed;
  But now I 've gotten for my reward
    The gallows-tree to tread.

22 'I charge ye all, ye mariners,
    When ye sail ower the faem,
  Let neither my father nor mother get wit
    But that I 'm coming hame!

23 ' I charge ye all, ye mariners,
 That sail upon the sea,
Let neither my father nor mother get wit
 This dog's death I 'm to die!

24 ' For if my father and mother got wit,
 And my bold brethren three,
O mickle wad be the gude red blude
 This day wad be spilt for me!

25 'O little did my mother ken,
 That day she cradled me,
The lands I was to travel in,
 Or the death I was to die!'

177

432. 44[1]. *Ciuill* is Seville.
433. 55[3]. *All that* is perhaps an error for
All they or *All these.*

178

Nine versions.
435. *A* 21. (*F* 5.) Cf. *D* (Foulis, 1755): —

'And ein wae worth ye, Jock my man!
 I paid ye weil your fee;
Why pow ye out my ground-wa-stane,
 Lets in the reek to me?

' And ein wae worth ye, Jock my man!
 For I paid you weil your hire;
Why pow ye out my ground-wa-stane,
 To me lets in the fire?'

'Ye paid me weil my hire, lady,
 Ye paid me weil my fee,
But now I 'm Edom of Gordon's man,
 Maun either do or die.'

So in *G* (Motherwell's MS.), sts. 13–14: —

' O wae be to thee, Carmichael,' she said,
 ' And an ill death may ye die!
For ye hae lifted the pavement-stane,
 And loot up the lowe to me.

' Seven years ye war about my house,
 And received both meat and fee:'
' And now I 'm Adam o Gordon's man,
 I maun either do or dee.'

179

439. 6[4]. Ritson's emendations are indicated
by ' '. They have of necessity been allowed to
stand.
440. 9[3]. *Corbyl.* Perhaps for *Corbyt*, which
is a Northern name.
441. 30. Rowland Emerson was perhaps a
kinsman of the bailiff. The family of Emerson
of Eastgate long exercised the offices of bailiff of
Walsingham (the chief borough of Weardale),
forester, etc.

180

442. 10. Half a page is torn away, and
about nine stanzas are lost. Douglas offers
Brown his daughter in marriage to betray the
king.
443. 28. John Hamilton, Archbishop of St
Andrews, must be the person whom Brown
slays for an attempt to poison the young king.
He was, however, hanged by his political enemies, April 7, 1571.

181

Two versions.
444. *A* 5. According to Sir James Balfour,
" the queen, more rashly than wisely, some few
days before had commended " Murray, "in the
king's hearing, with too many epithets of a
proper and gallant man." Balfour may have
had gossip, or he may have had a ballad, for his
authority; the suggestion deserves no attention.
444. *B* 1. Here the Countess of Murray is
treated as Huntly's sister.

182

Six versions.

183

Two versions.
446. *A.* After st. 4 *b* has the following
stanza (which ends the ballad): —

Light was the mirk hour
 At the day-dawing,
For Auchindoun was in flames
 Ere the cock-crawing.

184

448. 8. After this Scott inserts: —

For the Galliard, and the gay Galliard's men,
They neer saw a horse but they made it their ain.

The Galliard to Nithside is gane,
To steal Sim Crichton's winsome dun.

448. 21[1]. In the margin of the MS.: Will of
Kirkhill.

185

450. 10. Probably meant for Henry Lord
Scroop of Bolton, who was warden of the West
Marches for thirty years from 1563.
450. 14. Harribie was the place of execution at Carlisle.
450. 18. The Laird's Jock, in the opinion
of Mr. R. B. Armstrong, was a son of Thomas
of Mangerton, the elder brother of Gilnockie
(cf. No. 169).
452. 47[2]. The MS. has "steal the Laird
Jock horse" erroneously repeated from the line
above. Corrected from Caw (*b*).
452. 51[3, 4]. Wanting in *a*. Supplied from *b*.

187

Four versions.
459. 2. *C* (Percy Papers, as " collected from
the memory of an old person . . . in 1775 ")
has: —

Now Downy 's down the water gone,
 With all her cots unto her arms,
And she gave never over swift running
 Untill she came to Mengertown.

188

Seven versions.
461. 6[2] (cf. 14[2], 16[2]). Explained by *B* 10[2]:
he bragged for lower Liddesdale, was from
lower Liddesdale.

464. *B.* The following are the stanzas used by Scott (see **p. 461,** above) in his second version: —

2 'An ye wad be blythe an ye wad be sad,
    What better wad billie Archie be,
Unless I had thirty men to mysell,
    And a' to ride in our companie?

3 'Ten to had the horses' heads,
    And other ten to walk alee,
And ten to break up the strang prisoun
    Where billie Archie he does lie.'

4 Up bespak him mettled John Hall,
    The luve o Teviotdale ay was he;
'An I had eleven men to mysell,
    It 's ay the twalt man I wad be.'

5 Up bespak him coarse Ca'field,
    I wat and little gude worth was he
'Thirty men is few enow,
    And a' to ride in our companie.'

12 'There lives a smith on the water-side,
    Sae has he done thirty years and three:

. . . .

13 'O I have a crown in my pocket,
    And I 'll give it every groat to thee

    Gin thou shoe my little black mare for me.'

14 'The night is mirk, and vera pit-mirk,
    And wi candle-light I canna weel see;
The night is mirk, and vera pit-mirk,
    And there 'll never a nail ca right for me.'

15 'Shame fa you and your trade baith,
    Canna beet a gude fallow by your mysterie!
But lees me on thee, my little black mare,
    Thou 's worth thy weight o gowd to me.'

19 'My mare is young, and vera young,
    And in o the weel she will drown me;'
'But ye 'll take mine, and I 'll take thine,
    And soon thro the water we sall be.'

20 Then up bespak him coarse Ca'field,
    I wate and little gude worth was he;
'We had better lose ane than lose a' the lave,
    We 'll leave the prisoner, we 'll gae free.'

21 'Shame fa you and your lands baith,
    Wad ye een your lands to your born billie?
But hey! bear up, my little black mare,
    And yet thro the water we sall be.'

Of these stanzas, 12–15 are indifferent modern stuff.

464. 16⁴. 'And that was her gold-twist to be' is an emendation of Scott's, *gold-twist* meaning "the small gilded chains drawn about the chest of a war-horse."

191

Nine versions.
470. 2. *Screw:* Scroope. The second line is corrupt: read probably *crime* for *scrime.*
470. 9. *Garlard* for *Carlisle.*
470. 11⁴. Corrupt.
470. 13². *Rumary:* corrupt.

192

Five versions.
472. 4⁴. *her* should doubtless be *him* (so Scott). Similarly in 13⁴, 18⁴.

193

Two versions.
473. 2. After this in *B* (letter at Abbotsford): —

    And Crozier says he will do warse,
        He will do warse if warse can be;
    For he 'll make the bairns a' fatherless,
        And then the land it may lie lea.

473. 5. In *B:* —

    They 've taen frae him his powther-bag,
        And they 've put water i his lang gun;
    They 've put the sword into the sheathe
        That out again it 'll never come.

474. 11. In *B:* —

    O turn, O turn, O Johny Ha,
        O turn now, man, and fight wi me;
    If ever ye come to Troughend again,
        A good black I will gie to thee;
    He cost me twenty pounds o gowd
        Atween my brother John and me.

474. *A* 16 ff. *B* ends thus: —

    O fare ye weel, my married wife!
        And fare ye weel, my brother John!
    That sits into the Troughend ha
        With heart as black as any stone.

    O fare ye weel, my married wife!
        And fare ye weel now, my sons five!
    For had ye been wi me this day
        I surely had been man alive.

    O fare ye weel, my married wife!
        And fare ye weel now, my sons five!
    And fare ye weel, my daughter Jean!
        I loved ye best ye were born alive.

    O some do ca me Parcy Reed,
        And some do ca me Laird Troughend,
    But it 's nae matter what they ca me,
        My faes have made me ill to ken.

    The laird o Clennel wears my bow,
        The laird o Brandon wears my brand;
    Whae ever rides i the Border-side
        Will mind the laird o the Troughend.

194

Three versions.
475. *B* 9⁴. This is quite wrong as to the duration of their married life. Jean Livingston was but twenty-one years old when she was executed.

195

Two versions.
476. *A* 1². For *house* read *place*? Cf. *B* 11.
476. *A* 3. John, the eighth Lord Maxwell, was killed in a battle between the Maxwells and the Johnstones in 1593.
476. 9, 10. Douglas of Drumlanrig, Kirkpatrick of Closeburn, and Grierson of Lag fought on the side of Lord Maxwell in the battle of Dryfe Sands (mentioned above), and fled in the *sauve qui peut* with which it ended.
476. 11. *Robin,* etc.: properly Sir Robert Maxwell of Orchardton (cf. *B* 1), the speaker's cousin; but it is obvious that Lord John's brother Robert is meant.
476. 14. Maxwell's wife was no longer living.

196

Five versions,

478. 7. Cf. *C* 8. A fragment in the Kinloch MSS. (*E*) has : —

> Now wake, now wake you, Rothiemay !
> I dread you sleep oer soun ;
> The bed is burnin us about
> And the curtain 's faain down.

479. 26. This stanza involves an error. The third line corresponds to nothing that is known of the relations between John Gordon (Viscount Aboyne) and his wife (Sophia Hay). Perhaps the stanza comes from some other ballad.

479. 12. Chalmers really escaped, though lodged in the third story ; Colin Ivat (here called Irving) was burnt.

480. *C* 21. This recalls the fragment " Edinburgh castle, towne, and tower," etc. (p. 637).

197

Two versions.

481. 2. Sir Walter Scott (Sharpe's Ballad Book, 1880, p. 145) remarks : " I conceive Ballindalloch, being admitted by Grant, set upon him, and that there should be asterisks between the fourth line [the second stanza] and those which follow."

198

Two versions.

482. *A* 12. *B* (Buchan's Ballads) ends as follows : —

> Then they rade on, and further on,
> Till they came to the Crabestane,
> And Craigievar, he had a mind
> To burn a' Aberdeen.

> Out it speaks the gallant Montrose,
> Grace on his fair body !
> ' We winna burn the bonny burgh,
> We 'll even laet it be.'

> Then out it speaks the gallant Montrose,
> ' Your purpose I will break ;
> We winna burn the bonny burgh,
> We 'll never build its make.

> ' I see the women and their children
> Climbing the craigs sae hie ;
> We 'll sleep this night in the bonny burgh,
> And even lat it be.'

199

Four versions and a fragment.

200

Twelve versions and a fragment.

201

485. 3³. *b* has *Dornoch-haugh. Dranoch haugh* is the right reading.

203

Five versions.

204

Fifteen versions.

490. The song referred to in the Introduction is as follows : —

WALY, WALY, GIN LOVE BE BONY

a. Ramsay's Tea-Table Miscellany, the second volume, published before 1727 ; here from the Dublin edition of 1729, p. 176. b. Thomson's Orpheus Caledonius, second edition, 1733, I, 71 ; four stanzas in the first edition, 1725, No. 34.

> O WALY, waly up the bank !
> And waly, waly, down the brae !
> And waly, waly yon burn-side,
> Where I and my love wont to gae !

> I leand my back unto an aik,
> I thought it was a trusty tree ;
> But first it bowd, and syne it brak,
> Sae my true-love did lightly me.

> O waly, waly ! but love be bony
> A little time, while it is new ;
> But when 't is auld, it waxeth cauld,
> And fades away like morning dew.

> O wherefore shoud I busk my head ?
> Or wherefore shoud I kame my hair ?
> For my true-love has me forsook,
> And says he 'll never love me mair.

> Now Arthur-Seat shall be my bed,
> The sheets shall neer be fyl'd by me ;
> Saint Anton's well shall be my drink,
> Since my true-love has forsaken me.

> Martinmas wind, when wilt thou blaw,
> And shake the green leaves off the tree ?
> O gentle death, when wilt thou come ?
> For of my life I am weary.

> 'T is not the frost that freezes fell,
> Nor blawing snaw's inclemency ;
> 'T is not sic cauld that makes me cry,
> But my love's heart grown cauld to me.

> When we came in by Glasgow town,
> We were a comely sight to see ;
> My love was cled in the black velvet,
> And I my sell in cramasie.

> But had I wist, before I kissd,
> That love had been sae ill to win,
> I 'd lockd my heart in a case of gold,
> And pin'd it with a silver pin.

> Oh, oh, if my young babe were born,
> And set upon the nurse's knee,
> And I my sell were dead and gane !
> For a maid again I 'll never be.

490. 12. After this *B* (Kinloch MSS.) continues thus to the end : —

> ' What 's needs me value you, Jamie Douglas,
> More than you do value me ?
> The Earl of Mar is my father,
> The Duke of York is my brother gay.

> ' But when my father gets word o this,
> I trow a sorry man he 'll be ;
> He 'll send four score o his soldiers brave
> To tak me hame to my ain countrie.'

> As I lay owre my castell-wa,
> I beheld my father comin for me,
> Wi trumpets sounding on every side ;
> But they werena music at a' for me.

> ' And fare ye weel now, Jamie Douglas !
> And fare ye weel, my children three !

And fare ye weel, my own good lord!
For my face again ye shall never see.

'And fare ye weel now, Jamie Douglas!
And fare ye weel, my children three!
And fare ye weel now, Jamie Douglas!
But my youngest son shall gae wi me.'

What ails ye at yer youngest son,
Sits smilin at the nurse's knee?
I 'me sure he never knew any harm,
Except it was from his nurse or thee.'

. . . .

And when I was into my coaches set,
He made his trumpets a' to soun.

I 've heard it said, and it 's oft times seen,
The hawk that flies far frae her nest;
And a' the world shall plainly see
It 's Jamie Douglas that I love best.

I 've heard it said, and [it 's] oft times seen,
The hawk that flies from tree to tree;
And a' the world shall plainly see
It 's for Jamie Douglas I maun die.

205

491. 6. The cornet was Robert Graham, the "nephew" of Claverhouse, of whom so much is made in Old Mortality. There is no evidence beyond the name to show that he was a near kinsman of his captain. Cf. No. 206, st. 12.

206

492. 1–9. William Gordon of Earlston, a hot Covenanter, on his way to join the insurgents, fell in with some dragoons who were pursuing his already routed copartisans, and, resisting their attempt to make him prisoner, was killed. His son Alexander, a man of more temperate views, was at Bothwell Bridge, and escaped. Although Earlston in st. 4 is represented as bidding farewell to his father, the narrative with which the ballad begins can be understood only of the father. The last half of st. 9 must be spoken by Monmouth.
492. 12. For the cornet, see No. 205.

207
Four versions.

208
Ten versions.
494. 2. Here Derwentwater seems to be taken for a Scot. The name Derwentwater is preserved in most versions.
494. 8. Other versions show other omens. Thus in D (Kinloch MSS.), st. 6 : —

He set his ae fit on the ground,
The tither on the steed;
The ring upon his finger burst,
And his nose began to bleed.

495. A 10. After this we have in some versions a stanza like the following (B) : —

O then stood up an old gray-headed man,
With a pole-axe in his hand:

''T is your head, 't is your head, Lord Derwent-water,
'T is your head that I demand.'

209
Fourteen versions.
496. A 3. Cf. C (MS. at Abbotsford) : —

' What news, what news, my bonny boy?
What news hae ye frae Geordie ? '
' He bids ye sew his linen shirts,
For he 's sure he 'll no need many.'

496. 5. After this B (MS. at Abbotsford) has : —

When she cam to the water-side,
The cobles war na ready;
She 's turnd her horse's head about,
An in by the Queen's Ferry.

When she cam to the West Port,
There war poor folks manie;
She dealt crowns an the ducatdowns,
And bade them pray for Geordie.

When she cam to the Parliament Closs,
There amang our nobles many,
Cravats an caps war standing there,
But low, low lay her Geordie.

When she gaed up the tolbooth-stairs,
Amang our nobles manie,
The napkin 's tyed oer Geordie's face,
And the gallows makin ready.

210
Four versions.

212
Six versions.

214
Nineteen versions.
505. A 6. Cf. E 1. In some versions the subject of the dispute is who is the Rose of Yarrow. Thus in D, communicated to Percy by Robert Lambe, Norham, 1768 : —

There were three lords drinking of wine
On the bonny braes of Yarrow;
There fell a combat them between,
Wha was the rose of Yarrow.

Up then spak a noble lord,
And I wot it was bot sorrow :
I have as fair a flower,' he said,
' As ever sprang on Yarrow.'

505. 8². The words in ' ' are so distinguished in the MS., and are of course emendations.
505. 10. Versions differ as to who it is that stabs the hero in the back. The preponderance of tradition, however, is to the effect that he was treacherously slain by his wife's (love's) brother.
505. 11¹. *Now Douglas* is taken from Hamilton's ballad.
505. 14³. *wiped* : probably substituted for *drank* (cf. E 12³, etc.).
505. 15³. *her* : probably substituted for *his*.

215

Eight versions.
506. *A* 2. This stanza probably does not belong to the ballad.
507. 4. *E* (Buchan's Ballads) has: —

On Wednesday, that fatal day,
    The people were convening;
Besides all this, threescore and ten,
    To gang to the bride-steel wi him.

507. 9. *E* has: —

Then they rode on, and further on,
    Till they came to the kirk o Gamery;
And every one on high horse sat,
    But Willie's horse rade toomly.

507. 10. *E* has: —

Then out it speaks the bride hersell,
    Says, What means a' this mourning?
Where is the man amo them a'
    That shoud gie me fair wedding?

216

Three versions.
508. 18. Read, of course, as in 9: —

He raid in, an forder in,
    Till he came to the chin;
And he raid in, and forder in,
    Bat never mare came out agen.

508. 13. Here should follow something like *B* 15. Sts. 14, 15 would come in better after 18, and that arrangement is supported by *C* (Buchan's Ballads): —

The very hour this young man sank
    Into the pot sae deep,
Up it wakend his love Meggie
    Out o her drowsy sleep.

'Come here, come here, my mither dear,
    And read this dreary dream;
I dreamd my love was at our gates,
    And nane wad let him in.'

'Lye still, lye still now, my Meggie,
    Lye still and tak your rest;
Sin your true-love was at your yates,
    It's but twa quarters past.'

St. 16 seems to be adapted from No. 76 (*D* 26). It hardly fits the situation. Possibly all three stanzas (14–16) belong to that ballad.

217

Fourteen versions.
510. 6. After this in *D* (Motherwell's MS.) and some other versions: —

He put his fut into the stirrup
    And rade after his men,
And a' that his men said or did
    Was, Kind maister, ye 've taiglit lang.

'I hae rade east, I hae rade wast,
    And I hae rade owr the knowes,
But the bonniest lassie that I ever saw
    Was in the yowe-buchts, milkand her yowes.'

218

Two versions.

219

Four versions.

220

Two versions.

221

Twelve versions.
515. *A* 8 ff. Cf. *D* (MS. at Abbotsford) 14–16: —

'I came not here for sport,' he says,
    'Nor came I here for play;
But an I had ae word of your bride,
    I 'll horse and gae my way.'

The first time that he calld on her,
    Her answer was him Nay:
But the next time that he calld on her,
    She was not slow to gae.

He took her by the milk-white hand,
    And by the grass-green sleeve,
He 's pulld her on behind him,
    At the bridegroom speard nae leave.

515. *B* 9. Cf. *I* (Motherwell's MS.): —

Then rose up the young bridegroom,
    And an angry man was he:
'Lo, art thou come to fight, young man?
    Indeed I 'll fight wi thee.'

'O I am not come to fight,' he sayd,
    'But good fellowship to hae,
And for to drink the wine sae red,
    And then I 'll go away.'

222

Six versions.

225

Twelve versions.
521. *A* 6. We have the complete stanza in *D* (MS. at Abbotsford) and elsewhere: —

As they gaed oer yon high hill,
    The ladie often fainted;
'Oh, wae be to my gold,' she said,
    'This road for me invented!'

226

Nine versions.

227

524. 1. Version *h* begins as follows: —

As I came in by Carron sid,
    An in nou by Dumblain,
Ther I mett we Dugall Grame:
    He said he wad see me hame.
'My bonny Lisey Ballie,' etc.

228

Seven versions.
526. 1. *B* (Kinloch's Ballads) begins: —

The Lawland lads think they are fine,
    But the Hieland lads are brisk and gaucy
And they are awa, near Glasgow toun,
    To steal awa a bonnie lassie.

526. 3. In *B* the suitor retorts: —

'I have got cows and ewes anew,
    I 've got gowd and gear already;

Sae I dinna want your cows nor ewes,
  But I will hae your bonnie Peggy.'

And Peggy adds : —

' I 'll follow you oure moss and muir,
    I 'll follow you oure mountains many,
  I 'll follow you through frost and snaw,
    I 'll stay na langer wi my daddie.'

527. 13. *B* ends thus: —

' See ye no a' yon castles and towrs?
    The sun sheens owre them a sae bonnie ;
  I am Donald, the Lord of Skye,
    I think I 'll mak ye as blythe as onie.'

A' that Peggy left behind
  Was a cot-house and a wee kail-yardie ;
Now I think she is better by far
  Than tho she had got a Lawland lairdie.

229

Two versions.
527. 2 ff. Cf. *B* (Buchan's Ballads), sts. 2–
5 : —

When we had been married for some time,
  We walked in our garden green,
And aye he clapped his young son's head,
  And aye he made sae much o him.

I turnd me right and round about,
  And aye the blythe blink in my ee :
' Ye think as much o your young son
  As ye do o my fair body.

' What need ye clap your young son's head?
    What need ye make so much o him ?
What need ye clap your young son's head?
    I 'm sure ye gotna him your lane.'

' O if I gotna him my lane,
    Show me the man that helped me ;
  And for these words your ain mouth spoke
    Heir o my land he neer shall be.'

527. 4⁴, 5, 6. Wanting in *a* ; supplied from *b*.
527. 13. The reply of the boy is found in *b* :

O here am I, a bonny boy,
  That 's willin to win meat and fee,
That will go on to Earl Crawford's,
  And see an 's hairt be faen to thee.

In *B* Lady Crawford rides to her husband's
castle in person to see if the earl will pity her.
He shuts his gates and steeks his doors, and will
neither come down to speak with her himself
nor send his man. She retires weeping. The
earl in turn now goes to the castle where his lady
is lying, to see if she will pity him. She shuts
the gates and steeks the doors, and will neither
come down to speak with him nor send her
waiting-maid. Not the less she takes to her
bed, both she and Crawford die before morning,
and both are buried in one tomb.

230

528. 2⁴. *James* is an alternative reading for
John.
528. 3. Cowdenknows is perhaps Sir John
Home of Cowdenknows, named as one of the
curators of James Haitlie (a minor in 1607).
Earlstoun is not determinate. Bemerside is an

alternative reading for Earlstoun, and the laird
of Bemerside at the date of the slaughter was
the turbulent James Haig.

231

Eight versions.
529. 11. *B* (the Old Lady's MS.) has the
following instead of sts. 1–10 of *A* : —

Earell is a bonny place,
  Itt stands upon yon plain ;
The gratest faut about the toun,
  Earell's na a man.
For fat ye caa the danton o 'tt,
  According as ye ken,
For the pearting . . . . . . ,
  Lady Earel lays her lean.

Eearel is a bonny place,
  It stans upon yon plain ;
The rosses they grou read an whit,
  An the apples they grou green.

232

Nine versions.
531. *A* 11. *F* (Sharpe's version) and *G* (Kinloch MSS.) are not satisfied with this conclusion.
The footman is really a lord in disguise, the
Earl of Hume or of Cumbernauld. Thus in *F* :

Cumbernauld is mine, Annie,
  Cumbernauld is mine, Annie ;
And a' that 's mine, it shall be thine,
  As we sit at the wine, Annie.

233

Three versions.
532. 19, 20. In *B* (Jamieson, II, 382, from a
stall copy) : —

My sister stands at her bower-door,
  And she full sore does mock me,
And when she hears the trumpet sound, —
  ' Your cow is lowing, Nanny ! '

' O be still, my sister Jane,
  And leave off all your folly ;
For I 'd rather hear that cow low
  Than all the kye in Fyvie.'

Two versions.
534. *B* (Buchan's version) completes the
story thus (sts. 17–20) : —

' O farewell now, Helen, I 'll bid you adieu ;
  Is this a' the comfort I 'm getting frae you ?

' It was never my intention ye shoud be the waur ;
  My heavy heart light on Whitehouse o Cromar !

' For you I hae travelled full mony lang mile,
  Awa to Kinadie, far frae the West Isle.

' But now ye are married, and I am the waur ;
  My heavy heart light on Whitehouse o Cromar ! '

235

Fourteen versions.
534. 1. *C** (the Old Lady's MS.) begins : —

The Earl of Aboyn he 's carrlis an kind,
  An he is nou come frae Lonon ;
He sent his man befor,
  To tell of his hame-coming.

535. 19, 20. *B* (Buchan's Gleanings) ends thus : —

'My nobles all, ye 'll turn your steeds,
  That comely face [I] may see then;
Frae the horse to the hat, a' must be black,
  And mourn for bonny Peggy Irvine.'

When they came near to the place,
  They heard the dead-bell knellin,
And aye the turnin o the bell
  Said, Come bury bonny Peggy Irvine.

C* ends with this stanza : —

We must go to the North, to burry her corps,
  Aless for our hear coming!
I rather I had lost a' the lands of Aboyn
Or I had lost bonny Marg[ra]t Irvien!

236

Six versions.
  536. 12. After this *D* (Buchan's Ballads) has : —

When they had eaten and well drunken,
  And all men bound for bed,
The Laird o Drum and his lady gay
  In ae bed they were laid.

'Gin ye had been o high renown,
  As ye are o low degree,
We might hae baith gane down the streets
  Amang gude companie.'

'I tauld you ere we were wed
  You were far abeen my degree;
But now I 'm married, in your bed laid,
  And just as gude as ye.'

'Gin ye were dead, and I were dead,
  And baith in grave had lain,
Ere seven years were at an end,
  They 'd not ken your dust frae mine.'

238

Nine versions.
  538. 1. *B* (Sharpe's Ballad Book) begins thus : —

Four and twenty nobles sits in the king's ha,
Bonnie Glenlogie is the flower among them a'.

In came Lady Jean, skipping on the floor,
And she has chosen Glenlogie 'mong a' that was there.

She turned to his footman, and thus she did say :
Oh, what is his name? and where does he stay ?

'His name is Glenlogie, when he is from home;
He is of the gay Gordons, his name it is John.'

538. 7, 10. This uncalled-for language seems to have slipped in by a mere trick of memory from No. 65.

239

Two versions.
  540. 2. See note on No. 238, *A* 7.
  540. 3. In *B c* (Old Lady's MS.) we have : —

Achainace Gordon is a pritty man,
Bat Acchanace Gordon has na free land ;
For his land is laying wast, an his castell faaen doun,
So ye man take Salton, latt Achennecy be.

240

Four versions.
  541. 8. *A b* prefixes the following manufactured lines : —

His face it reddened like a flame,
He grasped his sword sae massy.

In *C* (Laing's Thistle of Scotland) the stanza runs : —

Who are they dare be so bold
  To cruelly use my lassie?
But I 'll take her to bonny Aboyne,
  Where oft she did caress me.

241

Three versions.

243

Eight versions.

244

Three versions.
  546. 1². The king was from home but lately *b*; The king from home he chanced to be *c*.
  547. 5. After this *b* has : —

Up then spak the king himsel,
  And an angry man I wot was he:
'For stealin o my jewels rare,
  Hatlie shall oer the barriers die.'

547. 13$^{1, 2}$. Two half-stanzas are wanting. They may be supplied from *b* : —

For this is spillin o noble blude,
  And shamein of my noble kin.

'Hold up, hold up,' Sir Fenwick he said,
  'Hold up, and ye sal justified be.'

In *B* (MS. at Abbotsford) we have : —

O hold your hand, my little pretty prince,
  And let my breath go out and in,
For spilling of my noble blood
  And shaming of my noble kin.

O hold your hand, my little pretty prince,
  And let my breath go out and in,
And there 's the key of my coffer,
  And you 'll find the king's jewels lying therein.

245

Five versions.
  548. 11, 12. Cf. *D* (Murison MS.), sts. 3, 4 : —

Whar will I get a bonnie wee boy
  That 'll tak my helm in han, O
Till I gang up to my high topmast
  An look oot for some dry lan?

He 'll get half o my gowd, an half o my gear,
  An the third pairt o my lan,
An gin he row me safe on shore
  He shall hae my daughter Ann.

548. 19. In *D* : —

O where is he, the bonnie wee boy
  That took my helm in han
Till I gied up to my high topmast
  An lookd oot for some dry lan?

246

Three versions.

248

551. 1. Probably suggested by No. 77.
551. 6. An imitation, or a corruption, of the bribe offered to the parrot in some versions of No. 4, or in No. 68, *A* 10, etc.

250

Five versions.

252

Five versions.
557. 8. Cf. No. 70, *B* 8; No. 71, 13.
558. 22. In *B* (Buchan's Ballads) : —

Now Willie 's taen a gay gold ring
And gave her presentlie ;
Says, Take ye that, ye lady fair,
A love-token from me.

558. 36. In *B* : —

Fine silk it was his sailing-clothes,
Gold yellow was his hair ;
It would hae made a hale heart bleed
To see him lying there.

558. 38. In *D* (Harris MS.) : —

' A priest, a priest,' the lady she cried,
' To marry my love an me ; '
' A clerk, a clerk,' her father cried,
' To sign her tocher free.'

254

Three versions.

257

Three versions.
563. 2. St. 2 of Buchan's version (*B*) may be quoted as a stop-gap : —

Thus I speak by Burd Isbel ;
She was a maid sae fair,
She laid her love on Sir Patrick
She 'll rue it for evermair.

564. 10. Cf. *B* : —

He 's done him down thro ha, thro ha,
Sae has he in thro bower ;
The tears ran frae his twa grey eyes,
And loot them fast down pour.

564. 20. A stanza may be supplied from *C* (Sharpe's papers) : —

Now she got frowning throw the closs,
And frowning on the floor,
And she has styled him, Patrick,
And he her, aunty dear.

564. 23. *B* has (st. 40) : —

' O how is this, Burd Isbel,' he said,
' So ill ye 've used me ?
What gart you anger my gude grand-aunt,
That I did send to thee ? '

258

565. 11. After this *b* has : —

The Highland hills are high, high hills,
The Highland hills are hie ;
They 're no like the pleasant banks o Tay,
Nor the bonnie town o Dundee.

260

Two versions.

265

573. 2². For *monie* read perhaps *menie* ' retinue.'

266

Two versions.
575. 15¹. Two months, Buchan ; but cf. st. 8.

267

Two versions.
576. For ' The Drunkard's Legacy' see Child, v, 19 f.
576. 3². There is probably a gap after this line.

269

Five versions.
583. 3⁴. He was an unwelcom gast. *B*.
583. 4. In *B* (the Old Lady's MS.) there is a longer dialogue, in which the king says ' Fra yer face the couller is gane,' and asks : —

' O have ye loved ? or have ye lang-sought ?
Or die ye goo we barn ? '
' It 's all for you, fair father,
That ye stayed so long in Spain.'

583. 6. *B* continues and ends : —

. . . .
It 's the morn befor I eat or drink
His heart-blude I sall see.'

He 's tean Bold Robien by the hand
Lead him across the green ;
His hear was leak the very threeds of **goud,**
His face shone leak the moon.

He 's tane out this bonny boy's hear[t]
Into a cupe of gold,
Had it to Lady Dayesë's bour,
Says, No[u], Dayesë, behold !

' O welcom to me my heart's delight !
Nou welcom to me my joy !
Ye have dayed for me, an I 'll day for ye,
Tho ye be but the kitchen-boy.'

She has tean out the coup of gold,
Lead it belou her head,
An she wish it we the tears ran doun fra her eays
An or midnight she was dead.

She has tean out the coup of gold,
Laid it belou her hear,
An she wish it we the tears ran don fra her eays
An alass ! spak never mare.

271

Two versions.
586. The first stanzas of *B* may be given since they are somewhat clearer : —

It was a worthy Lord of Lorn,
He was a lord of high degree,
He sent [his son] unto the schoole,
To learn some civility.

He learned more learning in one day
Then other children did in three ;
And then bespake the schoolmaster
Unto him tenderly.

'In faith thou art the honestest boy
  That ere I blinkt on with mine eye;
I hope thou art some easterling born,
  The Holy Ghost is with thee.'

He said he was no easterling born,
  The child thus answered courteously;
My father is the Lord of Lorn,
  And I his son, perdye.

The schoolmaster turned round about,
  His angry mood he could not swage;
He marvelled the child could speak so wise,
  He being of so tender age.

586. 9. *B* adds: —

'There's nere a doctor in all this realm,
  For all he goes in rich array,
I can write him a lesson soon
  To learn in seven years day.'

272

593. *a* was "printed for W. Thackery and
T. Passenger;" *b* "by and for A. M[il-
bourne]." The date of *a* is added by Wood.

273

595. *a* was "printed for F. Coles, T. Vere,
and W. Gilbertson;" *b* "for F. Coles, T. Vere,
and J. Wright;" *c* "by A. M[ilbourne]" (1670–
97).

274

Two versions.

275

Three versions.
601. 5. *C* (contributed to Johnson's Museum by Robert Burns) has: —

Three travellers that had tint their gate,
  As thro the hills they foor,
They airted by the line o light
  Fu straught to Johnie Blunt's door.

276

Two versions.
601. *a* was "printed for F. Coles, T. Vere,
and J. Wright;" *b* "for W. Thackeray and
T. Passinger."

277

Seven versions.

278

Two versions.

280

Five versions.
606. 3. *B* (Murison MS.) has: —

O I can love ye manyfold,
As Jacob loved Rachel of old,
And as Jessie loved the cups o gold;
  My dear, can ye believe me?
  As Jessie, etc.

C (Motherwell's MS.) has: —

As Judas loved a piece of gold,
As Jacob loved Rachel of old,
As Jacob loved Rachel of old,
  O laddie, I do love thee.

606. 8. In *B*: —

When they cam to yon grassy hill,
Where spotted flocks do feed their fill,
'I'll sit me doon an I'll greet a while,
  For the followin o my laddie.'

'It's ye'll tak aff yer beggin-weed,
An ye'll pit on the goons o red,
An ye'll gang back the road ye cam,
  For I canna bide yer greetin.'

'Betide me weel, betide me woe,
It's wi the beggar an I'll go,
An I'll follow him through frost an snow
  An I'll be the beggar's dawtie.'

606. 11, 12. In *B*: —

When they cam to yonder ha,
He knockit loud an sair did ca;
She says, My dear, we'll be foun in fa
  For knockin here sae loudly.

606. 15. *B* ends as follows: —

The streen ye was the beggar's bride,
An noo this nicht ye'll lie by my side,
Come weel, come woe, whateer betide,
  An ye'll be aye my dawtie.

D (Christie's Ballad Airs) ends thus: —

Yestreen she was the begger's bride,
As his wife she now stood by his side,
And for a' the lassie's ill misguide,
  She's now the young knight's lady.

283

Six copies (*a–f*) of a single version.
608. *c–f*, the traditional copies, were derived
originally from print; *c* is from *a*; *d–f* are from
another edition, not recovered, resembling *b*; *b*
was printed in The Manchester Songster, 1792.

285

610. *b* was "printed for F. Coles, T. Vere
and J. Wright" (1655–80); *c* "for F. Coles,
J. Wright, Tho. Vere, and W. Gilbertson" (the
earliest known ballad by the four together is
dated 1655).
610. 6². *aboard*: probably, 'alongside.'
610. 7. 'Amain' is strike (sails) in sign of
surrender. The French use the word derived
from their own language; the English say,
strike.

286

Three versions.
612. *B*. The different copies show many
variations.

287

613. "Printed by and for W. Onley." Dated
at the British Museum 1680 at the earliest.

288

Three versions.

289

Six versions.

292

618. 20^3. The word *leaves* is in all copies, but seems doubtful.

293

Four versions.

294

Two versions.
620. 6 . Cf. B 9^4, 10^4, 11^2.

295

Two versions.

305

Three versions.
632. 1^4. Cf. 16^2, 29^4. *b* has " wilde beastes."
632. 4^1. *ae* is supplied from 19^1 and *b*. So in 32^1.
633. 34. In *b*:

'Gar warn me Perthshire and Angus baith,
  Fife up and down and the Louthians three,
And graith my horse,' said the nobil king,
 'For to Ettricke Foreste hie will I me.'

634. $41^{3,4}$. Supplied from the copy in Herd's Scottish Songs. *b* has the same.
635. $72^{1,2}$. Scott has : —

And I have native steads to me,
  The Newark lee and Hangingshaw.

SOURCES OF THE TEXTS

SOURCES OF THE TEXTS

MANUSCRIPTS

MS. B. 14. 39, Library of Trinity College, Cambridge, 13th century. (No. 23.)

Rawlinson MS. D. 328, 15th century (before 1445). Bodleian Library. (No. 1.)

MS. F. f. 5. 48, Library of the University of Cambridge, c. 1450. (No. 119 a.)

One leaf of MS. in Bagford Ballads, vol. i., art. 6, British Museum, c. 1450. (No. 119 b.)

Sloane MS. 2593, British Museum, c. 1450. (Nos. 22, 115.)

MS. E. e. 4. 35, Library of the University of Cambridge, c. 1500. (No. 121.)

Rawlinson MS. C. 813, beginning of the 16th century. Bodleian Library. (No. 111.)

Cotton MS. Cleopatra, C. iv., British Museum, c. 1550. (No. 161 A a.)

MS. Ashmole 48, Bodleian Library, Oxford, 1550, or later. (No. 162.)

MS. in York Minster Library, 16th century. (No. 167 C).

Cotton MS. Vespasian, A. xxv, British Museum, end of 16th century. (No. 178.)

Harleian MS. 293, leaf 52, British Museum, about 1620. (No. 161 A b.)

Percy MS., British Museum, Additional MSS., 27879, c. 1650.

Philiphaugh MS. of No. 305, Edinburgh, 1689–1708 (?). Not now accessible : printed by Aytoun. A supposed transcript extant among the Philiphaugh papers is not older than 1848.

Fly-leaf of a volume printed at Edinburgh, 1670. Laing MSS., Div. ii, 358, Library of the University of Edinburgh. (Fragment, p. 637.)

Elizabeth Cochrane's Songbook, Collection of Songs English and Scots, 1730 (?). Harvard College Library.

Mrs Cockburn's MS. of No. 305, used by Scott, and described by him as " apparently of considerable antiquity." Edinburgh. Not now accessible.

Bishop Percy's papers. MS. copies of ballads from Rev. P. Parsons of Wye, Miss Fisher of Carlisle, Principal Robertson of Edinburgh, the Dean of Derry, George Paton of Edinburgh, Rev. Robert Lambe of Norham, Roger Halt, the Duchess Dowager of Portland, and others. In all about 33. 1766–80. Harvard College Library.

David Herd's MSS., two volumes folio, the second volume duplicating a portion of the first. 1776. British Museum. Additional MSS., 22311–12. (See Mr H. L. D. Ward's Catalogue of Romances, i, 531.)

MSS. of Mrs Brown of Falkland. 1783–1801.

(1) Jamieson-Brown MS., mostly taken down from the mouth of Mrs Brown by Professor Scott of Aberdeen about 1783. Laing MSS., Library of the University of Edinburgh.

(2) William Tytler's Brown MS. Fifteen ballads, with the airs : thirteen being revisions of pieces in (1). Presented by Mrs Brown to W. Tytler in 1783. Described by Anderson in a letter to Percy, Nichols's Illustrations, vii, 176 ff. The MS. has disappeared, but, excepting one, all the pieces it contained are substantially known from (1) or other sources.

(3) Alexander Fraser Tytler's Brown MS. Nine ballads sent A. F. T. by Mrs Brown in 1800 ; with the airs. Anderson, as above, vii, 179 f. Aldourie Castle, Inverness-shire.

Sir Walter Scott's collection, Abbotsford. 1783–1830.

(1) Small folio without title, Library, L 2 (Catalogue, p. 57). Two fragments.

(2) ' Scottish Songs,' 1795. Library, N 3 (Catalogue, p. 104). Seven ballads with airs and three fragments. All the ballads appear to be Mrs Brown's copies altered.

(3) Letters addressed to Sir Walter Scott, 1796–1831. Ballads enclosed have in most cases been removed, but some seven remain.

(4) ' Scotch Ballads, Materials for Border Minstrelsy,' a folio volume made up at a recent date from detached pieces to the number of above eighty.

(5) ' North Country Ballads ' in a quarto volume with the title ' Miscellanea Curiosa,' Library B 5 (Catalogue, p. 15).

(6) ' Miscellanies,' a folio with one ballad and a fragment.

Glenriddell MS., 1791. In volume xi of Robert Riddell's collection of Scottish Antiquities. (There is an earlier transcript of one of the ballads in vol. viii.) Library of the Society of Antiquaries of Scotland.

MS. described by Scott as the ' collection of an old lady's complete set of ballads.' In two portions, the first in 53 pages, on paper of 1805–6–7 ; the second in 10 pages, on paper of 1818. Contains thirty-two popular ballads and gives the titles of others known to the compiler. Obtained by Skene of Rubislaw in the north of Scotland (but obviously not so early as 1802–3 as endorsed by Scott on the cover of the Skene MS.), turned over to Scott by Skene, and in 1823 by Scott to C. K. Sharpe. In the possession of Mr Macmath.

Skene MS., nine separate quires, amounting in all to 125 pages, and containing thirty-six pieces. Almost all of these are found in the Old Lady's Collection, from which they appear to have been transcribed, but with misreadings and changes. 118 pages in the possession of Mr Alexander Allardyce of Edinburgh ; the remainder in the possession of Mr Macmath.

Pitcairn's MSS., 1817-25. Three volumes in the writing of Robert Pitcairn ; partly from printed sources. In the possession of the representatives of Mr James L. Mansfield, Edinburgh.

Charles Kirkpatrick Sharpe's Collection (besides the Old Lady's MS. and the Skene MS.). (1) 'Songs,' 12mo, in Sharpe's handwriting. (2) MS. of 32 pages, small 4to, on paper of 1822, not in Sharpe's hand. (3) MS. of 12 pages, on paper of 1820, not in Sharpe's hand. (4) An independent transcript by Sharpe of the pieces entitled by Scott ' North Country Ballads.' (5) Letters from Motherwell to Sharpe, enclosing ballads. (6) Single copies of ballads, not in Sharpe's hand. All in possession of Mr Macmath.

Motherwell's MS., 1825 and after. A folio, almost entirely in Motherwell's hand, containing, besides some pieces not indexed, 228 indexed ballads. Most of these are from the West of Scotland, but not a few were given Motherwell by Buchan and are duplicates of copies which occur in Buchan's MSS. In the possession of Mr Malcolm Colquhoun Thomson, Glasgow.

Motherwell's Note-Book, c. 1826-27. A small octavo containing various memoranda referring to ballads, including the whole, or a portion, of several copies. Formerly in the possession of Mr J. Wylie Guild.

Kinloch MSS., 1826 and after. Seven volumes, the fourth being an interleaved (printed) copy of Kinloch's Ancient Scottish Ballads with additions and variations. Vols. I, II, III, VII, are almost wholly in Kinloch's hand ; V, VI, are mostly in the writing of James Beattie, John Hill Burton, and Joseph Robertson. Harvard College Library.

Peter Buchan's MSS., about 1828. Two volumes, folio. British Museum, Additional MSS., 29408-9. For a description, see Mr Ward's Catalogue of Romances, etc., I, 537.

Mr David Scott of Peterhead possessed a volume entirely in Buchan's writing "which contains all [the ballads] that Buchan ever collected except some ' high-kilted ' ones in another volume." These two volumes are now in the Child Memorial Library of Harvard University. The " high-kilted " volume is entitled 'Secret Songs of Silence,' and its contents are not properly called ballads.

Joseph Robertson's MSS., 1829-32. Four small note-books, one entitled ' Journal of Excursions ; ' another, ' Adversaria ' ; also an annotated copy of The New Deeside Guide [1832]. In the possession of Dr Robertson's representatives.

John Hill Burton's MSS., 1829-30. Mostly in the Kinloch collection, but his daughter, Mrs Rodger, Aberdeen, has a small volume containing portions of two ballads.

Alexander Laing of Brechin's MS., 1829-35. ' Ancient Ballads and Songs, etc., etc., from

the recitation of old people . never published, 1829.' Three ballads and a fragment. Harvard College Library.

Robert White's Papers, 1829 and after. Ballads selected from his *collectanea* by Mr White of Newcastle-on-Tyne. Harvard College Library.

British Museum, Additional MSS., 20094. 1829. (No. 4.)

Campbell MSS., 1830 or earlier. ' Old Scottish Songs collected in the counties of Berwick, Roxburgh, Selkirk and Peebles.' 2 volumes. Collector unknown. At Marchmont House, Berwickshire.

' Scottish Songs and Ballads,' copied probably before 1830, by a granddaughter of Lord Woodhouselee, mostly from print or from A. F. Tytler's Brown MS., but containing two or three versions of popular ballads not found elsewhere.

Harris MS. Ballads learned by Amelia Harris in her childhood from an old nurse in Perthshire (the last years of the 18th century) ; taken down by her daughter, who has added a few of her own collecting. With an appendix of airs. Harvard College Library.

Joseph Robertson. An interleaved and annotated copy of The New Deeside Guide [1832] (of which J. R. was the author).

Gibb MS., 1860. Twenty-one ballads written down from the recitation of his mother by Mr James Gibb of Joppa, representing the form in which ballads were recited about the beginning of the century in Angus and Mearns. Harvard College Library.

David Louden's MS., 1873. Contains four popular ballads derived from reciters in Haddingtonshire. Harvard College Library.

Murison MS., about 1873. Some forty pieces collected by Mrs A. F. Murison in Old Deer, among which there are several traditional popular ballads. Harvard College Library.

A few detached ballads collected by Dr Alexander Laing of Newburgh-on-Tay. About 1873.

Findlay MSS. Two volumes, the first (only) containing several ballads and many fragments gathered from recitation by Rev. William Findlay, of Saline, Fifeshire, 1865-85. In the hands of the collector.

Macmath MS. Ballads and songs recently collected by Mr Macmath. In the possession of the collector.

" Common Place Book filled with a collection of Old Ballads of the 17th century," a MS. formerly belonging to J. Payne Collier, now in the British Museum. Contains thirty ballads written in a forged hand of the 19th century, some of the pieces being also spurious. Nos. 8 C, 137, 168 are in this MS.

Communications, noted in their places, of a single ballad or of several ballads, taken down or remembered by friends or correspondents in Europe and America, and several taken down by Professor Child himself. Child MSS., Harvard College Library.

PRINTED SOURCES

A Gest of Robyn Hode. Fragment without printer's name or date, but of the end of the 15th or beginning of the 16th century: the eleventh and last piece in a volume the other contents of which are nine pieces printed by Walter Chepman and Andrew Myllar — three of these purporting to be printed at Edinburgh in 1508 — and one other piece the printer of which is also unascertained. Advocates' Library, Edinburgh.

A Lytell Geste of Robyn Hode, etc. Wynken de Worde, London, n. d. (1492–1534). Library of the University of Cambridge.

Three fragments (one of which was attributed to Wynken de Worde by Ritson). Douce, Bodleian Library.

A Mery Geste of Robyn Hoode, etc. London, Wyllyam Copland, n. d. (1549–69). British Museum.

A Merry Iest of Robin Hood, etc. London, Printed for Edward White, n. d. (1577–1612). Bodleian Library.

The sources of the later Robin Hood ballads may more conveniently be entered here, than in regular course. Articles n. d. may of course not be in strict chronological order.

Broadside copies in the Wood, Pepys, Douce, Roxburghe, and Rawlinson collections.

Martin Parker, A True Tale of Robbin Hood. London, 1634 (?). British Museum, C. 39, a. 52. — The same. By Clark, Thackeray, and Passinger. London, 1686. Bodleian Library.

Robin Hoods Garland; or Delightful Songs, Shewing the Noble Exploits of Robin Hood, and his Yeomendrie. With new Edditions and Emendations. London, Printed for W. Gilbertson, at the Bible in Giltspur-street, without Newgate, 1663. (17 ballads.) Wood, Bodleian Library.

Robin Hoods Garland. Containing his merry Exploits, and the several Fights which he, Little John, and Will. Scarlet had, upon several occasions. Some of them never before Printed. [London,] Printed for F. Coles, T. Vere, and J. Wright. 1670. (16 Ballads.) Douce, Bodleian Library.

Robin Hood's Garland. Printed by C. Dicey in Bow Church Yard, n. d. (before 1741).[1]

Robin Hood's Garland, without place or printer. 1749. Percy Papers, Harvard College Library.

Robin Hood's Garland. Printed by W. & C. Dicey, in St Mary Aldermary Church Yard, Bow Lane, Cheapside, and sold at the Warehouse in Northampton, n. d. (c. 1753).[1]

The English Archer . . . Robin Hood. Paisley, printed by John Neilson for George Caldwell, Bookseller, near the Cross, 1786.[1]

The English Archer, or . . . Robin Hood. York, printed by N. Nickson in Feasegate, n. d.[1]

Robin Hood's Garland. Printed by L. How in Peticoat Lane, n. d.[1]

Robin Hood's Garland. London, J. Marshall & Co., Aldermary Churchyard, n. d. Harvard College Library.

Robin Hood's Garland. London. R. Marshall, in Aldermary Church Yard, Bow Lane, n. d. Harvard College Library.

Captain Delany's Garland. In a collection of folio sheet-ballads mostly dated 1775. Edinburgh (?). British Museum, 1346. m. 7. (9.)

Robin Hood's Garland. York, T. Wilson and R. Spence, n. d.[1]

Robin Hood's Garland. Preston, Printed and sold by W. Sergent, n. d.[1]

Robin Hood's Garland. Wolverhampton, Printed and sold by J. Smart, n. d.[1]

Adventures of . . . Robin Hood. Falkirk, Printed and sold by T. Johnston, 1808.[1]

The History of Robin Hood and the Beggar. Aberdeen. A. Keith (1810–35).[1]

Adam Bell, Clim of the Clough, and William of Cloudesly. Two fragments of an edition by John Byddell. London, 1536. Library of the University of Cambridge.

A fragment by a printer not identified, formerly in the possession of J. Payne Collier. (No. 116.)

Adambel, Clym of the cloughe, and Wyllyam of cloudesle. William Copeland, London, n. d. (1562–69. See Arber, Transcript, v, 25). British Museum.

Adam Bell, Clim of the Clough, and William of Cloudesle. London, Printed by James Roberts, 1605.[1]

[Thomas Ravenscroft.] Deuteromelia, or, The Second Part of Musicks Melodie or Melodius Musicke, etc. London, 1609.

[Thomas Ravenscroft.] Melismata, Musicall Phansies, fitting the Court, Cittie, and Countrey Humours. London, 1611.

Thomas Deloney. Pleasant History of John Winchcomb, in his younger years called Jacke of Newberie: reprint of the 9th edition, of London, 1633, by J. O. Halliwell. London, 1859

The History of the Houses of Douglas and Angus, written by Master David Hume of Godscroft. Edinburgh, 1644.

Broadsides: mostly of the second half of the 17th century.

Wood, Rawlinson, Douce collections. Bodleian Library. Here from the originals.

Pepys collection. Magdalen College Library, Cambridge. Mostly from the originals.

Roxburghe collection. British Museum. Here sometimes from originals, sometimes from The Roxburghe Ballads, Ballad Society. Vols. I, II, edited by William Chappell, London, 1871–80. Vols. IV–VII, edited by J. W. Ebsworth, 1883–93.

Bagford Collection. British Museum. Here from the Bagford Ballads, Ballad Society, edited by J. W. Ebsworth, 2 vols. Hertford, 1878.

Osterley Park Library, British Museum, c. 39, k. 6 (60). 1690 (?).

[1] Bodleian Library, Oxford.

Laing (Scottish) Broadsides, c. 1700. In the possession of Lord Rosebery.

A Scottish Broadside formerly in the possession of J. Maidment, c. 1700. (No. 162.) Harvard College Library.

"Ballard's Collection" (so cited by Percy).

Pepys Penny Merriments. Magdalen College Library, Cambridge.

The King's Pamphlets. British Museum, 669, f. 20, 55. 1657.

Wit Restord, in several select poems not formerly publisht. London, 1658 (in Facetiæ, Musarum Deliciæ, 1656, Wit Restord, 1658, and Wits Recreations, 1640. 2 vols. London, 1817).

Wit and Drollery, Jovial Poems. Corrected and amended, with New Additions. London, 1682.

Wit and Mirth, or, Pills to Purge Melancholy, being a collection of the best Merry Ballads and Songs, etc., [with airs]. London. [Ed. by Henry Playford,] four editions, London, 1699–1714, 5 vols.; [ed. by T. D'Urfey,] 6 vols. London, I–v, 1719, vi, 1720.

True Love Requited, or, The Bayliff's Daughter of Islington. Printed and sold in Aldermary Churchyard, Bow Lane, "1700 or a little later."

A Collection of Old Ballads, corrected from the best and most ancient copies extant. With introductions historical, critical, or humorous. 3 vols. London, I, II, 1723; III, 1725.

Allan Ramsay. The Ever Green, being a collection of Scots Poems, wrote by the ingenious before 1600. 2 vols. Edinburgh, 1724.

Allan Ramsay. The Tea-Table Miscellany, or a collection of Choice Songs, Scots and English. (Vol. I, Edinburgh, 1724; vol. II, 172–?; vol. III, 1727. 3 vols in one, Dublin, 1729; London, 1733. 9th edition, enlarged with a fourth volume, London, 1740. 11th edition, four volumes in one, London, 1750. David Laing's notes in the Musical Museum, ed. 1853, pp. 108* f., 382*, 393* f.) London, 1733, 3 vols in one; 1763, 4 vols in one.

W. Thomson. Orpheus Caledonius, or, a Collection of the best Scotch Songs. [London, 1725.] 1 vol. fol. Orpheus Caledonius, or, a Collection of Scots Songs. 2 vols, 8°, London, 1733.

Gill Morrice. An Ancient Scottish Poem, 2d ed. Robert & Andrew Foulis, 1755.

Young Waters. An Ancient Scottish Poem, never before printed. Robert & Andrew Foulis, Glasgow, 1755.

Edom of Gordon. An Ancient Scottish Poem, never before printed. Robert & Andrew Foulis, Glasgow, 1755.

Letter of Thomas Gray, June, 1757? (Gray's Works, ed. Gosse, II, 316. London, 1884.)

Thomas Percy. Reliques of Ancient English Poetry: consisting of Old Heroic Ballads, Songs, and other pieces of our Earlier Poets, together with some few of later date. 3 vols. London, 1765, 1767, 1775. 4th ed., 1794, ostensibly edited by Percy's nephew, with restoration of some original readings.

Garlands, etc., of the second half of the 18th century:

The Brown Girl's Garland. British Museum. 11621 c. 3. (10.)

The Duke of Gordon's Garland. British Museum. 11621 c. 2. (15.) Also, Harvard College Library.

The Glasgow Lasses Garland. British Museum. 11621 c. 3. (68.)

The Jovial Rake's Garland. (No. 104.) Bodleian Library.

Lord Roslin's Daughter's Garland. (No. 46.)

Lovely Jenny's Garland. (No. 91.)

Sir James the Rose's Garland. Harvard College Library.

The Rambler's Garland. B. M. 11621 c. 4. (57.)

A chap-book of Four New Songs and a Prophecy. 1745? (Here from The Scots Musical Museum, 1853, IV, 458.)

The Merry Cuckold and Kind Wife. Broadside. Printed and Sold at the Printing Office in Bow Church-Yard, London.

Five Excellent New Songs. Edinburgh, 1766. B. M. 11621. b. 6. (8.)

The Duke of Gordon's Daughter, 1775, in a collection of folio ballads. B. M. 1346, m. 8.

Sir James the Rose, stall-tract of about 1780. Abbotsford Library.

The Duke of Gordon's Daughter. C. McLachlan, Dumfries, 1785 (?).

Lord Douglas Tragedy, stall-copy of 1792.

[David Herd.] The Ancient and Modern Scots Songs, Heroic Ballads, etc., now first collected into one body from the various Miscellanies wherein they formerly lay dispersed, containing likewise a great number of Original Songs from Manuscripts never before published. Edinburgh, 1769.

[David Herd.] Ancient and Modern Scottish Songs, Heroic Ballads, etc., collected from memory, tradition and ancient authors. The second edition. 2 vols. Edinburgh, 1776.

John Pinkerton. Scottish Tragic Ballads. London, 1781.

John Pinkerton. Select Scotish Ballads. 2 vols. (vol. I, Tragic Ballads; vol. II, Comic Ballads). London, 1783.

[Joseph Ritson.] A Select Collection of English Songs, with their Original Airs, and a historical essay on the Origin and Progress of National Song. 3 vols. London, 1783. (The second edition, with Additional Songs, and occasional Notes. By Thomas Park. 3 vols. London, 1813.)

[Joseph Ritson.] "The Bishopric Garland, or Durham Minstrel. Being a choice collection of Excellent Songs relating to the above county. Stockton, 1784. A new edition, corrected, 1792." Reprinted by J. Haslewood in, Northern Garlands, edited by the late Joseph Ritson, Esq. London, 1810.

[George Caw.] The Poetical Museum. Containing Songs and Poems on almost every subject. Mostly from periodical publications. Hawick, 1784.

James Johnson. The Scots Musical Museum, in six volumes. Consisting of Six Hundred Scots Songs, with proper Basses for the Piano Forte, etc. Edinburgh [1787–1803]. (Second Edition, 1839.) Third Edition, with copious Notes and Illustrations of the Lyric Poetry and Music of Scotland, by the late William Stenhouse, [and] with additional Notes and Illustrations [by David Laing]. 4 vols. Edinburgh and London, 1853.

[Joseph Ritson.] Ancient Songs, from the time of King Henry the Third to the Revolution. London, 1790. ("Printed, 1787; dated 1790; published 1792." Second Edition. Ancient Songs and Ballads from the Reign of King Henry the Second to the Revolution. Collected by Joseph Ritson, Esq. 2 vols. London, 1829.)

Joseph Ritson. Pieces of Ancient Popular Poetry: from authentic manuscripts and old printed copies. London, 1791. 2d ed., London, 1833.

[Joseph Ritson.] "The Northumberland Garland, or Newcastle Nightingale. A matchless collection of Famous Songs. Newcastle, 1793." Reprinted by J. Haslewood in, Northern Garlands, edited by the late Joseph Ritson, Esq. London, 1810.

[Joseph Ritson.] Scotish Song. In two volumes. London, 1794.

[Joseph Ritson.] Robin Hood: A Collection of all the Ancient Poems, Songs, and Ballads, now extant, relative to that celebrated English Outlaw. To which are prefixed Historical Anecdotes of his Life. In two volumes. London, 1795. (Second edition, London, 1832.)

[J. Currie.] The Works of Robert Burns, with an Account of his Life, etc. 4th ed., 4 vols. London, 1803.

John Leyden. The Complaynt of Scotland, written in 1548. With a Preliminary Dissertation and Glossary. Edinburgh, 1801.

Walter Scott. Minstrelsy of the Scottish Border: consisting of Historical and Romantic Ballads collected in the Southern Counties of Scotland, with a few of modern date, founded upon local tradition. 3 vols. Vols. I, II, Kelso, 1802; vol. III, Edinburgh, 1803. 2d ed., Edinburgh, 1803; 3d, 1806; 4th, 1810. 4 vols. edited by J. G. Lockhart, with airs. Edinburgh, 1833.

The Edinburgh Magazine, or, Literary Miscellany. Edinburgh, 1803.

The Scots Magazine, vol. LXV, 1803; vol. LXXX, 1817; vol. LXXXIX, 1822. Edinburgh.

The Sporting Magazine, vol. XXV. London, 1805.

Robert Jamieson. Popular Ballads and Songs from Tradition, Manuscripts, and Scarce Editions; with translations of similar pieces from the Ancient Danish Language, and a few Originals by the Editor. 2 vols. Edinburgh, 1806.

John Finlay. Scottish Historical and Romantic Ballads, chiefly ancient. 2 vols. Edinburgh, 1808.

R. H. Cromek. Remains of Nithsdale and Galloway Song: with Historical and Traditional Notices relative to the manners and customs of the Peasantry. London, 1810.

R. H. Cromek. Select Scottish Songs, Ancient and Modern; with Critical Observations and Biographical Notices, by Robert Burns. 2 vols. London, 1810.

Gammer Gurton's Garland, or, The Nursery Parnassus. London, 1810.

John Bell. Rhymes of Northern Bards, being a curious collection of Old and New Songs and Poems peculiar to the counties of Newcastle upon Tyne, Northumberland, and Durham. Edited by John Bell, Jun. Newcastle upon Tyne, 1812.

[John Fry.] Pieces of Ancient Poetry from unpublished manuscripts and scarce books. Bristol, 1814.

H. Weber, R. Jamieson, W. Scott. Illustrations of Northern Antiquities, etc. Edinburgh, 1814.

Sir Egerton Brydges. Restituta, vol. I. London. 1814.

Alexander Campbell. Albyn's Anthology, or, a select collection of the Melodies and Local Poetry peculiar to Scotland and the Isles, hitherto unpublished. 2 vols. 1816, 1818.

R. H. Cromek. Reliques of Robert Burns. 4th ed. London, 1817.

James Hogg. The Jacobite Relics of Scotland, being the Songs, Airs, and Legends of the adherents to the House of Stuart. 2 vols. Edinburgh, 1819–21.

R. A. Smith. The Scotish Minstrel, a selection from the Vocal Melodies of Scotland, ancient and modern. 6 vols. Edinburgh [1820–24].

John Struthers. The British Minstrel, a selection of Ballads, ancient and modern, etc. 2 vols. London, 1822.

Robert Trotter. Lowran Castle, or, The Wild Boar of Curridoo, with other Tales, illustrative of the Superstitions, Manners, and Customs of Galloway. Dumfries, 1822.

[Alexander Laing.] Scarce Ancient Ballads, many never before published. Aberdeen, 1822.

Alexander Laing. The Thistle of Scotland, a selection of Ancient Ballads, with notes. Aberdeen, 1823.

[Charles Kirkpatrick Sharpe.] A Ballad Book. Edinburgh, 1823. Reprinted by E. Goldsmid, Edinburgh, 1883.

Davies Gilbert. Some Ancient Christmas Carols, with the Tunes to which they were formerly sung in the West of England. Together with two ancient Ballads, a Dialogue, etc. 2d edition. London, 1823.

William Hone. Ancient Mysteries. London, 1823.

[James Maidment.] A North Countrie Garland. Edinburgh, 1824. Reprinted by E. Goldsmid. Edinburgh, 1884.

The Common-Place Book of Ancient and Modern Ballad and Metrical Legendary Tales. An original selection, including many never before published. Edinburgh, 1824.

John Mactaggart. The Scottish Gallovidian Encyclopedia, or, the original, antiquated, and natural Curiosities of the South of Scotland. London, 1824.

David Webster. A Collection of curious Old Ballads and Miscellaneous Poetry. Edinburgh, 1824.

The Gentleman's Magazine. Vol. xcv, Part I. London, 1825.

Peter Buchan. Gleanings of Scotch, English, and Irish scarce old Ballads chiefly tragical and historical, etc. Peterhead, 1825.

Allan Cunningham. The Songs of Scotland, ancient and modern, with an introduction and notes, historical and critical, etc. 4 vols. London, 1825.

Stall copies, etc., mostly of uncertain date:
The Song of Bewick and Grahame. B. M. 11621. e. 1. (4.)
Bewick and Graham's Garland. M. Angus & Son, Newcastle.
A Jolly Book of Garlands collected by John Bell in Newcastle. Abbotsford Library.
Curious Tracts, Scotland. B. M. 1078. m. 24. A collection made by J. Mitchell at Aberdeen in 1828.
The Unfortunate Weaver, etc. (for No. 25). Greenock, [1810.] B. M. 11621. b. 7. (43.)
Stall or chap-book copies by M. Randall & C. Randall, Stirling; John Sinclair, Dumfries; W. Fordyce, Newcastle; T. Johnston, Falkirk; P. Buchan, Peterhead; Aberdeen, printed for the booksellers.
Recent Broadsides of Catnach, Pitts, Such.
Peggy Irvine. Stall-copy printed by J. Morren, Cowgate, Edinburgh.

Robert Chambers. The Popular Rhymes of Scotland, with illustrations, chiefly collected from oral sources. Edinburgh, 1826, 1870.

George R. Kinloch. Ancient Scottish Ballads, recovered from tradition and never before published, with notes, historical and explanatory, and an appendix containing the airs of several of the ballads. London and Edinburgh, 1827.

[George R. Kinloch.] The Ballad Book. Edinburgh, 1827. Reprinted by E. Goldsmid. Edinburgh, 1885.

Thomas Lyle. Ancient Ballads and Songs, chiefly from tradition, manuscripts, and scarce works, etc. London, 1827.

William Motherwell. Minstrelsy, Ancient and Modern, with an historical introduction and notes. Glasgow, 1827. (A copy with MS. entries by Motherwell.)

Peter Buchan. Ancient Ballads and Songs of the North of Scotland, hitherto unpublished, with explanatory notes. 2 vols. Edinburgh, 1828.

The Paisley Magazine, or, Literary and Antiquarian Miscellany. Paisley, 1828.

Robert Chambers. The Scottish Ballads, collected and illustrated. Edinburgh, 1829.

Sir N. H. Nicolas. History of the Battle of Agincourt. 2d ed. London, 1832.

[Joseph Robertson.] The New Deeside Guide, by James Brown. Aberdeen [1832].

Andrew Picken. Traditional Stories of Old Families. 2 vols. London, 1833.

William Sandys. Christmas Carols, Ancient and Modern, including the most popular in the West of England, and the airs to which they are sung, etc. London, 1833.

William Sandys. Christmastide, its history, festivities, and carols. London [18—].

Sir Cuthbert Sharpe. The Bishoprick Garland, or a collection of Legends, Songs, Ballads, etc., belonging to the county of Durham. London, 1834.

The Universal Songster, or, Museum of Mirth, forming the most complete, extensive, and valuable collection of Ancient and Modern Songs in the English language. 3 vols. London, 1834.

The Songs of England and Scotland. 2 vols. London, 1835.

Fisher's Drawing-Room Scrap-Book. London, 1835.

[E. V. Utterson.] A Little Book of Ballads. [Printed for the Roxburghe Club.] Newport, 1836.

J. E. Tyler. Henry of Monmouth, or, Memoirs of the Life and Character of Henry the Fifth. 2 vols. London, 1838.

The Loving Ballad of Lord Bateman. Illustrated by George Cruikshank. London, 1839.

Sir N. H. Nicolas. The Poetical Works of Robert Burns. Aldine Edition. 3 vols. London, 1839.

J. O. Halliwell. The Nursery Rhymes of England, collected principally from oral tradition. London, 1842 (vol. iv of the Percy Society Publications). 4th ed., 1846; 5th ed., 1853.

Alexander Whitelaw. The Book of Scottish Song; collected and illustrated with historical and critical notices, etc. (Glasgow, 1844.) Glasgow, Edinburgh, and London, 1855.

Alexander Whitelaw. The Book of Scottish Ballads; collected and illustrated with historical and critical notices. Glasgow, Edinburgh, and London. [1844] 1845.

J. O. Halliwell. Nugæ Poeticæ. Select Pieces of Old English Popular Poetry, illustrating the manners and arts of the fifteenth century. London, 1844.

R. Chambers. Twelve Romantic Scottish Ballads, with the original airs. Edinburgh, 1844.

[James Maidment.] A New Book of Old Ballads. Edinburgh, 1844.

T. Wright and J. O. Halliwell. Reliquiæ Antiquæ. Scraps from Ancient Manuscripts. 2 vols. London, 1845.

The New Statistical Account of Scotland, vol. v. Edinburgh and London, 1845.

James Henry Dixon. Scottish Traditional Versions of Ancient Ballads. (Vol. xvii of the Percy Society Publications.) London, 1845.

James Henry Dixon. Ancient Poems, Ballads and Songs of the Peasantry of England, taken down from oral recitation, and transcribed from private manuscripts, rare broadsides, and scarce publications. (Vol. xvii of the Percy Society Publications.) London, 1846.

M. A. Richardson. The Borderer's Table Book, or, Gatherings of the Local History and Romance of the English and Scottish Border. 8 vols. Newcastle-upon-Tyne and London, 1846.

James Paterson and Charles Gray. The Ballads and Songs of Ayrshire, illustrated with sketches historical, traditional, narrative, and biographical. 2 series. Ayr, 1846, 1847.

Frederick Sheldon. The Minstrelsy of the English Border, being a collection of Ballads, ancient, remodelled, and original, founded on well known Border legends. London, 1847.

John Matthew Gutch. A Lytyll Geste of Robin Hode, with other Ancient and Modern Ballads and Songs relating to this celebrated yeoman, etc. 2 vols. London, 1847.

The Scottish Journal. Vol. II, 1848.

The Edinburgh Topographical, Traditional, and Antiquarian Magazine. [Sept.-Dec. 1848.] Edinburgh, 1849.

J. O. Halliwell. Popular Rhymes and Nursery Tales; a sequel to the Nursery Rhymes of England. London, 1849.

J. O. Halliwell. Ballads and Poems respecting Hugh of Lincoln. Brixton Hill, 1849.

Abraham Hume. Sir Hugh of Lincoln, or, an examination of a curious tradition respecting the Jews, with a notice of the Popular Poetry connected with it. London, 1849.

Notes and Queries. London, 1850-.

Proceedings of the Society of Antiquaries of Scotland. Vol. I, 1852.

J. S. Moore. The Pictorial Book of Ancient Ballad Poetry of Great Britain, historical, traditional, and romantic, etc. London, 1853.

John Miller. Fly-Leaves, or Scraps and Sketches, literary, biographical, and miscellaneous. The Second Series. London, 1855.

William Chappell. Popular Music of the Olden Time. A collection of Ancient Songs, Ballads, and Dance Tunes, illustrative of the National Music of England, etc. 2 vols. London [1855-59].

Jabez Allies. The British, Roman, and Saxon Antiquities and Folk-Lore of Worcestershire. 2d ed. London, "1856" [1852?].

Robert Bell. Ancient Poems, Ballads, and Songs of the Peasantry of England, taken down from oral recitation, and transcribed from private manuscripts, rare broadsides, and scarce publications. London, 1857.

William E. Aytoun. The Ballads of Scotland. 2 vols. Edinburgh and London, 1858; 2d ed., revised and augmented, 1859.

James Maidment. Scotish Ballads and Songs. Edinburgh, London, and Glasgow, 1859.

R. Chambers. The Romantic Scottish Ballads: their Epoch and Authorship. London and Edinburgh, 1859.

Thomas Hughes. The Scouring of the White Horse. Cambridge [England], 1859.

Joshua Sylvester. A Garland of Christmas Carols, ancient and modern, including some never before given in any collection. London, 1861.

Mary (Wilson) Gordon. Christopher North. A Memoir of John Wilson. 2 vols. Edinburgh, 1862.

William Allingham. The Ballad Book. A selection of the choicest British Ballads. London, 1865.

Robert Hunt. Popular Romances of the West of England. First Series. London, 1865.

M. H. Mason. Nursery Rhymes and Country Songs, both tunes and words from tradition. London, n. d. [c. 1877].

William Henderson. Notes on the Folk-Lore of the Northern counties of England and the Borders. With an Appendix by S. Baring-Gould. London, 1866; new ed., 1879.

Llewellyn Jewitt. The Ballads and Songs of Derbyshire, with illustrative notes and examples of the original music, etc. London and Derby, 1867.

John W. Hales and Frederick J. Furnivall. Bishop Percy's Folio Manuscript. Ballads and Romances. 3 vols. and a supplement. London, 1867-68.

James Maidment. Scotish Ballads and Songs, Historical and Traditionary. 2 vols. Edinburgh, 1868.

W. H. Logan. A Pedlar's Pack of Ballads and Songs, with illustrative notes. Edinburgh, 1869.

Robert Chambers. Popular Rhymes of Scotland. New edition. London and Edinburgh. [1870].

Wm. Henry Husk. Songs of the Nativity, being Christmas Carols, Ancient and Modern, several of which appear for the first time in a collection. London [187-?].

Salopian Shreds and Patches. Vol. I. Shrewsbury, 1875.

Jahrbuch für Romanische u. Englische Sprache und Literatur. Vol. XV. Leipzig, 1876.

W. Christie. Traditional Ballad Airs, arranged and harmonized, etc., from copies obtained in the counties of Aberdeen, Banff, and Moray, etc. Edited, with the words for singing and with illustrative notes. 2 vols. Edinburgh, vol. I, 1876; vol. II, 1881.

Suffolk Notes and Queries, in The Ipswich Journal, 1877-78.

H. R. Bramley and J. Stainer. Christmas Carols, New and Old. London [187-?].

Folk-Lore Record. Vol. II. London, 1879.

Francis Hindes Groome. In Gipsy Tents. Edinburgh, 1880.

The Leisure Hour, February 14, 1880. London.

Walter W. Skeat. Specimens of English Literature, from the Ploughmans Crede to the Shepherdes Calender, etc. 3d ed. Oxford, 1880.

A Ballad Book. By Charles Kirkpatrick Sharpe, Esq. 1823. Reprinted with Notes and Ballads from the unpublished MSS. of Charles Kirkpatrick Sharpe, Esq., and Sir Walter Scott, Bart. Edited by the late David Laing. Edinburgh and London, 1880.

Aungervyle Society's Publications. A Garland of Old Historical Ballads. Edinburgh, 1881.

B. Harris Cowper. The Apocryphal Gospels. 5th ed. London, 1881.

J. C. Bruce and J. Stokoe. Northumbrian Minstrelsy. A collection of the Ballads, Melodies and Small-Pipe Tunes of Northumbria. Newcastle-upon-Tyne, 1882.

A. Nimmo. Songs and Ballads of Clydesdale. Edinburgh and Glasgow, 1882.

G. A. Sala. 'Sir Hugh,' in Illustrated London News, October 21, 1882. (Repeated in Living London, 1883.)

Charlotte Sophia Burne. Shropshire Folk-Lore, a sheaf of gleanings edited from the collections of Georgina F. Jackson. London, 1883–6.

Wm. W. Newell. Games and Songs of American Children. New York, 1883.

Edmund Venables. A Walk through Lincoln Minster. Lincoln, 1885.

W. H. Long. A Dictionary of the Isle of Wight Dialect, and of Provincialisms used, . . . with illustrative anecdotes and tales, etc. London and Newport, 1886.

Transactions of The New Shakspere Society, 1880–86. London, 1866.

A. H. Bullen. Carols and Poems from the 15th century to the present time. London, 1886.

Letters from and to Charles Kirkpatrick Sharpe, Esq. Ed. by Alexander Allardyce. 2 vols. Edinburgh and London, 1888.

Mrs Graham R. Tomson. Ballads of the North Countrie. London, 1888.

S. Baring-Gould and H. Fleetwood Sheppard. Songs and Ballads of the West. A collection made from the mouths of the People. 4 parts. London [1889(?)–91].

The Monthly Chronicle of North-Country Lore and Legend. Vol. III. Newcastle-on-Tyne and London, 1889.

The Folk-Lore Journal. Vols. VI, VII. London, 1888–9.

James Raine, Jr. A volume of English Miscellanies, illustrating the history and language of the Northern Counties of England. Surtees Society, No. 85. Durham, 1890.

Blackwood's Magazine. Vol. CXLVII. Edinburgh, 1890.

Margaret Warrender. Walks near Edinburgh. Edinburgh, 1890.

Longman's Magazine. Vol. XVII. London, 1890.

Journal of the Gypsy-Lore Society. Vol. II. London, 1890–91.

Frank Kidson. Traditional Tunes. A collection of Ballad Airs, chiefly obtained in Yorkshire and the South of Scotland, together with their appropriate words from broadsides or from oral tradition. Oxford, 1891.

Lucy E. Broadwood and J. A. Fuller Maitland. English County Songs, words and music. London and New York, 1893.

County Folk-Lore. Printed Extracts. No. 2. Suffolk. Collected and edited by the Lady Eveline Camilla Gurdon. Folk-Lore Society. London, 1893.

The Journal of American Folk-Lore. Vol. VII. Boston, 1894.

H. A. Kennedy. Professor Blackie : his Sayings and Doings. London, 1895.

Francis Hindes Groome. Two Suffolk Friends. Edinburgh and London, 1895.

GLOSSARY

GLOSSARY

[References are to page and stanza.]

A

a', aa, aw, all.

a', every.

a, abridgment of *have*.

a, I, in the phrase, *a wat* (a wait, a wite, a wot, etc.), I know, verily, assuredly. a's, I's, I shall, will.

a, of.

a, on, as in *a grefe*, *a blode*.

a, one.

a, ae, one single, as in *a warst*.

a, to.

a be, (with *let*) be.

abeen, abeene, aboon, abone, etc., above. his hose abeen his sheen, his stockings ungartered, falling above, over his shoes.

abide, abyde, stop, wait, withstand.
pret. abode, waited, endured.
p. p. abiden, abyden, awaited.

able, suitable.

ablins, aiblins, perhaps.

aboard, alongside ; or, *laid us aboard* may be *boarded us*.

aboone, aboun, abown. See abune.

about, been, been engaged in.

abowthe, about.

abune, aboone, aboon, abon, abone, abown, aboun, abeen, above (above them).

abyde. See abide.

abyden. See abide.

Acaron, 312, 32, being the oath of a Turk, may be taken as *Alcoran*.

acward, ackward stroke, described as a back-handed stroke. See aukeward.

aduise, observe.

ae, one, single.

ae, aye, always.

aevery, voracious, very hungry.

af, aff, off.

affronted, confronted, opposed.

aft, oft.

after, after (the way), along, on. after me, according to me, my advice.

agast of him, alarmed about him (the consequences to him).

agayn(e), ageyn, against. a-geyn euyn, towards evening.

agree, bring to agreement.

a-ȝon : comyn a-ȝon, came upon, encountered.

ahind, ahint, ahin, behind, over and above.

aiblins, ablins, perhaps.

aileth at. See at.

air, ayre, by air, by ayre, early, betimes.

airn, ern, iron.

airt, art, quarter of the heavens, point of the compass.

aith, oath.

a' kin, a' kin kind, all kind, every.

'al, al, 'ull, wull, will.

al : al so mote I the, absolutely.

alane, alone. See lane.

alang, along.

alean, alone.

alelladay, exclamation of grief.

alive. See born alive.

allacing, repeating of alace (alas).

alld, old.

allther, representing the ancient genitive plural of *all*, allther moste, allther best, best of all, etc.

along of, owing to.

alow, below.

alsua, also.

althocht, although.

amain(e), with force ; at once, quickly.

amain (Fr. amener), lower, strike.

a-married, married.

amense, amends.

amo, among.

an, one.

-an, -ane, -and, -en, etc., annexed to the definite form of the superlative of the adjective (preceded by *the, her*, etc.), or to numerals, or following separately, seems to be *an, one :* the firstan, nextan, firsten, nexten, that samen. The history of this usage has not been made out.

an, and, if.

ance, anse, once.

ancient, ancyent, ensign.

and, *superfluous*, as in " when that I was and a tiny little boy," and two other songs in Shakspere. The same usage in German, Swedish, and especially Dutch ballads.

and, if.

aneath, aneth, beneath. aneath the sun, sheltering the eyes with the hand.

anent, over against, in the face of.

anew, enough, enow.

angel(1), a gold coin, of value varying from 6s. 8d. to 10s.

angerly, angrily.

ankir, recluse, hermit.

anse, once.

answere your quarrel, be responsible for, take on me to settle, your difference.

ant, and.

ape : lead an ape in hell, penance for old maids.

applyed, plied.

ar, or, before.

archborde, 408, 23 ; 409, 29, may be a misspelling of *hachebord*. Barton grappled the ship to his archborde, from which we should infer that the word meant the side of the ship, as *hatch-bord* would naturally signify at p. 411, 70. But *archborde* might of itself mean the stern of the ship, a timber at the stern being still so called, and German *hackbord* meaning the upper part of the stern of a ship.

archery, collected archers.

armorie, seems to be employed in the sense of *armament*, *men at arms*.

armorye, armor.

art. See airt.

asay, *p. p.*, tried [read *asayed ?*]

asking, asken, askend, askent, boon, request.

assoyled, absolved.

aste, east.

astoned, astonied, astonished, amazed.

at, from: reade must rise at, 113, 34, 35. ails ye at, aileth thee at, with (what ail comes to you from me). I was at thee, (apud) with.

at, with ellipsis of *the door*, rappit at.

at, att, *pron. and conj.*, that.

a ta, at all.

attoure, outowr, over and above.

atweel, I wot well, assuredly.

atween, between. atween hands, meanwhile.

aucht, aught: wha 's aucht ? who is it owns ? whose is (are) ?

aught, *v.*: suld hae come and aught a bairn to me, had a (child by).

aukeward, awkwarde (stroke), backhanded. See acward.

auld son, without regard to absolute age. So auld dochter, auld son, of child just born and the only one, sometimes called young son immediately after.

aull, auld, old.

ava, of all, at all.

avayle, put down, doff.

avow, consent, own, confess.

avowe, *n.*, vow.

avowë, avower, patron, protector.

avoyd, begone.

aw, all.

awaite, awayte, lie in wait for. awayte me scathe, lie in wait to do me harm.

awenden, weened, imagined.

awet, know. Perhaps, await, descry.

awkwarde stroke, a backhanded stroke. See aukeward.

awsom, awful.

ayenst, against, towards, about.

ayon, ayont, beyond, over against, in the face of.

ayre, eare, ere, heir.

B

baa, ball.

bacheeleere, young knight devoted to the service of a lady.

bad, bade, ordered, offered.

bad, bade, baed, abode, stopped, waited for.

badgers, pedlars.

baed. See bad.

baffled, thwarted (perhaps, made a fool of), affronted, insulted, or disgraced.

bailie, municipal officer, alderman. See baylye.

bairn, barn, bern, child.

baked, backed.

bald, boldly, fiercely.

bale, ill, trouble, mischief, harm, calamity, destruction. See balys.

ballup, front or flap of breeches.

balow, lullaby, sing a lullaby to.

ban, bound (*pret.*)

ban, band, hinge, band.

ban, band, bande, bond, band, bond.

ban, bann, *v.*, curse.

band(e), bond, compact.

band-dogs, bandoggs, dogs that are kept chained (on account of their fierceness).

bane, destruction, death.

bangisters, people violent and regardless of law.

banis, slayers, murderers.

bargain, brawl, fight.

barm, lap.

barn, barne, bairn, child ; (A. S. bearn) child ; (A. S. beorn) man, fighting man.

barn-well, 196, 8, the well has no sense, and has probably been caught from 9, at the far well-washing.

baron, often simply knight.

barrine, bairn.

bassonet, basnet, basnit, a light helmet, shaped like a skull-cap.

bat, bet, but.

bath, both.

batit, bated.

batts, blows : burden of batts, all the blows (beating) he can bear.

baube, babe.

baubee, bawbee, halfpenny.

baucheld sheen, shoes twisted out of shape or down at the heels.

bay, by, in comparison with.

baylleful, destructive, deadly.

bayls, misfortunes, troubles. See bale.

baylye, bailiff, sheriff's officer (to execute writs, etc.) ; chief magistrate, mayor. See bailie.

bayne, perdition.

be, by.

beager, beggar.

bean, bone.

bear, bier.

bear, beer.

bear, barley.

beare (as the lawes will thee beare), have (mercy) for (as in *bear malice*, etc.).

beare, *pret.*, bare.

beared, buried.

bearing arrow, perhaps a very long arrow, such as required to be carried in the hand. Mr C. J. Longman suggests that a bearing arrow was probably what is now called a flight-arrow, — a thin, light arrow with a tapering point for long shooting.

bear-seed, barley ; bear-seed time seems to refer to barley-harvest.

became his courtisie, that is, his courtesy became him (as in Shakspere's " youth becomes the livery that it wears "). See become.

because, in order that.

become them well, look well in them (i. e., they became him well). See **became**.

bed, offered. See **bede**.

bed-head, the top of the box or case of a Scottish bed.

bedone, worked, ornamented.

bed-stock, the outer side of a bed, that farther from the wall.

bedyls, beadles, under-bailiffs, summoners.

beeds, (that beeds) string of beads.

beerly, **buirdly**, (bride) large and well made; stately; (cheer) great. See **bierly**.

beet, kindle, keep up. *p. p.* **bett**.

beette, *pret.* of **beat**.

beforne, before. 116, 15, before (morning).

beft, beat, beaten.

begane, **bigane**, overlaid, covered.

begeck, **begack**, give a, play a trick on, make a fool of. (A. S. *géac*, cuckoo, simpleton.)

begule, beguile.

behad, behold.

behear, hear.

behote, *pres.*, promise. thou behotë, didst promise.

beliue, **belyfe**, **b(e)lyue**, soon, immediately.

belle, bere the, stand foremost, take the lead.

bell-groat, groat for ringing bell.

belly-, **billie-blind.** See **Billie Blin.**

belted plaids, "properly twelve yards of tartan cloth worn round the waist, obliquely across the breast and left shoulder, and partly depending backwards, ut in bello gestatur."

belyfe, straightway. See **beliue**.

belyue. See **beliue**.

ben : good ben be here, God's (or good) benison (?). Probably corrupt.

ben, towards the inner apartment or parlor of the house, in, within.

benbow, **bende bowe**, bent bow, bow, simply, the bow being frequently not in actual use.

bend, where the way turned (?).

bended, bounded.

bent the way, took her course over.

bent, a coarse, reedy grass.

bent, **bents**, field, fields covered with bent grass.

ber, *pret.* of **bear**.

bern, **barn**, bairn (A. S. *bearn*), child.

berne (A. S. *beorn*, fighting man, brave, etc.), man.

be's, (it be 's) shall be.

bescro, beshrew, curse.

beside, in addition to.

bespeak : *pret.* bespa(c)ke, bespoke, bespake him, spake.

bespoke. See **well-bespoke**.

bestand, help, avail.

bested, **bestead**, circumstanced. ferre and frembde bested, in the position of one from a distance and a stranger.

bet, but.

bet, boot.

betaken, made over.

bete, better, second, relieve.

betook, took (simply).

bett, *pret.* of **beet**, kindle.

better (he rade and better rade), longer, farther still.

beuk, book.

bide, **byde**, stay. bide (a doulfou day), await, look for. bide it whoso may, await the result (?).

bidene, **bydene**, **bydeene**, successively, one after another; together; simultaneously, or *en masse*.

biek, bask.

bier, cry, lamentation.

bierly, **beerly** (bride), portly, stately. See **buirdly**.

big, **bigg**, build. *p. p.* buggin, bugn.

biggeall, beguile.

bigging, **biggin**, building, house, "properly of a large size, as opposed to a cottage."

bigly (Icelandic, *byggiligr*, habitable), commodious, pleasant to live in, frequent epithet of bower. of a bier : handsomely wrought.

bill, a paper. sworne into my bill, sworn in writing.

bill, bull.

billaments, habiliments (of head-gear).

billie, **billy**, comrade, brother; "a term expressive of affection and familiarity." See **bully**.

Billie Blin, **Bellie Blind**, a serviceable household demon.

binna, be not.

bird (burd), maid, lady.

birk, birch.

birl, **berl**, drink, ply with drink.

birnande, burning.

birtled, cut up.

bit, but. bit and, and also.

bitaihte, committed to.

bitten, taken in, cheated.

blabring, babbling.

bla 'd, bla it, blow it.

blaewort, corn bluebottle.

blan, **blane**, **blanne**, *pret.* of blin, stop, cease.

blate, dumfoundered, abashed, silly.

blaw, blow. *pret.* blow, *pres. p.* blawn (blawing).

blee, color, complexion.

bleed, blood.

bleeze, blaze.

blin, blind.

blin, **blyn**, **blinne** (belin), cease, stop. *pret.* blan.

blink, *n.*, look, glance. of the moon, gleam.

blink, to look; glance, emit, throw a glance, shine, glitter. blinkin ee, shining, twinkling. wha is this that blinks in Willie's ee? sends brightness into, whose brightness is reflected from.

blint, blinded.

bliss, bless.

block, exchange, bargain. lost the better block, had the worse in a bargain or dealing.

blood, **blude**, man (disrespectfully), fellow.

blow, *pret.*, blew.

blowe, blossom.

blowe (wynde), give vent to.

blowe (boste), give breath to, utter.

blude, bluid, blood. See blood.

blue, blew.

bluid is gude, good to dream of.

blume, bloom.

blutter, dirty.

blyue, belyfe, beliue, quickly, immediately.

board-floor, 144, 5, 6: should probably be bower-floor, as in 142, 6, 9.

bocht, bought.

bocking, vomiting, belching.

boddom, bottom.

bode, n., offer.

bode, p. p., bidden, invited.

bode-words, messages.

body: faith, faikine, of my body, truth of my body, either by my personal faith, or, by my body.

bokin, bodkin.

bold, bauld (of fire), sharp, brisk.

boldly (understand), freely, confidently, fully (verbiage).

bolts, rods, bars (to make a petticoat stand out).

bon, bone, boune, on the way, going. See boun.

bone, boon.

bone. See royal-bone.

bonie, bony, bonnie.

bonnetie, dimin. of bonnet.

boor, bore.

booting, making of boot or booty.

born alive: 'That I love best that's born alive,' i. e. of all that are born.

borough-town, borrow's toun, borrous-toun, etc. See borrows-town.

borowe, borrow, n., security, sponsor, vindicator.

borowe, borrow, v., set free, deliver, ransom.

borowehode, securityship.

borrows-town, borrous-toun, borough-town, borough, corporate town.

boskyd, busked, made ready. See busk.

bot, but. bot and : see but and.

bot, without. See but.

bote, boote, boot, help, use, advantage.

both, be (old plural).

bottle: be my bottle, 624, 1, hold my own, bear my full part, in drinking (?). Probably corrupt.

bottys, butts.

bouk, trunk, body.

boun, bowne, bune, bound, bownd, bowynd, bounded, v., make ready, go. bounded, set out, went. bound him to his brand, went, betook himself. was boon, boun, bound, going, on the way. how she is bune, going on.

boun, bon, bowne, bowen, bowyn, adj. (búinn, p. p. of Icelandic búa, to make ready): bound, ready. See boun, v.

bountieth, bounty, alms.

bourde, v., jest.

boustrouslie, boisterously, roughly.

bouted, bolted.

bow, bough.

bower, chamber.

bower, house, home. Often indistinguishable from the above.

bower-yett, house-gate.

bowne, bownd, bowyn. See boun.

boyt, both.

bra, braw, brave, fine, handsome. See braw.

bracken, braken, brachan, breckin, breaken, breckan, brecken, breachan, fern, brake.

brae, bra, bray, hillside, hill, river-bank. "Conjoined with a name, it denotes the upper part of a country, as the Braes of Angus." Jamieson.

brae, brow.

braid, breadth. Adj., broad.

braid (broad) letter, either a letter on a broad sheet or a long letter.

brain, mad.

brake, break, cause to break off, correct, cure.

braken, fern. See bracken.

branded (bull), of a brindled reddish brown color.

brank, n., caper, prance, gallop.

branken, branking, galloping.

branks, a sort of bridle; a halter with two pieces of wood, instead of a leathern strap or a cord, over the nose, the whole resembling a muzzle.

brash, sickness.

brast, burst, broke, broken.

brauches, brooches. But perhaps branches, the clothes embroidered with rings and sprigs.

braw, fine, handsome, finely dressed; (of a meeting) pleasant. See bra and braws.

brawn, calf of the leg.

bray, brae, hillside, hill.

brayde, breyde: at a brayde, in a moment, of a sudden.

breachan. See bracken.

bread, breadth.

bread, broad.

break, brake, cause to break off, correct, cure.

break, (till five minutes break) expire.

breaken. See bracken.

breast, in a, in one voice; in a breast (Scottish), sometimes, abreast, side by side.

breast, v.: breast a steed, mount, by bringing the breast to it.

breastplate, some part of a woman's attire, said here to be of steel instead of gold. Possibly a stomacher. "Curet, breastplate, or stomager." Huloet, 1552. "Torace, also a placket, a stomacher, or brest plate for the body." Florio.

breathed, 110, unto, 21, on, 22: does not seem to be the right word. Possibly breved, gave information to (but the word is antique for the text, and on in 22 would not suit).

brecham, a straw collar for a horse, also a packsaddle made of straw, so more probably here, carts not being used.

brechan, brichan, (Gael. breacan) plaid.

breckan, -en, -in. See bracken.

brede, 41, 7, to have the whims attributed to breeding women. Perhaps a corruption for wede, go mad.

bree, brie, brow, eyebrow.

bree, broth. See broo.

breek-thigh, thigh of his breeches.

breeme, fierce.

breist. See breast.

bren, brenn, brenne, burn. *p. p.* brent.

brent (brow), high and straight. Also, smooth, unwrinkled.

brest. See breast.

brest, burst.

brether, bretheren, brethern, bretherne, brothren, brethen, brothers, brethren.

bretther o degs: with a b. of d. ye 'll clear up my nags (the reading may be *bretlher . . . clean*): corrupt. " brathay an degs would mean with old cloth and torn rags: brathay (obsolete) worn out brats or clothes." W. Forbes.

breyde, n.: with abreyde, with a rush, in haste.

breyde, v., rushed, bounded.

brid-stell, bride-stool, seat in church where the bridegroom and bride sat before the beginning of the service.

brie, brow. See bree.

bried, bride.

brig, bridge.

bright, bryghte, sheen, beautiful.

brim, In, fa oure the brim, the brim of a precipice may be meant.

bring hame, give birth to.

brither, brother.

broad (brode arrow, brod arwe (aro)), an arrow with a forked or barbed head.

broad letter. See braid letter.

broad sow, a sow that has a litter (brod=breed).

brodinge, shooting up, sprouting.

broke, brook, enjoy.

broked cow, a cow that has black spots or streaks mixed with white in her face.

broken, bankrupt, ruined.

broken men, men under sentence of outlawry, or who lived as vagabonds and public depredators, or were separated from their clans in consequence of crimes. Jamieson.

broo, brue, bree, brie, brow.

broo, water in which something has been boiled.

brook, broke, bruik, enjoy.

broom-cow, branch of broom.

brough, borough, town.

brought hame. See bring hame.

brow3t, browt, browthe, brought.

browne sword, possibly, gleaming ; or artificially browned to prevent rust.

browst, brewage.

browt, browthe, brought.

bruik, enjoy, possess. See brook.

brume, broom.

brunt, burnt.

brusten, burst.

bryde, young woman.

bryk, breeches, hose.

bryng yow on your way, take, accompany.

brytlyng, bryttlynge, (breaking) cutting up.

bucht, bught, bought, n., a small pen, usually put up in the corner of the field, into which it was customary to drive the ewes when they were to be milked. Jamieson.

bugge, buy.

buggin, bugn, p. p. of big, build.

buik, buke, book.

buik, pret. of bake.

builded, *pret.*, sheltered, hid. (A. S. byldan, Scot. bield.)

buirdly, buirlie, beerly, bierly (bride), portly, stately, large and well made.

buke, buik, book.

buld, build, built.

bully, billy, brother, fellow, mate. See billie.

bullyship, comradeship.

burd, bird, damsel, maid, lady.

burd-alone, solitary, by himself.

burlow-beanie, Billy Blin, which see.

burn, brook.

burn-brae, hillside with a brook at the bottom.

burnyssht, shining, made bright.

busk, buss, 1. make ready. 2. dress, deck. 3. betake oneself, go.

buske, bush.

busker : corrupt ; *testament* in other copies.

buss, bush.

busshement, ambuscade.

but, *prep.*, without.

but, towards the outer apartment or kitchen, without, out. but it speaks, 621, 6, perhaps a corruption for *out*.

but and, bot and, but an, bat an, and also.

by, be, bay, about, concerning (as, by a knight I say my song) ; in comparison with, on comparing. kend thy friend by thy foe, in distinction from. by than, by the time that. by yere, distributively, a year. do them by, do without. ca'd by Andrew Lammie, called by the name of.

by and by, directly, immediately.

by, aby, pay for, atone for.

byckarte, *pret.* of bicker, attacked (the deer).

byd, must, am under necessity.

byddys, abides.

byde, wait.

bydene. See bidene.

bye fell, a rocky hill or piece of high land lying off or aside of the way.

bygane, gone by.

byre, cow-house.

bystode : hard bystode, hard pressed.

C

ca, caw, call, drive, strike.

ca'd by, called by the name of.

caddie. See cadie.

cadger, cauger, an itinerant huckster.

cadie, caddie, a young fellow who does errands, or any inferior kind of work.

cakers. See cawker.

call, cold.

call, v., address.

cam, *pret.* of come.

cammer, cambric.

camovine, camomile.

camric, cambric.

can, knows.

can, cann, auxiliary of the past tense, did. (Probably a corruption of gan.) cold, colde, could, cowde, did. cold be, were, was. cold see, saw, have seen. (An extension of the use of can, gan.)

cankerdly, crossly.

cankred, ill-humored, complaining, crabbed ; or possibly, crooked.

cannas, cannis, canies, canvas, coarse cloth.

cannel, candle.

canny, *adj.*, gentle, safe, cautious, clever, expert.

canny, cannie, cannilie, *adv.*, cautiously, attentively, carefully, expertly, gently, slowly, softly.

cantie, canty, merry.

capull-hyde, horse-hide.

care, car, cart.

care, *v.*, mind, object.

care-bed, almost, or quite, sick-bed.

carefull, full of care, sorrowful.

carket, carknet, necklace.

carl, carle, carel, carril, cerl, fellow, man of low condition, peasant.

carlin, carline, old woman ; of a wealthy woman, low-born woman, peasant woman.

carlish, churlish, uncivilized.

carnal, crow.

carp, carpe, talk. In, harp and (or) carp, carp seems to mean tell tales, probably sing or chant tales (ballads) to the harp.

carping, talk, tale.

carrlis, careless.

case : in case that, against the chance that, lest.

casey, cassie, causeway.

cast, *n.*, venture.

cast : *pret.*, coost, koost, cust, cuist, keist, kiest, kyst, kest. *p. p.* casten, castin, coosten, custan, caisten.

cast, project, intend. cast on sleepe, thrown into a sleep, fallen asleep.

casten, castin, *p. p.* of cast.

cauger. See cadger.

cavil, lot.

caw, cawd. See ca'.

cawker, calkin, the turned-down part of a horseshoe.

cawte, wary.

cerl. See carl.

cerstyn, Christian.

certyl, kirtle (man's garment).

césererá, intended for an imitation of the sound of bells.

chaffare, ware, merchandise.

chafts, chaps, jaws.

chalmer, chamer, chaumer, chamber.

chamber (thy words), restrain, suppress, be chary of.

channerin, fretting, petulant.

chap, knock, rap, tap.

chaperine, 169, 10, would make some sense as chapel, but the form is unaccountable except as a popular diminutive.

chartre of peace, grant of pardon, paper condoning past offences.

chase, follow up, hunt down. chase the wine, follow, keep up, like *follow strong drink.*

chaunter, 92, 6, usually, tube of the bagpipe, which would not be expected here. A book of chants would suit.

chays, hunting-ground.

chear. See chere.

chear, well to, have good cheer at.

cheepe. See chepe.

cheeped, chipped, broken.

chepe, cheepe, *n.*, bargain. better chepe, more cheaply. gret chepe ! great bargain !

chepe, *v.*, cheapen, bargain for, or buy.

chere, cheer, cheir, chier, chear, face, countenance, state of mind, bearing, behavior ; entertainment, repast.

cherish, *v.*, cheer.

chess, jess, strap ; properly, leather strap for a hawk's leg.

chess, chiss of farie, corrupt ; read, cheese o Fyvie.

cheue, *v.*, end.

cheverons, gloves.

cheys, choose.

child, chiel, chil, cheel, child, young fellow ; as an appellation. *pl.* chylderin.

childer, children.

chimly, chimney.

chin, chappit at the chin, gin, that is, pin. See gin, pin.

chine, chin.

chiss, chess, cheese.

chiven, play the, 310, 8 : "run away precipitately," Nares ; chiven, chivin, chub, or any shy fish. Cf. chivie, fearful.

choised, chosen.

chossen, *p. p.*, chosen.

christendom, christendame, christendoun. christening.

christentie, cristendie, christendom.

chrystall, rock-crystal, a variety of quartz.

church-style, the gate of the enclosure round a church.

chylderin. See child.

clade, clead, cleed, clad.

claes, claise, clothes.

claiding, cleadin, etc., clothing.

claith, garment.

clam, *pret.* of climb.

clap, pat, fondle, embrace.

clarry, claret.

clead, cleed, cleid, clied, clothe. *pret.* cled. *p. p.* clead.

cleadin, cleeding, cleiding, clieden, cliding, *n.*, clothing.

cleare, bright.

cleathe, clothe.

clecked, clekit, *pret.*, *p. p.*, hatched.

cleek, *n.* and *v.*, hook.

clef, *pret.* of cleave.

cleffe, cleave.

cleiding, clieden, clothing. See cleadin.

cleugh, clough, a hollow between steep banks, narrow glen or valley, high rocky bank.

clied. See clead.

clifting, clift, cleft, fissure.

clintin, crevice, fissure.

cloathe, garment.

clock, limper, hobbler.

clocken-hen, sitting hen.

Clootie, a name for the devil, from cloot, the half-hoof of a cloven-footed beast.

close, closs, enclosure, yard, and, before a house, courtyard. close parler, 435, 22 : securely enclosed, or fastened (?) 23 ; you are in close : one (not trustworthy) transcript has *to chose*, which would make easier sense. Saint Evron's closs, cloister (?)

closs. See close.

cloth and fee, clothing and wage. holde with cloth and fee, retained by presents of clothes and money.

clout-leather, clouting-leather, leather for mending, patching.

clouty, patched.

clunkers, clunkerts, clots of dirt.

clutt, clouted.

co, quo, quoth.

coad. See cod.

coate-armor, surcoat or tabard, embroidered with armorial bearings, worn over the armor as a personal distinction, and for identification, the face being concealed.

coble, boat (yawl, flat-bottomed boat).

cockward, old cock, fool.

cod, coad, pillow.

coffer, trunk or box, for clothes and valuables.

coft, bought.

cog, coug, boat, vessel.

coif, quoif, cap.

coil (of hay), cock.

cold, could, coud, understood.

cold, could, coud, did. See can.

cole, cowl, monk's hood, also frock, which last is intended here, for the king wears a broad hat and puts on a green garment when he casts off his cowl.

coled (high coled). See colld.

coll, cold.

collaine, collayne, collen, of Cologne steel.

colld, coled, cut, shaped, fashioned.

collen, of Cologne. See collaine.

com, come, *pret.* of come.

comd, *pret.* and *p. p.* of come.

come, *pret.* cam, com, come, coom, comd. *pret. pl.* come. *ptc. pres.* coomin. *p. p.* comen, commen, coom, comd.

come by (life), get, obtain, gain.

comen, commen, *p. p.* of come.

comfort, *p. p.* of comfort.

commaunded theym agayne : *come* has perhaps dropped out ; later editions, them to come.

compted, 277, 437, emendation for *commytted*.

comt, count.

comunye, communing.

comyn-bell, town bell.

conquess, conquer.

convay. See convoy.

conve, convoy, escort.

convenient, suitable.

convey. See convoy.

convoy, convay, *n.*, escort.

convoy, convey, *v.*, convey, escort, accompany part of the way homeward, or on a journey, see a friend off, a young woman home.

coot, queet, ankle.

cop, coppe, head.

corbie, raven.

cordain, cordevine, Cordovan leather.

cordin, cording, cord (and not whangs of leather).

cordiuant, *adj.*, of Spanish, Cordovan leather.

core, corrie, a hollow in a hill. Penman's Core, 634, 51, described as a hollow on the top of a high ridge of hills, might possibly be Penman score (score, a deep, narrow, ragged indentation on the side of a hill, South of Scotland).

coresed (hors), 261, 100, bodied (?) (later texts, coresse, corse).

corn, 125, 18, in Scotland, unground oats. (Here distinguished from white meal, which is usually oat-meal.)

corn-caugers, cadgers, hucksters, in corn.

corp, a vulgar singular of the supposed plural, corpse.

cors, curse.

corser, 269, 256, should probably be forser, coffer (text *g* has coffer).

cote of pie, corruption of courtepi, short cloak or gown.

couchd, lay, leaned.

coug, cog, boat.

could, did. See can.

councell, counsell, secret.

coup, cupe, cup.

courting, demonstration of affection, embracing.

courtrie, belonging to a court, courtiers.

couth, sound, word.

couent, convent.

cow, branch. See broom-cow, heather-cow, kow.

cowing, eating.

cowte, colt.

crabby (crabbed), provoking.

crack, crak, talk, brag. crackd (the Border-side), defied, challenged.

crack, crak, a moment of time.

crack fingers, in grief or perplexity

crak. See crack.

cramoisie, cramasie, crimson.

crap, crop, top.

crap, *pret.* of creep.

crawen, crawn, *p. p.* of craw, crow.

cray, cry.

creel, basket.

Cristiantë, Cristinty, Cristendie, Christendom.

croche, crouch.

croodlin, cooing.

cropped (knee), crooked.

cross, *v.*, oppose. *p. p.*, (the sheriff was) crost, balked.

crouse, crouselie, crously, briskly, merrily, jubilantly. See crowse.

crowen, *p. p.* of crow.

crowse, audacious. See crouse.

crowt, draw together, pucker up.

cruds, *n.*, curds.

cry, crye, proclaim, proclamation.

cry on, upo, call upon, summon. cryed out on Robyn Hode, cried out against, or, simply, cried out "R. H."

cryance, cowardice, faintheartedness (disposition to succumb).

cum, become.

cum, *pret.* of come.

cumand, *ptc.*, coming.

cumber, oppress, torment.

cumbruk, cambric.

cunnes: nones cunnes, of no kind. enes cunnes, of any kind.

cun thanke, am, feel, grateful.

curch, curche, kerchief, woman's head covering.

curn, quantity, parcel, pack.

curstlye, fiercely, savagely.

curst turne, malignant, spiteful, ferocious job, piece of work, feat.

curtal, having charge of, attached to, the vegetable garden of a monastery.

cust, pret. of cast.

custan, p. p. of cast.

cutted (friar), short-frocked (but apparently a corruption of curtal).

cutters, bravos, robbers.

D

'd (for 't), it.

dag-durk, dagger.

daggie, drizzling (dag, a slight rain).

daghter, daughter.

dail (dool), the grief, the ill consequences.

daily dight, beautifully adorned.

dale, dole.

damasee, damson plum.

dandoo, dun doe (?).

dane, done. dane him to, betaken himself. See do to.

dang, pret. of ding, beat, struck, knocked, thrust, shoved.

danger, (do danger) exercise of the power of a superior (?) ; violence (?).

dather, daughter.

daut, dawt, fondle, caress, make much of, pet.

daw, v., dawn. p. p. dawen.

dawtie, darling.

day, dayed, die, died.

dayly. See daily.

dea, die.

dead, deed, n., death.

deak, deck.

dean, done.

dearsome, costly.

dear vow, interjection of surprise or commiseration.

deas, pew (stone seat at the door of the church. Chambers). Same word as dais. See dice.

debate, quarrel.

deck-board, deck-buird, oer (over), overboard.

dee, do, be allowed, borne ; avail.

dee, deei, do.

dee, deei, die.

deed, death. See dead.

deed, indeed.

deed-thraw, death-throe.

deei, do, avail ; die.

deerlye (dight), expensively (ornamented).

deft, neat, nice-looking.

degree, rank, sort. served him in his ain degree, rendered him respect accordant with his rank. wee shall beare no degree, shall have no position, standing.

delit, delight.

demean, treat, maltreat ; treat as he deserves.

demed, judged.

den, small valley, glen, dingle.

den, done.

deputed, consigned, handed or delivered over (used of a fugitive carried back for trial).

dere, dear(e), injury.

dere-worthy, precious, dear.

derf (blowes), powerful.

dernë, secret, hidden, privy, obscure.

dey, dairy-woman.

deythe, dyth, dight, prepared.

di, do.

dice, deas, pew in a church.

did, 14, 3, used for should.

did him to. See do to.

did of. See do of.

die, do, din, dien, done.

dien. See den, die.

dight, dicht, dycht, deight, dyght, prepared. (dedys) dyght, done. dight (shoon), clean. dighted (wounds), dressed. (deerlye) dight, fitted out. dill was dight, grief was ordained.

dight, adv. : bird sang fu dight, readily, freely (strange use of the word).

dill, dule, grief.

din, dien, done.

dine, dinner, meal.

ding, beat, knock. ding down, lay low, overthrow. pret. dang, dung. p. p. dung, dang.

dinna, do not.

dinne, (noise), ado, trouble.

dis, does.

discreeue, 115, 3, should be disceuere, diskevere, discover, reveal.

disers, desires.

disgrate, unfortunate, out of fortune's favor.

disna, does not.

dip, deep.

dive, do.

diuel's mouth. He could not finde a priuy place, for all lay in the diuel's mouth, 239, 4 : as the devil's mouth is depicted wide open in painted windows, etc., Professor Skeat has suggested that meaning for the phrase.

do. See doo.

do, doe (mee thy hawkes), give, deliver.

do adowne, put down.

do away, have done with, stop.

do gladly, make yourself happy.

do (doe) of, off, put off.

do on, put on, don.

do to, do till, with reflexive pronoun, betake.

dois, does.

doited, stupid, doting.

döl, dule, grief.

don, down.

done upon, put on.

doo, dou, dow, dove.

dool, doll, dule, grief. See dail.

dorn, (sheets of) dornic, table-linen, ordinarily, from Dornick, the Dutch name for Tournay.

dou, dove. See doo.

dou, dow, can (of physical ability). (with negative) am unable from aversion, want of resolution, etc. dought, pret., was able, could.

he neere dought good day, 90, 32, he never was good for anything a good day. But we should expect *him* : never a good day profited him.

double-horsed, with horse carrying double.

doubt, doute, dout, *n.* and *v.*, fear.

douce, staid and sober.

douë, douey, dowie, dreary, melancholy.

doughetë, doughty man.

dought. See **dou.**

doulfou, doleful.

dounae. See **dou.**

dout, doute. See **doubt.**

dow, dou, doo, dove.

dow, do.

dow, downa, *v.* See **dou.**

dowie, dowy, sad, doleful, melancholy, wretched.

downcome of Robin Hood, with the, 377, 30, knocked down in R. Hood's fashion (?).

doyn, done.

doyt, doth (plural).

draff, refuse, dirt.

draps, drops.

draw, move.

draw till, draw on.

draw up wi, take up with, enter into intimacy, relations of love, with.

dray, dry.

dreaded, suspected.

drede, *n.*, doubt.

dre(e), dri, drie, drye, suffer, undergo, hold out, stand, be able. **drie to feel**, be compelled, come to feel.

dreel, gie a, stir up, put into a flurry, make scud.

dri. See **dree.**

drie, dri. See **dree.**

driep, drop.

drifts, droves.

droop and drowsie (of blood), 515, 13 : droop might be the Old English *drup*, sad, piteous, but a word indicating the quality or condition of the blood would be expected (as in German *trübe*, thick, muddy). The nearest is *drubly*, turbid, muddy. See **drousie.**

droped, drooped.

drousie : droop and drowsie, 515, 13, sluggish, perhaps slowly dripping.

drowsie. See **drousie.**

druken, drucken, *p. p.*, drunk, imbibed.

drumlie, -ly, perturbed, gloomy.

drunken, *p. p.* of drink. **drunken was**, had drunken.

drunkilie, 465, 25, merrily (as being tipsy with pleasure ?).

drussie, drowsy.

drye. See **dree.**

drywyng, driving.

dub, pool.

dubby, dirty, having many small pools.

duck, douk, dive.

duckers, doukers, divers.

du3ty, doughty, valiant.

dule, dool, grief.

dumpes, dumps, in the modern sense, but not inelegant.

dune out, worn out, used up.

dung, *pret.* of ding, beat, knock, strike. *p. p.*, beaten, worsted, overpowered, put down. **dung over**, knocked over.

dwine, pine, waste.

dyde adowne, put down.

dyd him to, betook himself.

dyght, (dedes that here be dyght) prepared, concerted.

dyght (to the deth), done, brought.

dyghtande, making ready (but seems to be intended for a past participle).

dyke, wall.

dyke, ditch.

dyne : garre me ones to dyne, give me my dinner, my fill, beat thoroughly.

dynt(e), dint, stroke, hit, lunge, shot (of spear, arrow).

dysheryte, dispossessed.

dyspyse, cause to be despised.

E

e, ae, only.

eaght, the, the eighth.

ean, eyes. See **ee.**

ear, eer, ever.

eare, ere, ayre, heir.

eare, *v.*, plough.

eased (of horses), cared for, attended to.

eather, other.

ee, eye. *Pl.* een, eeen. See **ean, eyen.**

ee (of a cup), may be eye, top, brim.

ee-bree, eyebrow.

een, one.

een, even.

eerie, eiry, weird, exciting superstitious dread.

eftsones, hereafter, another time.

eie, awe.

eight, eighth.

eihte, possession, valuable thing.

eild, age.

eiry. See **eerie.**

eke, also.

eke a, each (one).

eldern, eldren, eldrin, old.

eldrige, elridge (hill, king), elvish.

element, air, sky.

elephant, a species of scabious is so called, according to Halliwell.

Elfan, fairy-land.

elfin, elphin, elphan, *n.* and *adj.*, elf, elvish.

Elfins, the, fairy-land.

elflyn, of the elves.

Elizium, Elysian.

ell, ill, ull, *v.*, will.

elphan, elphin, *n.* and *adj.* See **elfin.**

eme, uncle. **emys**, uncle's.

end, en, end.

eneuch, enew, enough.

enter plea att my iollye, 380, 32, unintelligible: iollye should probably be iollytë. The king will have the head to serve some inscrutable purpose when he is making merry.

enterprise, *v.*, undertake.

entertain, take into service.

envye, ill-will, hostility, spite.

ere, eare, ayre, *n.*, heir.

ere, *v.*, heir.

ere, till.
ermeline, ermine.
esk, newt.
even cloth, smooth, with the nap well shorn.
even down, flat to the ground.
euery syde, each side of.
euerych, euerichone, euerechone, euerilkon, everlke ane, each, each one.
euyn, evening.
evyll, *adv.*, ill. euyll go, ill walk.
ew-bught. See bucht.
examine, put you to test.
eyen, eyn, eyne, eyes.
eylde het the, yield, requite thee for it.
eylyt, aileth.
eyre, *pl.*, years.

F

f, in northern Scotch, often for wh; as, *fa, faa,* who; *fan,* when; *far, faer,* where.
fa, fae, from.
fa, fall.
face, with a, with effrontery, boldness.
fache, fetch.
fact, offence, crime.
fadge: fat fadge, a lusty and clumsy woman.
fae, fay, fey, fee, fie, destined to die.
fae, frae, from.
faein, faen, fawn, fallen.
faem, fame, foam, sea.
faikine, faith.
fail, feall, fell, turf.
fain(e), fayn(e), glad, pleased, eager. for faine, for glad, for gladness.
fainly, joyfully, blithely.
fair, far.
fairlie, farlie, ferlie, wonder.
fait, faitt, fett, white.
faith and troth, to be, to be in the relation of men who have taken the engagement of mutual fidelity, sworn-brethren.
fald, fall, fauld, *n.*, fold.
fall, suit, become. well falls me, my luck is good.
fallow's deed, 93, 7-10, deed of a bad fellow seems unlikely. Possibly felloun's, or farlie, strange.
falsh, false.
falyf, fallow.
fame, faem, foam, sea.
fa'n, fallen.
fan, when.
fand, found.
fang, fastening. Perhaps North Scotch for whang.
far, fair.
fare, go. I fare you well, I bid you fare well. *pret.*, foor. *p. p.*, forn.
fare, go on, comport oneself.
fare, *n.*, going on, procedure. (in the modern sense) fortune, experience.
fared, favored. well-fared, well-(weel-)fard, weel-fart, well-(weel-)faird, weil-faurit, weill-(weel-)faurd, well-fard, well-favored, handsome.

farer, further.
farest, fairest.
farlies, farleys, ferlies, wonders, novelties.
far sought, was, required long to reach.
fas, false.
fa's, fall, 1st per. sing. pres.
fash, *n.* and *v.*, trouble.
fast, strenuously, intently, (weep) copiously. fast unto, close down to.
fat, fatt, what.
fate they could na fa, from it (fae it, frae it) they could not desist.
faun, fallen.
faund, found.
faurit, faurd. See fared.
fause, false.
fause fa thee, may treachery befall thee, be thy lot!
fave, five.
fawn, fallen.
fay, *adj.* See fae.
fay, faith.
fayne, glad, fond of, pleased with.
fe, feea, wage, etc. See fee.
feall. See fail.
fear, frighten.
fearder, feardest. See feart.
feare, in, together. See fere.
feart, feert, frightened. fearder, more frightened. feardest, most frightened.
feathern, feathers.
fecht, feght, *v.*, fight.
fedred, ifedred fre, feathered liberally, handsomely.
fee, fie, wealth, possessions, property, having, pay, wages, reward. gentylman of clothynge and of fee, entitled to a regular stipend. knightes fee, land of the value of £20 per annum (under Edward I, II). penny-fie, gift. See foster of the fe.
fee, *v.*, hire.
fee, fey, doomed. See fae.
feed, feid, feud.
feed, fode, fode, child, man.
feel, fell, very.
feere, fere, feire, feer, mate, consort (fere); fellow (contemptuously). See feires.
feert. See feart.
feght, fight. See fecht.
feid, feud. See feed.
feires, feiries, comrades, consorts. See feere.
felaushyp, abstract for concrete, our fellows.
felischepe, fellowship.
fell. See fail.
fell, high land, fit only for pastures, a wild hill.
fell (yard), severe, cutting; strange, prodigious; considerable.
fell, *v.*, kill.
fell, feel, very.
fells, befalls. well fells me, good for me!
felon (the kynggis), traitor, rebel.
fences: cock shall crow fences three, 100, 10, 11, evidently bouts, *coups;* but this usage has not been found elsewhere.
fend, *v.*, provision.
fend, defence.
fende, defend.

fer dayes, far on in the day.

ferd, fear.

ferder, farther.

fere (fere love), fair.

fere, feere, mate, consort.

fere, in, on, in company, together. See feare.

ferly, ferlie, ferley, farlie, marvel, wonder, news.

ferly, adj. (ferly strife), strange, extraordinary.

fesh, fess, fetch.

fet. See fett.

fett, fetch. pret., fet, fette.

fey, destined to death. See fae.

ffend : that ffend I Godys fforbod, 293, 72, seems to be a double expression for deprecation, — I inhibit, protest, God forbid (see forbode).

ff₂ttle, make ready.

ffeyt, faith.

ffooder, tun.

fforefend, avert, forbid.

ffarley, adj., strange.

ficht, fecht, feght, v., fight. pret., focht, foucht. p. p., foughten, feughten.

fie. See fee.

fie, doomed. See fae.

fieldert, fieldward, away (from where they were).

fill, full.

fill, follow, pursue.

filtt, p. p., filed.

fin, find.

finikin, fine, handsomely dressed.

firlot, the fourth part of a fou, which is a dry measure varying from two to six Winchester bushels (a Winchester bushel being of a slightly less capacity than the present imperial bushel).

fit, fitt, fyt, fytte, song, division of a song.

fit, foot, feet.

fit, ready.

fitches (of deer), flitches, sides.

fitt, foot.

fitted, footed.

fitted, ready, disposed.

fivesome, five together.

flattering (toung), fluttering, waggling.

flaugh, flaw, pret. of fly.

flaw, (tell me without a flaw) lie.

flay, frighten. See fley.

flay, fly. pret., flaw, flaugh.

flear, fleer, floor.

flee, fly.

fleed, flood.

fleer, floor.

fleet, flute.

fley, flay, frighten. pret., fleed, flied.

flice, fleece.

flinters, flinders, fragments.

flo, arrow.

flotterd, floated.

flow, moss with a spring in it, morass.

flud, flood.

focht, pret. of fecht, ficht, fight.

fode. See feed.

folde, pret., folded.

folle, foal.

fond : fond to see him sleep, 180, 26, doted, was foolishly happy (?). (But probably corrupt : E has, foudly seen thee sleep.)

food, man. See feed.

foote, goe two foote, 337, 6, corrupt for fold.

for, ffor, (ye, i. e. yes, for God, nay, for God), by.

for, where.

for no, phrase of refusal, obscurely elliptical, after the manner of why, no; or corruptly for fye, no.

forbode, forbott, ouer Goddes, God forbid, against God's prohibition. Elliptically, God's forbod ; see ffend.

forbye, forebye, near by. apart, aside.

forbye, forebye, forby, besides.

force, no, no matter.

forces : for a' her father's forces, 620, 11, in spite of all her father could do (?) .

forder, further.

fordoo, destroy.

forebye. See forbye.

forehammer, sledge-hammer, the large hammer, which strikes before the smaller.

foremost man, apparently the bridegroom's "best man."

forenent, fornent, over against, in the face of.

foret, forward.

forfaulted, forfeited.

forfoughen, tired out with fighting.

forgone, forgo.

foriete, forgotten.

forl, whorl, fly of a spinning-rock.

for-lee : she 'll come in att your formast an gee out att yer forlee, she 'll cross your bows and sail round you, coming out at your fore-lee or lee-bow.

forlorn, lost. (has him) forlorn, causatively, destroyed, killed ; destitute, deserted.

forren, foreign.

forsake, let go, part with, give up, renounce. forsake (that I haue promised), withdraw from. forsake this sorowe, decline to have to do with this sad matter.

forth, (in find forth, choose forth) out.

forthynketh, repenteth.

fortune be my chance, my hap it were.

forward, van.

foster of the fe, "a person who had for some service to the crown a perpetual right of hunting in a forest on paying to the crown a certain rent for the same." Halliwell.

fothe, foot.

fou. See firlot.

fou, how.

fou, fow, full, drunken.

foucht, pret., fought. p. p., foughten.

found, provided for.

foure-eared foole, as denoting a double ass (?).

fow, fou, full.

fowk, folk.

fra, free.

fraa, frae, fray, from. be frae, remain away from.

frame, succeed. sae weel we frame, we are doing, or beginning so well.

frayers, friars.

free, adj., is used in a great variety of senses,

and is often indefinite and hardly more than a rhyme word : bounteous, gracious, of noble birth or rank, independent, unrestricted, exempt, spirited, valorous, beautiful, precious, excellent in any way. The danger will be in assigning too positive a meaning to the word.

free, *adv.* : (arowes ifedred) fre, in handsome style.

freely, *adj.* : freely feed, of noble birth, or beautiful.

freke, freck, freake, freyke, bold man, man.

frem, foreign.

frembde, *adv.* : frembde bested, in the position of a stranger (other readings, frend, friend).

frese : frese your, our, bowes of ewe, 267, ₂₁₅ ; seems to be corrupt. The interpretation in Donaldson's Supplement to Jamieson, where " to frese a bow " (cited as if a phrase in full use) is said to mean unbend, slack, would be entirely inappropriate here, since three men are to make a desperate attack on two hundred and fifty (bende your bowes, st. ₂₁₈). **f g** have, bend we, the required sense. Chese will not do ; they have but one bow each. leese, loose is possible, or dress, or even, free.

frichtit, frighted.

frienged, fringed, gray, referring to mane and fetlocks, or perhaps to long fetlocks only.

frith, firthe, enclosed land, wood.

fue, few.

fue, full.

fule, fowl.

full, proud.

fun, fune, whun, whin, furze.

fur, furrow.

fute, whute, *v.*, whistle.

fynde, 395, ₂₄, Professor Skeat would read fyne, end.

fynly, goodly.

fyt, fytt, fytte. See fit.

G

ga, gaa, gaw, gall.

ga, gaa, go. See gang, gae.

ga, gaa, gave.

gabber reel, evidently a sprightly air. The root may be Icelandic *gabb*, mockery. Perhaps simply gabber, jabber.

gad, gaud, bar.

gae, gai, gay, ga, gaa, gee, gie, go. *pret.*, gaed, gade, gad, gaid, gied, gid, ged, good, gude. *p. p.*, gaen, gain, gane, gaed. *pres. p.*, gain, gan, gaen, gane, gaun, gawen, etc. See gang.

gae, *pret.* of gie, gave.

gae, gay, gey, *adv.*, (gay) pretty, rather.

gaed, gade, gad, gaid, *pret.* of gae, go.

gaed, *p. p.*, gone.

gaen, gain, gane, *p. p.* of gae, gone.

gaen, gain, *p. p.* of gie, give.

gaeng. See gang.

gai. See gae.

gaid. See gaed.

gain. See gaen.

gain, gaine, gaing, gan, gaen, gane, gaun, gawn, gawen, *pres. p.* of gae, ga, go.

gain (with ellipsis of will), serve, suffice. 205, ₁₅ : suit my case.

gaing. See gain, *pres. p.*

gair (of clothes). See gare.

gait, way, road. See gate.

Galiard, *sobriquet* of a freebooter of a gay (perhaps dissipated) character.

gallaly, galalie, galley, prolonged for metrical convenience.

gallows-pin. See pin.

gam, game.

gamon, amuse himself.

gan, gane. See gain, *pres. p.*

gan, gon, with infinitive, began, did.

gane, *p. p.* of gae, go.

gane, *p. p.* of gae, give.

gang, gange, gaeng, gieng, go, walk. *pret.*, yede, yeede, yeed, yed, ȝede, yode, yod, youd. *p. p.*, gaen, gain, gane, gaed, gade, gad, gaid, gude, good. *inf.* also, gon, gone. See gae.

gang, gae, go down : like the Scottish *be put down*, be hanged.

gantrees, barrel-stands.

gar, gaur, make do, cause.

garded, looked at.

gare, gair, gore, properly, a triangular piece of cloth inserted in a garment to give width at that part ; in Old English often coat or gown. low down by his (her) gare, is a frequently recurring expression which may be taken literally, down by that part of a garment where the gore would be, low by his knee. she hung 't (cup of wine) low down by her gare, 205, ₁₀ (recklessly and absurdly ; the cup is in her hand in the next stanza). In, frae my sark ye shear a gare, gare must be a strip large enough to make a bandage for the head.

ȝare, ready.

garl, gravel (suspicious word).

garlande, rose-garlonde, a circular wreath, apparently hung upon a wand or rod. In 280, ₃₁, this can be nothing more than an extemporized circlet of twigs.

garrett, watch-tower, look-out.

gars, garse, grass.

garthes, girths.

gast, guest.

gat, got.

gate, gait, get, way, road ; 457, ₁₁, ₁₅ (ford). water-gate, 468, ₁₂, round by the water. tuke the gate, started, departed.

gaud. See gad.

gaule, of the color of gall ; or gules, red.

gaun, gawn, gawen, going.

gaur, gar, make.

gaw. See ga.

gawen, gawn. See ga, and gaun.

gay. See gae.

gay, gae, gey, *adv.*, pretty, rather.

ge, ye.

ge, give. See gie.

gear, geare, geere, geir, gier, goods, property, often cattle ; fighting equipments ; business, affair ; (silken) gear, clothes.

geat. See get.

gecks, gien the, made a fool of.

gee, give. See gie.

gee, gie, *pret.*, gied, gid, ged. See gae.

geere. See gear.

geid, *pret.* of gie, give.

gein, *p. p.* of gie.

geir. See gear.

general, with the, people in general (in public).

genty, elegant of form or dress, but here refers to gentleness of disposition.

gereamarsey, gramercy.

gerss, grass.

gey, *adv.*, pretty, rather. See gay.

ghesting, guesting, lodging.

gie, go. See gae.

gie, gi, ge, gee, gae, geve, give. *pret.*, gae, ga, gaa, gaed, geed, geid, gied. *p. p.*, gin, gine, geen, gein, gien, gen, gane, gaen. gies over, is past.

gied, gid, ged, *pret.* of gae, gie, go.

gied, geed, geid, *pret.* of gie, give.

gien, gine, gin, gein, geen, gen, *p. p.* of gie, give. given (a blow) to.

gier. See gear.

gif, giff, if.

gill, a steep, narrow glen.

Gilliecrankie, a Gilliecrankie woman, a Highlander.

gillore, galore, in plenty.

gilt, money.

gimp, jimp, slender.

gin, gine, ginne, a contrivance, specially, the apparatus for fastening a door, the lever for raising the latch.

gin, (of time) against, towards, by the time that.

gin, *conj.*, if.

gin, gine, given.

gine, ginne, *n.* See gin.

girded out, guirded, cracked, let.

girdle, griddle.

girds, hoops.

girth was the gold-twist to be, 464, 16, girth should probably be graith, but admitting this, the sense is not clear, and further corruption may be suspected. We may understand, perhaps, that after the rescue the mare was to have a caparison of gilded chains. Or we may read, her graith was used the gold-twist to be.

gladdynge, gladdening.

glamer, glamour, glamourie, glaumry, a charm deluding the eye.

glashet, darted, flashed.

glasse, lantern, ship-light.

glaue, a cutting weapon fixed to the end of a pole.

glaumry. See glamer.

glazen, of glass.

glede, gleed(e), glowing coal, fire.

glee (glue), glove.

glent, glanced, went (perhaps, darted).

glister, shine.

gloamin, twilight, evening.

gloom, frown, morose look.

glove tee. See tee.

glue, glove.

go, goe, goo, gone, walk. goe vppon his death, pass upon the question of.

god, godde, property, goods.

God, often, the second person in the Trinity.

God a marsey, God amercy, God have mercy, gramercy, much thanks.

God's peny, an earnest-penny, to bind a bargain.

gogled, joggled, waggled.

golett of ʒe hode, throat, part covering the throat.

gon, gone, *inf.* of go.

gone, *subj.* of gon, go.

good, *pret.* of go.

Good-ben, 375, 10. If *ben* is to stand, it must be *benison* abridged. Good benison be here, quoth he, makes a satisfactory line.

good-brother, brother-in-law.

good b'w'ye, God be wi you, good-bye.

goodman, master of a house.

good-mother, mother-in-law.

good-son, son-in-law.

goodwife, mistress of a house, housewife.

gorgett, defence for the neck, here a part of a jack.

gorgett, a neckerchief.

gorney, journey.

goud, gowd, *n.* and *adj.*, gold.

gouden, gowden, golden.

gouernor, director, guardian.

gould, gold.

gowans, daisies.

gowany, covered with daisies.

gowd. See goud.

gowk, cuckoo, fool.

goy, joy.

graid, great.

grain, fork or branch of a tree.

grait, great.

graith, *v.*, make ready. *p. p.*, graithed, equipped in defensive armor. gowden-graithd before and siller-shod behind, 200, 4, properly, harnessed, but as the horse is silver-shod before and gold behind, shod seems to be meant here.

graithing (gowd), harness or caparison, behind horse. But see graith, *v.*

grammarye, grammeree, grammar, learning. 113, 36, 41, magic.

grat, *pret.* of greet, weep.

grat(e), great.

graveld green, 142, 1, a green with gravel walks (?) Probably corrupt.

greaf, grave.

greahondes, grehoundis, greyhounds.

grece, a fat hart.

gree: made the gree, paid my dues.

gree, prize, superiority.

greeme, (groom) young fellow. See grome.

greet, greit, weep, cry. *pret.*, grat.

greete, grit, gravel, sand.

greeting, weeping.

grefe, offence, displeasure. a-grefe, in displeasure.

grehoundis, greyhounds.

greit, greet, weep, cry.

gret, *pret.* of greet, address.

grett wurdes, high, haughty words.

grevis, groves. See grief.

grew, grow.

grew hound, grew(e)hund, Dr. J. A. H. Murray says Greek hound; "still called in Scotland a grewe, which was the older Scotch for Greek." Grew, Greek, is well known in Middle English, and *greyhound* (Icelandic greyhundr) may have been changed to *grewhound* under its influence.

grey (meal), barley-(bere-)meal, as distinguished from oat-meal (white meal).

griesly, grizly, frightful.

grievd, *pret.*, injured.

grimlie, grimly, grim, terrible.

grind, an apparent corruption for *graith, graithed*, accoutre, adorn.

grisel, grissell, gray horse.

grit, grite, gryte, great.

grith, (peace) remission of hostility, "charter of peace."

grizly, frightful.

grome, groom, greem, man, young fellow.

gross, big, burly.

ground, (the grounds o my pouches) bottom.

growende, growynd, ground.

grue, grew.

grumly, (of a seal) fierce-looking.

grun, ground.

gryming, sprinkling, thin covering.

grype, griffon (also vulture).

grysely, frightfully.

gude, guid, gueed(e), good.

gudemother, mother-in-law.

gudeson, stepson, son-in-law.

guid, good.

guide, gyde, *n.*, one who has charge, etc., custodian, escort, convoy. this sword shall be thy guide, shall settle thy case.

guide, *v.*, treat, use.

guilt, all of gilt, of gilding or gilt metal, all begilt.

gull, a fool.

gunies, guineas.

gurious (same as gruous, grugous), grim, grisly (or, ugly).

gurly, (sea) grim, surly, growling.

gyde, be þe munkis, take charge of the monk. See guide.

gyff, gif, if.

gyll, 238, 4, opprobrious term for woman, here referring to levity.

gyrde, *pret.*, girt.

gyst, gettest.

ȝare, ready.

ȝates, ȝatis, gates.

ȝe, yea.

ȝede, went.

ȝelpe, brag.

ȝeman, ȝoman, yeoman.

ȝete, ate.

ȝeue, give. ȝouyn, given.

ȝone, yon.

H

ha, hae, hay, have. See haet.

ha, haa, hall, house, manor-house.

hachebord, hatchbord, 409, 36, 411, 70, would most naturally be interpreted gunwale, or side of the ship, and so archborde, 408, 23. But in 36 Sir Andrew lies at the hache-bord (which is hached with gold), and stern would be a better meaning for hachebord in that place, the high stern of the old ship being a conspicuous place for a captain to lie. See archborde.

hached: the hache-bord is hached with gold, gilt (possibly inlaid).

haches, deck; properly a frame of crossbars laid over an opening in a ship's deck.

had, haad, hold. See haud.

hadden, *p. p.*, held.

hadno, had not.

hae, have. See ha.

haely. See haly.

haet, hayt, hath.

ha-house, manor-house.

haik ye up, keep you in suspense, "bear in hand," delude with false hopes (?).

hail. See hale.

hailing, denoting rapid motion, driving, rushing. See halling.

hailing at the ba', playing foot-ball. Hail the ba is, specifically, drive the ball to or beyond goal.

haill. See hale.

hair, hire.

halch, halch vpon, salute, bestow a salutation on.

hald. See hauld, hold.

hale, haill, hail, haylle, hell, whole, in sound condition; wholly.

halfendell, the half part.

halke, corner, hiding-place.

hall, house, manor-house. See ha.

hall, (either in archbord or in hall, he wold ouercome you, 409, 29) hull (?).

hall, hold.

halld. See hauld.

halled, hailed, saluted.

halling, come halling to the town. See hailing.

hallow, holy.

Hallowday, saints' day, All Saints.

hallow-seat, saint's place.

hals-bane, hass-bane, hause-bane, hase-bane, neck-bone.

haly, haely, hallow, holy.

halyde, hauled.

hame, bring hame, bear a child. See bring.

hand, att hand of, nearly, about.

hand for hand, in a fair match?

hand, lokyde at his hand, probably, shading his eyes with his hand; possibly, looked aside.

hand, on the upper side, uppermost.

hand, out of, 440, 25 : forthwith (?). The line seems to be corrupted; without resource, unable to help themselves, *hors de combat*, would give an easier sense if allowable. Should we read : as many as was, out of hand?

hang, *pret.* of hing, to hang.

hanging well, draw-well of which the bucket is raised and lowered by a pole or beam turning on an upright post (?). By some understood as, a well near the place of execution.

hankit, tied tight.

hansell : haffe hansell for the mare, 291, 32 : have a present, the more you buy (?) ; have the first purchase (which was thought lucky) for the larger part of the ware) (?). (Doubtful.) 383, 10 : reward.

hap, happing, cover, coverlet.

hap, v., cover, wrap.

happer, hopper.

happing. See hap.

harbengers, harbingers, officers who preceded the king in a progress to provide accommodation for the court.

harnessed (men), equipped.

harried, haryed, pret. and p. p., plundered.

harte of gre(e)ce, a fat hart.

hart-roote, term of affection.

has, hase, halls.

hase, hass, neck, throat. See hause.

hase-bane, hass-bane. See hause-bane.

hastëly, hastilye, immediately, soon, promptly.

hat, pret. of hit.

haud, had, hawd, howd, hold, keep. p. p., hadden.

haugh, low ground, properly on the border of a river.

hauld, hald, halld, hall, hold, place of shelter, stronghold, quarters. See hold.

hauld, gang by the, walk by taking hold of things.

hause, hase, hass, neck, throat.

hause-bane, hase-bane, hass-bane, hals-bane, neck-bone.

have in, had him in, had him in my possession.

hawd. See haud.

hay, for hae, has.

hay, went forth to view the hay, to see how the hay was coming on, as a way of taking the air.

haylle, whole, entire. See hale.

hayt, hath.

he, they.

he, hee, high.

header, heather.

heal, healle, hail, conceal.

healy, hooly, adj., gentle.

healy, heely, hooly, slowly, gently.

heans, hens.

hear, here.

heathen (child), unbaptized.

heathennest, heathendom.

heavë, heavy.

hee. See he.

heely, slowly. See healy.

heght, promised.

heihte, hight, hette, was, is, called.

heir, heire. See hear.

hele, heal, conceal.

hell, whole, staunch, tight. See hale.

hell, heel.

hend, hendë, heynd, hind, hindy, noble, gracious ; friendly, kindly ; civil. See hind.

hende, hind, young fellow.

hent, caught, took.

hepe, hip, berry of the wild rose.

herkens, imperative plurai, harken.

herowed, harried, despoiled. See harried, herry.

herry, harry, pillage, rob.

he se. See -s as sign of future.

het, eat.

het, hot.

hett, bid.

hette is called. See heihte.

heuch, heugh, steep hill or bank, glen with steep overhanging sides.

heved, head.

hey, interjection of pleasure, displeasure, pain, excitation.

heynd, friendly, kindly. See hend, hind.

heyt war howte ! heyt ! is a well-known call to horses (get up !), and war-oute is a term used in driving.

hi, have.

hich, high.

hie, hye, n., haste.

hie : she smiled hie, with a smile not confined to her mouth, but mounting higher.

hiean, hying.

hight, is, was, called.

hight, I promise. pret. heght, hight.

hilt, flayed.

hin-chill. See hind and child.

hind, hinde, hindy, hynde, adj., courteous, gracious, gentle, kindly. See hend.

hind, hynde, n., youth, chiel, callant, seems often to be used as an epithet, young (but this may possibly be hind, kindly courteous, etc., in some cases).

hindy. See hind.

hing, hang. pret. hang, hanget. p. p. hanged, hangit.

hingers, hangings.

hinnie, hinny, honey, term of affection.

hinnie-mark, honey-mark, mole ?

hired your han, 520, 14, if right, must mean, she would have paid you to do it. Other copies, kissed.

ho, who.

hoky-gren (burnt like), 140, 27 : hoakie, " a fire that has been covered up with cinders, when all the fuel has become red." Jamieson. A branch or stem in such a fire (?) or good to make such a fire with (?) Scott has, hollins grene.

hold, holde, hauld, housing, quarters, place of shelter, lodging. thirty horsses in one hold, perhaps place of keeping.

hold, holde, v., wager.

holde, retain (legally).

hollan, hollin, holland, linen.

Hollan, Hollans, boats, Dutch boats. Dutch fishing-luggers are to be seen in great numbers on the Scottish coast in summer.

hollen, hollin, holly.

hollin, holland.

holm, holme, houm, howm, low ground on a river-bank.

holpe, pret. of help.

holtes, woods.

holydame, by my, halidom. Originally halidom in oaths meant reliques of saints ; my halidom seems to be used in the sense of sacred oath.

hom, them.

hondert, hondreth, hondrith, hundred.

honey, term of endearment. See hinny.

hooding. See huddin.

hooly, hoolie, hollie, huly, slowly, softly. See healy.

hope, houp, sloping hollow between two hills.

hope, expect, think.

hore, hoar, gray.

hose, embrace, hug.

hosen, hose, stockings (not breeches).

hosens, stockings without feet.

hostler, innkeeper.

hou, how.

houk, dig. pret. and p. p. houked, houket, houkit, howket, etc.

houm, howm, holm, level low ground on a river-bank.

houp. See hope.

hour, whore.

housen, house (sing.).

housle, houzle, give the sacrament.

houzle, communion.

hoved, hung about, tarried.

how, howe, n., hollow, sometimes, plain.

how, adj., hollow.

howd, hold. See haud.

howk, howked, etc. See houk.

howm. See houm.

howyn, own.

huddle, (hide) cover, protect (Scot. hiddle, hide).

huggell, hug, or, perhaps, a variety of huddle.

huly, hooly, healy, slowly, softly.

humming, heady, strong, as causing a hum in the head.

hunder, hundre, hunner, huner, hundredth, hundred.

hunger, hungre, v., starve.

hunt's ha, hunting-house or lodge.

husbande, husbonde, farmer, husbandman; economist, manager.

hussyfskap, husseyskep, housewifery, 600, 3 (she was making puddings).

hy, hye, hyght, on, vpon, in a loud voice. on hy, hye, on high, up, erect. on hyght, on high.

hye, hie, n., haste.

hyghte, promise. hyght, p. p., promised; vowed.

hynd-chiel. See hind, adj.

hynde, n. See hind, n.

hynde, adj., gentle, or the like. See hind, adj.

hyne, (up) behind.

hyne, hence, away.

hypped, hopped.

I

(See also under J, Y.)

I, ay.

i, abridgment of in.

i, abridgment of with.

i-bouht, bought.

i-dyght, y-dyght, furnished, adjusted; made ready.

i-fedred, feathered.

i-flawe, flayed.

ilk, ilke, same. of that ilk, having a title the same as the surname: as, Wemys of Wemys. in that ilke, in that same; at that same moment.

ilk, ilka, each, either. ilkone, each one.

ilkone. See ilk.

ill, ell, ull, will.

ill-bukled, badly run down at the heel. See baucheld. (Unless ill be for old.)

ill-far'd, ill-favored.

im, am.

imy, in my.

in, an, and, if.

in one, anon, at once.

inclen, incline.

in-fere, together. See fere.

ingle, fire.

inn, inne, lodging.

i-nocked, nocked, notched.

inowe, enough.

instiled, styled, intitled.

intil, intill, into, in.

into, in. into (his age), at, of.

intoxicate, pret., intoxicated.

i-pyght, put.

ir, are.

ire, thro, 212, 17: seems to mean, as resenting the covering (not ballad-like).

irke with, tired, weary of.

is, has.

I'se, I shall. See s, se.

it, its.

ith, in the.

'ith, with.

ither, other; one another.

I wat, a wat, I wot, I wad, surely.

I wis, I wiss, assuredly.

i-wis, i-wisse, i-wys, surely, indeed.

I wist, for iwis, indeed.

iyen, iyn, eyen, eyes.

J

Jack, insolent fellow.

iacke, 411, 64: (here) coat of mail, cf. 58, 59, 60. An ordinary soldier's jack consisted of two folds of stout canvas, or some quilted material, with small pieces of metal enclosed. Fairholt.

iapis, japes, jests, waggery, trifling.

jaw, jawe, wave.

jelly (jolly), handsome, pleasant, jovial.

ietted, moved in state or with pride.

jimp, gimp, jump, adj., slender, slim.

jo, sweetheart.

jobbing (of faces), billing (like doves).

iollye, should probably be iollytë. See enter plea.

joukd, lurched forward.

jow (of bell), stroke.

jule, jewel.

jully-flowers, gilly-flowers.

jumbling, mudding, fouling.

justle, joust, tilt.

justler, jouster, tilter.

justling, jousting.

K

kail, kale, colewort; broth made of greens, especially of coleworts.

kaim, kame, keem, comb.

kaivle, lot.

kale. See kail.

kame, keem, comb.

kamen, combing.

kavil, kaivle, kevel, cavil, lot.

kay, key, kine.

keames, combs.

kebbuck, cheese.

keem, kem, kemb, kame, comb.

keen, v., ken, know.

keen(e), bold.

keep, catch. See kep.

keepit (a bower), frequented, lived in.

keepit, heeded, observed.

keist, kiest, kest, kyst, pret. of cast.

kell, a cap of network for women's hair.

kem, kemb, comb.

kemp, kempe, kempy, champion, fighting-man.

kempery(e), company of fighting men (or, if adjective, fighting).

kempy. See kemp.

ken, know. 375, 4, to make known.

kene, (cawte and kene) wise, shrewd, or, perhaps, brave.

kenna, know not.

kep, keep, cap, cape, catch, stop, intercept. she keppit him (received him) on a penknife (as he leaned over to her). pret. kept, kepd, kepped, kepit, keppit.

kepe I be, care I to be.

keping, 535, 20, meeting. The meaning is that he went to meet (come should be came) the body which was lying at the gates. There was no procession towards him.

kepping, keeping.

kerches, kerchiefs.

kest, keste, pret. of cast.

kettrin, cateran, Highland marauder.

kevel, kevil, lot.

key, kye, cows.

keys, (rang the keys) keys of her spinnet.

kickle, 365, 59, not easily managed, unsteady, Scot. kittle. (But perhaps we should read kick, since a verb would be expected.)

kilt, a skirt worn by Highlanders, reaching from the belly to the knees.

kilt, kelt, tuck up. p. p. kilt.

kin: a' kin kind, a' kin, all kind, equivalent to every.

kin, ken.

kind, kindly, kindred, native. kindly cock-ward, natural (born) fool.

king's felon, kynggis felon, kings ffelon, traitor, or rebel, to the king.

kinnen, coney, rabbit.

kintra, country.

kipeng, keeping.

kipple, couple, rafter.

kirk-shot, the fishings on the water where nets are shot, belonging to, or adjacent to, the kirk.

kirk-style, the gate of the enclosure round a church, or, the stile in the church-yard wall.

kirtle, kirtell, kyrtell, part of a man's dress, perhaps waistcoat; name given to a variety of articles of female attire, explained as jacket, corsage or waist, upper petticoat, a loose upper garment, tunic or short mantle, etc.

kist, chest, coffin.

kithe, a, of kith, of the same country, region, people.

knack fingers (in sign of grief), crack the finger-joints.

knaue, servant.

knave-bairn, male child.

knell, v., ring.

knet, pret. of knit, knitted, knotted.

knoe. See know.

knoke, knock.

knoppis, knobs.

know(e), knoe, knoll, hillock.

kod, kuod, quoth.

kow, bunch of twigs.

ky, kye, kyne, cows.

kyrtell. See kirtle.

kyst, cast.

kyth (and kin), home, country, people. See kithe.

kythe, be manifest, appear.

L

laa, law.

lack, lake, n. (think, hae, lack), reproach, discredit. what other ladies would think lack (but here lack may = laigh, and mean beneath them). tooke a lake, incurred a reproach or blame (?). of his friends he had no lack, corrupted from, of him his friends they had no lack (or the like).

lad-bairn, boy.

lad, pret. of lead.

lade, led, taken.

ladë, lady.

laek, v., like.

laid about, invested.

laid: laid her bye, lay down by her.

laidley, laily, laylë, layely, etc., loathly, loathsome.

laigh, low, mean.

laigh, leugh, n., low ground, lower part.

laily, lailly, layle, layly, layelly. See laidley.

lain, laine, leane, lene, len, conceal.

lain, alone. See lane.

laine, p. p., laid.

lair, lear, instruction.

lair, lear, lying-in.

laird, a landholder, under the degree of knight; the proprietor of a house, or of more houses than one.

laised, laced.

lait, late.

laith, loath. See leath.

lake, n. See lack.

lake, pit, cavity.

lake, laigh, of mean position.

lake-wake, leak-wake, lyke-wake, watching of a dead body.

lamar, lamer, lammer, amber.

land, country (opposed to town).

land-serg(e)ant, officer of the gendarmerie of the Borders, lieutenant.

landsman, land owner.

lane, lain, leen, lean, lone, alane, alone, annexed to the dative or genitive of the personal pronoun (as in Old Eng. him ane, hire ane), my, mine, thy, our, your, her, his, him, its : I alone, by myself, etc.

lap, lappe, wrap, roll.

lap, *pret.* of loup, leap.

lappen, *p. p.* of loup, leap.

lass-bairn, lassie-bairn, girl.

lassed, laced.

lat, let.

late, *pret.* of let, allow.

latten, *p. p.* of let.

lau, low.

lauch, *n.*, laugh.

lauch, lawhe, *v.*, laugh. *pret.* laugh, laughe, leuch, leugh, luke, lough, low, lowe, lowhe, laucht, lought.

laue, law.

launde, lawnde, plain ground in a forest ; " a small park within a forest, enclosed in order to take the deer more readily, or to produce fatter venison by confining them for a time."

launsgay, a kind of lance, javelin.

lave, leve, rest, remainder.

lauede ablode, swam in blood.

lav(e)rock, lark.

law, (Biddess-law) hill.

lawin(g), tavern-reckoning.

lawing, lying (reclining).

lawnde. See launde.

lax, relief.

lay, law, faith.

lay, land not under cultivation, grass, sward. lays, fields, plains, ground.

lay, *v.*, lie.

lay bay, put aside or behind, outsail.

layelly, loathsome. See laidley.

lay-land, lea land, untilled land ; simply plain, ground.

laylë, loathsome. See laidley.

layn (withouten), lie (i. e., truly).

layne, *v.*, lie.

layne, *v.*, lean.

lazar, -er, leper.

lea, lee, lie, loe, loi, loie, loy, loo, low, lue, *v.*, love.

lea, lee, lie, *mentiri.*

lea, leave.

lea, *n.* See lee.

leace, (withouten leace) falsehood.

lead, 448, 26 : lead their horses (?).

lead, led.

lead, laid.

lead(e), vat, boiler.

leaf, loaf.

leak, *adj.*, like.

leak, *v.*, like.

leal, leel, leil, liel, loyal, faithful, true ; virginal, chaste, veracious ; upright, honest.

lean, leane, lene, len, *v.*, conceal ; lie. See lain.

lear, instruction, learning, information. See lair.

leard, laird.

lease, leash, 177, 19, a thong or string (as if for bringing back the deer he should kill ?). a leash (of hounds), pack. a leash (of bucks), three.

leasing(e), leasynge, lesynge, leesin, falsehood.

leath, laith, loath.

leaugh, leugh, lewgh, leiugh, lieugh, low.

leave : gie them a' thier leave, take leave of them all.

leave, leeve, dear.

leave, live.

lede, leading, conduct.

ledës-man, lodesman, guide.

ledyt, *old imperative plural :* lead.

lee, lea, untilled ground, grass land, open plain, ground.

lee, *adj.*, the (this, a) lee-lang, lief-lang day, livelong. So lee, le, lei, ley, licht o the moon, as in die liebe sonne, der liebe mond, regen, wind, and other formulas in great variety.

lee, *v.*, lie, *mentiri.*

lee, *v.*, love. See lea, love.

leech, 566, 11, meant for leash, and so spelt in another copy.

leed, laid.

leedginge, leeching, doctoring.

leeft, *pret.*, lived.

lee-lang. See lee.

leems, 87, 7, gleams ; but *langs*, belongs, is the word required.

leen, lean, her, your leen, him leen, lone. See lane.

lees, leeze, me on thee, commend me to (originally leeve is me, dear is to me).

leese, lose.

leesome, lovely, pleasing ; pleasantly.

leeve, leve, leave, lefe, lieve, live, *adj.*, lovely, dear, pleasant. *comp.* leifer, leuer. (whether he were) loth or lefe (properly, him were), disagreeable or agreeable, unwilling or willing.

leeve, believe.

leeve, grant.

leeze. See lees.

lefe, pleasing, agreeable ; pleased.

leffe, remain.

leg, highwayman.

legg, league.

lei, ley, lei light o the moon. See lee, *adj.*

leil. See leal.

leiugh, low. See leaugh.

leman, lemman, beloved (of both sexes) ; lover, paramour ; love, mistress, loose woman.

lemanry, illicit love.

len, *v.*, lean. See lend.

len, lene, conceal. See lain.

lend, grant, give.

lende, dwell.

lene, conceal. See len.

lenger, lengre, longer.

lenght, length.

lere, cheek, face.

lere, learn.

lese, leese, lose.

lesse, false, falsehood.

lesynge, falsehood. See leasing(e).

let, lat, allow, leave ; omit, fail. *pret.* late, loot, lute, lett. *p. p.* latten, letten, lotten, looten, loot (?).

let, lette, hinder.

letten, *p. p.* of let, allowed ; left.

letters, letturs, letter.

leuch, luke, *pret.* of laugh.

leugh, *n.*, lower part.

leugh, *pret.* of laugh.

leutye, lewté, loyalty, faith.

leve, lave, *n.*, rest.

leue, *v.*, permit, grant.

leven, lawn, glade, open ground in a forest. See launde.

leuer, leifer, pleasanter, preferable, rather. See leeve.

lewde (lye), base, vile.

lewgh, low. See leaugh.

lewte. See leutye.

ley, lea, lee, land not under cultivation, simply land, plain, field ; lands and ley, arable land and pasture.

ley-land, land lying lea, not under cultivation. See lay-land.

ley licht. See lee.

leythe, light.

lian, lying.

licht, alight.

lichter, delivered. See lighter.

lichtlie, lichtly, lightly, make light of, treat, or speak of, with disrespect.

lick, take for one's self.

lidder, lither, lazy.

lie, ly, lye, reside, live.

lie, lee, lea, love. See lea.

lief-lang. See lee-lang, under lee.

lierachie, hubbub.

lieugh, low. See leaugh.

life, leaf.

lief : man of life, man alive.

lift, air, sky.

lig, ligge, lygge, lie.

light, *pret.*, lighted, alighted. See lyght.

light, 318, 1 : corruption of lith, listen.

lighter, of a bairn, delivered.

lightly, lightlie, lyghtly(e), quickly.

lightly, lichtlie, -ly, treat with disrespect.

like, liken, (like to be dead or to dee), in a condition, in a fair way, or likely.

likesome, pleasing.

lilt, to sing cheerfully.

lily, lilly, lilye, lillie, liley, lillie, (lea, lee, lie, leven) explained as "overspread with lilies or flowers," but clearly from A. S. léoflíc, Old Eng. lefly, etc., lovely, charming.

limmer, a term of opprobrium, or simply of dislike, wretch (*m.* or *f.*), rascal ; of a woman, jade.

lin. See linn.

Lin, Linn, Linne, Line, Lyne, a stock ballad-locality (like Linkum).

lin, stop.

lin'd, beat.

ling, lyng, a species of rush, or thin long grass, bent grass, Scotland ; in England, heath, furze.

lingcan, lichame, body.

Linkem. See Linkum.

linkin, linken, tripping, walking with a light step ; light of movement.

Linkum, an indefinite ballad-locality.

linn, lin, lynn(e), water-course, torrent, river, pool in a river.

linsey, linsey-woolsey.

lint, linen, linen mutch or cap.

lish, leash.

list, *n.*, inclination.

list, *v.*, desire, be disposed. *pret.* list. *impersonal*, me list.

lith, lyth, member, joint.

lith, lithe, lythe, hearken.

lither, bad. See lidder.

live, leave.

live best, are the best of those living.

lively, alive.

liuer, *adj.*, deliver, agile.

liuerance, payment for delivering.

livery-man, servant.

liues, 'lieves, believes.

liuor, deliver, hand over, surrender.

load, loaded (with liquor).

locked, lockit (in a glove), fastened.

lodesman. See ledesman.

lodging-maill, rent for lodging.

lodly, loathly, disgusting.

lodomy, laudanum.

loe, loie, loy, lou, *v.*, love. See lea.

loie, loy, love. See loe.

loke, look.

lome, lame man.

lone, a common, any free or uncultivated spot where children can play or people meet, even the free spaces about a house.

long, tall.

long of, owing to, the fault of.

loo, love, *pret.* lood.

lood, loud.

loof, loof, lufe, luve, palm of the hand.

looke, look up.

loon. See loun.

loord. See lourd.

loot, bend. See lout.

loot, *pret.* and *p. p.* of let, allowed, allowed to come.

looten, *p. p.* of let, allowed (to come).

lope, *pret.* of loup, leaped.

lord nor loun. In 143, 26, lord is a wrong reading ; rogue nor loun, or the like, is required.

lordane, lurden, dolt, clodpoll, etc.

lore, lorne, lost.

loset, loosed, delivered.

loss, lose.

lotten, *p. p.* of let, allowed.

loudly, loud.

lough, loughe, *pret.* of laugh.

lought, *pret.* of laugh.

louk, look.

loukynge, expectation, hope deferred.

loun, lown, lowne, loon, a person of low rank ; rogue ; often a mere term of general disparagement (as in, English loun); naughty girl; mistress, concubine, etc.

loup, leap. *pret.* lap, leap, leepe, lope, loup, louped. *p. p.* loupen, luppen.

loup, *pret.* of loup.

loupen, louped, *p. p.* of loup.

lourd, loord, *pret.* and *p. p.* of lour, prefer; verb made from lever, rather.

lout, loot, bow, bend, lean. *pret.* louted, looted. *p. p.* louted, lootit, louten.

louten, *p. p.* of lout, bent.

love-clapped, embraced lovingly, caressed.

loverd, lord.

louesome, lovely.

lov(e)ly, louelie, epithet of London. See leeve.

low, lowe, hill.

low, lowe, flame.

low, lowe, *pret.* of laugh.

lowe, (doggs) bite soe, a phrase for, take mean advantages.

lowse, loose, free.

lucettes, luces, pikes.

lue, loe, loo, lou, loie, lea, lee, lie, *v.*, love. See lea.

lufe, luve, leuve, loof, palm of the hand.

lugs, ears.

luid, loved.

luppen, *p. p.* of loup, leap.

lust, inclination, disposition.

luve, palm of the hand. See loof.

ly, lye, live, dwell. *pret.* lyed.

lyand, lying.

lybertye, (apoint) a place of, 231, 39; a place where the two can fight freely, without risk of interruption (?).

lye. See ly.

lyed, lay, lived. See ly.

lygge, lay. See lig.

lyghte, lyght, alighted.

lyghtly(e). See lightly.

lyke, please.

lyke-wake, watch of a dead body.

lynde, lyne, linden, tree.

lyne. See lin.

lyng, heath. See ling.

lynne. See linn.

lyste, me lyste, it would please me, I should like.

lyth, lithe, hearken.

lyth, member. See lith.

lyueray, present of clothes; purveyance of drink.

M

ma, 464, 15; 465, 27, 29: bit, whit.

Mable, booke of, some book of predictions, like Thomas Rymer's.

machr(e)l(l), mackerel.

made (men), raised.

mae, more.

maen, mane, meen, *n.*, moan.

magger of, in the, in spite of, maugre.

maick, make, mate.

maid, may, used loosely of a young wife. So κόρη, παρθένος, in Homer, of a young wife, and *puella* of a married woman often.

maik. See make.

mail, rent; black-mail.

mair, mare, more, bigger.

maist, almost.

make, maik, maicke, mate, consort; match, like.

male, trunk. male-hors, pack-horse.

malicen, mallasin, malison.

man, mane, maun, mun, must.

mane, maen, main(e), meane, meen, moan, complaint, lament; often nothing more than utterance, enunciation.

maney, meny, followers.

manhood, manhead, manheed, men (man) o your, men to your, i. e. if you are men (man) of true valor, willing to fight one by one; manly deed, exploit demanding courage.

manie, mennie, maunna, must not, may not.

mansworn, perjured.

manten, maintain.

marchandise, dealing.

march-man, one who lives on the march, or border.

March-parti, Marche-partes, Border-part, Border-parts, Border, Borders.

mare, more.

marie, mare.

marie. See mary.

mark, murky.

marke, merk, two thirds of a pound.

marke hym, commit himself by signing the cross.

marrow, (of man or woman) mate, husband, wife; match, equal in rank, equal antagonist.

mary, marie, marrie, marry, a queen's lady, maid-of-honor, maid (like abigail).

mary mild, marigold.

masar, maser, a drinking-vessel of wood, especially of knotty-grained maple, often mounted with bands or rings of precious metals.

mass: in the frequent formula, when bells were rung and mass was sung and a' men bound to bed, a domestic religious service at the end of the day.

mast, maste, mayst.

master-man, captain of a ship; chief.

masteryes, make, do feats of skill.

mat, matt, (mat he, ye, dee! wae mat fa, matt worth!) mot, in the sense of may.

maught, maugt, might.

maugre: maugre in theyr teethe, in spite of.

maun, must.

maunna, must not.

maw, sea-maw, sea-mew, gull.

maw, *v.*, mow.

may, mey, maid.

may, *optative*, frequently put after the subject, as, Christ thy speed may bee! thou mayst sune be! I may be dead ere morn!

may be, is, like *can be.*

mayne, strength.

maystry, mastery.

me, men, French *on.*

meal, bag.

mean, man of: meaning uncertain.

mean, meane, meen, v., moan, lament ; be-
moan, lament the state of. not to mean, not
to be pitied. See mane.

mean, n., moan. See meen.

meany, troop. See menë.

meat and fee, food and wages.

meaten, meeten, measured.

meatrif, abounding in food.

meed, mood, heart, state of feeling.

meed, warld's meed, 15, 14: seems to be corrupted from mate (make).

meen, v., moan, lament.

meen, mean, lamentation.

meen, moon.

meet, meete, even, equal ; scant, close.

meeten, meaten, measured, by measure. See
met.

meiht, mayst.

meikle, meickle, mickle, muckle, much,
great.

meisseine, spanker, or perhaps, Fr. misaine,
foresail.

mell, mall, wooden hammer, beetle.

mell, meddle.

menë, meany, meynë, maney, monie, followers, band.

menement, amendment.

mennie, manie, maunna, must not, may not.

menye, menyie, household, retinue, people.
See menë.

meri. See mery.

merk, marke, two thirds of a pound.

merk. See merkes.

merk, v., mark. merked them one, took their
aim at.

merkes, distances between the bounds.

merlion, merlyon, merlin, the smallest of British falcons.

merrilye, in good or valiant fashion.

merry (men). See mery.

mery, meri, merry, merrie, myrri, myrry
men, a standing phrase for followers, companions in arms.

Mess, an epithet said to be contemptuous for a
priest or parish minister (as one who says, or
said, mass).

met, mat, may. See mat.

met, pret. of mete, measured. p. p. met, mete.

methe, meat.

mett, meet.

met-yard, measuring-rod.

mey. See may.

mey, my.

meynë, retinue, suite, household, company,
body of people. See menë.

meythe, might.

micht, v., might.

micht 'll, might well.

mickle, great, much. See meikle.

midder, mideer, mider, mother.

middle-earth, earth (conceived as being the
middle of the universe).

middle stream, middle of the stream.

mild, (maidens) meek, gentle, demure. myld(e)
Mary, of the Virgin, lenient, compassionate.

millaine, of Milan steel.

min, mind, recollection.

mind o, on, remember. pret. mind, remind of.

minde : ffor the maydens loue that I haue most
minde, 115, 5: elliptical or corrupt. Comparing 116, 21 (where the MS. reads, wrongly,
most meed) we see that for is not to be taken
with minde. We must understand most in
mind or most mind to or of, or, possibly, minde
may be (from minnen, remember) had in
mind.

minge, utter. minged, didst name the name
of, mention (or, perhaps, only bore in mind).

minion, dainty.

minnie, minny, mother, dam.

mint to, put out the hand towards, move
towards. minted as, took a direction as if,
made as if.

mire, myre, swamp, bog.

Mirry-land toune, probably a corruption of
merry Lincoln.

miscarry me, get me into trouble; fail, disap-
point me (?).

misgae, misgave.

misgiding, ill treatment.

misguide, misgiding, ill treatment.

miss(e), v., omit, fail.

mister, myster, need, requirement, an exi-
gency. misters, sorts of.

mith, mithe, v., might. mith slain, might
[have] slain.

mold, molde, earth ; land, country ; ground.

Moll Syms, a well-known dance tune of the
sixteenth century.

mome, dolt.

monand, n., moaning.

monie, menie, company, suite. See menë.

monny, many.

montenans. See mountnaunce.

mood, giue me, 288, 23: though give me my God
(i. e. the consecrated host) looks like a bold
change, it is not improbable.

mool, mools. See moul.

moody-hill, moudie-hill, mould-hill, mole-
hill.

morn, morrow. the morn, to-morrow.

morning, mourning.

mornin's gift, morning gift, gift made the
morning after marriage.

mort, note on the horn to announce the death
of deer.

moss, muss, mose, bog.

mot, mote, may.

mote, meeting.

moten, molten.

mother-in-law, stepmother.

mothly, motley.

motion, proposal.

mou, moue, mow, mouth.

moudie-hill. See moody-hill.

mought, mote, may.

moul, mouls, mool, mools, mould, dust, ashes
(of the dead) ; earth of a grave.

mould-hill. See moody-hill.

mould-warpe, mole.

mountnaunce, montenans, amount.

mow, 313, 34: seems to be meant for mouth
(lip). But perhaps we may understand grimace
(for a tyrant to make faces at). See mou.

mucell. See muckle.

muck, dung.

muck the byre, carry out dung from the cow-house.

muckle, mukle, mucell, meikle, big, much.

muir, moor.

mullertd, miller.

mun, maun, man, must.

mune, moon.

muntit, p. p. of munt, mount.

muss, moss, bog. See moss.

myght neuer no tyme to sleepe, 277, 441: probably corrupt, and to be read, no tymë slepe; but the construction is not unknown.

myld, mylde. See mild.

myle: two myle way, the time it takes to go two miles.

myllan, Milan steel.

mylner, miller.

myneyeple, 395, 30: corruption of manople, a gauntlet protecting the hand and the whole forearm (?). Skeat.

myre. See mire.

myrke, mirk, mark, dark.

myrri, myrry. See mery.

myrthes can, knows pleasant stories.

mysaunter, mischance.

myster, need, occasion. See mister.

N

n, carried on from preceding word to following. noo nother, no noder, none other. a nother nether, an other. a naughtless, noughtless, an aughtless, good for nought. a noke, an oke. they nere, they nee, theyn ere, thyn ee. So, his nawn, her nain (nen), yer nane, as if from hisn, hern, yern. See nane.

na, nae, no, not. Frequently united with the preceding verb: hadna.

naesaid, refused.

nagie, nagy, little nag.

nags, notches, nicks.

nain, own. See n.

nan, none.

nane, nen, yer nane, my nane; etc.: own (n, originally, carried on from mine). See n.

nane, neen, none; adverbially, not, not at all. See none.

napkin (-ken, -kain), pocket handkerchief.

napskape, head-piece.

nar, nor. with comparative, for than. See nor.

nas, ne was, was not.

naught, naughtiness.

naw, na, no.

naw, nay.

nawn, own. See n.

naye: withowghten naye, undeniably, truly.

ne, no, not.

neads, needs.

nean, none.

near, neare, ner, nere, nearer.

near, 15, 14⁴: corrupt, as the repetition from the second verse shows; while (till) my days are near (to an end) would be extremely forced, in any case.

near, neer, never.

near-hand, adj., near, short. adv. (near-han), near, almost.

neast, neist, nist, nest, next.

neathing, nothing.

neave, fist.

nee, nigh.

needle-steik, needle-stitch, fastening or stitch with a needle.

neen, none. See nane.

neerice, nurse. See nourice.

neigh, v., (nigh) approach.

neist, niest, next.

ner, nere, nearer. See near.

nere, were [it] not.

nere: they nere, theyn ere, thine ear.

neshe, of delicate quality.

nest, next. See neast.

new-fa'n, new-fallen.

new-fangle, fond of novelties, capricious, inconstant.

next, nighest.

nicher, nicker, n. and v., neigh.

nicht, the, to-night.

nicked him of naye, nickd them wi nae, refused with nay.

nicker. See nicher.

nie, neigh.

nie, neigh, nigh.

niest, next, nearest.

night-coif, night-cap.

ning, nine.

nip, bit.

nires, norice, nurse. See nourice.

nist, nest, neast, next.

nit, knit, fasten.

nit, nut.

nit-broun, nut-brown.

no, not.

noble, nobellys, a gold coin of the value of one third of a pound.

noder, noo nother, none other. See n.

noghte, not.

nolt, nout, neat, neat cattle.

noo, now.

noorice. See nourice.

nor, nar, after a comparative, than.

nother. See noder.

noumbles, nowmbles: noumbles of the dere, of a do, frequently defined entrails; Palsgrave, praecordia, the numbles, as the heart, the splene, the lunges, and lyver. At least a part of the noumbles are the two muscles of the interior of the thighs of a deer.

nourice, nourrice, noorice, nourry, nurice, nury, nurse.

nout, nolt, neat cattle.

nouther, neither.

noy, grief.

nul, nule, will not.

nurice. See nourice.

nury. See nourice.

nyll, will not.

O

o, of. diel o there, devil (i. e. not a bit) of anything in that way (?).

o, on.
oerword, refrain.
of, on. In, seruyd (q. v.) him of bred, *for* is required, and *of*, which would signify *with*, cannot stand.
okerer, usurer.
old, auld, old son. See auld son.
on, of.
on, one.
on: wedded on, 22, 24, on the strength of (to have as a dowry).
on fere, in company.
on o, on.
one, a.
one, on.
onë, ony, onie, any.
ones, onys, once.
onfowghten, unfought, without fighting.
ony, onie, onë, any.
or, before. or eir, or or (doubling of before).
or, over.
order, ordre, rule of an order.
orders, prepares.
ordeyn, give order for, levy.
orghie, orgeis, a fish, large kind of ling.
osterne, austere.
other, *pl.* others.
ought, am under obligation. *pret.* and *p. p.*, owed.
our, owr, ower, over, too.
oure, ovr, *prep.*, over. See ower.
ousen, owsen, owsn, oxen.
out (beat out), out and out.
outehorne, a horn blown to call out citizens to the support of the civil authority.
outmet, *p. p.*, measured out.
out-oer, -our(e), -ower, -owre, -over, over, above, beyond.
out of hand, forthwith.
outrake, excursion, outing.
outspeckle, laughing-stock.
outthro, through to the opposite side.
outwood, wood outside (of a town?).
ouer all, everywhere.
ouer goddes forbode, forbott. See forbode.
overthrew us, 610, 8, threw us over.
ower, owre, oure, ovr, over. ower (a window), over against.
ower, owr, our, over, too.
owre, or, before.
owsn, owsen, ousen, oxen.
owthe, out.
owtlay, outlaw.
oxe-lig, ox-leg.

P

pa, paw.
pa. See palle.
pakets, packets.
palle, pale, paule, pa, fine cloth.
pallions, pavilions.
palmer, pilgrim ; tramp, vagabond, beggar.
paramour, lover, lady-love. the love was like paramour, 212, 8, like amorous passion (?). In 7, 4, the word should signify something eatable.

pardon, leave of absence.
part: God, Christ haue part(e) of the (me), perhaps, make thee an object of his care (as prendre part en, take an interest in) ; or, take thee for his, number thee among the saved.
part, quit, part from.
parti: vppone a parti, aside. March-parti, Marche-partes, Border-side.
party, be of part with.
Pasch, Pasche, Easter.
passage, occurrence, incident, adventure.
passe vppon, pass, go, on.
passe, 273, 357, extent (?).
pass for, care for.
pat, pot.
pat, patt, *pret.* of pit, put.
pavag, pauage, pawage, pavage, road-tax.
paw, a slight motion. neer played paw, never stirred again.
pay, *n.*, satisfaction.
pay, paye, *v.*, satisfy, please.
pay, beat.
peak, pick.
peak, peck.
peak-staff, pike-staff.
pearling, pearlin, lace.
pearting, parting, separation.
pecis, vessels (of silver), probably cups.
peel, pool.
peel, a tower, stronghold.
peeped, spoke faintly, whined.
peers, pears.
peit, a peat carried to school as a contribution to the firing.
pellettes, bullets.
penny-fee, -fie, gift of a penny, largess, pourboire.
peny: shete a peny, shoot for a penny.
pestilett, pistolet.
phat, what.
philabeg, kilt, skirt worn by Highlanders, reaching from belly to knee.
pick: pick a mill, sharpen the surface of a millstone when worn smooth by friction. picked a stane, dressed with a pick.
pick, *n.*, pitch.
pickle, a grain.
pickle, pick, collect.
picklory, name of a cloth.
pickman, pikeman.
pin, pinn, an implement for raising the fastening of a door. "The pin was always inside, hung by a latch, or leather point, the end of which was drawn through a small hole in the door to the outside. During the day-time, the pin was attached to a bar or sneck in such a way that when the latch was pulled the door was free to open. But at night the pin was disconnected from the door-fastening and hung loose, so that when the latch was pulled the pin rattled." W. Forbes. (See tirled.) knocked upon a pin, is probably corrupted from knocked at the ring ; if not, the meaning must be, knocked at the door at the place of the latch. that so priuilye knowes the pinn, implies that there was some secret connected with the pin which it is difficult to conceive

in an arrangement so simple as that described above ; but it is probable that complications were employed by the cautious. See gin.

pin, gallows-pin, gallou-pine, the projecting or horizontal beam of the gallows (?). Any projection upon which a rope could be fastened.

pinder, pindar, pinner, pounder.

pine, pyne, suffering, pain. (Goddës, Creystys) pyne, suffering, distress, passion.

piner-pig, an earthen vessel for keeping money.

pinner. See pinder.

pint, point.

pistol-pece, pistol.

pit, put. pit mee down, be my death. *pret. pat. p. p.* pitten, putten.

pith, hammer o the, 208, B 2 : sounds like nonsense. The smith's anvil being of gold and his bellows-cords of silk, his hammer should be of some precious material. To say his hammer was wielded with force would be out of keeping, and very flat at best.

pitt, put.

pitten, *p. p.* of pit, put.

place : in place, 434, 76, there.

plaid. See belted.

plaiden, coarse woollen cloth diagonally woven.

plain fields, open fields.

plat, *pret.* of plet : plaited, interfolded.

plate-jack, defensive upper garment laid with plates.

platen, plates, pieces.

play-feres, play-fellows.

plea, quarrel.

plea, enter plea att my iollye. See enter.

plead, contend.

plett, plait.

plewed, feathers plewed with gold, 225, 49 : not understood.

plight I lay, 570, 21, the pledge I did lay (?), condition in which I should lie (?). (Very obscurely expressed stanza.)

plight, *pret.,* plighted.

plooky, pimpled.

plough, pleugh, pleuch, plow (of land), as much land as one plough will till in a year.

plucke-buffet, they shote, 277, 424, taking and giving a buffet for missing. (This supposes pluck = take, get ; it may be the noun pluck, blow.)

plummet, of swords, pommel.

pock, bag.

poll : lighter than the poll, 571, 1, boll, lint-bow, the seed-pod of flax (?). Not probable.

poorly, feebly, faint-heartedly.

portly, of imposing appearance.

pot, deep place or pool in a river.

potewer, 47, 6 : read potener, pouch, purse.

powder, dust.

powther, powder.

prece, prese, prees, press, crowd ; thick of a conflict.

preen, *v.,* pin. See prin.

prees, prese. See prece.

preke, *n.* See pricke.

preke, *v.* See prekyd.

prese. See prece.

present, represent, act as representatives of.

presentting (wine), holding out the cup or glass towards the person saluted.

president, precedent.

prest, ready, in haste. (berdys sang) preste, freely, con amore.

prestly, quickly.

prevayle, avail.

prick(e), pry(c)ke, preke, rod or wand, used as a mark in shooting, pricke-wand ; a mark or butt generally.

pricked, *pret.,* stuck.

pricke-wande, a rod set up for a mark.

prime, pryme, the first canonical hour.

prin, *n.* and *v.,* pin.

process, occurrences, story of occurrences.

prossed, proceed.

prowed, proud.

pryce, prize.

prycke, *n.* See pricke.

prycked, sped.

pryckynge, spurring, riding briskly. In 267, 229, should probably be rakynge ; the yeomen are on foot.

pryke, *n.* See pricke.

pryme, prime, the first canonical hour, first hour of the day.

pu, pow, pull.

pudding-pricks, wooden skewers to fasten the end of a gut containing a pudding.

puggish, 221, 6, in a later copy, ragged. Mr. Ebsworth suggests the meaning, tramper's. (Cf. puggard, thief ; pugging, thieving.)

puir, pure, poor.

pusin, *n.* and *v.,* poison. *pret.* pusned.

put down. See putten down.

putten, putn, *p. p.* of put.

putten, put, down, hanged.

pyght, pitched (fixed in the ground the pole of).

pyke, pick.

pyne : (Goddës, Creystys) pyne, passion. See pine.

Q

quarrelld, *p. p.,* quarrelled with, found fault with.

quarterer, lodger.

queen, quean, queyne, quen, quien, woman, concubine.

queer, quir, choir.

queet, cweet, ankle.

quequer, quiver.

querry, quyrry, quarry, dead game.

quest, inquest.

questry-men, another, 470, 13, men constituting a quest, inquest ; but *another* raises a doubt whether we should not read *quest of,* as in 12 (-ry being caught from jury, above).

queyt, quit, requite.

quien. See queen.

quin, queen.

quite, reqite.

quite, free, clear, unpunished.

quoif, coif, cap.

quyrry, quarry, the slaughtered game.

quyte þe, acquit thyself, square the account.

R

race, course in justing.

race: castle-race, course in the castle-grounds, or contour of the castle (?).

rack, ford. "A very shallow ford, of considerable breadth: Teviotdale." Jamieson.

rad, afraid.

rader, rider.

radly, quickly.

raged, ragged.

raid, read, rede, *pret.* of ride.

raik. See rake.

rair, roar.

rair, rare.

rais, raise, rase, *pret.*, of rise.

rake, raik, reek, walk, move. raking on a rowe, advancing in a line; on a rowte, in a company.

rang, wrong.

rank, rawnke, wild, bold (turbulent), strong, violent; rude, boisterous; of spirit and courage, sturdy. rank robber, one who robs with violence, "strong thief."

ranshakled, ransacked.

rantan, ranten, rantin, making noisy merriment. See ranting, *adj.*

ranting, *n.*, raking.

ranting, rantin, rantan, ranten (laird, laddie), *adj.*, jovial, dissipated, wanton, rakish, "fast."

rap, *pret.* rapped, rappit, rappet, at, with ellipsis of the door.

rap, (of tears) to fall in quick succession.

rape, rope.

rase, *pret.* of rise. See rais.

rash, *n.*, rush.

rau, row. See rawe.

raught, reached, delivered.

rauked, searched, rummaged.

rawe, rewe, *n.*, row.

rawnke. See rank.

rawstye by the roote, 281, 56, rusty, soiled, foul, (with blood) at the end (?).

ray, *n.* and *v.*, array; make ready, saddle.

ray, *n.*, track.

raye, striped cloth.

raysse, riding, raid.

reacheles on, reckless of, heedless about.

read, *pret.* of ride.

read, rehearse, tell.

read (of dreams), interpret, give an issue to.

read, reade, rede, red, redd, *n.*, advice.

read, reade, red, *v.* advise. See riddle.

ready, direct; indubitable, certain.

reak, smoke. See reek.

rean, rin, run.

reap, ripe, search, rummage.

reapen, *p. p.* of reap.

rear, rare.

reas, praise. See roos.

reas, ryse, rouse.

reast, reest, roost.

reaths, quarters of a year.

reave, rave, rive, *pret.* of rive.

reavel(l)d, ravelled, disordered (of hair).

reaver, rever, riever, robber.

record, sma, little note.

red, redd, rede, *n.*, counsel, talk, tale. See read.

red, redd, rede, reid, *v.* advise.

red, to rid, clear out. red (the question), clear up, settle.

red river comb, 162, 19, 21: corrupted, as are other versions in this passage. See river.

redding-kaim, reeding-comb, comb (for disentangling).

rede. See red.

rede, *p. p.*, read, divined, discerned.

rede, *pret.* of ride; reden, they rode.

redly, quickly.

reeding-comb. See redding-kaim.

reef-tree, roof-tree, beam in the angle of a roof.

reek, reak, reik, *n.*, smoke.

reekit, smoked, smoky.

reest, reast, roost.

reet, root.

reign, 100, 1, (for rhyme) range (?) or rein (?).

reik, smoke. See reek.

reill, reel.

reiver, rever, riever, robber.

remeid, remedy.

remorse, compassion.

remoued, agitated.

renisht: renisht them to ride of twoe good renisht steeds, 111, 8; 113, 42 (42 emended from, on tow good renish, in conformity with 8): should have some such meaning as accoutred, but a derivation is not to be made out. Qy. [ha]renisht, harnessed?

renown (spake wi renown), force of authority (of prestige), or, with the air of a person of repute.

require, ask for. (Other texts, inquire.)

rest, *pret.* of rest.

restore, restore, because the morning-gift would revert to the father and be at his disposition, no son having been born.

reues, bailiffs.

rewe: be rewe, in a row, one after another, each of the whole class.

rewth, pity.

rid, ried, red.

riddle, resolve. riddle my riddle, resolve my dilemma.

ried, ride.

rien, riven.

riever, reiver, rever, robber.

rig, rigg, riggin, ridge.

rig-length, furlong?

riggin, ridge.

rigland, land under the plough, and so in rigs, ridges. rigland shire, a shire of such land.

rin, run.

ring (knocked at the, with the, ring, tinkled at the), the hammer of a door-knocker. But, perhaps, in the case of tinkling, the ring may have been gently drawn up and down or struck against the projecting bow or rod of a door-handle (often wound with a spiral), an operation which, when vigorously performed, is described as risping or rasping.

ring (game): to ride at the ring, to attempt,

while at full gallop, to carry off, on the point of a rod, a ring suspended on a cross-beam resting on two upright posts. (Jamieson.)

ring and the ba, a game in which a ring was thrown up, and a ball was to be thrown through before the ring fell. (Dr W. Gregor).

ripe, reap, rype, search, rummage, clear or clean out, rifle.

rise, branch.

rise, raise. *pret.* rose. See ryse.

rise, *pret.* of rise.

rive, rave, reave, *pret.* of rive, tear.

riued, arrived, travelled.

river-comb, red, 162, 19, 21: is river a corruption of *ivory*?

road, rode.

rock, roke, distaff.

rod, rode.

roddins, rowans, berries of mountain ash.

rode, rood.

roke, reek, vapor.

rood, rod (a measure).

rood, four and thirty stripes comen beside the rood, 116, 29 : referring to the scourging of Jesus (?).

room ye roun, move round so as to make room.

roos, rous, *v.*, to praise, laud, boast.

roosing, rosin, rousing, *n.*, praising, boasting, bragging.

rose-garlonde, 275, 398 : a "garland" appears to have been attached to the yerdes (397), and every shot outside of the garland was accounted a failure.

rosin, boasting. See roosing

rosses, roses.

rottens, rottons, rats.

roudes, haggard (*subst.*, an old wrinkled woman).

roun, rown, round, whisper.

round : so it went round, 499, 7, so much it came to (?).

roundlie, at a good pace.

round tables, a game.

rounin(g), *n.*, whispering.

rous, roos, reas, boast of.

rousing, *n.*, boasting. See roosing.

rout, *n.*, blow.

rout, *v.*, roar, bellow.

route, rowte, rowght, company, band, crowd. In 388, 33, perhaps mêlée, affray.

routh, plenty.

row, rough.

row, rowe, roll. *pret.* and *p. p.* rowed, rowd, rowit, rowt, rolled, wound.

rowe, on a, in a line, file.

row-footed, rough-footed.

rowght, company. ryall in rowght, 388, 33, kingly among men. See route.

rowght, wrought.

rowte. See route.

rowynde, round.

royal bone : uncertain, perhaps ivory.

royaltye, splendid display, or the like.

rub-chadler, rub-chandler, rubbish-barrel.

rudd, *n.*, (redness) complexion, face.

rudely, sturdily.

rue, cause to rue.

rugge, back.

rule, going on, taking on, noisy bewailing.

run : red run's i the rain, 191, 4, gives no sense.

rung, staff, pike-staff.

rung (of the noise of a cannon), *n.*, 482, 14, ring ; appears to have been altered, for rhyme, from ring, which is in two other copies.

ryall. See rowght.

ryght, straight, directly.

rynde : be rynde and rent, 389, 42, flayed. (But rynde should perhaps be *riven*.)

rype, *v.* See ripe.

ryse, rouse.

rysyt, riseth (old *imperat. pl.*), rise.

S

s, se, in I 'se, thou 's, etc., as a sign of the future tense. Properly a fragment of *shall*.

saa, *pret.*, saw.

sackless, sakeless, saikless, innocent.

sad, steadfast, firm, stanch.

sae, so.

safe, save.

safeguard, riding-skirt.

safly, softly.

saft, (of sleep) lightly.

saikless. See sackless.

saint, blest.

St Mary knot(t), a triple knot.

sair, sore.

sair, sare, sear, sere, serve.

sait, set.

sakeless. See sackless.

sall, shall. *pret.* sould.

sally rod, sallow, willow.

salued, greeted.

san, sane, sayn, syne, since.

sana. See sanna.

sanchoɔis of his bryk, 245, 13, apparently the fork of the breeches.

sanna, shall not.

sarbit, exclamation of sorrow.

sare, serve. See sair.

sark, shirt, shift.

sarsenent, sarcenet.

sarving, serving.

sat, saut, salt.

saugh, willow.

saul, soul.

saut, sat, salt.

sauyour : see (saw) my sauyour, attended mass, or, took the sacrament.

saw, *v.*, sow.

sawe, *p. p.* of see.

sawe, speech.

sawten, *v.*, *3 pl.*, assault, attack.

say, try.

say, saye, *pret.* of see.

sayn, san, sane, syne, since, then.

sayne, *strong participle of* say. In, I yow sayne, 389, 46, an auxiliary, *do* or *can*, must be omitted, or else we must read *saye*, as in 32, 34, 62, 65.

scaith, skaith, scath, *n.* and *v.*, hurt.

scales, discs worn as ornaments on the head.

scarson, scarcely up to.

scath, scaith, *n.*, harm.

scathe : awayte me scathe, lie in wait, seek an opportunity to do me harm.

scaur (Braidscaur), a bare and broken place on a steep hill ; also, cliff, precipice.

Scere-thorsday, Maundy Thursday, Thursday before Easter.

schane, *pret.*, shone.

schele, scheel, school.

schet, schette, *pret.* of schote, shoot.

schill. See shill.

scho, she.

schoote (his horsse) away, froo, discarded, sent off.

schrewde (arrow), accursed, pernicious, baneful.

sckill, reason, judgment. See skill.

scope, gag.

score. See core.

scorn, skorne, shame, humiliation, mortification. give the, this, a, scorn, put to shame, subject to humiliation (especially, by showing a preference as to marriage, or by slighting a woman). So, playd you the scorn, get the scorn.

scoup, *v.*, move hastily from one place to another, fly.

scouth, room, range.

scray, 294, 4, as to form suggests *scrag*, scrog ; but the meaning required is, branches, *branchage*, or even spray.

scread, shred, bit, piece.

screfë, screffë, shryvë, sheriff.

scrime, 470, 2 : seems to be corrupt ; possibly, crime ; pursuing the crime for pursuing the criminal.

scroggs, scrogs, stunted bushes, or perhaps trees ; underwood.

scug, shade, screen ; expiate.

se, sign of the future tense. See s.

se, *pret.* of see.

sea-ground, bottom of the sea.

sea-maw, gull.

seal, happiness, blessing.

seale, sail.

sear, serve. See sair.

seck, sack.

securly, surely.

see (*videre*), *pret.* say, saye, sey, se, see, seed. *p. p.* se.

see : save and se(e), protect.

see, well mot ye fare and see, 375, 3 : as here used, *see well* would have to mean, see prosperity ; but apparently there is a confusion of *well may you fare* and *God see you*, protect you (as in, save and see). well may you sit and see, lady, well may you sit and say, 187, 15 : (corrupted) nonsense.

see (sigh and see), apparently a doublet of sigh, as *ne* of *neigh* and *nigh*, *he* of *high*.

seed, *pret.* of see.

seek, seke, search, ask. *pret.* socht, asked for. *partic.* seekand, seeking.

seek, sick.

seeke to, unto, resort to.

seely, happy. seely court, fairy court.

seen, soon.

seen, syne, afterwards.

seene, I seene, ellipsis of have.

seke, search. See seek.

seke, to, at a loss.

seker, firm, resolute.

seld, sold.

selerer, the monk who has charge of the provisioning of a convent.

selkie, silkie, seal.

sell, self.

semblant, semblaunce, semblaunte, semblaunt, mien, look.

sembled, met.

sen, send, sent.

sen, since.

sent, sendeth.

sent (sent I me), assent.

sentence past, order given.

septer, scepter.

sere, serve. See sair.

serre, 116, 29, sair, sore ? (MS. serrett).

seruyd him of bred and cloth, 40, 1 : *for* would make an easier reading than *of*, which will have to be understood, on terms of (receiving food and clothing).

set, sit, become, suit. See become.

set her brest (and swom), brought her breast to a level with the water.

set (the monke to-fore the brest), assailed, shot at.

set (sete, and wrongly sat) a dynt on, vppon, of, inflicted a blow, stroke.

set by, lay aside, cease, let be.

sete, *n.*, suit, dress.

sett, take aim.

settle by, set you aside (?).

settled (gun), levelled, adjusted.

several, variously.

seyn, syen, syne, then, afterwards.

shadow, reflection (of the color of).

shaft their arrows on the wa, 466, 16 : so in both copies, unintelligible ; corrected by Scott to sharp.

shaftmont, shathmont, the measure from the top of the extended thumb to the extremity of the palm, six inches.

shame, the, euphemism for the Devil. shame a ma, devil a bit.

shames death, death of shame, shameful death.

shank, the projecting point of a hill, joining it with the plain.

share, cutting, portion.

shathmont. See shaftmont.

shaw, shawe, wood, thicket. See wode shawe. In Teviotdale, shawe is "a piece of ground which becomes suddenly flat at the bottom of a hill or steep bank." Jamieson.

shaw, sha, show.

she, 401, 4 ; spurious Highland dialect, representing *I, you, he, they*, and even *Highlander*, for which she, her, hernanesell have become a nickname. (The Gaelic having no word for the neuter it, the *masc.* e and *fem.* i do duty for the absent form. i in some Highland districts is largely used in speaking of sexless objects.)

sheaf, shefe, of arrows, bundle of twenty-four.

shealin, shiel, shielin, shielen, shieling, shield, herdsman's hut.

shear, several. (Scot. seir.)

sheave, shive, n., slice.

shed, a piece of ground on which corn grows, so called as being separate from adjacent land.

shed by (hair), parted, threw off from the face on both sides.

shedd, pret. See sheede.

shee, shie, shoe.

sheed, sheet.

sheede, shed, spill.

sheen, sheene, sheyne, shining, bright, beautiful. In, shawes been sheene, shadowes sheene, we must take sheene in the secondary sense, beautiful.

sheen, shene, shoes.

sheene, n., brightness, splendor.

shefe. See sheaf.

shend, put to shame, injure, destroy.

shent(e), p. p., hurt.

sheppd, shipped.

shete, shoot. shete a peny, shoot for a penny-stake. pret. shet, shyt.

sheugh, trench, ditch, furrow.

sheyne. See sheen.

shie, shoe. See shee.

shiel, shielen, shieling, shield. See shealin.

shill, schill, shrill.

shimmerd, glittered.

shin'd, pret. of shine.

shirife, shirrfe, shrife, sheriff. See screfe.

shirrs, shears.

shogged, moved away.

shon, schon, shone, shoon(e), shoun, shoes.

shooled, shovelled.

shoon(e), shoun, shoes. See shon.

shoon, shoun, soon.

shoot at sun and moon: they wish to have no mark measured, are ready to take any distance.

shope, created.

shortlye and anone, speedily.

shortsome, v., divert, while away the time, (opposed to langsum).

shot, reckoning.

shott, reckoning. See shot.

shot-window: the shot-window of recent times is one turning on a hinge, above, and extensible at various angles by means of a perforated bar fitting into a peg or tooth. Donaldson, Jamieson's Dictionary, 1882, notes that in the west of Scotland a bow-window is called an out-shot window. A bow-window would be more convenient in some of the instances.

shoudder-bane. See shoulder.

shouir, shower, throe, pang. See showr.

shoulder, looked over the left, apparently a gesture of vexation or of indignant perplexity.

shoun, shun, shoes. See shon.

shoun, soon.

shour, sure.

shouther, showther, shuder, shoulder.

shower. See showr.

showing-horne, 227, 78: shoeing-horn, a pun on the beggar's horn, whether as a means of sponging liquor, or of helping one to take in drink.

showr, shower, shouir, throe, paroxysm of pain.

shradds, coppices.

shrewde, shrewed, a term of vituperation; originally, cursed. thou art a shrewed dettour. thou arte a shrewde hynde, perhaps ironical (devilish pretty). shrewde wyle, clever.

shroggs, rods, wands (serving for prickes, marks).

shryuë, sheriff. See screfe.

shun, shoun, shoes.

shyt, pret., shot.

shyt, imperative, shut.

si, so.

siccan, sic, sick, sicke, sicken, such, such a.

siccer, sicker, securely, safely.

sich, sick, n., sigh.

sich, sick, v., sigh. pres. p. sichand, sichan, sichin.

sicht, sight.

sick, sicke, sicken, sicken-like, such.

sicker. See siccer.

sickles of ice, icicles.

side (keeping her flocks on yon side): ellipsis of hill, river, or the like.

side, adj., long, wide.

side be (mother-in-law side be), 120, 11: seems to mean, side by, by his side. Possibly, sud, should be.

sighan, sighend, pres. p. of sigh.

signots, ornaments, whether seals or not, attached to the ears by "grips." Three syg-nets hang at a gold ring, 476, 13, which is taken off, and was, therefore, a finger-ring.

sike, syke, ditch, trench, water-course, marshy bottom with a stream in it.

sikt, sighed.

silkie, selkie, seal.

silly: silly sisters, harmless, innocent (?). silly old man, silly old woman, etc., of a "puir body," palmer, beggar. In 608, 1, of a supposedly simple old man who turns out to be shrewd.

simmer, summer. simmer-dale, 175, 8, 9 (?).

simple, poor, scant.

sin, sun.

sin, sine, syne, since (temporal and causal), then.

sinder, sunder.

sindle, seldom.

sindry, several, sundry (people).

sine, then, since. See sin and syne.

single liverie, dress of a private soldier.

sir, title of parson.

sitt, p. p., seated.

skaith, skaeth, n., harm.

skaith, v., harm.

skerry, rocky.

skerry, skerrie, a rock or rocky islet in the sea.

skill, sckill, skylle, reason, discernment, knowledge. (a baron) of sckill, reasonable, of good judgment, etc. (that's but) skill, reason, something right and proper.

skinkled, sparkled.

skorne, disgrace, humiliation. See **scorn.**

skylle. See **skill.**

slack, a gap or narrow pass between two hills; low ground, a morass.

slade, a valley, ravine, plain. Cf. **slack.**

slae, sloe.

slawe, *p. p.* of slay. See **slo.**

slee, sly.

sleste, slist, sliced, split.

slet, *pret.* of slit.

slichting, slighting.

slight, demolish. (we'll fecht them) we'll slight them, 489, ₅, make light of (?).

slipe, sleep.

slist, sliced, split.

slo, sloe, sloo, slon, slay. *pret.* sloughe. *p. p.* slo, slowe, slone, slawe, y-slaw.

slode, *pret.* of slide, split.

sloe, sloo, slay. *pret.* sloughe. *p. p.* slowe, slone. See **slo.**

slogan, war-cry, gathering word of a clan.

sloken, slocken, quench.

slough-hounds, sleuth-hounds, blood-hounds.

sloughe, *pret.* of slo, slay.

slowe, *p. p.* of slo, slay.

sma, small. of linen, of fine texture.

smeek, smoke.

smirkling (smile), suppressed.

smoldereth, smothereth.

smooth, pass lightly over. smooth the breast for swimming, see **breast.**

snack, quick.

sned, cut, lop.

sneed, snood, fillet for a maiden's hair.

sneer, snort.

snell, of weather, wind, frost, sharp, keen. of a blast of a horn, shrill.

snoded, tied with a snood.

snood, a fillet with which a maiden's hair was bound up. See **sneed.**

soberly, quietly, making no noise.

socht, sought, *pret.,* asked for.

sodde, *pret.,* seethed, boiled.

soir, sore.

solaces, merry-makings, diversions.

soldan, sultan, any pagan king; hence, giant. See **soudan.**

some, *with singular,* some clean white sheet.

somers, sumpter-horses, pack-horses.

sone, at once.

sone so, as soon as.

sonsie, plump.

soom, soum, sume, swoom, swim.

scon, early.

sore, as, they mighten a had, on whatever hard terms.

sorowe, sorrow, sorry, sorrowful, sad.

sorraye, sorrow.

sorrowful, sorry, pitiful.

soud, sude, should.

soudan, sowdan, souden, soldan, sultan.

Soudron, Southron.

Soudronie, Southronry.

sough, sound.

sould, should.

soum, soom, sume, swim.

soun, sound.

soun (lead the bridle soun), steadily, so as not to cause a jolt by jerking it.

southen, southin, southern.

sowdan. See **soudan.**

sowens, flummery; "oat-meal sowr'd amongst water for some time, then boiled to a consistency, and eaten with milk or butter." Herd.

sowt, sought, peered, scanned.

sowt, south.

soyt, sooth.

spait, flood.

spald. See **spaul.**

spare, opening in a gown or petticoat.

sparred, shut.

spaul, spauld, spald, spole, shoulder.

spayed, spied.

spear, *v.,* spare.

spear, speer, speir, spier, sper, ask. See **spyrr.**

speed, prosperity, help.

speen, spoon.

speer, inquire. See **spyrr.**

speere, 577, ₂₀; "a hole in the wall of the house, through which the family received and answered the inquiries of strangers." Ritson. This may be conjectural. Speere, a screen (wall) between fire and door to keep off the wind is well known both in England and Scotland. But the Heir seems to be outside and could not look up at this speere.

speir, ask. See **spyrr.**

spendyd, a spear, spanned; hence, got ready, placed in rest.

spin, gar your blood, spirt.

spird, spurred.

spite, spital, hospital.

spleen, *v.,* regard with spleen, hatred.

spleene, *n.,* animosity.

splent (splint), armor of overlapping plates.

splinders, splinters.

spole, shoulder. See **spaul.**

sporne, *v.,* kick.

spreckl(e)d, speckled.

sprente, sprang, spurted.

spring, quick tune.

sprunks, fine, showily dressed women ?

spulyie, spuilye, spuilzie, *v.,* despoil.

spurn(e), *n.,* 397, ₆₅, ₆₆, kick. The word, though protected by rhyme and by occurring twice, is suspicious. If spurn could be taken as clash, encounter, collision, it might stand, but such a sense is forced. See note.

spurtle, stick for stirring porridge.

spyrr, spire, spier, speir, speer, spear, sper, ask, inquire. request.

squar, squer, squire.

squier, swire, neck.

st, as sign of the future. I'st, thoust, thou'st shee'st, she'st, you'st. (Only in English ballads.)

sta, *pret.* of steal.

sta, stall.

staen, stolen.

stage, at a, 284, 39, from a floor, story (?).

stage, stag.

stalle : in strete and stalle, 286, 89, station ; from the contrast with street, we may infer the meaning to be, when in movement (on the road) and when stationary, or housed.

stand, (of a court) sit.

stand out, stickle, scruple.

stand, na, ne, no(e), awe, stand not in awe.

stank, ditch.

stap, n. and v., step.

stap, stape, stop, stay, reside. will stap (to die), shrink, hesitate.

stap, stuff, cram.

stare (of hair), stand up.

stark, strong. stark and stoor, in a moral sense, wanting in delicacy, rude, violent, or indecent.

starn, stern, star.

start, spring, jump ; recoil, flinch, recede. pret. start, stert, sprang. See stert.

stawn, p. p. of steal.

stead, steed.

stead(e), steed(e). See stede.

steal, pret. sta, staw. p. p. stawn, stowen, stown, stoun, stelld.

stean : Marie's stean, a stone seat at the door of St Mary's Church.

stear, steer, stir, commotion.

steck. See steek.

stede, steed(e), stead(e), place, dwelling-place.

steed, stood.

steek, steck, steik, stick, shut, fasten.

steek, steik, n., stitch with the needle.

steer, steir, rudder.

steer, stear, disturbance.

steer, strong, robust.

steer, stir, move.

steik, n., stitch. See steek.

steik, v., shut. See steek.

steir, n., rudder. See steer.

stell, steel.

stelld, pret. of steal.

stelld, placed, planted.

stende : me stende, that people should stone.

sterne, stern (men).

stert, start, pret. of start, sallied, rushed.

steuen, voice. vnsett steven, time not previously fixed.

stiffe, unyielding, stanch.

still : had your still, hold your peace.

stime, styme, glimpse, ray, particle of light.

stint, stinte, stop.

stirred, 322, 49 : should probably be stirted (shrank, flinched). The other text has, started.

stirt, stirred.

stock, the outer side of a bed, opposite the wall (the bed, an enclosed box, being enterable at this side only).

stock (term of disparagement), a person wanting in vitality, sensibility, youth, or what not.

stonde, while, time. See stound(e).

stonyt, stoneth, old plural of the imperative.

stood him upon, was incumbent on. See stand.

stoode (my need stoode), existed.

stook, put into shocks.

stoor : stark and stoor, in a moral sense, rude, brutal.

store (buffets store), in plenty.

store (purse of gold and store), treasure. carryd the store (of constancy), the totality.

stoun, p. p. of steal.

stound(e), stonde, time ; point, moment of time.

stoup, pitcher, can, bucket.

stour, stoure, stowre, tumult, brawl, fight. stour (of thy hand), turbulence, destructiveness.

stout(e), haughty, high-mettled, bold, sturdy ; (traitor) audacious, unflinching.

stowen, stown, p. p. of steal. See stoun.

stowre, n. See stour.

stowre, adj., (originally, big) strong.

strack, struck.

strae, stray, stro. straw.

straik, streak, streek, stroke. (a sword) oer (on) a strae (strow), pass it over a straw to give it an edge. straik (streek) wi a (the) wan(d), of a measure, to even at the top by passing a stick over.

strait (a rope), straighten, stretch, tighten.

strand, stream. Sometimes hardly more than a rhyme-word. In, Scotland's strands, 186, 7, strand appears to be put for country, bounds ; and for nothing more definite than way, road, in he gaed in the strand, etc.

strang, strong.

strang, strange.

strange, backward, diffident.

stratlins, straddlings, stridings.

straucht, straught, adj. and adv., straight.

stray. See strae.

streak, straik, of whetting a sword by passing it over a straw. See stroak, strike, strip.

streek, streak, stretch. p. p. streeket, streekit, strickit, stretched, laid out, as dead.

streen, the streen, yestreen, yester-night.

strickit. See streek.

strike, of whetting a sword, etc., on a straw, or the ground. See stroak, streak, strip.

strinkled, sprinkled.

strip, of whetting a sword by passing it across straw, a stone, the ground ; replaced by stroak, streak, strike, draw. See stroak, etc.

stro, strow, strae, stray, straw.

stroak, stroke, of whetting a sword by passing it over a straw. See strip, streak, straik, strike.

stroke. See stroak.

stroke, 332, 13 : probably corrupt ; read streke, stretch (?).

stronge th(i)efe, strong thief, a thief using violence.

strook, pret. of strike.

strucken, p. p. of strike.

stubborn, truculent, fierce.

stude, stede, place.

study, studie, studdy, stithy, anvil.

sturdy (sturdy steel), stiff, rigid.

stye, pen, den ; a smaller thoroughfare, alley.

styrande, stirring, dislodging.

suan, swain.

suar, sure, trusty.

suar(e), *pret.*, swore.

such an a, such a.

sud, soud, suld, should.

sudne, should not.

suet, suit, sweat.

sugar-sops, defined in dictionaries as sugar-plums. Fletcher's Monsieur Thomas, ii, 3, "Dandle her upon my knee, and give her sugar-sops." By analogy, bits of bread or cake dipped in sugar juice.

suit, sweet.

sulle, sell.

sune, *adj.*, sound.

swack, nimble.

swads, swades: "swad in the North is a pescod-shell: thence used for an empty shallow-headed fellow." Also, a cant term for soldier.

swak. See swap.

swap, swak (swords, with swords), smite.

swarmd, climbed. (swarm, to climb a tree that has no side branches to help one.)

swarued, climbed.

swat, *pret.* of swe(a)t, swett(e).

swathed, swaddled (as it were) in blood.

sway: howsoeuer this geere will sway, whatever turn this business may take, however this affair may turn out.

swear, *pret.*, swore.

sweauen, sweuen, dream.

sweer, reluctant (to part with money).

swerers, quest of, jurors.

swet, swett, swette, *pret.* of swe(a)t. See swat.

sweven, sweauen, dream.

swick, blame.

swikele, deceptive, treacherous.

swilled, tossed about or shook, as in rinsing (but in this case to effect a mixture).

swimd, swimmed, *pret.* of swim.

swinke, labor.

swire, swyre, neck. "The declination of a mountain or hill, near the summit." (Jamieson.)

swith, quickly.

swoond, swound, *n.*, swoon.

syde, of a horn worn low. See side.

sygnets. See signots.

syke, sike, ditch, trench.

syne, sayn, san, sane, then, afterwards, since.

synsyne, since.

sypress, crape (veil).

syt, old contracted form of sitteth.

T

table, take vp the, take away: the tables were laid on trestles and easily handled, removed, and, as we often see in ballads, kicked over.

tack, took.

tacken, taiken, token.

tae, too.

tae, the tae, ae, one. See tane.

taen, tain, tane, tean, teyne, *p. p.*, taken.

taiken, tacken, token.

tain, taken.

tait. See tate.

take, talk.

take, hand over, give ; deliver a blow, strike.

take sworne, take an oath of, put under oath.

take truce, take trewes, pledges of good faith, for suspension of hostility. take peace, perhaps formed upon take truce.

take up (the table), clear away (remove the boards) ; see table. take up (dogs), stop, restrain, call off (?).

take with, take up with, put up with, submit to.

takle, takyll, arrow.

talbott, a species of hound.

talents. In 112, 17, talents probably refers to the weight or value of gold worn in massive ornaments. It is not likely that the lady wore coins.

tane, the tane, the tither, tother, the one, the other.

tane, taen, tean, teyne, *p. p.*, taken. tane sworn (I am), of one who has taken an oath.

targats, targits, tassels.

targe, charter, document.

tate, tait, teet, tet, tette, lock (of hair, of mane).

taucher, toucher, tocher, dowry. See toucher.

tauchy, greasy.

taul, tauld, told.

tay, tie.

teall, tale.

tean, taken.

tear begane this spurn, 397, 65. See note.

tee, tie.

tee, ti, to, too.

teem, toom, empty.

teemed, allowed.

teen, teene, tithe. See teind.

teene, tene, injury, wrath, vexation, annoyance, grief, trouble.

teet. See tate.

teind, teein, tiend, tene, teen, tithe.

teindings, tithings.

tell, till, to.

tempeng, tempen, tempting.

tene, *v.*, do harm to.

tene, *n.* See teene.

tenements, holdings (either of lands or houses).

tent, *n.*, heed.

tent, *v.*, take care of, guard, watch.

tet, tette. See tate.

tha, then. See tho.

thae, they, them, those, these.

that, *imperative particle*, anone that you tell me ! no peny that I se ! no ferther that thou gone !

that, *plur.*, that two lords.

the, thé, they.

the, thé, thee.

the day, to-day.

the morn, to-morrow.

the night, the nicht, to-night.

the streen, yestreen.

the, thee, then, thye, *v.*, thrive, prosper.

theek, *pret.* and *p. p.*, theekit, theekd ; thatched, roofed.

thegither, thegithar, thegether, together.

their. See thir.

then, v. See the, v.

there: the diel o there, 462, 26, seems to mean *of that*; but we have, devil be there, in 43, as an equivalent phrase.

there, there is, there are.

there down, downwards, down.

theretoo, besides.

thes, thus. See this.

they, the (frequent in Percy MS.).

thimber, heavy, massive.

think, thynk, seem. me thinke, me thynke, methink, methinketh, methinks.

think lang (A. S. lang thyncan, seem long). In Scottish, personal, with substitution of *think* for *seem*. think lang, find the time wearisome, suffer from *ennui*. I think lang, long for. I 'll never think lang, shall never be discontented.

thir, their, these, those.

this, *pl.*, this twa.

this, thes, thys, thus.

tho, then.

thoe, 384, 33 : those, they (possibly, then).

thole, thoule, bear, suffer. (472, 2 : like dree, be capable of.)

thother, the, tother, other.

thou, though.

thought lang. See think lang.

thoule, suffer, put up with. See thole.

thra, thrae, dialectic variety of fra, frae, from.

thrae, through.

thrall, bondage.

thrast, *pret.*, pressed.

thraw, twist, contort. *pret.* threw. *p. p.* thrawen, thrawin, thrawn.

thrawn, twisted. See thraw.

threefold oer a tree. See twofold.

threesome, three together.

threty, thirty.

threw, *pret.* of thraw, twisted, intertwined. Robin he lope, Robin he threw: may be, threw himself about, or twisted, twirled, showing his suppleness.

thrien, thrice.

thrild vpon (a pinn), tirled, rattled. See pin.

thrill, pierce, penetrate.

thristle-cock, throstle, thrush.

throly, strenuously, doggedly.

thronge, pressed, made his way.

throw, *intrans.* (fyer out of his eyen did throw), dart, shoot.

throwe, space of time.

þrumme, the extremity of a weaver's warp, from six to nine inches long, serving to hold arrows.

thryfte: euyll thryfte, ill thriving, ill speed, bad luck.

thye, thigh.

thye, thrive. See the, v.

ti, to, too.

tidding, tidings.

tide, tyde, time. into the tide, by the tide, at the time, now.

tiend, tithe. See teind.

tift, puff, whiff.

till, to.

till, v., entice.

timmer, timber, wooden.

tine, tyne, tayen, lose; to be lost, perish. *pret.* and *p. p.* tint, lost.

tinye, n. (a little tinye), bit.

tip, tippet (of horse's mane), tate, lock.

tirl at the pin, trill, rattle, at that part of the door-fastening which lifts the latch. See pin.

tithyngus, tidings.

to, two.

to, till.

tobreke, *subj.*, break, burst (apart). *p. p.* to-broke, broken up.

tocher, toucher, tougher, taucher, n. See toucher.

tod, fox.

to-hande, two-hand, two-handed.

tolbooth, tolbuith, tollbooth, prison, jail.

tolde, counted.

ton, tone, the, the one.

tooke, put. See take.

tooken vpon one part, engaged, enlisted, on the same side.

toom, teem, empty.

topcastle, top.

topps. "Among seamen tops are taken for those round frames of board that lye upon the cross-trees, near the heads of the masts, where they get up to furle or loose the topsails." Phillips.

tor (of saddle), pommel.

tor, tore, projection or knob at the corner of old-fashioned cradles (as also, ornamental balls surmounting the backs of chairs).

torne, turn, bout.

tortyll-tre, 292, 56, corruptly for trystell-tre.

to t', to the.

to-towe, too-too, a strong *too*.

toucher, tougher, taucher, n., tocher, dowry.

toucher, v., pay a dowry to.

toun, town, a farmer's steading or place (or, a small collection of houses).

toung, tongue.

touting, blowing.

tow, rope.

tow, let down by a rope.

towbooth. See tolbooth.

town. See toun.

trace, track, path, way.

trachled, tired out.

train, company.

traitorye, treachery.

tranckled, travelled.

trapand, *p. p.*, (of horse) treacherously dealt with.

tray, tree, injury, suffering, grief, vexation.

tray, try.

tread, tred, *pret.* and *p. p.* of tread.

tree, tre, wood ; the cross ; staff, straight piece of rough wood ; crooked tree, bow. of (a) myghttë tre, of strong wood. a trusti tree, 396, 40, perhaps shaft ; but the *a* is likely to be *of* and the meaning, of trusty wood. horse of tree, bridge, or, at least, tree-trunk.

tree. See tray.

trenchen tree, truncheon, cudgel, staff.

trew, true, trow, believe.

trews, trues, trousers.

treyffe, thrive.

triest, trist. See tryst.

trinkle, trickle.

tristil-tre. See trystell-tre.

trou, true.

trow, trew, true, believe, suppose.

trowt, trowet, troth.

true-love, lover, betrothed lover (often not to be distinguished from true love).

trues, trousers.

truff, turf.

trust, trow, believe, suppose (of the things one would rather not believe).

truste, trusty.

trusty tree, an obvious corruption of trystill-tree, a tree appointed for a meeting or assemblage. (Trusty also in later copies of Adam Bell and the Gest for trysty, trystell, which see).

trusyd, trussed, bound up.

tryst, tryste, n., appointment to meet.

tryst, tri(e)st, v., engage, induce, entice, to come, go with; prepare a way for coming, cause to come.

trystell-tree, trysty-tre, trystyll-tre, tristil-tre, a tree serving for a meeting-place (of Robin Hood's band).

trysty tre, tree fixed upon for rendezvous (trusty, trustie in later copies).

tua, two. But twa part, 548, 20, seems to mean second part, half, that is, it is more likely that an equal share should be offered.

tul, til, to. tul a, to have.

twa, two. twa part, see tua.

twafald (-fold), oer a tree, staff, bent double over a stick. See twofold.

twain, v., part. See twin.

twal, twelve.

twalmon, twalmont, twelvemonth.

twalt, twelt, twelfth.

twan, pret. of twine.

twaw, two.

twig, twitch, pull.

twin, twine, twyne, deprive; part with; separate; part, intrans.

twine, coarse linen, duck, crash; texture, yarn; towel.

twinkle, trinkle, trickle.

twinn, v. See twin.

twinn : part in twinn, in twain, in two.

twofold oer a staff, threefold oer a tree, 375, 9: the body being bent double over the staff, the whole presentation is, with the staff (tree), threefold. Corruptly, 337, 6, two foote on a staffe, the third vpon a tree. See also twafald.

tydand, tidings.

tyde. See tide.

tyndes, tynes, antlers.

tyne, v., to lose, to perish. See tine.

tyte, quickly. his backe did from his belly tyte, 379, 17 : a verb of the sense *fall away* may have dropped out after *did*, and is at any rate to be understood, unless *tyte* had that sense. A Scottish *tyte*, to totter, fall (tyte oer, fall over), is noted by Jamieson.

U

ugsome, exciting disgust or abhorrence.

ull, I ull, will.

unbeen : my barn's unbeen, 498, A 4, not thoroughly closed in or made tight (?). (been, well-provided, warm, dry and snug. A bein cask, water-tight, Jamieson.) a house is beind when thoroughly dried.

vnbethought him, bethought himself of.

unbigged, unbuilt.

unco, *adj.*, unknown, strange. unco squire, stranger. unco (lair, lear), extraordinary.

unco, *adv.*, unusually, very.

uncouth, vnkowth, vnkuth, vnketh, unknown, strange.

vndergoe, undertake.

vnder hand, shott it vnder hand. Dr Furnivall and Mr C. J. Longman suggest, putting the bow horizontally, in which case you shoot with the arrow under the left hand, instead of beside it, as in shooting with the bow vertical. Dr W. Hand Browne, of Johns Hopkins University, cites Ascham : " Men doubt yet, in looking at the mark, what way is best, above or beneth hys hand "; " a byg brested shafte for hym that shoteth *under hande*, bycause it will hobble ; " and remarks, " As he is here speaking only of taking aim, underhand shooting would seem to be done when the archer raised his bow high, and looked at the mark under the arrow-hand."

under night, in the night.

unkent, unknown.

vnketh, vnkouth, vnkuth, uncouth, unknown, stranger.

vnmackley, misshapen.

vnneth, unneath, with difficulty, scarcely.

unright(e), wrong.

unruly, 549, 1, unlucky, should probably be unseally.

unshemly, unseemly.

unthought, unthocht, onthought lang, haud, keep, keep from thinking long, wearying, from *ennui*. See think lang.

until, untill, unto, to.

unto, into, in.

vnto the same, after the same fashion.

vntyll, gates shut them vntyll, to, against.

vp chaunce, on, for, the chance.

up, (came) up.

upgive, avow, acknowledge, own up.

vpon, vppon, on.

upper hand, upper tier, above.

upstart, sprang up.

V

va(l)low, *v.*: vallow not the feed, value, care not for the feud which will ensue.

value (of an hour), amount.

vawward, vanward, vanguard, van.

veiwe, vew, vewe, yew.

venison, hunting (prerogative of).

vepan, weapon.

verament, truly.

vessell, *pl.*, vessels.

vew, vewe, veiwe, yew.

vild, vile.

virgus, verjuice, a kind of vinegar (green juice).

virr, vigor.

vo, vou, woe.

vouch it safe, grant, bestow (safe corrected from halfe).

voued, *pret.*, vowed.

voyded, made off.

vyld, wild.

W

wad, *n.*, pledge, in security ; forfeit.

wad, wade, would.

wad, wade, *v.*, wager ; engage (to fight).

wadded, of woad color, blue.

wadding, wadin, wedding.

wade, wad, *pret.* of wide, wade.

wadin. See wadding.

wae, wa, wo.

wae, *adj.*, unhappy.

waefou, woful.

wael, choice. See wale.

waft, weft, woof.

wafu, woful.

wair. See war.

wait, I wait, a wait, wate, I wot, know, indeed. See wat, and a = I.

wait, wayte, watch, lie in wait, seek an opportunity, to do.

waitmen, waiting-men (or possibly, wight men, strong men).

wake, watch (people set to watch me).

wake, *v.*, walk.

waken, waking.

wald, would.

wale, wael, walle, choice.

wale, weil, wile, wyle, choose.

walker, fuller.

wall, well, spring.

wall : green wall sea, green wall wave, apparently wave, despite tautology.

walle, wale, choice. See wale.

wallourt, wallowt, drooped, grew pallid.

wall-wight, waled wight, picked strong men (?). Perhaps for well-wight.

wallwood (swine), wild-wood.

walting, welting, edging.

waly, wallie, wally, exclamation of admiration.

waly, wally, interjection of lamentation.

wamb(e), wame, womb.

wan, one.

wan, dark-colored, pallid, colorless, white.

wan, wane, *pret.* of win.

wan, *p. p.* of win.

wan, wand, (willow) twigs.

wane, habitation. in my bower there is a wane, 14, 5 ; wane, says Jamieson, denotes not only a dwelling (Old Eng. wone), but " different apartments in the same habitation ; " if so, in my house there is a room, is the sense here.

wane, 395, 36, " quantity, multitude ; a single arrow out of a vast quantity." Skeat (quantity as in Chaucer's wone). This is unsatis-

factory, but no better interpretation has been suggested. Wain, in the sense of a vehicle for a missile, ballista, catapult, would be what is wanted.

wanna, did not win, go.

wannelld, was unsteady, staggered.

wanny, small wand, rod.

want, do without, dispense with. sae soon as we 've wanted him, had to do without.

wanton, free and easy, frolicsome.

wantonlie, -ly, gaily, merrily ; in easy, spirited style.

wap : horse will gie his head a wap, throw, toss.

wap, *v.*, wrap, lap. wap (halter oer horse's nose), lap, twine, perhaps throw.

wap, *v.*, throw. wappit (wings), beat, flapped.

war, ware : be war, ware, a, of, on, be aware, have a sight of.

war, waur, worse.

war, waur, were.

war, ware, expend, bestow. ware my dame's cauf's skin on thee, apply, use, my wife's (mother's) whip.

waran, warran, warrand, warraner, warrant, sponsor for, security ; safeguard.

ward, warde, prison, confinement.

warden pies, made of large pears called wardens.

wardle, world. wardle's make, see warld.

ware, sea-weed, alga marina (used for manure).

ware, were.

ware. See war.

warison, waryson, reward.

warld, world. warld's make, wordlye make, world's, earthly, mate, consort.

warldly. See warld.

warlock, wizard.

warn, surety, safeguard.

warn, *p. p.*, warned.

warran, warrand. See waran.

warraner. See waran.

warsle, *n.*, wrestle.

warsle, warsel, *v.*, wrestle. warsled, wrestled, struggled, bestirred himself.

waryson. See warison.

wa's, ways.

was. See wash.

wash. *pres.* was ; *pret.* wush ; *p. p.* washen, wushen, which see.

wast, west.

wat, wate, wait, watt, weet, wet, wit, wite, wyte, wis, wot, know. I wat, wate, a wat, a wite, etc., frequently nothing more than assuredly, indeed. *pret.* wist. *p. p.* wist, west.

wat, *pret.* and *p. p.* of weet, weit, to wet.

water, water-side. "the banks of a river, in the mountainous districts of Scotland the only inhabitable parts." Scott.

water-gate, street leading to the water, way along the water.

water-side. See water.

water-stoups, water-buckets or pitchers.

watt, know. See wat.

waught, draught.

wauk, walk.

wauk, watch, be awake.

wauken, waken.

waur, war, worse.

waur, were.

wavers wi the wind, is as restless, changeable (?).

way, the Milky Way.

waylawaye, alas.

wayte, wait, look out for ; watch, lie in wait, seek an opportunity, to do. *pret.* wayted, lay in wait for.

we, wee, with.

we, wee, little.

wea, woe.

wead, would.

weal, 397, 60, "clench so as to leave marks, mark with wales"(?). "Perhaps read wringe and wayle." Skeat.

wean, little one, child.

Wearie, the Devil.

weary, wearie, sad, unhappy, distressed ; vexatious, hateful, horrid, cursed.

weate, 410, 47, corrupt. Possibly, I weate, wit, know.

wed, wedd(e), wad, pledge, fine, forfeit. sette to wedde, put in pledge.

wed, proudest wed, proudest dressed (from wede).

wede, weed, clothing, garment.

wee, little ; short time.

weed. See wede.

weel, well. See well.

weel, well : weel fa ! good luck befall. for my weel, well, advantage. Euphemism for God : weel met thee save ! etc.

weel-fared, weel-fart, weil-faurit, etc., well-favored.

ween, whimper, whine, lament.

weer, war. See weir.

weet, *n.*, rain, shower of rain.

weete, weit, *v.*, wet.

weetie, rainy.

weil, wile, wale, choose. See wale.

weil, well, very. See well.

weir, weer, war.

weird, wierd, weer, *n.*, fate, fortune, destiny.

weird her a grit sin, destined, put her in the way of, a great sin.

welde, would.

well, euphemism for God. See weel.

well, will.

well, weel, weil, very, right, very good.

well and wellsome, should probably be wae and waesome (sad and woful).

well-a-woo, a variety of well-a-way.

well-bespoke, well spoken.

well-wight, very strong, sturdy, stalwart ; but, sometimes, brave.

welt, *pret.* of wield, disposed of.

welth(e), 277, 436, either, simply, his money, or, more probably, his well-being, his palmy days ; (rich) booty.

weme (of ring), belly, hollow. See wamb(e).

wen, win, get, go. *pret.* of win.

wenking, winking.

were, vulgar English, was.

werne, were.

werryed, worried.

werschepyd, showed respect to.

west, *p. p.*, wist.

westlin, westryn, western.

wet, wete, know.

wether (perhaps, whether), whither.

weynde, wend, go.

wha, whae, who.

wha 's (whae 's) aught. See aucht.

whall : white as whall, that is, whale's bone.

whang, thong.

whas, whose.

what an a, whaten a, whatna, whattna, whatten, what sort ? what (in particular) ? what a ! So, what for a ? what like a ?

wheder, whither.

whether, which of the two.

whether, whither.

whew, whue, whute, whistle.

whidderand, (of arrows) whizzing, moving with a whiz.

whight. See wight.

while, the other, the remaining time, henceforth (?).

while, for a while.

while, whyll(e), till.

whiles, at times.

whiles, whilest, whileste, whilste, whyllys, the whyles, while.

whilk, which.

whin, whun, fun, furze.

white bread, wheat bread.

white-fish (fait fish), haddock, cod, ling, etc., as distinguished from gray-fish, coal-fish ; in Banff, as opposed to salmon, trout, herring.

white-fisher, one who fishes for haddock, cod, etc. (as distinguished from salmon).

white-land, wheat-land.

white meal and gray, oat-meal as distinguished from barley-meal. But white meal, 124, 17 ; 125, 18, being contrasted with corn (oats), must there be wheat.

white money, monie, silver.

who would, if one would.

whue. See whute.

whummil, whimble, gimlet.

whun, fun, whin, furze.

whute, fute, whue, whew, *n.* and *v.*, whistle.

whyles, the whyles, while.

whyll(e), till. See while.

whyllys, while.

wiald, wield.

wicht. See wight.

wicker, wigger, willow.

wicker, twist.

wide, wade. *pret.* wade, wad.

widifu, widdifu, widifau, widdefu, one qualified to fill a widdie or halter.

widna, widne, would not.

wie, with.

wiell, well.

wierd. See weird.

wigger. See wicker.

wight, wyght, wicht, whight, strong ; but also, denoting bodily activity, brisk, sturdy. See well-wight.

wightdom, weight.

wightlye, with vigor, or briskness.

wight-men, waith-men, hunters.

wightsmen, wechtsmen, winnowers. wecht is "an instrument for winnowing corn, made of sheep's skin, in the form of a sieve, but without holes."

wighty, wight, strong. See wight.

wild-wood swine, steer, drunk as; a popular comparison like, drunk as a dog.

wile, vile.

wilfull, 280, 24: wilfull of my way, astray, lost; *and of my morning tyde* may be that he does not know the hour, or, he has lost his time as well as his road.

wile, wyle, weil, wale, choose.

will, *pret.* wald, walde, wad, wade, wild, wid, wud.

will, bewildered, at a loss what to do.

willinglye, at will, freely.

willy, willow.

win, wynne, won, wonne (hay), dry by airing.

win, wine, wynne, wen, won, make your way, arrive; get, go. *pret.* wan. *p. p.* wone, wan, win, wine, wen.

win your love aff me, detach your love from me.

wine, win, won.

windling sheet, winding-sheet.

winn, in your barn, do harvest work generally, dry corn, etc., by exposing to the air. (unless meant for winna, winnow.)

winna, winnë, will not.

winter, wynter, year(s).

wir, our.

wire-window, probably a window grated with bars.

wis, us.

wis, you wis, know.

wis, was.

wiss, *n.*, wish.

wiss, wis, *v.*, wish.

wiss, I wiss, perhaps for I wot (not i-wiss), wist, know.

wist, *pret.* of wiss, wish. See wiss.

wiste, wist, *pret.* of wat, etc. *p. p.* west.

wit, witt, *n.*, knowledge, information.

wite, I wite, I know, indeed. See wat, wyte.

wite, wyte, *n.*, blame.

wite, wyte, *v.*, blame.

with, wyth, by.

wither, wather, wether.

withouten, withowghten, without.

with that, on condition that.

witt, knowledge. See wit.

witted, minded.

wittering, information, indication.

witty, 301, 3, corruption of wight, wighty.

wo, woo, woe, sad, unhappy.

wod, would.

wod, wode, mad. See wood.

wode shawe: grene-wode shawe, greenwood shaw, thicket of the wood.

woe. See wo.

wolwarde, with skin against wool, that is, wearing a woolen fleece directly against the sk[..]

won, dwell.

won, win, get, go, come, arrive; gain, earn.

won, wone, one.

won, wonne, win (hay), dry by airing.

wonder, 426, 2, bewilderment, or disaster (?).

wone, number, plenty.

wonynge, wonning, dwelling.

woo, wool.

woo. See wo.

wood, woode, wode, wod, mad.

woodcock(e), tropically, fool, (from the bird's reputation for folly).

woodweele, wodewale, 279, 2 (MS. wood-weete), woodwale, woodlark (?). Generally explained as woodpecker; sometimes as thrush, red-breast.

woon, won, *v.*, dwell.

woor, wore.

word, att a, in short.

wordlye make, earthly mate, consort. See warld.

worrie, worry, *v.*, (of smoke, flame) choke.

worth: wo the worth, worth the! come, be, to thee. wae mat worth, may wo come to.

wou, how.

wouche, evil, harm.

wound, *pret.*, wounded.

wow, exclamation of distress, admiration, or sorrowful surprise.

wrack, ruin.

wraith, wroth.

wrak. See wrack.

wreck, sea-wreck, whatever is thrown up by the sea.

wreke, *p. p.*, avenged.

wrist, ankle, instep.

writer, writter, attorney (?).

writhe of, (*pret.* of writhe, twist) twisted off.

writs (things written), papers.

writter. See writer.

wrocht, wrought.

wrocken, wroken, *p. p.*, avenged.

wrongeous, unjust.

wrought, *p. p.*, rought, recked.

wrought, *pret.*, raught, reached.

wrthe, worthe.

wruched, thrown up (ruck, a heap, to gather in heaps); perhaps, thrown ashore as wrack.

wud, mad. See wood.

wud, would.

wush, *pret.* of wash.

wyght, *adj.*, strong, sturdy, active. See wight.

wyld, 394, 6, deer; or, perhaps, an adjective with noun to be supplied, of which there are several cases in the ballad.

wyle, choose. See wile.

wylie, wily.

wynd, alley, lane.

wynke, shut the eyes.

wynne, joy, pleasure.

wynne, *v.* See win.

wynter, winter, year(s).

wystly, observingly, thoughtfully.

wyte: I wyte, (I know) indeed, assuredly. See wit, wyte.

wyte, *n.* and *v.*, blame. See wite.

wyth, with, by.

wythowtten drede, without, beyond doubt. withowghten naye, beyond denial. wythowghten (withouten) stryffe (strife), beyond contestation.

X

xal, shall.
xalt, shalt.
xul, *sing.* and *pl.*, shall.

Y

(See also under ӡ, at the end of G and I.)

y, first y, ae, one. See a, ae.
yae, only, one. See a, ae.
yard, yerde, rod, stick.
yare, ӡare, ready.
yate, yeat, yett, gate. ӡates, ӡatis, gates.
ychon, each one.
ydyght, idyght, prepared, made, fabricated, adjusted; made ready.
yea, ye, you.
yeaman. See yeman.
yeard-fast, yird-fast, fixed firmly in the earth.
yebent, bent.
yede, yeede, yeed, yed, ӡede, yode, yod, *pret.* of gang, gae, go, went.
yee, eye.
ye feth, i faith.
yeffell, evil, ill.
yeffor. See yeuer.
yeft, gift.
yeldyde, surrendered.

yellow-fit, yellow-foot[ed].
yeman, yeaman, yeoman.
yemanr(e)y, yemenrey, yeomanry, yeomandree, yeomandrie, yeomendry, class or company of yeomen; what is in accordance with a yeoman's principles, idea or character.
yend, yond, yon.
yenoughe, enough.
yeomanry, yeomandrie, etc. See yeman-r(e)y.
yer, yere, your.
ye'r, ye are.
yerde. See yard.
yerl, yerle, yerlle, earl.
yerly, early.
ye'se, ye shall. See s.
yestreen, yesterday even, yesternight. See streen.
yet, yett, gate.
yeuer, yeffor, ever.
yield, grant, concede.
yill, ale.
yird-fast. See yeard-fast.
ylke, same. See ilk.
yll: with grete yll, in much distress.
ynowe, enough.
yode, yod, youd, *pret.* of gang, gae, go, went. See yede.
yon, that.
yonders, yonder.
yont, beyond. (lie) yond, yont, further off.
youd, went. See yode.
young son, of a babe just born; sometimes called auld son, being the oldest because the only one, 29, ӡ, 8, 9. See auld son, old son.
yowe-bucht. See bucht.
y-slaw, *p. p.* of slay.

INDEX

INDEX